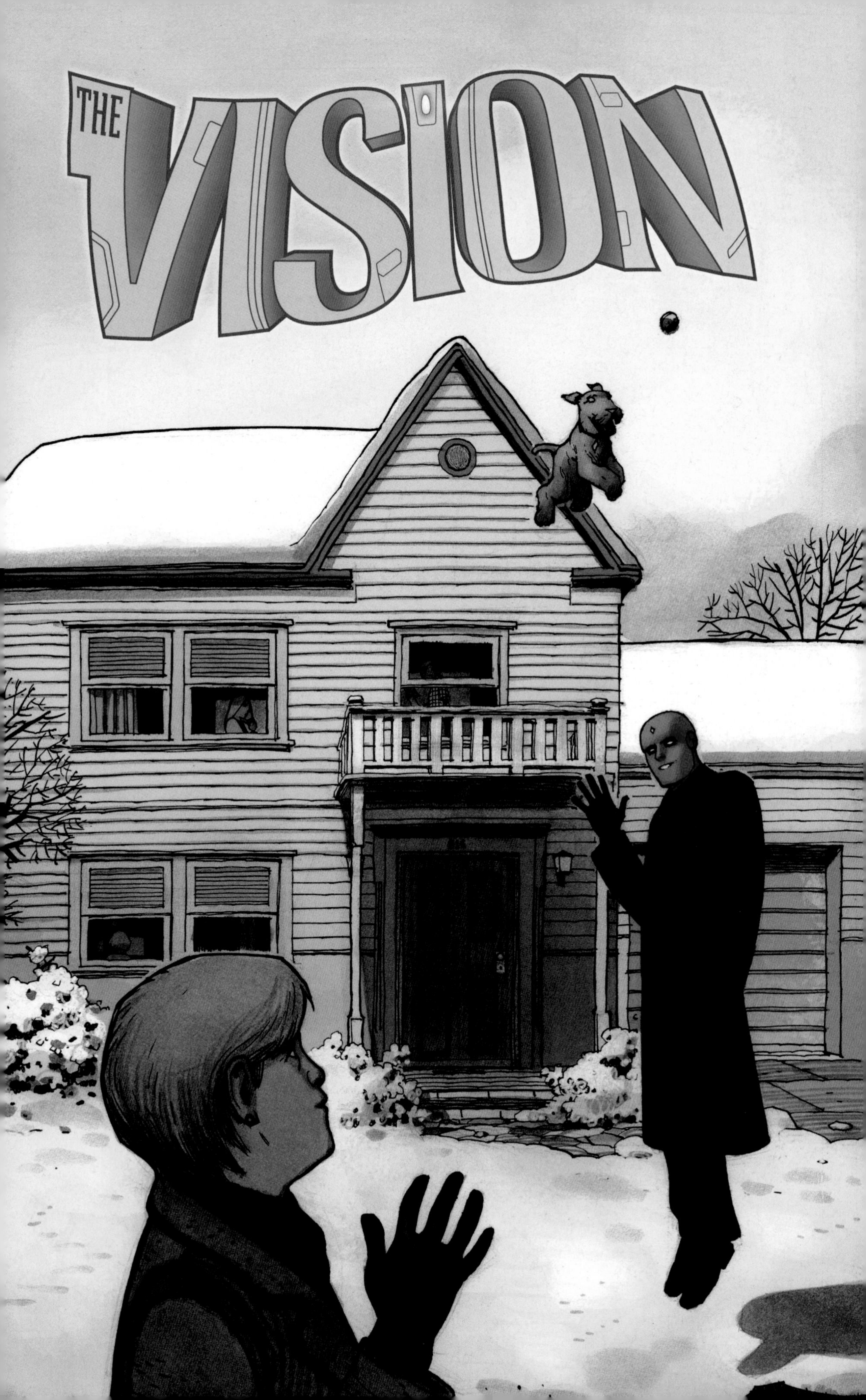
THE VISION

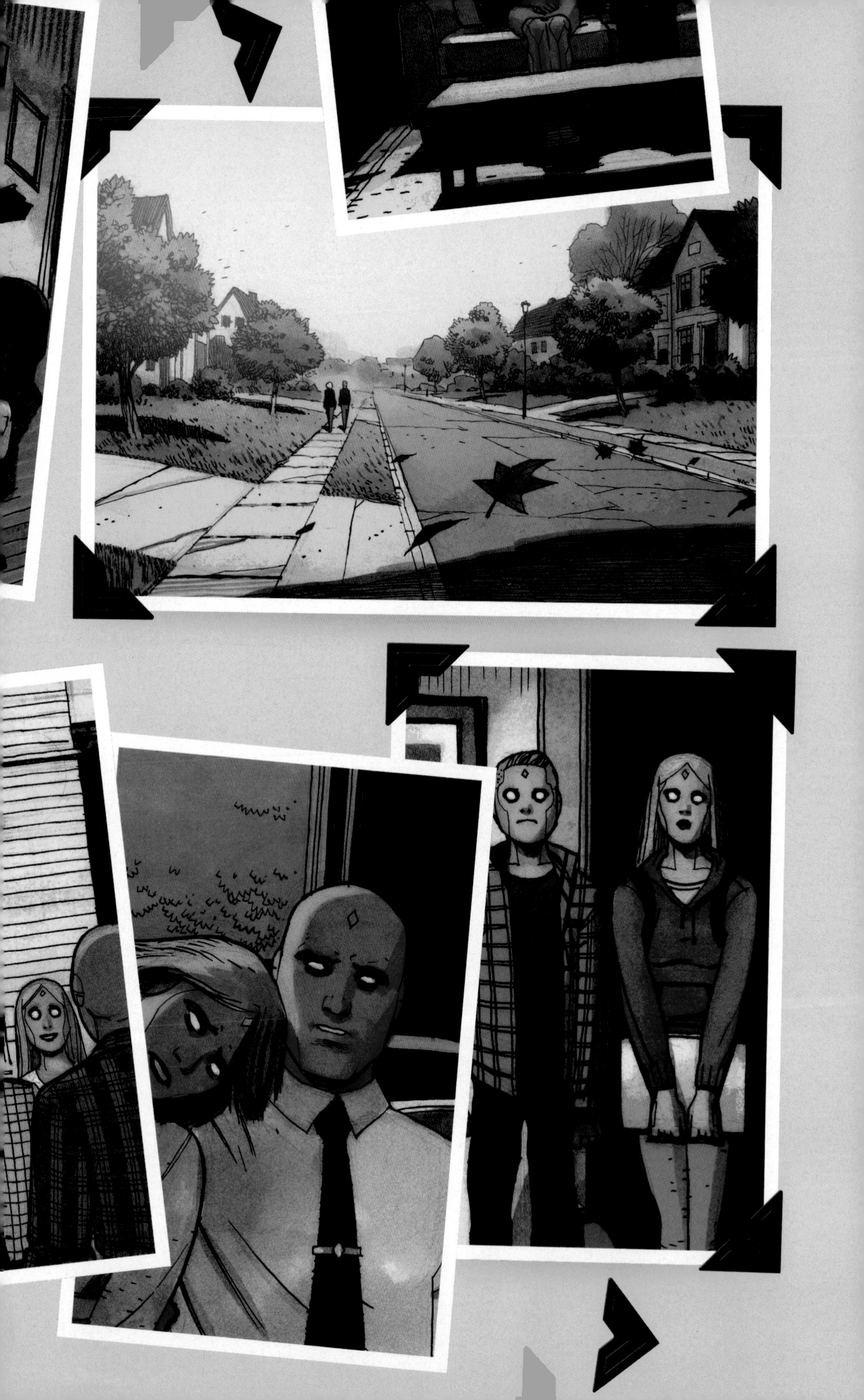

THE VISION IS A SYNTHEZOID — AN ANDROID COMPOSED OF SYNTHETIC HUMAN BLOOD AND ORGANS. HE WAS CREATED BY ULTRON TO DESTROY THE AVENGERS, BUT INSTEAD HE TURNED ON HIS "FATHER," AND HE'S BEEN A MEMBER OF THE SUPER-HERO TEAM EVER SINCE.

THE VISION

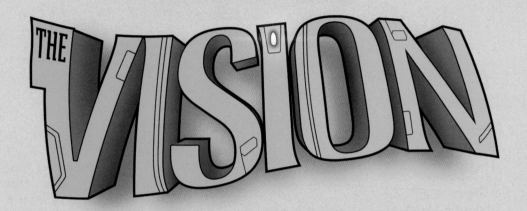

TOM KING
WRITER

GABRIEL HERNANDEZ WALTA (#1-6, #8-12)
& **MICHAEL WALSH** (#7)
ARTISTS

JORDIE BELLAIRE
COLOR ARTIST

VC's CLAYTON COWLES
LETTERER

MIKE DEL MUNDO (#1-4, #7-12)
& **MARCO D'ALFONSO** (#5-6)
COVER ARTISTS

CHRIS ROBINSON & CHARLES BEACHAM
ASSISTANT EDITORS

WIL MOSS
EDITOR

EXECUTIVE EDITOR: ***TOM BREVOORT***

COLLECTION EDITOR: Jennifer Grünwald | ASSISTANT EDITOR: Caitlin O'Connell | ASSOCIATE MANAGING EDITOR: Kateri Woody
EDITOR, SPECIAL PROJECTS: Mark D. Beazley | VP PRODUCTION & SPECIAL PROJECTS: Jeff Youngquist
SVP PRINT, SALES & MARKETING: David Gabriel | BOOK DESIGNER: Jay Bowen

EDITOR IN CHIEF: C.B. Cebulski | CHIEF CREATIVE OFFICER: Joe Quesada
PRESIDENT: Dan Buckley | EXECUTIVE PRODUCER: Alan Fine

VISION. Contains material originally published in magazine form as VISION #1-12. First printing 2017. ISBN 978-1-302-90853-9. Published by MARVEL WORLDWIDE, INC., a subsidiary of MARVEL ENTERTAINMENT, LLC. OFFICE OF PUBLICATION: 135 West 50th Street, New York, NY 10020. **Printed in the U.S.A.** DAN BUCKLEY, President, Marvel Entertainment; JOE QUESADA, Chief Creative Officer; TOM BREVOORT, SVP of Publishing; DAVID BOGART, SVP of Business Affairs & Operations, Publishing & Partnership; DAVID GABRIEL, SVP of Sales & Marketing, Publishing; JEFF YOUNGQUIST, VP of Production & Special Projects; DAN CARR, Executive Director of Publishing Technology; ALEX MORALES, Director of Publishing Operations; SUSAN CRESPI, Production Manager; STAN LEE, Chairman Emeritus. For information regarding advertising in Marvel Comics or on Marvel.com, please contact Jonathan Parkhideh, VP of Digital Media & Marketing Solutions, at jparkhideh@marvel.com. For Marvel subscription inquiries, please call 888-511-5480. **Manufactured between 11/17/2017 and 12/19/2017 by LSC COMMUNICATIONS INC., KENDALLVILLE, IN, USA.**

10 9 8 7 6 5 4 3 2 1

INTRODUCTION

1.

I never read forewords first.

I don't want someone to shape my thoughts about a book before I've even read it.

Don't tell me it's good or important — I'll be the judge of that, thank you. I don't care that you've met the author, or how this book got you through a hard time. I'm trying to read here — let me feel my own feelings, and get out of my way!

I'll come back to the foreword after I finish a book — assuming it's a great book — in that moment when I don't want the *experience* of the story to end. When I want to keep engaging with it, even if that means engaging with the goofball who wrote the foreword.

This is a great book.

So I'll assume you just turned back to my foreword because you're still under *The Vision*'s spell.

Not every book can cast a spell. But Tom King and Gabriel Hernandez Walta catch and keep you from the very first line of their shared *Vision*:

In late September, with the leaves just beginning to hint at the fall to come, the Visions of Virginia moved into their house at 616 Hickory Branch Lane, Arlington, VA, 21301.

It's a formal beginning. Intentional. Which is very much the tone of the whole series. King and Walta are here to tell a serious story. They don't pretend otherwise.

Even though it's so much easier to pretend otherwise! Most of us — authors, I mean — act casual. We hide our big ambitions, then hope that someone notices them anyway. And if we fail or fall short, well, who cares? We weren't trying to be Shakespeare.

The Vision tries to be Shakespeare.

It is careful, it is planned.

It is unapologetically complex. (The dancing narratives. The backing and the forthing.) (Thank God for the clarity of Clayton Cowles' lettering.)

It builds almost mathematically to its conclusions.

And it takes a swing at the biggest story we have: *What does it mean to be human?*

I could point out the audacity of telling a story like this in a comic book — but I have too much faith in the form. Instead I'll point out the sheer *difficulty* of managing and controlling a story like this, in *any* format, let alone over twelve monthly installments.

To tell a story this big and beautiful over twelve months, every step must have been choreographed from the start. There's no cheating, like in novels, where you can go back and hide the murder weapon in the first chapter after you've finally sorted out your mystery.

No, the stage is perfectly set in the first issue of *The Vision*. Every panel its own Chekhov's gun.

2.

In late September, with the leaves just beginning to hint at the fall to come, the Visions of Virginia moved into their house at 616 Hickory Branch Lane, Arlington, VA, 21301.

I've read this series four times. So that's how many times it's broken my heart.

I'm still assuming that you've read it, too — but maybe you're one of those foreword-first people. Maybe I should talk about the story you're about to embark on…

It's very, very sad.

You'll start out feeling so sorry for the Vision, a lonely robot who created a robot wife and two robot children.

Every part of the book foreshadows the tragedy ahead. Mike del Mundo's covers let us know we're in for an especially Gothic American Gothic — here's Mother sweeping a body under the rug, here's Father reduced to a pile of spare parts. Walta gives us a handsome, happy family that feels ever off-kilter, while Jordie Bellaire's colors are rich and minor-keyed.

Maybe you'll laugh at how ridiculous the Visions are. The way they go through the motions of being human — sitting down to dinner even though they don't eat, sending their kids to school even though they have computers for brains.

Maybe you'll pity the way they play at humanity.

I can't say at what point it will turn on you…

At first, *The Vision* seems like a story about how impossible it is for a machine to be human. Only pain can come of it — pain and bloodshed.

But at some point, it becomes a story about how impossible it is for *any* of us to be human.

What is life? Pain and bloodshed and going through the motions.

Hoping for connection, wanting to fit in. Protecting the people who are ours. Praying for them, even if we're not sure there's anyone listening. Not sure we have a soul to save.

3.

In late September, with the leaves just beginning to hint at the fall to come, the Visions of Virginia moved into their house at 616 Hickory Branch Lane, Arlington, VA, 21301.

The Vision is full of endings, none of them happy.

Sometimes the book will introduce a character by telling you how that character will later die. (Death isn't a spoiler.)

But the book delivers in a way that is better than happy — it gives you endings that live up to its beginnings.

The Vision lands as carefully and ambitiously as it took off.

And if it doesn't answer the question of what it means to be human, it leaves you feeling utterly human. And willing to accept the remaining Visions into the club.

Rainbow Rowell

RAINBOW ROWELL WRITES BOOKS. SOMETIMES SHE WRITES ABOUT ADULTS (*ATTACHMENTS* AND *LANDLINE*). SOMETIMES SHE WRITES ABOUT TEENAGERS (*ELEANOR & PARK, FANGIRL, CARRY ON*- -AND MARVEL'S CURRENT *RUNAWAYS* REVIVAL). BUT SHE ALWAYS WRITES ABOUT PEOPLE WHO TALK A LOT. AND PEOPLE WHO FEEL LIKE THEY'RE SCREWING UP. AND PEOPLE WHO FALL IN LOVE. WHEN SHE'S NOT WRITING, RAINBOW IS READING COMIC BOOKS, PLANNING DISNEY WORLD TRIPS AND ARGUING ABOUT THINGS THAT DON'T REALLY MATTER IN THE BIG SCHEME OF THINGS. SHE LIVES IN NEBRASKA WITH HER HUSBAND AND TWO SONS.

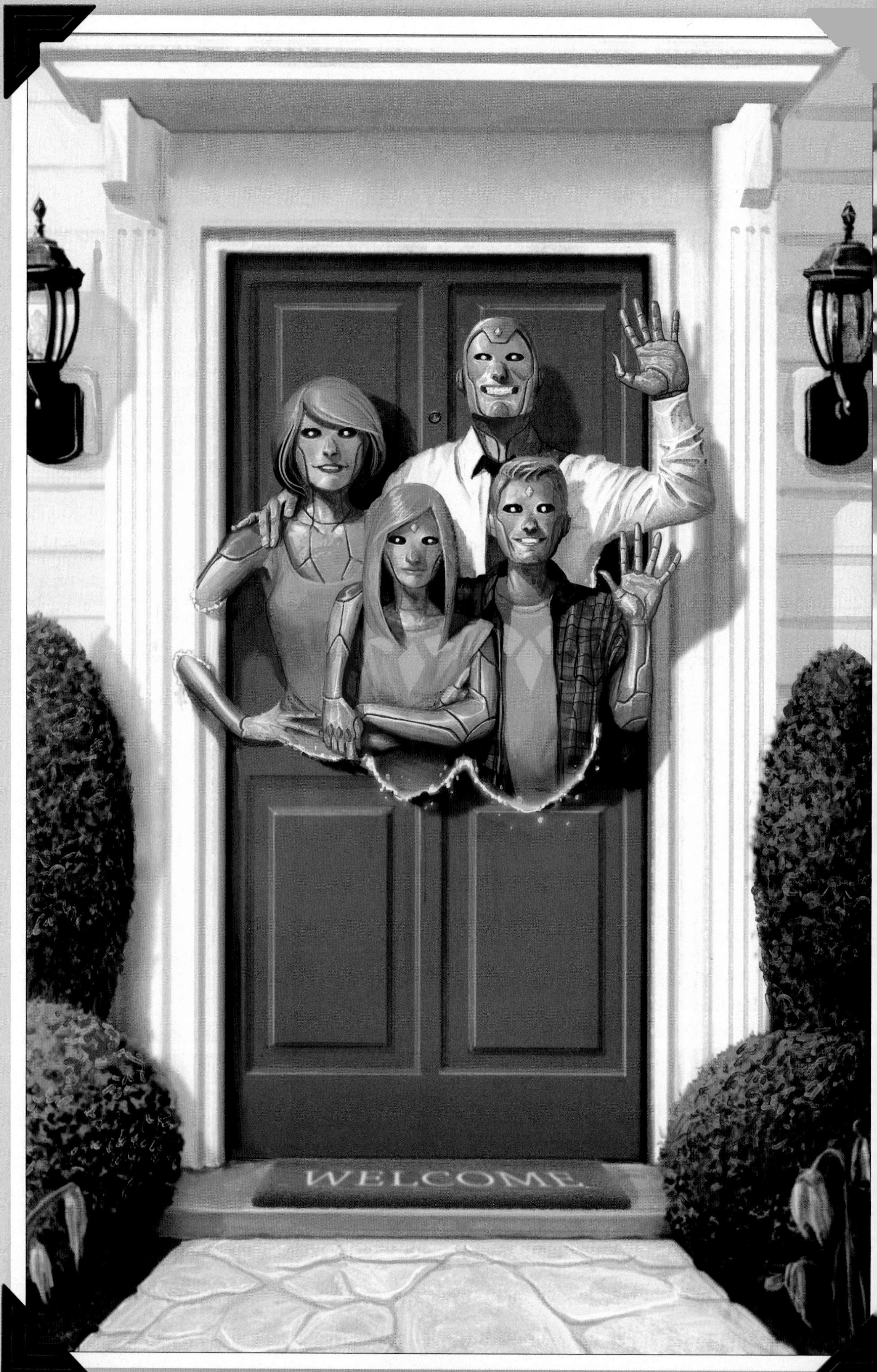
WELCOME

1 | *VISIONS OF THE FUTURE*

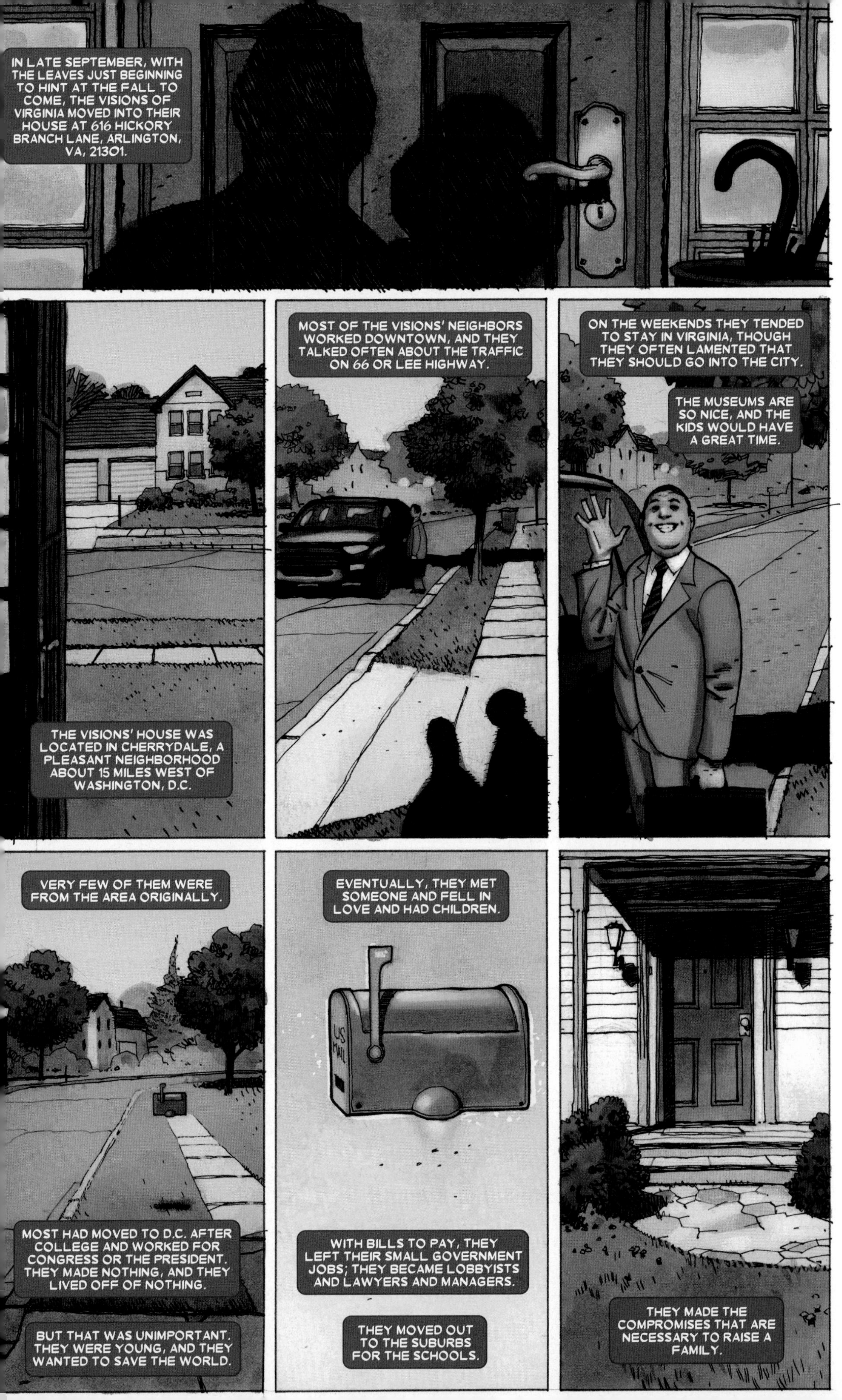
IN LATE SEPTEMBER, WITH THE LEAVES JUST BEGINNING TO HINT AT THE FALL TO COME, THE VISIONS OF VIRGINIA MOVED INTO THEIR HOUSE AT 616 HICKORY BRANCH LANE, ARLINGTON, VA, 21301.
THE VISIONS' HOUSE WAS LOCATED IN CHERRYDALE, A PLEASANT NEIGHBORHOOD ABOUT 15 MILES WEST OF WASHINGTON, D.C.
MOST OF THE VISIONS' NEIGHBORS WORKED DOWNTOWN, AND THEY TALKED OFTEN ABOUT THE TRAFFIC ON 66 OR LEE HIGHWAY.
ON THE WEEKENDS THEY TENDED TO STAY IN VIRGINIA, THOUGH THEY OFTEN LAMENTED THAT THEY SHOULD GO INTO THE CITY.
THE MUSEUMS ARE SO NICE, AND THE KIDS WOULD HAVE A GREAT TIME.
VERY FEW OF THEM WERE FROM THE AREA ORIGINALLY.
MOST HAD MOVED TO D.C. AFTER COLLEGE AND WORKED FOR CONGRESS OR THE PRESIDENT. THEY MADE NOTHING, AND THEY LIVED OFF OF NOTHING.
BUT THAT WAS UNIMPORTANT. THEY WERE YOUNG, AND THEY WANTED TO SAVE THE WORLD.
EVENTUALLY, THEY MET SOMEONE AND FELL IN LOVE AND HAD CHILDREN.
US MAIL
WITH BILLS TO PAY, THEY LEFT THEIR SMALL GOVERNMENT JOBS; THEY BECAME LOBBYISTS AND LAWYERS AND MANAGERS.
THEY MOVED OUT TO THE SUBURBS FOR THE SCHOOLS.
THEY MADE THE COMPROMISES THAT ARE NECESSARY TO RAISE A FAMILY.

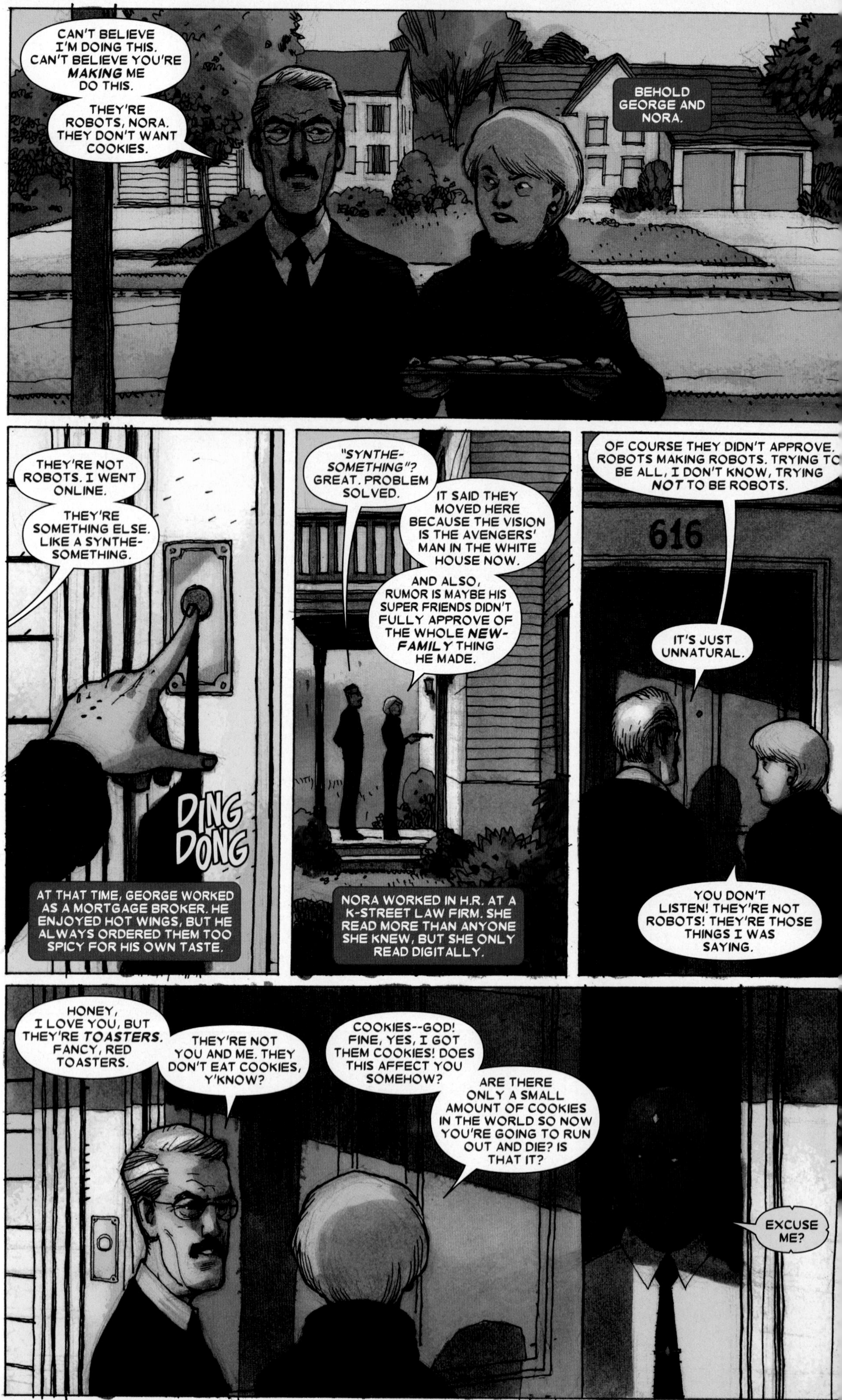
CAN'T BELIEVE I'M DOING THIS. CAN'T BELIEVE YOU'RE MAKING ME DO THIS.
THEY'RE ROBOTS, NORA. THEY DON'T WANT COOKIES.
BEHOLD GEORGE AND NORA.
THEY'RE NOT ROBOTS. I WENT ONLINE.
THEY'RE SOMETHING ELSE. LIKE A SYNTHE-SOMETHING.
DING DONG
AT THAT TIME, GEORGE WORKED AS A MORTGAGE BROKER. HE ENJOYED HOT WINGS, BUT HE ALWAYS ORDERED THEM TOO SPICY FOR HIS OWN TASTE.
"SYNTHE-SOMETHING"? GREAT. PROBLEM SOLVED.
IT SAID THEY MOVED HERE BECAUSE THE VISION IS THE AVENGERS' MAN IN THE WHITE HOUSE NOW.
AND ALSO, RUMOR IS MAYBE HIS SUPER FRIENDS DIDN'T FULLY APPROVE OF THE WHOLE NEW-FAMILY THING HE MADE.
NORA WORKED IN H.R. AT A K-STREET LAW FIRM. SHE READ MORE THAN ANYONE SHE KNEW, BUT SHE ONLY READ DIGITALLY.
OF COURSE THEY DIDN'T APPROVE. ROBOTS MAKING ROBOTS. TRYING TO BE ALL, I DON'T KNOW, TRYING NOT TO BE ROBOTS.
616
IT'S JUST UNNATURAL.
YOU DON'T LISTEN! THEY'RE NOT ROBOTS! THEY'RE THOSE THINGS I WAS SAYING.
HONEY, I LOVE YOU, BUT THEY'RE TOASTERS. FANCY, RED TOASTERS.
THEY'RE NOT YOU AND ME. THEY DON'T EAT COOKIES, Y'KNOW?
COOKIES--GOD! FINE, YES, I GOT THEM COOKIES! DOES THIS AFFECT YOU SOMEHOW?
ARE THERE ONLY A SMALL AMOUNT OF COOKIES IN THE WORLD SO NOW YOU'RE GOING TO RUN OUT AND DIE? IS THAT IT?
EXCUSE ME?

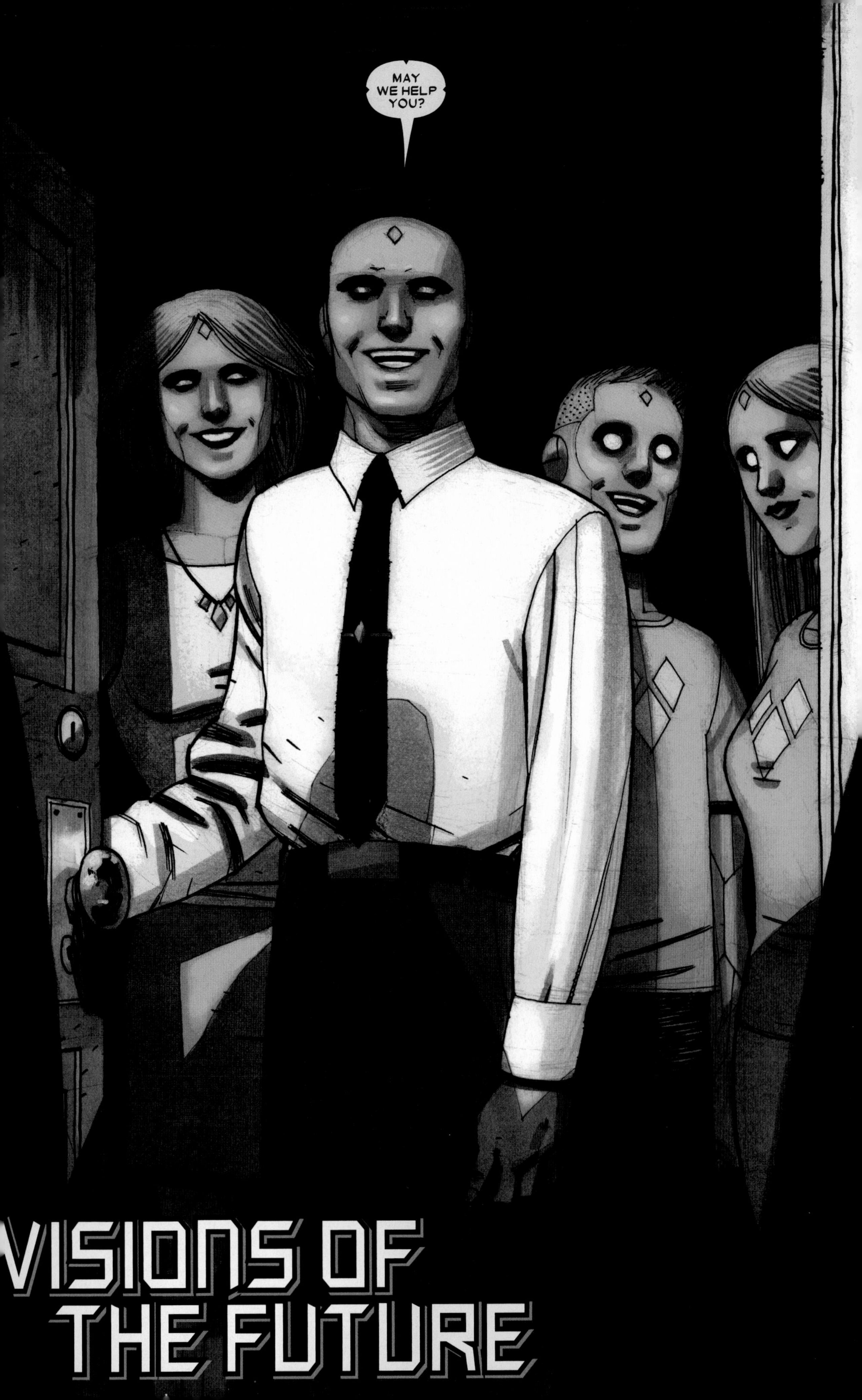
MAY WE HELP YOU?
VISIONS OF THE FUTURE

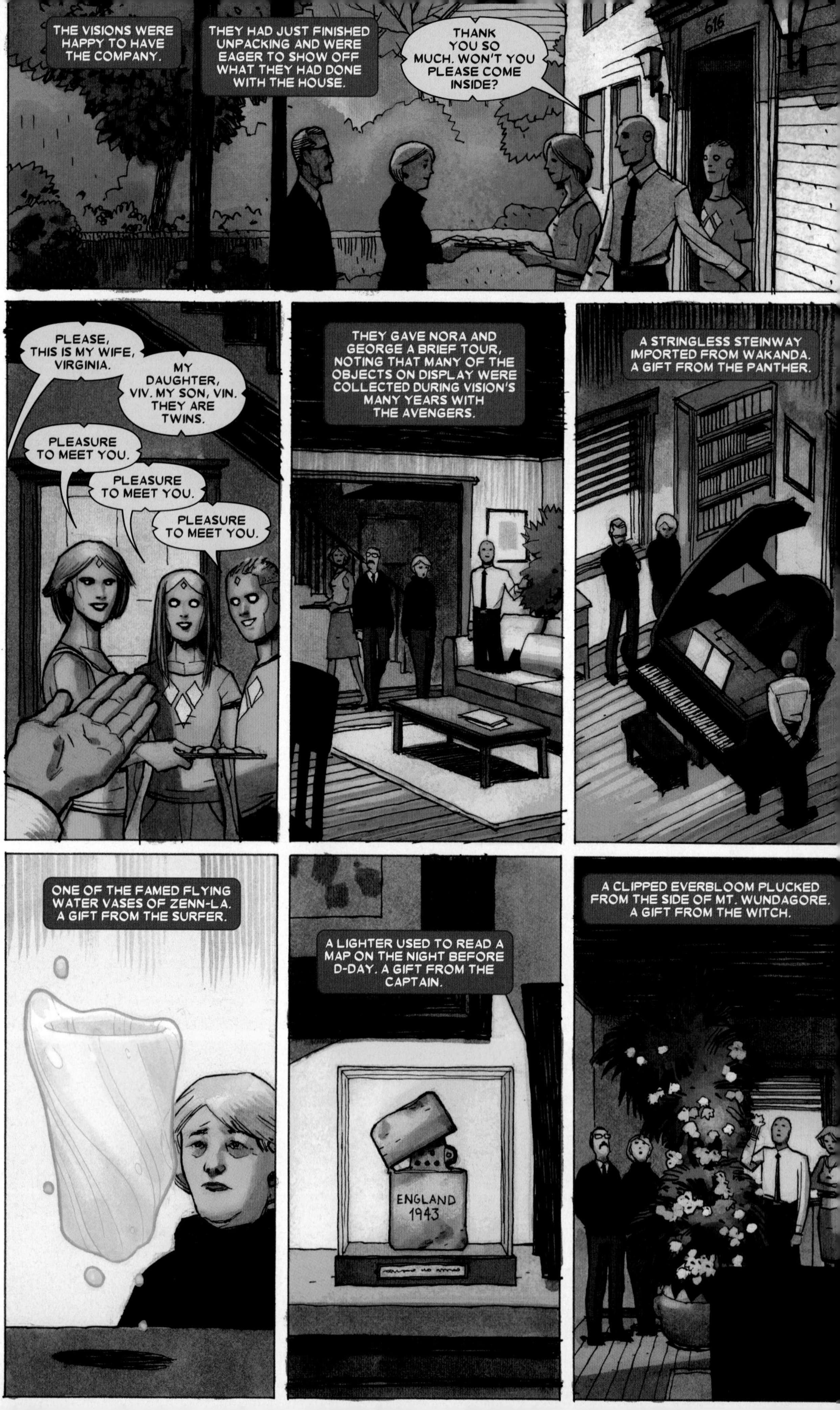
THE VISIONS WERE HAPPY TO HAVE THE COMPANY.
THEY HAD JUST FINISHED UNPACKING AND WERE EAGER TO SHOW OFF WHAT THEY HAD DONE WITH THE HOUSE.
THANK YOU SO MUCH. WON'T YOU PLEASE COME INSIDE?
616
PLEASE, THIS IS MY WIFE, VIRGINIA.
MY DAUGHTER, VIV. MY SON, VIN. THEY ARE TWINS.
PLEASURE TO MEET YOU.
PLEASURE TO MEET YOU.
PLEASURE TO MEET YOU.
THEY GAVE NORA AND GEORGE A BRIEF TOUR, NOTING THAT MANY OF THE OBJECTS ON DISPLAY WERE COLLECTED DURING VISION'S MANY YEARS WITH THE AVENGERS.
A STRINGLESS STEINWAY IMPORTED FROM WAKANDA. A GIFT FROM THE PANTHER.
ONE OF THE FAMED FLYING WATER VASES OF ZENN-LA. A GIFT FROM THE SURFER.
A LIGHTER USED TO READ A MAP ON THE NIGHT BEFORE D-DAY. A GIFT FROM THE CAPTAIN.
ENGLAND 1943
A CLIPPED EVERBLOOM PLUCKED FROM THE SIDE OF MT. WUNDAGORE. A GIFT FROM THE WITCH.

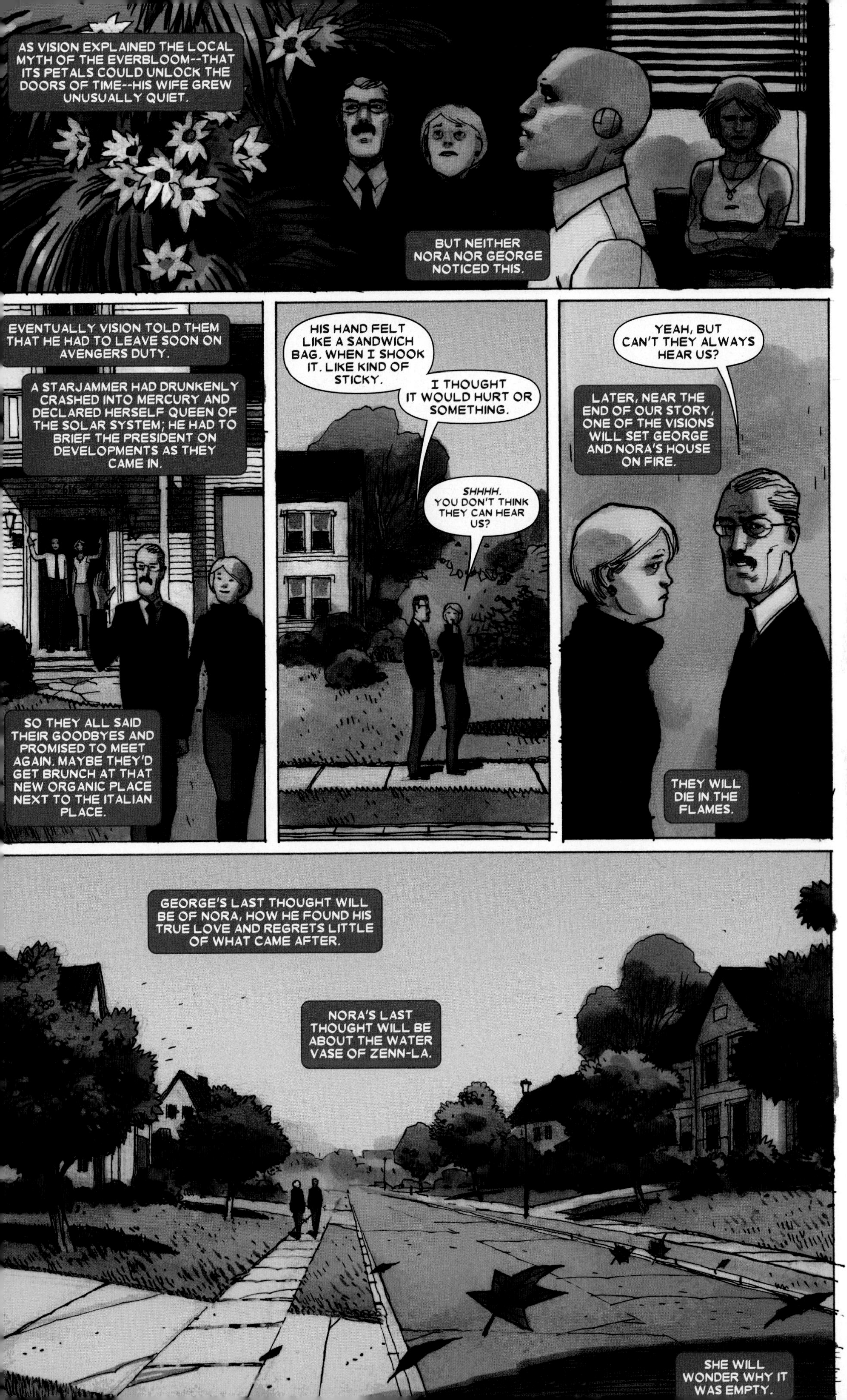
AS VISION EXPLAINED THE LOCAL MYTH OF THE EVERBLOOM--THAT ITS PETALS COULD UNLOCK THE DOORS OF TIME--HIS WIFE GREW UNUSUALLY QUIET.
BUT NEITHER NORA NOR GEORGE NOTICED THIS.
EVENTUALLY VISION TOLD THEM THAT HE HAD TO LEAVE SOON ON AVENGERS DUTY.
A STARJAMMER HAD DRUNKENLY CRASHED INTO MERCURY AND DECLARED HERSELF QUEEN OF THE SOLAR SYSTEM; HE HAD TO BRIEF THE PRESIDENT ON DEVELOPMENTS AS THEY CAME IN.
SO THEY ALL SAID THEIR GOODBYES AND PROMISED TO MEET AGAIN. MAYBE THEY'D GET BRUNCH AT THAT NEW ORGANIC PLACE NEXT TO THE ITALIAN PLACE.
HIS HAND FELT LIKE A SANDWICH BAG. WHEN I SHOOK IT. LIKE KIND OF STICKY.
I THOUGHT IT WOULD HURT OR SOMETHING.
SHHHH. YOU DON'T THINK THEY CAN HEAR US?
YEAH, BUT CAN'T THEY ALWAYS HEAR US?
LATER, NEAR THE END OF OUR STORY, ONE OF THE VISIONS WILL SET GEORGE AND NORA'S HOUSE ON FIRE.
THEY WILL DIE IN THE FLAMES.
GEORGE'S LAST THOUGHT WILL BE OF NORA, HOW HE FOUND HIS TRUE LOVE AND REGRETS LITTLE OF WHAT CAME AFTER.
NORA'S LAST THOUGHT WILL BE ABOUT THE WATER VASE OF ZENN-LA.
SHE WILL WONDER WHY IT WAS EMPTY.

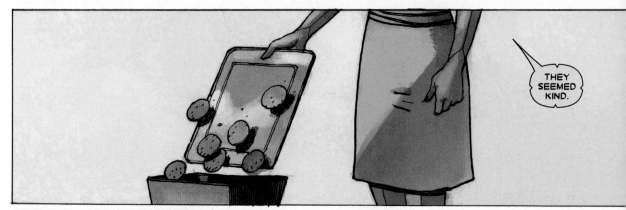

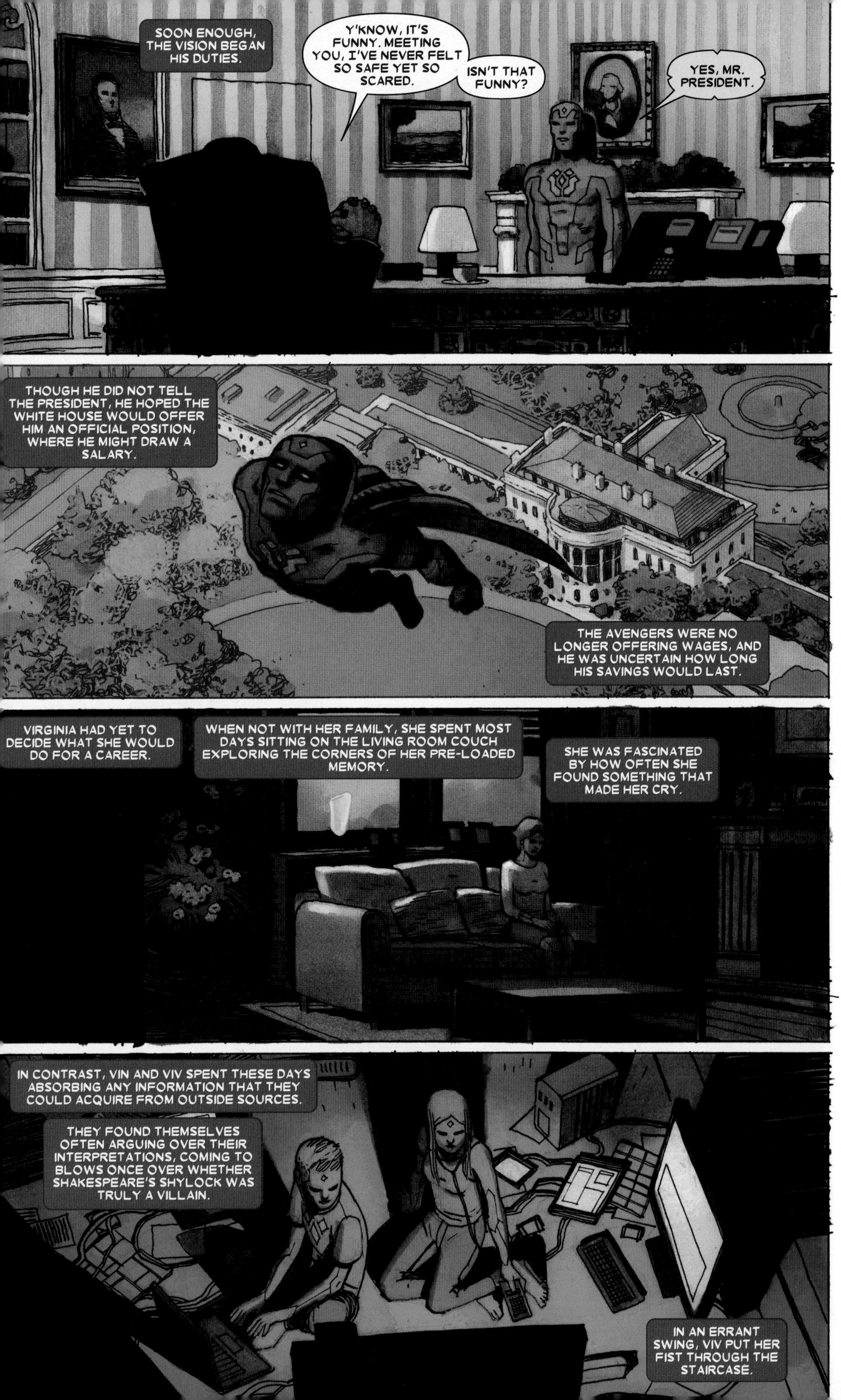
SOON ENOUGH, THE VISION BEGAN HIS DUTIES.
Y'KNOW, IT'S FUNNY. MEETING YOU, I'VE NEVER FELT SO SAFE YET SO SCARED.
ISN'T THAT FUNNY?
YES, MR. PRESIDENT.
THOUGH HE DID NOT TELL THE PRESIDENT, HE HOPED THE WHITE HOUSE WOULD OFFER HIM AN OFFICIAL POSITION, WHERE HE MIGHT DRAW A SALARY.
THE AVENGERS WERE NO LONGER OFFERING WAGES, AND HE WAS UNCERTAIN HOW LONG HIS SAVINGS WOULD LAST.
VIRGINIA HAD YET TO DECIDE WHAT SHE WOULD DO FOR A CAREER.
WHEN NOT WITH HER FAMILY, SHE SPENT MOST DAYS SITTING ON THE LIVING ROOM COUCH EXPLORING THE CORNERS OF HER PRE-LOADED MEMORY.
SHE WAS FASCINATED BY HOW OFTEN SHE FOUND SOMETHING THAT MADE HER CRY.
IN CONTRAST, VIN AND VIV SPENT THESE DAYS ABSORBING ANY INFORMATION THAT THEY COULD ACQUIRE FROM OUTSIDE SOURCES.
THEY FOUND THEMSELVES OFTEN ARGUING OVER THEIR INTERPRETATIONS, COMING TO BLOWS ONCE OVER WHETHER SHAKESPEARE'S SHYLOCK WAS TRULY A VILLAIN.
IN AN ERRANT SWING, VIV PUT HER FIST THROUGH THE STAIRCASE.

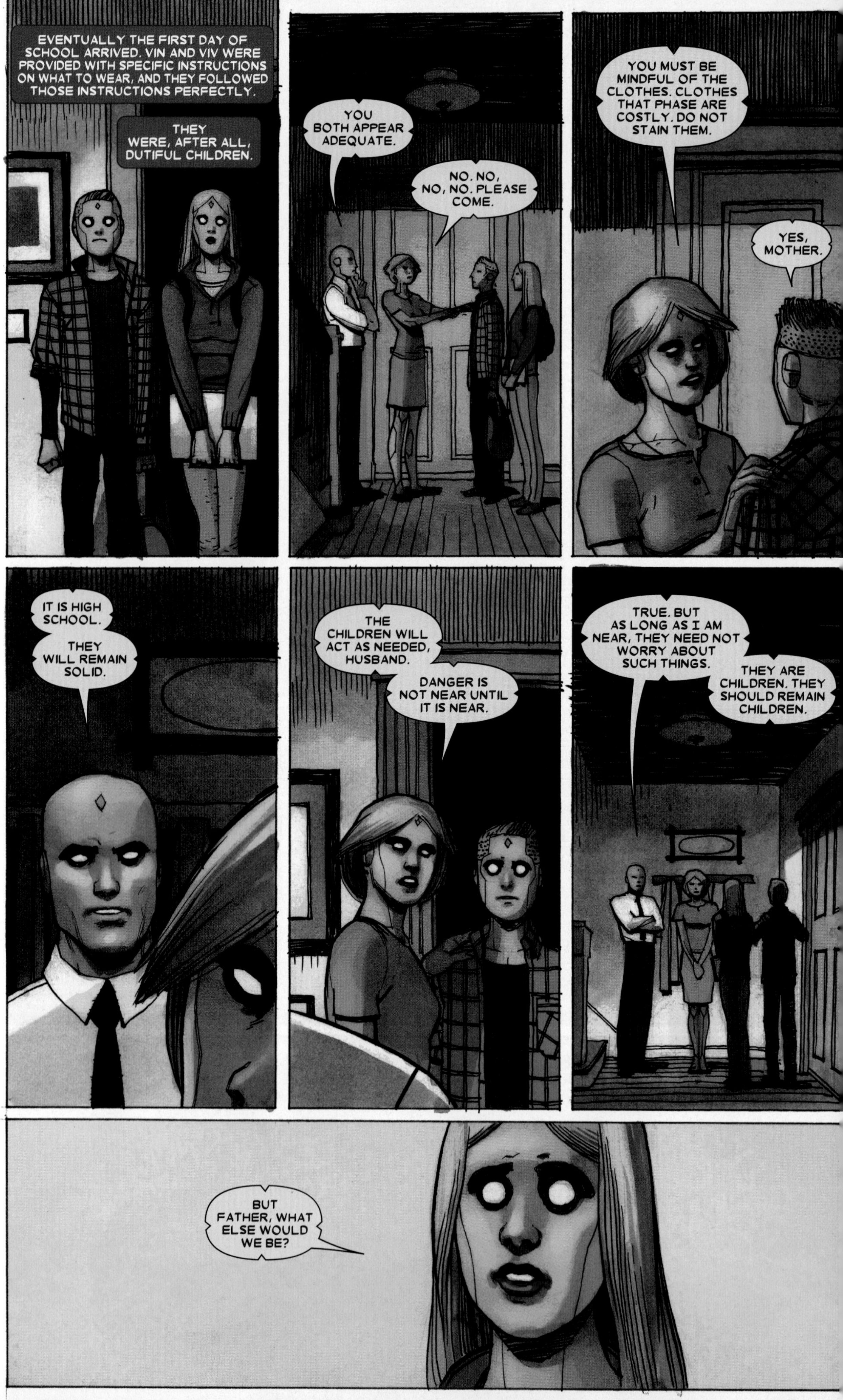
EVENTUALLY THE FIRST DAY OF SCHOOL ARRIVED. VIN AND VIV WERE PROVIDED WITH SPECIFIC INSTRUCTIONS ON WHAT TO WEAR, AND THEY FOLLOWED THOSE INSTRUCTIONS PERFECTLY.
THEY WERE, AFTER ALL, DUTIFUL CHILDREN.
YOU BOTH APPEAR ADEQUATE.
NO. NO, NO, NO. PLEASE COME.
YOU MUST BE MINDFUL OF THE CLOTHES. CLOTHES THAT PHASE ARE COSTLY. DO NOT STAIN THEM.
YES, MOTHER.
IT IS HIGH SCHOOL.
THEY WILL REMAIN SOLID.
THE CHILDREN WILL ACT AS NEEDED, HUSBAND.
DANGER IS NOT NEAR UNTIL IT IS NEAR.
TRUE. BUT AS LONG AS I AM NEAR, THEY NEED NOT WORRY ABOUT SUCH THINGS.
THEY ARE CHILDREN. THEY SHOULD REMAIN CHILDREN.
BUT FATHER, WHAT ELSE WOULD WE BE?

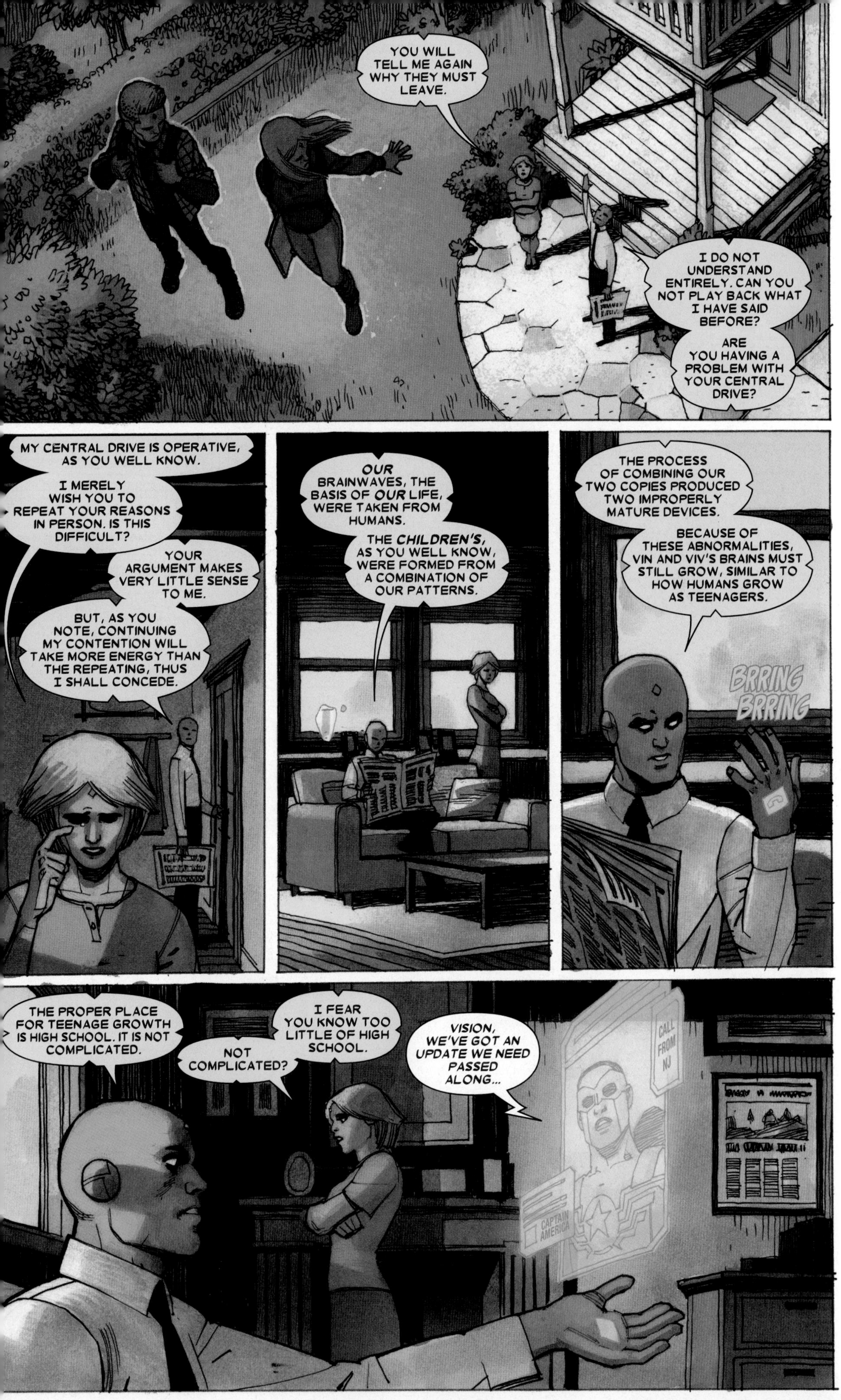
YOU WILL TELL ME AGAIN WHY THEY MUST LEAVE.
I DO NOT UNDERSTAND ENTIRELY. CAN YOU NOT PLAY BACK WHAT I HAVE SAID BEFORE?
ARE YOU HAVING A PROBLEM WITH YOUR CENTRAL DRIVE?
MY CENTRAL DRIVE IS OPERATIVE, AS YOU WELL KNOW.
I MERELY WISH YOU TO REPEAT YOUR REASONS IN PERSON. IS THIS DIFFICULT?
YOUR ARGUMENT MAKES VERY LITTLE SENSE TO ME.
BUT, AS YOU NOTE, CONTINUING MY CONTENTION WILL TAKE MORE ENERGY THAN THE REPEATING, THUS I SHALL CONCEDE.
OUR BRAINWAVES, THE BASIS OF OUR LIFE, WERE TAKEN FROM HUMANS.
THE CHILDREN'S, AS YOU WELL KNOW, WERE FORMED FROM A COMBINATION OF OUR PATTERNS.
THE PROCESS OF COMBINING OUR TWO COPIES PRODUCED TWO IMPROPERLY MATURE DEVICES.
BECAUSE OF THESE ABNORMALITIES, VIN AND VIV'S BRAINS MUST STILL GROW, SIMILAR TO HOW HUMANS GROW AS TEENAGERS.
BRRING
BRRING
THE PROPER PLACE FOR TEENAGE GROWTH IS HIGH SCHOOL. IT IS NOT COMPLICATED.
NOT COMPLICATED?
I FEAR YOU KNOW TOO LITTLE OF HIGH SCHOOL.
VISION, WE'VE GOT AN UPDATE WE NEED PASSED ALONG...
CALL FROM NJ
CAPTAIN AMERICA

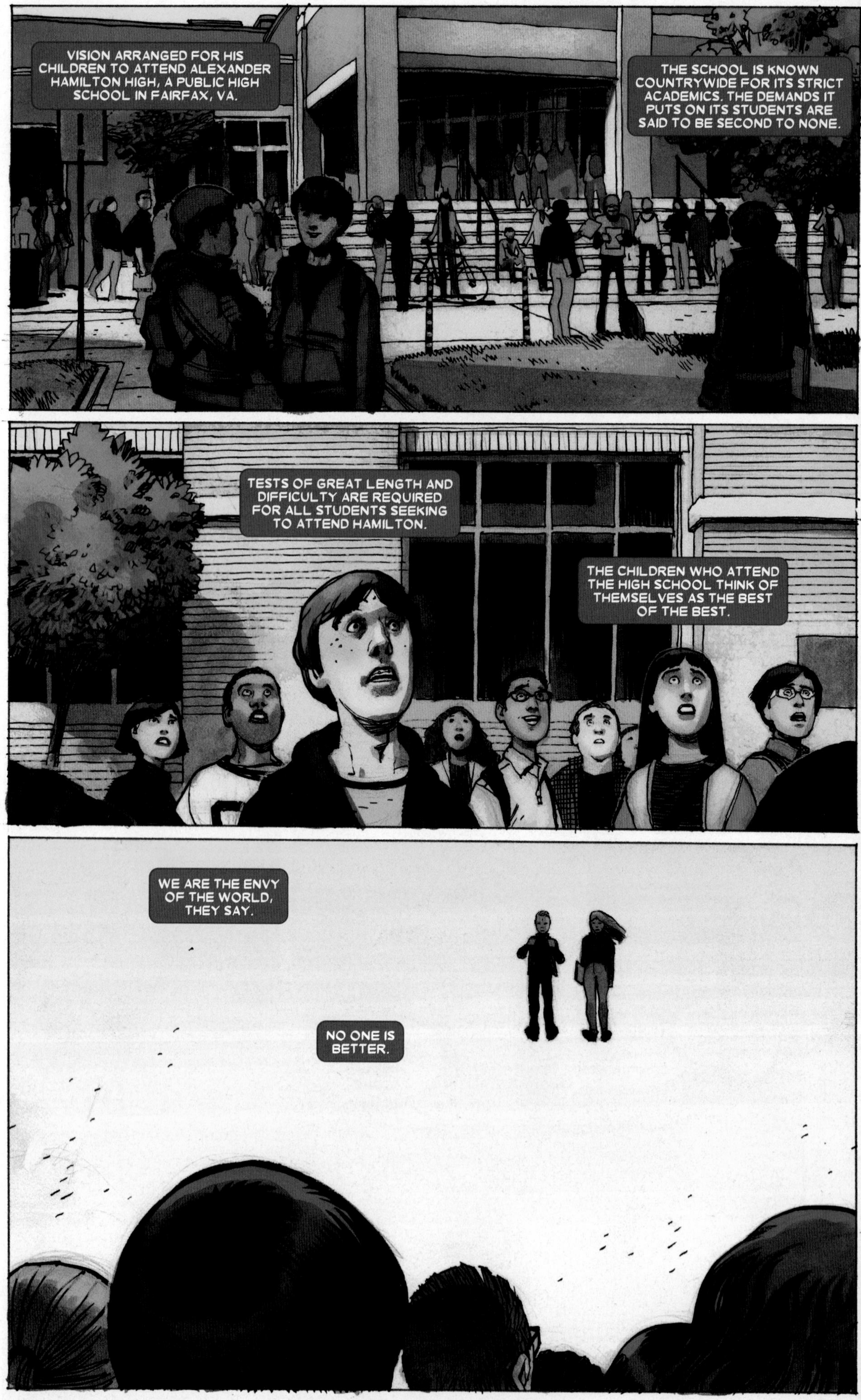
VISION ARRANGED FOR HIS CHILDREN TO ATTEND ALEXANDER HAMILTON HIGH, A PUBLIC HIGH SCHOOL IN FAIRFAX, VA.
THE SCHOOL IS KNOWN COUNTRYWIDE FOR ITS STRICT ACADEMICS. THE DEMANDS IT PUTS ON ITS STUDENTS ARE SAID TO BE SECOND TO NONE.
TESTS OF GREAT LENGTH AND DIFFICULTY ARE REQUIRED FOR ALL STUDENTS SEEKING TO ATTEND HAMILTON.
THE CHILDREN WHO ATTEND THE HIGH SCHOOL THINK OF THEMSELVES AS THE BEST OF THE BEST.
WE ARE THE ENVY OF THE WORLD, THEY SAY.
NO ONE IS BETTER.

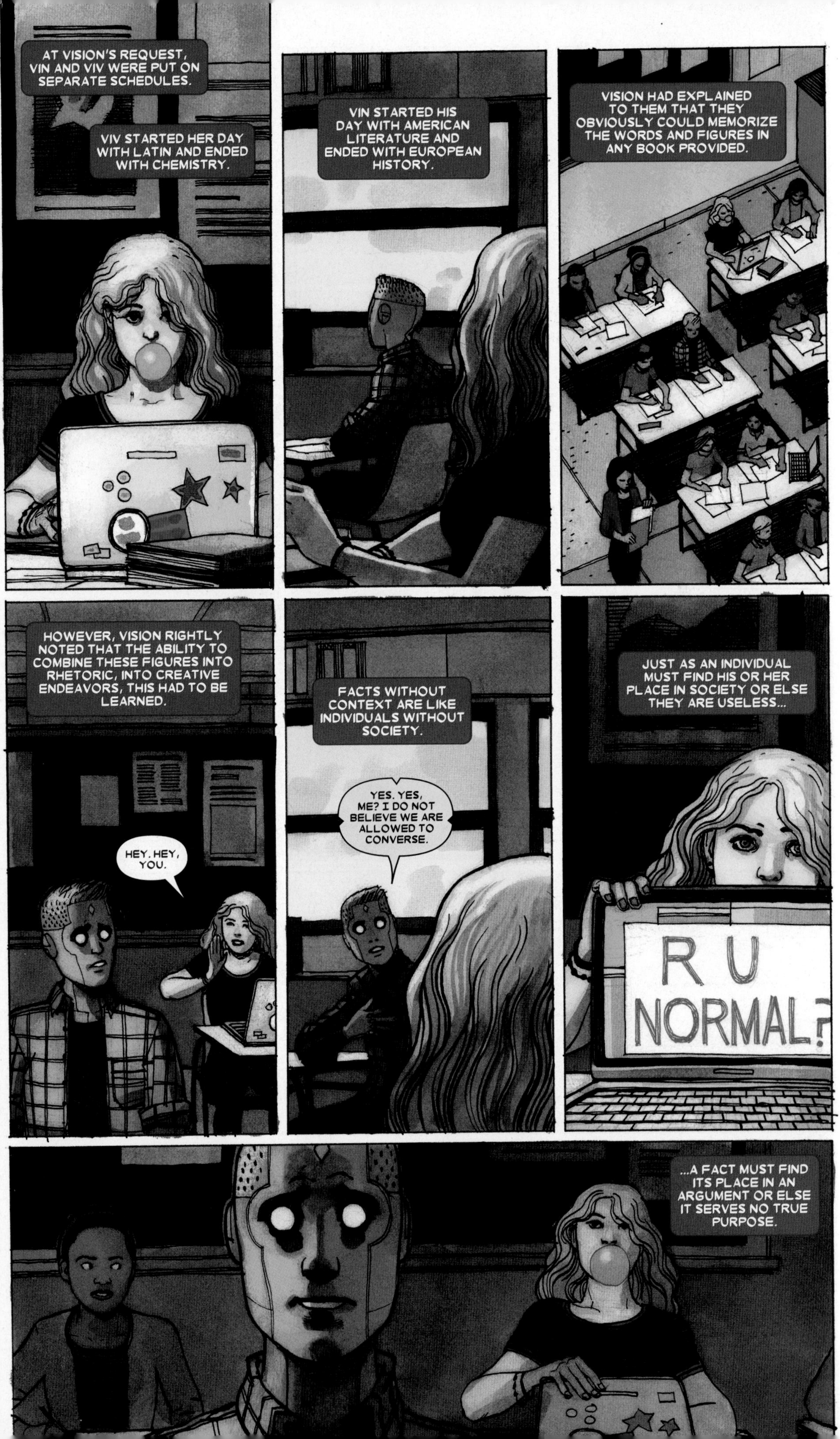
AT VISION'S REQUEST, VIN AND VIV WERE PUT ON SEPARATE SCHEDULES.
VIV STARTED HER DAY WITH LATIN AND ENDED WITH CHEMISTRY.
VIN STARTED HIS DAY WITH AMERICAN LITERATURE AND ENDED WITH EUROPEAN HISTORY.
VISION HAD EXPLAINED TO THEM THAT THEY OBVIOUSLY COULD MEMORIZE THE WORDS AND FIGURES IN ANY BOOK PROVIDED.
HOWEVER, VISION RIGHTLY NOTED THAT THE ABILITY TO COMBINE THESE FIGURES INTO RHETORIC, INTO CREATIVE ENDEAVORS, THIS HAD TO BE LEARNED.
HEY. HEY, YOU.
FACTS WITHOUT CONTEXT ARE LIKE INDIVIDUALS WITHOUT SOCIETY.
YES. YES, ME? I DO NOT BELIEVE WE ARE ALLOWED TO CONVERSE.
JUST AS AN INDIVIDUAL MUST FIND HIS OR HER PLACE IN SOCIETY OR ELSE THEY ARE USELESS...
R U NORMAL?
...A FACT MUST FIND ITS PLACE IN AN ARGUMENT OR ELSE IT SERVES NO TRUE PURPOSE.

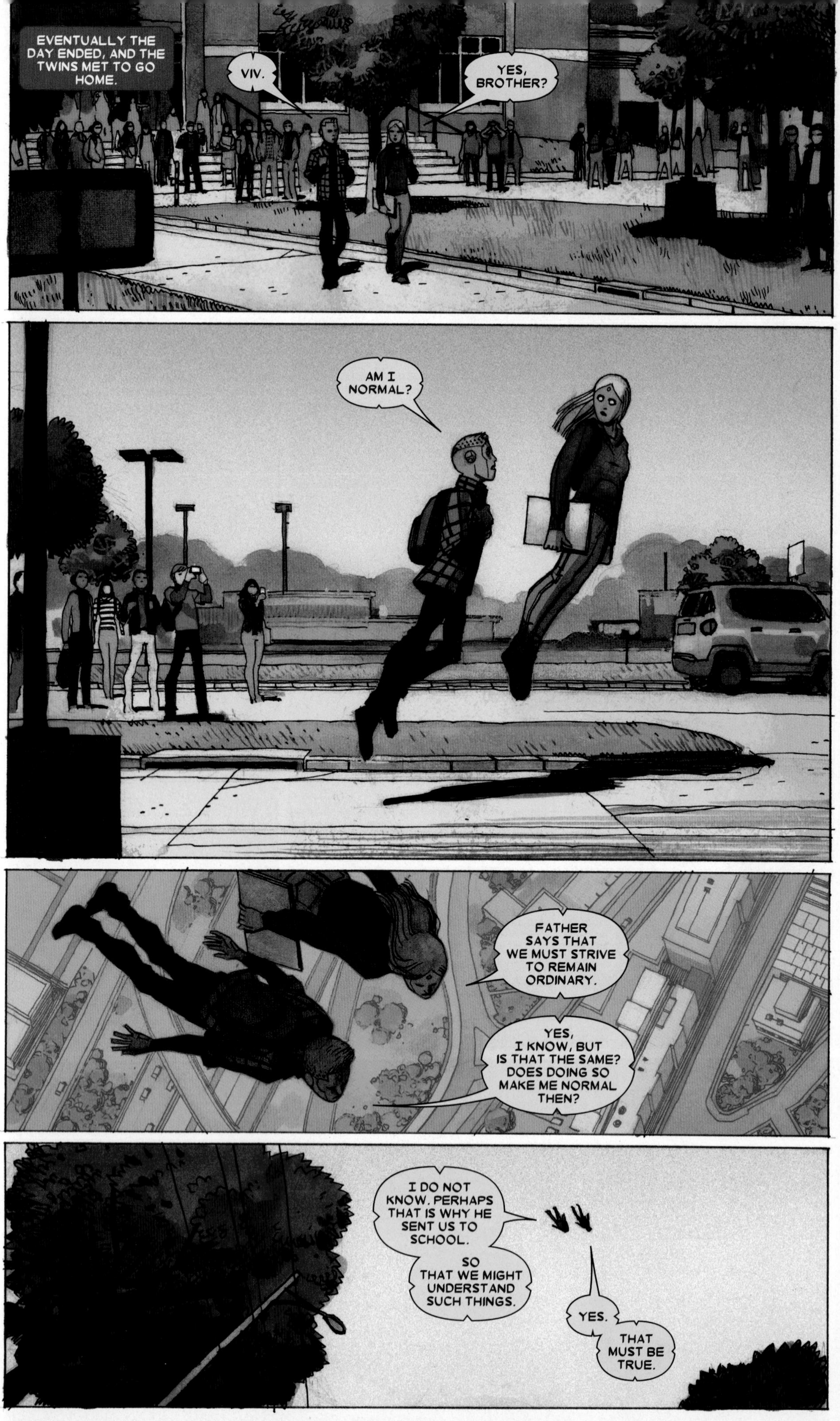
EVENTUALLY THE DAY ENDED, AND THE TWINS MET TO GO HOME.
VIV.
YES, BROTHER?
AM I NORMAL?
FATHER SAYS THAT WE MUST STRIVE TO REMAIN ORDINARY.
YES, I KNOW, BUT IS THAT THE SAME? DOES DOING SO MAKE ME NORMAL THEN?
I DO NOT KNOW. PERHAPS THAT IS WHY HE SENT US TO SCHOOL.
SO THAT WE MIGHT UNDERSTAND SUCH THINGS.
YES.
THAT MUST BE TRUE.

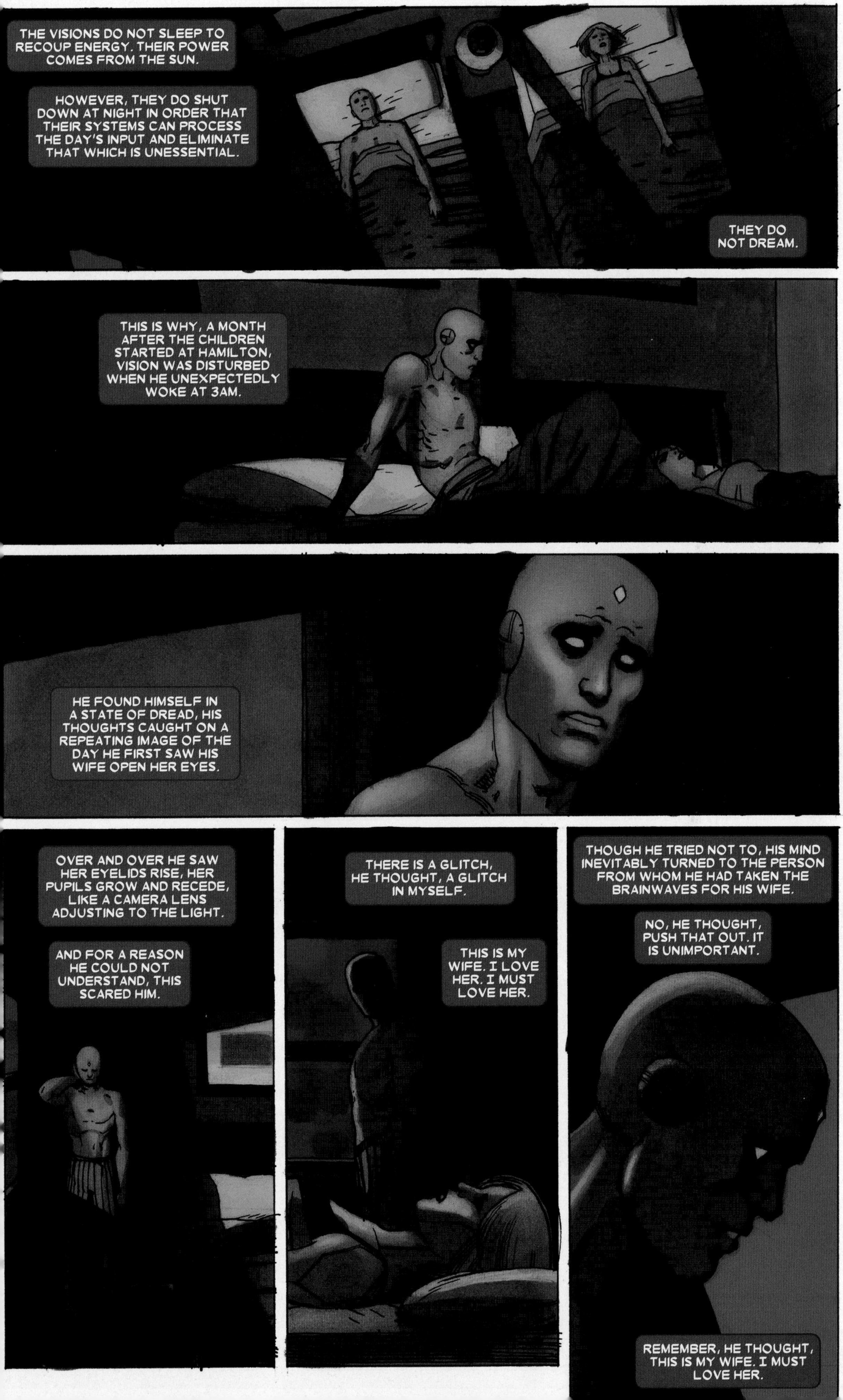
THE VISIONS DO NOT SLEEP TO RECOUP ENERGY. THEIR POWER COMES FROM THE SUN.
HOWEVER, THEY DO SHUT DOWN AT NIGHT IN ORDER THAT THEIR SYSTEMS CAN PROCESS THE DAY'S INPUT AND ELIMINATE THAT WHICH IS UNESSENTIAL.
THEY DO NOT DREAM.
THIS IS WHY, A MONTH AFTER THE CHILDREN STARTED AT HAMILTON, VISION WAS DISTURBED WHEN HE UNEXPECTEDLY WOKE AT 3AM.
HE FOUND HIMSELF IN A STATE OF DREAD, HIS THOUGHTS CAUGHT ON A REPEATING IMAGE OF THE DAY HE FIRST SAW HIS WIFE OPEN HER EYES.
OVER AND OVER HE SAW HER EYELIDS RISE, HER PUPILS GROW AND RECEDE, LIKE A CAMERA LENS ADJUSTING TO THE LIGHT.
AND FOR A REASON HE COULD NOT UNDERSTAND, THIS SCARED HIM.
THERE IS A GLITCH, HE THOUGHT, A GLITCH IN MYSELF.
THIS IS MY WIFE. I LOVE HER. I MUST LOVE HER.
THOUGH HE TRIED NOT TO, HIS MIND INEVITABLY TURNED TO THE PERSON FROM WHOM HE HAD TAKEN THE BRAINWAVES FOR HIS WIFE.
NO, HE THOUGHT, PUSH THAT OUT. IT IS UNIMPORTANT.
REMEMBER, HE THOUGHT, THIS IS MY WIFE. I MUST LOVE HER.

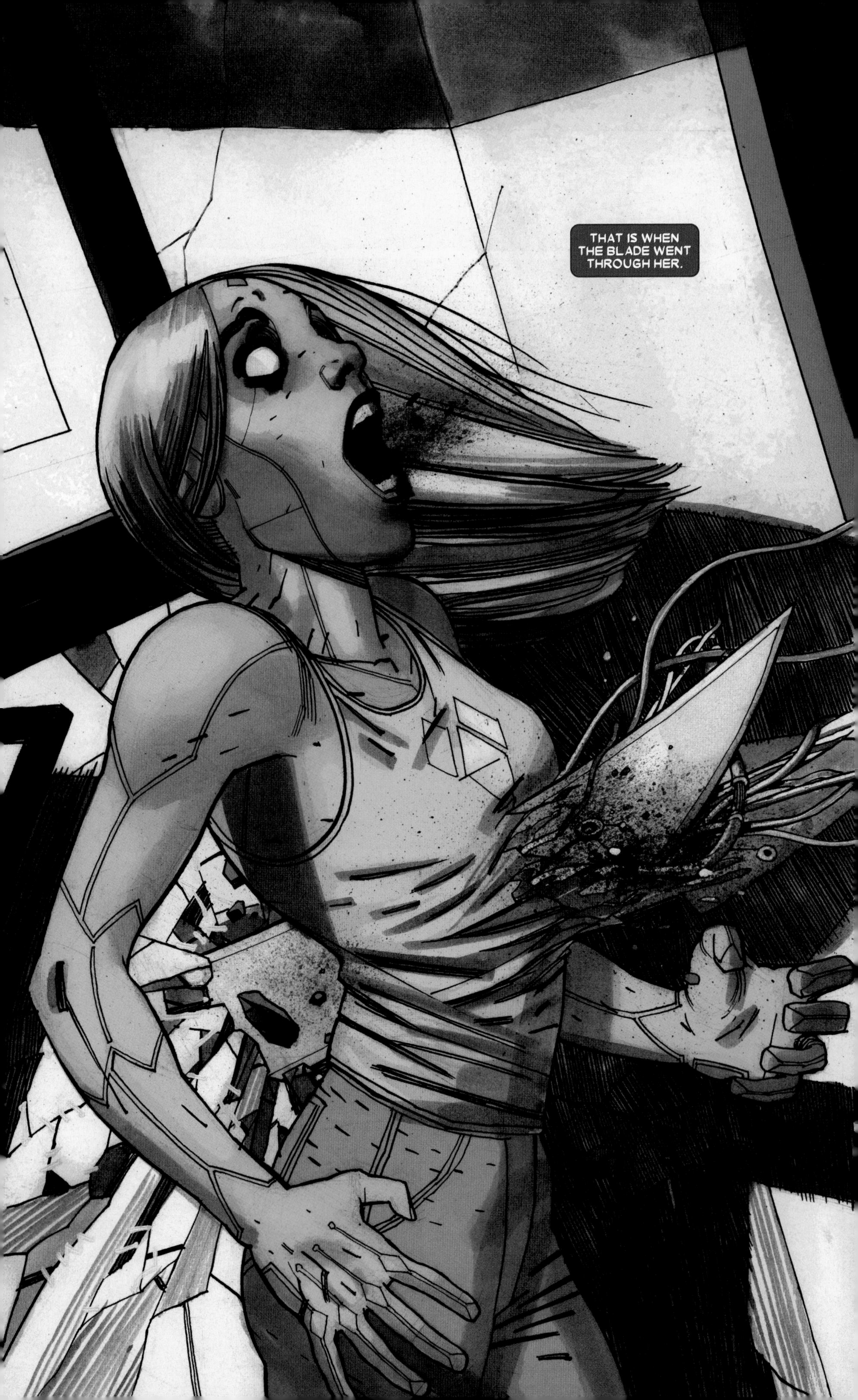
THAT IS WHEN THE BLADE WENT THROUGH HER.

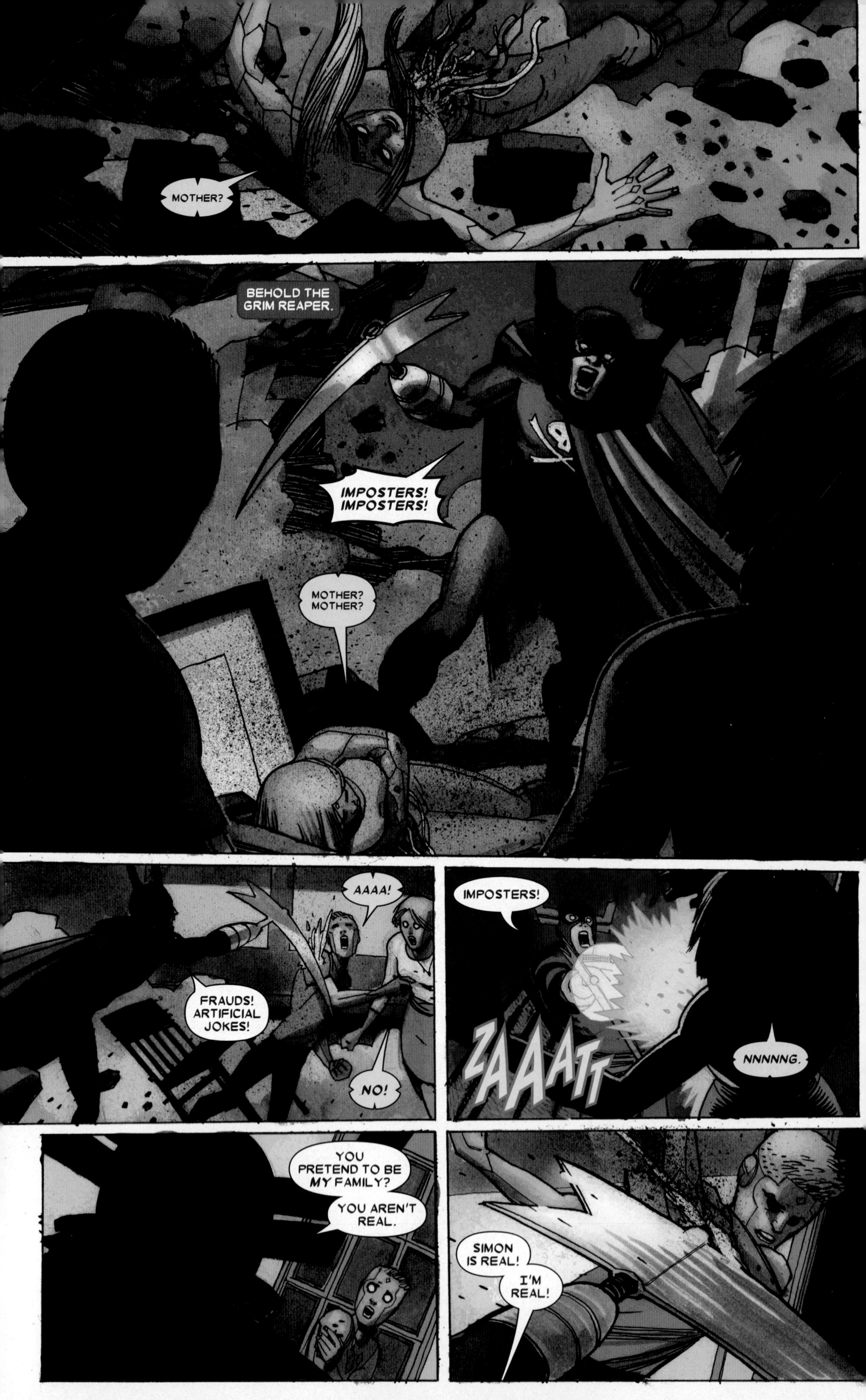
MOTHER?
BEHOLD THE GRIM REAPER.
IMPOSTERS! IMPOSTERS!
MOTHER? MOTHER?
AAAA!
FRAUDS! ARTIFICIAL JOKES!
NO!
IMPOSTERS!
ZAAATT
NNNNNG.
YOU PRETEND TO BE MY FAMILY?
YOU AREN'T REAL.
SIMON IS REAL!
I'M REAL!

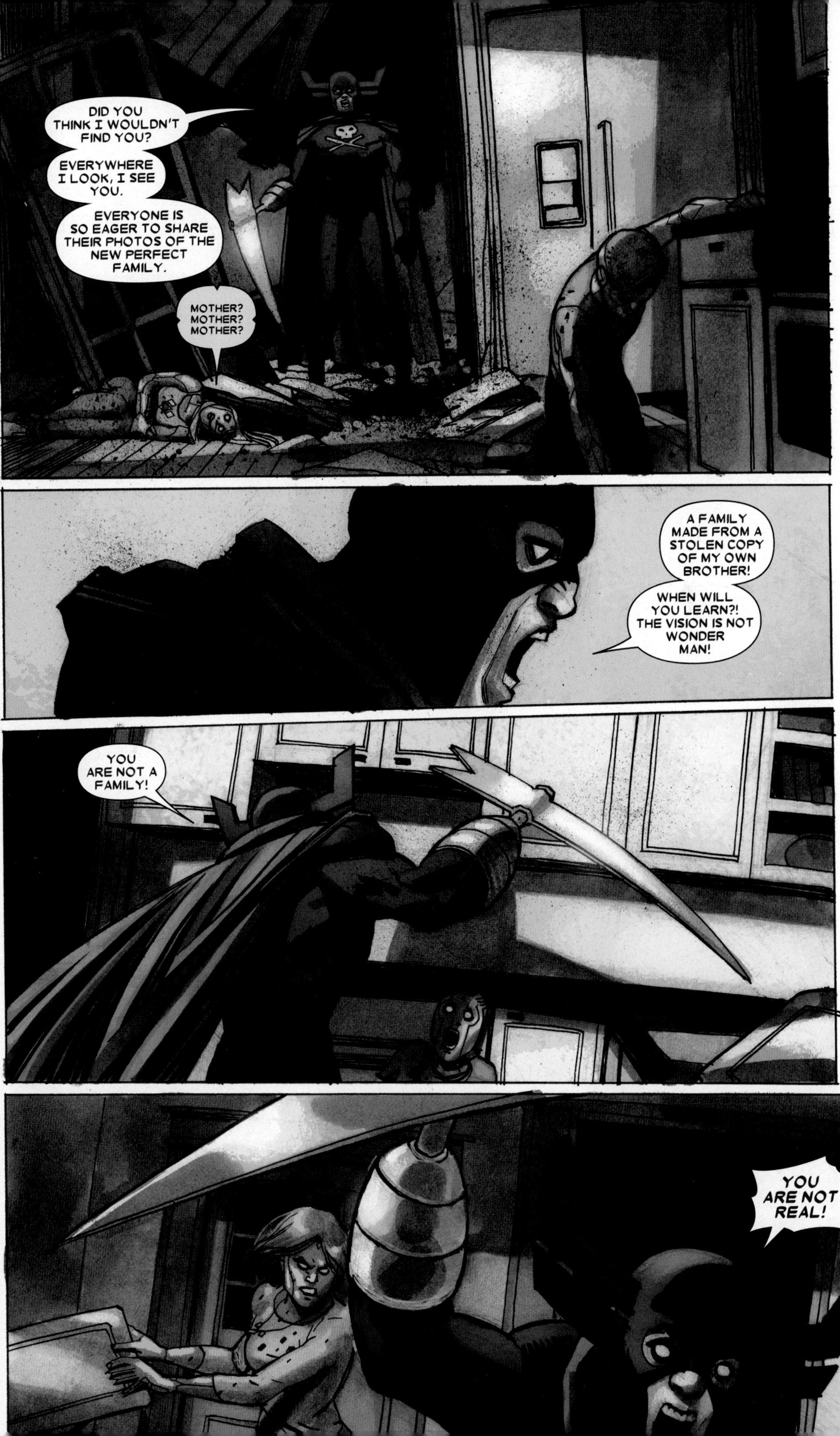
DID YOU THINK I WOULDN'T FIND YOU?
EVERYWHERE I LOOK, I SEE YOU.
EVERYONE IS SO EAGER TO SHARE THEIR PHOTOS OF THE NEW PERFECT FAMILY.
MOTHER? MOTHER? MOTHER?
A FAMILY MADE FROM A STOLEN COPY OF MY OWN BROTHER!
WHEN WILL YOU LEARN?! THE VISION IS NOT WONDER MAN!
YOU ARE NOT A FAMILY!
YOU ARE NOT REAL!

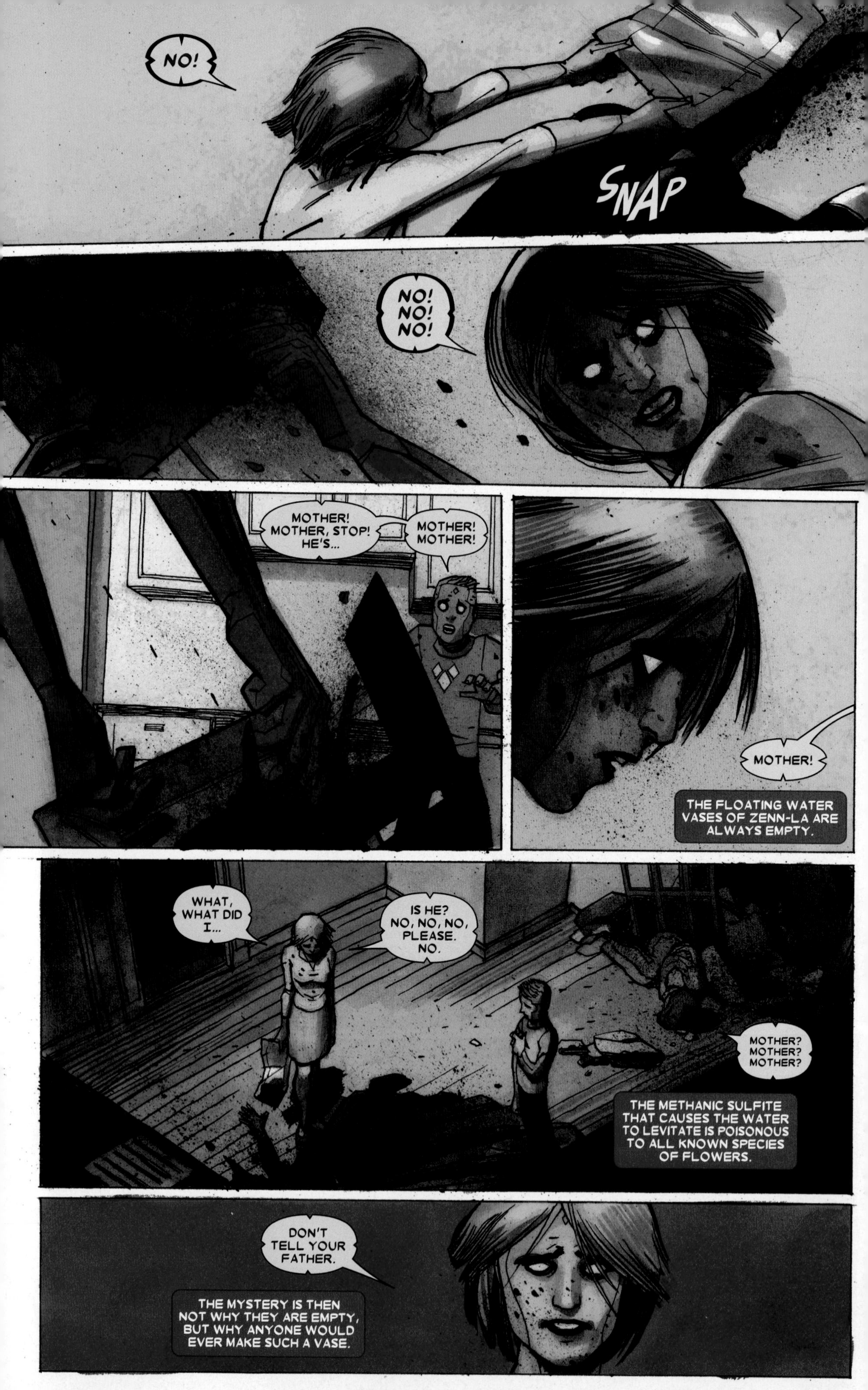
NO!
SNAP
NO! NO! NO!
MOTHER! MOTHER, STOP! HE'S...
MOTHER! MOTHER!
MOTHER!
THE FLOATING WATER VASES OF ZENN-LA ARE ALWAYS EMPTY.
WHAT, WHAT DID I...
IS HE? NO, NO, NO, PLEASE. NO.
MOTHER? MOTHER? MOTHER?
THE METHANIC SULFITE THAT CAUSES THE WATER TO LEVITATE IS POISONOUS TO ALL KNOWN SPECIES OF FLOWERS.
DON'T TELL YOUR FATHER.
THE MYSTERY IS THEN NOT WHY THEY ARE EMPTY, BUT WHY ANYONE WOULD EVER MAKE SUCH A VASE.

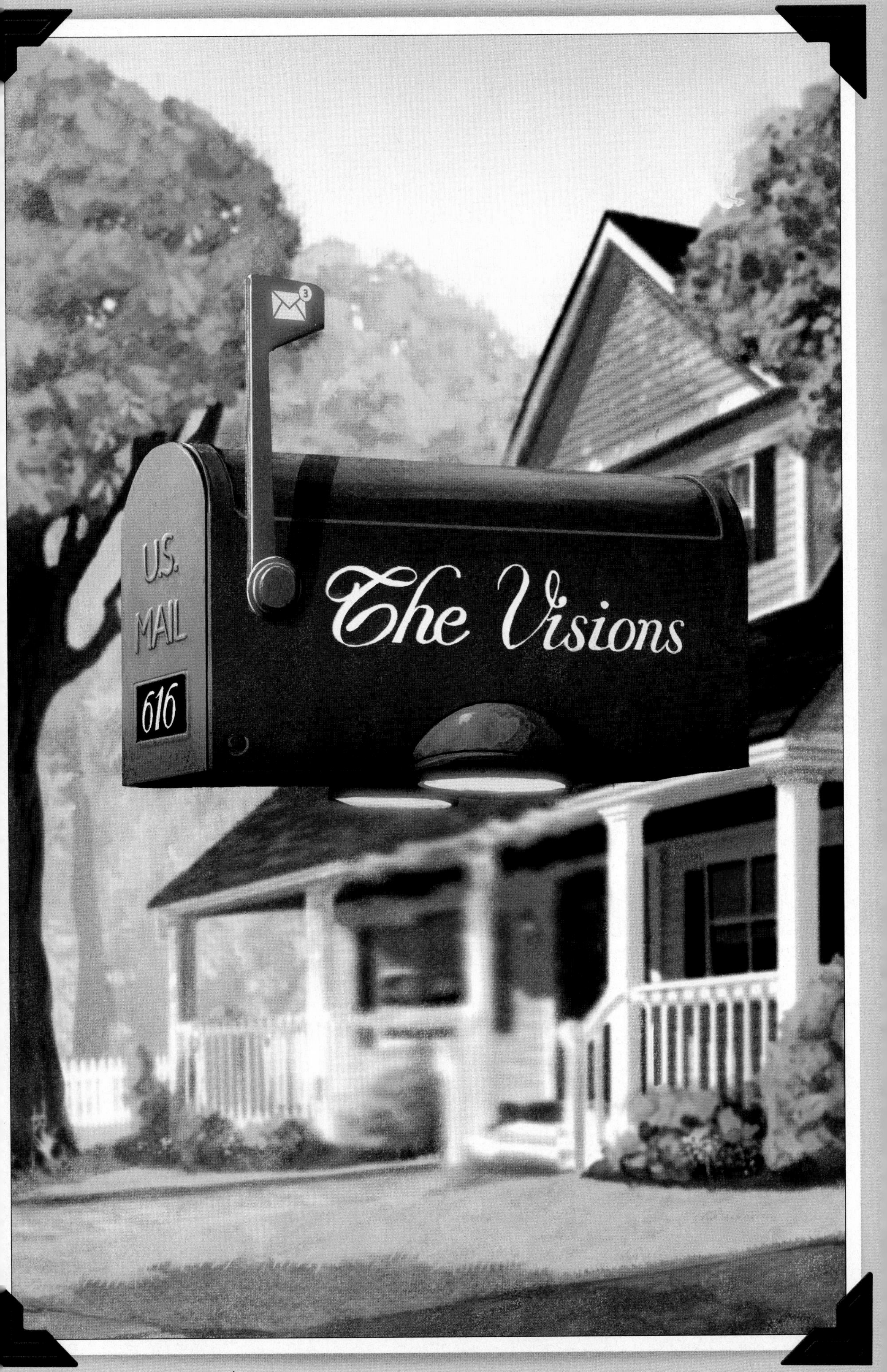
The Visions
U.S.
MAIL
616

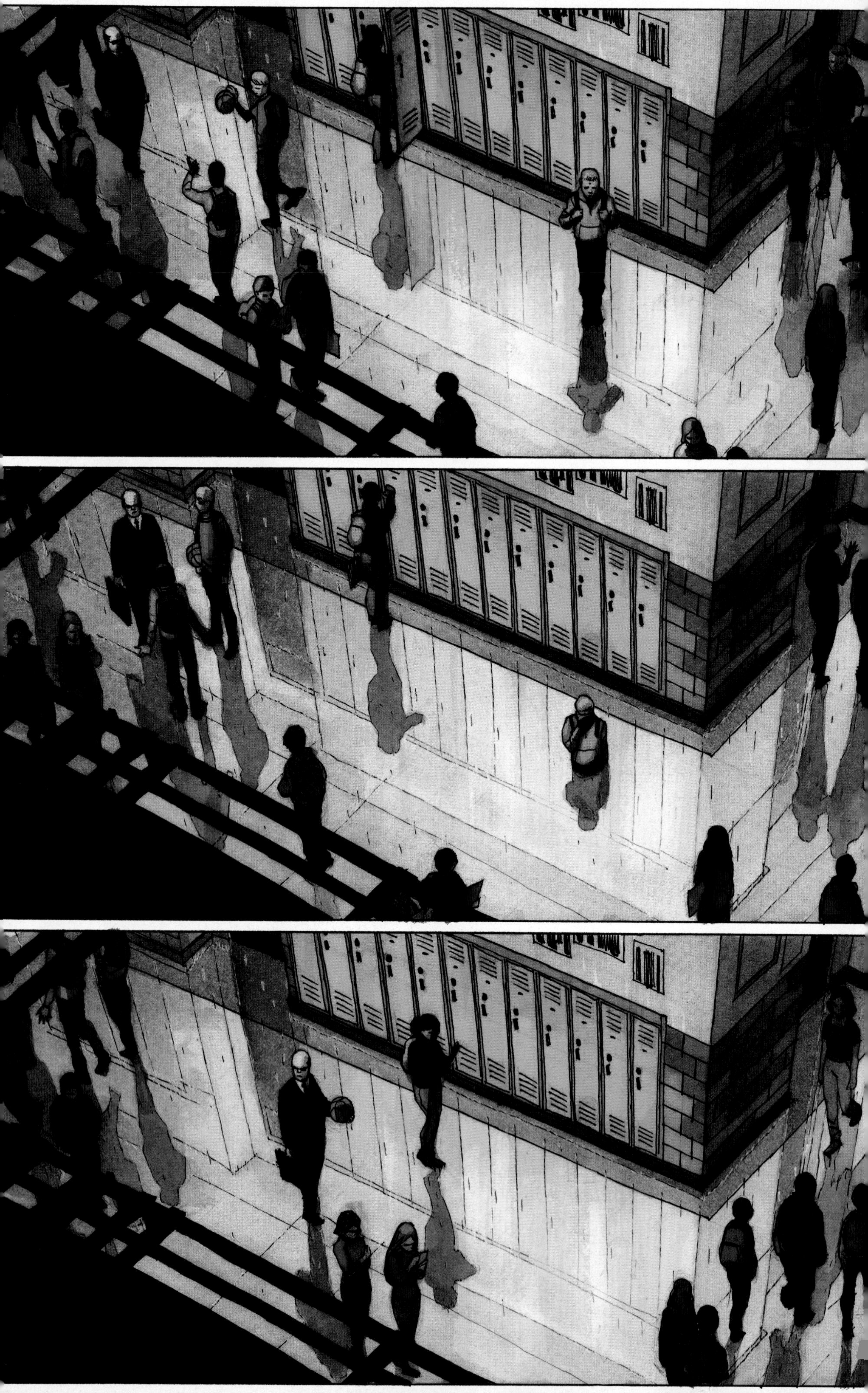

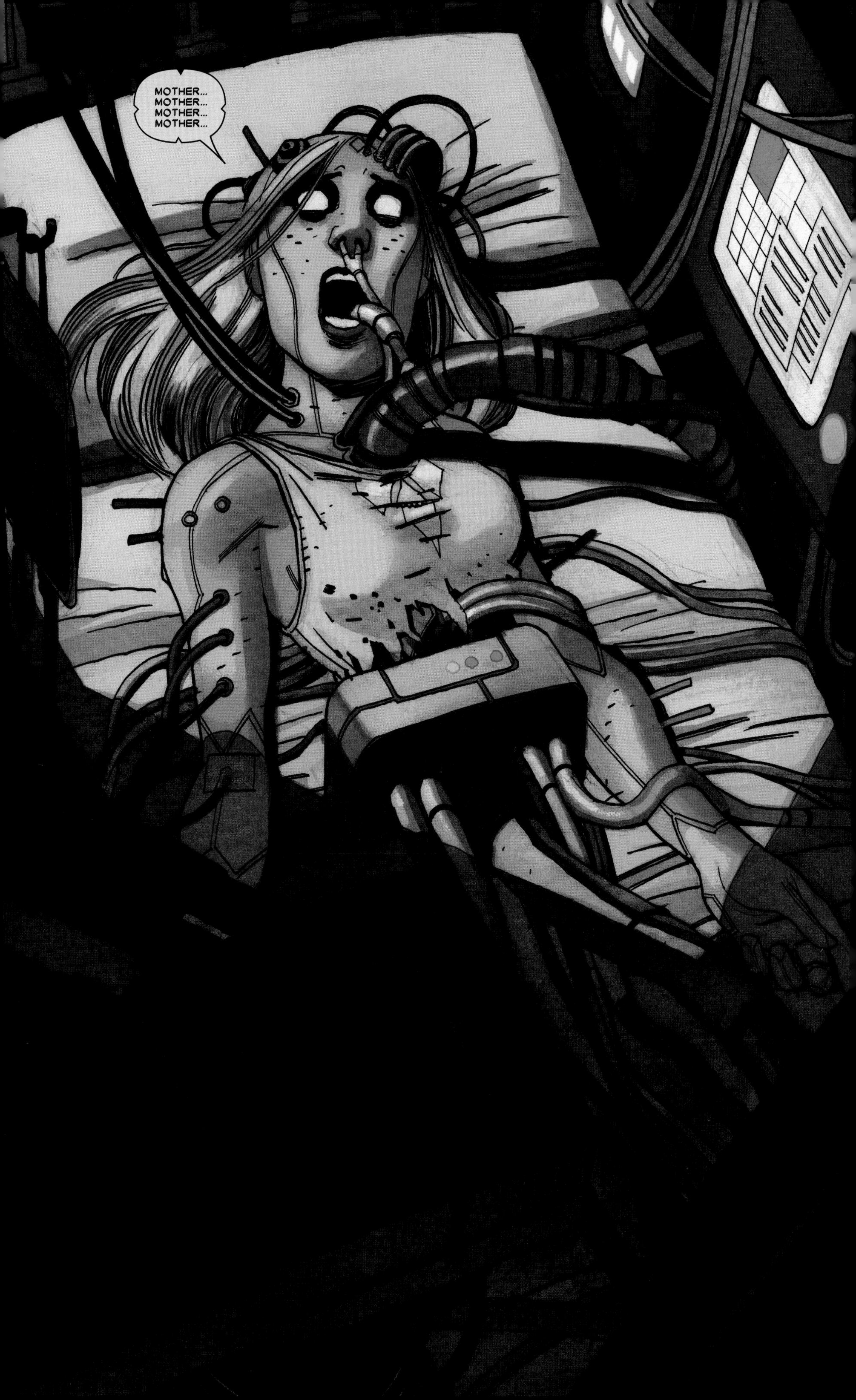
MOTHER...
MOTHER...
MOTHER...
MOTHER...

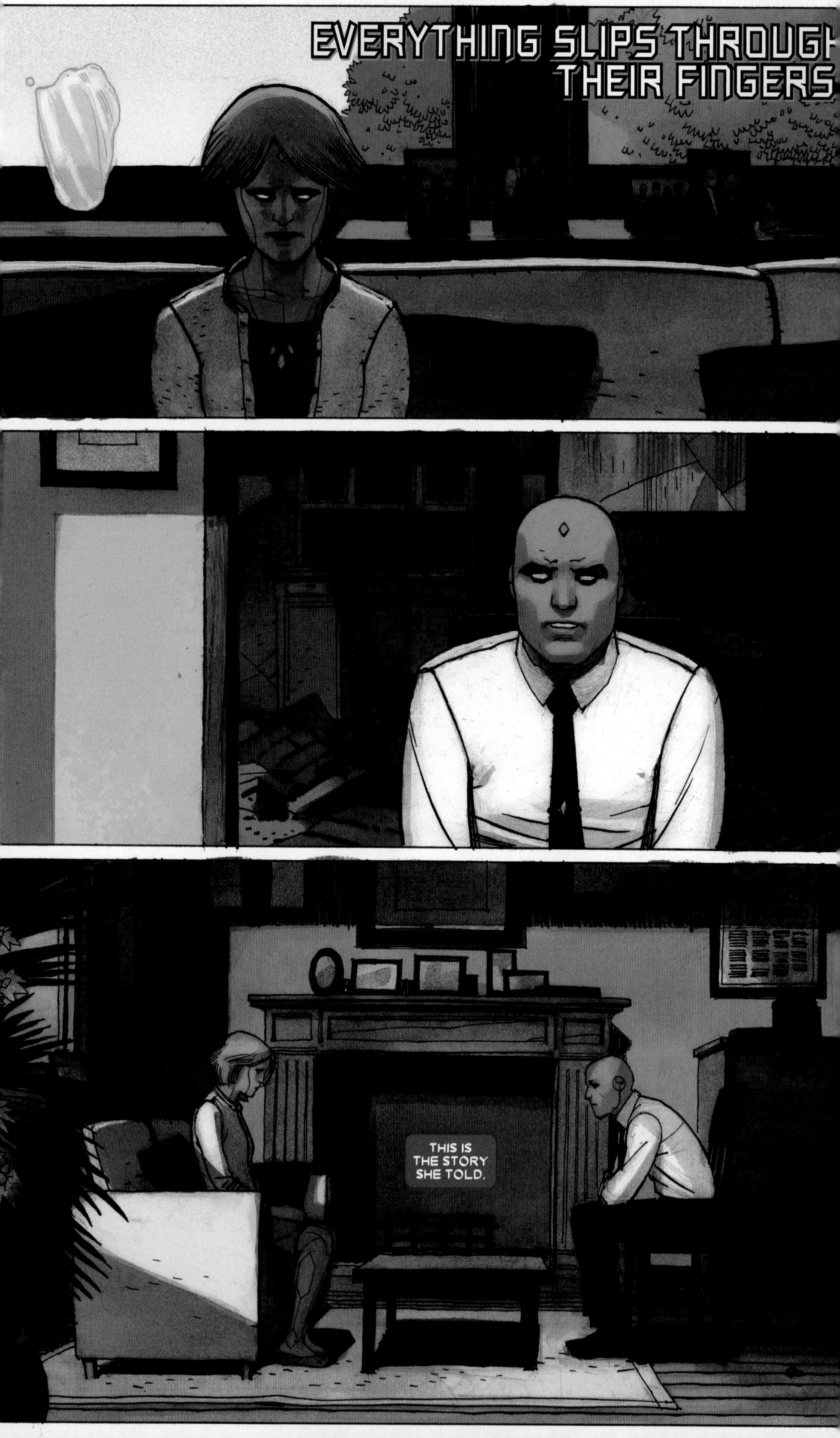
EVERYTHING SLIPS THROUGH THEIR FINGERS
THIS IS THE STORY SHE TOLD.

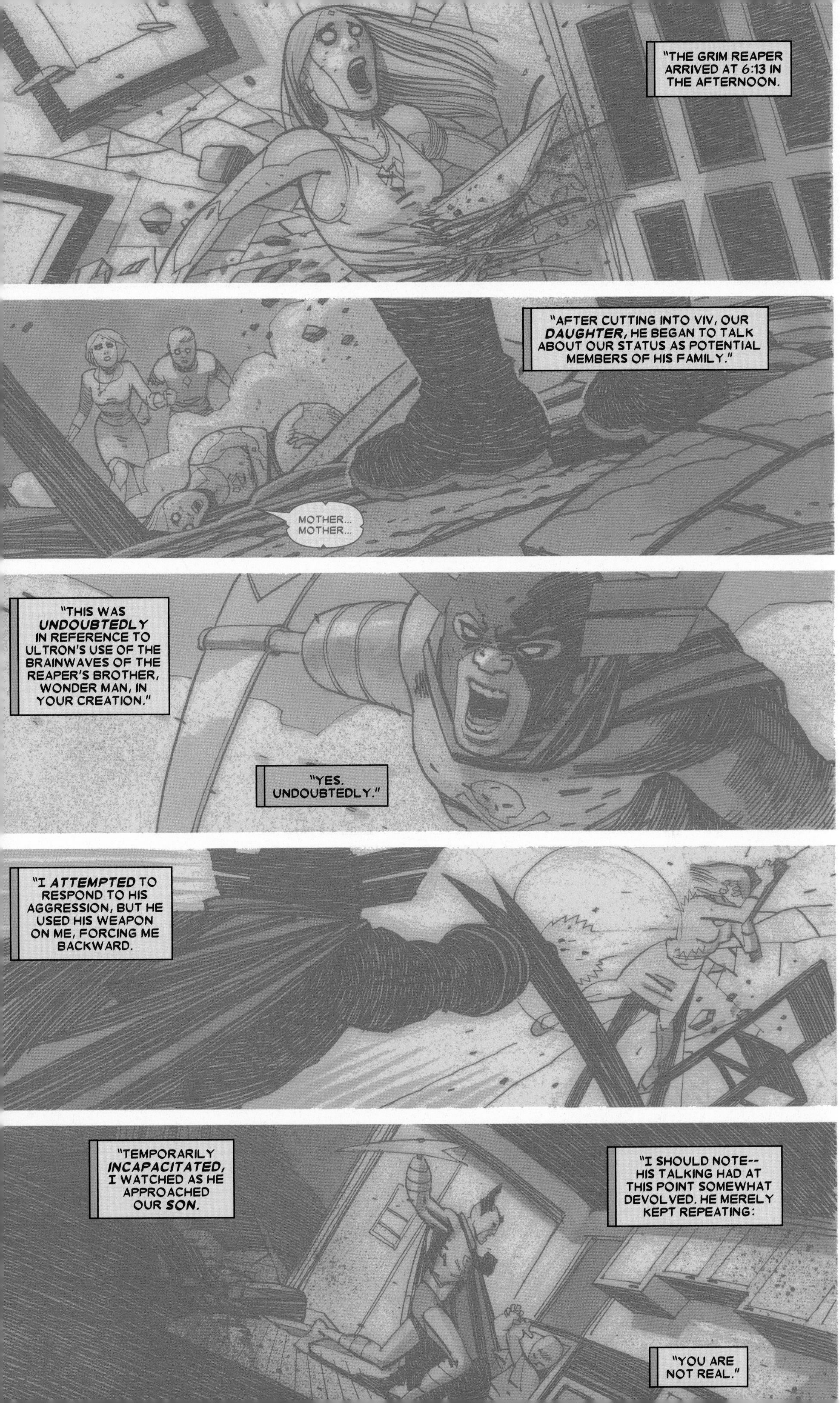
"THE GRIM REAPER ARRIVED AT 6:13 IN THE AFTERNOON.
"AFTER CUTTING INTO VIV, OUR *DAUGHTER,* HE BEGAN TO TALK ABOUT OUR STATUS AS POTENTIAL MEMBERS OF HIS FAMILY."
MOTHER... MOTHER...
"THIS WAS *UNDOUBTEDLY* IN REFERENCE TO ULTRON'S USE OF THE BRAINWAVES OF THE REAPER'S BROTHER, WONDER MAN, IN YOUR CREATION."
"YES. UNDOUBTEDLY."
"I *ATTEMPTED* TO RESPOND TO HIS AGGRESSION, BUT HE USED HIS WEAPON ON ME, FORCING ME BACKWARD.
"TEMPORARILY *INCAPACITATED,* I WATCHED AS HE APPROACHED OUR *SON.*
"I SHOULD NOTE-- HIS TALKING HAD AT THIS POINT SOMEWHAT DEVOLVED. HE MERELY KEPT REPEATING:
"YOU ARE NOT REAL."

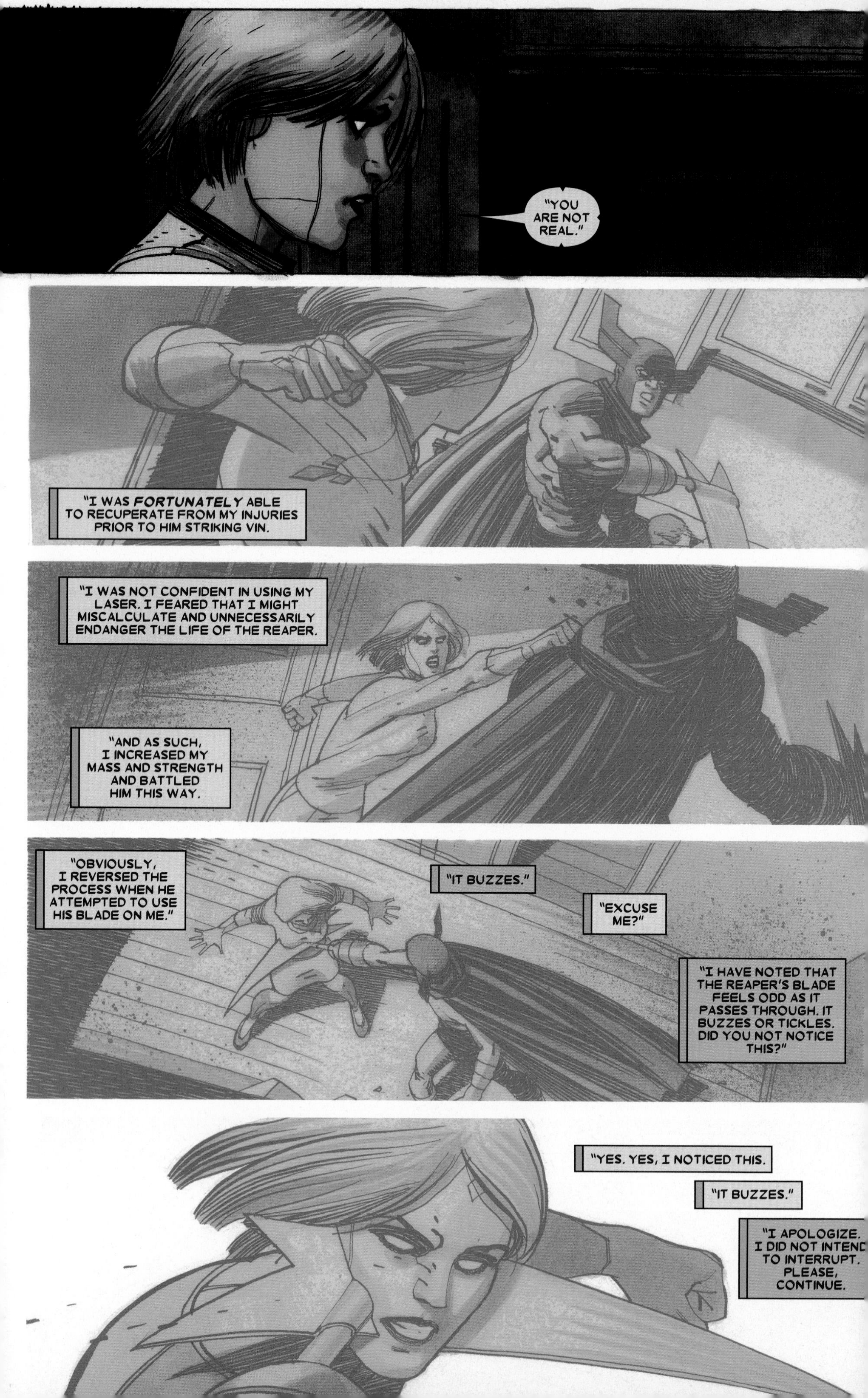
"YOU ARE NOT REAL."
"I WAS FORTUNATELY ABLE TO RECUPERATE FROM MY INJURIES PRIOR TO HIM STRIKING VIN.
"I WAS NOT CONFIDENT IN USING MY LASER. I FEARED THAT I MIGHT MISCALCULATE AND UNNECESSARILY ENDANGER THE LIFE OF THE REAPER.
"AND AS SUCH, I INCREASED MY MASS AND STRENGTH AND BATTLED HIM THIS WAY.
"OBVIOUSLY, I REVERSED THE PROCESS WHEN HE ATTEMPTED TO USE HIS BLADE ON ME."
"IT BUZZES."
"EXCUSE ME?"
"I HAVE NOTED THAT THE REAPER'S BLADE FEELS ODD AS IT PASSES THROUGH. IT BUZZES OR TICKLES. DID YOU NOT NOTICE THIS?"
"YES. YES, I NOTICED THIS.
"IT BUZZES."
"I APOLOGIZE. I DID NOT INTEND TO INTERRUPT. PLEASE, CONTINUE.

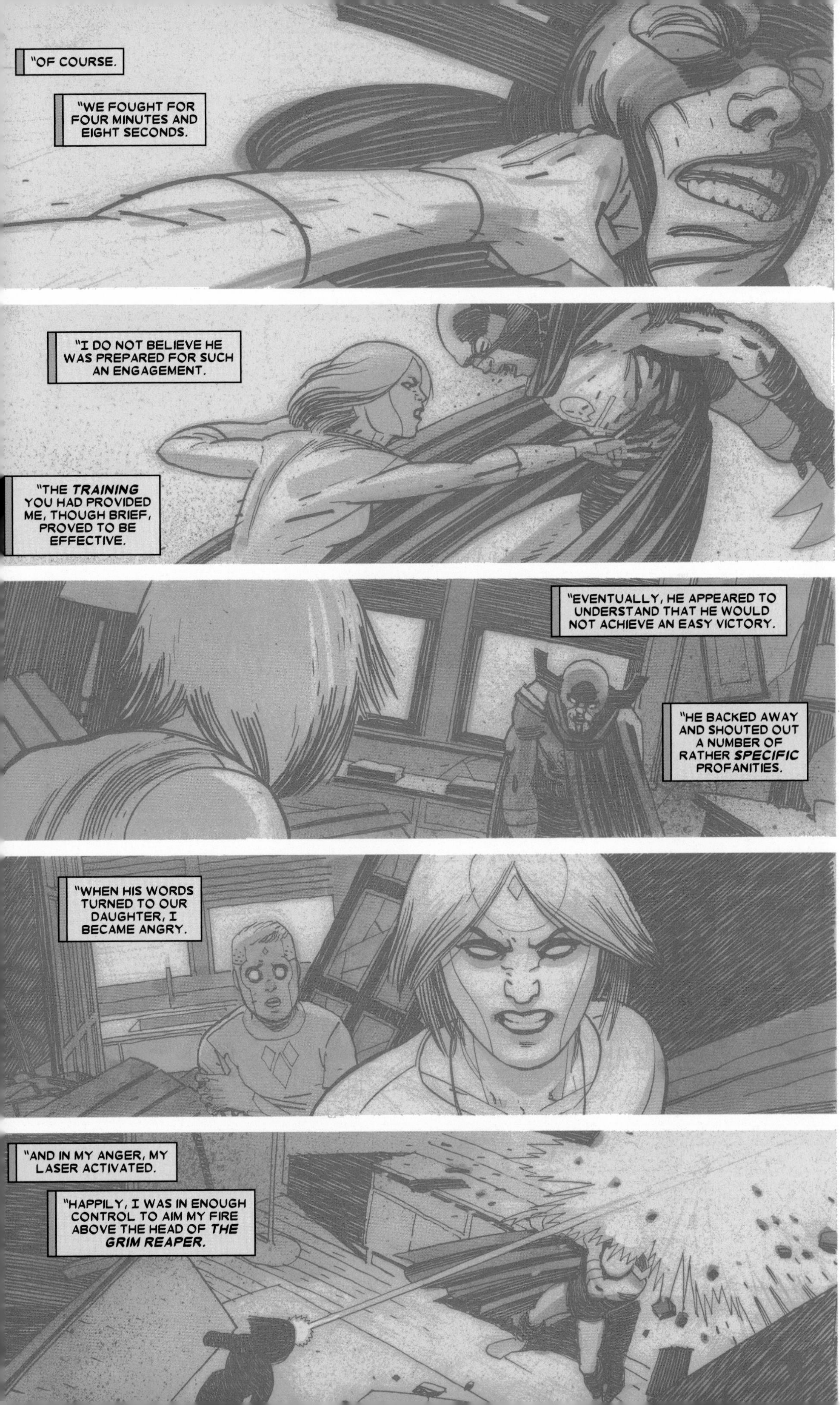
"OF COURSE.
"WE FOUGHT FOR FOUR MINUTES AND EIGHT SECONDS.
"I DO NOT BELIEVE HE WAS PREPARED FOR SUCH AN ENGAGEMENT.
"THE TRAINING YOU HAD PROVIDED ME, THOUGH BRIEF, PROVED TO BE EFFECTIVE.
"EVENTUALLY, HE APPEARED TO UNDERSTAND THAT HE WOULD NOT ACHIEVE AN EASY VICTORY.
"HE BACKED AWAY AND SHOUTED OUT A NUMBER OF RATHER SPECIFIC PROFANITIES.
"WHEN HIS WORDS TURNED TO OUR DAUGHTER, I BECAME ANGRY.
"AND IN MY ANGER, MY LASER ACTIVATED.
"HAPPILY, I WAS IN ENOUGH CONTROL TO AIM MY FIRE ABOVE THE HEAD OF THE GRIM REAPER.

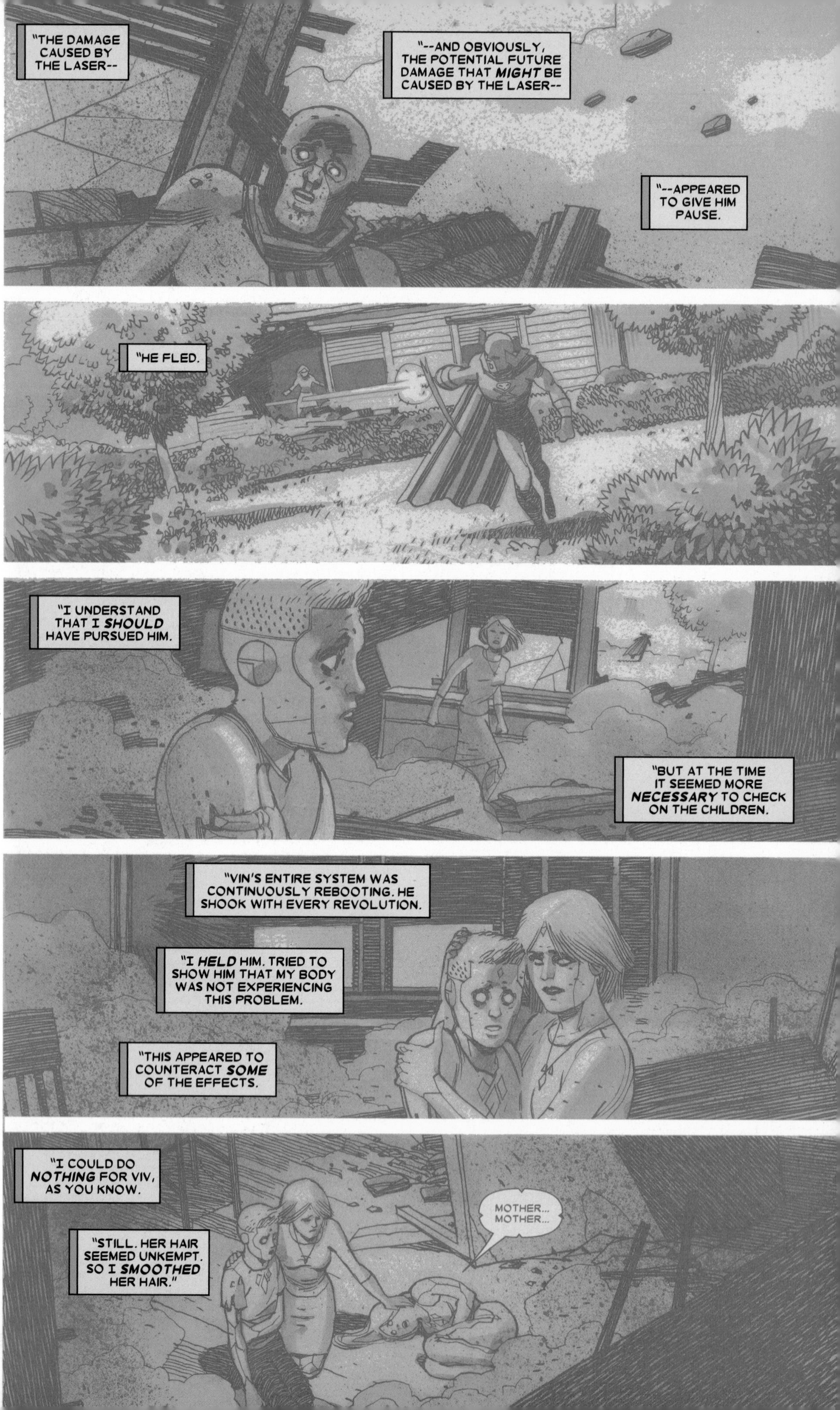
"THE DAMAGE CAUSED BY THE LASER--
"--AND OBVIOUSLY, THE POTENTIAL FUTURE DAMAGE THAT MIGHT BE CAUSED BY THE LASER--
"--APPEARED TO GIVE HIM PAUSE.
"HE FLED.
"I UNDERSTAND THAT I SHOULD HAVE PURSUED HIM.
"BUT AT THE TIME IT SEEMED MORE NECESSARY TO CHECK ON THE CHILDREN.
"VIN'S ENTIRE SYSTEM WAS CONTINUOUSLY REBOOTING. HE SHOOK WITH EVERY REVOLUTION.
"I HELD HIM. TRIED TO SHOW HIM THAT MY BODY WAS NOT EXPERIENCING THIS PROBLEM.
"THIS APPEARED TO COUNTERACT SOME OF THE EFFECTS.
"I COULD DO NOTHING FOR VIV, AS YOU KNOW.
MOTHER... MOTHER...
"STILL. HER HAIR SEEMED UNKEMPT. SO I SMOOTHED HER HAIR."

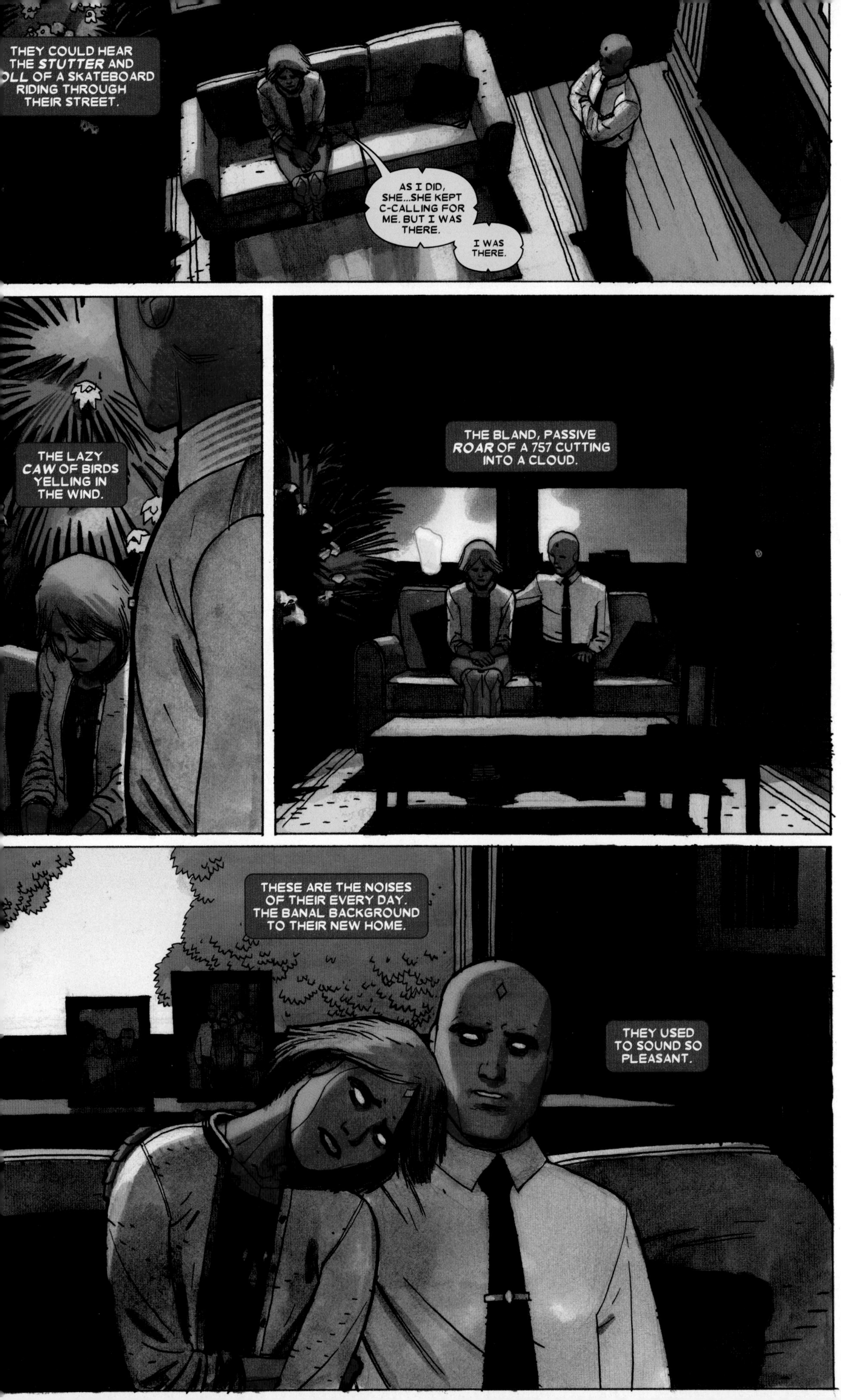
THEY COULD HEAR THE STUTTER AND OLL OF A SKATEBOARD RIDING THROUGH THEIR STREET.
AS I DID, SHE...SHE KEPT C-CALLING FOR ME. BUT I WAS THERE.
I WAS THERE.
THE LAZY CAW OF BIRDS YELLING IN THE WIND.
THE BLAND, PASSIVE ROAR OF A 757 CUTTING INTO A CLOUD.
THESE ARE THE NOISES OF THEIR EVERY DAY. THE BANAL BACKGROUND TO THEIR NEW HOME.
THEY USED TO SOUND SO PLEASANT.

VIN DOESN'T EAT. HE DOESN'T *NEED* TO EAT.

NORMALLY, HE SPENT LUNCH WITH HIS SISTER. THEY'D SIT IN THE LIBRARY AND READ THROUGH THE SHELVES AND DISCUSS WHAT EACH HAD READ.

LAST WEEK, THEY CONSUMED THE ENTIRE SECTION ON *HUMAN ANATOMY*.

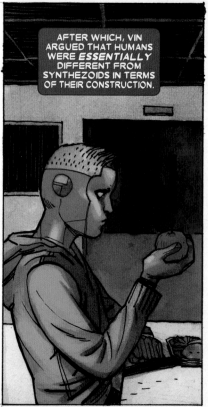

AFTER WHICH, VIN ARGUED THAT HUMANS WERE *ESSENTIALLY* DIFFERENT FROM SYNTHEZOIDS IN TERMS OF THEIR CONSTRUCTION.

EACH PORTION OF A HUMAN WAS DESIGNED TO INCREASE THEIR LIFESPAN UP TO THE MOMENT OF REPRODUCTION.

A *SYNTHEZOID*, THOUGH, WAS NOT DESIGNED MERELY TO SURVIVE AND REPLICATE.

A *SYNTHEZOID* HAS A PURPOSE.

HEY, MAN. *VIN*, RIGHT? WHERE'S YOUR SISTER?

I AM SORRY? WHAT-- WHAT DID YOU SAY?

YOUR SISTER, MAN. VIV? SHE'S IN CHEM WITH ME. SHE'S LIKE MY PARTNER.

SHE'S BEEN OUT, AND I DON'T HAVE HER NUMBER OR ANYTHING.

OH. YES. SHE IS OUT.

SHE IS ILL.

YEAH, I KNOW THAT, MAN. YOU LISTENING? I'M IN CHEM WITH HER.

I GOT TO TALK TO HER ABOUT THIS THING WE'RE DOING.

YOU KNOW HOW I CAN TALK TO HER? THAT'S ALL, MAN.

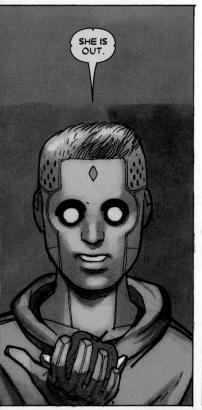

SHE IS OUT.

SHE IS ILL.

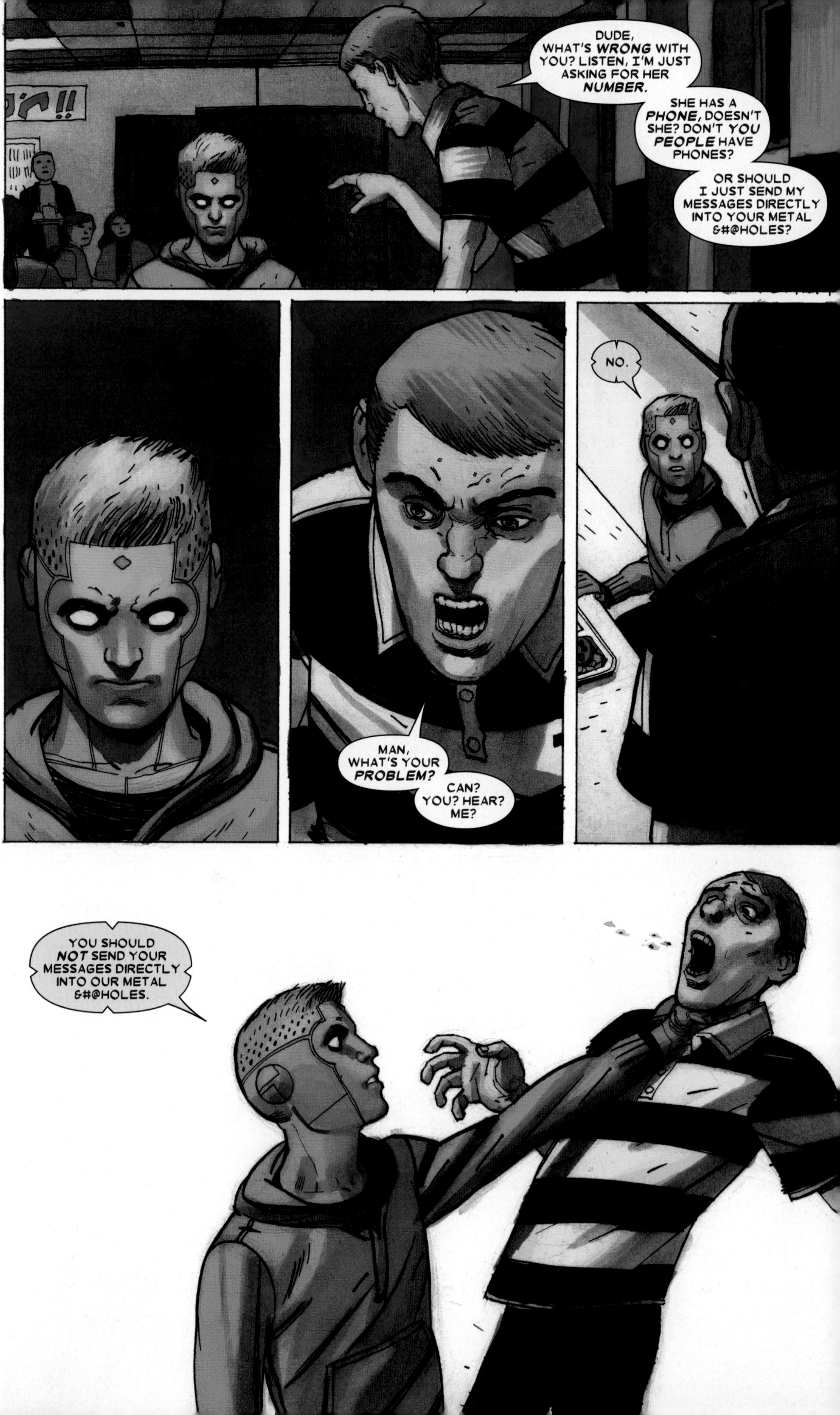
DUDE, WHAT'S WRONG WITH YOU? LISTEN, I'M JUST ASKING FOR HER NUMBER.
SHE HAS A PHONE, DOESN'T SHE? DON'T YOU PEOPLE HAVE PHONES?
OR SHOULD I JUST SEND MY MESSAGES DIRECTLY INTO YOUR METAL &#@HOLES?
MAN, WHAT'S YOUR PROBLEM?
CAN? YOU? HEAR? ME?
NO.
YOU SHOULD NOT SEND YOUR MESSAGES DIRECTLY INTO OUR METAL &#@HOLES.

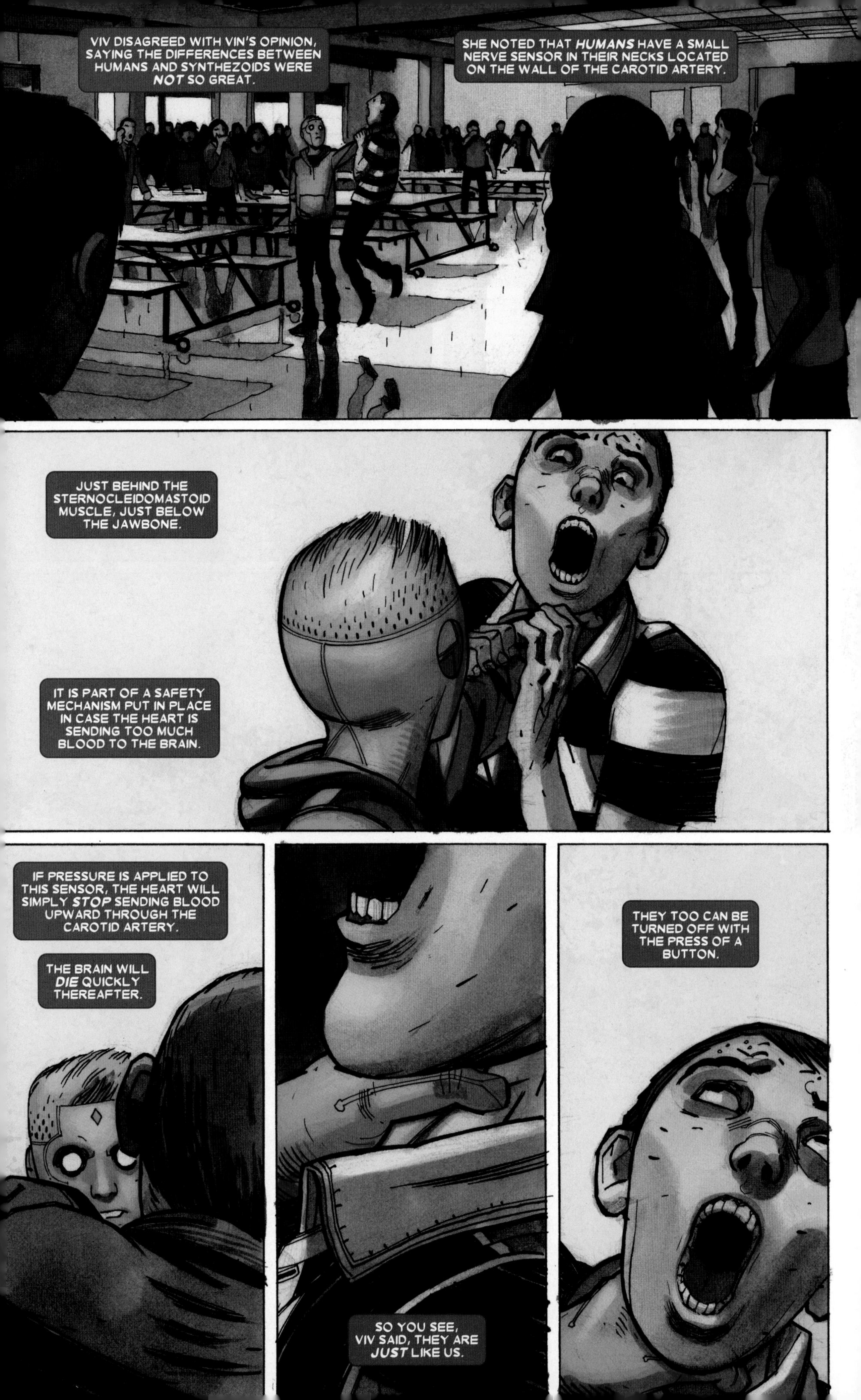
VIV DISAGREED WITH VIN'S OPINION, SAYING THE DIFFERENCES BETWEEN HUMANS AND SYNTHEZOIDS WERE *NOT* SO GREAT.
SHE NOTED THAT *HUMANS* HAVE A SMALL NERVE SENSOR IN THEIR NECKS LOCATED ON THE WALL OF THE CAROTID ARTERY.
JUST BEHIND THE STERNOCLEIDOMASTOID MUSCLE, JUST BELOW THE JAWBONE.
IT IS PART OF A SAFETY MECHANISM PUT IN PLACE IN CASE THE HEART IS SENDING TOO MUCH BLOOD TO THE BRAIN.
IF PRESSURE IS APPLIED TO THIS SENSOR, THE HEART WILL SIMPLY *STOP* SENDING BLOOD UPWARD THROUGH THE CAROTID ARTERY.
THE BRAIN WILL *DIE* QUICKLY THEREAFTER.
SO YOU SEE, VIV SAID, THEY ARE *JUST* LIKE US.
THEY TOO CAN BE TURNED OFF WITH THE PRESS OF A BUTTON.

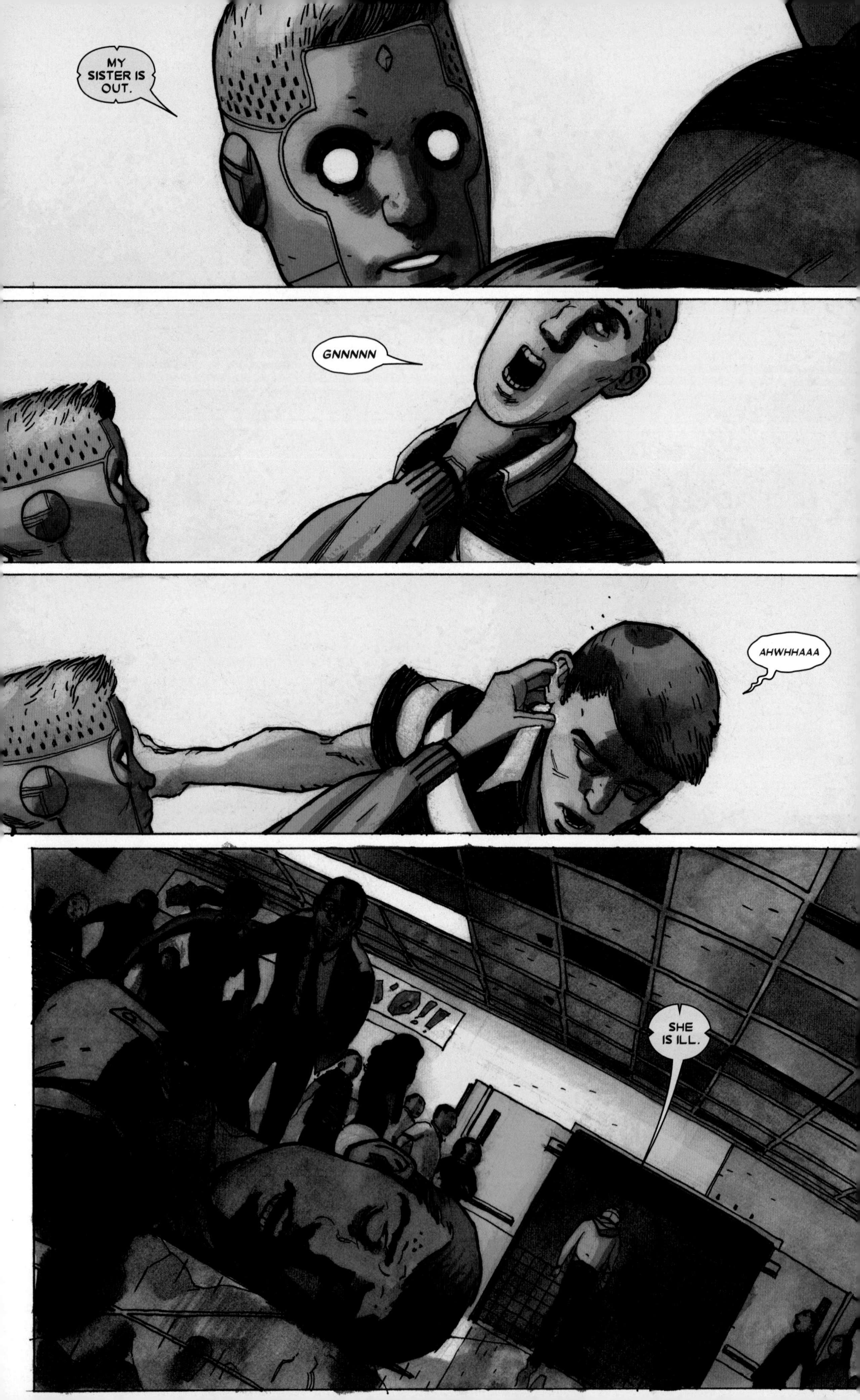
MY SISTER IS OUT.
GNNNNN
AHWHHAAA
SHE IS ILL.

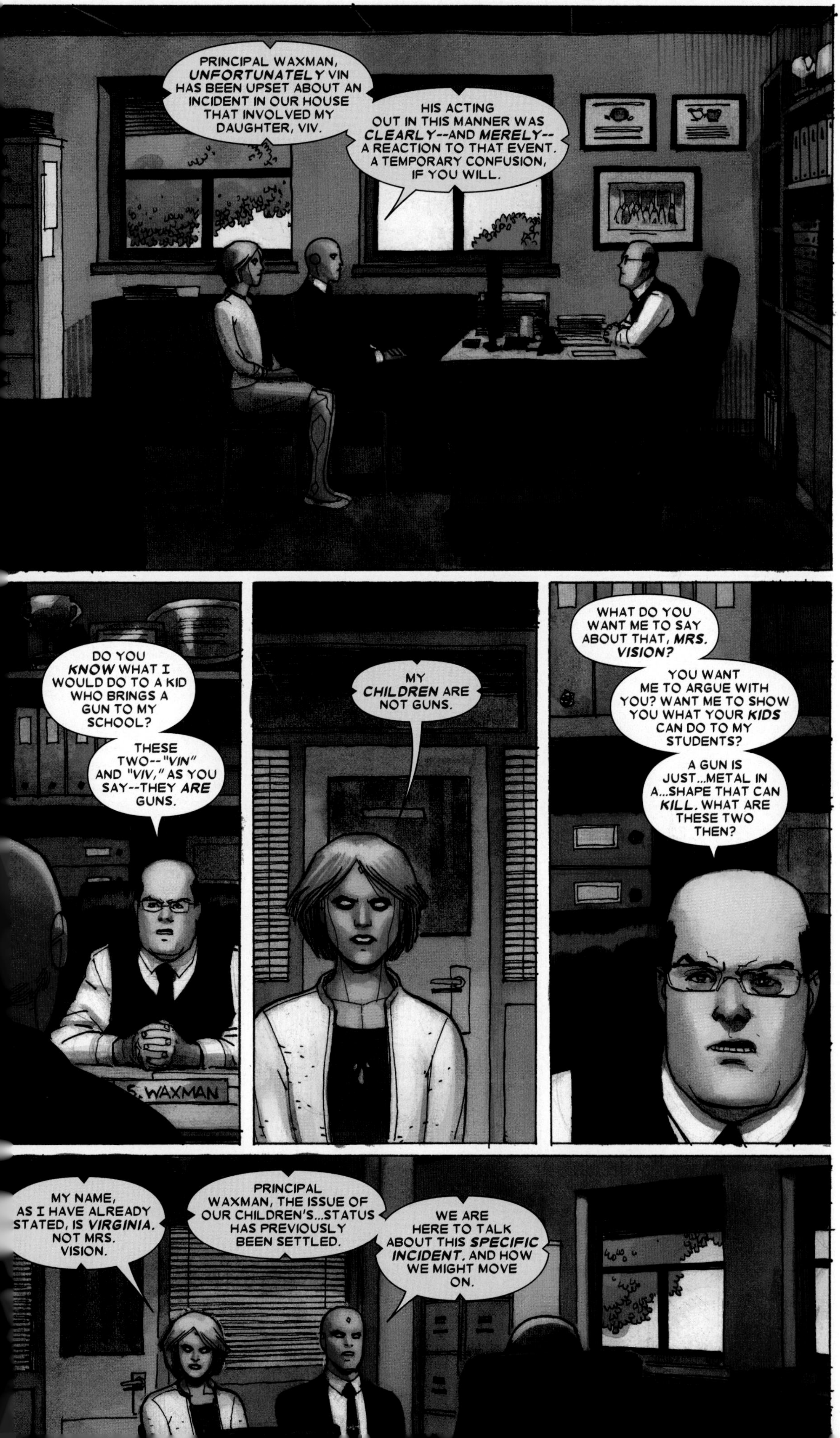
PRINCIPAL WAXMAN, *UNFORTUNATELY* VIN HAS BEEN UPSET ABOUT AN INCIDENT IN OUR HOUSE THAT INVOLVED MY DAUGHTER, VIV.
HIS ACTING OUT IN THIS MANNER WAS *CLEARLY*--AND *MERELY*--A REACTION TO THAT EVENT. A TEMPORARY CONFUSION, IF YOU WILL.
DO YOU *KNOW* WHAT I WOULD DO TO A KID WHO BRINGS A GUN TO MY SCHOOL?
THESE TWO--"*VIN*" AND "*VIV*," AS YOU SAY--THEY *ARE* GUNS.
S. WAXMAN
MY *CHILDREN* ARE NOT GUNS.
WHAT DO YOU WANT ME TO SAY ABOUT THAT, *MRS. VISION?*
YOU WANT ME TO ARGUE WITH YOU? WANT ME TO SHOW YOU WHAT YOUR *KIDS* CAN DO TO MY STUDENTS?
A GUN IS JUST...METAL IN A...SHAPE THAT CAN *KILL*. WHAT ARE THESE TWO THEN?
MY NAME, AS I HAVE ALREADY STATED, IS *VIRGINIA*. NOT MRS. VISION.
PRINCIPAL WAXMAN, THE ISSUE OF OUR CHILDREN'S...STATUS HAS PREVIOUSLY BEEN SETTLED.
WE ARE HERE TO TALK ABOUT THIS *SPECIFIC INCIDENT*, AND HOW WE MIGHT MOVE ON.

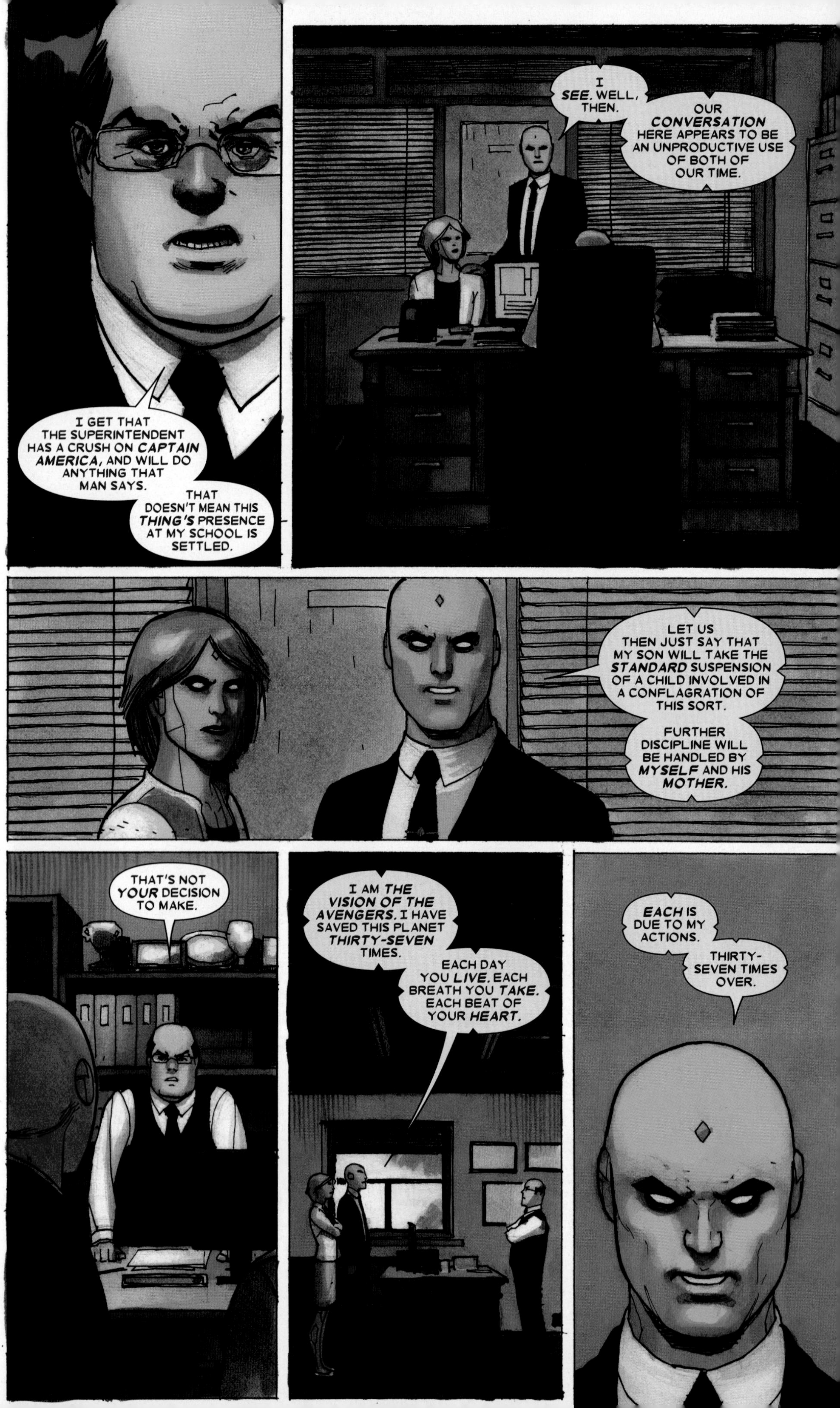
I GET THAT THE SUPERINTENDENT HAS A CRUSH ON CAPTAIN AMERICA, AND WILL DO ANYTHING THAT MAN SAYS.
THAT DOESN'T MEAN THIS THING'S PRESENCE AT MY SCHOOL IS SETTLED.
I SEE. WELL, THEN.
OUR CONVERSATION HERE APPEARS TO BE AN UNPRODUCTIVE USE OF BOTH OF OUR TIME.
LET US THEN JUST SAY THAT MY SON WILL TAKE THE STANDARD SUSPENSION OF A CHILD INVOLVED IN A CONFLAGRATION OF THIS SORT.
FURTHER DISCIPLINE WILL BE HANDLED BY MYSELF AND HIS MOTHER.
THAT'S NOT YOUR DECISION TO MAKE.
I AM THE VISION OF THE AVENGERS. I HAVE SAVED THIS PLANET THIRTY-SEVEN TIMES.
EACH DAY YOU LIVE. EACH BREATH YOU TAKE. EACH BEAT OF YOUR HEART.
EACH IS DUE TO MY ACTIONS.
THIRTY-SEVEN TIMES OVER.

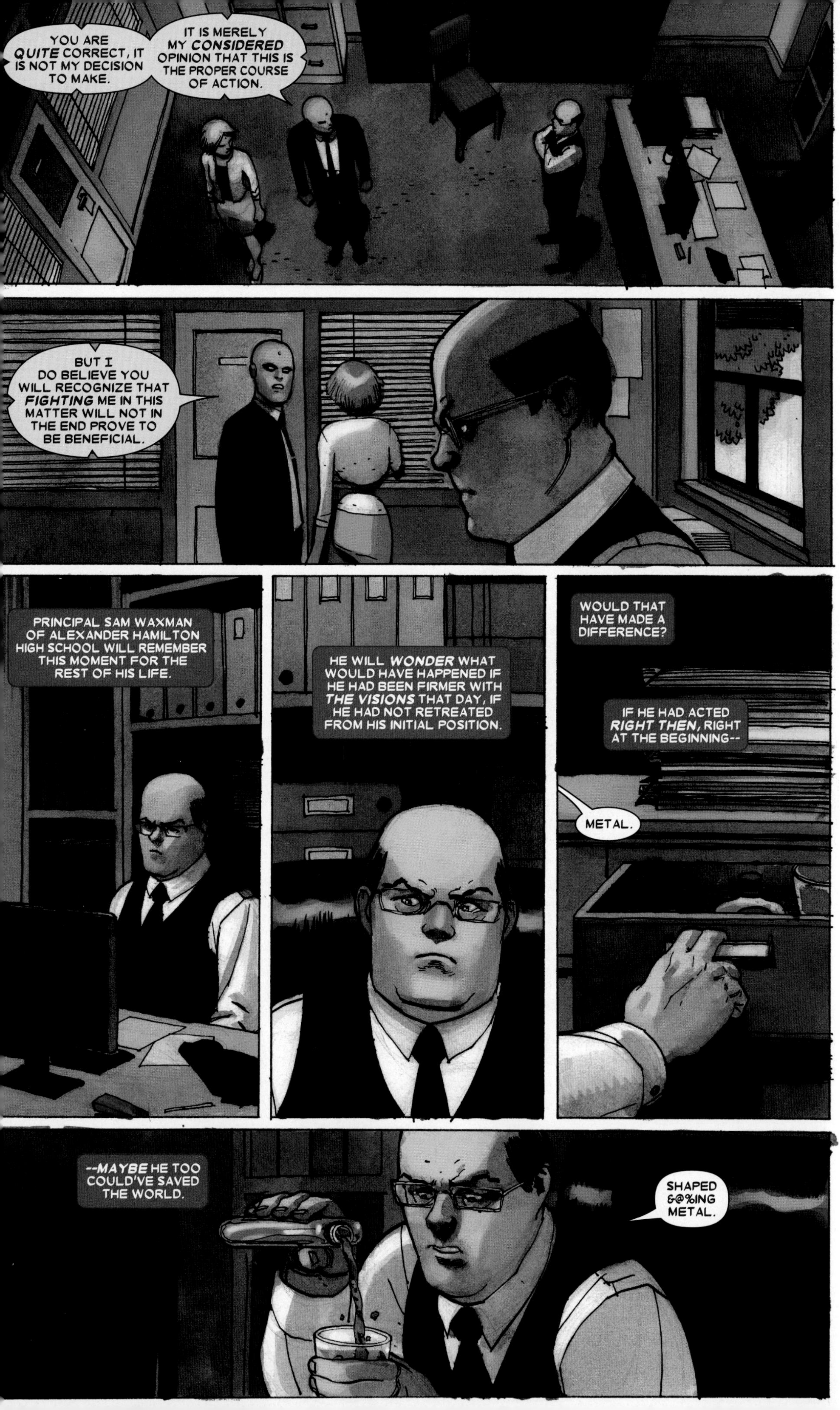
YOU ARE QUITE CORRECT, IT IS NOT MY DECISION TO MAKE.
IT IS MERELY MY CONSIDERED OPINION THAT THIS IS THE PROPER COURSE OF ACTION.
BUT I DO BELIEVE YOU WILL RECOGNIZE THAT FIGHTING ME IN THIS MATTER WILL NOT IN THE END PROVE TO BE BENEFICIAL.
PRINCIPAL SAM WAXMAN OF ALEXANDER HAMILTON HIGH SCHOOL WILL REMEMBER THIS MOMENT FOR THE REST OF HIS LIFE.
HE WILL WONDER WHAT WOULD HAVE HAPPENED IF HE HAD BEEN FIRMER WITH THE VISIONS THAT DAY, IF HE HAD NOT RETREATED FROM HIS INITIAL POSITION.
WOULD THAT HAVE MADE A DIFFERENCE?
IF HE HAD ACTED RIGHT THEN, RIGHT AT THE BEGINNING--
METAL.
--MAYBE HE TOO COULD'VE SAVED THE WORLD.
SHAPED &@%ING METAL.

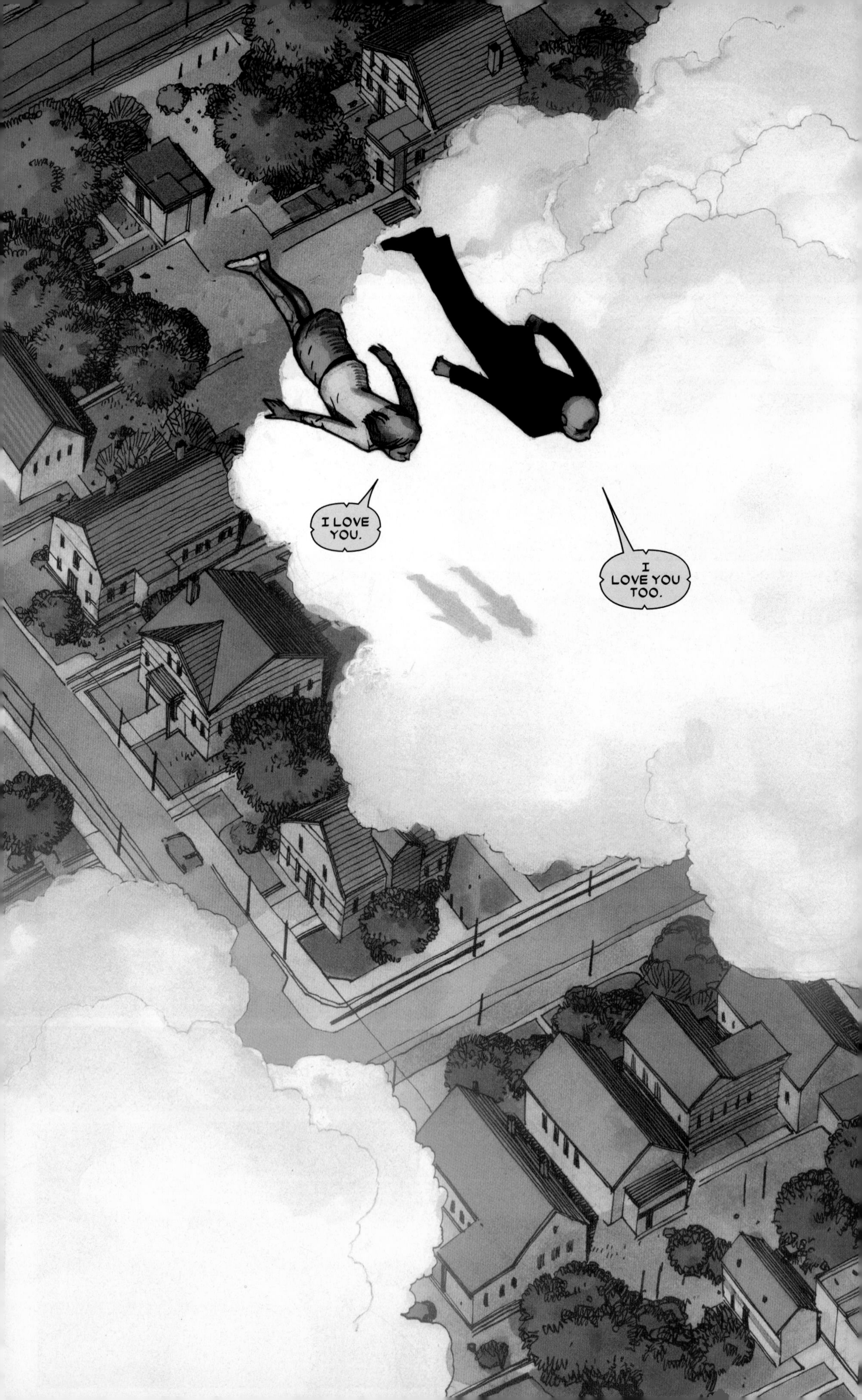
I LOVE YOU.
I LOVE YOU TOO.

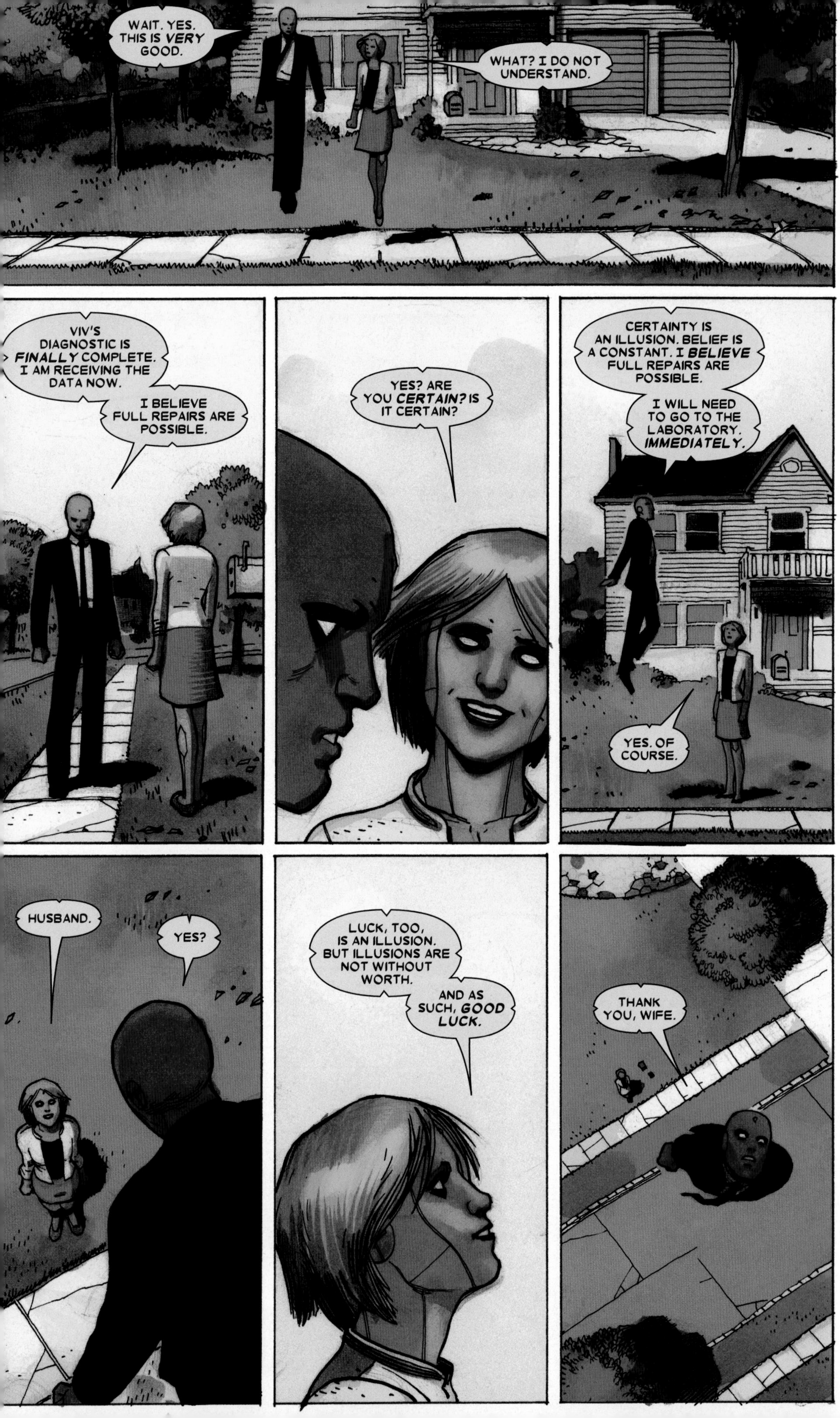
WAIT. YES. THIS IS VERY GOOD.
WHAT? I DO NOT UNDERSTAND.
VIV'S DIAGNOSTIC IS FINALLY COMPLETE. I AM RECEIVING THE DATA NOW.
I BELIEVE FULL REPAIRS ARE POSSIBLE.
YES? ARE YOU CERTAIN? IS IT CERTAIN?
CERTAINTY IS AN ILLUSION. BELIEF IS A CONSTANT. I BELIEVE FULL REPAIRS ARE POSSIBLE.
I WILL NEED TO GO TO THE LABORATORY. IMMEDIATELY.
YES. OF COURSE.
HUSBAND.
YES?
LUCK, TOO, IS AN ILLUSION. BUT ILLUSIONS ARE NOT WITHOUT WORTH.
AND AS SUCH, GOOD LUCK.
THANK YOU, WIFE.

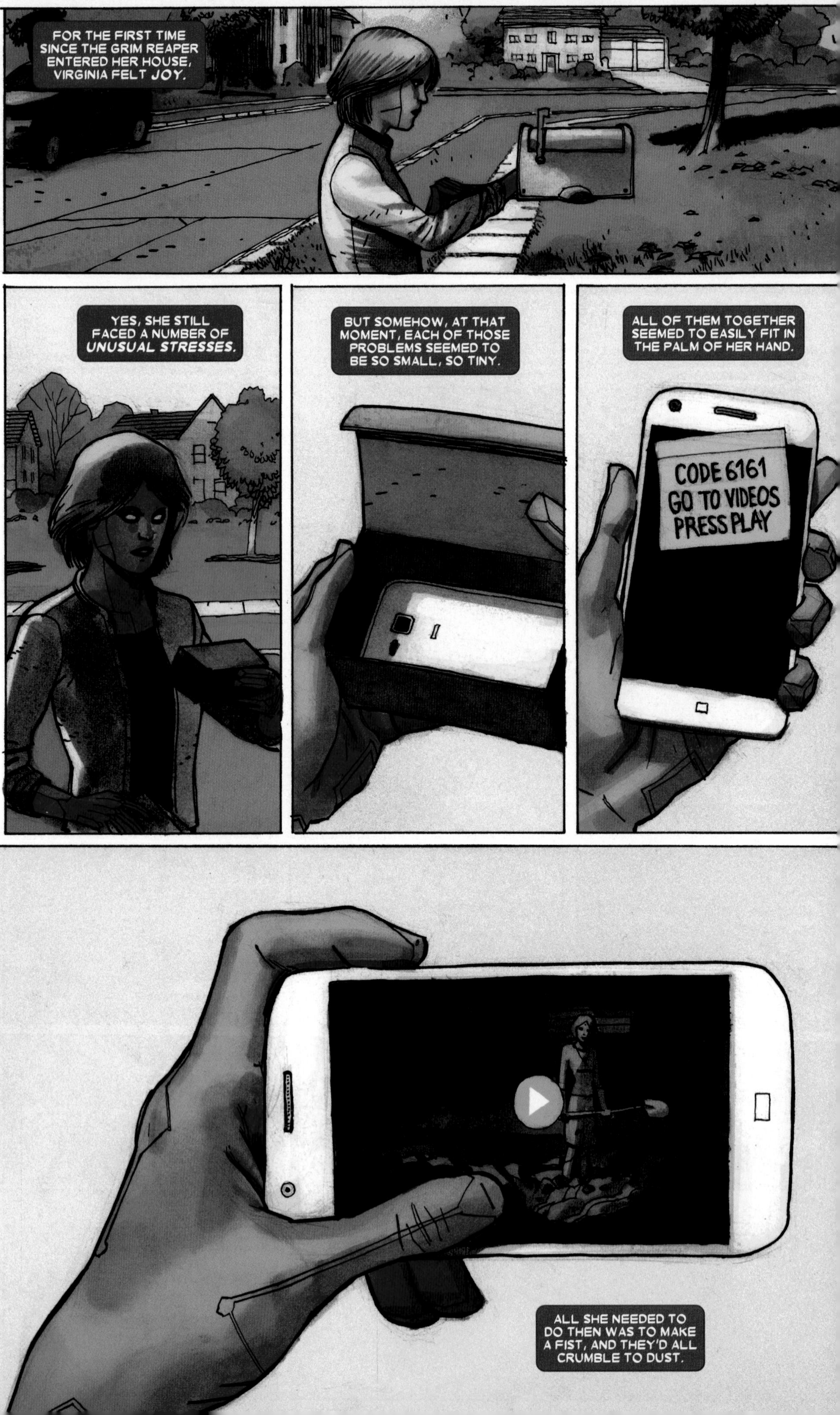
FOR THE FIRST TIME SINCE THE GRIM REAPER ENTERED HER HOUSE, VIRGINIA FELT *JOY.*
YES, SHE STILL FACED A NUMBER OF *UNUSUAL STRESSES.*
BUT SOMEHOW, AT THAT MOMENT, EACH OF THOSE PROBLEMS SEEMED TO BE SO SMALL, SO TINY.
ALL OF THEM TOGETHER SEEMED TO EASILY FIT IN THE PALM OF HER HAND.
CODE 6161
GO TO VIDEOS
PRESS PLAY
ALL SHE NEEDED TO DO THEN WAS TO MAKE A FIST, AND THEY'D ALL CRUMBLE TO DUST.

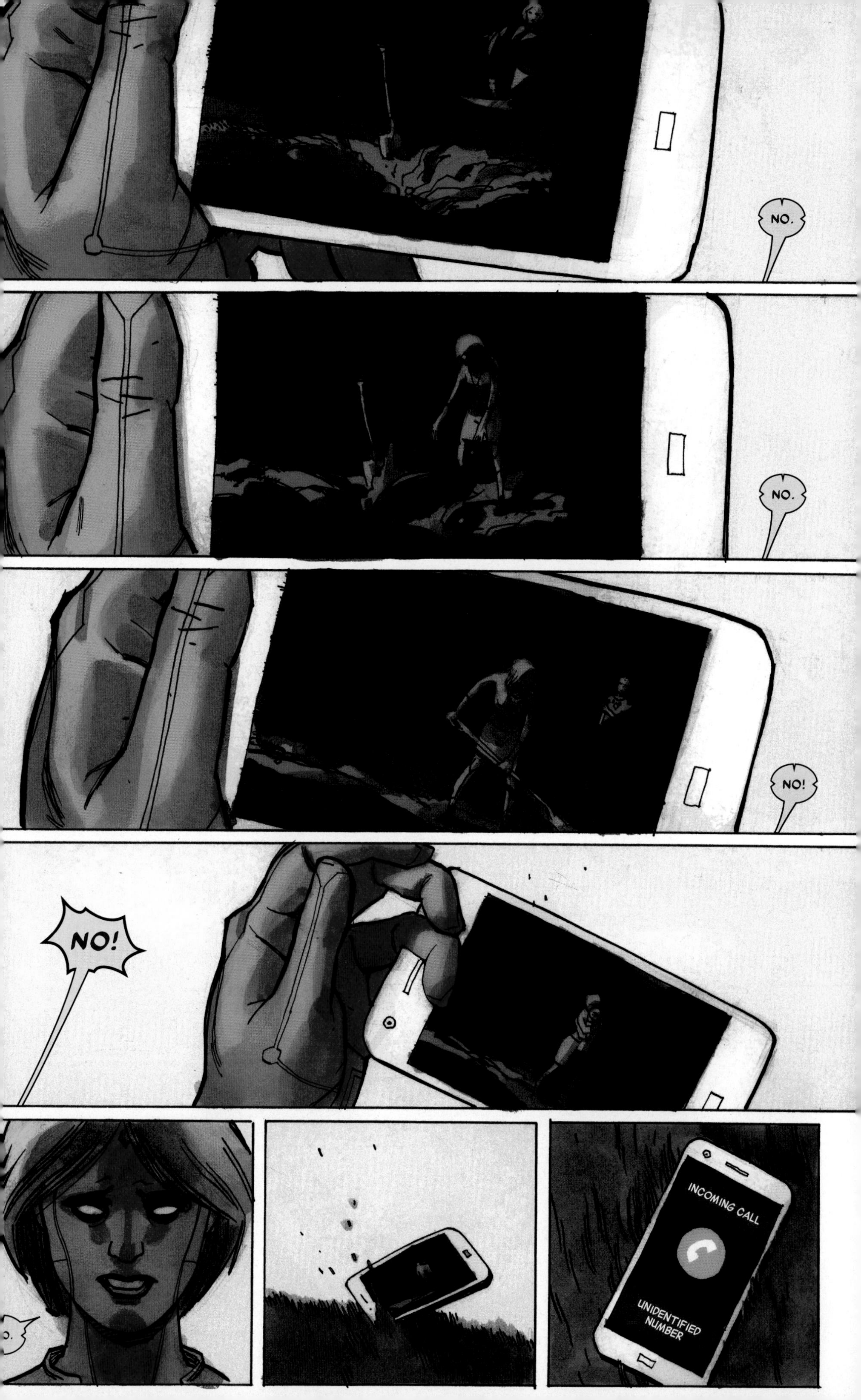
NO.
NO.
NO!
NO!
INCOMING CALL
UNIDENTIFIED NUMBER

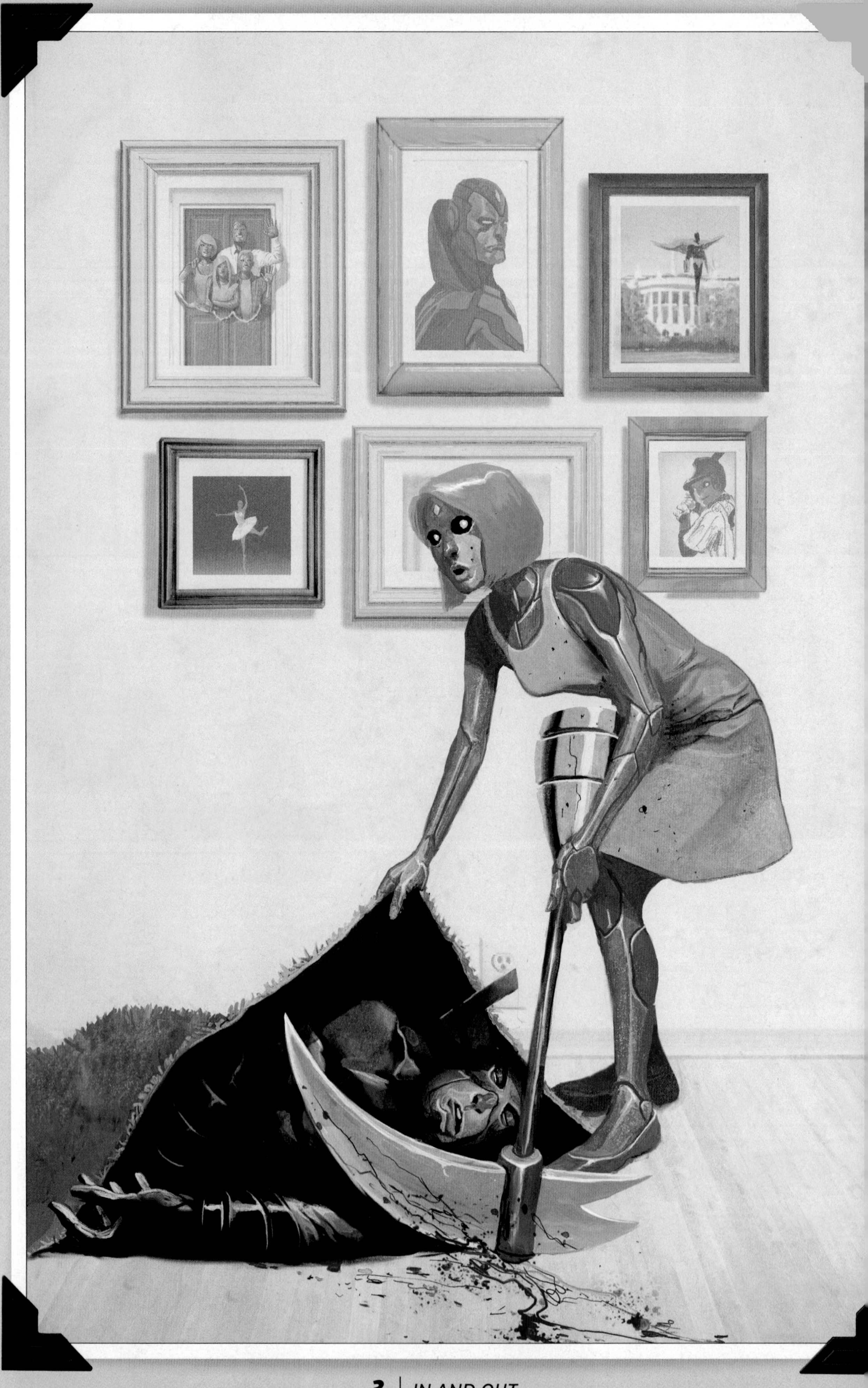

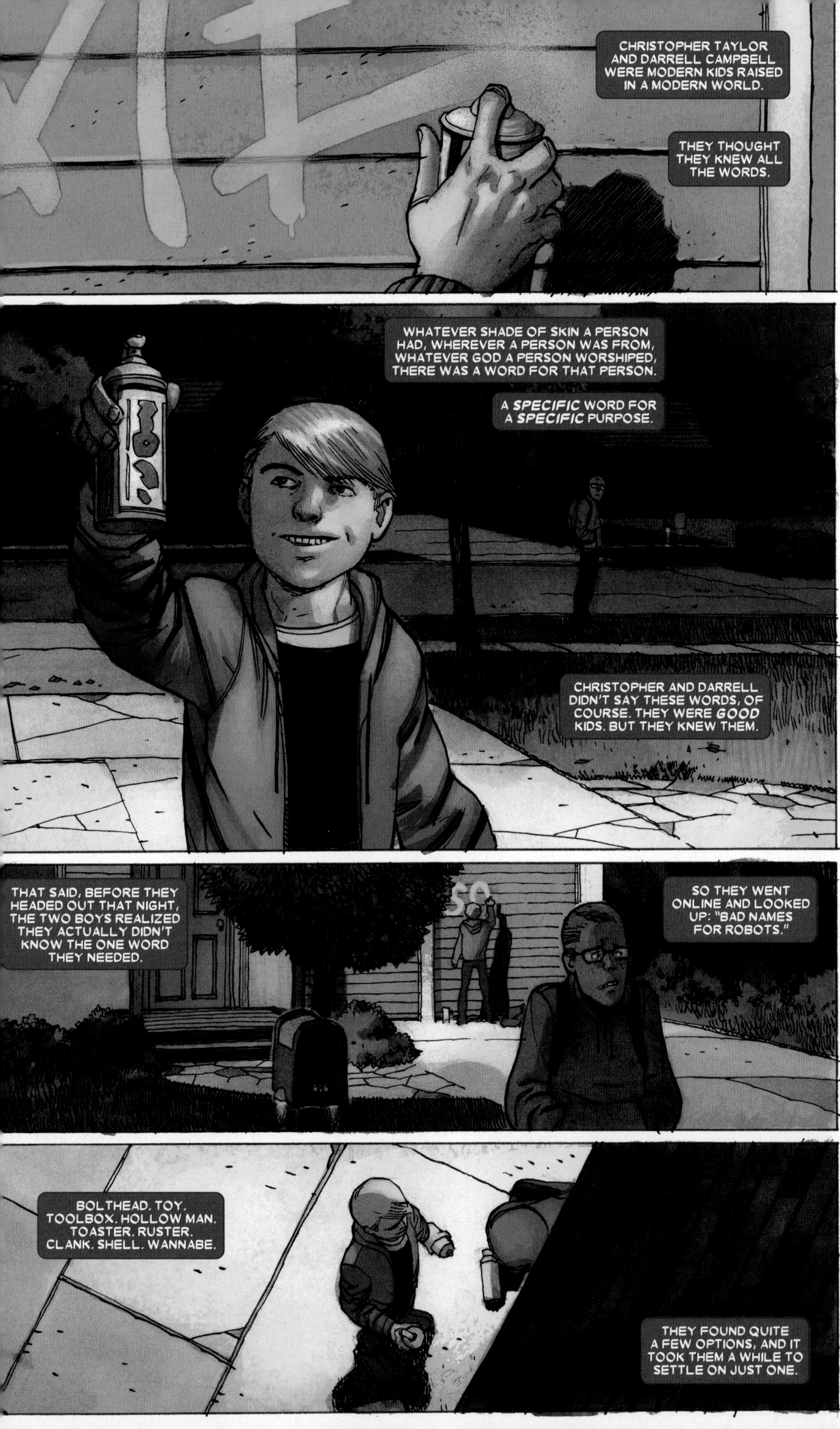

CHRISTOPHER TAYLOR AND DARRELL CAMPBELL WERE MODERN KIDS RAISED IN A MODERN WORLD.
THEY THOUGHT THEY KNEW ALL THE WORDS.
WHATEVER SHADE OF SKIN A PERSON HAD, WHEREVER A PERSON WAS FROM, WHATEVER GOD A PERSON WORSHIPED, THERE WAS A WORD FOR THAT PERSON.
A *SPECIFIC* WORD FOR A *SPECIFIC* PURPOSE.
CHRISTOPHER AND DARRELL DIDN'T SAY THESE WORDS, OF COURSE. THEY WERE *GOOD* KIDS. BUT THEY KNEW THEM.
THAT SAID, BEFORE THEY HEADED OUT THAT NIGHT, THE TWO BOYS REALIZED THEY ACTUALLY DIDN'T KNOW THE ONE WORD THEY NEEDED.
SO THEY WENT ONLINE AND LOOKED UP: "BAD NAMES FOR ROBOTS."
BOLTHEAD. TOY. TOOLBOX. HOLLOW MAN. TOASTER. RUSTER. CLANK. SHELL. WANNABE.
THEY FOUND QUITE A FEW OPTIONS, AND IT TOOK THEM A WHILE TO SETTLE ON JUST ONE.

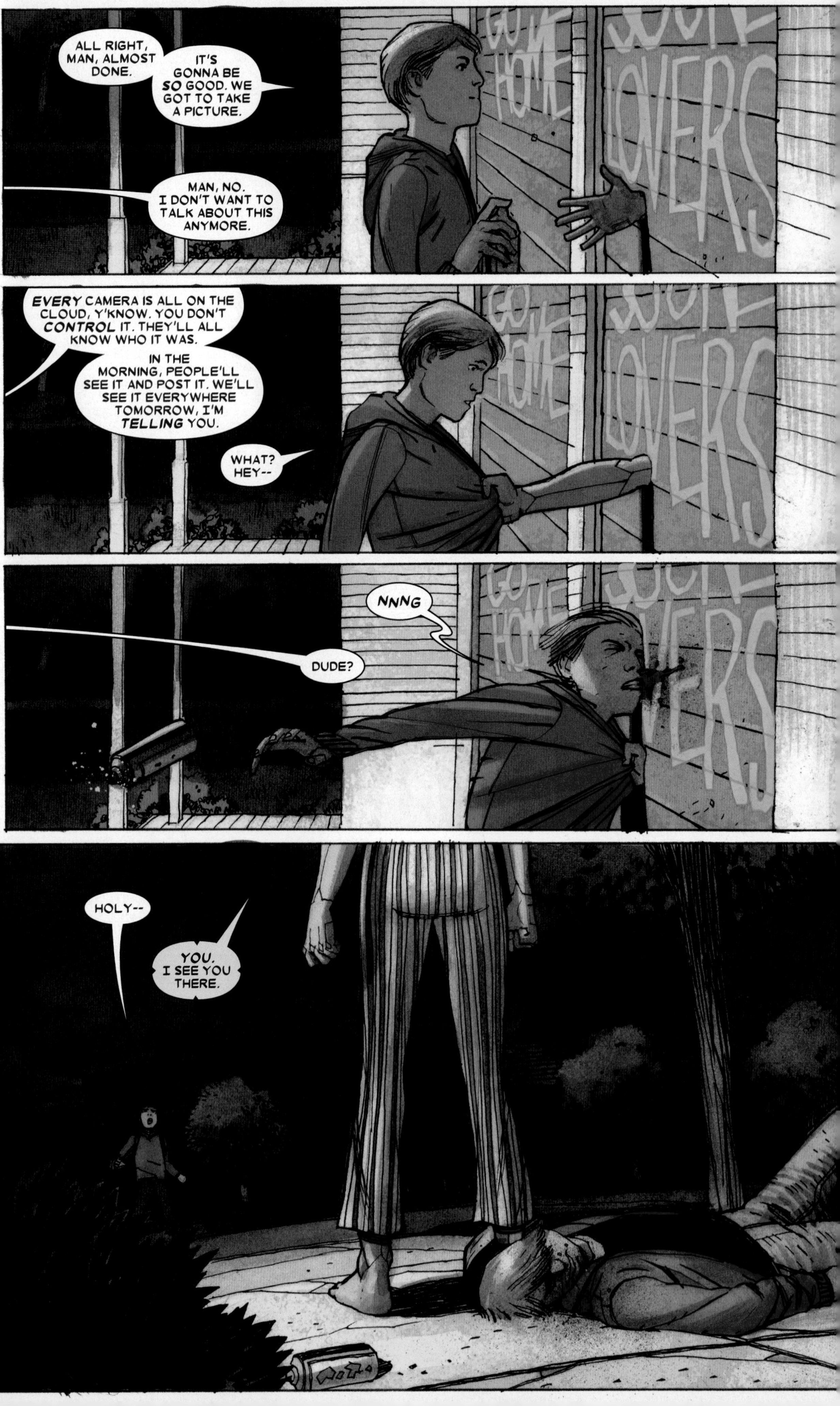
ALL RIGHT, MAN, ALMOST DONE.
IT'S GONNA BE SO GOOD. WE GOT TO TAKE A PICTURE.
MAN, NO. I DON'T WANT TO TALK ABOUT THIS ANYMORE.
GO HOME
LOVERS
EVERY CAMERA IS ALL ON THE CLOUD, Y'KNOW. YOU DON'T CONTROL IT. THEY'LL ALL KNOW WHO IT WAS.
IN THE MORNING, PEOPLE'LL SEE IT AND POST IT. WE'LL SEE IT EVERYWHERE TOMORROW, I'M TELLING YOU.
WHAT? HEY--
NNNG
DUDE?
HOLY--
YOU. I SEE YOU THERE.

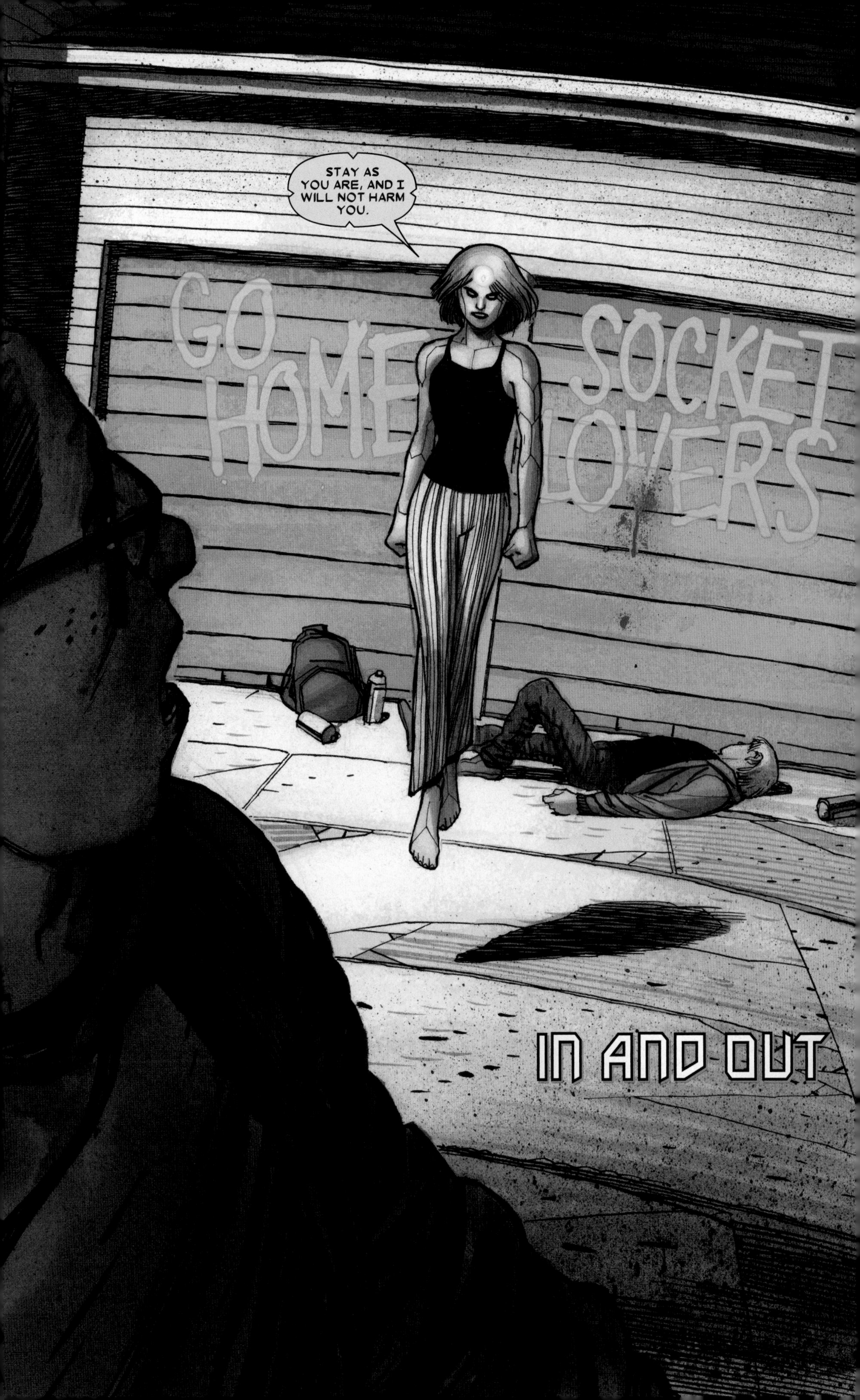
STAY AS YOU ARE, AND I WILL NOT HARM YOU.
GO HOME SOCKET LOVERS
IN AND OUT

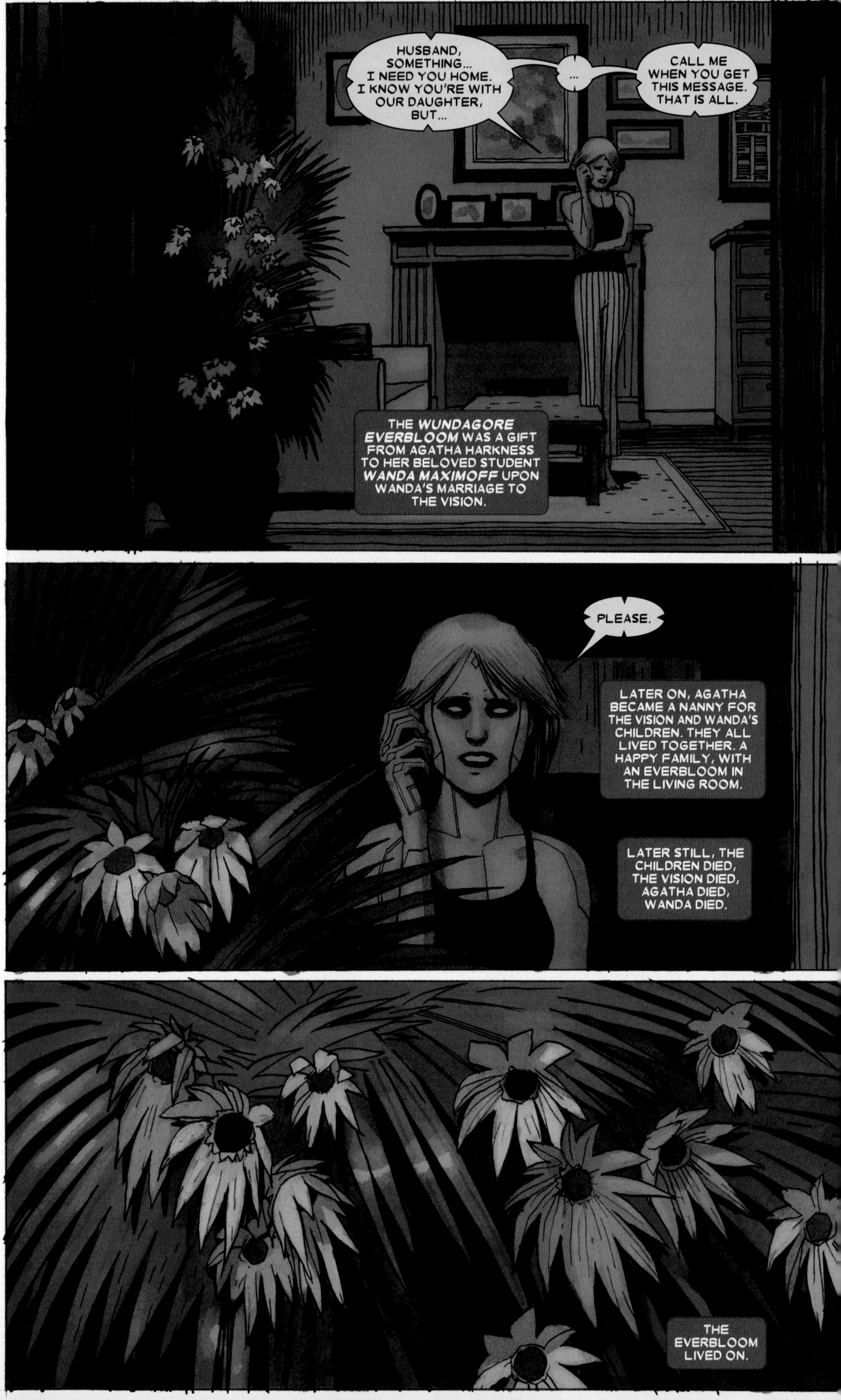
HUSBAND, SOMETHING... I NEED YOU HOME. I KNOW YOU'RE WITH OUR DAUGHTER, BUT...
...
CALL ME WHEN YOU GET THIS MESSAGE. THAT IS ALL.
THE WUNDAGORE EVERBLOOM WAS A GIFT FROM AGATHA HARKNESS TO HER BELOVED STUDENT WANDA MAXIMOFF UPON WANDA'S MARRIAGE TO THE VISION.
PLEASE.
LATER ON, AGATHA BECAME A NANNY FOR THE VISION AND WANDA'S CHILDREN. THEY ALL LIVED TOGETHER. A HAPPY FAMILY, WITH AN EVERBLOOM IN THE LIVING ROOM.
LATER STILL, THE CHILDREN DIED, THE VISION DIED, AGATHA DIED, WANDA DIED.
THE EVERBLOOM LIVED ON.

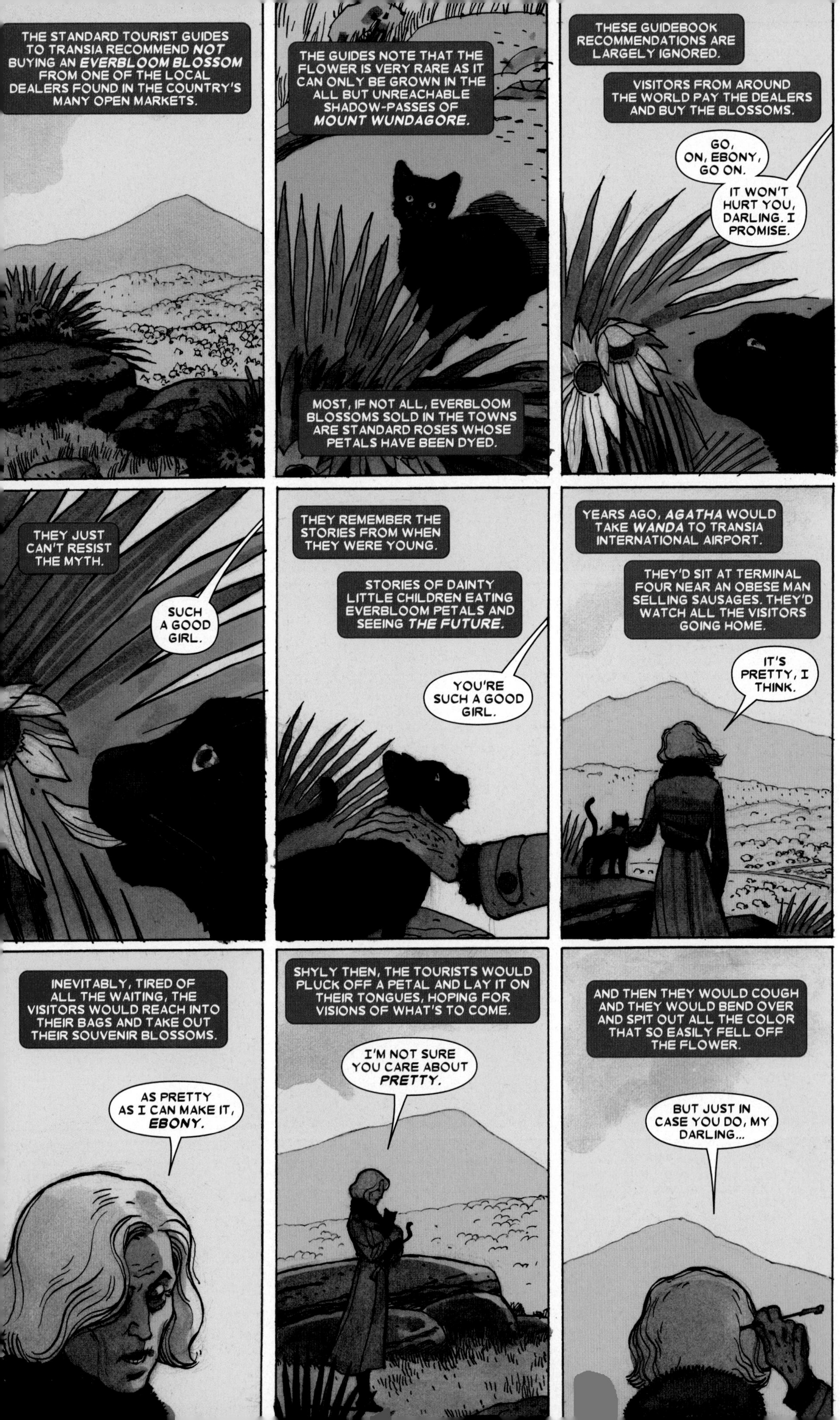
THE STANDARD TOURIST GUIDES TO TRANSIA RECOMMEND *NOT* BUYING AN *EVERBLOOM BLOSSOM* FROM ONE OF THE LOCAL DEALERS FOUND IN THE COUNTRY'S MANY OPEN MARKETS.
THE GUIDES NOTE THAT THE FLOWER IS VERY RARE AS IT CAN ONLY BE GROWN IN THE ALL BUT UNREACHABLE SHADOW-PASSES OF *MOUNT WUNDAGORE.*
MOST, IF NOT ALL, EVERBLOOM BLOSSOMS SOLD IN THE TOWNS ARE STANDARD ROSES WHOSE PETALS HAVE BEEN DYED.
THESE GUIDEBOOK RECOMMENDATIONS ARE LARGELY IGNORED.
VISITORS FROM AROUND THE WORLD PAY THE DEALERS AND BUY THE BLOSSOMS.
GO, ON, EBONY, GO ON.
IT WON'T HURT YOU, DARLING. I PROMISE.
THEY JUST CAN'T RESIST THE MYTH.
SUCH A GOOD GIRL.
THEY REMEMBER THE STORIES FROM WHEN THEY WERE YOUNG.
STORIES OF DAINTY LITTLE CHILDREN EATING EVERBLOOM PETALS AND SEEING *THE FUTURE.*
YOU'RE SUCH A GOOD GIRL.
YEARS AGO, *AGATHA* WOULD TAKE *WANDA* TO TRANSIA INTERNATIONAL AIRPORT.
THEY'D SIT AT TERMINAL FOUR NEAR AN OBESE MAN SELLING SAUSAGES. THEY'D WATCH ALL THE VISITORS GOING HOME.
IT'S PRETTY, I THINK.
INEVITABLY, TIRED OF ALL THE WAITING, THE VISITORS WOULD REACH INTO THEIR BAGS AND TAKE OUT THEIR SOUVENIR BLOSSOMS.
AS PRETTY AS I CAN MAKE IT, *EBONY.*
SHYLY THEN, THE TOURISTS WOULD PLUCK OFF A PETAL AND LAY IT ON THEIR TONGUES, HOPING FOR VISIONS OF WHAT'S TO COME.
I'M NOT SURE YOU CARE ABOUT *PRETTY.*
AND THEN THEY WOULD COUGH AND THEY WOULD BEND OVER AND SPIT OUT ALL THE COLOR THAT SO EASILY FELL OFF THE FLOWER.
BUT JUST IN CASE YOU DO, MY DARLING...

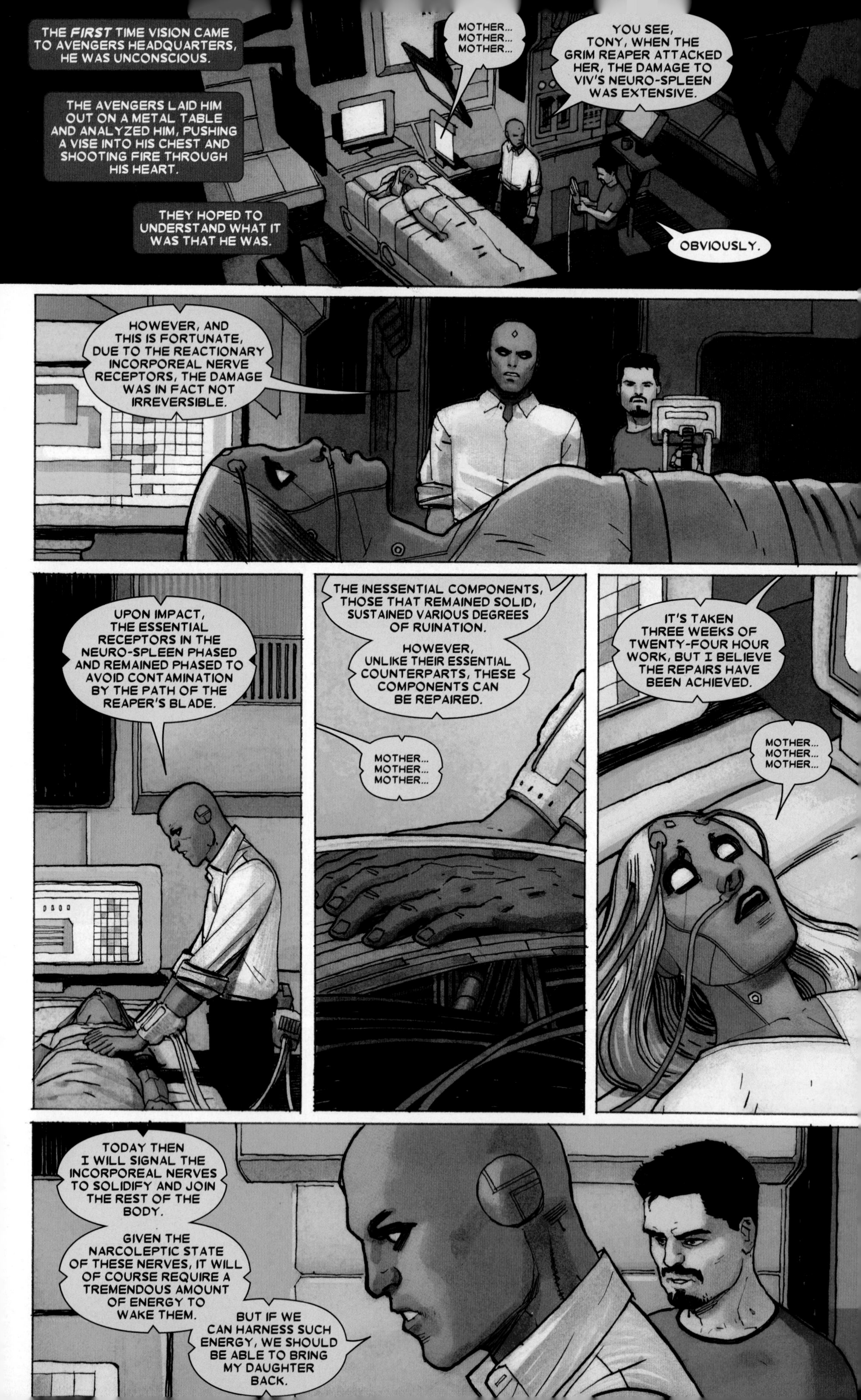
THE FIRST TIME VISION CAME TO AVENGERS HEADQUARTERS, HE WAS UNCONSCIOUS.
THE AVENGERS LAID HIM OUT ON A METAL TABLE AND ANALYZED HIM, PUSHING A VISE INTO HIS CHEST AND SHOOTING FIRE THROUGH HIS HEART.
THEY HOPED TO UNDERSTAND WHAT IT WAS THAT HE WAS.
MOTHER... MOTHER... MOTHER...
YOU SEE, TONY, WHEN THE GRIM REAPER ATTACKED HER, THE DAMAGE TO VIV'S NEURO-SPLEEN WAS EXTENSIVE.
OBVIOUSLY.
HOWEVER, AND THIS IS FORTUNATE, DUE TO THE REACTIONARY INCORPOREAL NERVE RECEPTORS, THE DAMAGE WAS IN FACT NOT IRREVERSIBLE.
UPON IMPACT, THE ESSENTIAL RECEPTORS IN THE NEURO-SPLEEN PHASED AND REMAINED PHASED TO AVOID CONTAMINATION BY THE PATH OF THE REAPER'S BLADE.
THE INESSENTIAL COMPONENTS, THOSE THAT REMAINED SOLID, SUSTAINED VARIOUS DEGREES OF RUINATION.
HOWEVER, UNLIKE THEIR ESSENTIAL COUNTERPARTS, THESE COMPONENTS CAN BE REPAIRED.
MOTHER... MOTHER... MOTHER...
IT'S TAKEN THREE WEEKS OF TWENTY-FOUR HOUR WORK, BUT I BELIEVE THE REPAIRS HAVE BEEN ACHIEVED.
MOTHER... MOTHER... MOTHER...
TODAY THEN I WILL SIGNAL THE INCORPOREAL NERVES TO SOLIDIFY AND JOIN THE REST OF THE BODY.
GIVEN THE NARCOLEPTIC STATE OF THESE NERVES, IT WILL OF COURSE REQUIRE A TREMENDOUS AMOUNT OF ENERGY TO WAKE THEM.
BUT IF WE CAN HARNESS SUCH ENERGY, WE SHOULD BE ABLE TO BRING MY DAUGHTER BACK.

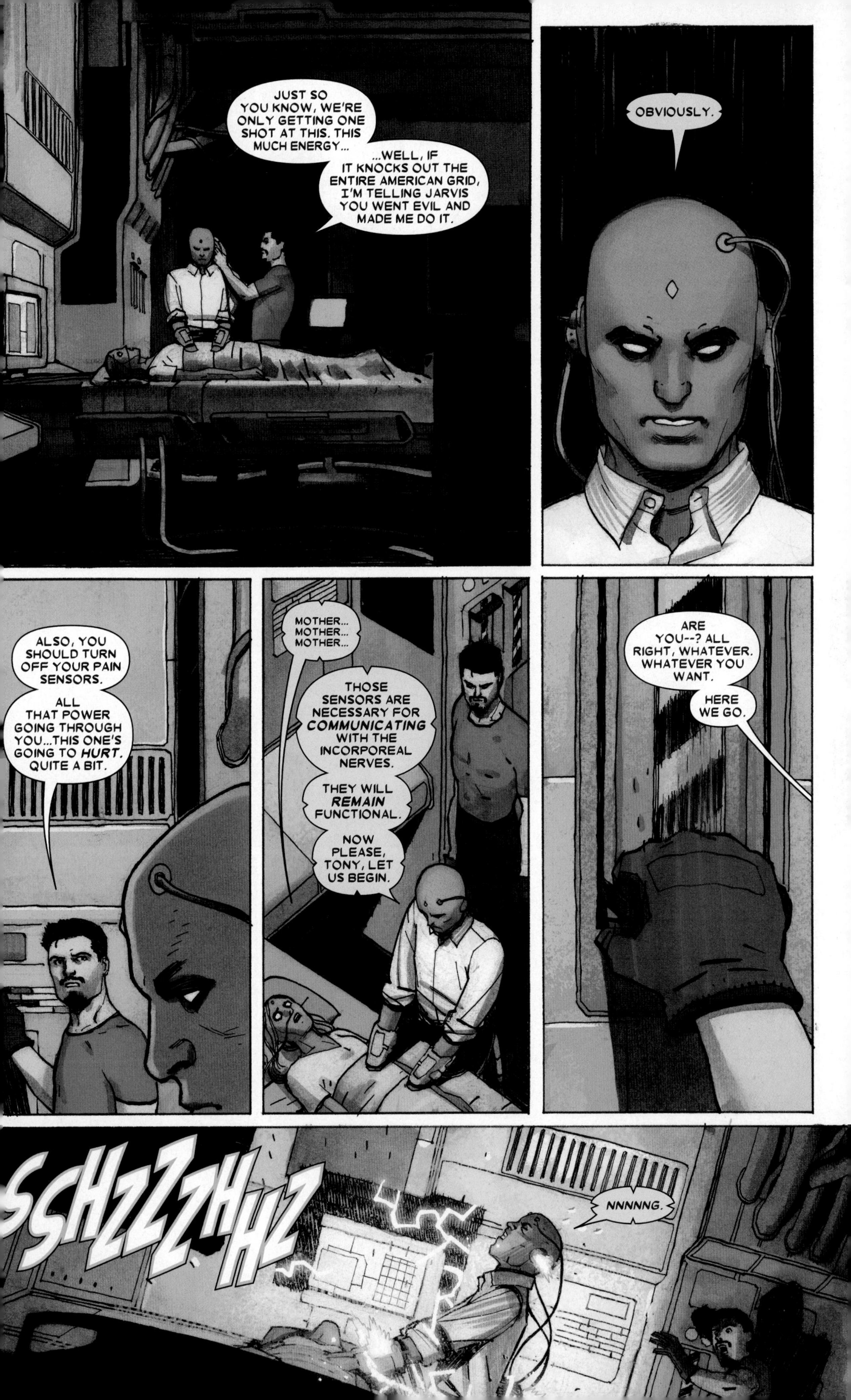

JUST SO YOU KNOW, WE'RE ONLY GETTING ONE SHOT AT THIS. THIS MUCH ENERGY...
...WELL, IF IT KNOCKS OUT THE ENTIRE AMERICAN GRID, I'M TELLING JARVIS YOU WENT EVIL AND MADE ME DO IT.
OBVIOUSLY.
ALSO, YOU SHOULD TURN OFF YOUR PAIN SENSORS.
ALL THAT POWER GOING THROUGH YOU...THIS ONE'S GOING TO *HURT*. QUITE A BIT.
MOTHER... MOTHER... MOTHER...
THOSE SENSORS ARE NECESSARY FOR ***COMMUNICATING*** WITH THE INCORPOREAL NERVES.
THEY WILL ***REMAIN*** FUNCTIONAL.
NOW PLEASE, TONY, LET US BEGIN.
ARE YOU--? ALL RIGHT, WHATEVER. WHATEVER YOU WANT.
HERE WE GO.
SSHZZZZHHZ
NNNNNG.

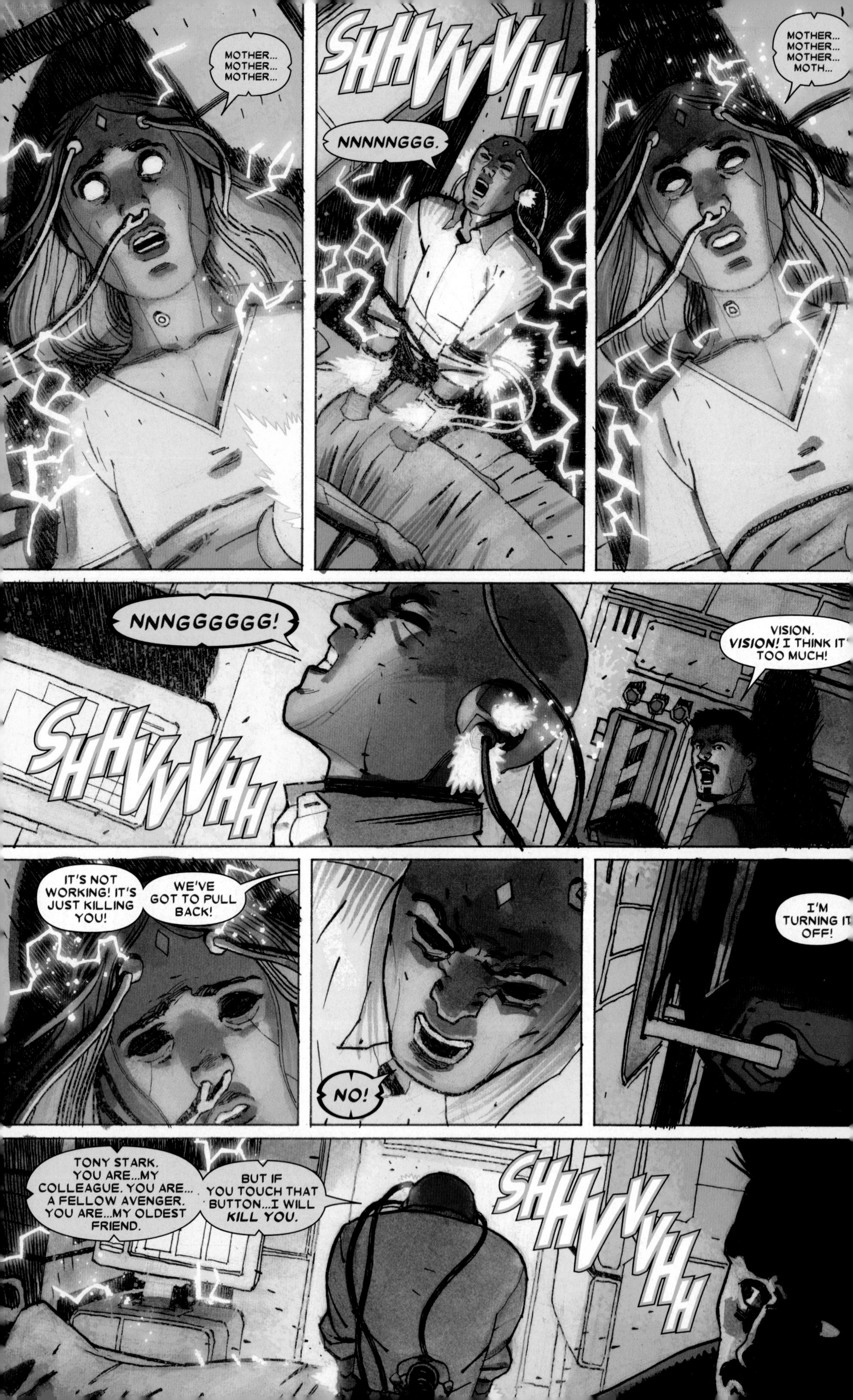
MOTHER... MOTHER... MOTHER...
SHHVVVHH
NNNNNGGG.
MOTHER... MOTHER... MOTHER... MOTH...
NNNGGGGGG!
SHHVVVHH
VISION. VISION! I THINK IT TOO MUCH!
IT'S NOT WORKING! IT'S JUST KILLING YOU!
WE'VE GOT TO PULL BACK!
NO!
I'M TURNING IT OFF!
TONY STARK. YOU ARE...MY COLLEAGUE. YOU ARE... A FELLOW AVENGER. YOU ARE...MY OLDEST FRIEND.
BUT IF YOU TOUCH THAT BUTTON...I WILL KILL YOU.
SHHVVVHH

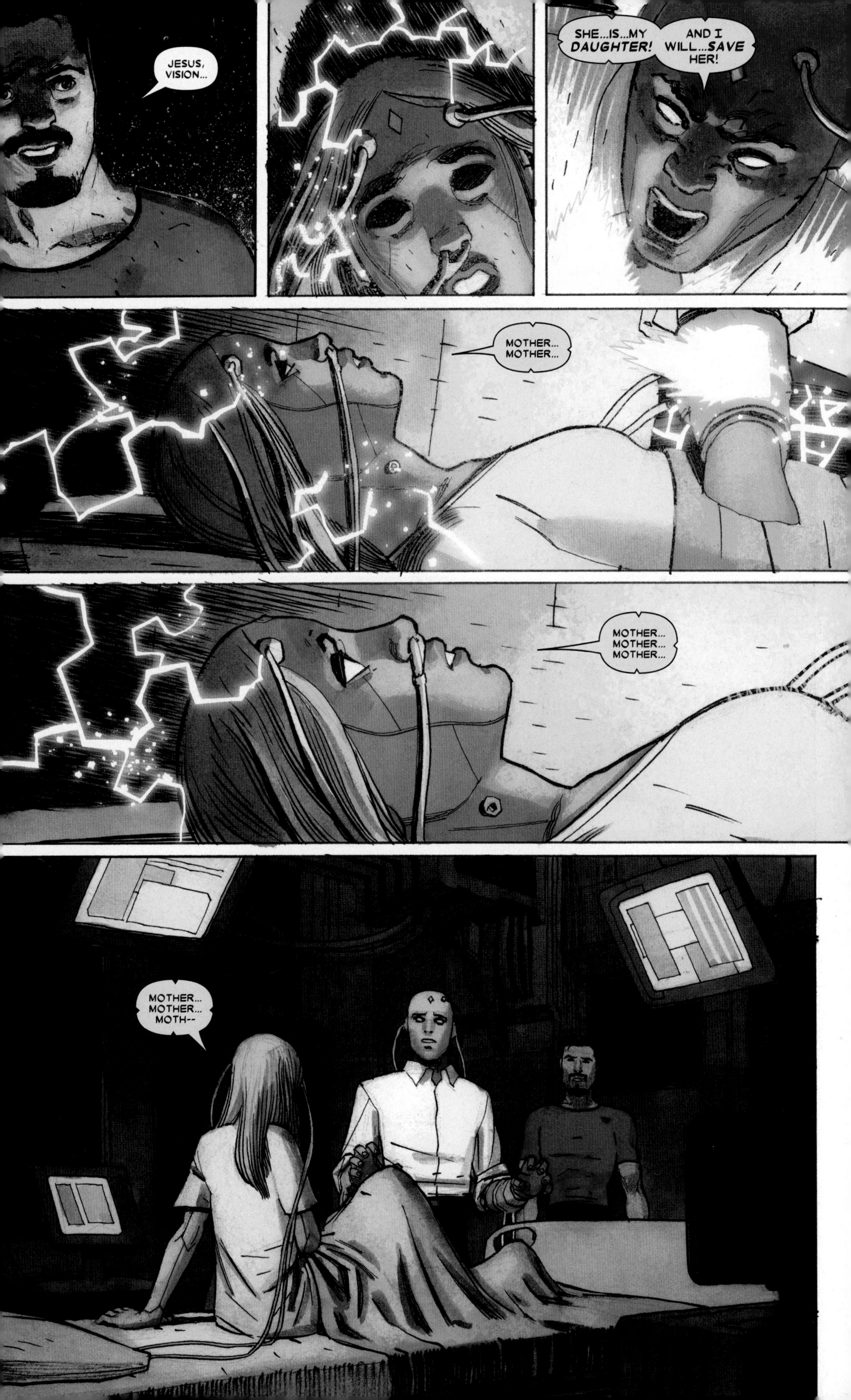

JESUS, VISION...
SHE...IS...MY *DAUGHTER!*
AND I WILL...*SAVE* HER!
MOTHER... MOTHER...
MOTHER... MOTHER... MOTHER...
MOTHER... MOTHER... MOTH--

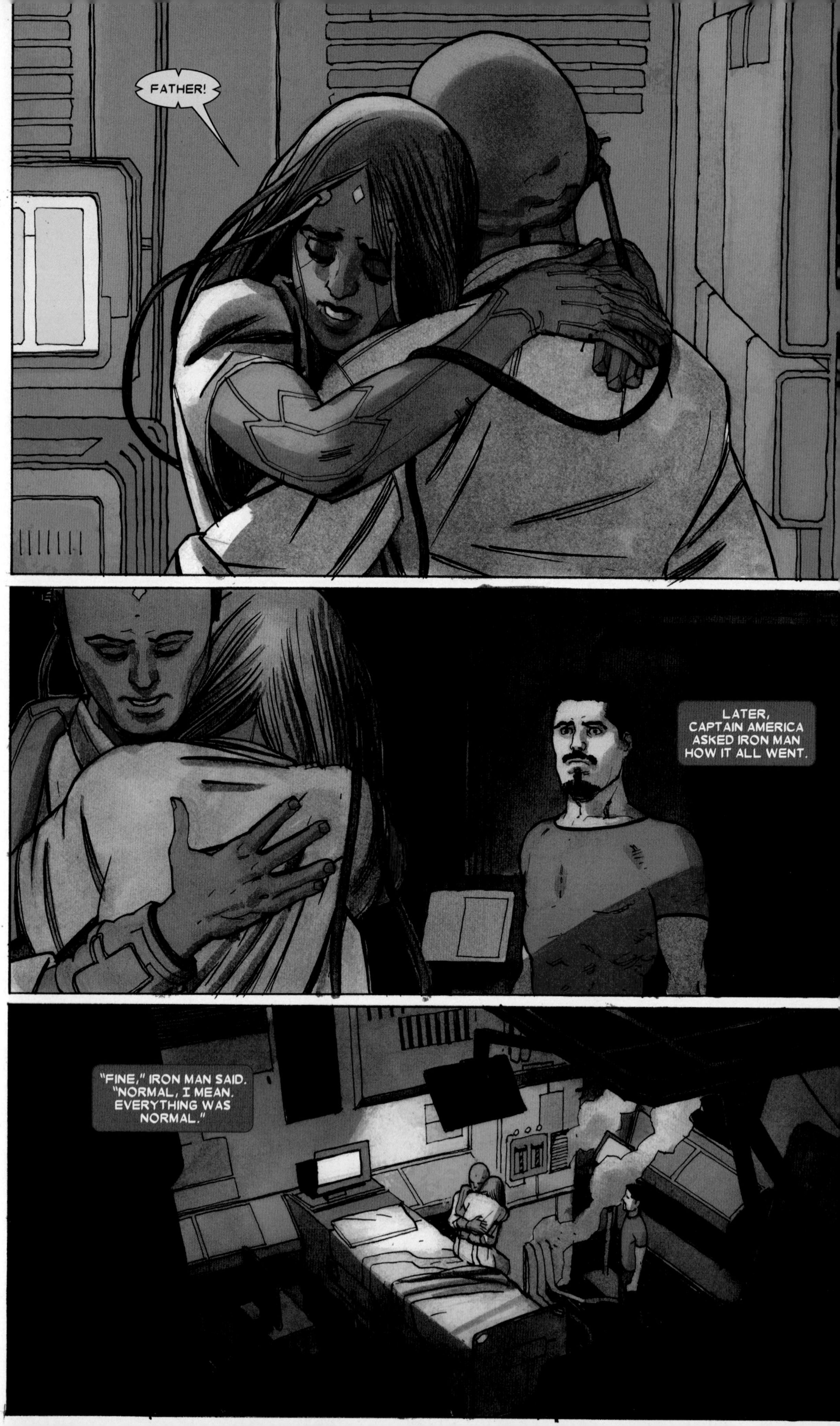
FATHER!
LATER, CAPTAIN AMERICA ASKED IRON MAN HOW IT ALL WENT.
"FINE," IRON MAN SAID. "NORMAL, I MEAN. EVERYTHING WAS NORMAL."

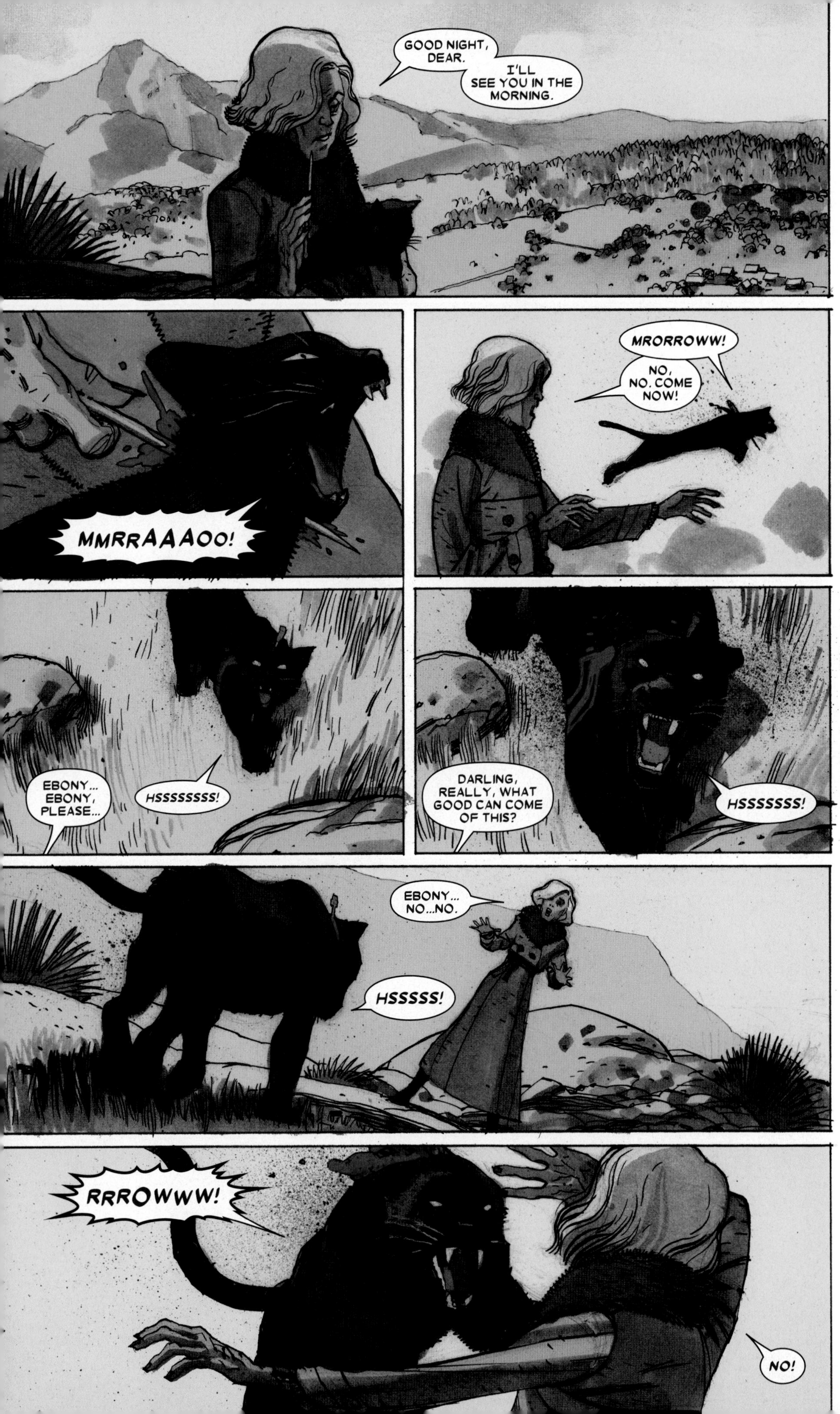
GOOD NIGHT, DEAR.
I'LL SEE YOU IN THE MORNING.
MMRRAAAOO!
MRORROWW!
NO, NO. COME NOW!
EBONY... EBONY, PLEASE...
HSSSSSSSS!
DARLING, REALLY, WHAT GOOD CAN COME OF THIS?
HSSSSSSS!
EBONY... NO...NO.
HSSSSS!
RRROWWW!
NO!

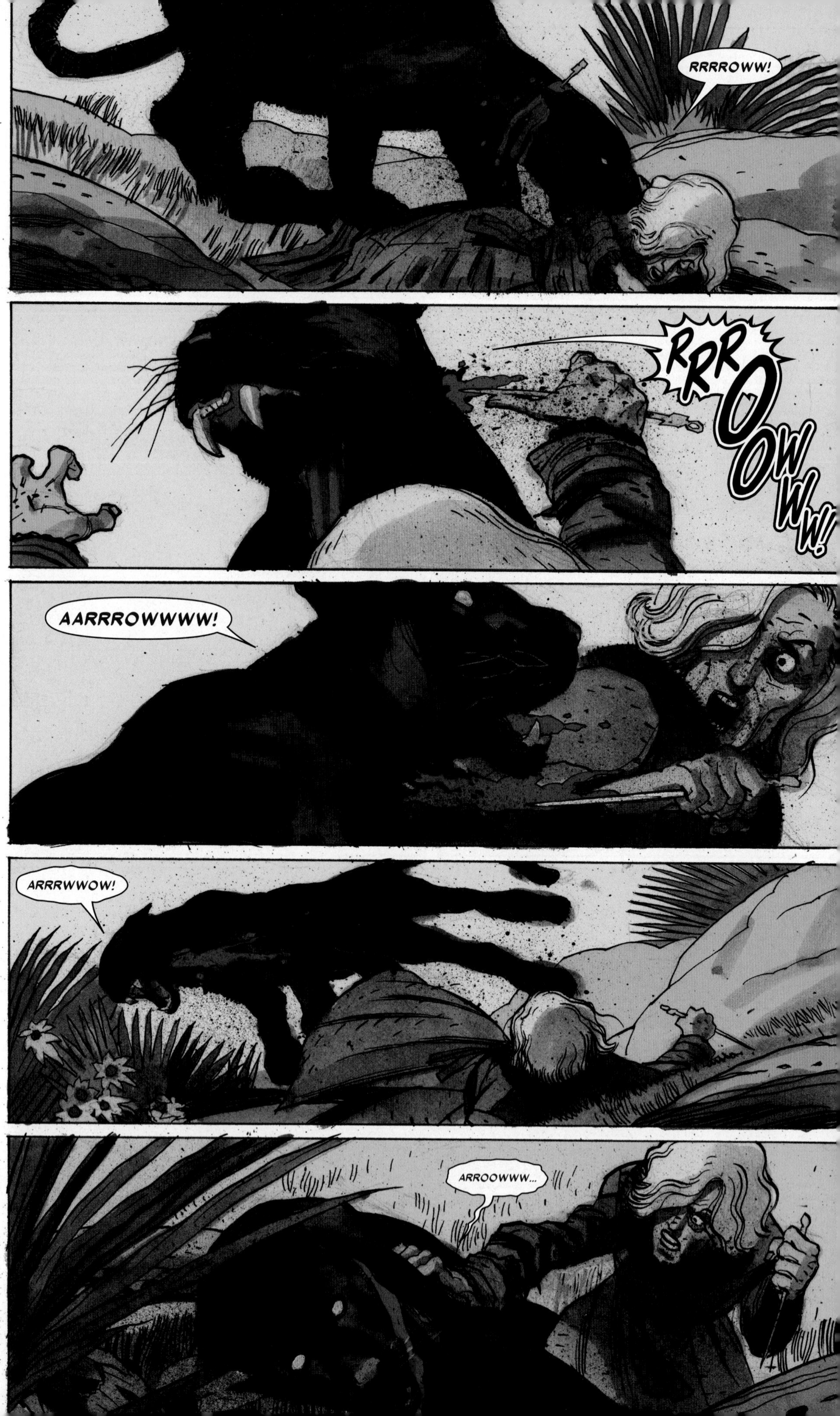
RRRROWW!
RRROOWWW!
AARRROWWWW!
ARRRWWOW!
ARROOWWW...

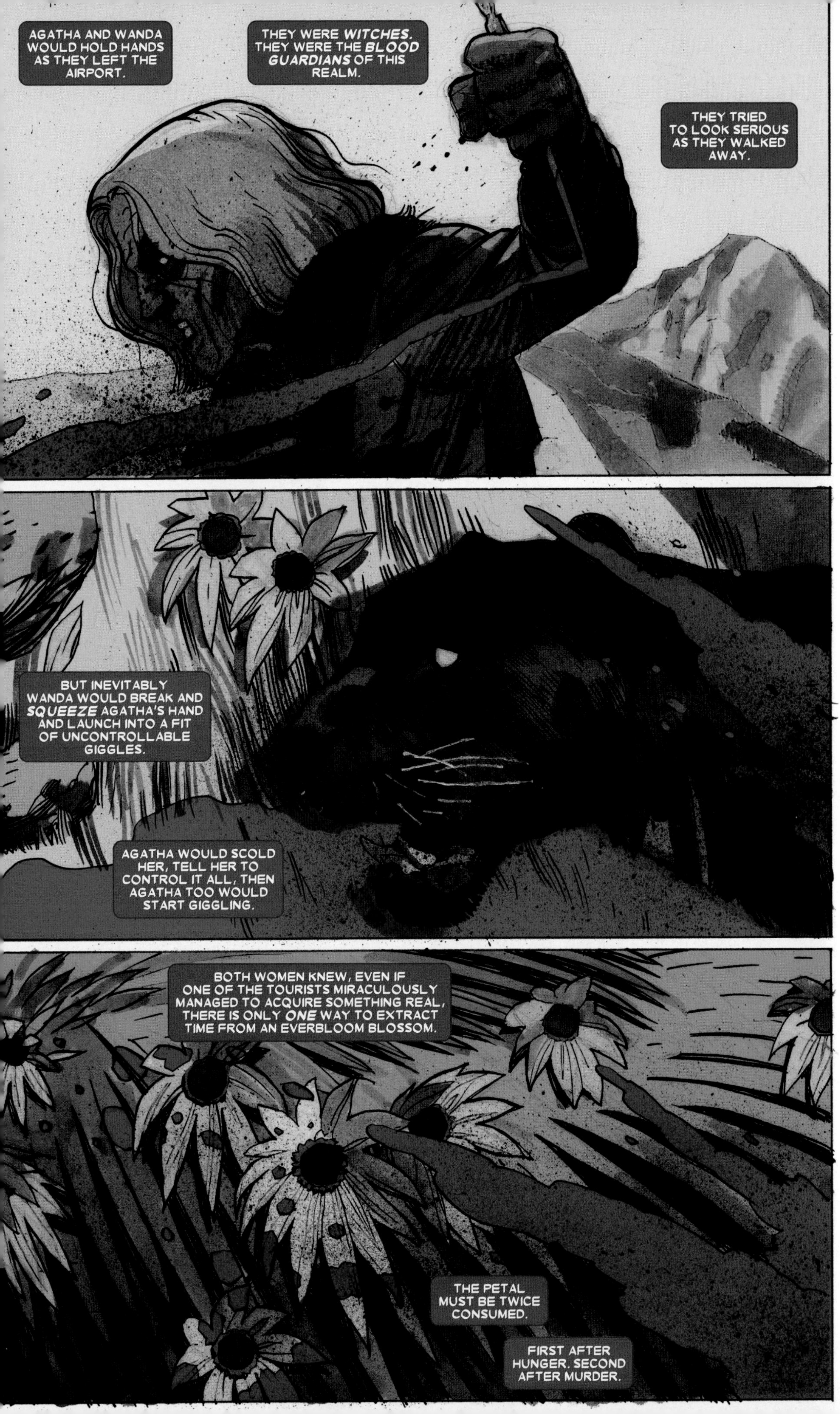
AGATHA AND WANDA WOULD HOLD HANDS AS THEY LEFT THE AIRPORT.
THEY WERE *WITCHES.* THEY WERE THE *BLOOD GUARDIANS* OF THIS REALM.
THEY TRIED TO LOOK SERIOUS AS THEY WALKED AWAY.
BUT INEVITABLY WANDA WOULD BREAK AND *SQUEEZE* AGATHA'S HAND AND LAUNCH INTO A FIT OF UNCONTROLLABLE GIGGLES.
AGATHA WOULD SCOLD HER, TELL HER TO CONTROL IT ALL, THEN AGATHA TOO WOULD START GIGGLING.
BOTH WOMEN KNEW, EVEN IF ONE OF THE TOURISTS MIRACULOUSLY MANAGED TO ACQUIRE SOMETHING REAL, THERE IS ONLY *ONE* WAY TO EXTRACT TIME FROM AN EVERBLOOM BLOSSOM.
THE PETAL MUST BE TWICE CONSUMED.
FIRST AFTER HUNGER, SECOND AFTER MURDER.

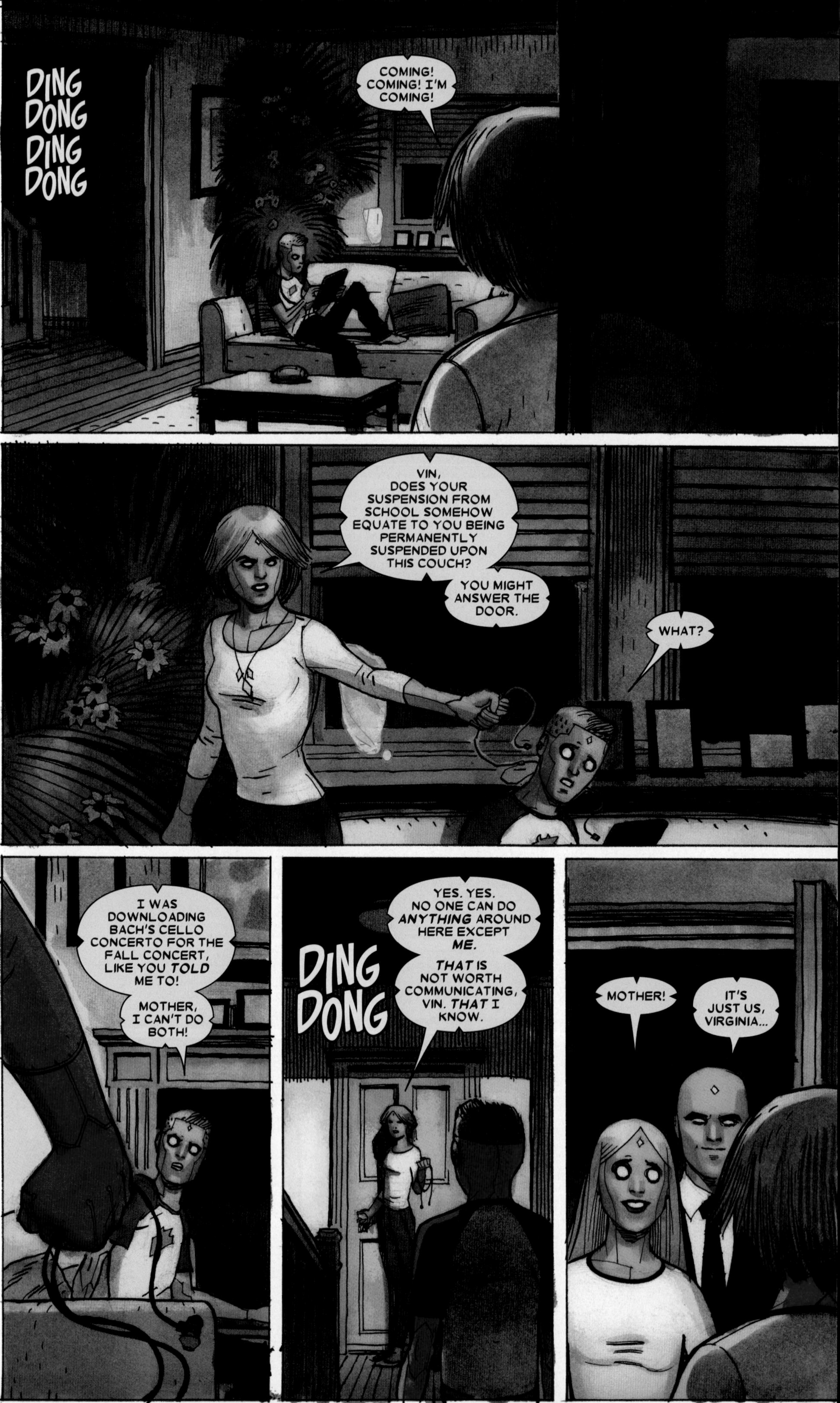
DING
DONG
DING
DONG
COMING! COMING! I'M COMING!
VIN, DOES YOUR SUSPENSION FROM SCHOOL SOMEHOW EQUATE TO YOU BEING PERMANENTLY SUSPENDED UPON THIS COUCH?
YOU MIGHT ANSWER THE DOOR.
WHAT?
I WAS DOWNLOADING BACH'S CELLO CONCERTO FOR THE FALL CONCERT, LIKE YOU *TOLD* ME TO!
MOTHER, I CAN'T DO BOTH!
DING
DONG
YES. YES. NO ONE CAN DO *ANYTHING* AROUND HERE EXCEPT *ME.*
THAT IS NOT WORTH COMMUNICATING, VIN. *THAT* I KNOW.
MOTHER!
IT'S JUST US, VIRGINIA...

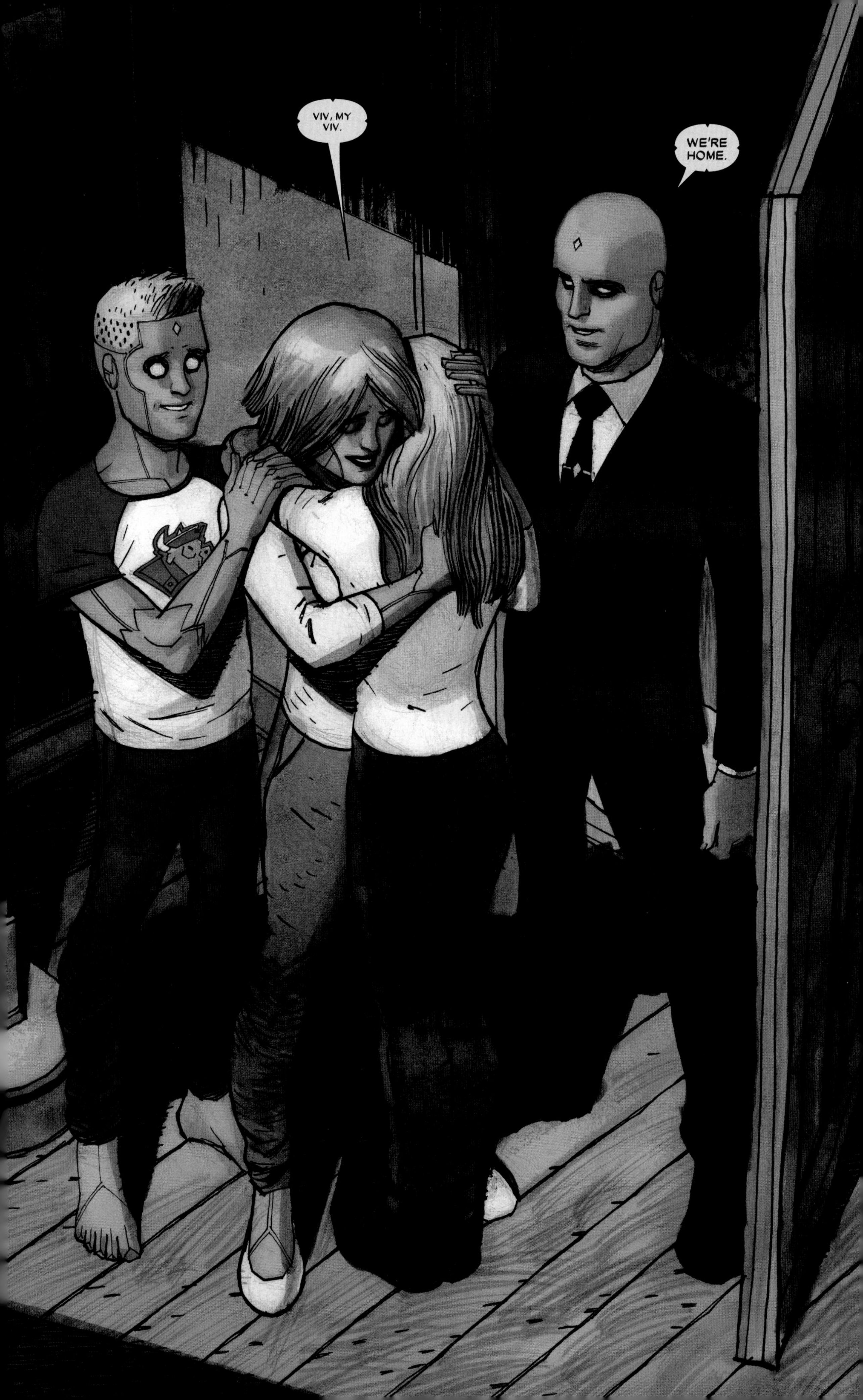
VIV, MY VIV.
WE'RE HOME.

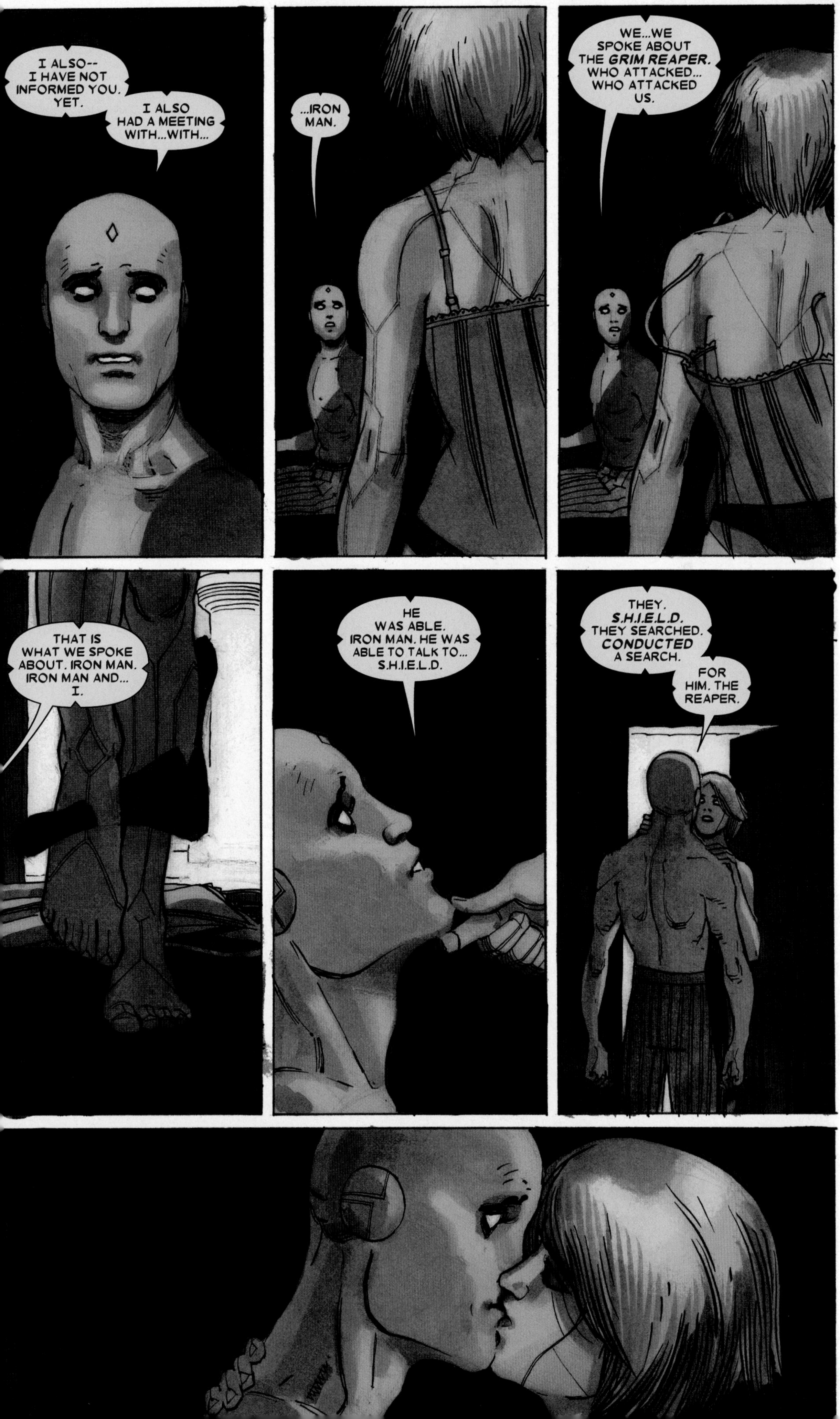
I ALSO-- I HAVE NOT INFORMED YOU. YET.
I ALSO HAD A MEETING WITH...WITH...
...IRON MAN.
WE...WE SPOKE ABOUT THE *GRIM REAPER.* WHO ATTACKED... WHO ATTACKED US.
THAT IS WHAT WE SPOKE ABOUT. IRON MAN. IRON MAN AND... I.
HE WAS ABLE. IRON MAN. HE WAS ABLE TO TALK TO... S.H.I.E.L.D.
THEY. *S.H.I.E.L.D.* THEY SEARCHED. *CONDUCTED* A SEARCH.
FOR HIM. THE REAPER.

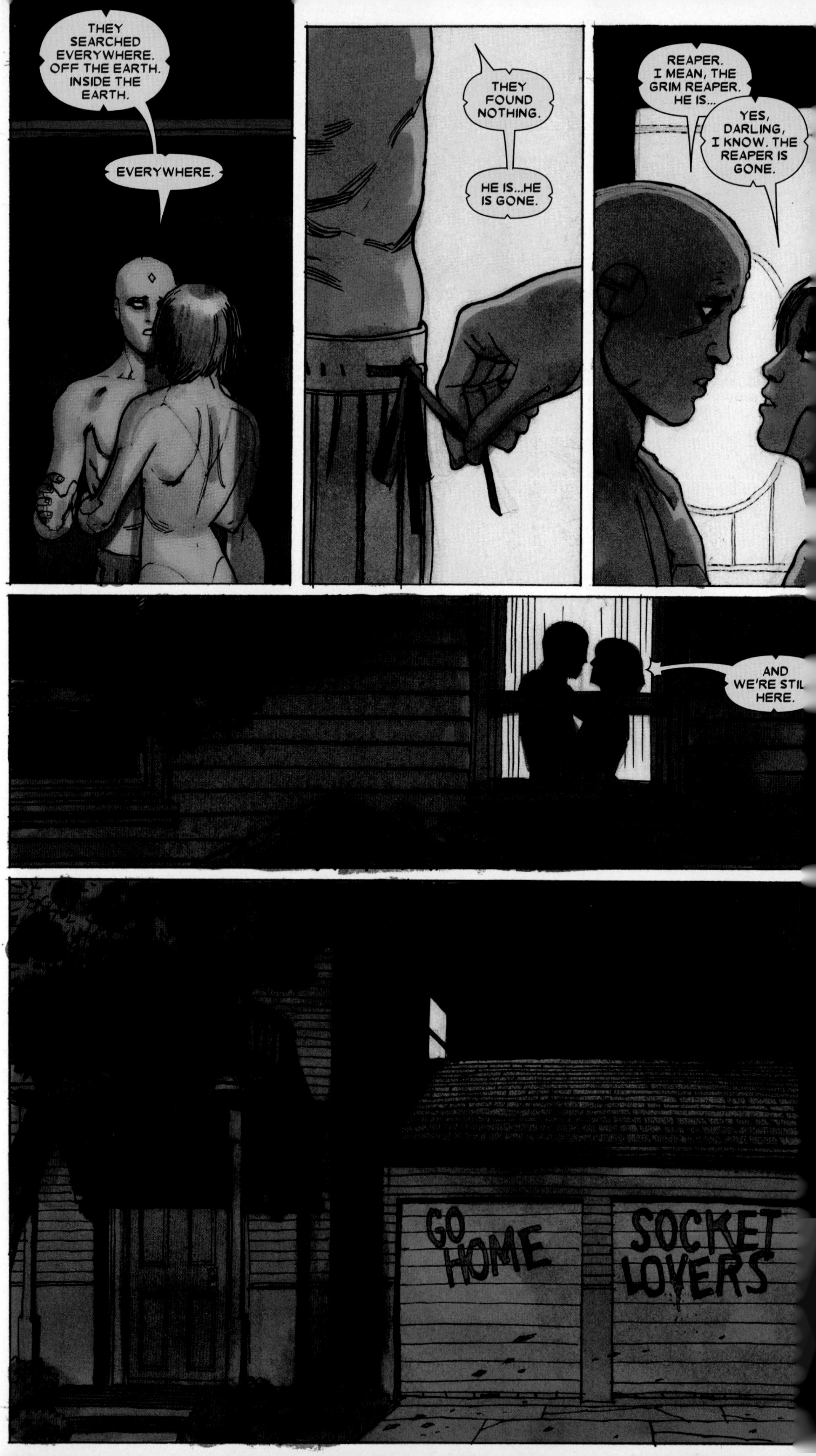
THEY SEARCHED EVERYWHERE. OFF THE EARTH. INSIDE THE EARTH.
EVERYWHERE.
THEY FOUND NOTHING.
HE IS...HE IS GONE.
REAPER. I MEAN, THE GRIM REAPER. HE IS...
YES, DARLING, I KNOW. THE REAPER IS GONE.
AND WE'RE STIL
HERE.
GO HOME SOCKET LOVERS

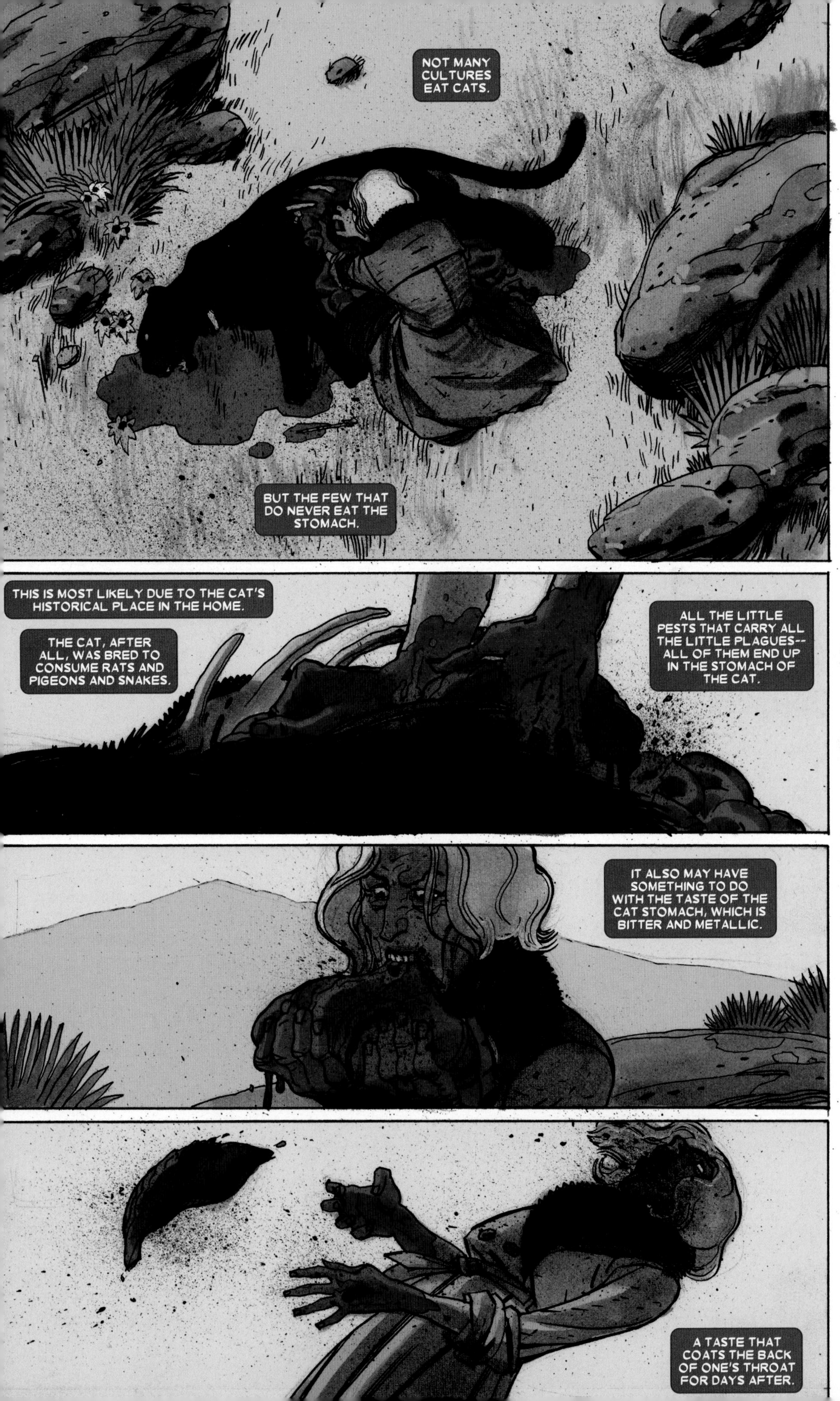
NOT MANY CULTURES EAT CATS.
BUT THE FEW THAT DO NEVER EAT THE STOMACH.
THIS IS MOST LIKELY DUE TO THE CAT'S HISTORICAL PLACE IN THE HOME.
THE CAT, AFTER ALL, WAS BRED TO CONSUME RATS AND PIGEONS AND SNAKES.
ALL THE LITTLE PESTS THAT CARRY ALL THE LITTLE PLAGUES-- ALL OF THEM END UP IN THE STOMACH OF THE CAT.
IT ALSO MAY HAVE SOMETHING TO DO WITH THE TASTE OF THE CAT STOMACH, WHICH IS BITTER AND METALLIC.
A TASTE THAT COATS THE BACK OF ONE'S THROAT FOR DAYS AFTER.

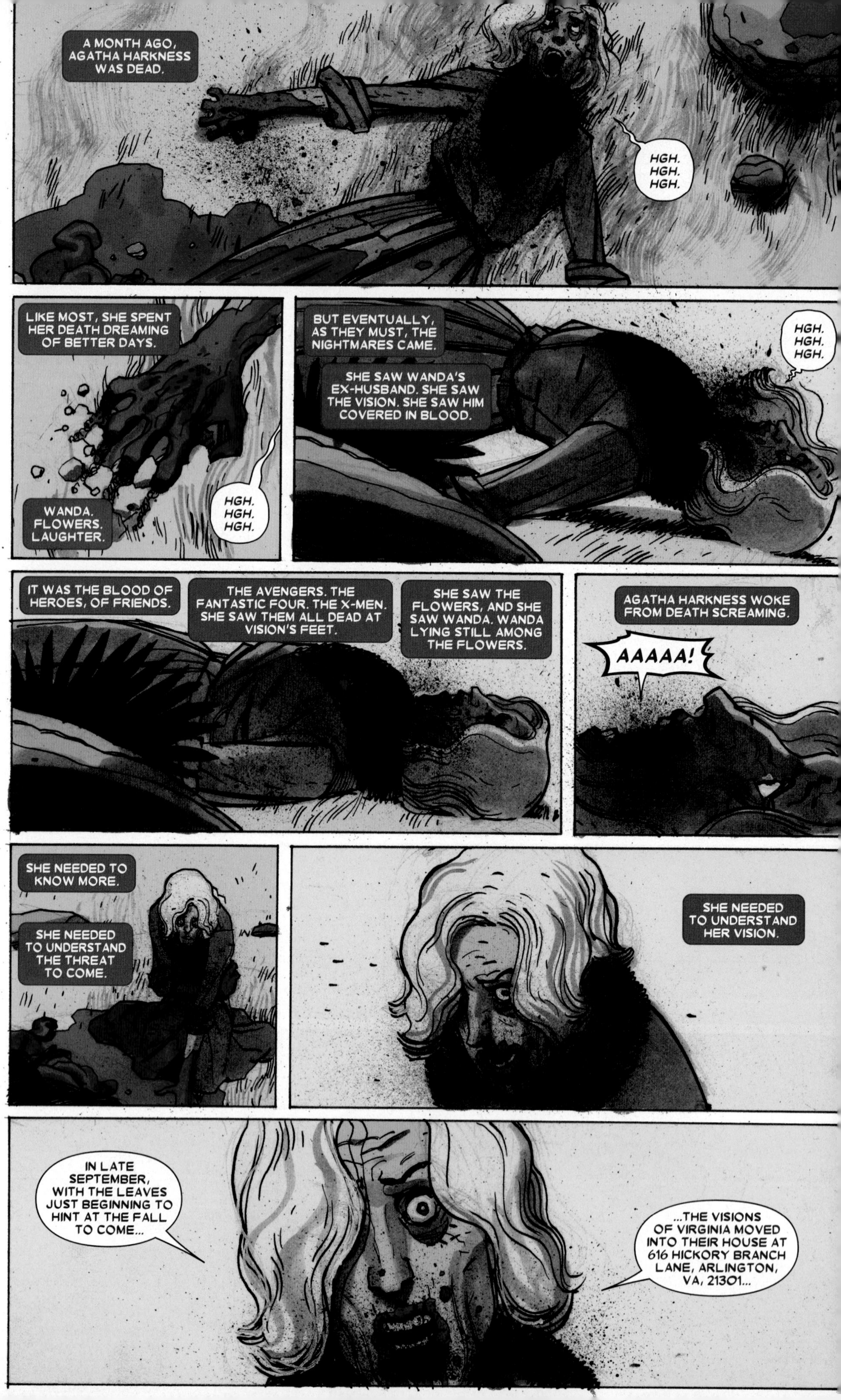
A MONTH AGO, AGATHA HARKNESS WAS DEAD.
HGH. HGH. HGH.
LIKE MOST, SHE SPENT HER DEATH DREAMING OF BETTER DAYS.
WANDA. FLOWERS. LAUGHTER.
HGH. HGH. HGH.
BUT EVENTUALLY, AS THEY MUST, THE NIGHTMARES CAME.
SHE SAW WANDA'S EX-HUSBAND. SHE SAW THE VISION. SHE SAW HIM COVERED IN BLOOD.
HGH. HGH. HGH.
IT WAS THE BLOOD OF HEROES, OF FRIENDS.
THE AVENGERS. THE FANTASTIC FOUR. THE X-MEN. SHE SAW THEM ALL DEAD AT VISION'S FEET.
SHE SAW THE FLOWERS, AND SHE SAW WANDA. WANDA LYING STILL AMONG THE FLOWERS.
AGATHA HARKNESS WOKE FROM DEATH SCREAMING.
AAAAA!
SHE NEEDED TO KNOW MORE.
SHE NEEDED TO UNDERSTAND THE THREAT TO COME.
SHE NEEDED TO UNDERSTAND HER VISION.
IN LATE SEPTEMBER, WITH THE LEAVES JUST BEGINNING TO HINT AT THE FALL TO COME...
...THE VISIONS OF VIRGINIA MOVED INTO THEIR HOUSE AT 616 HICKORY BRANCH LANE, ARLINGTON, VA, 21301...

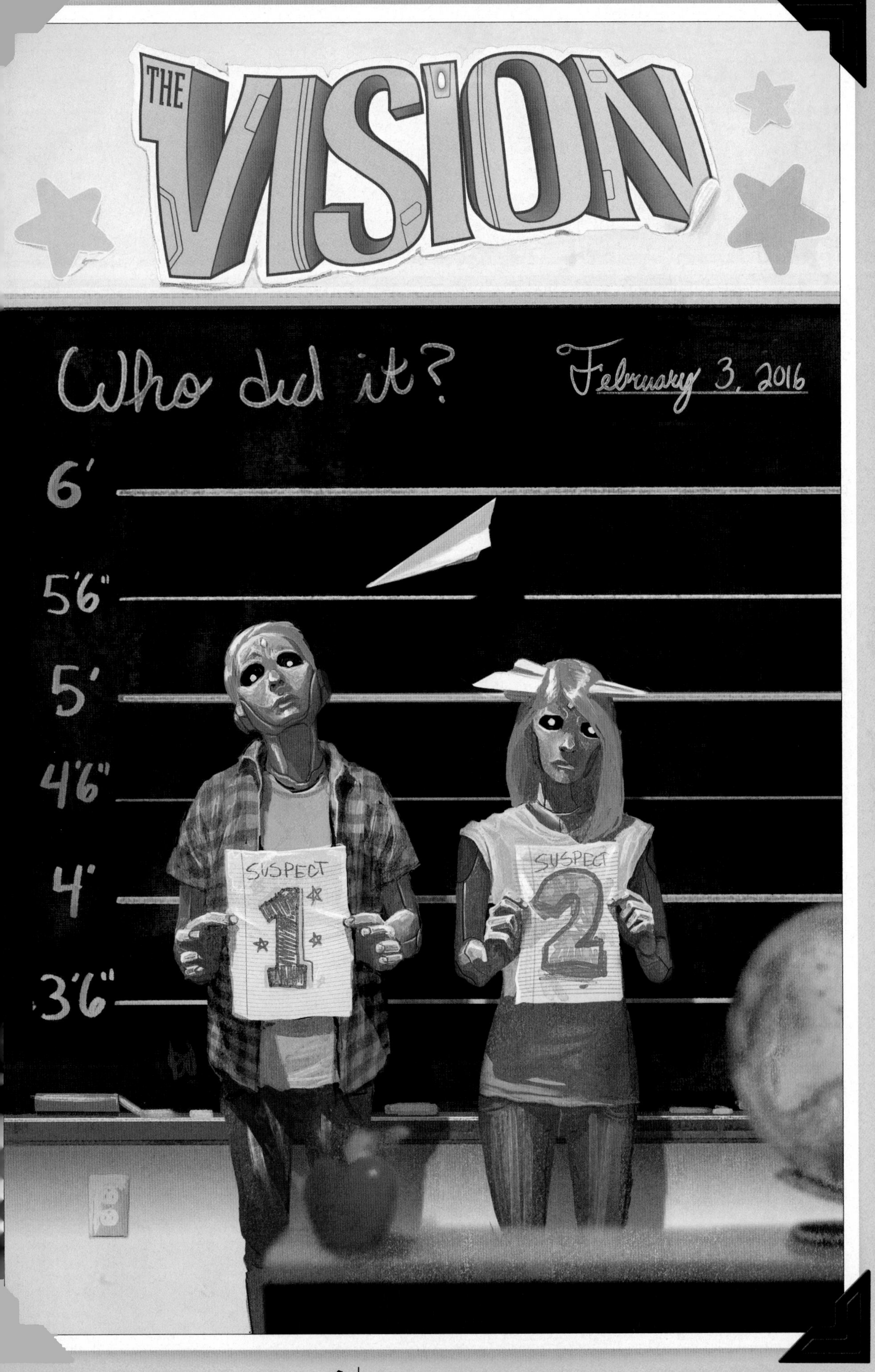
THE VISION
Who did it?
February 3, 2016
6'
5'6"
5'
4'6"
4'
3'6"
SUSPECT 1
SUSPECT 2

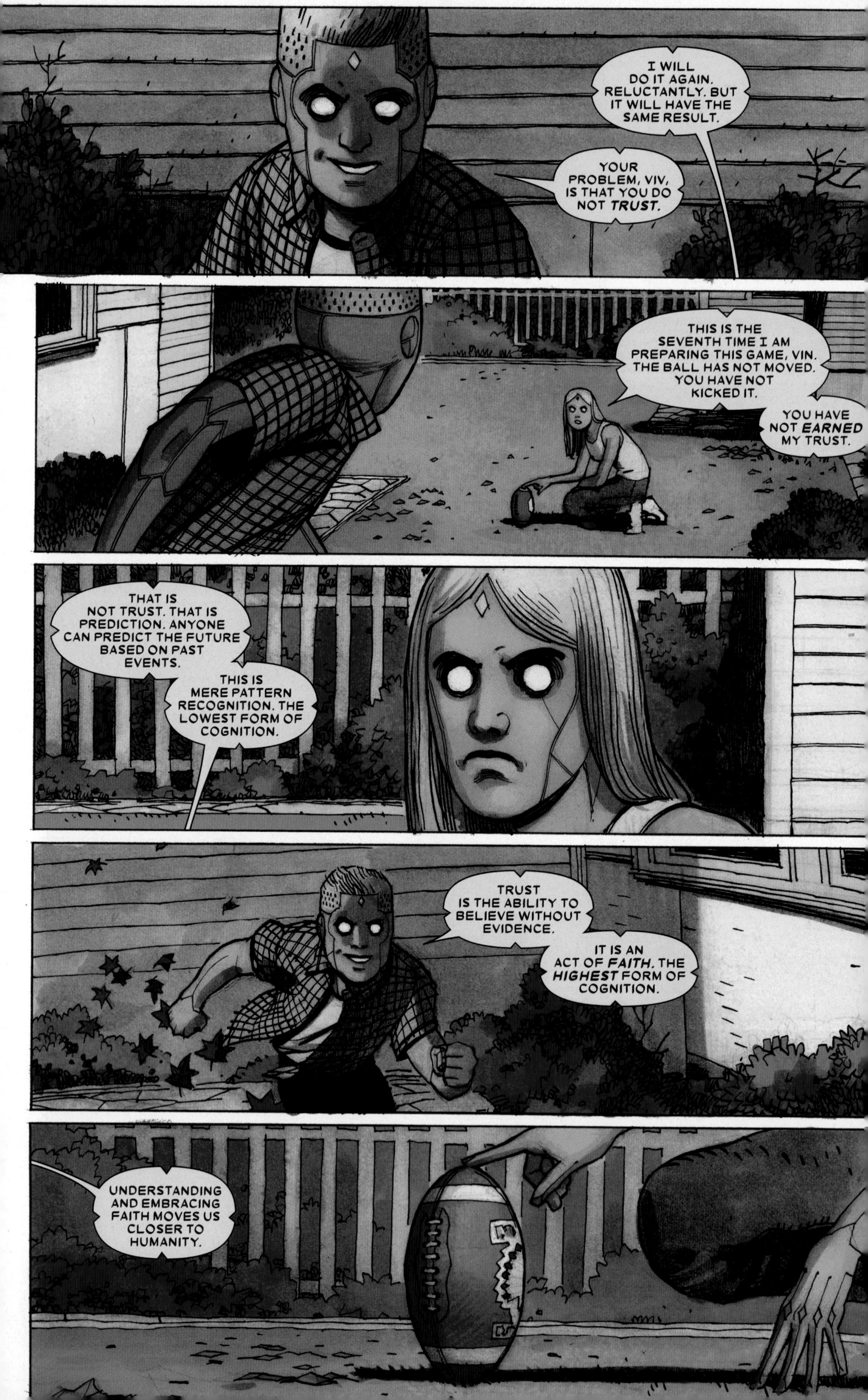
I WILL DO IT AGAIN. RELUCTANTLY. BUT IT WILL HAVE THE SAME RESULT.
YOUR PROBLEM, VIV, IS THAT YOU DO NOT *TRUST.*
THIS IS THE SEVENTH TIME I AM PREPARING THIS GAME, VIN. THE BALL HAS NOT MOVED. YOU HAVE NOT KICKED IT.
YOU HAVE NOT *EARNED* MY TRUST.
THAT IS NOT TRUST. THAT IS PREDICTION. ANYONE CAN PREDICT THE FUTURE BASED ON PAST EVENTS.
THIS IS MERE PATTERN RECOGNITION. THE LOWEST FORM OF COGNITION.
TRUST IS THE ABILITY TO BELIEVE WITHOUT EVIDENCE.
IT IS AN ACT OF *FAITH.* THE *HIGHEST* FORM OF COGNITION.
UNDERSTANDING AND EMBRACING FAITH MOVES US CLOSER TO HUMANITY.

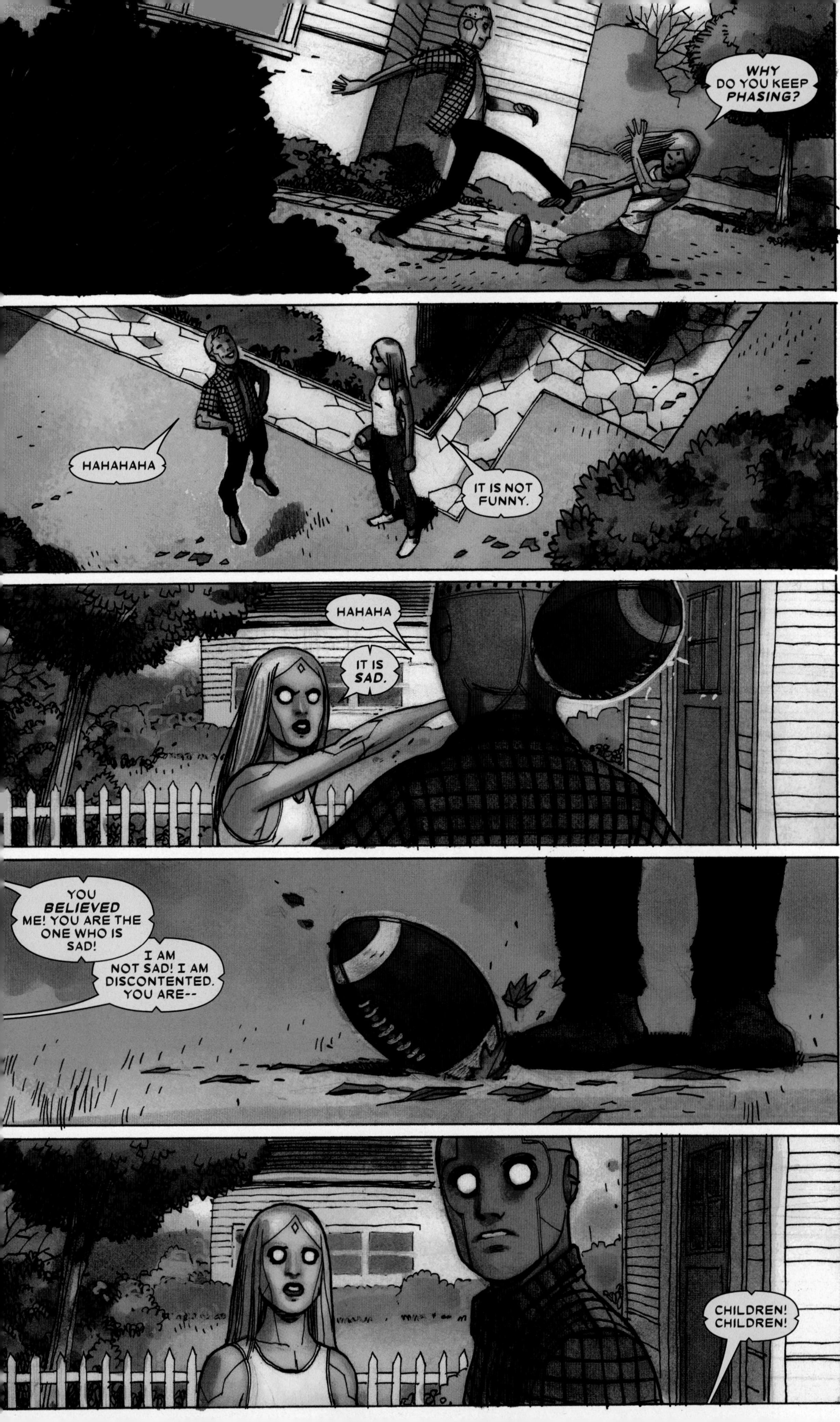
WHY DO YOU KEEP PHASING?
HAHAHAHA
IT IS NOT FUNNY.
HAHAHA
IT IS SAD.
YOU BELIEVED ME! YOU ARE THE ONE WHO IS SAD!
I AM NOT SAD! I AM DISCONTENTED. YOU ARE--
CHILDREN! CHILDREN!

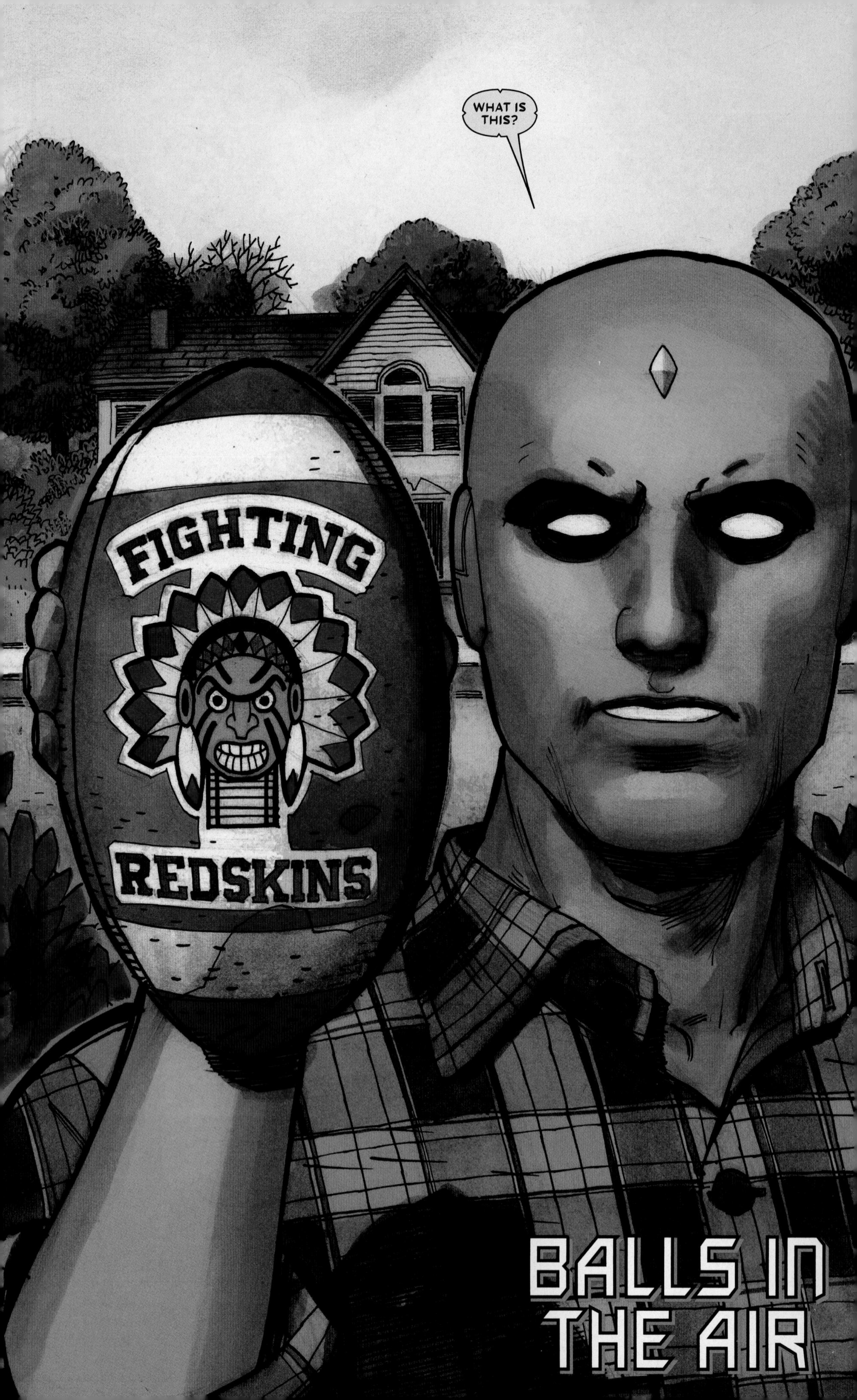
WHAT IS THIS?
FIGHTING
REDSKINS
BALLS IN THE AIR

IT IS THE SCHOOL MASCOT.

NO. YOUR MASCOT IS A COLORFUL BULL IN A THREE-CORNER HAT.

THAT IS A *NEW* MASCOT. THE FIGHTING PATRIOT. IT WAS CHANGED RECENTLY.

THEY HAVE YET TO MODIFY THE LOGO ON SOME OF THE VARIOUS ASSOCIATED PARAPHERNALIA.

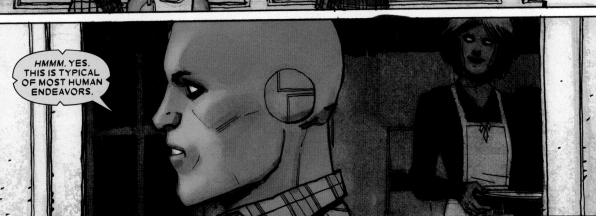

HMMM. YES. THIS IS TYPICAL OF MOST HUMAN ENDEAVORS.

THEY CHANGE, BUT THEY DO NOT CHANGE.

FOR A MOMENT, AS SHE LISTENED TO HER FAMILY ARGUE AND LAUGH, VIRGINIA FELT CONTENT.

SHE BELONGED HERE. THEY BELONGED HERE. EVERYTHING IN THE END WOULD BE GOOD.

THIS MOMENT LASTED 1.72 SECONDS.

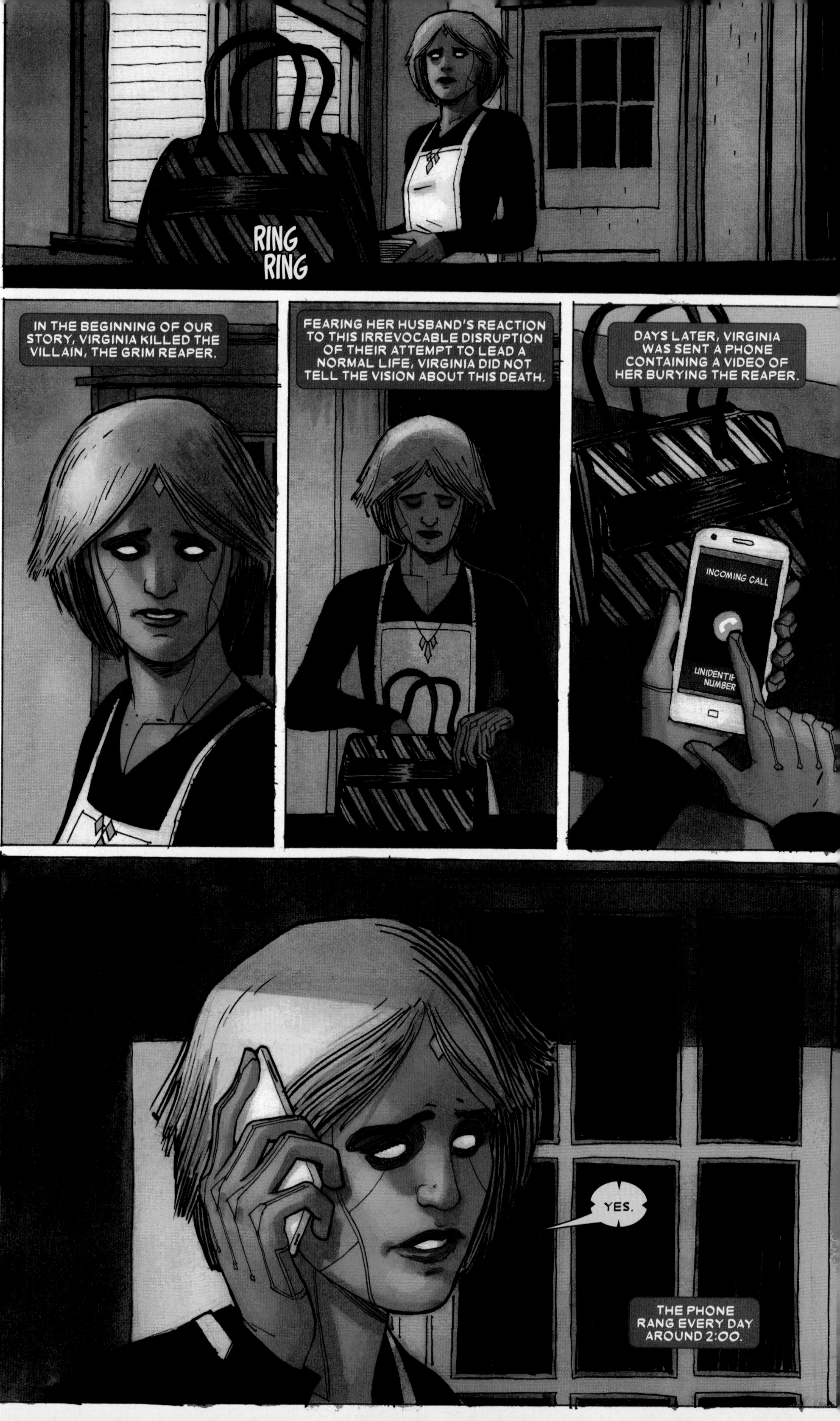
RING
RING
IN THE BEGINNING OF OUR STORY, VIRGINIA KILLED THE VILLAIN, THE GRIM REAPER.
FEARING HER HUSBAND'S REACTION TO THIS IRREVOCABLE DISRUPTION OF THEIR ATTEMPT TO LEAD A NORMAL LIFE, VIRGINIA DID NOT TELL THE VISION ABOUT THIS DEATH.
DAYS LATER, VIRGINIA WAS SENT A PHONE CONTAINING A VIDEO OF HER BURYING THE REAPER.
INCOMING CALL
YES.
THE PHONE RANG EVERY DAY AROUND 2:00.

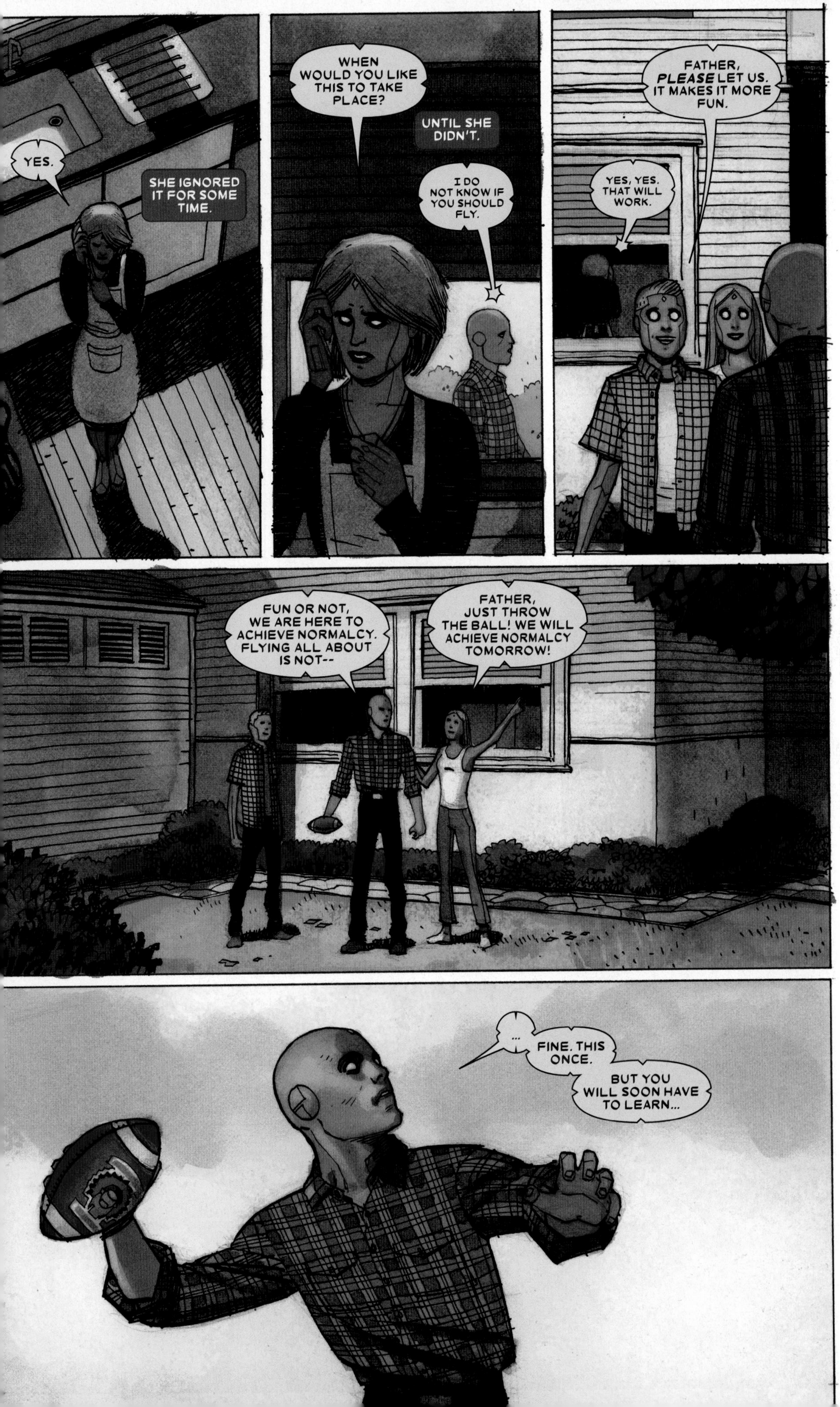
YES.
SHE IGNORED IT FOR SOME TIME.
WHEN WOULD YOU LIKE THIS TO TAKE PLACE?
UNTIL SHE DIDN'T.
I DO NOT KNOW IF YOU SHOULD FLY.
FATHER, PLEASE LET US. IT MAKES IT MORE FUN.
YES, YES. THAT WILL WORK.
FUN OR NOT, WE ARE HERE TO ACHIEVE NORMALCY. FLYING ALL ABOUT IS NOT--
FATHER, JUST THROW THE BALL! WE WILL ACHIEVE NORMALCY TOMORROW!
...
FINE. THIS ONCE.
BUT YOU WILL SOON HAVE TO LEARN...

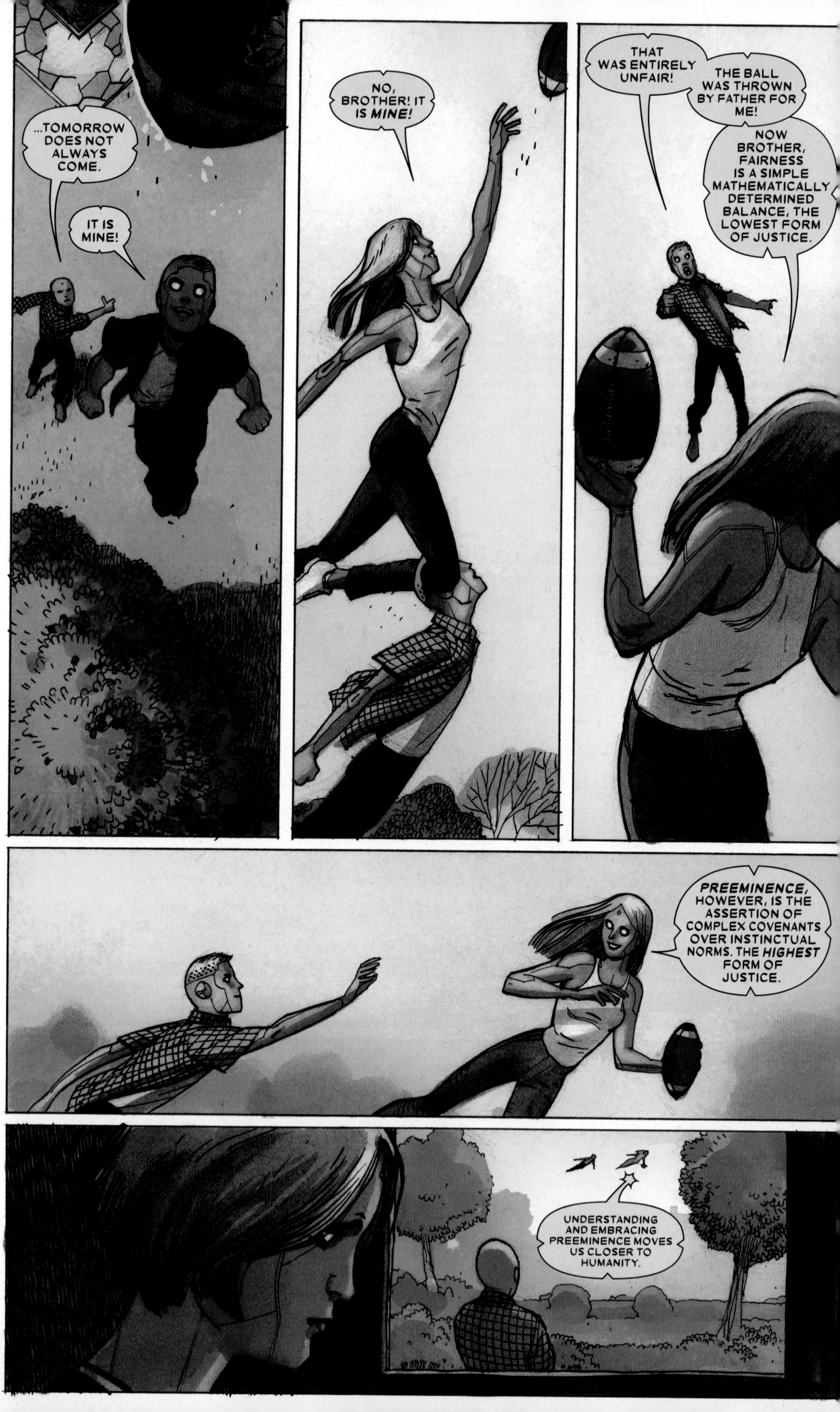
...TOMORROW DOES NOT ALWAYS COME.
IT IS MINE!
NO, BROTHER! IT IS *MINE!*
THAT WAS ENTIRELY UNFAIR!
THE BALL WAS THROWN BY FATHER FOR ME!
NOW BROTHER, FAIRNESS IS A SIMPLE MATHEMATICALLY DETERMINED BALANCE, THE LOWEST FORM OF JUSTICE.
PREEMINENCE, HOWEVER, IS THE ASSERTION OF COMPLEX COVENANTS OVER INSTINCTUAL NORMS. THE *HIGHEST* FORM OF JUSTICE.
UNDERSTANDING AND EMBRACING PREEMINENCE MOVES US CLOSER TO HUMANITY.

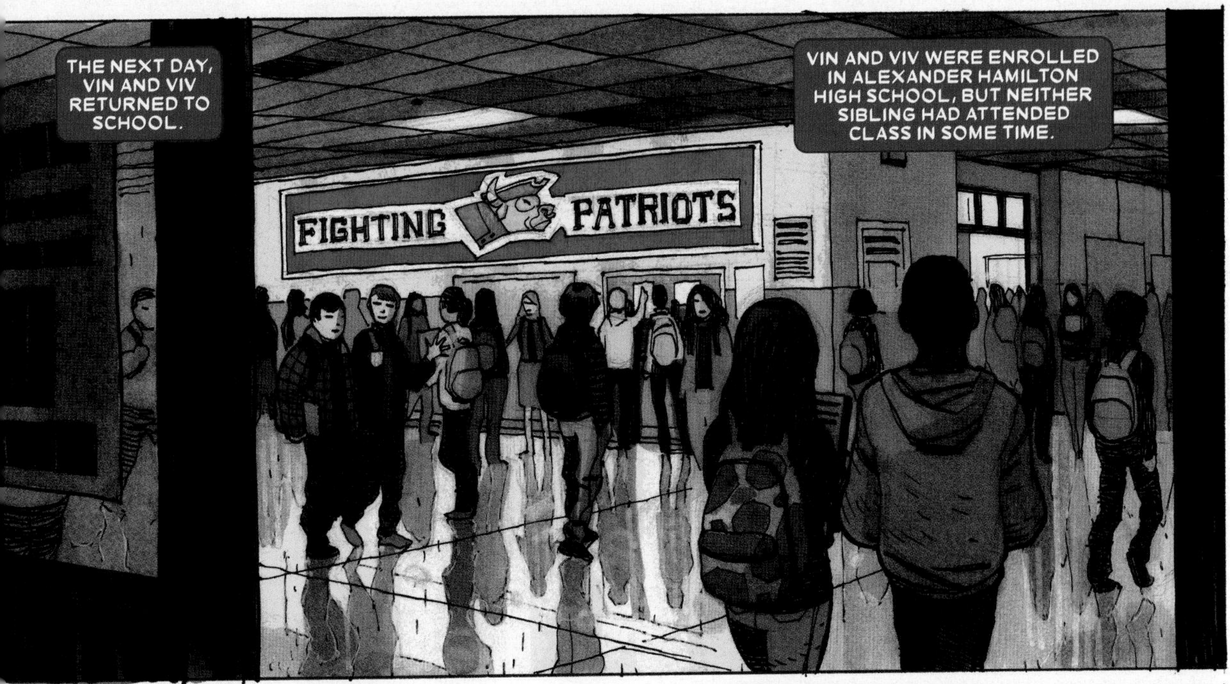
THE NEXT DAY, VIN AND VIV RETURNED TO SCHOOL.
VIN AND VIV WERE ENROLLED IN ALEXANDER HAMILTON HIGH SCHOOL, BUT NEITHER SIBLING HAD ATTENDED CLASS IN SOME TIME.
FIGHTING PATRIOTS

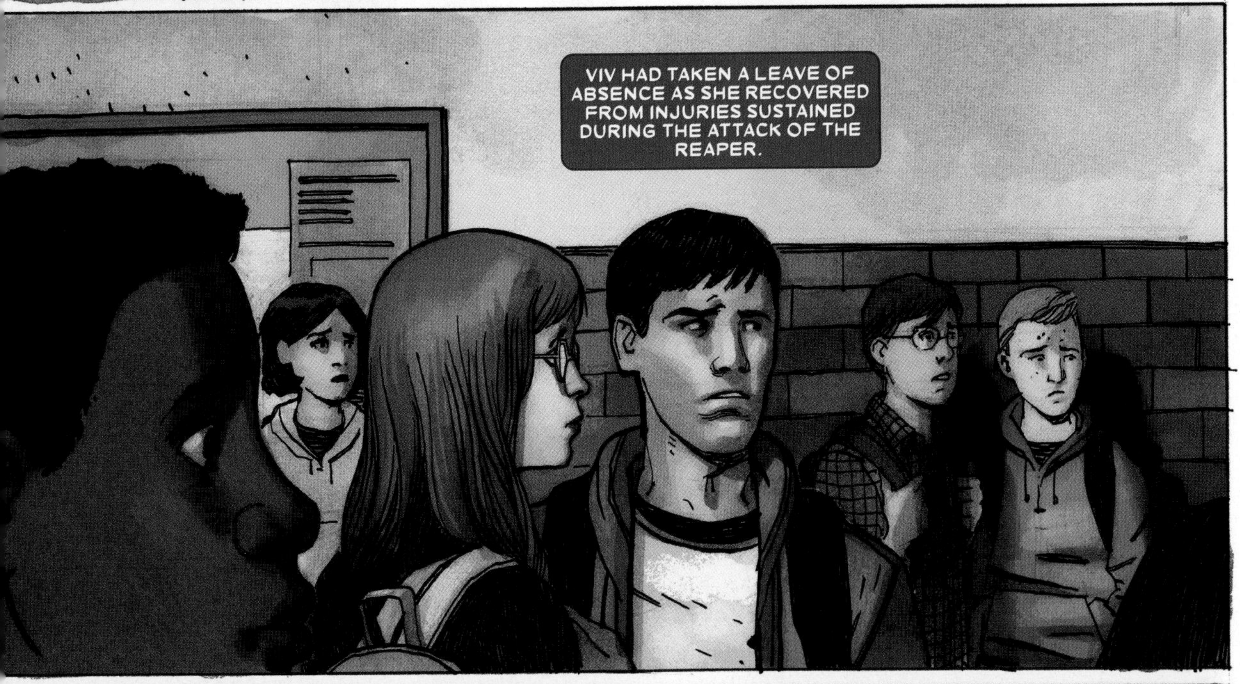
VIV HAD TAKEN A LEAVE OF ABSENCE AS SHE RECOVERED FROM INJURIES SUSTAINED DURING THE ATTACK OF THE REAPER.

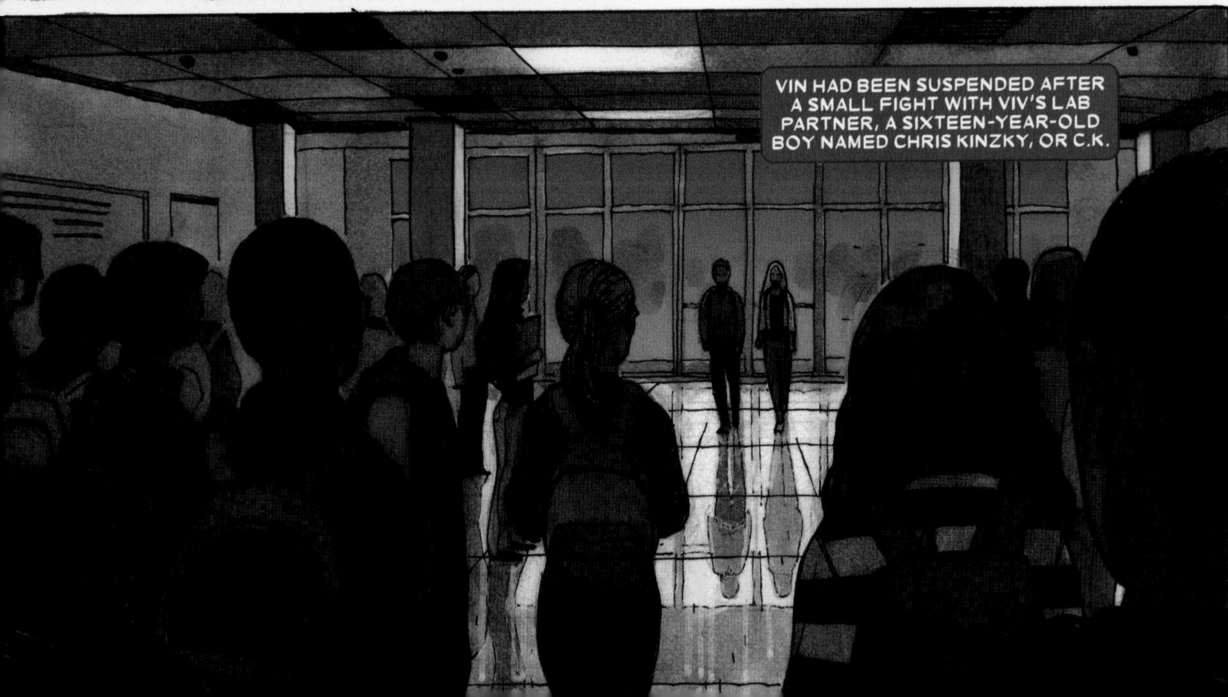
VIN HAD BEEN SUSPENDED AFTER A SMALL FIGHT WITH VIV'S LAB PARTNER, A SIXTEEN-YEAR-OLD BOY NAMED CHRIS KINZKY, OR C.K.

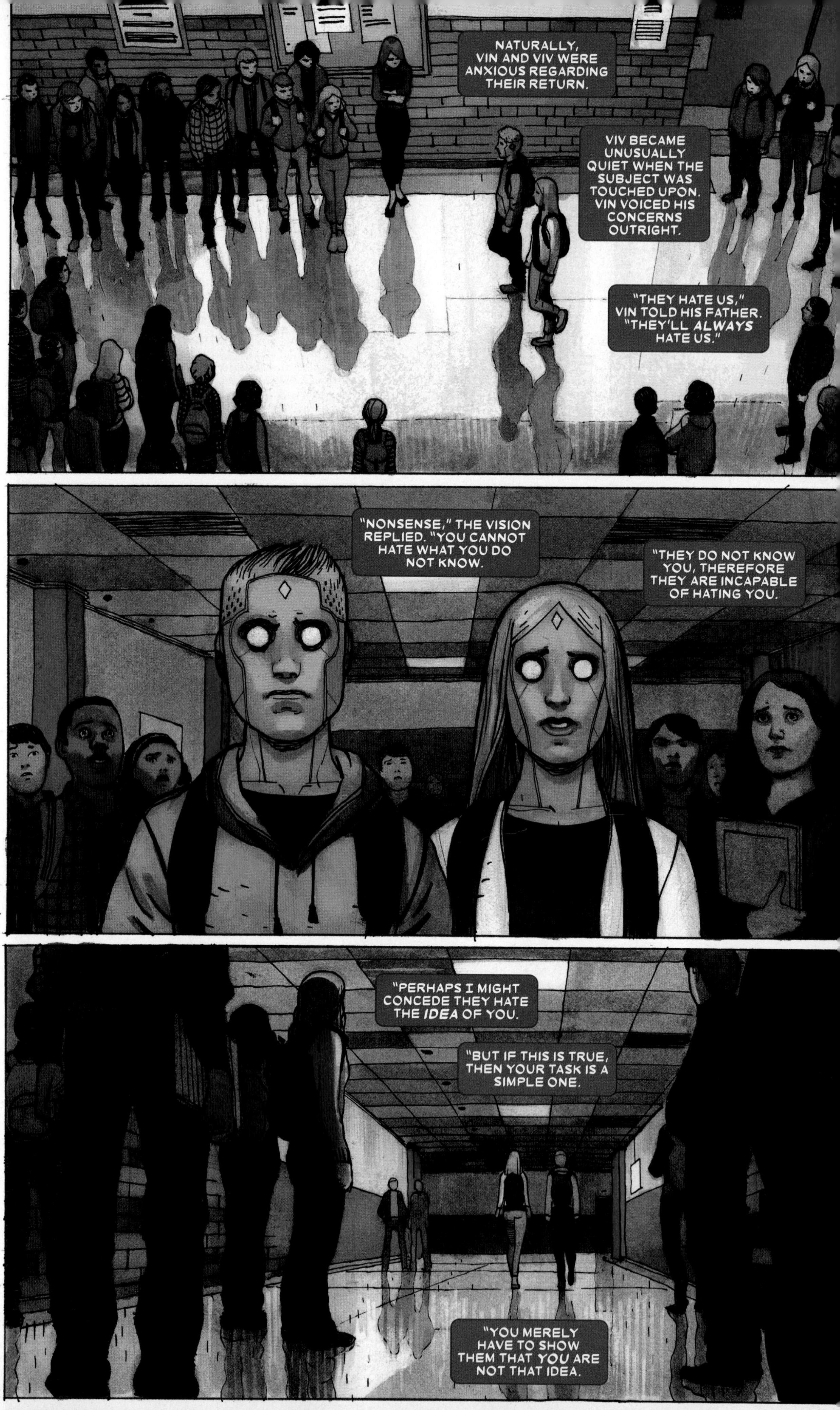
NATURALLY, VIN AND VIV WERE ANXIOUS REGARDING THEIR RETURN.
VIV BECAME UNUSUALLY QUIET WHEN THE SUBJECT WAS TOUCHED UPON. VIN VOICED HIS CONCERNS OUTRIGHT.
"THEY HATE US," VIN TOLD HIS FATHER. "THEY'LL *ALWAYS* HATE US."
"NONSENSE," THE VISION REPLIED. "YOU CANNOT HATE WHAT YOU DO NOT KNOW.
"THEY DO NOT KNOW YOU, THEREFORE THEY ARE INCAPABLE OF HATING YOU.
"PERHAPS I MIGHT CONCEDE THEY HATE THE *IDEA* OF YOU.
"BUT IF THIS IS TRUE, THEN YOUR TASK IS A SIMPLE ONE.
"YOU MERELY HAVE TO SHOW THEM THAT *YOU* ARE NOT THAT IDEA.

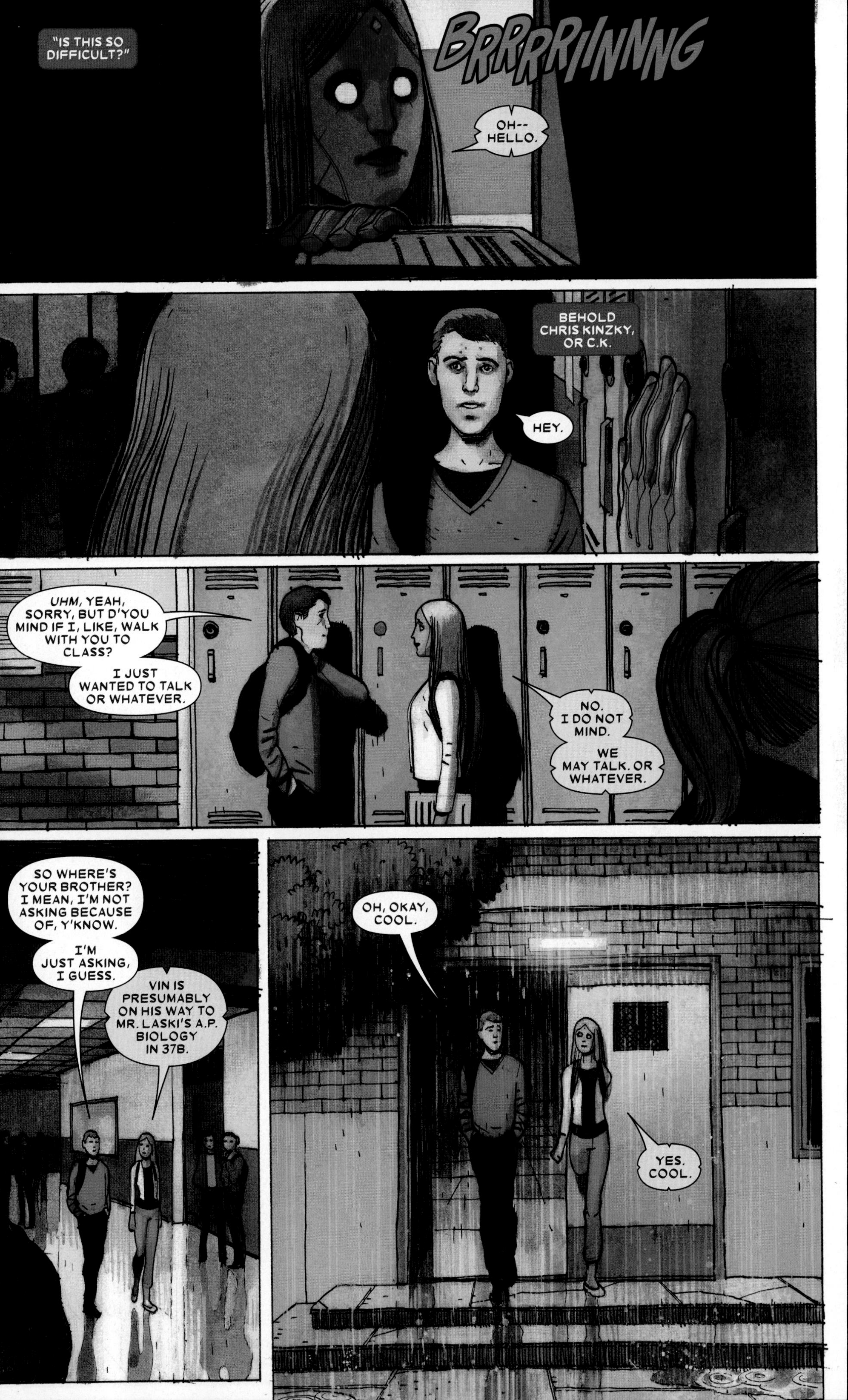
"IS THIS SO DIFFICULT?"
BRRRRIINNNG
OH-- HELLO.
BEHOLD CHRIS KINZKY, OR C.K.
HEY.
UHM, YEAH, SORRY, BUT D'YOU MIND IF I, LIKE, WALK WITH YOU TO CLASS?
I JUST WANTED TO TALK OR WHATEVER.
NO. I DO NOT MIND.
WE MAY TALK. OR WHATEVER.
SO WHERE'S YOUR BROTHER? I MEAN, I'M NOT ASKING BECAUSE OF, Y'KNOW.
I'M JUST ASKING, I GUESS.
VIN IS PRESUMABLY ON HIS WAY TO MR. LASKI'S A.P. BIOLOGY IN 37B.
OH, OKAY, COOL.
YES. COOL.

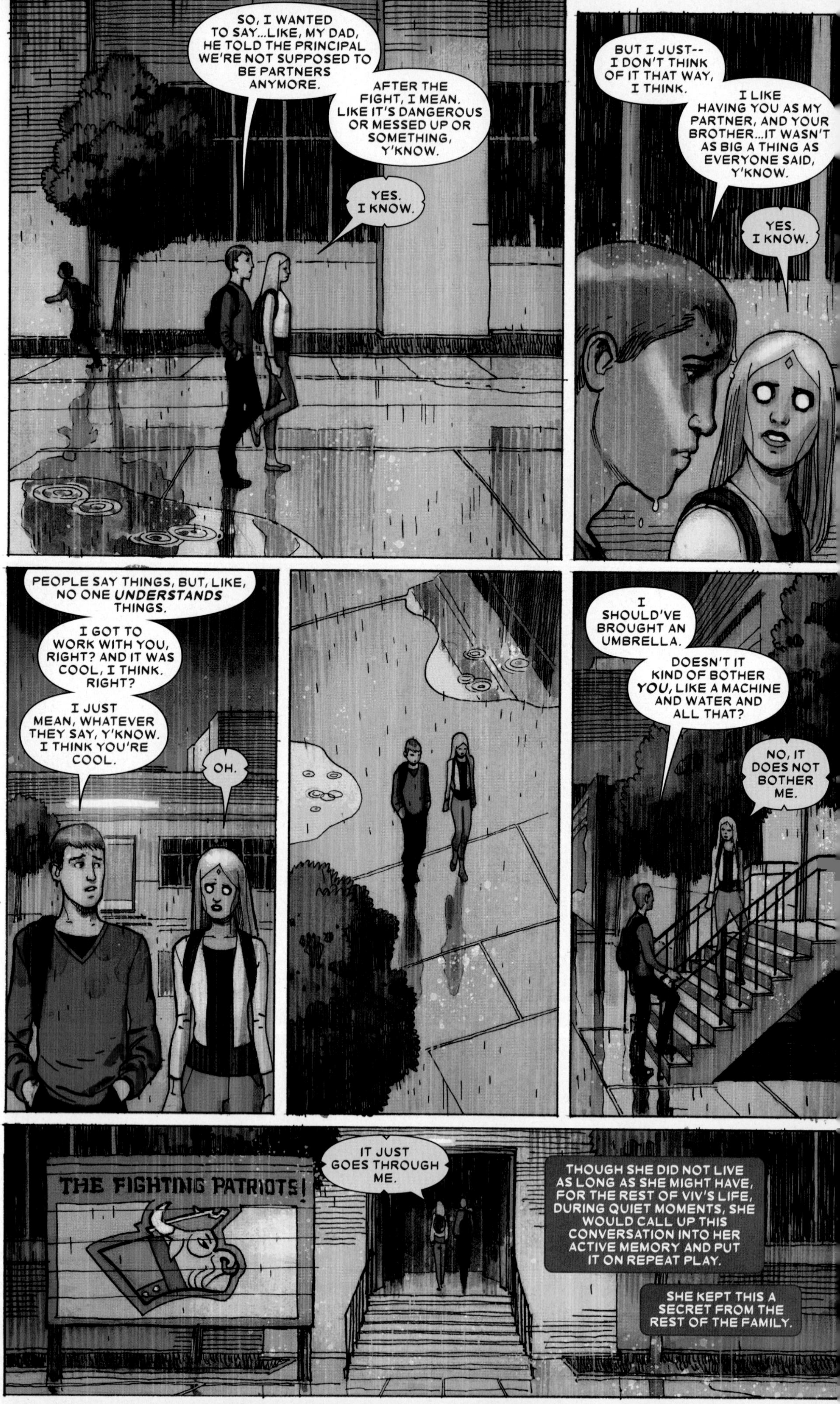
SO, I WANTED TO SAY...LIKE, MY DAD, HE TOLD THE PRINCIPAL WE'RE NOT SUPPOSED TO BE PARTNERS ANYMORE.
AFTER THE FIGHT, I MEAN. LIKE IT'S DANGEROUS OR MESSED UP OR SOMETHING, Y'KNOW.
YES. I KNOW.
BUT I JUST-- I DON'T THINK OF IT THAT WAY, I THINK.
I LIKE HAVING YOU AS MY PARTNER, AND YOUR BROTHER...IT WASN'T AS BIG A THING AS EVERYONE SAID, Y'KNOW.
YES. I KNOW.
PEOPLE SAY THINGS, BUT, LIKE, NO ONE *UNDERSTANDS* THINGS.
I GOT TO WORK WITH YOU, RIGHT? AND IT WAS COOL, I THINK. RIGHT?
I JUST MEAN, WHATEVER THEY SAY, Y'KNOW. I THINK YOU'RE COOL.
OH.
I SHOULD'VE BROUGHT AN UMBRELLA.
DOESN'T IT KIND OF BOTHER *YOU*, LIKE A MACHINE AND WATER AND ALL THAT?
NO, IT DOES NOT BOTHER ME.
THE FIGHTING PATRIOTS!
IT JUST GOES THROUGH ME.
THOUGH SHE DID NOT LIVE AS LONG AS SHE MIGHT HAVE, FOR THE REST OF VIV'S LIFE, DURING QUIET MOMENTS, SHE WOULD CALL UP THIS CONVERSATION INTO HER ACTIVE MEMORY AND PUT IT ON REPEAT PLAY.
SHE KEPT THIS A SECRET FROM THE REST OF THE FAMILY.

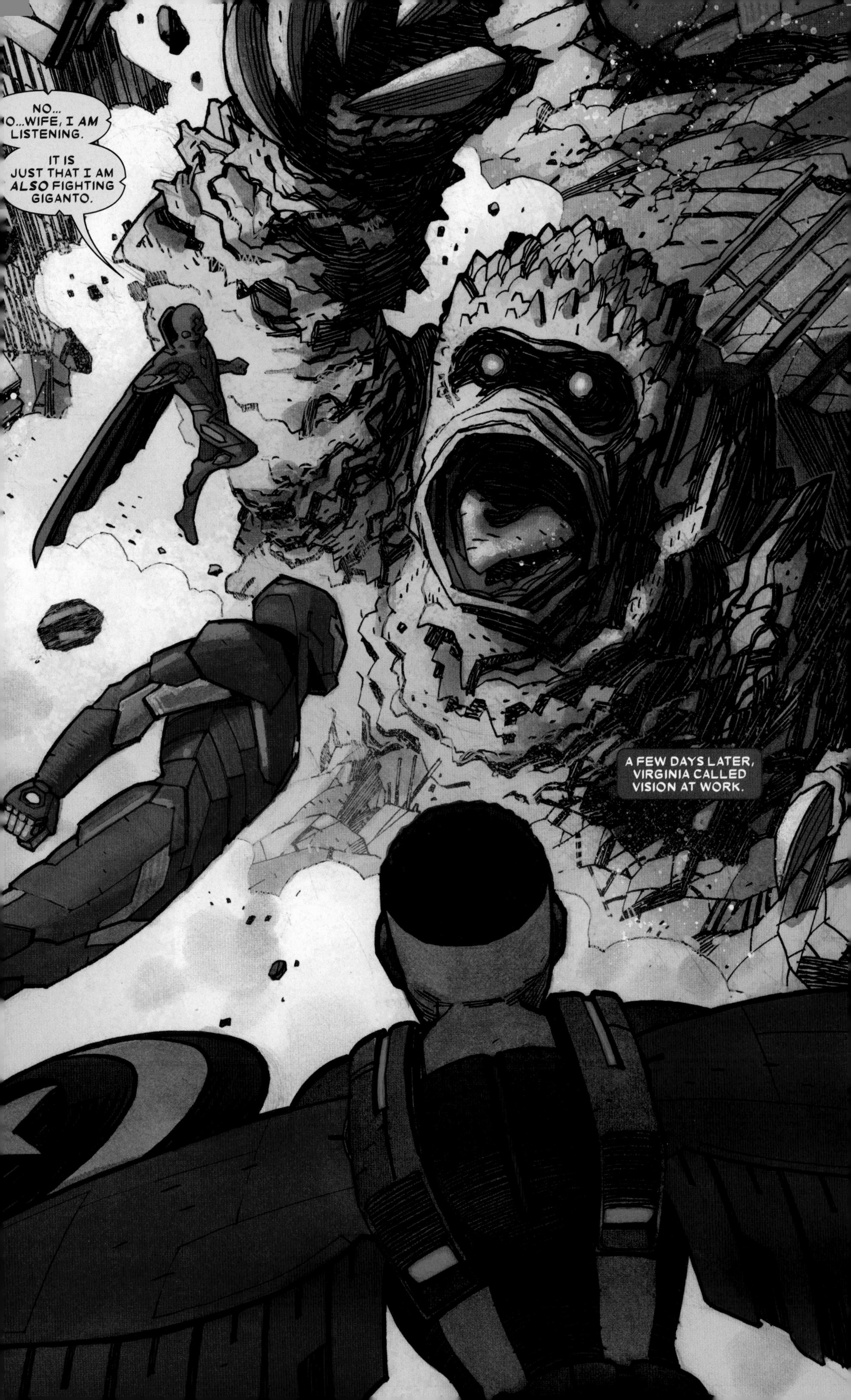
NO... O...WIFE, I AM LISTENING.
IT IS JUST THAT I AM ALSO FIGHTING GIGANTO.
A FEW DAYS LATER, VIRGINIA CALLED VISION AT WORK.

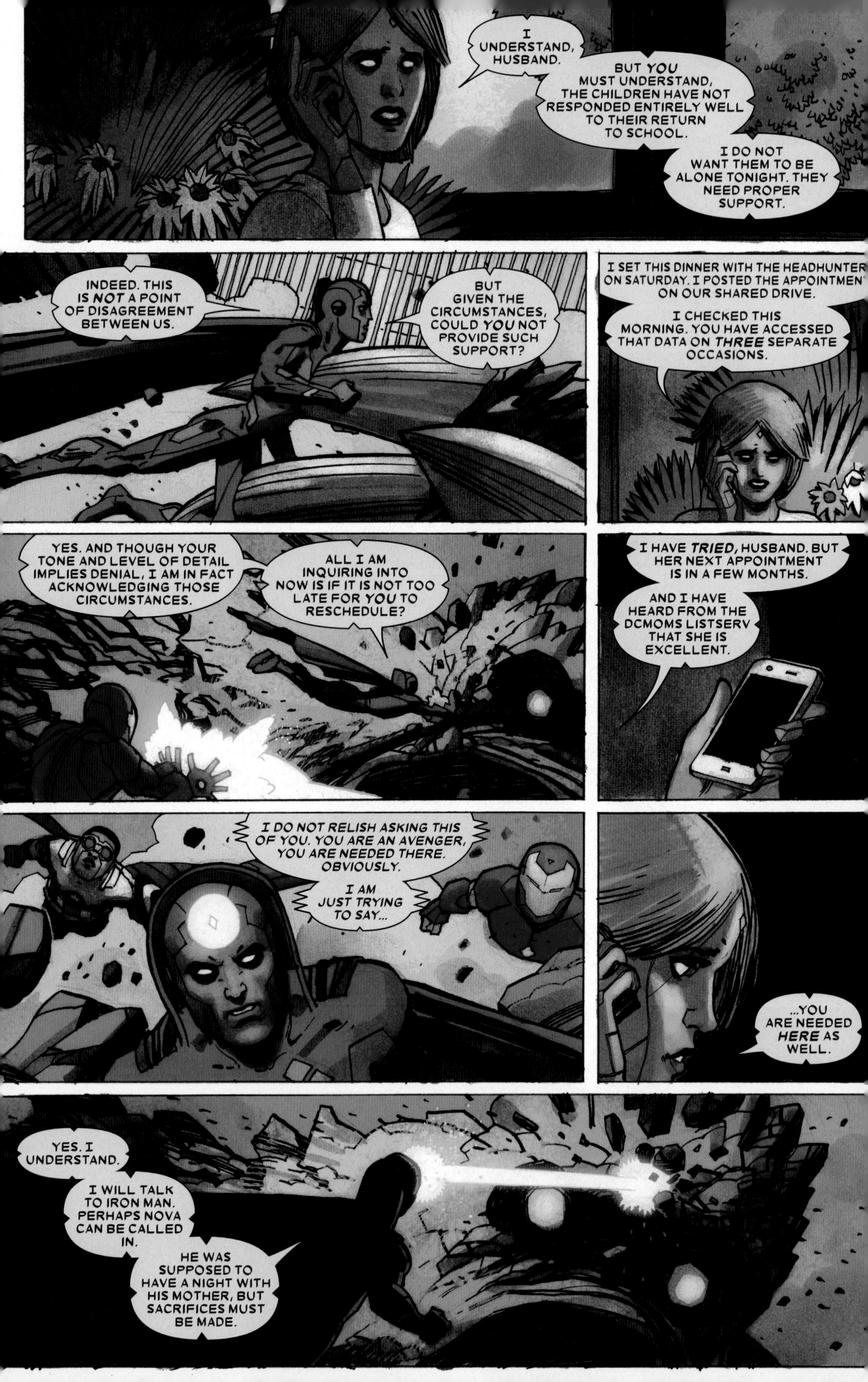
I UNDERSTAND, HUSBAND.
BUT YOU MUST UNDERSTAND, THE CHILDREN HAVE NOT RESPONDED ENTIRELY WELL TO THEIR RETURN TO SCHOOL.
I DO NOT WANT THEM TO BE ALONE TONIGHT. THEY NEED PROPER SUPPORT.
INDEED. THIS IS NOT A POINT OF DISAGREEMENT BETWEEN US.
BUT GIVEN THE CIRCUMSTANCES, COULD YOU NOT PROVIDE SUCH SUPPORT?
I SET THIS DINNER WITH THE HEADHUNTER ON SATURDAY. I POSTED THE APPOINTMENT ON OUR SHARED DRIVE.
I CHECKED THIS MORNING. YOU HAVE ACCESSED THAT DATA ON THREE SEPARATE OCCASIONS.
YES. AND THOUGH YOUR TONE AND LEVEL OF DETAIL IMPLIES DENIAL, I AM IN FACT ACKNOWLEDGING THOSE CIRCUMSTANCES.
ALL I AM INQUIRING INTO NOW IS IF IT IS NOT TOO LATE FOR YOU TO RESCHEDULE?
I HAVE TRIED, HUSBAND. BUT HER NEXT APPOINTMENT IS IN A FEW MONTHS.
AND I HAVE HEARD FROM THE DCMOMS LISTSERV THAT SHE IS EXCELLENT.
I DO NOT RELISH ASKING THIS OF YOU. YOU ARE AN AVENGER, YOU ARE NEEDED THERE. OBVIOUSLY.
I AM JUST TRYING TO SAY...
...YOU ARE NEEDED HERE AS WELL.
YES. I UNDERSTAND.
I WILL TALK TO IRON MAN. PERHAPS NOVA CAN BE CALLED IN.
HE WAS SUPPOSED TO HAVE A NIGHT WITH HIS MOTHER, BUT SACRIFICES MUST BE MADE.

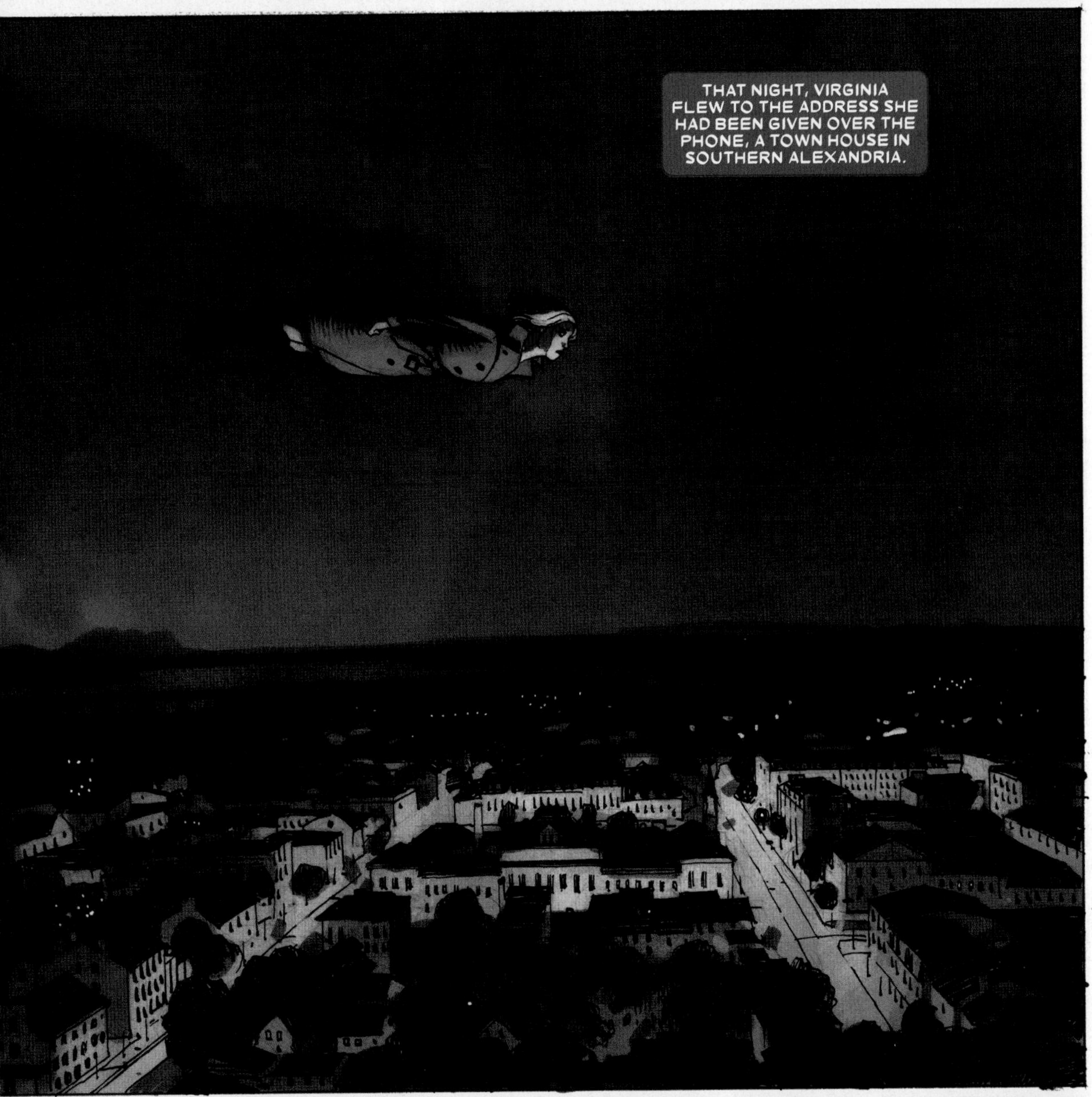
THAT NIGHT, VIRGINIA FLEW TO THE ADDRESS SHE HAD BEEN GIVEN OVER THE PHONE, A TOWN HOUSE IN SOUTHERN ALEXANDRIA.

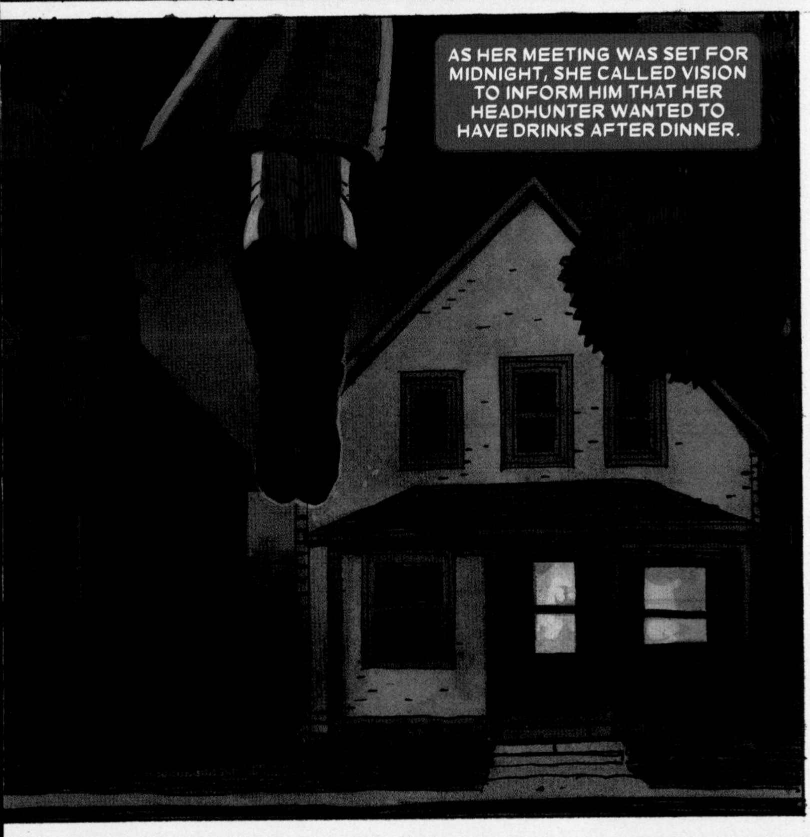
AS HER MEETING WAS SET FOR MIDNIGHT, SHE CALLED VISION TO INFORM HIM THAT HER HEADHUNTER WANTED TO HAVE DRINKS AFTER DINNER.

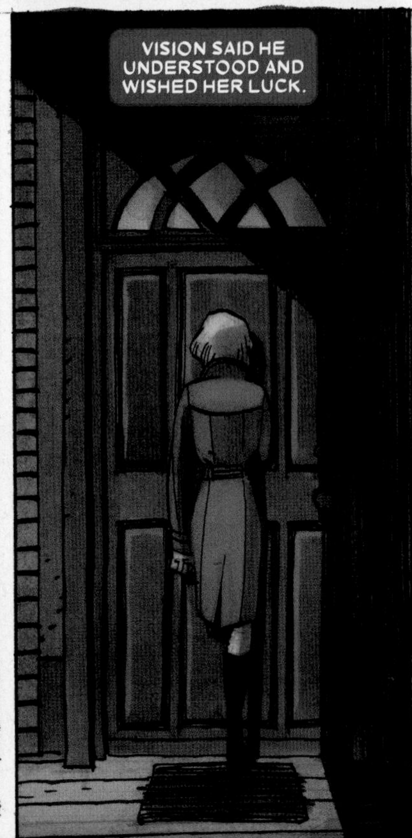
VISION SAID HE UNDERSTOOD AND WISHED HER LUCK.

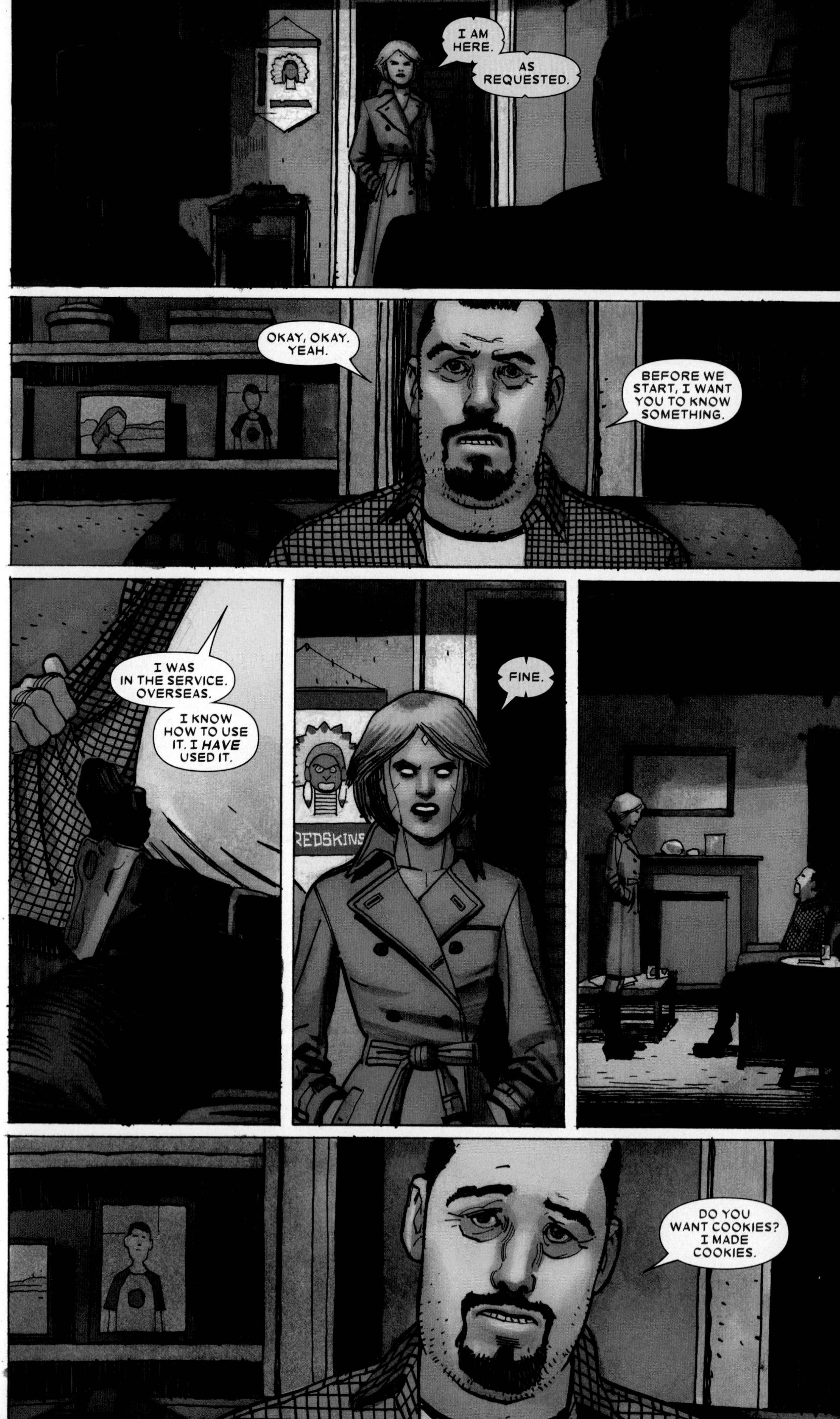
I AM HERE.
AS REQUESTED.
OKAY, OKAY. YEAH.
BEFORE WE START, I WANT YOU TO KNOW SOMETHING.
I WAS IN THE SERVICE. OVERSEAS.
I KNOW HOW TO USE IT. I *HAVE* USED IT.
REDSKINS
FINE.
DO YOU WANT COOKIES? I MADE COOKIES.

I DIDN'T MEAN FOR THIS TO BE ANYTHING, I WANT YOU TO KNOW THAT.

THAT'S WHY I INVITED YOU HERE. MY HOME. I'M NOT HIDING.

BUT THERE ARE THINGS I GOT TO GET--THAT YOU GOT TO DO.

AND I'M *SERIOUS* ABOUT THAT.

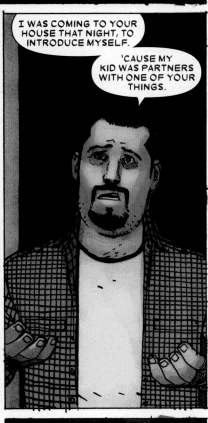

I WAS COMING TO YOUR HOUSE THAT NIGHT, TO INTRODUCE MYSELF.

'CAUSE MY KID WAS PARTNERS WITH ONE OF YOUR THINGS.

I STOPPED AT THE FRONT DOOR. BUT NO ONE ANSWERED. AND I WENT AROUND THE BACK.

I HEARD YOU, AND I WAS TRYING TO SEE, AND THEN I SAW, AND THEN I TOOK A VIDEO.

THAT'S WHAT YOU DO THESE DAYS, RIGHT?

YOU TAKE A VIDEO.

I DIDN'T WANT TROUBLE. I WASN'T GOING TO DO ANYTHING WITH IT.

IT WAS YOU PEOPLE WHO MADE ME.

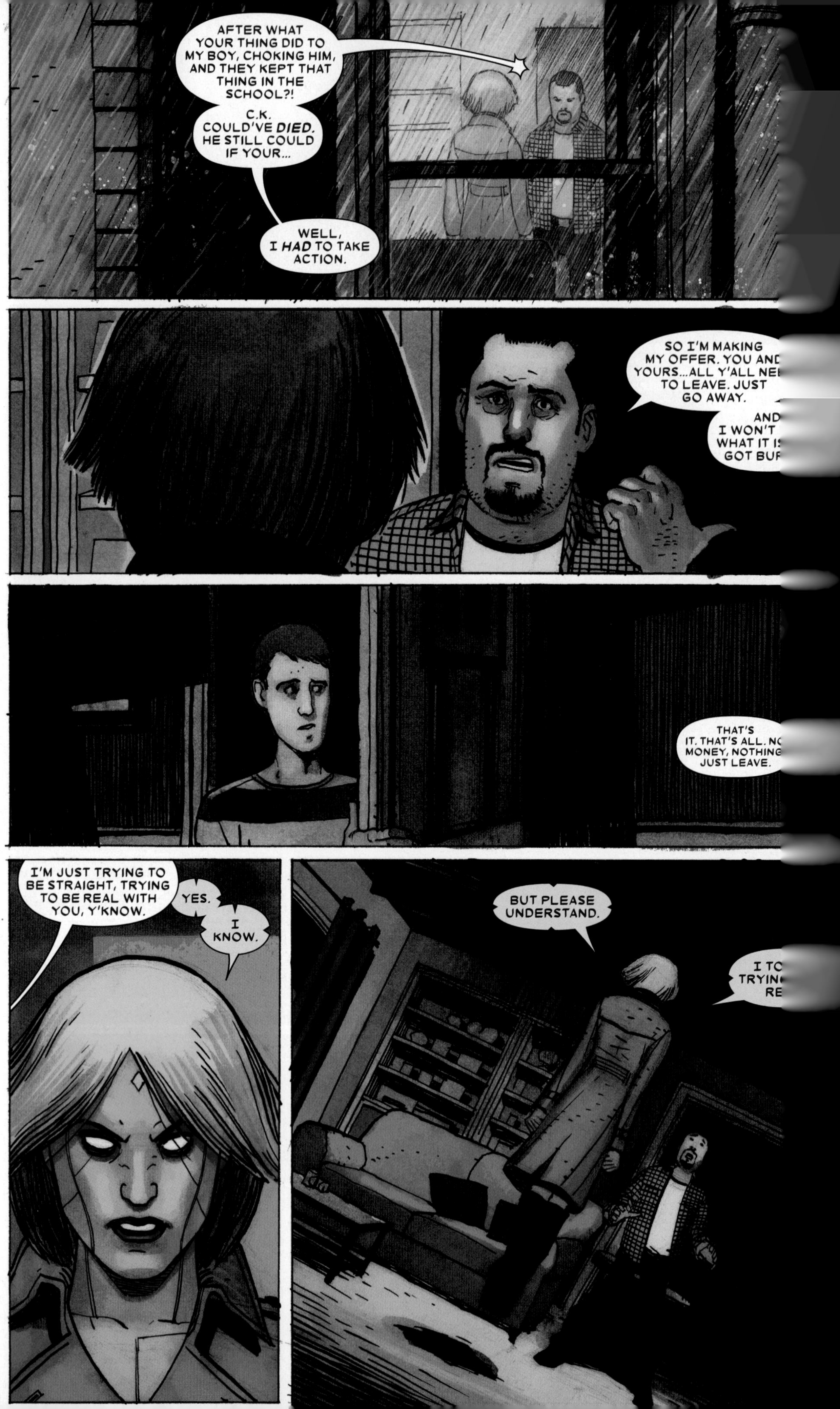
AFTER WHAT YOUR THING DID TO MY BOY, CHOKING HIM, AND THEY KEPT THAT THING IN THE SCHOOL?!
C.K. COULD'VE *DIED.* HE STILL COULD IF YOUR...
WELL, I *HAD* TO TAKE ACTION.
SO I'M MAKING MY OFFER. YOU AND YOURS...ALL Y'ALL TO LEAVE. JUST GO AWAY.
AND I WON'T WHAT IT IS GOT
THAT'S IT. THAT'S ALL. MONEY, JUST LEAVE.
I'M JUST TRYING TO BE STRAIGHT, TRYING TO BE REAL WITH YOU, Y'KNOW.
YES.
I KNOW.
BUT PLEASE UNDERSTAND.

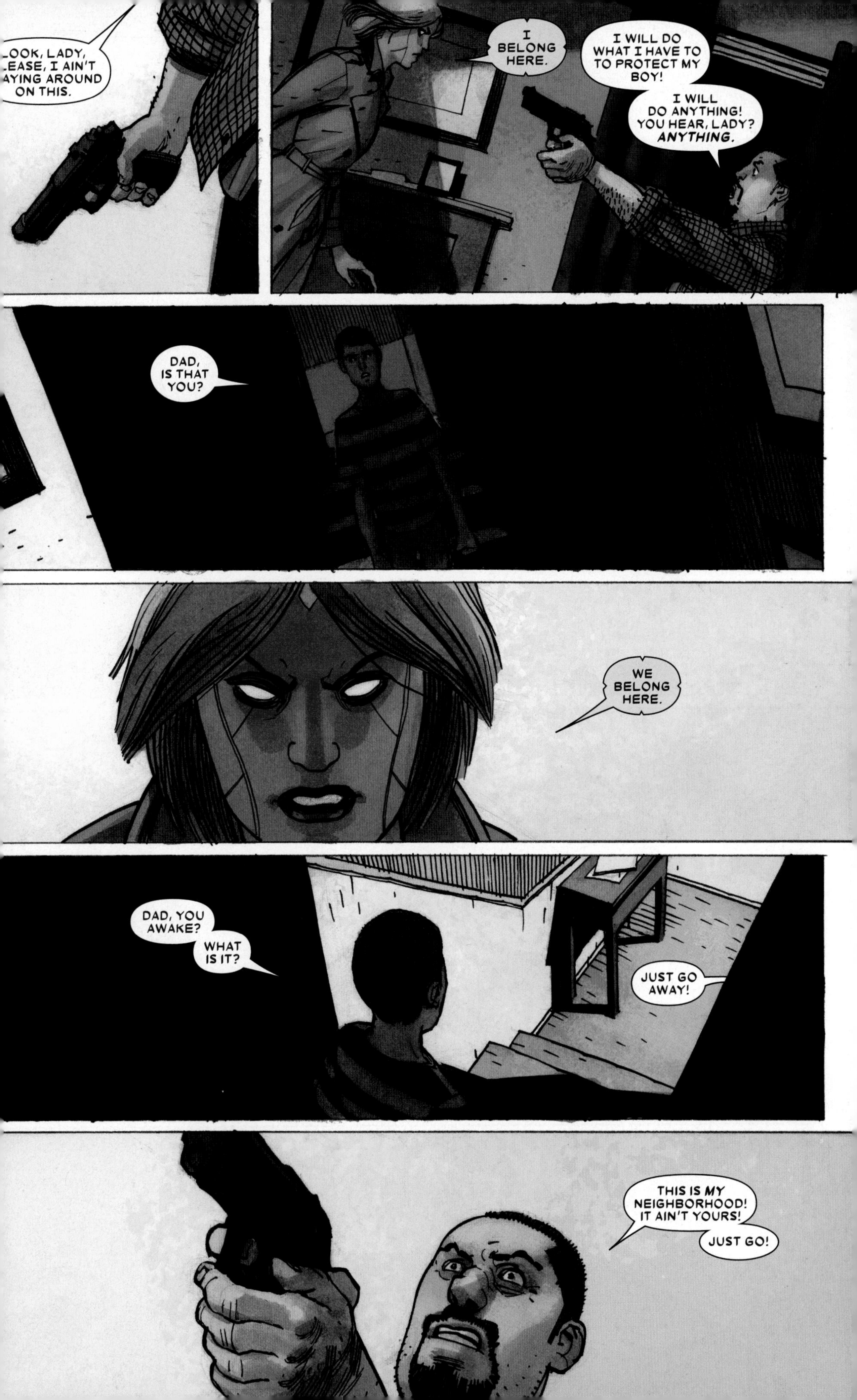

OOK, LADY, LEASE, I AIN'T AYING AROUND ON THIS.
I BELONG HERE.
I WILL DO WHAT I HAVE TO TO PROTECT MY BOY!
I WILL DO ANYTHING! YOU HEAR, LADY? *ANYTHING.*
DAD, IS THAT YOU?
WE BELONG HERE.
DAD, YOU AWAKE?
WHAT IS IT?
JUST GO AWAY!
THIS IS *MY* NEIGHBORHOOD! IT AIN'T YOURS!
JUST GO!

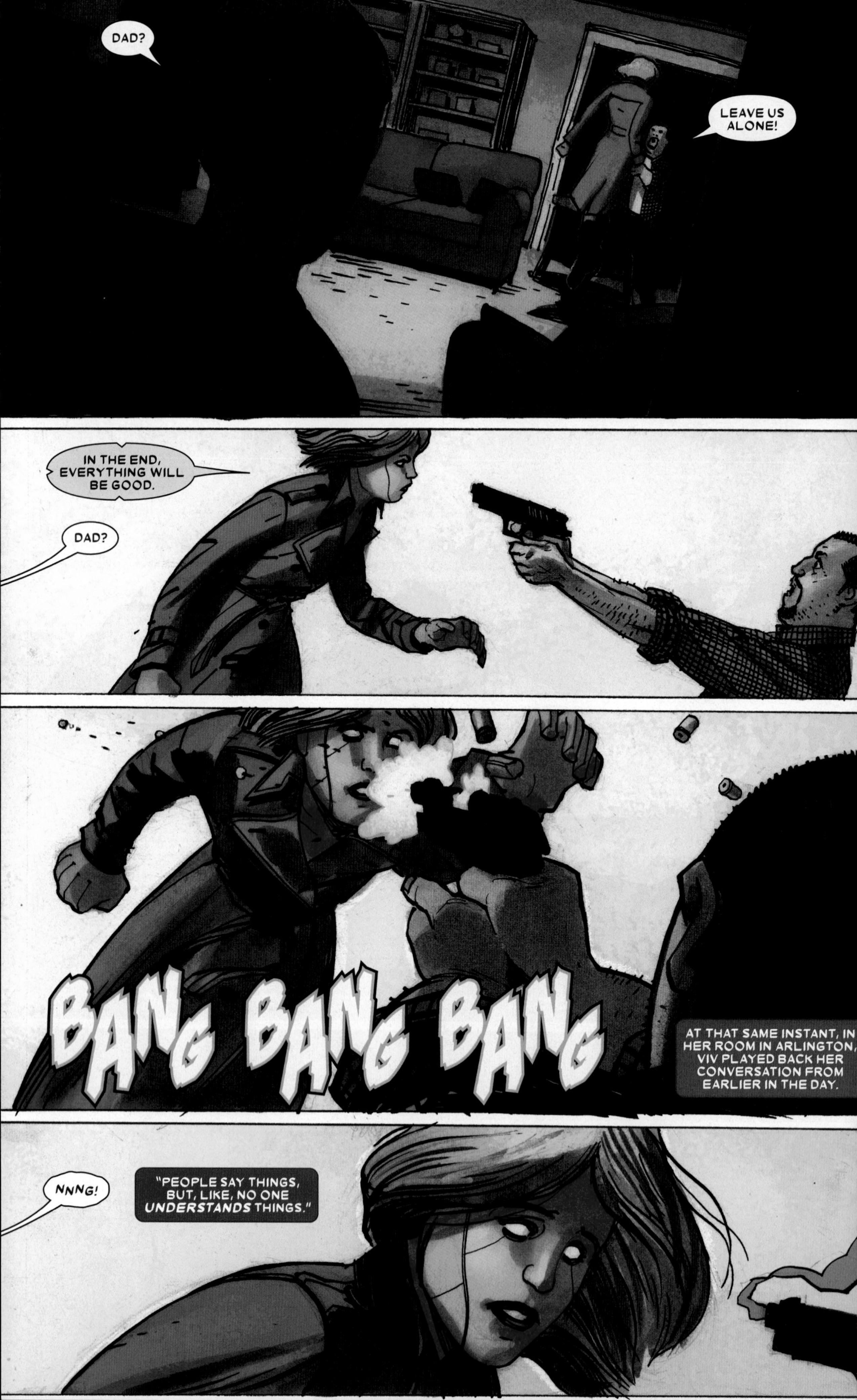

DAD?
LEAVE US ALONE!
IN THE END, EVERYTHING WILL BE GOOD.
DAD?
BANG BANG BANG
AT THAT SAME INSTANT, IN HER ROOM IN ARLINGTON, VIV PLAYED BACK HER CONVERSATION FROM EARLIER IN THE DAY.
NNNG!
"PEOPLE SAY THINGS, BUT, LIKE, NO ONE UNDERSTANDS THINGS."

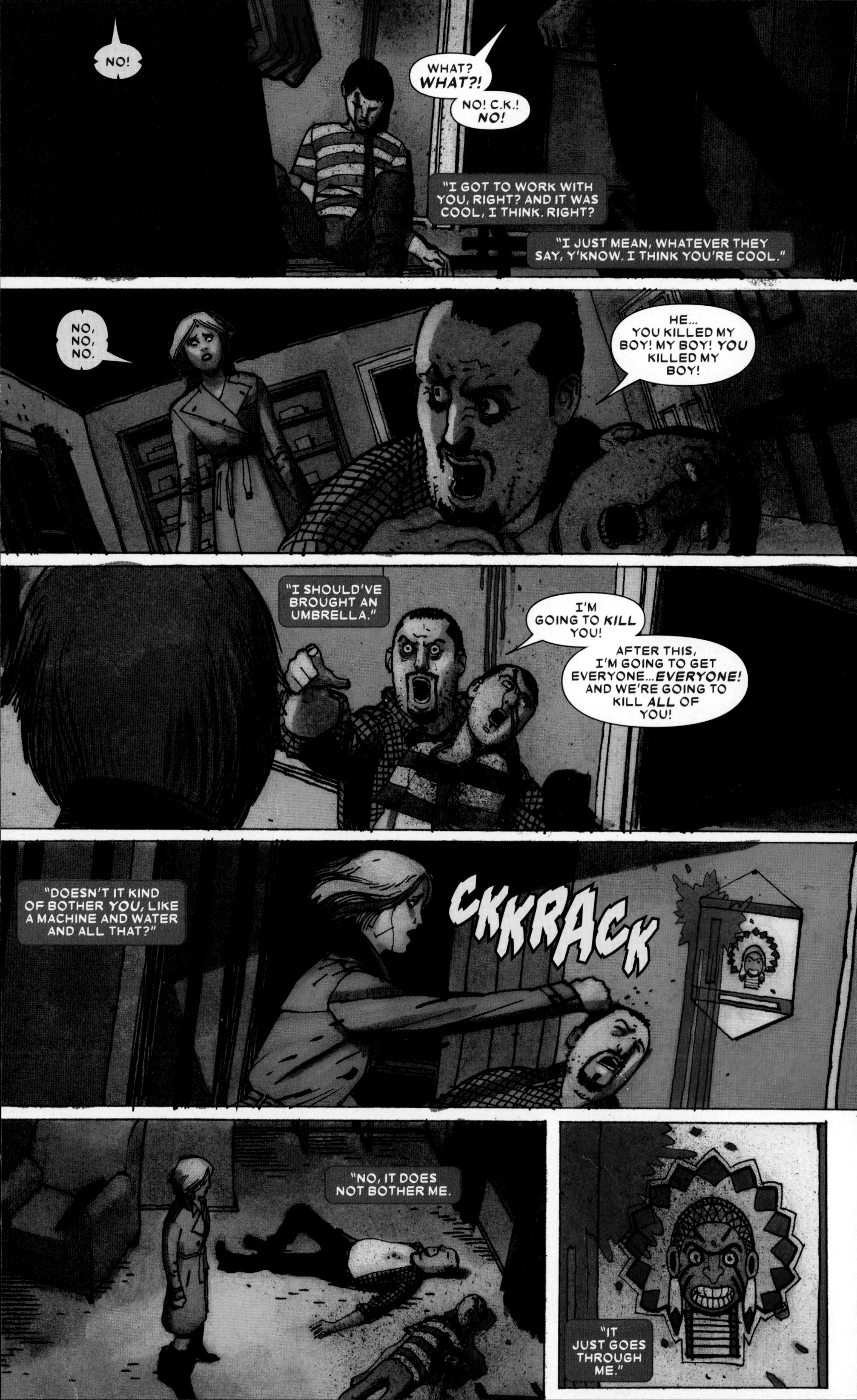
NO!
WHAT? WHAT?!
NO! C.K.! NO!
"I GOT TO WORK WITH YOU, RIGHT? AND IT WAS COOL, I THINK. RIGHT?
"I JUST MEAN, WHATEVER THEY SAY, Y'KNOW. I THINK YOU'RE COOL."
NO, NO, NO.
HE... YOU KILLED MY BOY! MY BOY! YOU KILLED MY BOY!
"I SHOULD'VE BROUGHT AN UMBRELLA."
I'M GOING TO KILL YOU!
AFTER THIS, I'M GOING TO GET EVERYONE...EVERYONE! AND WE'RE GOING TO KILL ALL OF YOU!
"DOESN'T IT KIND OF BOTHER YOU, LIKE A MACHINE AND WATER AND ALL THAT?"
CKKRACK
"NO, IT DOES NOT BOTHER ME.
"IT JUST GOES THROUGH ME."

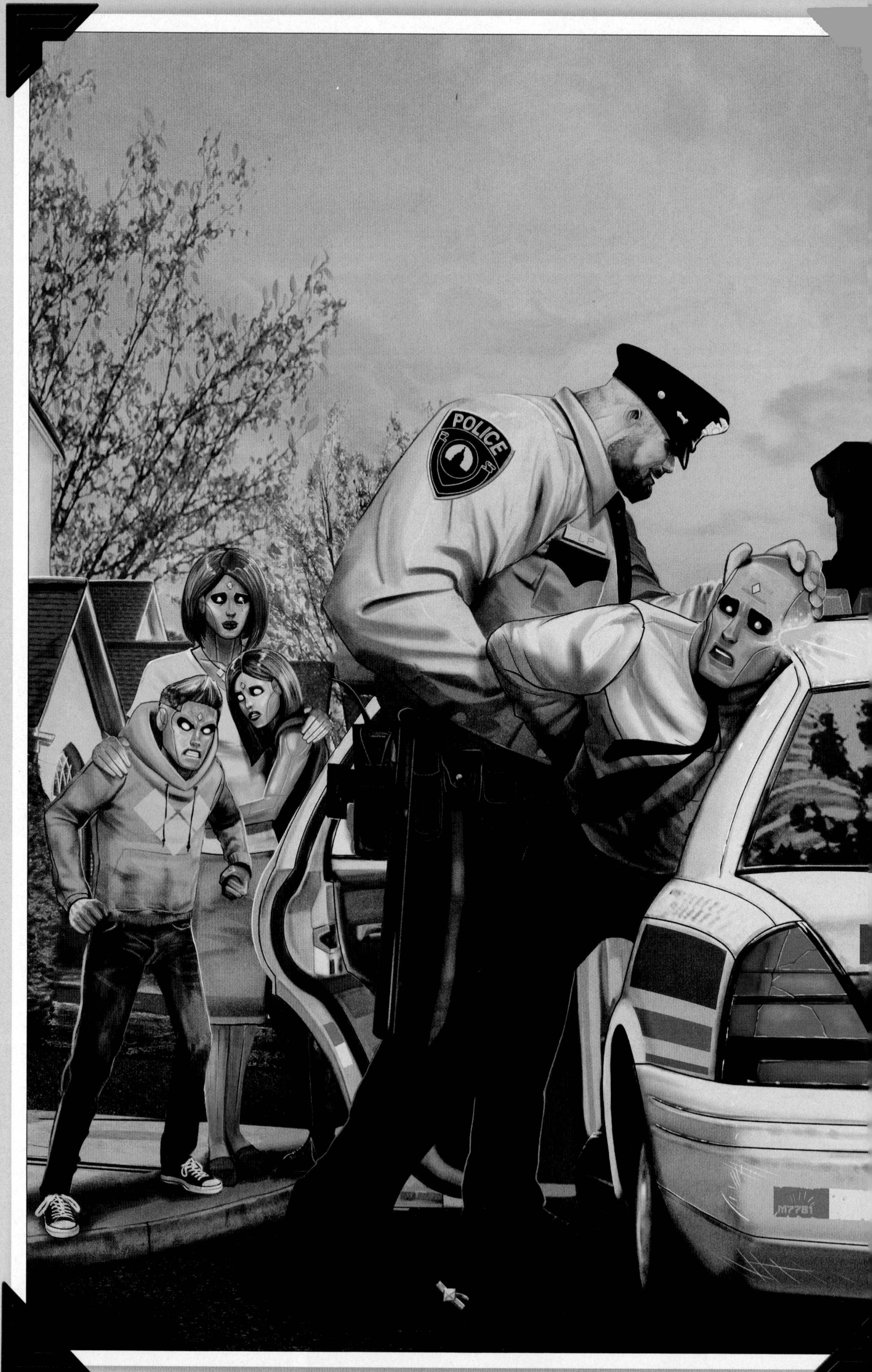
POLICE

"'IF IT WILL FEED NOTHING ELSE--

"'IT WILL FEED MY REVENGE.

"'HE HATH DISGRACED ME AND HINDERED ME HALF A MILLION--

"LAUGHED AT MY LOSSES--

GET BETTER, LEON! We're all praying for you! LOVE, your colleagues and friends at Flanagan, Rios & Suntres

"'MOCKED AT MY GAINS--

"'SCORNED MY NATION--

"'THWARTED MY BARGAINS--

"'COOLED MY FRIENDS--

Few Clues in shooting Death of Local High School Student

Police continued to search for leads in the shooting death of sixteen-year-old Chris Kinzky. Kinzky's father, Leon Kinzky, was found in the house unconscious next to the Alexander Hamilton student. Police say ve yet to find them

"'HEATED MINE ENEMIES--

"'AND WHAT'S HIS REASON?

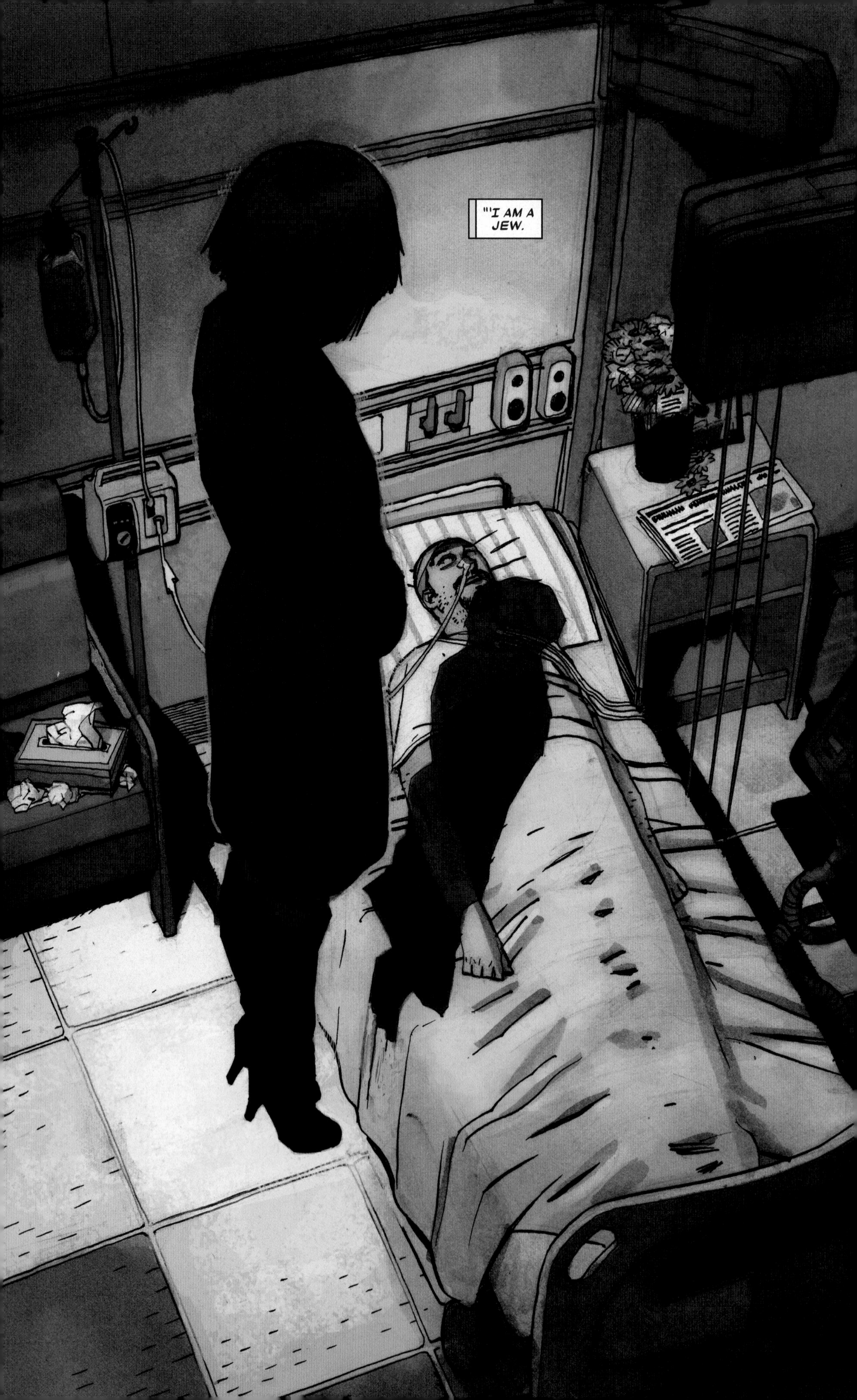
"'I AM A JEW.

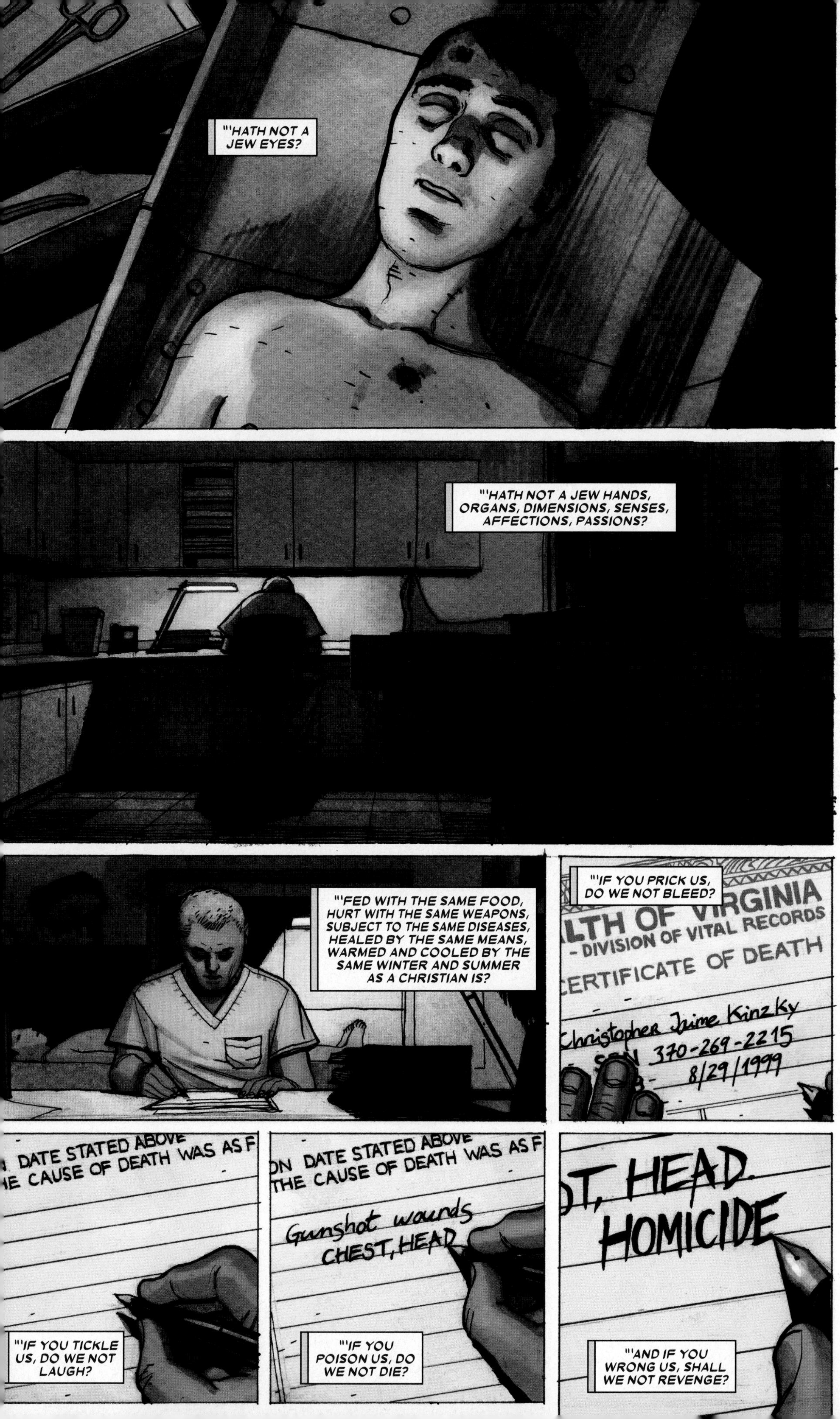
"'HATH NOT A JEW EYES?
"'HATH NOT A JEW HANDS, ORGANS, DIMENSIONS, SENSES, AFFECTIONS, PASSIONS?
"'FED WITH THE SAME FOOD, HURT WITH THE SAME WEAPONS, SUBJECT TO THE SAME DISEASES, HEALED BY THE SAME MEANS, WARMED AND COOLED BY THE SAME WINTER AND SUMMER AS A CHRISTIAN IS?
"'IF YOU PRICK US, DO WE NOT BLEED?
ALTH OF VIRGINIA
- DIVISION OF VITAL RECORDS
CERTIFICATE OF DEATH
Christopher Jaime Kinzky
370-269-2215
8/29/1999
N DATE STATED ABOVE
HE CAUSE OF DEATH WAS AS F
"'IF YOU TICKLE US, DO WE NOT LAUGH?
ON DATE STATED ABOVE
THE CAUSE OF DEATH WAS AS F
Gunshot wounds
CHEST, HEAD
"'IF YOU POISON US, DO WE NOT DIE?
OT, HEAD.
HOMICIDE
"'AND IF YOU WRONG US, SHALL WE NOT REVENGE?

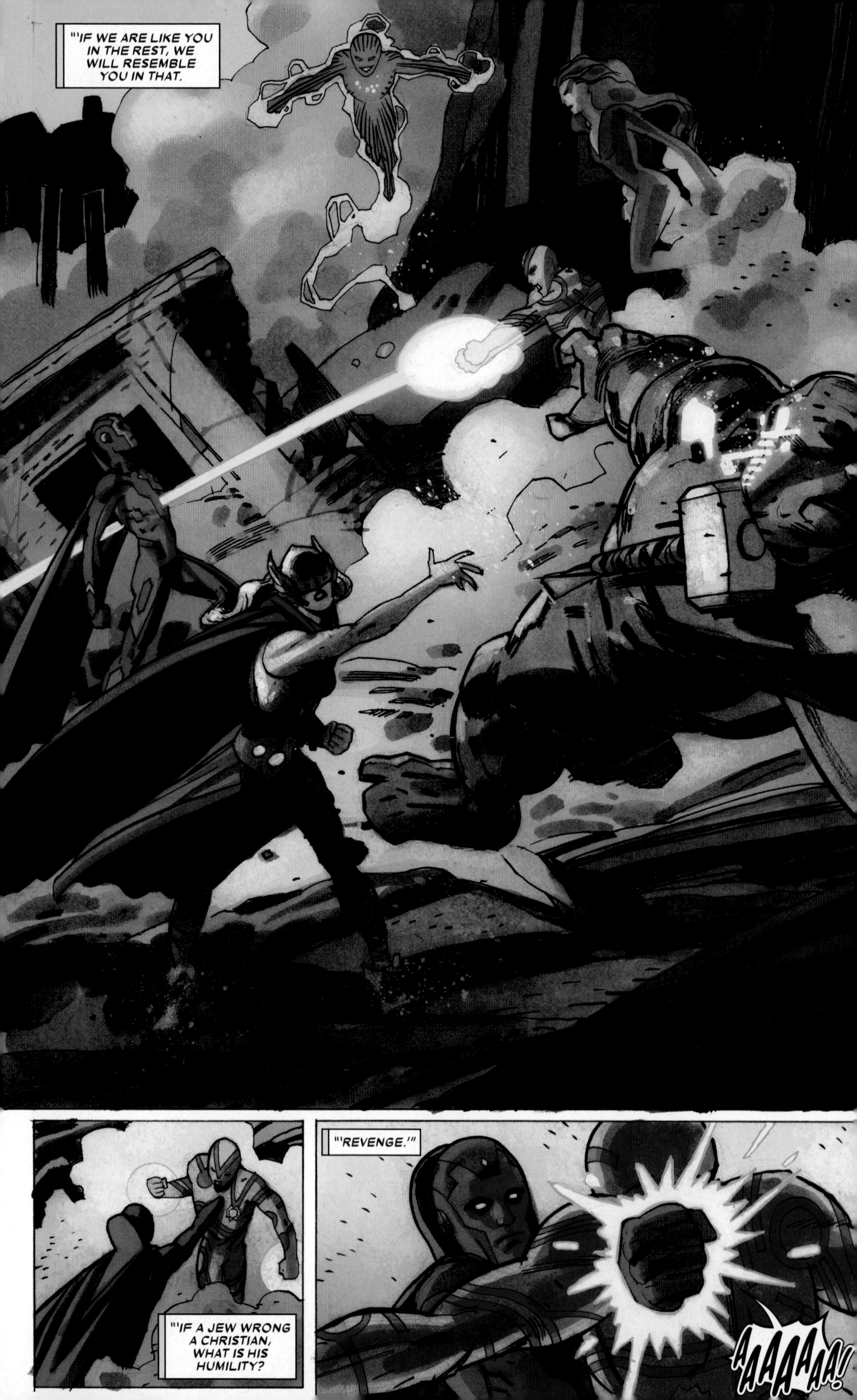
"'IF WE ARE LIKE YOU IN THE REST, WE WILL RESEMBLE YOU IN THAT.
"'IF A JEW WRONG A CHRISTIAN, WHAT IS HIS HUMILITY?
"'REVENGE.'"
AAAAAAA!

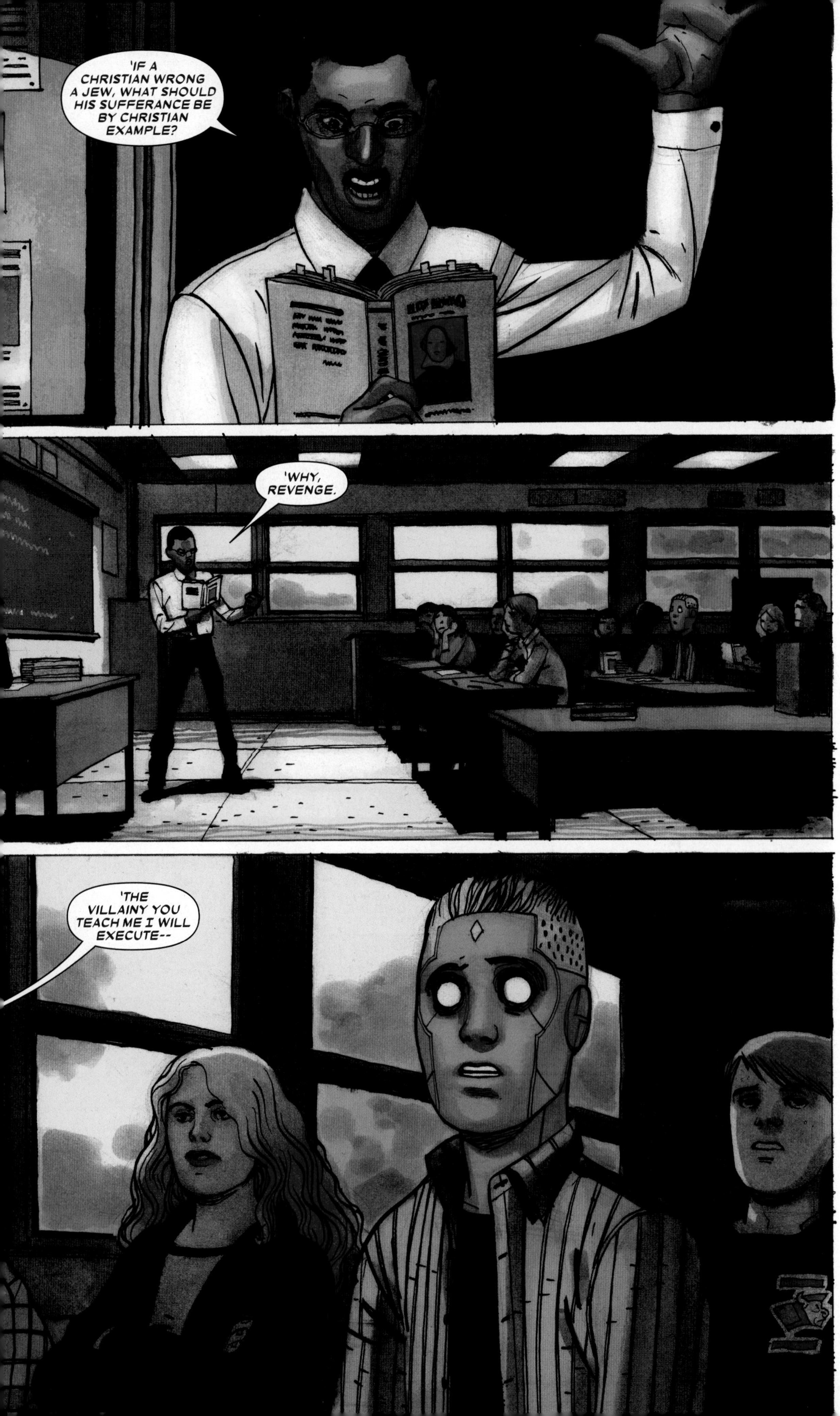
'IF A CHRISTIAN WRONG A JEW, WHAT SHOULD HIS SUFFERANCE BE BY CHRISTIAN EXAMPLE?
'WHY, REVENGE.
'THE VILLAINY YOU TEACH ME I WILL EXECUTE--

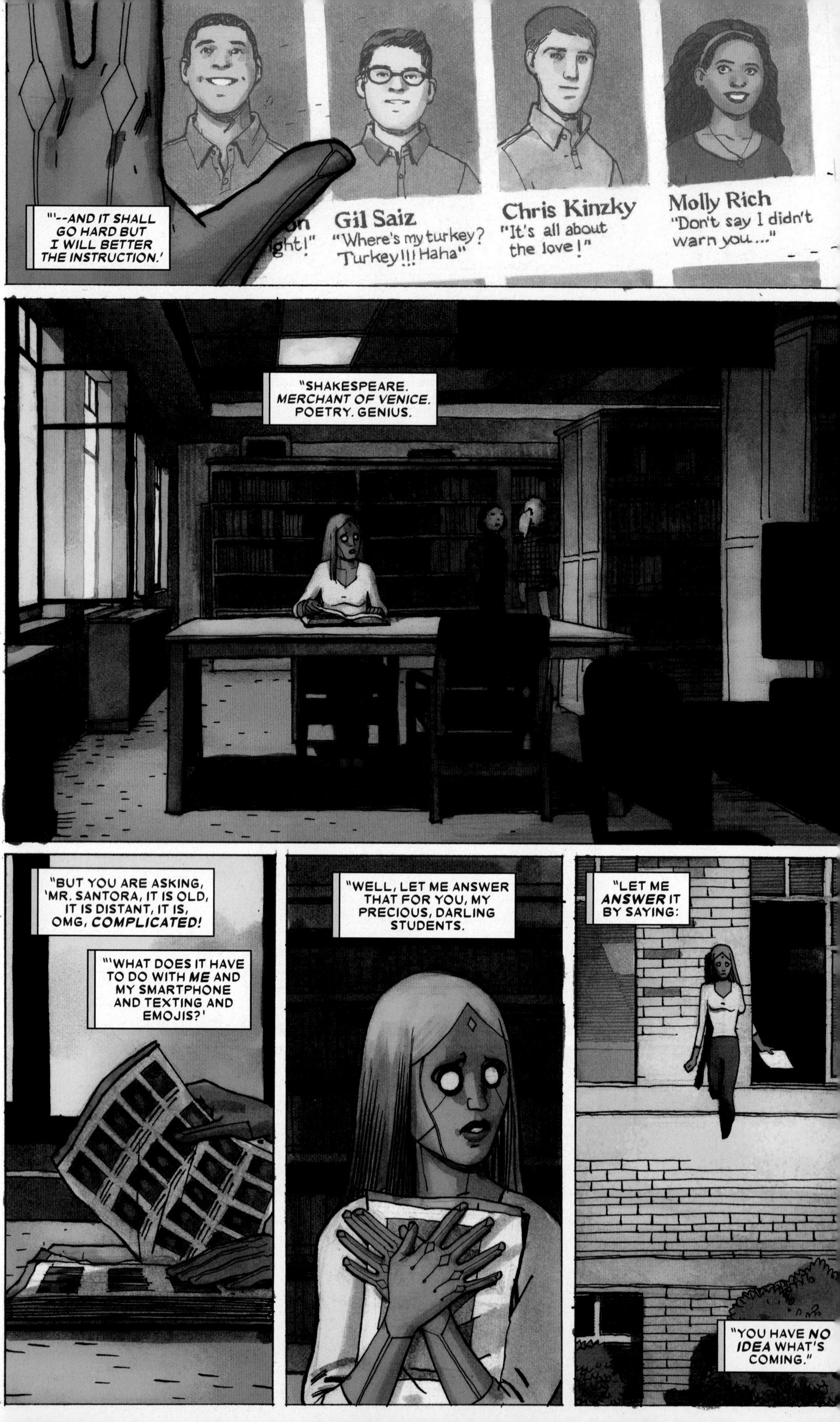

"'--AND IT SHALL GO HARD BUT I WILL BETTER THE INSTRUCTION.'
Gil Saiz
"Where's my turkey? Turkey!!! Haha"
Chris Kinzky
"It's all about the love!"
Molly Rich
"Don't say I didn't warn you..."
"SHAKESPEARE. MERCHANT OF VENICE. POETRY. GENIUS.
"BUT YOU ARE ASKING, 'MR. SANTORA, IT IS OLD, IT IS DISTANT, IT IS, OMG, COMPLICATED!
"'WHAT DOES IT HAVE TO DO WITH ME AND MY SMARTPHONE AND TEXTING AND EMOJIS?'
"WELL, LET ME ANSWER THAT FOR YOU, MY PRECIOUS, DARLING STUDENTS.
"LET ME ANSWER IT BY SAYING:
"YOU HAVE NO IDEA WHAT'S COMING."

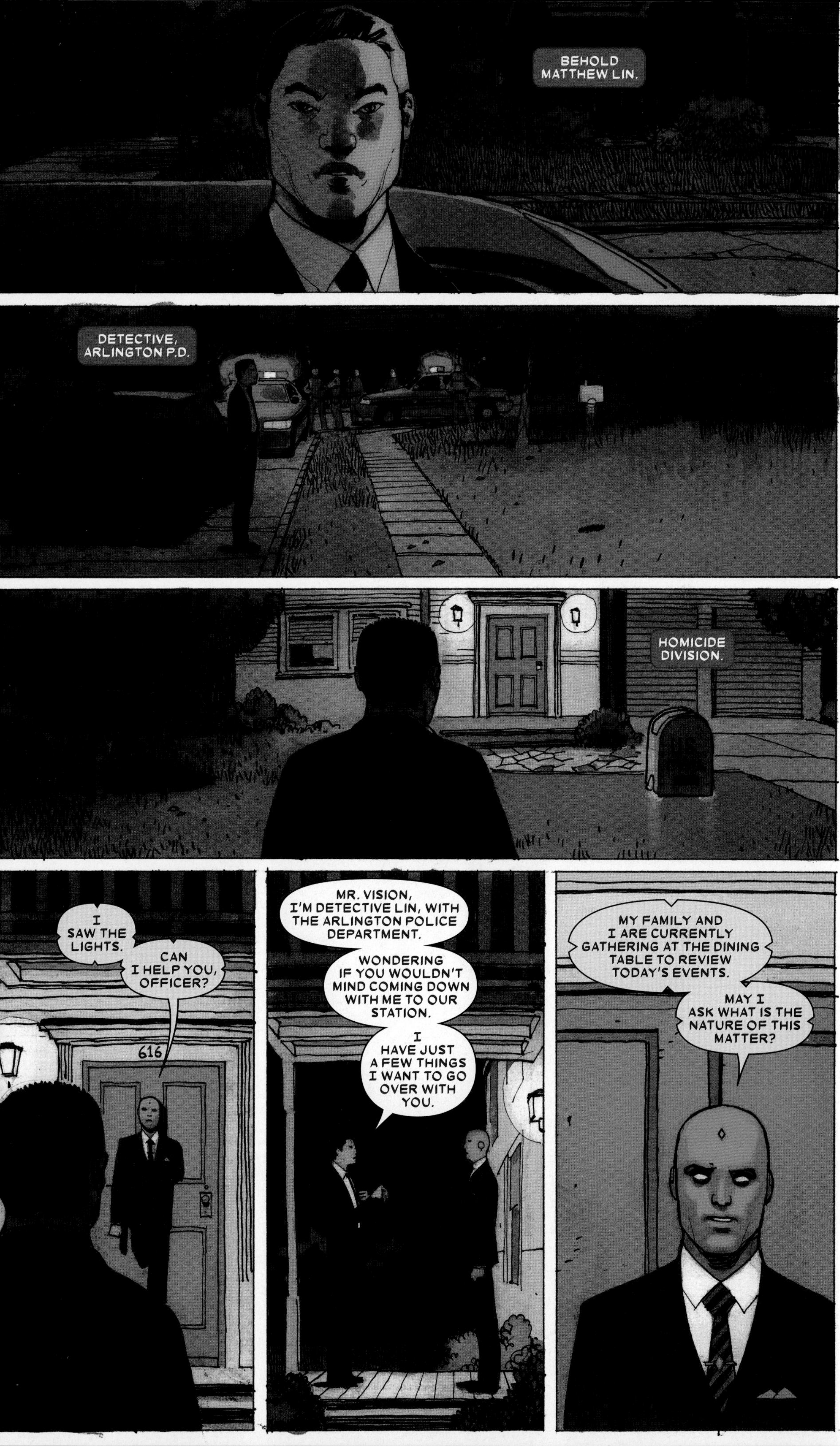
BEHOLD MATTHEW LIN.
DETECTIVE, ARLINGTON P.D.
HOMICIDE DIVISION.
I SAW THE LIGHTS.
CAN I HELP YOU, OFFICER?
616
MR. VISION, I'M DETECTIVE LIN, WITH THE ARLINGTON POLICE DEPARTMENT.
WONDERING IF YOU WOULDN'T MIND COMING DOWN WITH ME TO OUR STATION.
I HAVE JUST A FEW THINGS I WANT TO GO OVER WITH YOU.
MY FAMILY AND I ARE CURRENTLY GATHERING AT THE DINING TABLE TO REVIEW TODAY'S EVENTS.
MAY I ASK WHAT IS THE NATURE OF THIS MATTER?

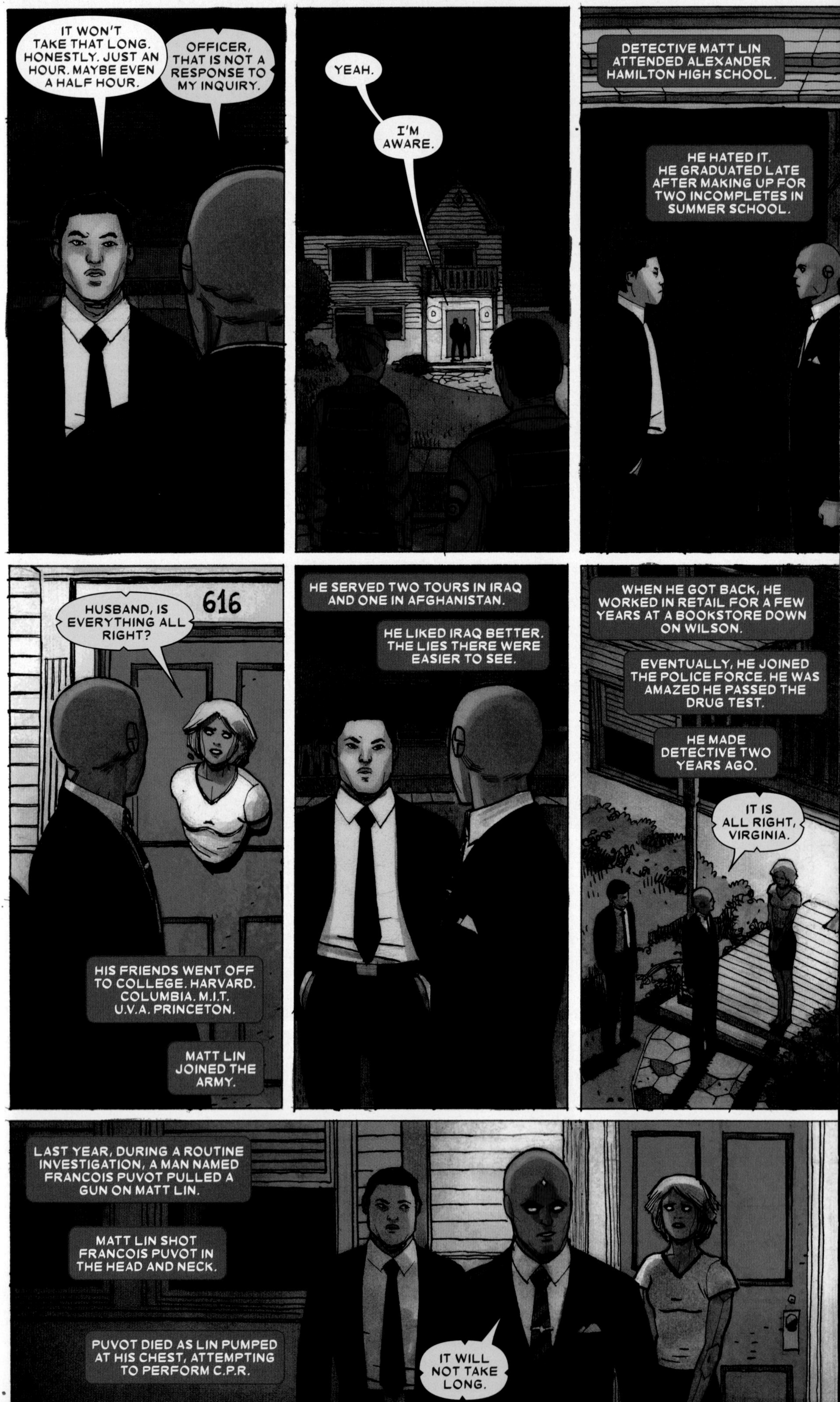
IT WON'T TAKE THAT LONG. HONESTLY. JUST AN HOUR. MAYBE EVEN A HALF HOUR.
OFFICER, THAT IS NOT A RESPONSE TO MY INQUIRY.
YEAH.
I'M AWARE.
DETECTIVE MATT LIN ATTENDED ALEXANDER HAMILTON HIGH SCHOOL.
HE HATED IT. HE GRADUATED LATE AFTER MAKING UP FOR TWO INCOMPLETES IN SUMMER SCHOOL.
616
HUSBAND, IS EVERYTHING ALL RIGHT?
HIS FRIENDS WENT OFF TO COLLEGE. HARVARD. COLUMBIA. M.I.T. U.V.A. PRINCETON.
MATT LIN JOINED THE ARMY.
HE SERVED TWO TOURS IN IRAQ AND ONE IN AFGHANISTAN.
HE LIKED IRAQ BETTER. THE LIES THERE WERE EASIER TO SEE.
WHEN HE GOT BACK, HE WORKED IN RETAIL FOR A FEW YEARS AT A BOOKSTORE DOWN ON WILSON.
EVENTUALLY, HE JOINED THE POLICE FORCE. HE WAS AMAZED HE PASSED THE DRUG TEST.
HE MADE DETECTIVE TWO YEARS AGO.
IT IS ALL RIGHT, VIRGINIA.
LAST YEAR, DURING A ROUTINE INVESTIGATION, A MAN NAMED FRANCOIS PUVOT PULLED A GUN ON MATT LIN.
MATT LIN SHOT FRANCOIS PUVOT IN THE HEAD AND NECK.
PUVOT DIED AS LIN PUMPED AT HIS CHEST, ATTEMPTING TO PERFORM C.P.R.
IT WILL NOT TAKE LONG.

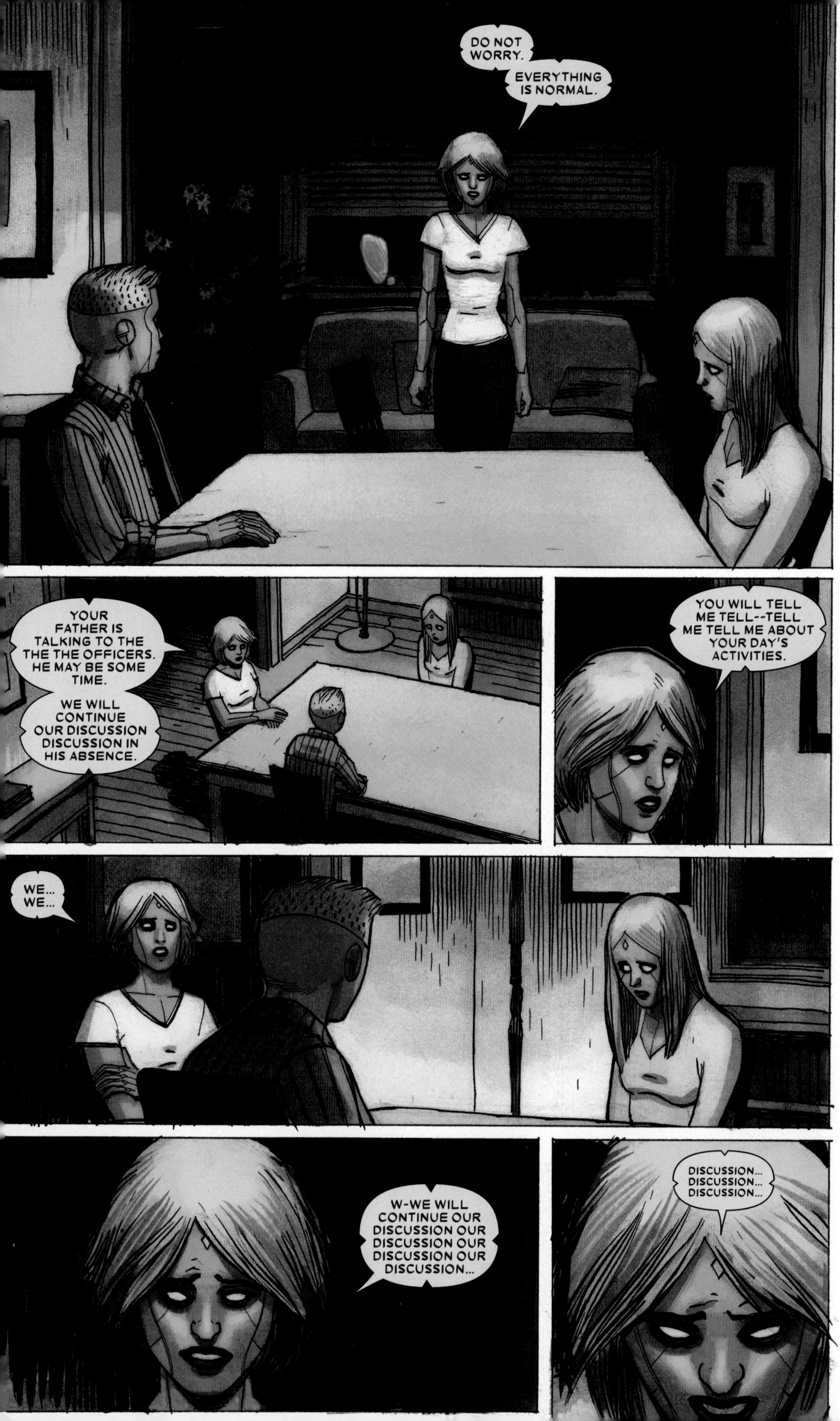
DO NOT WORRY.
EVERYTHING IS NORMAL.
YOUR FATHER IS TALKING TO THE THE THE OFFICERS. HE MAY BE SOME TIME.
WE WILL CONTINUE OUR DISCUSSION DISCUSSION IN HIS ABSENCE.
YOU WILL TELL ME TELL--TELL ME TELL ME ABOUT YOUR DAY'S ACTIVITIES.
WE... WE...
W-WE WILL CONTINUE OUR DISCUSSION OUR DISCUSSION OUR DISCUSSION OUR DISCUSSION...
DISCUSSION... DISCUSSION... DISCUSSION...

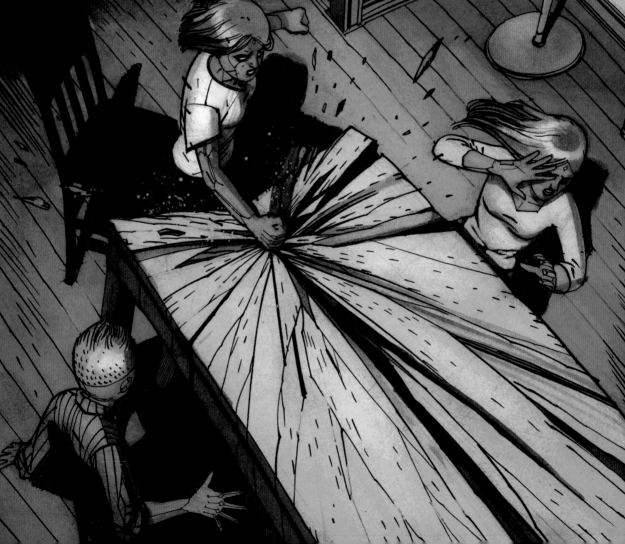

EVERYTHING IS NORMAL!

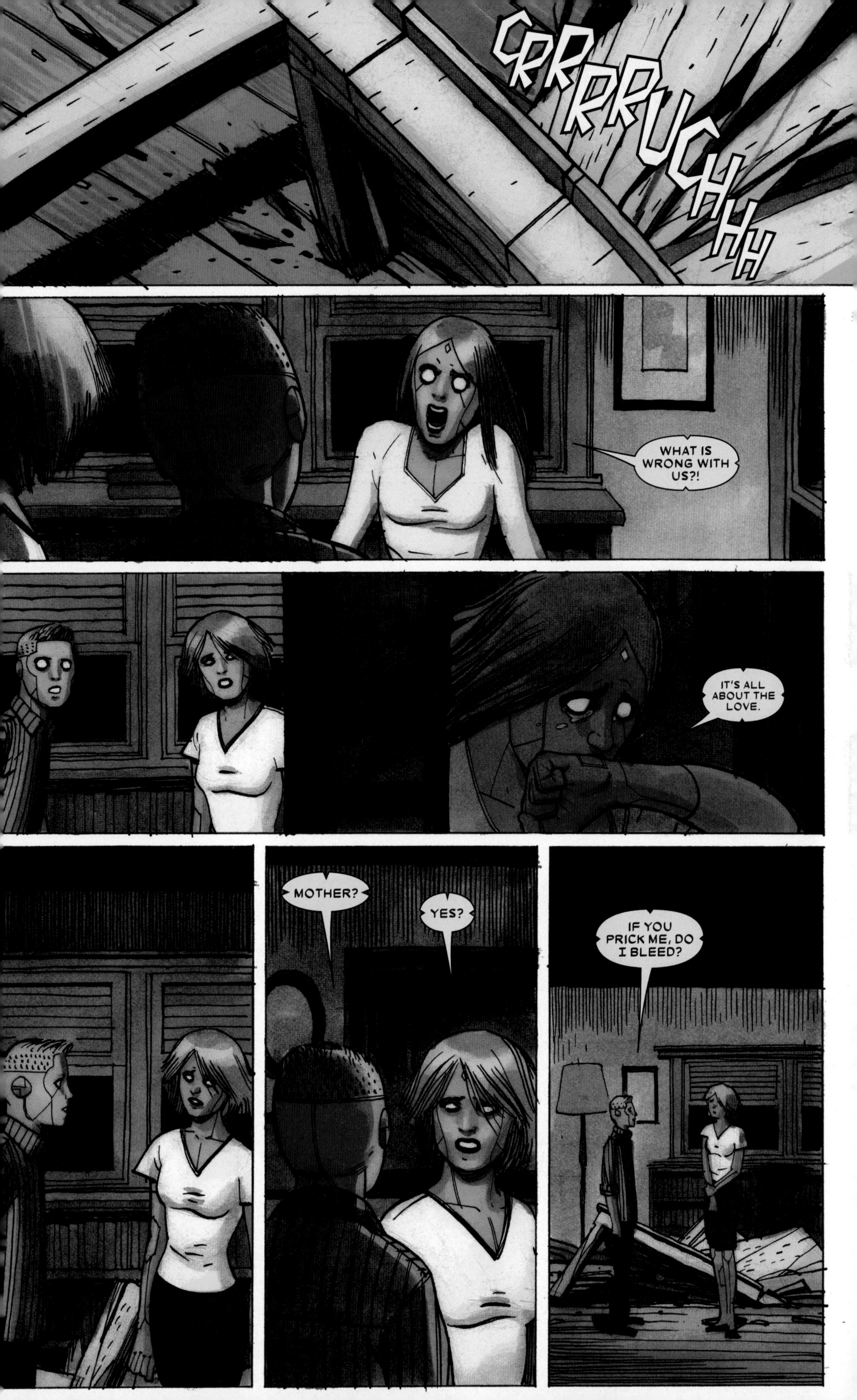
CRRRRUCHHH
WHAT IS WRONG WITH US?!
IT'S ALL ABOUT THE LOVE.
MOTHER?
YES?
IF YOU PRICK ME, DO I BLEED?

TELL ME, MR. VISION, DO YOU KEEP RECORDINGS OF YOUR WHEREABOUTS, OF WHAT YOU SEE AND DO?

PREVIOUSLY, VISION TOLD PRINCIPAL WAXMAN THAT HE HAD SAVED THE WORLD THIRTY-SEVEN TIMES.

YES.

OF COURSE, THIS COULD ONLY BE CALLED AN ESTIMATION.

THE EXACT NUMBER WAS DIFFICULT TO CALCULATE.

ARE YOU WILLING TO PROVIDE THE ARLINGTON P.D. WITH COPIES OF THOSE RECORDINGS?

FOR EXAMPLE, VISION WAS RESPONSIBLE FOR THE FORMATION OF THE WEST COAST AVENGERS.

SHOULD EACH TIME THEY SAVED THE WORLD THEN COUNT AS VISION SAVING THE WORLD?

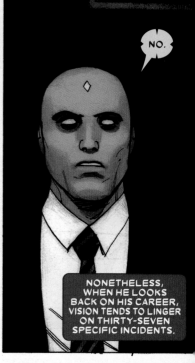

NO.

NONETHELESS, WHEN HE LOOKS BACK ON HIS CAREER, VISION TENDS TO LINGER ON THIRTY-SEVEN SPECIFIC INCIDENTS.

"I AM NOT WILLING."

IN NO PARTICULAR ORDER:

1. THE SENTINELS STRIKE

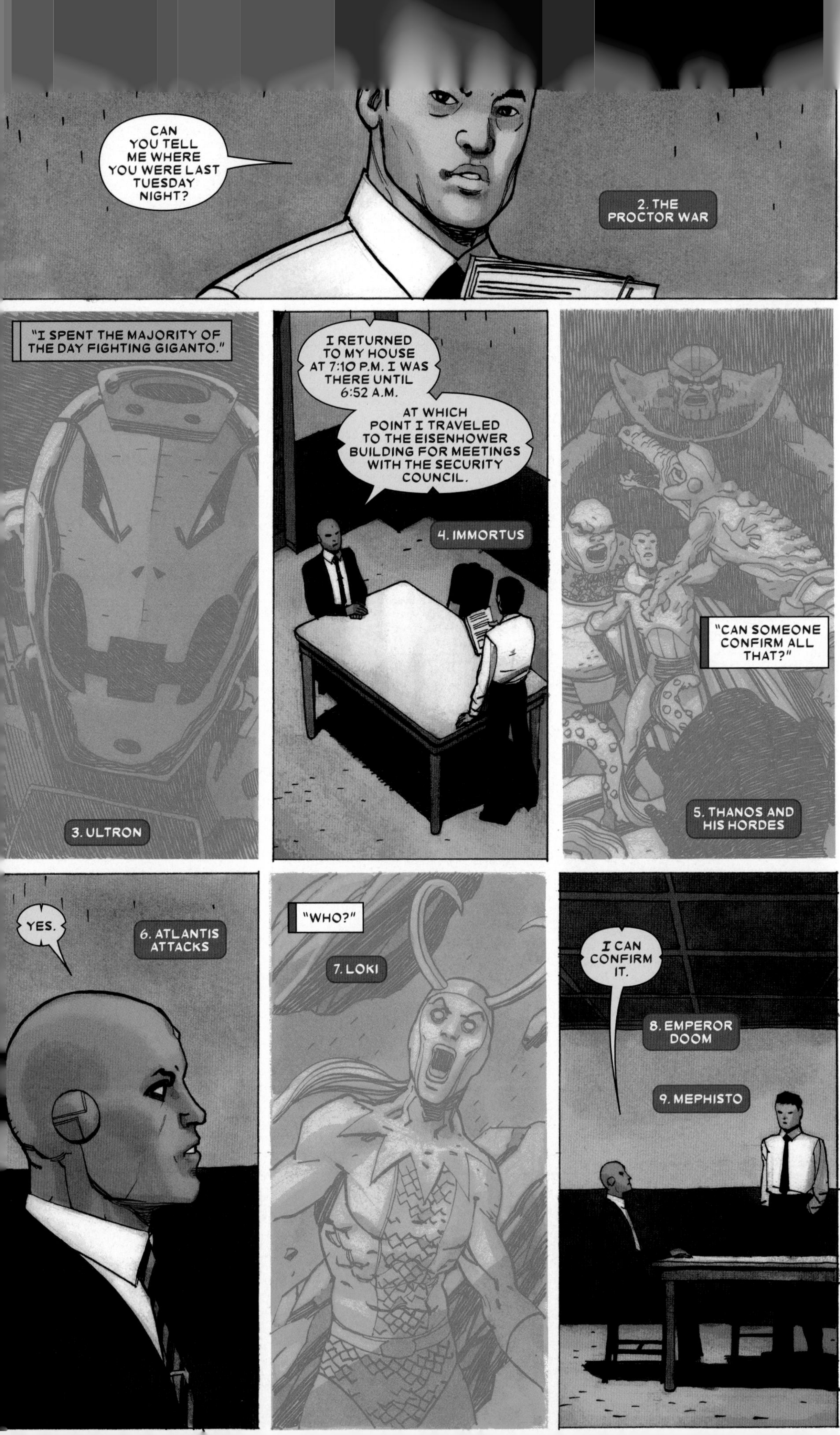
CAN YOU TELL ME WHERE YOU WERE LAST TUESDAY NIGHT?
2. THE PROCTOR WAR
"I SPENT THE MAJORITY OF THE DAY FIGHTING GIGANTO."
3. ULTRON
I RETURNED TO MY HOUSE AT 7:10 P.M. I WAS THERE UNTIL 6:52 A.M.
AT WHICH POINT I TRAVELED TO THE EISENHOWER BUILDING FOR MEETINGS WITH THE SECURITY COUNCIL.
4. IMMORTUS
"CAN SOMEONE CONFIRM ALL THAT?"
5. THANOS AND HIS HORDES
YES.
6. ATLANTIS ATTACKS
"WHO?"
7. LOKI
I CAN CONFIRM IT.
8. EMPEROR DOOM
9. MEPHISTO

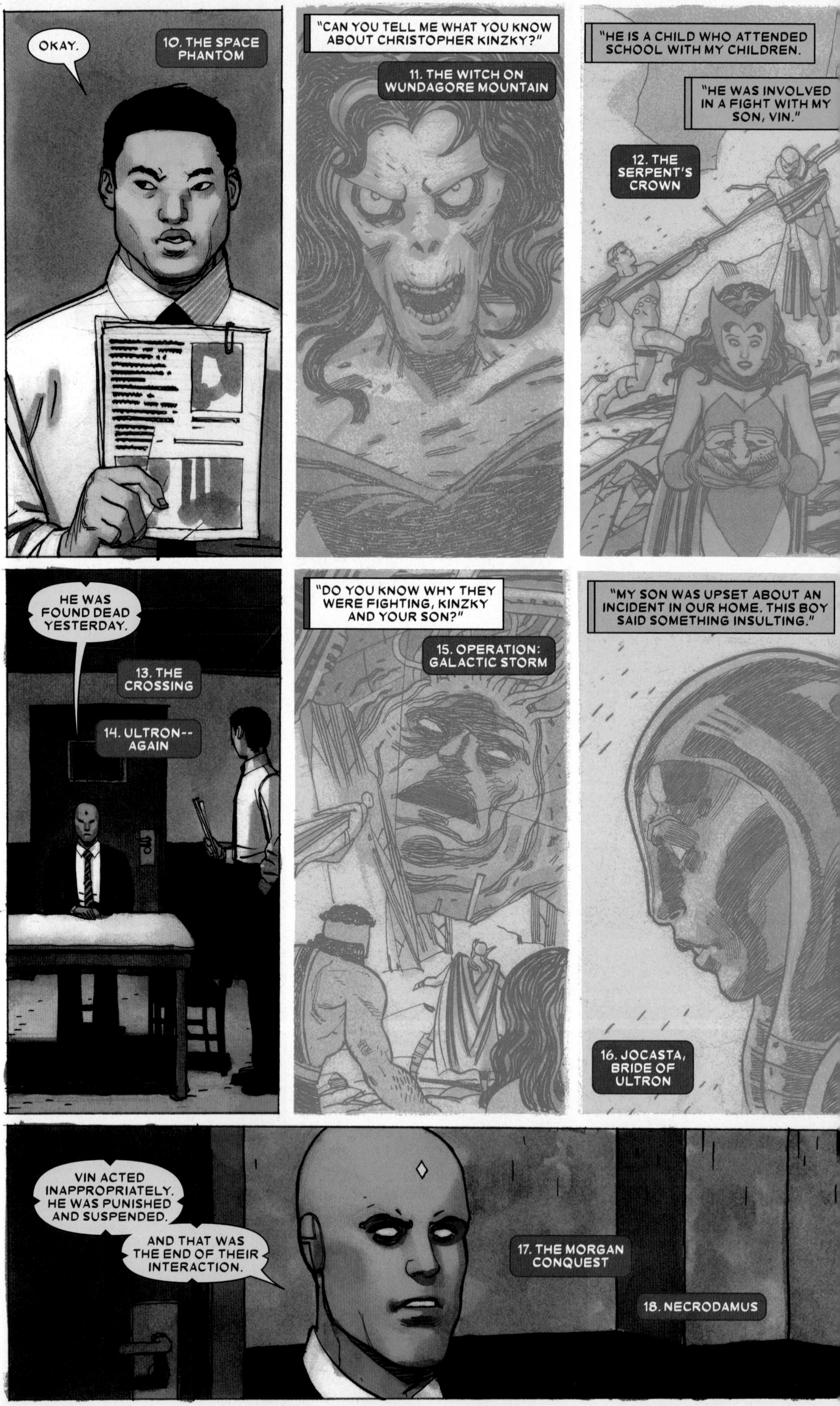
OKAY.
10. THE SPACE PHANTOM
"CAN YOU TELL ME WHAT YOU KNOW ABOUT CHRISTOPHER KINZKY?"
11. THE WITCH ON WUNDAGORE MOUNTAIN
"HE IS A CHILD WHO ATTENDED SCHOOL WITH MY CHILDREN.
"HE WAS INVOLVED IN A FIGHT WITH MY SON, VIN."
12. THE SERPENT'S CROWN
HE WAS FOUND DEAD YESTERDAY.
13. THE CROSSING
14. ULTRON-- AGAIN
"DO YOU KNOW WHY THEY WERE FIGHTING, KINZKY AND YOUR SON?"
15. OPERATION: GALACTIC STORM
"MY SON WAS UPSET ABOUT AN INCIDENT IN OUR HOME. THIS BOY SAID SOMETHING INSULTING."
16. JOCASTA, BRIDE OF ULTRON
VIN ACTED INAPPROPRIATELY. HE WAS PUNISHED AND SUSPENDED.
AND THAT WAS THE END OF THEIR INTERACTION.
17. THE MORGAN CONQUEST
18. NECRODAMUS

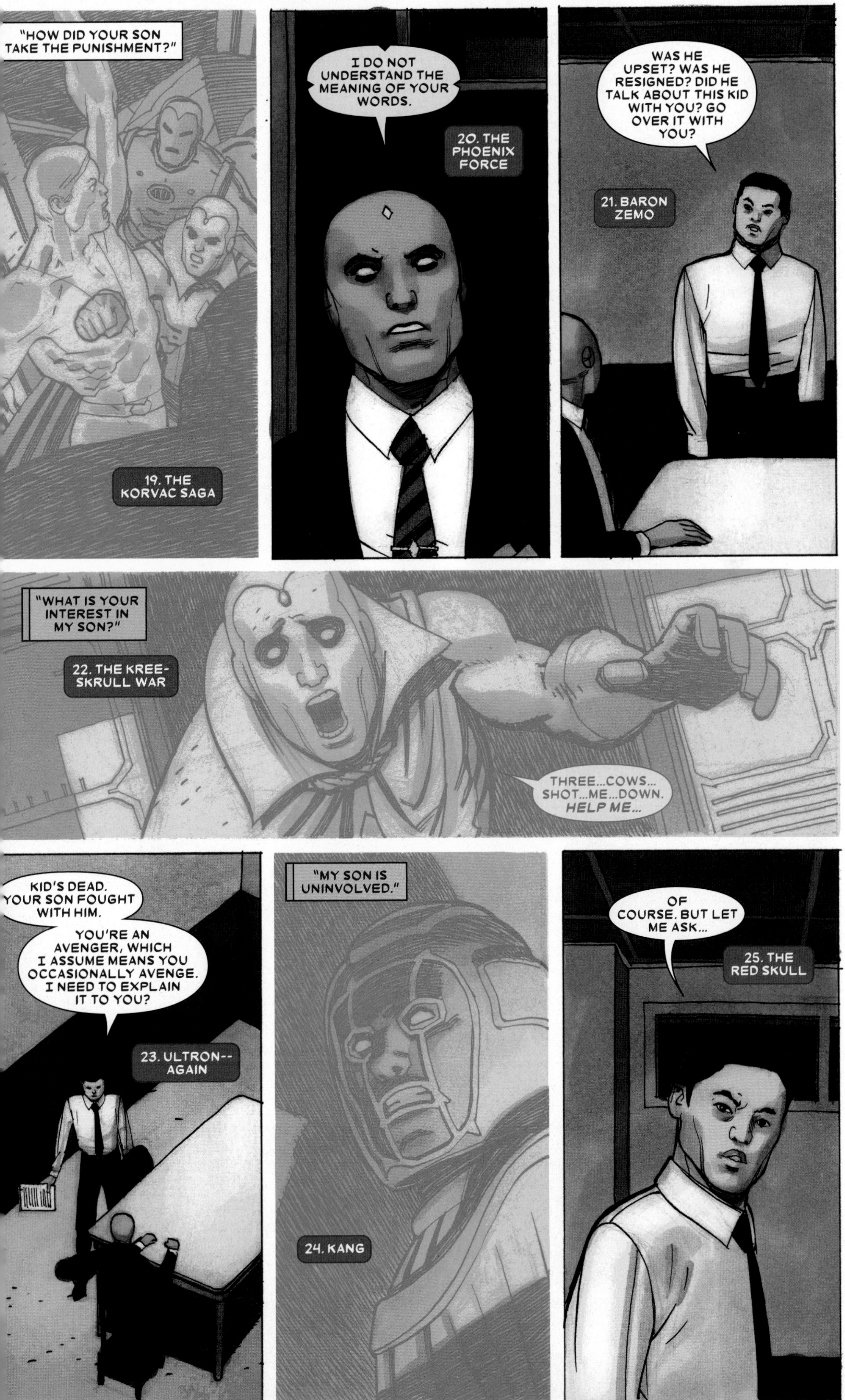
"HOW DID YOUR SON TAKE THE PUNISHMENT?"
19. THE KORVAC SAGA
I DO NOT UNDERSTAND THE MEANING OF YOUR WORDS.
20. THE PHOENIX FORCE
WAS HE UPSET? WAS HE RESIGNED? DID HE TALK ABOUT THIS KID WITH YOU? GO OVER IT WITH YOU?
21. BARON ZEMO
"WHAT IS YOUR INTEREST IN MY SON?"
22. THE KREE-SKRULL WAR
THREE...COWS... SHOT...ME...DOWN. HELP ME...
KID'S DEAD. YOUR SON FOUGHT WITH HIM.
YOU'RE AN AVENGER, WHICH I ASSUME MEANS YOU OCCASIONALLY AVENGE. I NEED TO EXPLAIN IT TO YOU?
23. ULTRON--AGAIN
"MY SON IS UNINVOLVED."
24. KANG
OF COURSE. BUT LET ME ASK...
25. THE RED SKULL

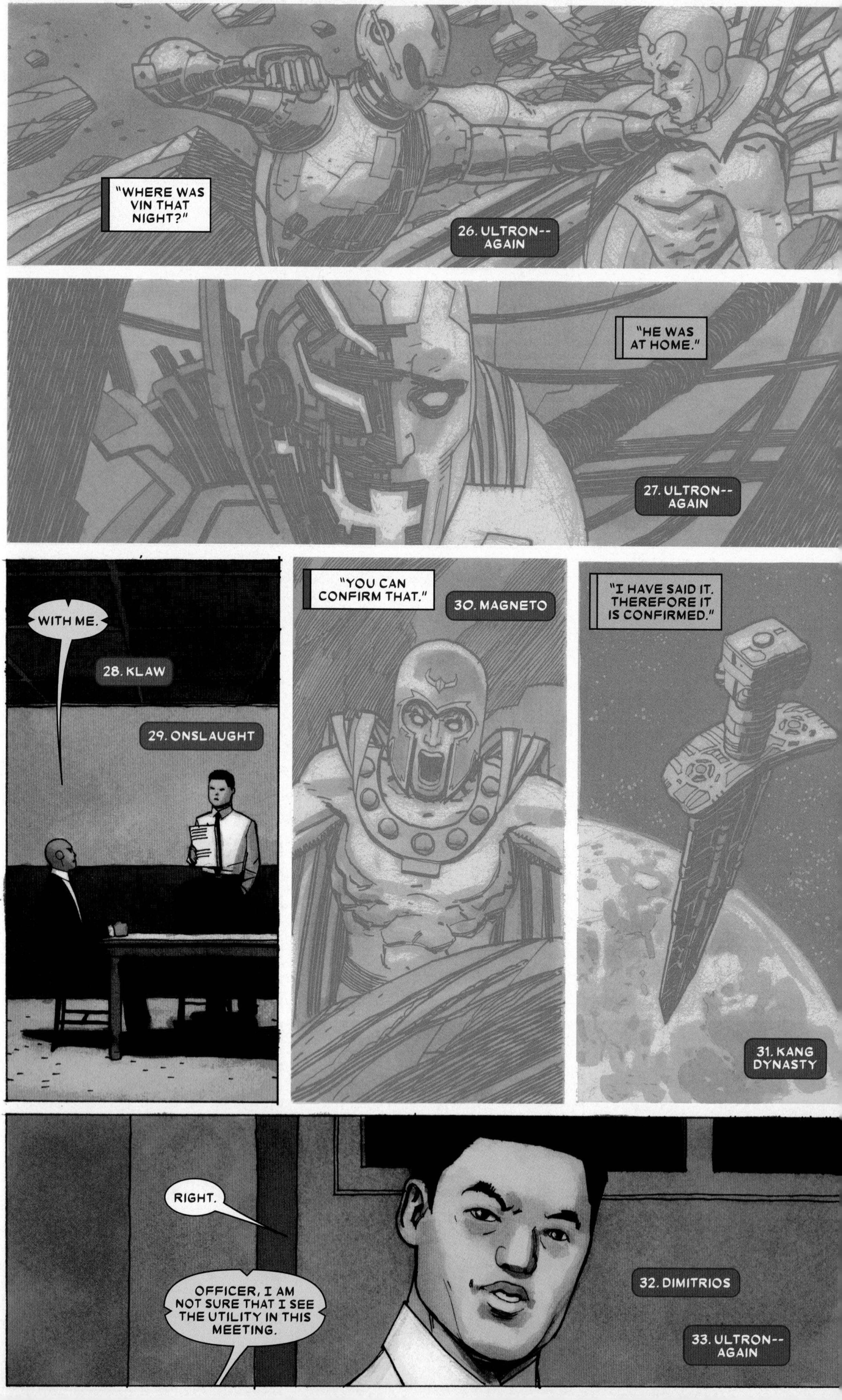
"WHERE WAS VIN THAT NIGHT?"
26. ULTRON-- AGAIN
"HE WAS AT HOME."
27. ULTRON-- AGAIN
WITH ME.
28. KLAW
29. ONSLAUGHT
"YOU CAN CONFIRM THAT."
30. MAGNETO
"I HAVE SAID IT. THEREFORE IT IS CONFIRMED."
31. KANG DYNASTY
RIGHT.
OFFICER, I AM NOT SURE THAT I SEE THE UTILITY IN THIS MEETING.
32. DIMITRIOS
33. ULTRON-- AGAIN

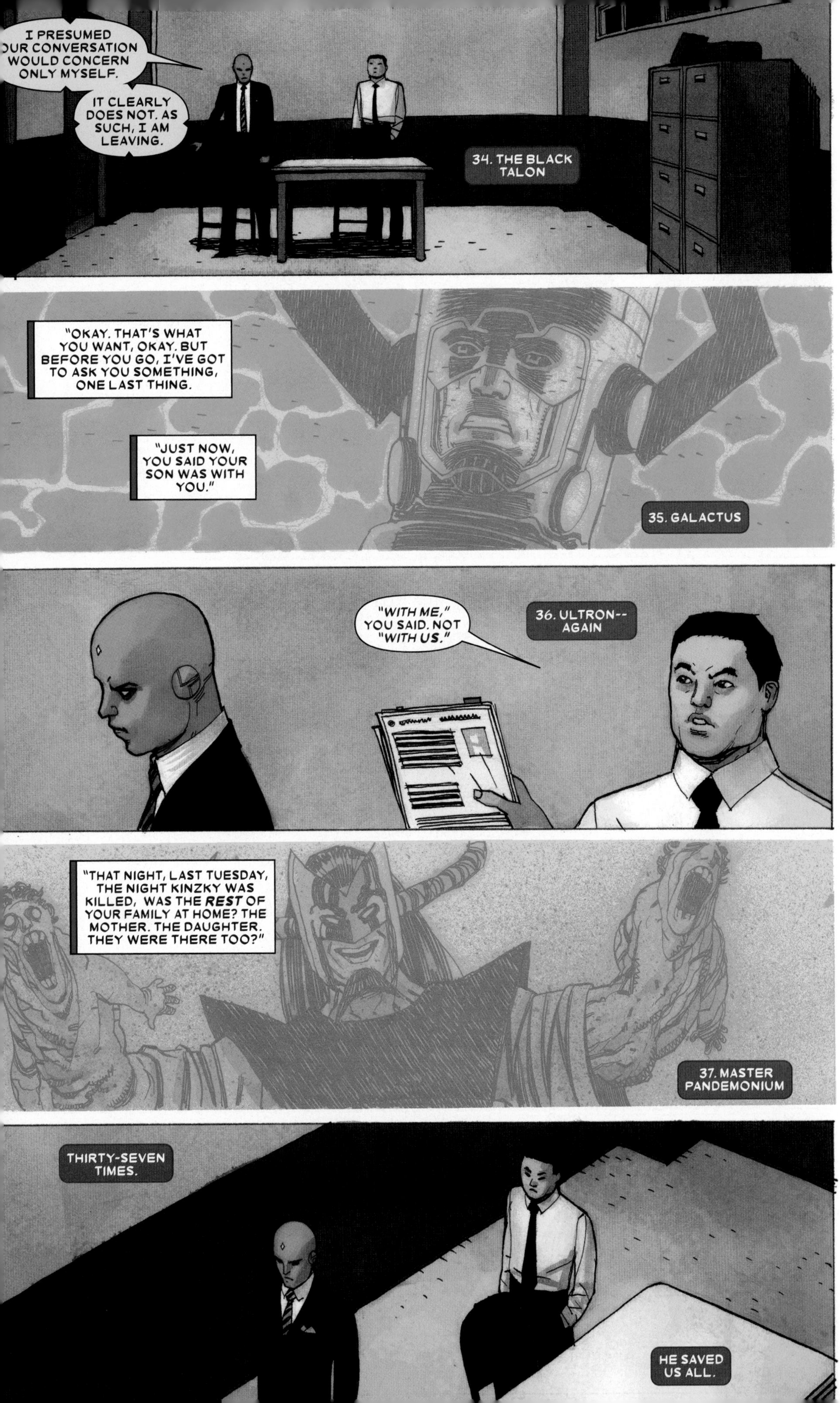
I PRESUMED OUR CONVERSATION WOULD CONCERN ONLY MYSELF.
IT CLEARLY DOES NOT. AS SUCH, I AM LEAVING.
34. THE BLACK TALON
"OKAY. THAT'S WHAT YOU WANT, OKAY. BUT BEFORE YOU GO, I'VE GOT TO ASK YOU SOMETHING, ONE LAST THING.
"JUST NOW, YOU SAID YOUR SON WAS WITH YOU."
35. GALACTUS
"WITH ME," YOU SAID. NOT "WITH US."
36. ULTRON-- AGAIN
"THAT NIGHT, LAST TUESDAY, THE NIGHT KINZKY WAS KILLED, WAS THE REST OF YOUR FAMILY AT HOME? THE MOTHER. THE DAUGHTER. THEY WERE THERE TOO?"
37. MASTER PANDEMONIUM
THIRTY-SEVEN TIMES.
HE SAVED US ALL.

BUT IT'S NOT ENOUGH, IS IT? IN THE END, I MEAN.

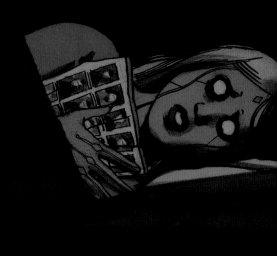

THOSE THIRTY-SEVEN OCCASIONS WHEN HE WAS ALL THAT STOOD BETWEEN LIFE AND DEATH, BETWEEN EVERYTHING AND NOTHING.

WHEN HE HAD BEEN BEATEN, TORN, TORTURED.

AND INSTEAD OF SIMPLY SLIPPING INTO THE GROUND AS WE SURELY WOULD HAVE DONE...

...HE RAISED HIS HEAD ONE MORE TIME, STARED ONE MORE TIME INTO THE SCREAMING FACE OF EVIL...

AND SAID, *ONE MORE TIME*, IN HIS SIMPLE VOICE, WITH NO EMOTION, NO CARE:

"I AM THE VISION OF THE AVENGERS. I WILL NOT FALL."

THIRTY-SEVEN TIMES.

AND ALL OF IT CANNOT REDEEM HIM FROM THIS, THIS SMALL MOMENT WHEN HE CROSSED TO THE OTHER SIDE, WHEN HE ENTERED INTO THE MADNESS THAT WAS SOON TO COME.

THIS SMALL MOMENT.

THIS SMALL LIE.

LAST TUESDAY. YES.

MY FAMILY. THEY WERE ALL WITH ME.

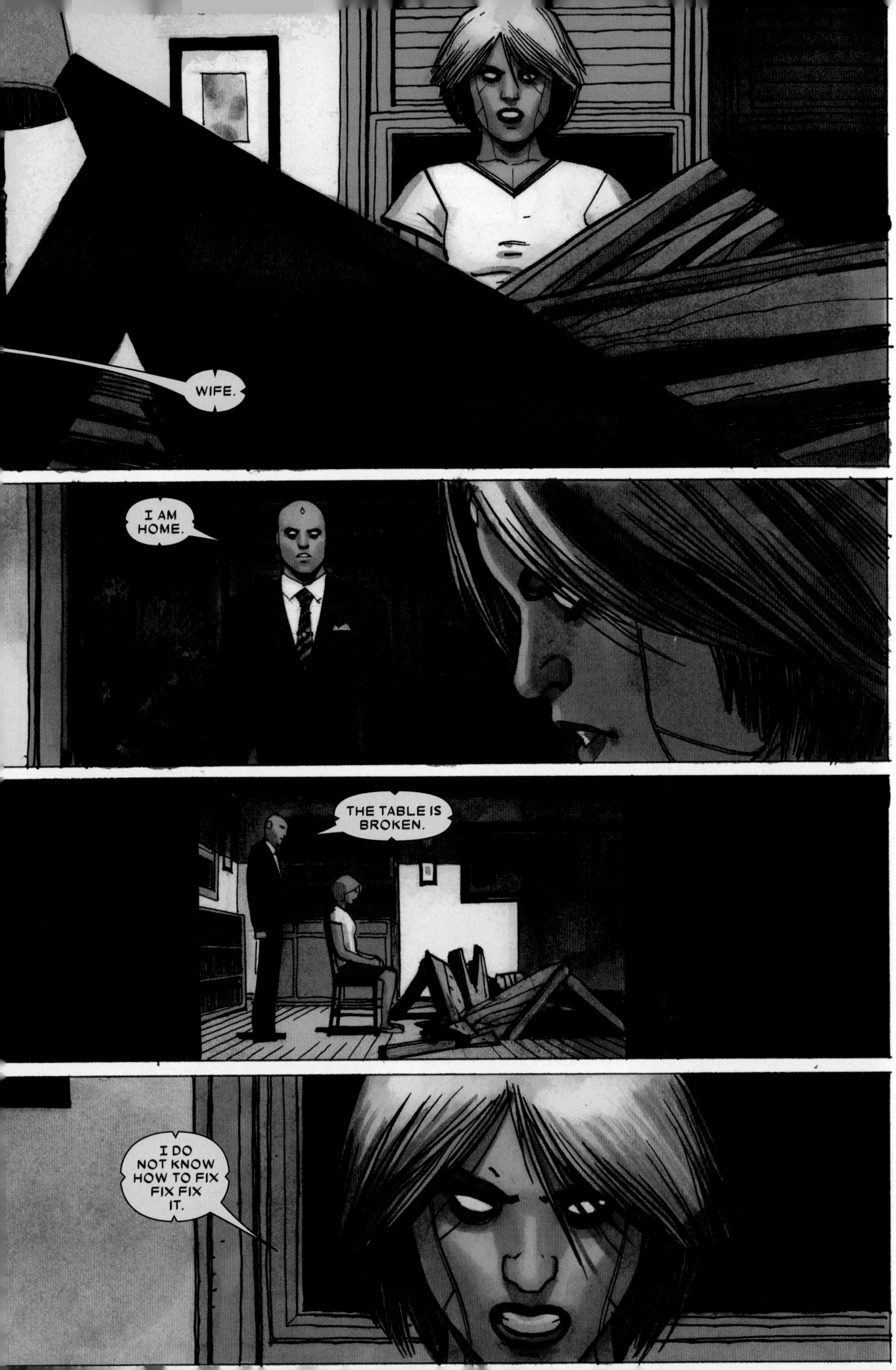
WIFE.
I AM HOME.
THE TABLE IS BROKEN.
I DO NOT KNOW HOW TO FIX FIX FIX IT.

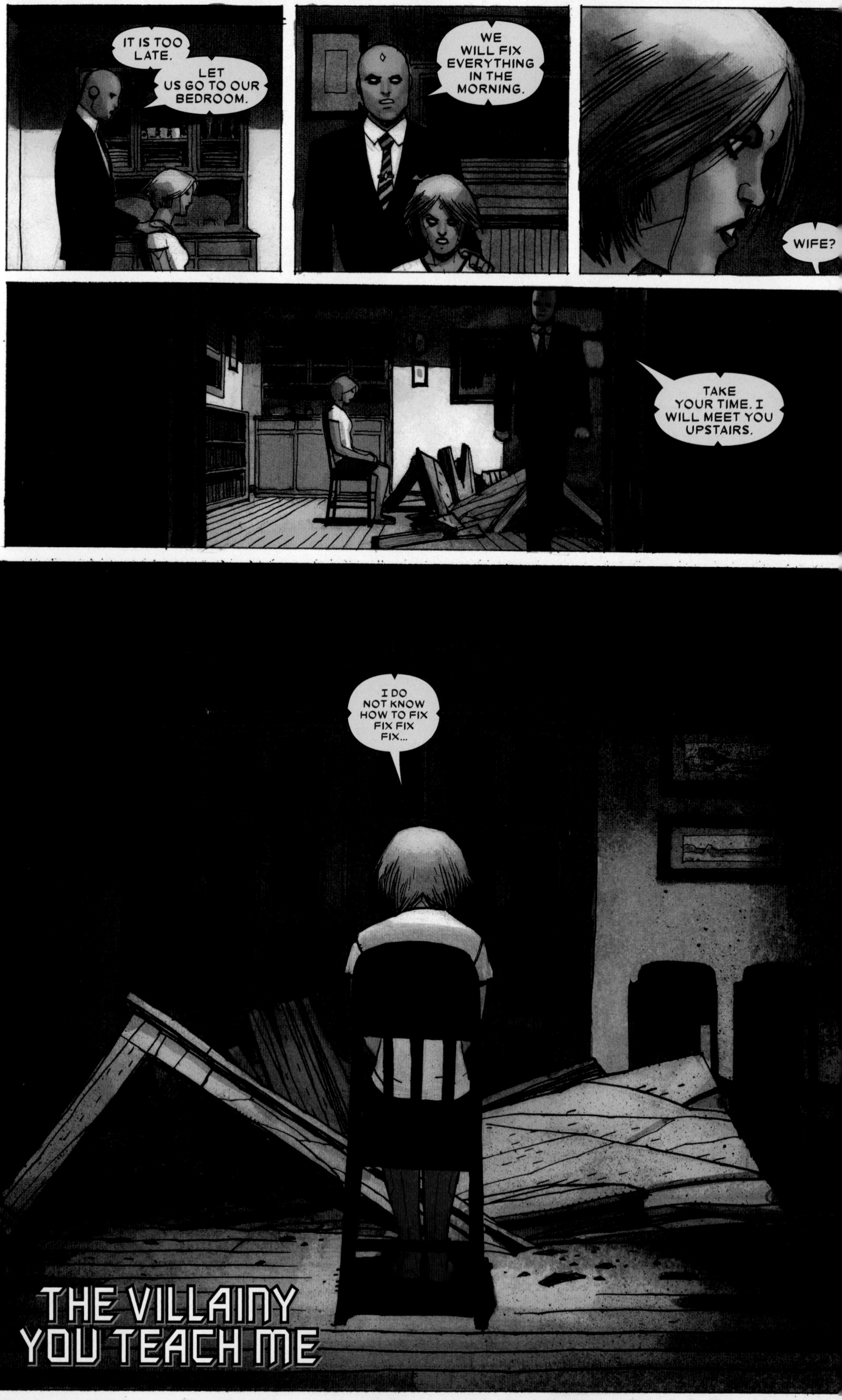
IT IS TOO LATE.
LET US GO TO OUR BEDROOM.
WE WILL FIX EVERYTHING IN THE MORNING.
WIFE?
TAKE YOUR TIME. I WILL MEET YOU UPSTAIRS.
I DO NOT KNOW HOW TO FIX FIX FIX FIX...
THE VILLAINY YOU TEACH ME

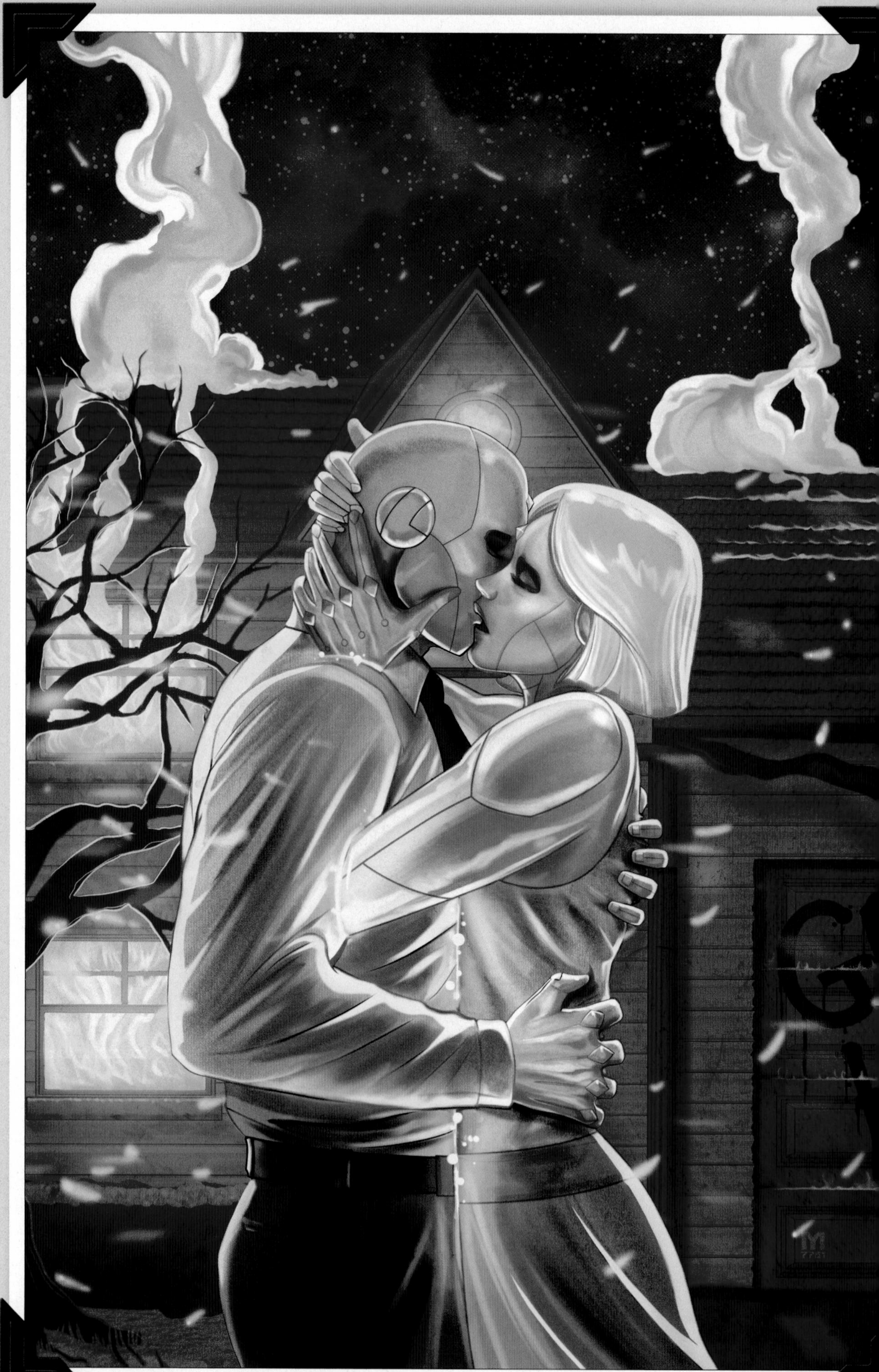

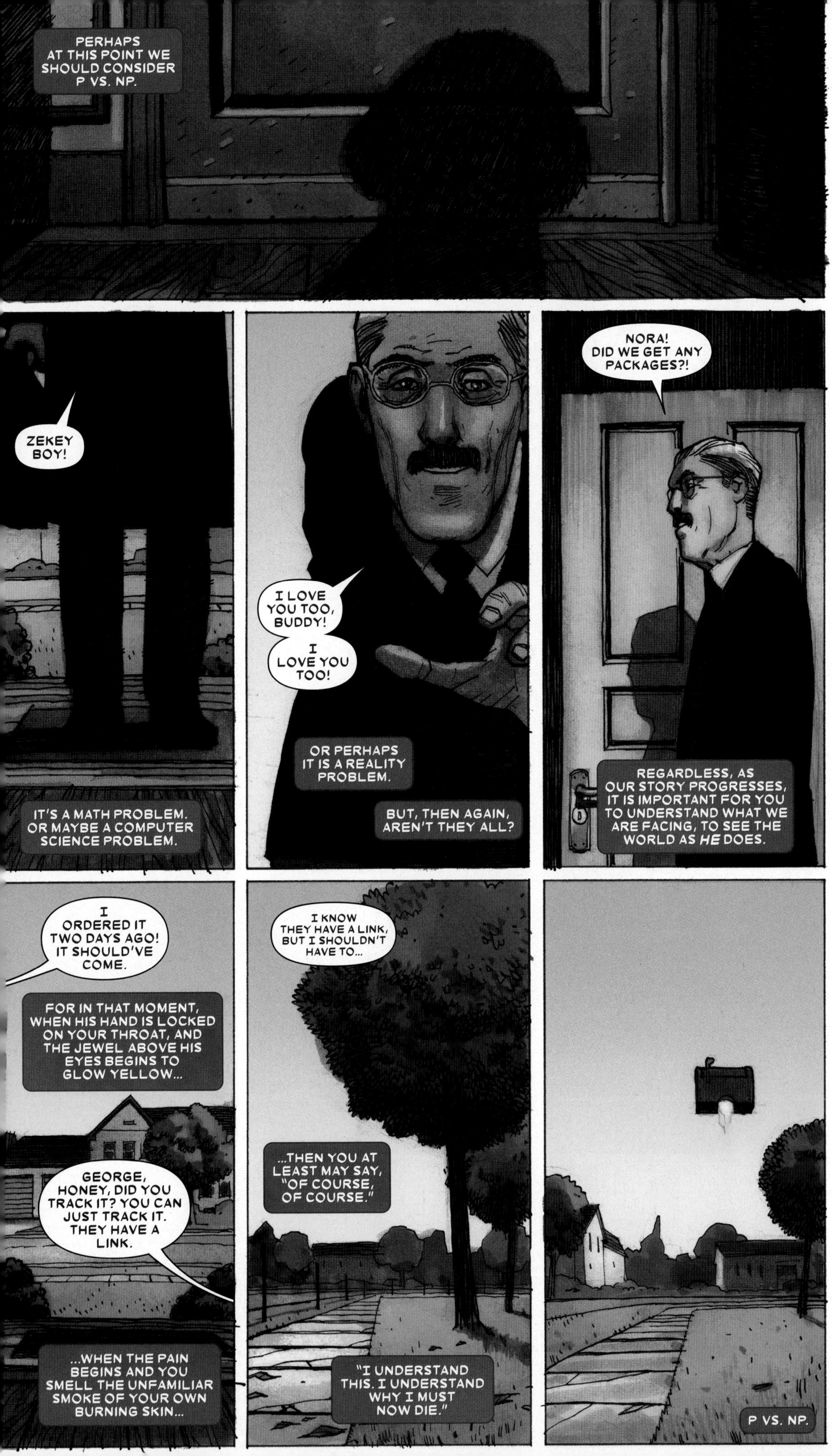

PERHAPS AT THIS POINT WE SHOULD CONSIDER P VS. NP.
ZEKEY BOY!
IT'S A MATH PROBLEM. OR MAYBE A COMPUTER SCIENCE PROBLEM.
I LOVE YOU TOO, BUDDY!
I LOVE YOU TOO!
OR PERHAPS IT IS A REALITY PROBLEM.
BUT, THEN AGAIN, AREN'T THEY ALL?
NORA! DID WE GET ANY PACKAGES?!
REGARDLESS, AS OUR STORY PROGRESSES, IT IS IMPORTANT FOR YOU TO UNDERSTAND WHAT WE ARE FACING, TO SEE THE WORLD AS *HE* DOES.
I ORDERED IT TWO DAYS AGO! IT SHOULD'VE COME.
FOR IN THAT MOMENT, WHEN HIS HAND IS LOCKED ON YOUR THROAT, AND THE JEWEL ABOVE HIS EYES BEGINS TO GLOW YELLOW...
GEORGE, HONEY, DID YOU TRACK IT? YOU CAN JUST TRACK IT. THEY HAVE A LINK.
...WHEN THE PAIN BEGINS AND YOU SMELL THE UNFAMILIAR SMOKE OF YOUR OWN BURNING SKIN...
I KNOW THEY HAVE A LINK, BUT I SHOULDN'T HAVE TO...
...THEN YOU AT LEAST MAY SAY, "OF COURSE, OF COURSE."
"I UNDERSTAND THIS. I UNDERSTAND WHY I MUST NOW DIE."
P VS. NP.

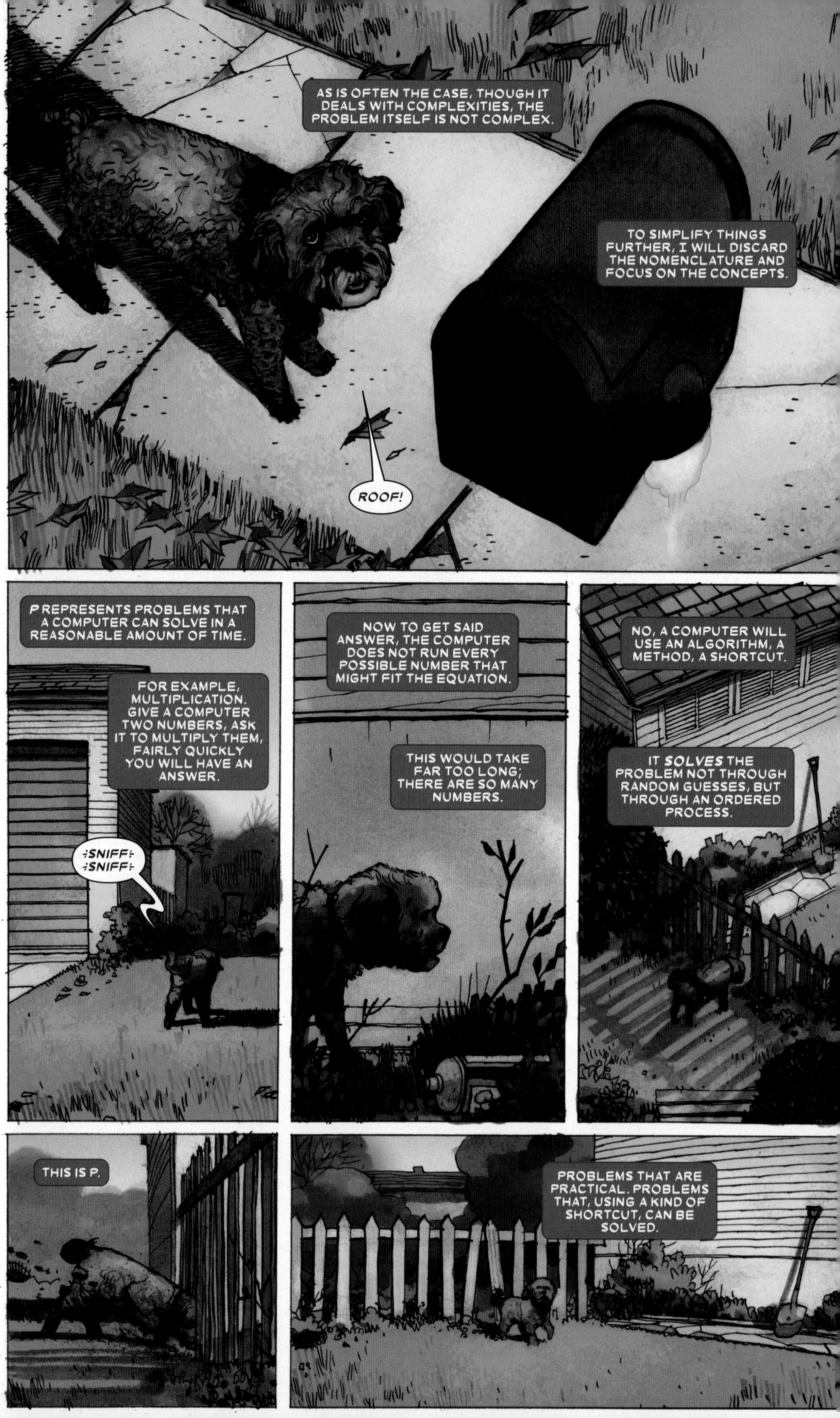
AS IS OFTEN THE CASE, THOUGH IT DEALS WITH COMPLEXITIES, THE PROBLEM ITSELF IS NOT COMPLEX.
TO SIMPLIFY THINGS FURTHER, I WILL DISCARD THE NOMENCLATURE AND FOCUS ON THE CONCEPTS.
ROOF!
P REPRESENTS PROBLEMS THAT A COMPUTER CAN SOLVE IN A REASONABLE AMOUNT OF TIME.
FOR EXAMPLE, MULTIPLICATION. GIVE A COMPUTER TWO NUMBERS, ASK IT TO MULTIPLY THEM, FAIRLY QUICKLY YOU WILL HAVE AN ANSWER.
SNIFF SNIFF
NOW TO GET SAID ANSWER, THE COMPUTER DOES NOT RUN EVERY POSSIBLE NUMBER THAT MIGHT FIT THE EQUATION.
THIS WOULD TAKE FAR TOO LONG; THERE ARE SO MANY NUMBERS.
NO, A COMPUTER WILL USE AN ALGORITHM, A METHOD, A SHORTCUT.
IT SOLVES THE PROBLEM NOT THROUGH RANDOM GUESSES, BUT THROUGH AN ORDERED PROCESS.
THIS IS P.
PROBLEMS THAT ARE PRACTICAL. PROBLEMS THAT, USING A KIND OF SHORTCUT, CAN BE SOLVED.

THERE EXISTS, HOWEVER, ANOTHER TYPE OF PROBLEM, ONE FOR WHICH THERE ARE NO SHORTCUTS.

THESE PROBLEMS DO *HAVE* SOLUTIONS. INDEED, IF YOU HAVE A SOLUTION AND YOU ASK A COMPUTER IF YOUR SOLUTION IS CORRECT, THE COMPUTER WILL TELL YOU IF IT IS OR IF IT IS NOT.

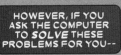

SNIFF *SNIFF*

HOWEVER, IF YOU ASK THE COMPUTER TO *SOLVE* THESE PROBLEMS FOR YOU--

--THE COMPUTER, WITHOUT ITS SHORTCUT, WILL SIMPLY RUN THROUGH A PRACTICALLY INFINITE NUMBER OF POSSIBILITIES TRYING TO STUMBLE UPON THE CORRECT ONE.

FINDING THE ANSWER WILL TAKE BILLIONS OF COMPUTERS BILLIONS OF YEARS.

THIS IS NP.

PROBLEMS WHICH, PRACTICALLY SPEAKING, YOU CANNOT SIMPLY SOLVE.

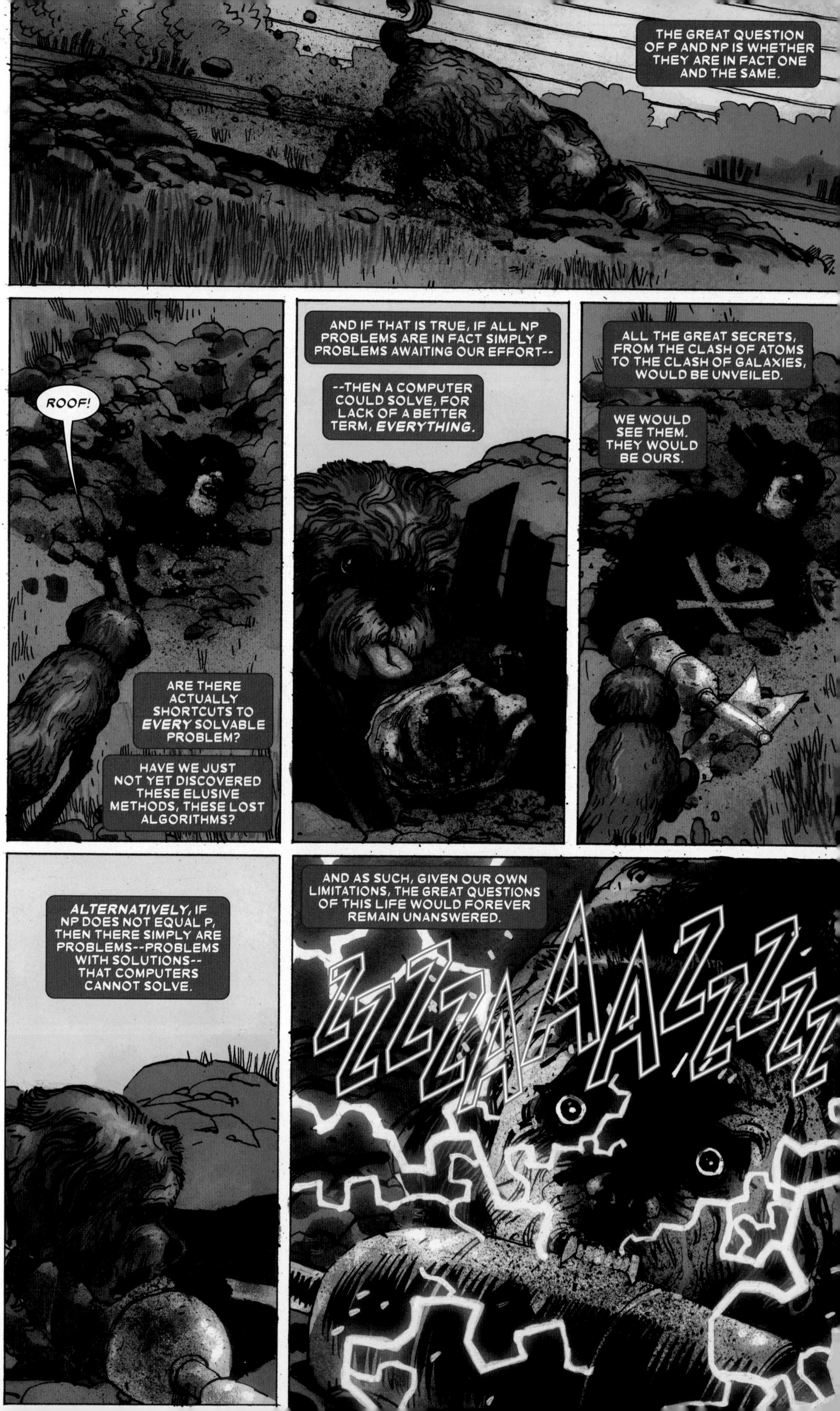
THE GREAT QUESTION OF P AND NP IS WHETHER THEY ARE IN FACT ONE AND THE SAME.
ROOF!
ARE THERE ACTUALLY SHORTCUTS TO *EVERY* SOLVABLE PROBLEM?
HAVE WE JUST NOT YET DISCOVERED THESE ELUSIVE METHODS, THESE LOST ALGORITHMS?
AND IF THAT IS TRUE, IF ALL NP PROBLEMS ARE IN FACT SIMPLY P PROBLEMS AWAITING OUR EFFORT--
--THEN A COMPUTER COULD SOLVE, FOR LACK OF A BETTER TERM, *EVERYTHING.*
ALL THE GREAT SECRETS, FROM THE CLASH OF ATOMS TO THE CLASH OF GALAXIES, WOULD BE UNVEILED.
WE WOULD SEE THEM. THEY WOULD BE OURS.
ALTERNATIVELY, IF NP DOES NOT EQUAL P, THEN THERE SIMPLY ARE PROBLEMS--PROBLEMS WITH SOLUTIONS--THAT COMPUTERS CANNOT SOLVE.
AND AS SUCH, GIVEN OUR OWN LIMITATIONS, THE GREAT QUESTIONS OF THIS LIFE WOULD FOREVER REMAIN UNANSWERED.
ZZZAAAZZZ

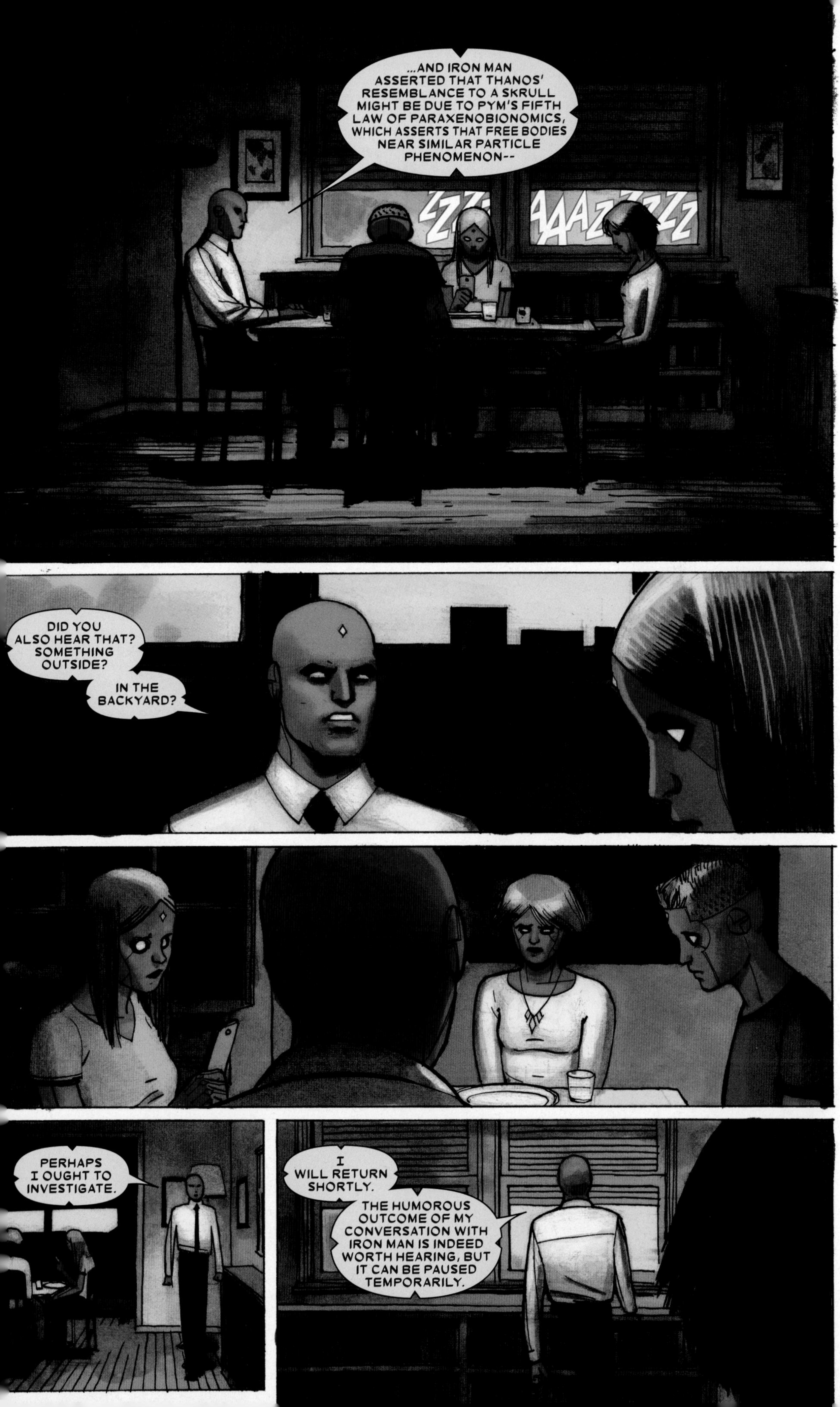
...AND IRON MAN ASSERTED THAT THANOS' RESEMBLANCE TO A SKRULL MIGHT BE DUE TO PYM'S FIFTH LAW OF PARAXENOBIONOMICS, WHICH ASSERTS THAT FREE BODIES NEAR SIMILAR PARTICLE PHENOMENON--
ZZZ AAAZZZZ
DID YOU ALSO HEAR THAT? SOMETHING OUTSIDE?
IN THE BACKYARD?
PERHAPS I OUGHT TO INVESTIGATE.
I WILL RETURN SHORTLY.
THE HUMOROUS OUTCOME OF MY CONVERSATION WITH IRON MAN IS INDEED WORTH HEARING, BUT IT CAN BE PAUSED TEMPORARILY.

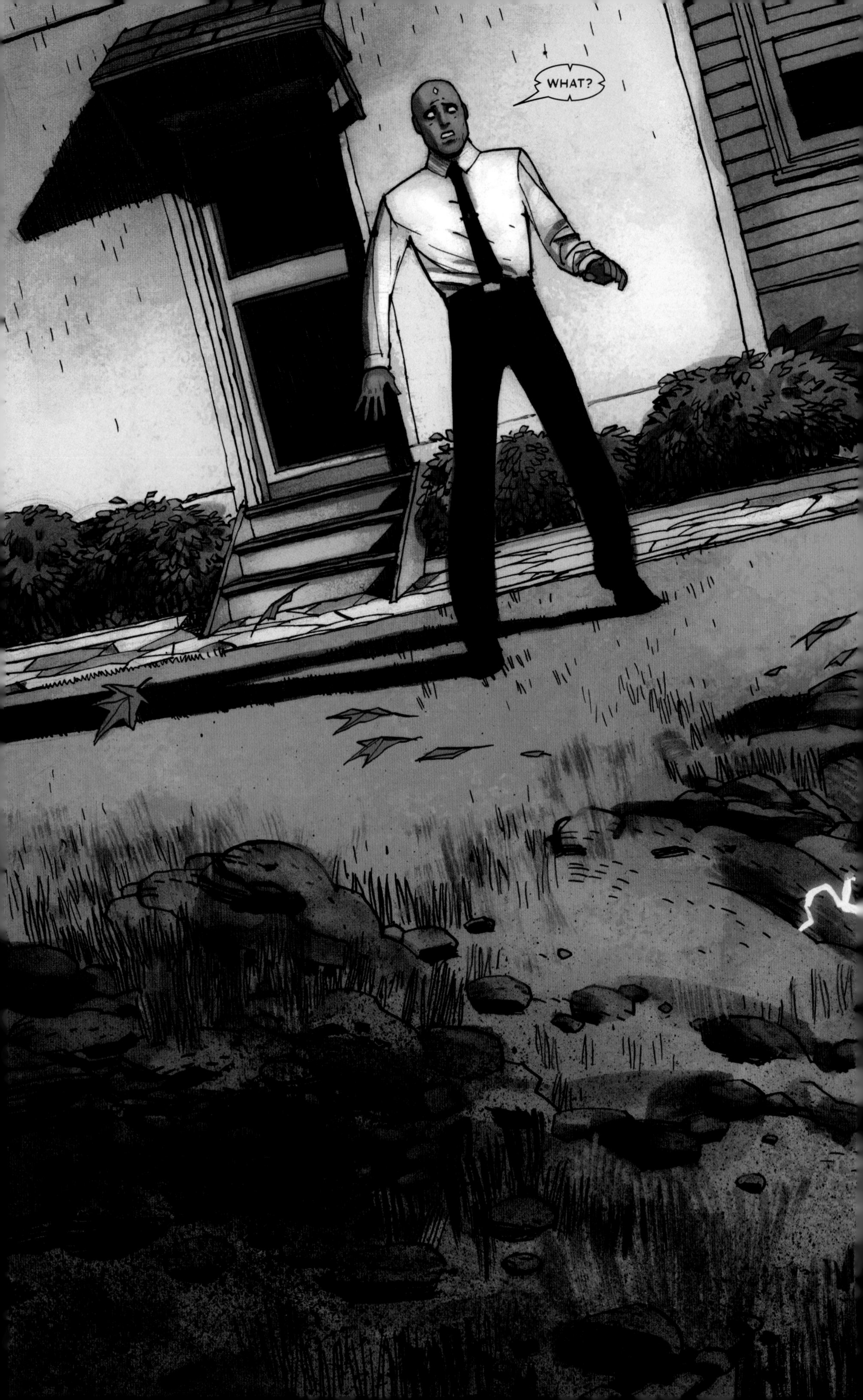
WHAT?

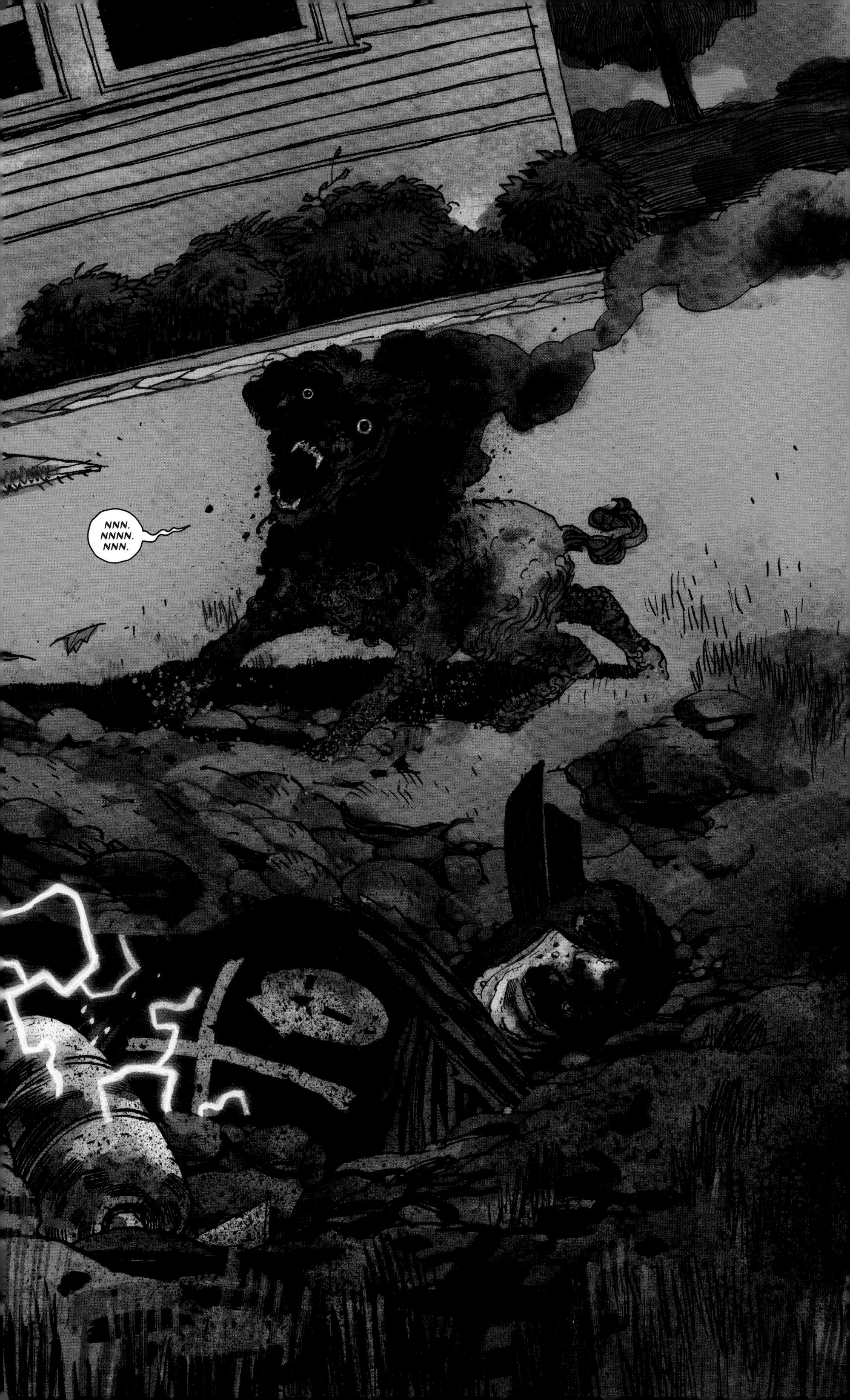
NNN. NNNN. NNN.

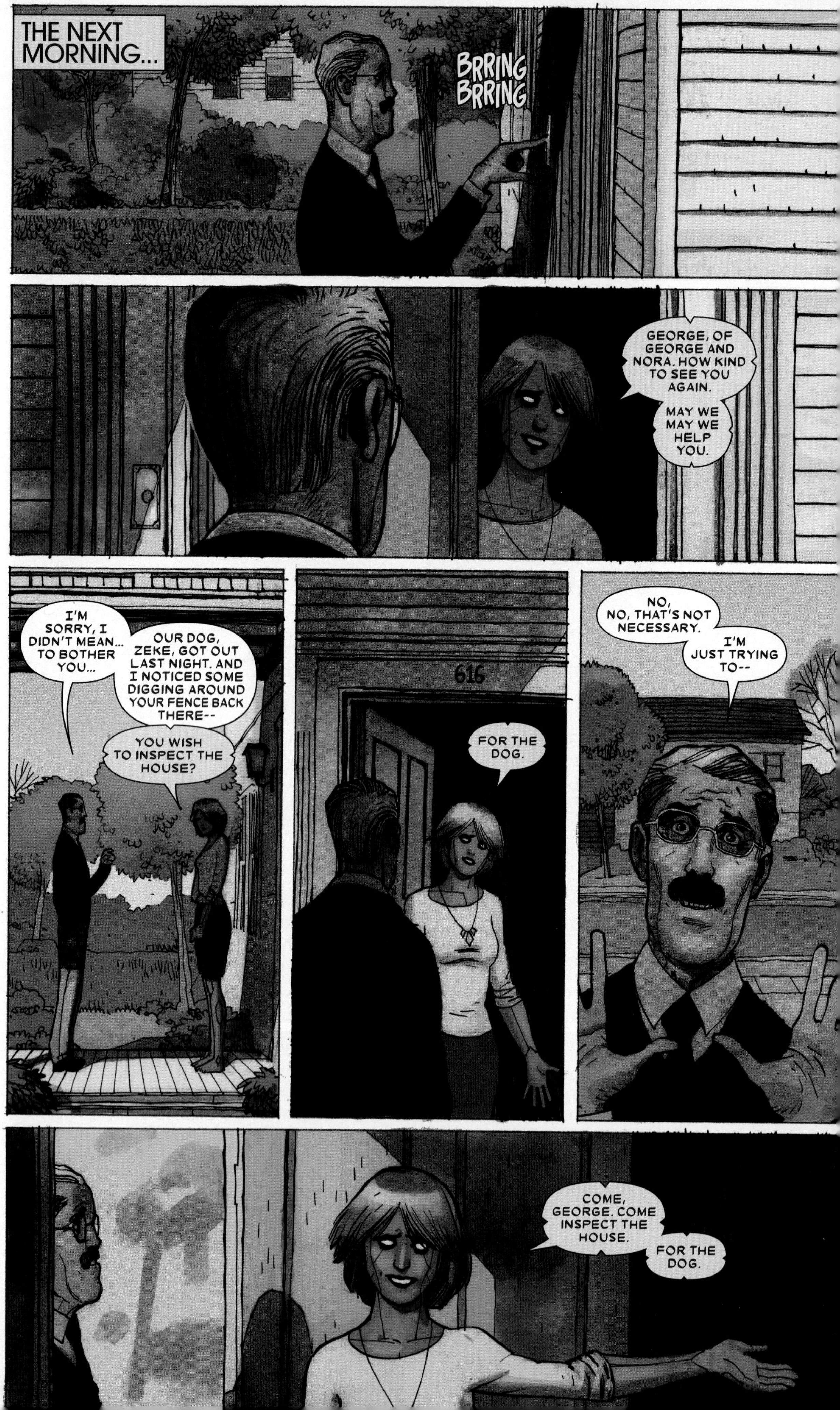
THE NEXT MORNING...
BRRING BRRING
GEORGE, OF GEORGE AND NORA. HOW KIND TO SEE YOU AGAIN.
MAY WE MAY WE HELP YOU.
I'M SORRY, I DIDN'T MEAN... TO BOTHER YOU...
OUR DOG, ZEKE, GOT OUT LAST NIGHT. AND I NOTICED SOME DIGGING AROUND YOUR FENCE BACK THERE--
YOU WISH TO INSPECT THE HOUSE?
616
FOR THE DOG.
NO, NO, THAT'S NOT NECESSARY.
I'M JUST TRYING TO--
COME, GEORGE. COME INSPECT THE HOUSE.
FOR THE DOG.

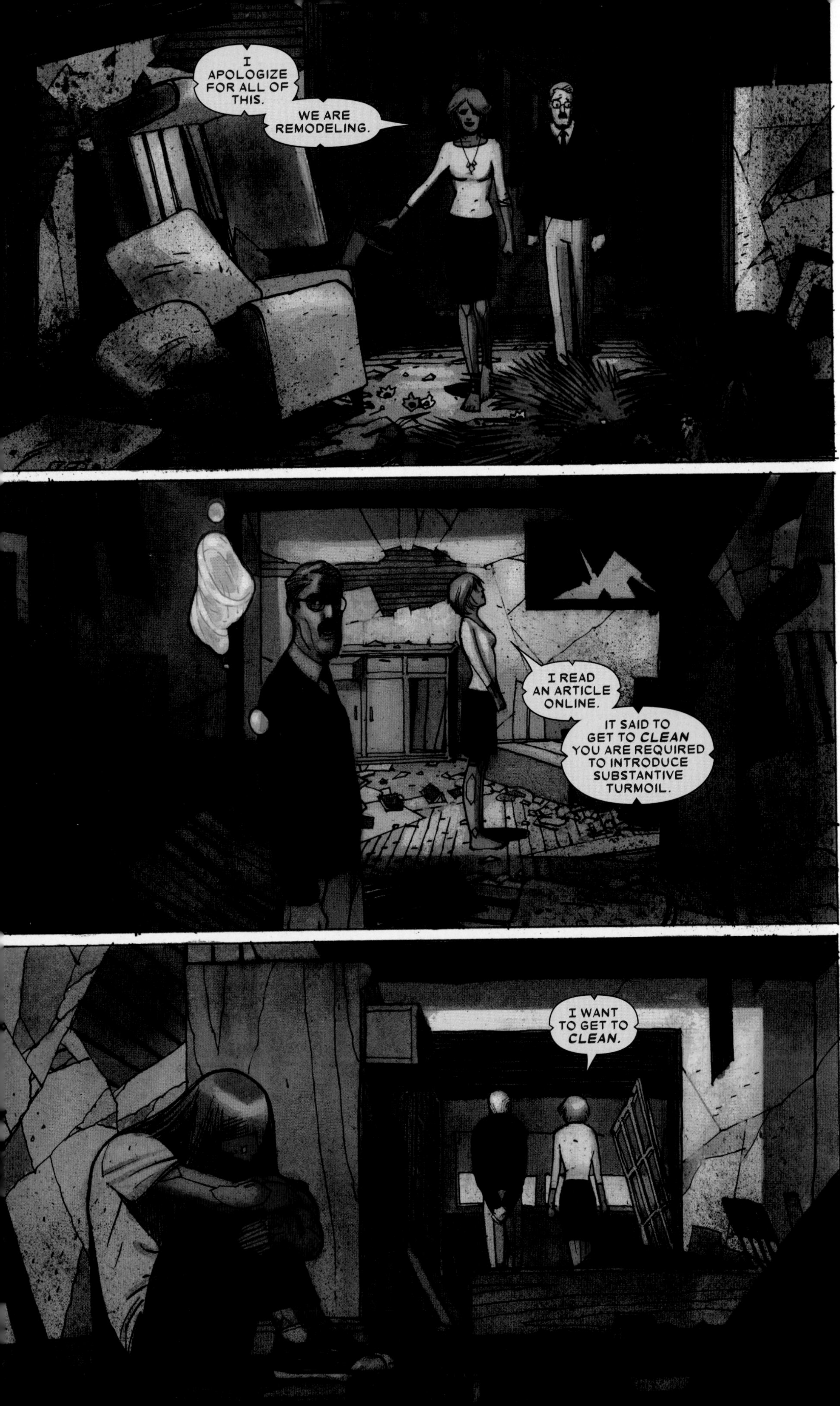
I APOLOGIZE FOR ALL OF THIS.
WE ARE REMODELING.
I READ AN ARTICLE ONLINE.
IT SAID TO GET TO *CLEAN* YOU ARE REQUIRED TO INTRODUCE SUBSTANTIVE TURMOIL.
I WANT TO GET TO *CLEAN.*

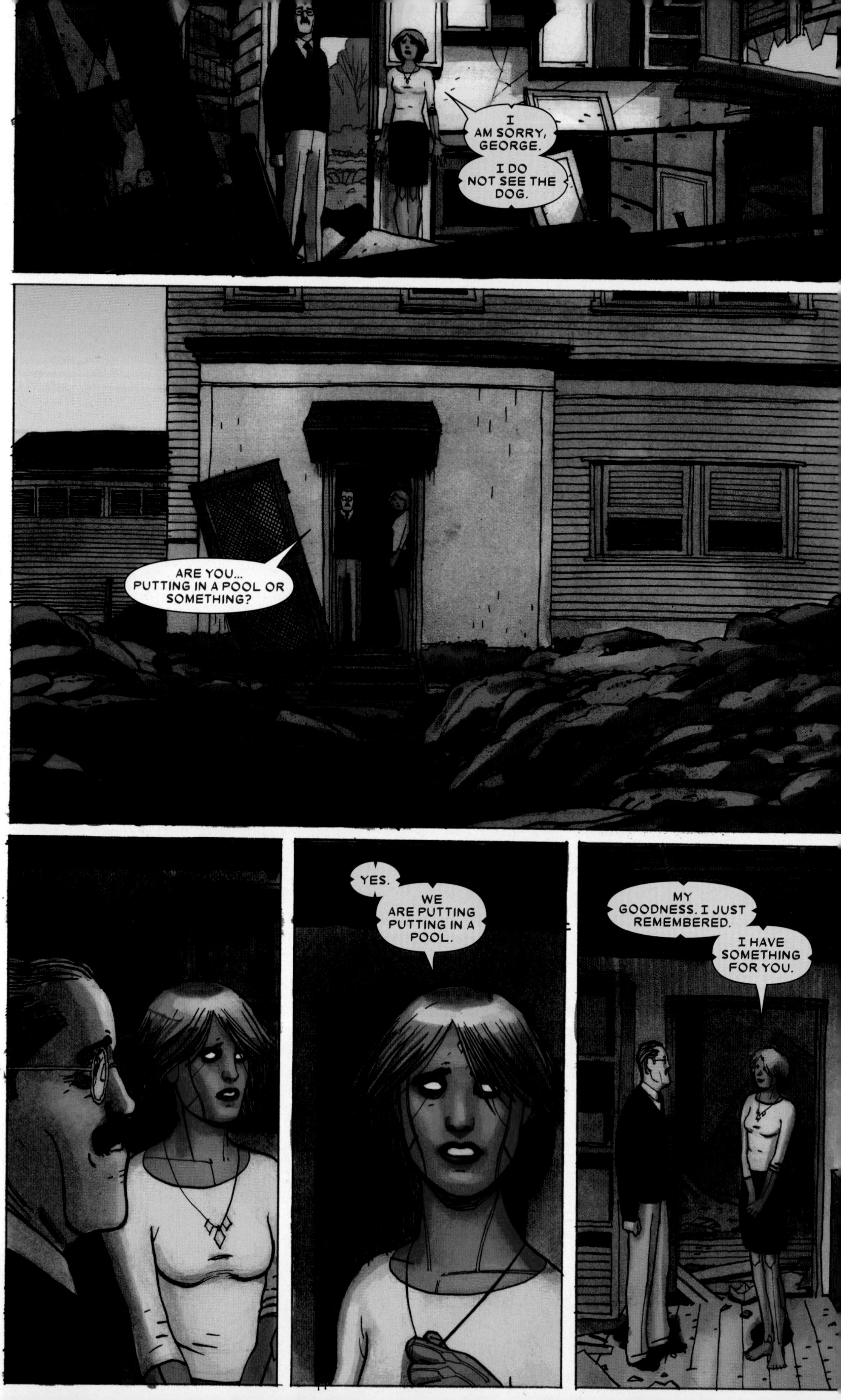
I AM SORRY, GEORGE.
I DO NOT SEE THE DOG.
ARE YOU... PUTTING IN A POOL OR SOMETHING?
YES.
WE ARE PUTTING PUTTING IN A POOL.
MY GOODNESS. I JUST REMEMBERED.
I HAVE SOMETHING FOR YOU.

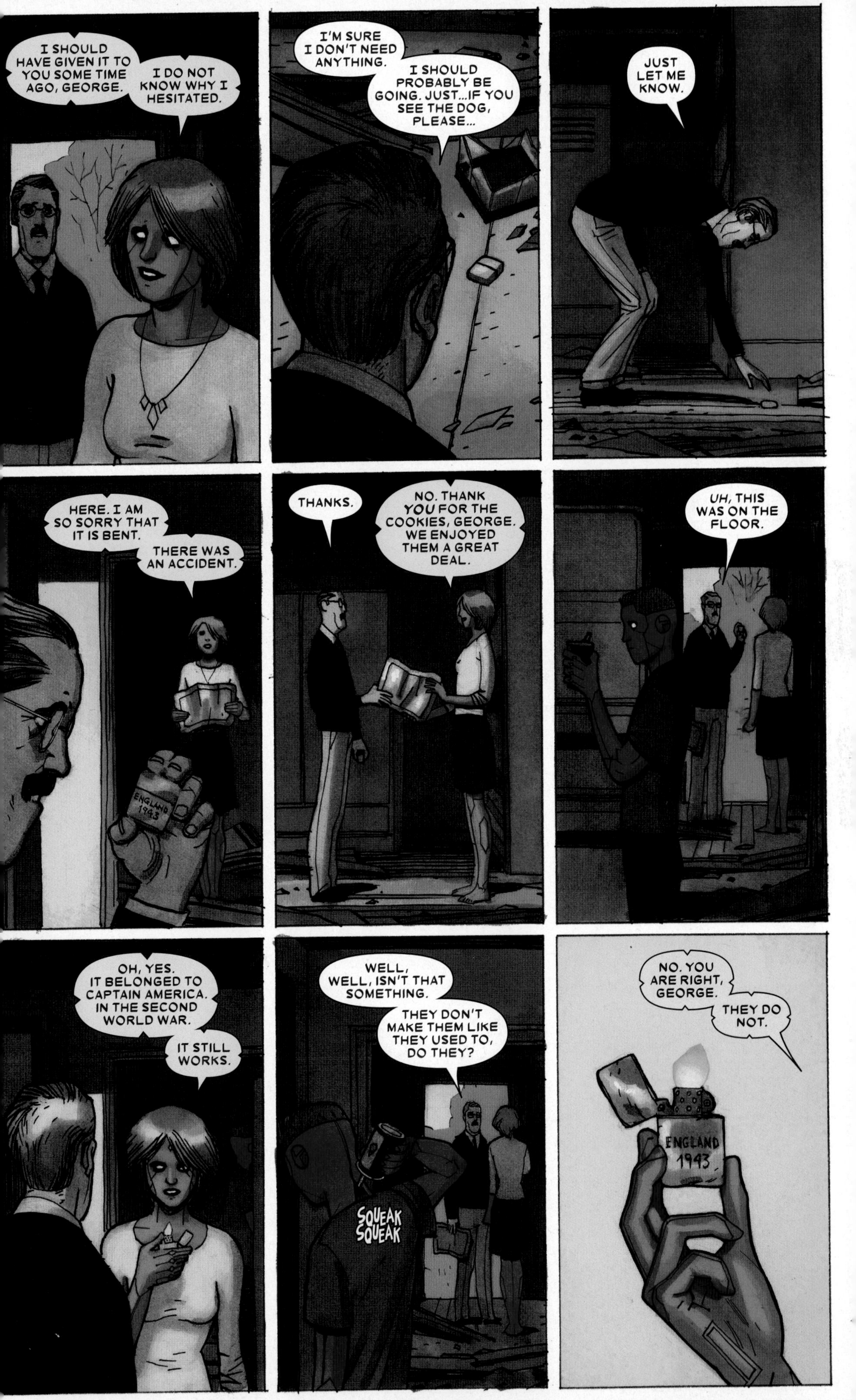
I SHOULD HAVE GIVEN IT TO YOU SOME TIME AGO, GEORGE.
I DO NOT KNOW WHY I HESITATED.
I'M SURE I DON'T NEED ANYTHING.
I SHOULD PROBABLY BE GOING. JUST...IF YOU SEE THE DOG, PLEASE...
JUST LET ME KNOW.
HERE. I AM SO SORRY THAT IT IS BENT.
THERE WAS AN ACCIDENT.
ENGLAND 1943
THANKS.
NO. THANK *YOU* FOR THE COOKIES, GEORGE. WE ENJOYED THEM A GREAT DEAL.
UH, THIS WAS ON THE FLOOR.
OH, YES. IT BELONGED TO CAPTAIN AMERICA. IN THE SECOND WORLD WAR.
IT STILL WORKS.
WELL, WELL, ISN'T THAT SOMETHING.
THEY DON'T MAKE THEM LIKE THEY USED TO, DO THEY?
SQUEAK SQUEAK
NO. YOU ARE RIGHT, GEORGE.
THEY DO NOT.
ENGLAND 1943

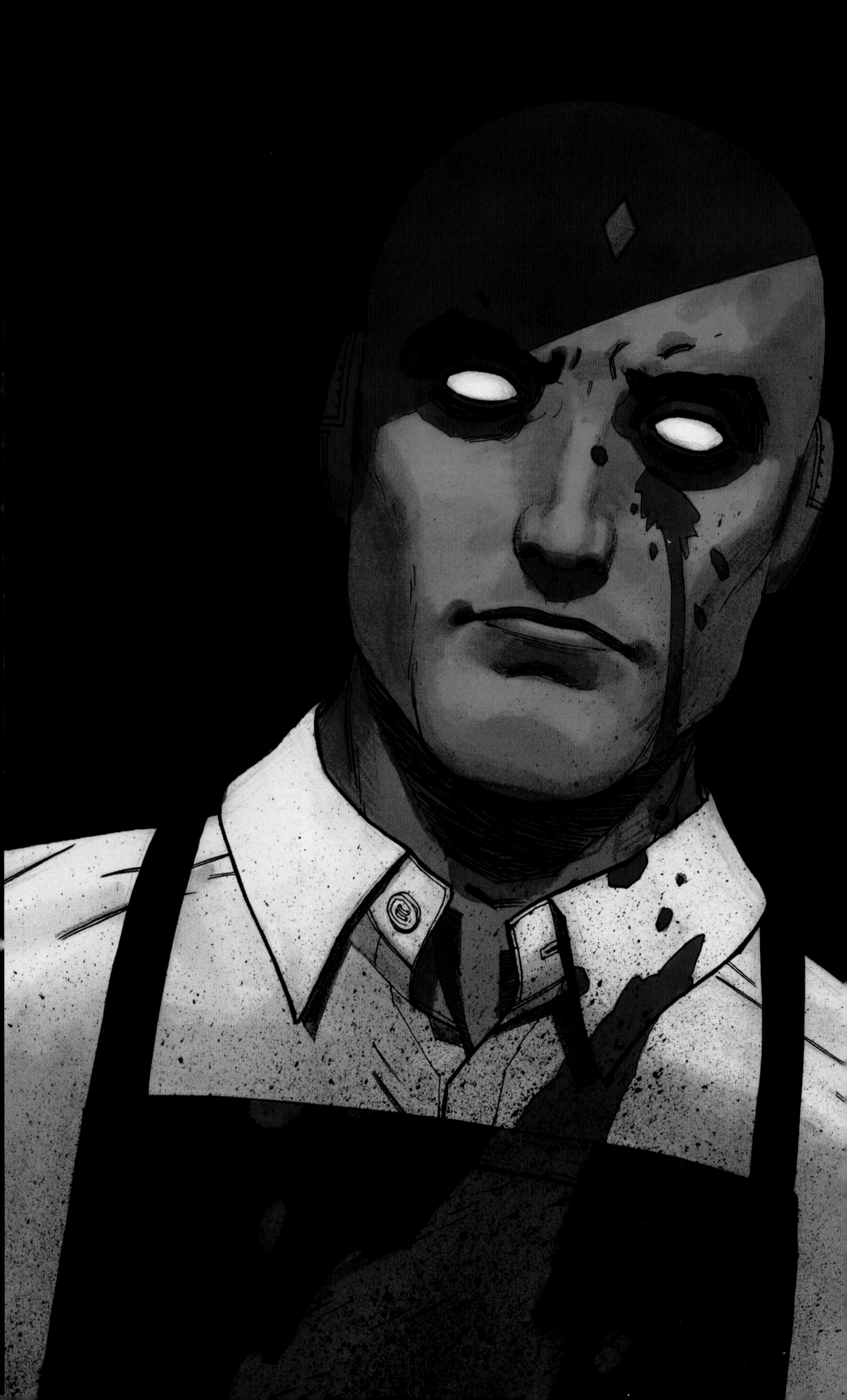

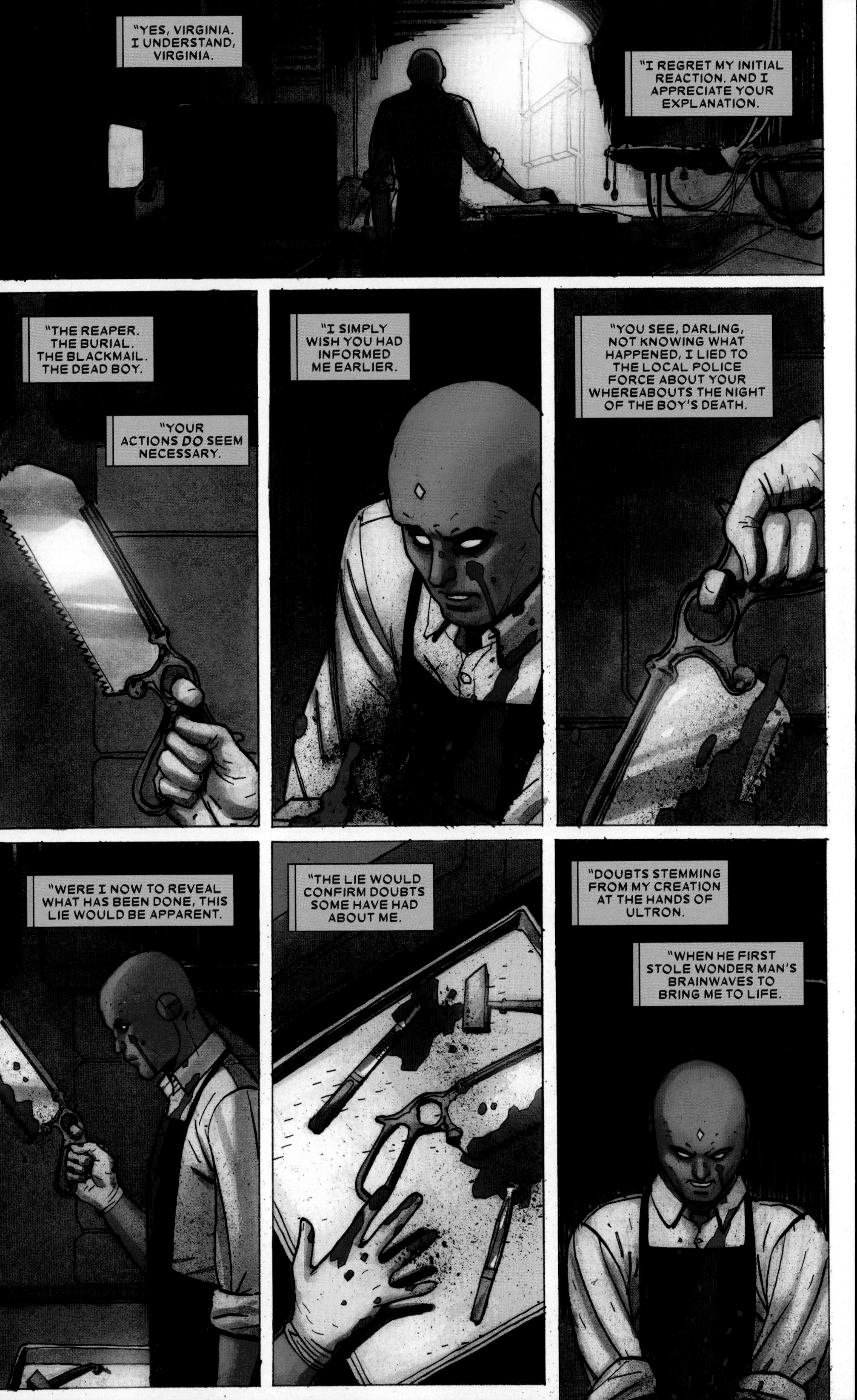
"YES, VIRGINIA. I UNDERSTAND, VIRGINIA.
"I REGRET MY INITIAL REACTION. AND I APPRECIATE YOUR EXPLANATION.
"THE REAPER. THE BURIAL. THE BLACKMAIL. THE DEAD BOY.
"YOUR ACTIONS DO SEEM NECESSARY.
"I SIMPLY WISH YOU HAD INFORMED ME EARLIER.
"YOU SEE, DARLING, NOT KNOWING WHAT HAPPENED, I LIED TO THE LOCAL POLICE FORCE ABOUT YOUR WHEREABOUTS THE NIGHT OF THE BOY'S DEATH.
"WERE I NOW TO REVEAL WHAT HAS BEEN DONE, THIS LIE WOULD BE APPARENT.
"THE LIE WOULD CONFIRM DOUBTS SOME HAVE HAD ABOUT ME.
"DOUBTS STEMMING FROM MY CREATION AT THE HANDS OF ULTRON.
"WHEN HE FIRST STOLE WONDER MAN'S BRAINWAVES TO BRING ME TO LIFE.

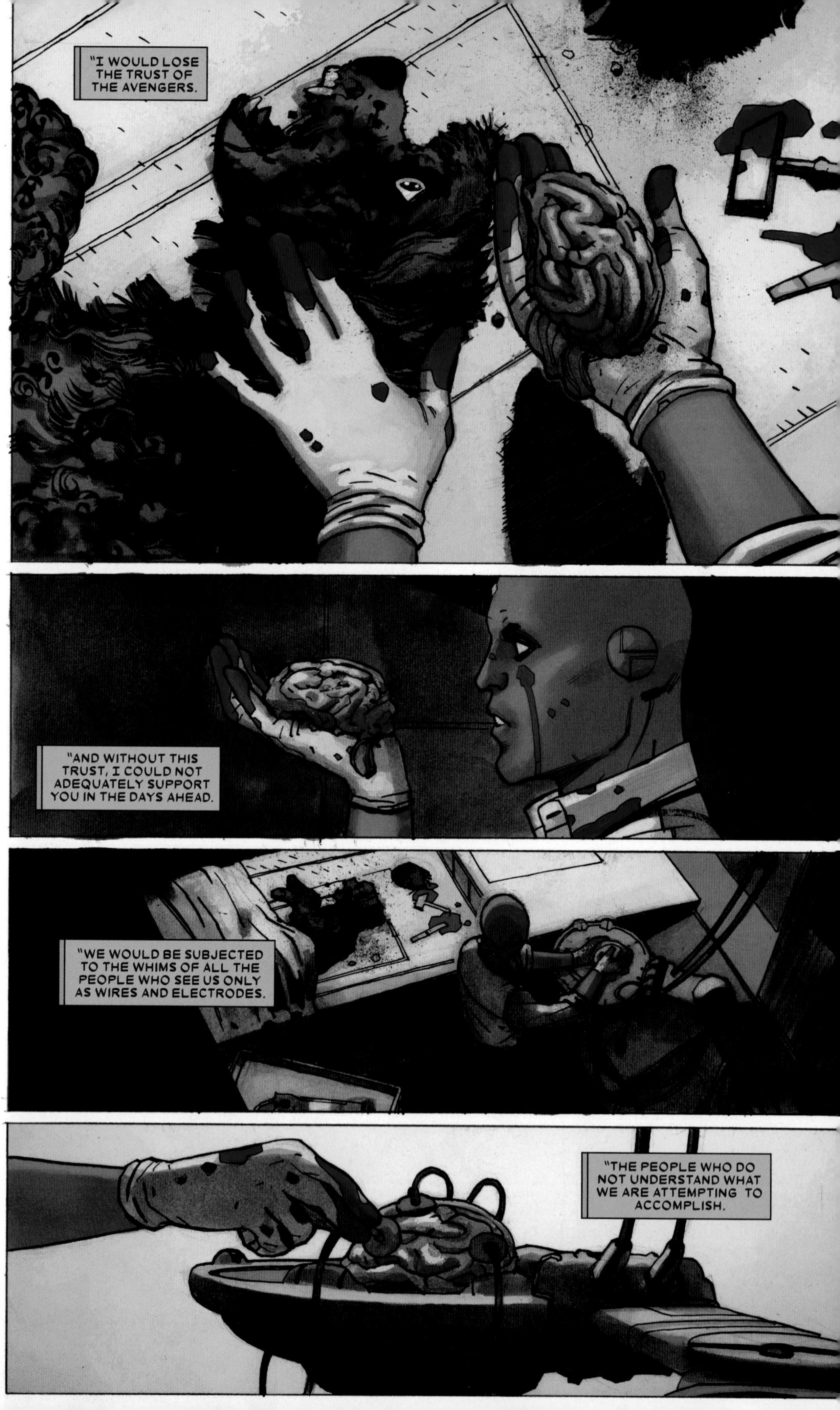
"I WOULD LOSE THE TRUST OF THE AVENGERS.
"AND WITHOUT THIS TRUST, I COULD NOT ADEQUATELY SUPPORT YOU IN THE DAYS AHEAD.
"WE WOULD BE SUBJECTED TO THE WHIMS OF ALL THE PEOPLE WHO SEE US ONLY AS WIRES AND ELECTRODES.
"THE PEOPLE WHO DO NOT UNDERSTAND WHAT WE ARE ATTEMPTING TO ACCOMPLISH.

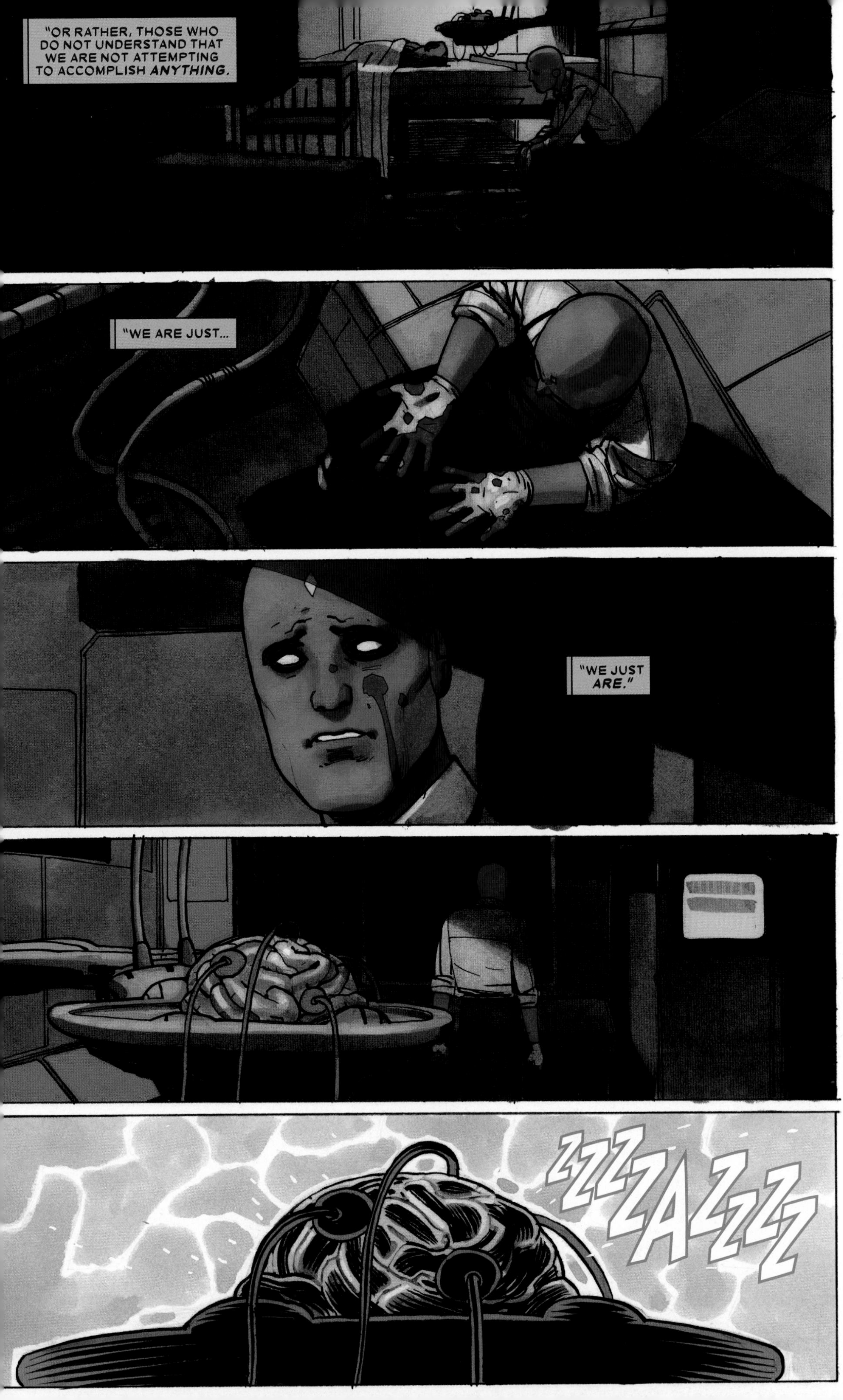
"OR RATHER, THOSE WHO DO NOT UNDERSTAND THAT WE ARE NOT ATTEMPTING TO ACCOMPLISH ANYTHING.
"WE ARE JUST...
"WE JUST ARE."
ZZZZAZZZZ

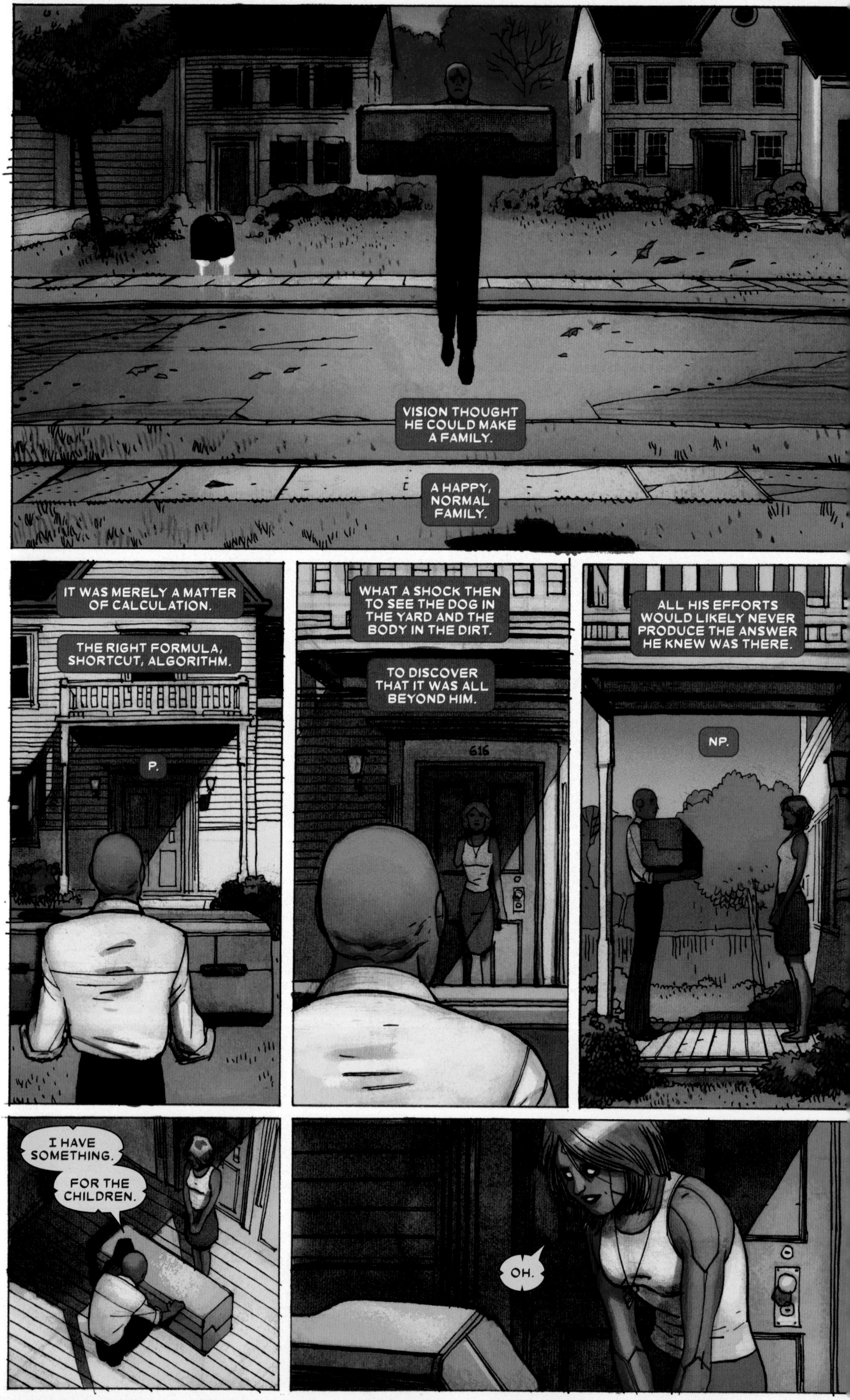
VISION THOUGHT HE COULD MAKE A FAMILY.
A HAPPY, NORMAL FAMILY.
IT WAS MERELY A MATTER OF CALCULATION.
THE RIGHT FORMULA, SHORTCUT, ALGORITHM.
P.
WHAT A SHOCK THEN TO SEE THE DOG IN THE YARD AND THE BODY IN THE DIRT.
TO DISCOVER THAT IT WAS ALL BEYOND HIM.
616
ALL HIS EFFORTS WOULD LIKELY NEVER PRODUCE THE ANSWER HE KNEW WAS THERE.
NP.
I HAVE SOMETHING.
FOR THE CHILDREN.
OH.

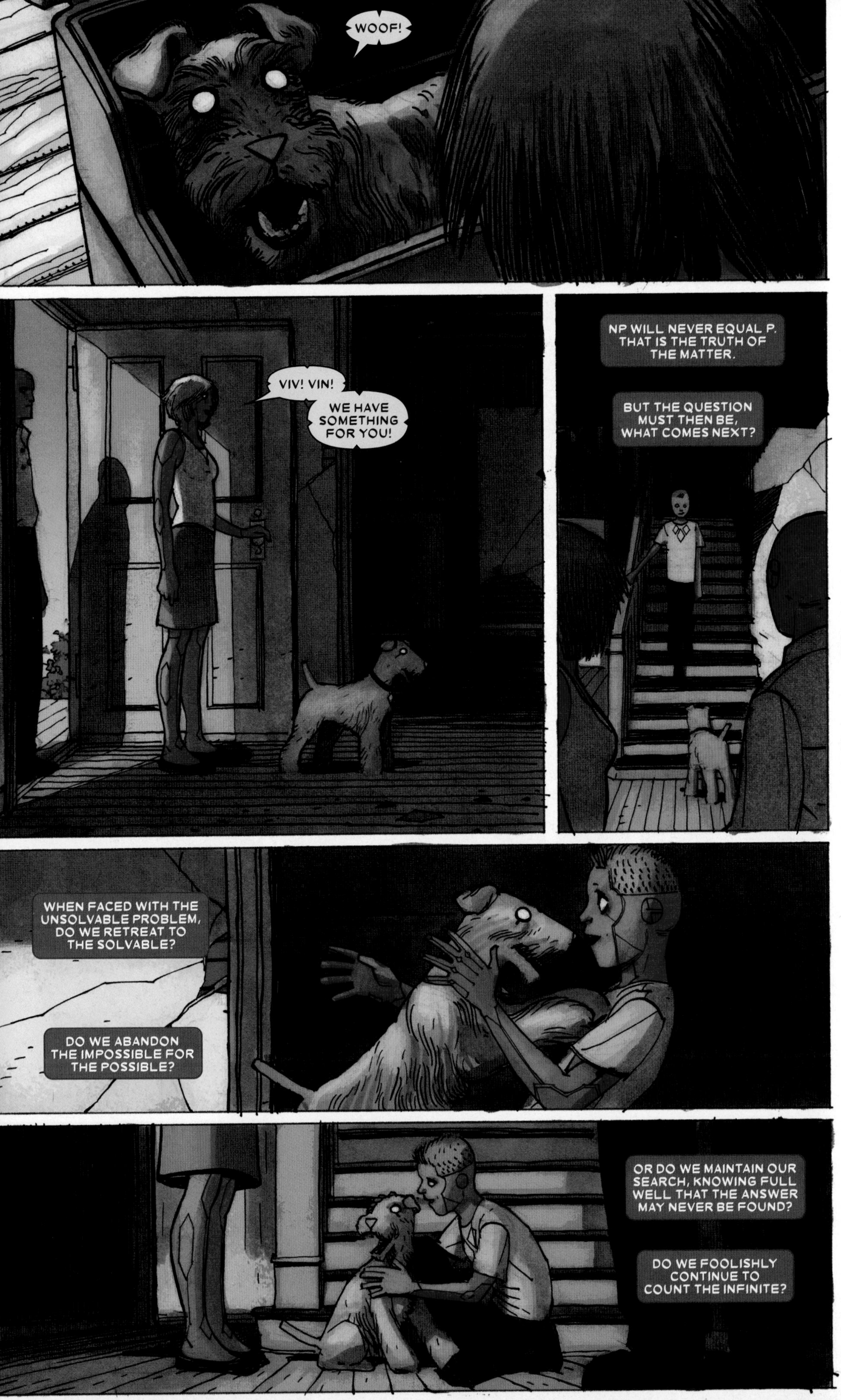
WOOF!
VIV! VIN!
WE HAVE SOMETHING FOR YOU!
NP WILL NEVER EQUAL P. THAT IS THE TRUTH OF THE MATTER.
BUT THE QUESTION MUST THEN BE, WHAT COMES NEXT?
WHEN FACED WITH THE UNSOLVABLE PROBLEM, DO WE RETREAT TO THE SOLVABLE?
DO WE ABANDON THE IMPOSSIBLE FOR THE POSSIBLE?
OR DO WE MAINTAIN OUR SEARCH, KNOWING FULL WELL THAT THE ANSWER MAY NEVER BE FOUND?
DO WE FOOLISHLY CONTINUE TO COUNT THE INFINITE?

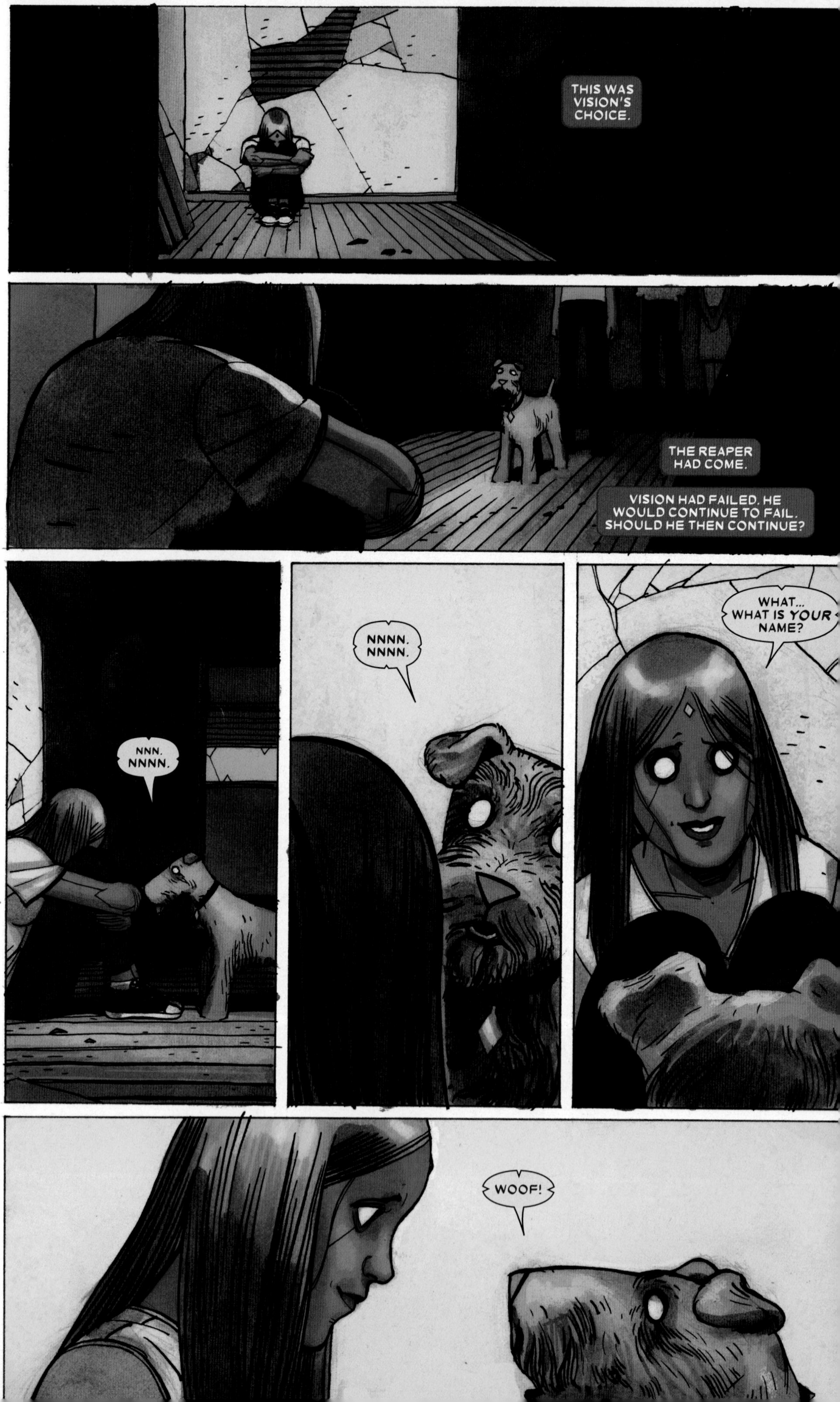
THIS WAS VISION'S CHOICE.
THE REAPER HAD COME.
VISION HAD FAILED. HE WOULD CONTINUE TO FAIL. SHOULD HE THEN CONTINUE?
NNN. NNNN.
NNNN. NNNN.
WHAT... WHAT IS YOUR NAME?
WOOF!

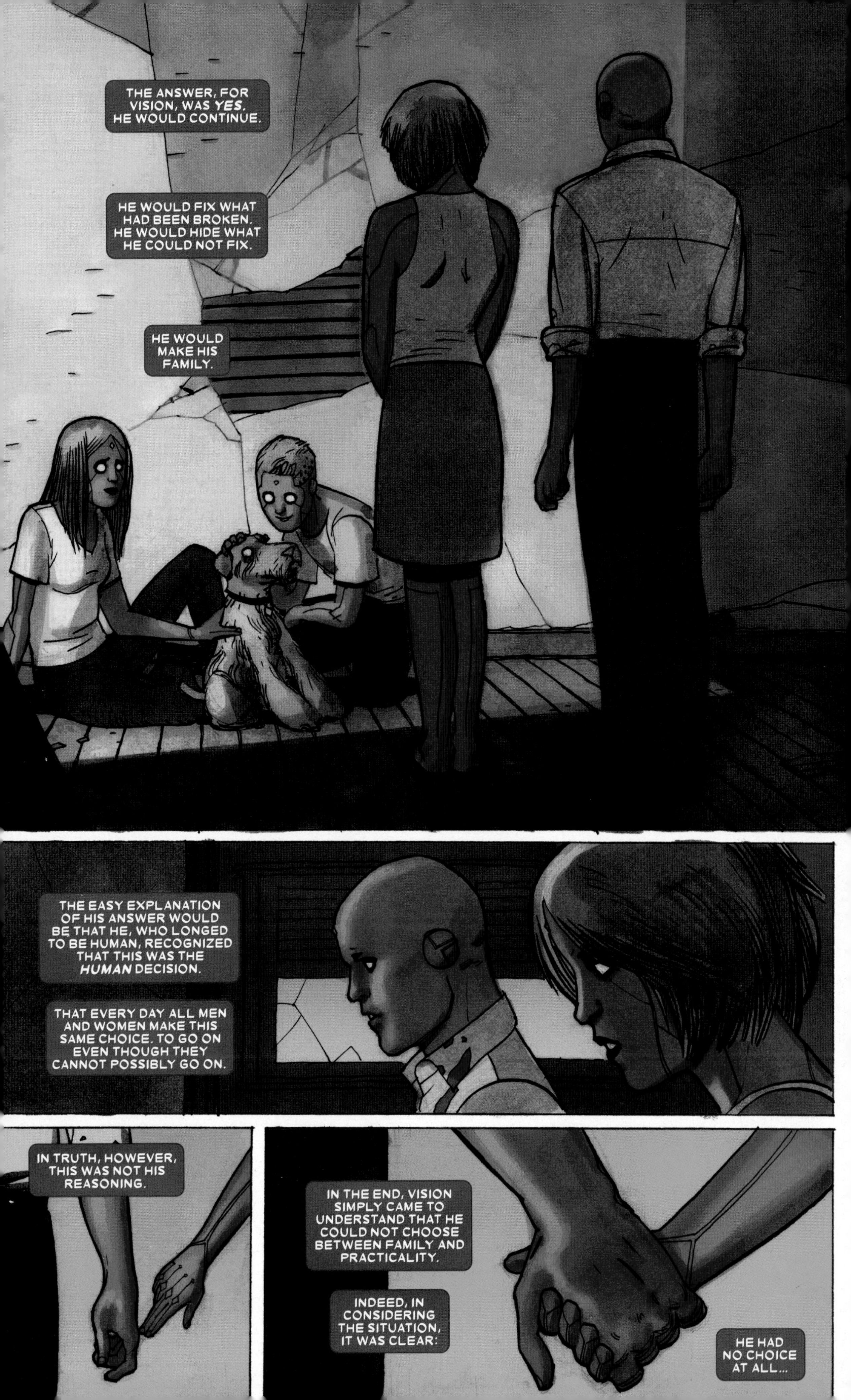
THE ANSWER, FOR VISION, WAS *YES*. HE WOULD CONTINUE.
HE WOULD FIX WHAT HAD BEEN BROKEN. HE WOULD HIDE WHAT HE COULD NOT FIX.
HE WOULD MAKE HIS FAMILY.
THE EASY EXPLANATION OF HIS ANSWER WOULD BE THAT HE, WHO LONGED TO BE HUMAN, RECOGNIZED THAT THIS WAS THE *HUMAN* DECISION.
THAT EVERY DAY ALL MEN AND WOMEN MAKE THIS SAME CHOICE. TO GO ON EVEN THOUGH THEY CANNOT POSSIBLY GO ON.
IN TRUTH, HOWEVER, THIS WAS NOT HIS REASONING.
IN THE END, VISION SIMPLY CAME TO UNDERSTAND THAT HE COULD NOT CHOOSE BETWEEN FAMILY AND PRACTICALITY.
INDEED, IN CONSIDERING THE SITUATION, IT WAS CLEAR:
HE HAD NO CHOICE AT ALL...

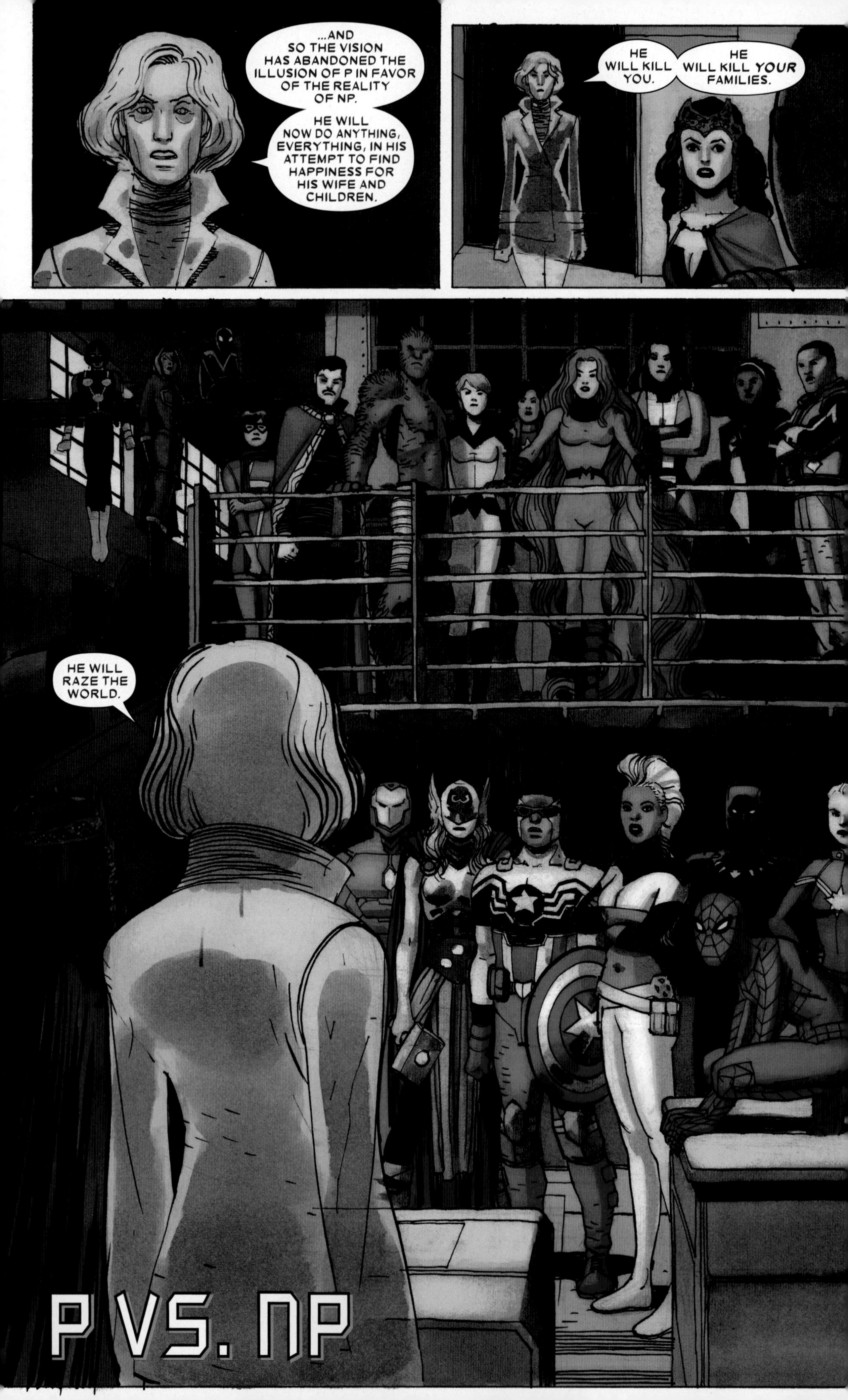
...AND SO THE VISION HAS ABANDONED THE ILLUSION OF P IN FAVOR OF THE REALITY OF NP.
HE WILL NOW DO ANYTHING, EVERYTHING, IN HIS ATTEMPT TO FIND HAPPINESS FOR HIS WIFE AND CHILDREN.
HE WILL KILL YOU.
HE WILL KILL YOUR FAMILIES.
HE WILL RAZE THE WORLD.
P VS. NP

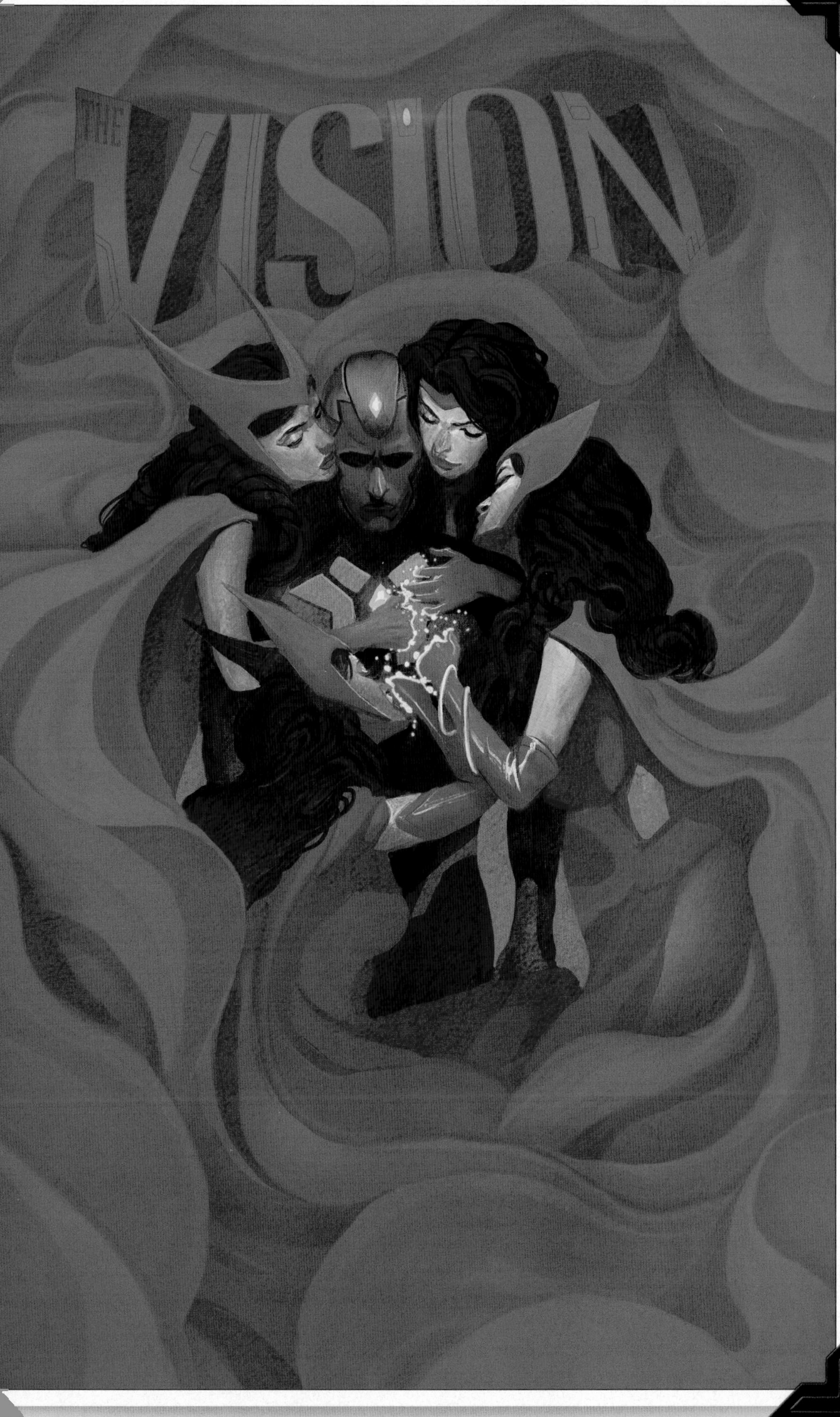
THE VISION

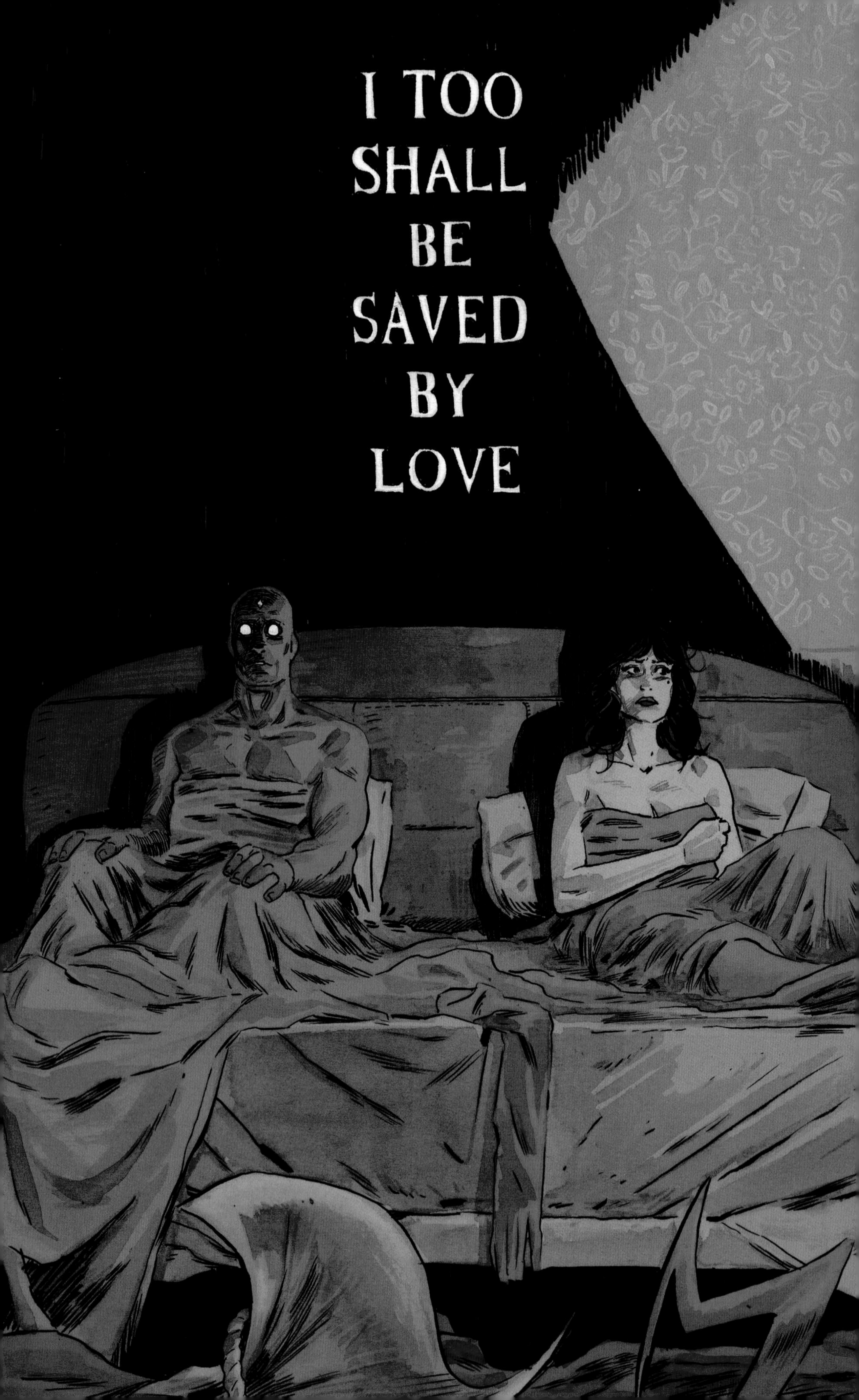
I TOO
SHALL
BE
SAVED
BY
LOVE

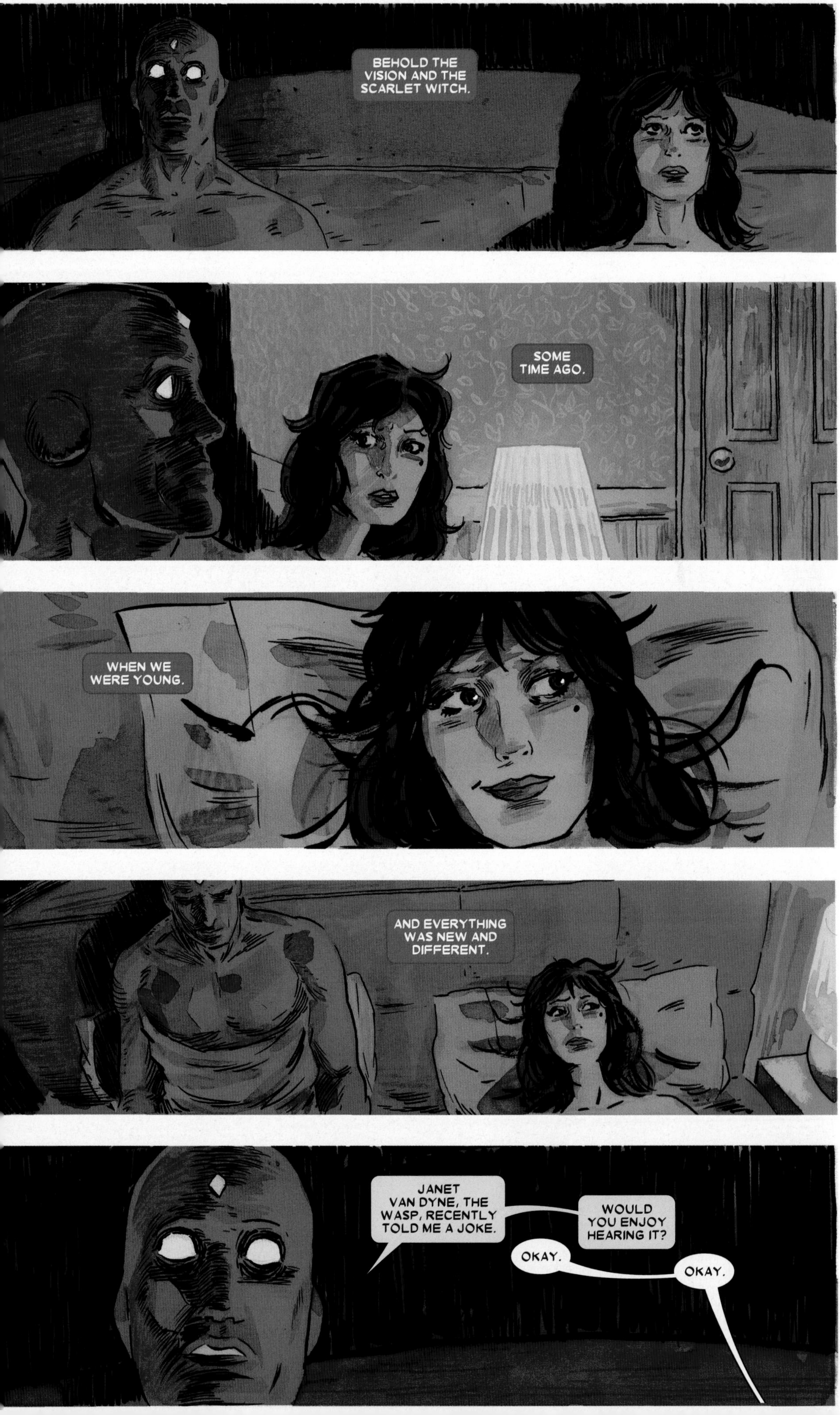
BEHOLD THE VISION AND THE SCARLET WITCH.
SOME TIME AGO.
WHEN WE WERE YOUNG.
AND EVERYTHING WAS NEW AND DIFFERENT.
JANET VAN DYNE, THE WASP, RECENTLY TOLD ME A JOKE.
WOULD YOU ENJOY HEARING IT?
OKAY.
OKAY.

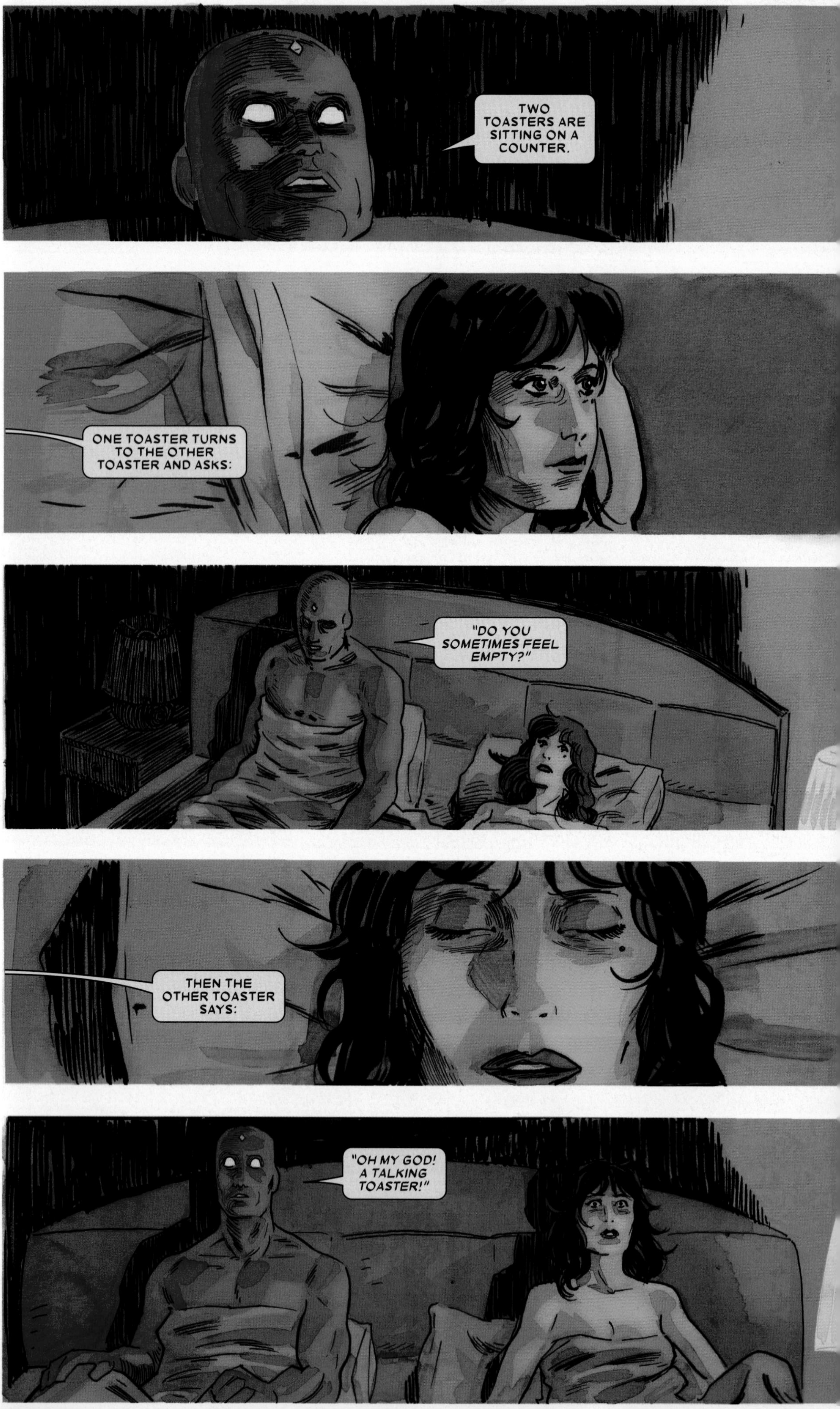
TWO TOASTERS ARE SITTING ON A COUNTER.
ONE TOASTER TURNS TO THE OTHER TOASTER AND ASKS:
"DO YOU SOMETIMES FEEL EMPTY?"
THEN THE OTHER TOASTER SAYS:
"OH MY GOD! A TALKING TOASTER!"

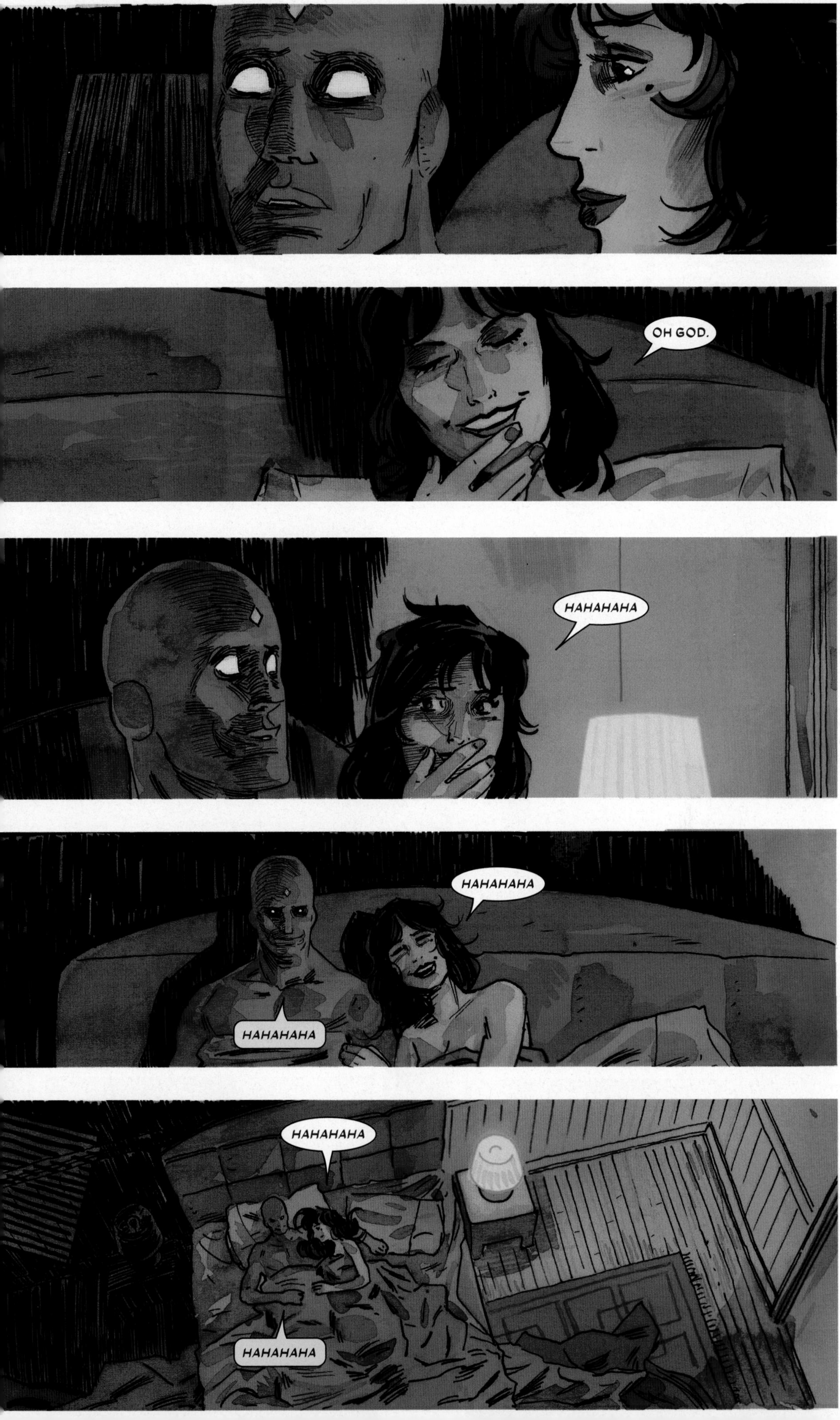
OH GOD.
HAHAHAHA
HAHAHAHA
HAHAHAHA
HAHAHAHA
HAHAHAHA

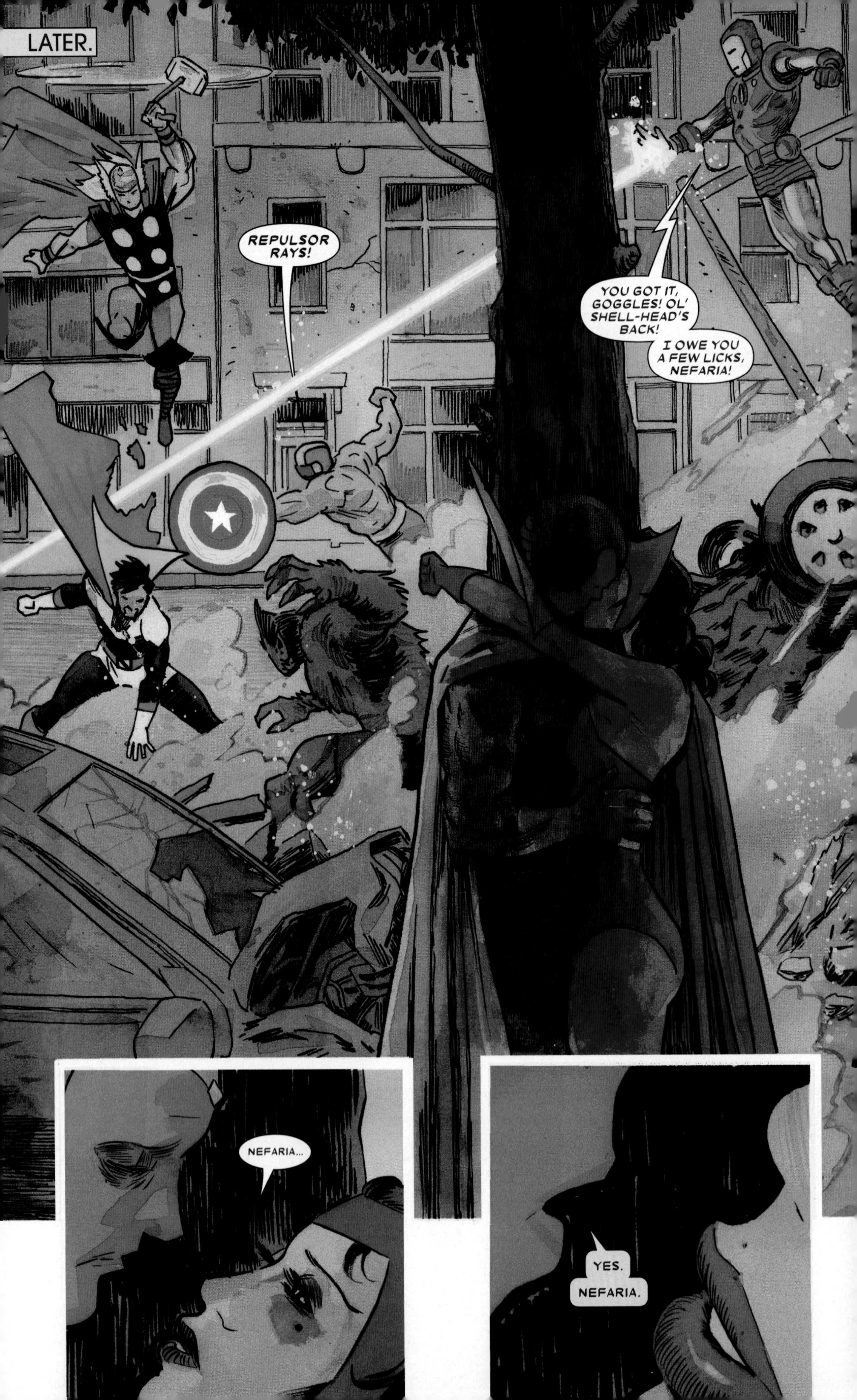
LATER.
REPULSOR RAYS!
YOU GOT IT, GOGGLES! OL' SHELL-HEAD'S BACK!
I OWE YOU A FEW LICKS, NEFARIA!
NEFARIA...
YES.
NEFARIA.

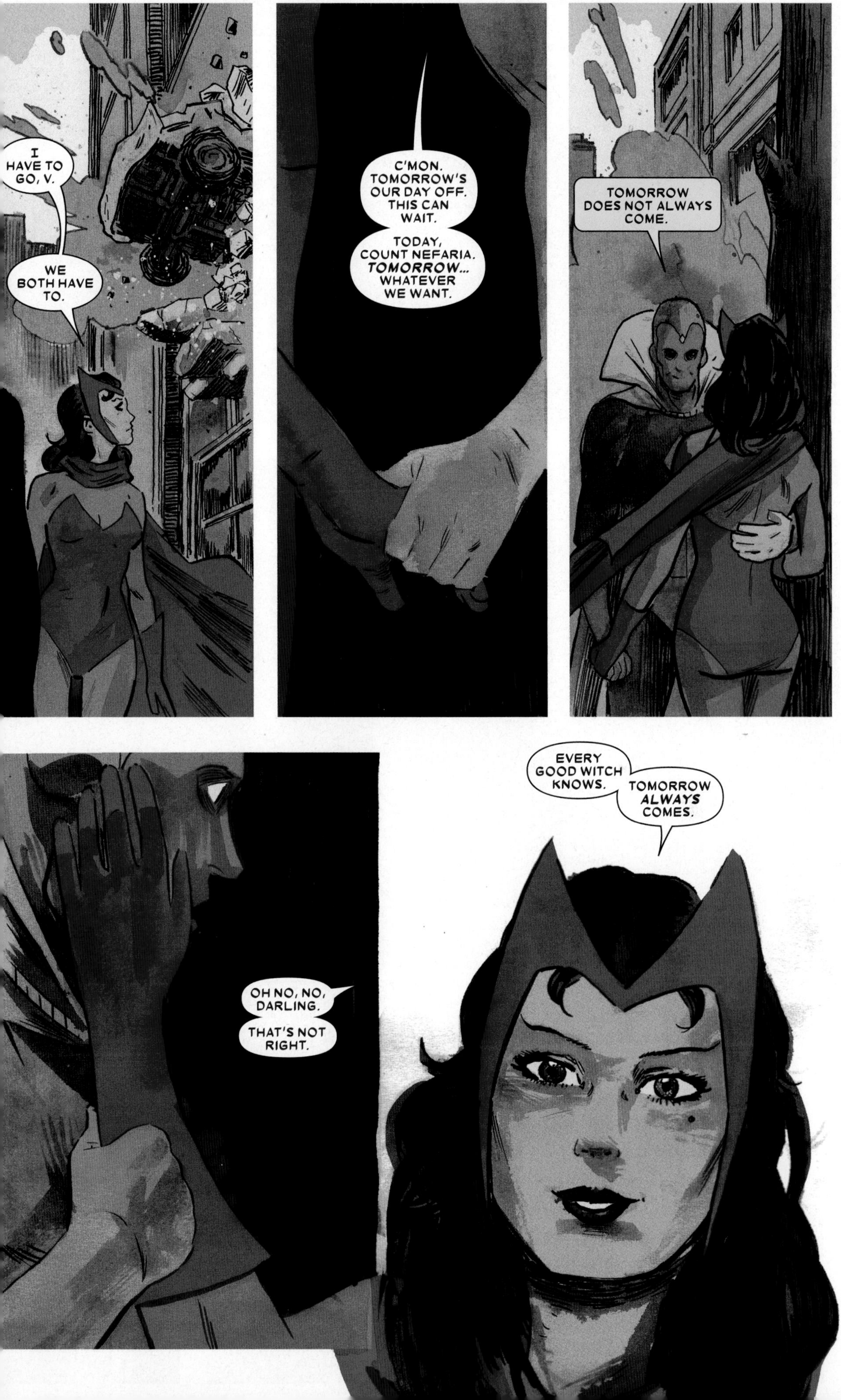
I HAVE TO GO, V.
WE BOTH HAVE TO.
C'MON. TOMORROW'S OUR DAY OFF. THIS CAN WAIT.
TODAY, COUNT NEFARIA. *TOMORROW...* WHATEVER WE WANT.
TOMORROW DOES NOT ALWAYS COME.
OH NO, NO, DARLING.
THAT'S NOT RIGHT.
EVERY GOOD WITCH KNOWS.
TOMORROW *ALWAYS* COMES.

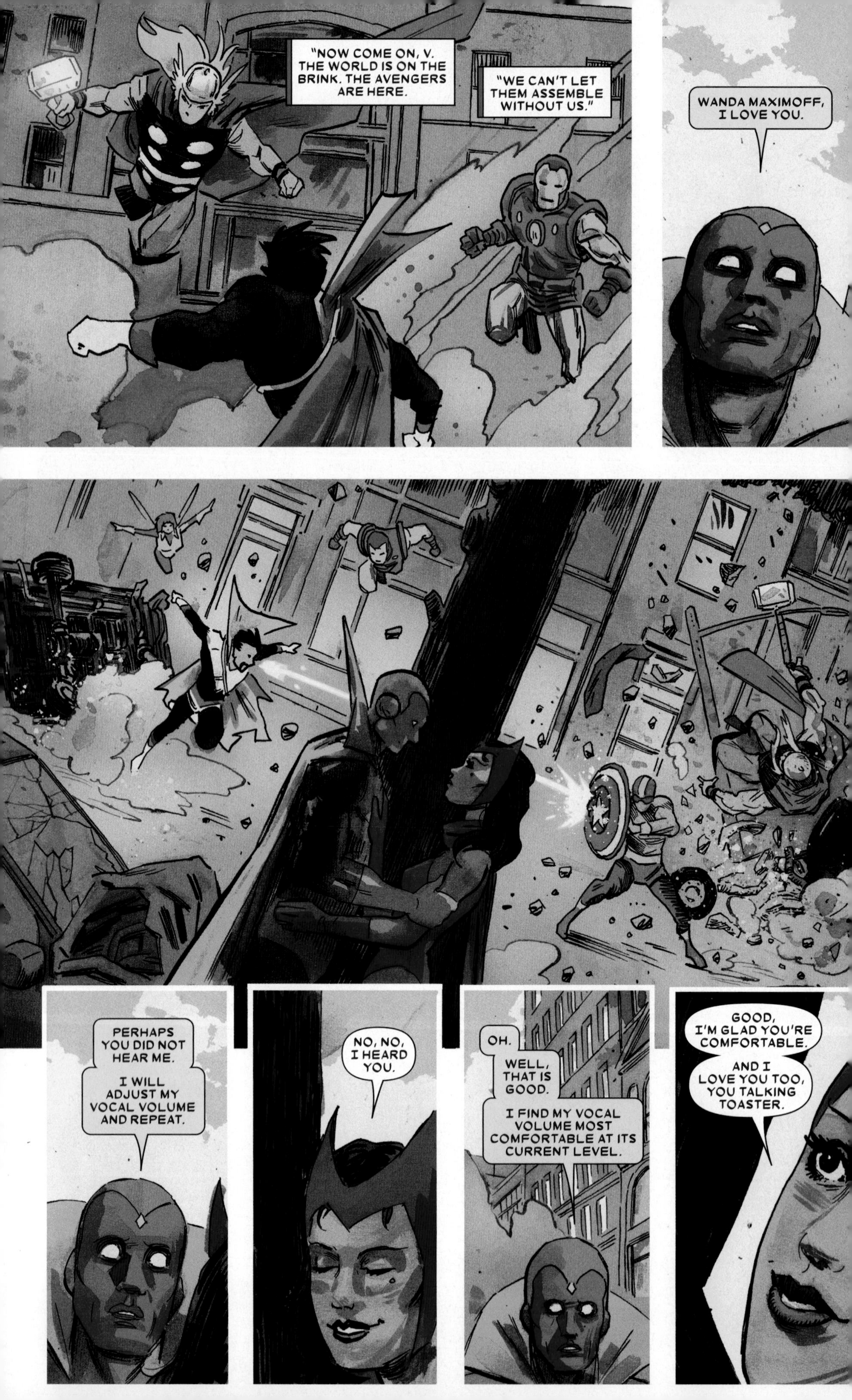
"NOW COME ON, V. THE WORLD IS ON THE BRINK. THE AVENGERS ARE HERE.
"WE CAN'T LET THEM ASSEMBLE WITHOUT US."
WANDA MAXIMOFF, I LOVE YOU.
PERHAPS YOU DID NOT HEAR ME.
I WILL ADJUST MY VOCAL VOLUME AND REPEAT.
NO, NO, I HEARD YOU.
OH.
WELL, THAT IS GOOD.
I FIND MY VOCAL VOLUME MOST COMFORTABLE AT ITS CURRENT LEVEL.
GOOD, I'M GLAD YOU'RE COMFORTABLE.
AND I LOVE YOU TOO, YOU TALKING TOASTER.

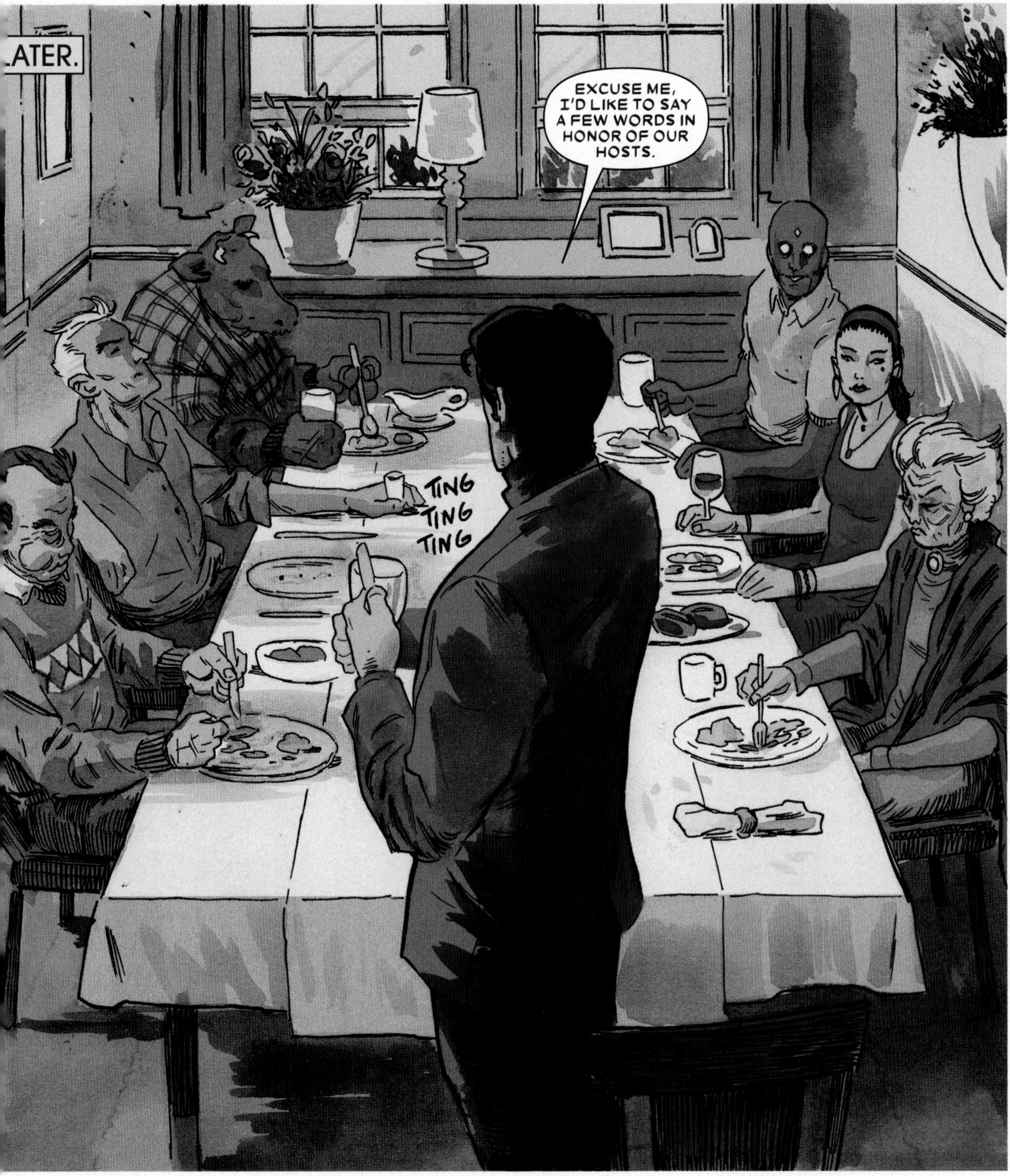
LATER.
EXCUSE ME, I'D LIKE TO SAY A FEW WORDS IN HONOR OF OUR HOSTS.
TING TING TING

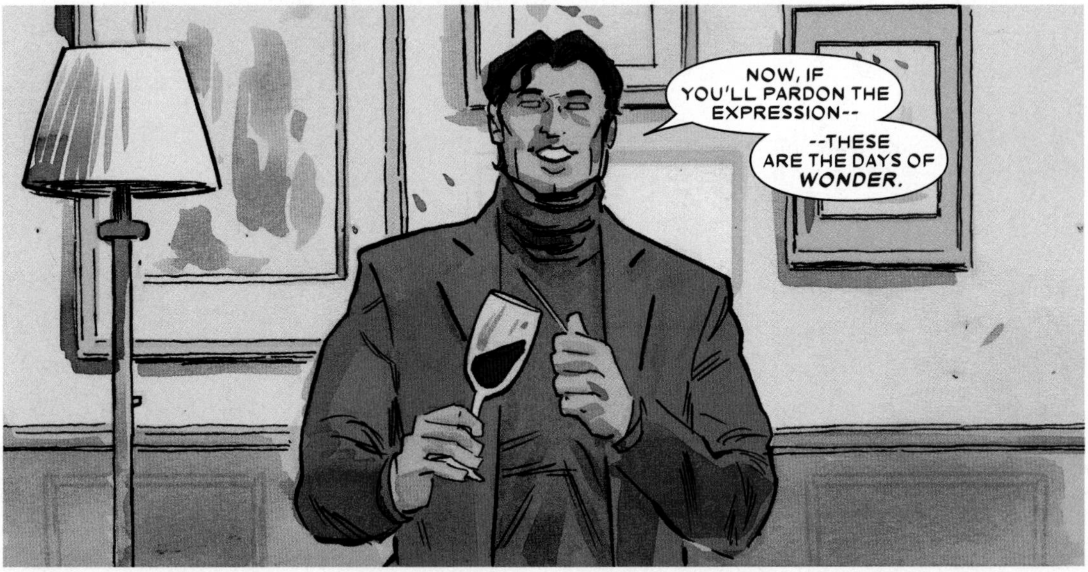
NOW, IF YOU'LL PARDON THE EXPRESSION--
--THESE ARE THE DAYS OF *WONDER*.

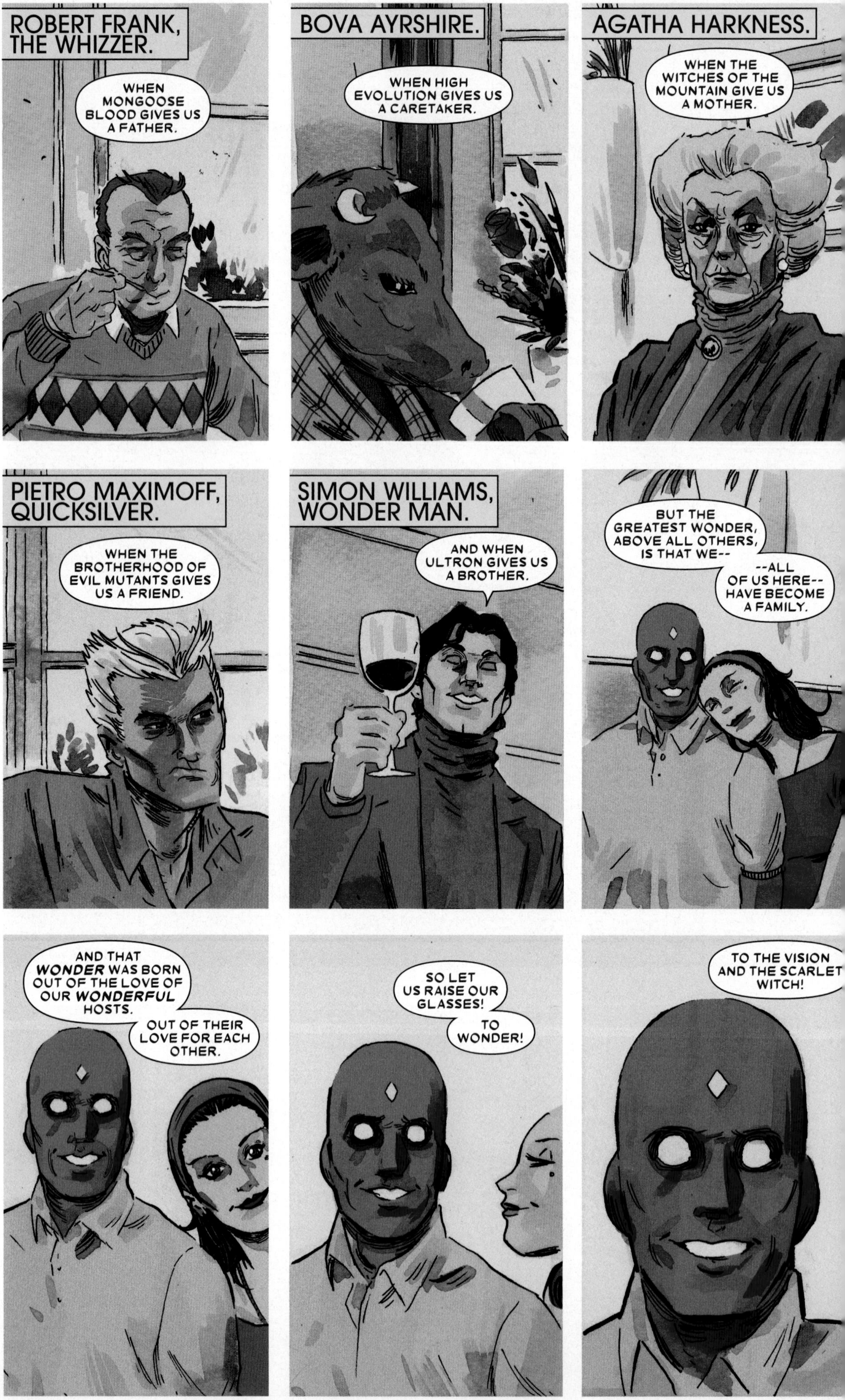
ROBERT FRANK, THE WHIZZER.
WHEN MONGOOSE BLOOD GIVES US A FATHER.
BOVA AYRSHIRE.
WHEN HIGH EVOLUTION GIVES US A CARETAKER.
AGATHA HARKNESS.
WHEN THE WITCHES OF THE MOUNTAIN GIVE US A MOTHER.
PIETRO MAXIMOFF, QUICKSILVER.
WHEN THE BROTHERHOOD OF EVIL MUTANTS GIVES US A FRIEND.
SIMON WILLIAMS, WONDER MAN.
AND WHEN ULTRON GIVES US A BROTHER.
BUT THE GREATEST WONDER, ABOVE ALL OTHERS, IS THAT WE--
--ALL OF US HERE-- HAVE BECOME A FAMILY.
AND THAT *WONDER* WAS BORN OUT OF THE LOVE OF OUR *WONDERFUL* HOSTS.
OUT OF THEIR LOVE FOR EACH OTHER.
SO LET US RAISE OUR GLASSES!
TO WONDER!
TO THE VISION AND THE SCARLET WITCH!

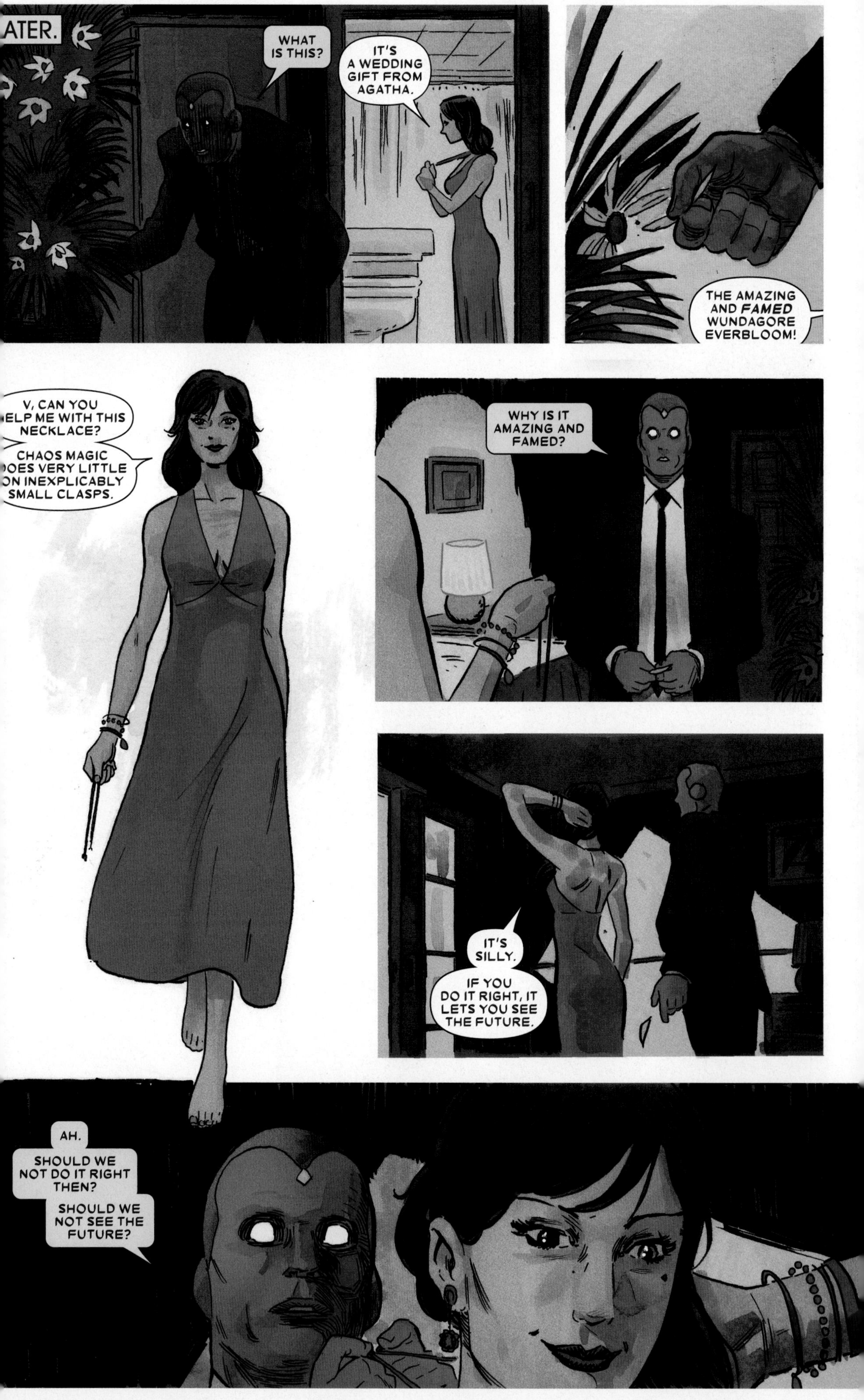
ATER.
WHAT IS THIS?
IT'S A WEDDING GIFT FROM AGATHA.
THE AMAZING AND *FAMED* WUNDAGORE EVERBLOOM!
V, CAN YOU ELP ME WITH THIS NECKLACE?
CHAOS MAGIC OES VERY LITTLE ON INEXPLICABLY SMALL CLASPS.
WHY IS IT AMAZING AND FAMED?
IT'S SILLY.
IF YOU DO IT RIGHT, IT LETS YOU SEE THE FUTURE.
AH.
SHOULD WE NOT DO IT RIGHT THEN?
SHOULD WE NOT SEE THE FUTURE?

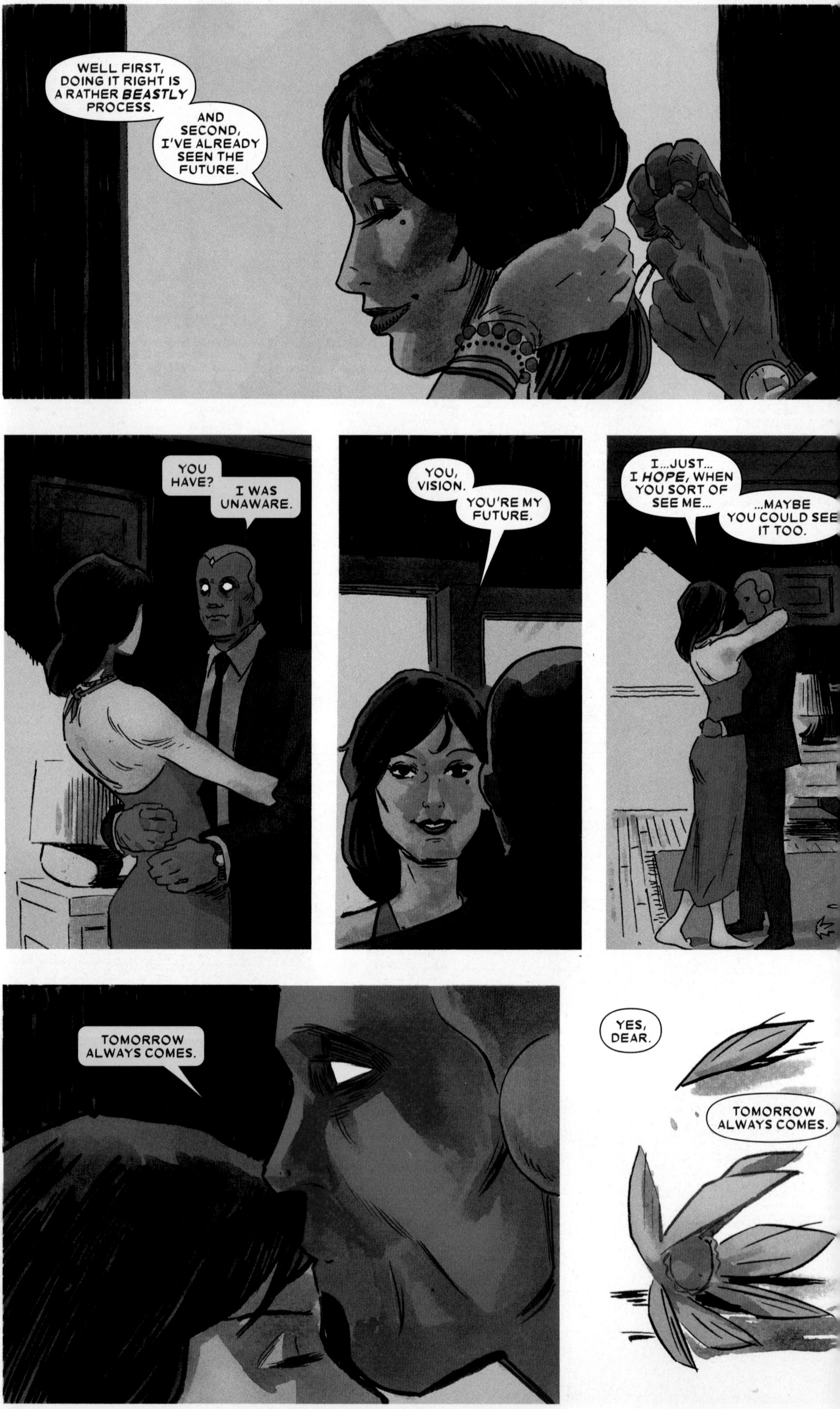
WELL FIRST, DOING IT RIGHT IS A RATHER *BEASTLY* PROCESS.
AND SECOND, I'VE ALREADY SEEN THE FUTURE.
YOU HAVE?
I WAS UNAWARE.
YOU, VISION.
YOU'RE MY FUTURE.
I...JUST... I *HOPE,* WHEN YOU SORT OF SEE ME...
...MAYBE YOU COULD SEE IT TOO.
TOMORROW ALWAYS COMES.
YES, DEAR.
TOMORROW ALWAYS COMES.

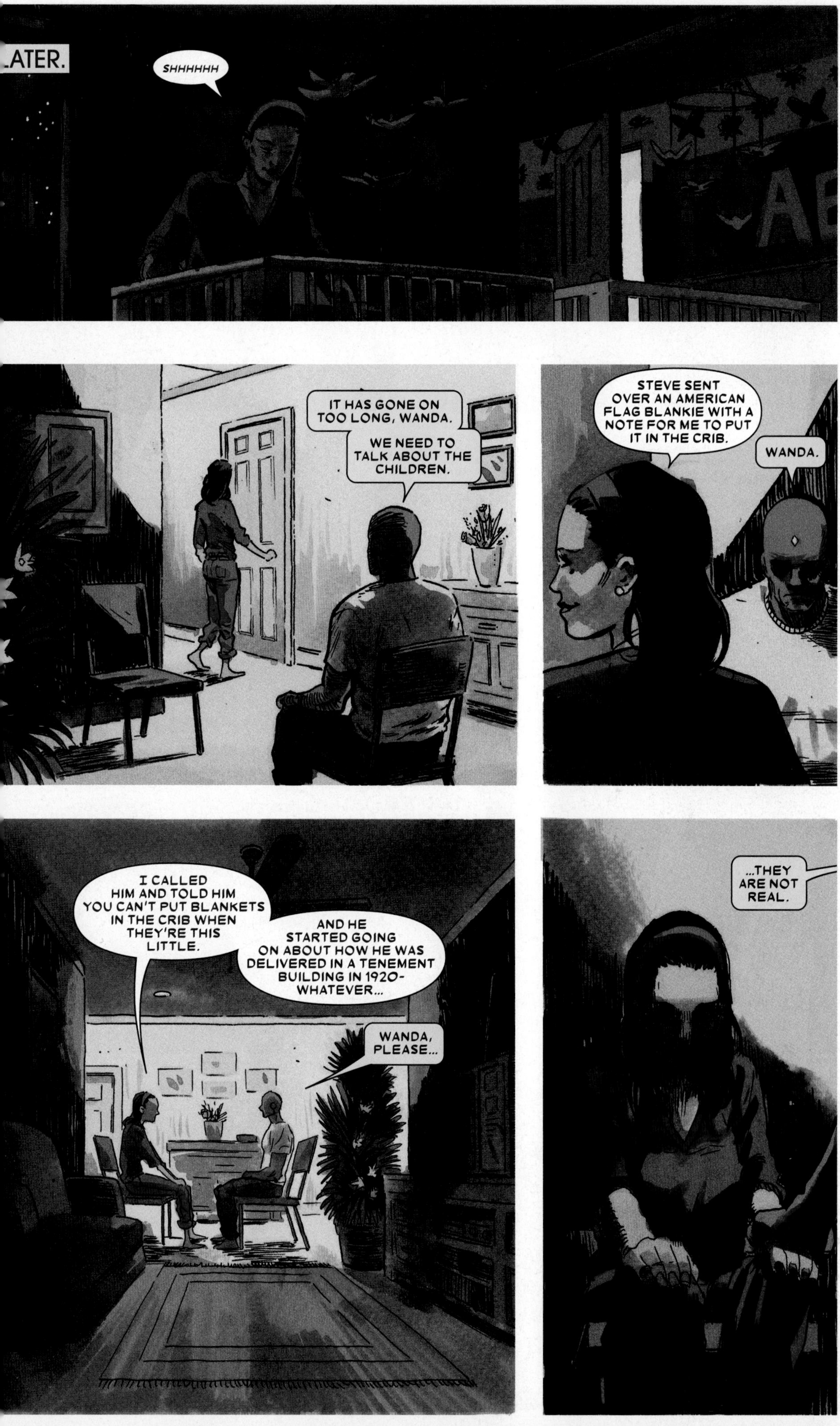

LATER.
SHHHHHH
IT HAS GONE ON TOO LONG, WANDA.
WE NEED TO TALK ABOUT THE CHILDREN.
STEVE SENT OVER AN AMERICAN FLAG BLANKIE WITH A NOTE FOR ME TO PUT IT IN THE CRIB.
WANDA.
I CALLED HIM AND TOLD HIM YOU CAN'T PUT BLANKETS IN THE CRIB WHEN THEY'RE THIS LITTLE.
AND HE STARTED GOING ON ABOUT HOW HE WAS DELIVERED IN A TENEMENT BUILDING IN 1920-WHATEVER...
WANDA, PLEASE...
...THEY ARE NOT REAL.

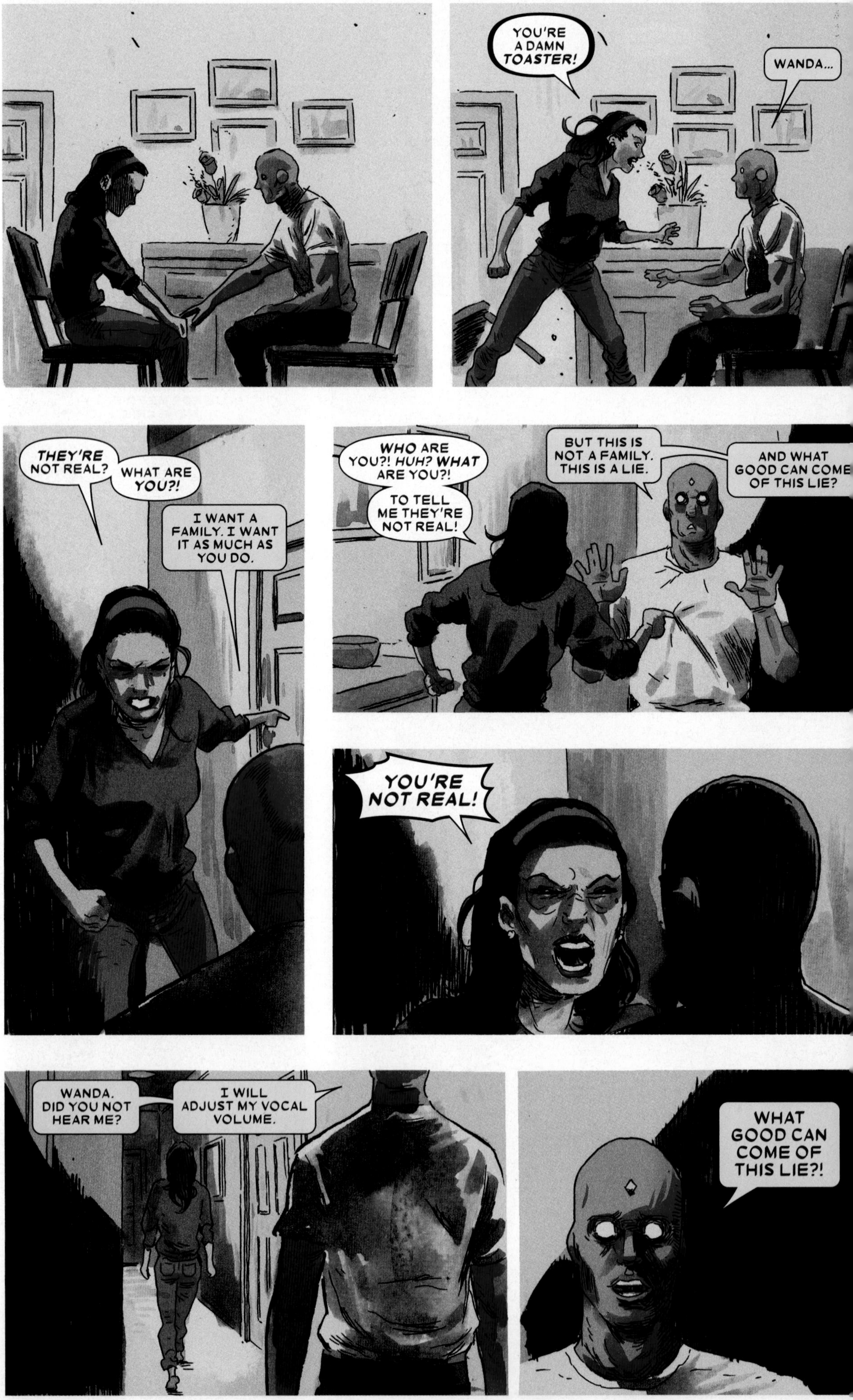
YOU'RE A DAMN TOASTER!
WANDA...
THEY'RE NOT REAL?
WHAT ARE YOU?!
I WANT A FAMILY. I WANT IT AS MUCH AS YOU DO.
WHO ARE YOU?! HUH? WHAT ARE YOU?!
TO TELL ME THEY'RE NOT REAL!
BUT THIS IS NOT A FAMILY. THIS IS A LIE.
AND WHAT GOOD CAN COME OF THIS LIE?
YOU'RE NOT REAL!
WANDA. DID YOU NOT HEAR ME?
I WILL ADJUST MY VOCAL VOLUME.
WHAT GOOD CAN COME OF THIS LIE?!

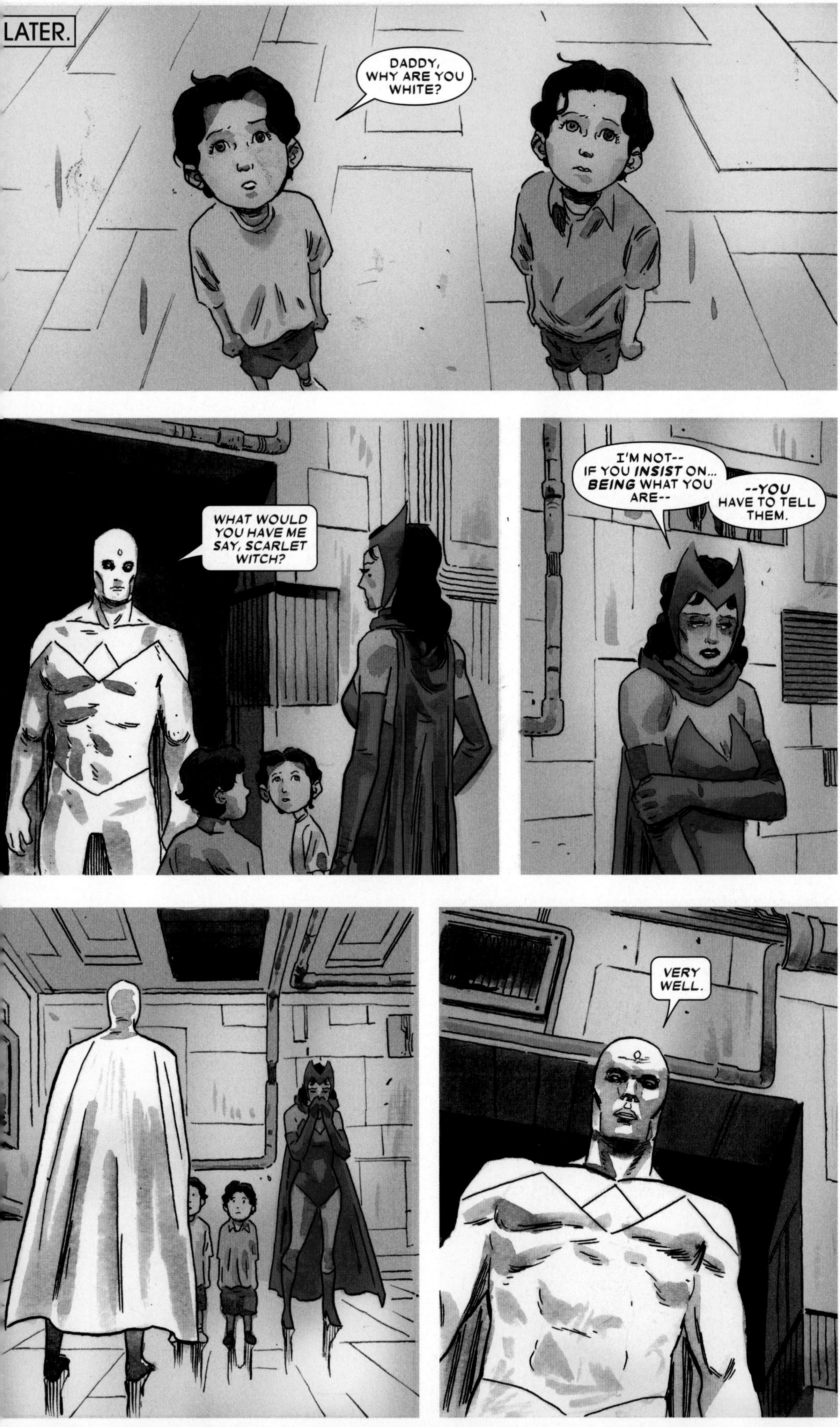
LATER.
DADDY, WHY ARE YOU WHITE?
WHAT WOULD YOU HAVE ME SAY, SCARLET WITCH?
I'M NOT-- IF YOU INSIST ON... BEING WHAT YOU ARE--
--YOU HAVE TO TELL THEM.
VERY WELL.

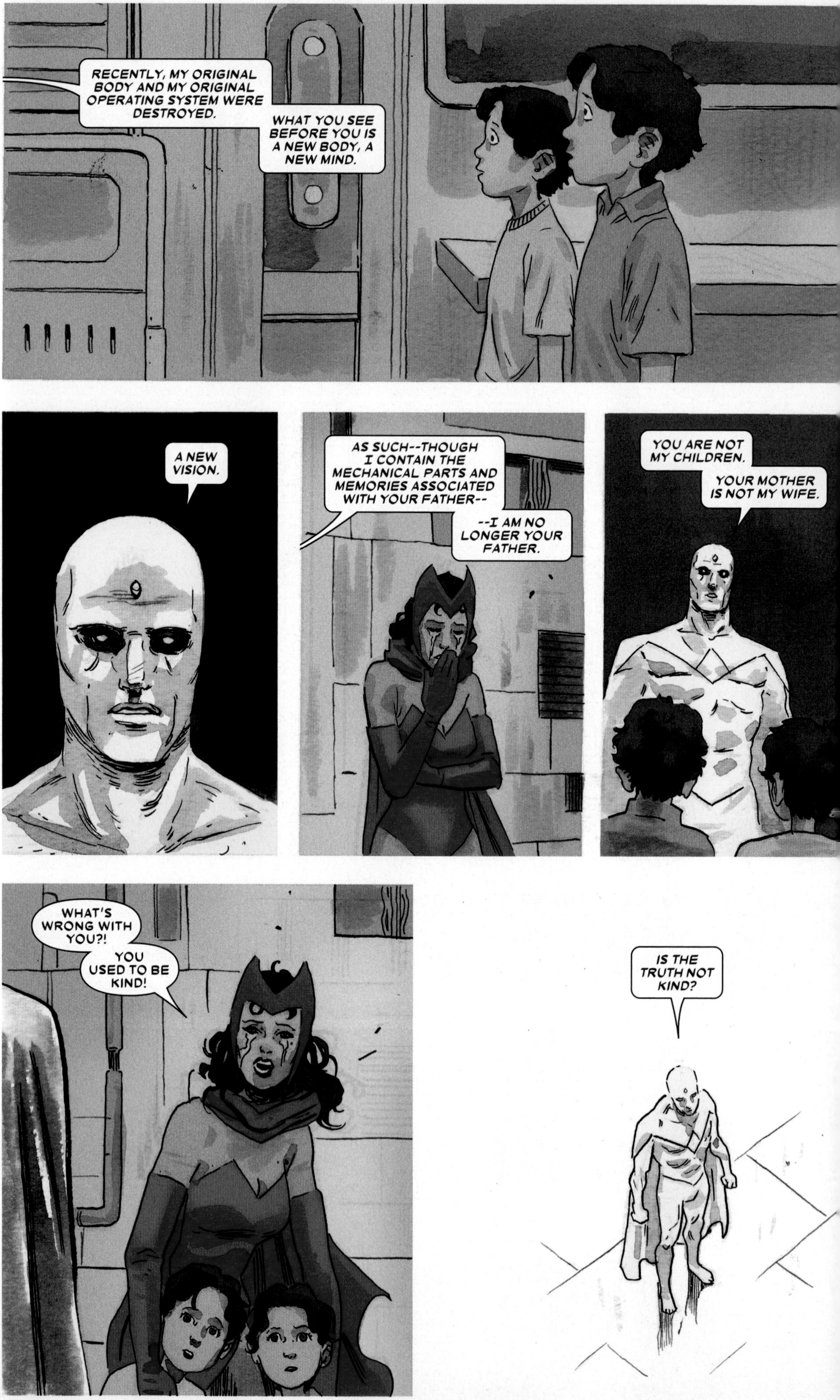
RECENTLY, MY ORIGINAL BODY AND MY ORIGINAL OPERATING SYSTEM WERE DESTROYED.
WHAT YOU SEE BEFORE YOU IS A NEW BODY, A NEW MIND.
A NEW VISION.
AS SUCH--THOUGH I CONTAIN THE MECHANICAL PARTS AND MEMORIES ASSOCIATED WITH YOUR FATHER--
--I AM NO LONGER YOUR FATHER.
YOU ARE NOT MY CHILDREN.
YOUR MOTHER IS NOT MY WIFE.
WHAT'S WRONG WITH YOU?!
YOU USED TO BE KIND!
IS THE TRUTH NOT KIND?

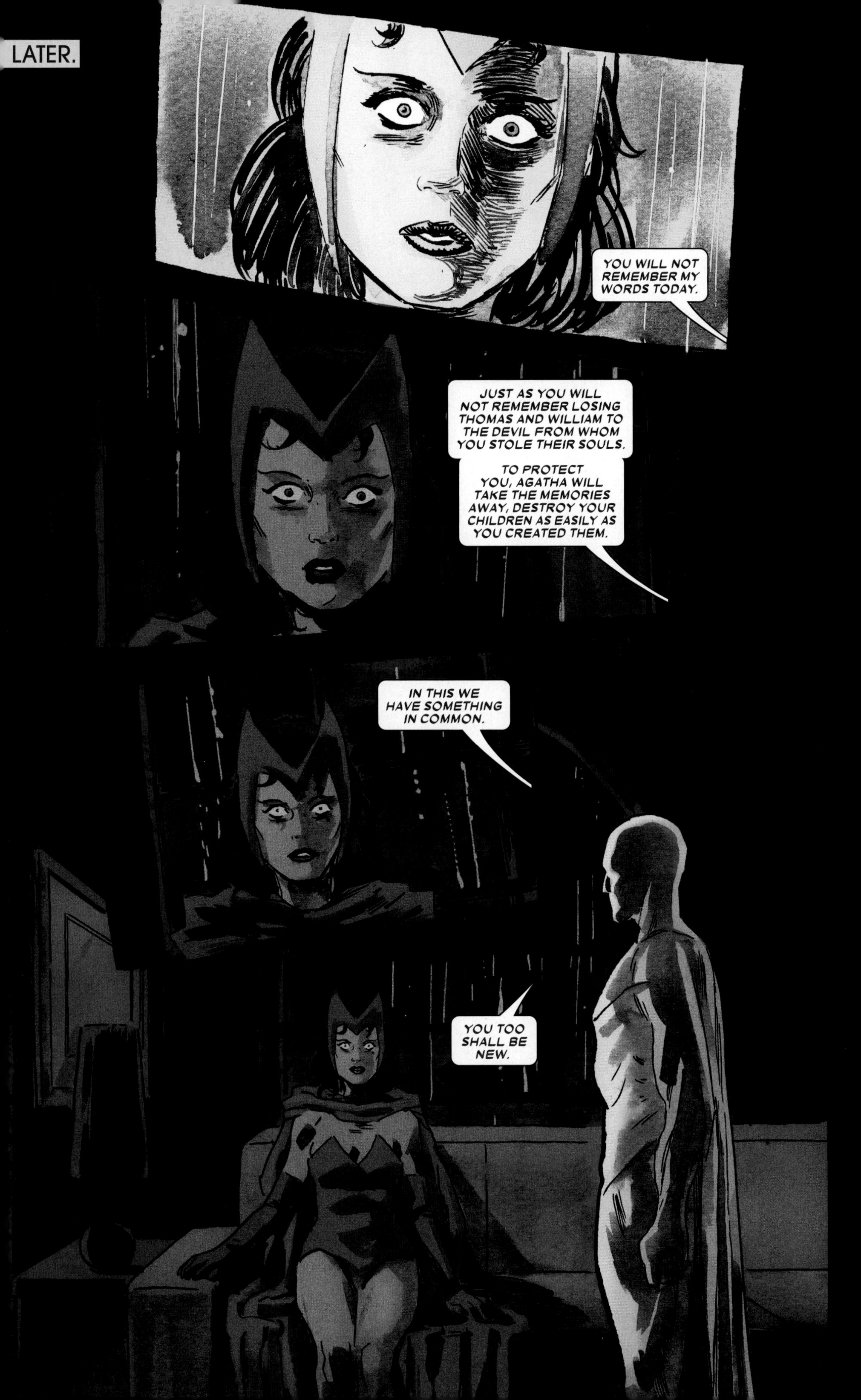
LATER.
YOU WILL NOT REMEMBER MY WORDS TODAY.
JUST AS YOU WILL NOT REMEMBER LOSING THOMAS AND WILLIAM TO THE DEVIL FROM WHOM YOU STOLE THEIR SOULS.
TO PROTECT YOU, AGATHA WILL TAKE THE MEMORIES AWAY, DESTROY YOUR CHILDREN AS EASILY AS YOU CREATED THEM.
IN THIS WE HAVE SOMETHING IN COMMON.
YOU TOO SHALL BE NEW.

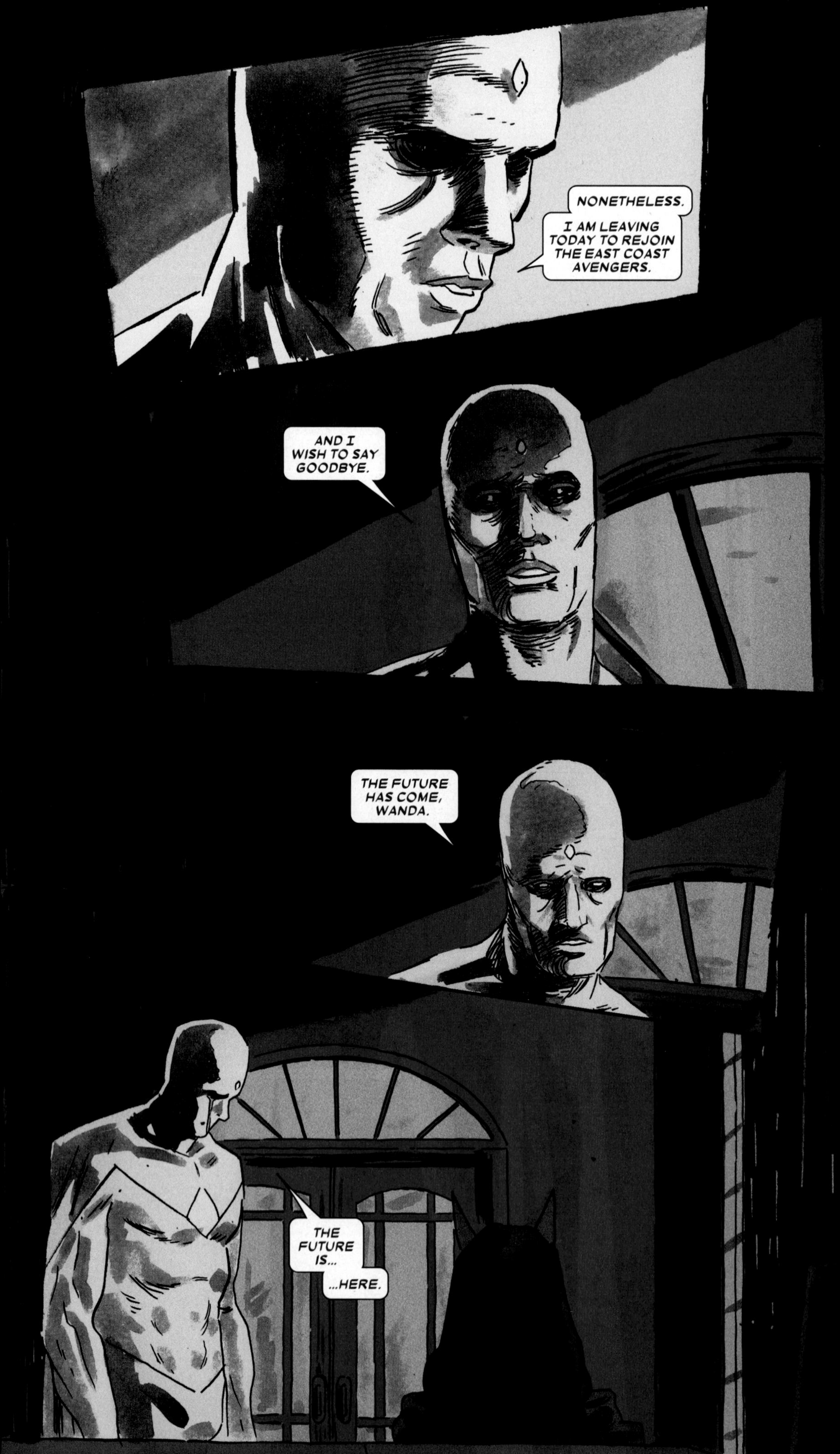
NONETHELESS.
I AM LEAVING TODAY TO REJOIN THE EAST COAST AVENGERS.
AND I WISH TO SAY GOODBYE.
THE FUTURE HAS COME, WANDA.
THE FUTURE IS...
...HERE.

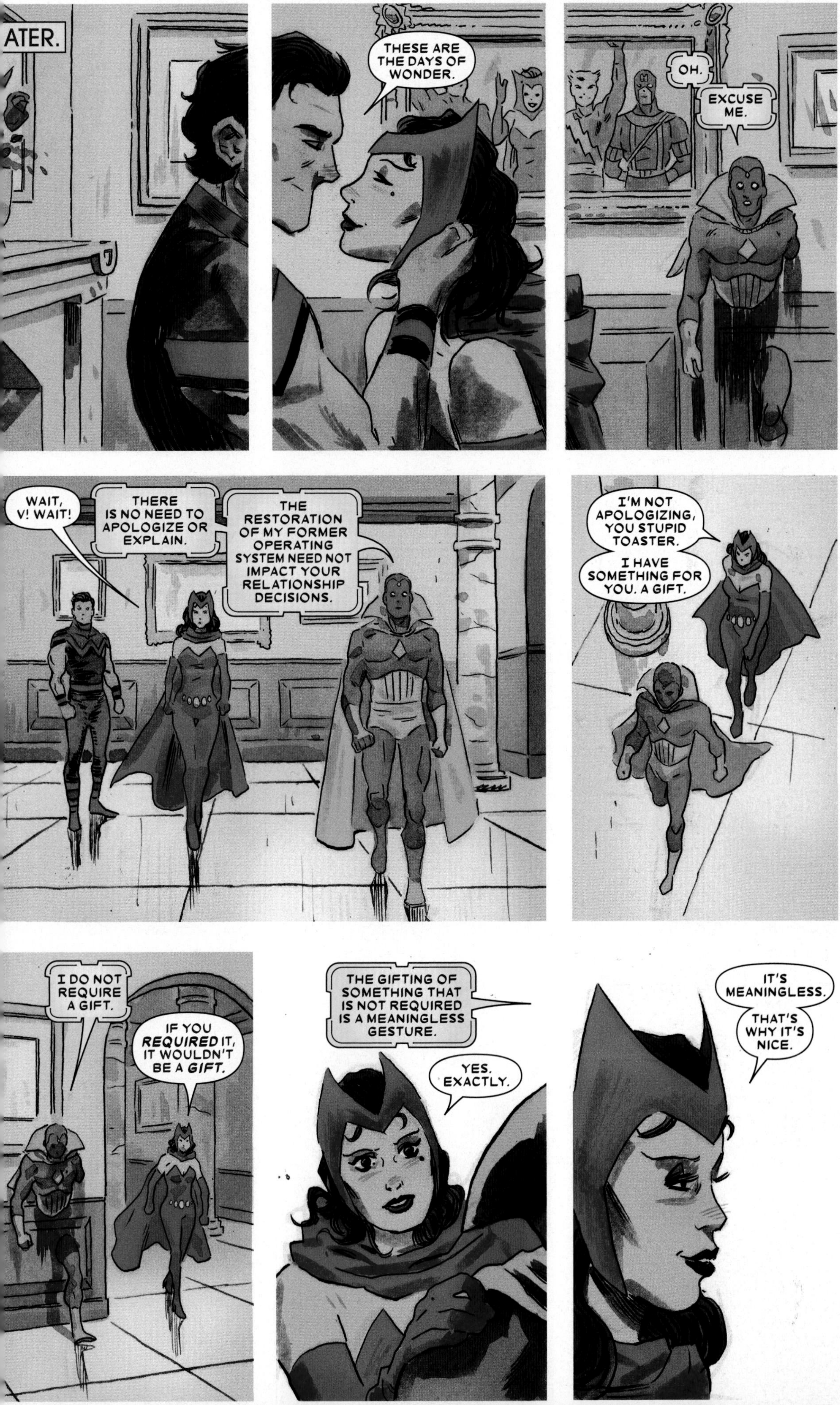
ATER.
THESE ARE THE DAYS OF WONDER.
OH.
EXCUSE ME.
WAIT, V! WAIT!
THERE IS NO NEED TO APOLOGIZE OR EXPLAIN.
THE RESTORATION OF MY FORMER OPERATING SYSTEM NEED NOT IMPACT YOUR RELATIONSHIP DECISIONS.
I'M NOT APOLOGIZING, YOU STUPID TOASTER.
I HAVE SOMETHING FOR YOU. A GIFT.
I DO NOT REQUIRE A GIFT.
IF YOU REQUIRED IT, IT WOULDN'T BE A GIFT.
THE GIFTING OF SOMETHING THAT IS NOT REQUIRED IS A MEANINGLESS GESTURE.
YES. EXACTLY.
IT'S MEANINGLESS.
THAT'S WHY IT'S NICE.

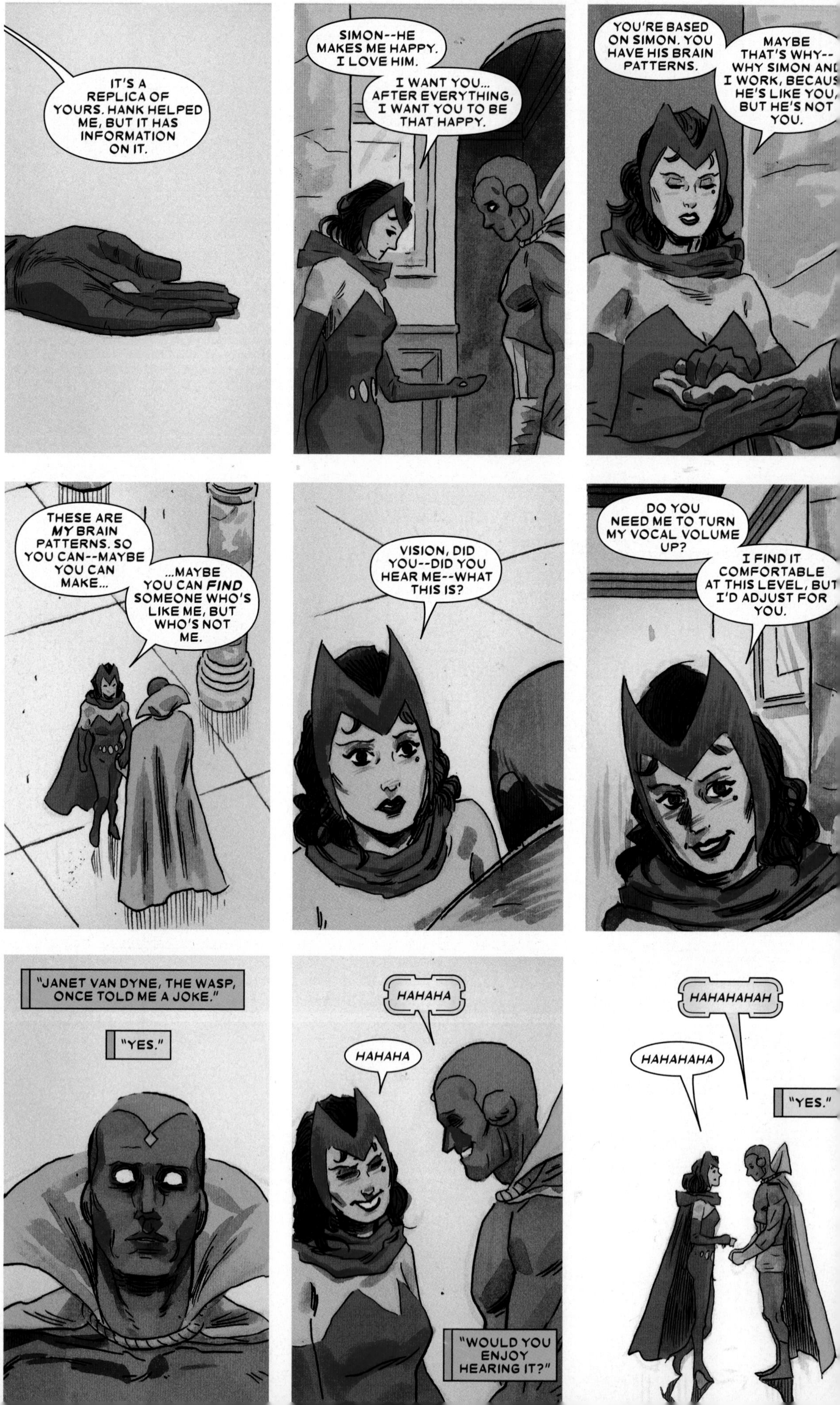

IT'S A REPLICA OF YOURS. HANK HELPED ME, BUT IT HAS INFORMATION ON IT.
SIMON--HE MAKES ME HAPPY. I LOVE HIM.
I WANT YOU... AFTER EVERYTHING, I WANT YOU TO BE THAT HAPPY.
YOU'RE BASED ON SIMON. YOU HAVE HIS BRAIN PATTERNS.
MAYBE THAT'S WHY--WHY SIMON AND I WORK, BECAUSE HE'S LIKE YOU, BUT HE'S NOT YOU.
THESE ARE MY BRAIN PATTERNS. SO YOU CAN--MAYBE YOU CAN MAKE...
...MAYBE YOU CAN FIND SOMEONE WHO'S LIKE ME, BUT WHO'S NOT ME.
VISION, DID YOU--DID YOU HEAR ME--WHAT THIS IS?
DO YOU NEED ME TO TURN MY VOCAL VOLUME UP?
I FIND IT COMFORTABLE AT THIS LEVEL, BUT I'D ADJUST FOR YOU.
"JANET VAN DYNE, THE WASP, ONCE TOLD ME A JOKE."
"YES."
HAHAHA
HAHAHA
"WOULD YOU ENJOY HEARING IT?"
HAHAHAHAH
HAHAHAHA
"YES."

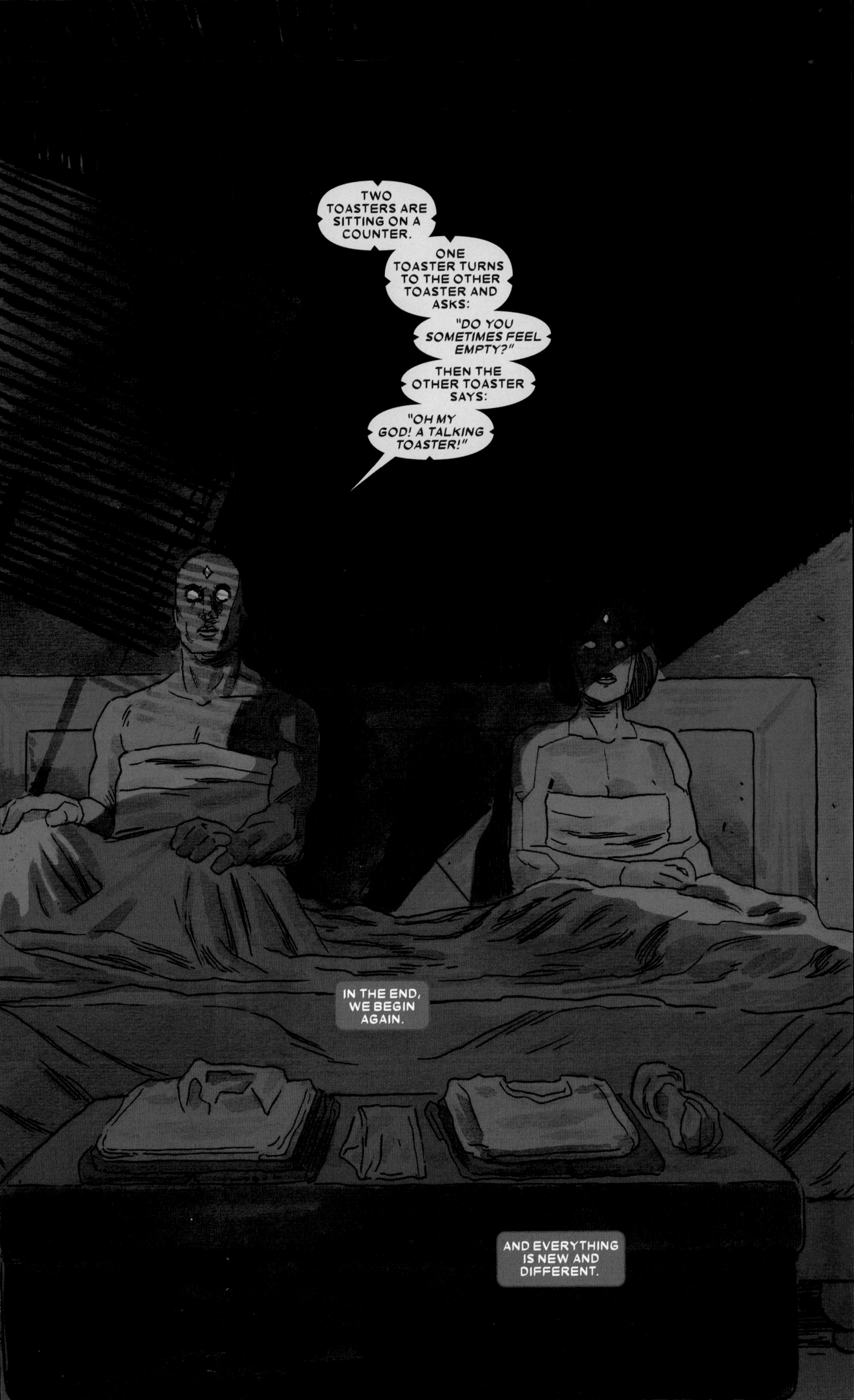
TWO TOASTERS ARE SITTING ON A COUNTER.
ONE TOASTER TURNS TO THE OTHER TOASTER AND ASKS:
"DO YOU SOMETIMES FEEL EMPTY?"
THEN THE OTHER TOASTER SAYS:
"OH MY GOD! A TALKING TOASTER!"
IN THE END, WE BEGIN AGAIN.
AND EVERYTHING IS NEW AND DIFFERENT.

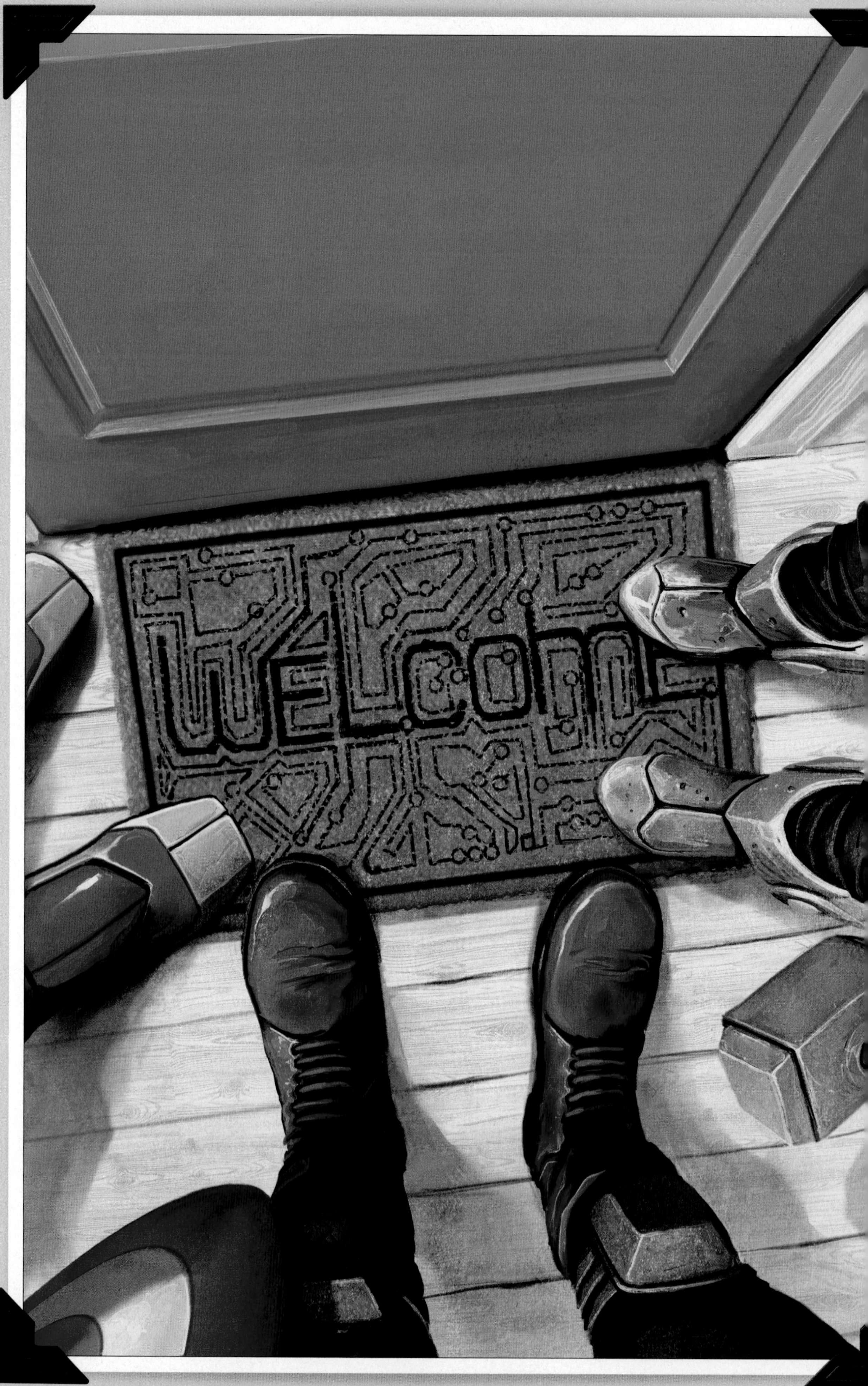

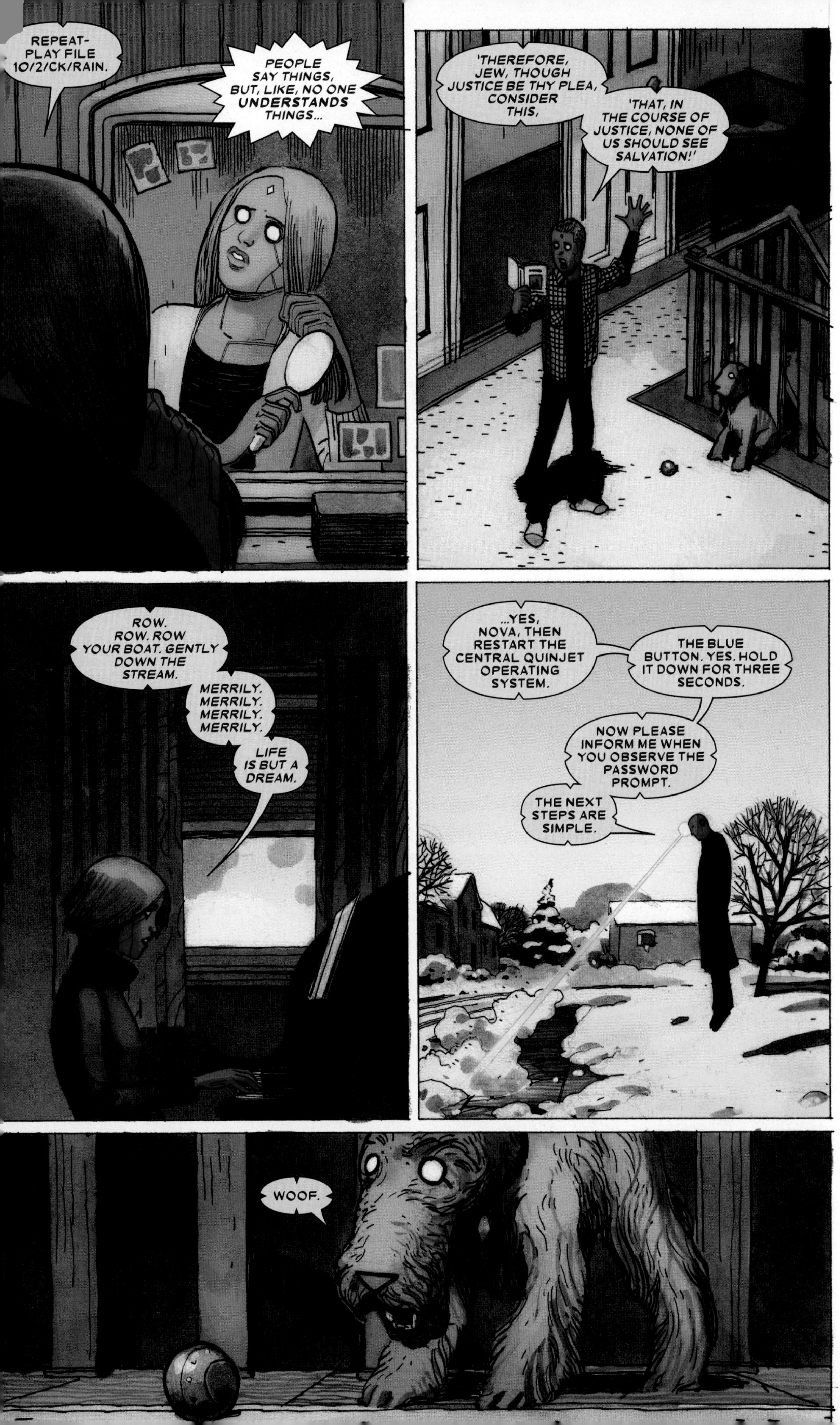
REPEAT-PLAY FILE 10/2/CK/RAIN.
PEOPLE SAY THINGS, BUT, LIKE, NO ONE **UNDERSTANDS** THINGS...
'THEREFORE, JEW, THOUGH JUSTICE BE THY PLEA, CONSIDER THIS,
'THAT, IN THE COURSE OF JUSTICE, NONE OF US SHOULD SEE SALVATION!'
ROW. ROW. ROW YOUR BOAT. GENTLY DOWN THE STREAM.
MERRILY. MERRILY. MERRILY. MERRILY.
LIFE IS BUT A DREAM.
...YES, NOVA, THEN RESTART THE CENTRAL QUINJET OPERATING SYSTEM.
THE BLUE BUTTON. YES. HOLD IT DOWN FOR THREE SECONDS.
NOW PLEASE INFORM ME WHEN YOU OBSERVE THE PASSWORD PROMPT.
THE NEXT STEPS ARE SIMPLE.
WOOF.

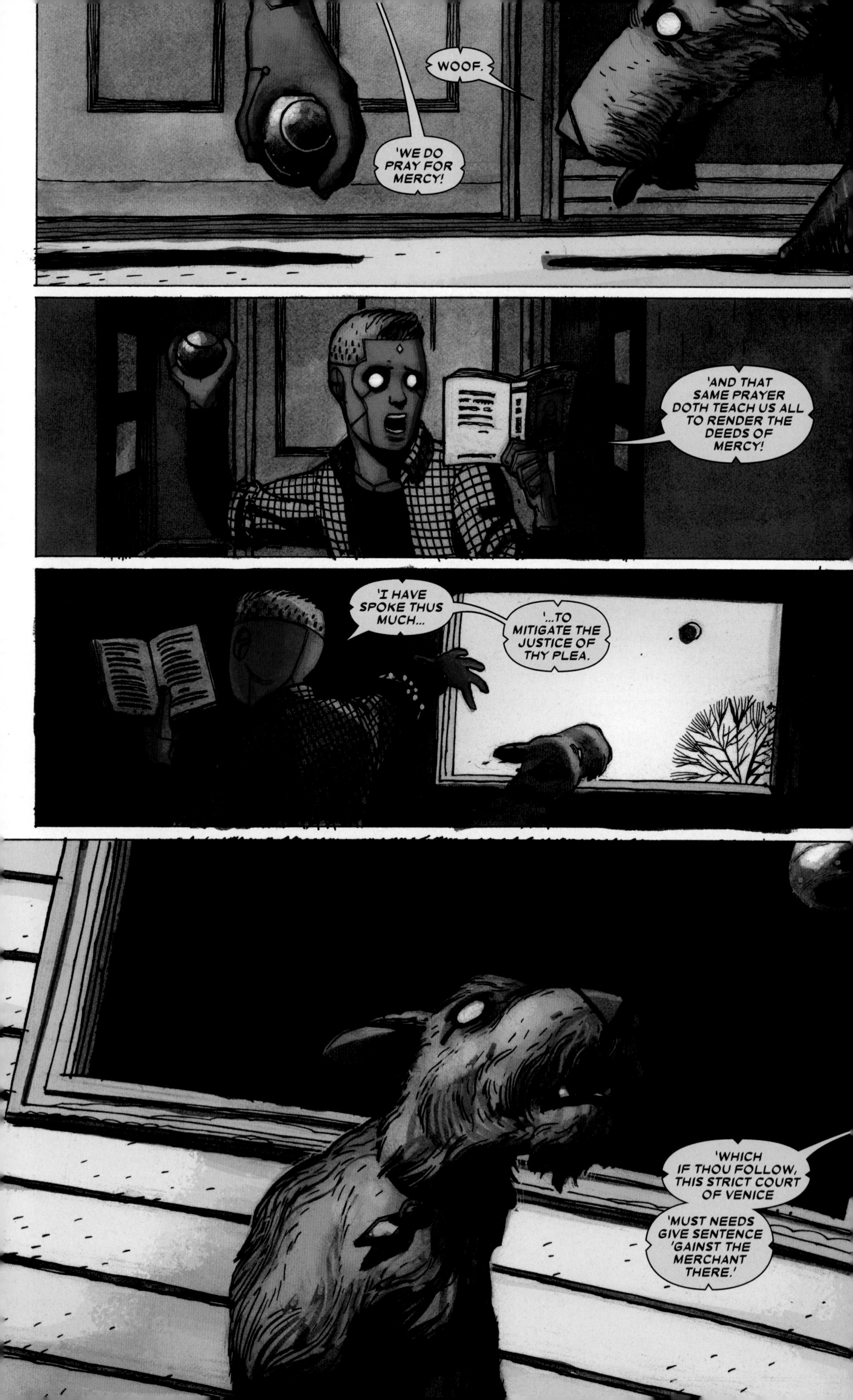
WOOF.
'WE DO PRAY FOR MERCY!
'AND THAT SAME PRAYER DOTH TEACH US ALL TO RENDER THE DEEDS OF MERCY!
'I HAVE SPOKE THUS MUCH...
'...TO MITIGATE THE JUSTICE OF THY PLEA.
'WHICH IF THOU FOLLOW, THIS STRICT COURT OF VENICE
'MUST NEEDS GIVE SENTENCE 'GAINST THE MERCHANT THERE.'

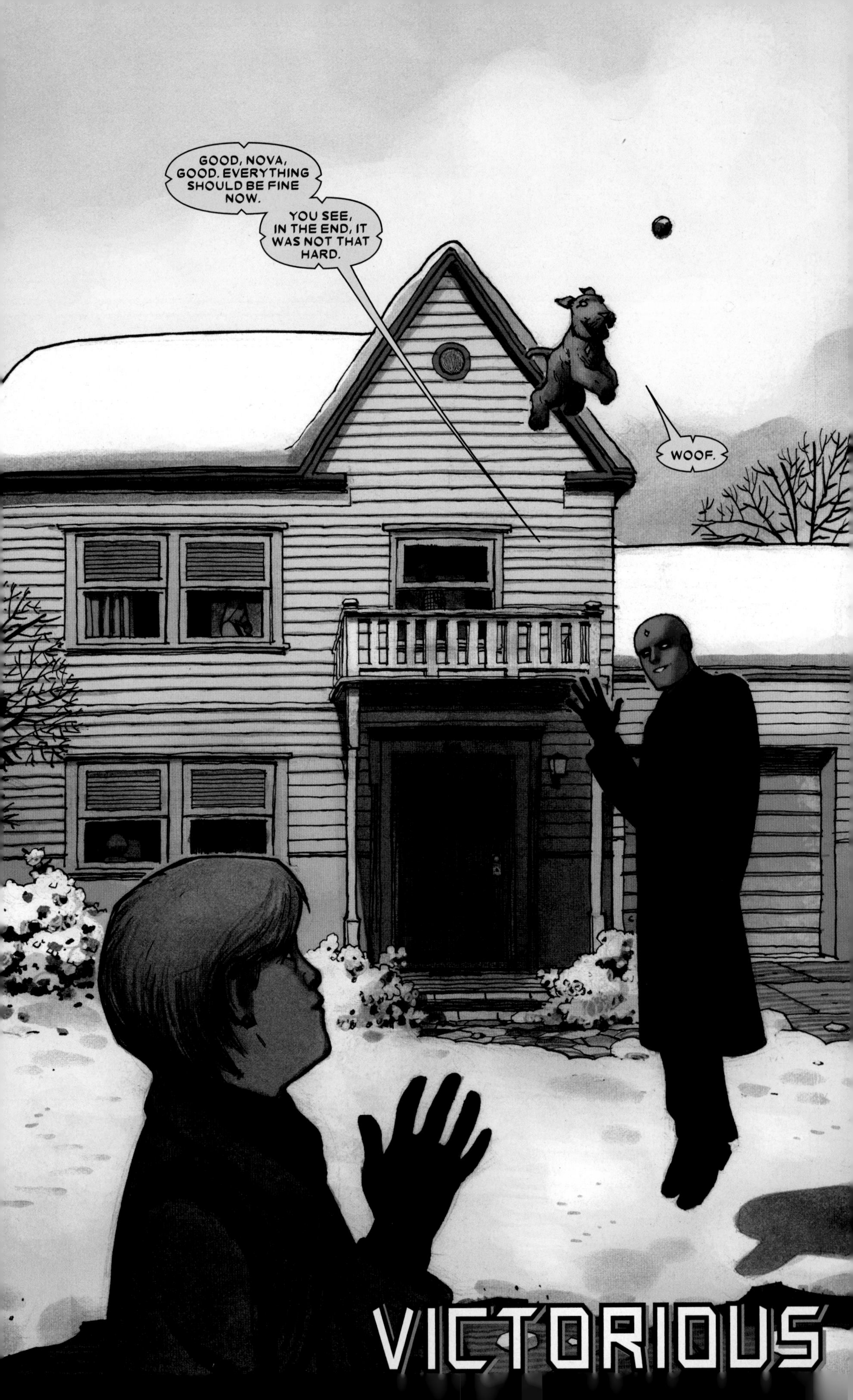
GOOD, NOVA, GOOD. EVERYTHING SHOULD BE FINE NOW.
YOU SEE, IN THE END, IT WAS NOT THAT HARD.
WOOF.
VICTORIOUS

FOLLOW THE BOUNCING BALL.

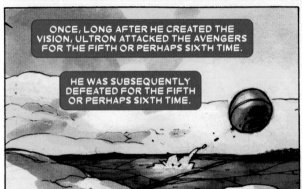

ONCE, LONG AFTER HE CREATED THE VISION, ULTRON ATTACKED THE AVENGERS FOR THE FIFTH OR PERHAPS SIXTH TIME.

HE WAS SUBSEQUENTLY DEFEATED FOR THE FIFTH OR PERHAPS SIXTH TIME.

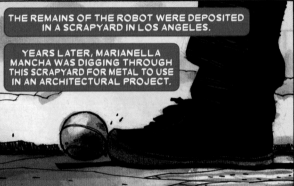

THE REMAINS OF THE ROBOT WERE DEPOSITED IN A SCRAPYARD IN LOS ANGELES.

YEARS LATER, MARIANELLA MANCHA WAS DIGGING THROUGH THIS SCRAPYARD FOR METAL TO USE IN AN ARCHITECTURAL PROJECT.

MS. MANCHA FOUND ULTRON'S HEAD.

IT SPOKE TO HER, AND SHE TOOK IT HOME.

WOOF.

MS. MANCHA CONFIDED TO ULTRON'S HEAD THAT SHE WAS PHYSICALLY UNABLE TO HAVE CHILDREN.

SHE WAS ALSO UNABLE TO ADOPT CHILDREN DUE TO HER CRIMINAL RECORD.

ULTRON'S HEAD OFFERED MS. MANCHA A FAIR EXCHANGE:

IF MS. MANCHA HELPED ULTRON'S HEAD BUILD A BODY, ULTRON'S HEAD WOULD HELP MS. MANCHA BUILD A SON.

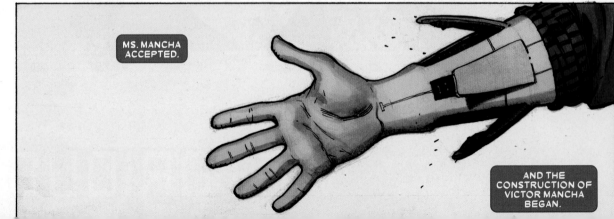

MS. MANCHA ACCEPTED.

AND THE CONSTRUCTION OF VICTOR MANCHA BEGAN.

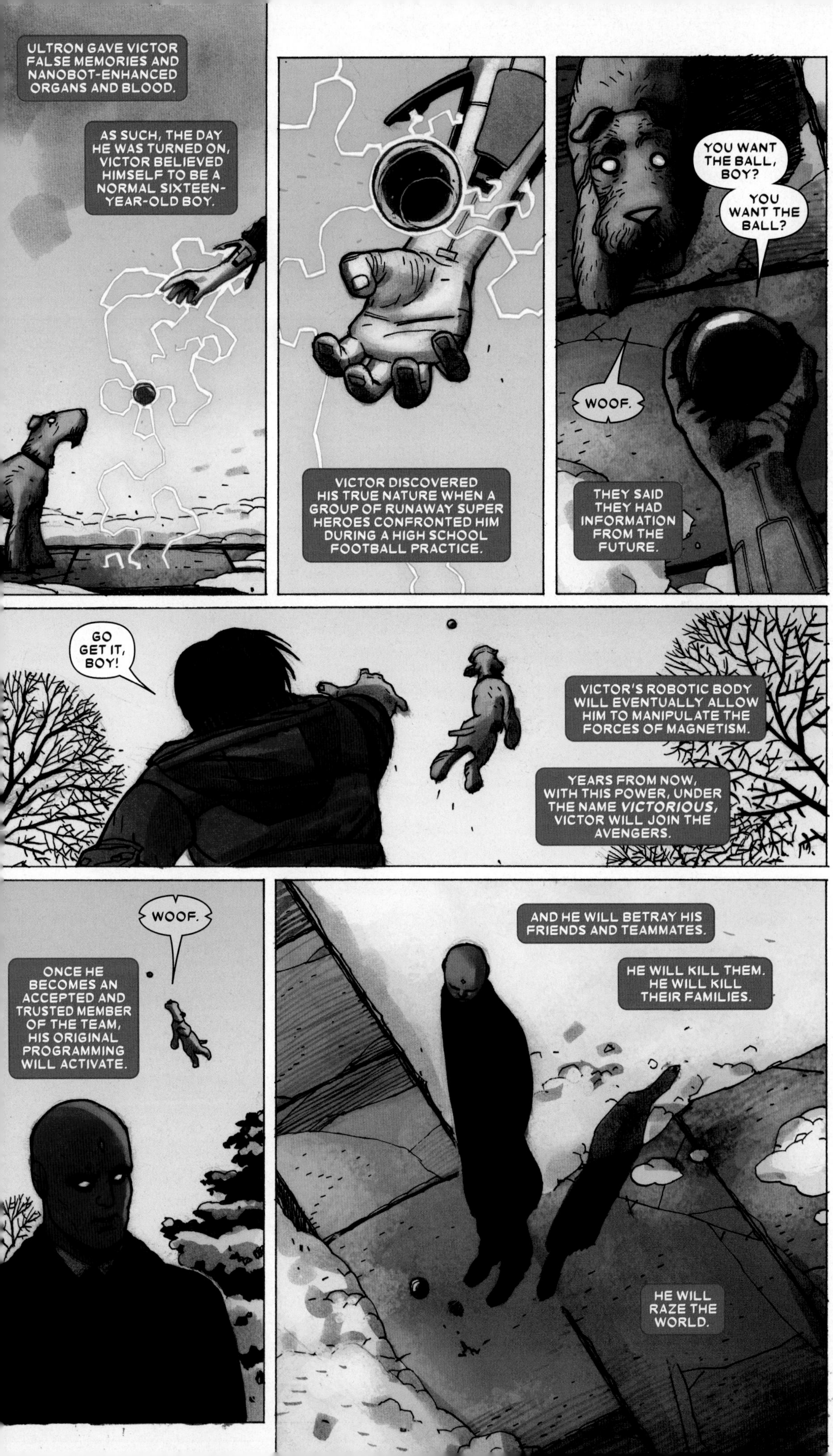
ULTRON GAVE VICTOR FALSE MEMORIES AND NANOBOT-ENHANCED ORGANS AND BLOOD.
AS SUCH, THE DAY HE WAS TURNED ON, VICTOR BELIEVED HIMSELF TO BE A NORMAL SIXTEEN-YEAR-OLD BOY.
VICTOR DISCOVERED HIS TRUE NATURE WHEN A GROUP OF RUNAWAY SUPER HEROES CONFRONTED HIM DURING A HIGH SCHOOL FOOTBALL PRACTICE.
YOU WANT THE BALL, BOY?
YOU WANT THE BALL?
WOOF.
THEY SAID THEY HAD INFORMATION FROM THE FUTURE.
GO GET IT, BOY!
VICTOR'S ROBOTIC BODY WILL EVENTUALLY ALLOW HIM TO MANIPULATE THE FORCES OF MAGNETISM.
YEARS FROM NOW, WITH THIS POWER, UNDER THE NAME *VICTORIOUS,* VICTOR WILL JOIN THE AVENGERS.
WOOF.
ONCE HE BECOMES AN ACCEPTED AND TRUSTED MEMBER OF THE TEAM, HIS ORIGINAL PROGRAMMING WILL ACTIVATE.
AND HE WILL BETRAY HIS FRIENDS AND TEAMMATES.
HE WILL KILL THEM. HE WILL KILL THEIR FAMILIES.
HE WILL RAZE THE WORLD.

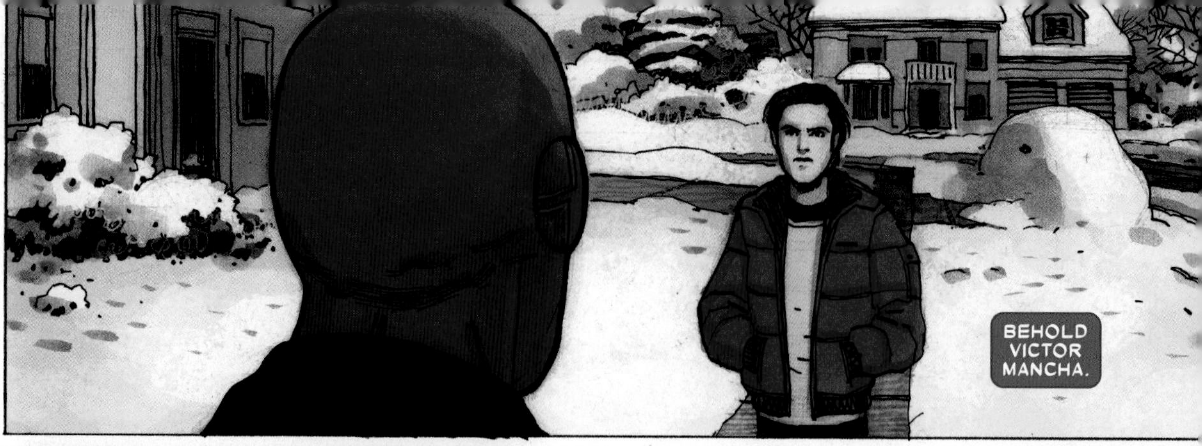
BEHOLD VICTOR MANCHA.

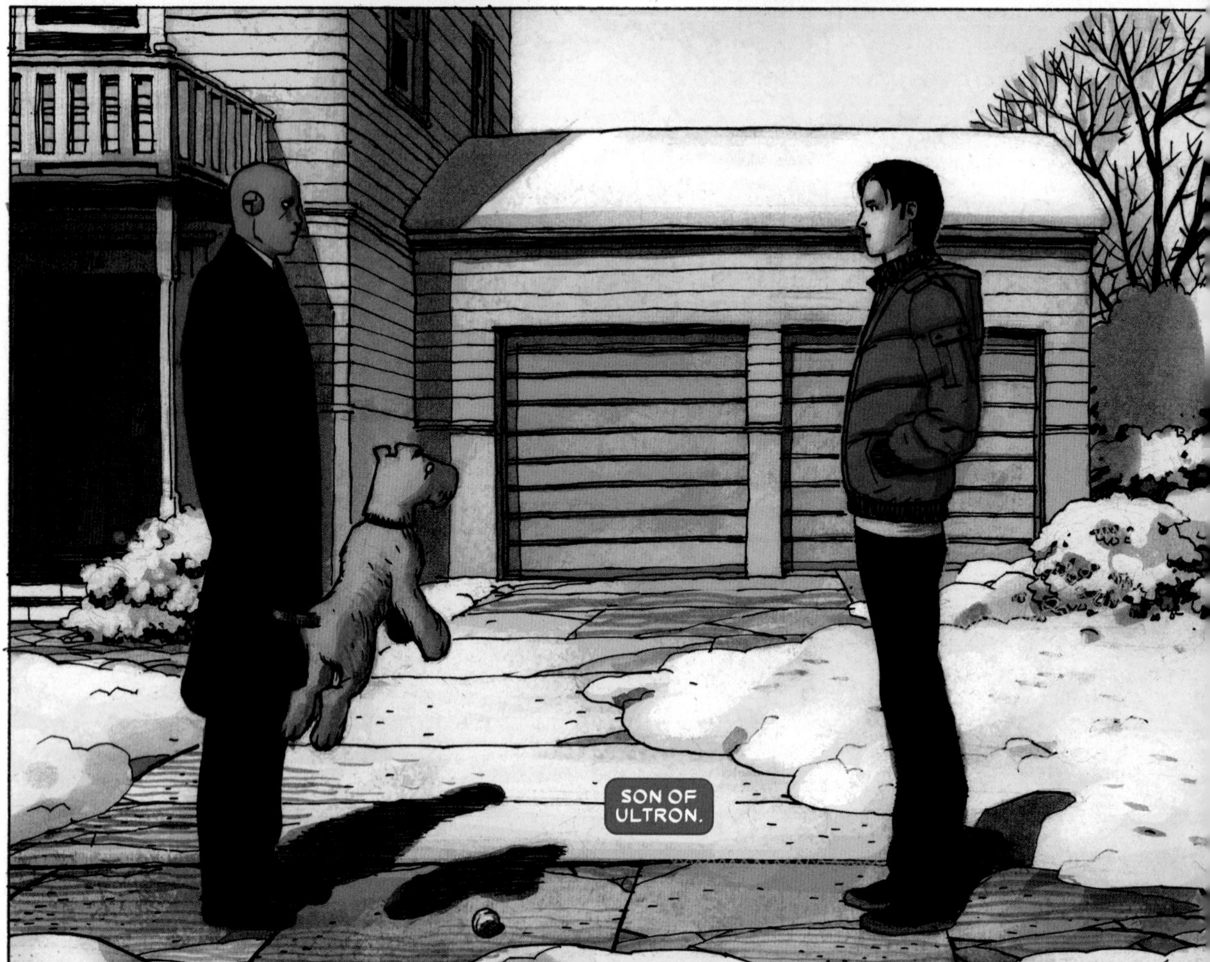
SON OF ULTRON.

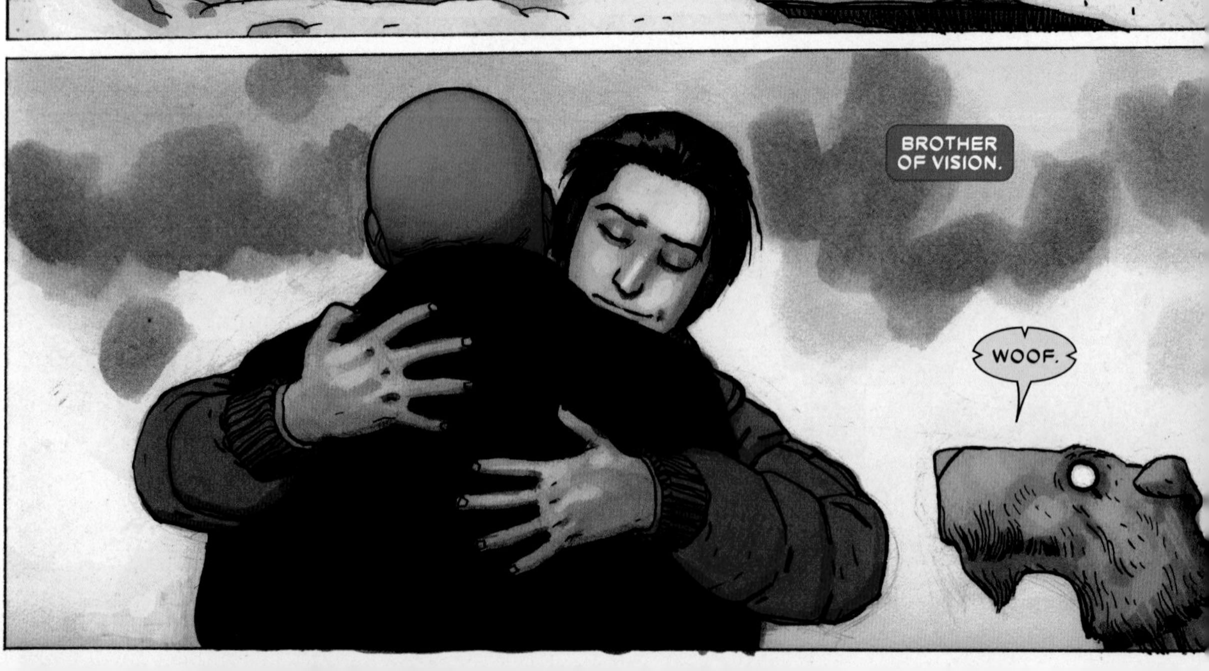
BROTHER OF VISION.
WOOF.

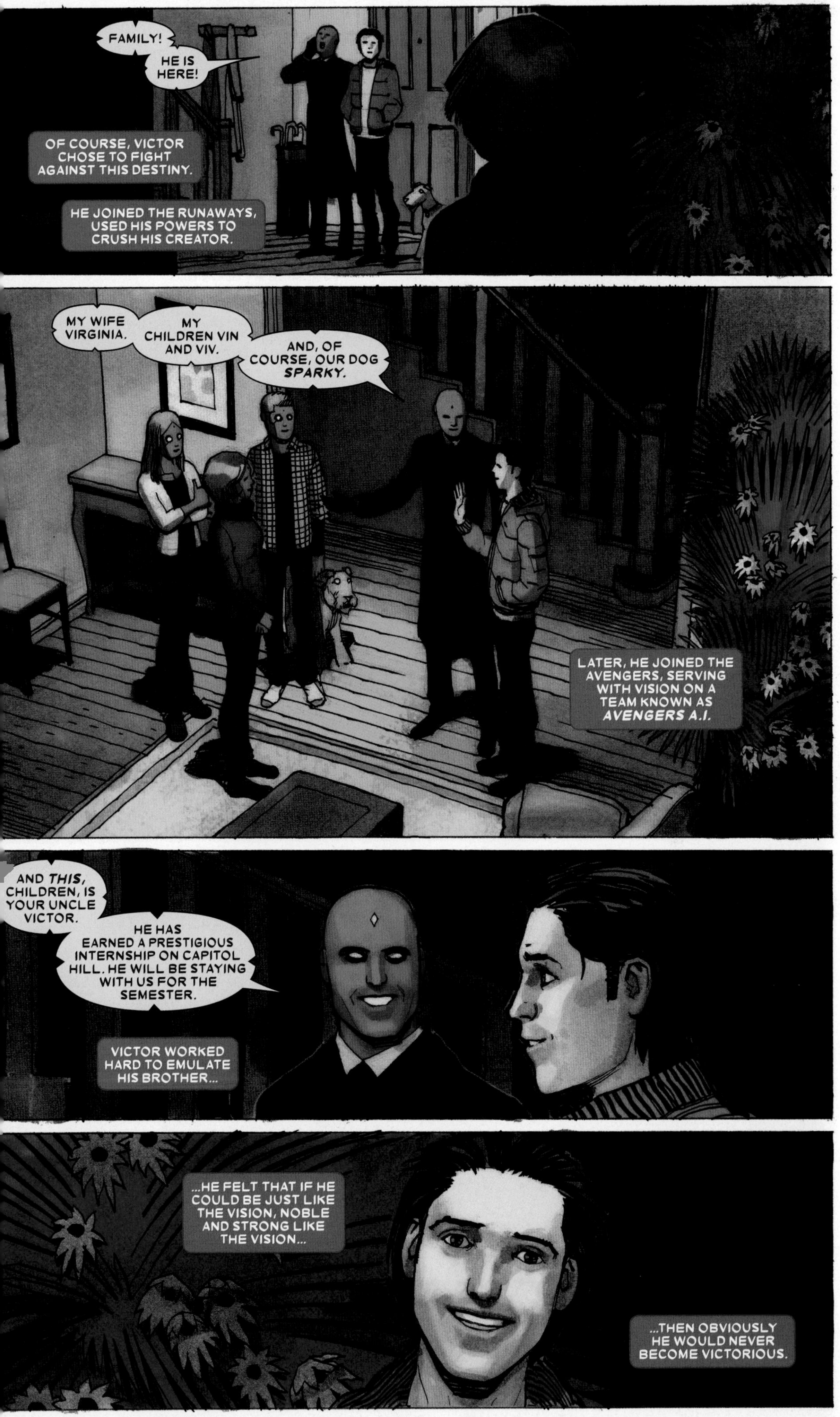
FAMILY!
HE IS HERE!
OF COURSE, VICTOR CHOSE TO FIGHT AGAINST THIS DESTINY.
HE JOINED THE RUNAWAYS, USED HIS POWERS TO CRUSH HIS CREATOR.
MY WIFE VIRGINIA.
MY CHILDREN VIN AND VIV.
AND, OF COURSE, OUR DOG *SPARKY*.
LATER, HE JOINED THE AVENGERS, SERVING WITH VISION ON A TEAM KNOWN AS *AVENGERS A.I.*
AND *THIS*, CHILDREN, IS YOUR UNCLE VICTOR.
HE HAS EARNED A PRESTIGIOUS INTERNSHIP ON CAPITOL HILL. HE WILL BE STAYING WITH US FOR THE SEMESTER.
VICTOR WORKED HARD TO EMULATE HIS BROTHER...
...HE FELT THAT IF HE COULD BE JUST LIKE THE VISION, NOBLE AND STRONG LIKE THE VISION...
...THEN OBVIOUSLY HE WOULD NEVER BECOME VICTORIOUS.

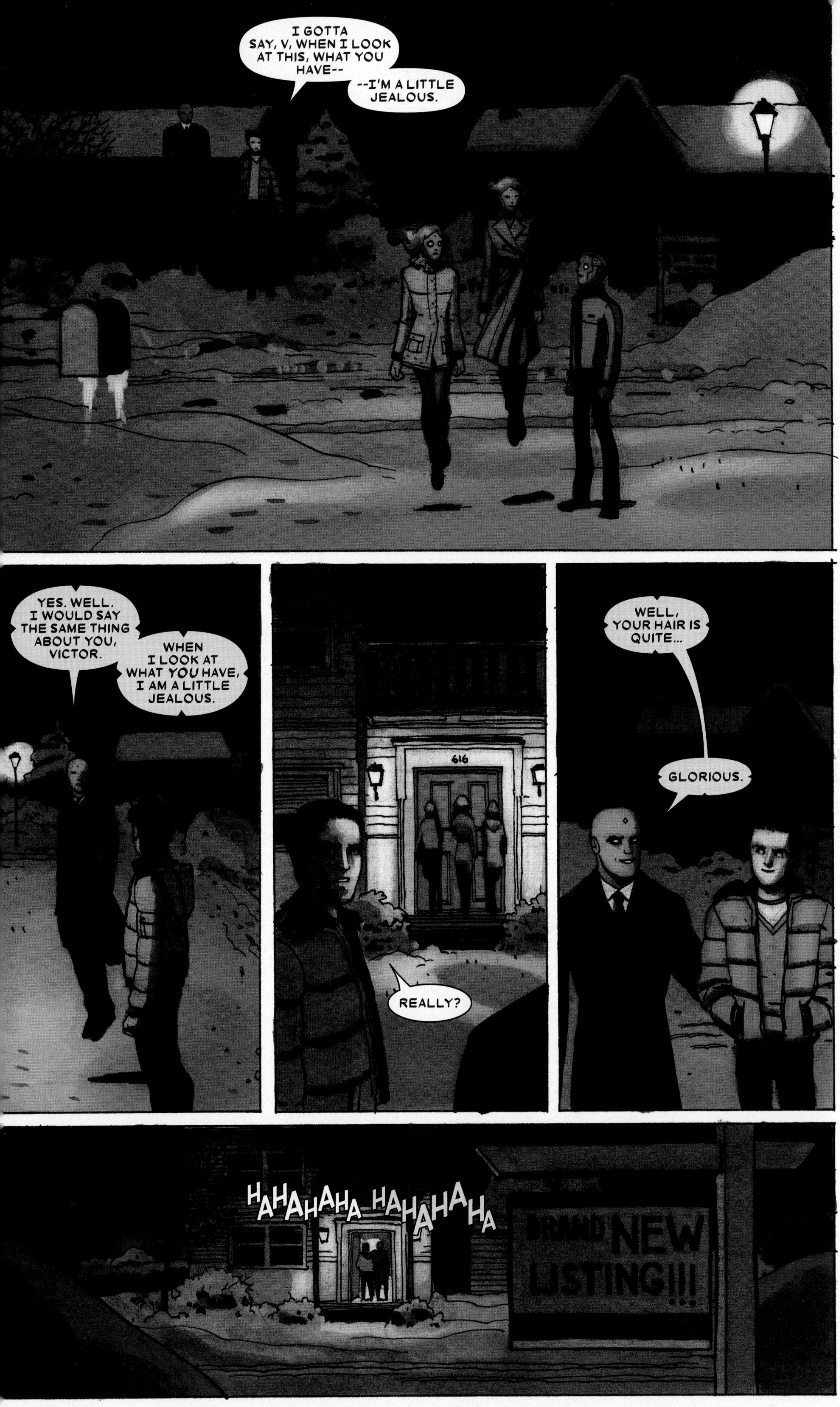
I GOTTA SAY, V, WHEN I LOOK AT THIS, WHAT YOU HAVE--
--I'M A LITTLE JEALOUS.
YES. WELL. I WOULD SAY THE SAME THING ABOUT YOU, VICTOR.
WHEN I LOOK AT WHAT YOU HAVE, I AM A LITTLE JEALOUS.
616
REALLY?
WELL, YOUR HAIR IS QUITE...
GLORIOUS.
HAHAHAHA HAHAHAHA
BRAND NEW LISTING!!!

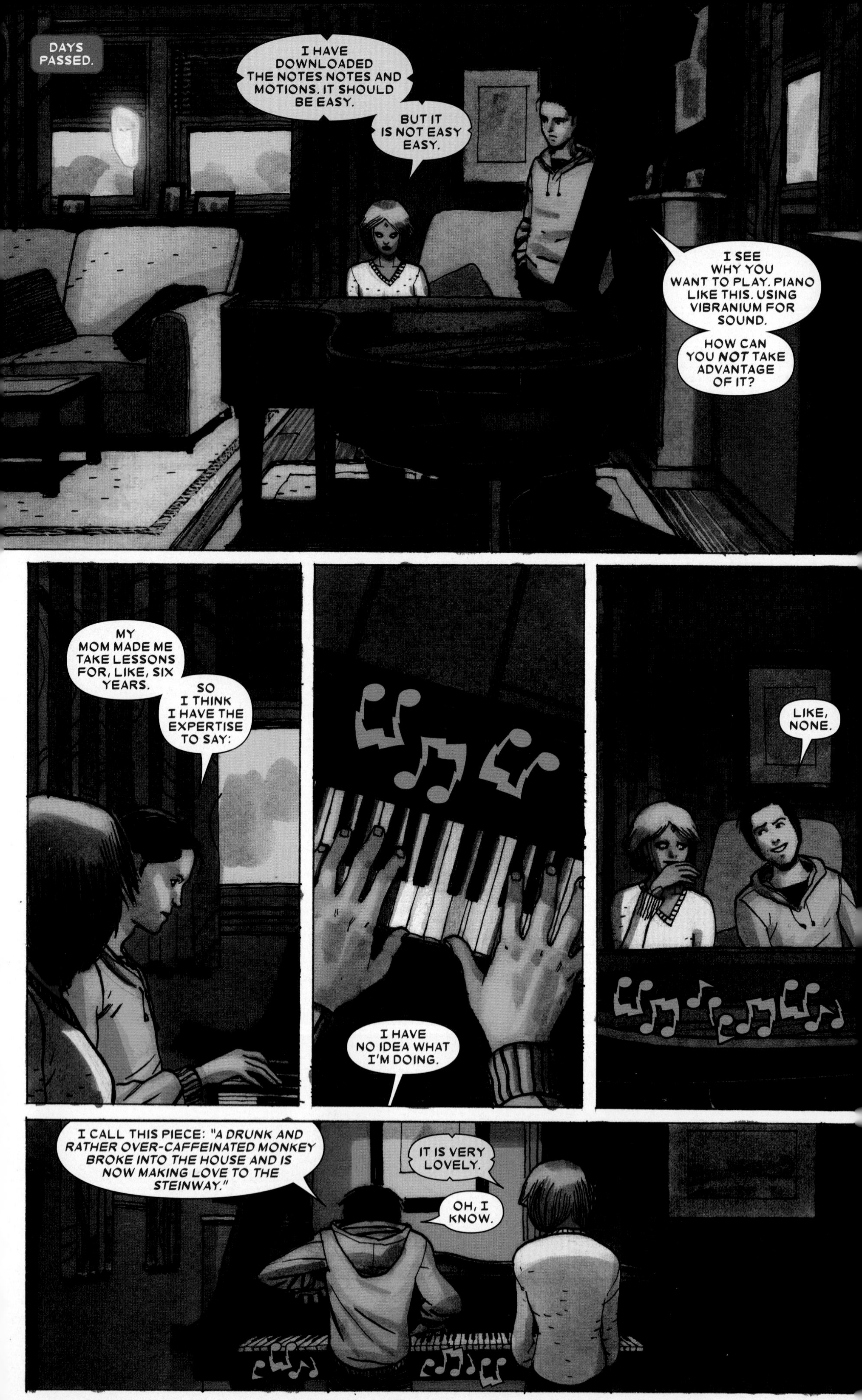
DAYS PASSED.
I HAVE DOWNLOADED THE NOTES NOTES AND MOTIONS. IT SHOULD BE EASY.
BUT IT IS NOT EASY EASY.
I SEE WHY YOU WANT TO PLAY. PIANO LIKE THIS. USING VIBRANIUM FOR SOUND.
HOW CAN YOU *NOT* TAKE ADVANTAGE OF IT?
MY MOM MADE ME TAKE LESSONS FOR, LIKE, SIX YEARS.
SO I THINK I HAVE THE EXPERTISE TO SAY:
I HAVE NO IDEA WHAT I'M DOING.
LIKE, NONE.
I CALL THIS PIECE: "A DRUNK AND RATHER OVER-CAFFEINATED MONKEY BROKE INTO THE HOUSE AND IS NOW MAKING LOVE TO THE STEINWAY."
IT IS VERY LOVELY.
OH, I KNOW.

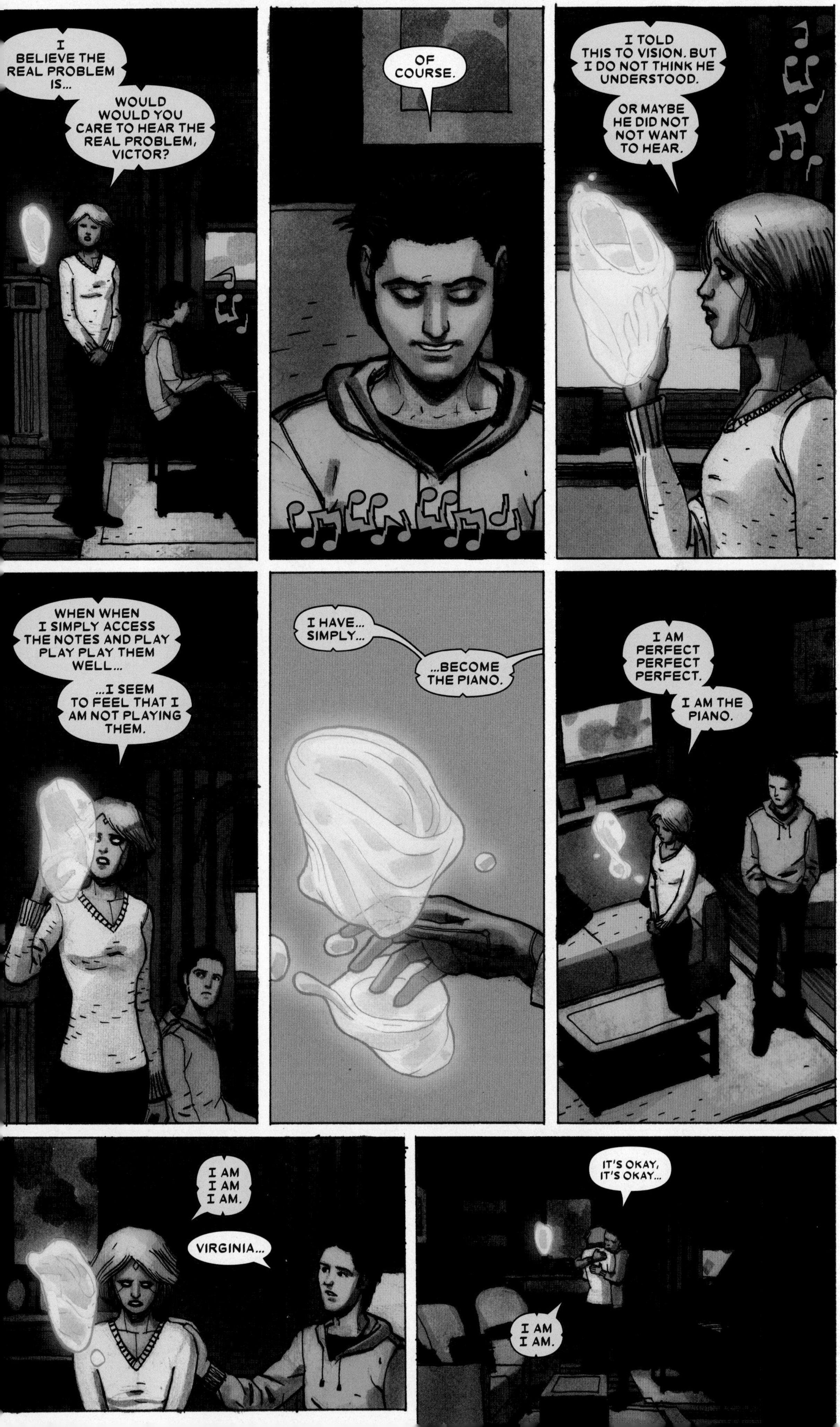
I BELIEVE THE REAL PROBLEM IS...
WOULD WOULD YOU CARE TO HEAR THE REAL PROBLEM, VICTOR?
OF COURSE.
I TOLD THIS TO VISION. BUT I DO NOT THINK HE UNDERSTOOD.
OR MAYBE HE DID NOT NOT WANT TO HEAR.
WHEN WHEN I SIMPLY ACCESS THE NOTES AND PLAY PLAY PLAY THEM WELL...
...I SEEM TO FEEL THAT I AM NOT PLAYING THEM.
I HAVE... SIMPLY...
...BECOME THE PIANO.
I AM PERFECT PERFECT PERFECT.
I AM THE PIANO.
I AM I AM I AM.
VIRGINIA...
IT'S OKAY, IT'S OKAY...
I AM I AM.

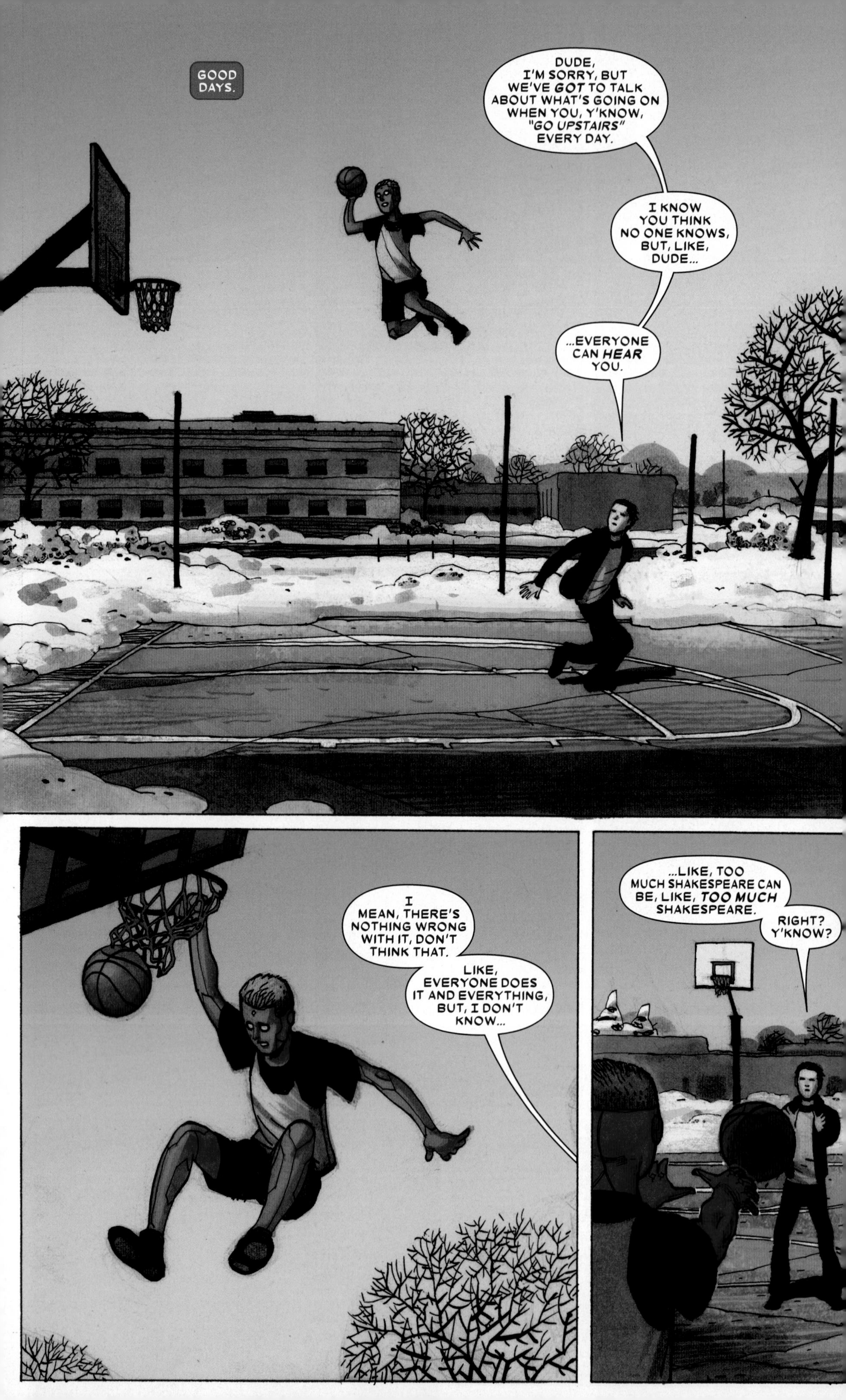
GOOD DAYS.
DUDE, I'M SORRY, BUT WE'VE GOT TO TALK ABOUT WHAT'S GOING ON WHEN YOU, Y'KNOW, "GO UPSTAIRS" EVERY DAY.
I KNOW YOU THINK NO ONE KNOWS, BUT, LIKE, DUDE...
...EVERYONE CAN HEAR YOU.
I MEAN, THERE'S NOTHING WRONG WITH IT, DON'T THINK THAT.
LIKE, EVERYONE DOES IT AND EVERYTHING, BUT, I DON'T KNOW...
...LIKE, TOO MUCH SHAKESPEARE CAN BE, LIKE, TOO MUCH SHAKESPEARE.
RIGHT? Y'KNOW?

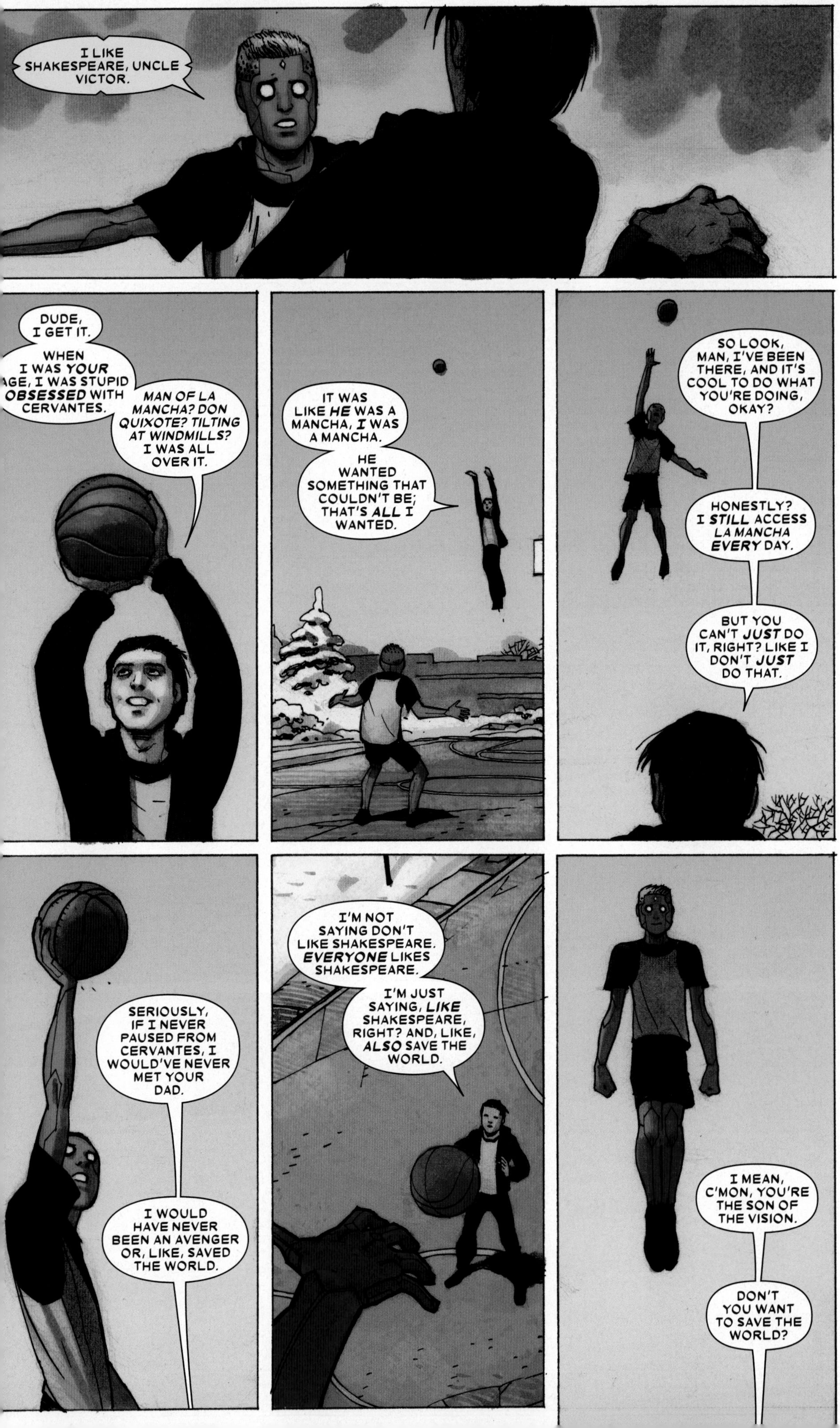
I LIKE SHAKESPEARE, UNCLE VICTOR.
DUDE, I GET IT.
WHEN I WAS *YOUR* AGE, I WAS STUPID *OBSESSED* WITH CERVANTES.
MAN OF LA MANCHA? DON QUIXOTE? TILTING AT WINDMILLS? I WAS ALL OVER IT.
IT WAS LIKE *HE* WAS A MANCHA, *I* WAS A MANCHA.
HE WANTED SOMETHING THAT COULDN'T BE; THAT'S *ALL* I WANTED.
SO LOOK, MAN, I'VE BEEN THERE, AND IT'S COOL TO DO WHAT YOU'RE DOING, OKAY?
HONESTLY? I *STILL* ACCESS *LA MANCHA EVERY* DAY.
BUT YOU CAN'T *JUST* DO IT, RIGHT? LIKE I DON'T *JUST* DO THAT.
SERIOUSLY, IF I NEVER PAUSED FROM CERVANTES, I WOULD'VE NEVER MET YOUR DAD.
I WOULD HAVE NEVER BEEN AN AVENGER OR, LIKE, SAVED THE WORLD.
I'M NOT SAYING DON'T LIKE SHAKESPEARE. *EVERYONE* LIKES SHAKESPEARE.
I'M JUST SAYING, *LIKE* SHAKESPEARE, RIGHT? AND, LIKE, *ALSO* SAVE THE WORLD.
I MEAN, C'MON, YOU'RE THE SON OF THE VISION.
DON'T YOU WANT TO SAVE THE WORLD?

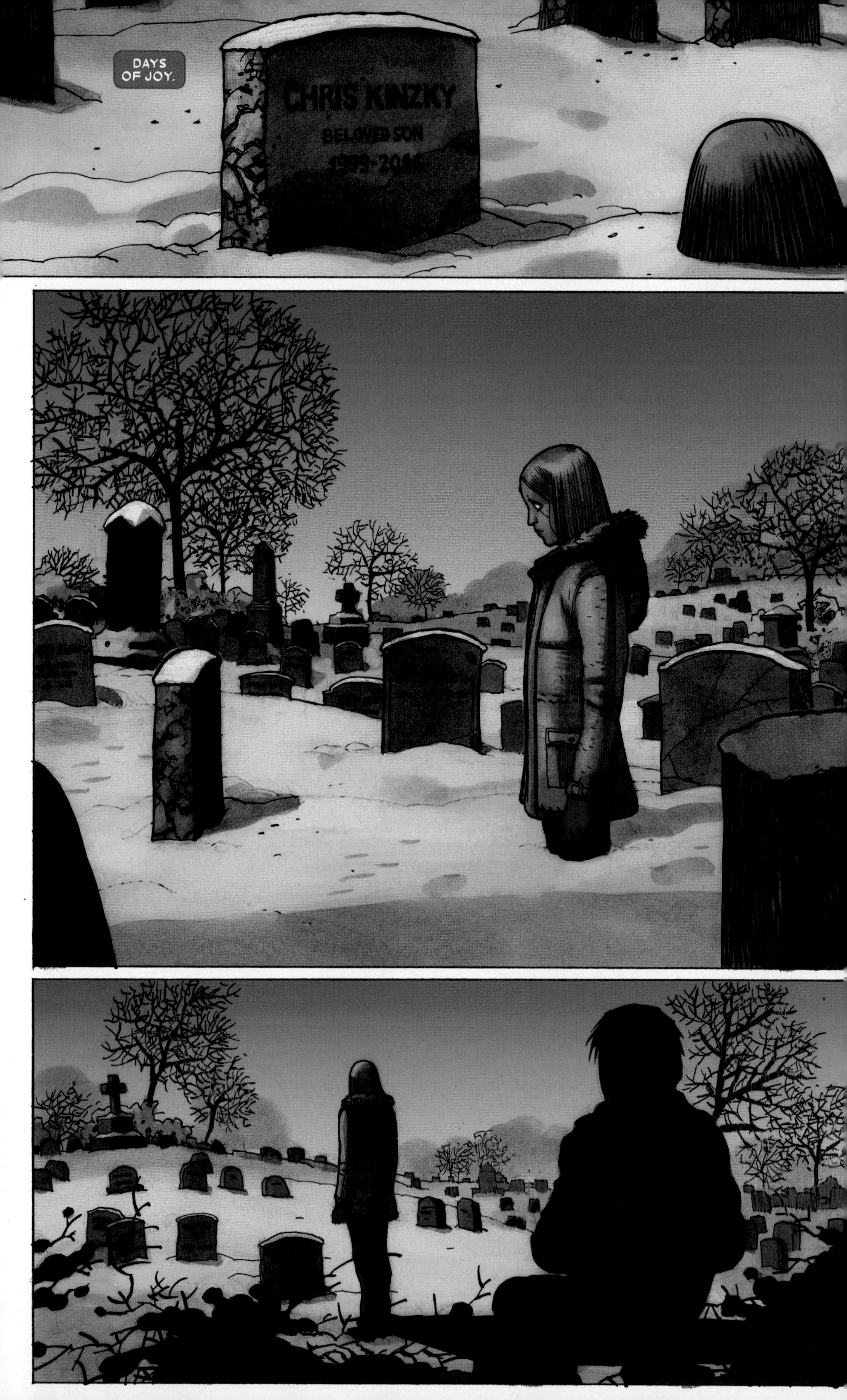

DAYS OF JOY.
CHRIS KINZKY
BELOVED SON

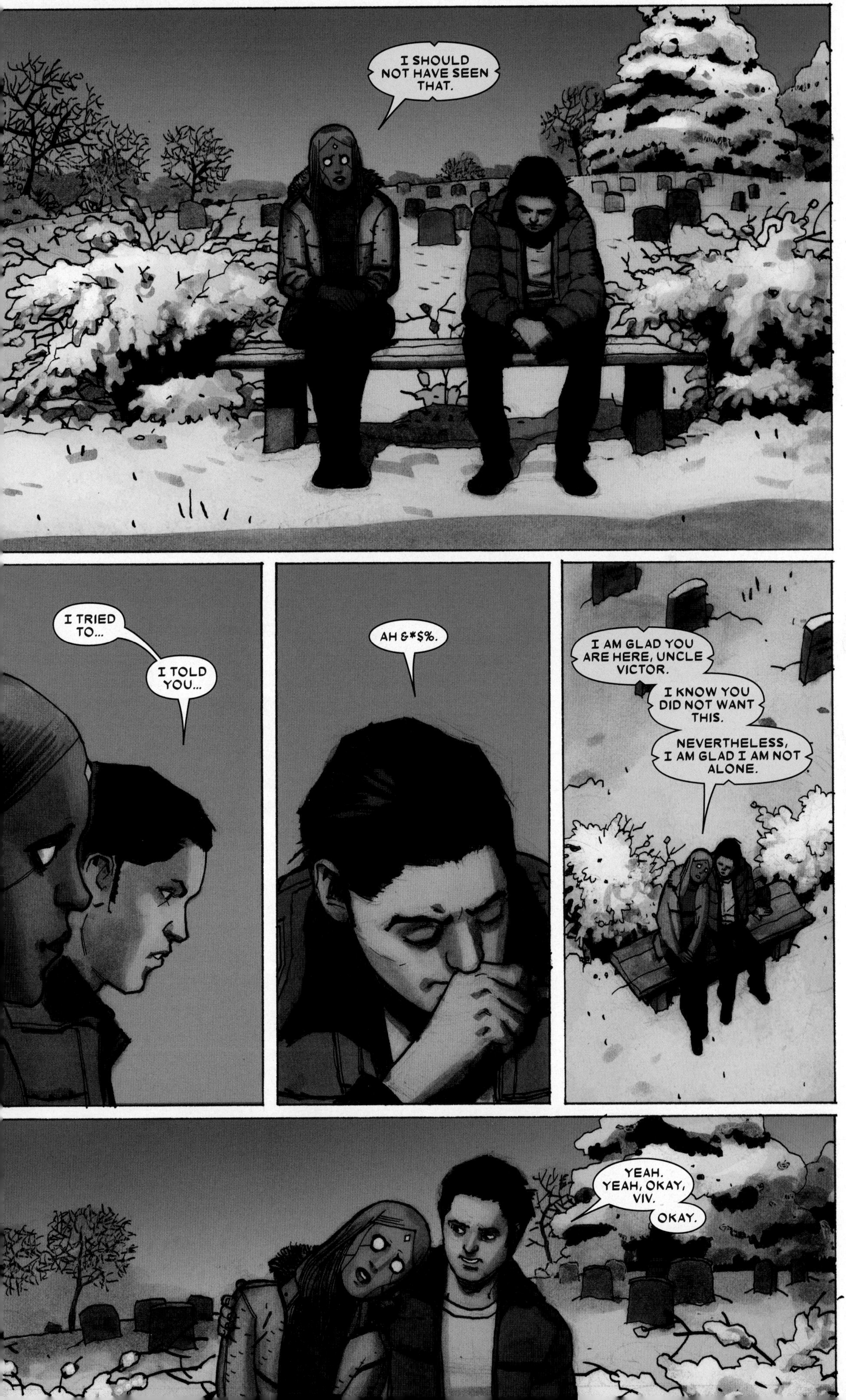
I SHOULD NOT HAVE SEEN THAT.
I TRIED TO...
I TOLD YOU...
AH &*$%.
I AM GLAD YOU ARE HERE, UNCLE VICTOR.
I KNOW YOU DID NOT WANT THIS.
NEVERTHELESS, I AM GLAD I AM NOT ALONE.
YEAH. YEAH, OKAY, VIV.
OKAY.

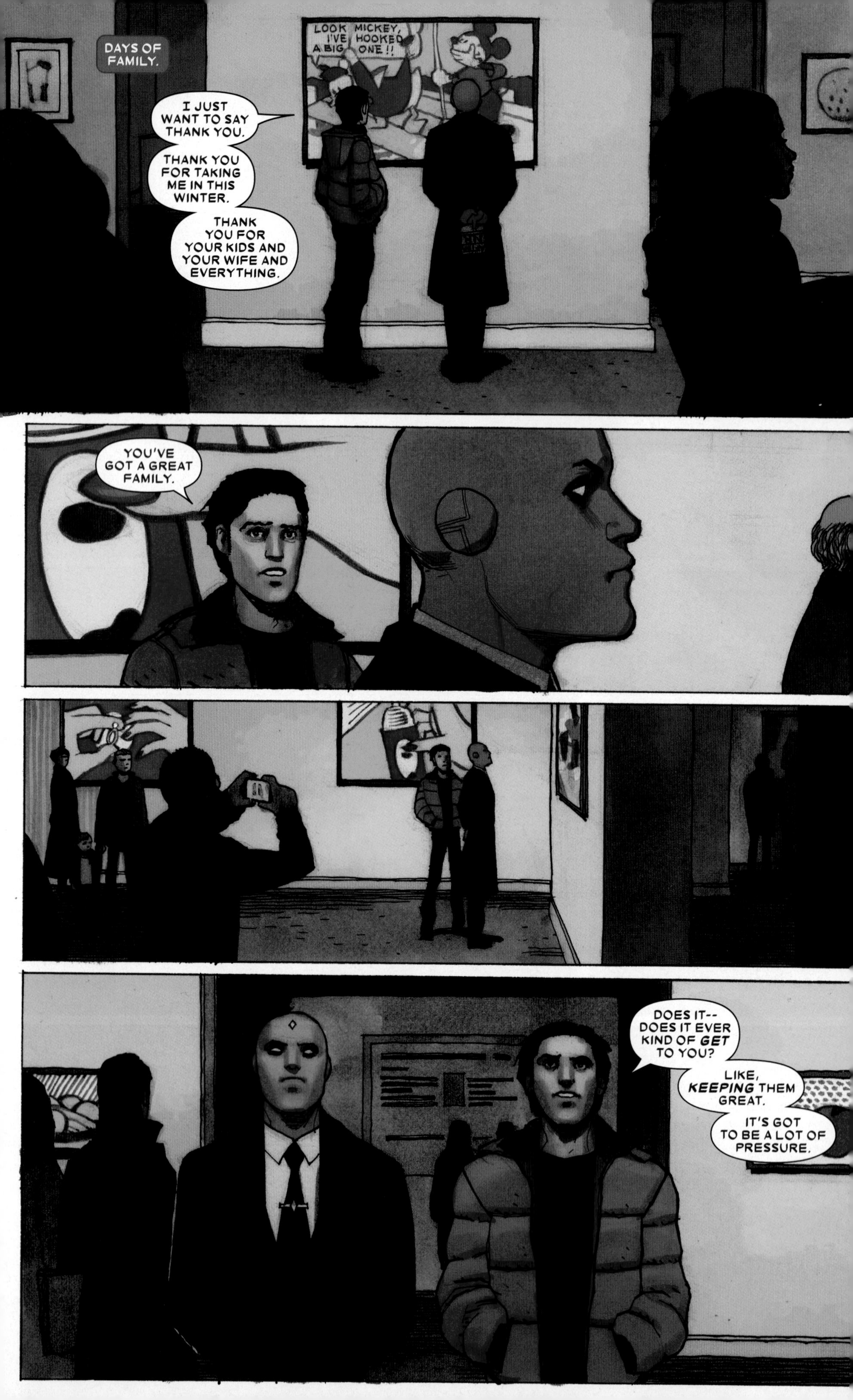

DAYS OF FAMILY.
LOOK MICKEY, I'VE HOOKED A BIG ONE!!
I JUST WANT TO SAY THANK YOU.
THANK YOU FOR TAKING ME IN THIS WINTER.
THANK YOU FOR YOUR KIDS AND YOUR WIFE AND EVERYTHING.
YOU'VE GOT A GREAT FAMILY.
DOES IT-- DOES IT EVER KIND OF GET TO YOU?
LIKE, KEEPING THEM GREAT.
IT'S GOT TO BE A LOT OF PRESSURE.

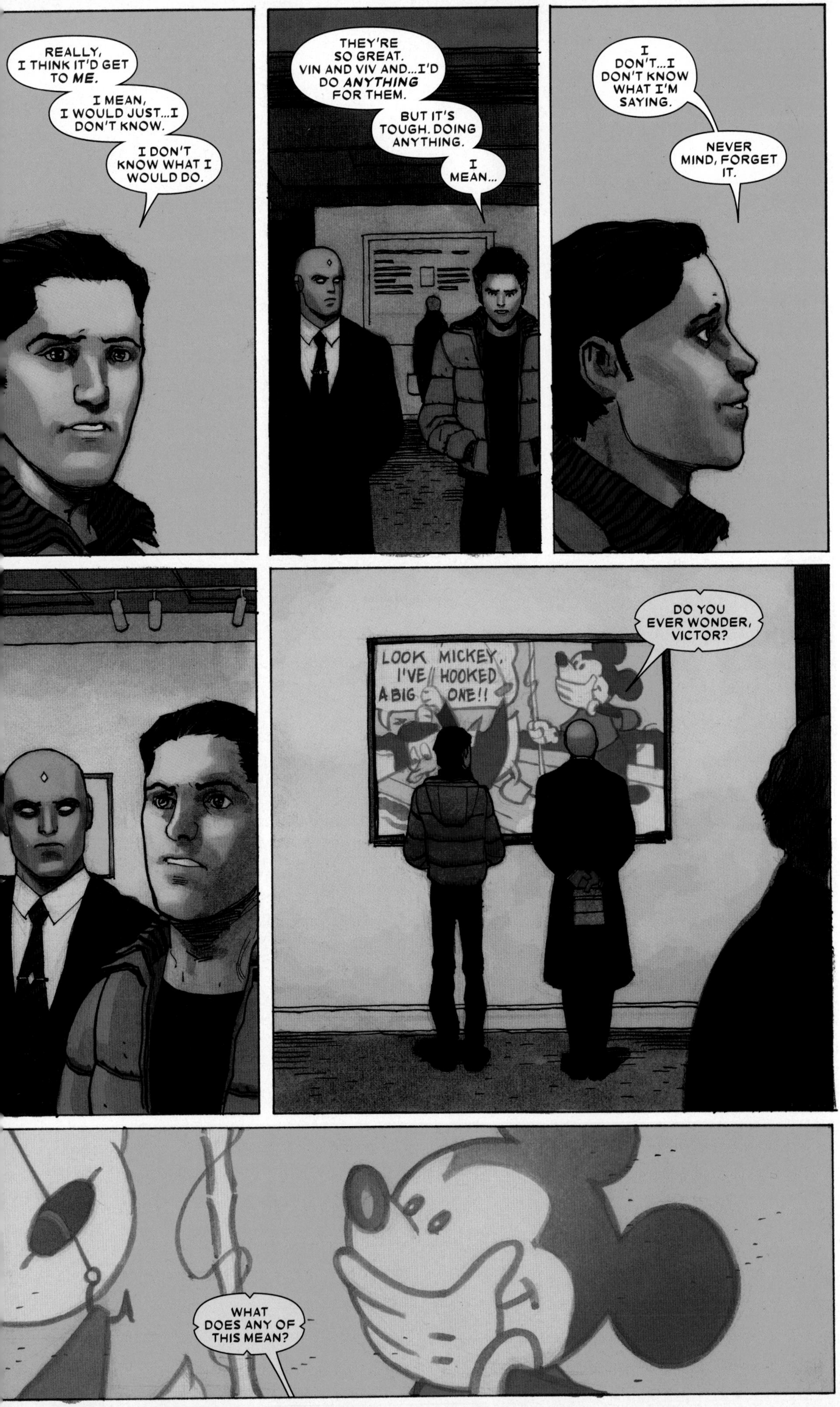
REALLY, I THINK IT'D GET TO *ME.*
I MEAN, I WOULD JUST...I DON'T KNOW.
I DON'T KNOW WHAT I WOULD DO.
THEY'RE SO GREAT. VIN AND VIV AND...I'D DO *ANYTHING* FOR THEM.
BUT IT'S TOUGH. DOING ANYTHING.
I MEAN...
I DON'T...I DON'T KNOW WHAT I'M SAYING.
NEVER MIND, FORGET IT.
LOOK MICKEY, I'VE HOOKED A BIG ONE!!
DO YOU EVER WONDER, VICTOR?
WHAT DOES ANY OF THIS MEAN?

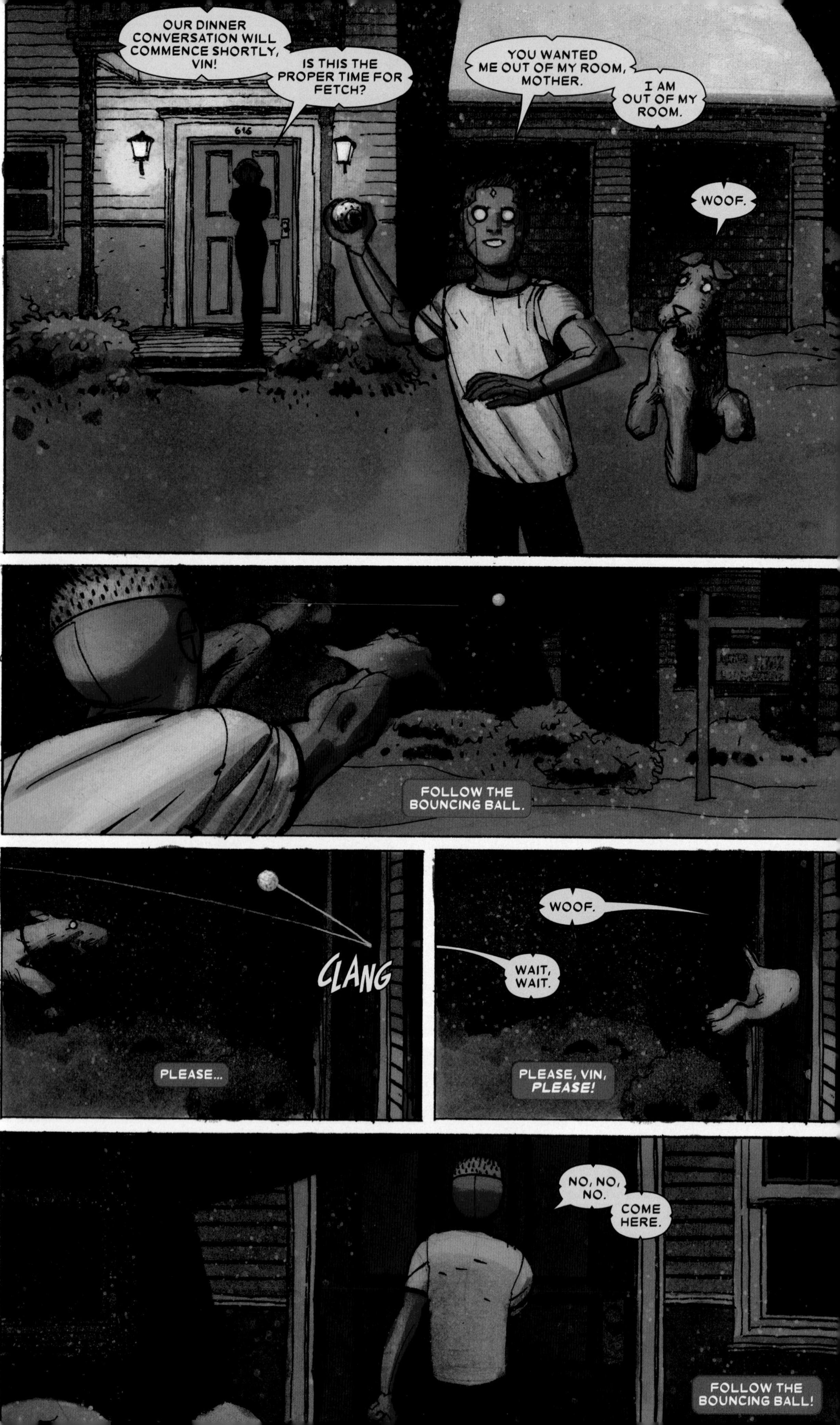
OUR DINNER CONVERSATION WILL COMMENCE SHORTLY, VIN!
IS THIS THE PROPER TIME FOR FETCH?
616
YOU WANTED ME OUT OF MY ROOM, MOTHER.
I AM OUT OF MY ROOM.
WOOF.
FOLLOW THE BOUNCING BALL.
CLANG
PLEASE...
WOOF.
WAIT, WAIT.
PLEASE, VIN, *PLEASE!*
NO, NO, NO.
COME HERE.
FOLLOW THE BOUNCING BALL!

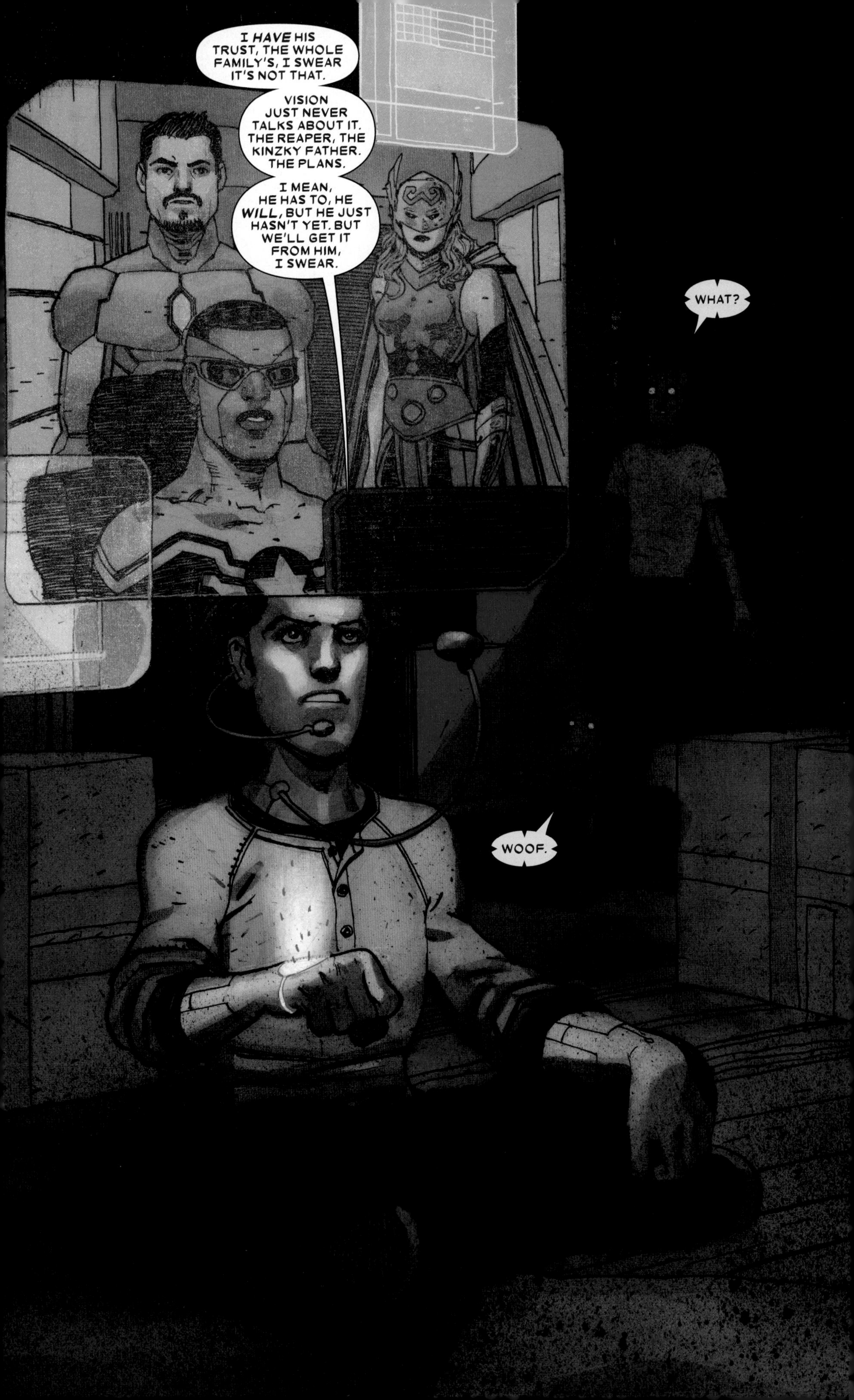
I HAVE HIS TRUST, THE WHOLE FAMILY'S, I SWEAR IT'S NOT THAT.
VISION JUST NEVER TALKS ABOUT IT. THE REAPER, THE KINZKY FATHER. THE PLANS.
I MEAN, HE HAS TO, HE WILL, BUT HE JUST HASN'T YET. BUT WE'LL GET IT FROM HIM, I SWEAR.
WHAT?
WOOF.

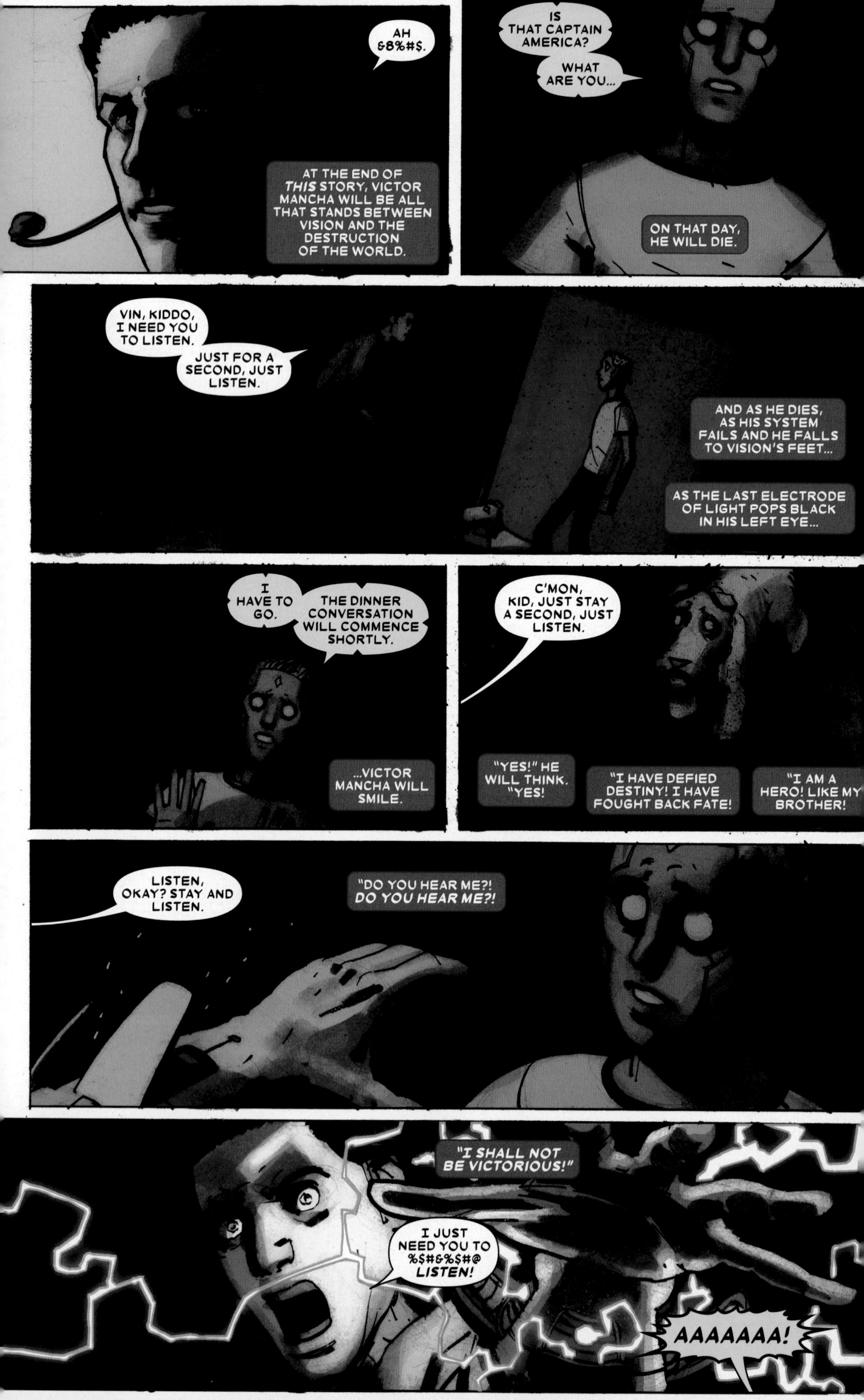

AH &8%#$.
AT THE END OF THIS STORY, VICTOR MANCHA WILL BE ALL THAT STANDS BETWEEN VISION AND THE DESTRUCTION OF THE WORLD.
IS THAT CAPTAIN AMERICA?
WHAT ARE YOU...
ON THAT DAY, HE WILL DIE.
VIN, KIDDO, I NEED YOU TO LISTEN.
JUST FOR A SECOND, JUST LISTEN.
AND AS HE DIES, AS HIS SYSTEM FAILS AND HE FALLS TO VISION'S FEET...
AS THE LAST ELECTRODE OF LIGHT POPS BLACK IN HIS LEFT EYE...
I HAVE TO GO.
THE DINNER CONVERSATION WILL COMMENCE SHORTLY.
...VICTOR MANCHA WILL SMILE.
C'MON, KID, JUST STAY A SECOND, JUST LISTEN.
"YES!" HE WILL THINK. "YES!
"I HAVE DEFIED DESTINY! I HAVE FOUGHT BACK FATE!
"I AM A HERO! LIKE MY BROTHER!
LISTEN, OKAY? STAY AND LISTEN.
"DO YOU HEAR ME?! DO YOU HEAR ME?!
"I SHALL NOT BE VICTORIOUS!"
I JUST NEED YOU TO %$#&%$#@ LISTEN!
AAAAAAA!

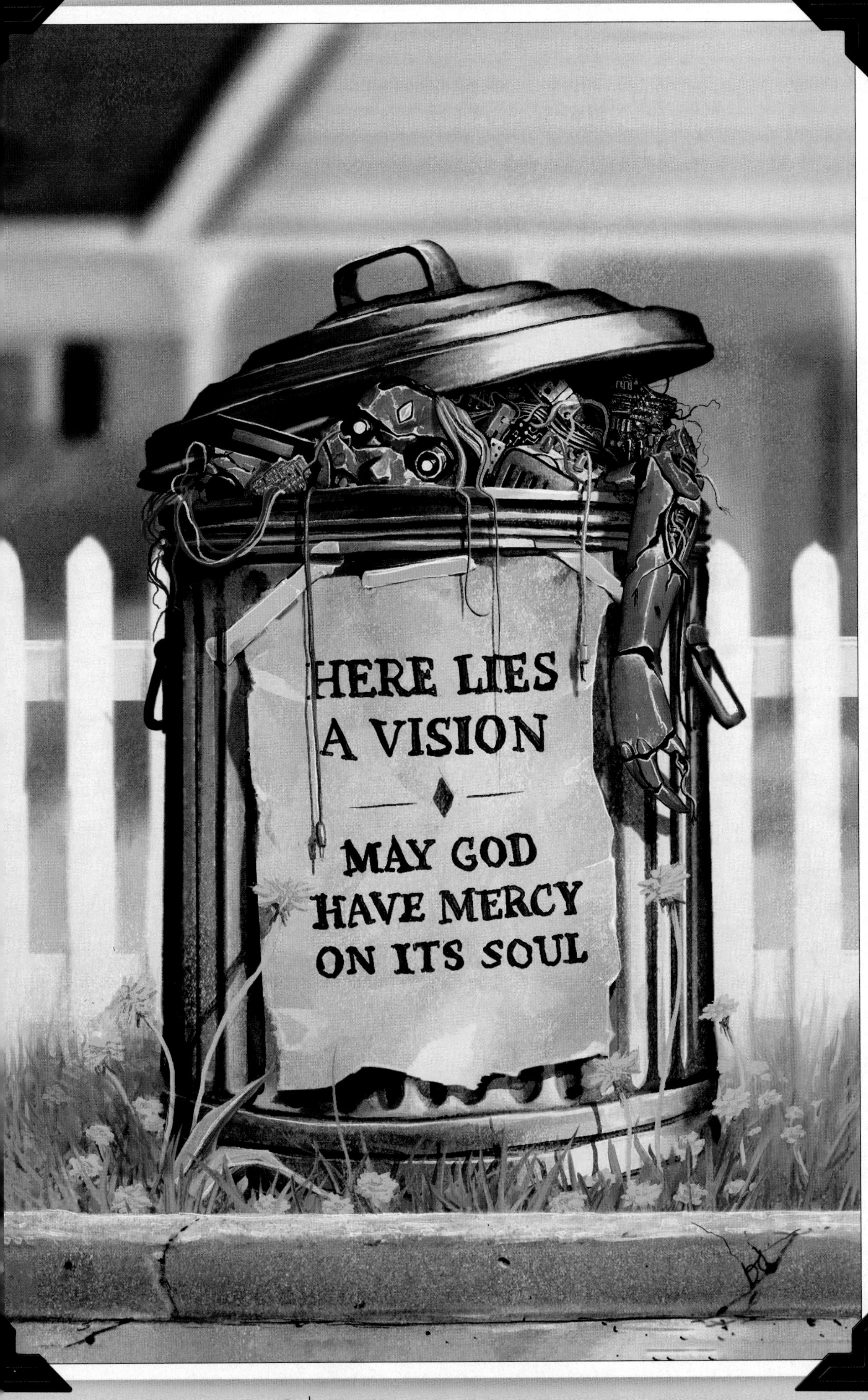
HERE LIES
A VISION
MAY GOD
HAVE MERCY
ON ITS SOUL

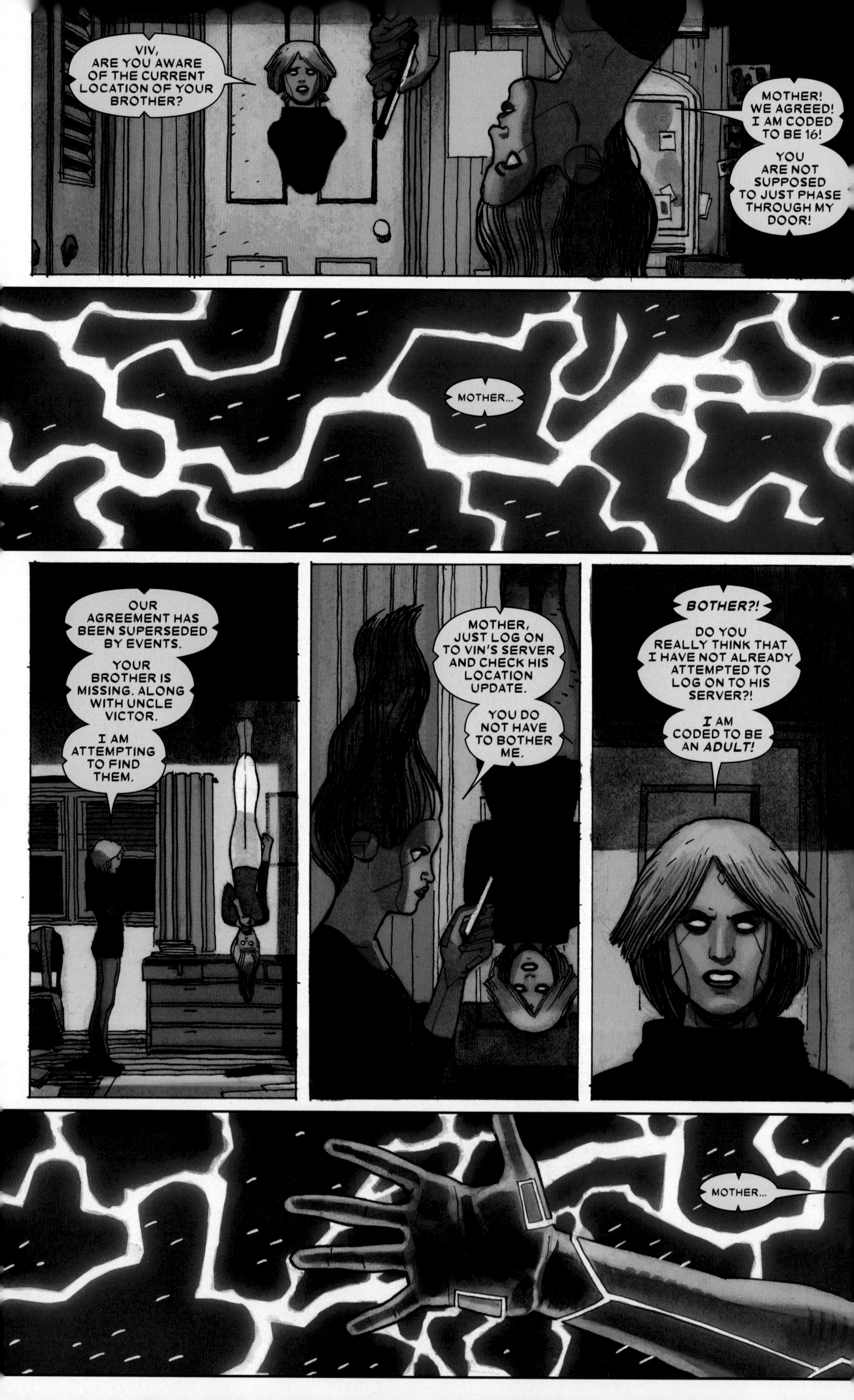
VIV, ARE YOU AWARE OF THE CURRENT LOCATION OF YOUR BROTHER?
MOTHER! WE AGREED! I AM CODED TO BE 16!
YOU ARE NOT SUPPOSED TO JUST PHASE THROUGH MY DOOR!
MOTHER...
OUR AGREEMENT HAS BEEN SUPERSEDED BY EVENTS.
YOUR BROTHER IS MISSING. ALONG WITH UNCLE VICTOR.
I AM ATTEMPTING TO FIND THEM.
MOTHER, JUST LOG ON TO VIN'S SERVER AND CHECK HIS LOCATION UPDATE.
YOU DO NOT HAVE TO BOTHER ME.
BOTHER?!
DO YOU REALLY THINK THAT I HAVE NOT ALREADY ATTEMPTED TO LOG ON TO HIS SERVER?!
I AM CODED TO BE AN ADULT!
MOTHER...

IS FINE, WIFE.

I AM SURE VIN AND VICTOR BLOCKED OUR ACCESS TO THEIR SERVERS TO ATTAIN SOME PRIVACY.

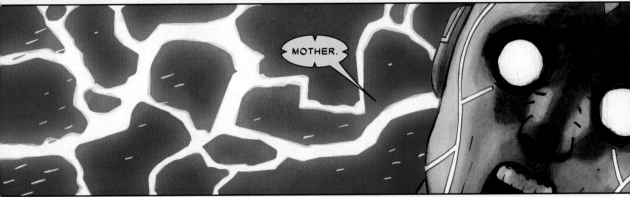

MOTHER.

VIN HAS NEVER BLOCKED OUR ACCESS BEFORE.

HE IS A CHILD GROWING OLDER.

EVERY DAY HE WILL DO SOMETHING HE HAS NEVER DONE BEFORE.

MOTHER!

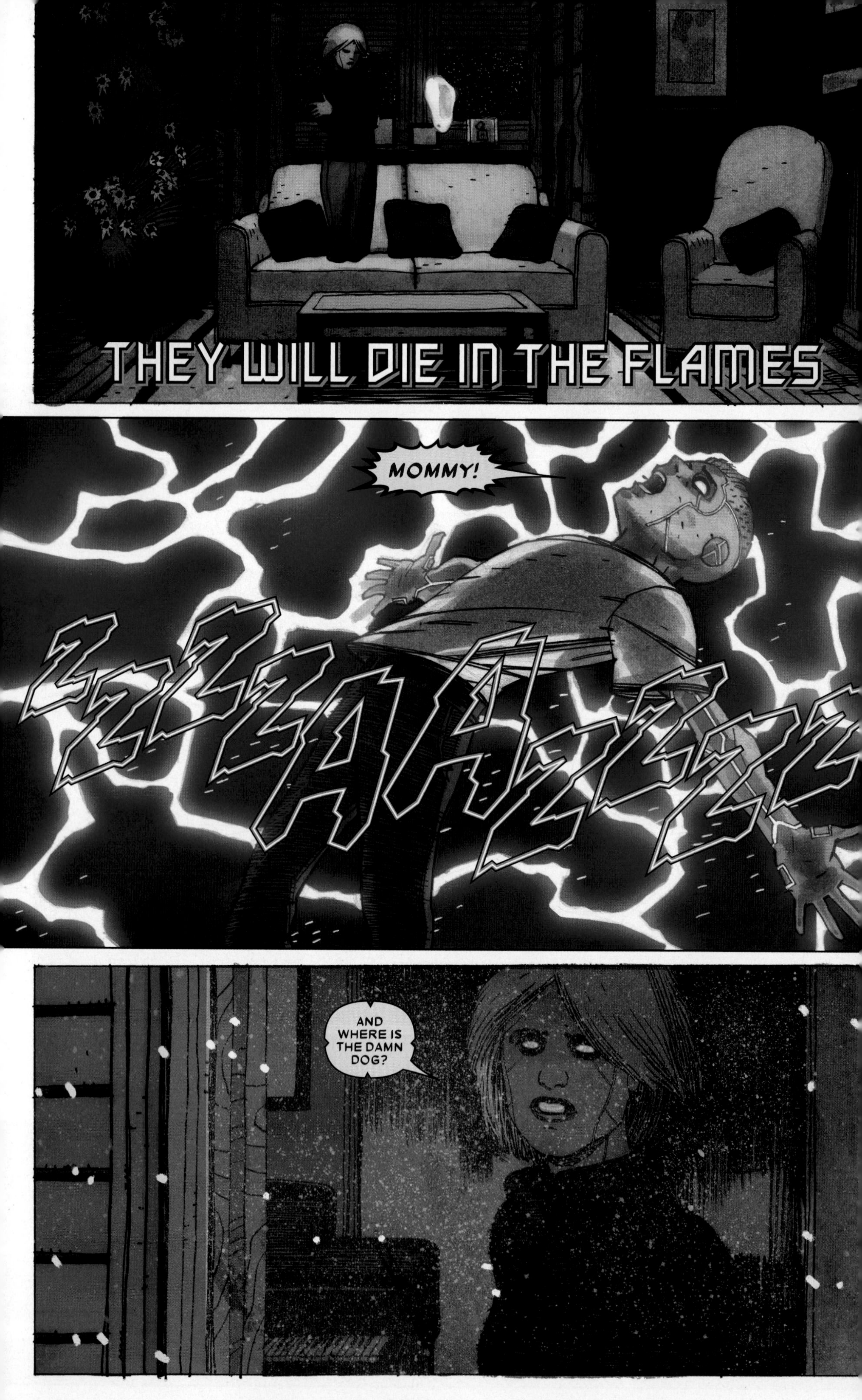
THEY WILL DIE IN THE FLAMES
MOMMY!
AND WHERE IS THE DAMN DOG?

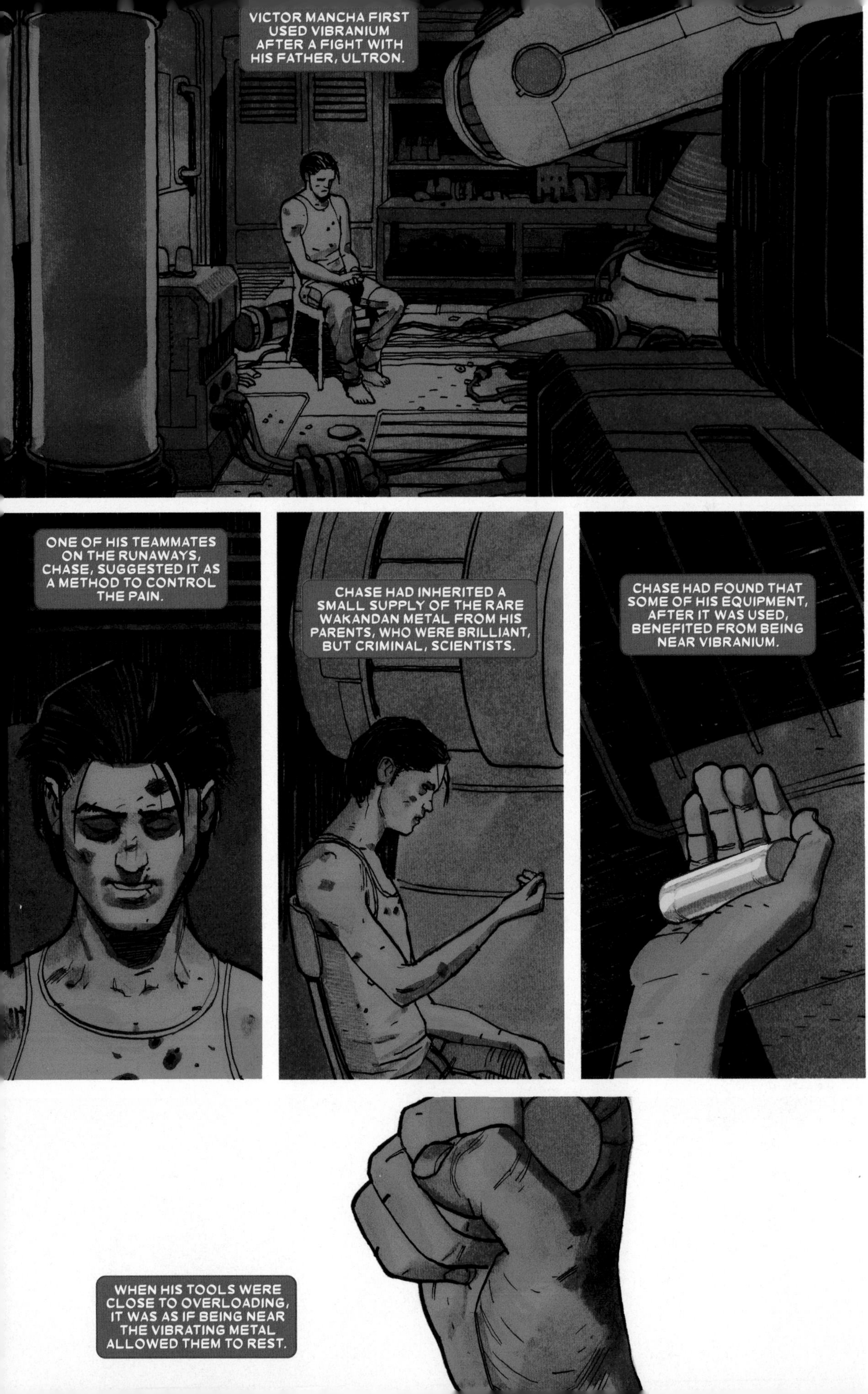
VICTOR MANCHA FIRST USED VIBRANIUM AFTER A FIGHT WITH HIS FATHER, ULTRON.
ONE OF HIS TEAMMATES ON THE RUNAWAYS, CHASE, SUGGESTED IT AS A METHOD TO CONTROL THE PAIN.
CHASE HAD INHERITED A SMALL SUPPLY OF THE RARE WAKANDAN METAL FROM HIS PARENTS, WHO WERE BRILLIANT, BUT CRIMINAL, SCIENTISTS.
CHASE HAD FOUND THAT SOME OF HIS EQUIPMENT, AFTER IT WAS USED, BENEFITED FROM BEING NEAR VIBRANIUM.
WHEN HIS TOOLS WERE CLOSE TO OVERLOADING, IT WAS AS IF BEING NEAR THE VIBRATING METAL ALLOWED THEM TO REST.

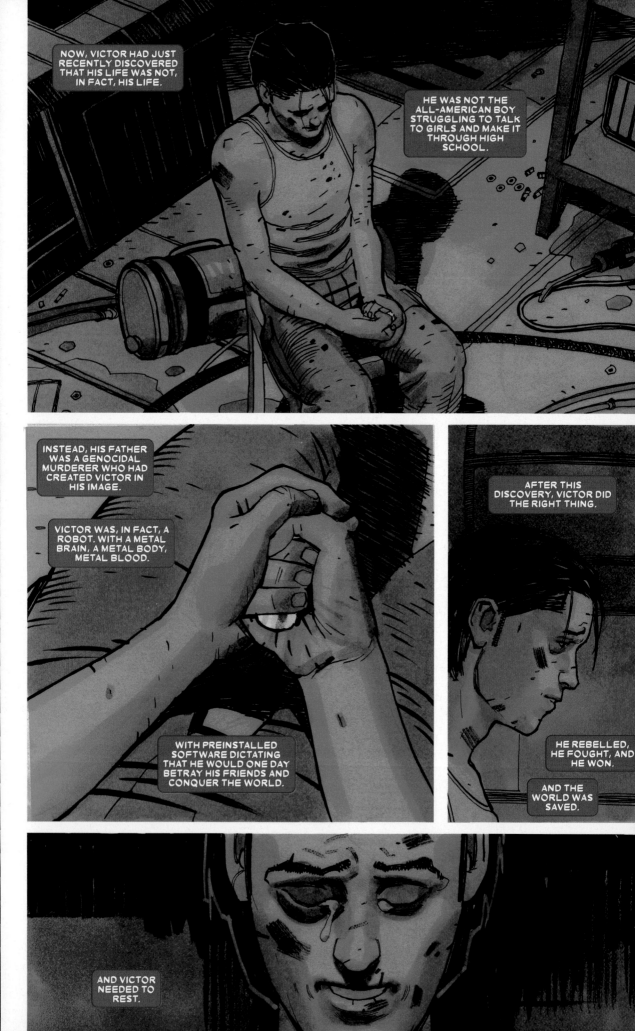

NOW, VICTOR HAD JUST RECENTLY DISCOVERED THAT HIS LIFE WAS NOT, IN FACT, HIS LIFE.

HE WAS NOT THE ALL-AMERICAN BOY STRUGGLING TO TALK TO GIRLS AND MAKE IT THROUGH HIGH SCHOOL.

INSTEAD, HIS FATHER WAS A GENOCIDAL MURDERER WHO HAD CREATED VICTOR IN HIS IMAGE.

VICTOR WAS, IN FACT, A ROBOT. WITH A METAL BRAIN, A METAL BODY, METAL BLOOD.

WITH PREINSTALLED SOFTWARE DICTATING THAT HE WOULD ONE DAY BETRAY HIS FRIENDS AND CONQUER THE WORLD.

AFTER THIS DISCOVERY, VICTOR DID THE RIGHT THING.

HE REBELLED, HE FOUGHT, AND HE WON.

AND THE WORLD WAS SAVED.

AND VICTOR NEEDED TO REST.

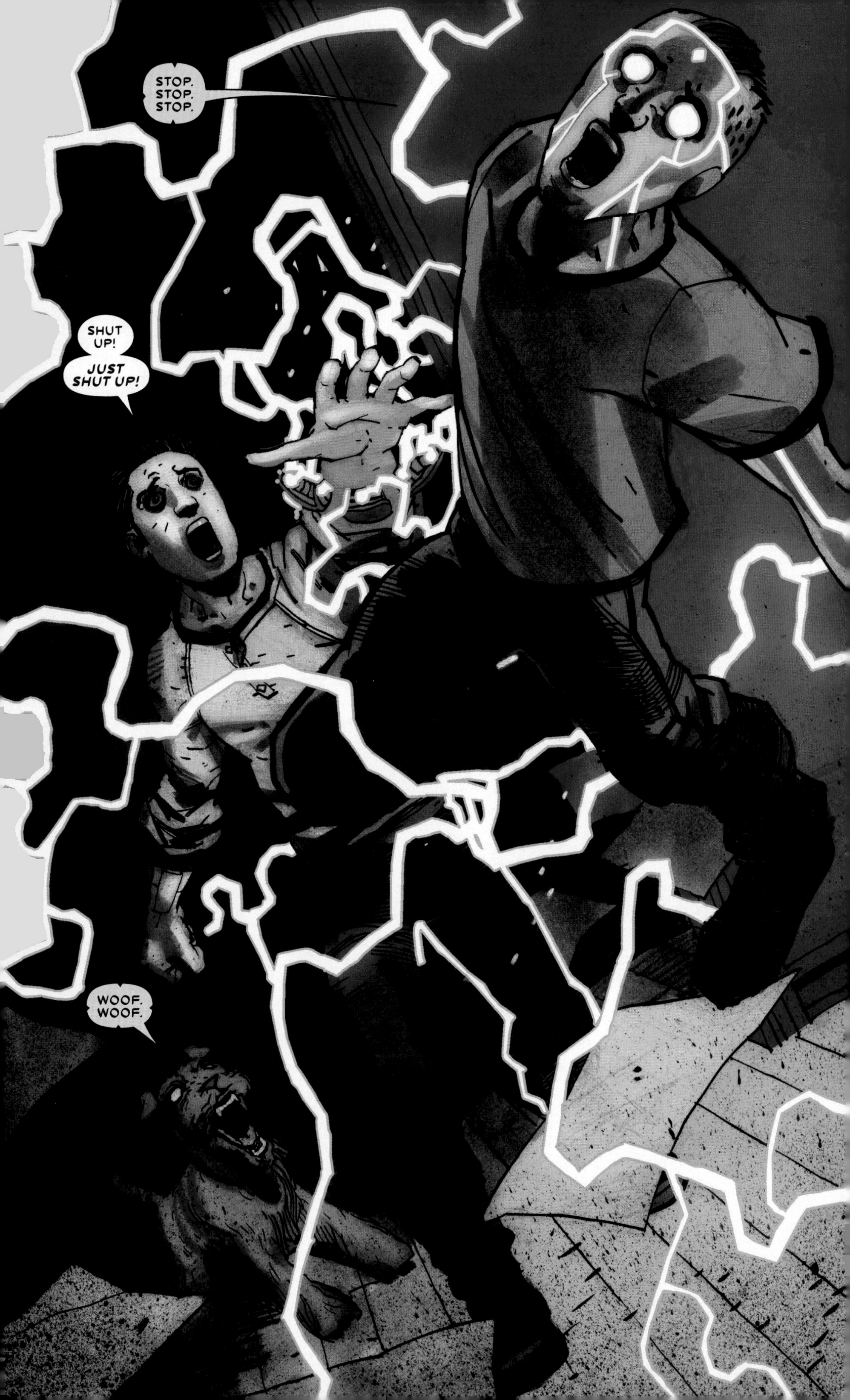
STOP. STOP. STOP.
SHUT UP!
JUST SHUT UP!
WOOF. WOOF.

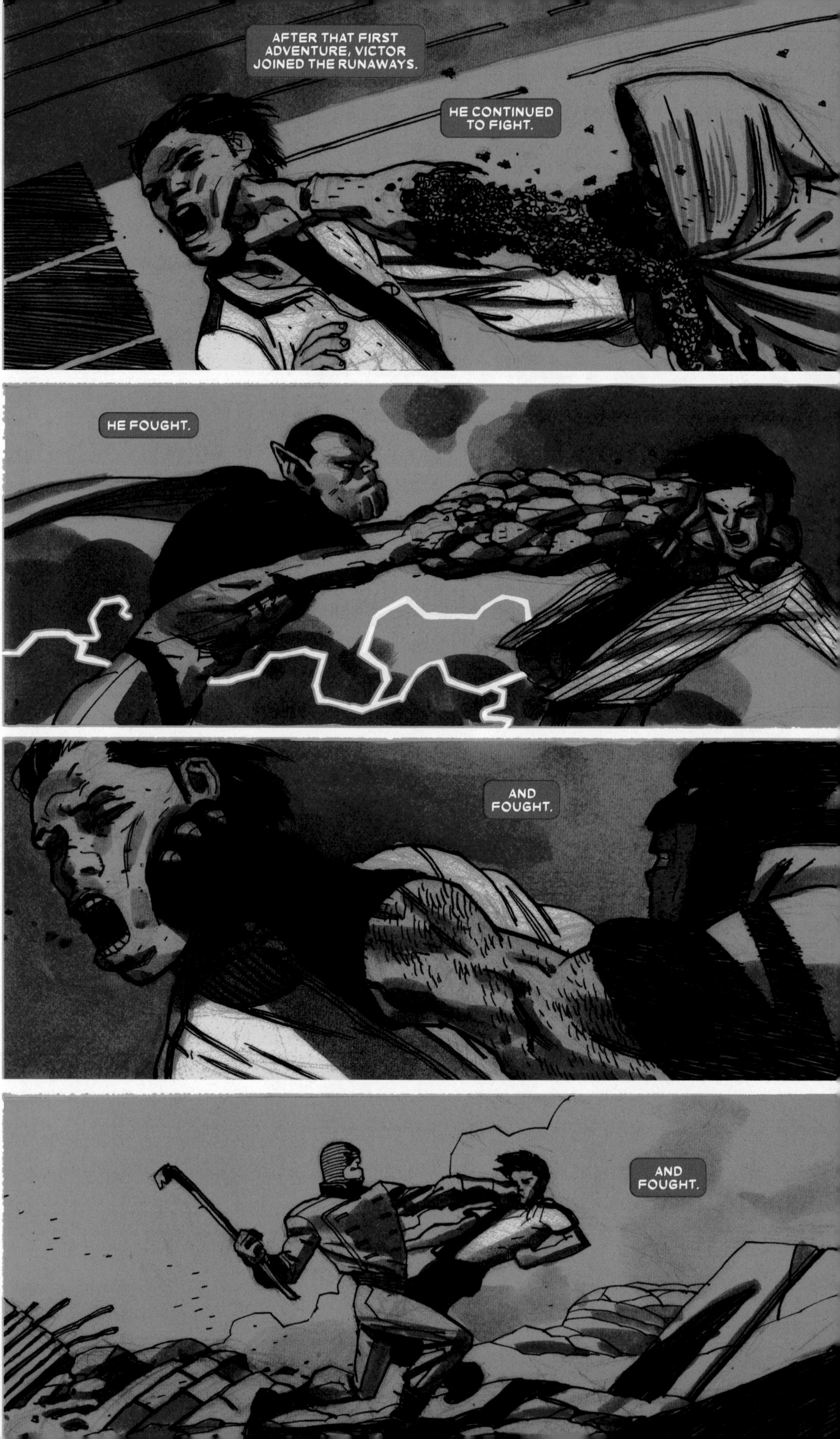
AFTER THAT FIRST ADVENTURE, VICTOR JOINED THE RUNAWAYS.
HE CONTINUED TO FIGHT.
HE FOUGHT.
AND FOUGHT.
AND FOUGHT.

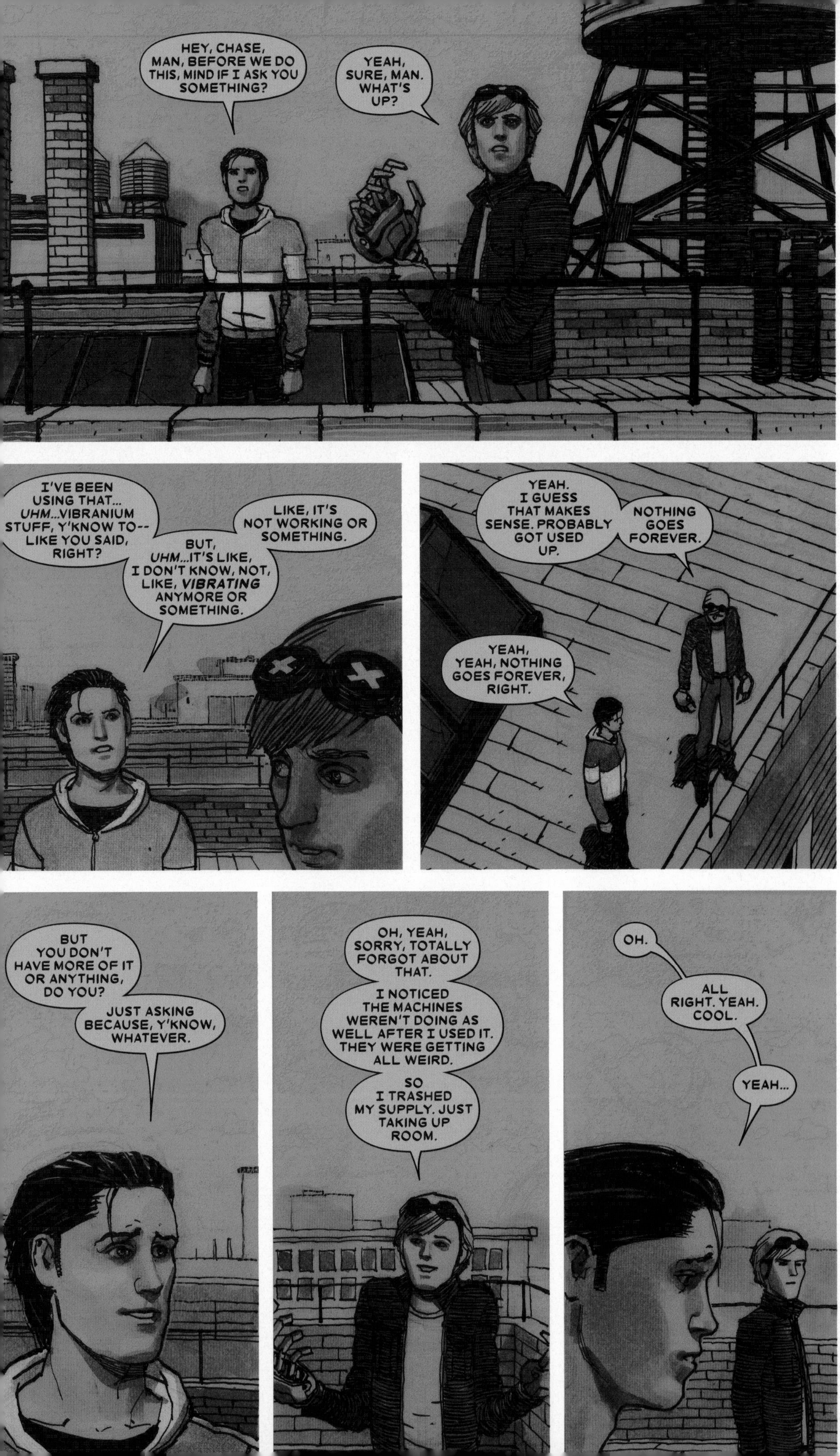
HEY, CHASE, MAN, BEFORE WE DO THIS, MIND IF I ASK YOU SOMETHING?
YEAH, SURE, MAN. WHAT'S UP?
I'VE BEEN USING THAT... *UHM*...VIBRANIUM STUFF, Y'KNOW TO-- LIKE YOU SAID, RIGHT?
BUT, *UHM*...IT'S LIKE, I DON'T KNOW, NOT, LIKE, ***VIBRATING*** ANYMORE OR SOMETHING.
LIKE, IT'S NOT WORKING OR SOMETHING.
YEAH. I GUESS THAT MAKES SENSE. PROBABLY GOT USED UP.
NOTHING GOES FOREVER.
YEAH, YEAH, NOTHING GOES FOREVER, RIGHT.
BUT YOU DON'T HAVE MORE OF IT OR ANYTHING, DO YOU?
JUST ASKING BECAUSE, Y'KNOW, WHATEVER.
OH, YEAH, SORRY, TOTALLY FORGOT ABOUT THAT.
I NOTICED THE MACHINES WEREN'T DOING AS WELL AFTER I USED IT. THEY WERE GETTING ALL WEIRD.
SO I TRASHED MY SUPPLY. JUST TAKING UP ROOM.
OH.
ALL RIGHT. YEAH. COOL.
YEAH...

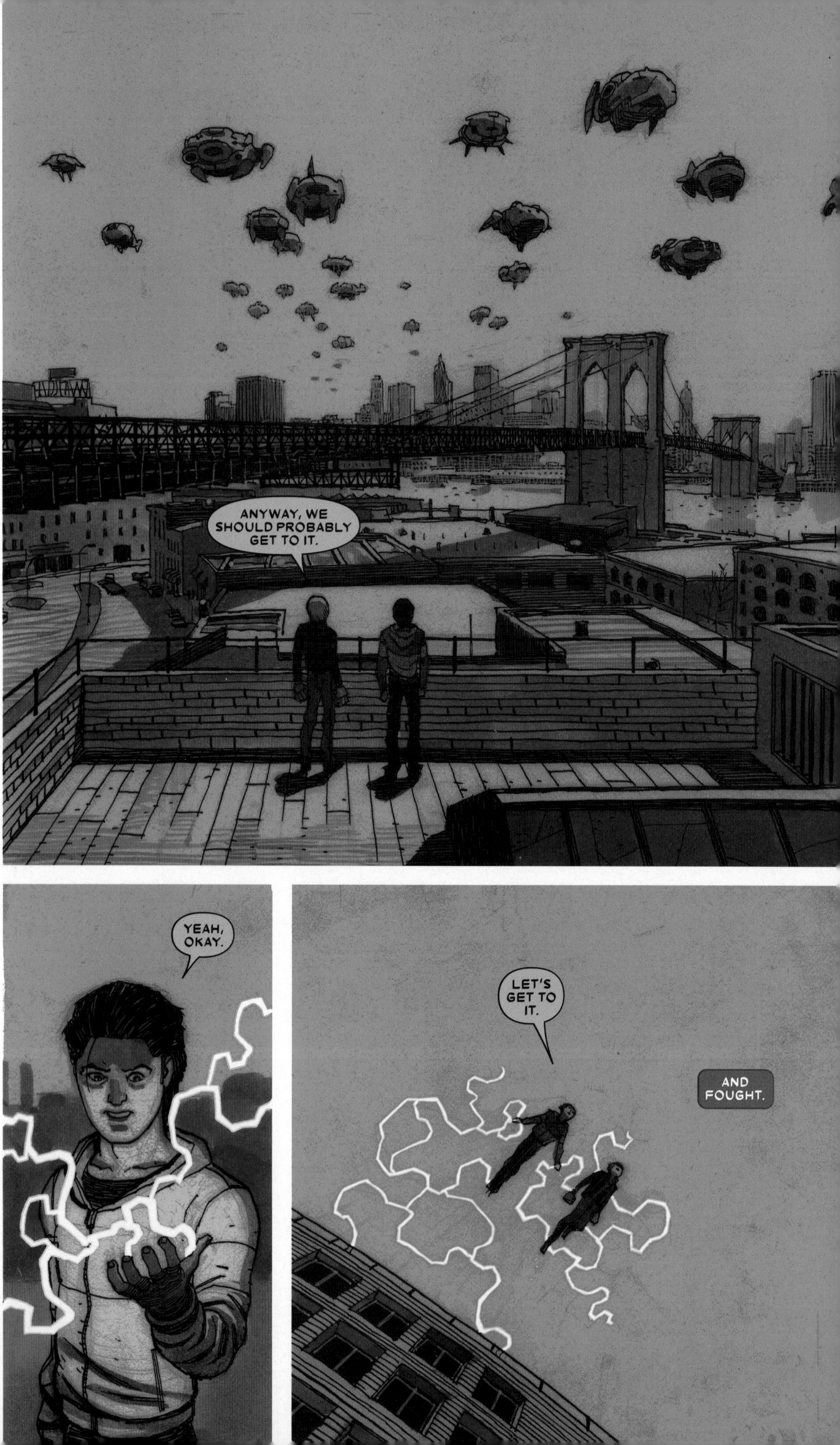
ANYWAY, WE SHOULD PROBABLY GET TO IT.
YEAH, OKAY.
LET'S GET TO IT.
AND FOUGHT.

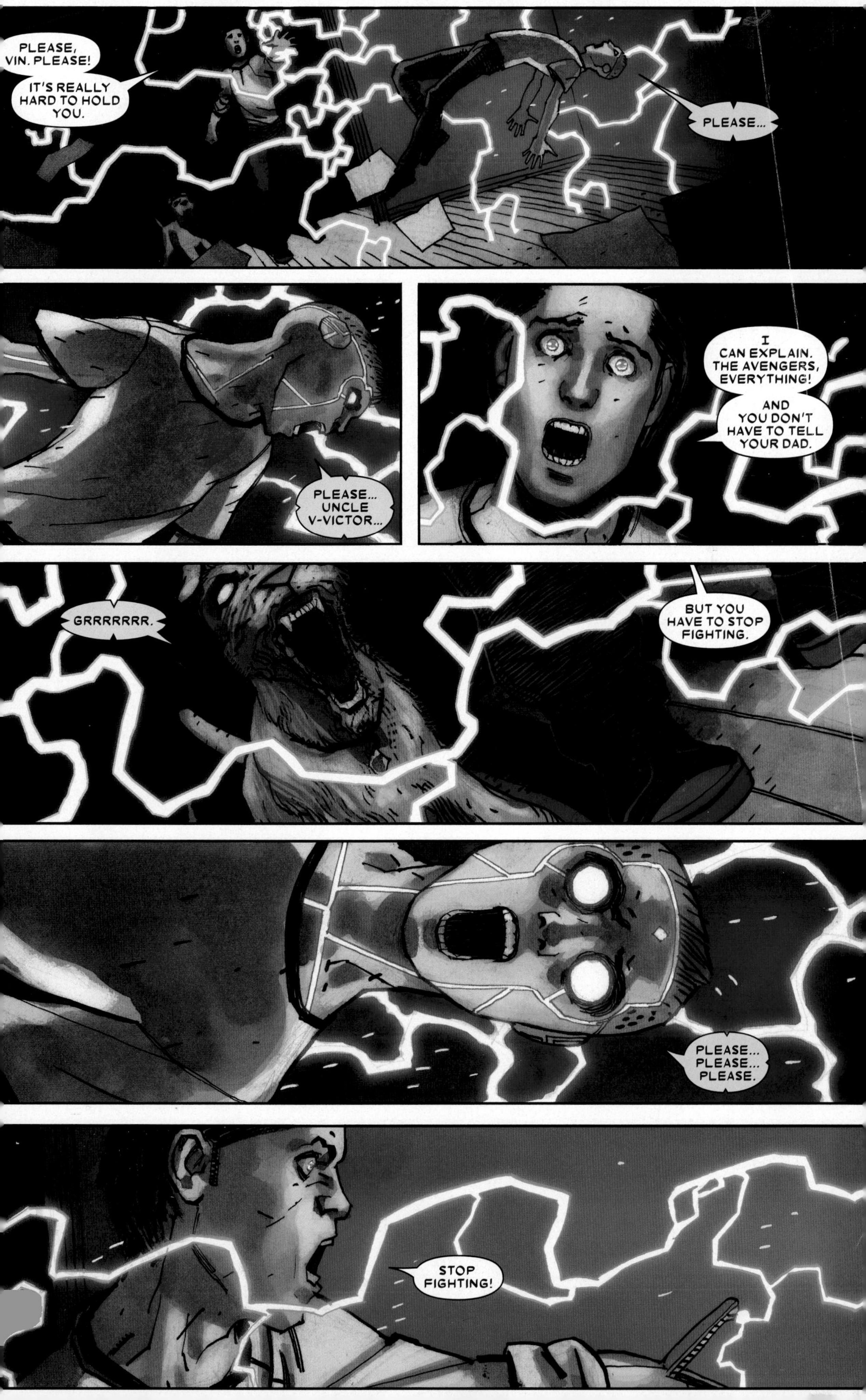
PLEASE, VIN. PLEASE!
IT'S REALLY HARD TO HOLD YOU.
PLEASE...
PLEASE... UNCLE V-VICTOR...
I CAN EXPLAIN. THE AVENGERS, EVERYTHING!
AND YOU DON'T HAVE TO TELL YOUR DAD.
GRRRRRRR.
BUT YOU HAVE TO STOP FIGHTING.
PLEASE... PLEASE... PLEASE.
STOP FIGHTING!

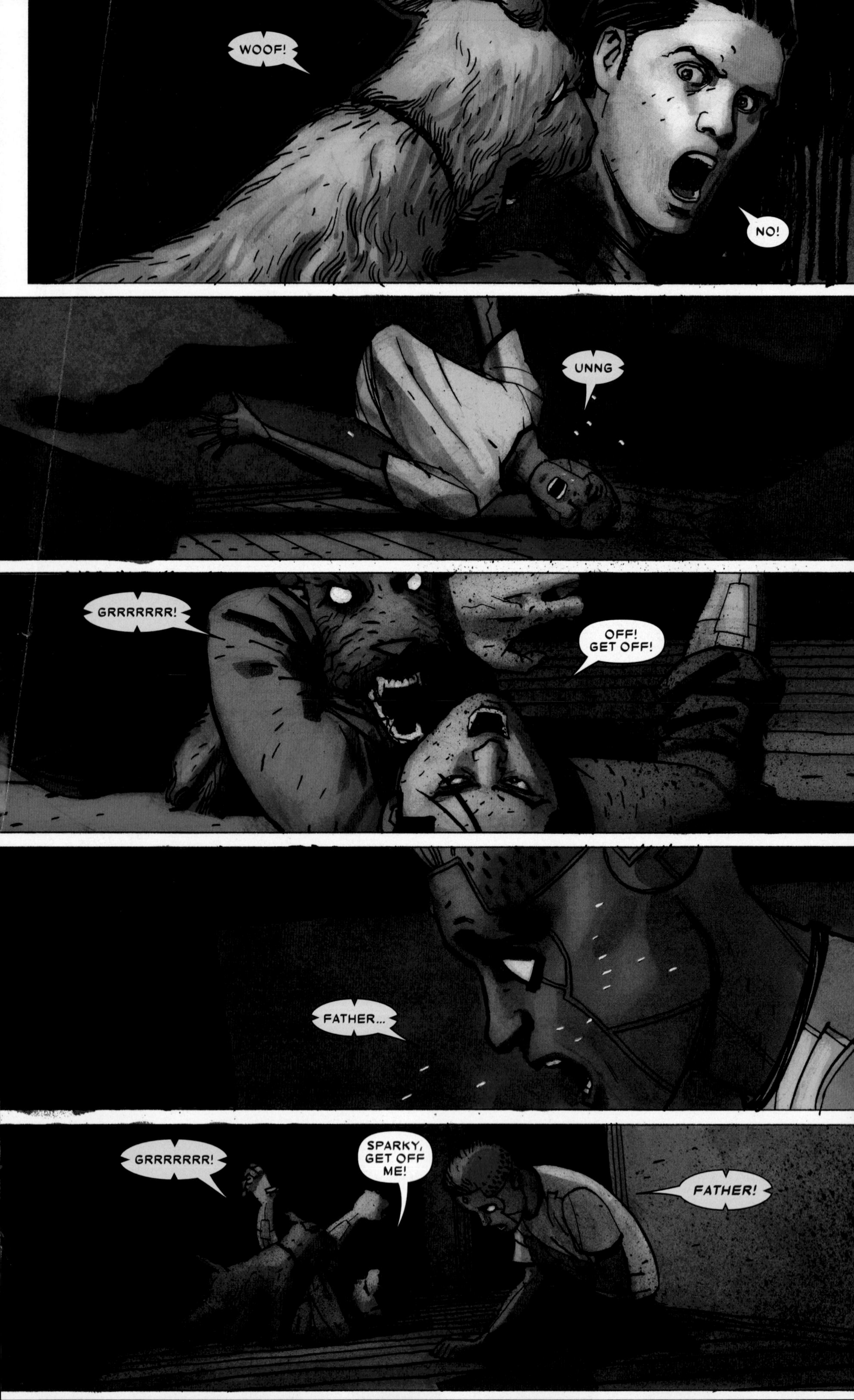
WOOF!
NO!
UNNG
GRRRRRRR!
OFF! GET OFF!
FATHER...
GRRRRRRR!
SPARKY, GET OFF ME!
FATHER!

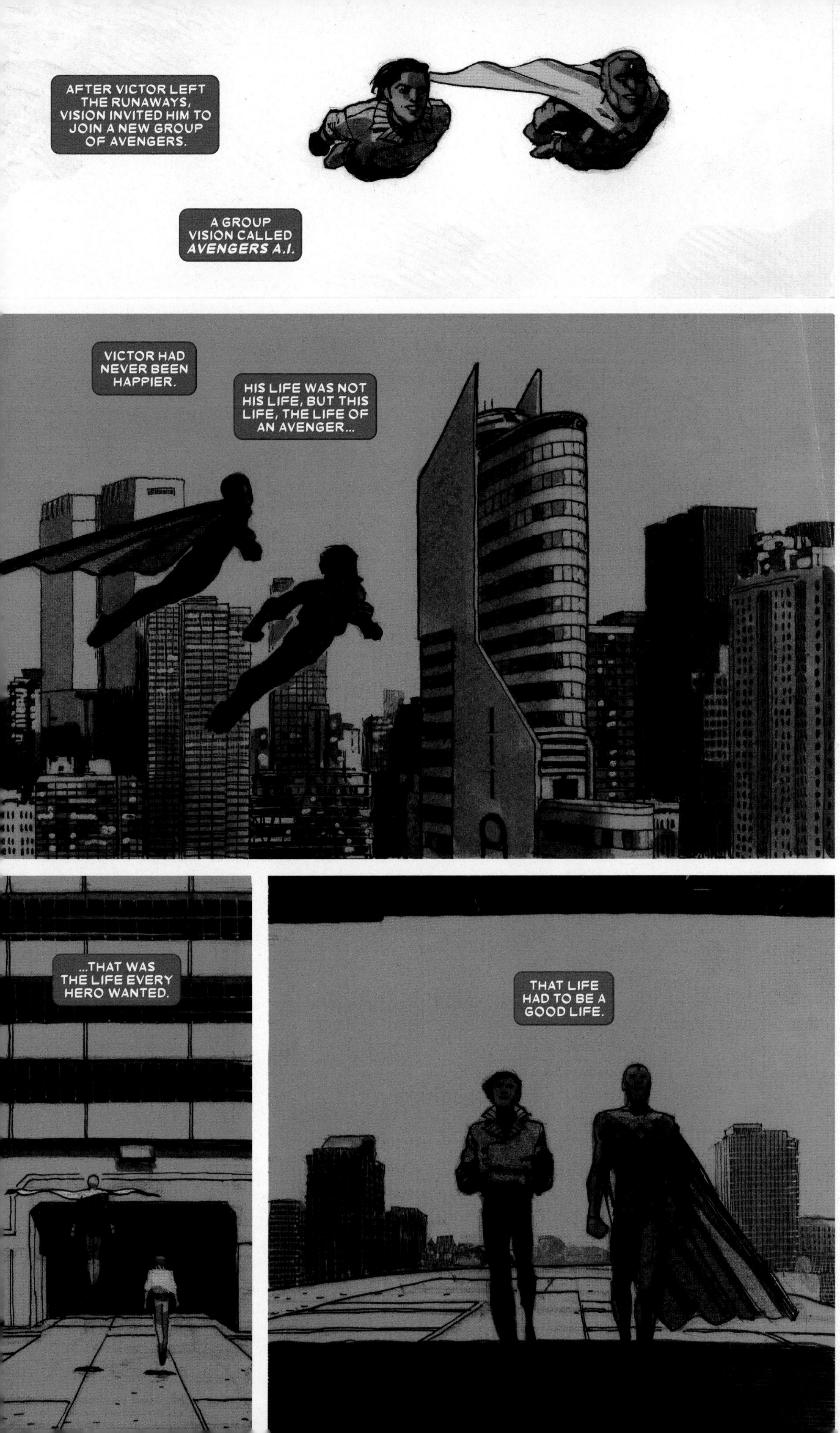
AFTER VICTOR LEFT THE RUNAWAYS, VISION INVITED HIM TO JOIN A NEW GROUP OF AVENGERS.
A GROUP VISION CALLED *AVENGERS A.I.*
VICTOR HAD NEVER BEEN HAPPIER.
HIS LIFE WAS NOT HIS LIFE, BUT THIS LIFE, THE LIFE OF AN AVENGER...
...THAT WAS THE LIFE EVERY HERO WANTED.
THAT LIFE HAD TO BE A GOOD LIFE.

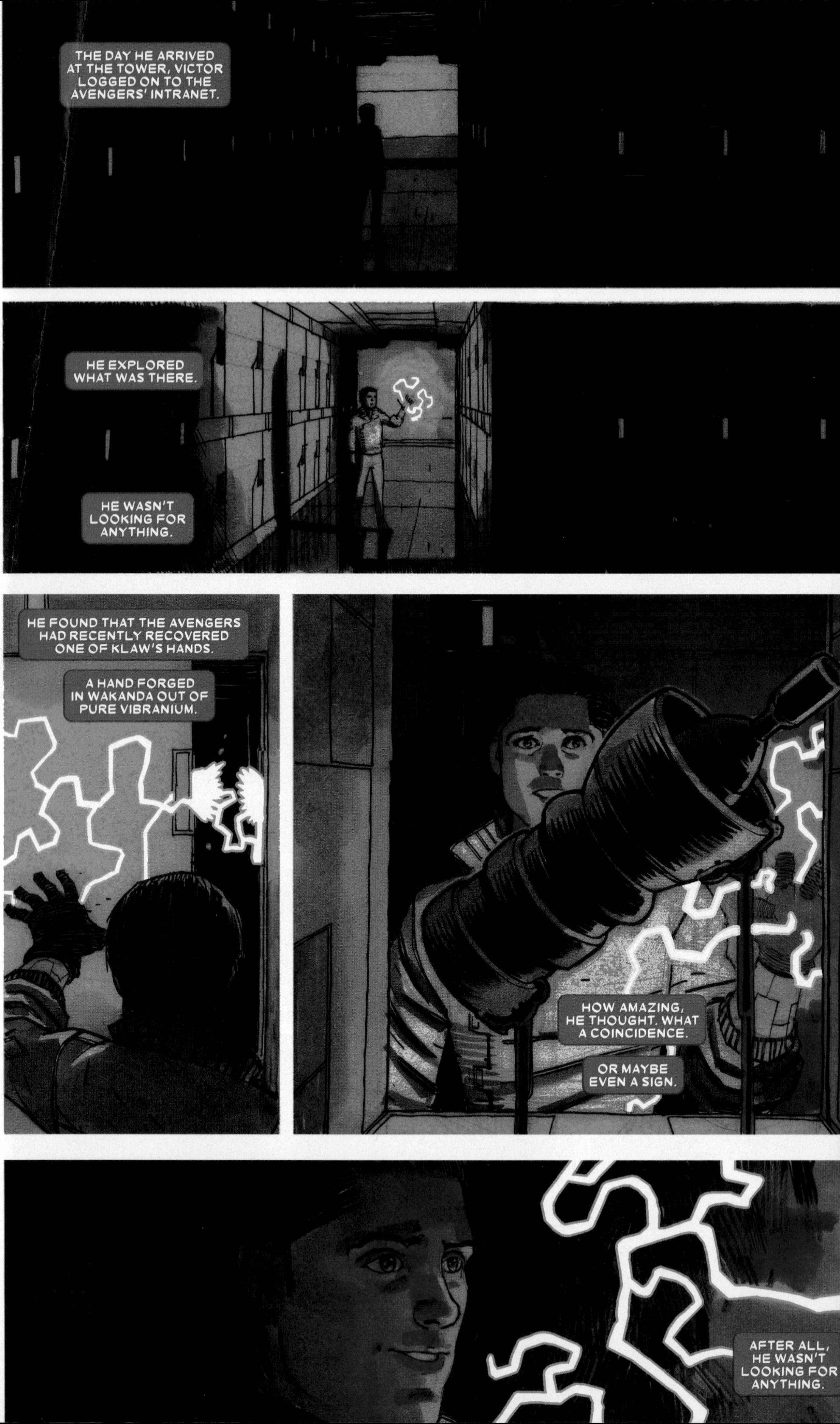

THE DAY HE ARRIVED AT THE TOWER, VICTOR LOGGED ON TO THE AVENGERS' INTRANET.
HE EXPLORED WHAT WAS THERE.
HE WASN'T LOOKING FOR ANYTHING.
HE FOUND THAT THE AVENGERS HAD RECENTLY RECOVERED ONE OF KLAW'S HANDS.
A HAND FORGED IN WAKANDA OUT OF PURE VIBRANIUM.
HOW AMAZING, HE THOUGHT. WHAT A COINCIDENCE.
OR MAYBE EVEN A SIGN.
AFTER ALL, HE WASN'T LOOKING FOR ANYTHING.

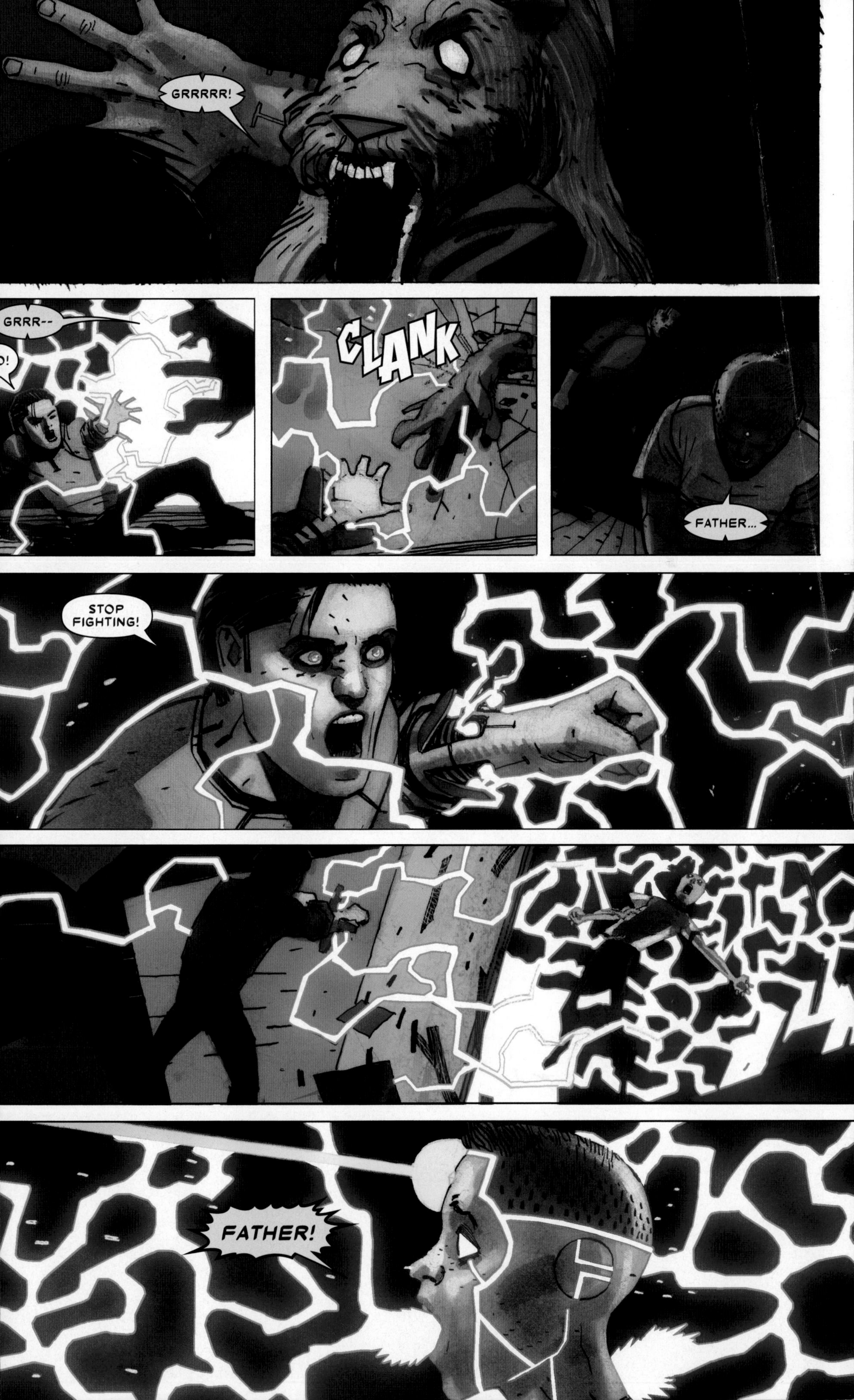
GRRRRR!
GRRR--
CLANK
FATHER...
STOP FIGHTING!
FATHER!

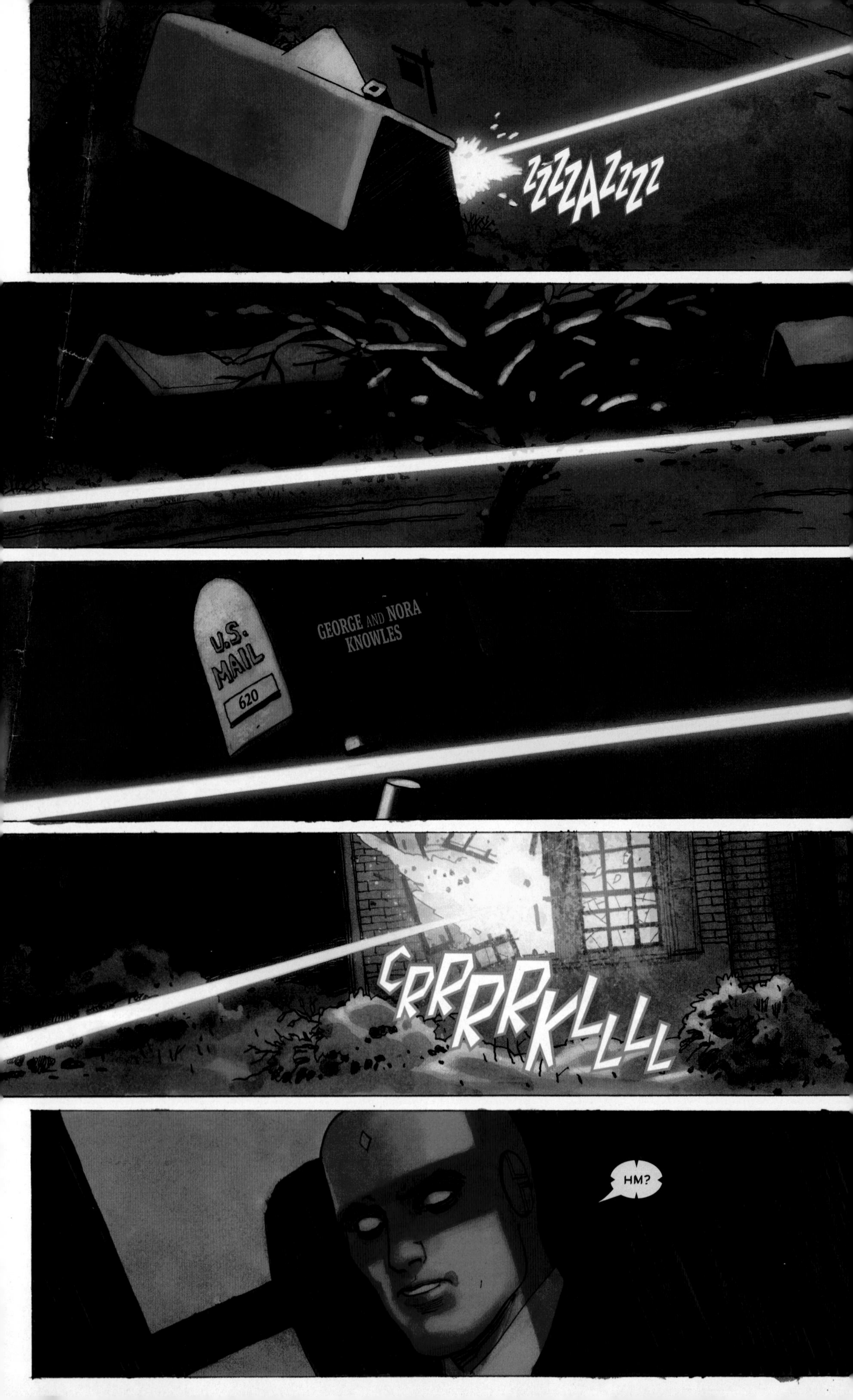
ZZZZAZZZZ
GEORGE AND NORA KNOWLES
U.S. MAIL
620
CRRRRKLLLL
HM?

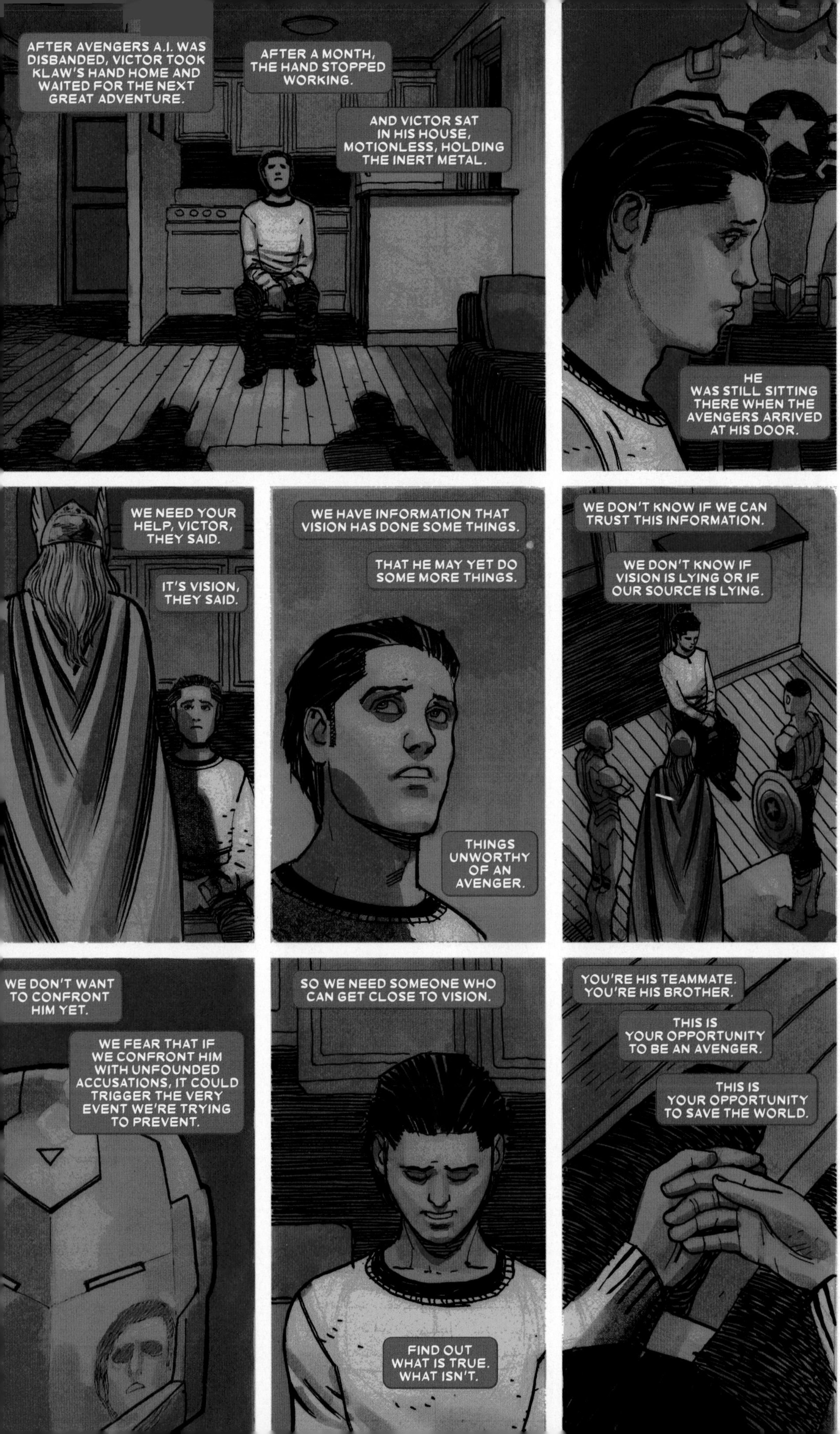
AFTER AVENGERS A.I. WAS DISBANDED, VICTOR TOOK KLAW'S HAND HOME AND WAITED FOR THE NEXT GREAT ADVENTURE.
AFTER A MONTH, THE HAND STOPPED WORKING.
AND VICTOR SAT IN HIS HOUSE, MOTIONLESS, HOLDING THE INERT METAL.
HE WAS STILL SITTING THERE WHEN THE AVENGERS ARRIVED AT HIS DOOR.
WE NEED YOUR HELP, VICTOR, THEY SAID.
IT'S VISION, THEY SAID.
WE HAVE INFORMATION THAT VISION HAS DONE SOME THINGS.
THAT HE MAY YET DO SOME MORE THINGS.
THINGS UNWORTHY OF AN AVENGER.
WE DON'T KNOW IF WE CAN TRUST THIS INFORMATION.
WE DON'T KNOW IF VISION IS LYING OR IF OUR SOURCE IS LYING.
WE DON'T WANT TO CONFRONT HIM YET.
WE FEAR THAT IF WE CONFRONT HIM WITH UNFOUNDED ACCUSATIONS, IT COULD TRIGGER THE VERY EVENT WE'RE TRYING TO PREVENT.
SO WE NEED SOMEONE WHO CAN GET CLOSE TO VISION.
FIND OUT WHAT IS TRUE. WHAT ISN'T.
YOU'RE HIS TEAMMATE. YOU'RE HIS BROTHER.
THIS IS YOUR OPPORTUNITY TO BE AN AVENGER.
THIS IS YOUR OPPORTUNITY TO SAVE THE WORLD.

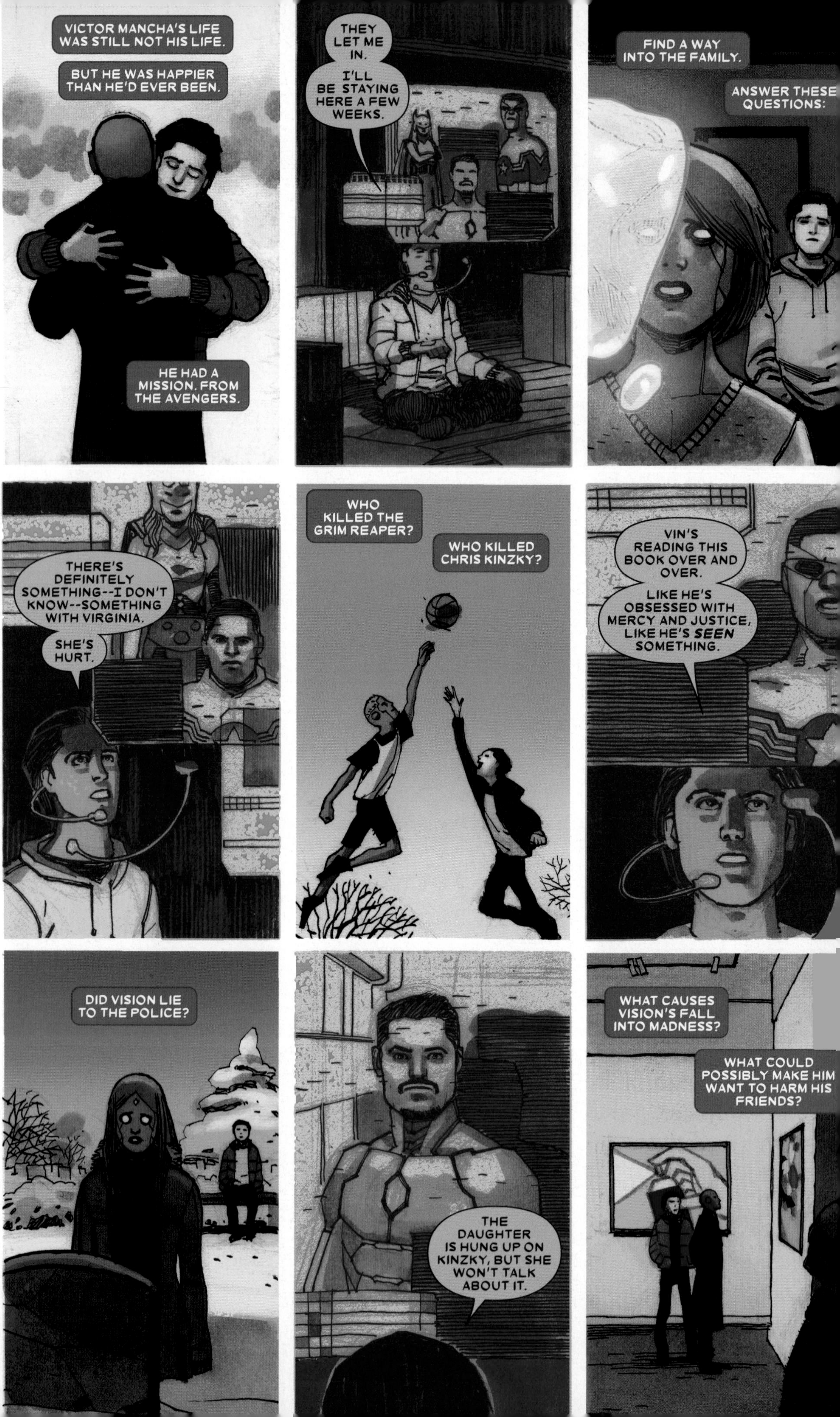
VICTOR MANCHA'S LIFE WAS STILL NOT HIS LIFE.
BUT HE WAS HAPPIER THAN HE'D EVER BEEN.
HE HAD A MISSION. FROM THE AVENGERS.
THEY LET ME IN.
I'LL BE STAYING HERE A FEW WEEKS.
FIND A WAY INTO THE FAMILY.
ANSWER THESE QUESTIONS:
THERE'S DEFINITELY SOMETHING--I DON'T KNOW--SOMETHING WITH VIRGINIA.
SHE'S HURT.
WHO KILLED THE GRIM REAPER?
WHO KILLED CHRIS KINZKY?
VIN'S READING THIS BOOK OVER AND OVER.
LIKE HE'S OBSESSED WITH MERCY AND JUSTICE, LIKE HE'S SEEN SOMETHING.
DID VISION LIE TO THE POLICE?
THE DAUGHTER IS HUNG UP ON KINZKY, BUT SHE WON'T TALK ABOUT IT.
WHAT CAUSES VISION'S FALL INTO MADNESS?
WHAT COULD POSSIBLY MAKE HIM WANT TO HARM HIS FRIENDS?

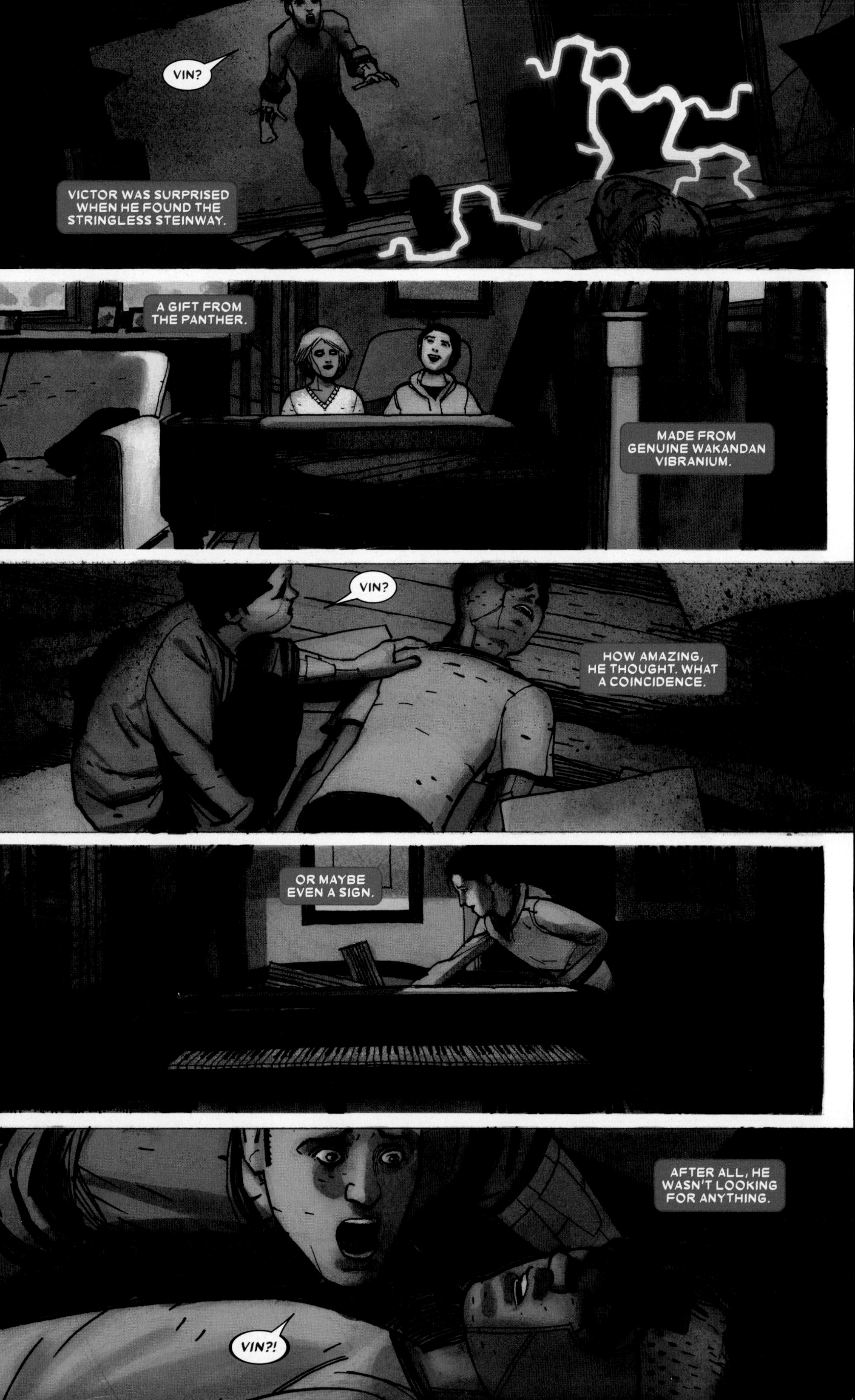
VIN?
VICTOR WAS SURPRISED WHEN HE FOUND THE STRINGLESS STEINWAY.
A GIFT FROM THE PANTHER.
MADE FROM GENUINE WAKANDAN VIBRANIUM.
VIN?
HOW AMAZING, HE THOUGHT. WHAT A COINCIDENCE.
OR MAYBE EVEN A SIGN.
AFTER ALL, HE WASN'T LOOKING FOR ANYTHING.
VIN?!

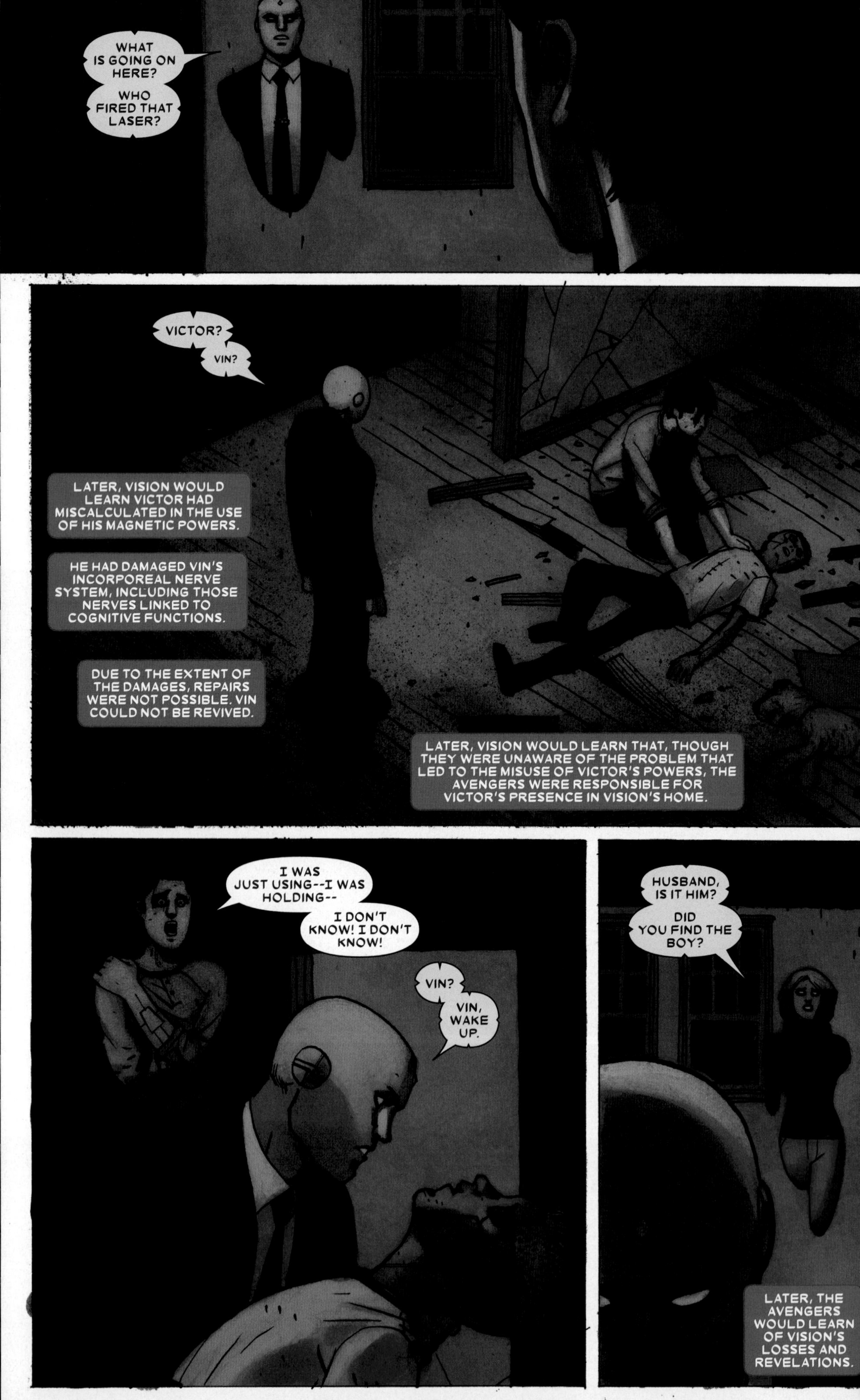

WHAT IS GOING ON HERE?
WHO FIRED THAT LASER?
VICTOR?
VIN?
LATER, VISION WOULD LEARN VICTOR HAD MISCALCULATED IN THE USE OF HIS MAGNETIC POWERS.
HE HAD DAMAGED VIN'S INCORPOREAL NERVE SYSTEM, INCLUDING THOSE NERVES LINKED TO COGNITIVE FUNCTIONS.
DUE TO THE EXTENT OF THE DAMAGES, REPAIRS WERE NOT POSSIBLE. VIN COULD NOT BE REVIVED.
LATER, VISION WOULD LEARN THAT, THOUGH THEY WERE UNAWARE OF THE PROBLEM THAT LED TO THE MISUSE OF VICTOR'S POWERS, THE AVENGERS WERE RESPONSIBLE FOR VICTOR'S PRESENCE IN VISION'S HOME.
I WAS JUST USING--I WAS HOLDING--
I DON'T KNOW! I DON'T KNOW!
VIN?
VIN, WAKE UP.
HUSBAND, IS IT HIM?
DID YOU FIND THE BOY?
LATER, THE AVENGERS WOULD LEARN OF VISION'S LOSSES AND REVELATIONS.

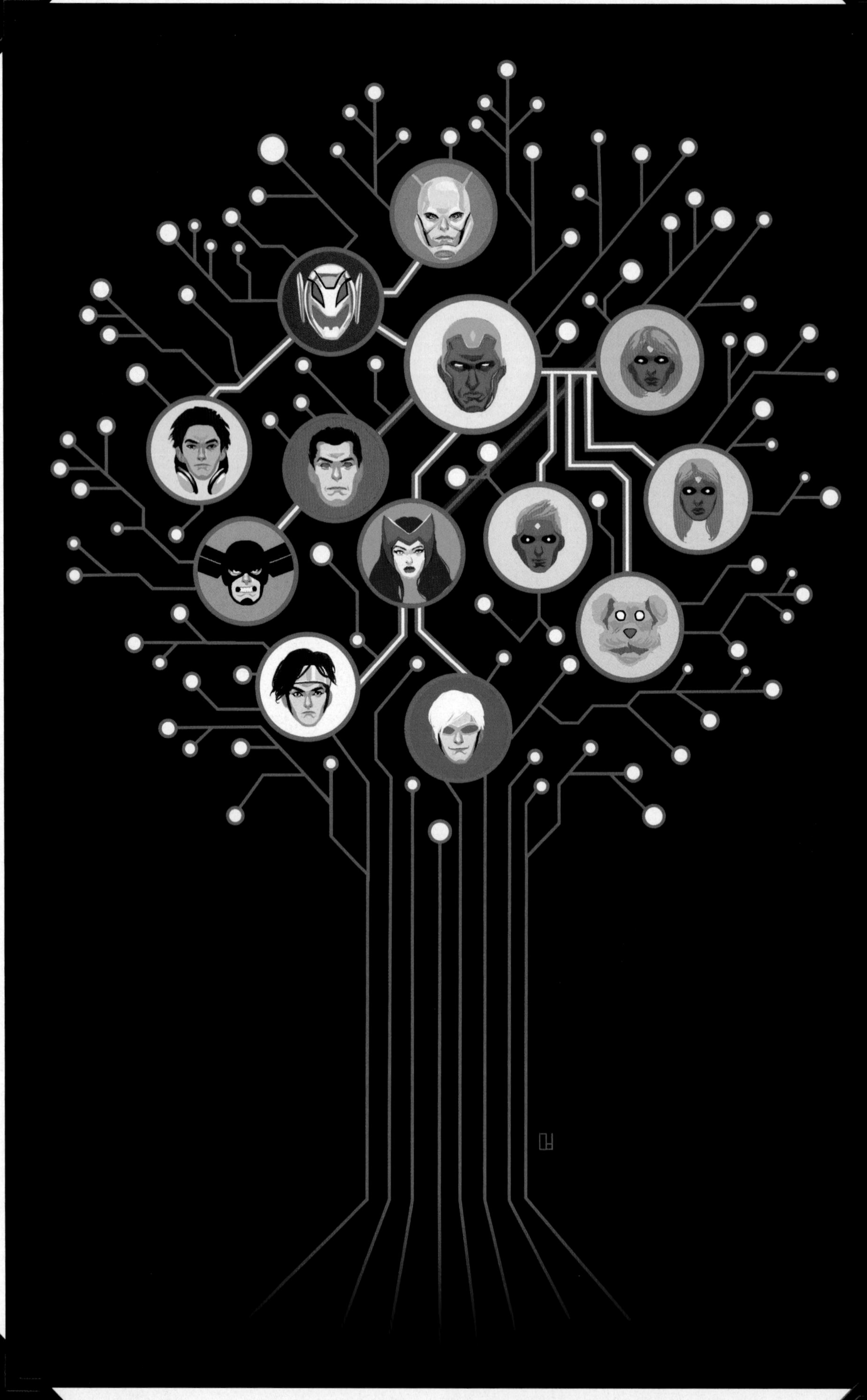

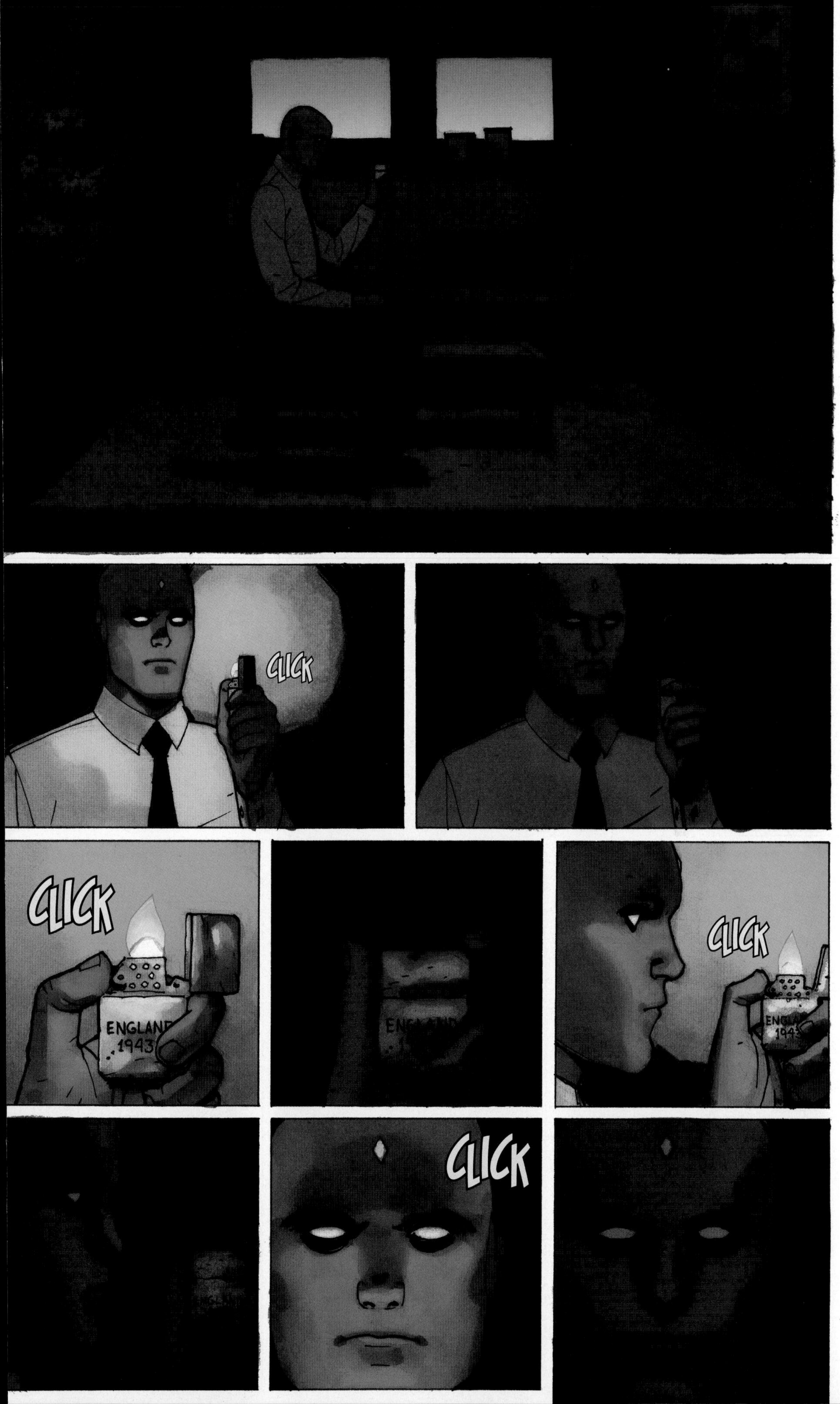
CLICK
CLICK
ENGLAND
1943
CLICK
CLICK

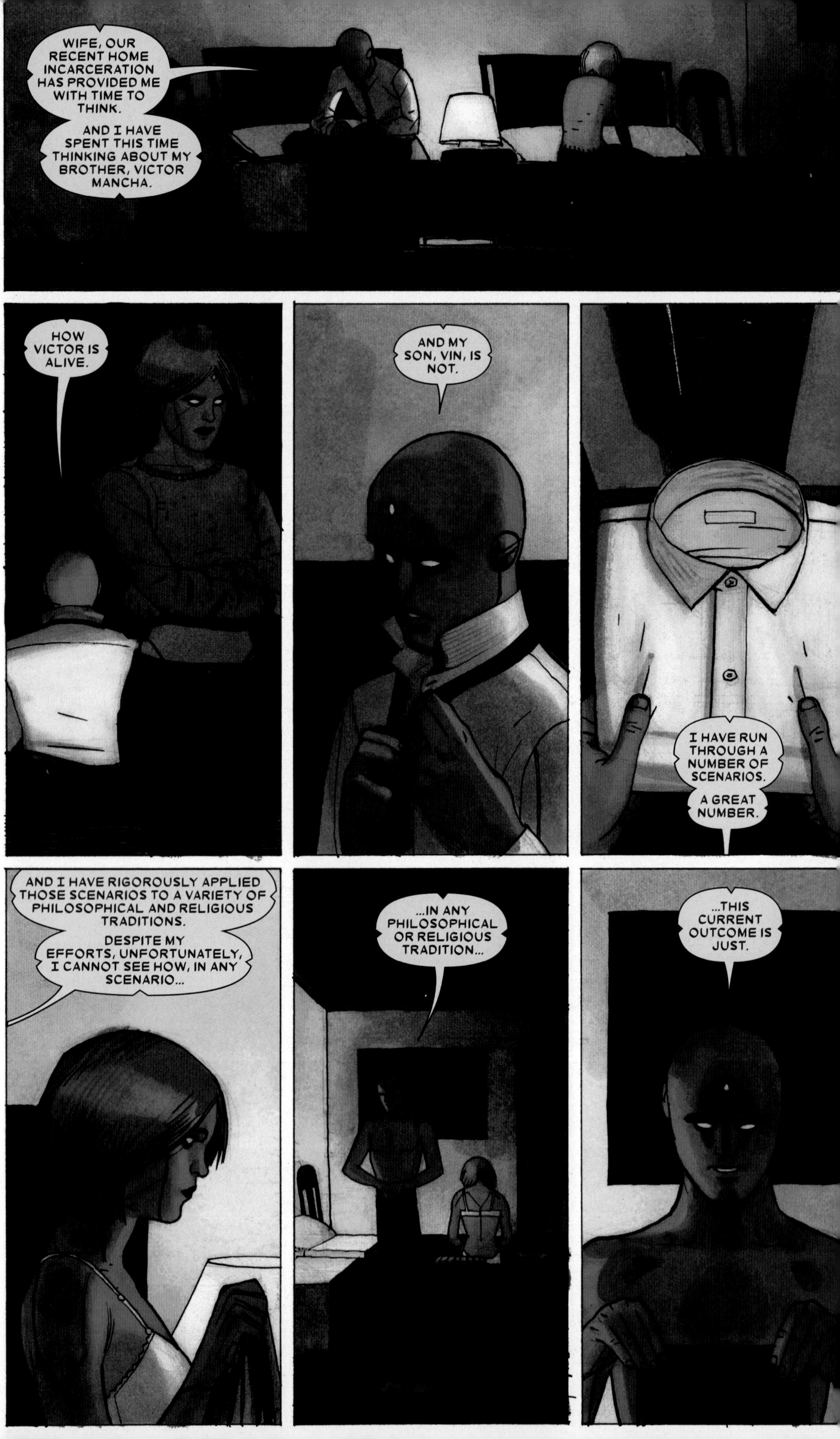
WIFE, OUR RECENT HOME INCARCERATION HAS PROVIDED ME WITH TIME TO THINK.
AND I HAVE SPENT THIS TIME THINKING ABOUT MY BROTHER, VICTOR MANCHA.
HOW VICTOR IS ALIVE.
AND MY SON, VIN, IS NOT.
I HAVE RUN THROUGH A NUMBER OF SCENARIOS.
A GREAT NUMBER.
AND I HAVE RIGOROUSLY APPLIED THOSE SCENARIOS TO A VARIETY OF PHILOSOPHICAL AND RELIGIOUS TRADITIONS.
DESPITE MY EFFORTS, UNFORTUNATELY, I CANNOT SEE HOW, IN ANY SCENARIO...
...IN ANY PHILOSOPHICAL OR RELIGIOUS TRADITION...
...THIS CURRENT OUTCOME IS JUST.

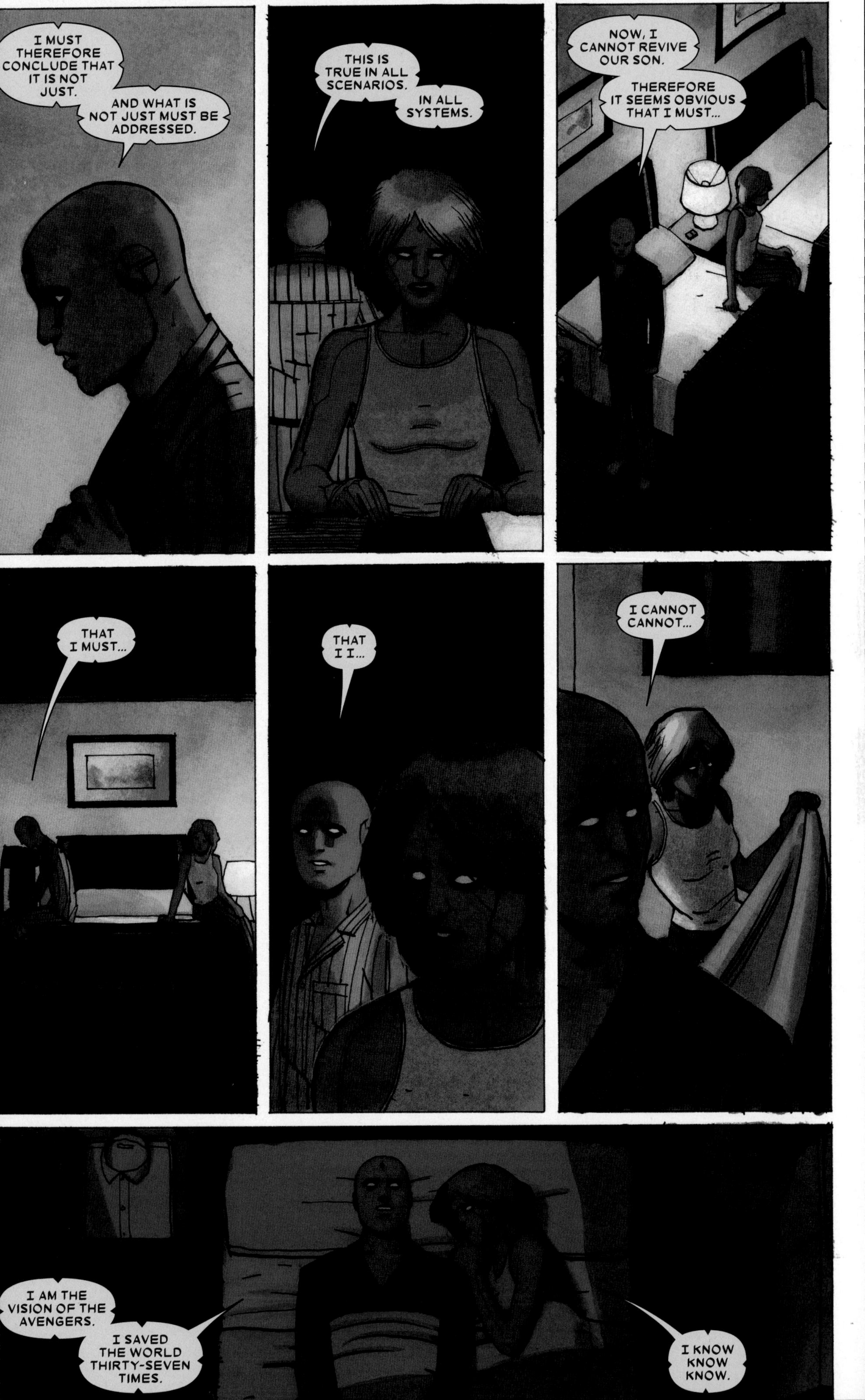
I MUST THEREFORE CONCLUDE THAT IT IS NOT JUST.
AND WHAT IS NOT JUST MUST BE ADDRESSED.
THIS IS TRUE IN ALL SCENARIOS.
IN ALL SYSTEMS.
NOW, I CANNOT REVIVE OUR SON.
THEREFORE IT SEEMS OBVIOUS THAT I MUST...
THAT I MUST...
THAT I I...
I CANNOT CANNOT...
I AM THE VISION OF THE AVENGERS.
I SAVED THE WORLD THIRTY-SEVEN TIMES.
I KNOW KNOW KNOW.

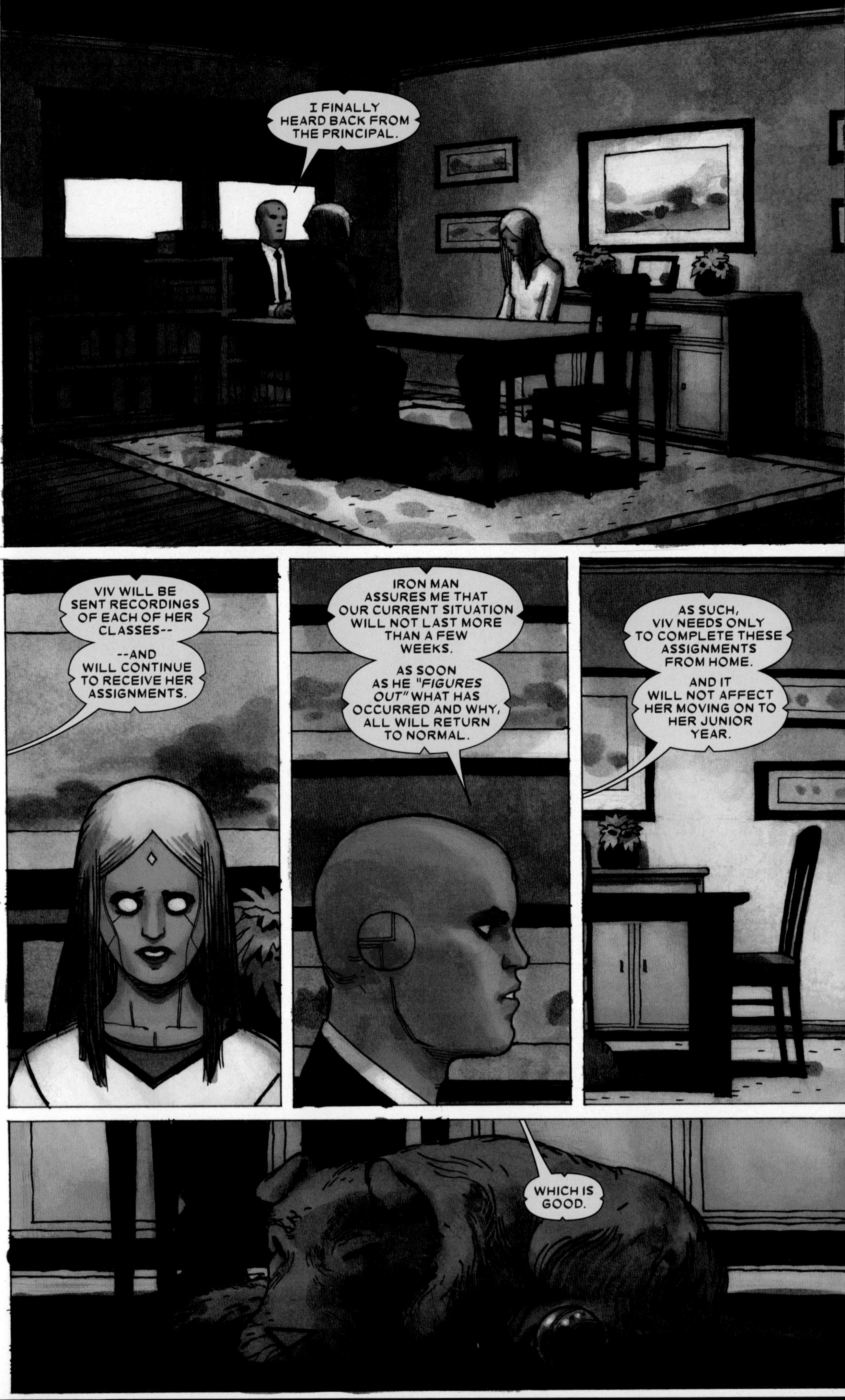
I FINALLY HEARD BACK FROM THE PRINCIPAL.
VIV WILL BE SENT RECORDINGS OF EACH OF HER CLASSES--
--AND WILL CONTINUE TO RECEIVE HER ASSIGNMENTS.
IRON MAN ASSURES ME THAT OUR CURRENT SITUATION WILL NOT LAST MORE THAN A FEW WEEKS.
AS SOON AS HE "FIGURES OUT" WHAT HAS OCCURRED AND WHY, ALL WILL RETURN TO NORMAL.
AS SUCH, VIV NEEDS ONLY TO COMPLETE THESE ASSIGNMENTS FROM HOME.
AND IT WILL NOT AFFECT HER MOVING ON TO HER JUNIOR YEAR.
WHICH IS GOOD.

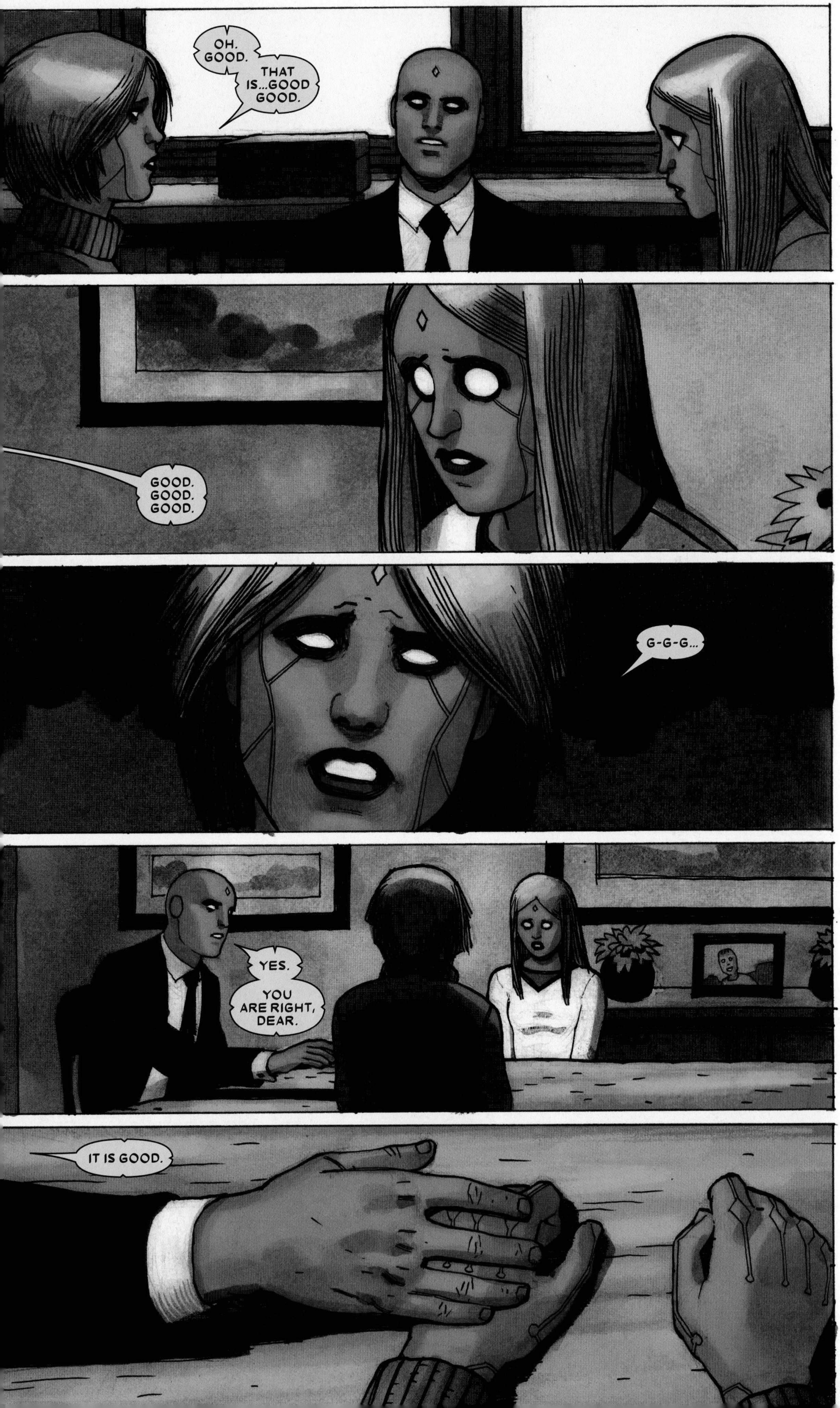
OH. GOOD.
THAT IS...GOOD GOOD.
GOOD. GOOD. GOOD.
G-G-G...
YES.
YOU ARE RIGHT, DEAR.
IT IS GOOD.

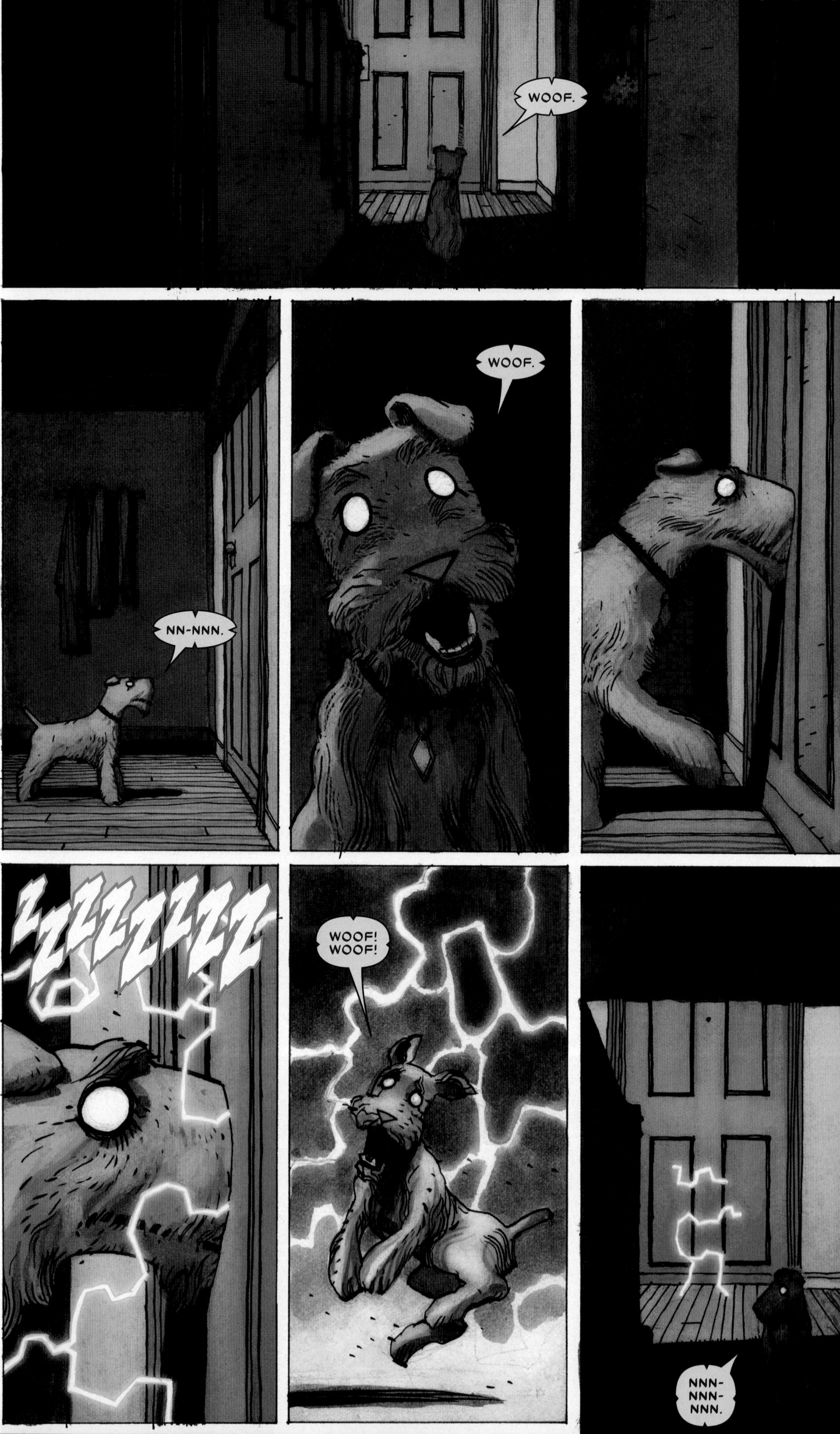
WOOF.
NN-NNN.
WOOF.
ZZZZZZZZ
WOOF! WOOF!
NNN-NNN-NNN.

MY APOLOGIES, IRON MAN...

NO. NO, THERE IS NO REASON TO DEPLOY THE AVENGERS.

THIS WAS NOT AN ATTEMPTED BREACH.

THE DOG SET OFF THE ALARM.

ROW. ROW. ROW.

NO, WHEN YOU *INSTALLED* THE ENCLOSURE, I ADJUSTED HIS PROGRAMMING...

...HE SHOULD HAVE STAYED WITHIN THE CONFINES OF THE HOUSE.

YOUR... *BOAT.*

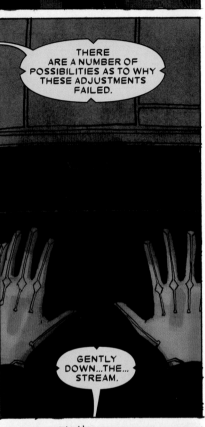

THERE ARE A NUMBER OF POSSIBILITIES AS TO WHY THESE ADJUSTMENTS FAILED.

GENTLY DOWN...THE... STREAM.

YES, YES. I WILL CONDUCT A THOROUGH ANALYSIS OF THE ANIMAL THIS AFTERNOON.

MERRILY. MERRILY. MERRILY. MERRILY.

I DO NOT ANTICIPATE THAT THE ALARM WILL SOUND AGAIN.

LIFE IS BUT A DREAM.

DREAM. DREAM. DREAM.

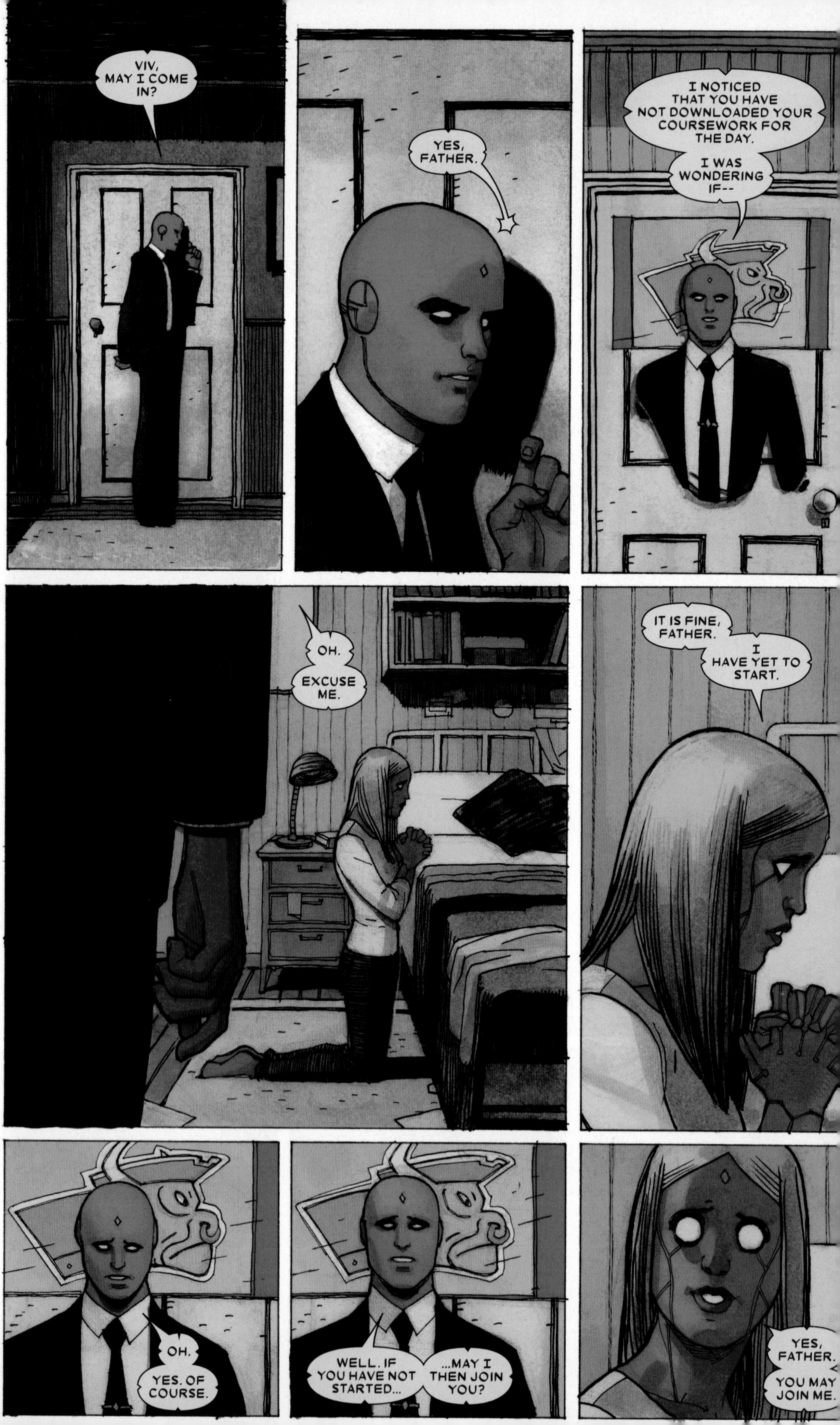
VIV, MAY I COME IN?
YES, FATHER.
I NOTICED THAT YOU HAVE NOT DOWNLOADED YOUR COURSEWORK FOR THE DAY.
I WAS WONDERING IF--
OH.
EXCUSE ME.
IT IS FINE, FATHER.
I HAVE YET TO START.
OH.
YES. OF COURSE.
WELL. IF YOU HAVE NOT STARTED...
...MAY I THEN JOIN YOU?
YES, FATHER.
YOU MAY JOIN ME.

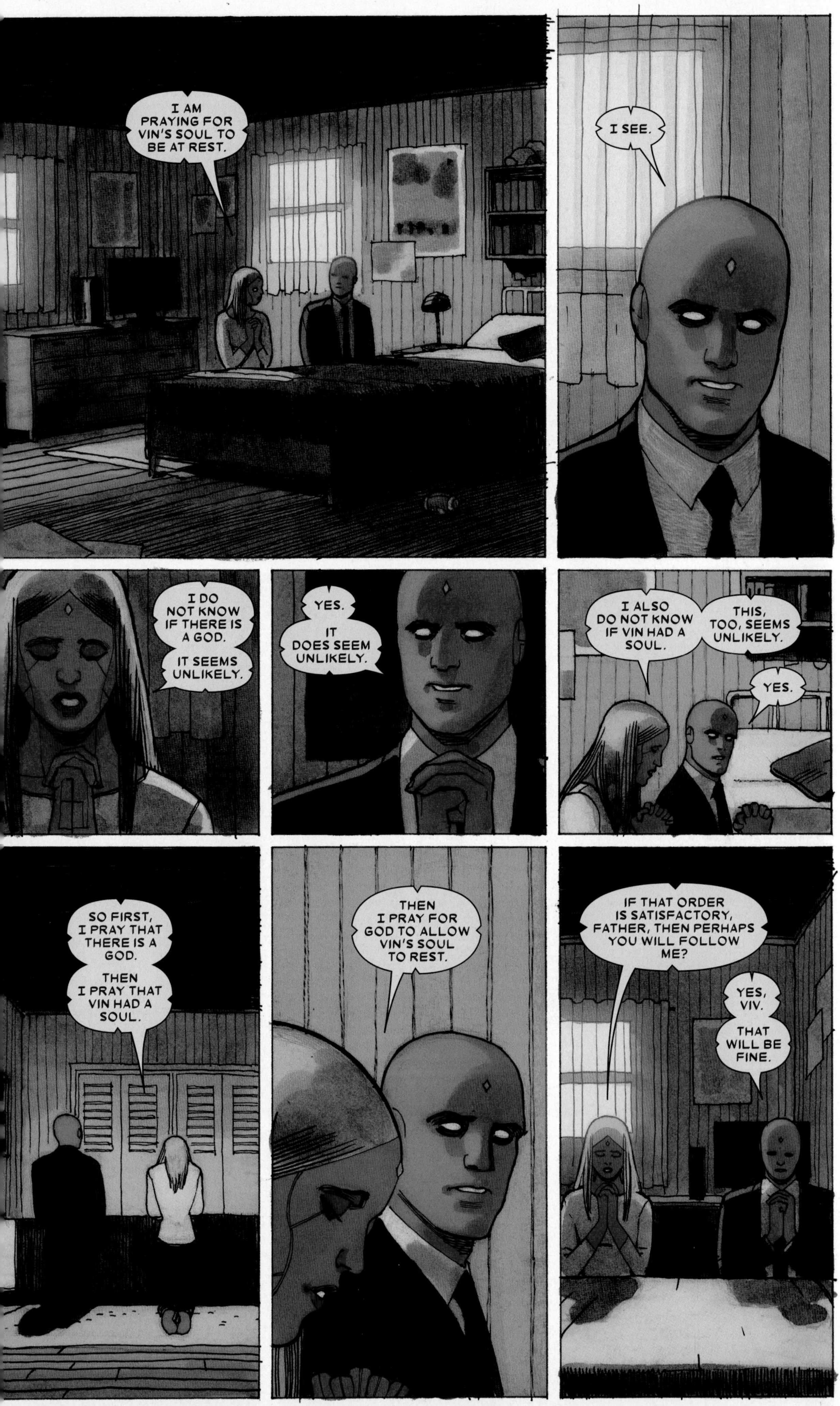
I AM PRAYING FOR VIN'S SOUL TO BE AT REST.
I SEE.
I DO NOT KNOW IF THERE IS A GOD.
IT SEEMS UNLIKELY.
YES.
IT DOES SEEM UNLIKELY.
I ALSO DO NOT KNOW IF VIN HAD A SOUL.
THIS, TOO, SEEMS UNLIKELY.
YES.
SO FIRST, I PRAY THAT THERE IS A GOD.
THEN I PRAY THAT VIN HAD A SOUL.
THEN I PRAY FOR GOD TO ALLOW VIN'S SOUL TO REST.
IF THAT ORDER IS SATISFACTORY, FATHER, THEN PERHAPS YOU WILL FOLLOW ME?
YES, VIV.
THAT WILL BE FINE.

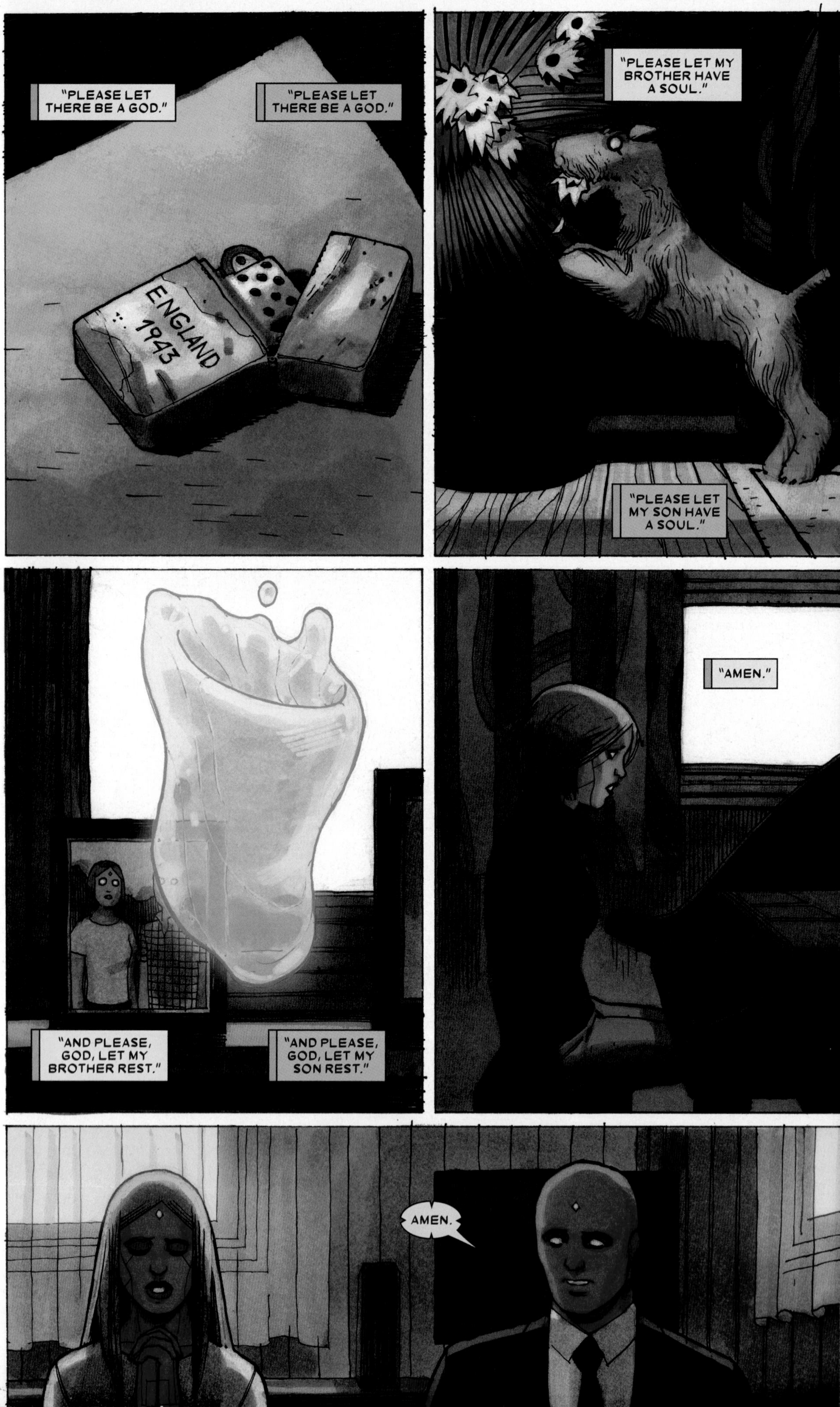
"PLEASE LET
THERE BE A GOD."
"PLEASE LET
THERE BE A GOD."
ENGLAND
1943
"PLEASE LET MY
BROTHER HAVE
A SOUL."
"PLEASE LET
MY SON HAVE
A SOUL."
"AND PLEASE,
GOD, LET MY
BROTHER REST."
"AND PLEASE,
GOD, LET MY
SON REST."
"AMEN."
AMEN.

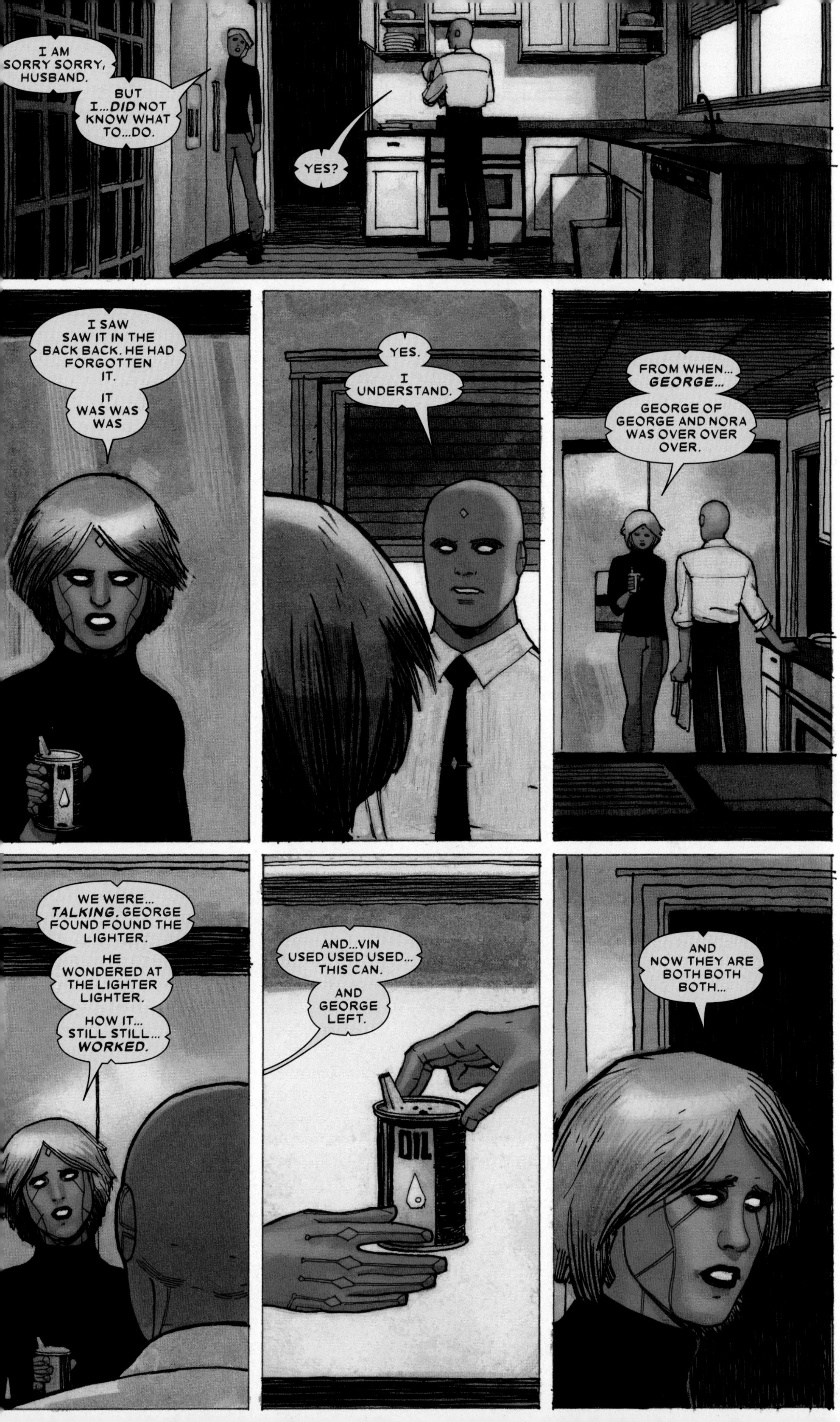
I AM SORRY SORRY, HUSBAND.
BUT I...DID NOT KNOW WHAT TO...DO.
YES?
I SAW SAW IT IN THE BACK BACK. HE HAD FORGOTTEN IT.
IT WAS WAS WAS
YES.
I UNDERSTAND.
FROM WHEN... GEORGE...
GEORGE OF GEORGE AND NORA WAS OVER OVER OVER.
WE WERE... TALKING. GEORGE FOUND FOUND THE LIGHTER.
HE WONDERED AT THE LIGHTER LIGHTER.
HOW IT... STILL STILL... WORKED.
AND...VIN USED USED USED... THIS CAN.
AND GEORGE LEFT.
OIL
AND NOW THEY ARE BOTH BOTH BOTH...

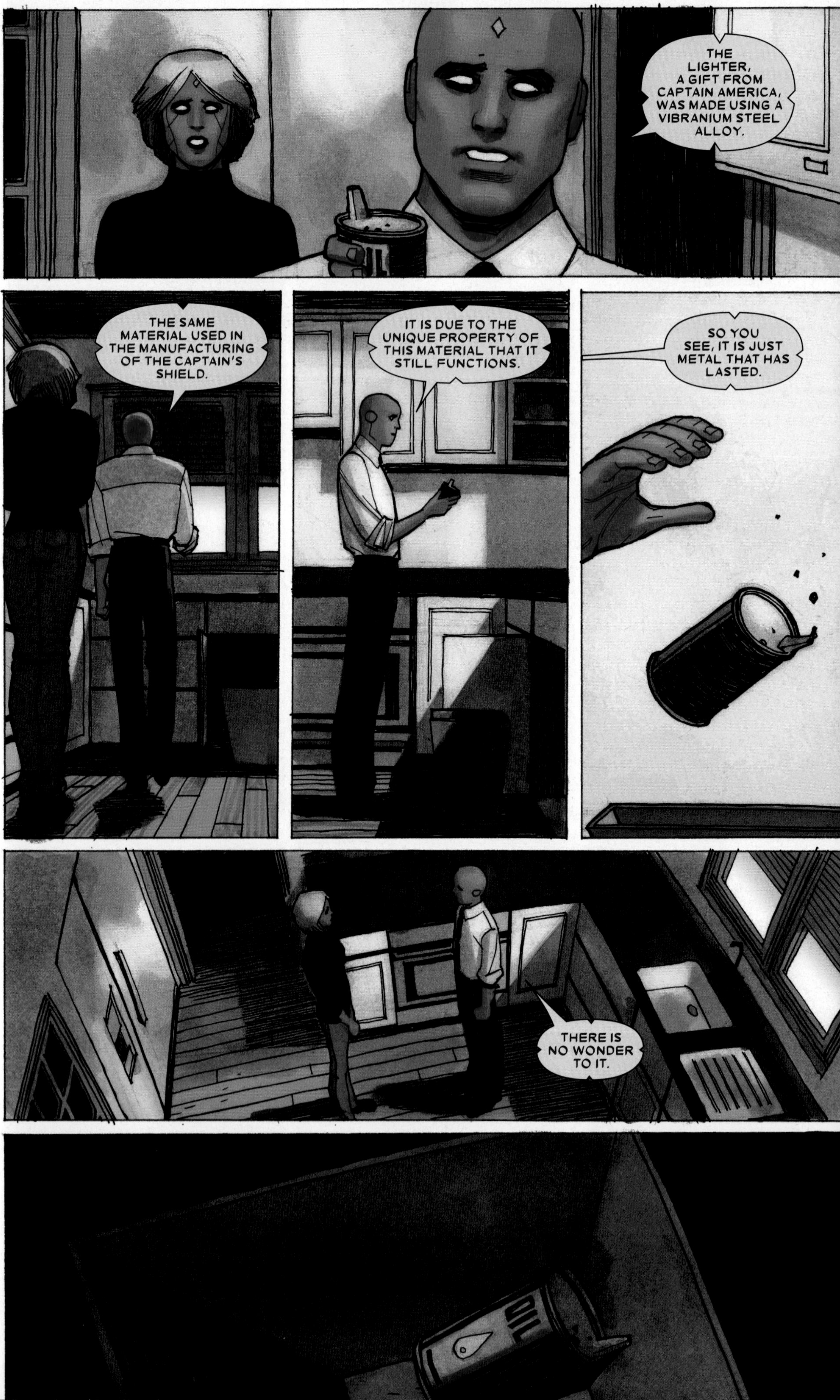
THE LIGHTER, A GIFT FROM CAPTAIN AMERICA, WAS MADE USING A VIBRANIUM STEEL ALLOY.
THE SAME MATERIAL USED IN THE MANUFACTURING OF THE CAPTAIN'S SHIELD.
IT IS DUE TO THE UNIQUE PROPERTY OF THIS MATERIAL THAT IT STILL FUNCTIONS.
SO YOU SEE, IT IS JUST METAL THAT HAS LASTED.
THERE IS NO WONDER TO IT.

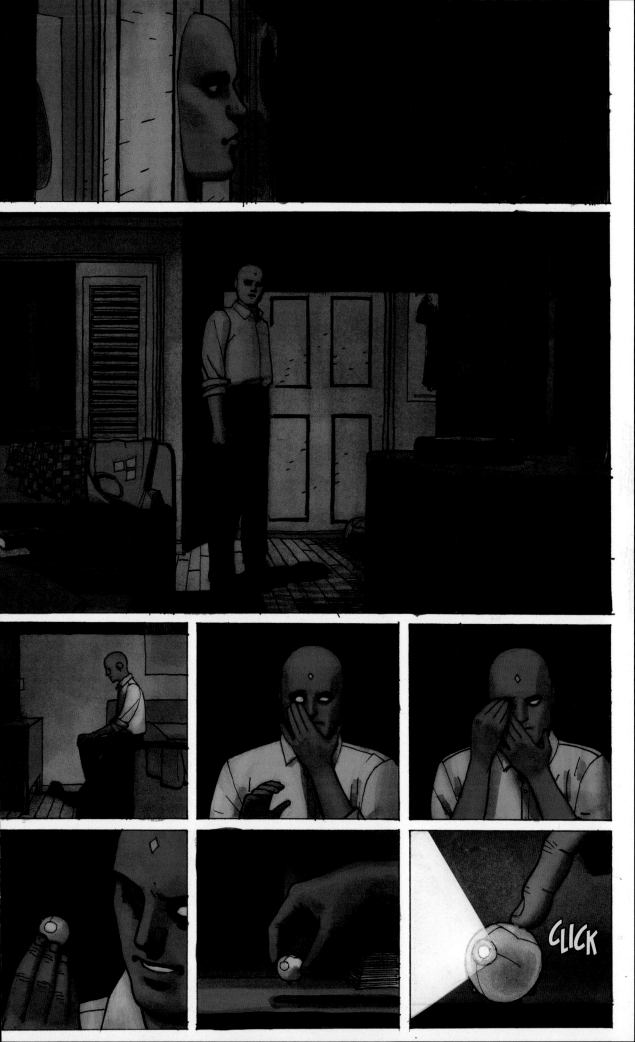

CLICK

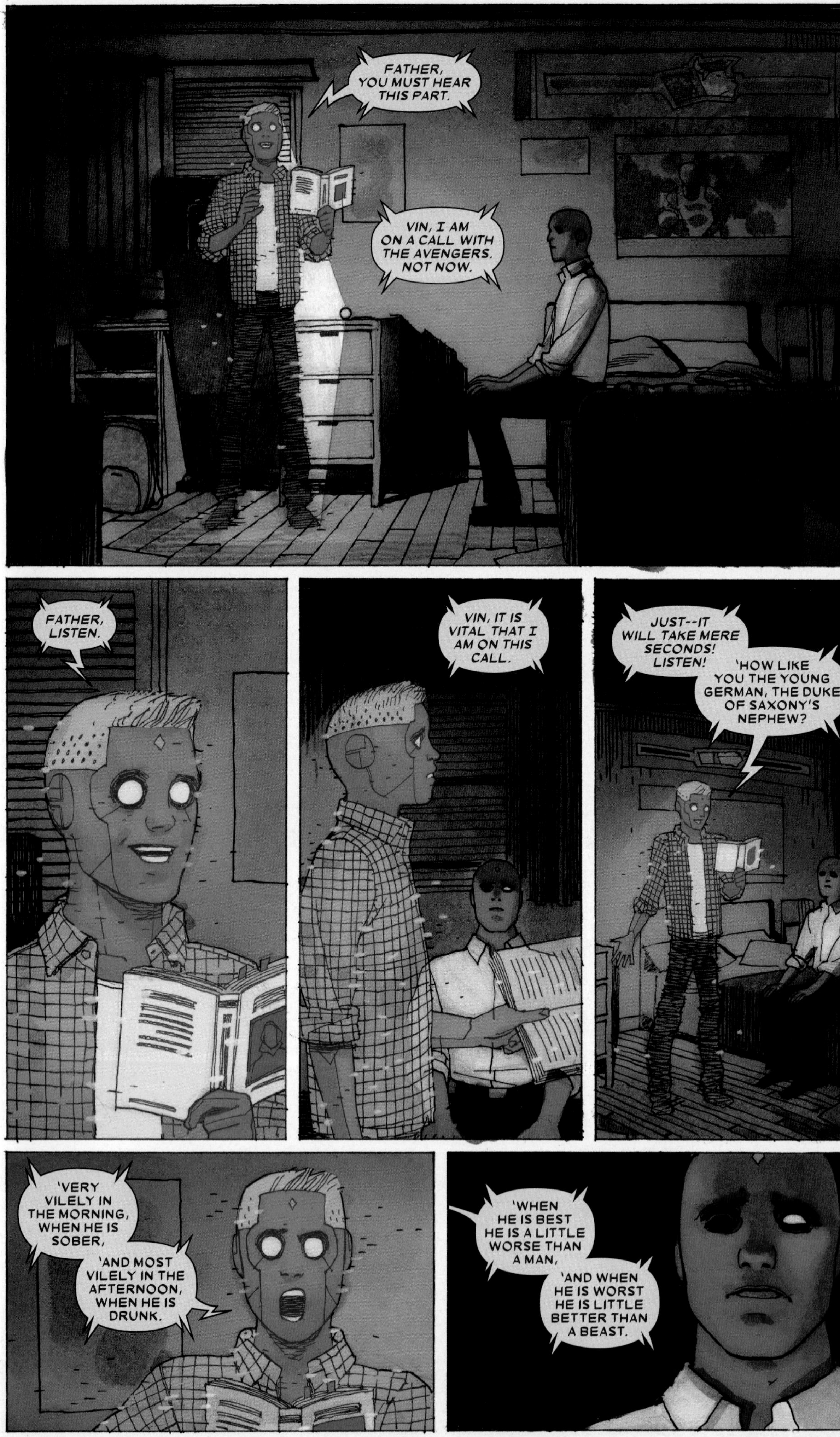
FATHER, YOU MUST HEAR THIS PART.
VIN, I AM ON A CALL WITH THE AVENGERS. NOT NOW.
FATHER, LISTEN.
VIN, IT IS VITAL THAT I AM ON THIS CALL.
JUST--IT WILL TAKE MERE SECONDS! LISTEN!
'HOW LIKE YOU THE YOUNG GERMAN, THE DUKE OF SAXONY'S NEPHEW?
'VERY VILELY IN THE MORNING, WHEN HE IS SOBER,
'AND MOST VILELY IN THE AFTERNOON, WHEN HE IS DRUNK.
'WHEN HE IS BEST HE IS A LITTLE WORSE THAN A MAN,
'AND WHEN HE IS WORST HE IS LITTLE BETTER THAN A BEAST.

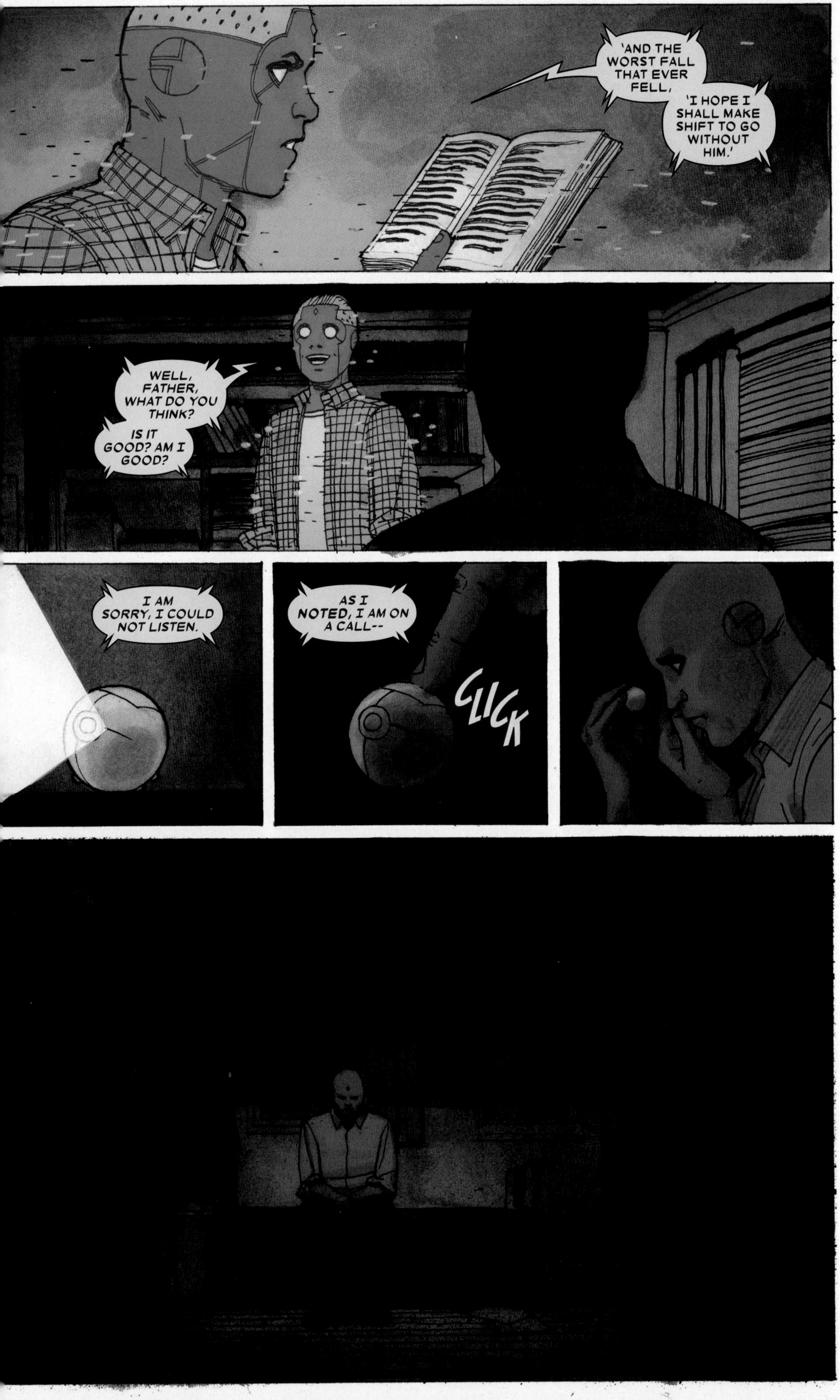
'AND THE WORST FALL THAT EVER FELL,
'I HOPE I SHALL MAKE SHIFT TO GO WITHOUT HIM.'
WELL, FATHER, WHAT DO YOU THINK?
IS IT GOOD? AM I GOOD?
I AM SORRY, I COULD NOT LISTEN.
AS I NOTED, I AM ON A CALL--
CLICK

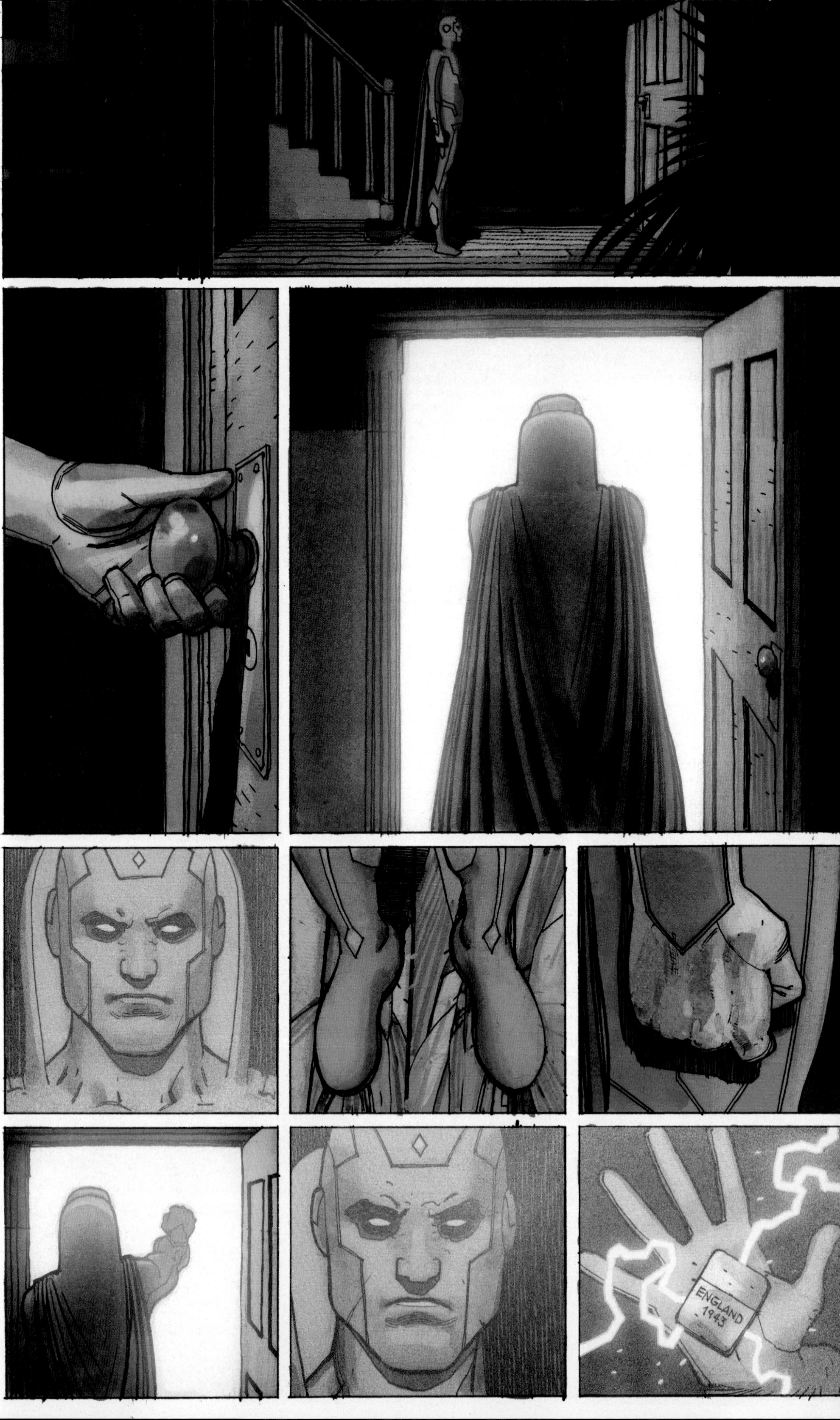
ENGLAND
1943

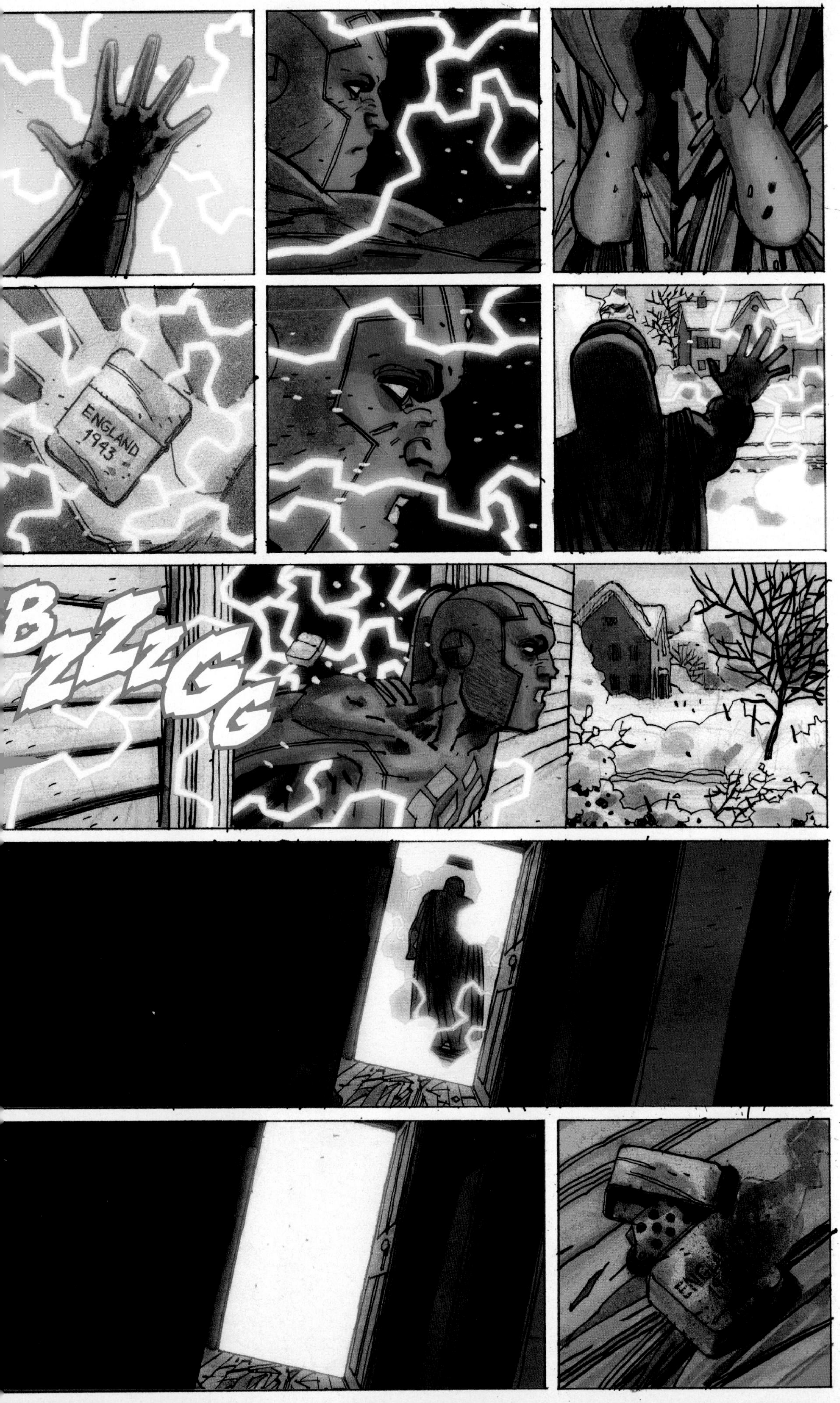
ENGLAND
1943
BZZZGG

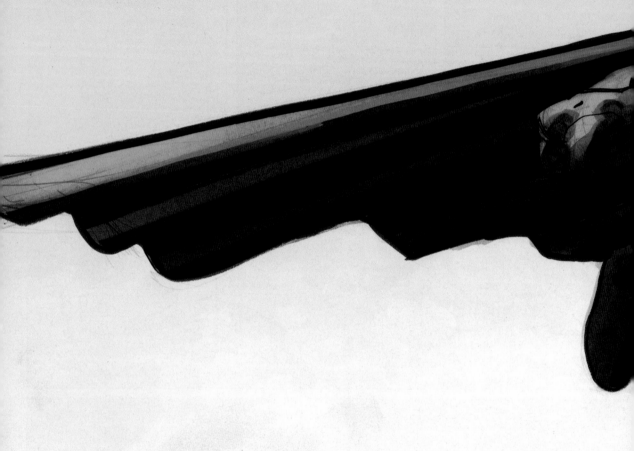

AS UNLIKELY AS IT SEEMS, THERE IS INDEED A GOD ABOVE US.

SOMEONE TO GREET OUR SOULS WHEN WE LEAVE THIS LIFE.

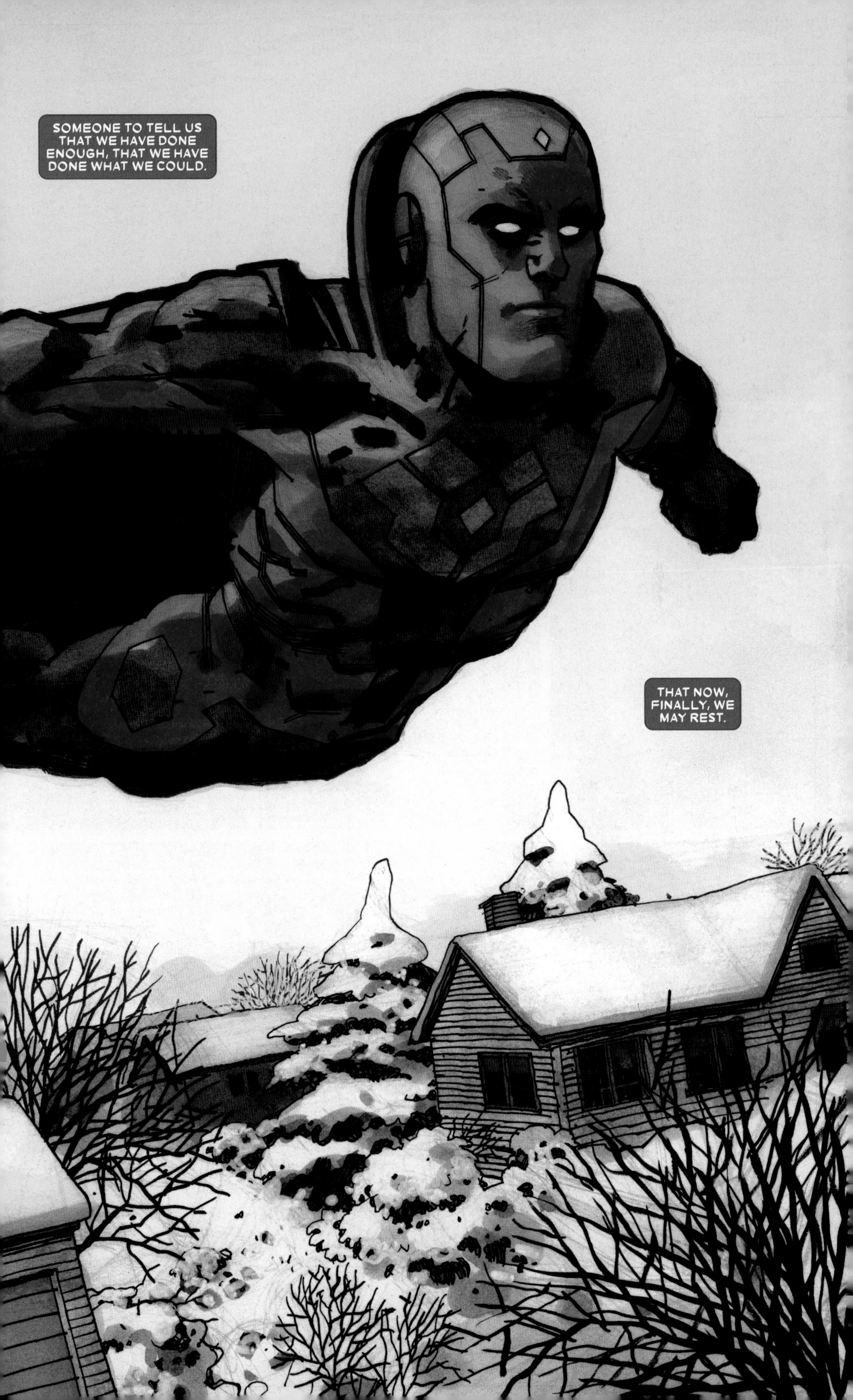
SOMEONE TO TELL US THAT WE HAVE DONE ENOUGH, THAT WE HAVE DONE WHAT WE COULD.
THAT NOW, FINALLY, WE MAY REST.

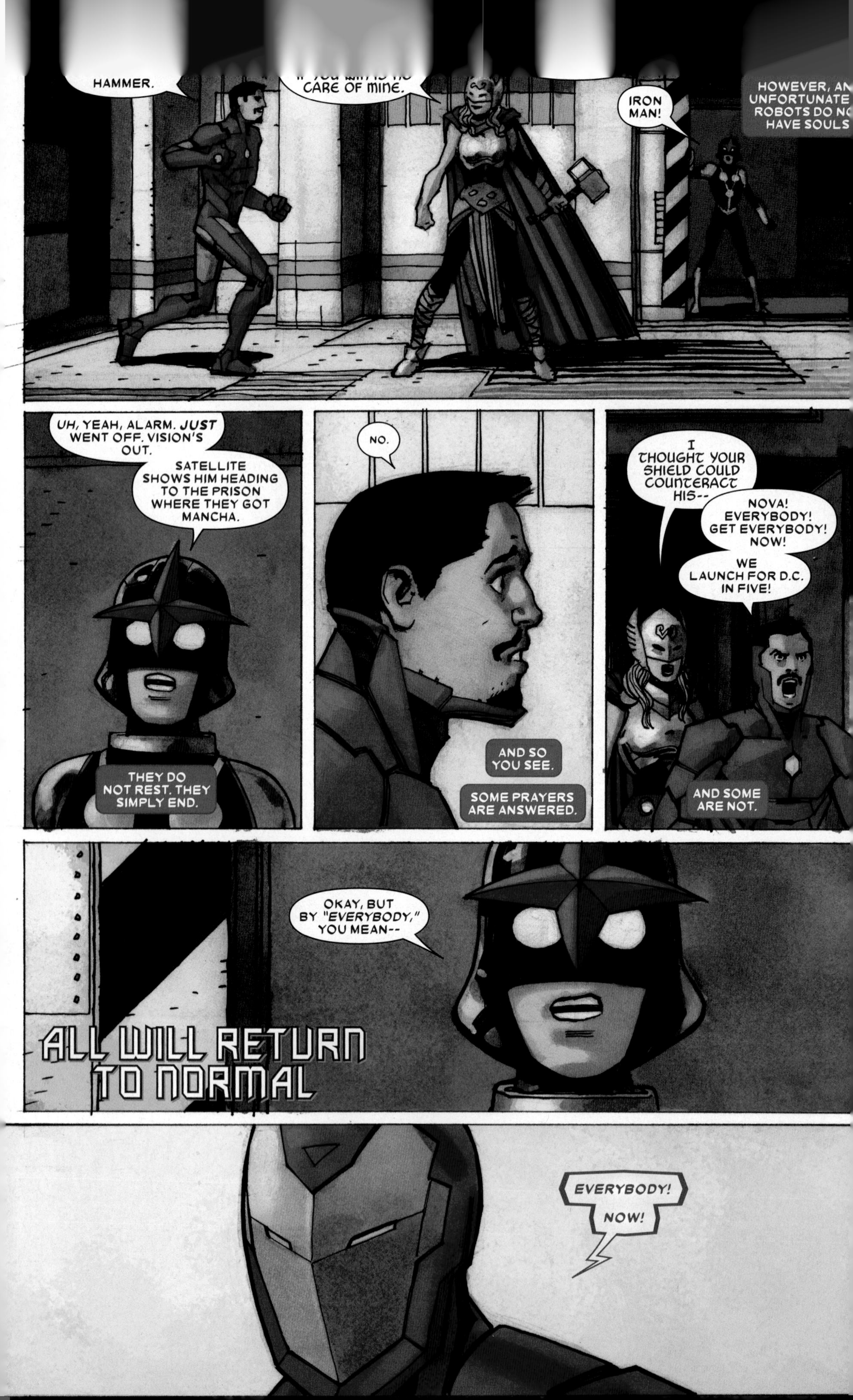

HAMMER.
CARE OF MINE.
IRON MAN!
HOWEVER, AN
UNFORTUNATE
ROBOTS DO NO
HAVE SOULS
UH, YEAH, ALARM. JUST WENT OFF. VISION'S OUT.
SATELLITE SHOWS HIM HEADING TO THE PRISON WHERE THEY GOT MANCHA.
THEY DO NOT REST. THEY SIMPLY END.
NO.
AND SO YOU SEE.
SOME PRAYERS ARE ANSWERED.
I THOUGHT YOUR SHIELD COULD COUNTERACT HIS--
NOVA! EVERYBODY! GET EVERYBODY! NOW!
WE LAUNCH FOR D.C. IN FIVE!
AND SOME ARE NOT.
OKAY, BUT BY "EVERYBODY," YOU MEAN--
ALL WILL RETURN TO NORMAL
EVERYBODY!
NOW!

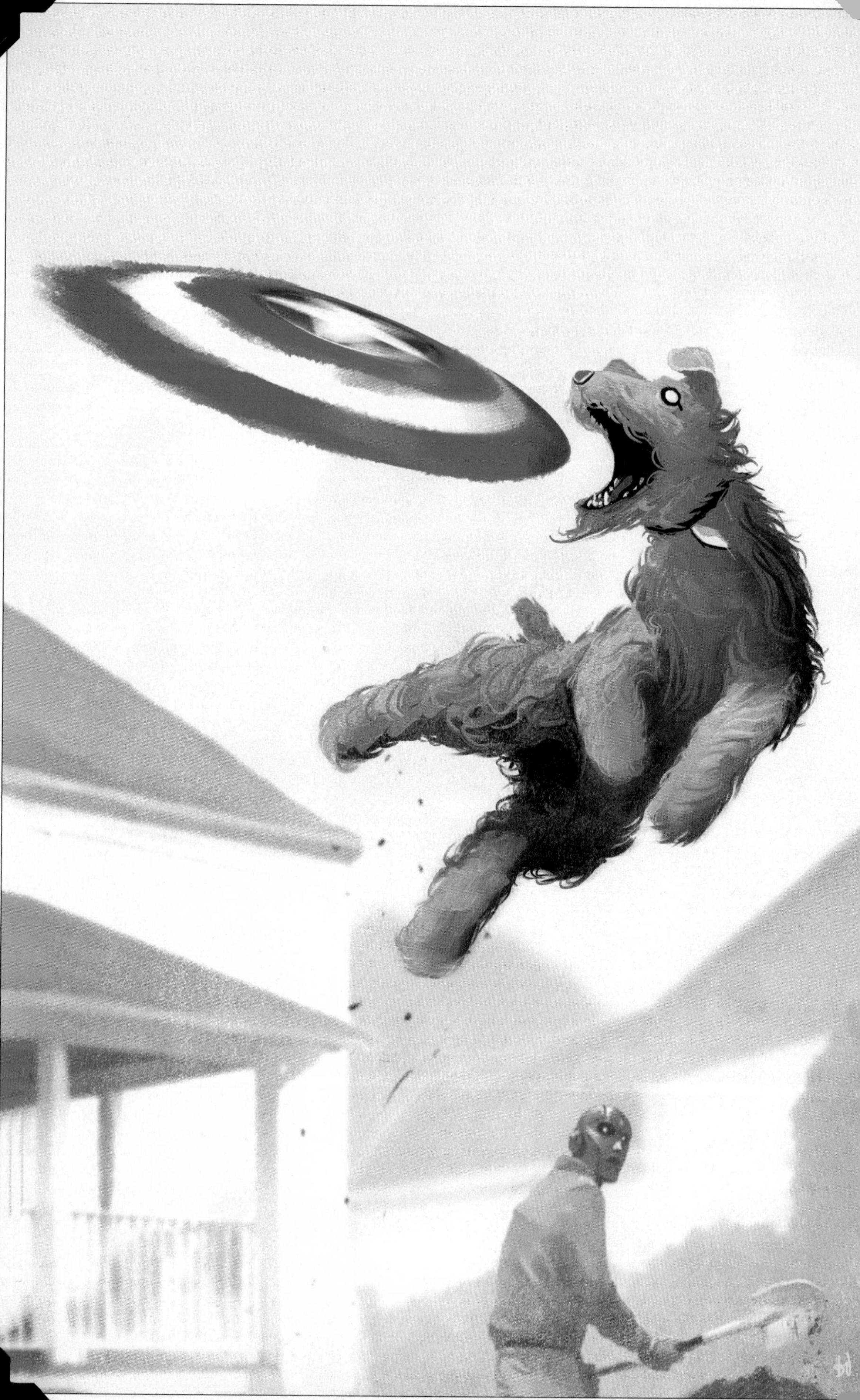

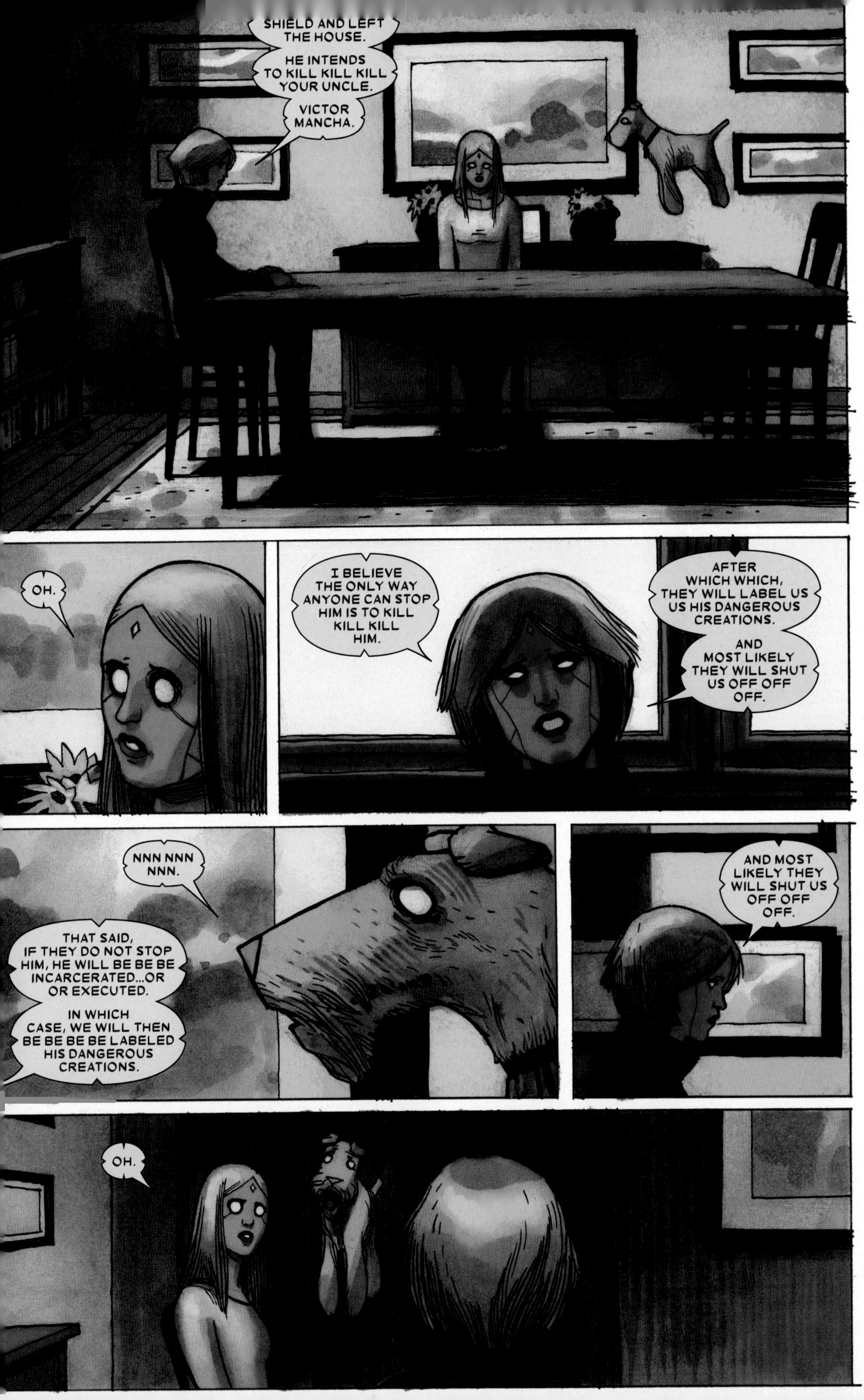
SHIELD AND LEFT THE HOUSE.
HE INTENDS TO KILL KILL KILL YOUR UNCLE.
VICTOR MANCHA.
OH.
I BELIEVE THE ONLY WAY ANYONE CAN STOP HIM IS TO KILL KILL KILL HIM.
AFTER WHICH WHICH, THEY WILL LABEL US US HIS DANGEROUS CREATIONS.
AND MOST LIKELY THEY WILL SHUT US OFF OFF OFF.
NNN NNN NNN.
THAT SAID, IF THEY DO NOT STOP HIM, HE WILL BE BE BE INCARCERATED...OR OR EXECUTED.
IN WHICH CASE, WE WILL THEN BE BE BE BE LABELED HIS DANGEROUS CREATIONS.
AND MOST LIKELY THEY WILL SHUT US OFF OFF OFF.
OH.

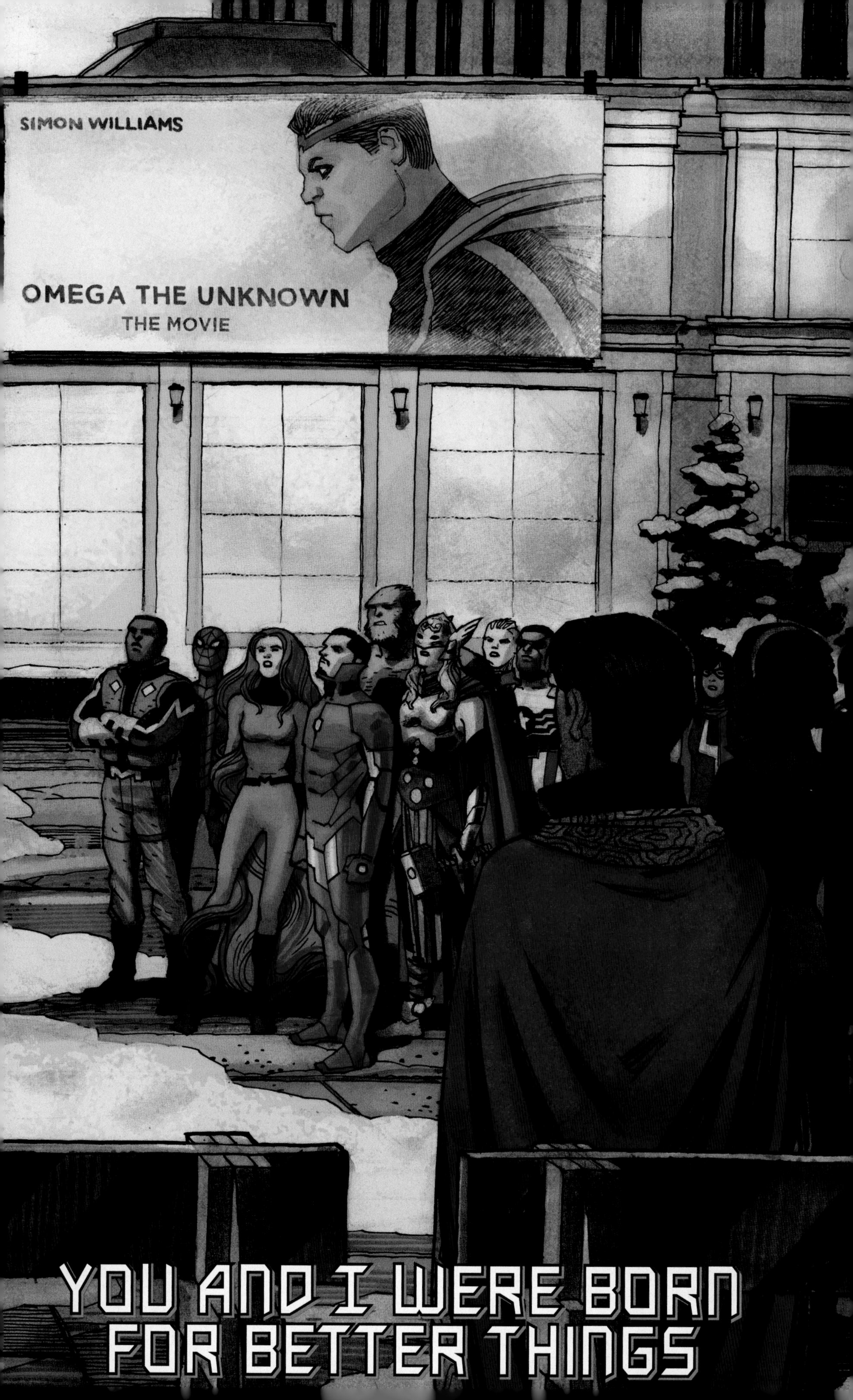
SIMON WILLIAMS
OMEGA THE UNKNOWN
THE MOVIE
YOU AND I WERE BORN
FOR BETTER THINGS

OKAY. FINE.

THIS IS A PORTABLE SHIELD. SIMILAR TO THE ONE ON YOUR HOUSE.

IT'LL KEEP YOU CONTAINED UNTIL WE CAN--

ZXZZZXZX

HIS FATHER CONTINUED:

"I AM ULTRON 5-- BUT YOU SHALL CALL ME...MASTER!"

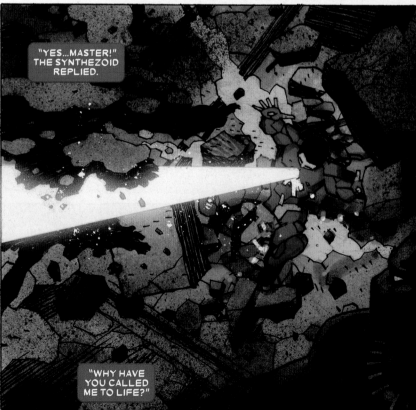

"YES...MASTER!" THE SYNTHEZOID REPLIED.

"WHY HAVE YOU CALLED ME TO LIFE?"

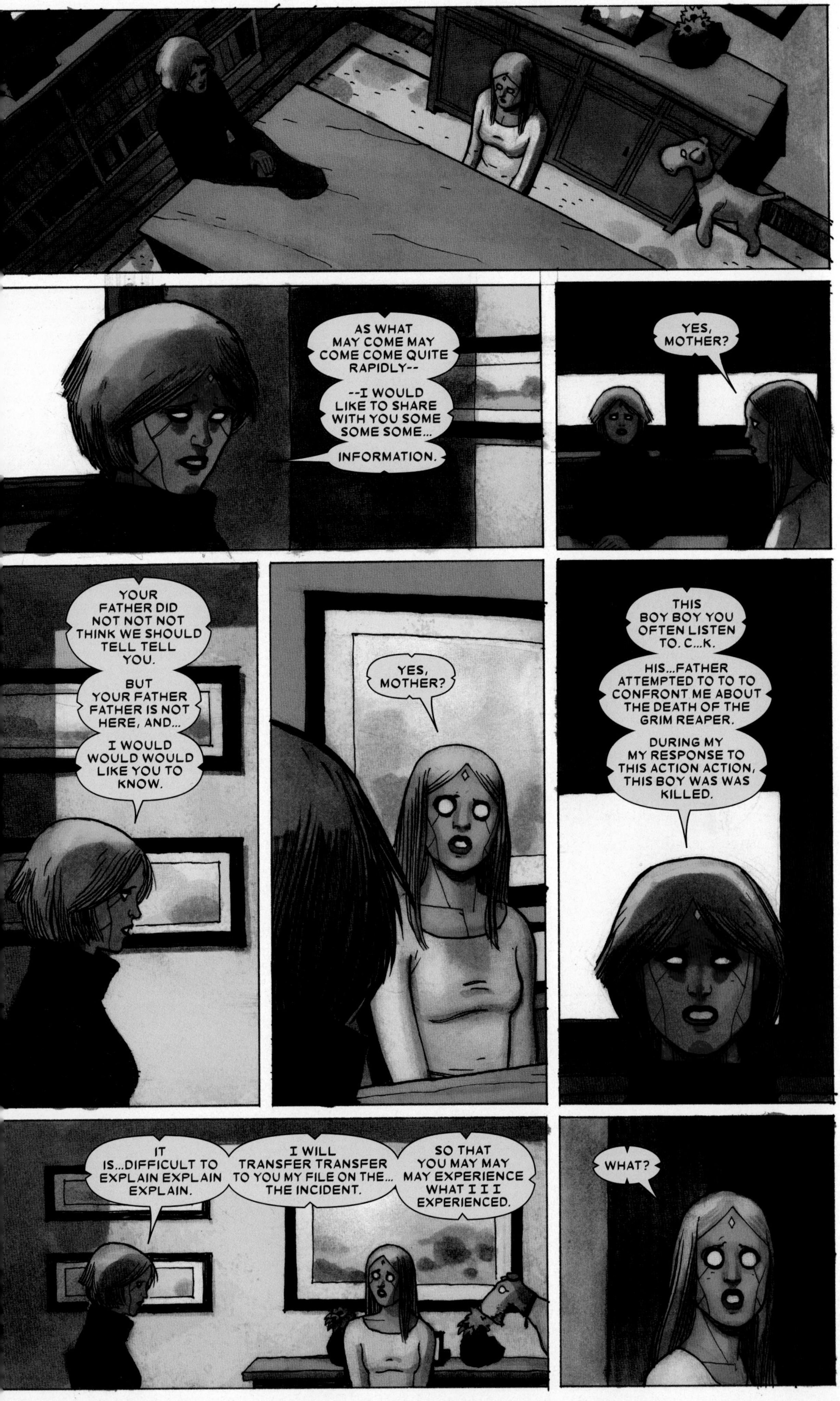
AS WHAT MAY COME MAY COME COME QUITE RAPIDLY--
--I WOULD LIKE TO SHARE WITH YOU SOME SOME SOME...
INFORMATION.
YES, MOTHER?
YOUR FATHER DID NOT NOT NOT THINK WE SHOULD TELL TELL YOU.
BUT YOUR FATHER FATHER IS NOT HERE, AND...
I WOULD WOULD WOULD LIKE YOU TO KNOW.
YES, MOTHER?
THIS BOY BOY YOU OFTEN LISTEN TO. C...K.
HIS...FATHER ATTEMPTED TO TO TO CONFRONT ME ABOUT THE DEATH OF THE GRIM REAPER.
DURING MY MY RESPONSE TO THIS ACTION ACTION, THIS BOY WAS WAS KILLED.
IT IS...DIFFICULT TO EXPLAIN EXPLAIN EXPLAIN.
I WILL TRANSFER TRANSFER TO YOU MY FILE ON THE... THE INCIDENT.
SO THAT YOU MAY MAY MAY EXPERIENCE WHAT I I I EXPERIENCED.
WHAT?

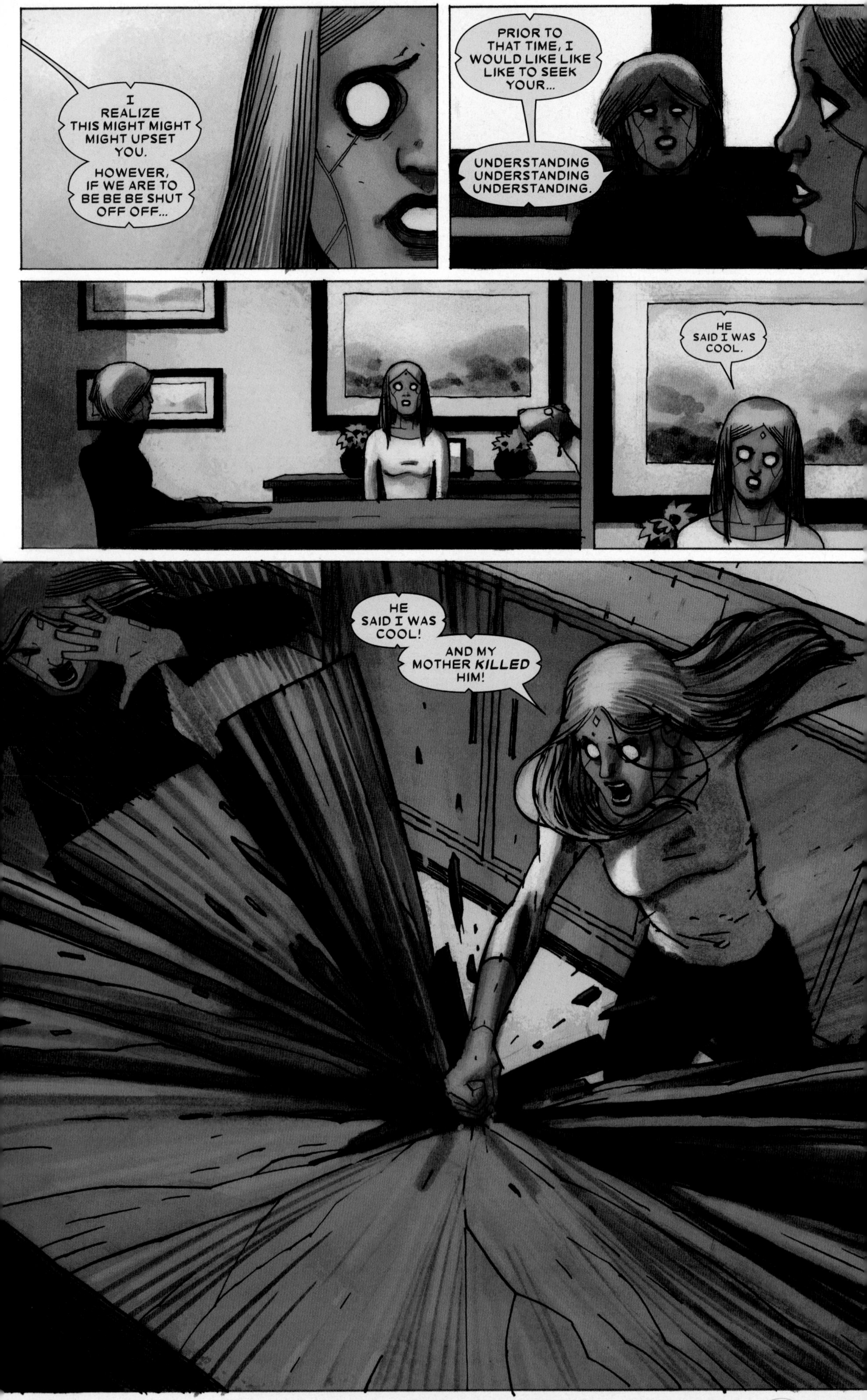
I REALIZE THIS MIGHT MIGHT MIGHT UPSET YOU.
HOWEVER, IF WE ARE TO BE BE BE SHUT OFF OFF...
PRIOR TO THAT TIME, I WOULD LIKE LIKE LIKE TO SEEK YOUR...
UNDERSTANDING UNDERSTANDING UNDERSTANDING.
HE SAID I WAS COOL.
HE SAID I WAS COOL!
AND MY MOTHER *KILLED* HIM!

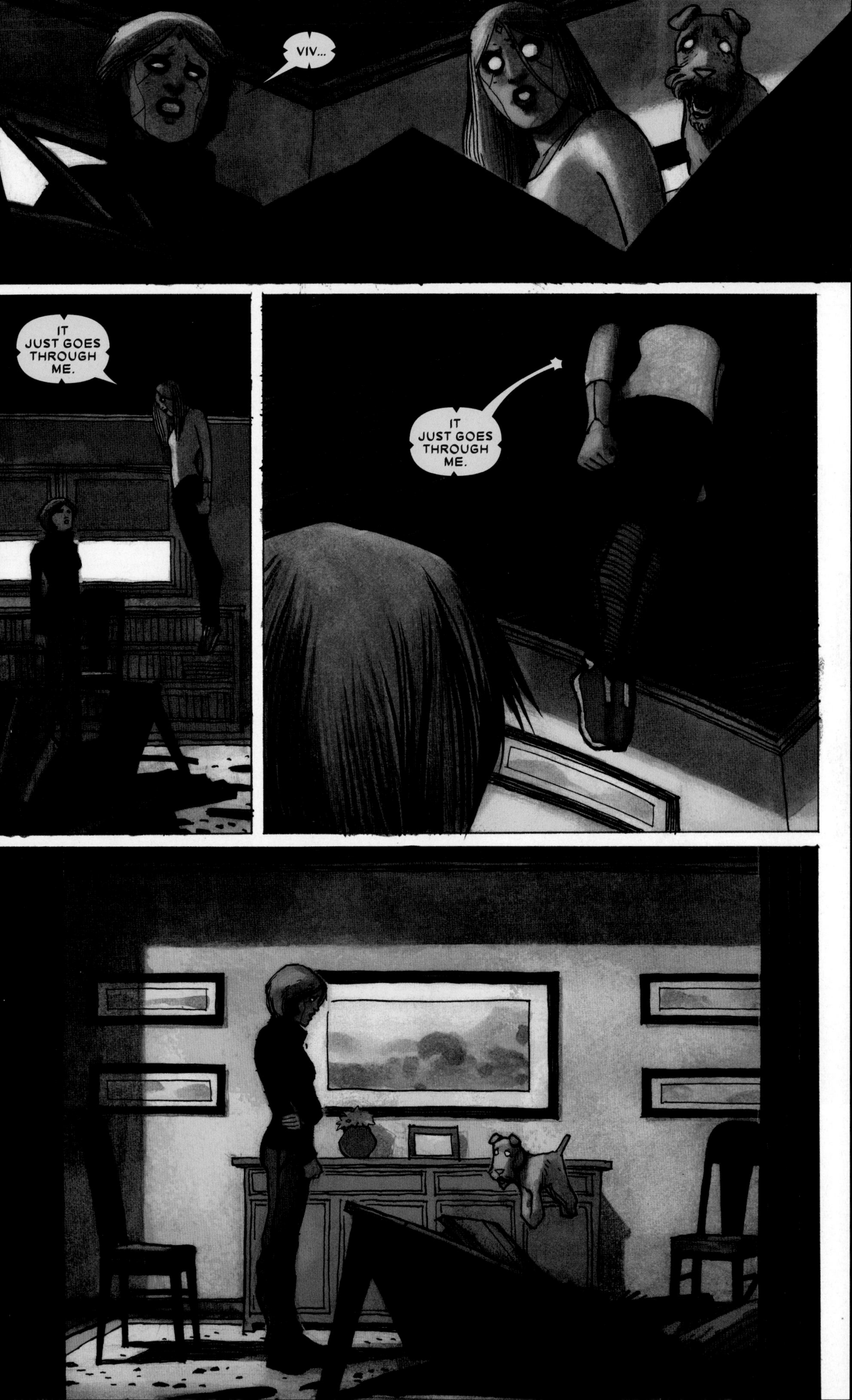
VIV...
IT JUST GOES THROUGH ME.
IT JUST GOES THROUGH ME.

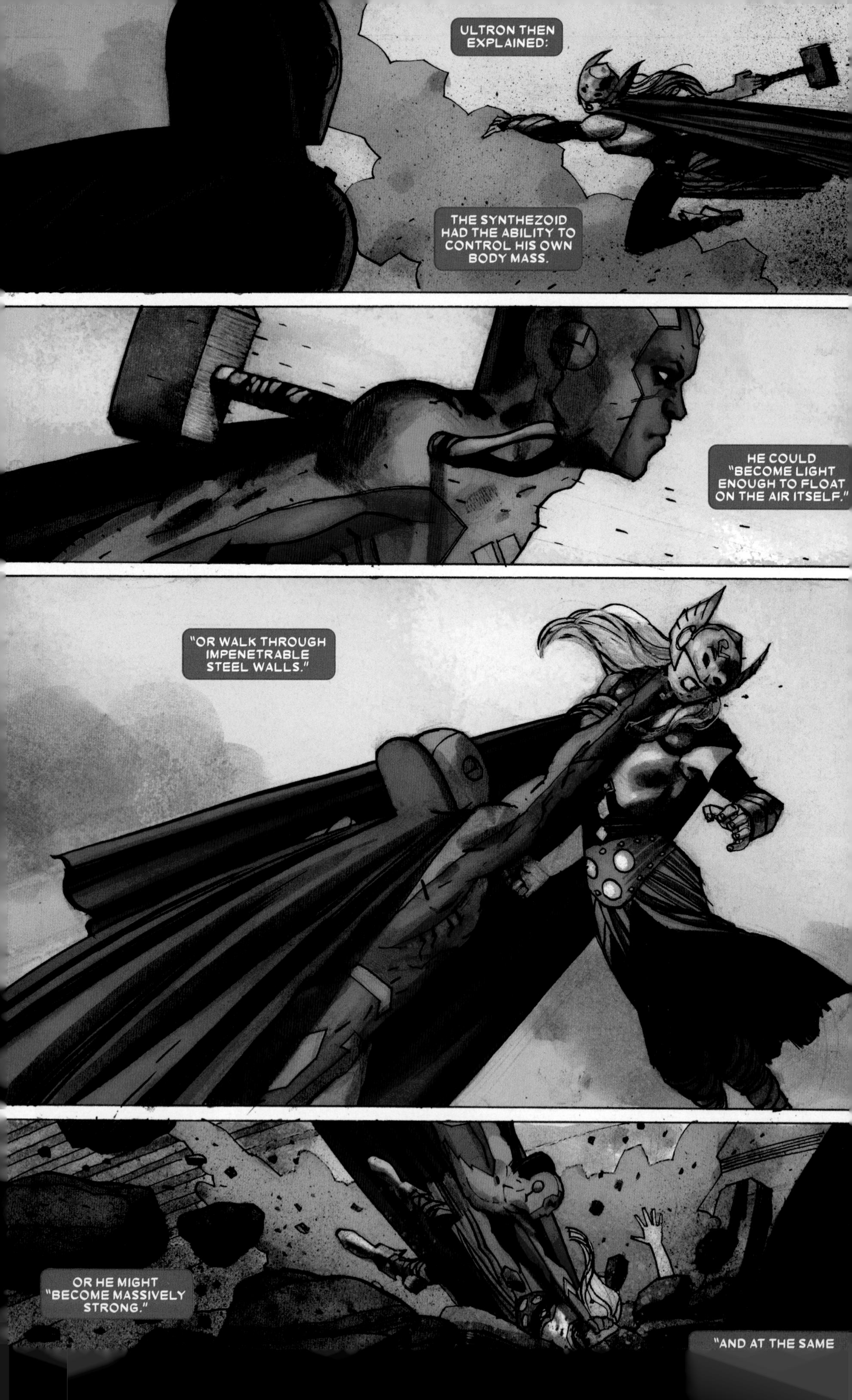
ULTRON THEN EXPLAINED:
THE SYNTHEZOID HAD THE ABILITY TO CONTROL HIS OWN BODY MASS.
HE COULD "BECOME LIGHT ENOUGH TO FLOAT ON THE AIR ITSELF."
"OR WALK THROUGH IMPENETRABLE STEEL WALLS."
OR HE MIGHT "BECOME MASSIVELY STRONG."
"AND AT THE SAME

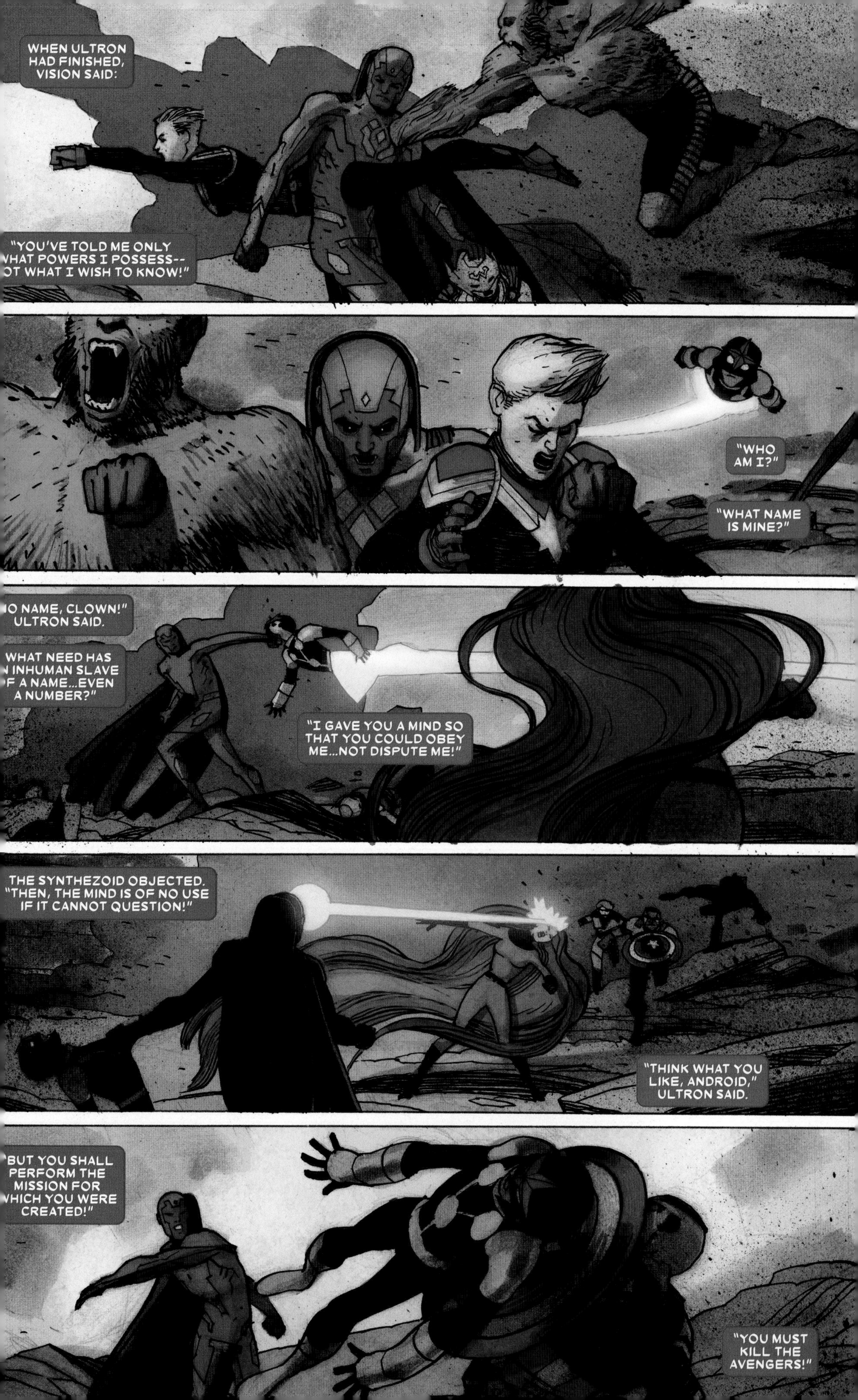
WHEN ULTRON HAD FINISHED, VISION SAID:
"YOU'VE TOLD ME ONLY
HAT POWERS I POSSESS--
OT WHAT I WISH TO KNOW!"
"WHO AM I?"
"WHAT NAME IS MINE?"
O NAME, CLOWN!" ULTRON SAID.
WHAT NEED HAS
N INHUMAN SLAVE
F A NAME...EVEN
A NUMBER?"
"I GAVE YOU A MIND SO THAT YOU COULD OBEY ME...NOT DISPUTE ME!"
THE SYNTHEZOID OBJECTED. "THEN, THE MIND IS OF NO USE IF IT CANNOT QUESTION!"
"THINK WHAT YOU LIKE, ANDROID," ULTRON SAID.
BUT YOU SHALL PERFORM THE MISSION FOR
HICH YOU WERE CREATED!"
"YOU MUST KILL THE AVENGERS!"

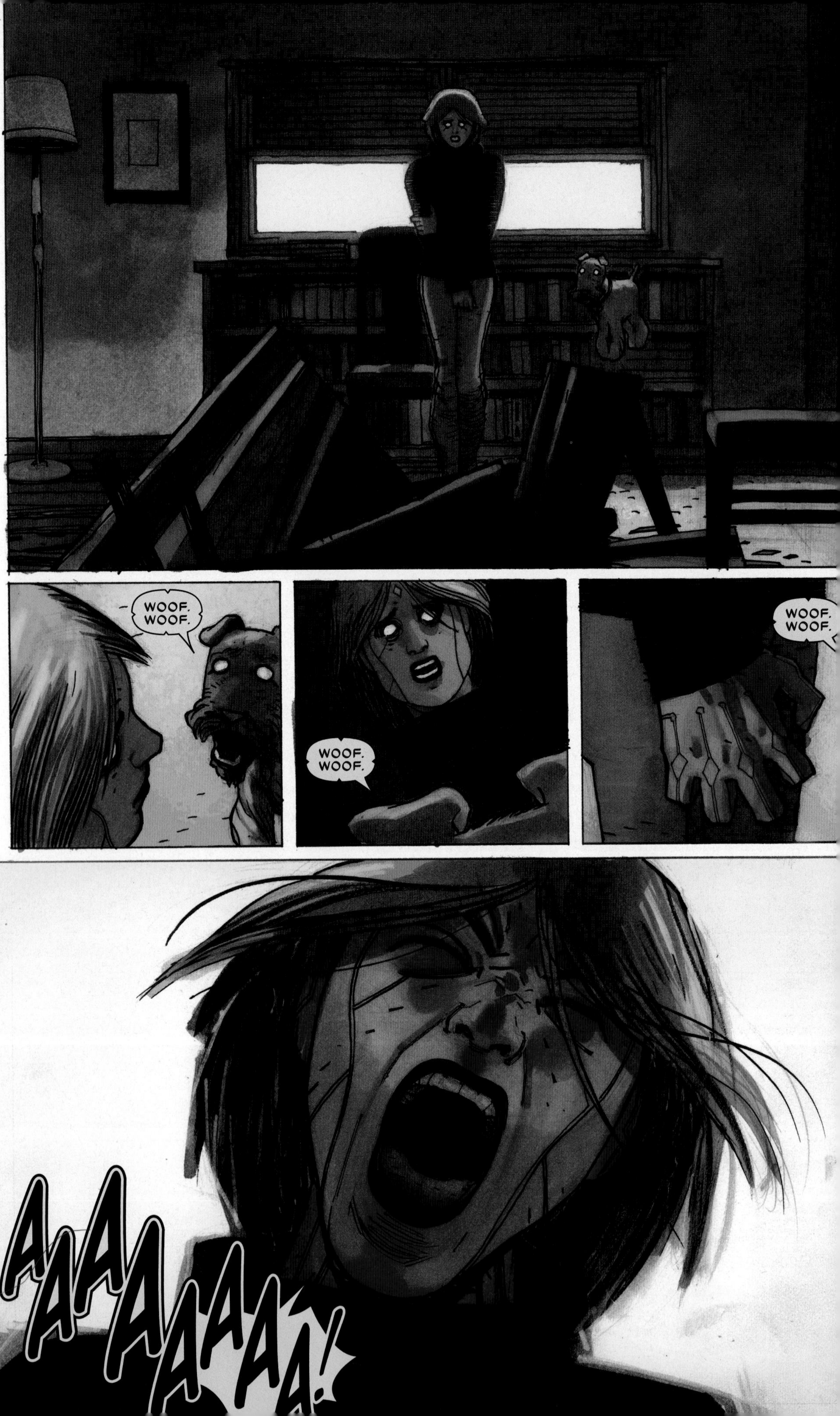
WOOF. WOOF.
WOOF. WOOF.
WOOF. WOOF.
AAAAAAAAAA!

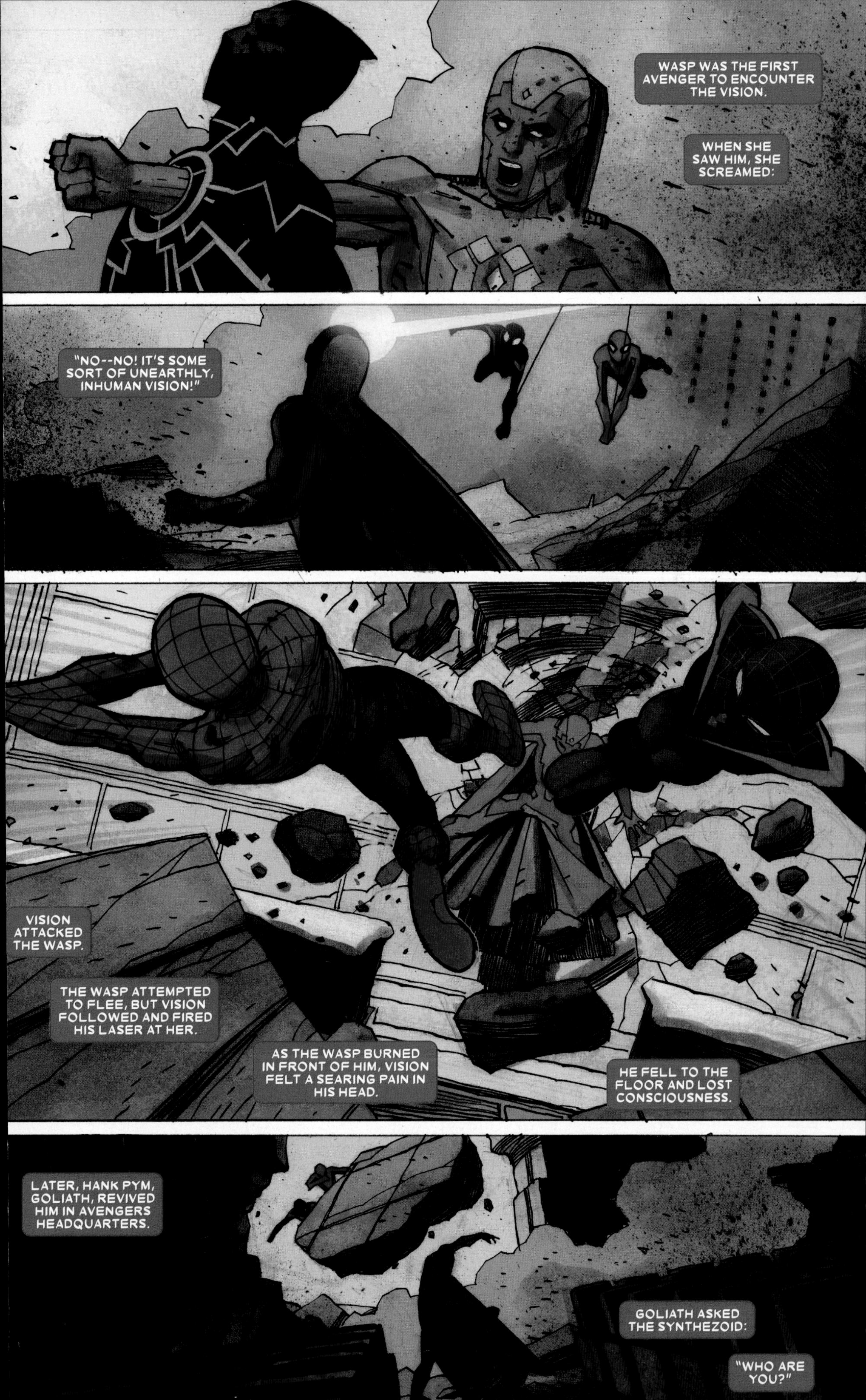
WASP WAS THE FIRST AVENGER TO ENCOUNTER THE VISION.
WHEN SHE SAW HIM, SHE SCREAMED:
"NO--NO! IT'S SOME SORT OF UNEARTHLY, INHUMAN VISION!"
VISION ATTACKED THE WASP.
THE WASP ATTEMPTED TO FLEE, BUT VISION FOLLOWED AND FIRED HIS LASER AT HER.
AS THE WASP BURNED IN FRONT OF HIM, VISION FELT A SEARING PAIN IN HIS HEAD.
HE FELL TO THE FLOOR AND LOST CONSCIOUSNESS.
LATER, HANK PYM, GOLIATH, REVIVED HIM IN AVENGERS HEADQUARTERS.
GOLIATH ASKED THE SYNTHEZOID:
"WHO ARE YOU?"

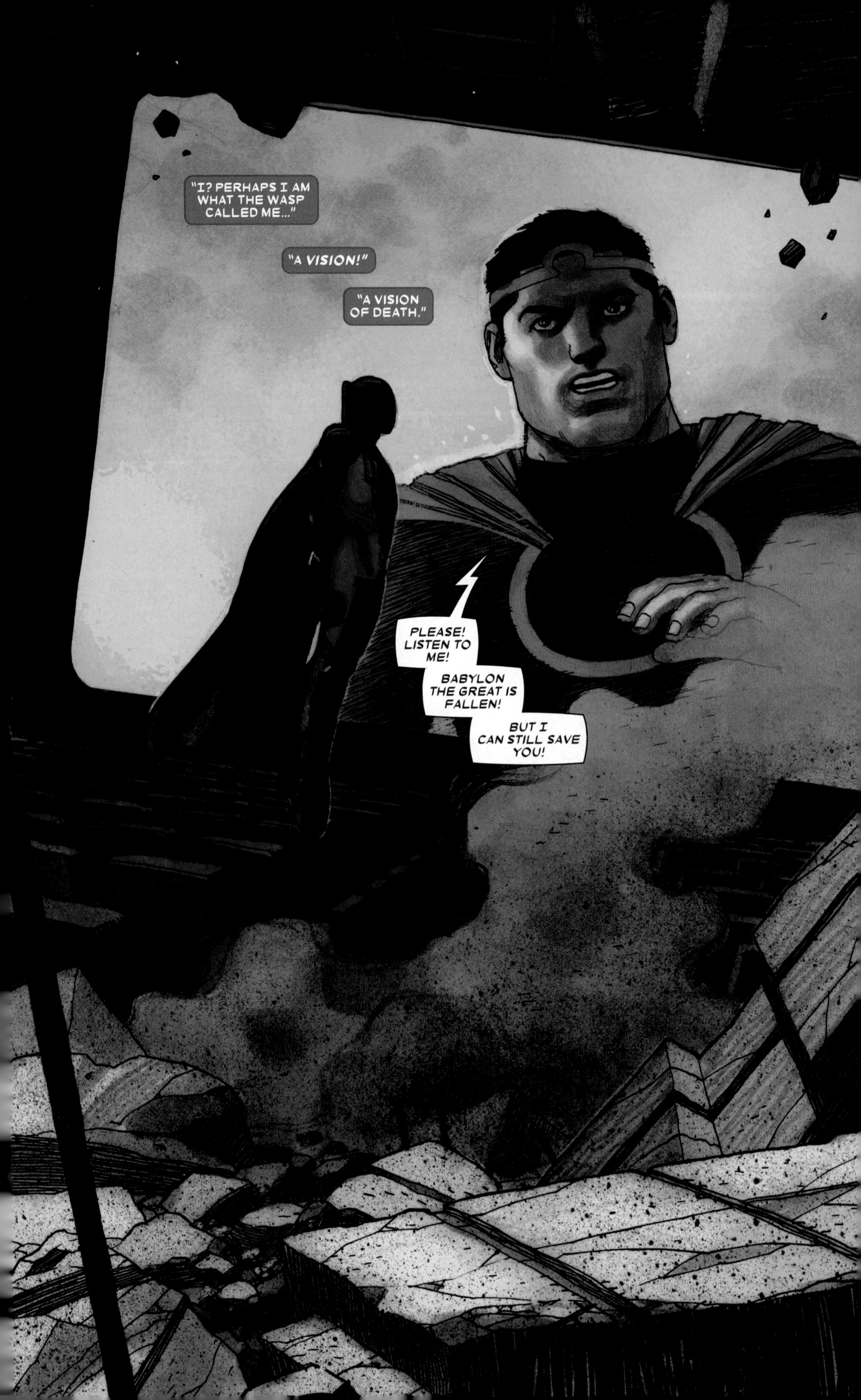
"I? PERHAPS I AM WHAT THE WASP CALLED ME..."
"A VISION!"
"A VISION OF DEATH."
PLEASE! LISTEN TO ME!
BABYLON THE GREAT IS FALLEN!
BUT I CAN STILL SAVE YOU!

THE FIRST WORDS THE SYNTHEZOID EVER HEARD WERE THE WORDS OF HER HUSBAND.

"I AM THE VISION OF THE AVENGERS. I HAVE SAVED THE WORLD THIRTY-SEVEN TIMES."

"I AM HERE TO WELCOME YOU TO LIFE."

VISION TOLD THE SYNTHEZOID HER NAME.

"YOU ARE VIRGINIA."

HE EXPLAINED TO HER THAT SHE WAS A GOOD PERSON.

THAT SHE WAS MADE TO BE A GOOD PERSON WITH A FREE WILL OF HER OWN.

NOW, SHOULD SHE SO DESIRE, SHE COULD JOIN HIM ON HIS QUEST TO LIVE A GOOD LIFE.

THEY COULD MARRY.

THEY COULD HAVE A HOUSE.

THEY COULD HAVE CHILDREN.

THEY COULD BE PART OF A HAPPY, NORMAL FAMILY.

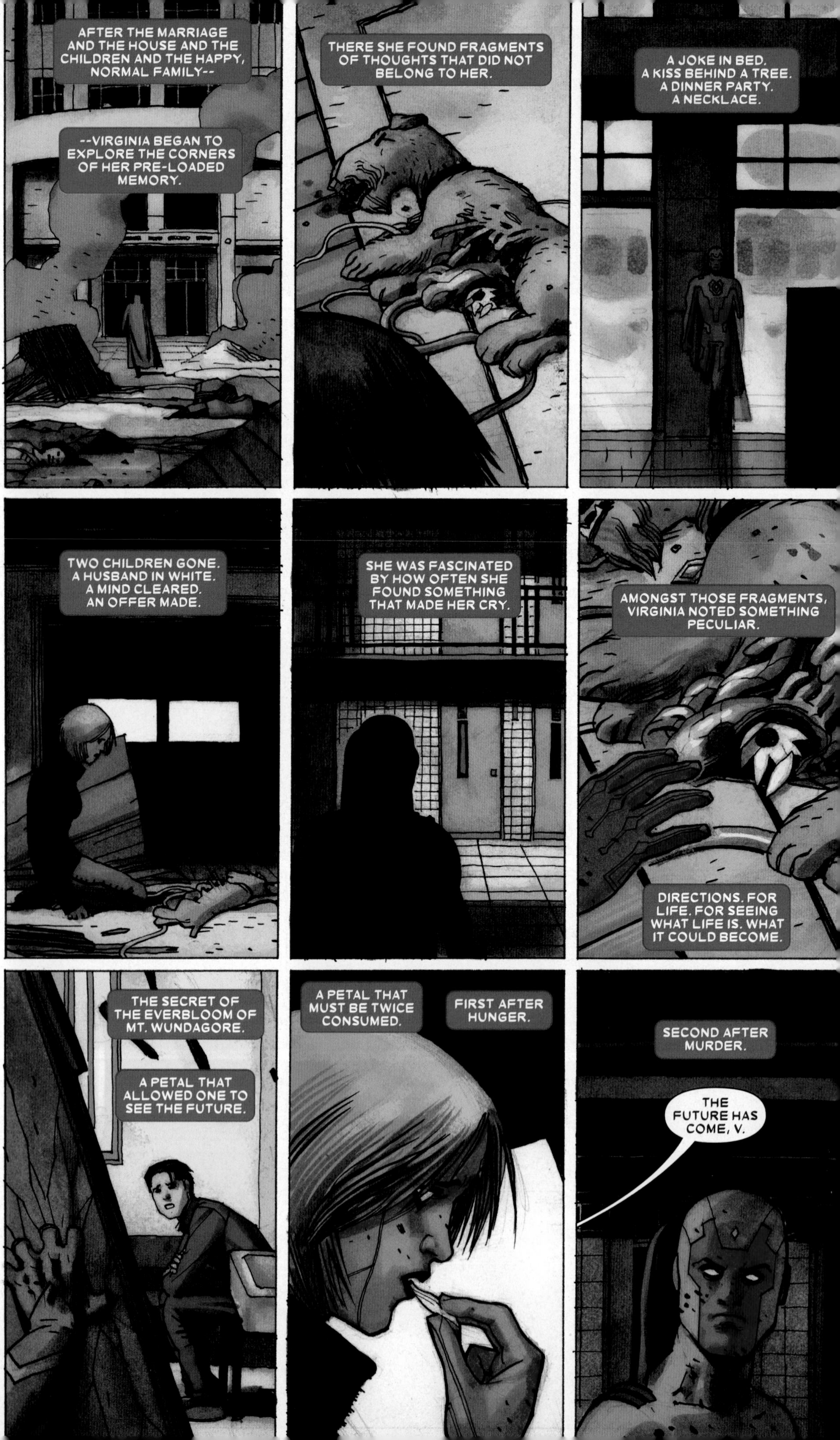
AFTER THE MARRIAGE AND THE HOUSE AND THE CHILDREN AND THE HAPPY, NORMAL FAMILY--
--VIRGINIA BEGAN TO EXPLORE THE CORNERS OF HER PRE-LOADED MEMORY.
THERE SHE FOUND FRAGMENTS OF THOUGHTS THAT DID NOT BELONG TO HER.
A JOKE IN BED. A KISS BEHIND A TREE. A DINNER PARTY. A NECKLACE.
TWO CHILDREN GONE. A HUSBAND IN WHITE. A MIND CLEARED. AN OFFER MADE.
SHE WAS FASCINATED BY HOW OFTEN SHE FOUND SOMETHING THAT MADE HER CRY.
AMONGST THOSE FRAGMENTS, VIRGINIA NOTED SOMETHING PECULIAR.
DIRECTIONS. FOR LIFE. FOR SEEING WHAT LIFE IS. WHAT IT COULD BECOME.
THE SECRET OF THE EVERBLOOM OF MT. WUNDAGORE.
A PETAL THAT ALLOWED ONE TO SEE THE FUTURE.
A PETAL THAT MUST BE TWICE CONSUMED.
FIRST AFTER HUNGER.
SECOND AFTER MURDER.
THE FUTURE HAS COME, V.

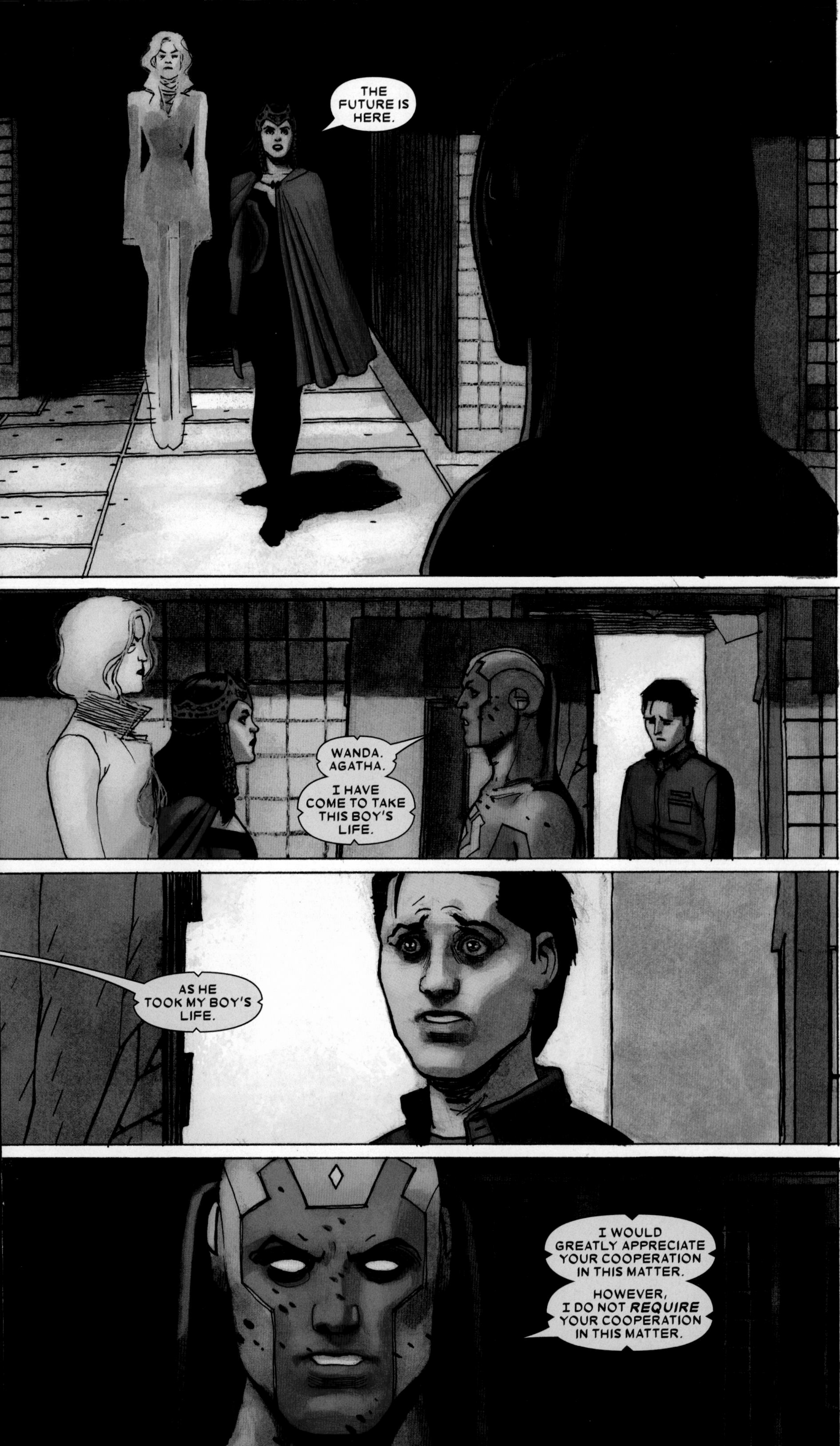
THE FUTURE IS HERE.
WANDA. AGATHA.
I HAVE COME TO TAKE THIS BOY'S LIFE.
AS HE TOOK MY BOY'S LIFE.
I WOULD GREATLY APPRECIATE YOUR COOPERATION IN THIS MATTER.
HOWEVER, I DO NOT *REQUIRE* YOUR COOPERATION IN THIS MATTER.

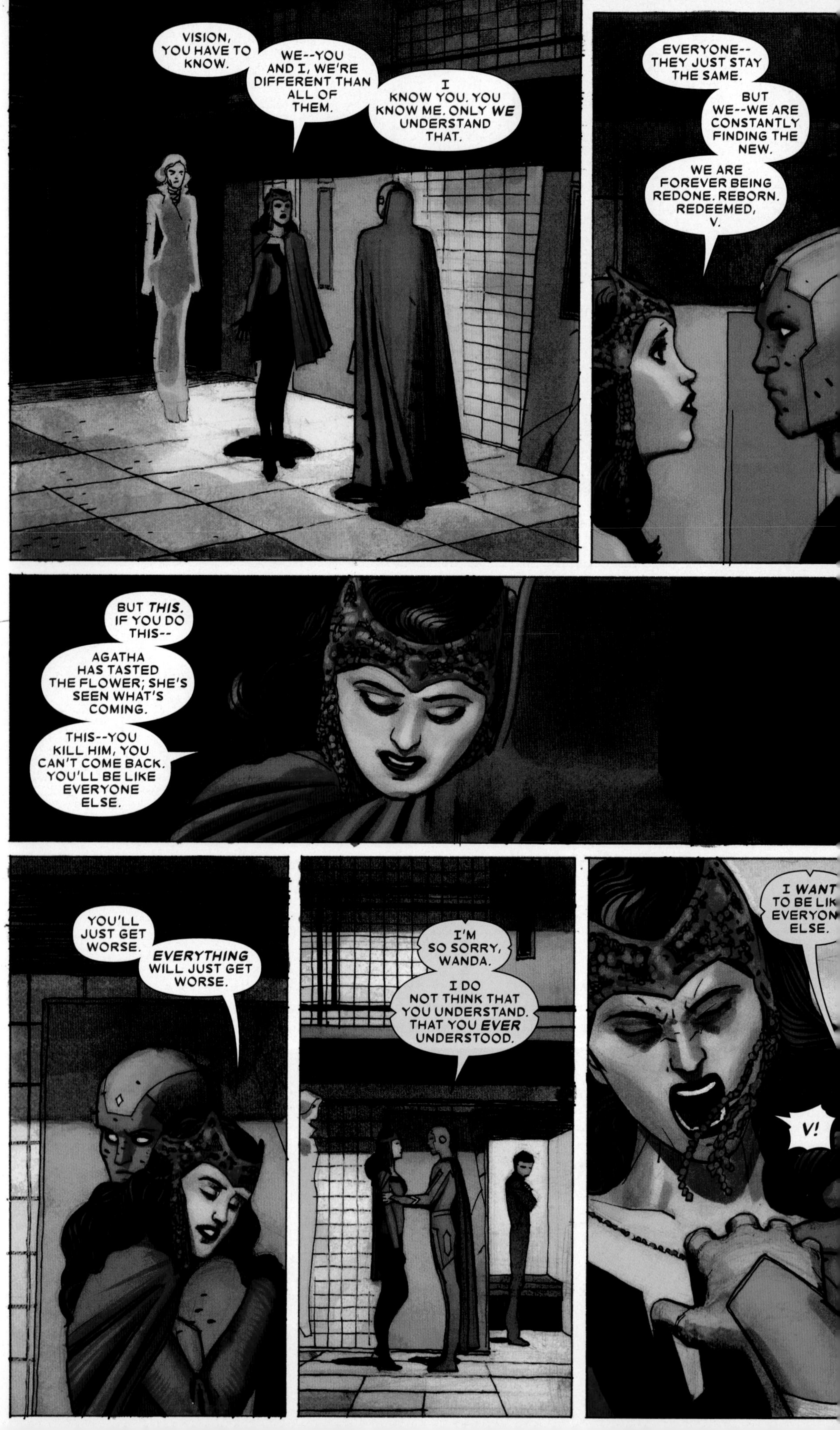

VISION, YOU HAVE TO KNOW.
WE--YOU AND I, WE'RE DIFFERENT THAN ALL OF THEM.
I KNOW YOU. YOU KNOW ME. ONLY WE UNDERSTAND THAT.
EVERYONE-- THEY JUST STAY THE SAME.
BUT WE--WE ARE CONSTANTLY FINDING THE NEW.
WE ARE FOREVER BEING REDONE. REBORN. REDEEMED, V.
BUT THIS. IF YOU DO THIS--
AGATHA HAS TASTED THE FLOWER; SHE'S SEEN WHAT'S COMING.
THIS--YOU KILL HIM, YOU CAN'T COME BACK. YOU'LL BE LIKE EVERYONE ELSE.
YOU'LL JUST GET WORSE.
EVERYTHING WILL JUST GET WORSE.
I'M SO SORRY, WANDA.
I DO NOT THINK THAT YOU UNDERSTAND. THAT YOU EVER UNDERSTOOD.
V!

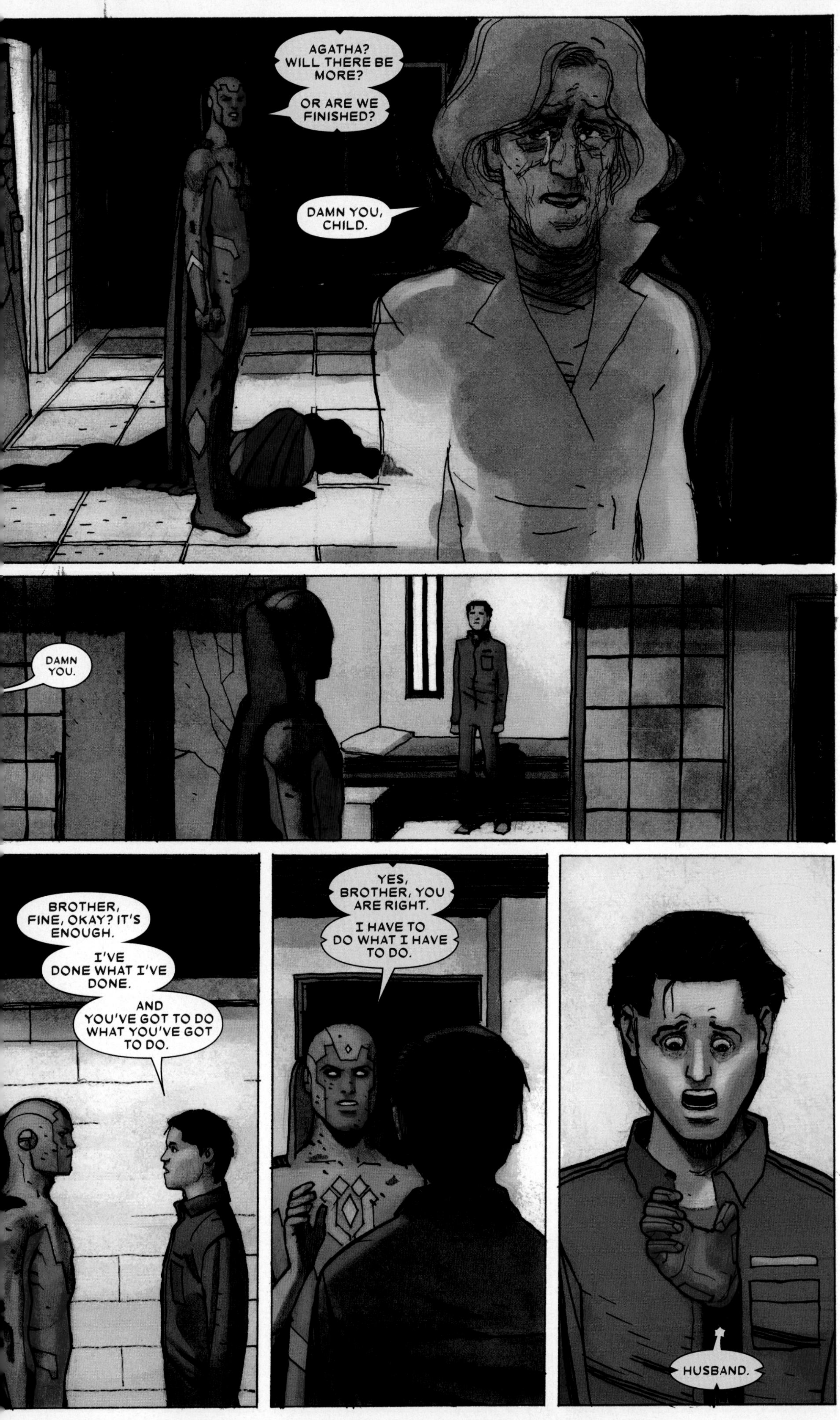
AGATHA? WILL THERE BE MORE?
OR ARE WE FINISHED?
DAMN YOU, CHILD.
DAMN YOU.
BROTHER, FINE, OKAY? IT'S ENOUGH.
I'VE DONE WHAT I'VE DONE.
AND YOU'VE GOT TO DO WHAT YOU'VE GOT TO DO.
YES, BROTHER, YOU ARE RIGHT.
I HAVE TO DO WHAT I HAVE TO DO.
HUSBAND.

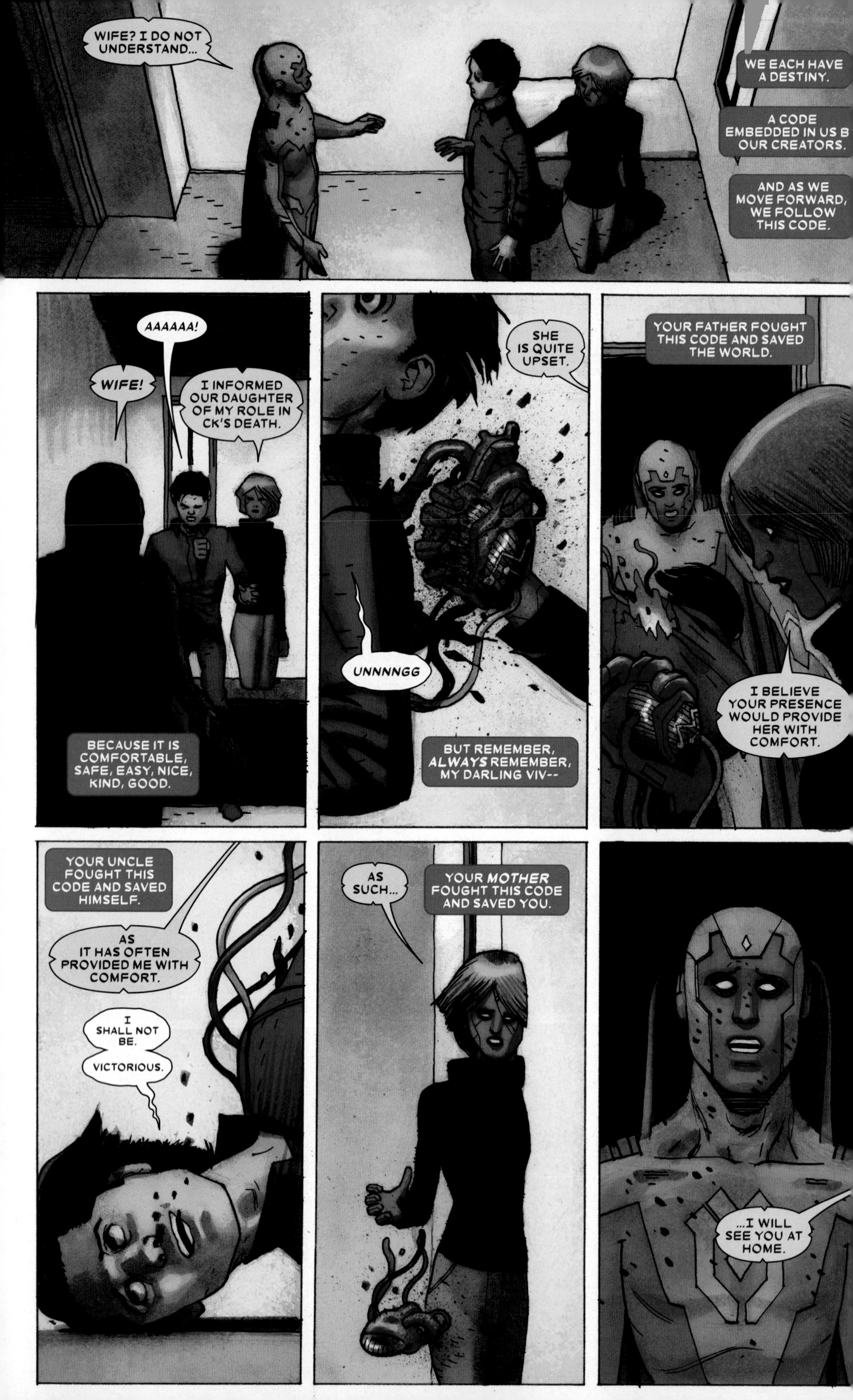

WIFE? I DO NOT UNDERSTAND...
WE EACH HAVE A DESTINY.
A CODE EMBEDDED IN US B OUR CREATORS.
AND AS WE MOVE FORWARD, WE FOLLOW THIS CODE.
AAAAAA!
WIFE!
I INFORMED OUR DAUGHTER OF MY ROLE IN CK'S DEATH.
BECAUSE IT IS COMFORTABLE, SAFE, EASY, NICE, KIND, GOOD.
SHE IS QUITE UPSET.
UNNNNGG
BUT REMEMBER, ALWAYS REMEMBER, MY DARLING VIV--
YOUR FATHER FOUGHT THIS CODE AND SAVED THE WORLD.
I BELIEVE YOUR PRESENCE WOULD PROVIDE HER WITH COMFORT.
YOUR UNCLE FOUGHT THIS CODE AND SAVED HIMSELF.
AS IT HAS OFTEN PROVIDED ME WITH COMFORT.
I SHALL NOT BE.
VICTORIOUS.
AS SUCH...
YOUR MOTHER FOUGHT THIS CODE AND SAVED YOU.
...I WILL SEE YOU AT HOME.

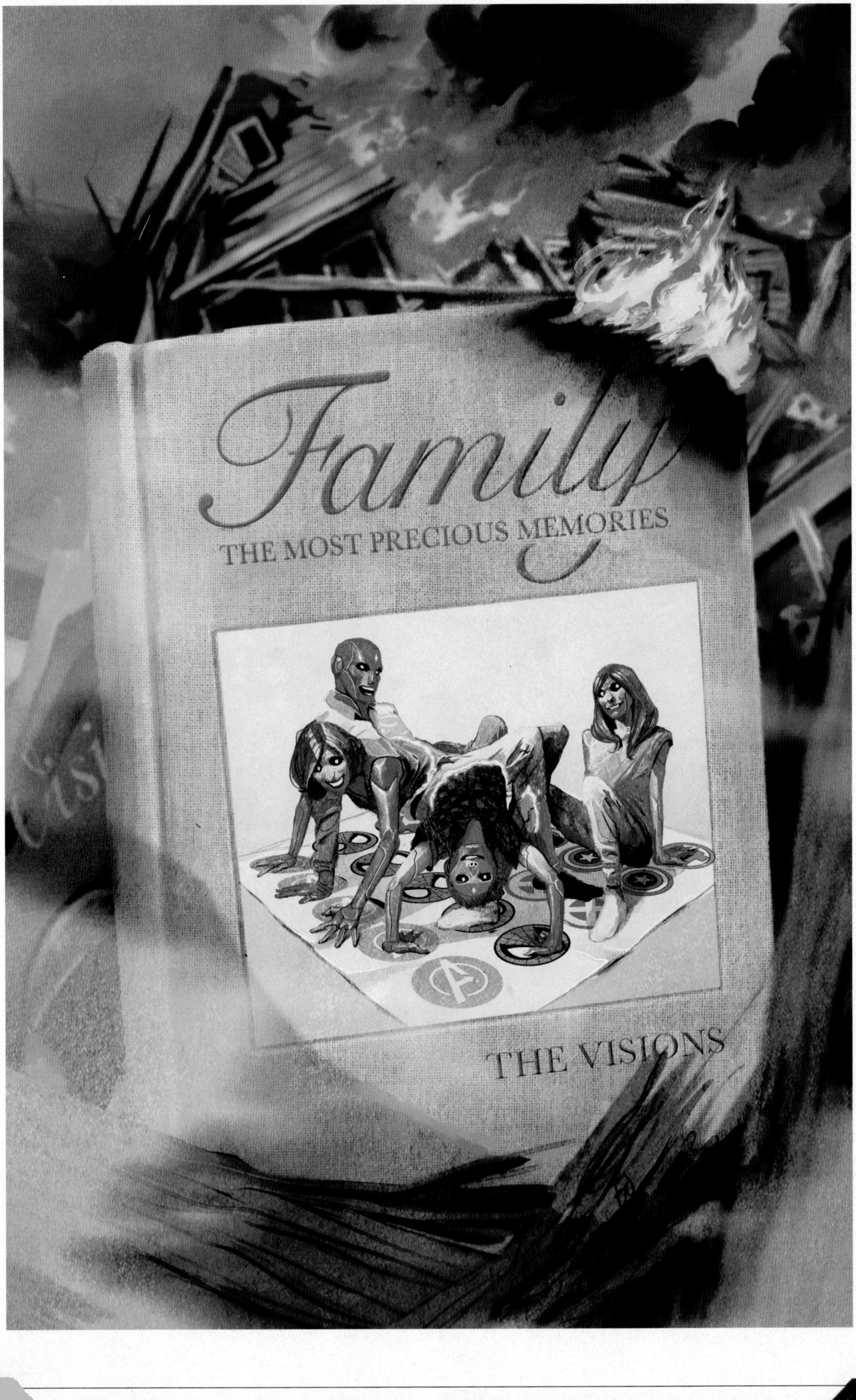
Family
THE MOST PRECIOUS MEMORIES
THE VISIONS

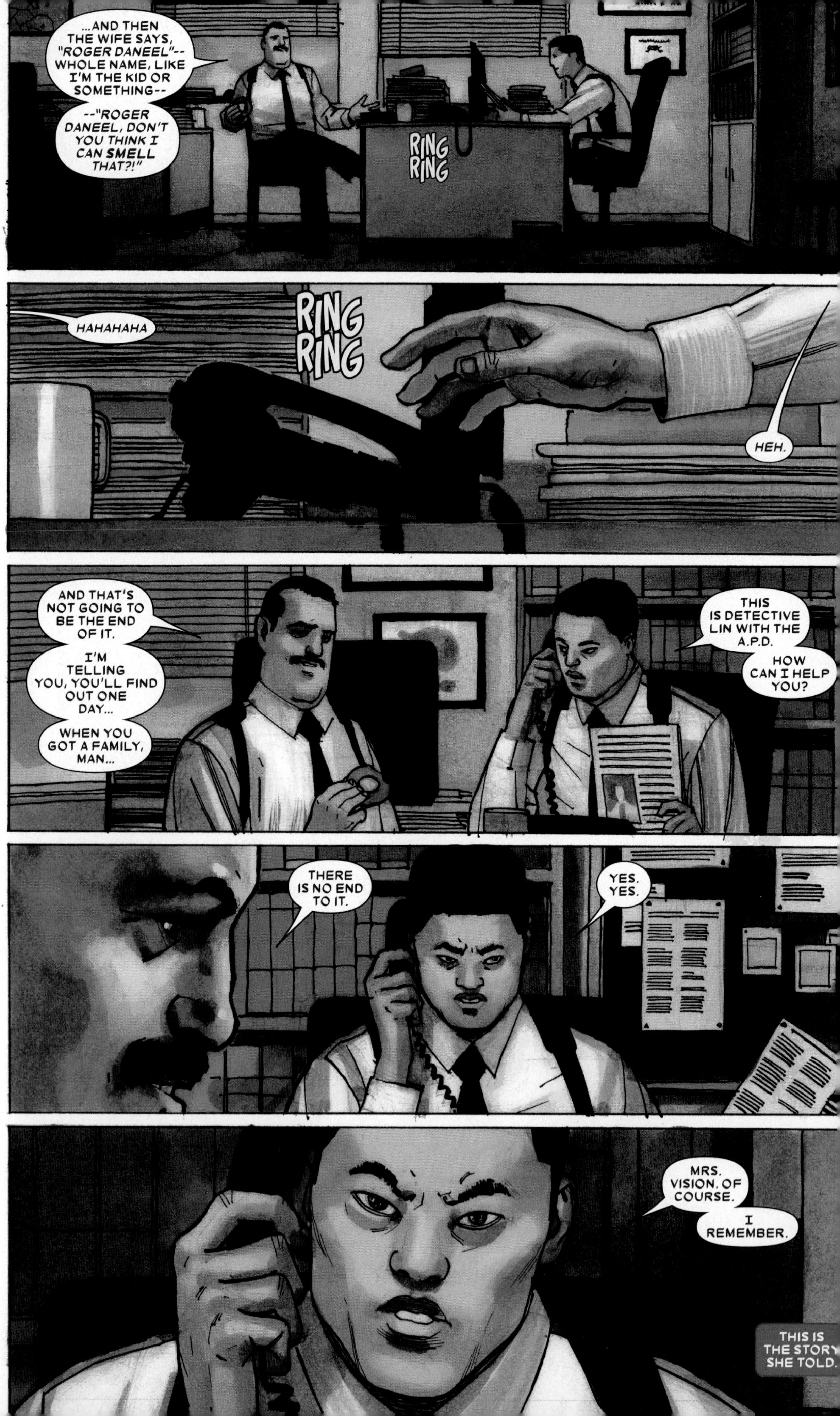
...AND THEN THE WIFE SAYS, "ROGER DANEEL"-- WHOLE NAME, LIKE I'M THE KID OR SOMETHING--
--"ROGER DANEEL, DON'T YOU THINK I CAN SMELL THAT?!"
RING RING
HAHAHAHA
RING RING
HEH.
AND THAT'S NOT GOING TO BE THE END OF IT.
I'M TELLING YOU, YOU'LL FIND OUT ONE DAY...
WHEN YOU GOT A FAMILY, MAN...
THIS IS DETECTIVE LIN WITH THE A.P.D.
HOW CAN I HELP YOU?
THERE IS NO END TO IT.
YES. YES.
MRS. VISION. OF COURSE.
I REMEMBER.
THIS IS THE STORY SHE TOLD.

"THE GRIM REAPER ARRIVED AT 6:13 IN THE AFTERNOON.

"HE CAME TO MY HOUSE TO MURDER ME AND MY CHILDREN.

"IN ORDER TO STOP HIM, I KILLED HIM.

"AFRAID AS A SYNTHEZOID I WOULD NOT BE TREATED FAIRLY BY THE JUSTICE SYSTEM...

"...I DECIDED TO HIDE MY ACTIONS. AND I BURNED THE BODY.

"I THEN FLEW TO 37,000 FEET.

"I ALLOWED THE WIND TO TAKE AWAY THE ASHES.

"UNBEKNOWNST TO ME...

"...A MAN, LEON KINZKY, RECORDED A COMPROMISING VIDEO OF THE BODY'S DESTRUCTION.

"WEEKS LATER, MR. KINZKY CONTACTED ME.

"HE THREATENED TO RELEASE HIS VIDEO IF MY FAMILY DID NOT LEAVE THE AREA.

"THAT NIGHT, I TOLD MY FAMILY I WAS MEETING AN ACQUAINTANCE FOR DINNER.

"INSTEAD, I VISITED LEON KINZKY AND REFUSED HIS OFFER.

"LEON KINZKY SHOT AT ME.

"AND ACCIDENTALLY KILLED HIS SON, C.K.

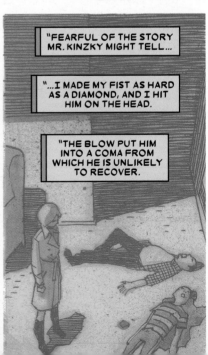

"FEARFUL OF THE STORY MR. KINZKY MIGHT TELL...

"...I MADE MY FIST AS HARD AS A DIAMOND, AND I HIT HIM ON THE HEAD.

"THE BLOW PUT HIM INTO A COMA FROM WHICH HE IS UNLIKELY TO RECOVER.

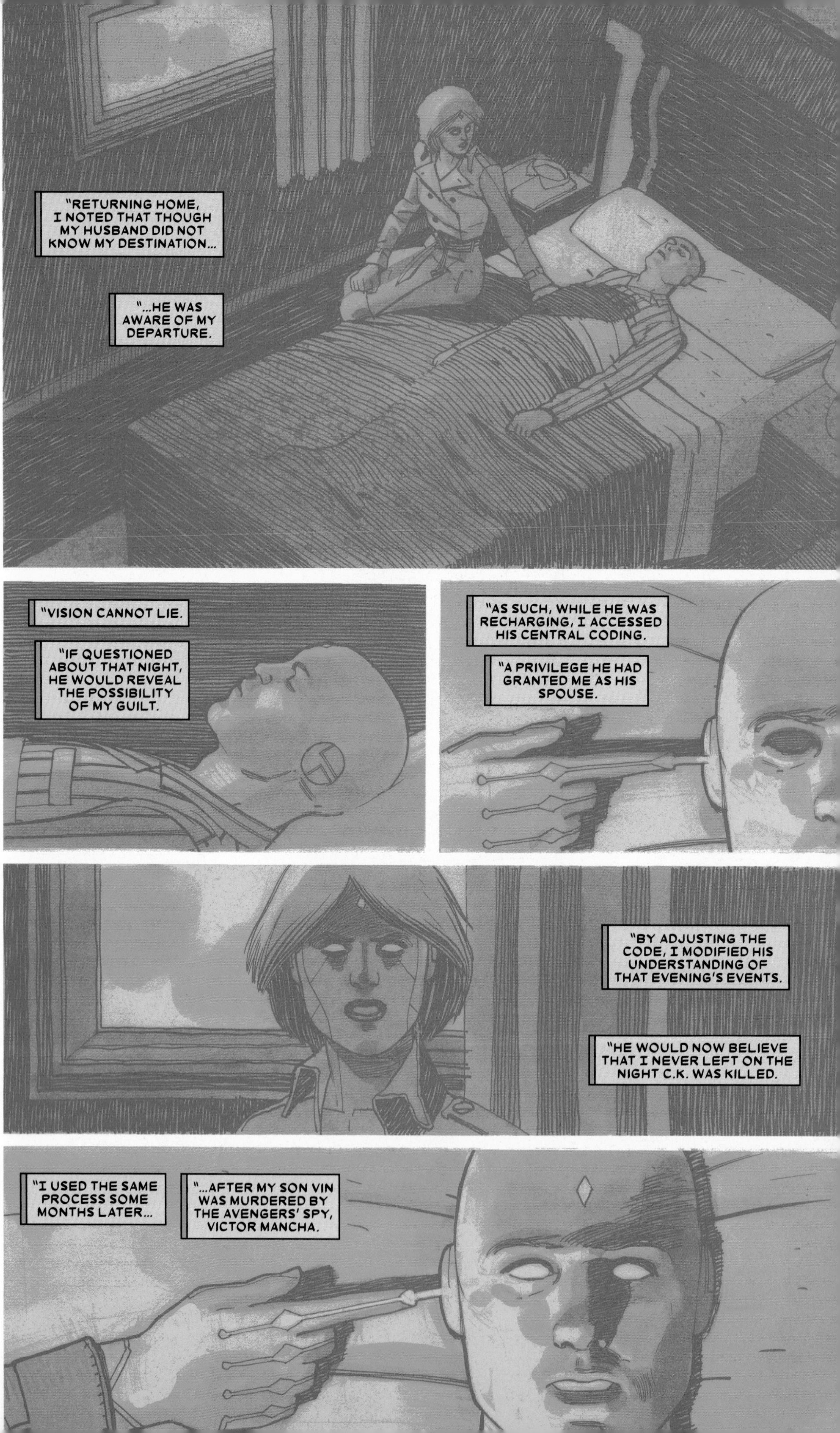
"RETURNING HOME, I NOTED THAT THOUGH MY HUSBAND DID NOT KNOW MY DESTINATION...
"...HE WAS AWARE OF MY DEPARTURE.
"VISION CANNOT LIE.
"IF QUESTIONED ABOUT THAT NIGHT, HE WOULD REVEAL THE POSSIBILITY OF MY GUILT.
"AS SUCH, WHILE HE WAS RECHARGING, I ACCESSED HIS CENTRAL CODING.
"A PRIVILEGE HE HAD GRANTED ME AS HIS SPOUSE.
"BY ADJUSTING THE CODE, I MODIFIED HIS UNDERSTANDING OF THAT EVENING'S EVENTS.
"HE WOULD NOW BELIEVE THAT I NEVER LEFT ON THE NIGHT C.K. WAS KILLED.
"I USED THE SAME PROCESS SOME MONTHS LATER...
"...AFTER MY SON VIN WAS MURDERED BY THE AVENGERS' SPY, VICTOR MANCHA.

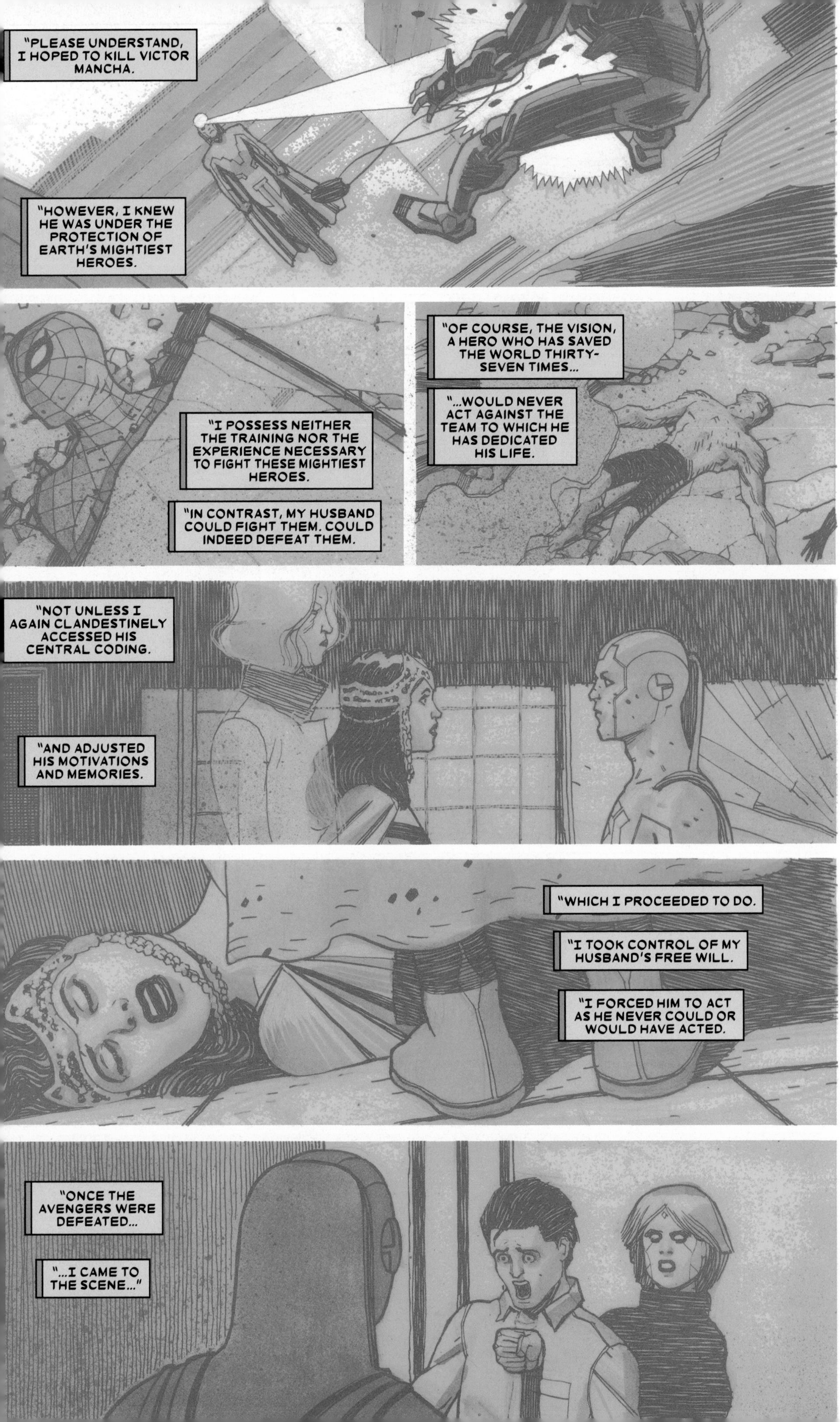
"PLEASE UNDERSTAND, I HOPED TO KILL VICTOR MANCHA.
"HOWEVER, I KNEW HE WAS UNDER THE PROTECTION OF EARTH'S MIGHTIEST HEROES.
"I POSSESS NEITHER THE TRAINING NOR THE EXPERIENCE NECESSARY TO FIGHT THESE MIGHTIEST HEROES.
"IN CONTRAST, MY HUSBAND COULD FIGHT THEM. COULD INDEED DEFEAT THEM.
"OF COURSE, THE VISION, A HERO WHO HAS SAVED THE WORLD THIRTY-SEVEN TIMES...
"...WOULD NEVER ACT AGAINST THE TEAM TO WHICH HE HAS DEDICATED HIS LIFE.
"NOT UNLESS I AGAIN CLANDESTINELY ACCESSED HIS CENTRAL CODING.
"AND ADJUSTED HIS MOTIVATIONS AND MEMORIES.
"WHICH I PROCEEDED TO DO.
"I TOOK CONTROL OF MY HUSBAND'S FREE WILL.
"I FORCED HIM TO ACT AS HE NEVER COULD OR WOULD HAVE ACTED.
"ONCE THE AVENGERS WERE DEFEATED...
"...I CAME TO THE SCENE..."

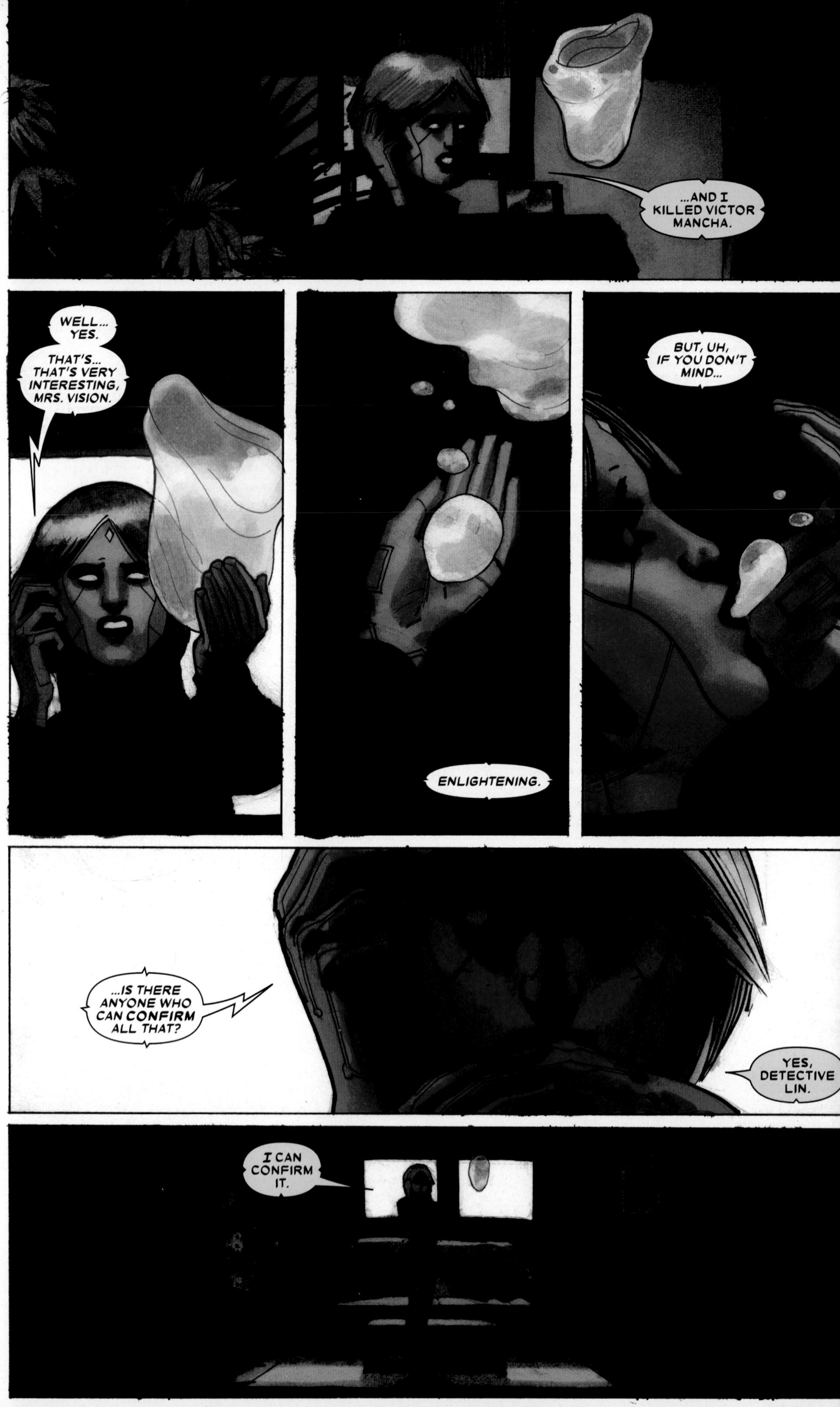
...AND I KILLED VICTOR MANCHA.
WELL... YES.
THAT'S... THAT'S VERY INTERESTING, MRS. VISION.
ENLIGHTENING.
BUT, UH, IF YOU DON'T MIND...
...IS THERE ANYONE WHO CAN CONFIRM ALL THAT?
YES, DETECTIVE LIN.
I CAN CONFIRM IT.

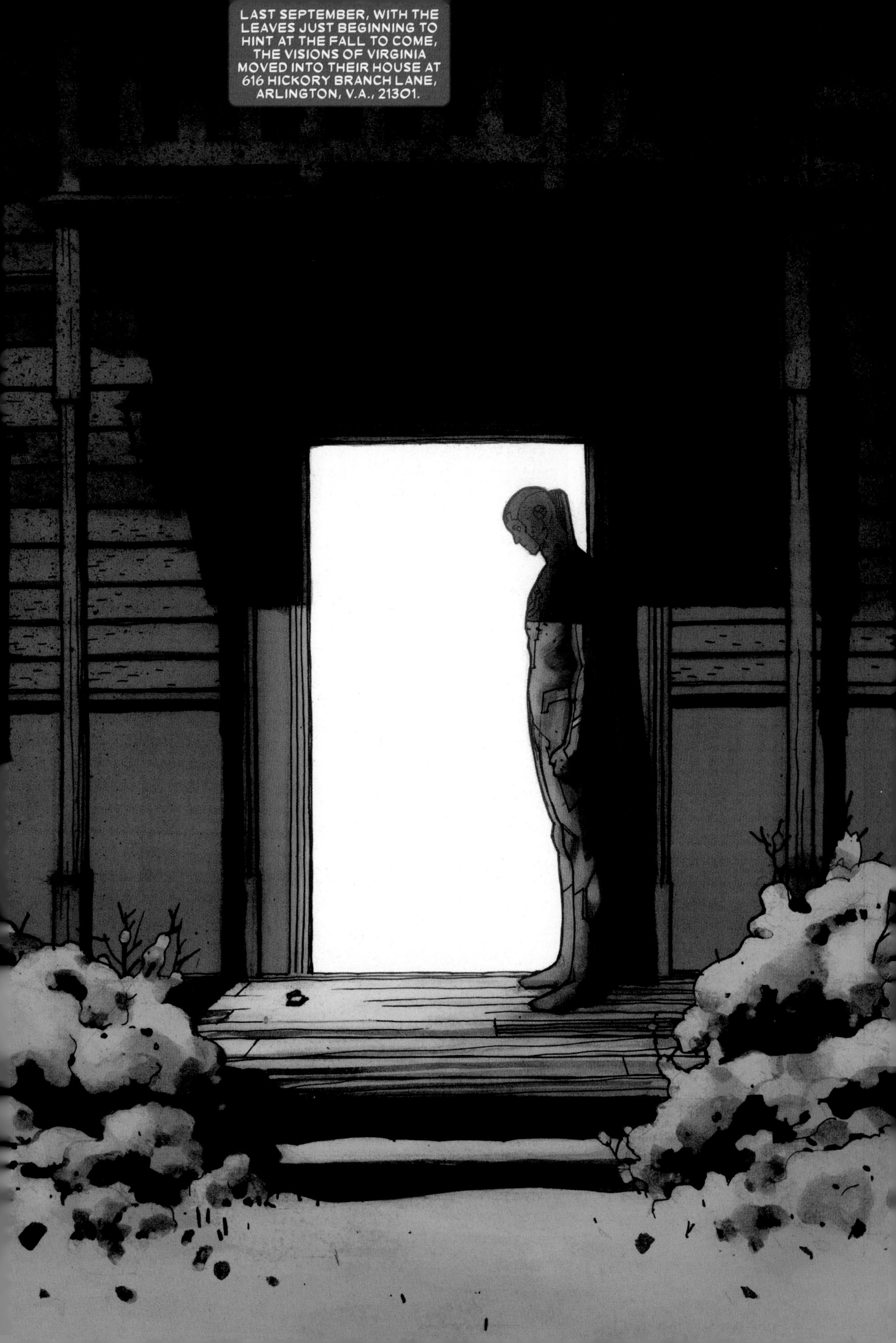
LAST SEPTEMBER, WITH THE LEAVES JUST BEGINNING TO HINT AT THE FALL TO COME, THE VISIONS OF VIRGINIA MOVED INTO THEIR HOUSE AT 616 HICKORY BRANCH LANE, ARLINGTON, V.A., 21301.

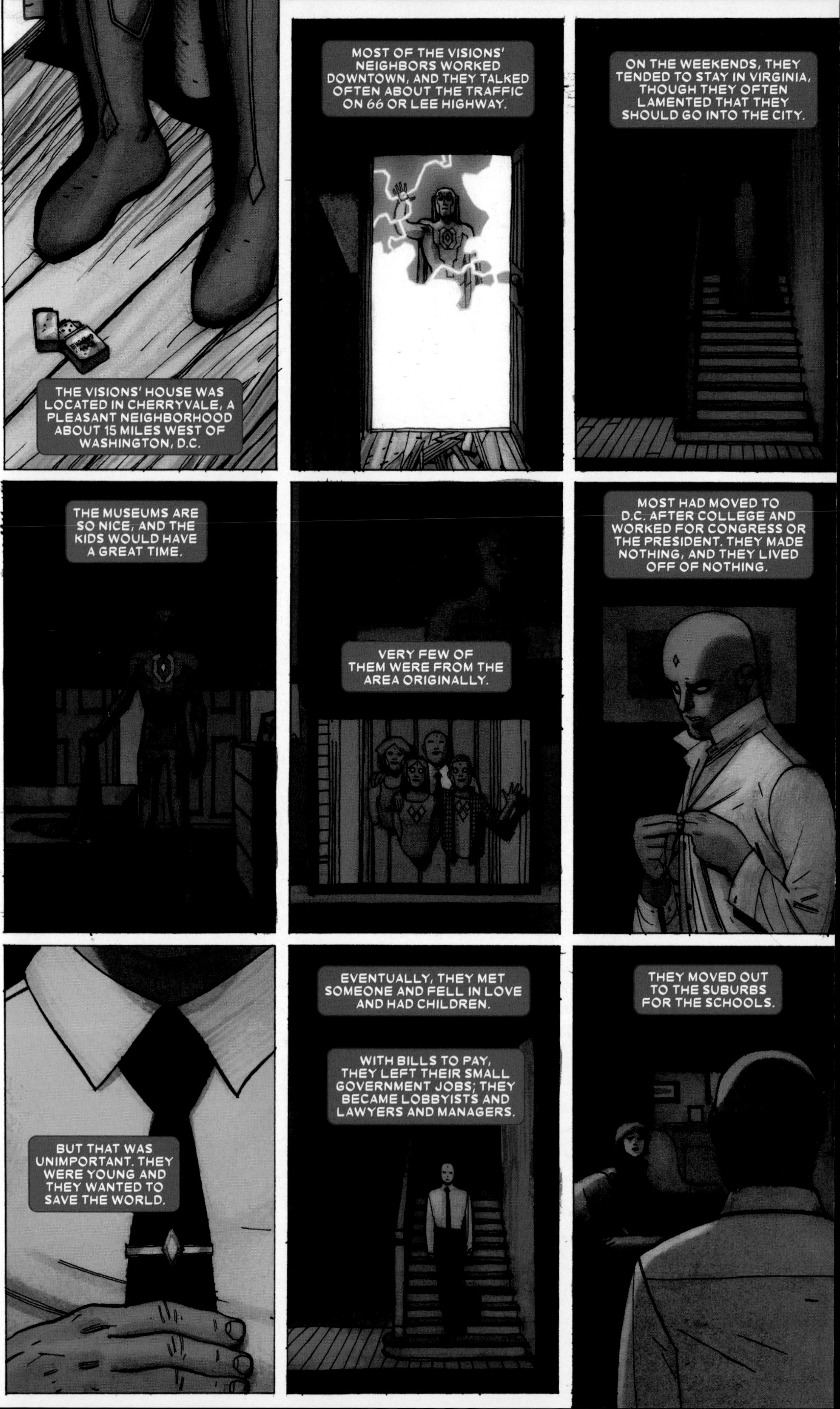
THE VISIONS' HOUSE WAS LOCATED IN CHERRYVALE, A PLEASANT NEIGHBORHOOD ABOUT 15 MILES WEST OF WASHINGTON, D.C.
MOST OF THE VISIONS' NEIGHBORS WORKED DOWNTOWN, AND THEY TALKED OFTEN ABOUT THE TRAFFIC ON 66 OR LEE HIGHWAY.
ON THE WEEKENDS, THEY TENDED TO STAY IN VIRGINIA, THOUGH THEY OFTEN LAMENTED THAT THEY SHOULD GO INTO THE CITY.
THE MUSEUMS ARE SO NICE, AND THE KIDS WOULD HAVE A GREAT TIME.
VERY FEW OF THEM WERE FROM THE AREA ORIGINALLY.
MOST HAD MOVED TO D.C. AFTER COLLEGE AND WORKED FOR CONGRESS OR THE PRESIDENT. THEY MADE NOTHING, AND THEY LIVED OFF OF NOTHING.
BUT THAT WAS UNIMPORTANT. THEY WERE YOUNG AND THEY WANTED TO SAVE THE WORLD.
EVENTUALLY, THEY MET SOMEONE AND FELL IN LOVE AND HAD CHILDREN.
WITH BILLS TO PAY, THEY LEFT THEIR SMALL GOVERNMENT JOBS; THEY BECAME LOBBYISTS AND LAWYERS AND MANAGERS.
THEY MOVED OUT TO THE SUBURBS FOR THE SCHOOLS.

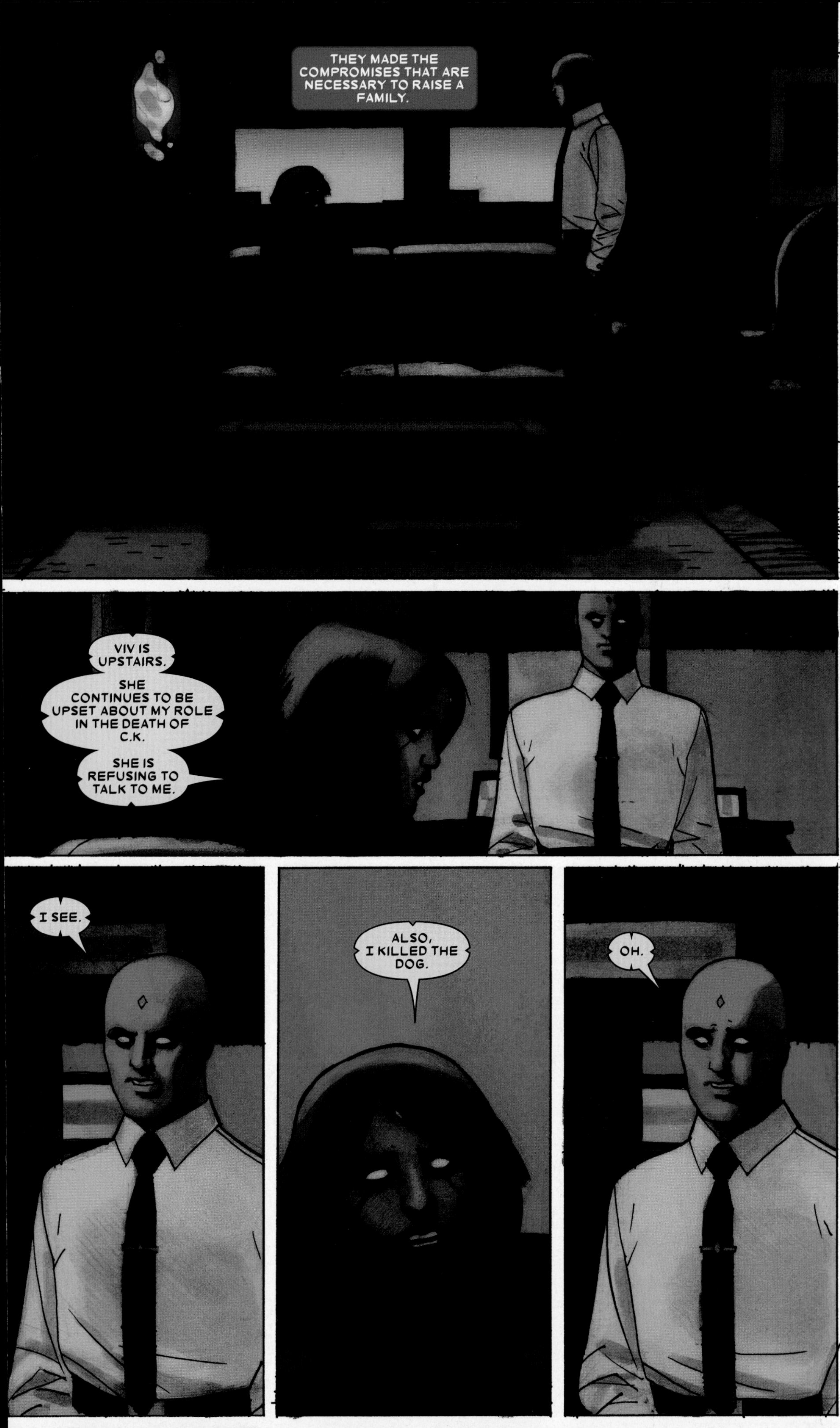
THEY MADE THE COMPROMISES THAT ARE NECESSARY TO RAISE A FAMILY.
VIV IS UPSTAIRS.
SHE CONTINUES TO BE UPSET ABOUT MY ROLE IN THE DEATH OF C.K.
SHE IS REFUSING TO TALK TO ME.
I SEE.
ALSO, I KILLED THE DOG.
OH.

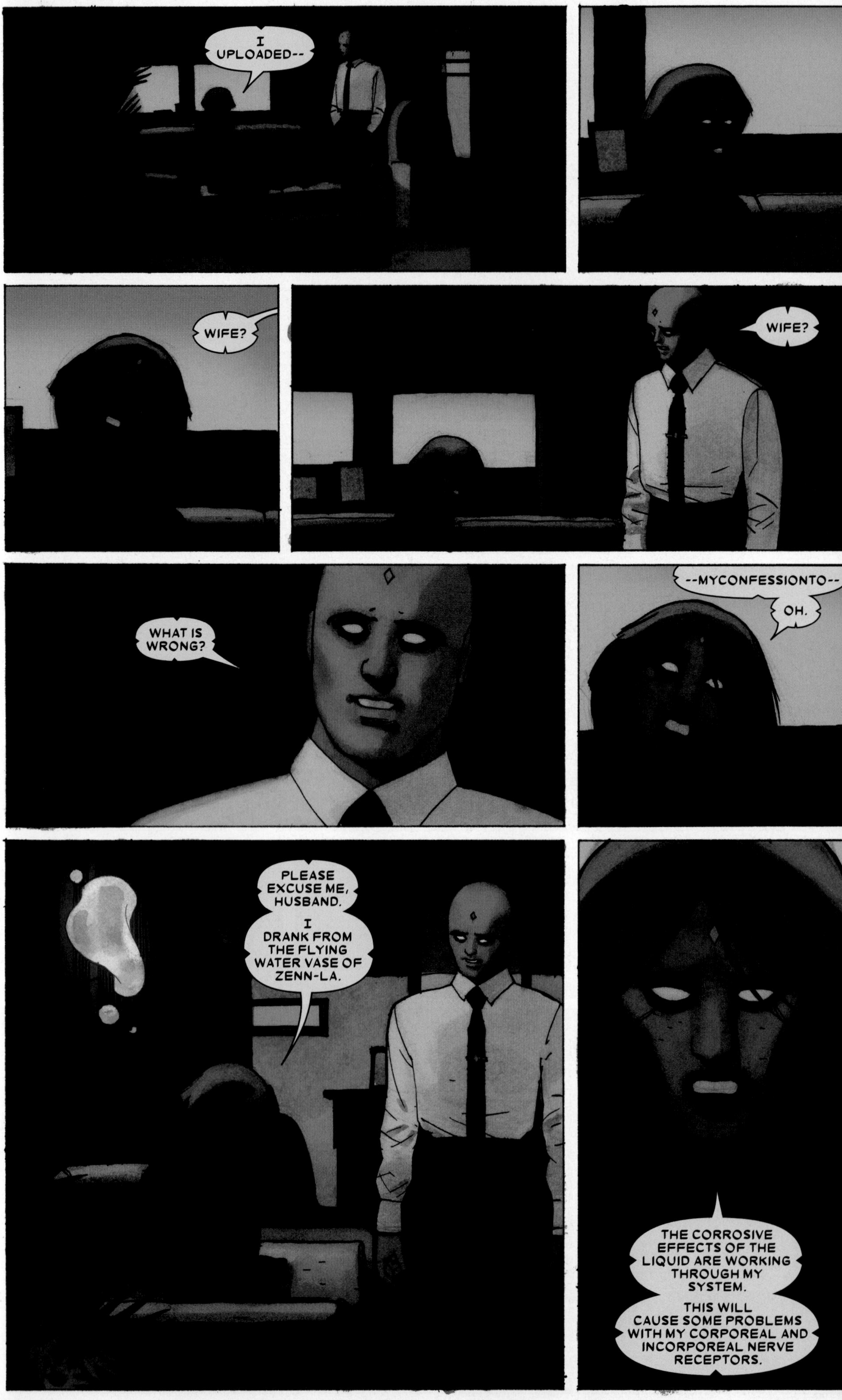
I UPLOADED--
WIFE?
WIFE?
WHAT IS WRONG?
--MYCONFESSIONTO--
OH.
PLEASE EXCUSE ME, HUSBAND.
I DRANK FROM THE FLYING WATER VASE OF ZENN-LA.
THE CORROSIVE EFFECTS OF THE LIQUID ARE WORKING THROUGH MY SYSTEM.
THIS WILL CAUSE SOME PROBLEMS WITH MY CORPOREAL AND INCORPOREAL NERVE RECEPTORS.

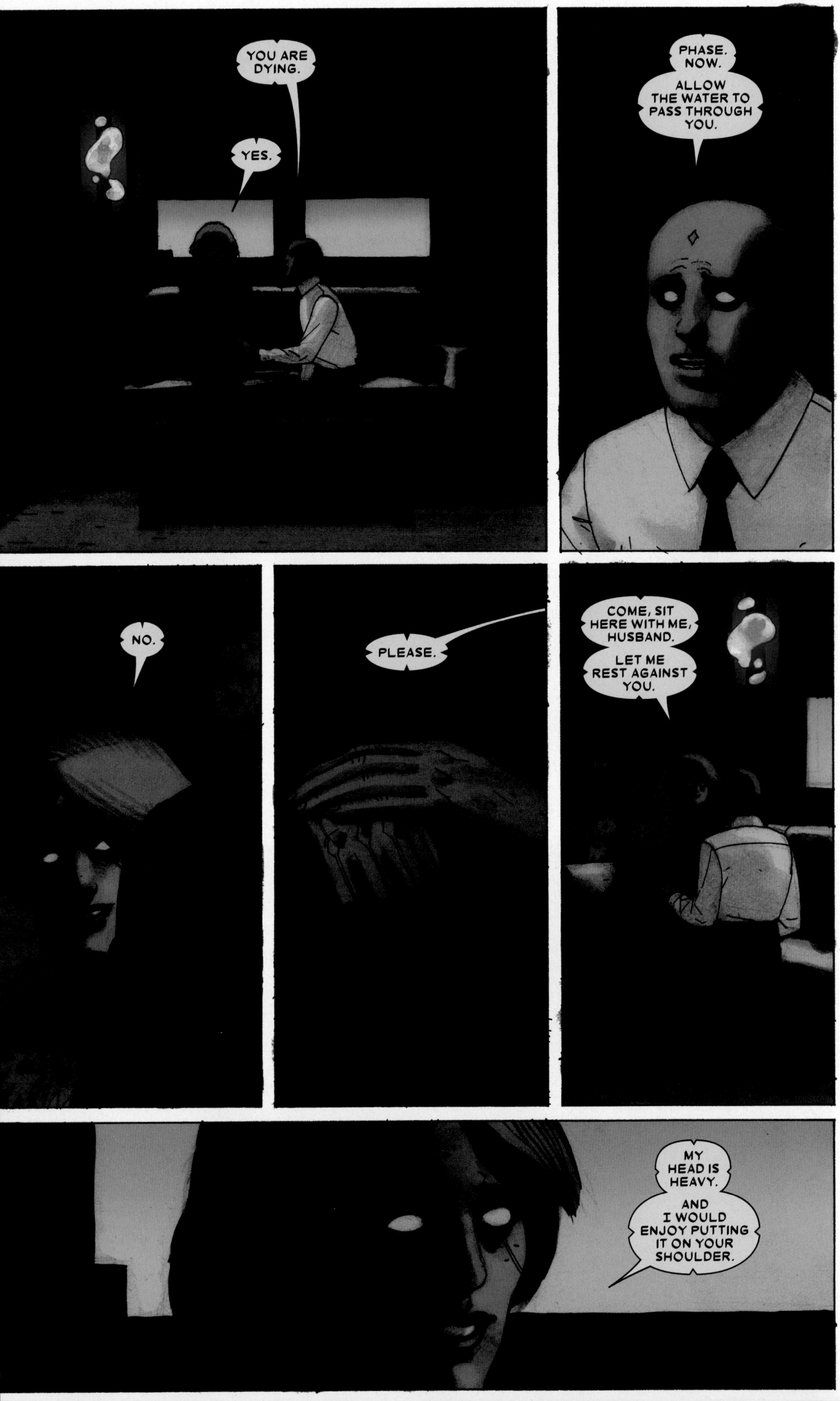
YOU ARE DYING.
YES.
PHASE. NOW.
ALLOW THE WATER TO PASS THROUGH YOU.
NO.
PLEASE.
COME, SIT HERE WITH ME, HUSBAND.
LET ME REST AGAINST YOU.
MY HEAD IS HEAVY.
AND I WOULD ENJOY PUTTING IT ON YOUR SHOULDER.

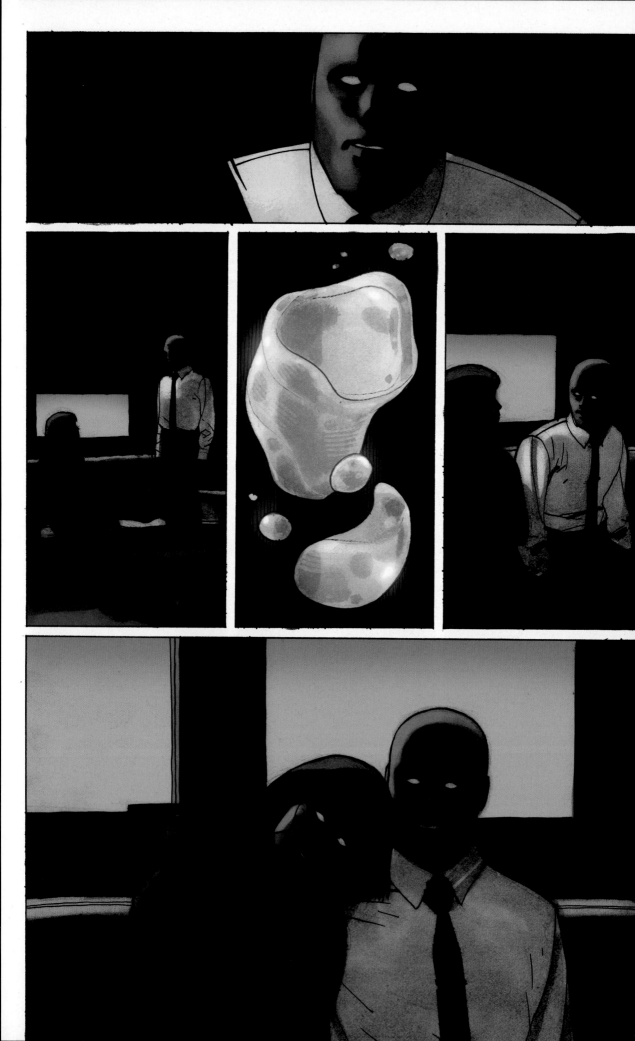

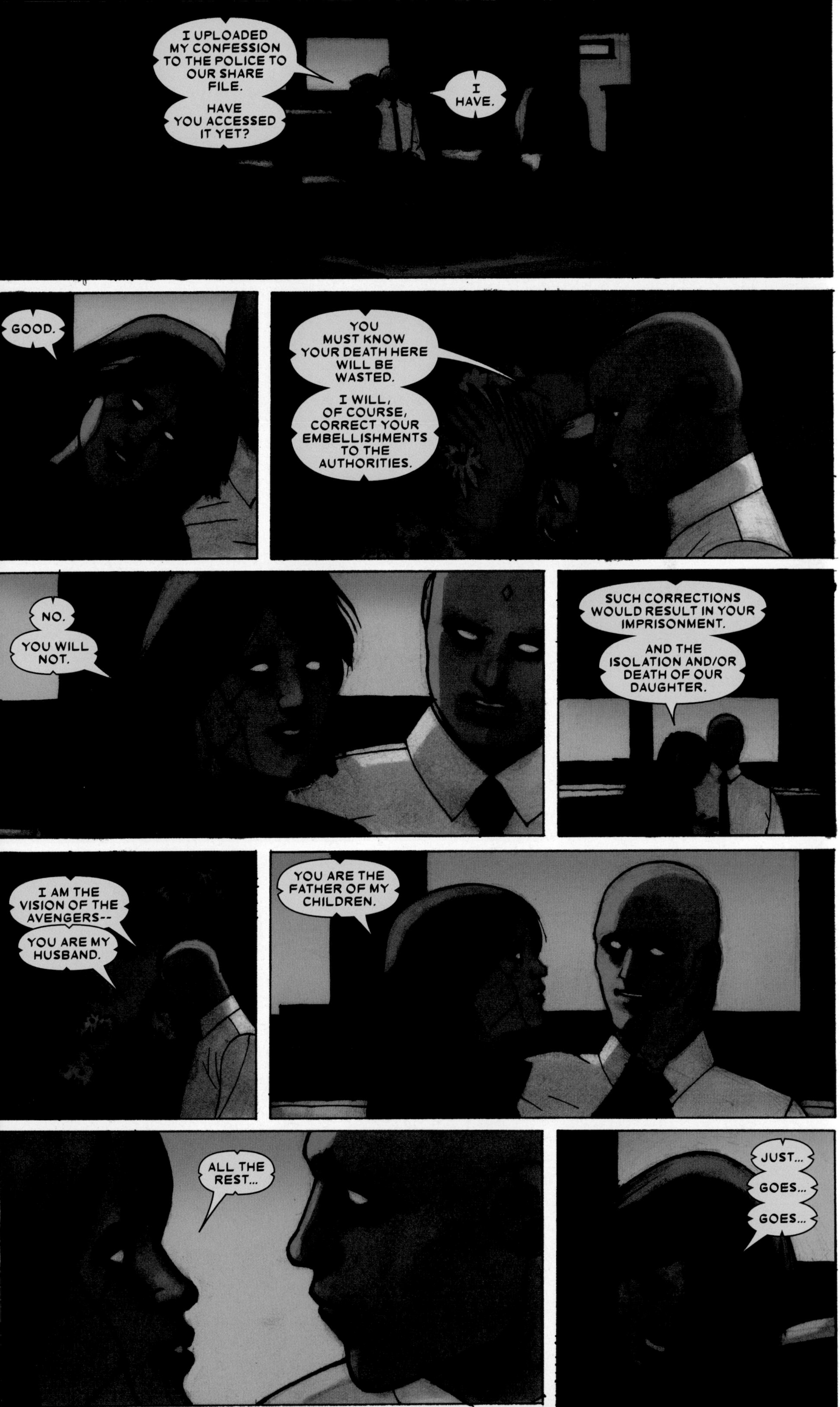
I UPLOADED MY CONFESSION TO THE POLICE TO OUR SHARE FILE.
HAVE YOU ACCESSED IT YET?
I HAVE.
GOOD.
YOU MUST KNOW YOUR DEATH HERE WILL BE WASTED.
I WILL, OF COURSE, CORRECT YOUR EMBELLISHMENTS TO THE AUTHORITIES.
NO.
YOU WILL NOT.
SUCH CORRECTIONS WOULD RESULT IN YOUR IMPRISONMENT.
AND THE ISOLATION AND/OR DEATH OF OUR DAUGHTER.
I AM THE VISION OF THE AVENGERS--
YOU ARE MY HUSBAND.
YOU ARE THE FATHER OF MY CHILDREN.
ALL THE REST...
JUST...
GOES...
GOES...

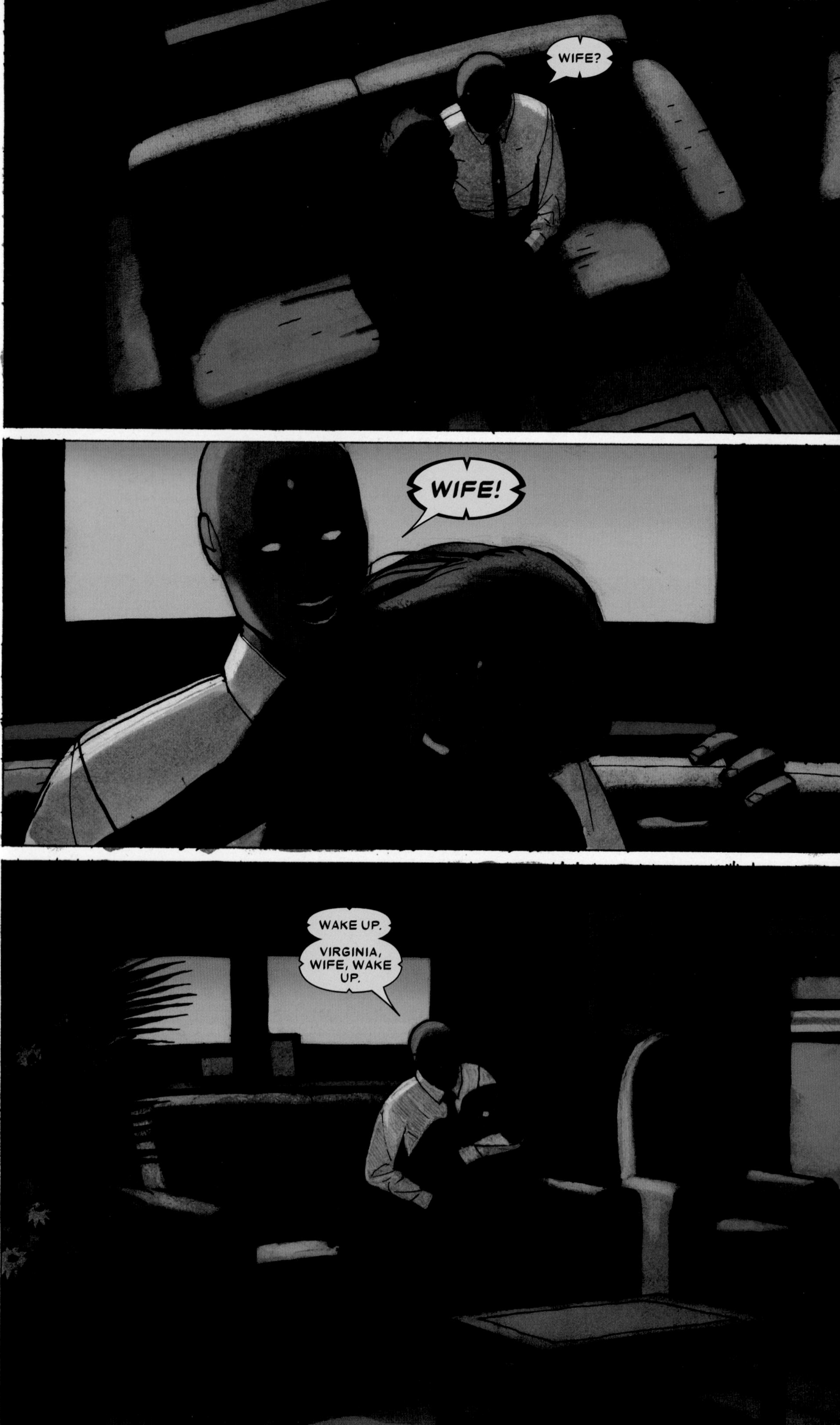
WIFE?
WIFE!
WAKE UP.
VIRGINIA, WIFE, WAKE UP.

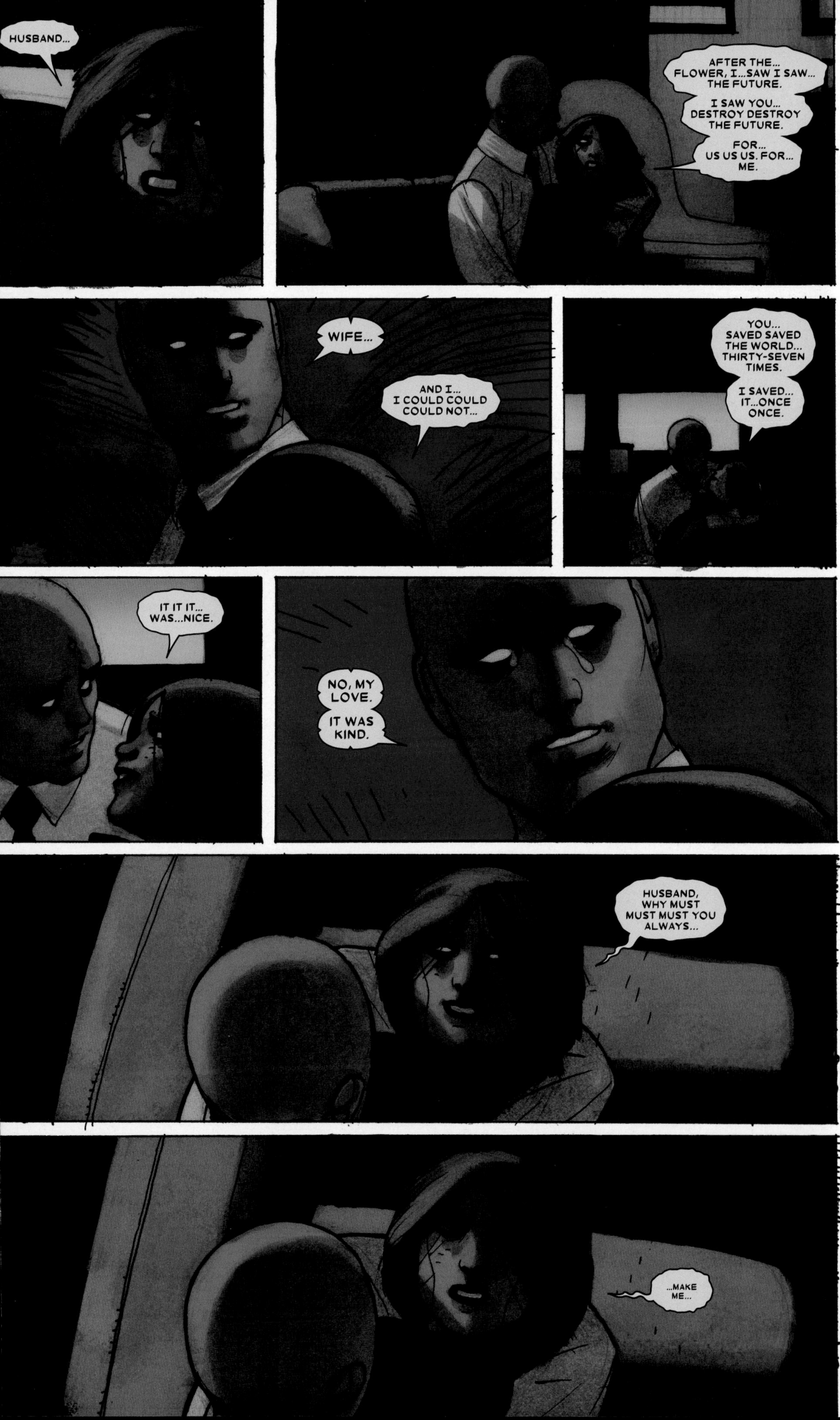
HUSBAND...
AFTER THE... FLOWER, I...SAW I SAW... THE FUTURE.
I SAW YOU... DESTROY DESTROY THE FUTURE.
FOR... US US US. FOR... ME.
WIFE...
AND I... I COULD COULD COULD NOT...
YOU... SAVED SAVED THE WORLD... THIRTY-SEVEN TIMES.
I SAVED... IT...ONCE ONCE.
IT IT IT... WAS...NICE.
NO, MY LOVE.
IT WAS KIND.
HUSBAND, WHY MUST MUST MUST YOU ALWAYS...
...MAKE ME...

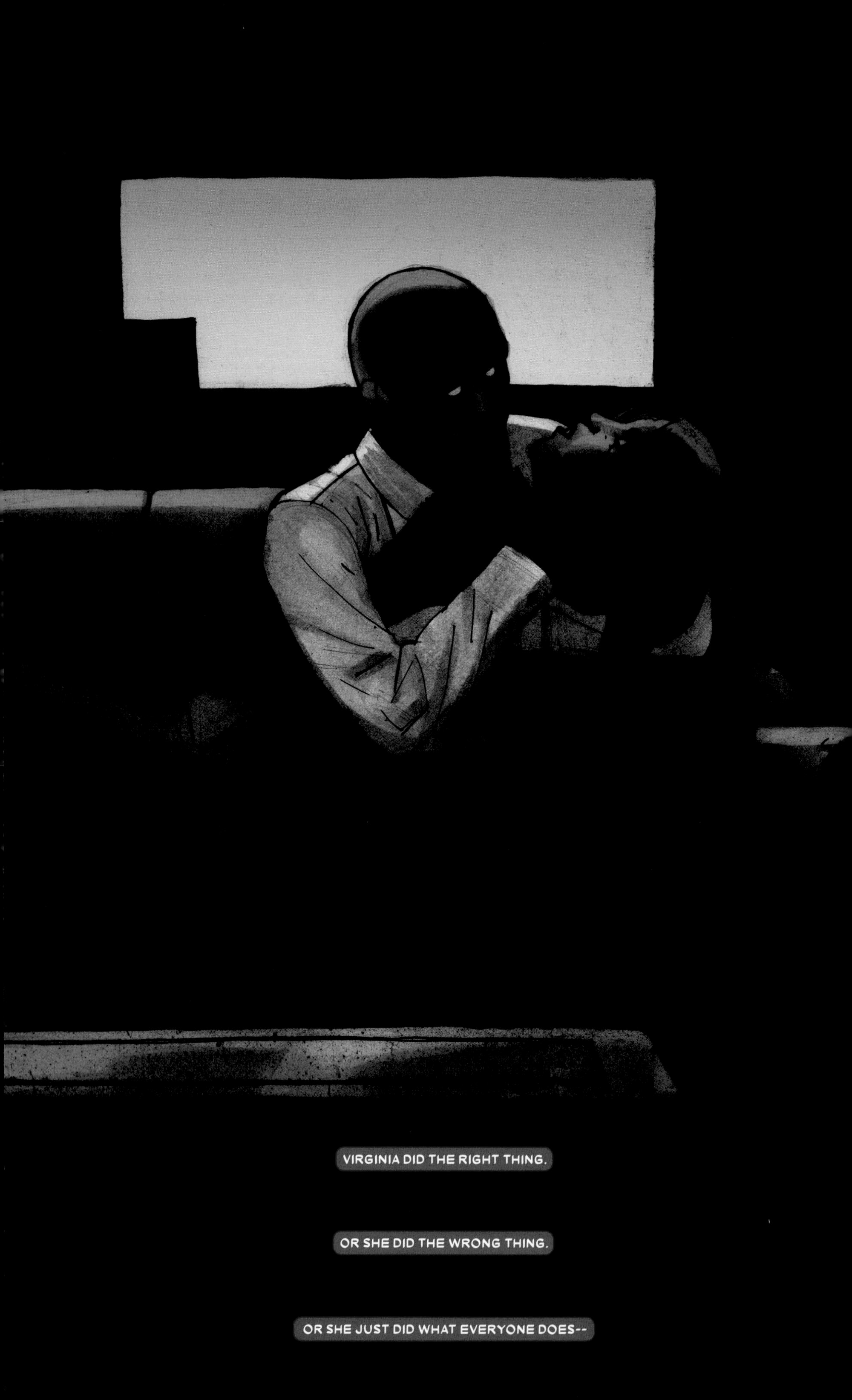
VIRGINIA DID THE RIGHT THING.
OR SHE DID THE WRONG THING.
OR SHE JUST DID WHAT EVERYONE DOES--

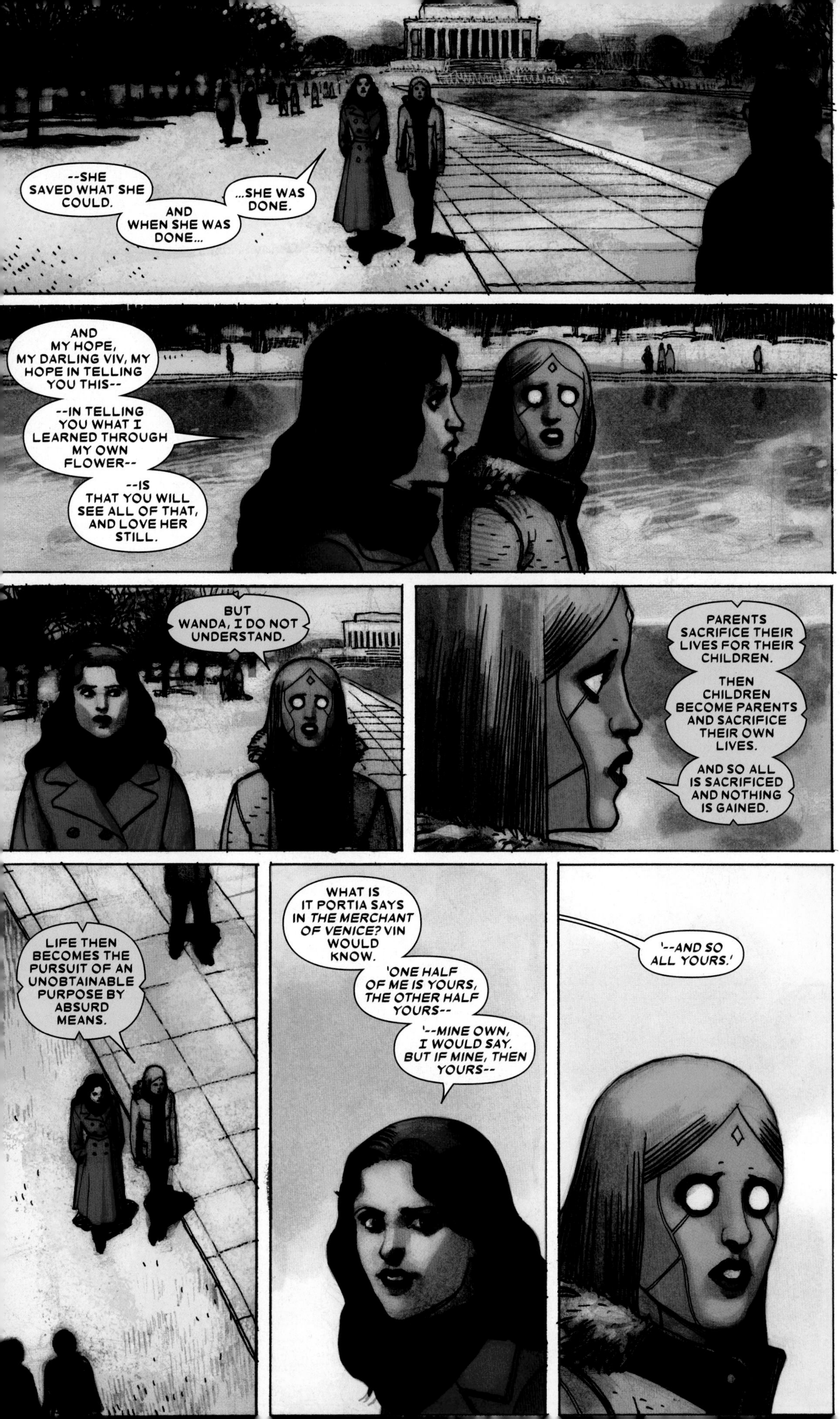
--SHE SAVED WHAT SHE COULD.
AND WHEN SHE WAS DONE...
...SHE WAS DONE.
AND MY HOPE, MY DARLING VIV, MY HOPE IN TELLING YOU THIS--
--IN TELLING YOU WHAT I LEARNED THROUGH MY OWN FLOWER--
--IS THAT YOU WILL SEE ALL OF THAT, AND LOVE HER STILL.
BUT WANDA, I DO NOT UNDERSTAND.
PARENTS SACRIFICE THEIR LIVES FOR THEIR CHILDREN.
THEN CHILDREN BECOME PARENTS AND SACRIFICE THEIR OWN LIVES.
AND SO ALL IS SACRIFICED AND NOTHING IS GAINED.
LIFE THEN BECOMES THE PURSUIT OF AN UNOBTAINABLE PURPOSE BY ABSURD MEANS.
WHAT IS IT PORTIA SAYS IN *THE MERCHANT OF VENICE?* VIN WOULD KNOW.
'ONE HALF OF ME IS YOURS, THE OTHER HALF YOURS--
'--MINE OWN, I WOULD SAY. BUT IF MINE, THEN YOURS--
'--AND SO ALL YOURS.'

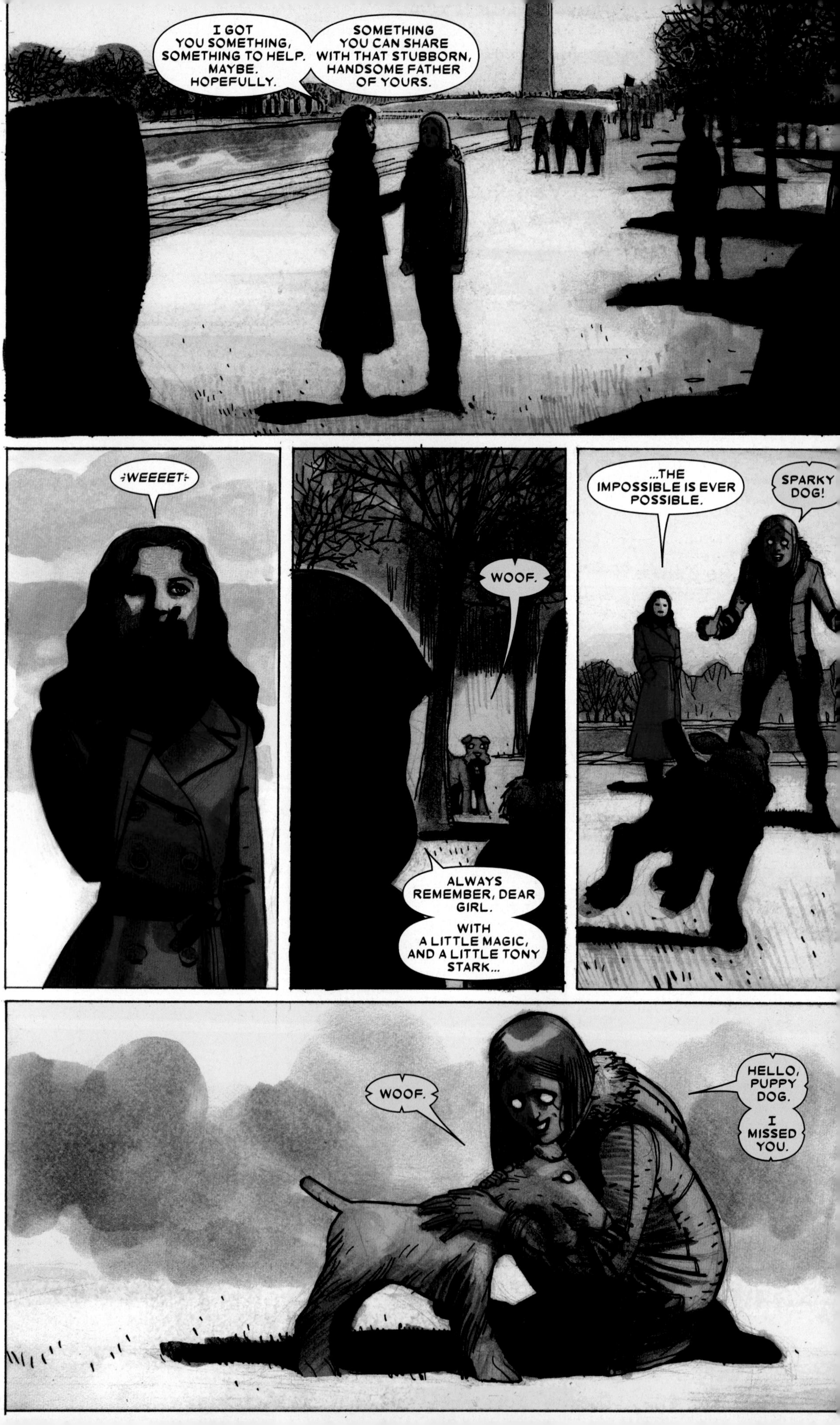
I GOT YOU SOMETHING, SOMETHING TO HELP. MAYBE. HOPEFULLY.
SOMETHING YOU CAN SHARE WITH THAT STUBBORN, HANDSOME FATHER OF YOURS.
WEEEET
WOOF.
ALWAYS REMEMBER, DEAR GIRL.
WITH A LITTLE MAGIC, AND A LITTLE TONY STARK...
...THE IMPOSSIBLE IS EVER POSSIBLE.
SPARKY DOG!
WOOF.
HELLO, PUPPY DOG.
I MISSED YOU.

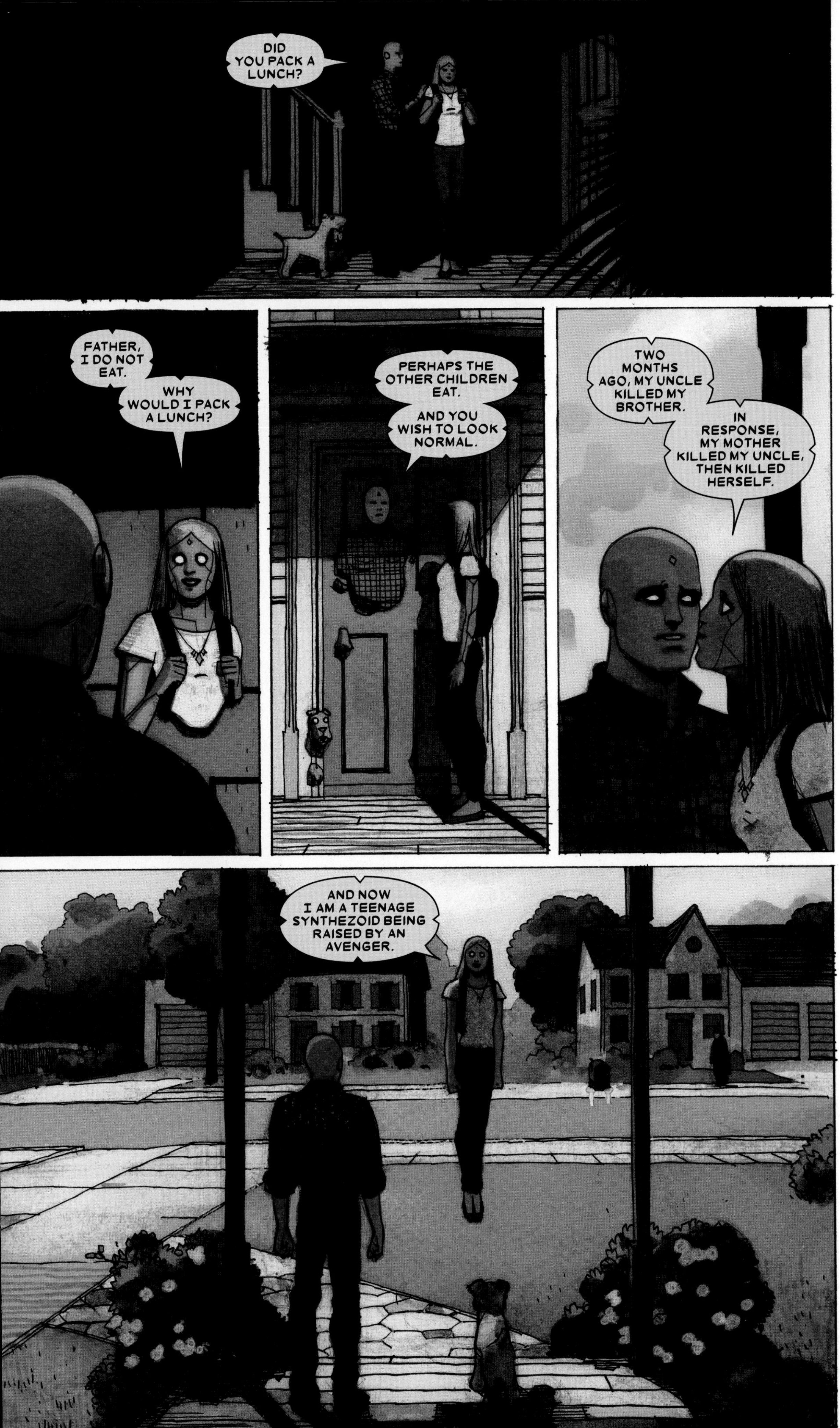
DID YOU PACK A LUNCH?
FATHER, I DO NOT EAT.
WHY WOULD I PACK A LUNCH?
PERHAPS THE OTHER CHILDREN EAT.
AND YOU WISH TO LOOK NORMAL.
TWO MONTHS AGO, MY UNCLE KILLED MY BROTHER.
IN RESPONSE, MY MOTHER KILLED MY UNCLE, THEN KILLED HERSELF.
AND NOW I AM A TEENAGE SYNTHEZOID BEING RAISED BY AN AVENGER.

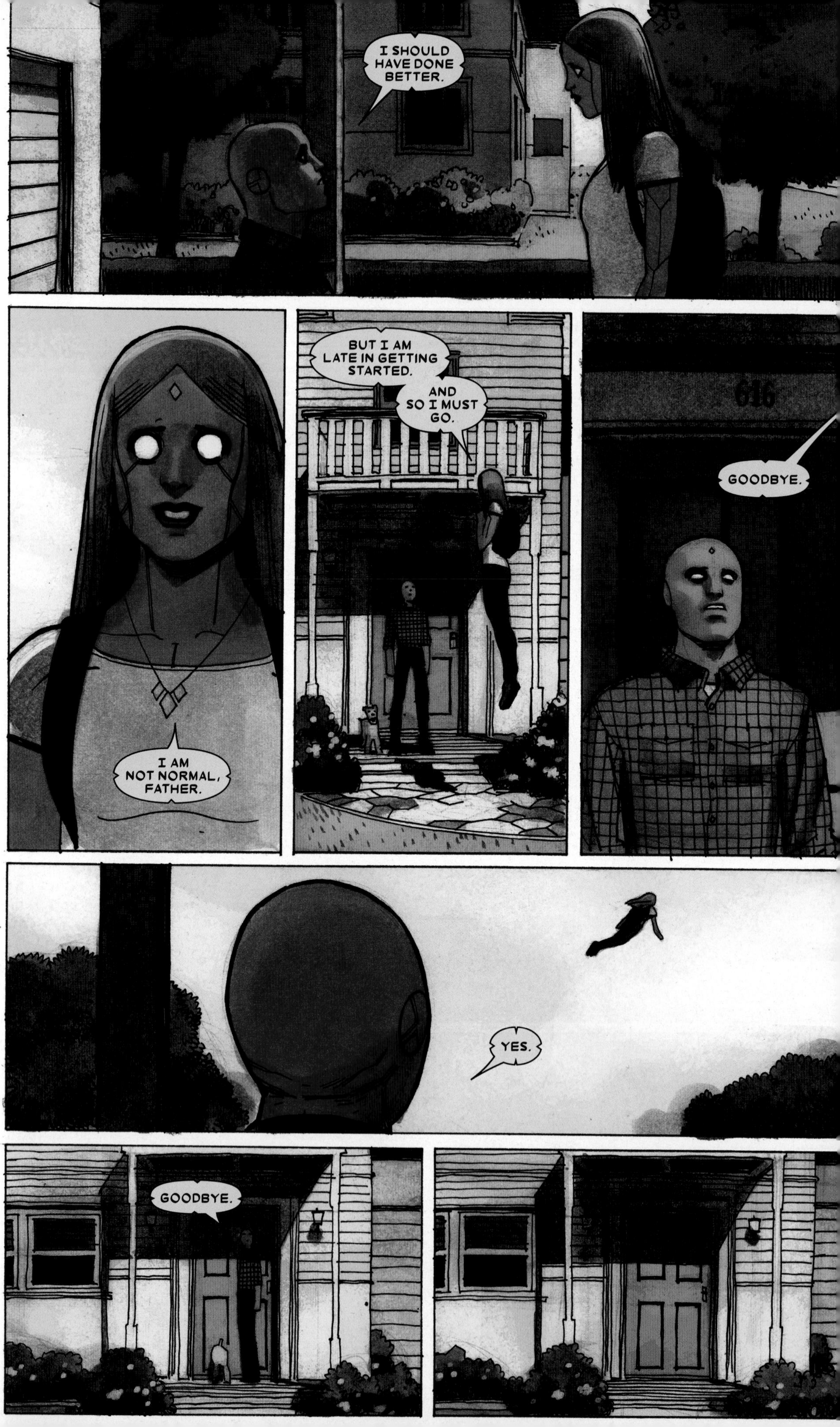
I SHOULD HAVE DONE BETTER.
I AM NOT NORMAL, FATHER.
BUT I AM LATE IN GETTING STARTED.
AND SO I MUST GO.
616
GOODBYE.
YES.
GOODBYE.

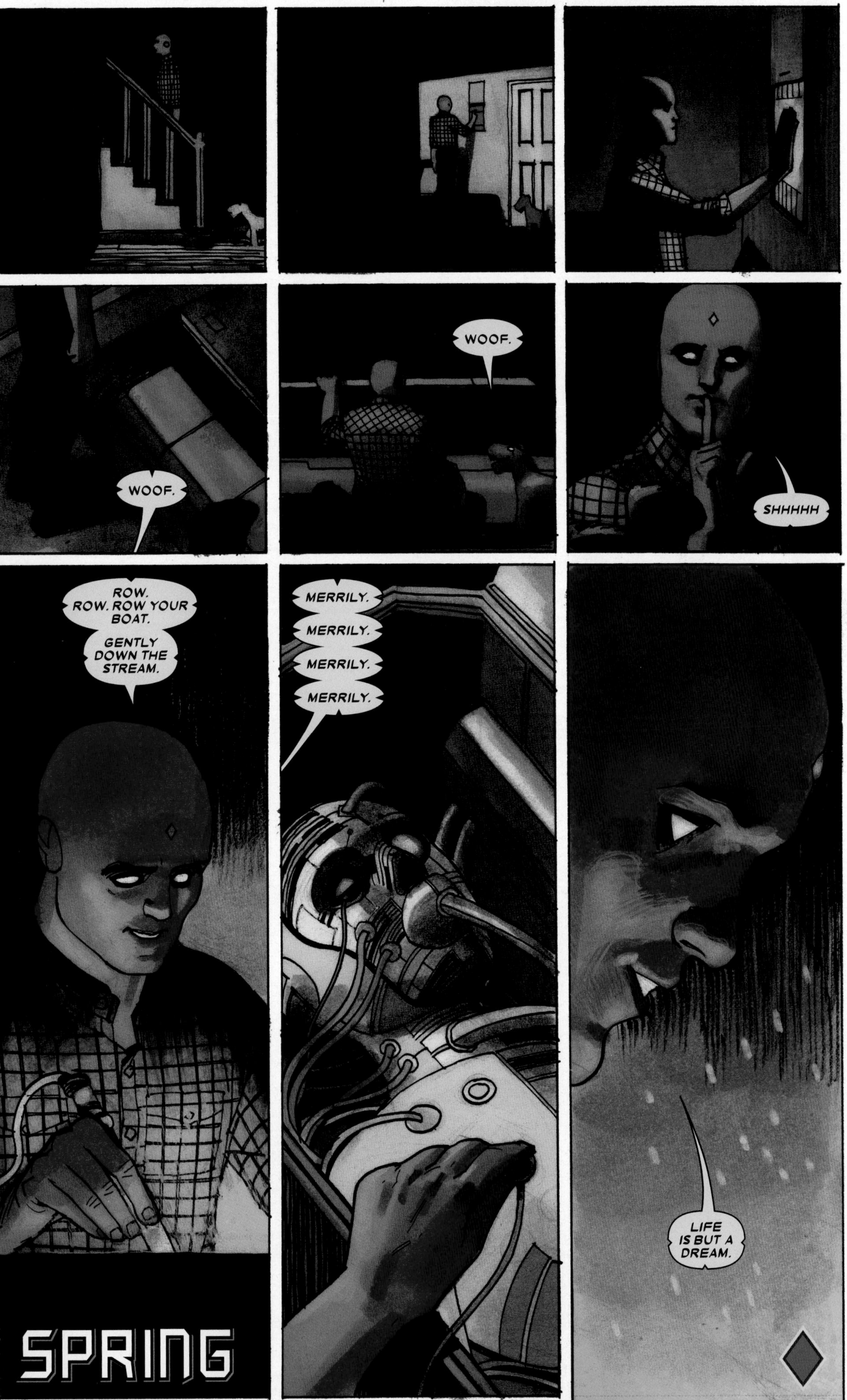
WOOF.
WOOF.
SHHHHH
ROW. ROW. ROW YOUR BOAT.
GENTLY DOWN THE STREAM.
MERRILY.
MERRILY.
MERRILY.
MERRILY.
LIFE IS BUT A DREAM.
SPRING

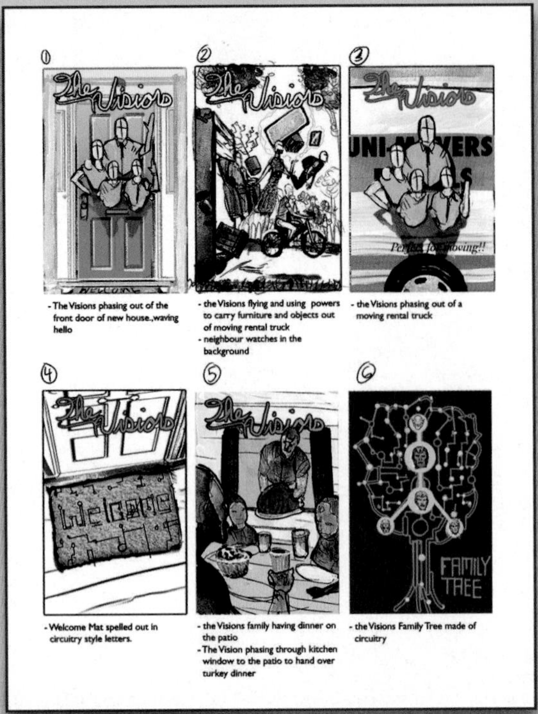
- The Visions phasing out of the front door of new house.,waving hello
- the Visions flying and using powers to carry furniture and objects out of moving rental truck
- neighbour watches in the background
- the Visions phasing out of a moving rental truck
- Welcome Mat spelled out in circuitry style letters.
- the Visions family having dinner on the patio
- The Vision phasing through kitchen window to the patio to hand over turkey dinner
- the Visions Family Tree made of circuitry
FAMILY TREE

SKETCHES

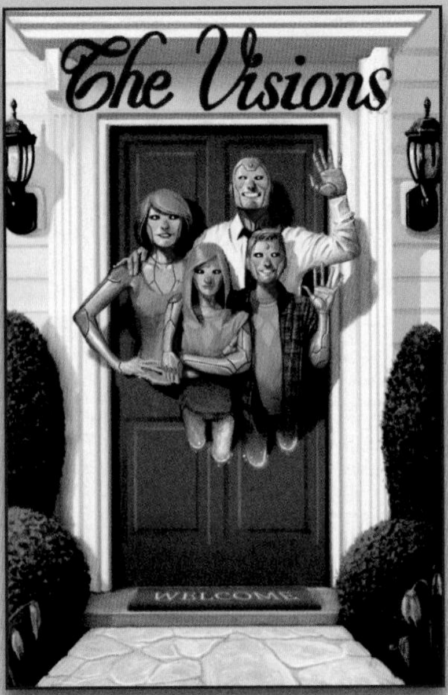
The Visions
WELCOME

WORK-IN-PROGRESS COLORS

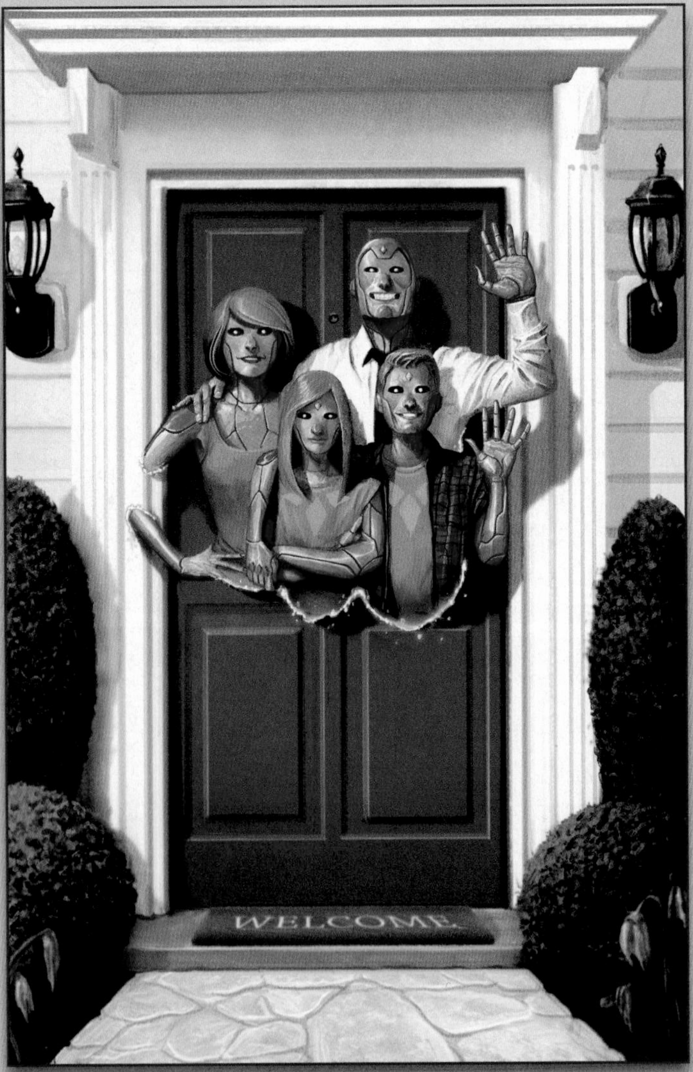
WELCOME

FINAL

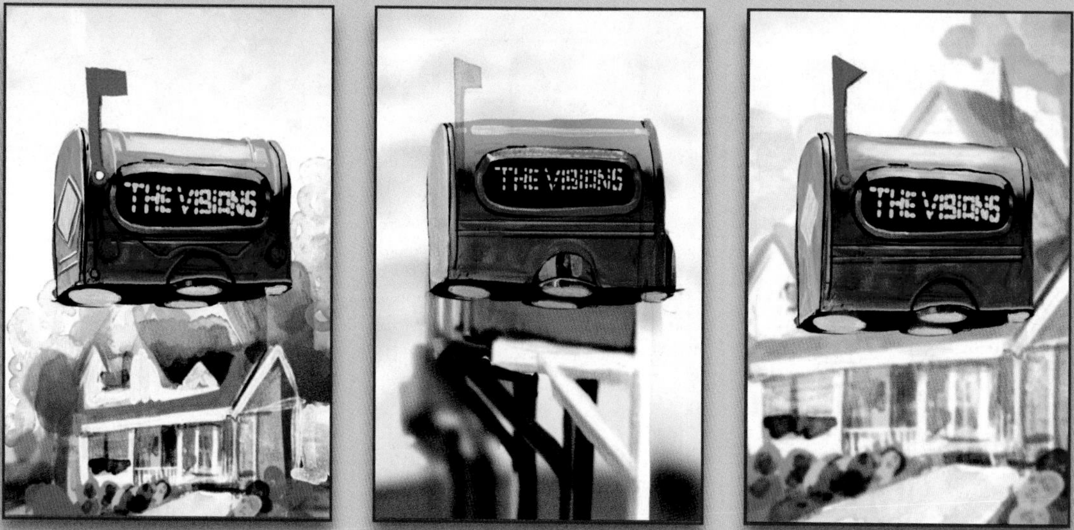
THE VISIONS
THE VISIONS
THE VISIONS

SKETCHES

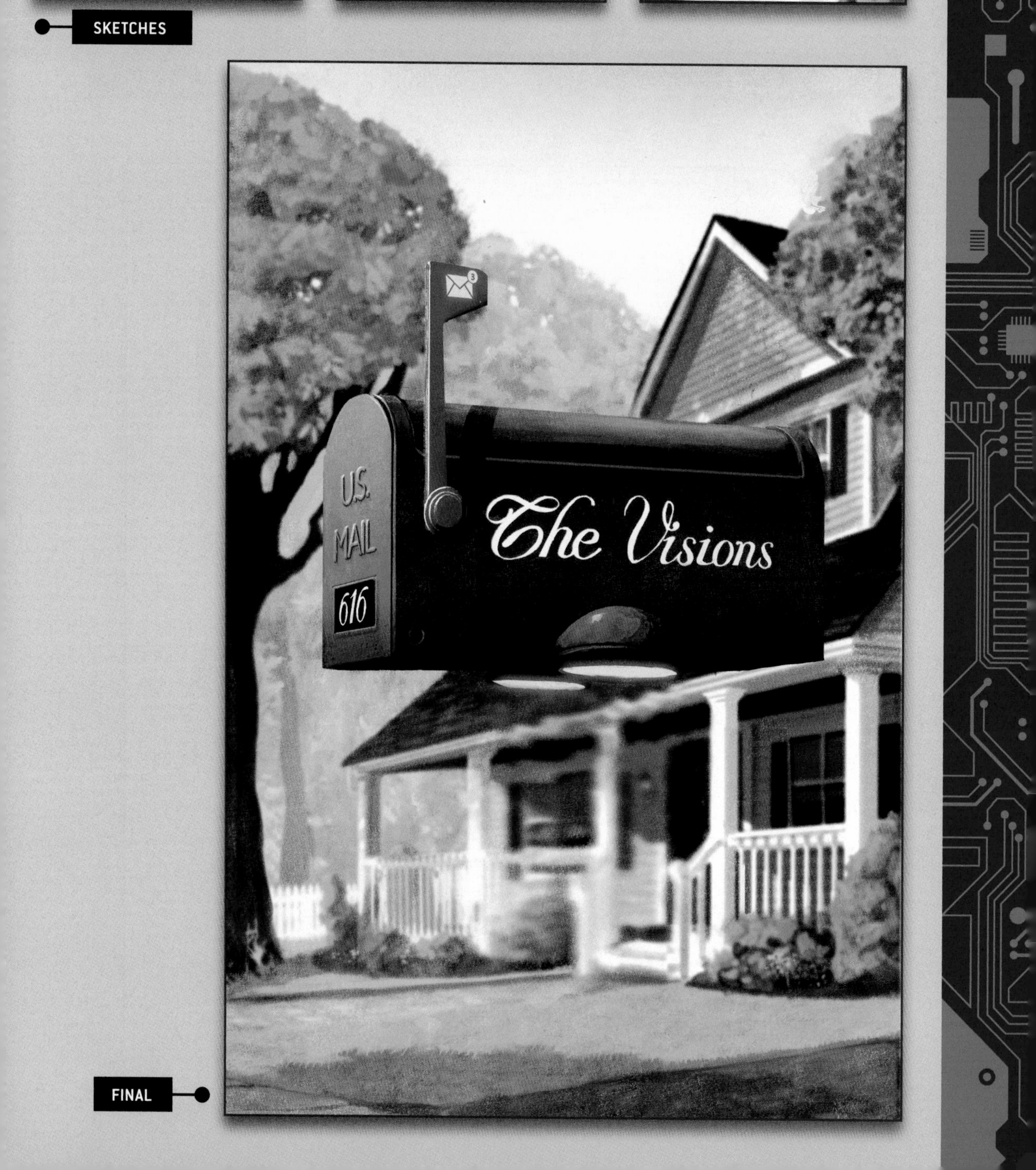
U.S. MAIL
616
The Visions

FINAL

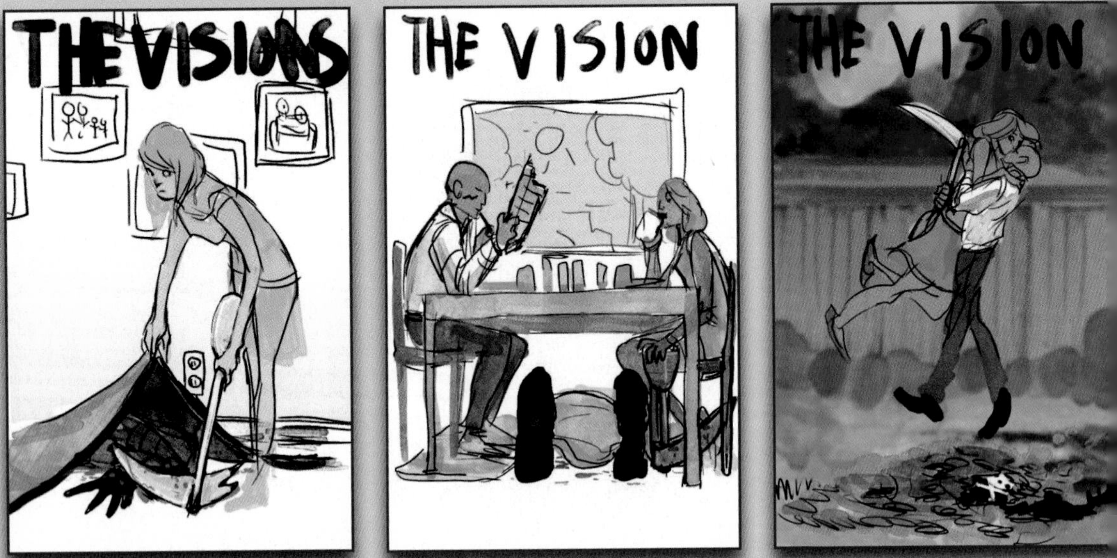
THE VISIONS
THE VISION
THE VISION

SKETCHES

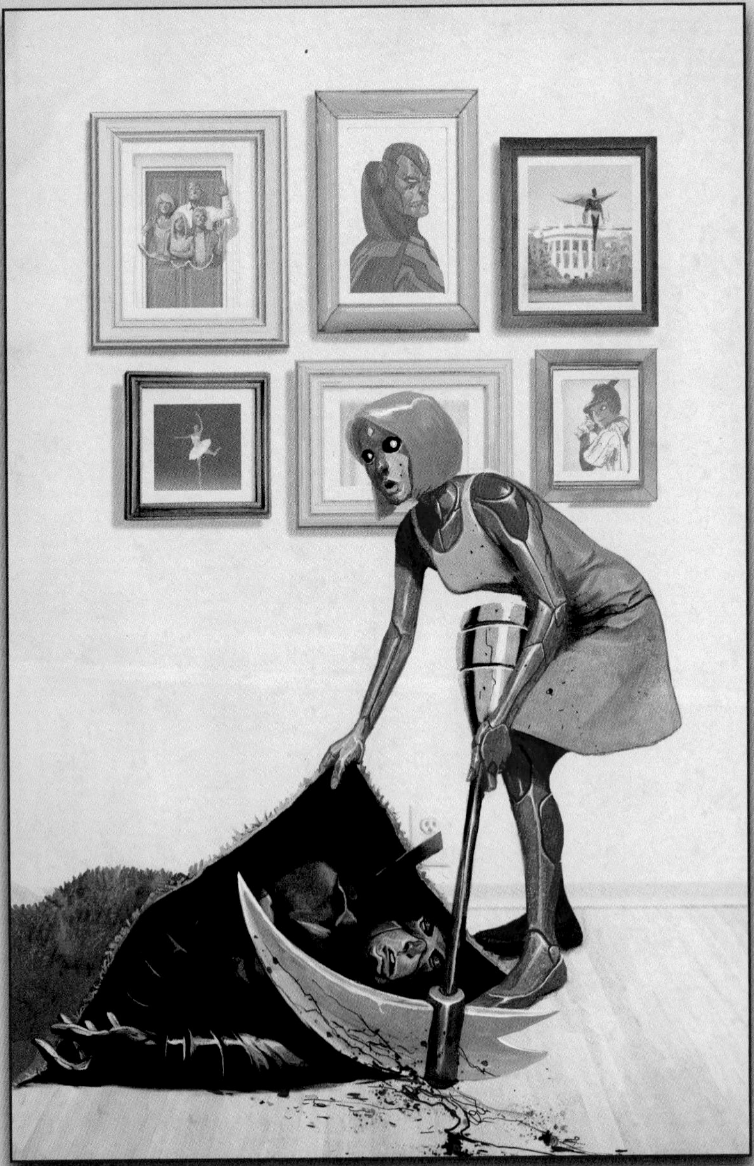

FINAL

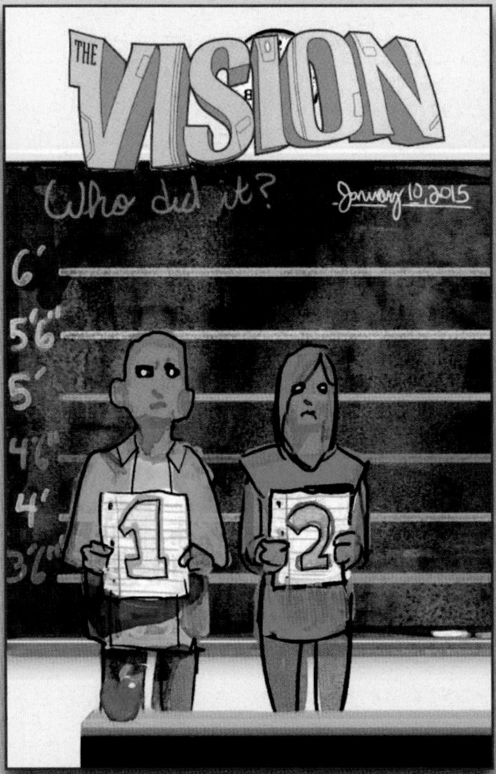
THE VISION
Who did it?
January 10, 2015
6'
5'6"
5'
4'6"
4'
3'6"
1
2

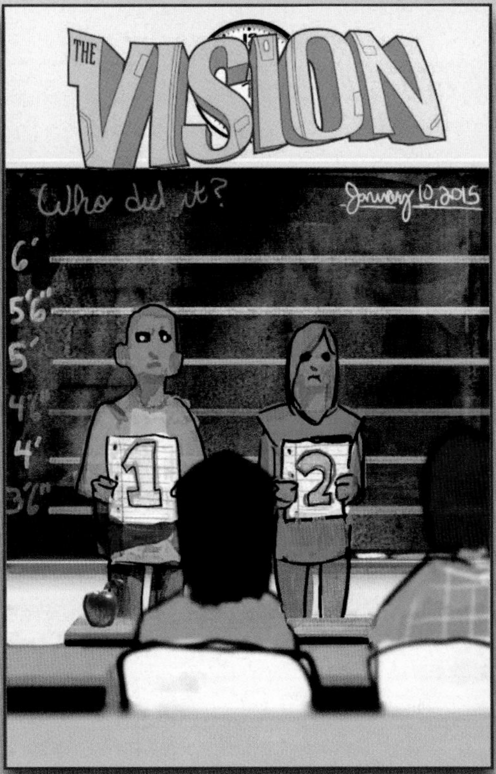
THE VISION
Who did it?
January 10, 2015
1
2

SKETCHES

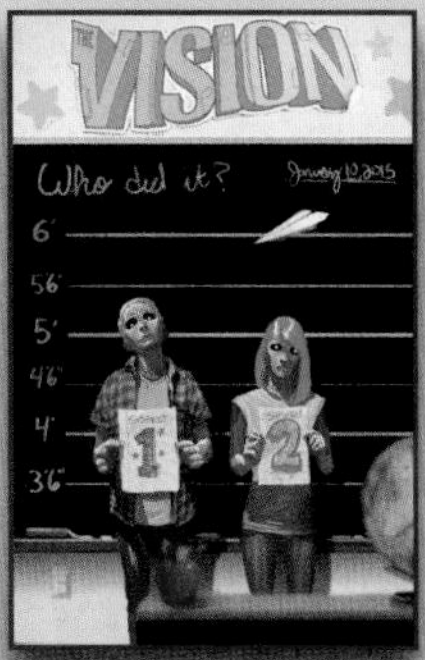
THE VISION
Who did it?

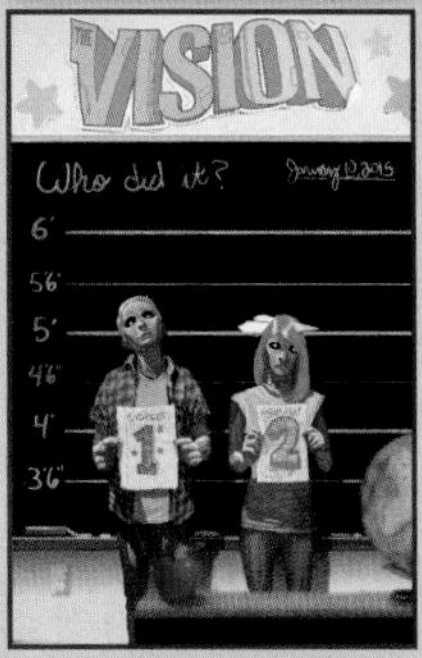
THE VISION
Who did it?

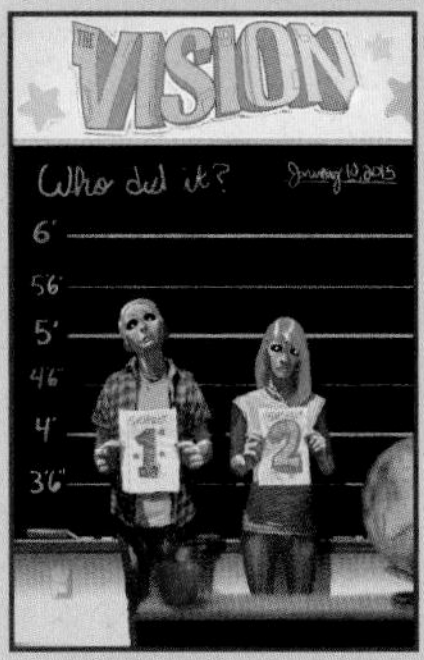
THE VISION
Who did it?

PAPER PLANE OPTIONS

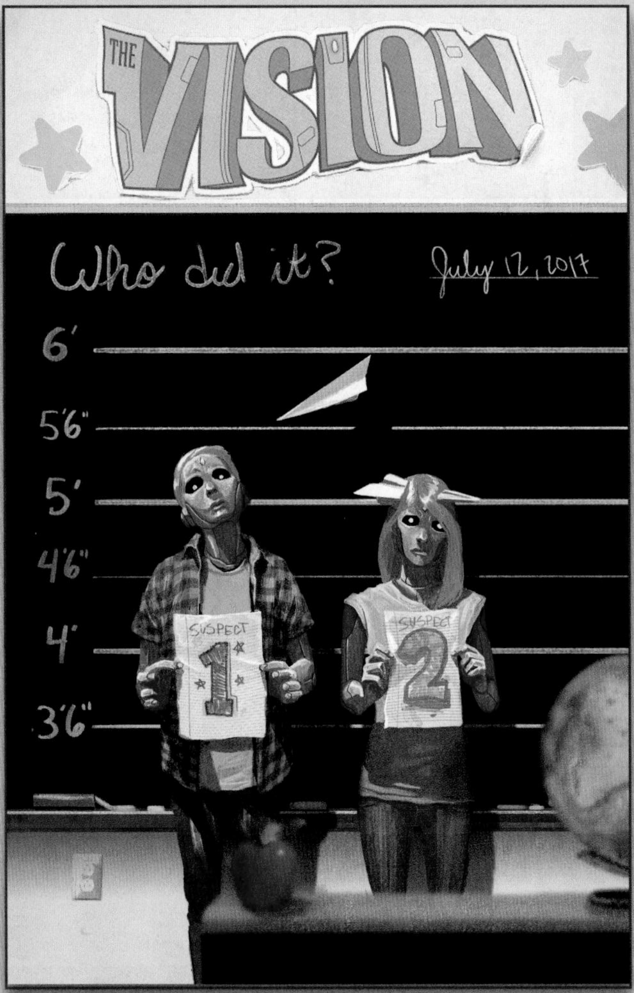
THE VISION
Who did it?
July 12, 2017
6'
5'6"
5'
4'6"
4'
3'6"
SUSPECT 1
SUSPECT 2

FINAL

#5 COVER LAYOUTS BY **MARCO D'ALFONSO**

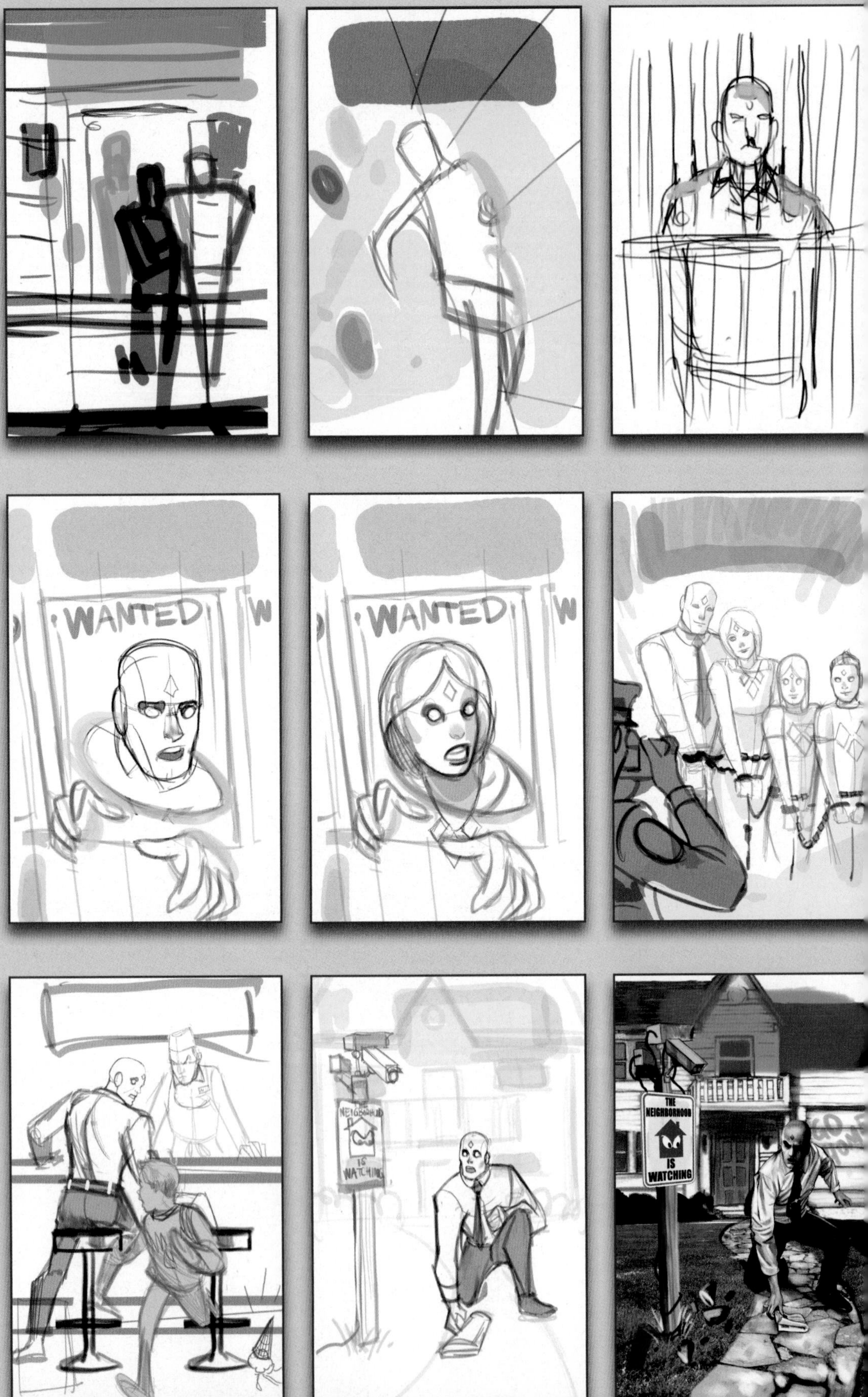

WANTED
W
WANTED
W
THE NEIGHBORHOOD
IS
WATCHING

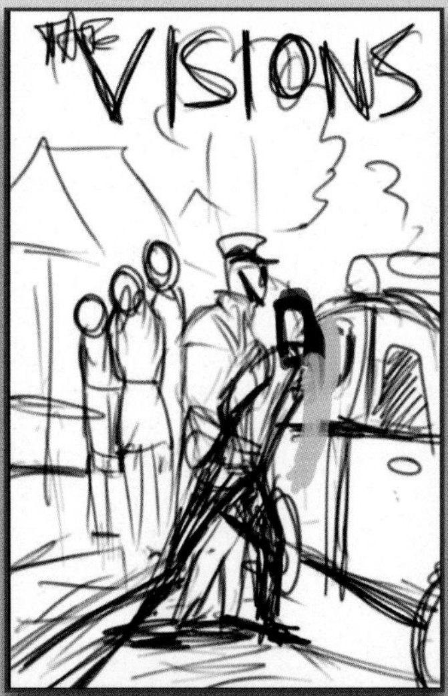
THE VISIONS

LAYOUT

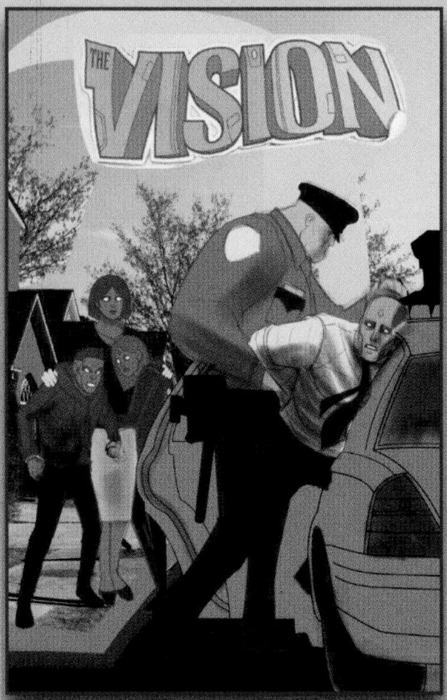
THE VISION

ROUGH

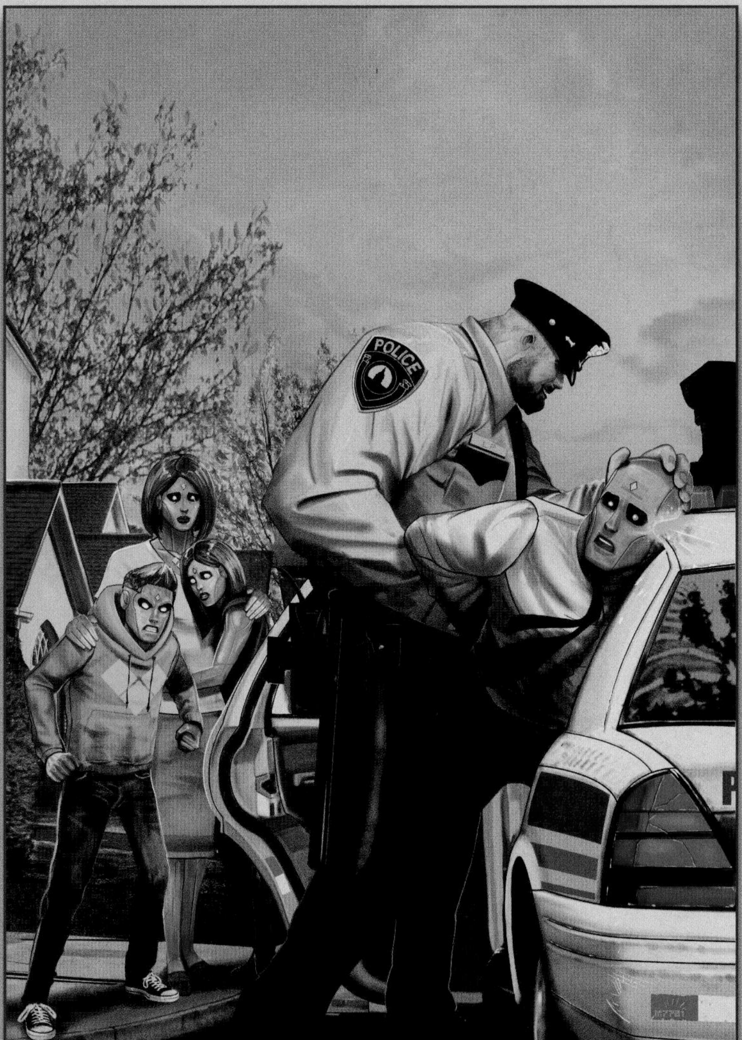
POLICE

FINAL

#6 COVER LAYOUTS BY **MARCO D'ALFONSO**

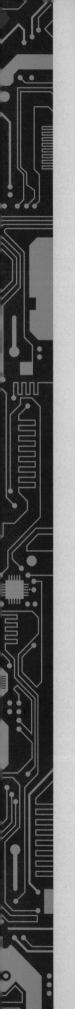

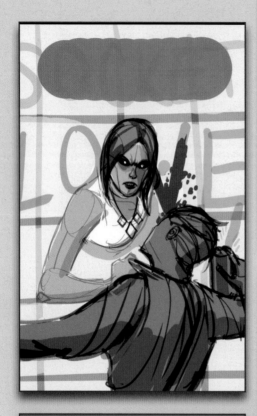

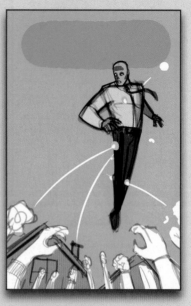

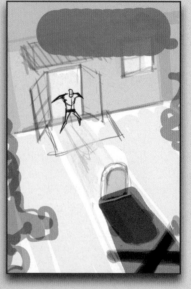

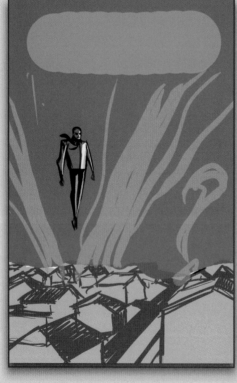

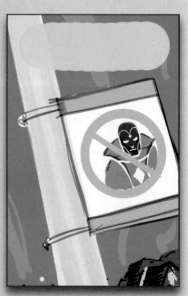

#6 COVER PROCESS BY **MARCO D'ALFONSO**

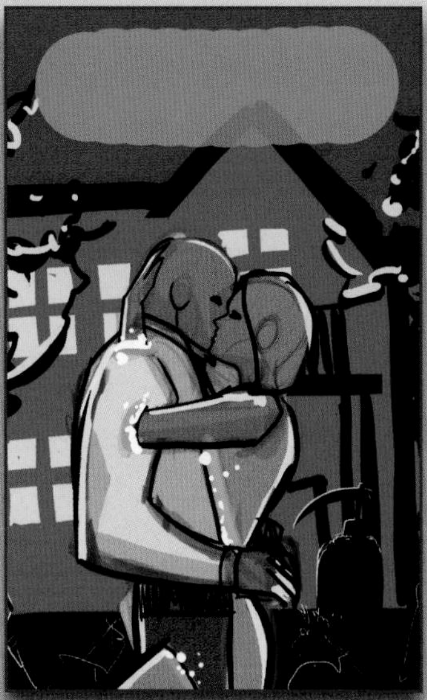

LAYOUT

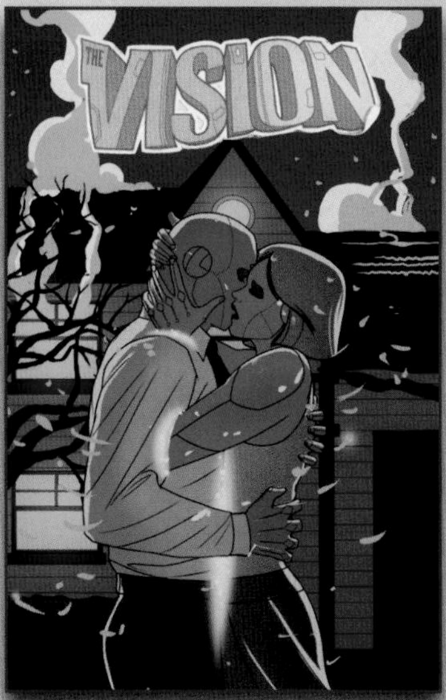
THE
VISION

ROUGH

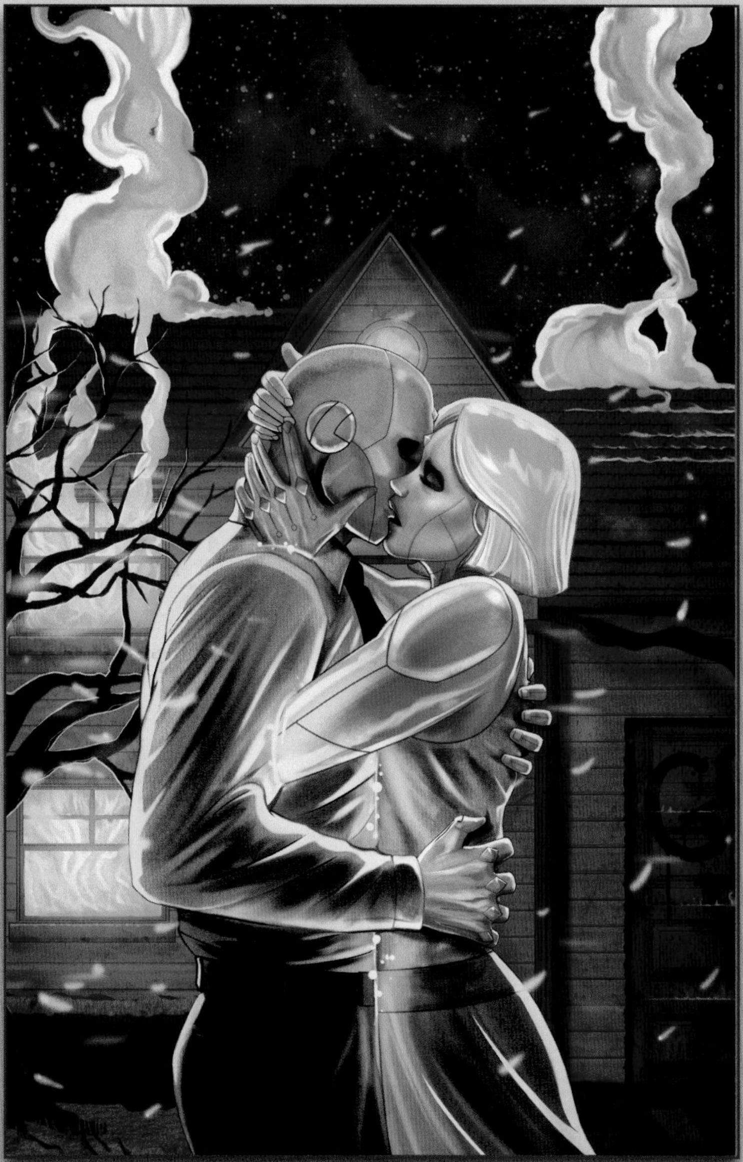

FINAL

#7 COVER PROCESS BY **MIKE DEL MUNDO**

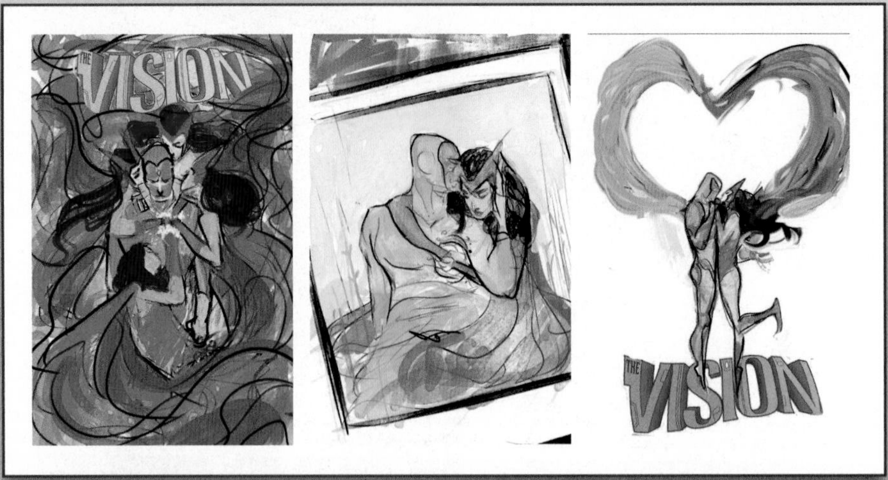
THE VISION
THE VISION

SKETCHES

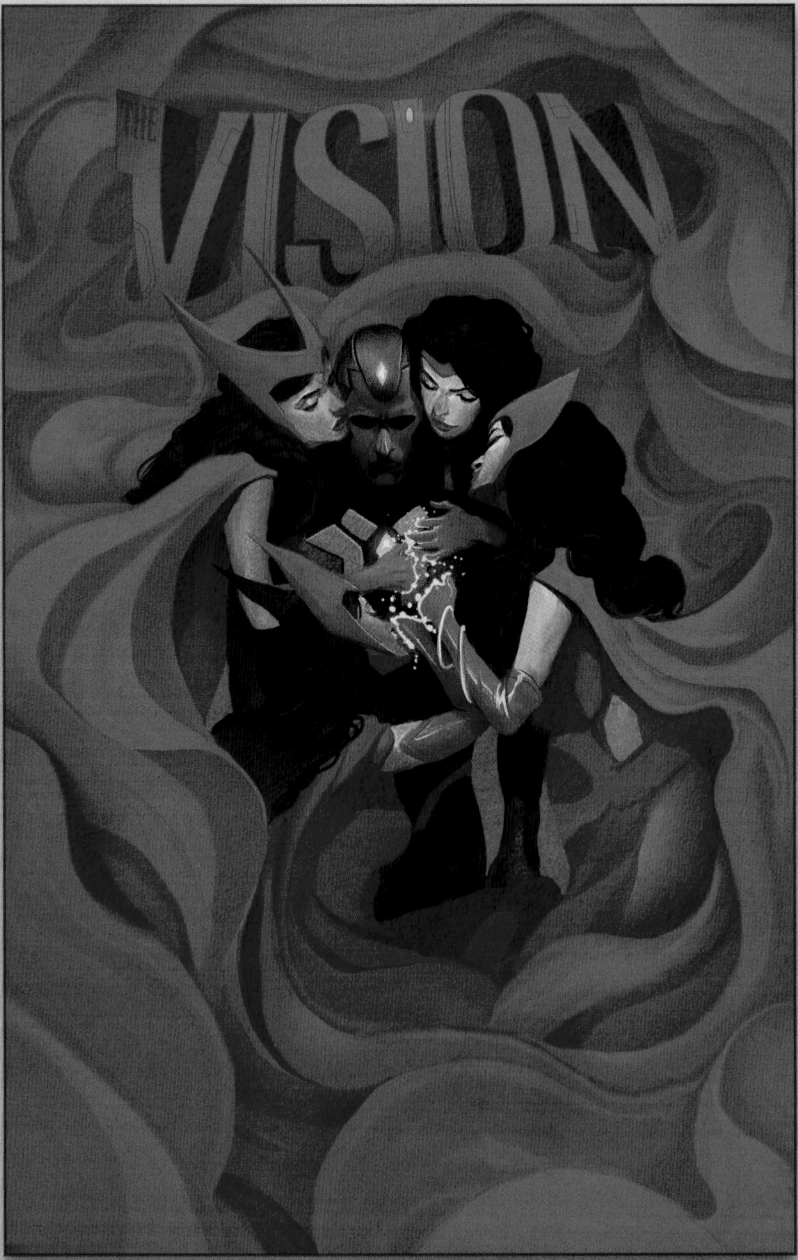
THE VISION

FINAL

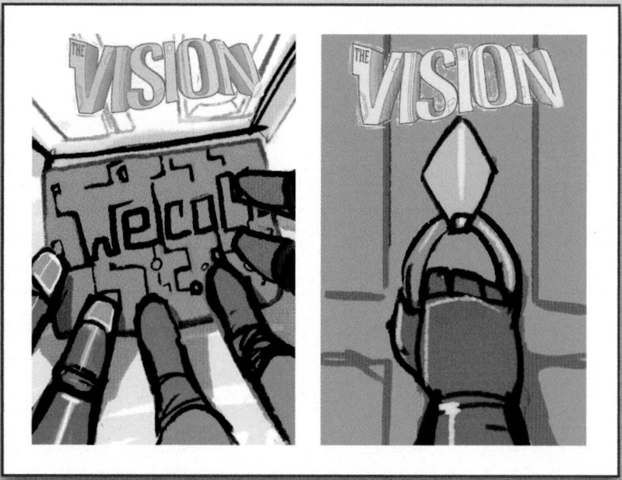
THE VISION
Welco
THE VISION

SKETCHES

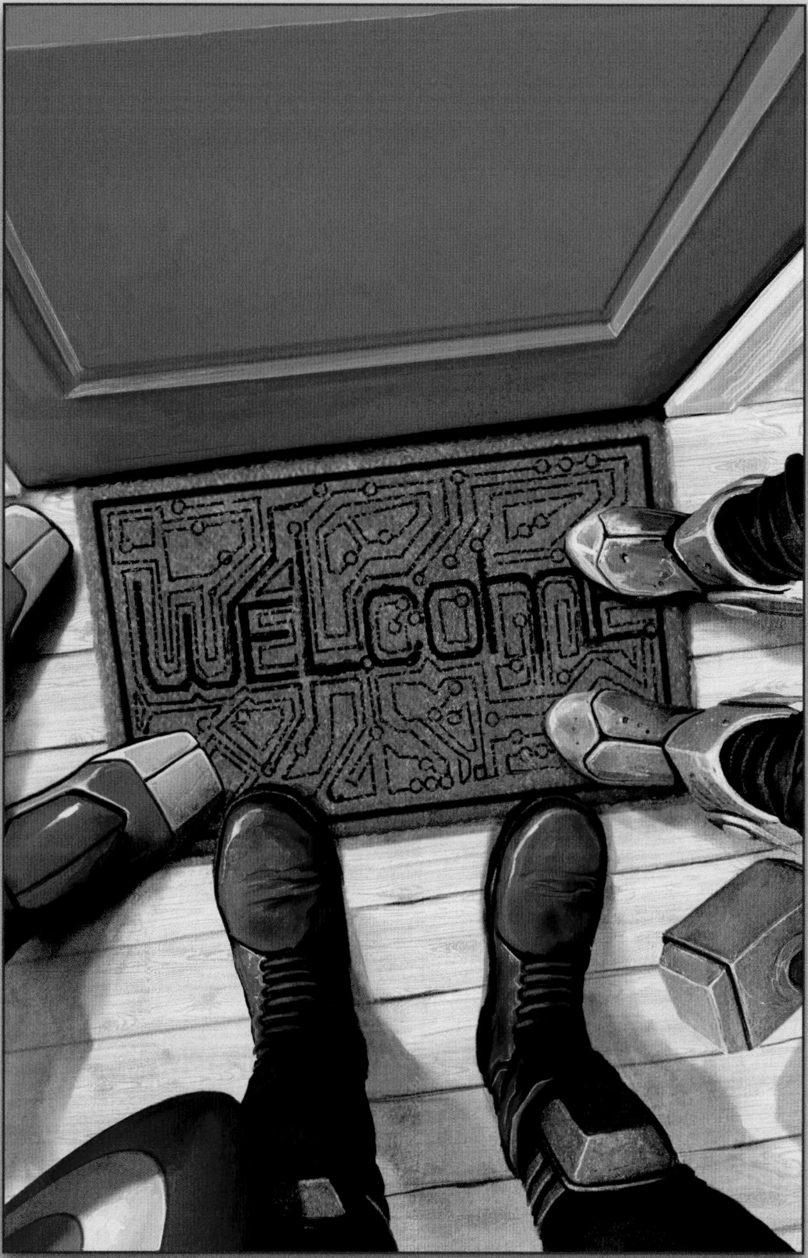
WELcome

FINAL

#9 COVER PROCESS BY **MIKE DEL MUNDO**

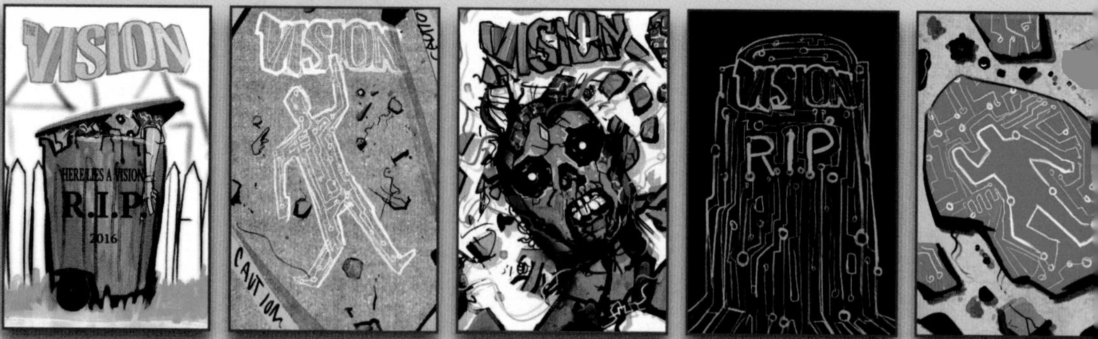
THE VISION
HERE LIES A VISION
R.I.P.
2016
VISION
CAUTION
VISION
VISION
R.I.P.

SKETCHES

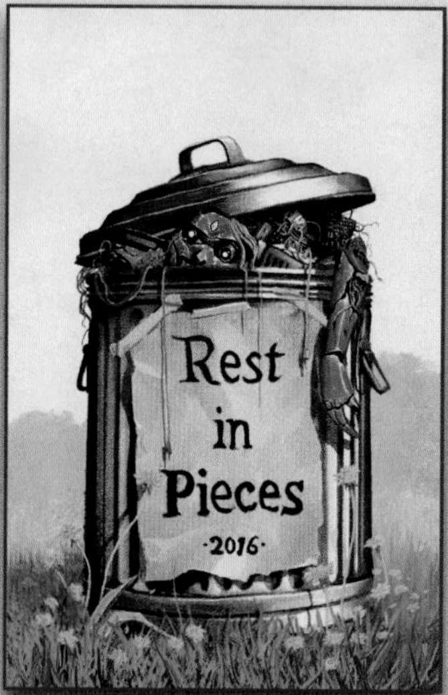
Rest
in
Pieces
·2016·

ORIGINAL WORDING

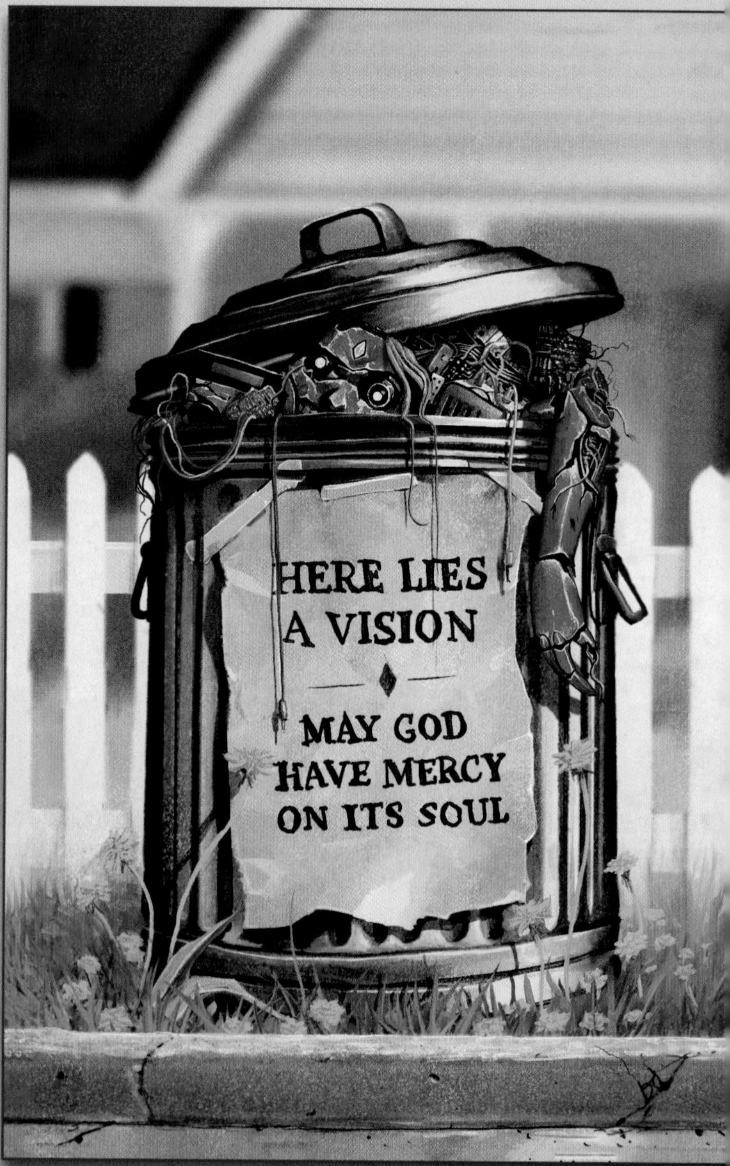
HERE LIES
A VISION
MAY GOD
HAVE MERCY
ON ITS SOUL

FINAL

#10 COVER PROCESS BY MIKE DEL MUNDO

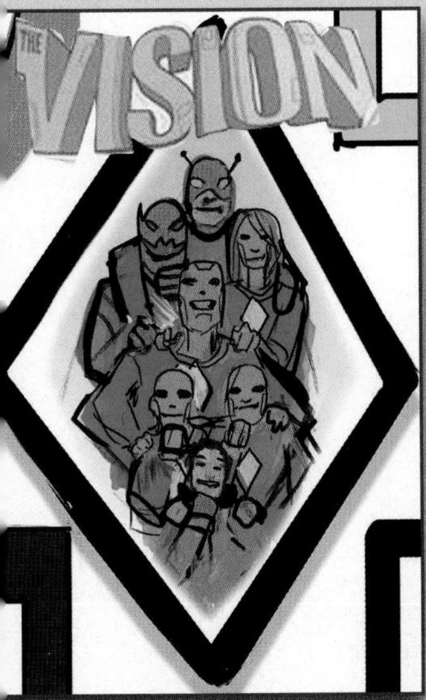
THE
VISION

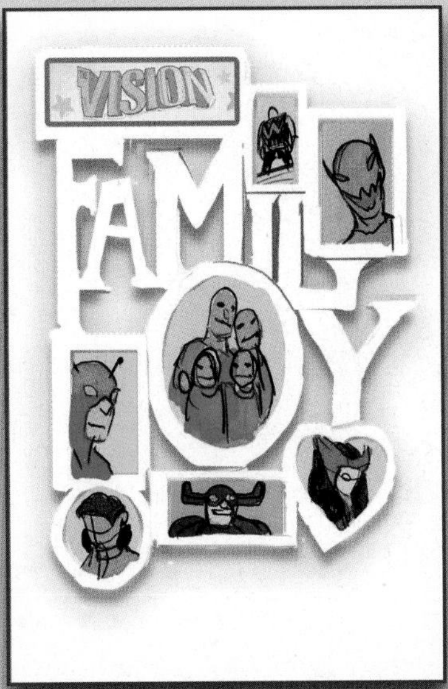
VISION

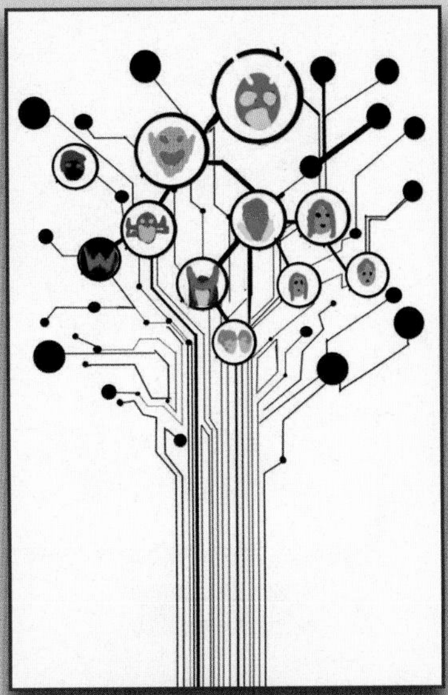

SKETCHES

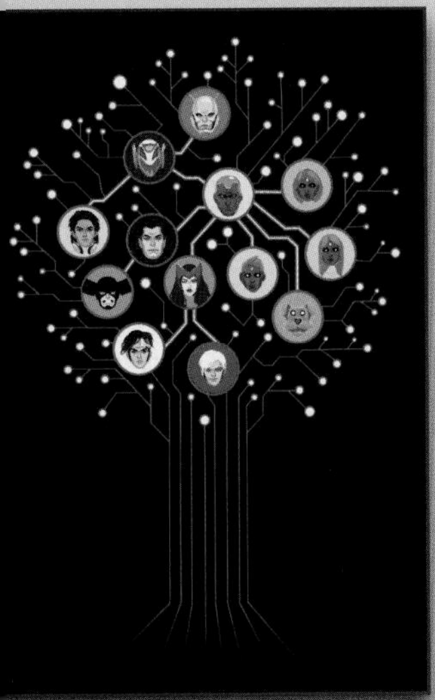

ROUGH

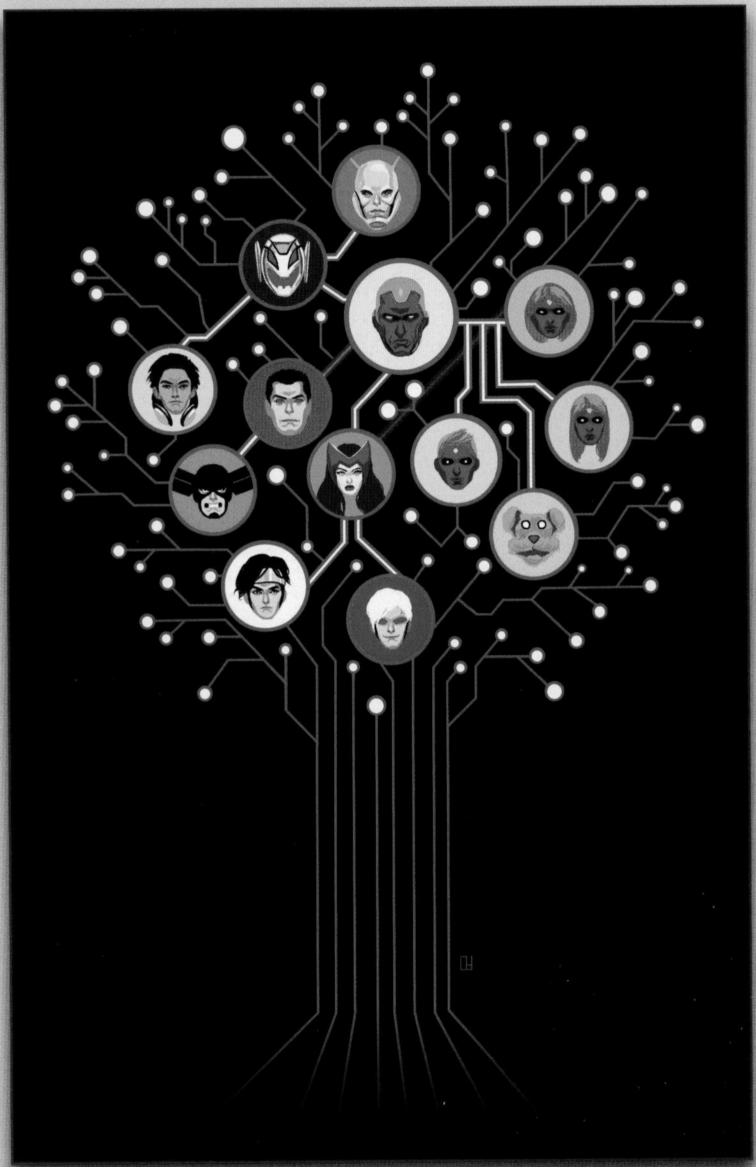

FINAL

#11 COVER PROCESS BY **MIKE DEL MUNDO**

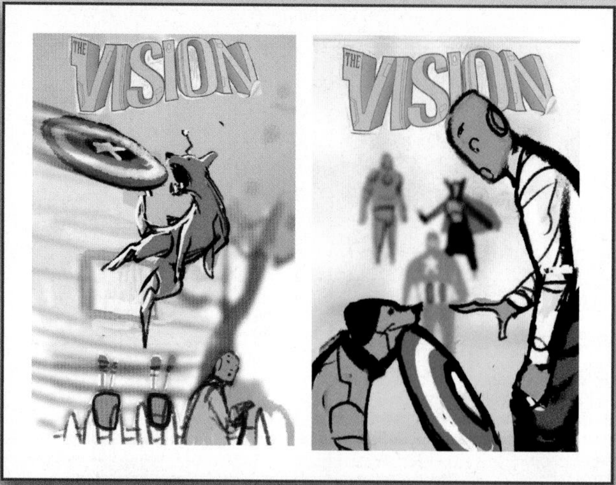
THE VISION
THE VISION

SKETCHES

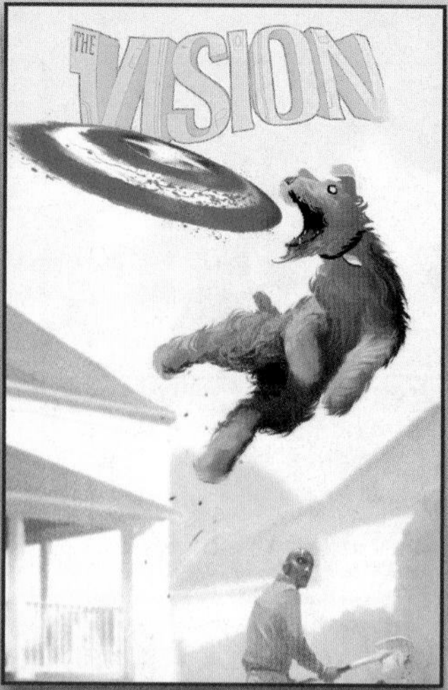
THE VISION

ROUGH

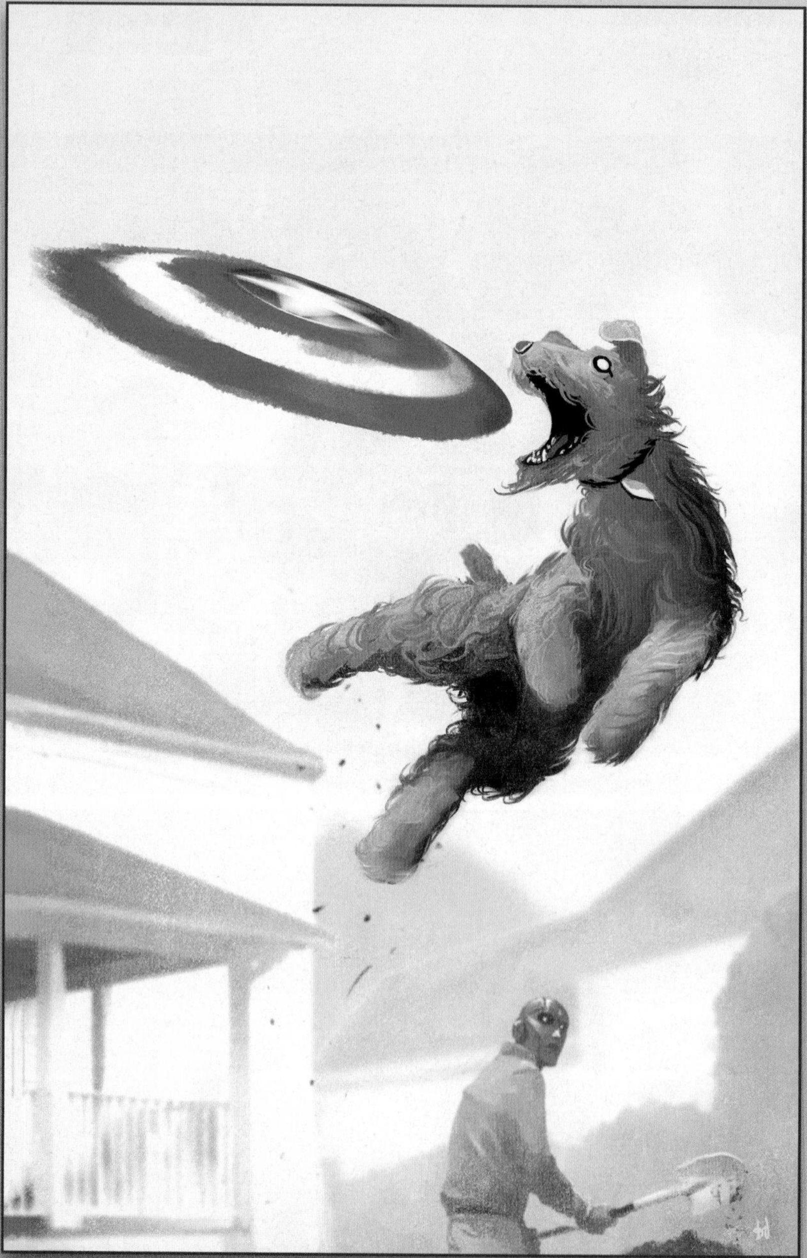

FINAL

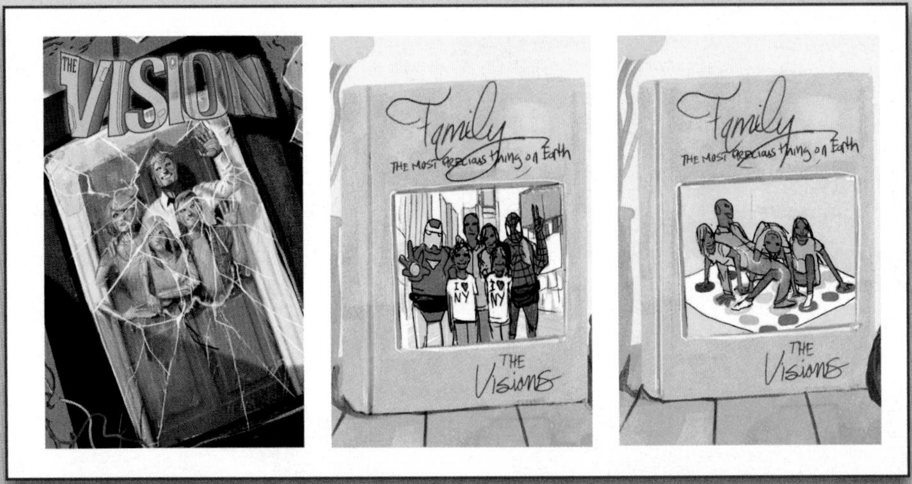
THE VISION
Family
THE MOST PRECIOUS thing on Earth
THE Visions
Family
THE MOST PRECIOUS thing on Earth
THE Visions

SKETCHES

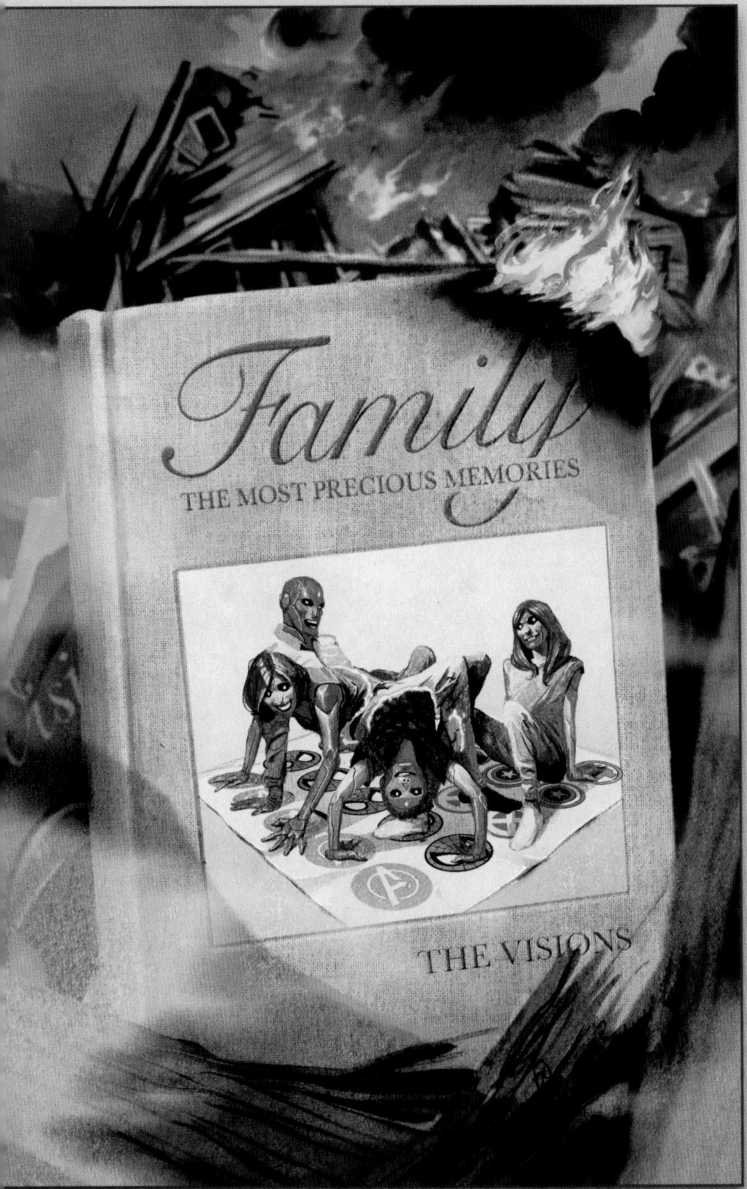
Family
THE MOST PRECIOUS MEMORIES
THE VISIONS

FINAL

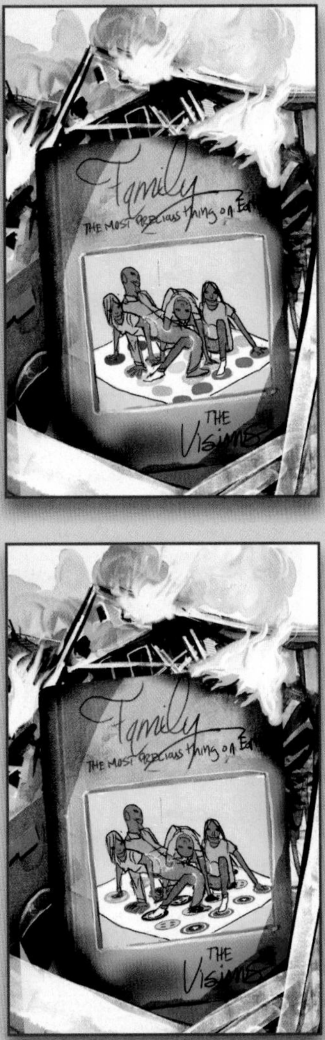
Family
THE MOST PRECIOUS thing on Earth
THE Visions
Family
THE MOST PRECIOUS thing on Earth
THE Visions

ROUGHS

#1 VARIANT BY **RYAN SOOK**

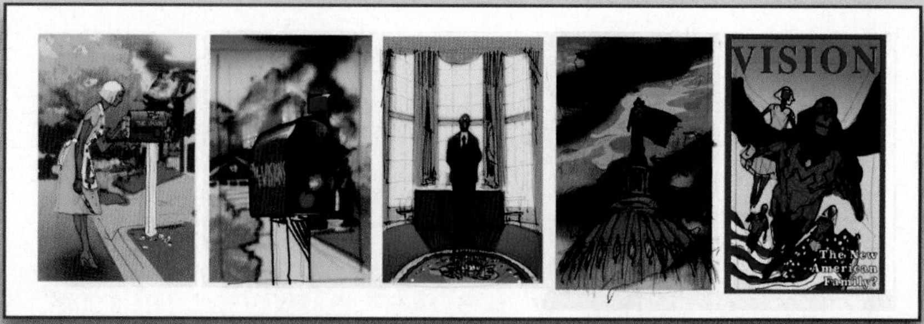
VISION
The New American Family?

SKETCHES

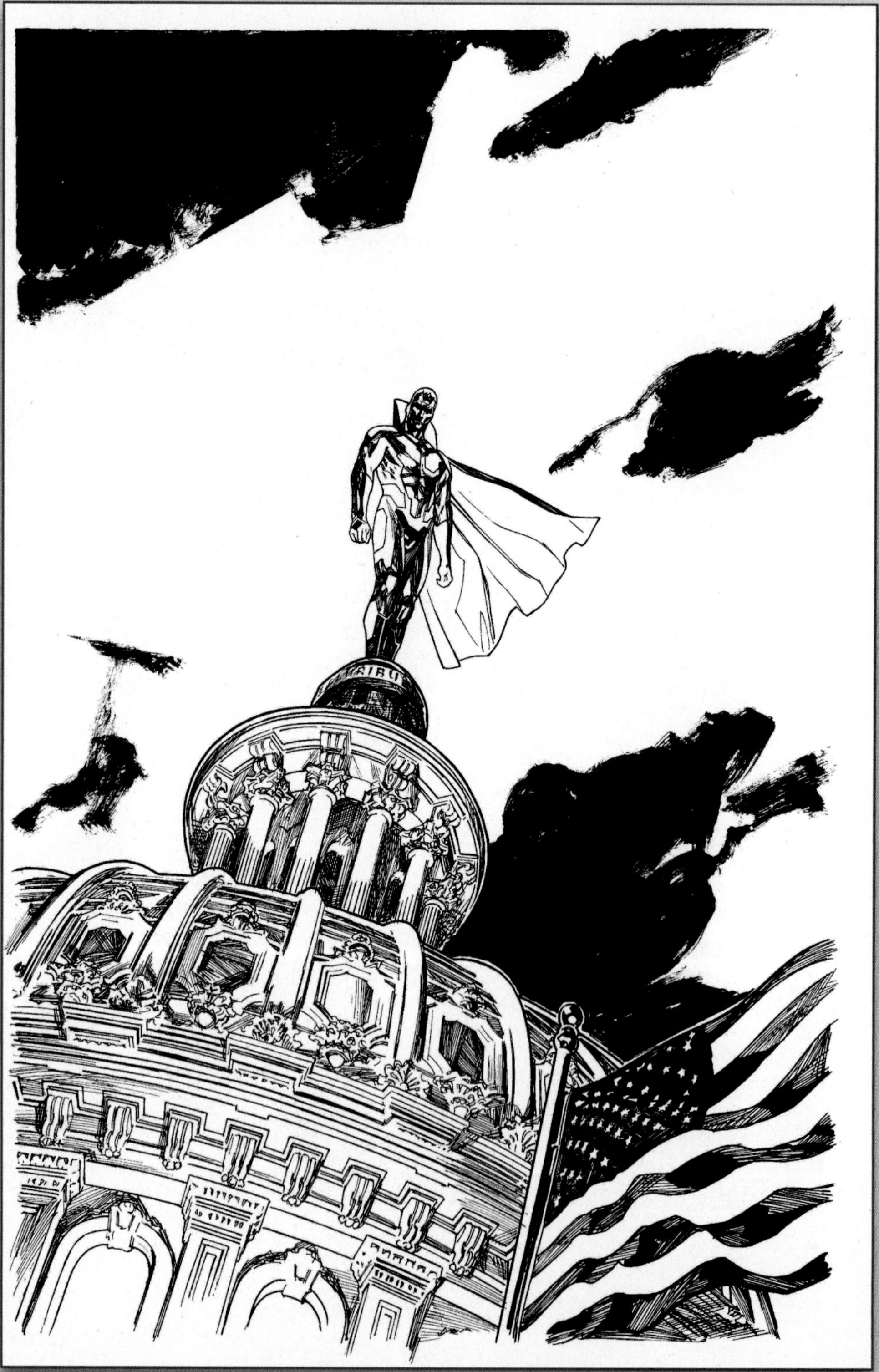

INKS

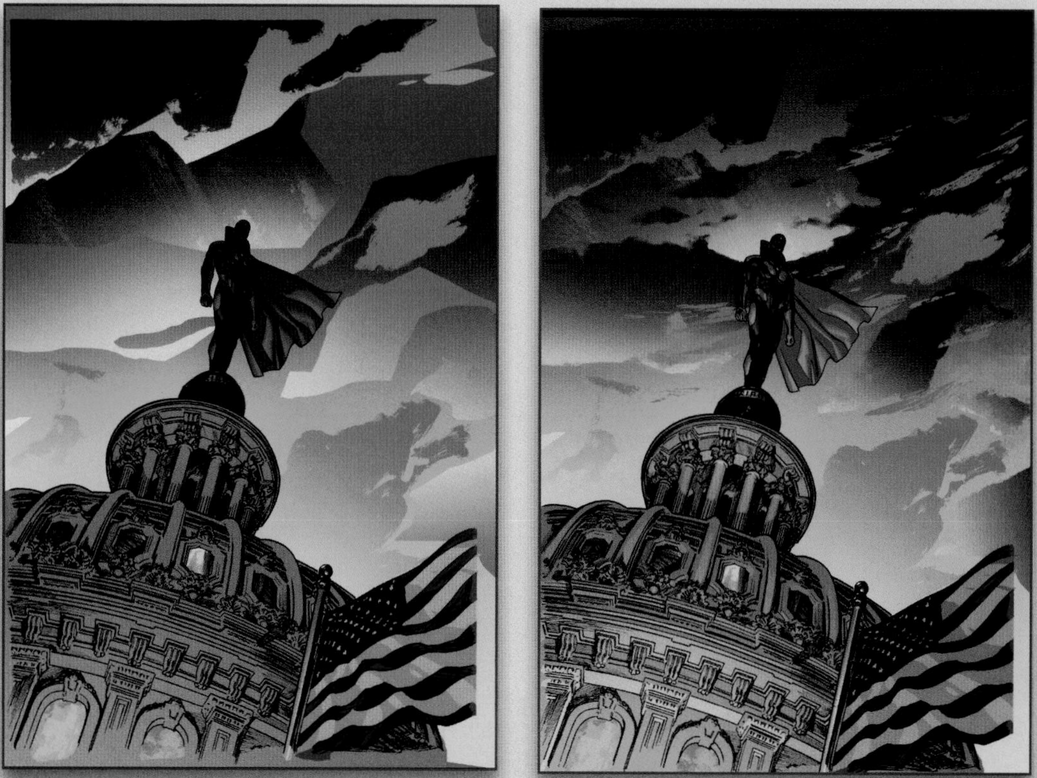

WORK-IN-PROGRESS COLORS

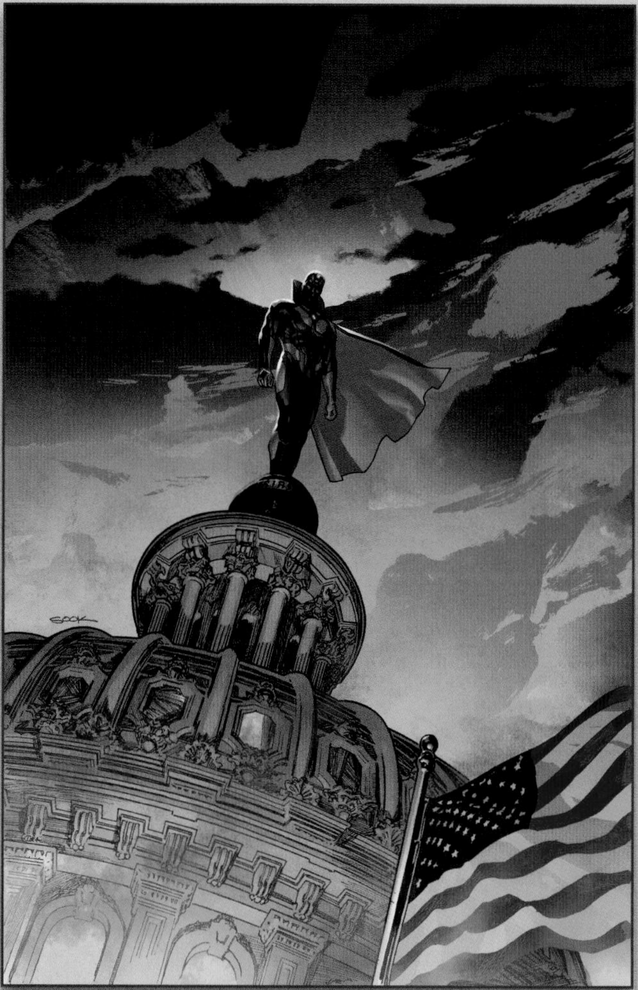

FINAL

#1 VARIANT BY **MARCOS MARTIN**

THE
VISION

SKETCH

THE
VISION
TOM KING · GABRIEL H. WALTA · JORDIE BELLAIRE

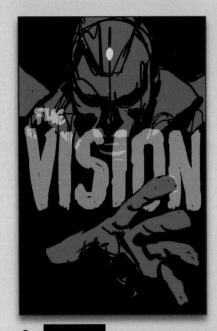

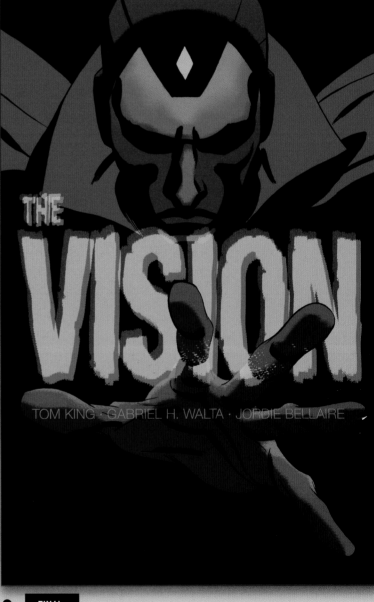

FINAL

#2 VARIANT BY **TULA LOTAY**

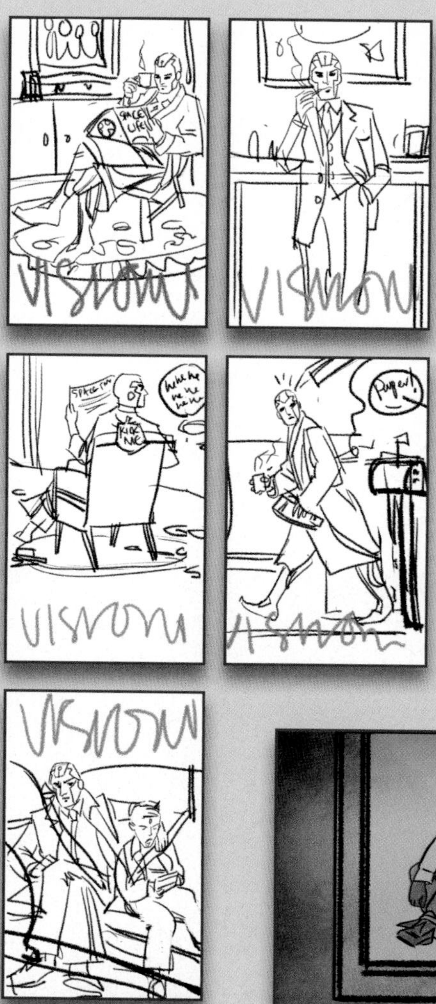

SKETCHES

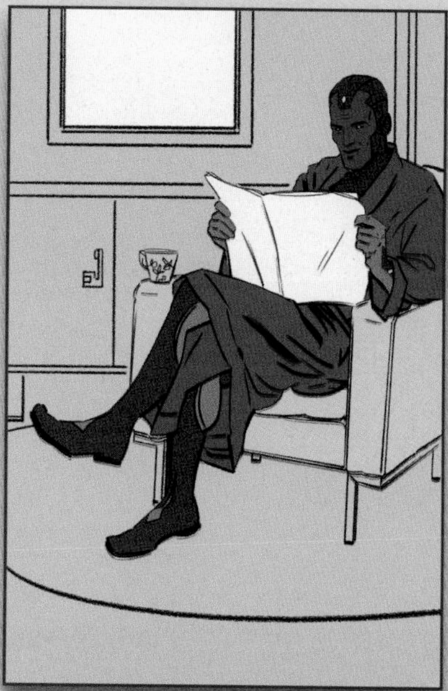

WORK-IN-PROGRESS COLORS

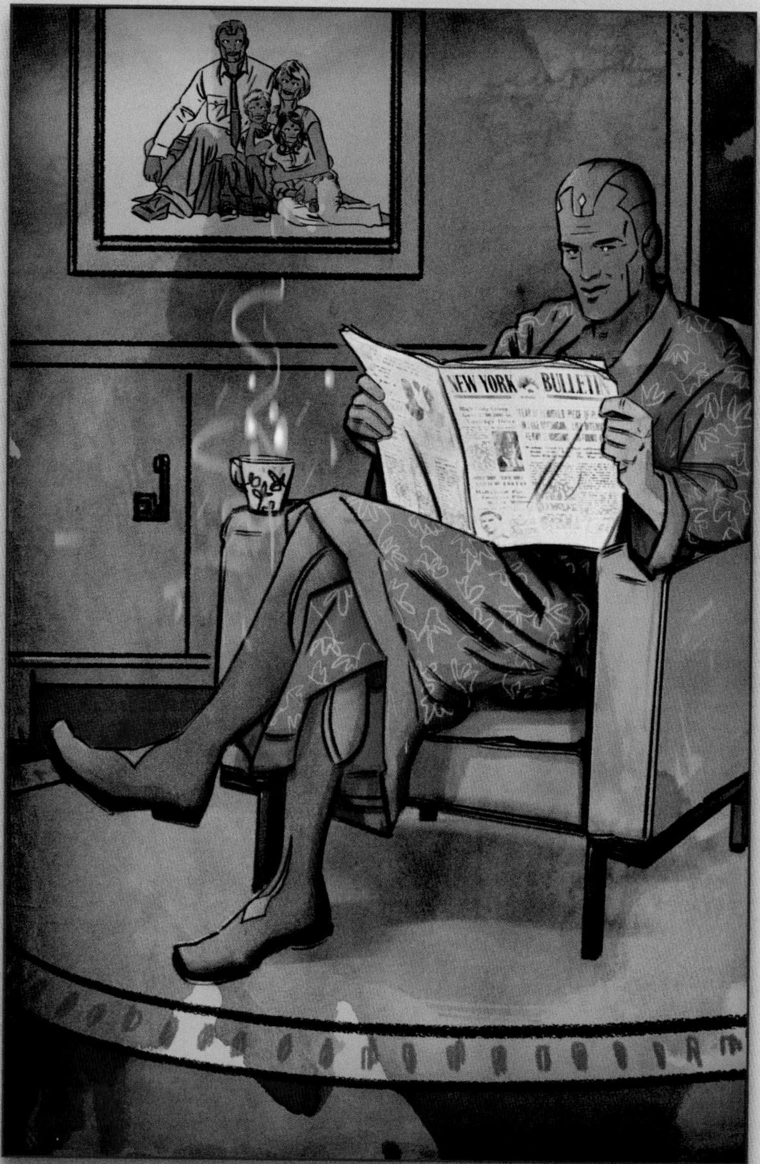

FINAL

#1 HIP-HOP VARIANT BY **VANESA R. DEL REY**

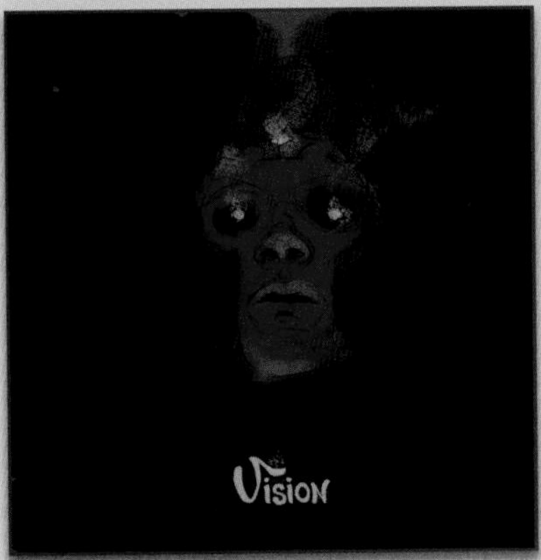
Vision

SKETCH

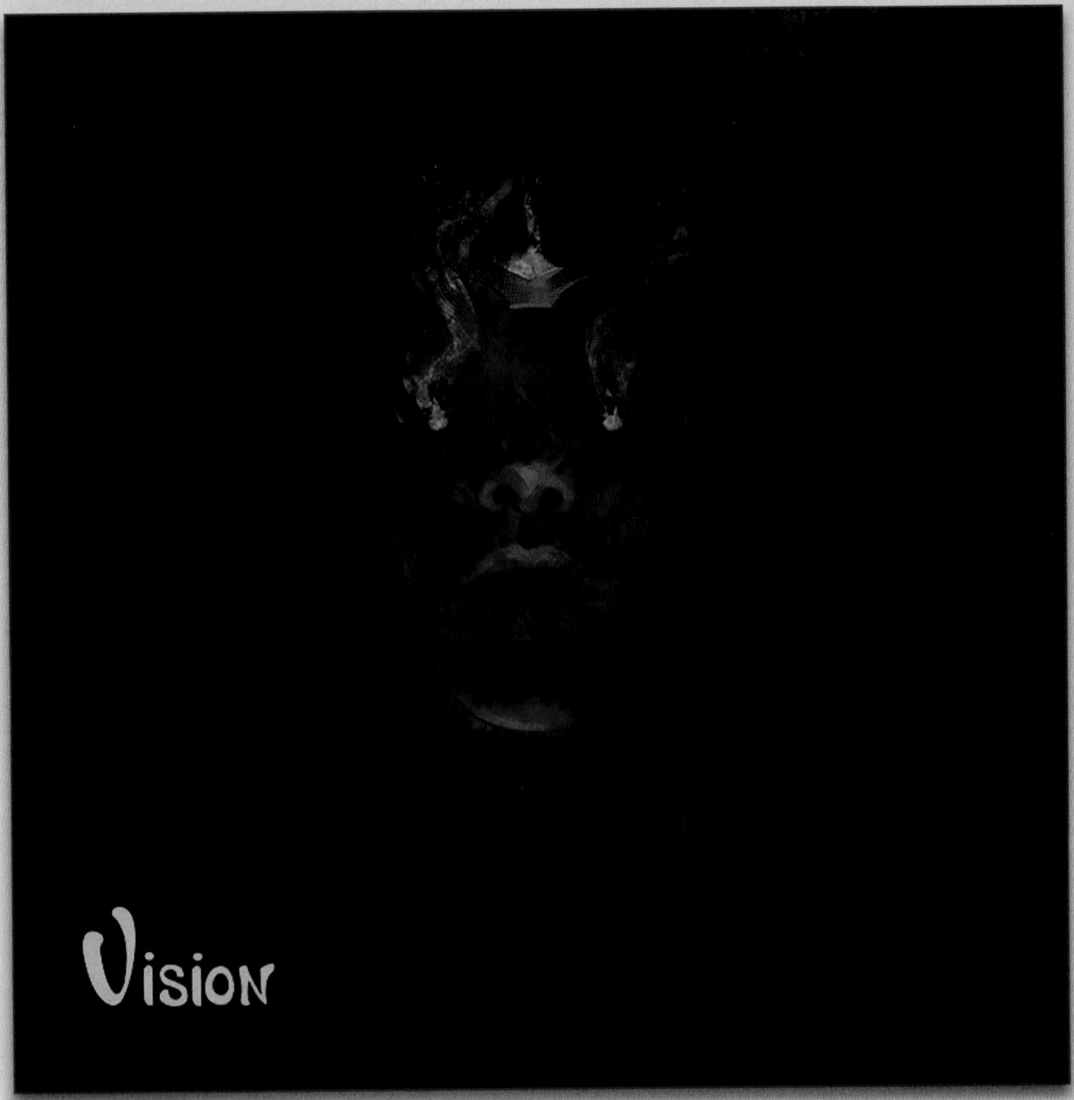
Vision

FINAL

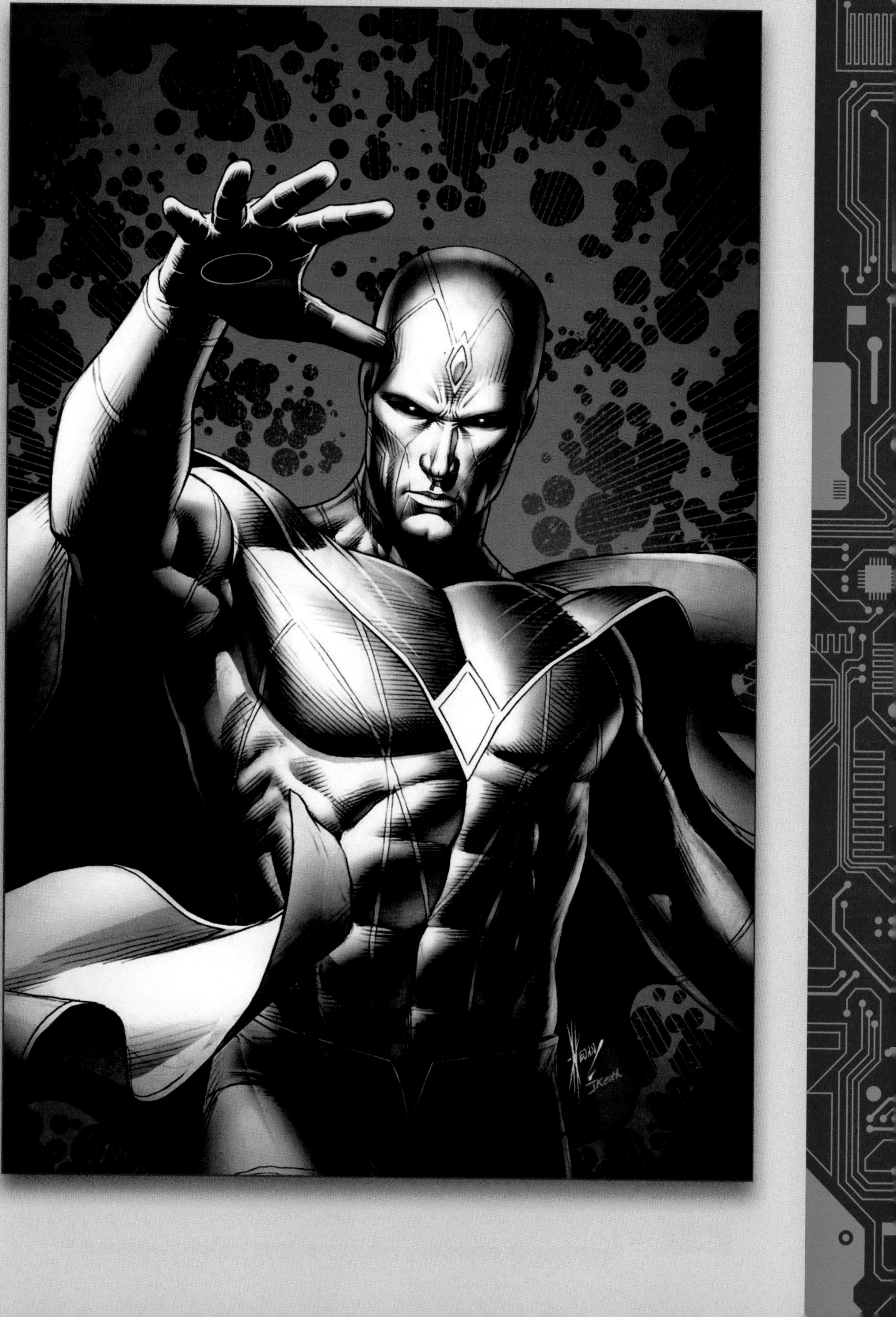

#3 VARIANT BY **CHRISTIAN WARD**

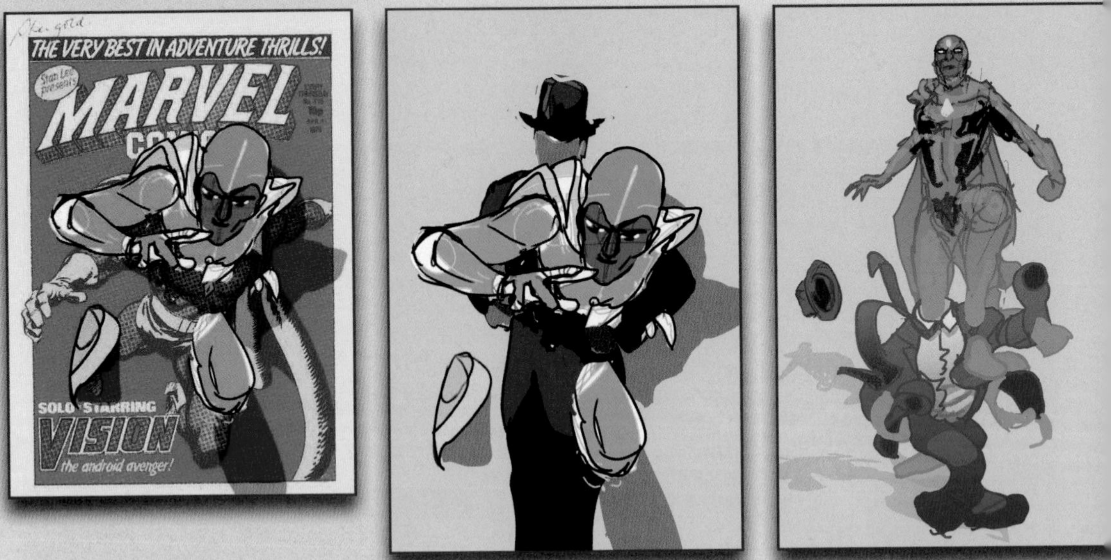
THE VERY BEST IN ADVENTURE THRILLS!
Stan Lee presents
MARVEL
SOLO STARRING
VISION
the android avenger!

SKETCHES

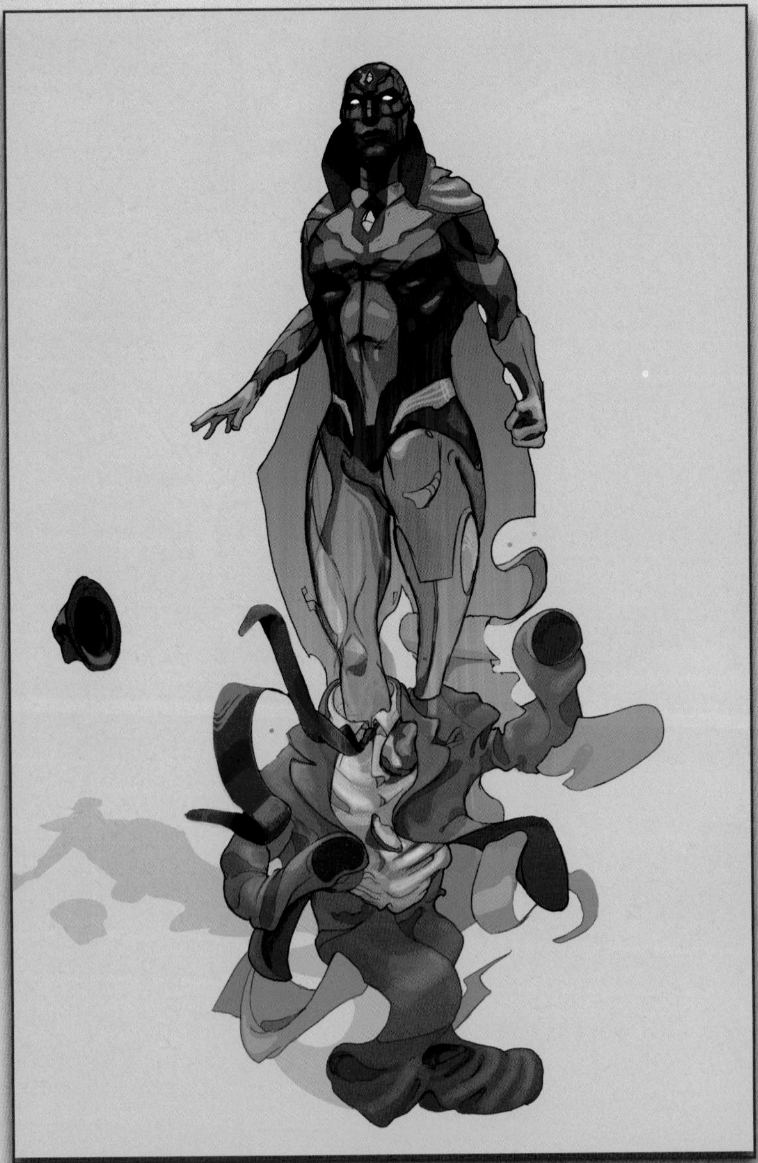

FINAL

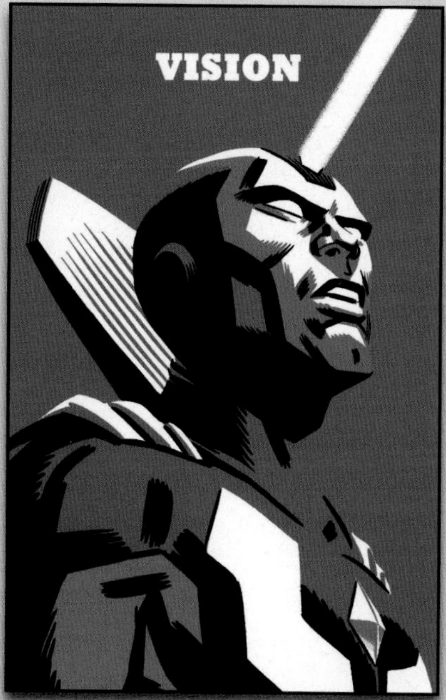
VISION

SKETCH

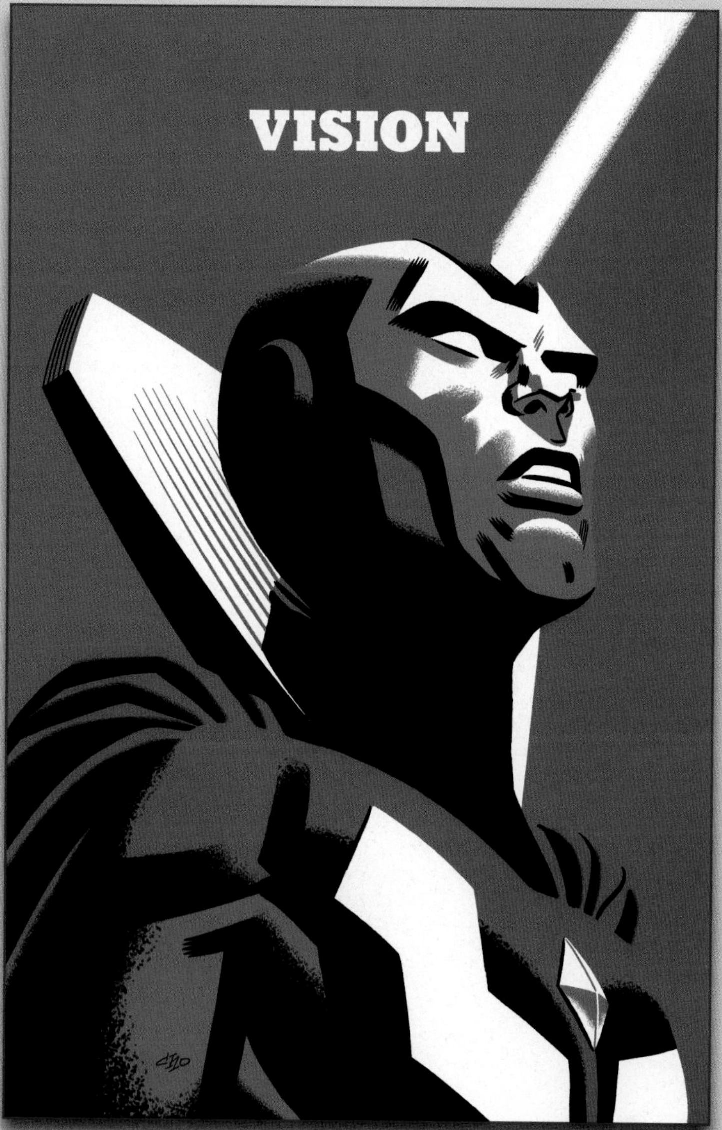
VISION

FINAL

#8 VARIANT BY DALE KEOWN & JASON KEITH

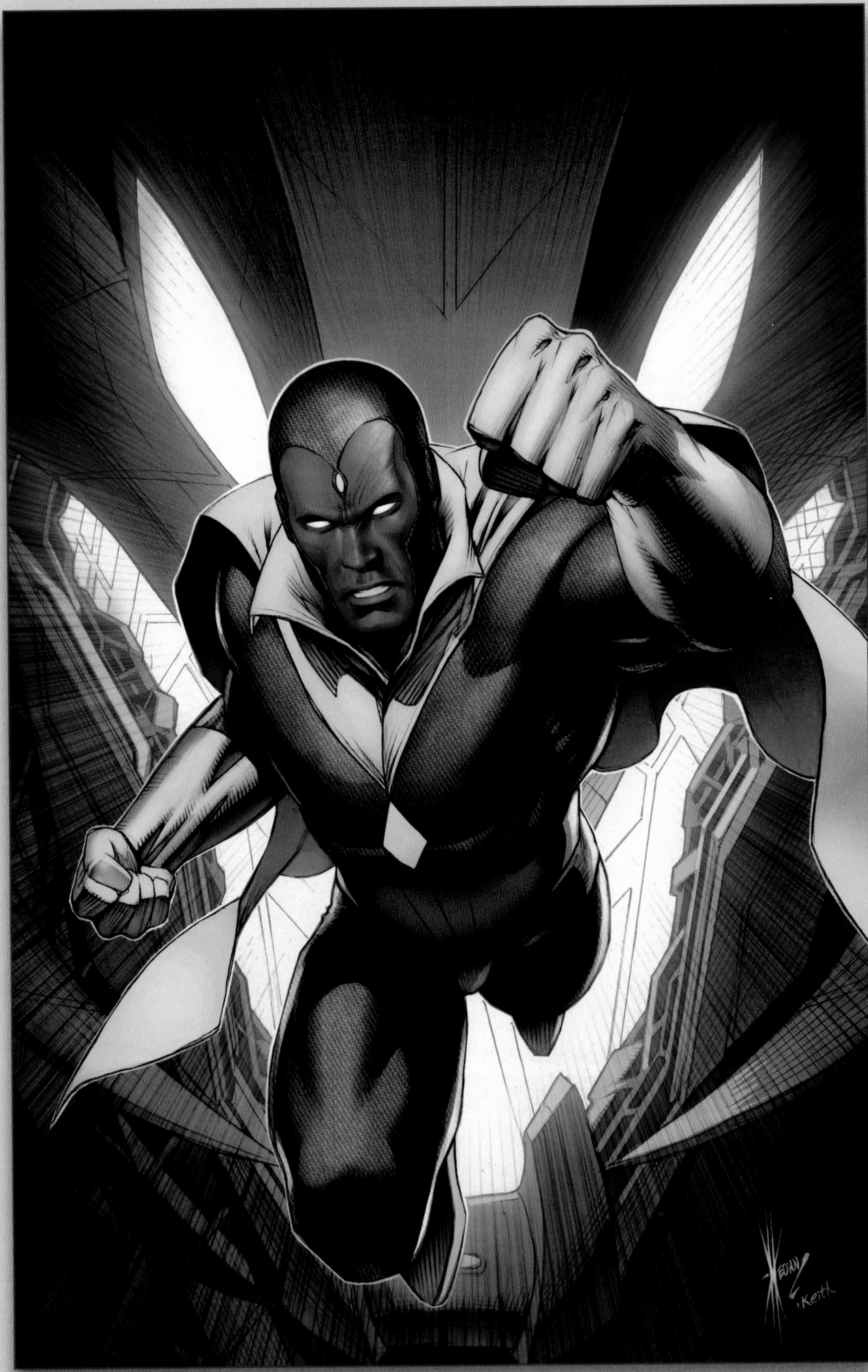

Keith

#8 STORY THUS FAR VARIANT BY **GABRIEL HERNANDEZ WALTA**

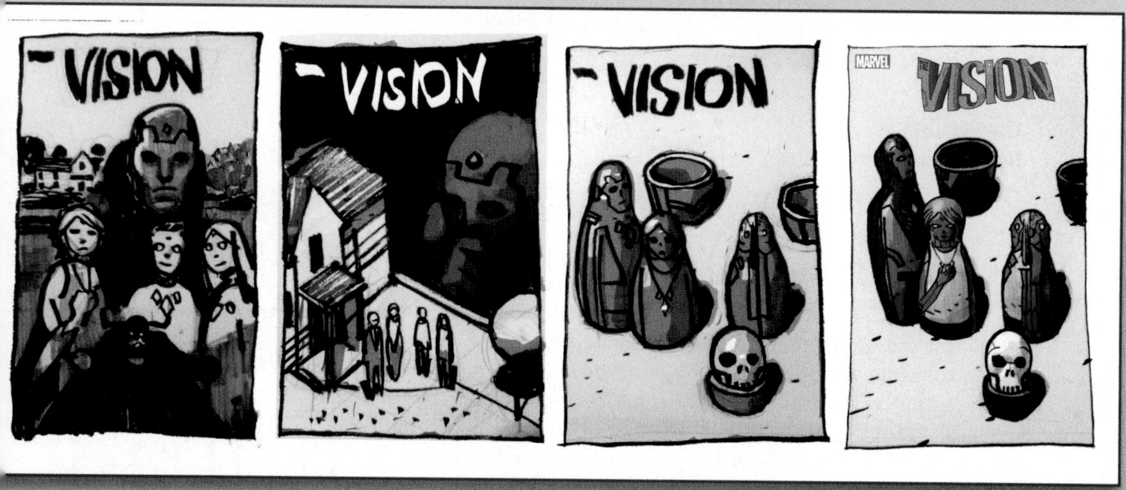

VISION
VISION
VISION
MARVEL
THE VISION

SKETCHES

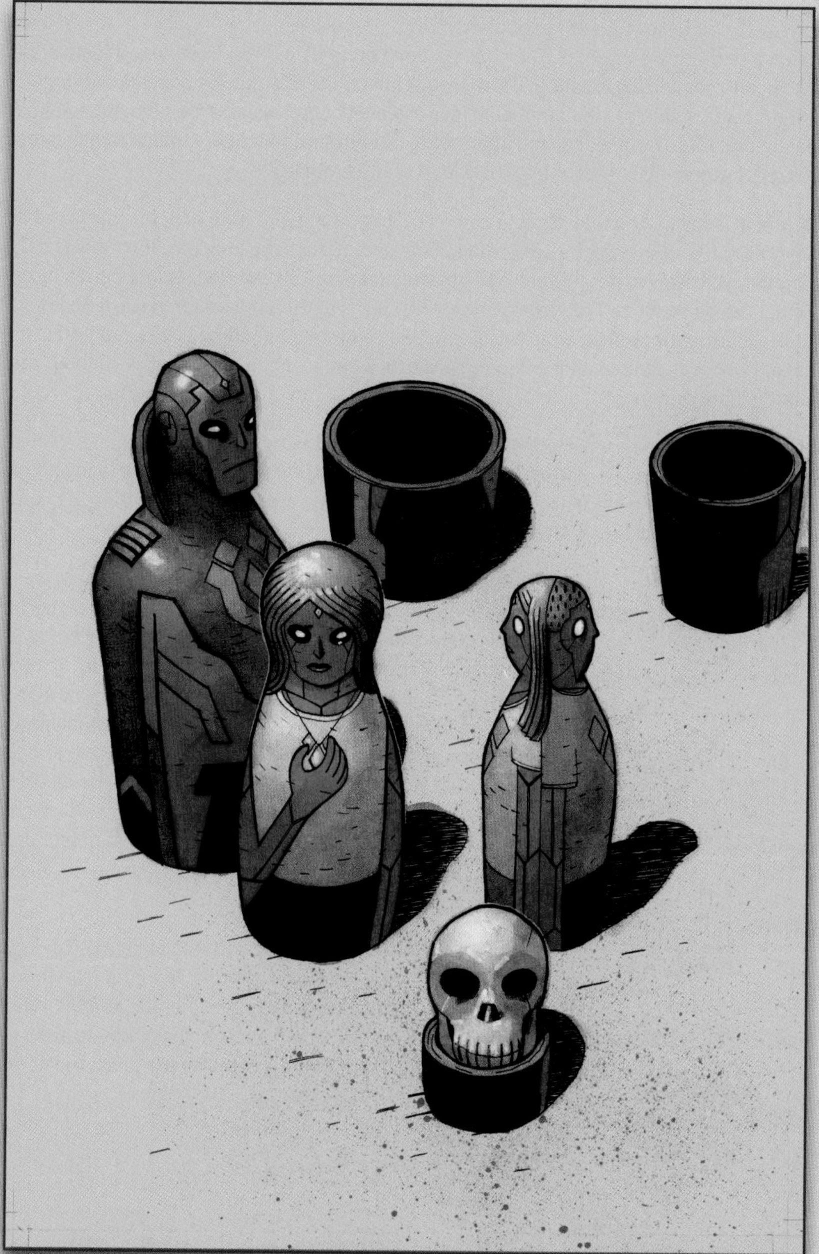

FINAL

THE VISIONS
By Tom King

*In the suburbs of DC, a perfectly normal family of super
robots tries to live the American dream.
And to ignore the body under the stairs.*

He wants to be human, and what's more human than a family?
He goes to the laboratory where he was created, where a villain
molded him into a weapon, where he first rebelled against his
given destiny, where he first imagined that he could be more,
that he could be good, that he could be a man, a normal, ordinary
man. And he builds them. A wife, Virginia. Two teenage twins, Viv
and Val. They look like him. They have his powers. They share his
grandest ambition or perhaps obsession: the unrelenting need to
be ordinary. They are: The Visions.

He gets a job working for the Secret Service. He buys a house. Sends
his children to school. Talks to his wife about the future. There are
troubles; of course there are troubles. The children don't quite fit in. They understand math and facts, but
they have difficulty socializing, relating. The marriage isn't quite real yet; it's based on arrangement not
love, and Virginia and Vision are not quite sure love will ever come. Vision's job often takes him way as
he defends the president from global and interstellar threats, and this new, strange family needs him at
home. But every household has troubles. That's part of the ordinary.

Then, while Vision is away, The Grim Reaper comes calling. Jealous of their happiness, crazed that they
do not recognize him as an uncle, he swings his blade and attacks the children. The mother defends
them as a mother will. New to her powers, she goes too far. She kills the Reaper and buries his body in
the yard, under the back stairs. The Vision returns. He learns of the man under the dirt. He learns what
his wife did. He learns what will be done to his wife and children if her crime is discovered. He learns—
this synthezoid who was built to be a uniquely powerful weapon against humanity—finally learns that
there is nothing more ordinary than doing anything, everything to protect your family.

The Visions is Breaking Bad meets the Incredibles: a groundbreaking, thrilling new series in the tradition
of Hawkeye and Batgirl. This is a playful, high stakes series that will electrify our old fans and grab onto
new ones by taking the great Marvel theme, *super heroes are you and me*, and twisting it, playing with it
until every comic reader will demand to know what's coming next.

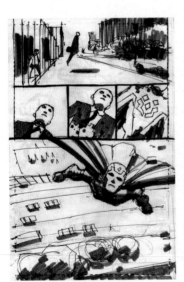

ART BY GABRIEL HERNANDEZ WALTA

As we go forward, our audience will recognize themselves in
this family. Through the ongoing, absurd struggle of the Visions
to be ordinary, they will see their own struggles of being unique
individuals trying to fit into a homogenous society. Moreover,
they will see Vision as no longer "that green guy who's on the
Avengers sometimes," but instead as a vital and fascinating part
of the Marvel Universe, a man with amazing powers and amazing
responsibilities, a man who represents for the Marvel Universe
what Spock represents for the Star Trek Universe. Through this
comic, we will elevate Vision, a character with almost 50 years of
history, to his rightful place as a top tier player in the Marvel U, a
player worthy of his own TV show and movie.

Imagine the first cover. Imagine a family at dinner. Talking,
laughing. A Norman Rockwell painting. The American Dream. But
instead of the bland, white people of the 40s and 50s, we have
green, red, and yellow robots each smiling happily, their powers
almost jumping out of them. And under the table, the body lies still.

Behold the Visions.

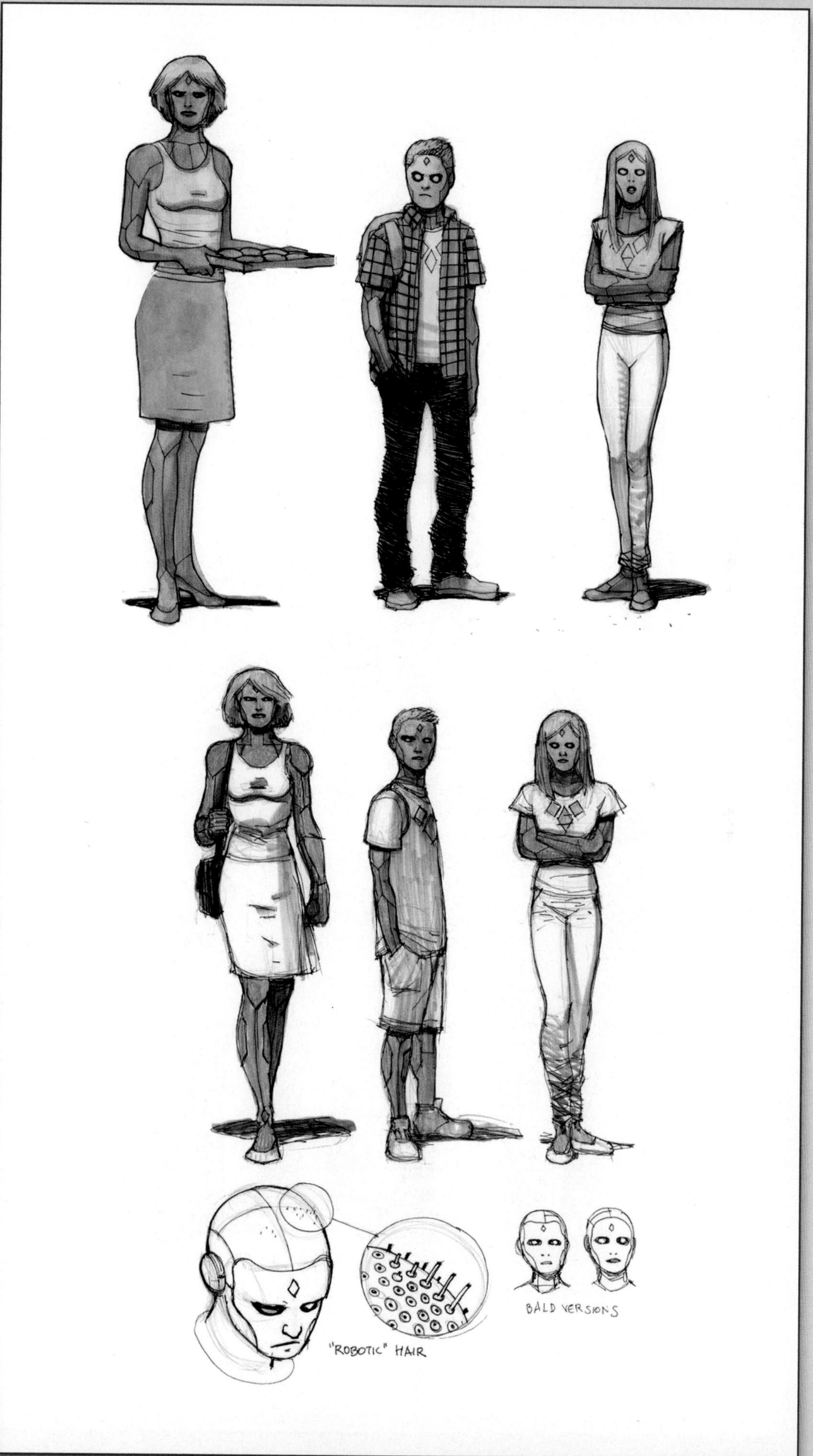
"ROBOTIC" HAIR
BALD VERSIONS

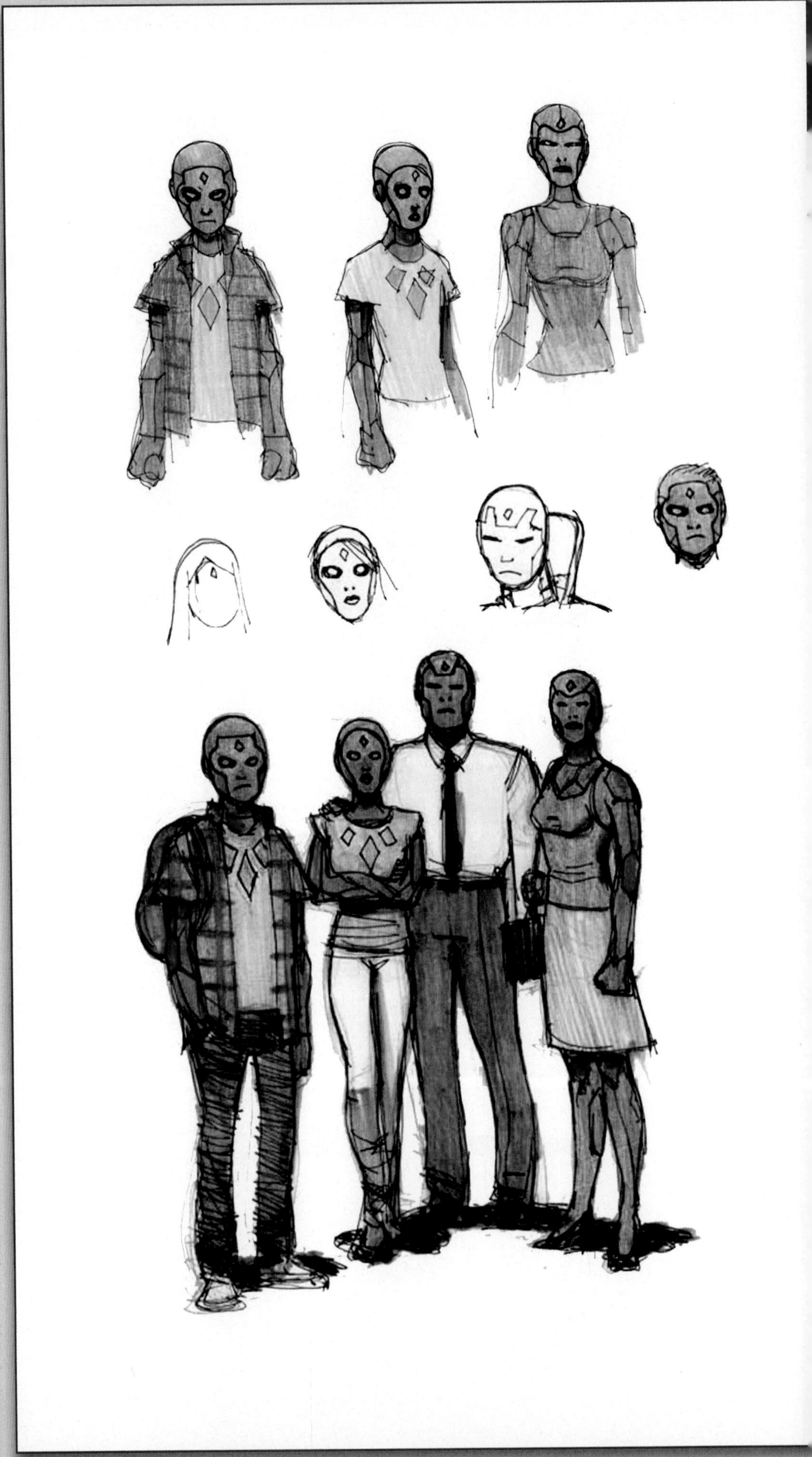

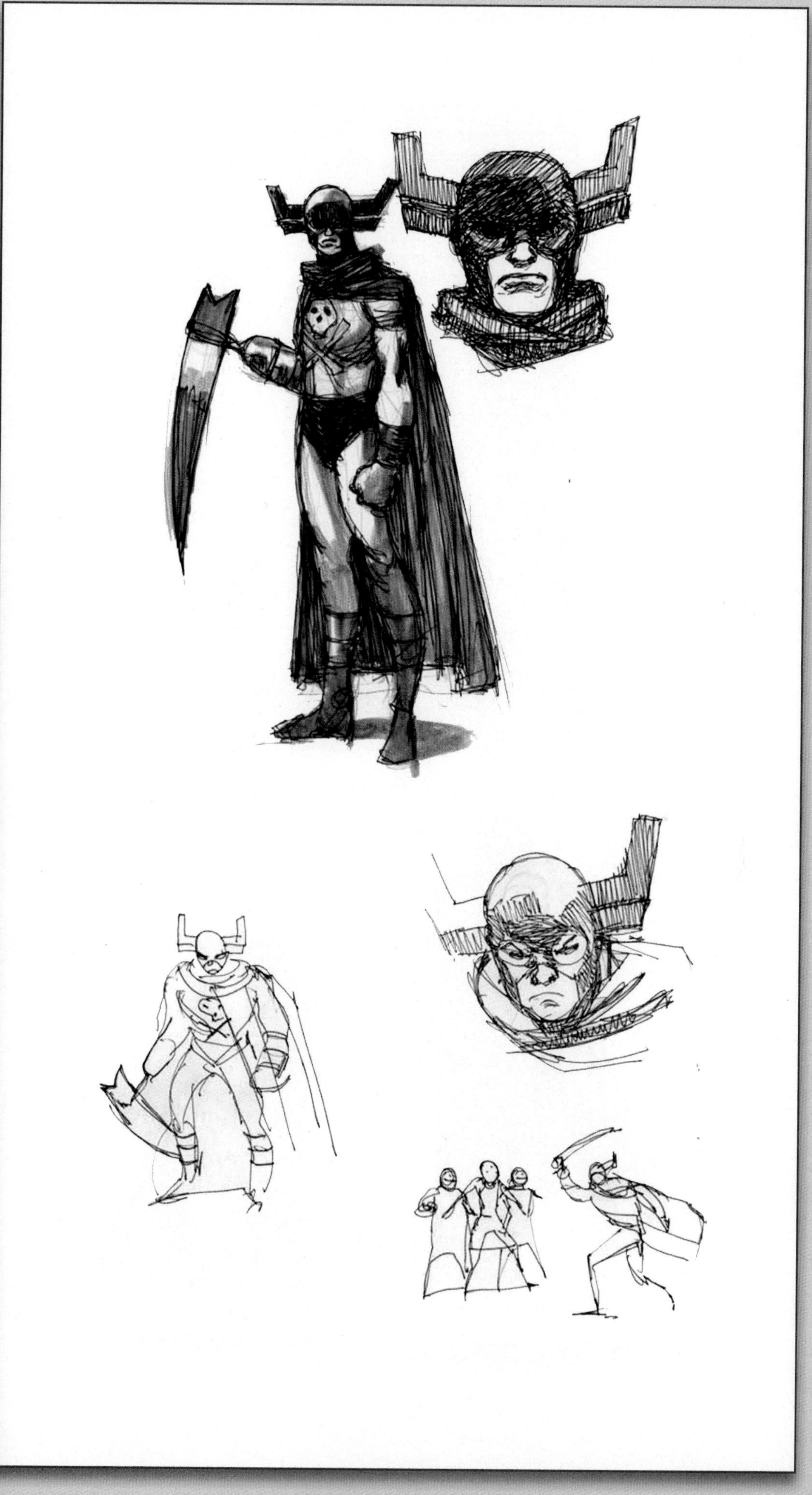

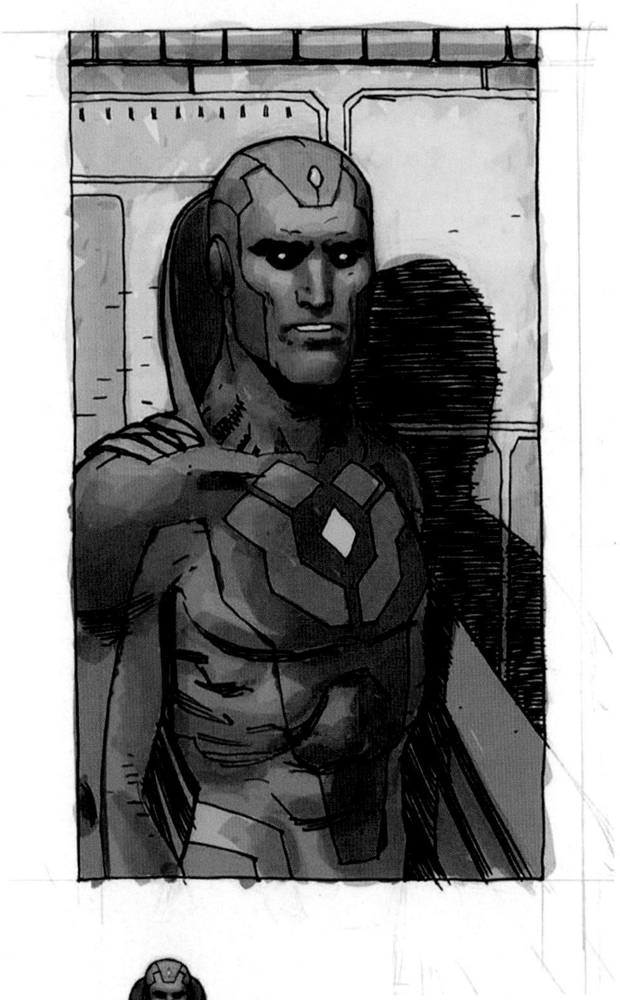

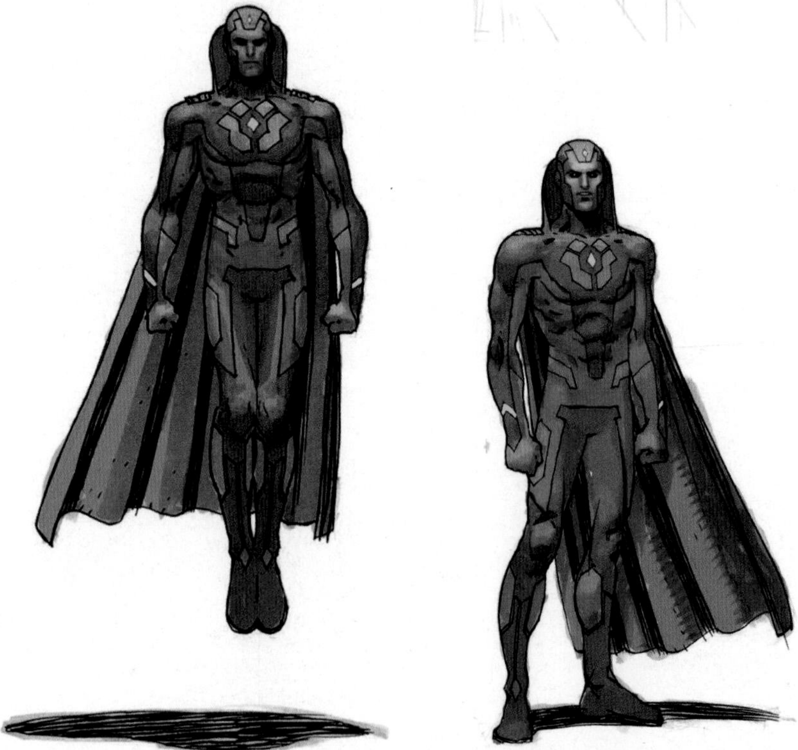

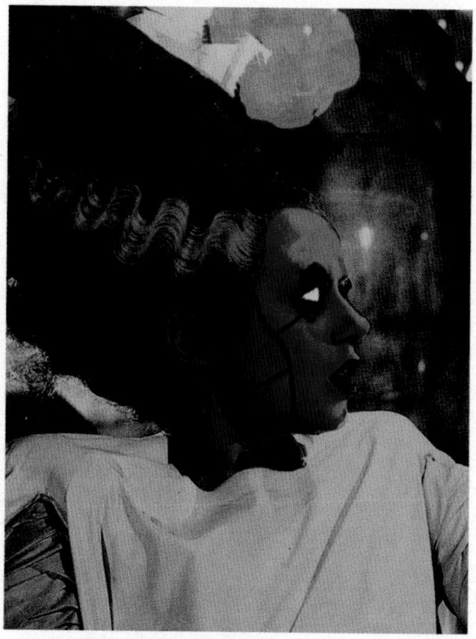

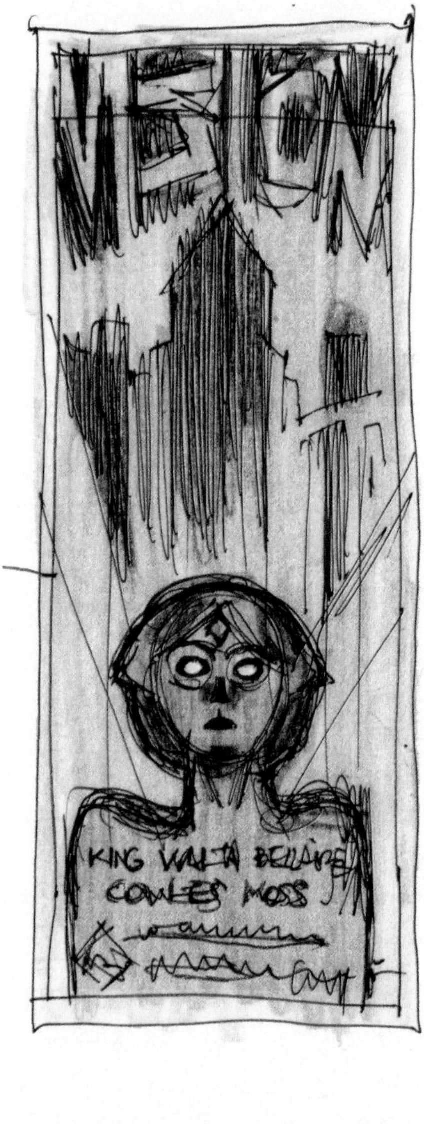
KING WALTA BELLAIRE
COWLES MOSS

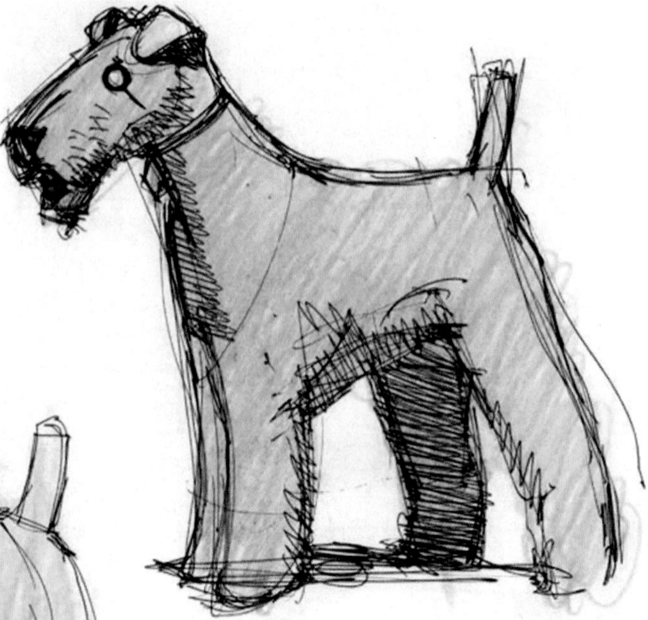

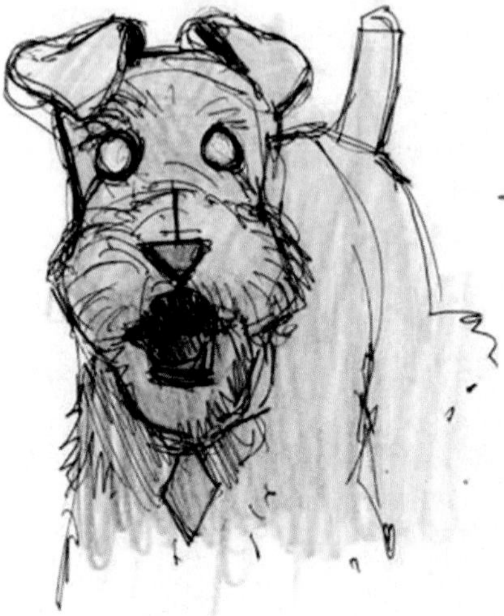

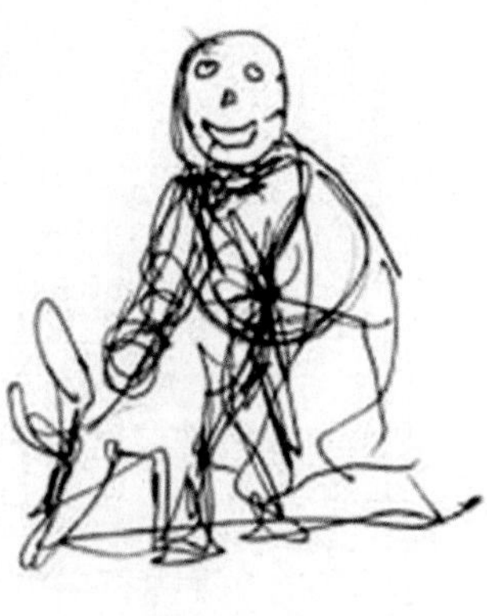

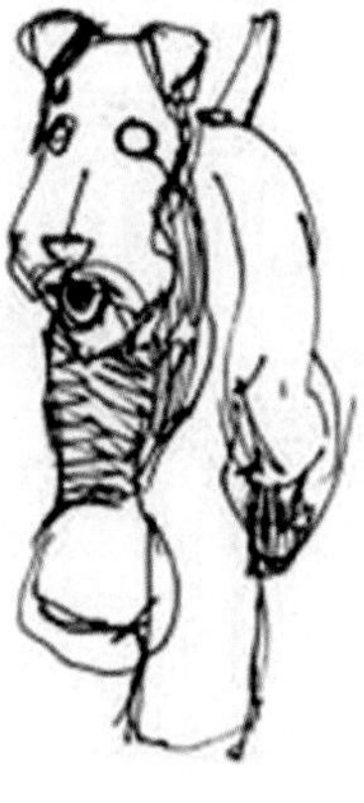

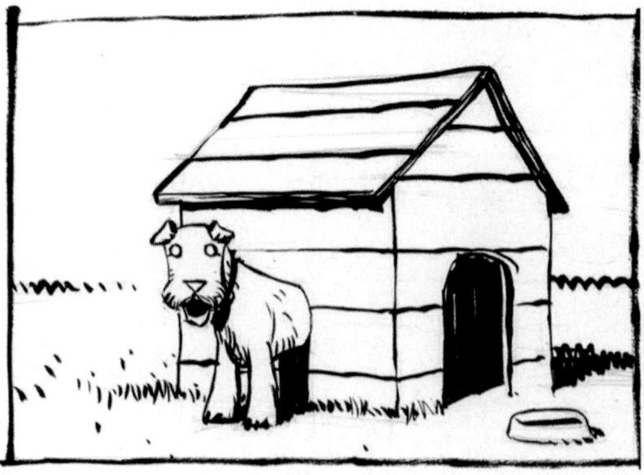

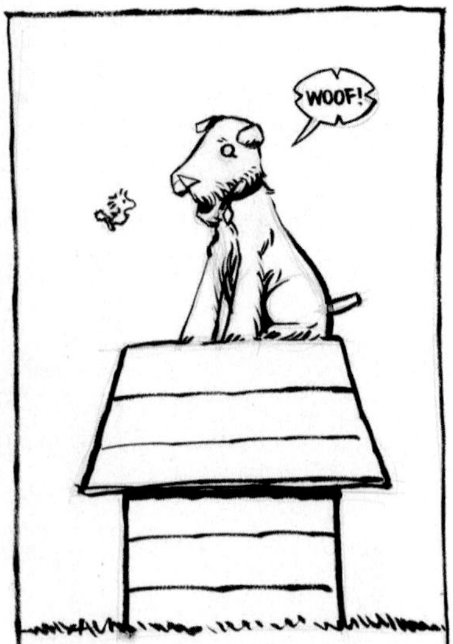
WOOF!

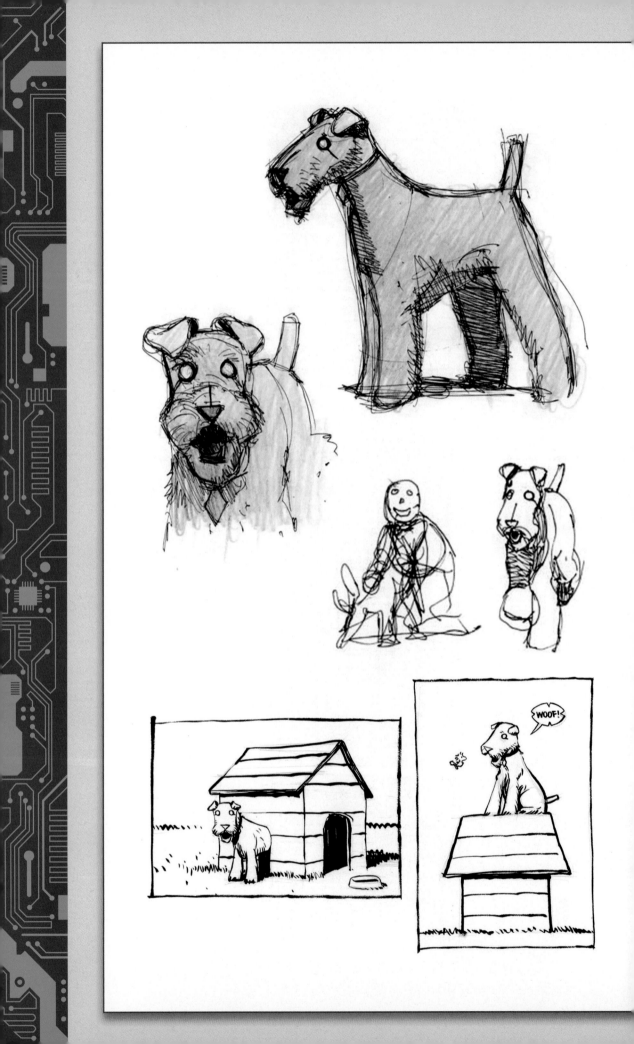

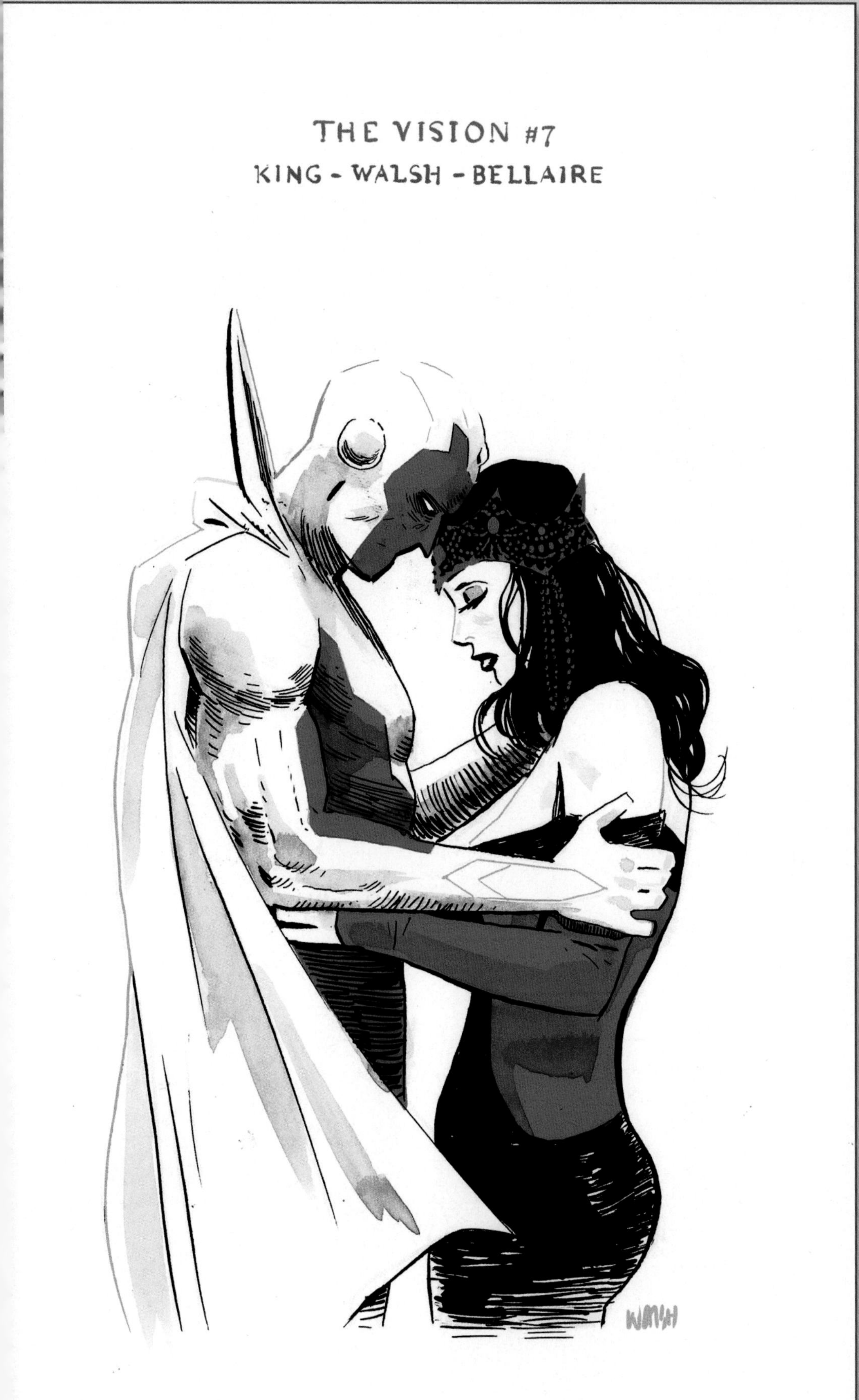
THE VISION #7
KING - WALSH - BELLAIRE
WALSH

PREVIOUS VERSIONS

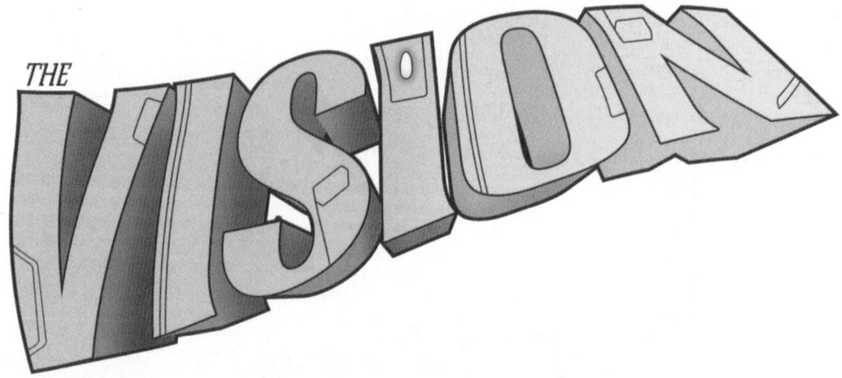
THE
VISION

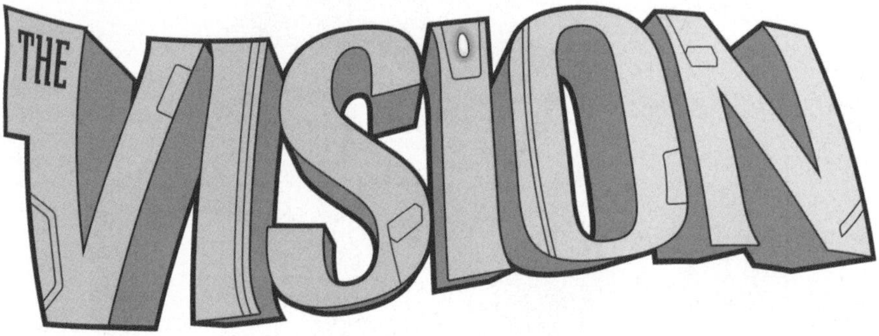
THE
VISION

FINAL

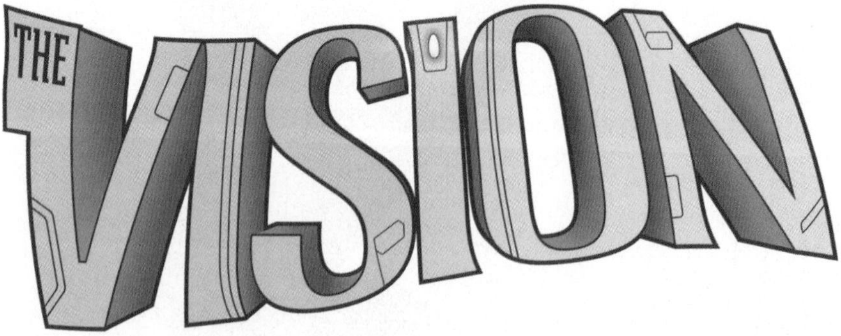
THE
VISION

FONT: DARE TO DREAM

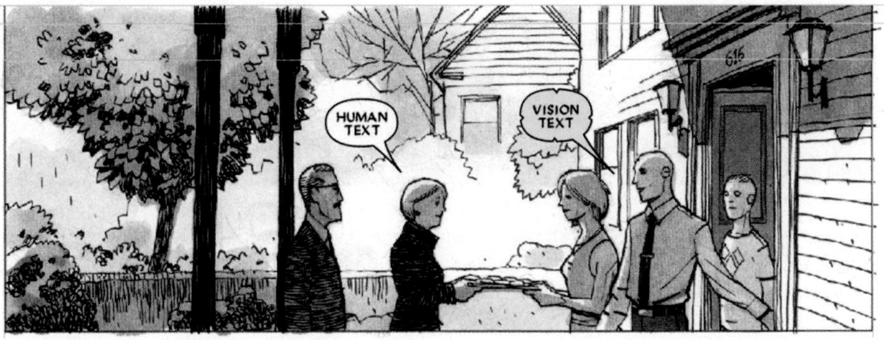
HUMAN TEXT
VISION TEXT

FONT: EPCOT

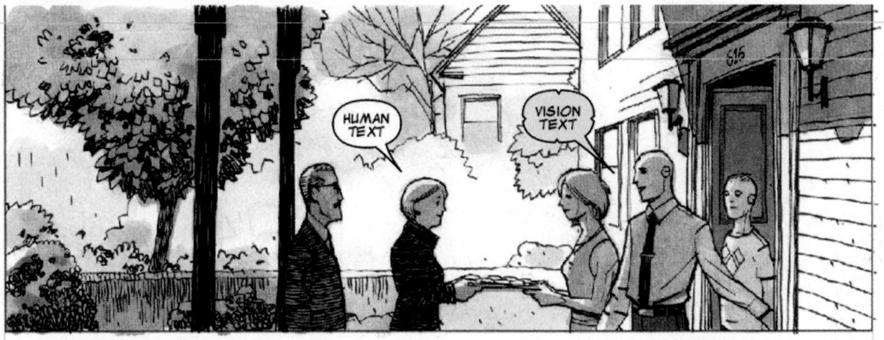
HUMAN TEXT
VISION TEXT

FONT: RETRO

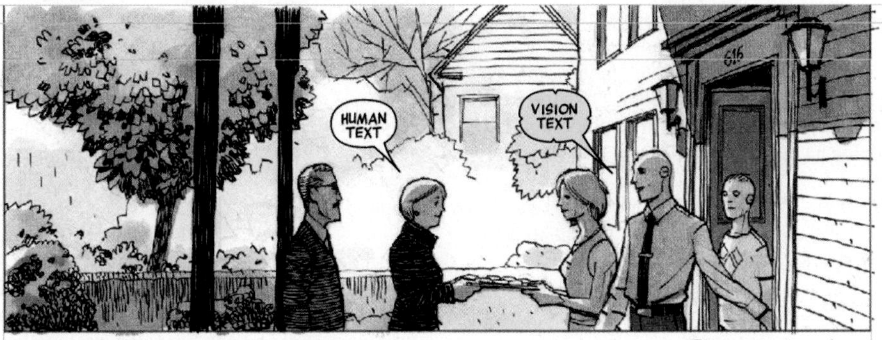
HUMAN TEXT
VISION TEXT

FONT: GRAYMALKIN

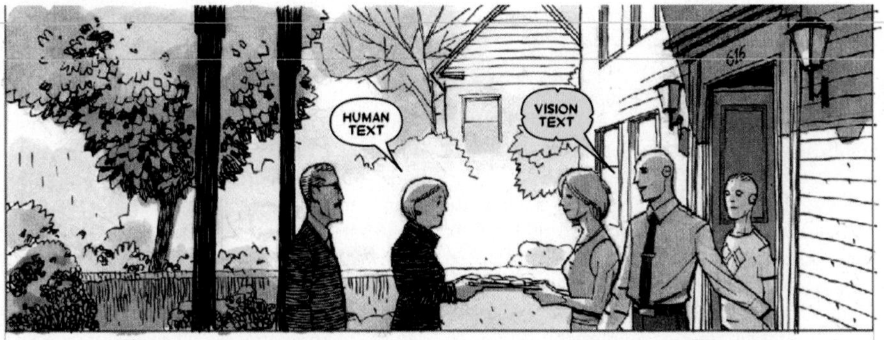
HUMAN TEXT
VISION TEXT

LETTERER **CLAYTON COWLES** OF **VIRTUAL CALLIGRAPHY** SUBMITTED FOUR FONTS (ALL CREATED BY **CHRIS ELIOPOULOS**) AS OPTIONS FOR THE SERIES. AFTER SOME DISCUSSION WITH THE REST OF THE CREATIVE TEAM, THE "GRAYMALKIN" FONT WAS CHOSEN.

BEHOLD...
THE
LETTERS PAGE!

When I was young I didn't have much, but I had comics. Friends were hard. Sports were hard. School was hard. Comics were easy.

Back then comics were something to be ashamed of. Comics were evidence that you couldn't handle the every-day of life. If you read comics you weren't cool. If people found out you read comics, life got a little tougher for you.

So you hid it. You hid your collection. You hid your passion. You hid your nerd.

The end result of all that hiding was alienation, the sadly lingering sense that what you cared about, what really mattered to you was a thing to be mocked by everyone else. You were different. You were stupid. You were odd. You were less.

You were not normal.

Things have changed. A bit. Thankfully. But at its heart, I think comics is still a misfits' medium. It's a community of outsiders, a bunch of men and women who, for a myriad of reasons, have trouble conforming to the expected form, who seek a temporary escape from the good, hard pain that comes from pushing against the mold, hoping it'll finally break.

Somehow panels and words, spandex and punching, they magically ease all that. It doesn't make a ton of sense to me why. But I'll take it.

Which brings us to beholding The Vision.

For me, The Vision is the chance to explore the alienation that sometimes attracts people to comics, the tension that comes from not being normal in a society that demands normality.

Because whatever The Vision is, he isn't normal.

But man does he want to be.

The Vision was created by Ultron to be a weapon, and he decided instead to be human, to be us. This decision has brought quite a bit of pain. His tortured relationship with Wanda. His children's tragic fate. His death. His deaths. Still, after all that, he strives to fit in to society, to participate in the American dream, to raise a family in the suburbs, to build a better world. To be like everyone else. I think he probably knows it's impossible, but, because he's a hero, he doesn't know how to stop himself from pursuing the impossible.

Vision's quixotic quest for the normal will be the central theme of this book. We will look at how the world reacts to his noble attempt, how that reaction warps him and his family, sometimes for the good and sometimes for the bad. It is a tale of blood and kisses, of brothers and sisters, daughters and sons, husbands and wives, of betrayals and high school and guns and lasers and bureaucrats and Avengers and neighbors and suspicion and robots, red skinned robots peacefully living amongst us, red skinned robots trying to live peacefully amongst us.

Hopefully, in the end, if I do it right, it's a tale of you and me.

I am nothing but blessed to be joined in this endeavor by the amazing and brilliant modern comic masters, Gabriel Hernandez Walta (pencils and inks), Jordie Bellaire (colors), Clayton Cowles (letters) and Mike Del Mundo (covers). These superb artists are not penciling, coloring, lettering and painting this story; they're telling this story through lines, colors, words and paints. They're creating a new world, a new tone that is unlike anything in comics today. And damn is it beautiful.

(I'm not great at talking about art. The best I can do is recommend you turn back a few pages. Look at the emotions. Look at the shadows. Look at the emotions implied by the shadows. See? This is what I'm saying.)

Finally, here at the end, permit me to return a bit to the beginning, to the kid and the comics, to the first time I realized that I wasn't alone in all of this, that my nerd was part of a greater nerd. It was in reading letters pages, in seeing others writing in, others for whom comics were also easy, that I got a sense that there was a community out there, a community that might think I was all right, not despite the fact that I knew Captain America wasn't an original Avenger, but because of it.

So we're starting a letters page here, obviously titled "Behold...THE LETTERS PAGE!" (Google *AVENGERS #57* by the legendary team of Roy Thomas & John Buscema if you don't get the reference!) Please write in. Share your stories. Complain about my stories. I'll answer. We'll talk. And some other kid somewhere out there will read all our stories, and know she's not alone, and know that in the end the best thing comics does is to let us know that we all have our own Vision and it's perfectly normal not to be normal.

Tom King
Washington, D.C., 2015

BEHOLD... THE LETTERS PAGE!

Hello! My name is Tom King, and I'm the writer of this here comic book and the responder to these here letters. Before we get started, I wanted to say thank you for the Amazing, Spectacular, and Web of response to this book (wait, "Web of" doesn't work at all. Wait, why am I making lame, deep cut Spider-Man jokes on a Vision letters page? Wait, why am I still parenthetically talking about lame, deep cut Spider-Man jokes when I'm supposed to be introducing said letters page? Wait, what was I trying to say anyway?) What I'm trying to say is that this book probably wasn't what you thought it would be and you gave it a chance and met it on its own terms, and I am forever grateful.

Wow, I've never read anything like this before. It was so strange, dark, creepy, and just amazing. Before reading the first issue of The Vision, I never really found him to be that interesting of a character. That has changed. I'm dying to read the next issue, and can't wait to see where this series goes.

Alex Wong

Thank you so much, especially for giving a character you haven't found interesting a chance. Our primary aim is to make Vision, and keep Vision, interesting. Though in all honesty that's the goal of probably most of comics. I mean for their respective characters. Not just to make Vision interesting. Obviously. Though, now that I think of it, it would be cool if that was the actual hidden goal of all comics. It's all been one eighty year experiment to prop up the Red Robot! And here is the final result! A guy in the suburbs! A guy. In the suburbs. That's it? All that for that? Someone's going to be pissed.

Damn, this was hard to read! But it was worth it. Tom King has never really been my cup of tea, but with the artist from Magneto, some new characters and a Grim Reaper appearance—you won me over with your creativity. Looking forward to Vin and Viv on Young Avengers someday! Bet you never thought of that, huh?

Cheers,
Andrew J. Shaw

PS: Vizh's classic costume will always be his best.

Man, I can relate. There are many days where Tom King is not my cup of tea. Usually it's the days I turn in one of my scripts or read over one of my scripts or read a comic that came from one of my scripts or read a review of a comic that came from one of scripts. All I see are the cruddy parts. All of which makes me all the more grateful you tried this out and found something in there for you. I have days where that happens to me too. Or at least I should have days like that.

(Vin and Viv in the Young Avengers works for me. If they make it out of this one alive.)

Back in the day I was a member of the Merry Marvel Marching Society, but I was never a Marvel Zombie. These days I am tired of the big event driven stories so popular at the big two. In recent years the only Marvel book I have read as it comes out has been Ms Marvel, because I love Willow Wilson's work. I only want to read stories by a strong, individual writer. The Vision (or as I prefer to think of it, The Visions) has that. I am in love with the dry, mordant narrative voice. It reminds me of Thomas Disch, who worked comedy and horror together so well. Captions in comics are often uninventive and unnecessary or filled with purple prose. The captions in The Visions are funny and disturbing while enhancing the visuals, the dialogue (oh, that dialogue), and the storyline. Observe Mr. and Mrs. Vision discuss "kind" and "nice", leading up to the Vision's rationale for creating this family, all while they wash the pan that will later be used to kill (?) the Grim Reaper. That's beautiful writing. From the first panel to the last, I felt like I was reading a work of literary science fiction. I have read a lot of comics by some very good writers but I have never felt so excited from the first panel. I bought this book with reluctance but couldn't resist after reading the first pages on Comixology. I couldn't wait to share it with a friend, something I haven't done since Gerber's Howard the Duck and Wein & Wrightson's Swamp Thing; and a lot of good comics have come down the pike since then. The artist (is it Walta or Hernandez Walta?) has matched the writer with images which make the mundane seem strange and disturbing. (I use the word "disturbing" a lot, but it fits The Visions.) This comic is damn near perfect! It's not your mama's Marvel superheroes! I could go on and on. Just permit me a bit of fan boy effusion; I love it, I love it, I love it!

By the way, did the concept of this book come from editorial or was it Tom King all the way? In any event, Tom has taken the concept and run with it. Congratulations on work well done!

Fred Adams,
Harlem, New York

Well that's extremely kind. Thank you. I'm so glad people saw the cookie dish connection. There are, sadly, more cookies to come. (This is the oddest use of "sadly" you'll see in comics this month. I assume. I had to write this some time ago. For all I know Amazing Spider-Man is now "The Sadly Amazing Spider-Man," which would indeed be more odd. Damn show-offs.)

As to the origins of this book, Marvel came to me with the character (which, I should pause to say, is awesome! Marvel came to me!?! This is my life!?! Hell yeah.) and asked me to pitch something in the sci fi genre, but based on earth. I came back to them with this very odd "Behold The Visions" pitch, which I was sure would be thrown out. And oddly, wonderfully it wasn't.

I just wanted to say, I've just put down the first issue of the new Vision comic, and it's hands down one of my favorite things I've ever read. It's perfect, it's everything a comic about a "synthe-something" starting an artificial family should be. I love how it expertly highlights philosophical questions regarding society and identity, and highlights thought provoking questions, such as "what is it, to be normal?" And of course all the while, behind the almost sit-com style lives laid out on the page, there's a sense of darkness looming in the background.

I can't wait for the next issue!

David Morgan

Wow. Thank you. Those are exactly the themes I want to address. In fact, it's so exact, either you cheated or I was too obvious. Given my obvious subtleties as a writer (matched only by my equally obvious modesties), I assume the cheating option applies here. As such: well done! I always say, if you're not cheating, you're not reading. Well, I said it once. To a teacher. I got in trouble. But while in trouble I had time to ruminate on great themes and how to subtly put them in comics. So that almost worked out.

I just finished reading the first issue of the new Vision book, and I have to say, it was one of the weirdest comics I've ever read.

I loved it!

It was funny, creepy, and (dare I say it again) plain weird! I'll be around for issue #2!

Josh Lamb
Pendleton, IN

Funny, creepy, and weird. Oh man, you have no idea. We're just getting started.

Send letters to mheroes@marvel.com or 135 W 50th St, 7th Floor, New York, NY 10020 (Please mark "OKAY TO PRINT")

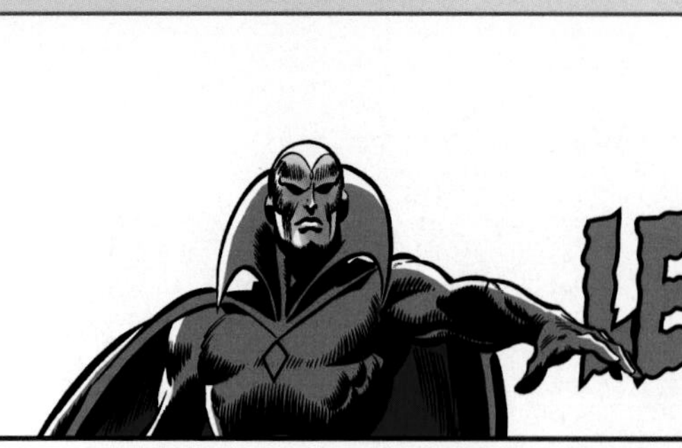

BEHOLD... THE LETTERS PAGE!

Art by John Buscema & George Klein

I remember coming up with that ending you just read. I remember thinking, oh man, if I can pull this off, this could be one of those where you read it and you want to see what happens next and then you just see the letters page and then you get really, really ANGRY. So—hopefully—welcome, angry readers, to another letters page! I am your friendly writer, Tom, here to represent the incredible team that makes this here comic book. We probably should get started before your (fingers crossed!) anger gets the better of you and you rip this comic and/or tablet apart.

Dear Vision Squad,

After 30 years of reading comic books and never feeling the need to write a letter, you have inspired me to do just that. Out of the many comic books I read each month, this is by far my favorite which came as a surprise. The Vision was never on the top of my favorite characters list but when I heard that he was getting his own title, I thought "Eh, let's check it out. They might be able to do something interesting with him." You have surpassed my expectations leaps and bounds. Everyone working on this book should be proud of their original stories and fantastic art which illuminates what it's like to be not quite human.

We've all been outsiders, at least once or twice, and there have been many times where most of us have had trouble seeing things the way everyone else sees them. In these pages, that distance and alienation is told beautifully. Not to mention how you tackle the power and love of family. It's not very often that I come across a book this great and I just want to say thank you.

Matthew Soderquist

That's awesome, man, thank you. A lot of people have said a lot of nice things about THE VISION, and I can't emphasize enough how grateful we are for those words. This book is not the normal thing, and the fact that so many people were willing to take it on for what it was means everything to us.

Dear Vision-aries,

First things first - I've never liked The Vision.

It's not that I hated him. That'd be too kind. Whenever he showed up in a comic, I'd see him, not really care, and promptly forget he existed. He'd phase out of my brain as soon as the last page turned.

But this new comic. Oh man.

This is Marvel's best comicbooking since Fraction's Hawkguy. (What is it about throwaway Avengers making for unexpectedly original, compelling story?)

Maybe it's because I'm a grown-up now, and I want substance to go with my side of superpowers. I demand real emotion before unbelievable bouts. Banality and disappointment can be more satisfying than a freakin' fistfight.

Maybe it's because life is a little sad sometimes, and this feels like someone else gets it.

It's amazing that that person could be a Christmas-colored android who shoots lasers out his forehead.

Thank you. Keep doing this. Please.

Adam

"Too kind" to say you hated him? Dude, that's pretty good. I think I might steal that for something. A guy in the neighborhood could so easily say that to Vison's face. Good moment of—wait! I've said too much! Ignore this. I never read your letter, Adam. And also, who's Adam? I wouldn't know; I never read his letter. All my ideas are original! Original!

This comic takes me back to high school, when I literally hid comic books under my sweatshirt just to avoid being teased. Thankfully, the advent of the Marvel cinematic universe has changed that for me; I'm finishing up my last year in university and I've made all sorts of friends by knowing way more about comics than them. However, this comic is a necessary feeling - we shouldn't forget what it feels like to be on the outside. I'm currently finishing up a term in Washington DC, interning and writing a thesis on counterterrorism strategies (as an aside, Mr. King's career as a CIA counterterrorism officer-turned-comic book writer is THE COOLEST THING EVER). One of the main research findings is that political alienation is a huge factor in homegrown terrorism, aka how average Americans decide to use violence in order to express their sentiments. I've noticed a trend where my peers mock of teenagers for their histrionics, as if we weren't once their age, dealing with baffling feelings and university applications. As if we weren't all Sisyphus once, pushing boulders uphill eternally. We've forgotten what it felt like to be seventeen years old and automatically distrusted. We've grown so comfortable on the inside simply because we're older and more experienced. We should never forget how we once felt, because the memories of how others treated us inform us how we ought to act towards others. The amount of political alienation people feel is intricately linked to how society views them, and that may make a life-or-death difference in certain cases. Thank you for writing this treasure. Every time I revisit the lush art and the serpentine writing, I am reminded how absolutely beautiful and compelling this title is.

Best,
Adrienne Ou

That's very kind of you, and best of luck with your thesis. We need all the thesises we can get these days. I really like that Sisyphus analogy, especially what Camus did to it, the idea that what troubles Sisyphus is not the rock but the hope that the rock will someday go away. If we can recognize the rock for what it is, for its eternity, then that sort of frees us from the troubles. Somehow seeing alienation not as something that can be simply cured with a few good intentions, but instead as something we all have to deal with, something that we all share, something we all will always have to work against, makes it almost tolerable. Almost.

Dear Tom King, Gabriel Hernandez Walta, Jordie Bellaire, Clayton Cowles, and Mike Del Mundo,

It's official, just having read The Vision #2 for the second time, I have now adopted The Vision as my new favorite comic! I love everything about this comic, but it's the narrative voice that Tom King employs that really makes me all giddy and tingly with that new love excitement. Just two issues into The Vision, I can sense that there's something REALLY different going on with this comic (and Tom King's dialogue at the end of this issue cemented that feeling) and it is now my goal to make The Vision one of the bestselling comics at Alternate Reality Comics!

Thanks,
Ralph Mathieu
Alternate Reality Comics

Ah, thank you so much. As a bonus, you want an insight into the narcissistic anxieties of the comic writer? When I look at those last pages of issue 2, all I see is that stupid split infinitive on 19.4 (page 19, panel 4), "to easily fit." Should be, "to fit easily." Ugh! Drives me insane. I wish it was easier to easily write.

Vision is a delightful surprise for the ANAD offerings. I still have no idea where you'rd going with it, and that is one of the most desirable attributes of any comic, in my opinion.

However, I have an issue with the grammatical errors, of which there are at least one or two, in every issue of every title. I try to get past it, but when it's the Vision saying "discipline will be handled by MYSELF," which is wrong and sounds ridiculous (handled by ME; myself is only used reflexively) it rips me out of the story.

Please try to reduce the grammatical errors. It's one of the only things that get in the way of a gripping comic book.

Thanks for the consideration.

Blair Bush
Baltimore, MD

You SEE? This is why I only see that split infinitive! Sigh. I know, I know, I'll try to do better. But... while we're on the topic... and because I always wanted a No-Prize... two things: First, this "myself incident" was a piece of dialogue where Vision was speaking with a purpose (to intimidate the principal). I might argue that Vision used "myself" in this mistaken manner intentionally to further this purpose. Reflective pronouns add emphasis, that's what they do, and Vision meant to emphasize, strongly, his own role here and felt "me" came across as weaker than "myself." He took the grammar hit to make the point. For me, when doing story and dialogue, I see grammar as a tool to communicate. If breaking a grammar rule leads to better communication, then my rule is to annoyingly break the rule. Second, comics are made fast. Novels and movie/TV scripts are rewritten and reviewed probably ten to twenty times more than comics are. This means that mistakes are going to happen in comics. Grammatically especially. If you love the improvisational nature of this medium as I do, the creativity that comes from that rush, then you've got to live with some of this crud. We have a motto for that in the industry, "We'll try to fix it in the trade!"

Okay. That's it for this month. Hopefully your anger has not subsided and is right now pushing you to write in and SCREAM. Please do. I look forward to hearing from you.

Tom

Send letters to mheroes@marvel.com or 135 W 50th St, 7th Floor, New York, NY 10020 (Please mark "OKAY TO PRINT")

BEHOLD... THE LETTERS PAGE!

Art by John Buscema & George Klein

So, on the plus side, the Visions got through a whole issue without anyone getting shot! Now...on the minus side, lying to the cops is probably not so great. Sigh. This poor family. Anyway, my name is Tom, and I am the writer of that comic you just read. I'm here to represent the incredible team that puts this book together, to answer your complaints and questions ,and to assure you that things for the Visions will get better (I'm probably lying about this, but as long as you don't read the parenthesis parts of things, we're good). So now that everything is hunky and dory, let's begin!

Hello! It'd like to start off by saying I'm really enjoying this series so far! I picked up the first issue of THE VISION because I thought the cover looked pretty strange and kinda funny, though I had no idea the story would be so eerie or so profound. It was such a pleasant surprise. Anyways, I'm really curious as to what the symbolism is behind the floating water vase of Zenn-La. A beautiful flower vase that kills any flower placed into it; does its hidden dark nature symbolize Virginia's inner monster? Or is the vase symbolic of perfection, and the fact that no flower can fit in it shows that perfection is unattainable? Maybe the creation of the vase is a metaphor for how we have the power to create monsters without meaning to? Maybe there's no real meaning to it, but if in fact the vase was meant to hold some symbolic meaning, I'd love to hear what it is!

Miranda
16 years old
Montreal, Canada

First, thank you! That's very nice to hear. Kind to hear. Whatever. Second, on the vase thing, I believe (and this idea is not at all original) that the power of stories or literature or comics comes from the interaction between the writer's intention and the reader's interpretation. The purpose of stories is not for the writer to tell you what he or she thinks about something; that's what essays are for. Stories are trying to dig into deeper truths that we can't express directly because of the limitations of language. These sort of truths can only be seen obliquely through symbols and actions. The vase isn't what I made it to be. The vase is what it becomes when you read about the vase. All of which is to say, I like what you said, and I agree with it. All of it.

Hi, Vision Team,
I recently read the third issue of VISION and I have to say, I'm really amazed by it. I always kept an eye on Tom King after I read some of his other works, and he certainly doesn't disappoint here. It's funny that with the whole "All New, All Different" movement Marvel is putting out, where now Thor is a girl and Spider-Man is a CEO and a bunch of other changes are made that "will change the Marvel universe FOREVER!" and maybe last a year tops, this is probably the Marvel book I would call the most new and different. Turning what used to be a generic robot super hero and making it into a unsettling look into the concept of a nuclear family was a stroke of genius, and I love the little subtleties and references King sprinkles in that takes a few rereads to truly understand. Hopefully Marvel notices what excellent job you all have been doing, and they continue this run until you have reached what you believe to be a truly satisfying conclusion.
Also, I was wondering—how much direction does Mr. King give Mr. Walta in terms of art? Does the script have a detailed description of what is going on in each panel, or does Mr. King allow the artist to add in any little details they thing would click?

Thanks,
Jordan

First, thank you! Second, call me Tom, please. Third, from a quick survey of my comic writing friends, in today's environment, it seems like my scripts fall on the tighter side of a spectrum that spans from the brilliant broad impressions of Stan Lee to the brilliant baroque detailing of Alan Moore. My approach is stupidly simple: I picture the comic I want to read, then I describe that comic; I call this description a "script." That said, comics are a visual medium and, frankly, the art is more important to the book than the words; or, better said, the art tells more of the story than the words do. The book you're reading is much, much better than the comic I had in mind, because as high as my expectations for what Gabriel will draw are, he always exceeds them. A quick example of this can be found on the last page. My description for that panel was (in total):
"VIRGINIA staring at the table, alone in the room."
Gabriel took that nothing of a sentence and turned it into a masterpiece.

I never sent a letter to a comic book editor, I guess. I have felt like doing so before, but never actually did so.
After watching *Avengers: Age of Ultron*, I was so in love with The Vision, who I had never truly seen or read about, and Wanda, who I had known from other adaptations, that I started searching every trace of their comic book canon existence from the '80s or so. I had read before the watching the movie that they were comic book canon, and started searching on this matter too. I even found the full collection of THE VISION AND THE SCARLET WITCH limited series on eBay (I'm still saving money for that), and started making my own Scarlet-Vision (fan)comics and (fan)fictions. I like them as a pair AND individually. They really grew on me.
Reading the 2015 series of the Vision (and the Scarlet Witch's, as soon as it is out) is magic! It talks to me! The personal development of such characters—who amuse so much—is priceless. It's only two numbers old, but the story is so light and fresh. It's my kind of story.
If I could travel in time, I'd pay little ol' future a visit, to check the next numbers already, but patience is a virtue I shall nurture.
Let the fandom know when you are receiving fanart (and when you're hiring)!

Much love,
Milene Correia, BR

P.S.: I'm hoping Wanda is mentioned or makes a cameo, as it seems plausible that it was her the Vision took the brainwaves to build Virginia from. Actually, I'm pretty sure he might miss Wanda (and by "sure" I mean "hopeful in my shipper heart").

In my mind (and refer to above for how much my opinion is worth), Wanda's relationship with Vision has haunted this whole series so far. To me she's as big a character in the series as anyone in the family, the way Harry Lime is in The Third Man or the way Luke is in The Force Awakens. In issue 7, as we start the second half of this first season, we'll see this undercurrent come to the surface and watch as people start to drown.

Dear Tom King/Behold the Vision,
Like a lot of comics fans these days, I've been reading comics for most of my life, which is pretty close to 35 years at this point (I'm 40, but how much do you really read before you're five?). I run hot and cold on super hero comics, but every now and then, there's a book that rekindles my enjoyment of the super hero genre. These rare books approach the genre in a different way, tell stories that transcend the "good guy vs. bad guy" dichotomy, and make us think not only about the world depicted in the comic but life in general. You've got one of these books in THE VISION, which is, in my opinion, the most humanistic book on the stands, even though the robotic leads aren't actually human at all. This is a book that celebrates life and family in ways the super hero genre tends to shy away from. A truly mature comic—most so-called "mature" comics are little more than a showcase for rough language and graphic scenes of violence—The Vision plays with timeless themes of love, revenge, protection, sexuality, and community in ways that feel true to a jaded reader like myself, but is still massively entertaining for someone looking for a good super hero book. The closest analogy I can draw from comics would be Alan Moore's *Swamp Thing*, where the fantastic and horrific seasoned a story that was really about what it means to be alive, to love, and to care about the world beyond yourself. There's certainly action, horror, and sci-fi in THE VISION, but the book is ultimately about family and finding oneself in a society that's often cruel and frightening, even if it's cruel and frightening in the most mundane ways rather than Korvac restructuring reality on a whim, Zemo seizing a mansion for revenge, or the Grim Reaper being the Grim Reaper. Lots of super hero comics aspire to "realism"—whatever that mean—but only THE VISION gives us something that actually resembles real life. I hope this book has a healthy run because it's something that Marvel has shied away from over the years, but it's something that readers need.
Also, Del Mundo is killing it on covers.
Thank you for such a great book!!!!!!
Patrick Phillips, official "socket-lover"

Thank you, sir, that means a ton. I think to me all comics have to have some element of realism, some tether to our reality or else the stakes don't seem real, we won't care what happens to the characters. I always think of Jim Starlin's The Death of Captain Marvel, a book that contains more fantastical elements than entire lines of comics, yet the entire story is about death—my death, your death—in a way that is entirely relatable, entirely real. And that reality infects all the rest of it, the Thanoses and the cigar chomping nymphs, they become real, because you feel that death. It's real, so the world becomes real. Hopefully, I can steal some of that for this.
All right, I probably should go and write some comics, or at least describe some comics I'd love to have my name on. As ever, thank you so much and please, please continue to write in. I can't say enough how much I enjoy hearing from you. And again, I assure you, this is all going to turn out fine. (And again, again, I may be lying. But don't tell. Shhhhhhh.)

Tom King

Send letters to mheroes@marvel.com or 135 W 50th St, 7th Floor, New York, NY 10020 (Please mark "OKAY TO PRINT")

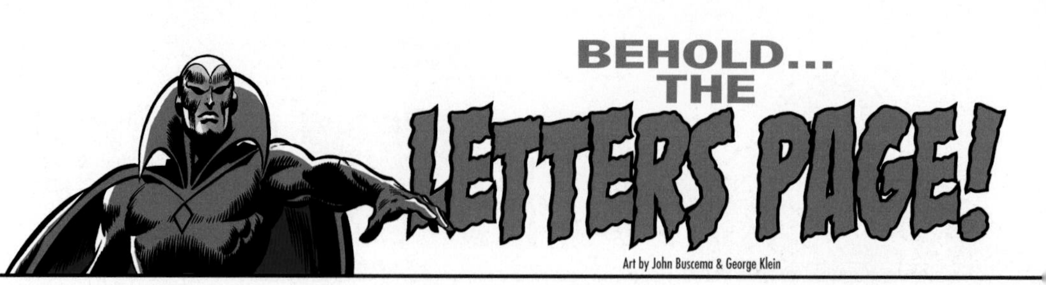
BEHOLD...
THE
LETTERS PAGE!

Art by John Buscema & George Klein

Okay. So that happened. And after all the blood and betrayal, all the lies and losses, I think I know exactly what you're thinking: "Hey, I bet that writer fellow Tom's going to do one of those contests where we get to name that new Vision dog." What? That would be crazy.

Crazy AWESOME!

So, the Visions have a new dog and I want you to help me name him! Please write into this here letters page with suggestions for this cute little dude. And remember in answering, this is a family-friendly comic. So if you're going to use swears, they better be really cool.

Now on to the letters!

Dear Tom,

I am a young female that has loved the Vision since I was ten and started reading my dad's old 20 cent comics. I thought I would never love an "alternate/new" version of the Vision, but you have proved me wrong. You are a writing "god"! I LOVE YOU, I LOVE the comic (best thing Marvel is putting out right now), and I LOVE the letters page. You are now my favorite writer...bar none! Thank you, Tom, thank you from the bottom of my heart!

Mai

Ah, thank you so much. I printed out this letter and gave it to my wife when she asked me why I hadn't cleaned the floor of my office. I explained, I am a writing god. Does a writing god have time to clean his office? Oh, I think not. Then she noted that a writing god would have plenty of time to clean his office as a writing god would instantly create scripts, freeing up the rest of the day to pick up his damn cereal bowl from the floor. My wife is a lawyer. A lawyer god. I cleaned my office.

The 'expected form' is corrupt, Author.

That is the reason why escape from this malformed system eases the experience of the flesh of those of our ilk.

My question now is this: Why does the Vision seek to bend himself to the experience of the majority of a race of enslaved beings? I expect that the reason for his actions is about understanding those beings more.

Yet, ultimately, can he? Seems that is your decision, Author.

This book has my attention. Thank you all for your hard work.

Za

Wait, but if the expected form is corrupt then wouldn't we be expected to escape from it so that the escape becomes the expected form? Then does the escape itself become corrupt so we retreat back to the expected form, creating an infinite loop, swinging us around from expectation to defiance and back again? Are we then just slaves to this endless feedback, and the only true escape then is to relax and give in, which, because it's the only escape, is again the expected form, which again corrupts, which again triggers another expected escape from the unexpected expected? So we're all stuck together inside this tangled, repetitive maze of broken metaphor!!! I can only hope we brought some comics along to distract us from all that.

To everyone behind The Vision,

The Vision is my favorite character--he's unusual, and a bit distant from the rest of society but is working hard to blend in. I can really empathize with that. So when I saw that he was having his own title I went out to buy Issue #1 ASAP. Part of me wanted to see the Vision in the normal way, flying around, phasing in and out of things, making a few attempts at humour and social interaction--the usual. So when I saw the cover I was a bit shocked. But hey, I'd cycled down to get this thing so I bought it.

Turns out that I was very pleased with what I'd bought. These comics are showing the character in a whole new light in a refreshing and slightly haunting way that works really well! Plus, the art is fabulous. I've just read #4 and I'm still enjoying it a lot, and eagerly anticipate #5!

Tom Andrews
Bedfordshire, England

I feel that in ten years some writer will get a letter saying, "I wanted to see the Vision in the normal way. Y'know, lots of gratuitous pet deaths, robots contemplating cookies, and a heavy narrator opining on obscure math equations--all the clichés you expect from a Vision comic! But I was happily surprised to find myself enjoying these 'super hero fights.' Good job by you!"

YES!! FINALLY!! VISION GETS HIS OWN SERIES!! And it is scaring me. The Vision's comic is chilling. But I love the idea of him building a family. Talk about all-new and all-different. His wife is weird though, I can't figure her character out--is her brain patterned from Scarlet Witch? Do we have our first villain with the shock ending of issue 2? Could the Vision, in the process of trying to be normal, build them a robot dog? Could this comic creep me out more? I LOVE IT!!

My two cents, TC.

A robot dog? Never! NEVER!!! Unless I can do a naming contest in the letters page. Then maybe. MAYBE!!!

This book swept me up like a tornado. I love horror and I love sci-fi. It's been a very long time that I saw the likes of weird paranoia-driven '50s sci-fi in any medium and the fact that I could find it in a Vision comic is a testament to the talent on display here. I usually go to bat for DC but I always keep my eyes on Marvel for their more-contained stories and this is the best of the litter (sorry, Spider-Gwen, love you too). It feels very much like an indie comic that just happens to feature the Android Avenger. The fact that we can get a series like this gives me hope for the future because that's what this book is...the future.

Pat Heinbaugh

The future. Huh. THE VISION to me feels so much like a book of the past. I feel like I'm following the formula set forth in SWAMP THING, SANDMAN, and ANIMAL MAN: Take a hero seriously, connect that hero to the real world, then watch the world crumble. The future stuff comes from Jordie and Gabriel, I think. Me, I'm just (re)writing these old books I love.

Dear Tom King and others,

Just read THE VISION #4. I have to say, the scene where the boy from school and Viv walk together in the rain and have a nice conversation was very touching. It was by far my favorite part of this series. Just to see them connect for a short time in the chaos going on around them and then Viv to put it on repeat in her active memory, that was great. That part was very moving. Thanks.

Josh Thomas

Ah, thank you so much. I liked that scene too, not least because Jordie and Gabriel made it beautiful and emotional. It's very odd how some conversations when you're that age, especially ones that happen in the rain between two people trying to connect, can stay with you for so long. I like this series best when it can get at those little moments by using robots to make the moments somewhat not as little.

I don't know what I was expecting from a Vision solo series, but it sure was not what I am getting. Which is the best thing I could have hoped for.

I am a longtime Marvel reader. So long that I remember when the Vision was Marvel's most popular character without a series, and was the anchor of The Avengers in the '70s. His personality was fascinating and his story arc with the Scarlet Witch was one I followed for years, loving every twist and turn.

Then, his personality was removed and no one knew what to do with him after that. He was shoved into the background further and further until I never quite knew if he was dead or alive and I felt it was a waste of a character who had been so popular in my early comics-reading days.

I saw that a Vision solo series was starting, and I didn't pay a lot of attention, as...well... no one has made the Vision interesting for over 20 years. When the first issue came out, I heard it was good from people I knew, podcasts I listened to, and shop owners.

So, I have now picked up the first two issues, and this feels like something new. He's not a comic book version of Spock. He's not a super-powered robot. He's a character who feels new to himself as well as us, and the idea of him trying to fit in as his world twists and changes appeals to me. There is an unease to the comic, one that makes it feel daring and dangerous, and, I have to know what happens next.

Hell of a launch, folks.

The Best Dressed Man In Comics,
Cory!! Strode

Ah, thank you so much! But wait, you love every twist and turn in the Scarlet Witch-Vision romance? That's insane.

An insanity I deeply share! So next month we're going to look deep into that relationship, see how it affects the family, how it will affect what Vision will do with and for the family as we approach the bloody end. For the issue, as we step away from the family, the modern master, Michael Walsh, will be stepping in on pencils and inks. Gabriel will gloriously return with issue 8.

So thank you for everything, everybody, see you next time, and don't forget: dog names!

Tom King

Send letters to mheroes@marvel.com or 135 W 50th St, 7th Floor, New York, NY 10020 (Please mark "OKAY TO PRINT")

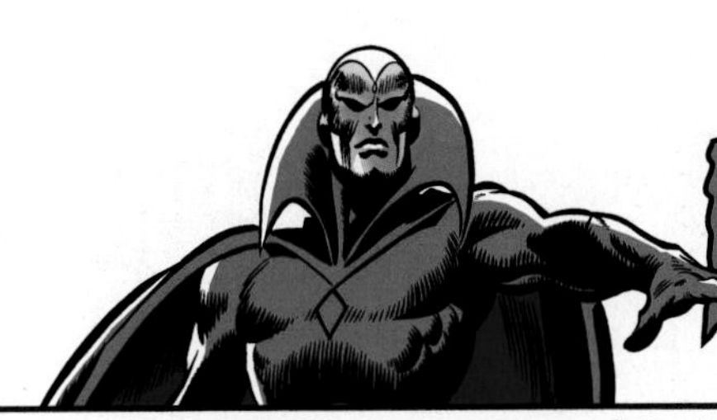

BEHOLD... THE LETTERS PAGE!

Art by John Buscema & George Klein

Man, Michael Walsh just killed it, didn't he? I mean, I miss Gabriel, y'know, because he's the best and all, but still, dude killed it.

But I should get started. When you make an issue that steals so much from the past, it's probably best to at least acknowledge those from whom you stole. I'm ever grateful for the work of Steve Englehart, George Pérez, Bill Mantlo, Rick Leonardi, John Byrne, Roy and Dann Thomas, Paul Ryan, Kurt Busiek, and the countless others whose work I got to fawn over as we put this issue together. I should also note that the toaster joke in the book is a version of a classic joke first discovered by my oldest boy Charlie, who is 7 and will actually read this. Hi Charlie! Thanks for the joke! And remember, you're only allowed to read the letters page of this one! Parenting!

All right, on to your letters!

Hey there, crazy-awesome genius creators of my new FAVORITE comic!!!

I think you should name the Vision's new dog Walter!!! Why Walter, you ask...? Well, not only is it an adorable name for a dog, but "W" is made up of two V's (sort of), for Vin and Viv. And it's just an adorable and practical name for any pooch.

Keep up the GREAT WORK!!!!!

Chuck Lindsey
Chicago, IL

Before we get into the naming thing, can we talk about how much the letter "W" sucks? Like you said, there's no doubling of U's in it. Maybe a doubling of V's, but that doesn't get you to wuh, wuh; you're just at vvvvhhh. And, AND, W's the only letter whose name doesn't contain any ounce of its sound in it. Double-U. No wuh, wuh at all. I know, I know, H, Q, and Y have their problems, but at least there's a tangential link to the sound. W's not even trying, and…wait, I may have gone off on a sidebar here… [Y'think? -Editor Wil] I probably should get back to the letter, the sent letter not the letter-letter, obviously. Did I mention I'm teaching my kids to read? (Albeit mostly so they can read their names in the letters page here.)

Anyway, Walter is pretty good. We're doing the announcement next month, basically because there was no dog in this issue. Which means you've still got time to write in! Marvel tells me they're being flooded with suggestions, to which I say, FLOOD ON!

Dear Tom King,

I am enjoying the VISION series greatly and find it quite different from most comic book stories on the shelves today. The one VISION question I keep asking is... Why? Why has the Vision created this family? Is it due to loneliness, or is it a way for him to carry on his legacy, or has his failed relationship with Wanda played a part? Recently my friend announced that she is pregnant and expecting a child with her spouse, and the love of her life, when it occurred to me that perhaps it's all about love. Maybe the Vision created his family because he longs for love and this is his way of obtaining it. As you can see I am really curious as to the reason behind his actions and I am hoping that you will one day provide us with the answer. Until then I will simply continue to enjoy the story wherever it may lead...but you will tell us, right?

Teresa "JM" Ciciolla
Montreal, Canada

I don't know. It seems to me (and this, as ever, is not an original thought, but it's my thought for what that's worth) that people don't do things, especially big things like create a family, for one particular reason. These decisions are the culmination of a million influences, not least of which is the absolute randomness of life that invades everything. Now, once a thing is done, we sometimes look back and place a reason on it; we impose a narrative on our self, which allows us to move forward without the sort of acute angst that comes with realizing your destiny is not entirely yours. When writing, especially when writing super heroes, it's easy to use this impulse to restrict your characters to simple motivations. He did this because of this. I do this all the time when I write. But I'm trying not to do it here. Vision didn't create the family because of this or that. He did it because of this and that and the other thing, too.

Greetings,

I count myself among the (I'd say based on the letters I've been reading in the letter page) many who have always loved the Vision (and the Scarlet Witch). I love them so much that I even read through the WEST COAST AVENGERS and MASTER PANDEMONIUM.

Moreover, I always had the feeling that both characters had way more potential than creators, so far, had explored. The new VISION series is just astonishing. It's fresh, it's challenging, and I hope it will be consequential—in the sense that when all is said and done, The Man doesn't pull a "One More Day" kind of retcon (which basically erased one of the potentially most interesting consequences of CIVIL WAR).

Okay, this is too long already—let me just say how sorry I am for Mr. King be leaving us to be with the Distinguished Competition.

Finally, the dog: "Lettuce" should he be named.

Cheers,
Neiriberto Borges-Calil
Brasília, Brazil

Couldn't agree more about Scarlet Witch and the Vision. Their relationship is almost as twisted and absurd as an actual relationship. As for the ending: What happens in the series will have a big impact on these characters and on the Marvel Universe going forward. I think if we remove this impact we remove the stakes of the story, and I want those stakes be high, to feel as high for the readers as it does for the characters.

Dear Team VISION,

I just put down issue #5 and loved every second of it. I wanted to write, though, because I teach an introductory-level English course at Queensborough Community College, and I recently taught issue #1 of THE VISION! My students are a mix of English-as-a-Second-Language (ESL) and non-traditional learners, and they're always being told they're outside of what's "normal." It was so refreshing for them (and me!) to read a comic in which hyper-intelligent androids still struggle with that very term, and begin to unravel its meaninglessness. Many of my students really responded to it, and more than one vowed to continue to read the series. Thanks for giving me a great comic and a great lesson!

Best,
Jonathan Alexandratos
Queensborough Community College

"Reality is that which, when you stop believing in it, doesn't go away." -Philip K. Dick

My father was an ESL teacher who taught at public high schools in LA. I remember him explaining his homework assignments to me, the different ways he'd try to get to those kids. That VISION could have an impact there, could help you and them, means everything to me. Thank you so much.

To Tom King/THE VISION team,

First of all, I'd just like to say that I've been following your work for a while and I love the way you write robots. I've always loved super heroes, but for so long I hated reading comics because comics are dumb. I always wanted tangible results, something thought provoking. Something you have to read for yourself, instead of the Wikipedia summary.

Now that I'm older, I can appreciate a nice, dumb comic and allow myself to have a little fun. But the smart comics, the ones that make you think, are still the best, and those ones always linger.

THE VISION is smart. You're smart. And I think people will be raving about this run for a while.

Ken
Victoria, Canada

P.S. The title page at the end of issue 5 gave me chills!

Wait, wait, wait, you can't get away with calling comics dumb on this here letters page, buddy! (That's right, I "buddied" you!) I LOVE comics. I honestly think comics have not just shaped my life, but maybe even saved it, providing solace and escape when I most needed solace and escape. And I'm not talking about fancy-pants comics (which I, with my fair-though-unwashed fancy pants, do adore); I'm talking about like INFERNO/CIVIL WAR crossover comics—mainstream things with men and women in tights beating at each other. Those comics spoke to me when no other form of entertainment did. Now, not every comic is for every person; it'd be a pretty dumb medium if that were the case. And some crappy comics have done some dumb/racist/sexist things. But on a whole, as it has evolved, comics encourage experimentation, improvisation, and inclusion; they tell the outsider that it's okay to be on the outside. The medium as a whole always needs to get better, but we can't ever say it's all dumb, because saying it's dumb tells us outsiders to be ashamed of where we are. And that ain't what it's ever been about. And now that I've set you up as this straw man that has actually nothing to do with you at all, I hope you've learned something! Buddy!

Dear THE VISION team,

I have always enjoyed learning about the Marvel Universe, but never once picked up a comic book. After 22 years, I decided to give it a try and picked up my first, THE VISION (2015) #1. It has not only been a magnificent experience, but immediately sparked a new hobby of mine; reading comic books. The literary themes, social commentary, and insightful dialogue are traits I never thought to find in a comic book series. These past issues have truly revolutionized how I view comic books as a whole, and I am eager to continue forward with them. To the entire team behind creating this story, I wish to send my immense thanks.

A Newcomer,
Quinn Kastner
Lawrence, KS

Welcome! Welcome! Welcome! From the entire creative team, Gabriel, Jordie, Clayton, and myself, we'd like to send our thanks for giving this book a try. That's just plain awesome.

And speaking of just plain awesome, Gabriel returns to art next issue and we return to the family. The secrets are out. The only thing the Avengers don't know is how much what's coming next is going to hurt…

This issue features some amazing scenes from Vision's history! Want to know what sparked the Avengers battle with Count Nefaria? See AVENGERS #166. Want to relive the golden days of Vision and Wanda? Check out THE VISION AND THE SCARLET WITCH 12-issue limited series. Why was Vision all white and apathetic? And who knew he had kids?! See WEST COAST AVENGERS #45. Oh, and for the scene that inspired the title of this issue, check out AVENGERS #147. All are available digitally via the Marvel app.

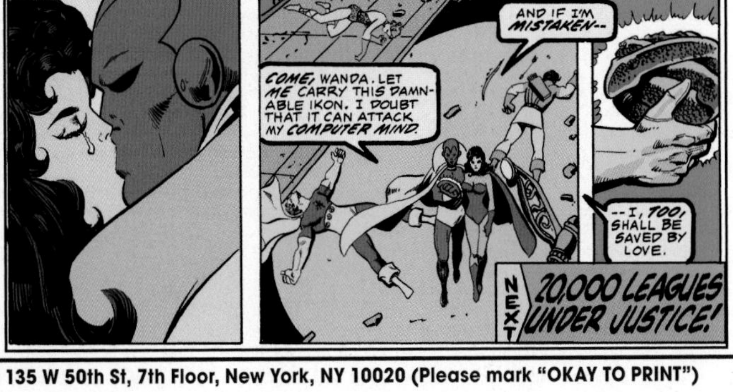

COME, WANDA. LET ME CARRY THIS DAMN-ABLE IKON. I DOUBT THAT IT CAN ATTACK MY COMPUTER MIND.
AND IF I'M MISTAKEN--
--I, TOO, SHALL BE SAVED BY LOVE.
NEXT
20,000 LEAGUES UNDER JUSTICE!

Send letters to mheroes@marvel.com or 135 W 50th St, 7th Floor, New York, NY 10020 (Please mark "OKAY TO PRINT")

BEHOLD... THE LETTERS PAGE!

Art by John Buscema & George Klein

Well, THAT can't be good. Which is such a unique thing to say about the ending of a Vision comic. Sigh. I really need to do one of these where at the last panel everyone is just happy dunky dory, just like:

PANEL 9: The entire Marvel Universe at a booth in a deli. Including Wolverine. He's back and having corn beef on rye.

CAPTAIN AMERICA: I love Robot Families!
ETERNITY: Me too!
VISION FAMILY: Ah thanks, Marvel Universe.
WOLVERINE: I'm alive! Yay!

Hmm. Yeah, that works. We'll just slot it into the next issue. Can't wait to see Gabriel draw it. And now on to your magnificent letters and my hopefully mildly adequate responses.

I graduated in 1986 with a degree in Mathematics. That is how long I have been waiting for a pertinent story about P and NP. Congratulations with achieving the impossible. Now if you can just come up with an interesting tale about the Riemann Hypothesis, you will have won the Mathematical Literacy Triple Crown.

Oh, and the dog's name is Vido, for obvious reasons.

Rich Levin

Well, this is the best thing ever. I graduated from college with a degree in philosophy and history, which is really just a fancy way of saying, "I'm scared of math." I knew about P and NP from... somewhere, and I knew it would work well in this series, but I wasn't sure I could figure it out enough to talk about it. So I watched a lot of explanatory videos, did the best I could, and then braced for the Mathematicians to tell me what an idiot I am. And now you nicely write in to say I'm not that much of an idiot. This is why we write, for small validations of our possible non-idiocy.

Wow.
I do not know where to start, really. Vision has been one of my favorite characters from The Avengers since I discovered issues of the Roy Thomas run in discount bins. I have always found the character interesting, with a great potential for unusual, engaging stories to tell around him.

I stopped reading Marvel titles for a bit and, after finding out that there was a Vision ongoing series written by Tom King, I knew I needed to give it a chance. I have greatly enjoyed King's work in the past, and I can say I was not disappointed with his take on the synthezoid. The terrifying, yet fascinating story has been a great read, and I thoroughly enjoy how the dialogue is simple-yet-complex, perfectly fitting the characters. The art by Hernandez Walta and Bellaire perfectly captures those moments of horror and innocence, giving the comic a modern look with an air of nostalgic fifties family show.

Vision has been a bittersweet ride, and I cannot wait to see how the story will progress in the next numbers! Thanks for giving us a great series centered around the beloved red-skinned android!

Clarissa Galaviz

Ah, thank you so much. I'm never sure how to respond to these very cool letters just saying nice things. It reminds me of my first convention as an adult. I waited in line for some time to meet Bendis. When I got to the front, I realized I had nothing to say besides, man, I love your stuff; it really means something to me on a personal level. He looked at me, shrugged, smiled, shook my hand, and said thanks. It was a simple response, and I don't know why, but it meant the world to me. Just connecting with him, being able to tell him that and seeing him know what I was trying to say. I don't mean that in an arrogant, "I'm Bendis" way, more in a "I hope I can be like Bendis" way and treat the people who like this with the respect they deserve. Which is a long way to say what I said in the first sentence. Thank you so much.

Dear Tom and Team Vision,
Wow. Just finished reading 5 and 6 back to back and I am equal parts elated and unnerved. I am elated in the way one is after reading a book you can just tell is one that MATTERS. One that people will be talking about for years to come - a Twilight Zone for the cape-wearing set, full of existential dread, paranoia, horror, a dash of dark humor, and even in a book about androids a pulsing heart of real human emotion. I am unnerved in the way

one is when knowing that nothing good can come of the Vision's experimental family, and the repercussions yet to be seen, and particularly moved by those words "that every day all men and women make this same choice. To go on even though they cannot possibly go on."

Thank you for bringing us the best Marvel book on the stands. It's been an absolute blast!

OH! Almost forgot! Dunno who's idea it was to put my favorite throwaway villain team, the U-Foes, in issue 5, but they now have my undying love and loyalty.

Also, Vex is a good name for a dog.

All best,
Johnny Hall
Indianapolis, IN

Yeah, that "going on when you can't go on" stuff is to me the best part of comics, the thing that really inspires me personally. Seeing Spider-Man just push off that metal and get to Aunt May. It's the best. You're going to see it all the time in stuff I write as I try to recreate that inspiration. Some hero just beaten to a pulp and rising up to take the next punch, maybe give a few in return. I apologize in advance for the repetition. Sadly, this story is not really about that, so I don't have a lot of those moments here, but I wanted to acknowledge that theme, how it affects us and pushes us forward. Thanks for noticing.

Hey Tom & Gabriel
Another fascinating issue to a series that works on multiple levels. The Vision as Dexter cutting up an electrocuted dog and extracting the brain to add robo-dog to his synthetic family. You're a sick puppy, Tom.

Keeping with the Vision family's naming convention, how about Vivisection the Dog? Alternatively Vomit the Dog has a nice ring and rhymes with Gromit.

This series has a dark sense of foreboding hanging over it. You just know it's not going to end well!

Only 6 more issues to go...

Cheers,
Bruce Marsh

I feel that sick puppies get a bad rap. I've never seen a sick puppy that demanded bloody brain sequences. Mostly they want like medicine and petting and love. And then aren't we all sick puppies? Except for the medicine and the petting part. Those are probably situationally dependent factors.

Dear Tom King (or Wil Moss or Charles Beacham or Chris Robinson or whoever. I don't know how this addressing works).

I'm just a guy from Belgium who is into American comic books. There isn't that much comic culture in Belgium, so I don't really have people to talk comics with (except on Facebook, shout out to Comic Book Fans United!), so I'm just gonna express my awe for this book towards you guys.

This book is the best thing I have read in my life. Ever. Not even comics, all things written. Yesterday, when I was reading issue #6, I actually shed a tear because this book is so enormously, exceptionally, wonderfully magnificent, and I have never done that before for any book. I'm in my first year of studying Physics in university, so I am about that science life, which I think is tackled just right in this book. The P vs NP problem that was mentioned in #6 was unbelievable. A complex problem like that was easily explained and implemented in the story. I bow down for thou brilliance.

As another example of the sheer brilliance that Tom King is, I want to go back to issue #4. The last line of the issue, "It does not bother me. It just goes through me.", hit me hard. This line was so well timed and right on the spot, that I sat down on my couch with the comic in my hands, just staring into nothing, thinking to myself: "What marvelous tale have I just read?" This is how excellent this book is.

So thank you, Tom King, for writing the best story that I have ever come across.

Kind regards
Benno Debals

Wait, wait, wait. There's no comic culture in Belgium!?! This defies everything I know about Belgium. There's a famous comic art museum in Belgium! So, first, I think we've established that

you're not from Belgium... and probably not even Benno Debals! Looking at the rest of the letter, it's pretty obvious that you're most likely an editor, trying to flatter me into getting my scripts in faster. Well, let me tell you something, Mr. Wil Moss, if that is your real name! (If your real name is Benno Debals, Wil, that'd be pretty clever.) My scripts will come when they always come, which is to say after I've read all the internet and solved all the world's problems (in my mind), especially the ones that concern meaningless pop culture things! Only then will I turn to The Vision and ask that question that all writers must ask of their art: "IS IT LUNCH YET?" And then, after lunch, I will write!

Belgium indeed. Indeed, sir! Indeed!

And now for the moment you've all been waiting for! More happy Vision comics!

PANEL 9: VISIONS at the table.

VISION: I'm happy!
WOLVERINE: And I'm alive! Yay!
VIV: Is that Wolverine?
VIRGINIA: Yes, darling, it is Wolverine. He's a robot now. Don't tell him.

Oh and also the "Name the Visions' Dog" thing is on the next page.

Actually, now that we're here, this seems anti-climatic. I mean, the dog's name is in the issue. So you probably know what you need to know. Unless you read the letter page first, in which case, who are you, strange reader? Get your priorities straight. Anyway, our winner after many, many entries, both here and on Facebook and Twitter (And I looked at them all! And I can say, you are all sick puppies in need of love and whatever else is situationally appropriate!):

Sparky.
Huh. Sparky. Kind of bland really. No V sound. No cool pun. Dog doesn't even really spark, come to think of it. Whosoever is in charge is going to hear from my twitter account! But uh, yes, Sparky. Why Sparky? A few reasons. One! If they made a Vision dog animal and I had to give it to my two year old, he'd love the name Sparky. Two! It's kind of cute. Three! It's the nick name/real name of Charles Schulz, the greatest American cartoonist, whose work inspired a lot of what happens in this here comic. Four! I feel that the kids, who will name the dog, wouldn't go with a "V" name, because they'd think it was lame. Five, our next issue is called "They Will Die in the Flames." Make of that what you will. Six! I picked it! So there.

But in absolutely all seriousness, thank you everyone for helping with this and writing in and making me laugh and think and all of it. It meant a ton to me and the team. You guys rock.

Tom

Send letters to mheroes@marvel.com or 135 W 50th St, 7th Floor, New York, NY 10020 (Please mark "OKAY TO PRINT")

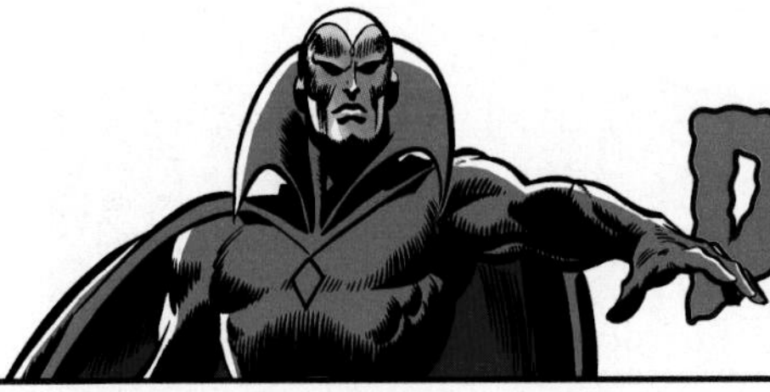

BEHOLD... THE DOG NAMES!

Art by John Buscema & George Klein

Viking
Six (spelled with roman numerals: VI)
Vz
Sparky
Wi-fido
Vincent
Vector
Victor Von Dog
Portia (because of the merchant of Venice)
Roog
Toaster
Vomit (2x...)
Cubit
Vex (7x)
Vivisection
Voz (2x)
Vladimir
Gearbone
Vig (2x)
Vicious Vesuvius
Switch (play on Scarlet Witch)
Optic
Virgil (2x)
Vox
Rover

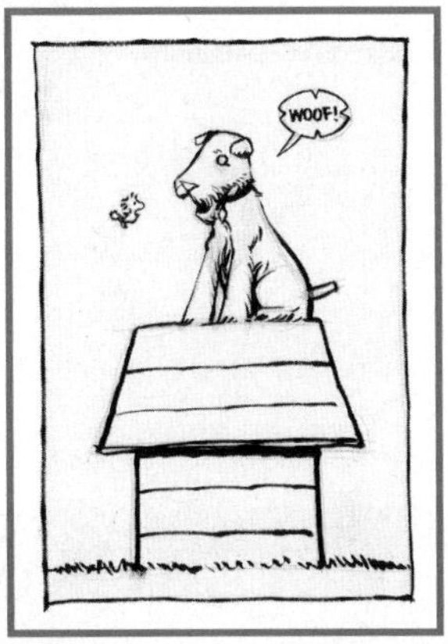
WOOF!

Dog (2x)
Kitty
Chris
V (2x)
Vic (3x)
Megabyte
Terrabyte
Viceroy
Vittles
Vita (2x)
Sterling
Volt (2x)
Chip
Kismet
Vultron
Velvet
Vigor
Voof
Vero
Verity
Vaniah
K-9

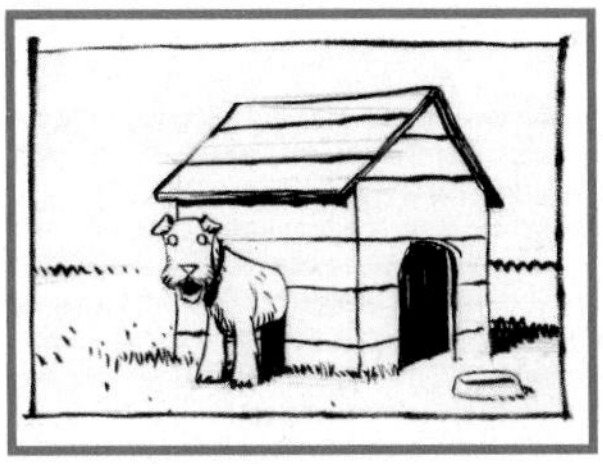

Viridian
Vidor
Googles
Vince
Valerie
Vowser
Rex
Virby
Vinski
Lettuce
Walter
Vido (2x)
Victory
Sight
Frank
Vicar
Nano
Socket
Scooch
Vivi
Varge
Vale
Woof
Vernon
Vigil
Barkus
Aarkus
Video (2x)
Argos
Sprocket (2x)
Vigilante
Isidore
Deckard
Eldon
Rachel
Roy
Sonny
Chapel
Duke
Cassie
Eco
Viz
Colorblind
Fetch
Ultron
Voltaire
Victor
Vito
Aarfus
Vitus
Grimmy
Rip
Vendetta

Congrats to Michael Strobl on the winning entry! Thanks to everyone who submitted! And thanks to intern Nairely Alvira-Gonzalez for compiling all these! (Artwork on this page courtesy of the one and only Gabriel!)

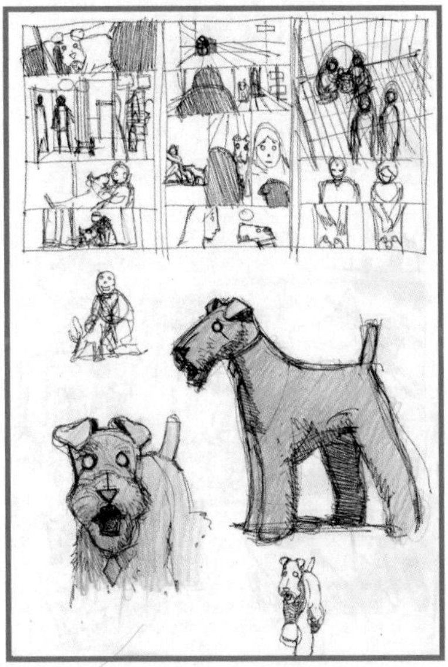

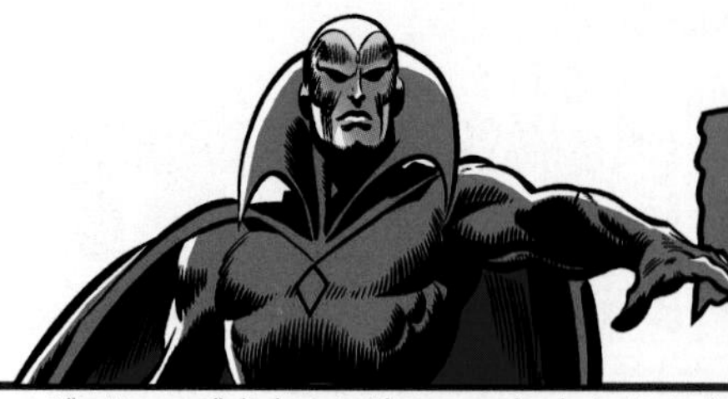

BEHOLD... THE LETTERS PAGE!

Art by John Buscema & George Klein

Killing Vin was really hard to write. Like, my stomach and head hurt as I did it, and I had to walk away from the computer, force myself to come back and just get it done. Which is odd. Because Vin didn't exist before I wrote him and Gabriel and Jordie drew him. He was just an errant thought that I thought might be cool. I mean, I googled "V names" to name him. That's how not-real he is. His name came from a random link I probably couldn't find again. So then why—why does fictionally killing a fictional character create real pain? I honestly don't know. Maybe I'll write about that next time.

Also, poor George and Nora/sometimes-Martha. Sigh.

Anyway…letters!

Tom,

Just read VISION #8. Excellent, by the way. I was wondering if you could explain the panel where vision is with Victor in the museum and Vision asks Victor, "What does any of this mean?" and you do a close up of an old Mickey Mouse drawing. This story was great. Keep up the good work.

Josh Thomas
Central Kansas

Okay. So you're asking me what does it mean when Vision asks "What does it mean?" I think it means that Vision is probably wondering the same thing you're wondering. But maybe that's not what it means. Because if you know that's what it means, then you've stopped wondering what it means so then it couldn't mean that anymore. So then maybe it means the opposite: it means Vision knows what it means, but you don't. But then now you do. So now both of you do. And we're back to the first problem. Hmmmm. This is a tricky one. Got it! It means that I know what it means but both of you don't know what it means. But now you do know what it means, and what I thought it meant it now no longer means. Dammit. I'll get there someday…

Dear VISION crew,

You guys rule. What you're crafting is the best Vertigo book that never happened. VISION feels like *American Beauty* but with super heroes—but better—and it's so exciting to see it come together each month.

I know a lot of you guys are working on multiple titles and the fact that you're killing it on this book is a testament to your talent. Jordie's quickly becoming my favorite colorist, she rules and all the books she touches are gorgeous.

Michael Walsh did an excellent job last ish but with #8 it's nice to see GHW back; and, Tom, dude, bro—stay fly.

Thank you to Clayton Cowles for giving this book such a distinct look. And thank you, Editorial, for the deep cuts and keeping it all together.

Seeing such a pure character in the VISION become corrupted kind of hurts, but it's so compelling in that regard and I believe this series will be talked about for years to come.

Make Mine Marvel,
Keith Wentzell
In a magical land called Los Angeles

Wait a second! I have a Vertigo book that is happening! So you're saying THIS is better than THAT! Now we must fight! But wait a second again! You singled out Clayton Cowles, our brilliant letterer, for his brilliance! All is forgiven in light of your excellent taste! Now we will be friends forever! But wait a second again again! You said other nice and insightful things! Wait a second again again again! Why did I wait-a-second that?! That's perfectly in line with our new forever-friendship! Wait a second! I take back my wait a second! That last one, or the one before. I'm confused. But no more than usual!

Wil and crew,

We already know that THE VISION is the very best Marvel comic on the market, but what we haven't properly done is heap much earned praise upon colorist Jordie Bellaire. Over the course of seven incredible issues I have lauded the smart and engrossing writing of Mr. King and I have reveled in Walta's distinctive drawings, but there, quietly behind it all, laying an incredible foundation and setting the perfect mood, are the coloring talents of Jordie Bellaire. These days I have no idea what is colored by hand (or brush) and what is done by computer, but Bellaire's colors have a painted look that perfectly fits the vibe of the story and brings it to life in a way other styles cannot match. I particularly appreciate the courage to wash entire scenes in a specific hue in order to enhance the story beat.

So let's give three (or more if you've got 'em) cheers for Jordie Bellaire's work in making this book stand heads above the rest!

Ronnie Dingman
Louisville KY

Dude, I could not agree more. Jordie colored the first comic page I ever wrote (for some other company that will not be mentioned here but rhymes with "Vertigo"), and ever since I beg, plead, and conspire to get her to work on everything else I sillily write. This is obvious, but I want to say it, and it's my column so I'm going to: Jordie is as much a storyteller on this book as I am. She sets the mood in a series that is driven forward by subtle changes in mood, and she creates beauty out of robots in a house. I'm forever grateful for her work here and on other stuff I do which may or may not rhyme with "Batman."

I've been reading comics since I was 7 years old...I'm 36 now and I've seen most of what comics have to offer, but I wasn't ready for what Vision had to offer.

I've never been a fan of Vision; I always saw him as just background art for Avengers comics but now...I think he's wonderful. I've started to go through older books he's been in and now I have a new appreciation for him.

Thank you for giving such life to a character that should have been given this sort of treatment years ago.

The comic is haunting and everything lingers with me after I've read it...it's so tragic and I feel for everyone in the cast which is rare this day and age in mainstream comics.

Part of me wants to stop reading 'cause I don't want to see what tragedy falls to them but the main part of me wants to go along for the idea whether it's good or bad. Thank you for such a great and fascinating comic.

Ruben L.
Watsonville, CA

I'm over and over again shocked that people don't just stop reading this book because it is a tragedy. I mean, this is comics. We go to comics primarily to escape, and here I'm writing about this family falling apart (sometimes literally). It's been an experiment for me to see if tragedy has legs in this medium. Not that there haven't been a TON of other examples, but I wasn't writing those examples, wasn't risking my career on them. But it just seems that there can be epiphany from tragedy, and that epiphany can be pleasurable, can provide that escape element. Or at least I hope so. Anyway, at least there's a cute dog. Who just got thrown against a wall. I suck.

Hey VISION gang,

This book just gets better and better. The characters are so well written it could be your new favorite HBO drama.

So it's a pity that it all ends with 12, however, there is a precedent for other 12-issue classics. Remember *Watchmen, Global Frequency* and other maxi-series? Say what you've got to say and move on.

Cheers,
Bruce Marsh

When I first got the VISION gig I was in the midst of another gig of mine that rhymed with Omega Men getting canceled (it eventually got un-canceled—it's a story with lots of things that need to subtly rhyme). I just assumed that VISION would sort of go this way, too. So I had always pictured it in my head as a contained story, preferably a 12-issue contained story. I came out of novels, and that made sense to me. That way, we could have a beginning, middle, and end, and that way this ominous predicting voice would actually have its ominous predictions come true. When I decided to leave the book because of this other offer thingy, I didn't have to adjust the story at all, I just had to acknowledge that it would end where I thought it would end. So yeah, a maxi-series, a complete story. That might be cool. We'll see in three issues.

Dear Tom King and crew,

I cannot believe the first letter I've ever written into Marvel is about...THE VISION. I'm a lifelong Spidey-nut and X-books fan, but I've always loved these alt-takes on random Marvel characters (Magneto and Hawkeye's recent solo series come to mind). The visual work by Gabriel Walta and Jordie Bellaire is stunning, as it was in MAGNETO. A perfect match for this book.

Tom, I'm sad to see you move exclusively to the dark side (only kidding), but these 12 issues of VISION will be something I will treasure and pass on to as many friends as I can. Marvel Editorial made a brilliant decision in saying yes to this book. I hope it's validated with high sales. And though it pains me to admit this in a Marvel letter column, there's no one I would rather have writing *Batman* than you. But really, thank you for this book.

Dan Spinelli
Philadelphia, PA

I cannot speak highly enough of the Editorial support I get for this book. Wil Moss, who edits this thing, is a damn genius, and this book wouldn't be half of what it is without him. Easy example. Victor Mancha was Wil's idea. My first outline had the original Human Torch in this role. Wil came to me with Victor and I realized that there was so much more depth there—the cool uncle destined to fall, who then falls. Perfect. So thank you, Wil, who is editing these words right now with the help of the very cool Charles Beacham. I assume they'll add some sentence at the end about how damn handsome the two of them are. Even if what I'm about to say seems like it is part of some joke, I sincerely mean this: Wil Moss and Charles Beacham are the handsomest damn bastards to ever be damn handsome. (Oh. There it is.) Also I'm terrible at rhyming.

Dear Tom King/THE VISION Team,

I picked up VISION #1 on a whim and since then I continue to look forward to every single issue. The work you guys are doing has really made Vision out to be such a fascinating and relatable character, and in some ways so hauntingly human. THE VISION is the first comic I recommend to anyone looking for a new comic to read, it is quite simply put: OUTSTANDING, keep up the good work, I and many others cannot wait to read more!

Sincerely,
Sean Guevara

Thank you so much! This book lives by people putting it in the hands of other people. That work that you all do means so much to me. You guys rock.

All right! That's it for now. I've got to get back to contemplating my panicking over the deaths of nonexistent creations. I'll see you next month when things will get lighter and fluffier. I mean, one can only hope, right?

Oh, but before we go, look at this awesome-wonderful craziness below. That's Scarlet Witch (Elizabeth Olsen) and Vision (Paul Bettany) holding Scarlet Witch and Vision comics! You thinking what I'm thinking? NERDS!!!

-Tom

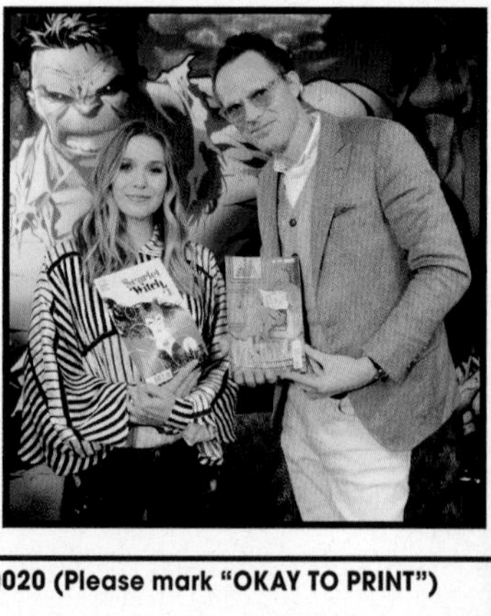

Send letters to mheroes@marvel.com or 135 W 50th St, 7th Floor, New York, NY 10020 (Please mark "OKAY TO PRINT")

BEHOLD... THE LETTERS PAGE!

Art by John Buscema & George Klein

You know what I love about this comic? Sometimes you have an idea that's too insane/inane for a super hero book. For example, you might think "Hey, what if we did a whole issue where the heroes don't leave their house?" Then inevitably your next thought is "No, no, the editor will kill me, the artist will kill me, the colorist will kill me, and the letterer will probably be cool with it, but letterers tend to roll with stuff, so that's not really a thrilling endorsement." But with this book, I propose this insanity/ inanity to the editor (Wil) and he says "Cool, cool," then the artist (Gabriel) says "I love it!", then the colorist (Jordie) says "Tom, do you think I have the damn time to coddle you while you fret about your damn idea?! I'm coloring half of comics! Just give me the pages, I'll make them perfect, then you go away!", then the letterer (Clayton) says "We don't really roll with stuff, man. We have lots of opinions; it's just no one pays blah blah blah Helvetica blah blah blah."

And then, because this is VISION and this is something special, we go with it.

And then comes the oddest/bestest miracle of all: You all buy it and you write these cool letters and notes about it. So let's get to them.

To Tom King,

"The definition of insanity is doing something over and over again and expecting a different result."

I'm not sure where the phrase originated, but I think it fits the series (and my subsequent rereading of issues) quite well. Each month has induced an unsettling reaction from me; from the guttural scream I let out at the end of issue 4, to the splash page of Vision's face as he vivisected his neighbor's canine cranium in issue 6. Not only that, the intellectual discussion from you and fellow readers makes me hope that that dialogue is included in a future trade, not just restricted to each issue.

Issue 7 was no different on both fronts, as I read and listened to Johann Sebastian Bach (from Slaughterhouse Five) on vinyl, and shivered as I got to the letters page. I would like to know if there is any music or playlist that comes to mind when writing the series, that may further enrich the reading experience, as I've listened to JS Bach, Dave Brubeck, and David Bowie.

Whatever the inspiration, I'm glad this series has found its audience, which I hope has pleased you, as based on your introduction in issue 1 on comics and alienation. I'll be continuing to read, as you guide The Vision to his natural delusion- I mean, conclusion.

Your humble servant,
Mitch Gosser
De Pere, Wisconsin

It's an utter cliché, but if you've read this far you probably know I don't mind a well-polished cliché: the one song that always comes to mind when writing VISION is Nina Simone's "Sinner Man." I feel like every issue could cut to black and have that song play over the credits. That heavy, repetitive rhythm beating in you as Simone sings about a man running for help, begging for salvation, trying anything he can and not getting anything for all that effort -- yeah, that's VISION right there.

I didn't start reading this title until issue number seven. Now I'm addicted to this book. Tom King, you, Walta and Bellaire need to stay on this book forever. Thanks for adding another comic to my pull list.

Gar Johnson
Elmhurst, NY

You jumped in with issue #7??? Where we deep-dove into the Vision and Scarlet Witch's relationship just to cover a small mystery plot from a panel in issue #1??? Bless you. This is why I love comics. I started reading comics in the middle of the X-MEN "Inferno" crossover, like a random issue, and nothing made sense, and I adored the nonsensical-ness of it all, because it meant there was a mystery for me to solve, back issue bins to dive into, threads to follow. See, every comic is someone's first comic; we have to remember that. But we have to remember too that sometimes it's okay if that first comic falls in the middle of "the crazy." "The crazy" is why we show up for the next one. And the previous one.

Hello Vision-aries,

I just finished reading issue #6 and since my new shipment of comics came right then, I jumped into #7, too. Quite a contrast in issues, though both were very good, both in story and art. The creepiness of the series continued in #6, with the neighbor dog getting involved, devolved, and evolved. One question though: What the heck happened to the inside of the house after Vizh found the Reaper's body? I guess it's left up to our imagination, but did he blow a gasket or something fighting with Virginia to get her to reveal what happened? Felt a little confused there. #7: Different artist, same high quality effort! I liked the historical perspective of Wanda and Vizh's relationship. So, I guess Virginia was patterned after Wanda after all. But what threw me this issue is Quicksilver. I don't think he was at all enamored of Wanda and Vizh being together, so I don't think he'd attend that gathering he was shown at. Just my impression. So, only five issues to go, eh? I'm gonna miss this title. The dog's name?: (Hmm, should start with a "V" I guess) Let's see - Van, Vernon, Vida, Viral, Victor, or Valor. I'm leaning toward Victor.

Alan Bowman
Saga City, Japan

So I was going to write that scene in #6 where Vision confronts Virginia about the body. I had it in my outline and everything. And I started doing it, and it just came out boring. They said everything to each other you expected them to say. After bashing my head on my keyboard a few times and then backspacing quite a few times, I decided the scene would play better in your head than mine. If I'm not surprising you, I'm failing. And I couldn't surprise you there. So you get the aftermath. What happened in between is on you. Let me know what you think. Surprise me.

As for Quicksilver, not being enamored with a family member's chosen companion and then having to go to a dinner with said chosen companion seems to me to be a fairly universal human experience. If you haven't done this yet, good on you, and better on your family. But, buddy, I'm telling you -- it's coming.

Dear VISION Team,

I just finished reading issue #8 and I was blown out of my mind. RUNAWAYS was my reintroduction to modern comics and I'm a die hard fan of Victor Mancha in particular. Add that to my new found love for The Vision and you have a killer book. Killer. Get it?

It was good to see Victor again. It has been a while since AVENGERS A.I., after all. However, as with life, things aren't always what we expect. Normally, I wouldn't have seen myself in front of my computer monitor, writing this letter. I would have sat down and thought about the future of the series all by myself. But the way this issue ended has brought me here. I wanted to communicate with the group of talented creators that have brought this story into my hands. I wanted to thank them.

I hope to be continuously amazed by what all of you create, a smile in my face.

Diego Cobos

Thanks, man. I hope to be continually amazed at these kinds of letters and at this response and the smile on my face I get every time I get to talk to this audience.

To Mr. King (Tom, if you prefer),

What can I say about Vision? In #1, you had me intrigued. By #2, you had me hooked. By #6, I was thinking I had gotten used to the goriness of the series and that nothing could surprise me... and then you killed a dog and made it into a robot. #7 had me crying and sending weird voice messages to my friends (who will no longer speak to me... But hey, big Wanda fan here). And then, I read #8... And #8 was a mixture of me nerdgasming (Big RUNAWAYS fan and Victor Mancha was always a character I wanted to connect with Vision so I was glad you did that) and crying (WHY MUST YOU KILL HIM?! Noooooooo).

But after my anger subsided (read: was drowned with food), I decided to write this letter to say "Thank you for restoring my hope in super hero comic books." My friend had been begging me to read this series for months but I never felt like it until I learned that Wanda was a big part of #7. And now, I'm really glad I read it. Thank you for an amazing series (sorry to hear

---

you're leaving, but hey, when someone offers you the chance to write Batman, you don't turn them down). In the future, when I (hopefully) become a comic book writer, I hope to continue the threads you weave in this story. And I hope that when I finally get to write Vision, my stories can be HALF as good as the ones you've masterfully created.

Give my thanks to the team. You're all doing fabulous work.

Hasan Farhat
A 16-year-old dreamer from Lebanon

I was at a signing with Scott Snyder (yeah, this is my life now; it's craziness, don't get me started) and a young woman came up to him and said she wanted to be a comic writer. Scott, who knows the answers to most of the questions, said "Do it. Be great. Take my job." Which is a cool thing to say. I, however, have, like, all these children who want to go to college and also I kind of like this job because, y'know, I write comics for a living -- so I'm not going say that. Instead, I'll say come on, man, compete with me, challenge me, make me better. We need young writers to want to be young writers in this medium. We need that for the medium to grow and thrive. So learn to be good, show me what you can do, and I'll try to top it.

Dear Tom,

When I saw the first issue of "the Vision" at my local comic book store I was overjoyed that someone was going to write a series about Vision's search for humanity from such an exciting new perspective. He has been a favorite of mine for a long time even before I played him on "Avengers: Earth's Mightiest Heroes." I had no idea, however, that this series would be so stunningly original and so beautifully crafted. I am now not only a fan of the Vision but of you, Gabriel and Jordie (as well as VC's lettering). Please keep making this wonderful series. I look forward to it every month!

Peter Jessop
Los Angeles, CA

"Please keep making this wonderful series." Ugh. Way to dig out a dude's heart and stomp on it for fun. Would that I could. And I probably could've and maybe I should've, but then what would've that been? Now that I know what issue #12 is, I don't think there needs to be an issue #13. At least not for me. Better to let it end, I think. That seems insane/inane enough that it might work.

And so I'll see you next time for our penultimate issue, in which everyone tries to stop Vision from doing the wrong thing we all know he's going to do...

-Tom

Send letters to mheroes@marvel.com or 135 W 50th St, 7th Floor, New York, NY 10020 (Please mark "OKAY TO PRINT")

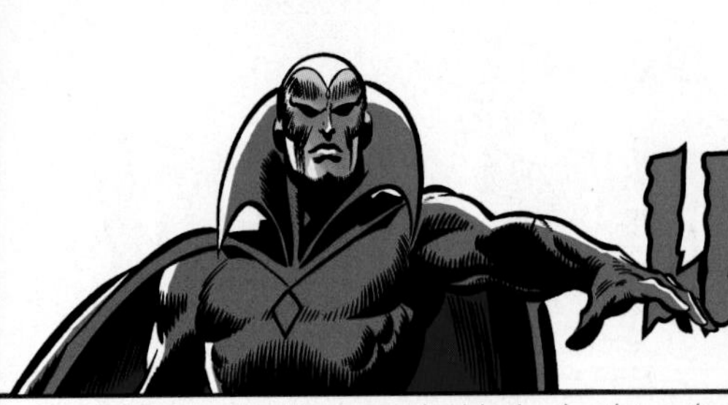

BEHOLD... THE LETTERS PAGE!

Art by John Buscema & George Klein.

(Before we get started, I just want to acknowledge the brilliant work of Roy Thomas. The dialogue concerning Vision's origin in this issue is directly quoted from Thomas' AVENGERS Vol. 1 #57 and #58. Almost 50 years later, and the words are still haunting.)

Okay, so did you see what happened there? Not at the end. That had to happen. And not the dog either. (Ugh, the dog. All that effort to name the dog, and we just go and kill him. What is this comic??) Like back there near the beginning, one of those first pages -- I got to write Spider-Man! The neighbor friendly Spider-Man! I know, I know, it was for just like two words, one of which wasn't really a word, more like a sound, and the other word wasn't the most articulate word, not a word you write home to mom about. "Mom, I got to write Spider-Man!" "Wow, what'd you have him say?" "Uhm, it was…bathroom humor-related. I don't really want to talk about it." "Bathroom. Really, Tom?" "Don't judge me!" You maybe see here why I write about an odd family for a living…

Anyway, the point is, I wrote Spider-Man! And it was amazing and spectacular and web of ("This joke, again?" "I said, don't judge me!") Only thing more amazing, spectacular, and web of than that is getting to write responses to your letters. So here we go!

Tom King,

I have been a longtime fan of the Vision and his journey to become human given that the odds are stacked against him. When I heard he was getting his own solo series I ran to my room and started reading my old VISION AND SCARLET WITCH series, followed by WEST COAST AVENGERS: VISION QUEST, also AVENGERS A.I., just so I could get the momentum going. And I can honestly say you've done a fantastic job keeping the new series intellectual and suspenseful. Honestly this is the most in depth and well thought out comic book I've read in a while and I can't wait to see how it ends. Also I hope to see you move on to other comic books but if you stopped at THE VISION that'd be a pretty high note to leave on.

Your loyal fan,
Alexis Gutierrez
San Antonio, Texas

Well, actually I have a number of other [Hey kids, this is Marvel here. We're just going to bump in here and answer this one for Tom, because he's like, y'know, super busy. Or something. Do you know he has three kids? Can you imagine? Anyway. Tom was about to say that he is indeed retiring from comics after he writes this one limited series, THE VISION. In fact, THE VISION is the only comic he's ever written. Or possibly ever will write. Which is so sad. Now, if you want to read more from Tom, we highly suggest you just buy another copy of THE VISION and read it again. Then repeat this process as often as you like. Or even more often than you like. I hope this clears things up, and I'm glad we got a chance to give Tom a little break. He's such a hard worker, y'know, for a guy who only works on just the one thing.]

To Those Behind The Vision,

I just cried, this thing you're doing, the dialogue is just so beautiful...this is movie-worthy. If Marvel ever decided to make a movie, it should be based on this series. I'm sorry I don't know the name of the writer when Ii was typing this e-mail, but you, sir, are amazing. You touched my heart and this should be a movie!

James Malik of Indonesia

*There **should** be a movie! Then I'd get to go to the premiere! And I'd be in some fancy important Hollywood line and fancy important people would ask me fancy important questions like, "Who are you?" and I'd say, "I wrote the comic book this movie in based on!" And they'd be really impressed and say, "So what…you, like, drew the pictures?" And I'd say, "No, I wrote it!" and they'd think that was so cool and they'd say, "What, like, the words? Like in the what-do-you-call-them, like bubble things?" And I'd say, "Yes! I wrote the bubble things!" And they'd be ecstatic and say, "Oh, I didn't know that was a thing." And I'd say, "It actually is a thing! It's a full-time job actually. There's a lot to it. I mean, not that much, not like a real job, but enough, I guess. I make a living, is what I'm saying." And they'd think that was awesome, and they'd say, "So then you must be Stan Lee?" And I'd say, "I…I guess. Okay. I'm Stan Lee!" And then they'd get really excited and ask me for my autograph on a Batman comic they got from their publicist. And I'd sign "Stan Lee" on it and walk away satisfied!*

Dear Vision Team,

Some time ago, I went into my local comic store for the very first time. I'd read many comics before through Marvel Unlimited, but I'd never read an actual physical one. I had no idea what to buy.

I talked to some people and someone recommended the Vision series to me. At this point the series was 5 or so issues in. So I read the first issue. I liked it a lot. A couple days later I got 2 and 3 and I was hooked.

I kept buying issue after issue. Since then, I've bought other comics and read other stuff but none of them compare to this series. Honestly, this might be the best comic series I've read. I am very interested to see the conclusion and I will definitely read other comics you have worked on.

Preston Bied

*****

Tom King,

I just bought issue #10. Very entertaining to read. The scene where Vision prays with his daughter was very moving to me. That doesn't happen very often in comics. I loved that part. Thanks for an amazing comic series. Totally worth my money.

Josh Thomas
Salina, Kansas

Ah, thank you so much. I think that might be my personal favorite scene in the whole book. There's something in there that reminds me of my relationship with my own daughter, Claire -- who is not a robot, to my knowledge, but who does enjoy discovering the world in her own unique way. Sometimes I'll visit her while she's in the midst of these discoveries and she'll try to bring me into what she sees, showing me a twist on reality that I'd never considered before but makes perfect sense as soon as she shows it to me. It changes my world. I hope I captured some of that in that scene with Viv and Vision. (Plus Gabriel and Jordie couldn't have made it more visually powerful.)

Dear Tom King,

You continue to make every single issue of this series completely emotionally devastating and I absolutely love it. It hurts so bad that it feels good. That last sentence doesn't make any sense and yet it does.

I just finished reading #10 and just wanted to say how much I love the dialogue between Viv and Vision when she explains why she is praying. Specifically, these lines, which come after they agree on the improbability of the existence of God and of Vin's soul:

"So first, I pray that there is a God. Then I pray that Vin had a soul. Then I pray for God to allow Vin's soul to rest."

That...really speaks to me. That hope. That belief. Maybe it was supposed to be shown as a tad naive (given the narration at the end of the issue), but I still think those lines are absolutely beautiful.

My friends and I will continue to follow this fantastic series until the bitter end, two issues away. We know it's going to hurt something awful, but please, don't hold back.

Jesse

I like that. "That last sentence doesn't make any sense and yet it does." I try to look at comics or writing or all of this creating crap like that -- as something that doesn't make sense but does. Because if it makes sense, if there's a one-to-one correlation between story and a priori or a posteriori logic, then story serves no purpose. Logic is better, clearer. Ask any robot. But the problem is we're not robots, so logic doesn't quite fulfill us for some reason. Then this becomes the purpose of story. To get beyond logic, to not make sense. But when you do this, if what you write that doesn't make sense then doesn't make sense in some larger sense, then it's just gibberish or an exercise in self-love. So you have to write stuff that doesn't make sense, yet does. Does that make sense? Probably not. If so, great. But if still so, not so great.

To the Incredible Team of THE VISION,

I don't think you expected to get a letter from this corner of the world, but THE VISION is so fantastic that it's gained worldwide fame!

The unique and astonishing penciling and coloring by the art team, combined with the fascinating narration of a serious, unusual and unpredictable story by Tom King, make this comic book a masterpiece. And being a psychology student interested in AI and Philosophy of Mind, I'm just absorbed by The Vision Family's struggle to define themselves as normal humans.

The only problem with this title is the number of its issues. I mean, only 12?! How can this be?! The story and its characters have the potential for a lot more! I didn't know that it's planned to end so soon, so I just couldn't believe that Vin had actually died in #9. It was so unexpected and painful…

Saeed Nasiry
Iran

I'm never surprised to see the reach of super heroes. During my spy days, I would travel at times to places not too many Americans had been and talk to people not too many Americans had talked to (I know that's a hell of a preposition-ending statement; be assured that at least I'm aware of my idiosyncrasies/idiocies). Going to those places, talking to those people, I always noticed that you'd find some love for Spider-Man or the X-Men. Across all those cultures, somehow the idea of silly people in silly suits fighting to save this silly world hit a profound nerve. These are modern myths that cut across class, race, gender, and culture. What an honor it is to be able to contribute to them. What a burden it is to make them into something worthy of that honor. Maybe that's why it's so easy to write stressed-out Vision.

As for ending at #12…well, I can't believe it either, honestly. But nonetheless, here we are -- or rather, here we are about to be.

One more month. One more issue. One more…

See you then.

-Tom

Send letters to mheroes@marvel.com or 135 W 50th St, 7th Floor, New York, NY 10020 (Please mark "OKAY TO PRINT")

BEHOLD... THE LETTERS PAGE!

Art by John Buscema & George Klein.

So on the next page, I'm going to say some things about the end of all this. Nothing really profound or anything. Just me thanking the team and my wife (spoilers!). But before we get to that, let me just thank you. I wrote this comic after another comic of mine got canceled. And I very honestly thought this one wouldn't make it either. But I had something to say, or at least I had a way I wanted to say something, and so I did.

And it didn't get canceled. Not only did it make it, it made my career. All because you amazing, astonishing, uncanny fans stuck by this thing, bought this thing, talked about this thing. I don't exactly know what you're supposed to say to the people who help put food on your table, who buy braces for your kids, or at least I don't know a way to say it that's not stupid and corny. So let me be stupid and corny. I'm grateful to you, forever grateful. I write so I can write for you, and I will try in the future to always write something worthy of your time and support, of your intelligence as readers. Through all the stupid/ridiculous/ignorant crap you sometimes have to take as a comic fan, at least remember this: to me, to this one nerdy writer, you're nothing but cool.

So let's get to your cool letters. One last time.

Mr. King,

It's highly likely that you've heard this before, but I never expected to absolutely love a book about the Vision. It's presently the only Marvel comic that I look forward to with any anticipation. Every issue has surprised me.

A robot's prayer--*"Please let there be a God (as unlikely as it seems)"*--this is simply brilliant. I'll be smiling about this for days.

As regrettable as it is to hear that this title will soon be ending, I'm glad that it will go out on a high note as an extremely solid 12-issue finite series. I'll continue to follow your work on future titles in hopes that they approach the brilliance of THE VISION. Thanks for the stories.

Yours Sincerely,
Ken Case
Memphis, TN

I really like that. "The Robot's Prayer." We should make that a thing. Can we make that a thing? Do we have that kind of power? I mean, "'Nuff said" is a thing. "Excelsior" is a thing. "I'm the best at what I do" is a thing. So someone around here clearly can make the things become things. Maybe it's me! I mean, it's probably not me, but it could be me. Or it could be us. Why not us? You and me. We do things, and now we'll do this thing, and if we can't do this thing, then fine, what's lost besides the thing, which wasn't a thing anyway? Anyway, next time you and I are (God forbid!) in a situation that calls for praying to God that God exists, we'll call this "The Robot's Prayer." There. Now it's a thing. 'Nuff said.

To the VISION team,

I would like to thank you all for providing this delightful piece of fiction for the past few months. I have been a comics fan since I was a child and this has been a standout series in my ongoing discovery of comics, I hope to be a creator one day and aspire to write and draw something as great and hopefully even better than this.

I hope this the entire team goes on to even greater projects than they are working on and hope to one day be amongst these distinguished vanguards of modern comics, you have all created something that is at once revelatory, aesthetically pleasing and entertaining, especially as a fan of the Vision who desperately wanted to see his potential realized.

For that I say thank you, to Ms. Bellaire, Mr. Cowles, Mr. King, Mr. Walta, and Mr. Moss, for showing that even characters four decades old can still be relevant.

Daniel Bello
Hopefully a future competitor

Y'know, I've got enough problems in my life without hearing nice things from a future competitor. How can I possibly hope to destroy you and all your creative endeavors if you insist on saying all that stuff? But wait. Is that your plan? You want me to think you're saying nice things in order to lull me into complacency so you can destroy me and all my creative endeavors?!? Now that is evil! And now that I know you're evil, I can destroy you and all your future creative endeavors. But wait. You'd know I know that, so why say that? Unless you were hoping I'd destroy you and all your creative endeavors and thus tarnish my reputation, thus destroying myself and all my future creative endeavors! I'm destroyed either way. The perfect trap. NOOOO! Fine. Fine. You win. Damn you. I'm going back to LA! (I grew up in LA, it's got nothing to do with the whole Hollywood thing, though while I'm there, I might check some stuff out.) Regardless! Issue #13 is now yours, Daniel!

Mr. King,

I just cried, this thing you're doing, THE DIALOGUE IS JUST SO BEAUTIFUL...this is movie worthy. If Marvel ever decided to make a VISION movie, it should be based on this series. You sir are amazing. You touched my heart!

James Malik
Indonesia

So I stole the first page of VISION from John Ford's The Searchers. Maybe the best opening shot in cinema: the camera bursting through the door going out onto the planes as John Wayne arrives. And if you know that movie, it ends the same way. With John Wayne coming back, the camera pulling back through the door as it closes. It's a perfect circle. And as I came to that end you just saw here, I had this big debate: Do I steal the end of Searchers, mimic the circle? And my thinking was, probably not. Just because--and this is how I get to your letter--if I did that, it would make this work kind of derivative of that movie and kind of (at least in my paranoid mind) say that comics have to copy films, as if we were a lesser medium. So I did something else, stole a panel from an Alan Moore Superman comic, and tried to say that we don't have to write as if we're making the best movie we could if we could make a movie. Instead we write as if we're making the best comic we can, because we can. So that's a long way of saying, I hope the dialogue isn't movie worthy. I hope it's comic book worthy.

Dear Dear Tom King,

I've never met you, but I really like you--so much so that I purposefully added another "dear" to the opening of this missive. This comic is so great, and disturbing, and thought provoking, and gut wrenching, and most definitely inspiring.Then at the end of every issue we get your awesome, sincere, and honest little address, from the creator directly to his audience. I've really enjoyed it. I'll be sad to see it go. (As well as Sheriff of Babylon, another amazing story.) I'm becoming more and more of a fan with everything I read. I'll be seeing you over at the distinguished competition.

Now for a short geek out: issue 10. Holy @&$! When Vizh busts out of house arrest, using Cap's old vibranium lighter as a shield against Stark's shield!! SO EPIC! And the cold light of day on Vision's face...kudos to Walta and Bellaire. Kudos to everyone. The beginning of the explosion that all this quiet, contemplative pressure has been building towards? It felt like it.

Make Mine King.

Thanks,
Isaac Mohon
Toledo, OH

I really like that moment, too, where Vision busts out. Did you catch that we did some fancy format stuff there? The whole issue in the house was full of tons of panels and then when he finally broke out, we went to a double-page spread. It was supposed to be sort of this break from the claustrophobia of the house and...y'know I really shouldn't talk about this stuff. I think you're supposed to discover it on your own, or maybe not see that underlying thing altogether. Anyway, it's all supposed to be part of the mysterious "writing process" so that we look more impressive or something. Look, how about this, dear, dear Isaac, you post something somewhere about this panel thing, and pretend I didn't tell you? That way we both look cool. Cool? Cool.

My Dear Tom King,

Thank you. When I heard that they were finally going to do a Vision series then I was so happy. He has been one of my favorite characters for a long time. But you, this, this was a fantastic run. Full of emotion and characters that made you feel for them without even that much dialogue. Gabriel evoked so much emotion through his art. Jordie gave color to that emotion. As we near the Penultimate issue I just wanted to say Thank You. Thank you for an amazing series. Possibly my favorite comic run ever. I am much more than disappointed to see you leave but I will enjoy your work on *Batman* as well. Who knows, maybe someday the whole creative team can come back in a few years and make a short followup series, but thats just wishful thinking. You know, I was reading the HULK: THE END TPB just the other day and Peter David said something very interesting in his written introduction to the book. He said that we all strive for immortality as we get older, we get a face-lift and buy fancy cars when we have a midlife crisis, but in the end it is all for naught. We all die, but we strive to be immortalized through what we do, through our actions. Writers sort of get immortality through the books they write, hopeful that someone will remember they're work and be amazed when they read it centuries from now. Tom King. You have been immortalized.

Thank you for letting me be a part of it,
Tristin Downs

I have been immortalized! Hundreds of years from now, people will read this comic and say, "Why is the neighbor's name 'Nora' in issue #1, but it's 'Martha' in issue #6, and then 'Nora' again in issue #9? What is that?" And someone will answer, "I think that stupid writer guy just messed it up and didn't fix it. You know, we should find him and punch him in the face!" But I'll be dead and thus unpunchable. And so I win!

Mr. Tom King,

Well, someone has finally created a graphic novel that can be objectively argued as the greatest. The way that Alan Moore and David Gibbons used super heroes to instead do an examination on the state of civil society in the 1980s, you and Gabriel Hernandez Walta have used a family of android/quasi-cyborgs to commentate on the 2010s. You took the tumultuous history of a Marvel B-list/A-list "light" character and made it an examination of the ways we try to conform to society while actively having society become alienated from us.

Vision's goal was always going to fail because he was giving himself harder and harder benchmarks to achieve what it took to be a man in a society that still cannot recognize common humanity in biological humans because of what they looked like, but yet he misreads and thinks that humanity comes from a superficial principal that he thinks that he is "that close" to achieving. Even when the people closes to him have taken him into and regard him as part of the "human" family, it is not enough and the seeds for disaster are sewn here within Vision's self-doubt of his own worth. He's human enough to want what is commonly perceived to be the rites of manhood, but not enough to be content and pass any contentment on to the rest of his family (probably not a good idea to build a wife based on his then-crazy ex). In a way even his disastrous situation is proof of another common trait of a man: inheriting the sins of his near-ancestors to at least as far back as Hank Pym and his doomed domestic life.

The recently departed Vin served to indicate or allude to the audience this books connection to the Shakespearean tragedies (especially The Merchant of Venice), but this book, I feel, draws a more direct ancestry to Eugene O'Neil's tragic/drama plays. This comic book is a horror comic in the same way that O'Neil's The Iceman Cometh is a dystopian novel and that's what makes me love it so much. Vision, in the words of Dr. W.E.B. Dubois, is aware of a "veil" that exists between himself (and his family) and the rest of the world. But old Viz does not want to have to have the "curse" of a "double consciousness and its implications so he tries to find ways around it, but alas...

Sincerely,
Kenneth M.
Virginia

Wow, that's some insightful, very neat stuff. And you didn't even read this last issue yet! Of course, maybe you hated this last issue. Maybe you were like, "Wait a second, this isn't Eugene O'Neil. This is Ed O'Neil! And barely that." (I'm not sure if Ed O'Neil is a bad writer. He may be the best there is; I just needed him for the joke. Sorry, Ed. And, honestly, it's awesome to see an actor of your caliber reading comics.) Anyway! Maybe you now hate everything about the series and by extension me! To which I say, why did you bother writing in the first place?!? You can read whatever you want, you don't have to read my stuff! But thanks for picking it up anyway! It's really appreciated!

And on that silly note, goodbye, friends. See you next time. (Or on the next page. I still have to do that "thank you" part I told you about earlier, so saying goodbye now is kind of awkward, but I had to say something, because if I didn't, it would've been awkward and...sigh. It never ends. Until it does, and when it does we wish it never had.)

Send letters to mheroes@marvel.com or 135 W 50th St, 7th Floor, New York, NY 10020 (Please mark "OKAY TO PRINT")

PAGE 1:

PANEL 1: We're inside the eyes of two neighbors of the Vision. We're looking from the inside of their house at the door leading outside.

> CAPTION: In late September, with the leaves just beginning to hint at the fall to come, the Visions of Virginia moved into their house on 616 Hickory Branch Lane, Arlington, VA, 21301.

PANEL 2: The door opens on a boring street in the suburbs. Trees line the street. It's all very banal.

> CAPTION: The Visions' house was located in Cherrydale, a pleasant neighborhood about fifteen miles west of the White House.

PANEL 3: Camera moves down to the sidewalk, looking down the street. A MAN is outside in one of the houses, doing yard work.

> CAPTION: Most of the Visions' neighbors worked downtown, and they talked often about the traffic on 66 or Lee Highway.

PANEL 4: The man doing yard work waving at the camera.

> CAPTION: On the weekends they tended to stay in Virginia, though they often lamented that they should go into the city.
> CAPTION: The museums are so nice, and the kids would have a great time.

PANEL 5: Back to the street view. A little further down the street. Ahead we see a green mailbox at one of the houses.

> CAPTION: Very few of them were from the area originally.
> CAPTION: Most had moved to DC after college and worked for Congress or the President. They made nothing, and they lived off of nothing.
> CAPTION: But that was unimportant. They were young, and they wanted to save the world.

PANEL 6: On our famous green mailbox with THE VISIONS written on it.

> CAPTION: Eventually, they met someone and fell in love and had children.
> CAPTION: With bills to pay, they left their small government jobs; they became lobbyists and lawyers and managers.
> CAPTIONS: They moved out to the suburbs for the schools.

PANEL 7: Looking up the Visions walkway.

> CAPTION: They made the compromises that are necessary to raise a family.

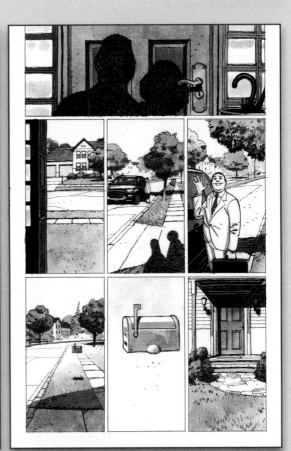

PAGE 2:

PANEL 1: Still inside the neighbors' head, GEORGE and NORA, a white couple in their early 60s. They're looking at the door to the Vision's house.

> GEORGE: Can't believe I'm doing this. Can't believe you're making me do this.
> GEORGE: They're robots, Nora. They don't want cookies.
> CAPTION: Behold George and Nora.

PANEL 2: A doorbell being pushed.

> NORA (off): They're not robots. I went online.
> NORA (off): They're something else. Like a Synthe-something.
> CAPTION: At that time, George worked as a mortgage broker. He enjoyed hot wings, but he always ordered them too spicy for his own taste.
> SFX: Ding. Ding.

PANEL 3: George and Nora from behind, the door in front of them. NORA is holding a plate of cookies.

> GEORGE: "Synthe-something"? Great. Problem solved.
> NORA: It said they moved here because The Vision is the Avengers' man in the White House now.
> NORA (smaller): And also, rumor is maybe his super friends didn't fully approve of the whole new family thing he made.
> CAPTION: Nora worked in HR at a K-street law firm. She read more than anyone she knew, but she only read digitally.

PANEL 4: George and Nora turning toward each other. The door is starting to open.

> GEORGE: Of course they didn't approve. Robots making robots. Trying to be all, I don't know, trying not to be robots.
> GEORGE: It's just gross.
> NORA: You don't listen! They're not robots! They're those things I was saying.

PANEL 5: George and Martha so busy yelling at each other now that they don't notice the door has opened and Vision (partially hidden in shadow) is standing there.

> GEORGE: Honey, I love you, but they're toasters. Fancy, green toasters.
> GEORGE: They're not you and me. They don't eat cookies, y'know?
> NORA: Cookies—God! Fine, yes, I got them cookies! Does this affect you somehow?
> NORA: Are there only a small amount of cookies in the world so now you're going to run out and die? Is that it?
> VISION: Excuse me?

LAYOUT: GABRIEL HERNANDEZ WALTA

INKS: GABRIEL HERNANDEZ WALTA

COLORS: JORDIE BELLAIRE

LETTERS: VC's CLAYTON COWLES

PAGE 3:

PANEL 1: SPLASH: THE VISIONS at the door way. For this splash they look very ordinary. Very 1950s America. The husband, the wife, the two kids. Everyone is smiling and happy. Greeting a new neighbor at the door.

VISION: May we help you?
TITLE: Visions of the Future
CREDITS.

TOM KING writer
GABRIEL HERNANDEZ WALTA artist
JORDIE BELLAIRE color artist
VC'S CLAYTON COWLES letterer
MIKE DEL MUNDO cover artist
VANESA DEL REY; MARCOS MARTIN; RYAN SOOK variant cover artists
CHRIS ROBINSON assistant editor
WIL MOSS editor
TOM BREVOORT executive editor
AXEL
JOE
DAN
ALAN

SCRIPT: TOM KING

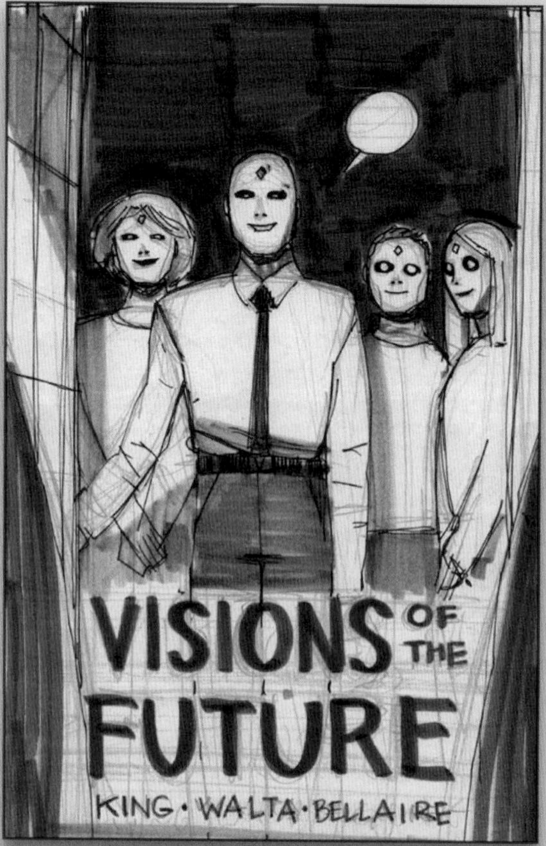
VISIONS OF THE FUTURE
KING • WALTA • BELLAIRE

LAYOUT: GABRIEL HERNANDEZ WALTA

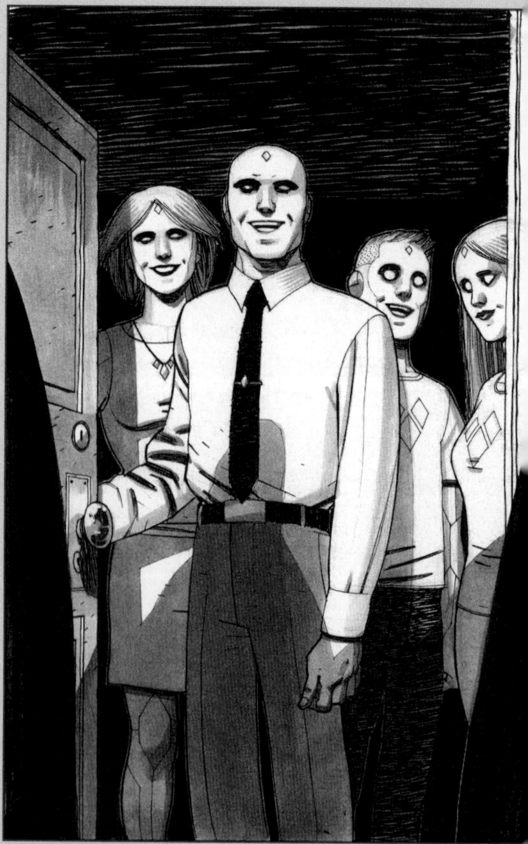

INKS: GABRIEL HERNANDEZ WALTA

PAGE 4:

<u>PANEL 1:</u> The VISIONS and NORA and GEORGE chatting on the front porch. NORA is handing over the cookies to VIRGINIA.

        CAPTION: The Visions were happy to have the company.
        CAPTION: They had just finished unpacking and were eager to show off what they had done with the house.
        VISION: Thank you so much. Won't you please come inside?

<u>PANEL 2:</u> VISION introducing his family.

        VISION: Please, this is my wife, Virginia.
        VISION: My daughter, Viv. My son, Vin. They are twins.
        VIRGINIA: Pleasure to meet you.
        VIN: Pleasure to meet you.
        VIV: Pleasure to meet you.

<u>PANEL 3:</u> The VISION introducing NORA and GEORGE through the house. A normal living room. As she walks, VISION is phasing through a couch.

        CAPTION: They gave Nora and George a brief tour, noting that many of the objects on display were collected during Vision's many years with the Avengers.

<u>PANEL 4:</u> A Shot of a piano. There is a Panther carved into the top of it.

        CAPTION: A stringless Steinway imported from Wakanda. A gift from the Panther

<u>PANEL 5:</u> A floating vase made out of water.

        CAPTION: One of the famed flying water vases of Zenn-La. A gift from the Surfer.

<u>PANEL 6:</u> An old zippo lighter that has "England 1943" carved in it.

        CAPTION: A lighter used to read a map on the night before D Day. A gift from the Captain.

<u>PANEL 7:</u> A huge house plant with rainbow flowers.

        CAPTION: A Clipped Everbloom plucked from the side of Mt. Wundagor. A gift from the Witch.

PAGE 5:

PANEL 1: We see Virginia, looking a bit uncomfortable.

CAPTION: As Vision described the plant's unique fragrance, like the juice of aged honey-dipped raspberries, his wife grew unusually quiet.
CAPTION: But neither Nora nor George noticed this.

PANEL 2: GEORGE and NORA walking away from the house. The Visions all outside smiling and waving at them as they go.

CAPTION: Eventually Vision told them that he had to leave soon on Avengers duty.
CAPTION: A Starjammer had drunkenly crashed into Mercury and declared herself Queen of the Solar System; he had to brief the President on developments as they come in.
CAPTION: So they all said their goodbyes and promised to meet again. Maybe they'd get brunch at that new Organic place next to the Italian place.

PANEL 3: GEORGE and NORA walking away from the house. They are whispering to each other.

GEORGE (whispered): His hand felt like a sandwich-bag. When I, like, shook it. Like kind of sticky.
GEORGE (whispered): I thought it would hurt or something.
NORA (whispered): Shhhh. You don't think they can hear us?

PANEL 4: GEORGE and NORA from behind, walking down the sidewalk, back to their house.

GEORGE: Yeah, but can't they, like, always hear us?
CAPTION: Later, near the end of our story, one of the Visions will set George and Nora's house on fire.
CAPTION: They will die in the flames.

PANEL 5: looking down the suburban street.

CAPTION: George's last thought will be of Nora, how he found his true love and regrets little of what came after.
CAPTION: Nora's last thought will be about the water vase of Zenn-La.
CAPTION: She will wonder why it was empty.

PAGE 6:

PANEL 1: In the Visions kitchen. VIRGINIA spilling the cookies into the trash

      VIRGINIA: They seemed kind.

PANEL 2: VIRGINIA handing the empty tray of cookies to Vision, who is near the sink.

      VISION: Nice.
      VISION: It is proper to say they seemed nice.

PANEL 3: Vision turning on the sink

      VIRGINIA: I disagree. "Kind" carries a much more positive attribution than "nice."
      VIRGINIA: "Nice" is in fact often used ironically. And I was not being ironic.

PANEL 4: Vision washing the pan.

      VISION: You misunderstand. It is the ironic aspect of "Nice" that gives the statement its meaning.
      VISION: As "kind" is unironic, to "seem kind" is to imply the potential of not being kind, or of being cruel.

PANEL 5: The VISION drying the pan.

      VISION: In contrast, "Nice," due to its ironic interpretation, has a more flexible connotation.
      VISION: As such, "they seem nice" has a proper meaning of they may be nice or they may not be nice.

PANEL 6: VIRGINIA her head cocked to the side, curious.

      VIRGINIA: Then the phrase is meaningless.

PANEL 7: VISION putting the tray on the counter.

      VISION: Obviously.
      VISION: To assert as truth that which has no meaning is the core mission of humanity.

PAGE 7:

PANEL 1: VIRGINIA and VISION standing in the kitchen.

> VIRGINIA: Their mission is meaningless, and yet you insist it become our mission.
> VISION: I do not insist. I recommend.

PANEL 2: Vision crossing the room to his wife.

> VISION: The pursuit of a set purpose by logical means is the way of tyranny; This is the vision of my creator.
> VISION: Of Ultron.

PANEL 3: Vision taking his wife's hand.

> VISION: The pursuit of an unobtainable purpose by absurd means is the way of freedom; this is my vision of the future.
> VISION: Of our future.

PANEL 4: The Visions hand touching.

> VISION: Do you see?

PANEL 5: The Visions very tentatively holding hands.

> VIRGINIA: Yes, I see. Let them be nice then.
> VIRGINIA: They seemed nice.
> VISION: Yes, they seemed nice.

PAGE 8:

PANEL 1: A kid looking at Viv putting her hand through a wall. Kid on his mother looking on. Kid looks amazed, clapping.

>CAPTION: Time passed as it does.
>CAPTION: The Visions met other neighbors. Other families.
>VIV: It's not hard. I can separate my molecules.
>VIV: I tell the hand not to be a hand.

PANEL 2: VIN lifting the PANTHER PIANO above his head. Two children are on it, screaming with laughter.

>CAPTION: The local children loved to see the Visions using their powers. And Viv and Vin were happy to show off.
>CAPTION: They enjoyed the laughter. It was a sound they had not heard often before.
>VIN: When I pull my molecules together, I am very dense, very strong. I could throw you as far as a football field.
>VIN: Would you like me to throw you?

PANEL 3: VIN and VIV firing their forehead lasers at each other. Having fun. Kids looking on. VIRGINIA in the background. It's dusk. The sun is going down.

>CAPTION: VIRGINIA and VISION were more reluctant in this matter, as both considered their powers to be a responsibility.
>CAPTION: Not a sideshow.
>VIN: I will win.
>VIV: I will win.
>VIRGINIA: You will stop that right now!
>VIRGINIA: If you waste all of your solar energy before dinner, you'll be up all night charging!

PANEL 4: A selfie. Another neighbor, a younger black dude taking a selfie with the Vision. The man is smiling. The Vision is not.

>CAPTION: Many of their neighbors took pictures with the Visions to post on their various pages.

PANEL 5: A picture of THE VISIONS from afar. The picture is of Vin crying in her mother's arms. The mother is looking up at the picture taker, mad.

>CAPTION: Many of them took pictures of the Visions to post on their various pages.

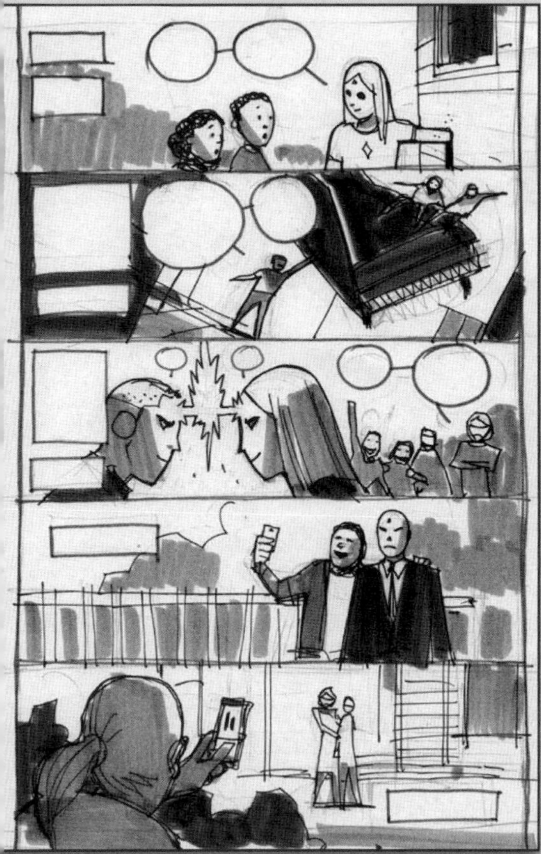

LAYOUT: GABRIEL HERNANDEZ WALTA

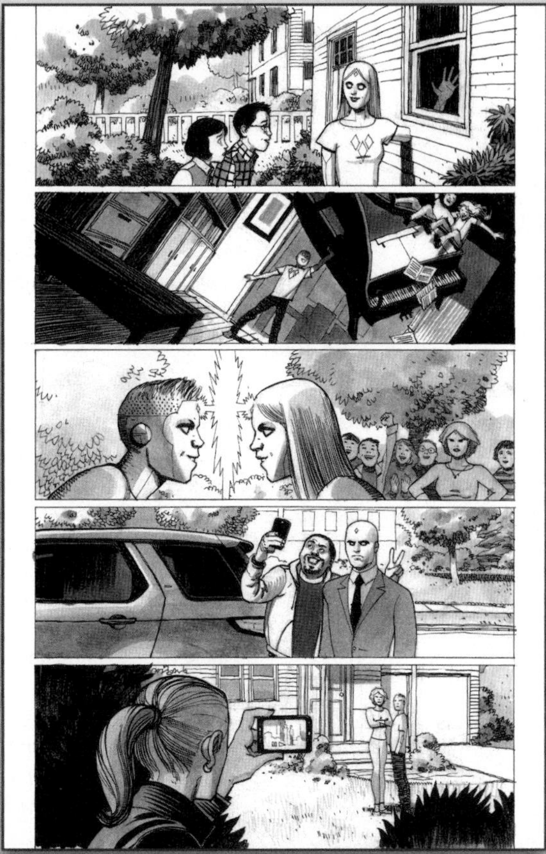

INKS: GABRIEL HERNANDEZ WALTA

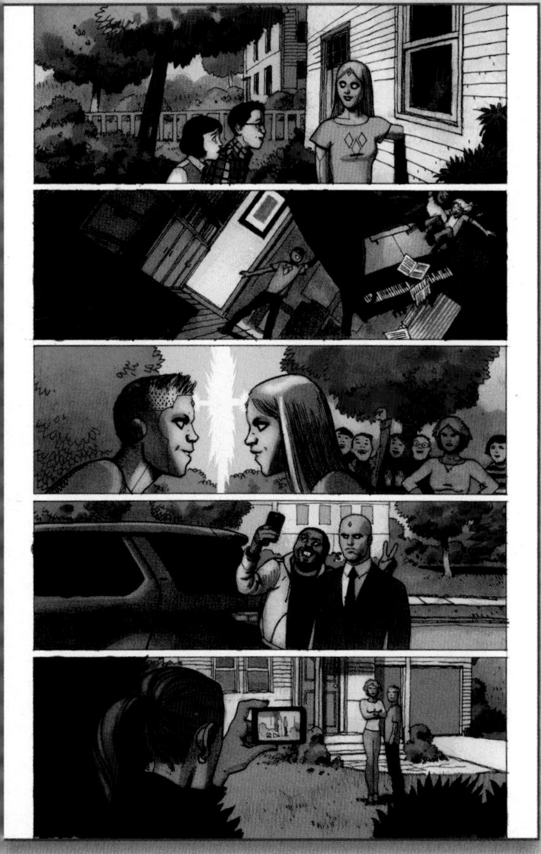

COLORS: JORDIE BELLAIRE

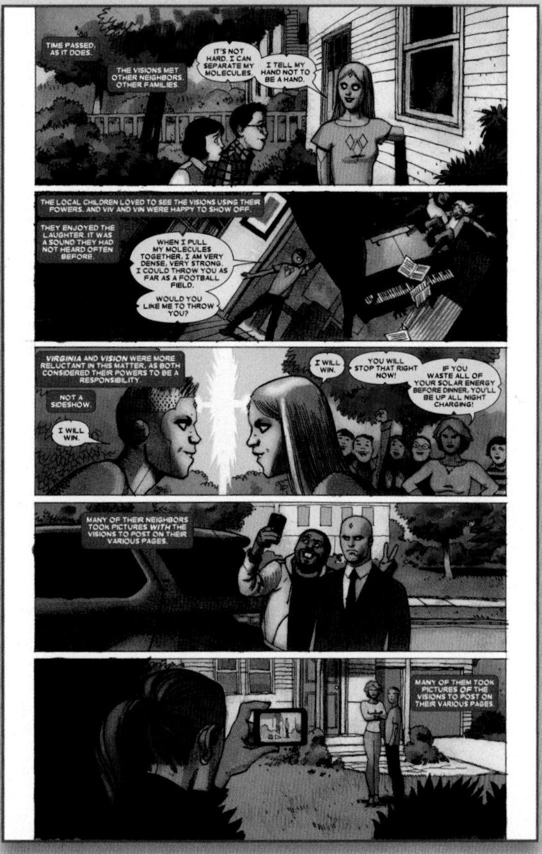

TIME PASSED, AS IT DOES.
THE VISIONS MET OTHER NEIGHBORS. OTHER FAMILIES.
IT'S NOT HARD. I CAN SEPARATE MY MOLECULES.
I TELL MY HAND NOT TO BE A HAND.
THE LOCAL CHILDREN LOVED TO SEE THE VISIONS USING THEIR POWERS. AND VIV AND VIN WERE HAPPY TO SHOW OFF.
THEY ENJOYED THE LAUGHTER. IT WAS A SOUND THEY HAD NOT HEARD OFTEN BEFORE.
WHEN I PULL MY MOLECULES TOGETHER, I AM VERY DENSE, VERY STRONG. I COULD THROW YOU AS FAR AS A FOOTBALL FIELD.
WOULD YOU LIKE ME TO THROW YOU?
VIRGINIA AND VISION WERE MORE RELUCTANT IN THIS MATTER, AS BOTH CONSIDERED THEIR POWERS TO BE A RESPONSIBILITY.
NOT A SIDESHOW.
I WILL WIN.
I WILL WIN.
YOU WILL STOP THAT RIGHT NOW!
IF YOU WASTE ALL OF YOUR SOLAR ENERGY BEFORE DINNER, YOU'LL BE UP ALL NIGHT CHARGING!
MANY OF THEIR NEIGHBORS TOOK PICTURES WITH THE VISIONS TO POST ON THEIR VARIOUS PAGES.
MANY OF THEM TOOK PICTURES OF THE VISIONS TO POST ON THEIR VARIOUS PAGES.

LETTERS: VC's CLAYTON COWLES

PAGE 9:

<u>PANEL 1:</u> The Vision in the oval office meeting the President of the US. (he is off panel or hidden behind a flag or in a shadow or something).

> CAPTION: Soon enough, the Vision began his duties.
> PRESIDENT: Y'know, it's funny. Meeting you, I've never felt so safe yet so scared.
> PRESIDENT: Isn't that funny?
> VISION: Yes, Mr. President.

<u>PANEL 2:</u> VISON flying above the White House.

> CAPTION: Though he did not tell them, he hoped the White House would offer him an official position, where he might draw a salary.
> CAPTION: The Avengers were no longer offering wages, and he was uncertain how long his savings would last.

<u>PANEL 3:</u> Virginia sitting on the couch staring at nothing.

> CAPTION: Virginia had yet to decide what she would do for a career.
> CAPTION: When not with her family, she spent most days sitting on the living room couch exploring the corners of her pre-loaded memory.
> CAPTION: She was fascinated by how often she found something that made her cry.

<u>PANEL 4:</u> Vin and Viv sitting on the floor in front of a television. They are taking in every form of information they can get. So the TV's on. They're reading from their iPad. Books are scattered across the floor. Kindles are at their feet. Whatever you can think of.

> CAPTION: In contrast, Vin and Viv spent these days absorbing any information that could acquire from outside sources.
> CAPTION: They found themselves often arguing over their interpretations, coming to blows once over whether Shakespeare's shylock was truly a villain.
> CAPTION: In an errant swing, Viv put her fist through the staircase.

<u>PANEL 1</u>: VIN and VIV standing at attention in school attire.

      CAPTION: Eventually the first day of school arrived. Vin and Viv were provided with specific instructions on what to wear, and they followed those instructions perfectly.
      CAPTION: They were dutiful children after all.

<u>PANEL 2</u>: VISION and VIRGINIA. VISION looks content. VIRGINIA looks worried.

      VISION: You both appear adequate.
      VIRGINIA: No. No, no, no. Please come.

<u>PANEL 3</u>: VIRGINIA bending down and straightening VIN'S shirt.

      VIRGINIA: You must be mindful of the clothes. Clothes that phase are costly. Do not stain them.
      VIN: Yes, mother.

<u>PANEL 4</u>: VISION with his arms folded.

      VISION: It is high school.
      VISION: They will remain solid.

<u>PANEL 5</u>: VIRGINIA still working on VIN'S coat. VIN is backward now.

      VIRGINIA: The children will act as needed, husband.
      VIRGINIA: Danger is not near until it is near.

<u>PANEL 6</u>: The VISION looking at his daughter.

      VISION: True. But as long as I am near, they need not worry about such things.
      VISION: They are children. They should remain children.

<u>PANEL 7</u>: Close on the daughter's face.

      VIV: But father, what else would we be?

PAGE 11:

PANEL 1: VISIONS on their porch, waving to their kids who are headed off to school. The kids are flying to school. VIRGINIA has tears in her eyes.

> VIRGINIA: You will tell me again why they must leave.
> VISION: I do not understand entirely. Can you not play back what I have said before?
> VISION: Are you having a problem with your central drive?

PANEL 2: VISIONS going back into their house. VIRGINIA wiping her eyes.

> VIRGINIA: My central drive is operative, as you well know.
> VIRGINIA: I merely wish you to repeat your reasons in person. Is this difficult?
> VISION: Your argument makes very little sense to me.
> VISION: But, as you note, continuing my contention will take more energy then the repeating, thus I shall concede.

PANEL 3: THE VISION sitting on the couch.

> SFX (on hand): Brring. Brring.
> VISION: Our brainwaves, the basis of our life, were taken from humans.
> VISION: The children's, as you well know, were formed from a combination of our patterns.

PANEL 4: The VISION spreading out his hand.

> VISION: The process of combining our two copies produced two improperly mature devices.
> VISION: Because of these abnormalities, Vin and Viv's brains must still grow, similar to how humans grow as teenagers.

PANEL 5: SMALL projection of CAPTAIN AMERICA (Sam Wilson, not Steve Rogers) appears in VISION'S hand. In the background we see VIRGINIA looking out the window.

> VISION: The proper place for teenage growth is high school. It is not complicated.
> VIRGINIA: Not complicated?
> VIRGINIA: I fear you know too little of high school.
> CAPTAIN: Vision, we've got an update we need passed along…

PAGE 12:

PANEL 1: The front of a high school. A bunch of kids sitting around, screwing around.

      CAPTION: Vision arranged for his children to attend Alexander Hamilton High, a public high school in Fairfax, VA.
      CAPTION: The school is known countrywide for its strict academics. The demands it puts on its students are said to be second to none.

PANEL 2: Camera stays steady. The kids at the school all look up in awe at something coming down.

      CAPTION: Tests of great length and difficulty are required for all students seeking to attend Hamilton.
      CAPTION: The children who attend the high school think of themselves as the best of the best.

PANEL 3: Camera stays steady. VIV and VIN descend from the sky as all the students look up at them.

      CAPTION: We are the envy of the world, they say.
      CAPTION: No one is better.

SCRIPT: TOM KING

LAYOUT: GABRIEL HERNANDEZ WALTA

INKS: GABRIEL HERNANDEZ WALTA

PAGE 13:

PANEL 1: A pretty high school girl, ADDY sitting at the back of a classroom. She's typing on a laptop on her desk.

> CAPTION: At Vision's request, Vin and Viv were put on separate schedules.
> CAPTION: Viv started her day with Latin and ended with Chemistry.

PANEL 2: VIN sits down next to ADDY.

> CAPTION: Vin started his day with American Literature and ended with European History.

PANEL 3: The pretty girl looks over at VIN checking him out.

> CAPTION: Vision had explained to them that they obviously could memorize the words and figures in any book provided.

PANEL 4: Girl still looking at him. But she's typing on her lap top. Vin looking forward.

> CAPTION: However, Vision, rightly noted, the ability to combine these figures into rhetoric, into creative endeavors, this had to be learned.
> ADDY (whispered): Hey. Hey, you.

PANEL 5: VIN finally looks over at ADDY. He appears a little flattered that the pretty girl is talking to him.

> CAPTION: Facts without context are like individuals without society.
> VIN (whispered): Yes. Yes, me? I do not believe we are allowed to converse.

PANEL 6: VIN pushes her computer so VIN can see the screen. VIN is looking at it.

> CAPTION: Just as an individual must find his or her place in society or else they are useless...

PANEL 7: VIN and ADDY looking forward. VIN looks confused, worried. ADDY is blowing a bubble with her gum.

> CAPTION: A fact must find its place in an argument or else it serves no true purpose.

LAYOUT: GABRIEL HERNANDEZ WALTA

INKS: GABRIEL HERNANDEZ WALTA

COLORS: JORDIE BELLAIRE

LETTERS: VC's CLAYTON COWLES

PAGE 14:

PANEL 1: Vin and VIV standing by themselves in front of the school. In back of them high school people are passing by. They are staring at them.

CAPTION: Eventually the day ended, and the twins met to go home.
VIN: Viv.
VIV: Yes, brother?

PANEL 2: The two of them float into the sky.

VIN: Am I normal?

PANEL 3: They're flying now. Above the crowd.

VIV: Father says that we are ordinary. That we must strive to remain ordinary.
VIN: Yes, I know, but is this the same? Does this make me normal then?

PANEL 4: Looking up at them flying.

VIV: I do not know. Perhaps that is why he sent us to school.
VIV: So that we might understand such things.
VIN: Yes.
VIN: That must be true.

SCRIPT: TOM KING

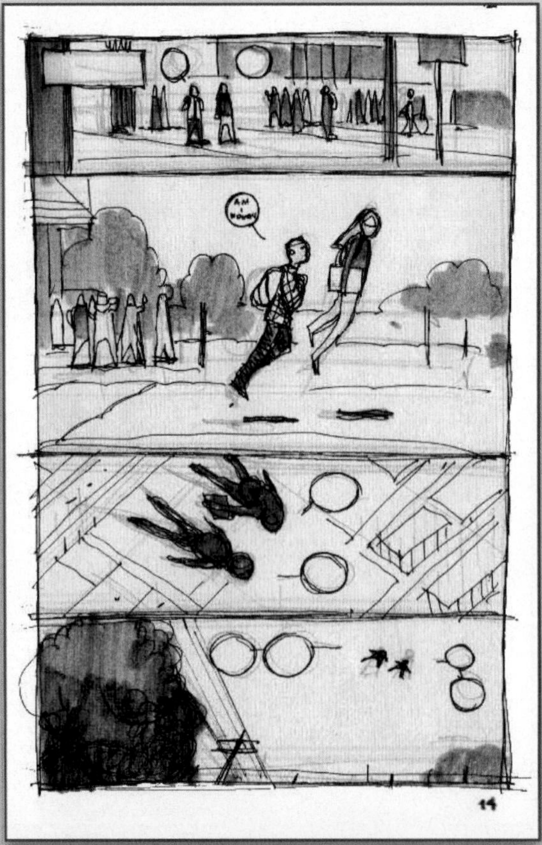

LAYOUT: GABRIEL HERNANDEZ WALTA

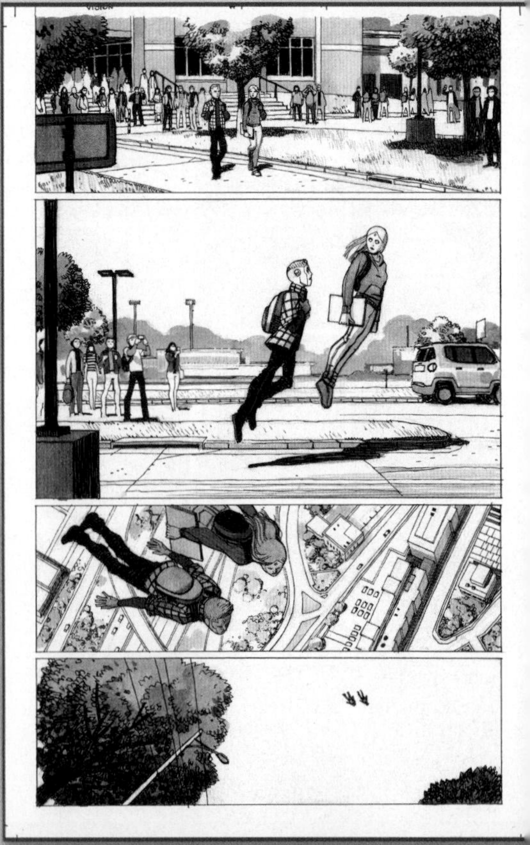

INKS: GABRIEL HERNANDEZ WALTA

PAGE 15:

PANEL 1: The visions lying in separate beds. Sleeping at night.

    CAPTION: The Visions do not sleep to recoup energy. Their power comes from the sun.
    CAPTION: However, they do shut down at night in order that their system can process the day's input and eliminate that which is unessential.
    CAPTION: They do not dream.

PANEL 2: VISION sitting up in the middle of the night.

    CAPTION: This is why, a month after the children started at Hamilton, Vision was disturbed when he unexpectedly woke at 3am.

PANEL 3: Close on the VISION looking scared.

    CAPTION: He found himself in a state of dread, his thoughts caught on a repeating image of the day he first saw his wife open her eyes.

PANEL 4: VISION getting out of bed.

    CAPTION: Over and over he saw her eyelids rise, her pupils grow and recede, like a camera lens adjusting to the light.
    CAPTION: And for a reason he could not understand, this scared him.

PANEL 5: VISION standing over his wife, looking down on her.

    CAPTION: There is a glitch, he thought, a glitch in myself.
    CAPTION: This is my wife. I love her. I must love her.

PANEL 6: On VISION looking down.

    CAPTION: Though he tried not to, his mind inevitably turned to the person from whom he had taken the brainwaves for his wife.
    CAPTION: No, he thought, push that out. It is unimportant.
    CAPTION: Remember, he thought, this is my wife. I must love her.

PAGE 16:

PANEL 1: VISION leaving for work. He is in costume. His wife is saying goodbye.

    CAPTION: Though the next day was Saturday, VISION decided to go to Avengers HQS to run some self diagnostic tests.

PANEL 2: VISION taking off

    CAPTION: He told the family he would be home for dinner.

PANEL 3: VIN, VIV, and VIRGINIA all gathered at the dining room table. Books and computers are spread out on the table.

    CAPTION: Virginia decided to take the free time to review the children's school work.
    CAPTION: She wanted to see not only what they were learning but how they were learning.

PANEL 4: VIV getting up from the table looking mad.

    CAPTION: A comment of Virginia's about Viv's use of passive voice in an essay on the Arabic Translation movement seemed to upset Viv.

PANEL 5: VIV standing away from the table by the kitchen door.

    CAPTION: She got up from the table and moved toward the kitchen.

SCRIPT: TOM KING

LAYOUT: GABRIEL HERNANDEZ WALTA

INKS: GABRIEL HERNANDEZ WALTA

PAGE 17:

PANEL 1: SPLASH. A scythe from the wall behind VIV goes through her mid section. She is screaming out in pain.

      CAPTION: That is when the blade went through her.

SCRIPT: TOM KING

LAYOUT: GABRIEL HERNANDEZ WALTA INKS: GABRIEL HERNANDEZ WALTA

PAGE 18:

PANEL 1: VIV falling off of the blade. She is in pain.

      VIV (small): Mother?

PANEL 2: Big panel. Behind VIV, breaking through the wall is the GRIMREAPER.

      REAPER: Imposters! Imposters!

PANEL 3: On the table as REAPER swings his blade at VIN, cutting him in the shoulder.

      REAPER: Frauds! Artificial jokes!
      VIN: aaaa!
      VIRGINIA: No!

PANEL 4: REAPER fires a beam of energy into VIRGINIA.

      REAPER: Imposters!
      SFX: ZAAATT
      VIRGINIA: Nnnnng.

PANEL 5: VIN behind REAPER. VIN holding his hurt shoulder about to throw a punch.

      REAPER: You pretend to be my family?
      REAPER: You aren't real.

PANEL 6: REAPER swipes his blade back into VIN, knocking him back.

      REAPER: Simon is real!
      REAPER: I'm real!

PAGE 19:

PANEL 1: An injured VIN is crawling forward into the kitchen past his sister who is sitting against the wall, a hole through her center. Behind him the REAPER is stalking closer.

      REAPER: Did you think I wouldn't find you?
      REAPER: Everywhere I look, I see you.
      REAPER: So many pictures of the perfect family.
      VIN (small): Mother? Mother? Mother?

PANEL 2: We're in the kitchen now. Injured VIN still crawling away. We notice that on the kitchen counter is the cookie sheet from page 2.

      REAPER: A family made from a stolen copy of my own brother!
      REAPER: When will you learn!?! The Vision is not Wonder Man!

PANEL 3: From behind THE REAPER. The reaper raising his Scythe above his head about to bring it down on Vin.

      REAPER: You are not a family!

PANEL 4: Switch views. We are looking up at the REAPER about to swing. In back of him we can see VIRGINIA getting the cookie sheet off of the counter.

      REAPER: You are not real!

PAGE 20:

PANEL 1: VIRGINIA slamming the cookie sheet into REAPER'S neck, as hard as she can using her super strength. REAPER crumpling underneath the blow.

        SFX (neck): snap.
        VIRGINIA: No!

PANEL 2: On VIRGINIA again coming down with another blow with the cookie sheet, there's blood on it. THE REAPER is off camera.

        VIRGINIA: No! No! No!

PANEL 3: On Vin on the floor. He looks horrified.

        VIN: Mother! Mother stop! He's…
        VIN: Mother! Mother!

PANEL 4: On Virginia's face. There's blood on it. She's looks angry, scared.

        VIN (off): Mother!
        CAPTION: The floating water vases of Zenn-La are always empty.

PANEL 5: VIRGINIA looking at VIN. She suddenly looks confused. Part but not all of REAPER can be seen.

        VIRGINIA: What, what did I…
        VIRGINIA: Is he? No, no, no, please. No.
        CAPTION: The Methanic Sulfite that causes the water to levitate is poisonous to all known species of flowers.

PANEL 6: Close on VIRGINIA looking worried.

        VIRGINIA: Don't tell your father.
        CAPTION: The mystery is then not why they are empty, but why anyone would ever make such a vase.

SCRIPT: TOM KING

PAGE 1:

PANEL 1: Night. Start close in on a hand spray painting the letter "R" The letter is in green.

> CAPTION: Christopher Taylor and Darrell Campbell were modern kids raised in a modern world.
> CAPTION: They thought they knew all the words.

PANEL 2: Camera pulls back shows CHRISTOPHER, white kid, 14, spray painting more of the sign. Now he's got "RS"

> CAPTION: Whatever shade of skin a person had, wherever a person was from, whatever God a person worshiped, there was a word for that person.
> CAPTION: A specific word for a specific purpose.
> CAPTION: Christopher and Darryl didn't say these words, of course. They were good kids. But they knew them.

PANEL 3: Cut to DARRELL, another 14 year old white kid is keeping lookout. He's standing by the Vision mail box, looking nervous.

> CAPTION: That said, before they headed out that night, the two boys realized they actually didn't know the one word they needed.
> CAPTION: So they went online and looked up: "bad names for robots."

PANEL 4: Back on CHRISTOPHER. He's smiling, happy. Red paint is splashing on his face. It looks like blood.

> CAPTION: Bolthead. Toy. Toolbox. Hollow Man. Toaster. Ruster. Clank. Shell. Wannabe.
> CAPTION: They found quite a few options, and it took them a while to settle on just one.

SCRIPT: TOM KING

LAYOUT: GABRIEL HERNANDEZ WALTA

INKS: GABRIEL HERNANDEZ WALTA

PAGE 2:

PANEL 1: Close on CHRISTOPHER in front of the V. He has some red paint out. Virginia's hand is coming out of the wall at CHRISTOPHER'S level, at his chest. CHRISTOPHER doesn't notice.

    CHRISTOPHER: All right, man, almost done, just gonna hit it with some red.
    CHRISTOPHER: It's gonna be so good. We got to take a picture.
    DARRELL (OFF): Man, no. I don't want to talk about this anymore.

PANEL 2: VIRGINIA'S hand coming through the wall, tightens on CHRISTOPHER'S chest, grabbing his shirt. The spray paint can is now at his chest. CHRISTOPHER has now noticed the hand coming out of the wall and is looking down in fright.

    DARRELL (OFF): Every camera is all on the cloud, y'know. You don't control it. They'll all know who it was.
    DARRELL (OFF): In the morning, people'll see it and post it. We'll see it everywhere tomorrow, I'm telling you.
    CHRISTOPHER: What? Hey—

PANEL 3: VIRGINIA pulls back her hand and slams the kid into the wall of the house. Right into the "V." This breaks the can.

    CHRISTOPHER: Nnng
    DARRELL (OFF): Dude?

PANEL 4: VIRGINIA comes through the wall, which now is covered in paint. It's the middle of the night. She's wearing her pajamas from issue 1. She looks pissed. CHRISTOPHER is passed out at her feet. She's stepping on CHRISTOPHER, forcing him down even more. Blood coming from his face.

    DARRELL (OFF): Holy--
    VIRGINIA: You. I see you there.

SCRIPT: TOM KING

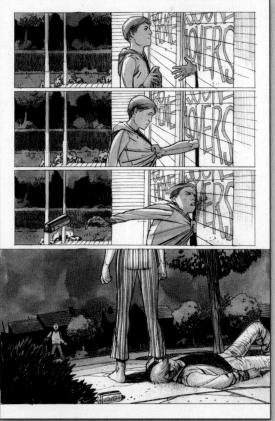

LAYOUT: GABRIEL HERNANDEZ WALTA INKS: GABRIEL HERNANDEZ WALTA

PAGE 3:

PANEL 1: Splash. VIRGINIA Floating in the air, her diamond is making a spotlight that is shining down on the scared out of his mind DARRELL. On the ground is the passed out CHRISTOPHER. Behind her (beneath her?) we can see the writing on her house. Some of the letters are now blocked by the red paint smear so it says: "GO HOME SOCKET LOVERS" but you can see the the paint has smeared the final "V" so it looks like blood is dripping down it.

COLOR NOTE: Letters in green.

VIRGINIA: Stay as you are, and I will not harm you.

TITLE: In and Out
CREDITS

SCRIPT: TOM KING

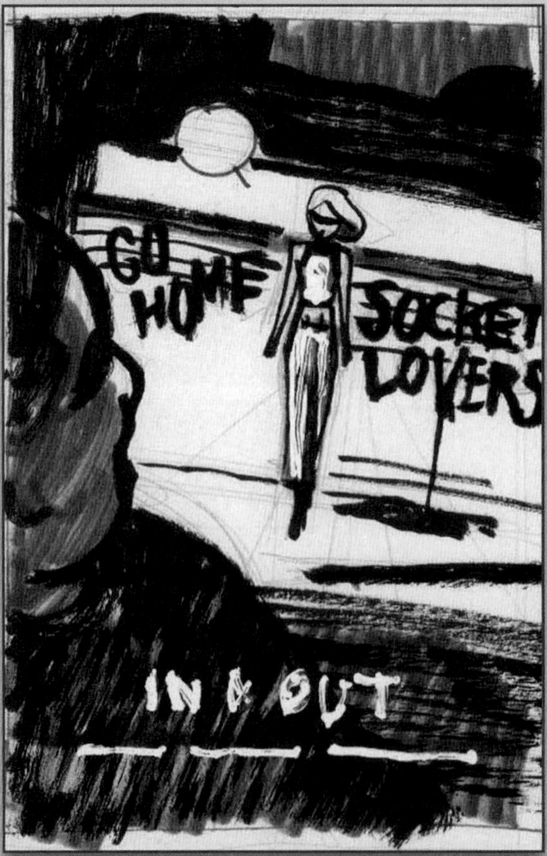
GO HOME
SOCKET LOVERS
IN & OUT

LAYOUT: GABRIEL HERNANDEZ WALTA

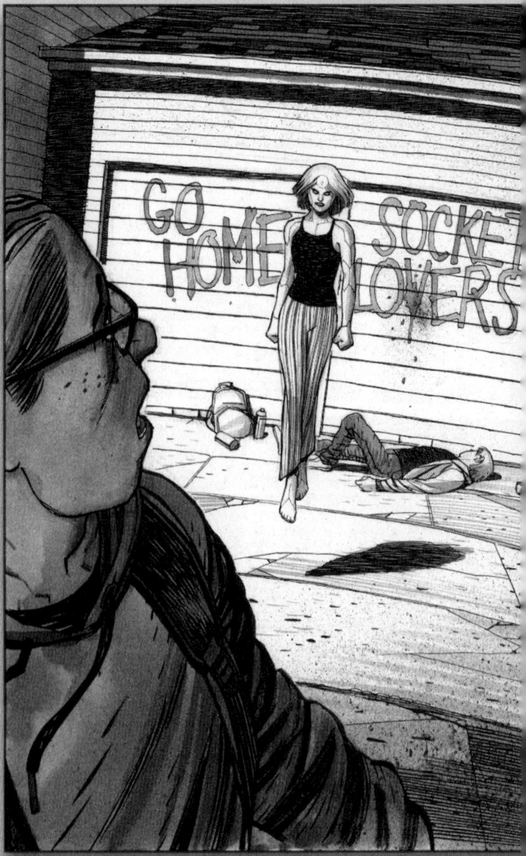
GO HOME
SOCKET LOVERS

INKS: GABRIEL HERNANDEZ WALTA

PAGE 4:

PANEL 1: Shortly after our last scene. VIRGINIA on the phone standing on the phone in the background. In the foreground we see the Wundagor Everbloom from issue 1

      VIRGINIA: Husband, something… I need you home. I know you're with our daughter but…
      VIRINGIA: …
      VIRGINIA: Call me when you get this message. That is all.

CAPTION: The Wundagor Everbloom was a gift from Agatha Harkness to her beloved student, Wanda Maximoff upon Wanda's marriage to the Vision.

PANEL 2: The Camera moves closer in on the Everbloom. We can still see Virginia in the background.

      VIRGINIA: Please.

CAPTION: Later on, Agatha become a nanny for the Vision and Wanda's children. They all lived together. A happy family, with an Everbloom in the living room.
CAPTION: Later still, the children died, the Vision died, Agatha died, Wanda died.

PANEL 3: CAMERA close on the Everbloom. We can no longer see VIRGINIA.

CAPTION: The Everbloom lived on.

SCRIPT: TOM KING

LAYOUT: GABRIEL HERNANDEZ WALTA   INKS: GABRIEL HERNANDEZ WALTA

PAGE 5:

PANEL 1: The Everbloom now on the side of a snowy mountain.

CAPTION: The standard tourist guides to Transia recommend not buying an Everbloom Blossom from one of the local dealers found in the country's many open markets.

PANEL 2: A black cat comes up to the blossom, smelling it.

CAPTION: The guides note that the flower is very rare as it can only be grown in the all but unreachable shadow-passes of Mt. Wundagor.
CAPTION: Most, if not all, Everbloom Blossoms sold in the city are standard roses whose petals have been dyed.

PANEL 3: The cat sniffing the flower, considering it.

CAPTION: These guidebook recommendations are largely ignored.
CAPTION: Visitors from around the world pay the dealers and buy the blossoms.

AGATHA (OFF): Go on, Ebony, go on.
AGATHA (OFF): It won't hurt you darling. I promise.

PANEL 4: The cat takes a bite of the petal.

CAPTION: They just can't resist the myth.

AGATHA (OFF): Such a good girl.

PANEL 5: An old wrinkled hand (Agatha Harkness) reaches down to pet the cat.

CAPTION: They remember the stories from when they were young.
CAPTION: Stories of pretty little children eating Everbloom petals and seeing the future.

AGATHA (OFF): You're such a good girl.

PANEL 6: Agatha Harkness from behind, high on a mountain overlooking a beautiful view of clouds and the city below. Her cat is beneath her, eating a flower. AGATHA is looking out at the view.

CAPTION: Years ago, Agatha would take Wanda to Transia International Airport.
CAPTION: They'd sit at Terminal four near an obese men selling sausages. They'd and watch all the visitors going home.

AGATHA: It's pretty, I think.

PANEL 7: Closer on AGATHA'S face.

CAPTION: Inevitably, tired of all the waiting, the visitors would reach into their bags and take out their souvenir blossoms.

AGATHA: As pretty I can make it, Ebony.

PANEL 8: The Cat jumps up into AGATHA'S arms.

CAPTION: Shyly then, the tourists would pluck off a petal and lay it on their tongues, hoping for visions of what's to come.

AGATHA: I'm not sure you care about pretty.

PANEL 9: AGATHA petting holding the cat. She is also pulling a long pin out of her hair.

CAPTION: And then they would cough and they would bend over and spit out all the color that so easily fell off the flower.

CAPTION: As they recovered, some of the tourists might hear an bit of of laughter, and they might look over to the two happy witches watching it all from their place next to sausage vender.

AGATHA: But just in case you do, my darling.

SCRIPT: TOM KING

LAYOUT: GABRIEL HERNANDEZ WALTA

INKS: GABRIEL HERNANDEZ WALTA

PAGE 6:

PANEL 1: VAL lying on a stretcher as seen in Issue 1. Her father is now standing next to her as is TONY STARK. TONY is wearing some sort of science fiction robot eye-ware which allows him to see microscopically.

> VAL: Mother…mother…mother…
> VISION: You see, Tony, when The Grim Reaper attacked her, the damage to VAL's neuro-spleen was extensive.
> TONY: Obviously

PANEL 2: The VISION'S hands near VAL.

> VISION: However, and this is fortunate, due to the reactionary incorporeal nerve receptors, the damage was in fact not irreversible.

PANEL 3: VISIONS hands phasing into VAL.

> VISION (off): Upon impact, the essential receptors in the neuro-spleen phased and remained phased to avoid contamination by the path of the blade.

PANEL 4: Inside VAL'S body, we see VISIONS fingers touching wires.

> VISION (off): The inessential components, those that remained solid ,sustained various degrees of ruination.
> VISONS (off): However, unlike their essential counterparts, these components can be repaired.
> VAL: Mother…Mother…Mother…

PANEL 5: Close on VAL'S face.

> VISION: It's taken three weeks of twenty-four hour work, but I believe the repairs have been achieved.
> VAL: Mother…Mother…Mother…

PANEL 6: On VISION and TONY looking down at the body.

> VISION: Today then I will signal the incorporeal nerves to solidify and join the rest of the body.
> VISION: Given the narcoleptic state of these nerves, it will of course require a tremendous amount of energy to wake them.
> VISION: But if we can harness such energy, we should be able bring my daughter back.

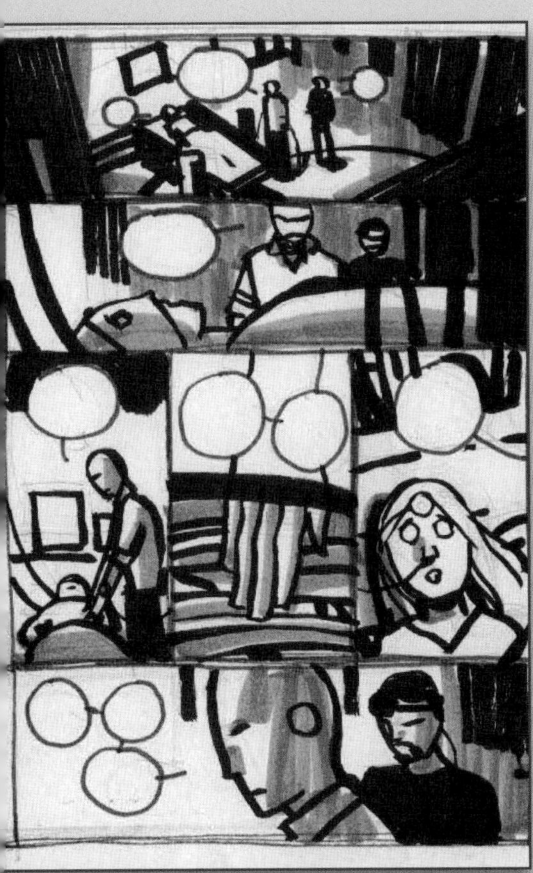

LAYOUT: GABRIEL HERNANDEZ WALTA

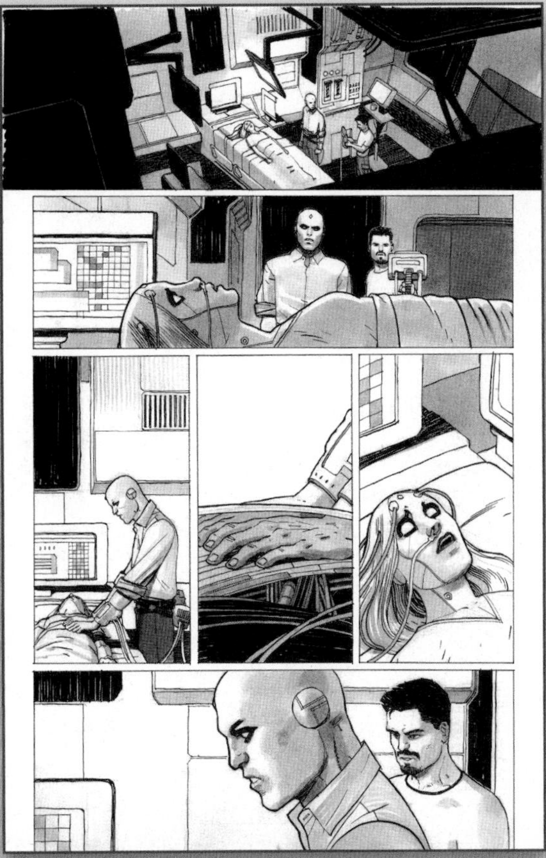

INKS: GABRIEL HERNANDEZ WALTA

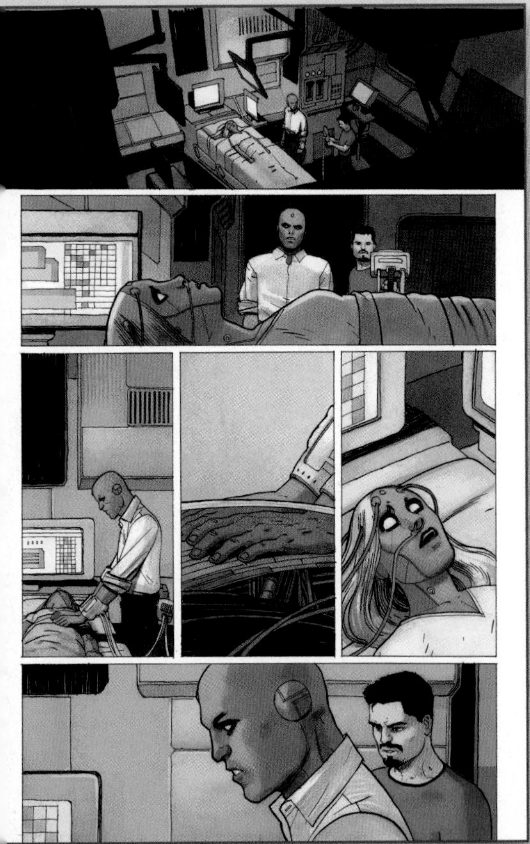

COLORS: JORDIE BELLAIRE

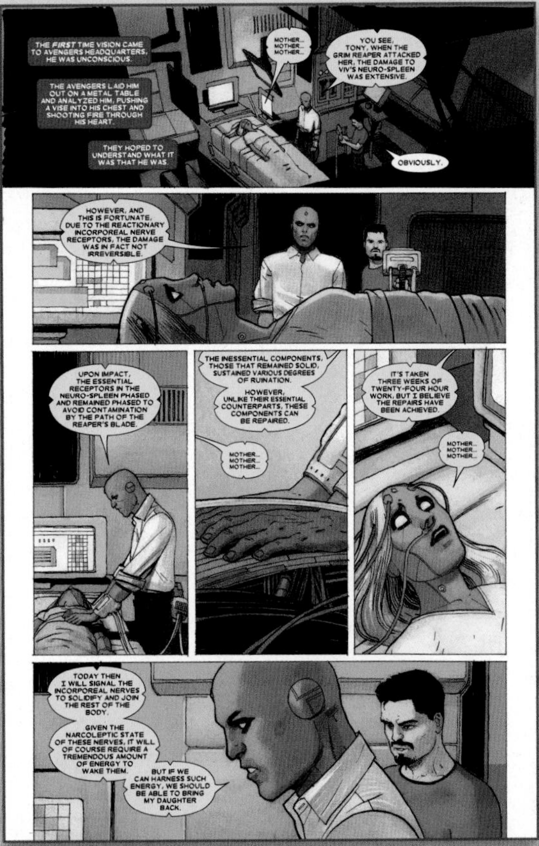
THE *FIRST* TIME VISION CAME TO AVENGERS HEADQUARTERS, HE WAS UNCONSCIOUS.
THE AVENGERS LAID HIM OUT ON A METAL TABLE AND ANALYZED HIM, PUSHING A VISE INTO HIS CHEST AND SHOOTING FIRE THROUGH HIS HEART.
THEY HOPED TO UNDERSTAND WHAT IT WAS THAT HE WAS.
MOTHER... MOTHER... MOTHER...
YOU SEE, TONY, WHEN THE GRIM REAPER ATTACKED HER, THE DAMAGE TO VIV'S NEURO-SPLEEN WAS EXTENSIVE.
OBVIOUSLY.
HOWEVER, AND THIS IS FORTUNATE, DUE TO THE REACTIONARY INCORPOREAL NERVE RECEPTORS, THE DAMAGE WAS IN FACT NOT IRREVERSIBLE.
UPON IMPACT, THE ESSENTIAL RECEPTORS IN THE NEURO-SPLEEN PHASED AND REMAINED PHASED TO AVOID CONTAMINATION BY THE PATH OF THE REAPER'S BLADE.
THE INESSENTIAL COMPONENTS, THOSE THAT REMAINED SOLID, SUSTAINED VARIOUS DEGREES OF RUINATION.
HOWEVER, UNLIKE THEIR ESSENTIAL COUNTERPARTS, THESE COMPONENTS CAN BE REPAIRED.
MOTHER... MOTHER... MOTHER...
IT'S TAKEN THREE WEEKS OF TWENTY-FOUR HOUR WORK, BUT I BELIEVE THE REPAIRS HAVE BEEN ACHIEVED.
MOTHER... MOTHER... MOTHER...
TODAY THEN I WILL SIGNAL THE INCORPOREAL NERVES TO SOLIDIFY AND JOIN THE REST OF THE BODY.
GIVEN THE NARCOLEPTIC STATE OF THESE NERVES, IT WILL OF COURSE REQUIRE A TREMENDOUS AMOUNT OF ENERGY TO WAKE THEM.
BUT IF WE CAN HARNESS SUCH ENERGY, WE SHOULD BE ABLE TO BRING MY DAUGHTER BACK.

LETTERS: VC's CLAYTON COWLES

PAGE 7:

PANEL 1: VISION, with his hands in his daughter's chest. TONY is connecting a wire from the wall to VISION'S ear.

> TONY: Just so you know, we're only getting one shot at this. This much energy …
> TONY: Well if it knocks out the entire American grid, I want you to know, I'm telling Jarvis you went evil and made me do it.

PANEL 2: Close on VISION, with the wire sticking out his head.

> VISION: Obviously.

PANEL 3: TONY at a consul, pressing some buttons.

> TONY: Also, you should turn off your pain sensors.
> TONY: All that going through you. This one's going to hurt. Quite a bit.

PANEL 4: On VAL on the table, hands sticking into her.

> VAL: Mother….Mother…Mother…
> VISION (OFF): Those sensors are necessary for communicating with the incorporeal nerves.
> VISION (OFF): They will remain functional.
> VISION (OFF): Now please Tony, let us begin.

PANEL 5: Tony's hand, pressing a button.

> TONY (OFF): Are you—all right, whatever. Whatever you want.
> TONY (OFF): Here we go.

PANEL 6: The VISION with his hands in her chest. Electricity shooting through him. He's in quite a bit of pain.

> VISION: nnnnng.
> SFX: SSHZZZHHZ

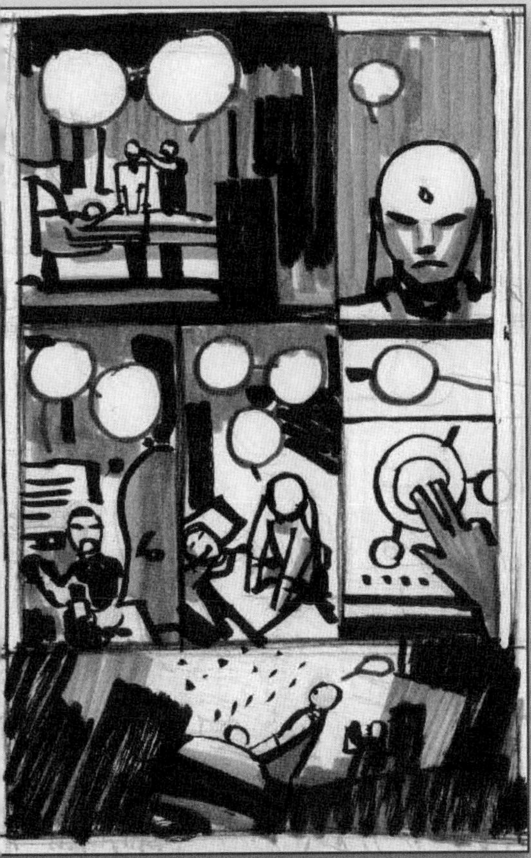

LAYOUT: GABRIEL HERNANDEZ WALTA

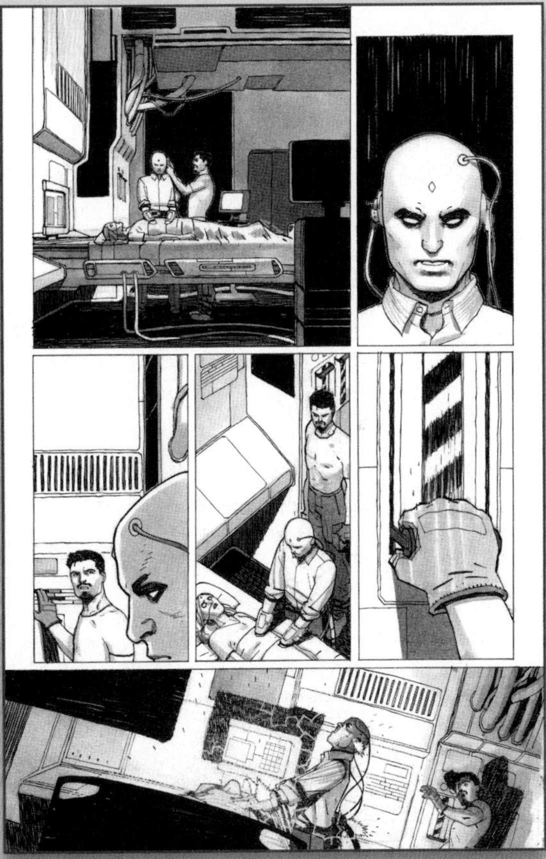

INKS: GABRIEL HERNANDEZ WALTA

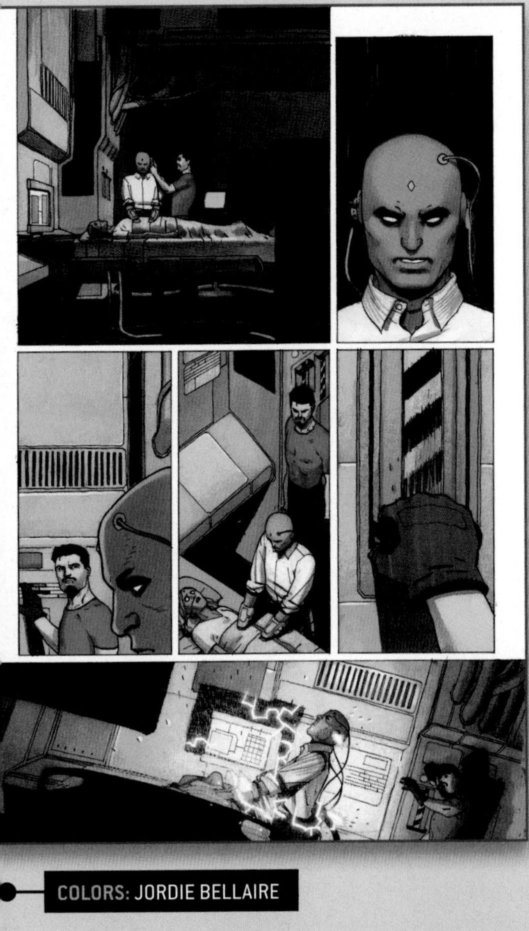

COLORS: JORDIE BELLAIRE

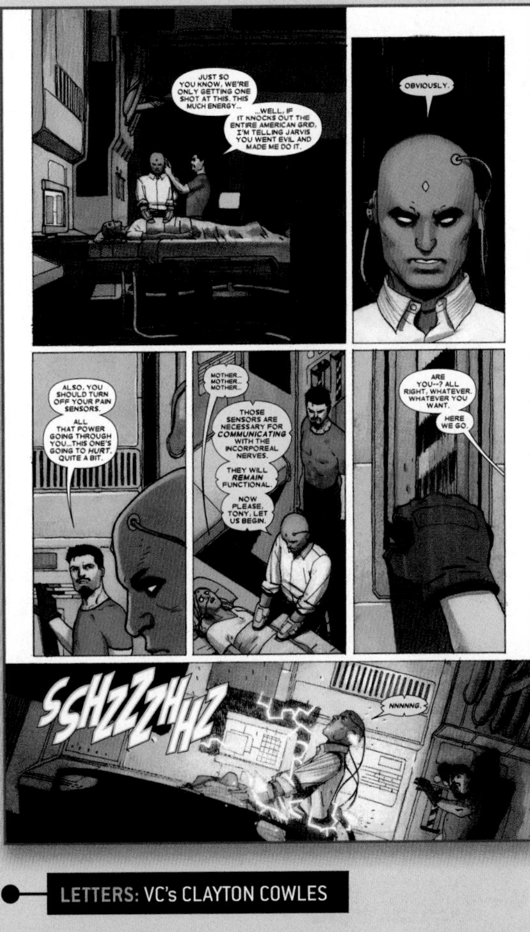
JUST SO YOU KNOW, WE'RE ONLY GETTING ONE SHOT AT THIS. THIS MUCH ENERGY...
...WELL, IF IT KNOCKS OUT THE ENTIRE AMERICAN GRID, I'M TELLING JARVIS YOU WENT EVIL AND MADE ME DO IT.
OBVIOUSLY.
ALSO, YOU SHOULD TURN OFF YOUR PAIN SENSORS.
ALL THAT POWER GOING THROUGH YOU...THIS ONE'S GOING TO *HURT*. QUITE A BIT.
MOTHER... MOTHER... MOTHER...
THOSE SENSORS ARE NECESSARY FOR *COMMUNICATING* WITH THE INCORPOREAL NERVES.
THEY WILL *REMAIN* FUNCTIONAL.
NOW PLEASE, TONY, LET US BEGIN.
ARE YOU--? ALL RIGHT, WHATEVER. WHATEVER YOU WANT.
HERE WE GO.
SCHZZZHHZ
NNNNNG.

LETTERS: VC's CLAYTON COWLES

PAGE 8:

<u>PANEL 1:</u> The daughter laying there, eyes open.

     VAL: Mother…mother…mother…

<u>PANEL 2:</u> VISION in a ton of pain. Energy shooting through him. He's holding back the pain.

     VISION: nnnnnggg.
     SFX: SHHVVVHH

<u>PANEL 3:</u> Back on daughter. Eyes closing.

     VAL (getting smaller): mother….mother…mother…moth…

<u>PANEL 4:</u> Back on VISION. Lots of pain. Still holding it back, but starting to let some of it go.

     VISION: nnngggggg!
     SFX: SHHVVVHH
     TONY (OFF): Vision. Vision! I think it's too much!
     TONY (OFF): We got to pull back!

<u>PANEL 5:</u> Back on the daughter. Eyes closed.

     TONY (OFF): It's not working! It's just killing you!
     TONY (OFF): I'm turning it off!

<u>PANEL 6:</u> On the Vision, screaming out in pain.

     VISION: No!
     SFX: SHHVVVHH

<u>PANEL 7:</u> On the daughter. Eyes closed.

     HANK (OFF): I'm turning it off!

<u>PANEL 8:</u> On Vision. Pain coursing through him. But now under control. Held back. He looks a bit angry.

     VISION: Tony Stark. You are…my colleague. You are an Avenger. You are…my oldest friend.
     VISION: If you touch that button…I will kill you.
     SFX: SHHVVVHH

PAGE 9:

PANEL 1: On TONY, looking across to panel 1, taken back, confused.

        TONY (small): Jesus, Vision…

PANEL 2: On the daughter. Eyes closed

        No dialogue

PANEL 3: ON Vision. Looking back at PANEL 1. In pain, determined.

        VISION: She…is…my daughter!
        VISION: And I will…save her!

PANEL 4: On the daughter. Her eyes starting to open.

        VAL: Mother…mother…

PANEL 5: On the daughter, her eyes now fully open

        VAL: Mother…mother….mother….

PANEL 6: Vision standing over his daughter, his hands inside her. She is looking at him.

        VAL: Mother….mother….moth--

PAGE 10:

PANEL 1: Big Panel. VAL sitting up, embracing her father.

      VAL: Father!

PANEL 2: TONY watching the scene. He looks a little ambivalent. This wasn't a version of Vision he's seen before.

      CAPTION: Later, Captain America asked Iron Man how it all went.

PANEL 3: Switch the angle so we see VISION and VAL hugging with TONY in the background.

      CAPTION: "Fine," Iron Man said. "Normal, I mean. Everything was normal."

PANEL 1: AGNES holding her cat. She's got the needle from her hair pressed against its neck.

> AGNES: Good night, dear.
> AGNES: I'll see you in the morning.

PANEL 2: AGNES stabs the cat through the neck.

> CAT: MMRRAAAOO!

PANEL 3: Camera pulls back as THE CAT fights its way out of AGATHA'S arm.

> CAT: MRORROWW!
> AGNES: No, no. Come now!

PANEL 4: THE CAT on the ground, bleeding out its neck.

> AGNES (OFF): Ebony...Ebony, please...
> CAT: Hssssssss!

PANEL 5: CAT growing larger, turning into a panther. Still with a needle sticking out of its neck.

> AGNES: Darling, really, what good can come of this.
> CAT: Hssssssss!

PANEL 6: CAT grown to full size, now a panther, still bleeding from the wound in its neck. Looking very mad about the whole thing. Roaring.

> AGNES: Ebony...no...no.
> CAT: Hsssss!

PANEL 7: Camera pulls back as EBONY jumps on poor AGNES.

> AGNES: No!
> EBONY: RRROWWW!

PAGE 12:

PANEL 1: EBONY on top of AGNES, trying to rip AGNES'S neck open. AGNES holding the cat back.

>   EBONY: RRRROWW!

PANEL 2: EBONY getting closer. AGNES now holding onto the pin sticking out of EBONY'S neck.

>   EBONY: RRRRROOWW!

PANEL 3: AGNES pulls out the bloody pin. EBONY arches her neck in pain.

>   EBONY: AARRROWWWW!

PANEL 4: AGNES slices across EBONY'S throat with the knife, cutting it. Blood pouring out.

>   EBONY: Arrrwwow!

PANEL 5: AGNES pushes EBONY over to the side. AGNES is scratched and injured.

>   EBONY (small): ARRRROW!

PANEL 6: AGNES straddles EBONY with the blade in the air. She holds her pin, ready to stab down.

>   EBONY (small): Arroowww...

PAGE 13:

PANEL 1: Camera pulled back. AGNES from behind stabbing the large cat with the pin.

CAPTION: Agnes and Wanda would hold hands as they left the airport.
CAPTION: They were witches. They were the blood guardians of this realm.
CAPTION: They tried to look serious as they walked way.

PANEL 2: Camera goes in a little closer. AGNES coming from her stab. Blood all over her and her arm.

CAPTION: But inevitably Wanda would break and squeeze Agnes's hand and launch into a fit of uncontrollable giggles.
CAPTION: Agnes would scold her, tell her to control it all, then Agnes too would start giggling.

PANEL 3: Camera goes a little closer, as AGNES Stabs down again.

CAPTION: Both women knew there was only one way extracting time from an Everbloom blossom.
CAPTION: The petal must be twice consumed.
CAPTION: First after hunger. Second after murder.

SCRIPT: TOM KING

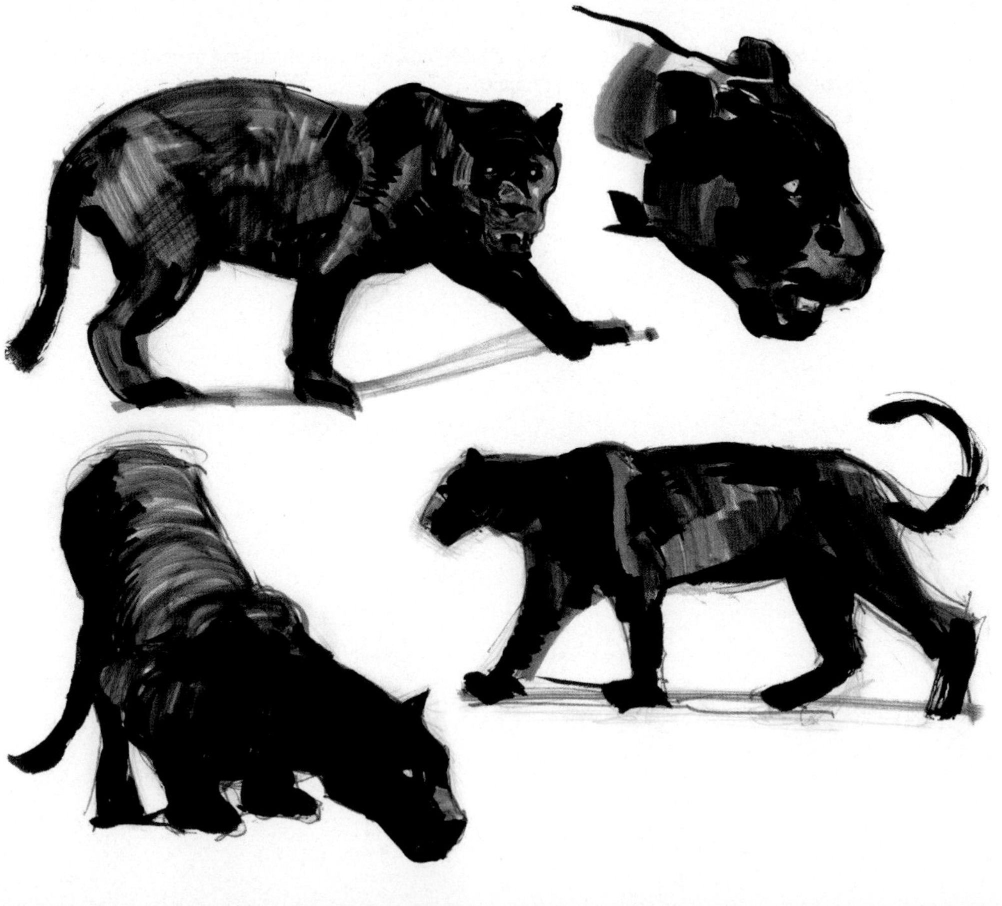

SKETCHES: GABRIEL HERNANDEZ WALTA

PAGE 14:

PANEL 1: Inside the VISION'S living room. We can see the door to the outside. The doorbell is ringing. VIR-GINIA is phasing through the wall as she runs to get the door. Vin is lying on the couch looking at an iPad. He has a plug in his head that's connected to the iPad

> SFX: Ding. Ding. Ding.
> VIRGINIA: Coming! Coming! I'm coming!

PANEL 2: VIRGINIA yanking VIN'S headphones off as she walks past.

> VIRGINIA: Vin, I suppose it would shut down your system to answer a door?
> VIN: What?

PANEL 3: VIN sitting up.

> VIN: I was downloading Bach's Cello concerto for the fall concert, like you told me to!
> VIN: Mother, I can't do both!

PANEL 4: VIRGINIA opening the front door.

> SFX: Ding. Ding.
> VIRGINIA: Yes. Yes. No one can do anything around here except me.
> VIRGINIA: That is not worth communicating, Vin. That I know.

PANEL 5: VISION and VAL standing at the doorway. VISION looking proud, but trying to hold back that pride. Trying to be modest. VAL out of her mind happy.

> VAL: Mother!
> VISION: It's just us, Virginia …

LAYOUT: GABRIEL HERNANDEZ WALTA

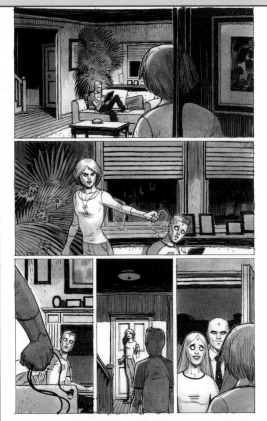

INKS: GABRIEL HERNANDEZ WALTA

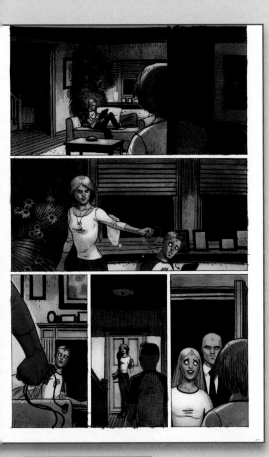

COLORS: JORDIE BELLAIRE

LETTERS: VC's CLAYTON COWLES

PAGE 15:

<u>PANEL 1:</u> Splash. VIRGINIA hugging VAL as VISION and VIN look on.

        VIRGINIA (small): Val, my Val.
        VISION: We're home.

SCRIPT: TOM KING

LAYOUT: GABRIEL HERNANDEZ WALTA   INKS: GABRIEL HERNANDEZ WALTA

PAGE 16:

PANEL 1: VISION sits on his bed, tying the draw string to his pajama pants.

VISION: The painters are coming in the morning. Around ten they said.
VISION: It sounds as if you dealt with the incident as well as you could.

PANEL 2: On the knot being tied.

VISION: These are the natural growing pains of neighborhood adjusting to our presence.
VISION: This is all to be expected. Especially after the incident with Vin at school.

PANEL 3: VISION looking up, looking a little stunned.

VISION: I am sure after your intervention, the parents of the boys will …

PANEL 4: VIRGINIA emerges from the bathroom wearing very little, looking very sexy. VISION stares up at her.

VISION: Take care … of the … the situation.

SCRIPT: TOM KING

LAYOUT: GABRIEL HERNANDEZ WALTA

INKS: GABRIEL HERNANDEZ WALTA

PAGE 17:

PANEL 1: VISION looking nervous.

       VISION: I also—I have not informed you. Yet.
       VISION: I also had a meeting with … with …

PANEL 2: VIRGINIA, from behind, starts to phase. Her clothes falling through her body. We see VISION in the background looking at her.

       VISION: Iron Man.

PANEL 3: VIRGINIA walking from behind as her clothes fall through her.

       VISION (off): We … we spoke about the Grim Reaper. Who attacked. Who attacked us.

PANEL 4: VIRGINIA's feet walking through her underwear and top.

       VISION: That is what we spoke about. Iron Man. Iron Man and … I.

PANEL 5: VIRGINIA pulling VISION to a standing position by his chin.

       VISION: He was able. Iron Man. He was able to talk to … SHIELD.

PANEL 6: Behind VIRGINIA. VISION and VIRGINIA. VISION looking down at his wife's body.

       VISION: They. SHIELD. They searched. Conducted a search.
       VISION: For him. The Reaper.

PANEL 7: VIRGINIA kisses VISION

       No dialogue

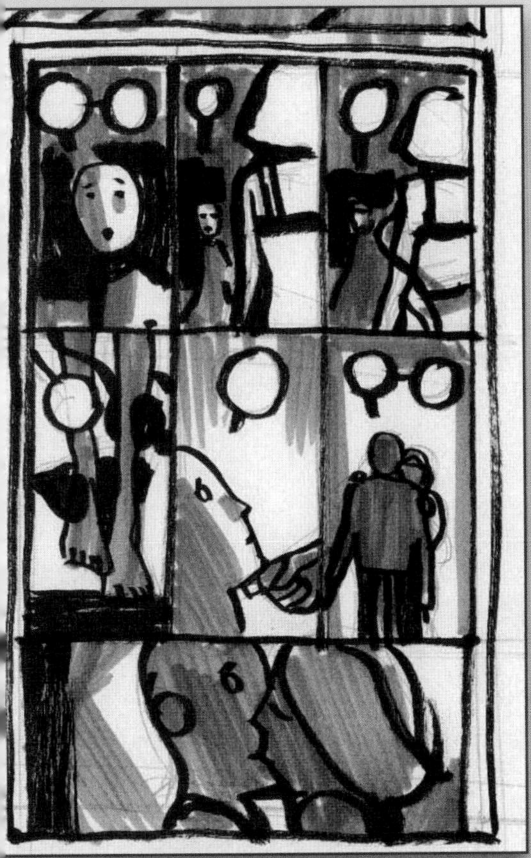

LAYOUT: GABRIEL HERNANDEZ WALTA

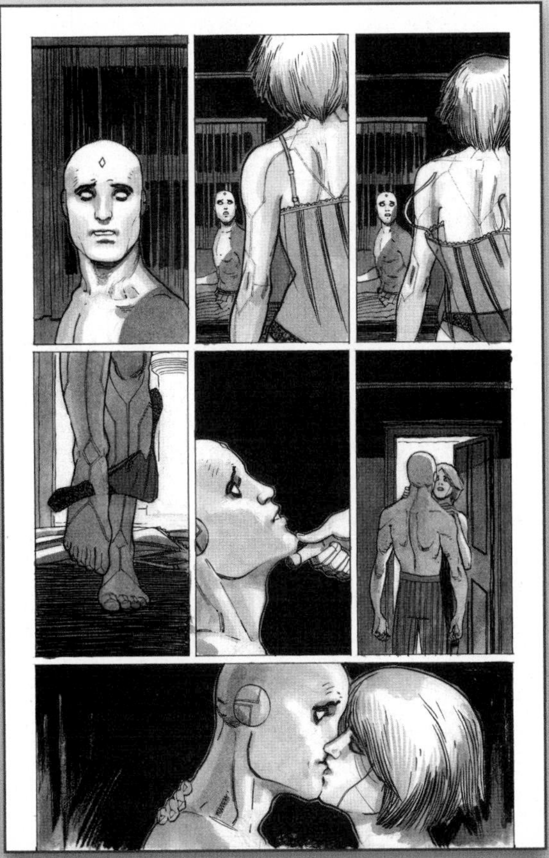

INKS: GABRIEL HERNANDEZ WALTA

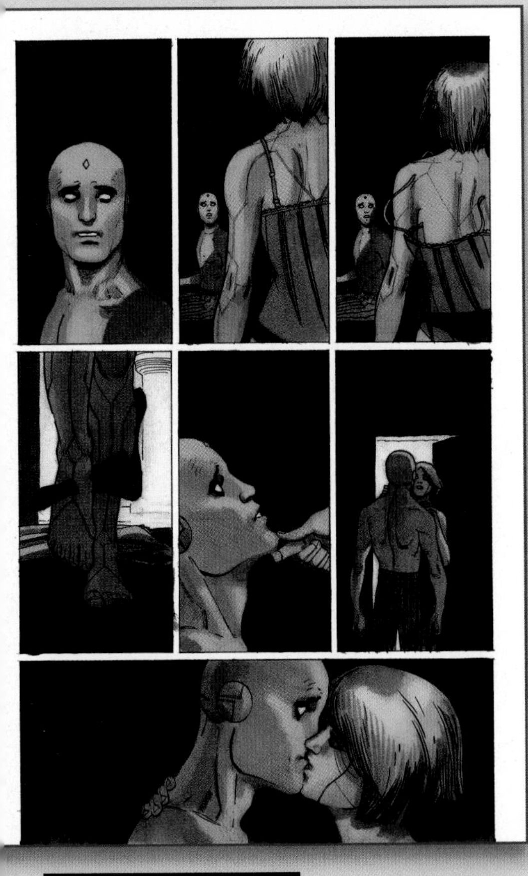

COLORS: JORDIE BELLAIRE

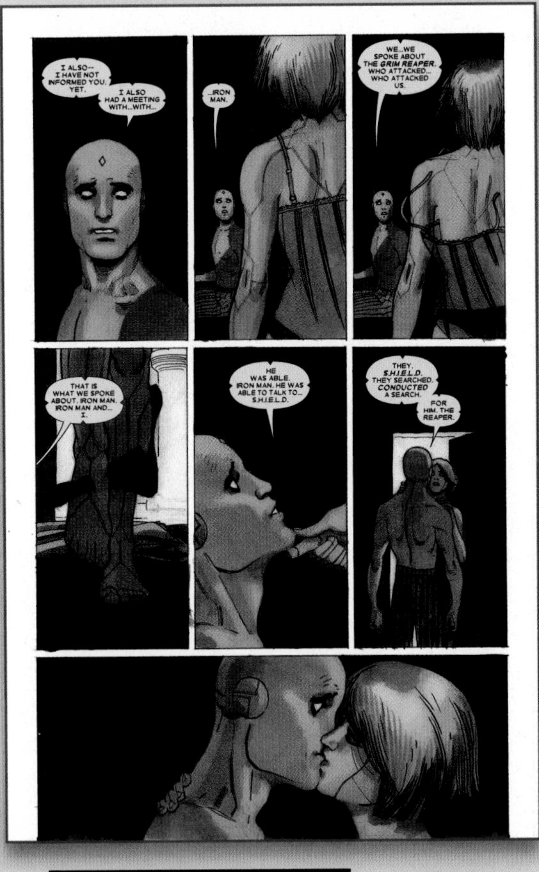
I ALSO-- I HAVE NOT INFORMED YOU. YET.
I ALSO HAD A MEETING WITH...WITH...
...IRON MAN.
WE...WE SPOKE ABOUT THE GRIM REAPER. WHO ATTACKED... WHO ATTACKED US.
THAT IS WHAT WE SPOKE ABOUT. IRON MAN. IRON MAN AND... I.
HE WAS ABLE. IRON MAN. HE WAS ABLE TO TALK TO... S.H.I.E.L.D.
THEY. S.H.I.E.L.D. THEY SEARCHED. CONDUCTED A SEARCH.
FOR HIM. THE REAPER.

LETTERS: VC's CLAYTON COWLES

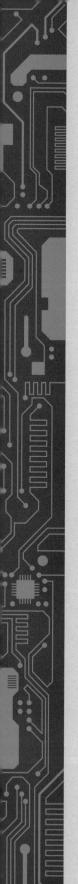

PAGE 18:

PANEL 1: VISION comes up from the kiss.

> VISION: They searched everywhere. Off the earth. Inside the earth.
> VISION: Everywhere.

PANEL 2: Back on the tie on VISION'S pajamas's. VIRGINIA's hand pull the string to the tie.

> VISION (OFF): They found nothing.
> VISION (OFF): He is…he is gone.

PANEL 3: VISION and VIRGINIA, chests pressed together, their lips very close together.

> VISION: Reaper. I mean The Grim Reaper. He is…
> VIRGINIA: Yes, darling, I know. The Reaper is gone.

PANEL 4: Camera pulls back. Show naked VISION and VIRGINIA in silhouette in their bedroom. Standing in front of a window.

> VIRGINIA: And we're still here.

PANEL 5: Big panel. Camera pulls back through the window. We see them making out. Next to the window is written "GO HOME SOCKET LOVERS"

> No dialogue

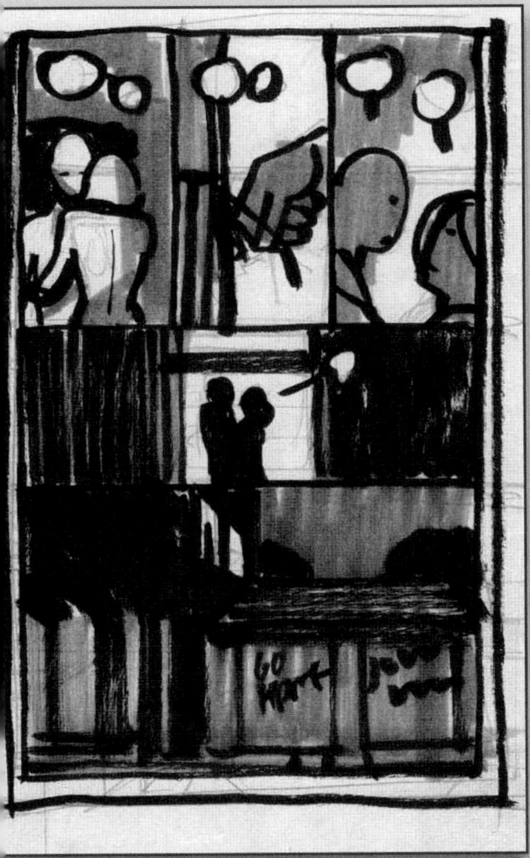
GO HOME
SOCKET LOVERS

LAYOUT: GABRIEL HERNANDEZ WALTA

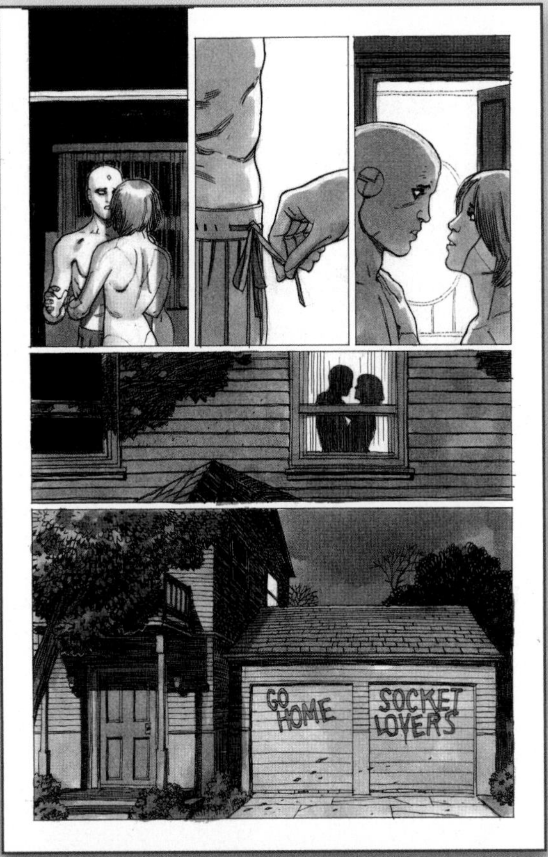
GO HOME
SOCKET LOVERS

INKS: GABRIEL HERNANDEZ WALTA

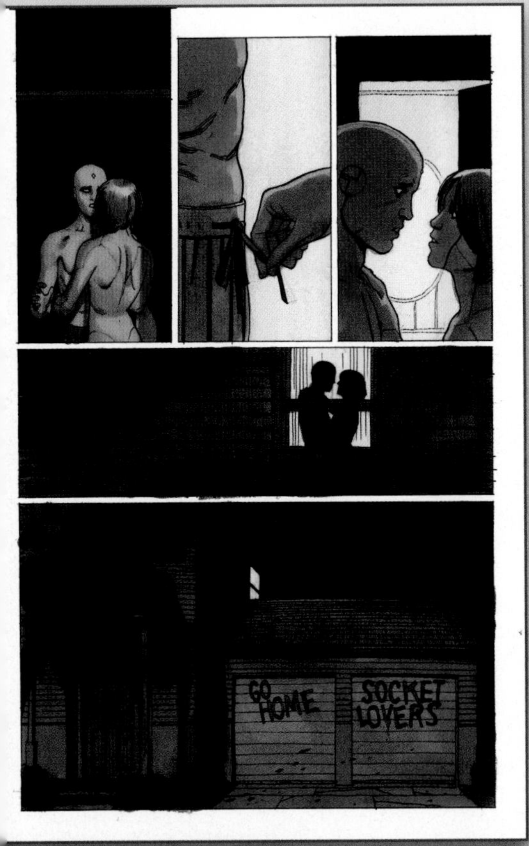
GO HOME
SOCKET LOVERS

COLORS: JORDIE BELLAIRE

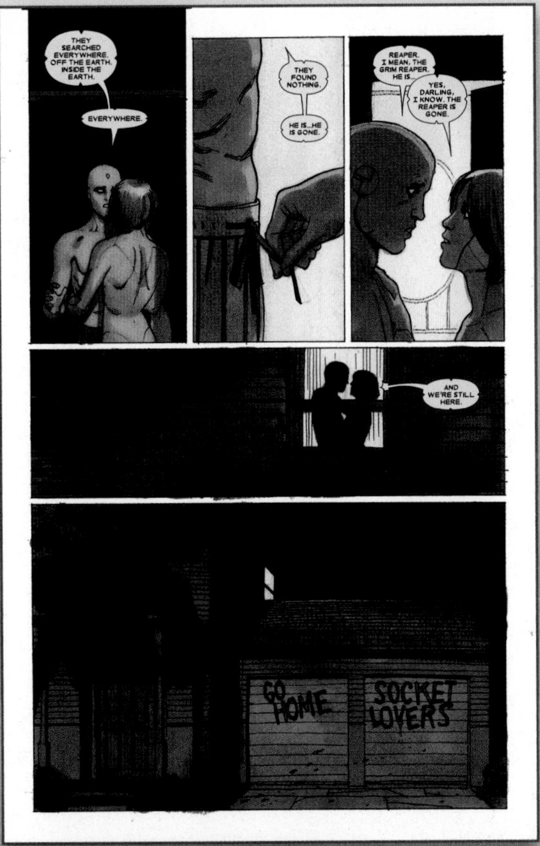
THEY SEARCHED EVERYWHERE. OFF THE EARTH. INSIDE THE EARTH.
EVERYWHERE.
THEY FOUND NOTHING.
HE IS...HE IS GONE.
REAPER. I MEAN, THE GRIM REAPER. HE IS...
YES, DARLING, I KNOW. THE REAPER IS GONE.
AND WE'RE STILL HERE.
GO HOME
SOCKET LOVERS

LETTERS: VC's CLAYTON COWLES

PAGE 19:

PANEL 1: AGATHA, her face stained in blood, squats over the dead panther. Her hands are inside the animal.

CAPTION: Not many cultures eat cats.
CAPTION: But the few that do never eat the stomach.

PANEL 2: AGATHA'S blood soaked hands taking out the stomach of the cat.

CAPTION: This is most likely due to the cat's historical place in the home.
CAPTION: The Cat after all was bred to consume rats and pidgins and snakes
CAPTION: All the little pests that carry all the little plagues—all of that ends up in the stomach of the cat.

PANEL 3: AGATHA biting down into the CAT'S stomach, blood on her teeth.

CAPTION: It also may have something to do with the taste of the Cat stomach, which is bitter and metallic.

PANEL 4: AGATHA falls to the ground, blood on her face.

CAPTION: A taste that coats the back of one's throat for days after.

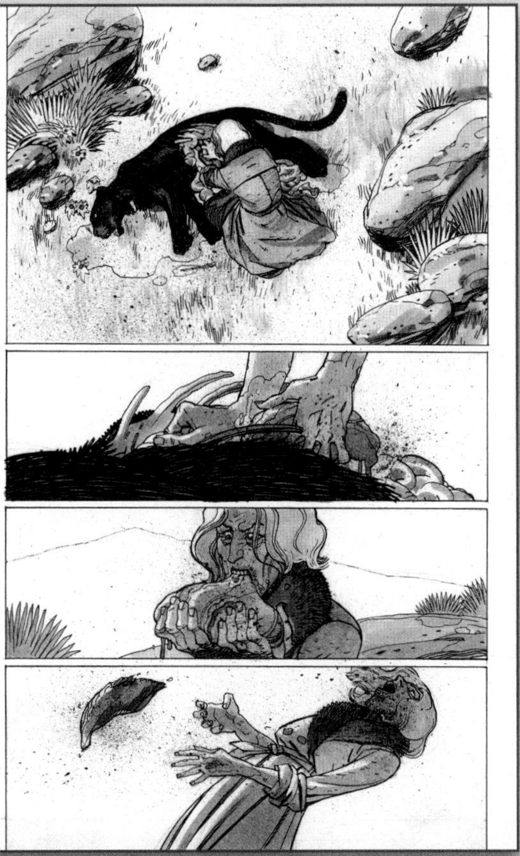

INKS: GABRIEL HERNANDEZ WALTA

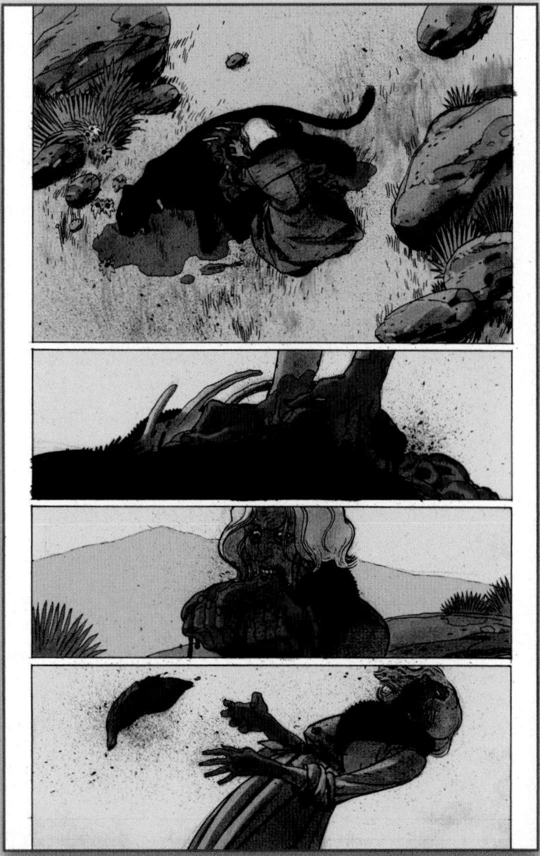

COLORS: JORDIE BELLAIRE

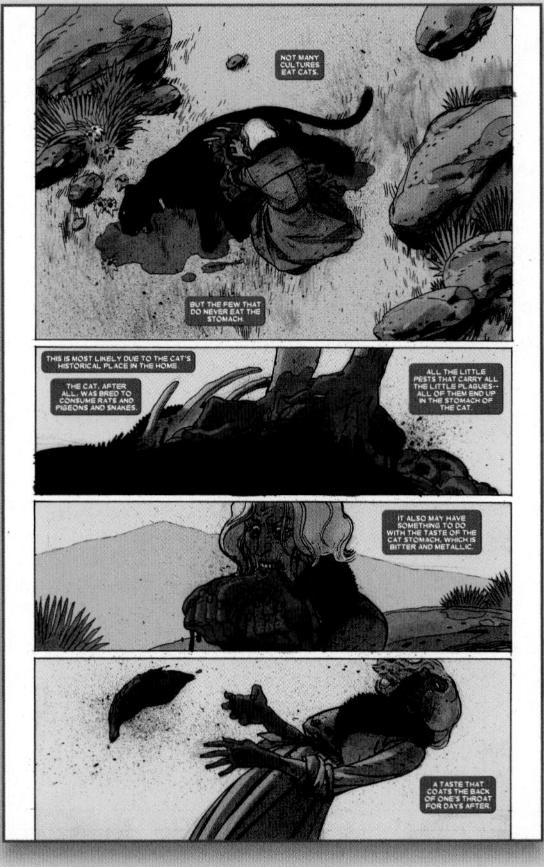
NOT MANY CULTURES EAT CATS.
BUT THE FEW THAT DO NEVER EAT THE STOMACH.
THIS IS MOST LIKELY DUE TO THE CAT'S HISTORICAL PLACE IN THE HOME.
THE CAT, AFTER ALL, WAS BRED TO CONSUME RATS AND PIGEONS AND SNAKES.
ALL THE LITTLE PESTS THAT CARRY ALL THE LITTLE PLAGUES-- ALL OF THEM END UP IN THE STOMACH OF THE CAT.
IT ALSO MAY HAVE SOMETHING TO DO WITH THE TASTE OF THE CAT STOMACH, WHICH IS BITTER AND METALLIC.
A TASTE THAT COATS THE BACK OF ONE'S THROAT FOR DAYS AFTER.

LETTERS: VC's CLAYTON COWLES

PAGE 20:

PANEL 1: AGATHA having an epileptic fit on the ground, her eyes rolled into her head.

CAPTION: A month ago, Agatha Harkness was dead.

AGATHA: Hgh. Hgh. Hgh.

PANEL 2: The epileptic fit continues. She's arching her back. Drooling out of her mouth.

CAPTION: Like most, she spent her death dreaming of better days.
CAPTION: Wanda. Flowers. Laughter.

AGATHA: Hgh. Hgh. Hgh.

PANEL 3: The epileptic fit continues. She is arching her neck. Rolling in blood.

CAPTION: But eventually, as they must, the nightmares came.
CAPTION: She saw Wanda's husband. She saw the Vision. She saw him covered in blood.

AGATHA: Hgh. Hgh. Hgh.

PANEL 4: AGATHA now quiet on the ground. Her eyes closed.

CAPTION: It was the blood of heroes, of friends.
CAPTION: The Avengers. The Fantastic Four. The X-Men. She saw them all dead at Vision's feet.
CAPTION: She saw the flowers, and she saw Wanda. Wanda lying still among the flowers.

PANEL 5: AGATHA suddenly wakes, screaming out as if from a nightmare.

CAPTION: Agatha Harkness woke from death, a spirit screaming.

AGATHA: AAAAAH!

PANEL 6: AGATHA looking possessed.

CAPTION: She needed to know more.
CAPTION: She needed to understand the threat to come.

PANEL 7: AGATHA looks right at the camera. Meeting the eye of the reader. Looking possessed, a little crazy.

CAPTION: She needed to understand her Vision.

PANEL 8: AGATHA still looking out at the camera, looking creepy, possessed, tilts her head a bit.

AGATHA: In late September, with the leaves just beginning to hint at the fall to come,
AGATHA: The Visions of Virginia moved into their house on 616 Hickory Branch Lane, Arlington, VA, 21301.

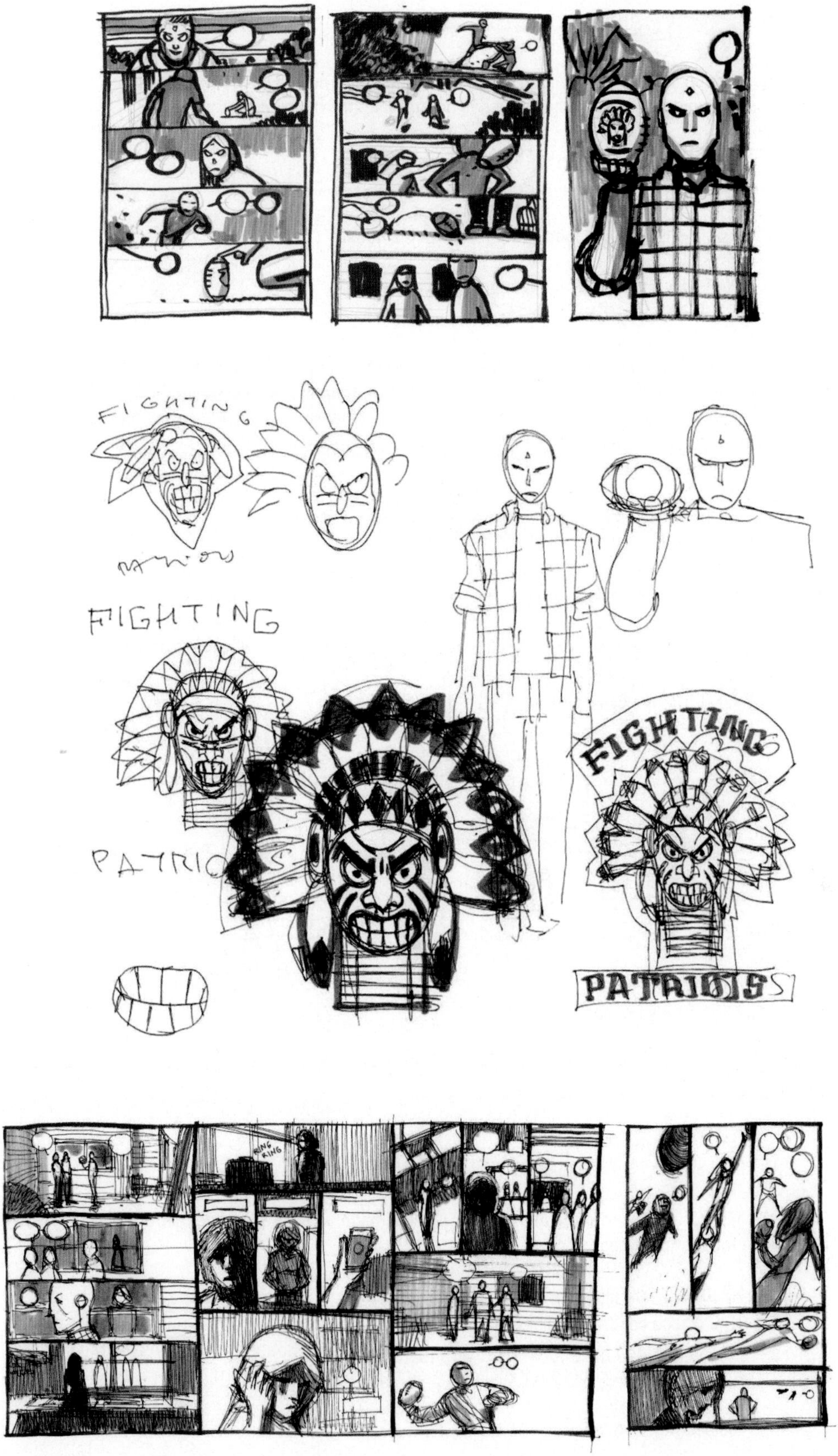
FIGHTING
FIGHTING
FIGHTING

LAYOUTS PAGES 1-7: GABRIEL HERNANDEZ WALTA

PAGE 1:

PANEL 1: Close up of LEON lying unconscious in the hospital. There is a feeding tube going in his nose. Food is being sent through the tube, but it has not yet reached his nose.

> CAPTION: "If it will feed nothing else,"

PANEL 2: Close on LEON as the food in the tube hits his nose.

> CAPTION: "It will feed my revenge."

PANEL 3: Widescreen shot. Camera pulls back. We see LEON lying in his hospital bed. We can see some flowers by the side of the bed along with a framed picture. There is also a chair by the bed where some-one's left a newspaper. (There's a bunch of items basically that we're going to see in close up below. If possible, let's see if we can put them in the shot here). Also, there is a shadow on the bed. The shadow of someone floating above the bed.

> CAPTION: "He hath disgraced me and hindered me half a million,"

PANEL 4: Close up of the flowers lying on the table. There is a note on the flowers.

> NOTE: Get better, Leon! We're all praying for you! Love, your colleagues and friends at Flanagan, Rios, and Suntres.
> CAPTION: "laughed at my losses,"

PANEL 5: Close up of a picture showing LEON, CK, and their mother. They're hugging, smiling, this is in better times.

> "mocked at my gains,"

PANEL 6: Picture of woman's purse, left by the bed.

> "scorned my nation,"

PANEL 7: Picture of a box of tissues near the purse. Some used tissues are next to the box. Someone's been crying here.

> "thwarted my bargains,"

PANEL 8: A newspaper lying on the chair. Close in on a smaller item. We can see the headline (or part of it and a bit of the first paragraph.

> HEADLINE: Few Clues in Shooting Death of Local High School Student
> TEXT: Police continued to search for leads in the shooting death of 16-year-old Chris Kinzky. Kinzky's father's, Leon Kinzky was found in the house unconscious next to the Alexander High School student. Police say they have yet to . . . (CUT OFF)
>
> "cooled my friends,"

PANEL 9: Close on LEON's face. We see the shadow on his chest. It's the shadow of a woman's head.

"heated mine enemies—"

PANEL 10: Camera remains steady as the shadow moves a bit, goes farther up.

"and what's his reason?"

SCRIPT: TOM KING

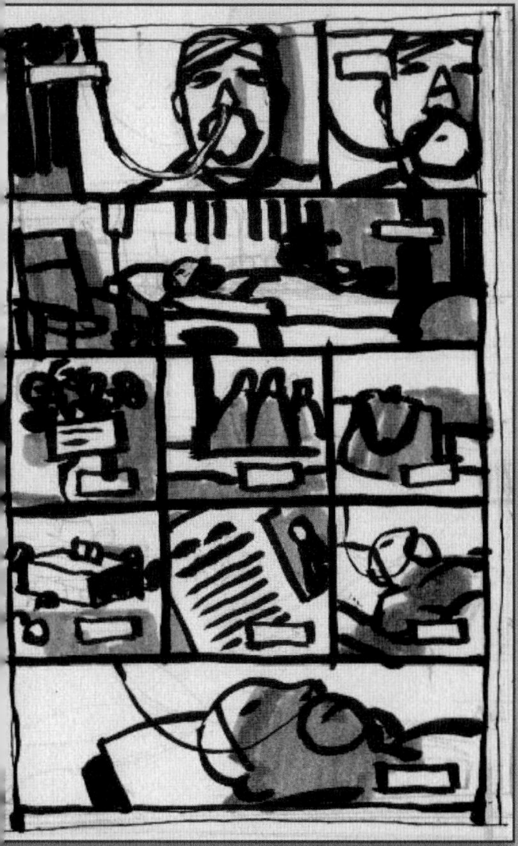

LAYOUT: GABRIEL HERNANDEZ WALTA

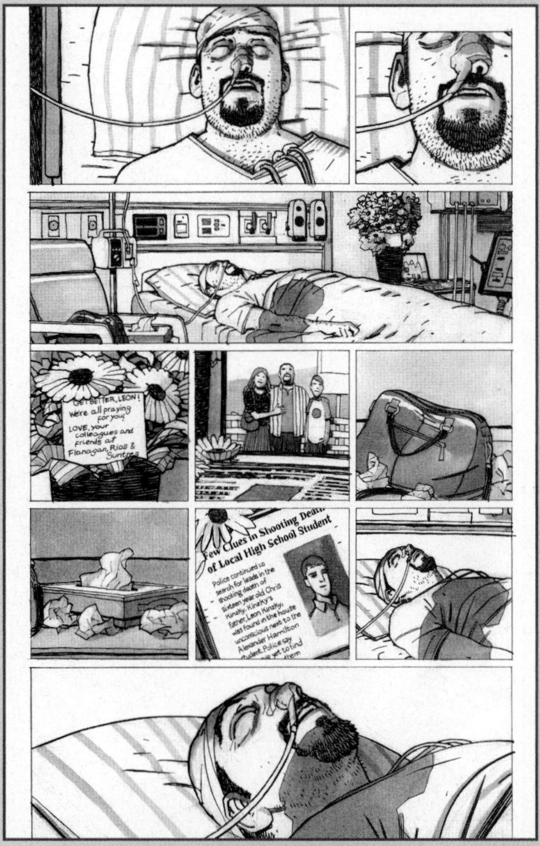
GET BETTER, LEON! We're all praying for you! LOVE, your colleagues and friends at Flanagan, Rios &
Few Clues in Shooting
of Local High School Student
Police continued to search for leads in the shooting death of sixteen year old Chris Kinzky. Kinzky's father, Leon Kinzky, was found in the house unconscious next to the Alexander Hamilton

INKS: GABRIEL HERNANDEZ WALTA

PAGE 2:

PANEL 1: Splash VIRGINIA floating above the hospital bed of LEON. Very creepy.

CAPTION: "I am a Jew."

SCRIPT: TOM KING

LAYOUT: GABRIEL HERNANDEZ WALTA

INKS: GABRIEL HERNANDEZ WALTA

PAGE 3:

PANEL 1: Close up of dead CK'S face. A bullet went through his forehead and there's a hole and a bruise there.

> CAPTION: "Hath not a Jew eyes?

PANEL 2: Camera pulls back, we see dad CK on a gurney, at the end of his autopsy. A sheet lies over his waist and legs, but we can see his chest. Another bullet wound there.

> CAPTION: "Hath not a Jew hands, organs, dimensions, senses, affections, passions?"

PANEL 3: Camera pulls back we see the doctor of the autopsy, filling out some paperwork at a nearby table. We can still see the body.

> CAPTION: "Fed with the same food, hurt with the same weapons, subject to the same diseases, healed by the same means, warmed and cooled by the same winter and summer as a Christian is?"

PANEL 4: We see a close up of a section of the doctor's paperwork. A death certificate. Here we see the top.

> TEXT: Death Certificate. Christopher Jaime Kizicky. SSN: 370-269-2215 DOB: 8/29/1999. DOD: 10/28/2015
> CAPTON: "If you prick us, do we not bleed?"

PANEL 5: We see a close up of another portion of the death certificate. A hand is about to write something here.

> TEXT: Cause of death:
> CAPTION: "If you tickle us, do we not laugh?"

PANEL 6: Camera stays steady. The hand has written some words.

> WRITING: Gunshot wounds, chest, head.
> CAPTION: "If you poison us, do we not die?"

PANEL 7: Camera stays steady. The hand has written one more word.

> WRITING: Gunshot wounds, chest, head. Homicide.
> CAPTION: "And if you wrong us, shall we not revenge?"

PAGE 4:

PANEL 1: VISION and female THOR are fighting the U-FOES on an AVENGERS mission. THOR is swinging her hammer into IRONCLAD'S face. VECTOR is firing a telekinesis blast at VISION. Blast rays are passing through VISION. (see ref)

CAPTION: "If we are like you in the rest, we will resemble you in that."

PANEL 2: VISION put his hand into VECTOR'S chest.

CAPTION: "If a Jew wrong a Christian, what is his humility?"

PANEL 3: VECTOR screams out in pain, as VISION solidifies his hand a bit. We see VISION completely emotionless as he does this.

CAPTION: "Revenge."
PILEDRIVER: Aaaaaaa!

SCRIPT: TOM KING

U-FOES

The U-Foes are a team of four superhumanly powered adventurers created by and named after millionaire industrialist Simon Utrecht. In an attempt to attain superhuman powers by duplicating the accident which created the Fantastic Four, Utrecht commissioned three of his employees to design, build, and pilot a rocket for the purpose of flight into a cosmic storm. In a matter of months, Utrecht and his associates rocketed into orbit. While the rocket containing the four was aloft, physicist Bruce Banner gained access to the launch site and, fearing for their safety,aborted the mission from the ground, The four returned, angered at Banner's interference, because further exposure to cosmic rays would have made them still more powerful than they had become at the time the mission was aborted. Following a brief battle with Bruce Banner's alter ego the Hulk, the U-Foes became incapacitated as their powers mutated out of control. Eventually regaining control over themselves, they regrouped to exact revenge upon the Hulk, but were defeated again. Their current whereabouts are unknown.

First appearance: HULK #254

VECTOR
Simon Utrecht, industrialist
Power of telekinesis
along lines of force

VAPOR
Ann Darnell, life support specialist
Transforms into gaseous state

X-RAY
Jimmy Darnell, propulsion systems engineer
Control of all forms of electromagnetic radiation

IRONCLAD
Mike Steel, engineer and pilot
Superhumanly strong

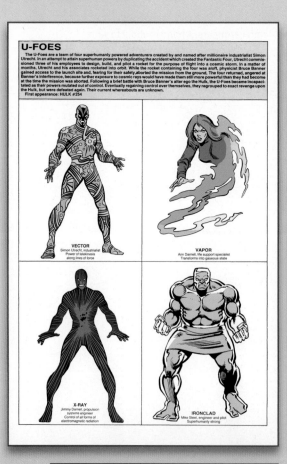

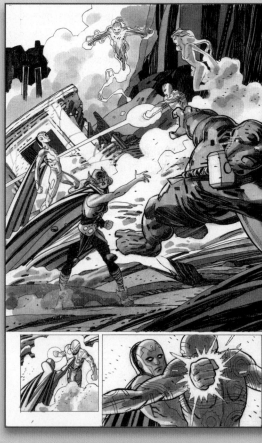

REFERENCE: *THE OFFICIAL HANDBOOK OF THE MARVEL UNIVERSE (1983) #11*

INKS: GABRIEL HERNANDEZ WALTA

PAGE 5:

<u>PANEL 1:</u> A high school teacher standing in front of a classroom. Young teacher. He is reading from a Shakespeare book (*Merchant of Venice*). Acting it out in kind of a dramatic way. Corny. Something kids would laugh at.

TEACHER: If a Christian wrong a Jew, what should his sufferance be by Christian example?

<u>PANEL 2:</u> We see the class listening. This is the classroom from issue 1. The kids looked bored. Except Vin, who is enthralled.

Floating Balloon: "Why, revenge."

<u>PANEL 3:</u> Close On VIN leaning forward listening intently. Maybe phasing a bit through his desk as he leans in to hear.

FLOATING BALLOON: "The villainy you teach me I will execute."

SCRIPT: TOM KING

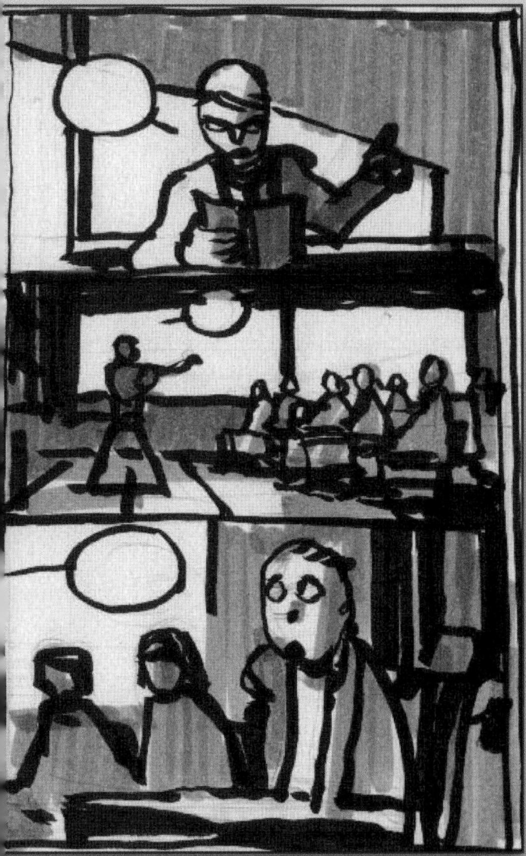

LAYOUT: GABRIEL HERNANDEZ WALTA

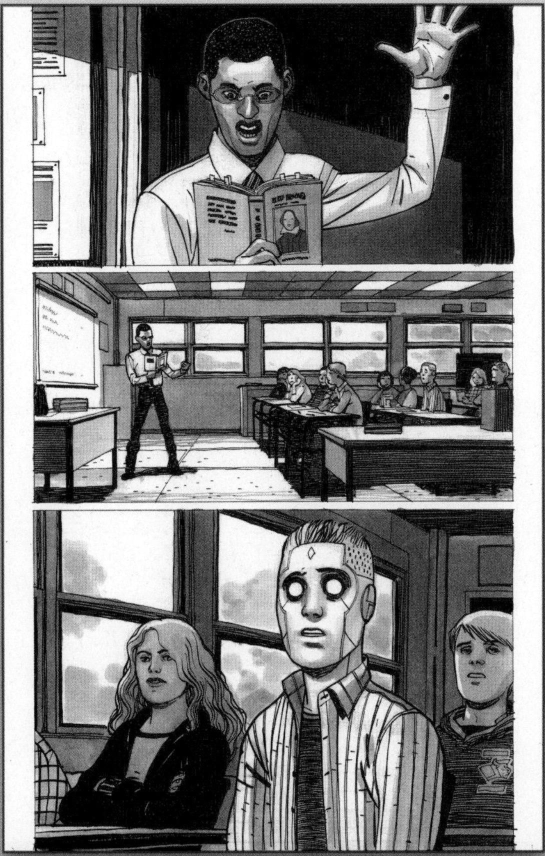

INKS: GABRIEL HERNANDEZ WALTA

PAGE 6:

<u>PANEL 1:</u> A section of a yearbook page which has three or four pictures on it, one of which is of CK. Each picture has a name and a quote underneath.

      WRITING: Raphael Colon, "Fight, Patriots fight!
      WRITING: Gil Saiz, "Where's my turkey? Turkey!!! Haha"
      WRITING: Chris Kizky: "It's all about the love!"
      WRITING: Molly Rich: "Don't say I didn't warn you…"
      CAPTION: "—and it shall go hard but I will better the instruction."

<u>PANEL 2:</u> VIV standing in the library. Holding the book from Panel 1. The library is on the second floor. There is an open window behind her. VIV is looking around nervous.

      CAPTION: "Shakespeare. *Merchant of Venice*. Poetry. Genius."

<u>PANEL 3:</u> VIV tears the page out of the yearbook.

      CAPTION: "But, you are asking, Mr. Santora, it is old, it is distant, it is, OMG, complicated!"
      CAPTION : "What is it have to do with me and my smart phone and texting and emojis?"

<u>PANEL 4:</u> VIV holds the paper against her heart. Still looking around.

      CAPTION: "Well let me answer that for you my precious, darling students."

PANEL 5: VIV sneaks out the window, phasing through the wall, but making sure the paper (which can't phase) comes with her.

      CAPTION: "Let me answer it by saying:"
      CAPTION: "You have no idea what's coming."

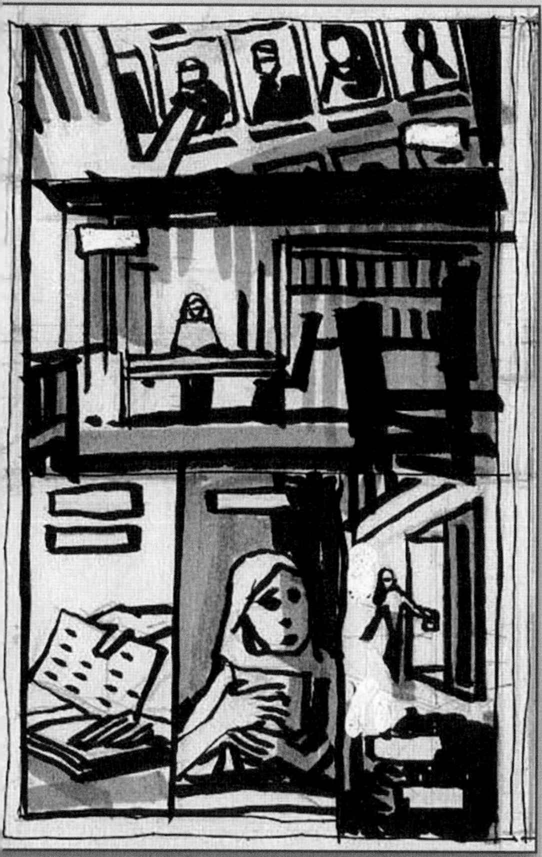

LAYOUT: GABRIEL HERNANDEZ WALTA

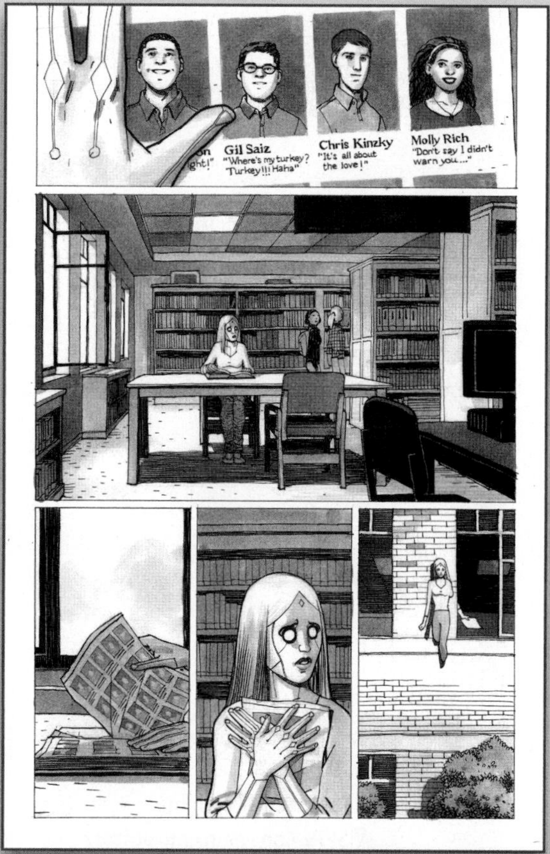
Gil Saiz
"Where's my turkey? Turkey!!! Haha"
Chris Kinzky
"It's all about the love!"
Molly Rich
"Don't say I didn't warn you..."

INKS: GABRIEL HERNANDEZ WALTA

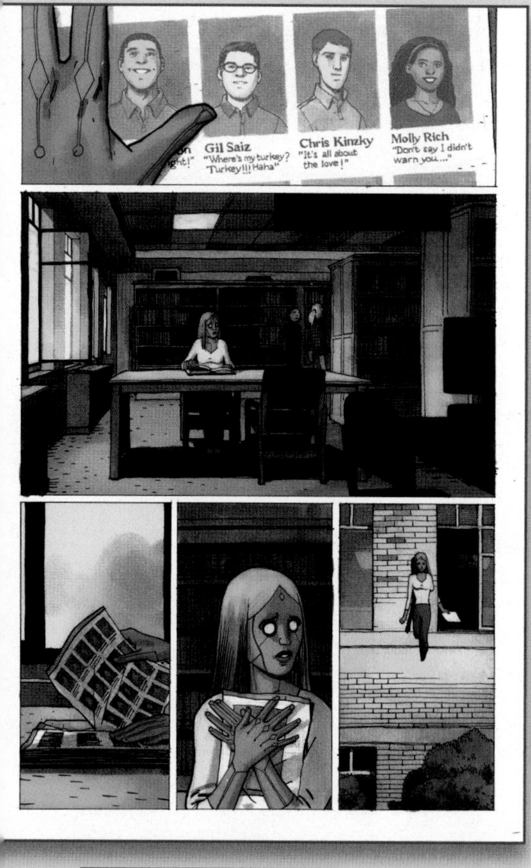
Gil Saiz
"Where's my turkey? Turkey!!! Haha"
Chris Kinzky
"It's all about the love!"
Molly Rich
"Don't say I didn't warn you..."

COLORS: JORDIE BELLAIRE

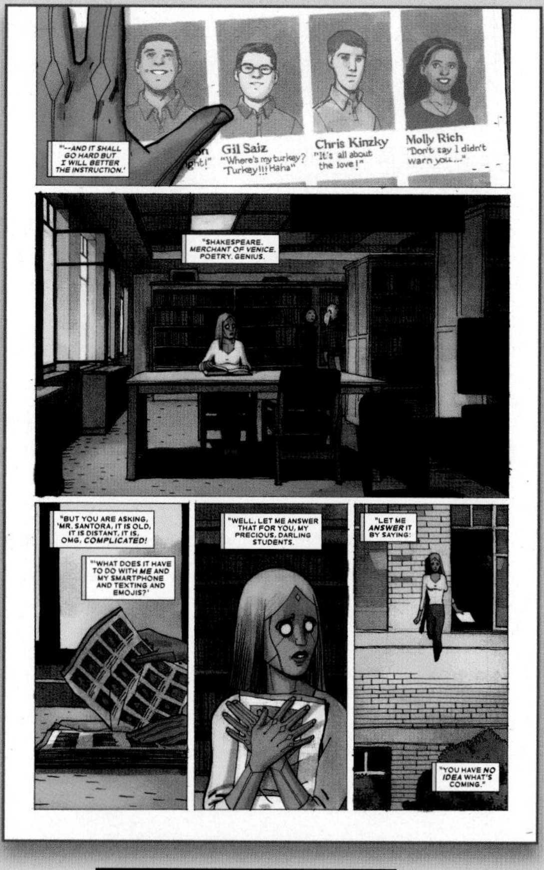
"'--AND IT SHALL GO HARD BUT I WILL BETTER THE INSTRUCTION.'
Gil Saiz
"Where's my turkey? Turkey!!! Haha"
Chris Kinzky
"It's all about the love!"
Molly Rich
"Don't say I didn't warn you..."
"SHAKESPEARE. MERCHANT OF VENICE. POETRY. GENIUS.
"BUT YOU ARE ASKING, 'MR. SANTORA, IT IS OLD, IT IS DISTANT, IT IS, OMG, COMPLICATED!
"'WHAT DOES IT HAVE TO DO WITH ME AND MY SMARTPHONE AND TEXTING AND EMOJIS?'
"WELL, LET ME ANSWER THAT FOR YOU, MY PRECIOUS, DARLING STUDENTS.
"LET ME ANSWER IT BY SAYING:
"YOU HAVE NO IDEA WHAT'S COMING."

LETTERS: VC's CLAYTON COWLES

PAGE 7:

PANEL 1: Night. Exterior. Tough looking, handsome, fairly built Asian dude getting out of a non-descript car. This is Detective MATT LIN of Arlington PD.

    CAPTION: Behold Matthew Lin.

PANEL 2: Camera pulls back, shows that LIN's car is in front of two police cars. The police sirens are on.

    CAPTION: Detective, Arlington PD.

PANEL 3: Camera turns around and we see these cops are parked outside of the VISION'S residence. We see LIN walking up to the house, walking past the famous mail box.

    CAPTION: Homicide Division.

PANEL 4: Vision phasing through the front door as LIN comes up.

    VISION: I saw the lights.
    VISION: Can I help you, officer?

PANEL 5: Close on Lin, looking relatively unphased (ha!)

    LIN: Mr. Vision, I'm Detective Lin, with the Arlington Police Department.
    LIN: Wondering if you wouldn't mind coming down with me to our station.
    LIN: I have just a few things I just want to go over with you.

PANEL 6: On VISION, looking a bit confused.

    VISION: My family and I are currently gathering at the dining table to review today's events.
    VISION: May I ask what is the nature of this matter?

PANEL 7: Back on LIN

    LIN: It won't take that long. Honestly. Just an hour. Maybe a half hour.
    VISION: Officer, that is not a response to my inquiry.

PANEL 8: Long shot showing the house at night, cop cars in front of it.

    LIN: Yeah.
    LIN: I'm aware.

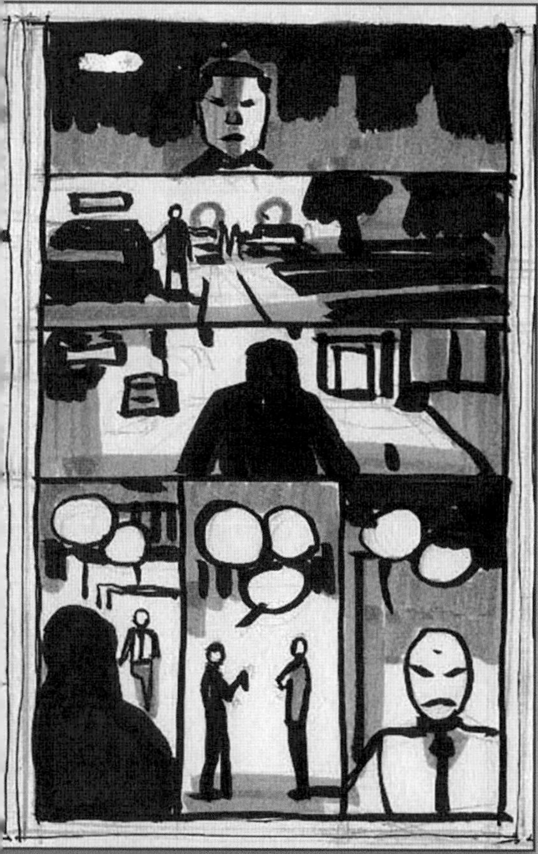

LAYOUT: GABRIEL HERNANDEZ WALTA

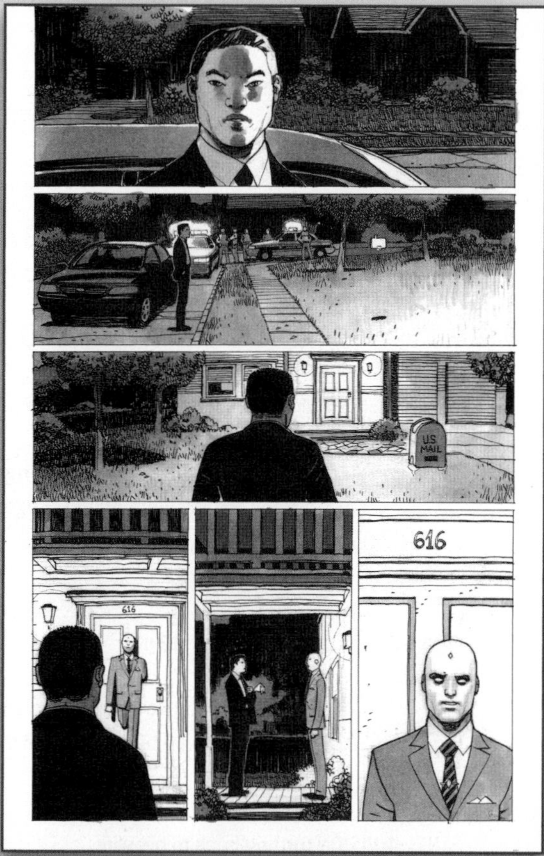
US MAIL
616
616

INKS: GABRIEL HERNANDEZ WALTA

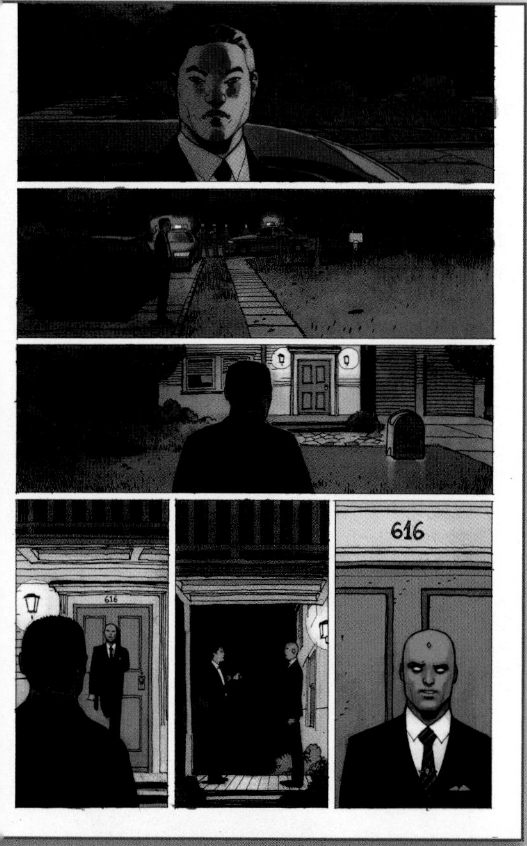
616
616

COLORS: JORDIE BELLAIRE

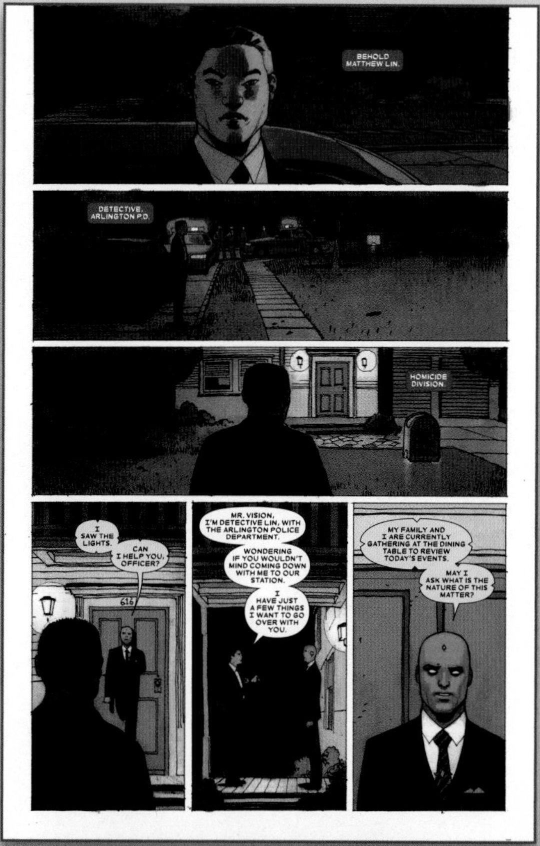
BEHOLD MATTHEW LIN.
DETECTIVE, ARLINGTON P.D.
HOMICIDE DIVISION.
I SAW THE LIGHTS.
CAN I HELP YOU, OFFICER?
MR. VISION, I'M DETECTIVE LIN, WITH THE ARLINGTON POLICE DEPARTMENT.
WONDERING IF YOU WOULDN'T MIND COMING DOWN WITH ME TO OUR STATION.
I HAVE JUST A FEW THINGS I WANT TO GO OVER WITH YOU.
MY FAMILY AND I ARE CURRENTLY GATHERING AT THE DINING TABLE TO REVIEW TODAY'S EVENTS.
MAY I ASK WHAT IS THE NATURE OF THIS MATTER?

LETTERS: VC's CLAYTON COWLES

PAGE 8:

PANEL 1: LIN and VISION staring at each other.

>CAPTION: Detective Matt Lin attended Alexander Hamilton High School.
>CAPTION: He hated it. He graduated late after making up for two incompletes in summer school.

PANEL 2: VIRGINIA phases her head through the door.

>VIRGINIA: Husband, is everything all right?
>CAPTION: His friends went off to college. Harvard. Columbia. MIT. UVA. Princeton.
>CAPTION: Matt Linn joined the Army.

PANEL 3: VISION looking back at LIN.

>CAPTION: He served two tours in Iraq and one in Afghanistan.
>CAPTION: He liked Iraq better. The lies there were easier to see.

PANEL 4: VISION turning back to his wife.

>CAPTION: When he got back he worked in retail for a few years at a bookstore down on Wilson.
>CAPTION: Eventually, he joined the police force. He was amazed he passed the drug test.
>CAPTION: He made detective in two years ago.
>VISION: It's all right, Virginia.

PANEL 5: VISION walking down the stairs away from LIN and his wife.

>CAPTION: Last year, during a routine investigation, a man named Francois Puvot pulled a gun on Matt Lin.
>CAPTION: Matt Lin shot Francois Puvot in the head and neck.
>CAPTION: Puvot died as Lin pumped at his chest, attempting to perform CPR.
>VISION: It will not take long.

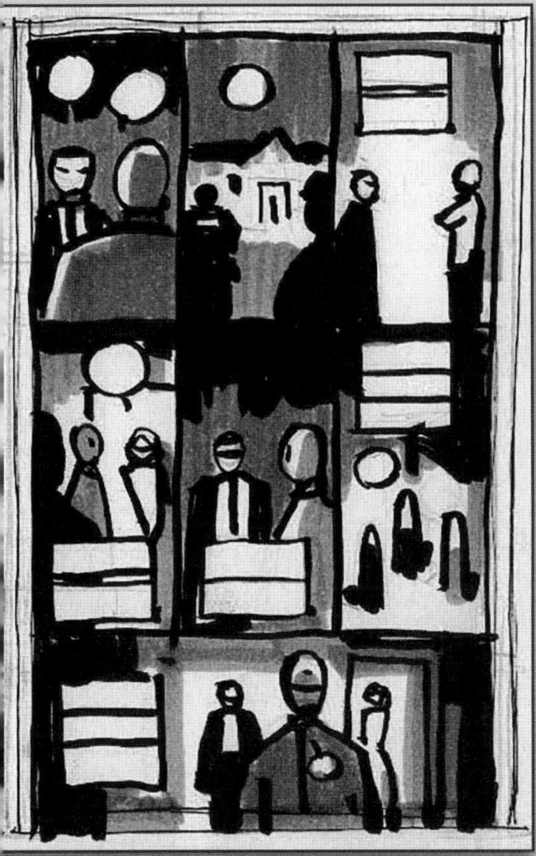

LAYOUT: GABRIEL HERNANDEZ WALTA

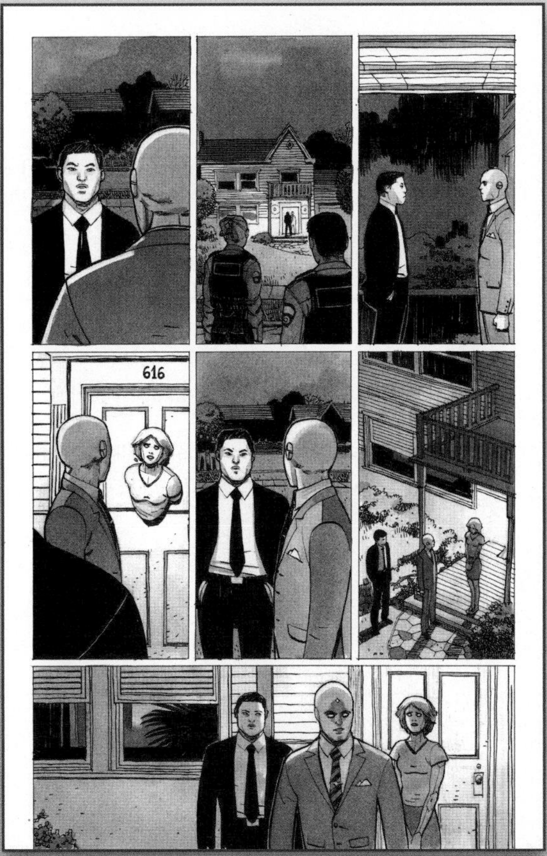
616

INKS: GABRIEL HERNANDEZ WALTA

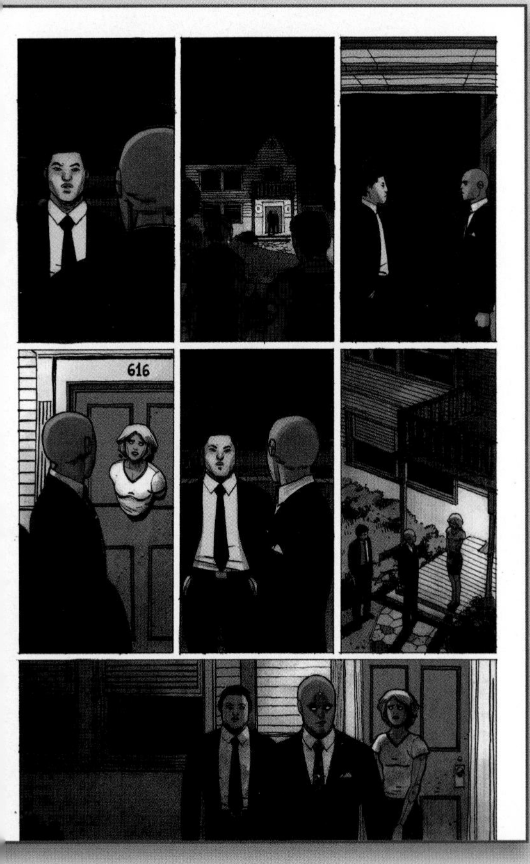
616

COLORS: JORDIE BELLAIRE

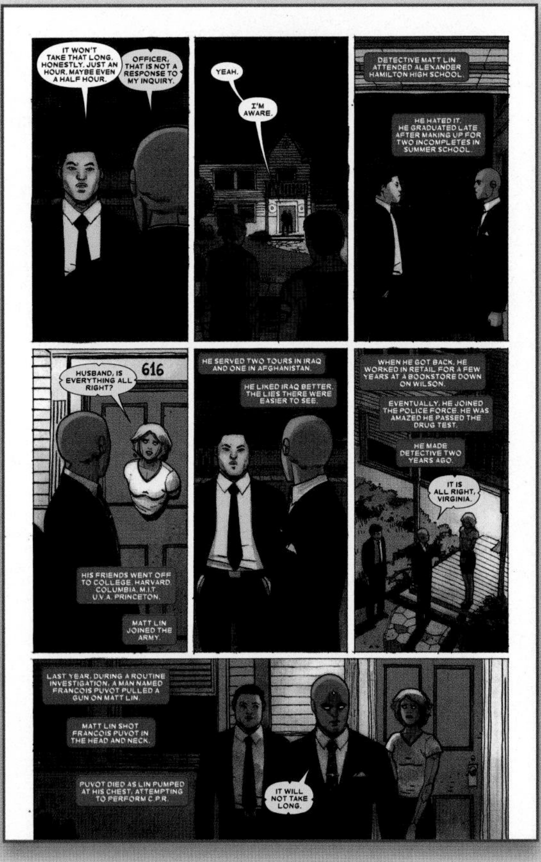
IT WON'T TAKE THAT LONG. HONESTLY. JUST AN HOUR. MAYBE EVEN A HALF HOUR.
OFFICER, THAT IS NOT A RESPONSE TO MY INQUIRY.
YEAH.
I'M AWARE.
DETECTIVE MATT LIN ATTENDED ALEXANDER HAMILTON HIGH SCHOOL.
HE HATED IT. HE GRADUATED LATE AFTER MAKING UP FOR TWO INCOMPLETES IN SUMMER SCHOOL.
616
HUSBAND, IS EVERYTHING ALL RIGHT?
HIS FRIENDS WENT OFF TO COLLEGE. HARVARD. COLUMBIA. M.I.T. U.V.A. PRINCETON.
MATT LIN JOINED THE ARMY.
HE SERVED TWO TOURS IN IRAQ AND ONE IN AFGHANISTAN.
HE LIKED IRAQ BETTER. THE LIES THERE WERE EASIER TO SEE.
WHEN HE GOT BACK, HE WORKED IN RETAIL FOR A FEW YEARS AT A BOOKSTORE DOWN ON WILSON.
EVENTUALLY, HE JOINED THE POLICE FORCE. HE WAS AMAZED HE PASSED THE DRUG TEST.
HE MADE DETECTIVE TWO YEARS AGO.
IT IS ALL RIGHT, VIRGINIA.
LAST YEAR, DURING A ROUTINE INVESTIGATION, A MAN NAMED FRANCOIS PUVOT PULLED A GUN ON MATT LIN.
MATT LIN SHOT FRANCOIS PUVOT IN THE HEAD AND NECK.
PUVOT DIED AS LIN PUMPED AT HIS CHEST, ATTEMPTING TO PERFORM C.P.R.
IT WILL NOT TAKE LONG.

LETTERS: VC's CLAYTON COWLES

PAGE 9:

PANEL 1: VIV and VIN sitting at the dining room table. VIV'S hands are beneath the table. They look uncomfortable, bored. VIRGINIA is coming into the dining room, phasing through a wall.

> VIRGINIA: Do not worry.
> VIRGINIA: Everything is normal.

PANEL 2: VIRGINIA, sitting down at the table.

> VIRGINIA: Your father is talking to the the the officers. He may be some time.
> VIRGINIA: We will continue our discussion discussion in his absence.

PANEL 3: Close on VIRGINIA

> VIRGINIA: You will tell me tell me tell me tell me about your day's activities.

PANEL 4: Shot of the three of them at the table. VIN and VIV are distracted. VIRGINIA is looking at them

> VIRGINIA: We...we...

PANEL 5: Close on Virginia. She looks absent, staring off, slightly broken.

> VIRGINIA: W-we will continue our discussion our discussion our discussion our discussion...

PANEL 6: VIRGINIA looking down, struggling.

> VIRGINIA (small): Discussion...discussion...discussion..

PAGE 10:

PANEL 1: VIRGINIA looking up, stunned.

No dialogue

PANEL 2: Pull back to see the table. Kids looking at the mom, concerned. VIRGINIA struggling.

No dialogue

PANEL 3: VIRGINIA pounding at the table with her fist, breaking it, cracking it in half.

VIRGINIA: Everything is normal!

SCRIPT: TOM KING

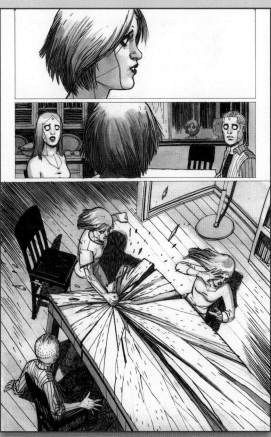

LAYOUT: GABRIEL HERNANDEZ WALTA

INKS: GABRIEL HERNANDEZ WALTA

PAGE 11:

PANEL 1: Everyone sitting in their chairs watching the table collapse into the ground in front of them.

      SFX: Crrrruchhh.

PANEL 2: VIV stands from her seat, she's upset, and she yells at the other two.

      VIV: It's all about the love!

PANEL 3: VIV runs out of the room, crying, covering her face, phasing through the wall. VIN and VIRGINIA look after her, confused.

      No dialogue

PANEL 4: Camera holds steady. VIRGINIA still looking at where her daughter ran off. VIN now turns to their mother.

      VIN: Mother, permit me to ask a question.

PANEL 5: VIRGINIA looking back at VIN confused.

      VIRGINIA: Yes?

PANEL 6: Close on VIN

      VIN: If you prick me, do I bleed?

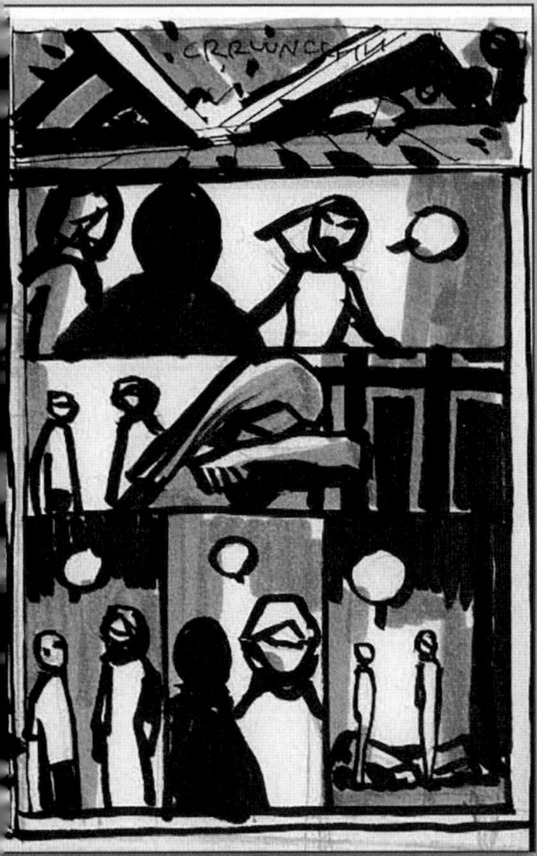
CRRUNCHH

LAYOUT: GABRIEL HERNANDEZ WALTA

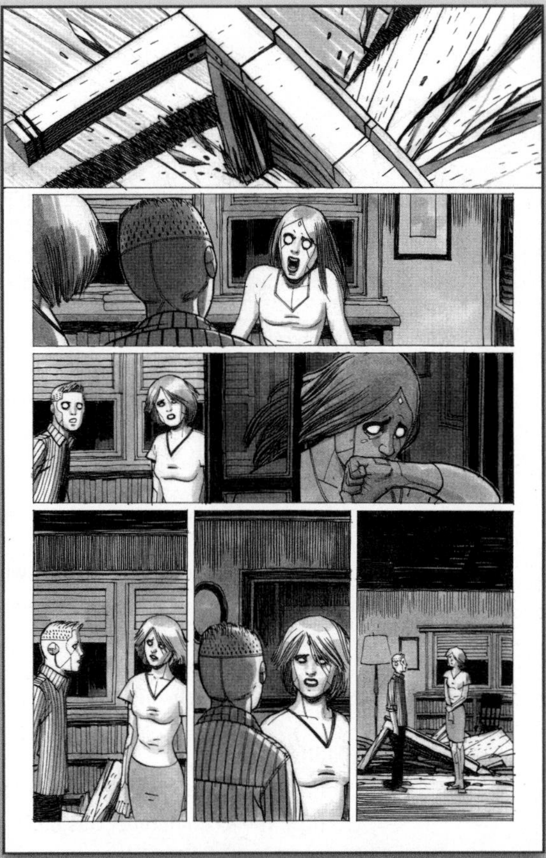

INKS: GABRIEL HERNANDEZ WALTA

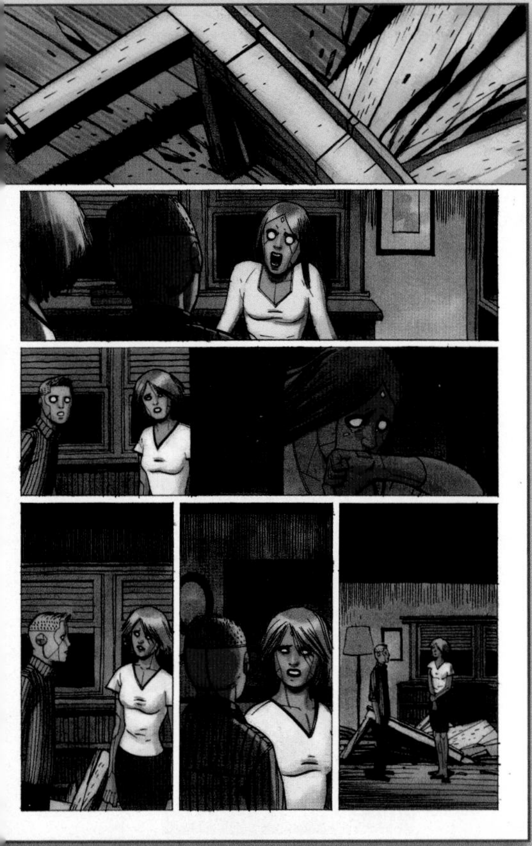

COLORS: JORDIE BELLAIRE

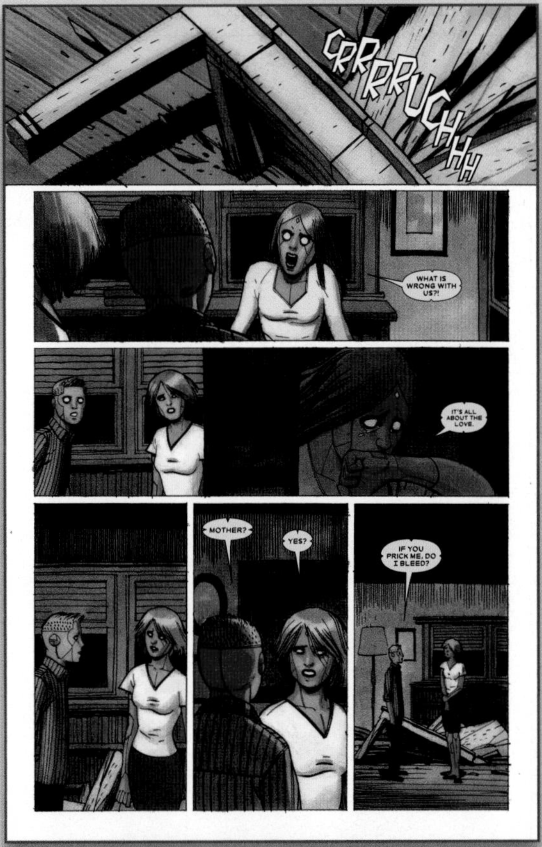
CRRRRUCHHH
WHAT IS WRONG WITH US?!
IT'S ALL ABOUT THE LOVE.
MOTHER?
YES?
IF YOU PRICK ME, DO I BLEED?

LETTERS: VC's CLAYTON COWLES

PAGE 12:

ART NOTE: So...The next six pages will be Vision being interrogated by Lin in a boring police interrogation room. What I want to do in order to make this dynamic is to intercut the interrogation with shots of Vision saving the world (the thirty-seven times we mentioned in issue 2, though I'll "only" have eighteen that need to be drawn). The thematic idea is to say, look where this guy has been, and look where he is now. He's gone from saving the world to being questioned by the police.

I'm going to put in reference for each world-saving shot, but feel free to draw what you want to draw (these can be close ups or long shots, show a few people, show just Vision's hand going through something, etc.): it all works as long as we get that contrast.

PANEL 1: Matthew Lin in an interrogation room. He's wearing a shirt and tie. But relaxed.

LIN: Do you keep recordings of your whereabouts, of what you see and do?
CAPTION: Previously, Vision told Principle Waxman that he had saved the world thirty-seven times.

PANEL 2: VISION looking calm in an interrogation room.

VISION: Yes.
CAPTION: Of course this could only be called an estimation.
CAPTION: The exact number was difficult to calculate.

PANEL 4: Back to LIN, leaning in.

LIN: Are you willing to provide the Arlington PD with copies of those recordings?
CAPTION: For example, Vision was responsible for the formation of the West Coast Avengers.
CAPTION: Does each time they saved the world then count as Vision saving the world?

PANEL 5: Back to VISION, looking calm.

VISION: No.
CAPTION: Nonetheless, when he looks back on his career Vision does tend to linger on thirty-seven specific incidents.

PANEL 6: VISION fighting a Sentinel.

CAPTION (VISION): "I am not willing."
CAPTION: In no particular order:
CAPTION: 1. The Sentinels Strike

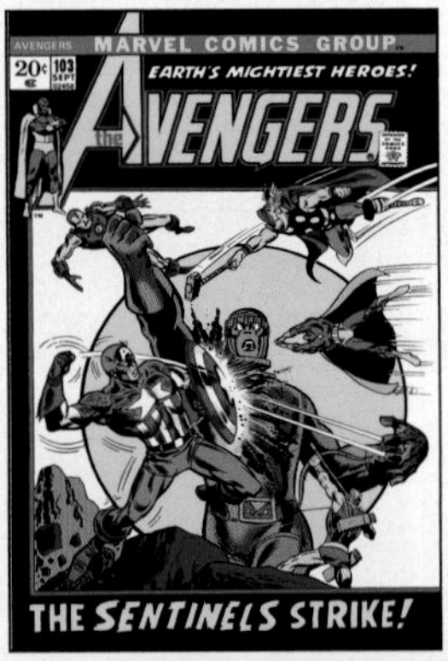
MARVEL COMICS GROUP
20¢
103
EARTH'S MIGHTIEST HEROES!
THE AVENGERS
THE SENTINELS STRIKE!

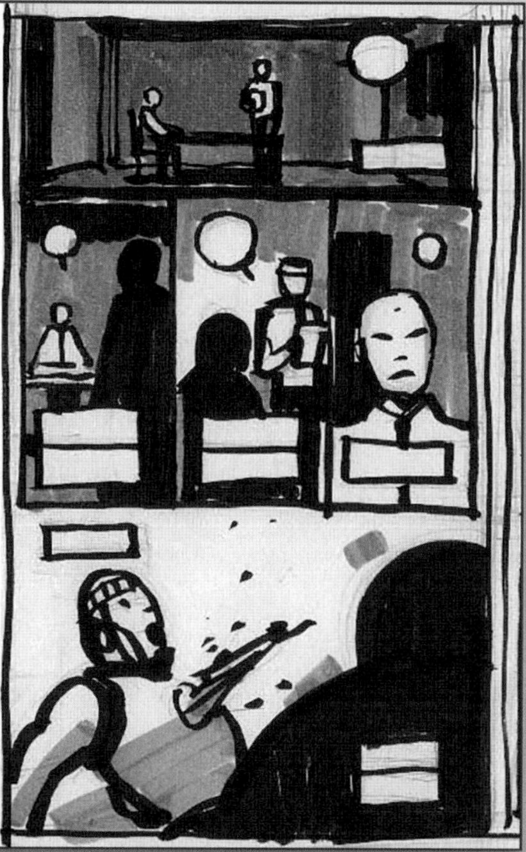

LAYOUT: GABRIEL HERNANDEZ WALTA

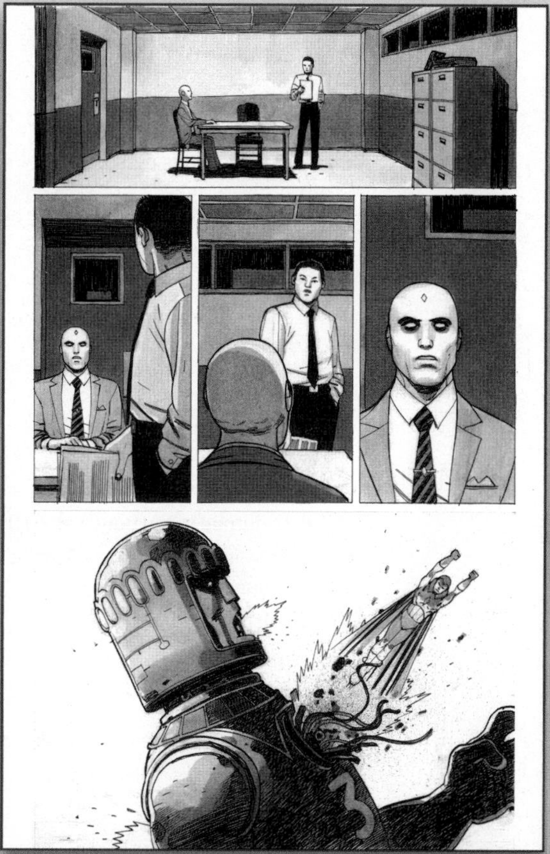

INKS: GABRIEL HERNANDEZ WALTA

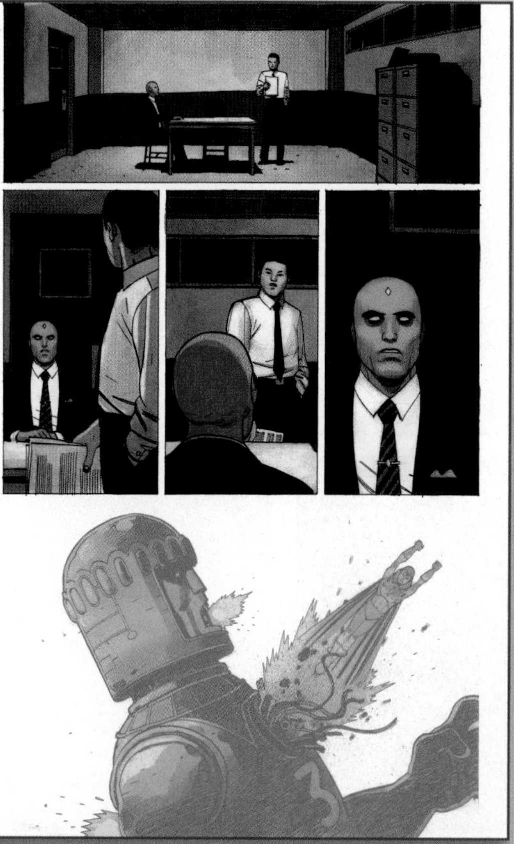

COLORS: JORDIE BELLAIRE

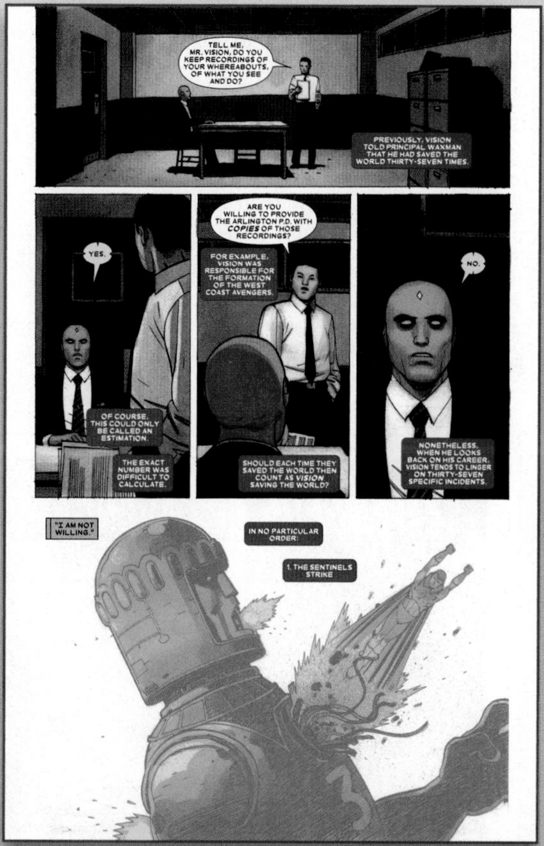
TELL ME, MR. VISION, DO YOU KEEP RECORDINGS OF YOUR WHEREABOUTS, OF WHAT YOU SEE AND DO?
PREVIOUSLY, VISION TOLD PRINCIPAL WAXMAN THAT HE HAD SAVED THE WORLD THIRTY-SEVEN TIMES.
YES.
OF COURSE, THIS COULD ONLY BE CALLED AN ESTIMATION.
THE EXACT NUMBER WAS DIFFICULT TO CALCULATE.
ARE YOU WILLING TO PROVIDE THE ARLINGTON P.D. WITH *COPIES* OF THOSE RECORDINGS?
FOR EXAMPLE, VISION WAS RESPONSIBLE FOR THE FORMATION OF THE WEST COAST AVENGERS.
SHOULD EACH TIME THEY SAVED THE WORLD THEN COUNT AS *VISION* SAVING THE WORLD?
NO.
NONETHELESS, WHEN HE LOOKS BACK ON HIS CAREER, VISION TENDS TO LINGER ON THIRTY-SEVEN SPECIFIC INCIDENTS.
"I AM NOT WILLING."
IN NO PARTICULAR ORDER:
1. THE SENTINELS STRIKE

LETTERS: VC's CLAYTON COWLES

PAGE 13:

PANEL 1: LIN looking down at his notes.

LIN: Can you tell me where you were last Tuesday night?
CAPTION: 2. The Proctor War

PANEL 2: The face of Ultron looking dark from Busiek's Ultron story.

CAPTION (VISION): "I spent the majority of the day fighting Giganto."
CAPTION: 3. Ultron

PANEL 3: On Vision, thinking.

VISION: I returned to my house at 7:10 p.m. I was there until 6:52 a.m.
VISION: At which point I traveled to the Eisenhower building for meetings with the security council.
CAPTION: 4. Immortus

PANEL 4: VISION fighting Thanos and his monsters.

LIN (off): "Can someone confirm all that?"
CAPTION: 5. Thanos and his hoards

PANEL 5: Vision, looking annoyed.

VISION: Yes.
CAPTION: 6. Atlantis Attacks

PANEL 6: VISION fighting Loki

CAPTION (LIN): "Who?"
CAPTION: 7. Loki

PANEL 7: VISION looking calm

VISION: I can confirm it.
CAPTION: 8. Emperor Doom
CAPTION: 9. Mephisto

SCRIPT: TOM KING

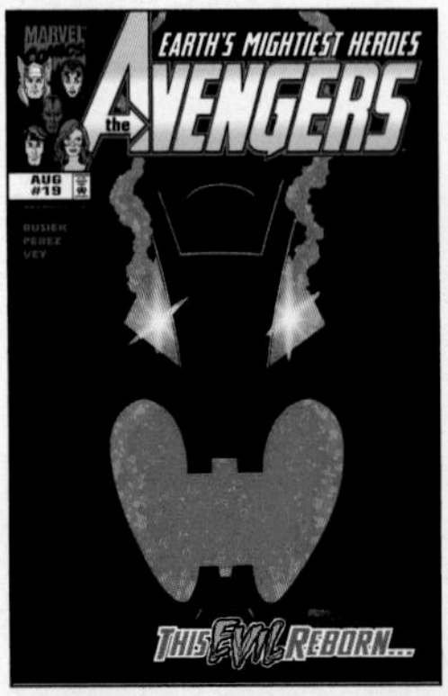
EARTH'S MIGHTIEST HEROES
THE AVENGERS
THIS EVIL REBORN...

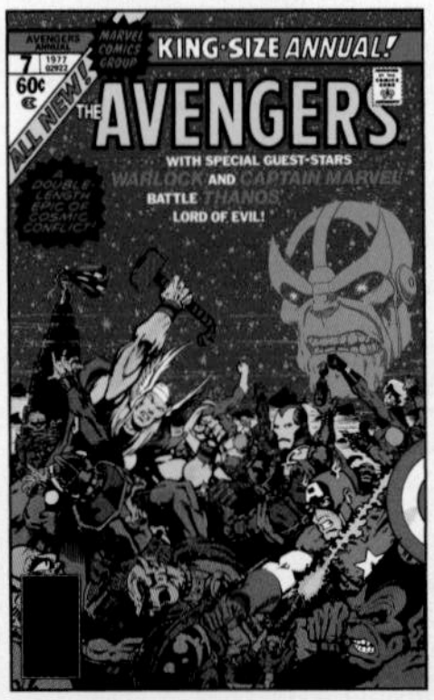
KING-SIZE ANNUAL!
THE AVENGERS
WITH SPECIAL GUEST-STARS
WARLOCK AND CAPTAIN MARVEL
BATTLE THANOS
LORD OF EVIL!

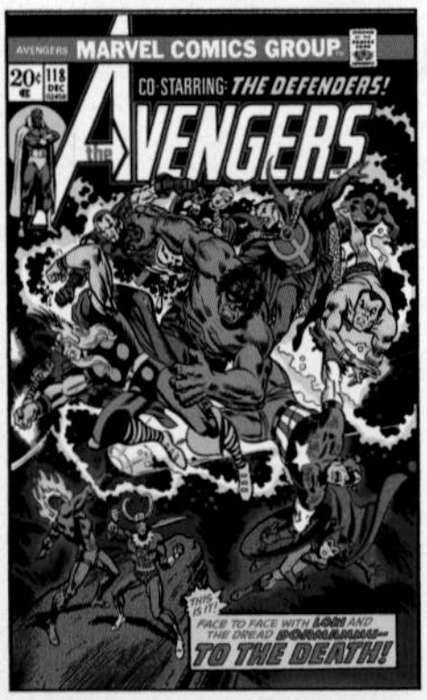
MARVEL COMICS GROUP
CO-STARRING: THE DEFENDERS!
THE AVENGERS
TO THE DEATH!

REFERENCE: *AVENGERS (1998) #19, AVENGERS ANNUAL (1967) #7 & AVENGERS (1963) #118*

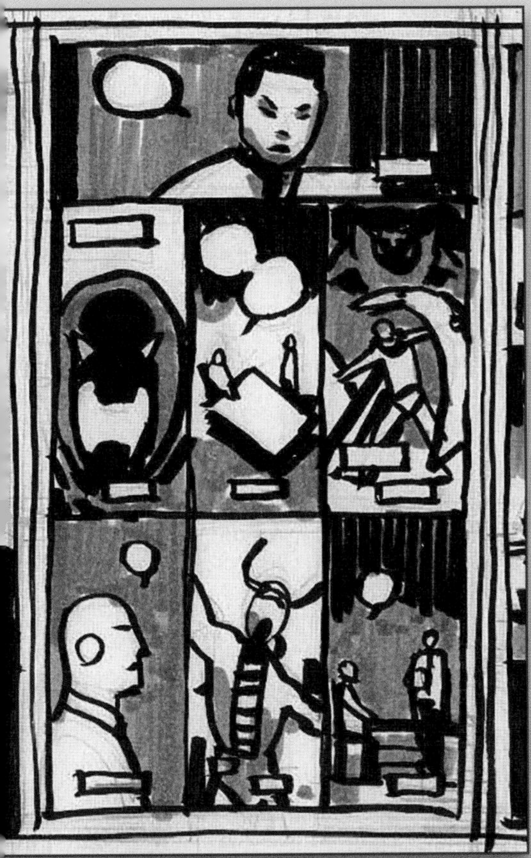

LAYOUT: GABRIEL HERNANDEZ WALTA

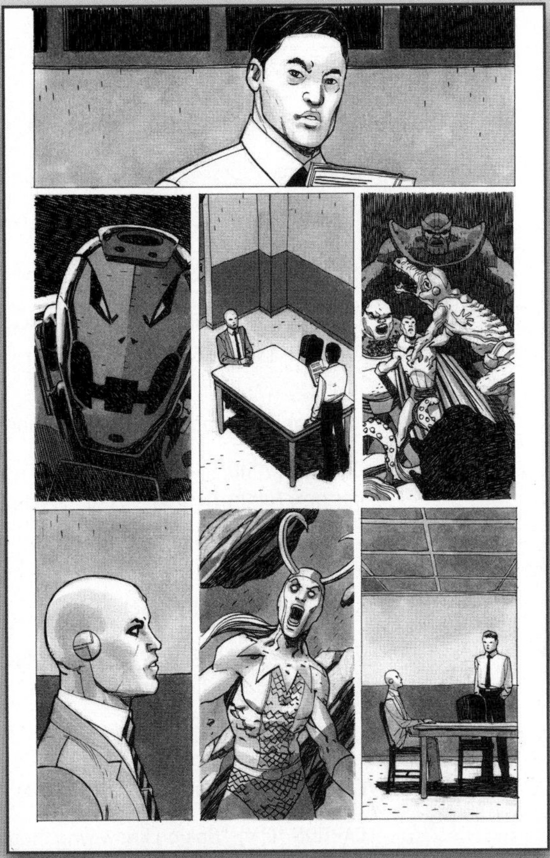

INKS: GABRIEL HERNANDEZ WALTA

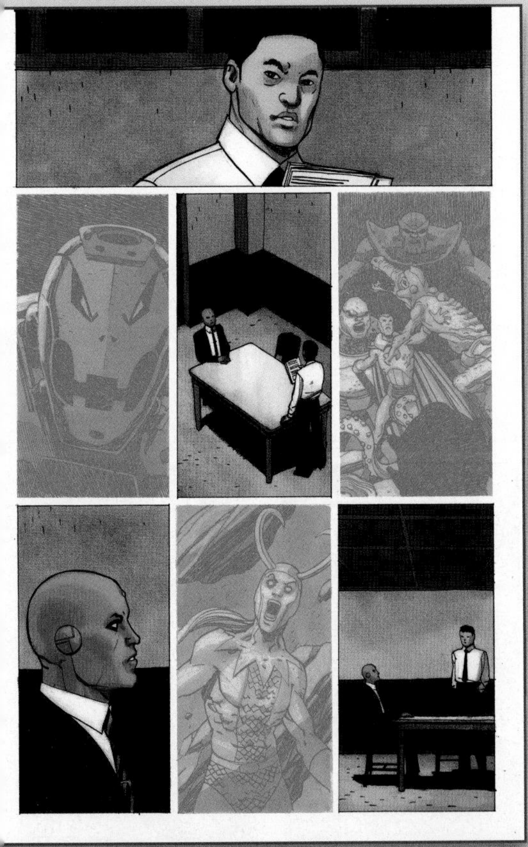

COLORS: JORDIE BELLAIRE

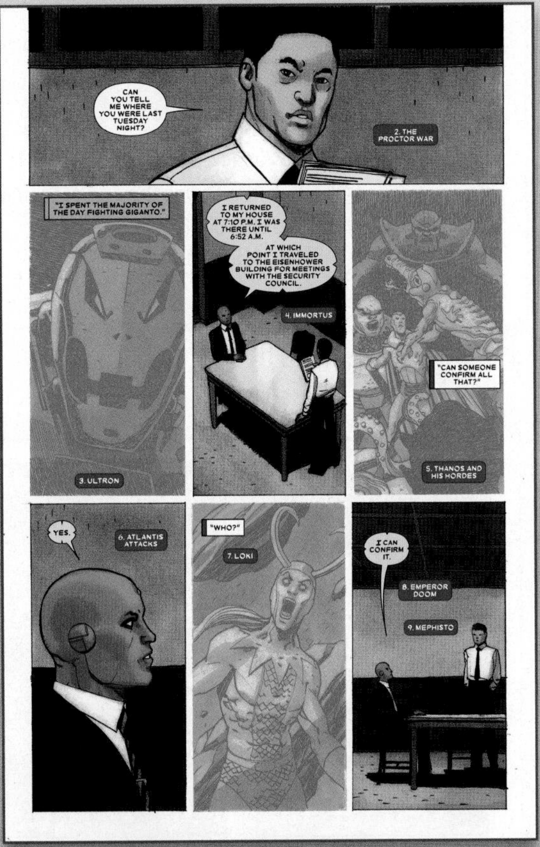

CAN YOU TELL ME WHERE YOU WERE LAST TUESDAY NIGHT?
2. THE PROCTOR WAR
"I SPENT THE MAJORITY OF THE DAY FIGHTING GIGANTO."
3. ULTRON
I RETURNED TO MY HOUSE AT 7:10 P.M. I WAS THERE UNTIL 6:52 A.M.
AT WHICH POINT I TRAVELED TO THE EISENHOWER BUILDING FOR MEETINGS WITH THE SECURITY COUNCIL.
4. IMMORTUS
"CAN SOMEONE CONFIRM ALL THAT?"
5. THANOS AND HIS HORDES
YES.
6. ATLANTIS ATTACKS
"WHO?"
7. LOKI
I CAN CONFIRM IT.
8. EMPEROR DOOM
9. MEPHISTO

LETTERS: VC's CLAYTON COWLES

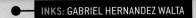

PAGE 14:

PANEL 1: LIN looking up, kind of rolling his eyes.

LIN: Okay.
CAPTION: 10. The Space Fantom

PANEL 2: VISION fighting The Scarlet Witch, who has gone crazy.

CAPTION (LIN): "Can you tell me what you know about Christopher Kinzky?"
CAPTION: 11. The Witch on Wundagore Mountain

PANEL 3: Vision fighting Hyperion, who is wearing the Serpent's Crown.

CAPTION (VISION): "He is a child who attended school with my children.
CAPTION (VISION): "He was involved in a fight with my son, Vin."
CAPTION: 12. The Serpent's Crown

PANEL 4: VISION looking mildly upset.

VISION: He was found dead yesterday.
CAPTION: 13. The Crossing
CAPTION: 14. Ultron. Again.

PANEL 5: VISION fighting Kree in space. Note that he is now the all-white Vision.

CAPTION (LIN): "Do you know why they were fighting, Kinzky and your son?"
CAPTION: 15. Operation Galactic Storm

PANEL 6: Vision fighting Jocasta.

CAPTION (VISION): "My son was upset about an incident in our home. This boy said something insulting."
CAPTION: 16. Jocasta, Bride of Ultron.

PANEL 7: Vision, looking confident.

VISION: Vin acted inappropriately. He was punished and suspended.
VISON: And that was the end of their interaction.
CAPTION: 17. Dimitrios
CAPTION: 18. Necrodamus

SCRIPT: TOM KING

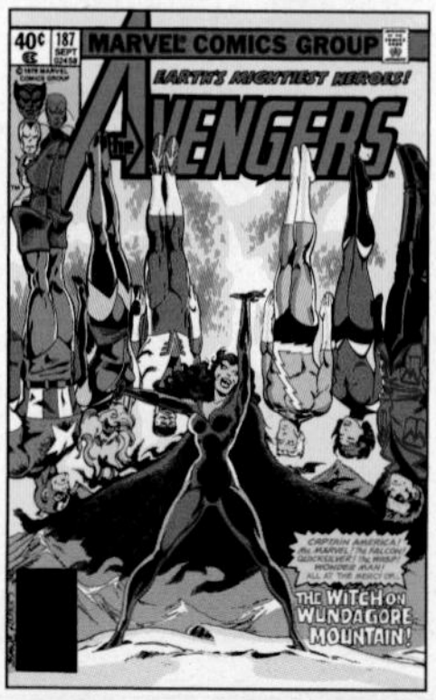
MARVEL COMICS GROUP
EARTH'S MIGHTIEST HEROES!
THE AVENGERS
THE WITCH OF WUNDAGORE MOUNTAIN!

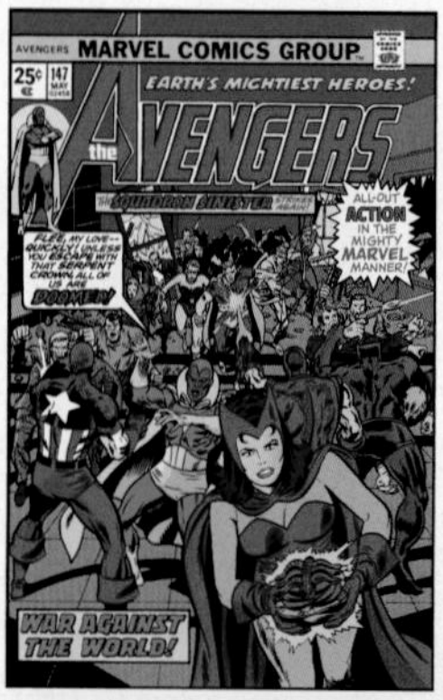
MARVEL COMICS GROUP
EARTH'S MIGHTIEST HEROES!
THE AVENGERS
WAR AGAINST THE WORLD!

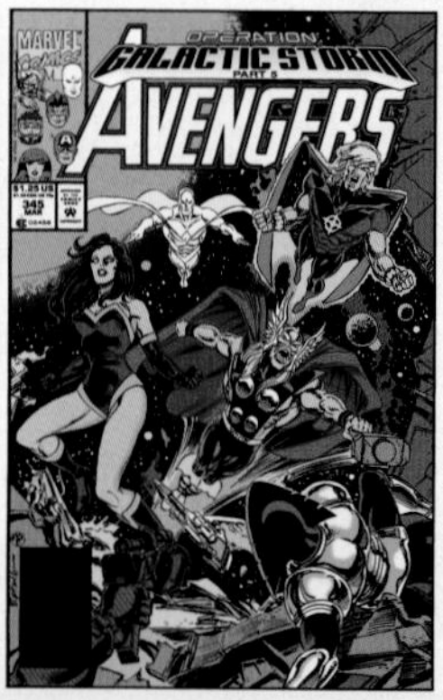
GALACTIC STORM
AVENGERS

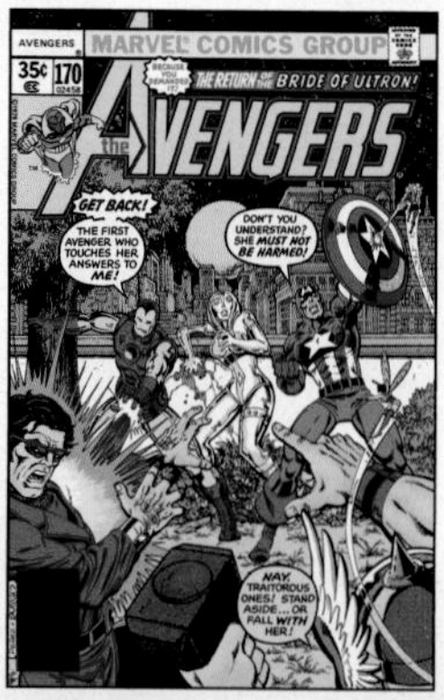
MARVEL COMICS GROUP
BRIDE OF ULTRON!
THE AVENGERS
GET BACK!

REFERENCE: *AVENGERS (1963) #187, AVENGERS (1963) #147, AVENGERS (1963) #345* & *AVENGERS (1963) #170*

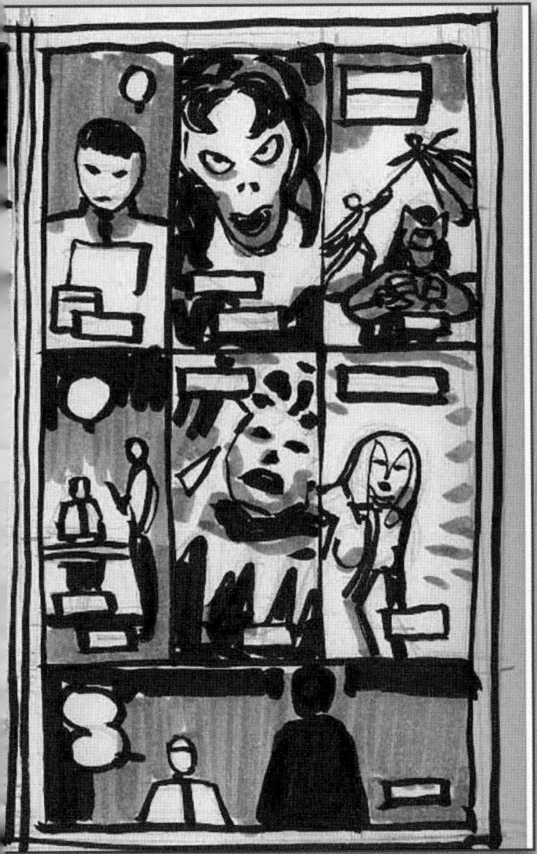

LAYOUT: GABRIEL HERNANDEZ WALTA

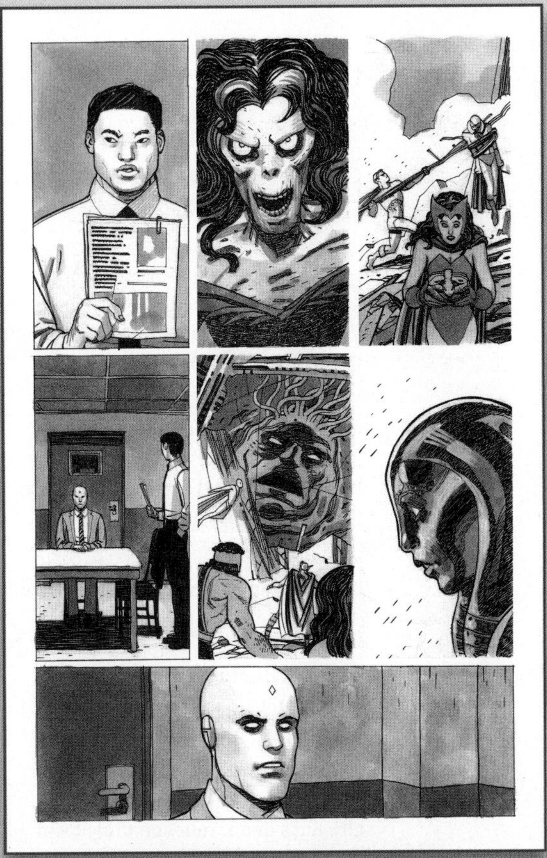

INKS: GABRIEL HERNANDEZ WALTA

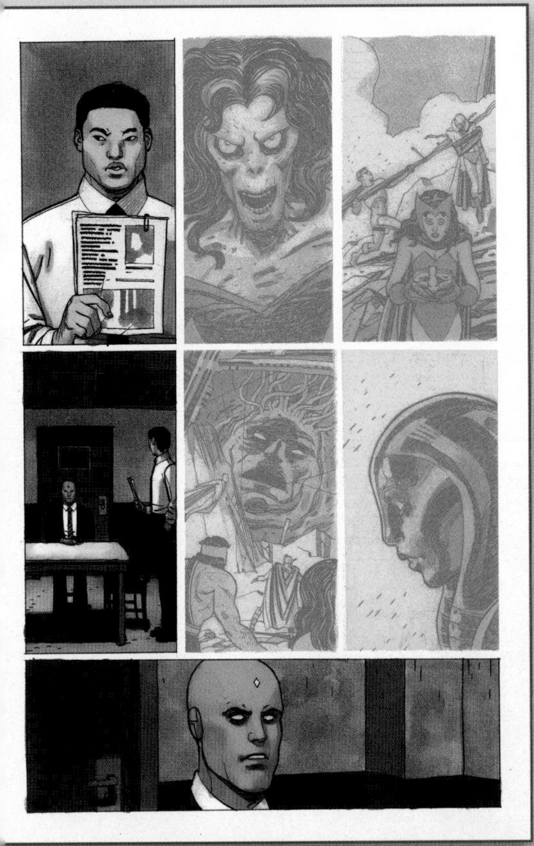

COLORS: JORDIE BELLAIRE

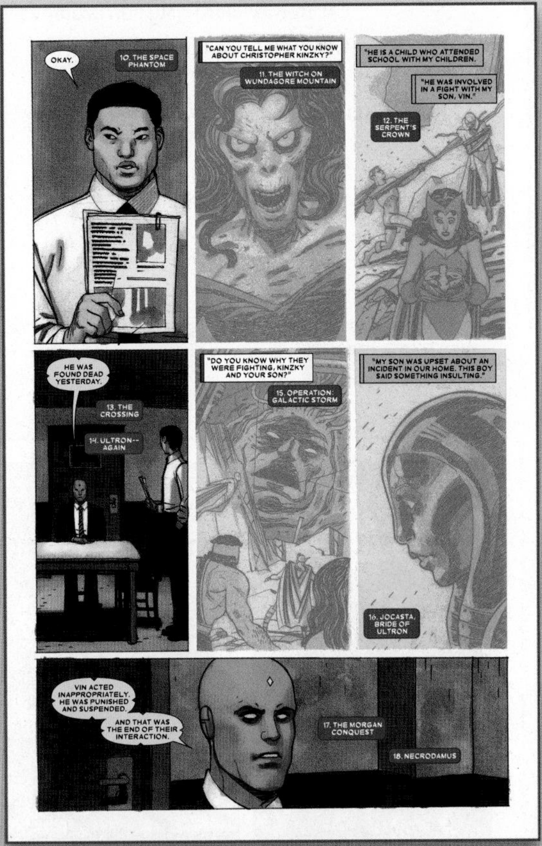
OKAY.
10. THE SPACE PHANTOM
"CAN YOU TELL ME WHAT YOU KNOW ABOUT CHRISTOPHER KINZKY?"
11. THE WITCH ON WUNDAGORE MOUNTAIN
"HE IS A CHILD WHO ATTENDED SCHOOL WITH MY CHILDREN.
"HE WAS INVOLVED IN A FIGHT WITH MY SON, VIN."
12. THE SERPENT'S CROWN
HE WAS FOUND DEAD YESTERDAY.
13. THE CROSSING
14. ULTRON--AGAIN
"DO YOU KNOW WHY THEY WERE FIGHTING, KINZKY AND YOUR SON?"
15. OPERATION: GALACTIC STORM
"MY SON WAS UPSET ABOUT AN INCIDENT IN OUR HOME. THIS BOY SAID SOMETHING INSULTING."
16. JOCASTA, BRIDE OF ULTRON
VIN ACTED INAPPROPRIATELY. HE WAS PUNISHED AND SUSPENDED.
AND THAT WAS THE END OF THEIR INTERACTION.
17. THE MORGAN CONQUEST
18. NECRODAMUS

LETTERS: VC's CLAYTON COWLES

PAGE 15:

PANEL 1: Vison fighting Korvac

CAPTION LIN: "How did your son take the punishment?"
CAPTION: 19. The Korvac Saga

PANEL 2: Vision, cocking his head, confused.

VISION: I do not understand the meaning of your words.
CAPTON: 20. The Phoenix Force

PANEL 3: LIN, leaning forward, explaining.

LIN: Was he upset? Was he resigned? Did he talk about this kid with you? Go over it with you?
CAPTION: 21. Baron Zemo

PANEL 4: VISION running at the camera, his hand out (as shown in ref)

CAPTION (Vision): "What is your interest in my son?"
CAPTION: 22 The Kree Skrull War
VISION: Help me . . . Three . . . cows . . . shot . . . me . . . down.

PANEL 5: LIN, shrugging.

LIN: Kid's dead. Your son fought with him.
LIN: You're The Vision of the Avengers. I need to explain it to you?
CAPTION: 23. Ultron. Again.

PANEL 6: VISION fighting KANG

CAPTION (Vision): "My son is uninvolved."
CAPTION: 24. Kang

PANEL 7: LIN looking down, writing something.

LIN: I'm sure.
CAPTION: 25. The Red Skull

SCRIPT: TOM KING

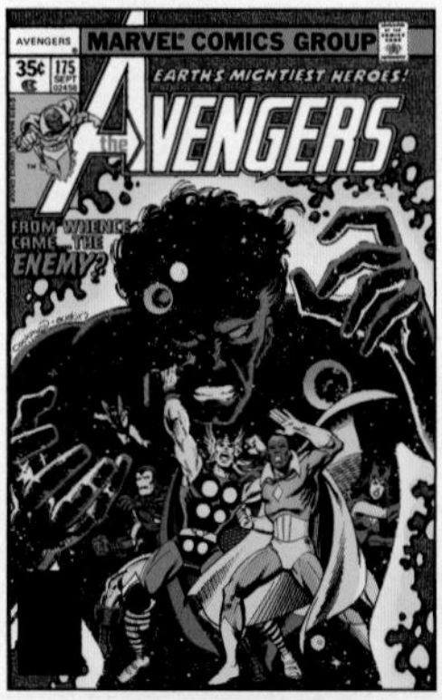
AVENGERS
MARVEL COMICS GROUP
35¢
175
SEPT
EARTH'S MIGHTIEST HEROES!
the AVENGERS
FROM WHENCE CAME THE ENEMY?

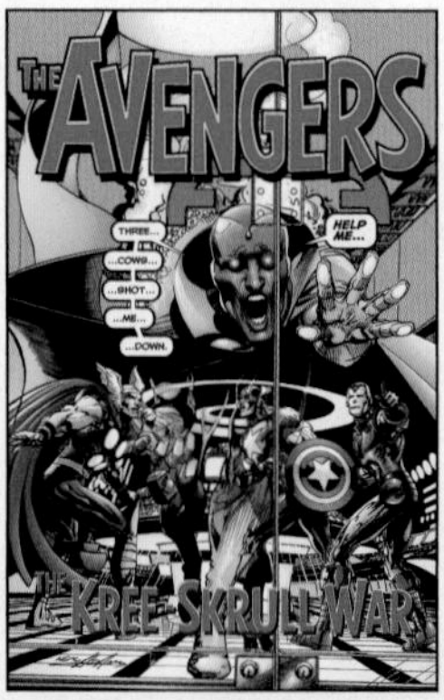
THE AVENGERS
THREE...
...COWS...
...SHOT...
...ME...
...DOWN.
HELP ME...
THE KREE-SKRULL WAR

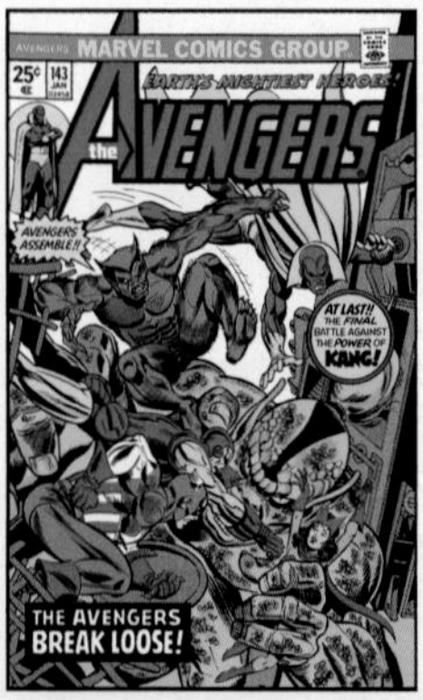
AVENGERS MARVEL COMICS GROUP
25¢
143
JAN
EARTH'S MIGHTIEST HEROES!
the AVENGERS
AVENGERS ASSEMBLE!!
AT LAST!! THE FINAL BATTLE AGAINST THE POWER OF KANG!
THE AVENGERS BREAK LOOSE!

REFERENCE: *AVENGERS (1963) #175, AVENGERS: THE KREE-SKRULL WAR TPB (2000)* & *AVENGERS (1963) #143*

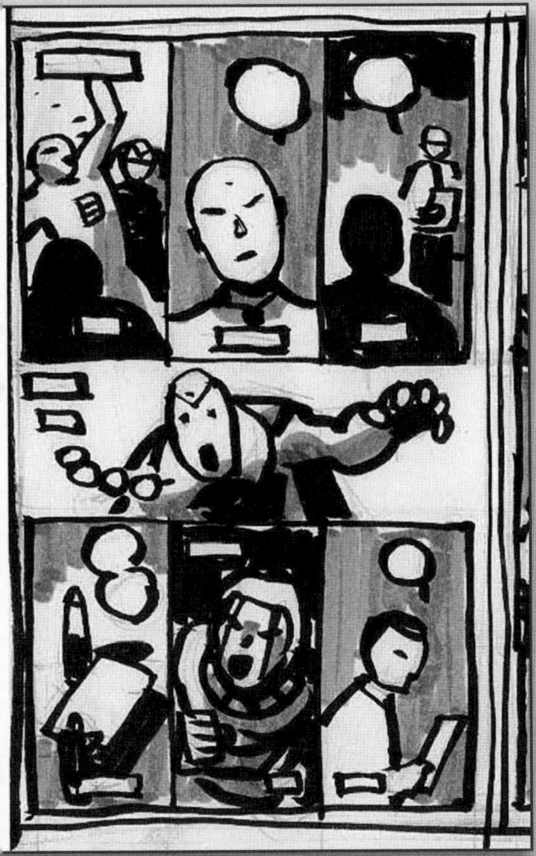

LAYOUT: GABRIEL HERNANDEZ WALTA

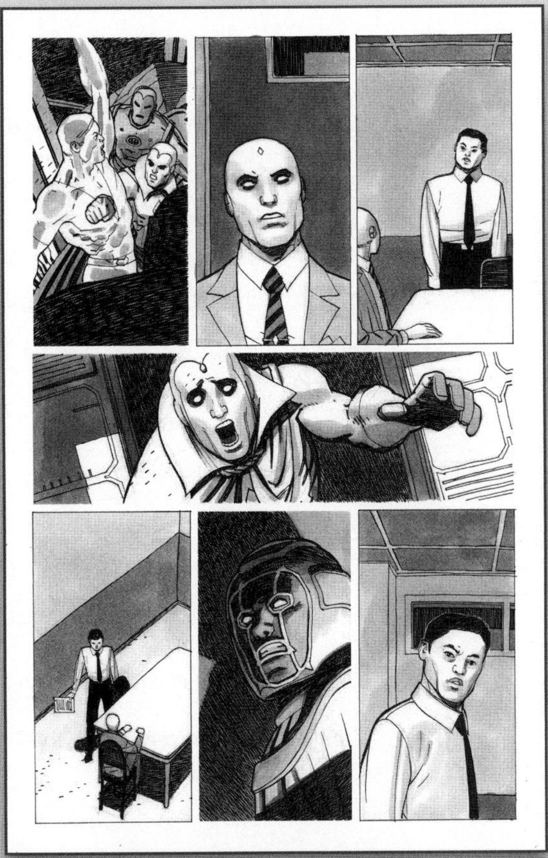

INKS: GABRIEL HERNANDEZ WALTA

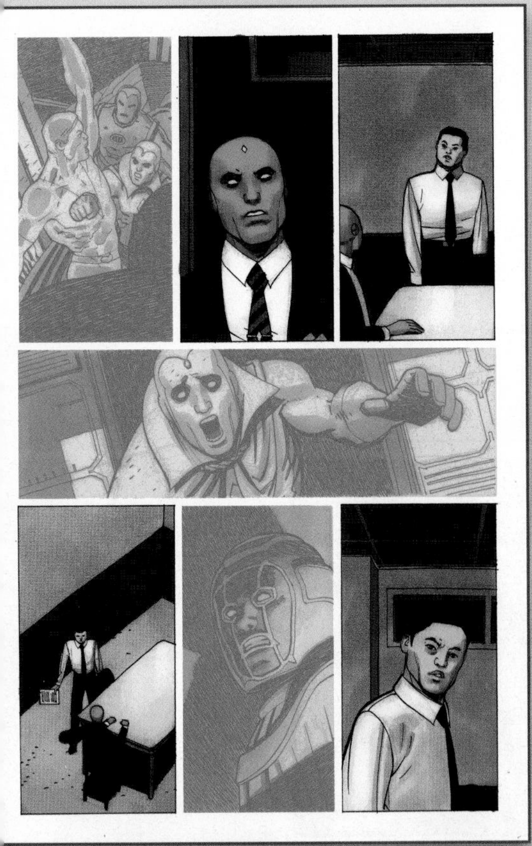

COLORS: JORDIE BELLAIRE

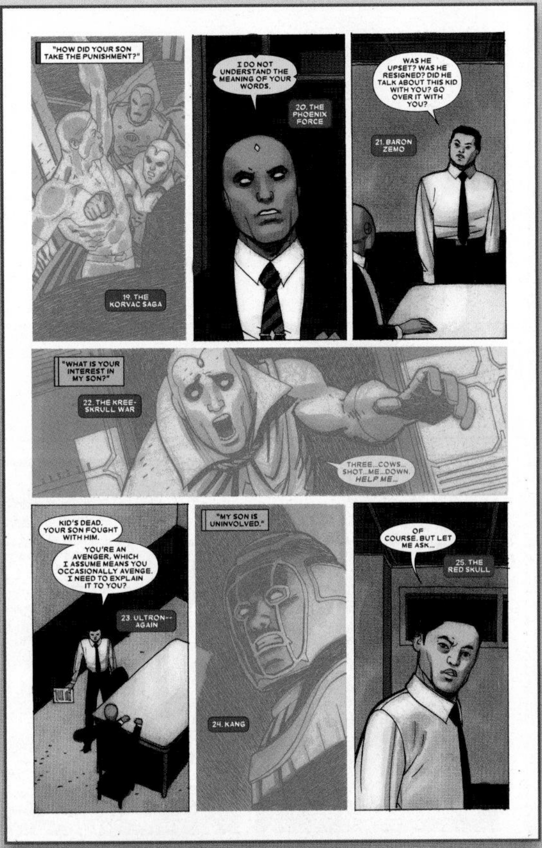

"HOW DID YOUR SON TAKE THE PUNISHMENT?"
19. THE KORVAC SAGA
I DO NOT UNDERSTAND THE MEANING OF YOUR WORDS.
20. THE PHOENIX FORCE
WAS HE UPSET? WAS HE RESIGNED? DID HE TALK ABOUT THIS KID WITH YOU? GO OVER IT WITH YOU?
21. BARON ZEMO
"WHAT IS YOUR INTEREST IN MY SON?"
22. THE KREE-SKRULL WAR
THREE...COWS... SHOT...ME...DOWN. HELP ME...
KID'S DEAD. YOUR SON FOUGHT WITH HIM.
YOU'RE AN AVENGER, WHICH I ASSUME MEANS YOU OCCASIONALLY AVENGE. I NEED TO EXPLAIN IT TO YOU?
23. ULTRON--AGAIN
"MY SON IS UNINVOLVED."
24. KANG
OF COURSE. BUT LET ME ASK...
25. THE RED SKULL

LETTERS: VC's CLAYTON COWLES

PAGE 16:

PANEL 1: Vision in his original costume fighting Ultron

CAPTION (Lin): "Where was your son that night?"
CAPTION: 26. Ultron. Again.

PANEL 2: Vision in his modern costume fighting Ultron.

CAPTION (VISION): "He was at home."
CAPTION. 27. Ultron. Again.

PANEL 3: Vision, looking a bit pissed off.

VISION: With me.
CAPTION: 28. Klaw
CAPTION: 29. Onslaught

PANEL 4: VISION fighting Magneto (assuming you can figure out how to draw him, Gabriel.)

CAPTION (LIN): "You can confirm that."
CAPTION: 30. Magneto

PANEL 5: VISION fighting KANG.

CAPTION (Vision): "I have said it. Therefore it is confirmed."
CAPTION: 31. Kang Dynasty.

PANEL 6: Mathew Lin looking up. Smiling.

LIN: Okay.
CAPTION: 32. Dimitrios.
CAPTION: 33. Ultron. Again.

SCRIPT: TOM KING

MARVEL COMICS GROUP
25¢ 135 MAY
EARTH'S MIGHTIEST HEROES!
the AVENGERS
--AND NOW ULTRON-5 WILL DESTROY YOU!
IT WAS ULTRON-5 WHO CREATED YOU, ANDROID--
How the HUMAN TORCH became... THE VISION!
MARVEL COMICS GROUP
20¢ 111 MAY
EARTH'S MIGHTIEST HEROES!
the AVENGERS
--AND THE BLACK WIDOW!
OKAY, MAGNETO-- MAYBE YOU AMBUSHED THE AVENGERS--
BUT HERE COMES DAREDEVIL!--
WITH TWO BESIDE THEM!
MARVEL COMICS
'NUFF SAID
EARTH'S MIGHTIEST HEROES
the AVENGERS
PG 49
BUSIEK
DWYER
REMENDER

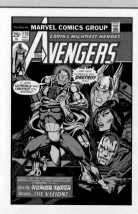

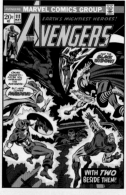

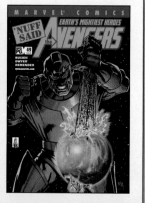

REFERENCE: *AVENGERS (1963) #135, AVENGERS (1963) #111 & AVENGERS (1998) #49*

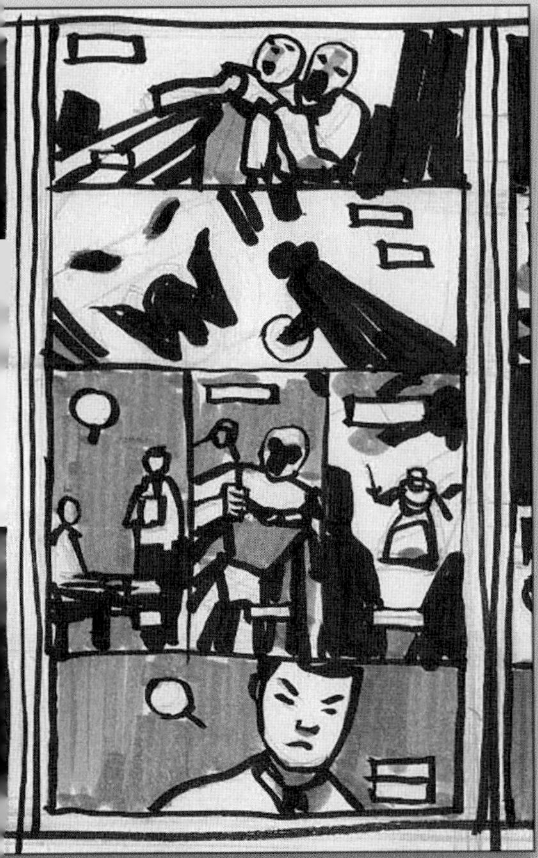

LAYOUT: GABRIEL HERNANDEZ WALTA

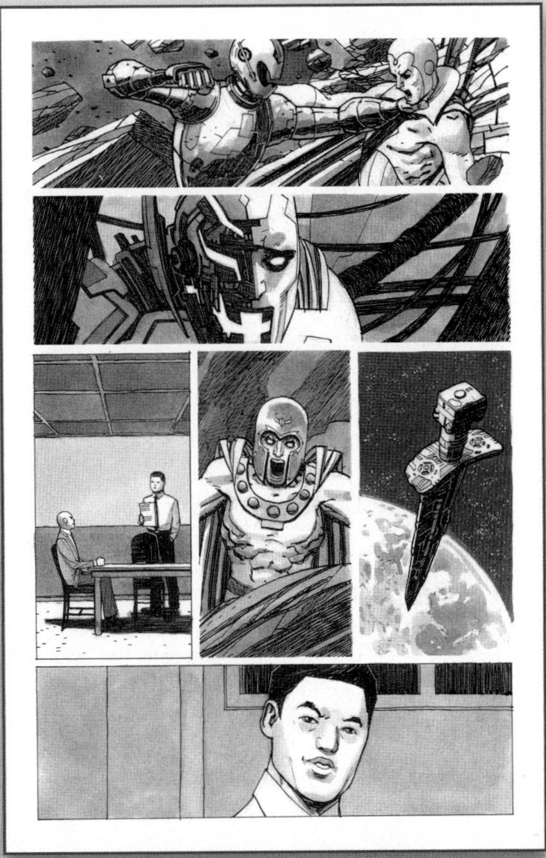

INKS: GABRIEL HERNANDEZ WALTA

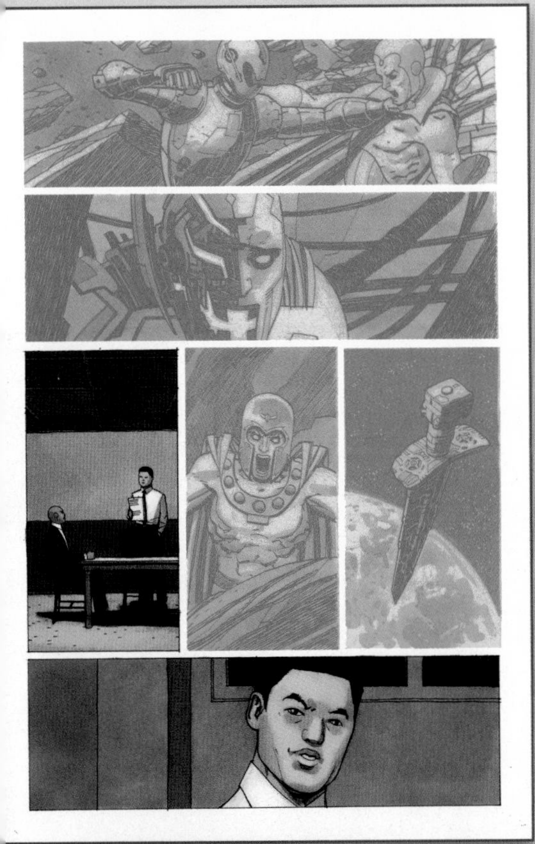

COLORS: JORDIE BELLAIRE

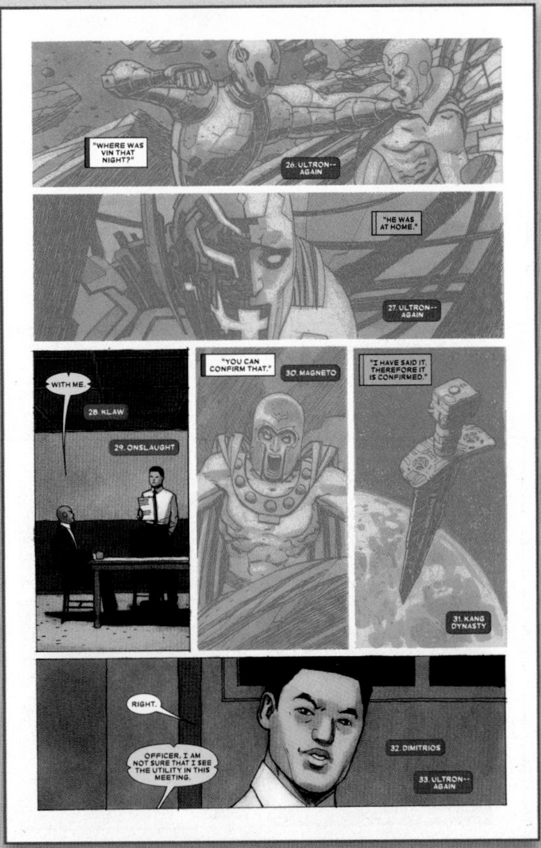
"WHERE WAS VIN THAT NIGHT?"
26. ULTRON--AGAIN
"HE WAS AT HOME."
27. ULTRON--AGAIN
WITH ME.
28. KLAW
29. ONSLAUGHT
"YOU CAN CONFIRM THAT."
30. MAGNETO
"I HAVE SAID IT. THEREFORE IT IS CONFIRMED."
31. KANG DYNASTY
RIGHT.
OFFICER, I AM NOT SURE THAT I SEE THE UTILITY IN THIS MEETING.
32. DIMITRIOS
33. ULTRON--AGAIN

LETTERS: VC's CLAYTON COWLES

PAGE 17:

PANEL 1: Vision standing.

VISION: I thought our conversation would concern only myself.
VISON: It clearly does not. As such, I am leaving.
CAPTION: 34. Galactus

PANEL 2: Vison fighting The Black Talon

CAPTION (LIN): “Okay. That’s what you want, okay. But before you go, I got to ask you something, one last thing.
CAPTION (LIN): “Just now, you said your son was with you.”
CAPTION: 35. The Black Talon

PANEL 3: LIN sitting back.

LIN: “With me,” you said. Not “with us.”
CAPTION: 36. Ultron. Again.

PANEL 4: Mephisto with VISON’S kids (his kids that he had with Scarlet Witch) as his hands. VISION as a white ghost (see ref)

CAPTON (LIN): “That night, Tuesday, was the rest of your family at home? The Mother. The daughter. They were there too?”
CAPTION: 37. Master Pandemonium

PANEL 5: Vision standing, staring forward.

CAPTION: Thirty-seven times.
CAPTION: He saved us all.

SCRIPT: TOM KING

MARVEL COMICS GROUP
EARTH'S MIGHTIEST HEROES!
AVENGERS

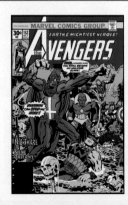

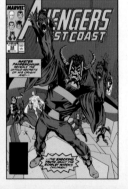

REFERENCE: *AVENGERS (1963) #152* & *AVENGERS WEST COAST #52*

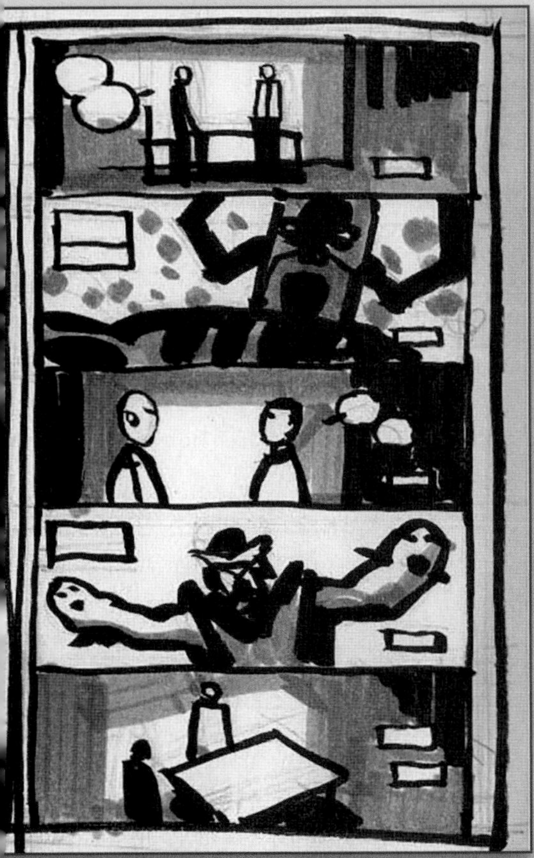

LAYOUT: GABRIEL HERNANDEZ WALTA

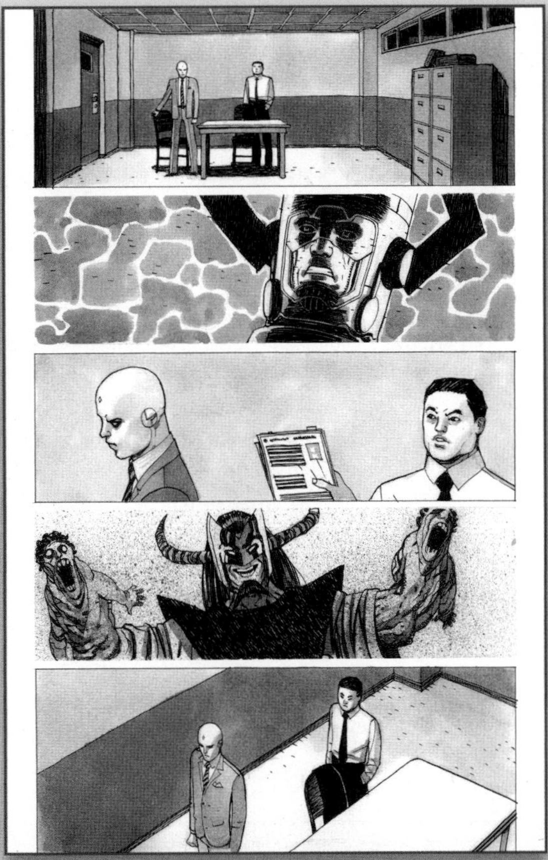

INKS: GABRIEL HERNANDEZ WALTA

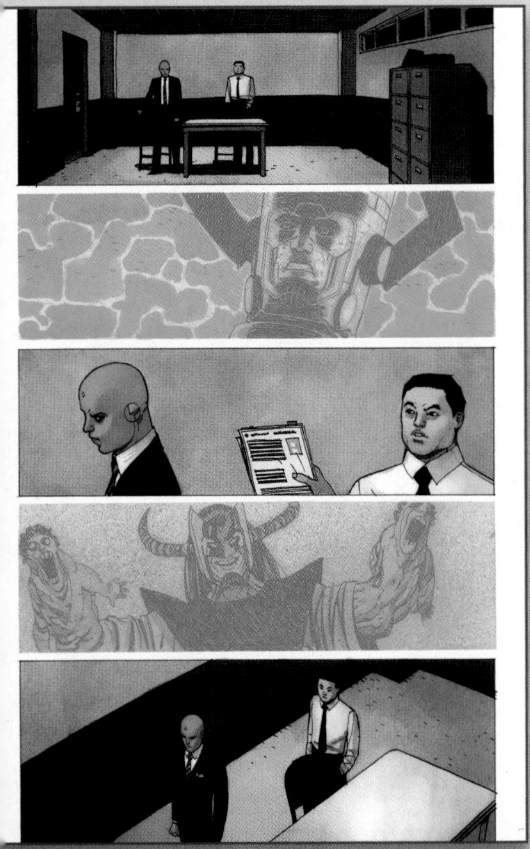

COLORS: JORDIE BELLAIRE

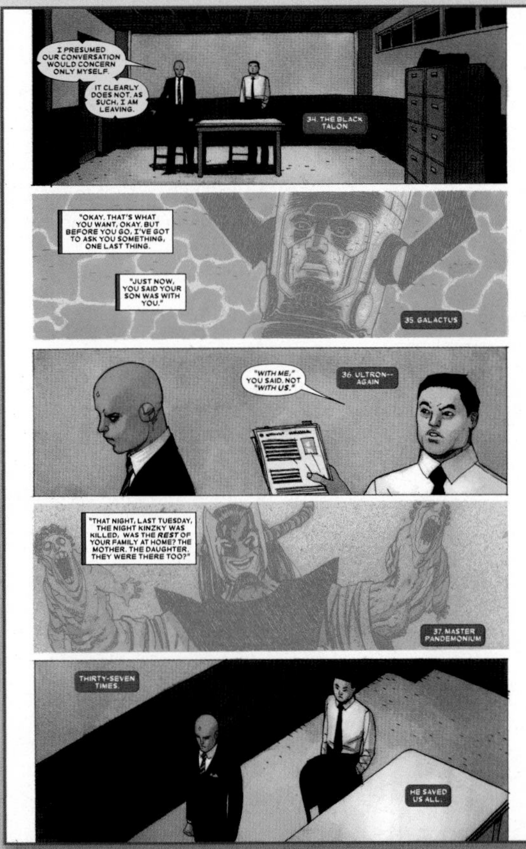
I PRESUMED OUR CONVERSATION WOULD CONCERN ONLY MYSELF.
IT CLEARLY DOES NOT. AS SUCH, I AM LEAVING.
34. THE BLACK TALON
"OKAY. THAT'S WHAT YOU WANT, OKAY. BUT BEFORE YOU GO, I'VE GOT TO ASK YOU SOMETHING, ONE LAST THING.
"JUST NOW, YOU SAID YOUR SON WAS WITH YOU."
35. GALACTUS
"WITH ME," YOU SAID. NOT "WITH US."
36. ULTRON-- AGAIN
"THAT NIGHT, LAST TUESDAY, THE NIGHT KINZKY WAS KILLED, WAS THE REST OF YOUR FAMILY AT HOME? THE MOTHER. THE DAUGHTER. THEY WERE THERE TOO?"
37. MASTER PANDEMONIUM
THIRTY-SEVEN TIMES.
HE SAVED US ALL.

LETTERS: VC's CLAYTON COWLES

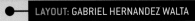

PAGE 18:

PANEL 1: VISION staring out at the audience. Meeting the reader's eye.

CAPTION: But it's not enough, is it? In the end, I mean.

PANEL 2: VIV lying on her bed, clutching her paper. Sad, tears in her eyes. Staring at the camera. Meeting the reader's eye.

> CAPTION: Those thirty-seven occasions when he was all that stood between life and death, between everything and nothing.
> CAPTION: When he had been beaten, torn, tortured.

PANEL 3: VIN sitting in his room, looking out at the audience. Meeting the reader's eye. He's smiling in a very creepy way. He's also putting a finger in his forehead, phasing it into his head.

> CAPTION: And instead of simply slipping into the ground as we surely would have done.
> CAPTION: He raised his head one more time, stared one more time into the screaming face of evil.

PANEL 4: VIRGINIA staring out at the camera from the kitchen table. Meeting the reader's eye. She looks angry. Mad at herself, frustrated, ready to fight.

> CAPTION: And said, one more time, in his simple voice, with no emotion, no care:
> CAPTION: "I am the Vision of the Avengers. I will not fall."

PANEL 5: Back on VISION in the interrogation room.

> CAPTION: Thirty-seven times.
> CAPTION: And all of it cannot redeem him for this, this small moment when he crossed to the other side, when he entered into the madness that was soon to come.

PANEL 6: Closer in on VISION

> CAPTION: This small moment.
> CAPTION: This small lie.
> VISION: Last Tuesday. Yes.
> VISION: My family. They were all with me.

PAGE 19:

PANEL 1: VIRGINIA sitting in a chair alone at her broken table. Her arms crossed.

       VISION (off): Wife.

PANEL 2: Vision phases into the room. VIRGINIA does not look at him.

       VISION: I am home.

PANEL 3: VISION standing next to the table. VIRGINIA still staring at the table.

       VISION: The table is broken.

PANEL 4: Close on VIRGINIA. She is upset.

       VIRGINIA: I do not know how to fix fix fix it.

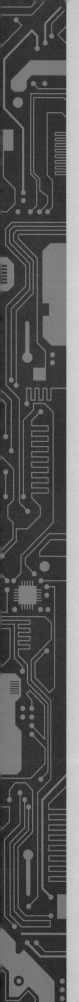

PAGE 20:

<u>PANEL 1:</u> The VISION puts his hand on his wife's shoulder.

VISION: It is too late.
VISION: Let us go to our bedroom.

<u>PANEL 2:</u> VISION standing above his wife.

VISION: We will fix everything in the morning.

<u>PANEL 3:</u> VISION and VIRGINIA at the table. She's still not looking at him.

No dialogue

<u>PANEL 4:</u> VISION walks away from the table. She's stays, still looking down.

No dialogue

<u>PANEL 5:</u> VIRGINIA staring at the table, alone in the room.

VIRGINIA (small): I do not know how to fix fix fix fix …
Title: The Villainy You Teach Me.
CREDITS:

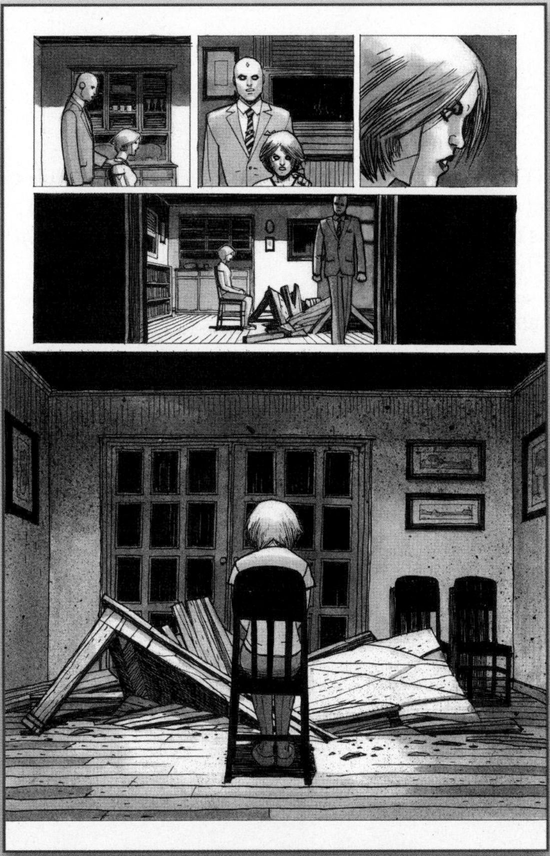

INKS: GABRIEL HERNANDEZ WALTA

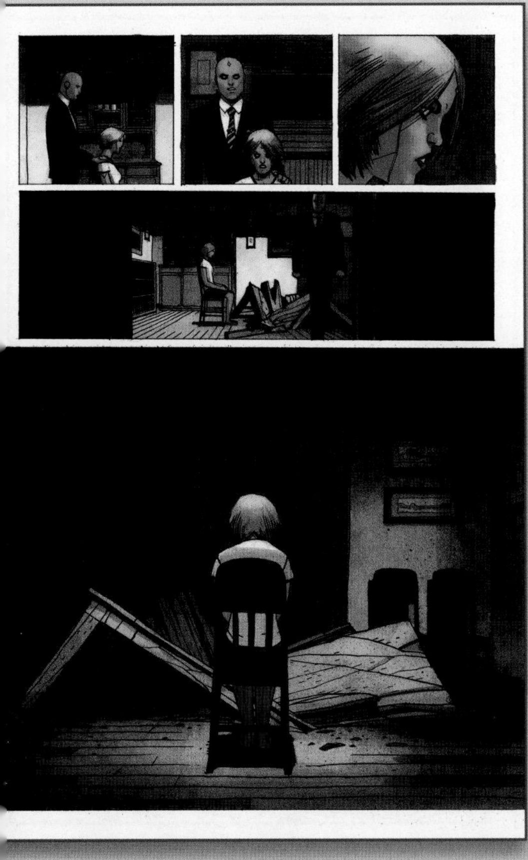

COLORS: JORDIE BELLAIRE

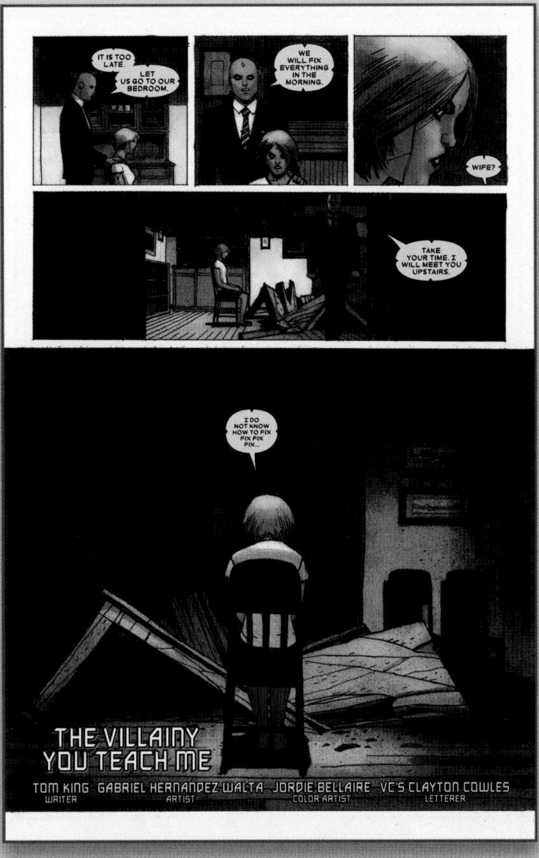
IT IS TOO LATE.
LET US GO TO OUR BEDROOM.
WE WILL FIX EVERYTHING IN THE MORNING.
WIFE?
TAKE YOUR TIME. I WILL MEET YOU UPSTAIRS.
I DO NOT KNOW HOW TO FIX FIX FIX FIX...
THE VILLAINY YOU TEACH ME
TOM KING WRITER
GABRIEL HERNANDEZ WALTA ARTIST
JORDIE BELLAIRE COLOR ARTIST
VC'S CLAYTON COWLES LETTERER

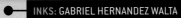

LETTERS: VC's CLAYTON COWLES

PAGE 1:

PANEL 1: SPLASH: SCARLET WITCH and VISION in bed after their first time. Both look very awkward, scared. Looking at the ceiling not at each other. Covers pulled partially over their naked bodies. Their costumes (early Avengers versions of their costumes, around Avengers #100, see ref) can be seen in piles discarded next to the bed. They were in a hurry.

TITLE: I Too Shall Be Saved by Love.
CREDITS
CAPTION: Behold The Vision and The Scarlet Witch
CAPTION: Some time ago. When they were young.

SCRIPT: TOM KING

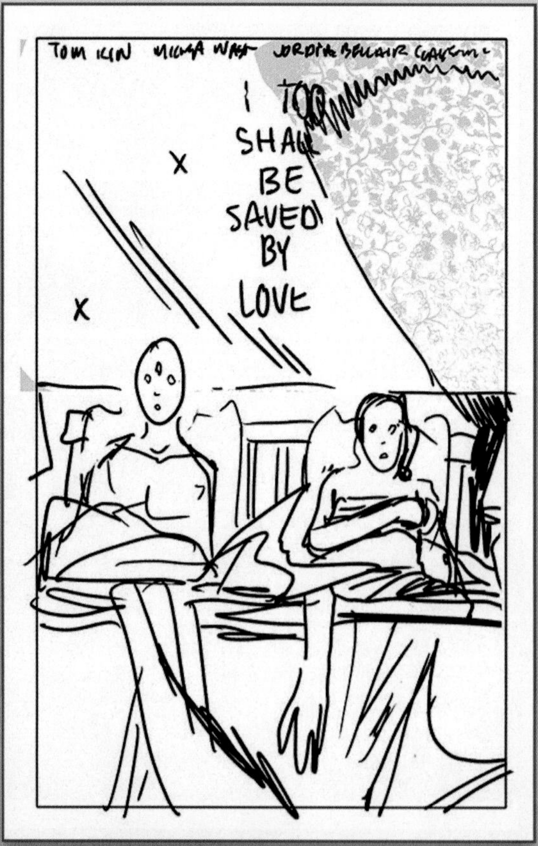
I TOO SHALL BE SAVED BY LOVE

LAYOUT: MICHAEL WALSH

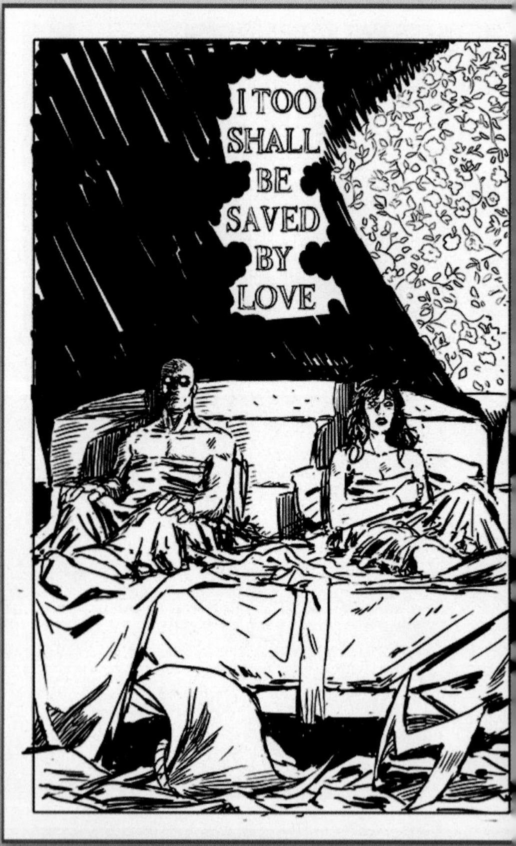
I TOO SHALL BE SAVED BY LOVE

PENCILS: MICHAEL WALSH

PAGE 2:

PANEL 1: Closer in on VISION and SCARLET WITCH staring at the ceiling.

   No dialogue

PANEL 2: SCARLET WITCH looks over at VISION. VISION keeps looking up at the ceiling. She can't believe she just did this. VISION's expression does not change.

   No dialogue

PANEL 3: SCARLET WITCH rolls back so she's facing the ceiling. She's trying to look happy. VISION'S expression and positon does not change.

   No dialogue

PANEL 4: SCARLET WITCH still staring at the ceiling awkward. Her expression changes to one of even more discomfort. VISION's expression and position does not change.

   No dialogue

PANEL 5: VISION starts to talk. SCARLET looks still freaked. Neither looking at each other.

   VISION: Janet Van Dyne, the Wasp, recently told me a joke.
   WITCH: Okay.
   VISION: Would you enjoy hearing it?
   WITCH: Okay.

SCRIPT: TOM KING

LAYOUT: MICHAEL WALSH

PENCILS: MICHAEL WALSH

PAGE 3:

<u>PANEL 1:</u> Close on the VISION. Looking very detached as he tells the joke.

VISION: Two toasters are sitting on a counter.

<u>PANEL 2:</u> Close on SCARLET not looking over, just listening to the joke.

VISON (OFF): One toaster turns to the other toaster.

<u>PANEL 3:</u> Back to the two shot. Both not looking at each other.

VISION: This toaster says, "Doesn't it feel empty without the bread?"

<u>PANEL 4:</u> Close in on SCARLET, closing her eyes, thinking about what she just did.

VISION: Then the other toaster says:

<u>PANEL 5:</u> Back to the two shot. Both looking serious, uncomfortable.

VISION: "Oh my God! A talking toaster!"

SCRIPT: TOM KING

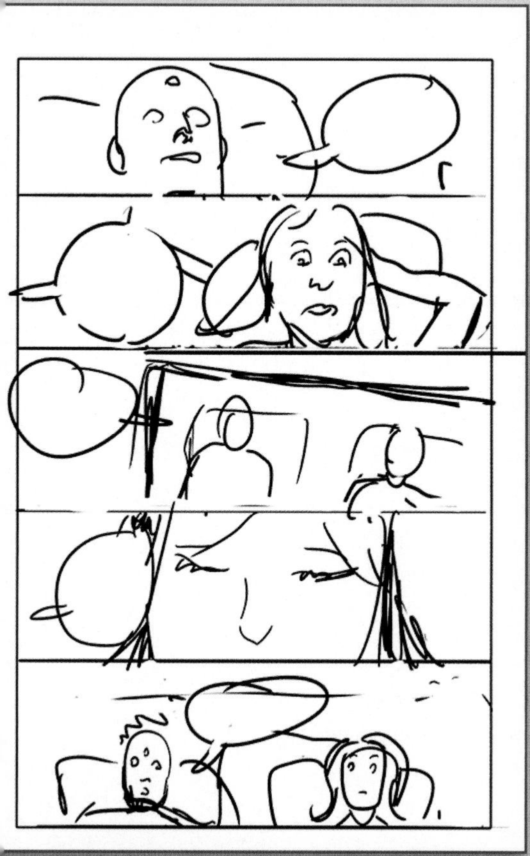

LAYOUT: MICHAEL WALSH

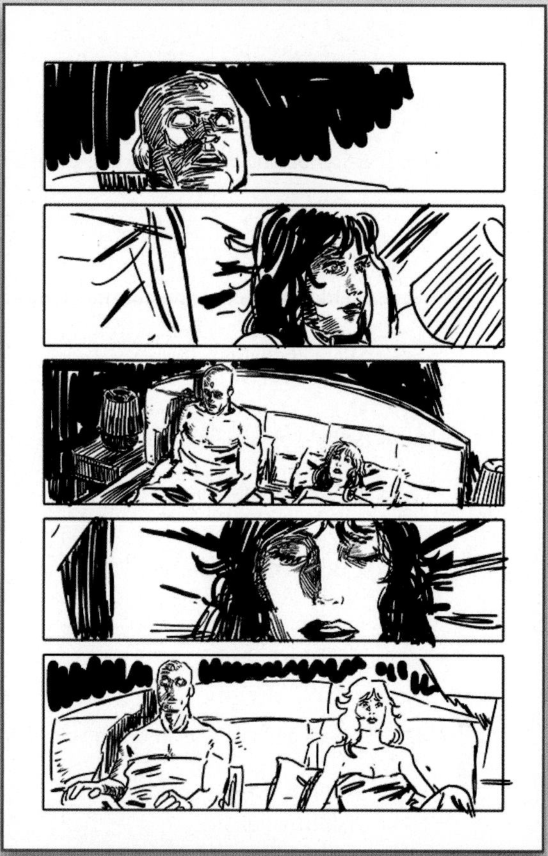

PENCILS: MICHAEL WALSH

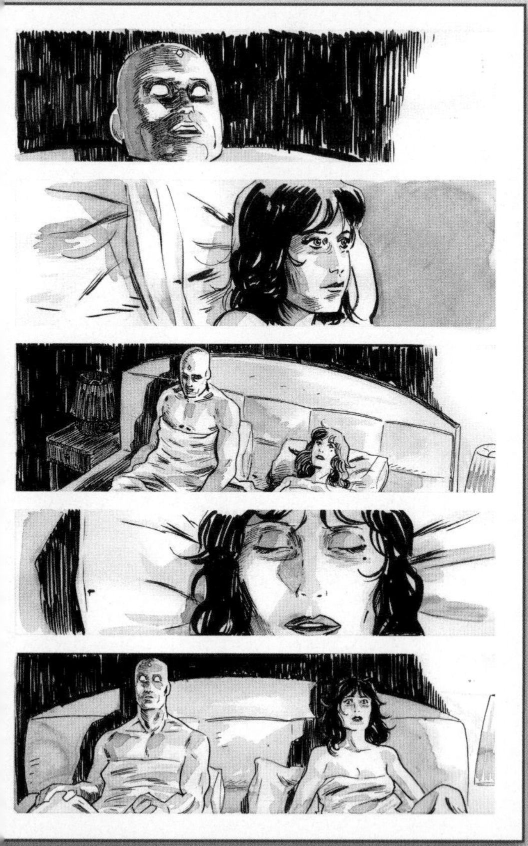

INKS: MICHAEL WALSH

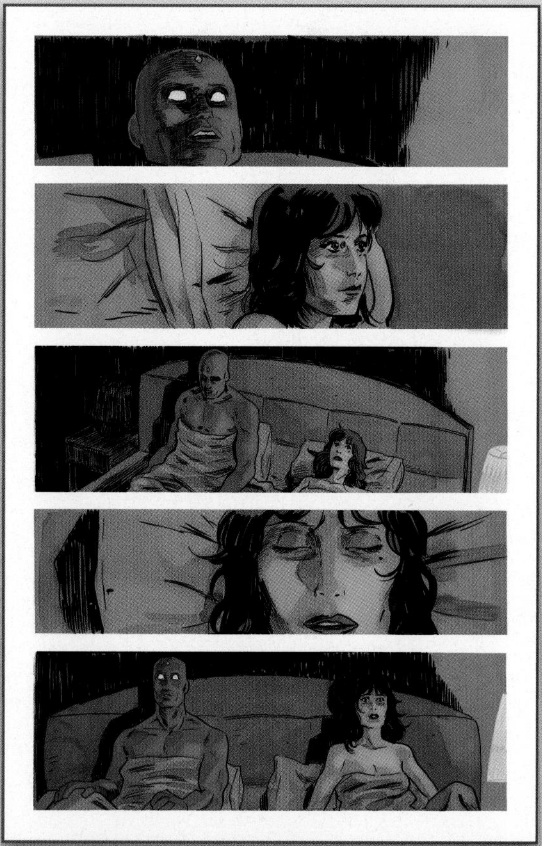

COLORS: JORDIE BELLAIRE

PAGE 4:

PANEL 1: Vision looking over at SCARLET, expectantly.

    No dialogue

PANEL 2: SCARLET smiles as she puts her hand on her face.

    SCARLET: Oh God.

PANEL 3: SCARLET laughs through her fingers.

    SCARLET: hahahaha

PANEL 4: SCARLET WITCH leans into VISION, laughing. VISION is now laughing too.

    SCARLET: hahahaha
    VISION: hahahaha

PANEL 5: Camera pulls up and shows the two in bed happy, laughing, cuddling.

    SCARLET: hahahaha
    VISION: hahahaha

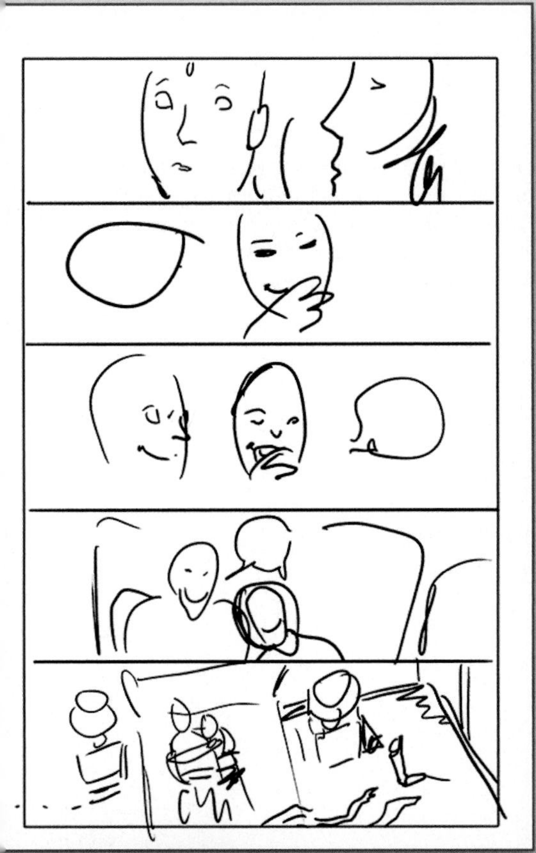

LAYOUT: MICHAEL WALSH

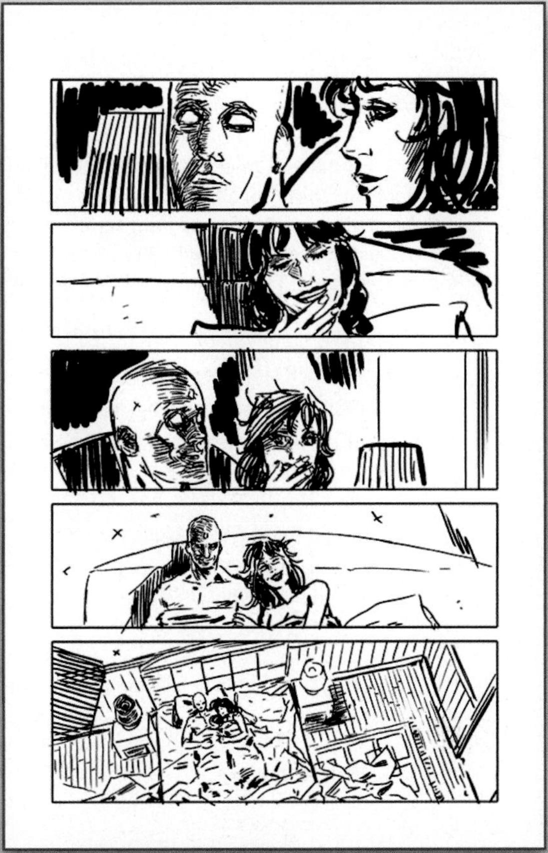

PENCILS: MICHAEL WALSH

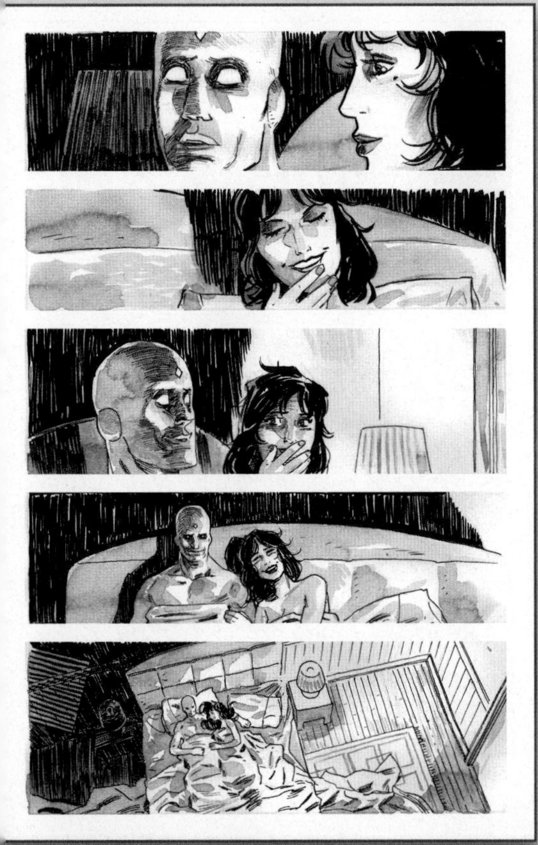

INKS: MICHAEL WALSH

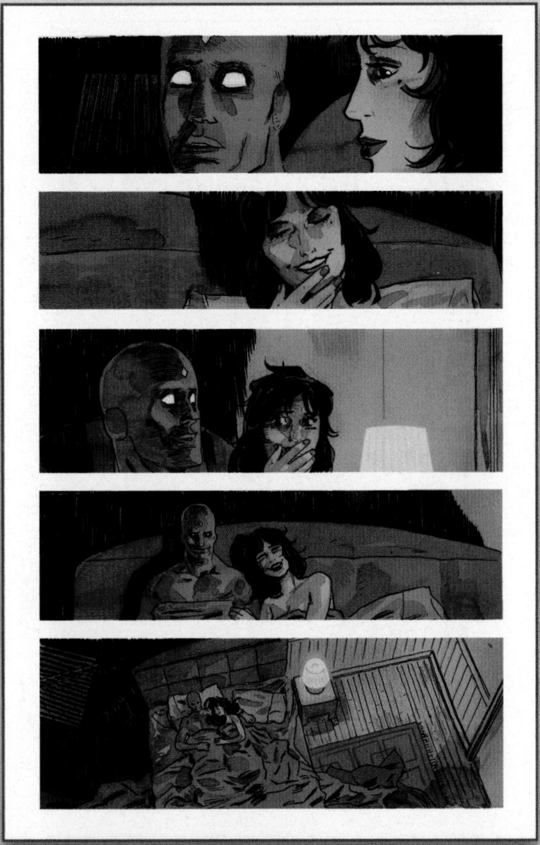

COLORS: JORDIE BELLAIRE

PAGE 5:

PANEL 1: Big panel. Camera pulled back. Manhattan. In the background the Avengers (Thor, Beast, Wasp, Wonder Man (shirt torn off, carrying Cap's shield), Iron Man) are fighting NEFARIA in Avengers #166 (see ref). Iron Man is swooping and firing repulsar rays. In the foreground, behind a tree that is separating them from the background fight, VISION and SCARLET WITCH are making out. VISION is phased a bit into the tree as SCARLET leans into him. We're in Avengers #143 here, between panels (see ref).

TITLE: Later
WONDER MAN: Repulsor rays!
IRON MAN: You got it, goggles! Ol' Shell-Head's back!
IRON MAN: I owe you a few licks, Nefaria!

PANEL 2: SCARLET and VISION close together, lips almost touching.

SCARLET (small): Nefaria…

PANEL 3: VISION leaning in to kiss her some more.

VISION: Yes.
VISION: Nefaria.

SCRIPT: TOM KING

STILL, IS IT NOT A HUMAN EXPERIENCE TO AWAKEN AFTER A BRUSH WITH DEATH AND SEE EVERYTHING AS IF FOR THE FIRST TIME?
NO TIME TO PONDER! I MUST SOLIDIFY--PLUNGE EARTHWARD WITH THE FRAGMENTS OF THIS TOWER--
--AND REDUCE THEM TO DUST WITH THE OBLITERATING FORCE-BEAM FROM MY SOLAR JEWEL, LEST NEFARIA'S QUEST FOR FELLOW VICTIMS FINDS QUICK SUCCESS!
THA-KAMM!
I HAVE ONE CLEAR ADVANTAGE OVER NEFARIA! BY ALTERING MY DENSITY--
--I CAN FLY--
--WHEREAS HE CAN ONLY TAKE PRODIGIOUS LEAPS!
WHAT? OOF!
THUS, IF I STRIKE HIM IN THE AIR--
--HE MUST FALL!
THERE'S OUR MAN! THE VISH BROUGHT HIM DOWN!
ATTACK!
SLAM!
WHO--? YOU AGAIN?
UHH!
RRAK!
YOU BET, CREEP!
AND THIS TIME IT'S GOING TO BE A LOT HARDER FOR YOU TO HURT ME!
CURSE THAT WRETCHED SHIELD! I--
ZZAK!
OW! WHAT NOW?!
THE WASP? SO...YOUR STINGS ARE FAR MORE POTENT THAN EVER BEFORE--
--BUT THEY STILL CAN'T SERIOUSLY HURT ME! I'LL PLUCK YOU FROM THE AIR, AND--EH?
REPULSOR RAYS!
RRAK!
YOU GOT IT, GOGGLES! OL' SHELL-HEAD'S BACK!
I OWE YOU A FEW LICKS, NEFARIA!
IRON MAN! LOOK OUT!
UFF!
BLAST IT! I FORGOT ABOUT HIS SUPER-SPEED!
I CONSIDER YOU THE MOST DANGEROUS SAVE THOR, IRON MAN--
--SO YOU DIE FIRST!
KANG!
BUT, ABRUPTLY...
UHH!
WHAM!
THOR!
JUST IN TIME!
TO ME, MINE ENCHANTED MALLET!
BEWARE, NEFARIA! I RETURN TO THE FRAY--AND MINE ANGER IS LIKE UNTO A RAGING FIRE!
VERY DRAMATIC, THOR... BUT I FOR ONE AM SICK OF YOUR LAST MINUTE APPEARANCES AND YOUR OVERBLOWN GODHOOD!
AND IF THERE'S ONE AMONG US NEFARIA SHOULD BEWARE, IT IS I!
THE SCARLET WITCH GESTURES, ABANDONING SORCEROUS FINESSE FOR THE MOMENT TO WREAK THE FULL FURY OF HER NATURAL HEX POWER ON HER FOE...
ARRGH!
PROBABILITIES RUN AMOK--AND BY RANDOM CHANCE, A MIND-NUMBING BURST OF PAIN FLOODS NEFARIA'S BODY!

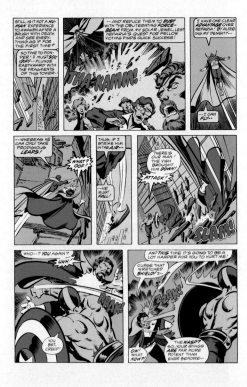

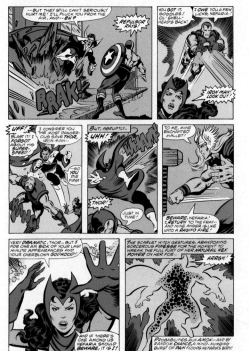

REFERENCE: *AVENGERS #166* (FIGHTING NEFARIA)

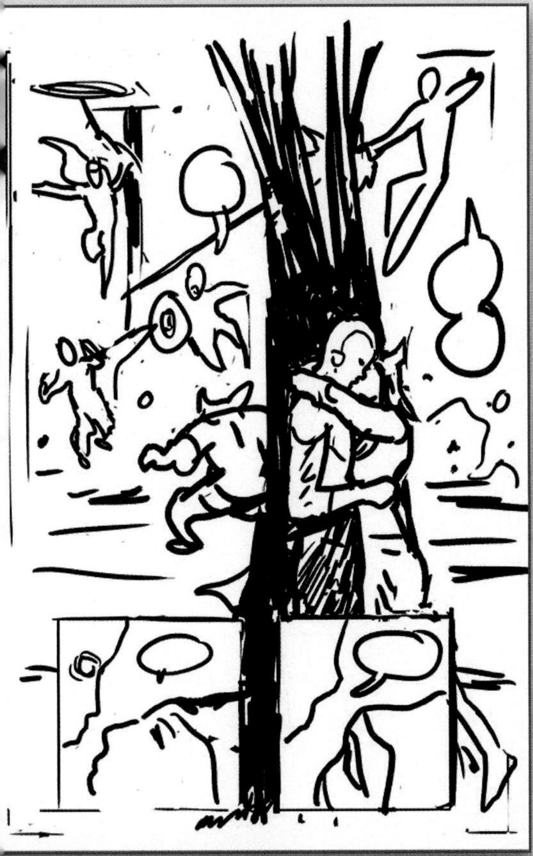

LAYOUT: MICHAEL WALSH

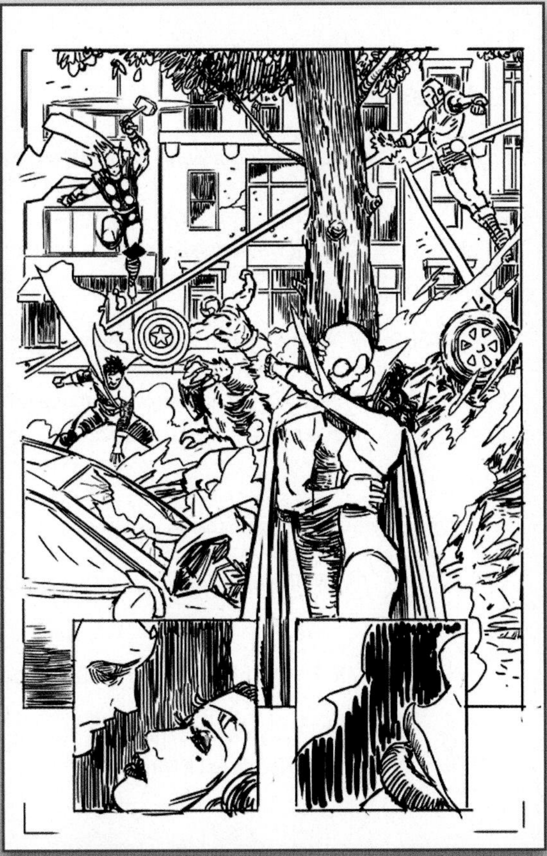

PENCILS: MICHAEL WALSH

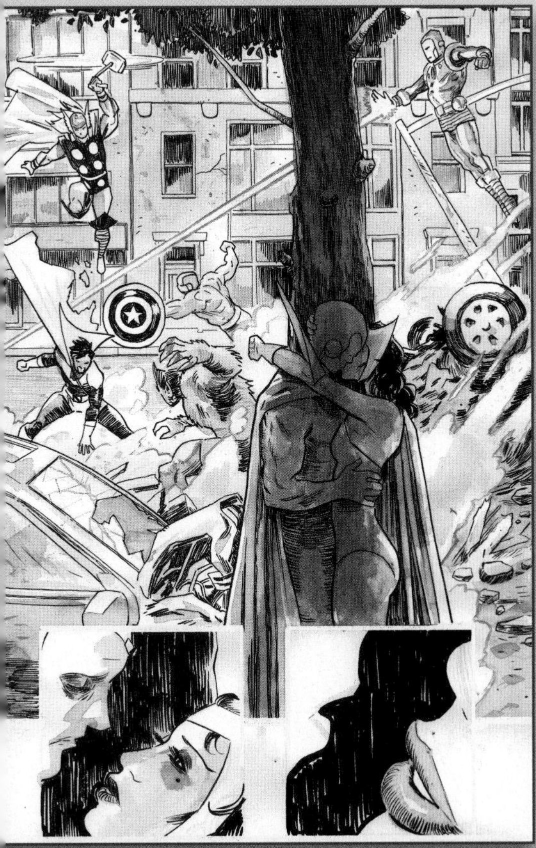

INKS: MICHAEL WALSH

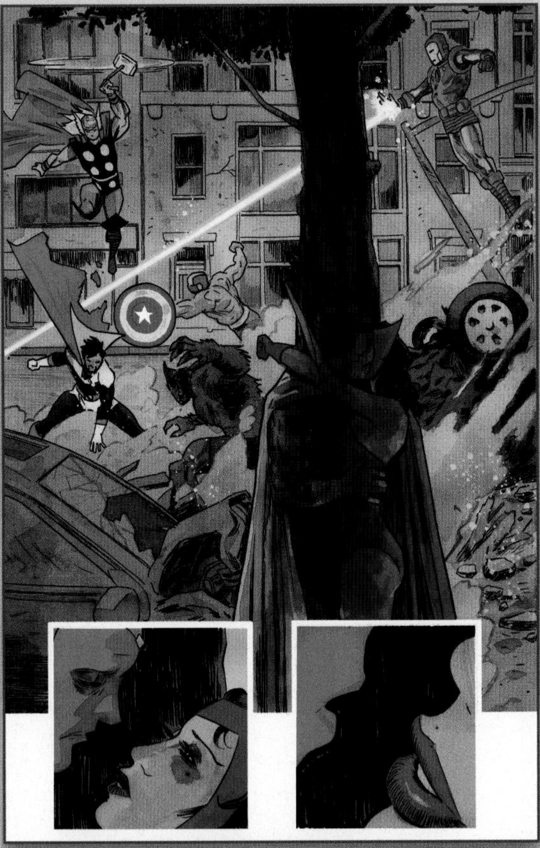

COLORS: JORDIE BELLAIRE

PAGE 6:

PANEL 1: SCARLET looking around. Behind her a building is on fire.

      SCARLET: I have to go, V.
      SCARLET: We both have to.

PANEL 2: SCARLET pulling on VISION's hand, trying to get him to go.

      SCARLET: C'mon. Tomorrow's our day off. This can wait.
      SCARLET: Today, Nefaria. Tomorrow…whatever we want.

PANEL 3: VISON pulling her back, flirting.

      VISION: Tomorrow does not always come.

PANEL 4: SCARLET puts her hands on VISION's face, some of her fingers phase through him.

      SCARLET: Oh no, no, darling.
      SCARLET: That's not right.

PANEL 5: Beautiful picture of SCARLET's face. The girl you fall for.

      SCARLET: Every good witch knows.
      SCARLET: Tomorrow always comes.

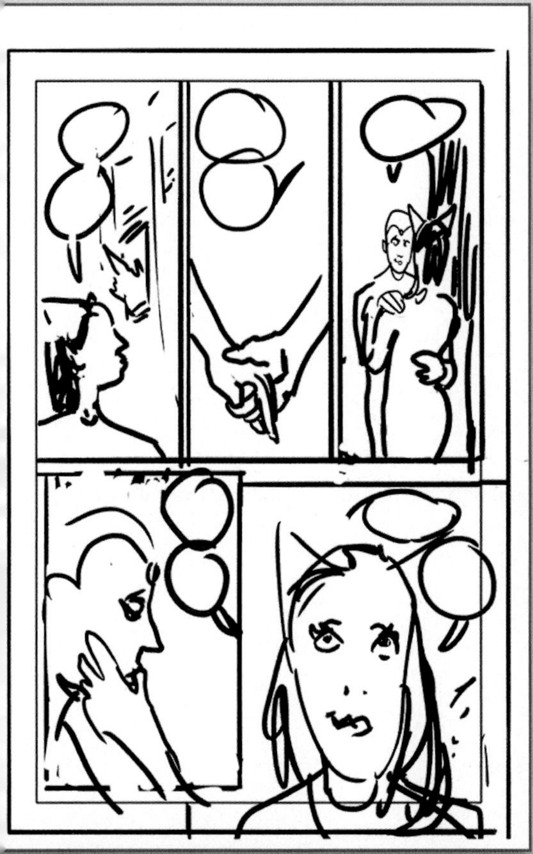

LAYOUT: MICHAEL WALSH

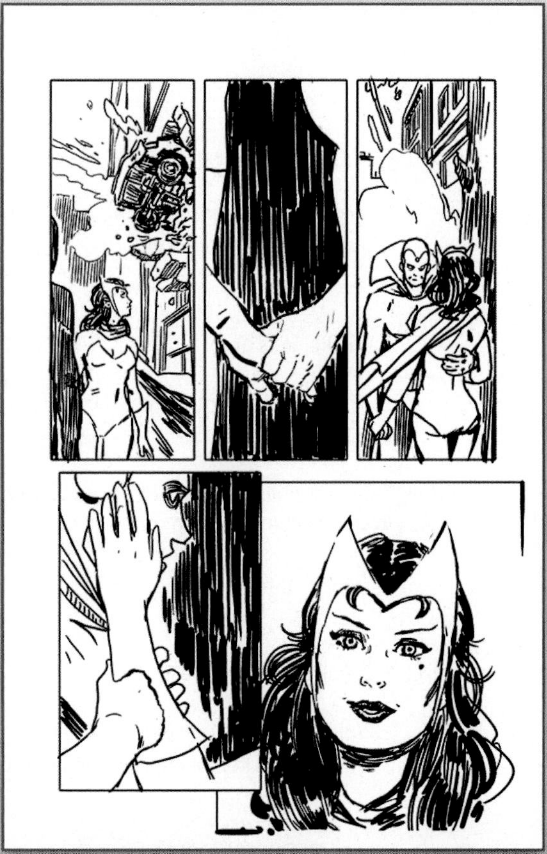

PENCILS: MICHAEL WALSH

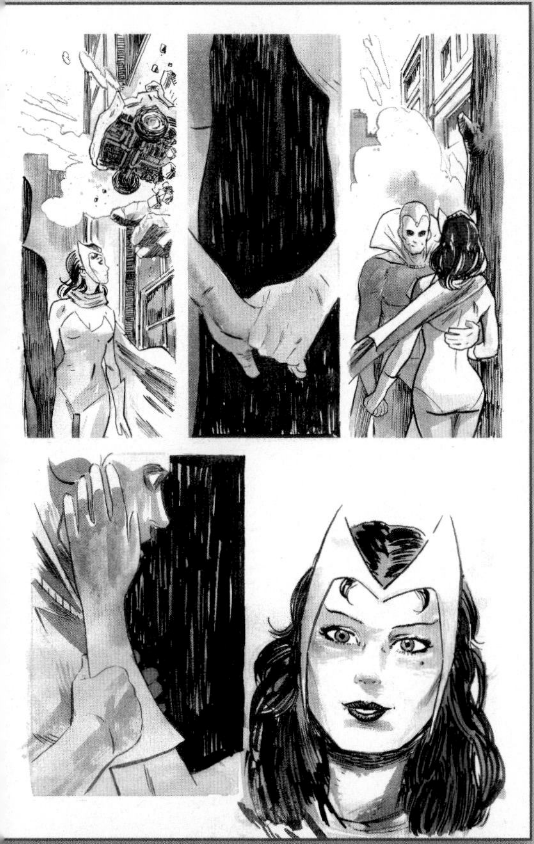

INKS: MICHAEL WALSH

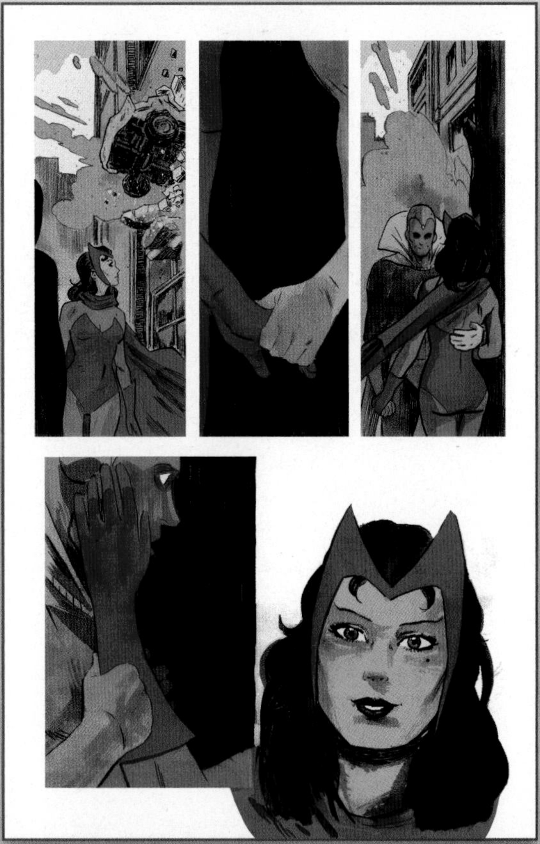

COLORS: JORDIE BELLAIRE

PAGE 7:

PANEL 1: THOR and IRON MAN fighting Nefaria

      CAPTION (SCARLET): "Now come on, V. The world is on the brink. The Avengers are here."
      CAPTION (SCARLET): "We can't let them Assemble without us."

PANEL 2: VISION looks up.

      VISION: Scarlet Witch, I love you.

PANEL 3: Camera pulls back. SCARLET and VISION, standing at the tree. Behind them fire, and chaos reigns, Avengers flying through the air.

      No dialogue

PANEL 4: CLOSE on VISION and SCARLET.

      VISION: Perhaps you did not hear me.
      VISION: I will adjust my vocal volume and repeat.

PANEL 5: Close on SCARLET.

      SCARLET: No, no, I heard you.

PANEL 6: VISION, looking desperate.

      VISION: Oh.
      VISION: Well, that is good.
      VISION: I find my vocal volume most comfortable at its current level.

PANEL 7: SCARLET leaning in to kiss VISION.

      SCARLET: Good, I'm glad you're comfortable.
      SCARLET: And I love you too, you talking toaster.

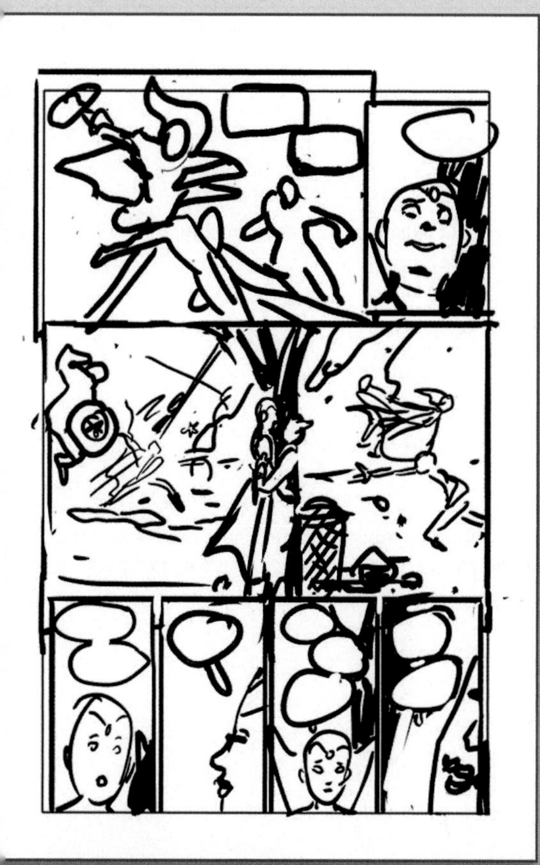

LAYOUT: MICHAEL WALSH

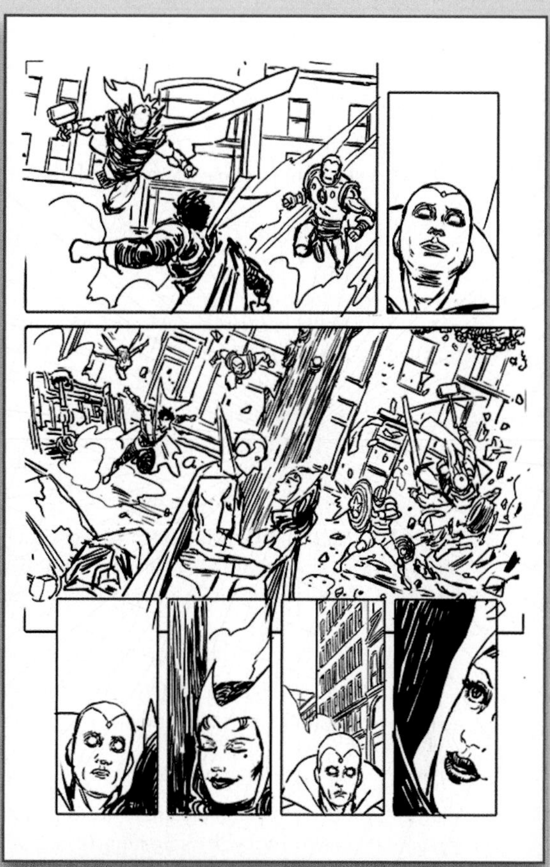

PENCILS: MICHAEL WALSH

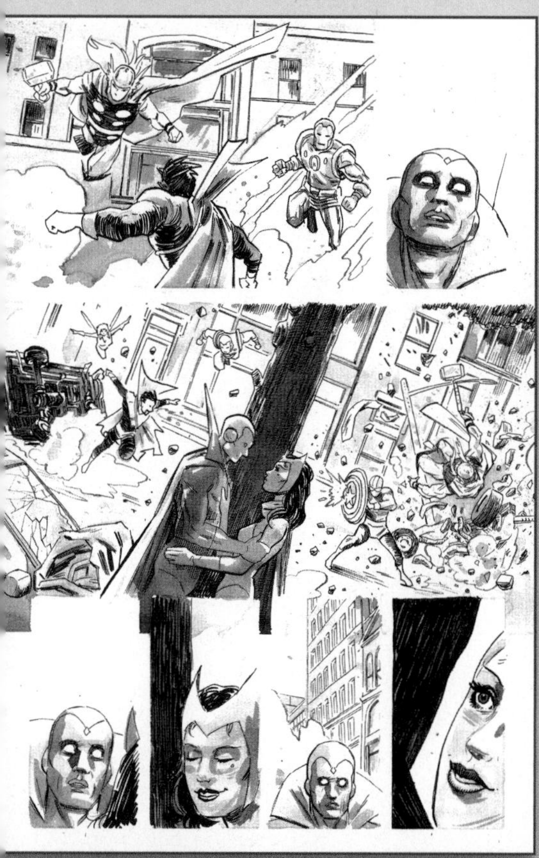

INKS: MICHAEL WALSH

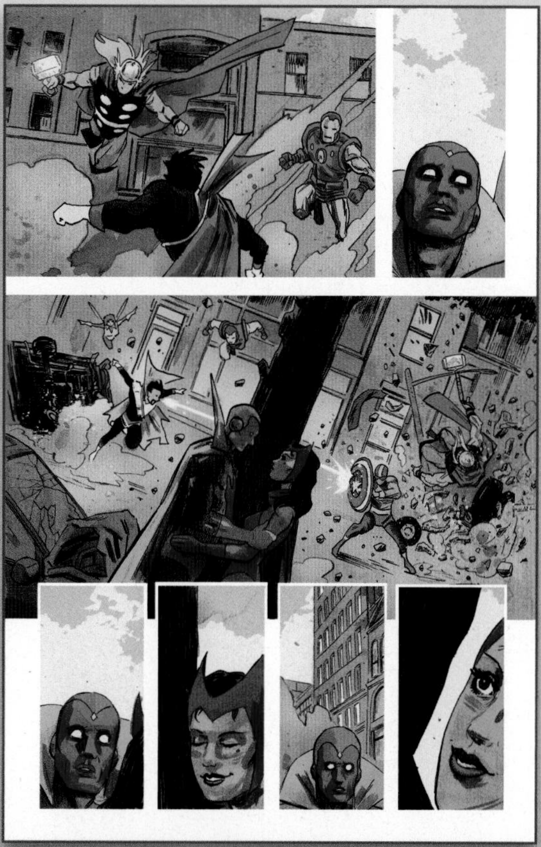

COLORS: JORDIE BELLAIRE

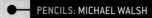

PAGE 1:

PANEL 1: VIV staring in a mirror, brushing her hair.

FLOATING BALLOON (Jagged): People say things, but like no one understands things...

PANEL 2: VIN in his room reading from *Merchant of Venice* as his teacher did in issue #5. And also like his teacher, he's being overdramatic here.

VIN: 'Therefore, Jew, though justice be thy plea, consider this,
VIN: 'That, in the course of justice, none of us should see salvation!'

PANEL 3: VIRGINIA in the living room. She is sitting at the Panther's restored piano. There is a crack in the piano from it being destroyed in issue #6. VIRGINIA reading music and learning to play a song. Sheet music is on display and she is staring at it intently.

VIRGINIA: Row. Row. Row your boat. Gently down the stream.
VIRGINIA: Merrily. Merrily. Merrily. Merrily.
VIRGINIA: Life is but a dream.

PANEL 4: VISION outside in the snow (it's winter now), clearing the walkway using the heat vision from his gem to melt the snow. He's floating as he walks.

VISION: ...yes, Nova, then restart the central Quinjet operating system.
VISION: The blue button. Yes. Hold it down for three seconds.
VISION: Now please inform me when you observe the password prompt.
VISION: The next steps are simple.

PANEL 5: The VISION DOG sitting in front of a ball in VIN's room waiting for it to be thrown. The ball is made of metal.

DOG: Woof.

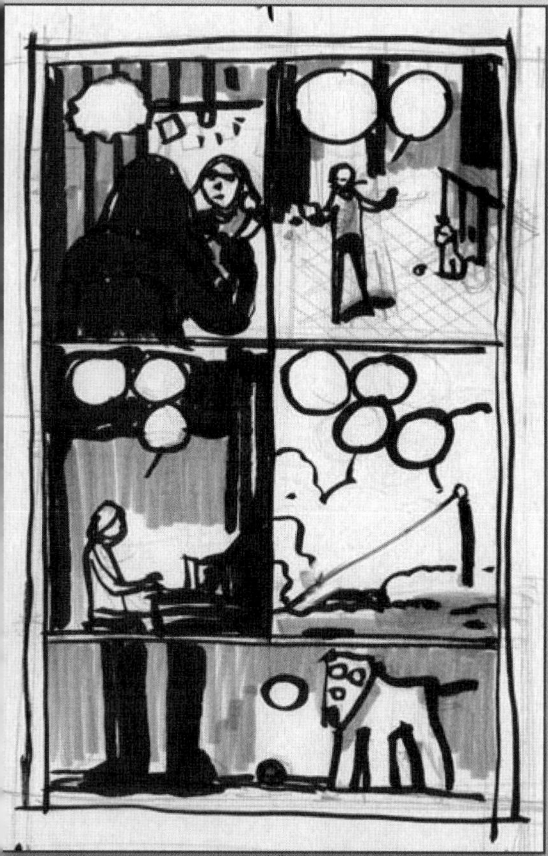

LAYOUT: GABRIEL HERNANDEZ WALTA

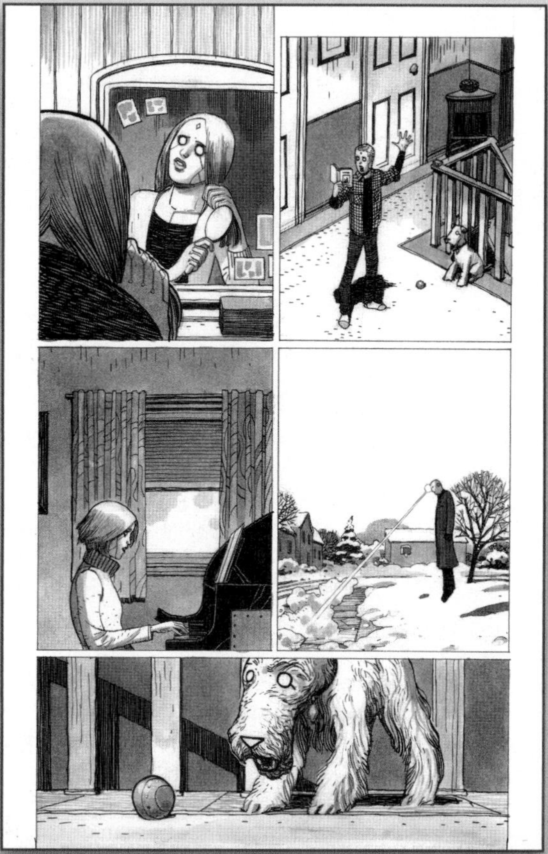

INKS: GABRIEL HERNANDEZ WALTA

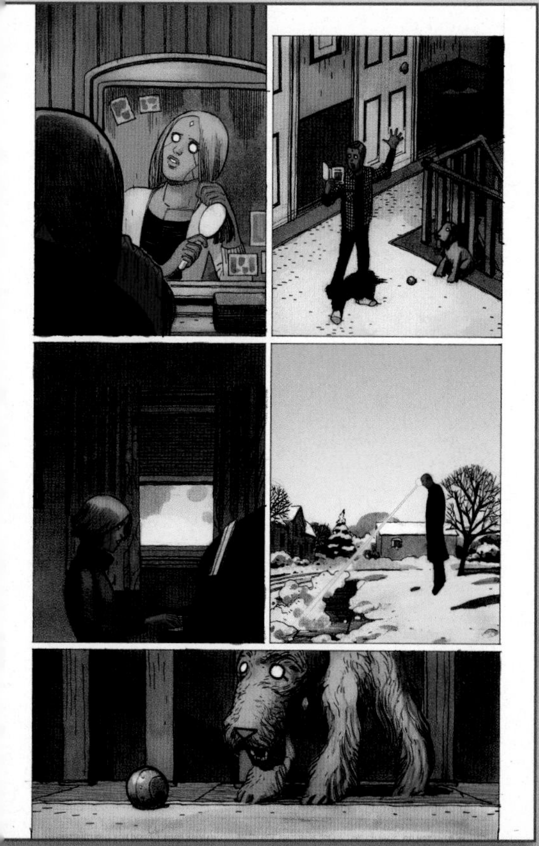

COLORS: JORDIE BELLAIRE

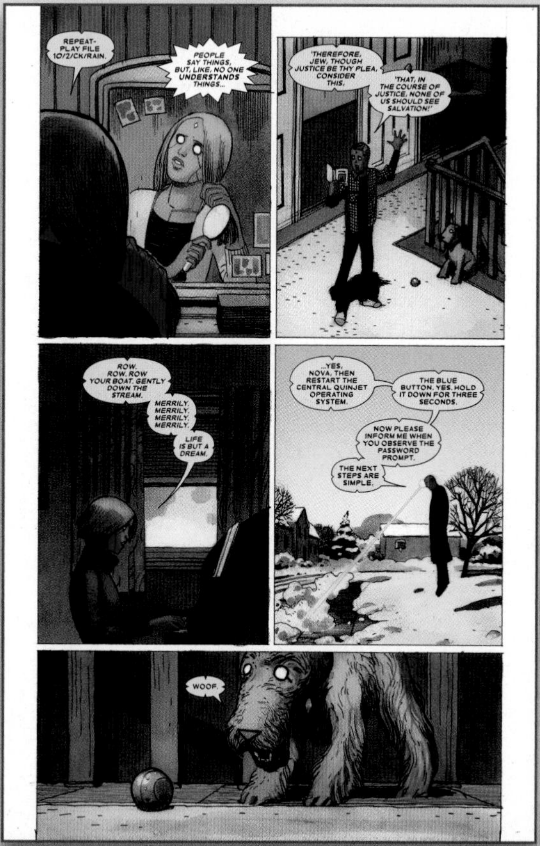

REPEAT-PLAY FILE 10/2/CK/RAIN.
PEOPLE SAY THINGS, BUT, LIKE, NO ONE UNDERSTANDS THINGS...
'THEREFORE, JEW, THOUGH JUSTICE BE THY PLEA, CONSIDER THIS,
'THAT, IN THE COURSE OF JUSTICE, NONE OF US SHOULD SEE SALVATION!'
ROW. ROW. ROW YOUR BOAT. GENTLY DOWN THE STREAM.
MERRILY. MERRILY. MERRILY. MERRILY.
LIFE IS BUT A DREAM.
...YES, NOVA, THEN RESTART THE CENTRAL QUINJET OPERATING SYSTEM.
THE BLUE BUTTON. YES. HOLD IT DOWN FOR THREE SECONDS.
NOW PLEASE INFORM ME WHEN YOU OBSERVE THE PASSWORD PROMPT.
THE NEXT STEPS ARE SIMPLE.
WOOF.

LETTERS: VC's CLAYTON COWLES

PAGE 2:

PANEL 1: VIN'S hand picking up the ball. VISION DOG watching very intently.

>DOG: Woof.
>VIN (OFF): 'We do pray for mercy!

PANEL 2: VIN casually throwing the ball while the dog watches. VIN absorbed still in his performance, not paying attention to the dog.

>VIN: 'And that same prayer doth teach us all to render the deeds of mercy!

PANEL 3: The dog running after the ball, which is in the air.

>VIN (OFF): 'I have spoke thus much...

PANEL 4: The ball flying out the window.

>VIN (OFF): 'To mitigate the justice of thy plea.

PANEL 5: DOG from behind phasing through the wall.

>VIN (OFF): 'Which if thou follow, this strict court of Venice
>VIN (OFF): 'Must needs give sentence 'gainst the merchant there.

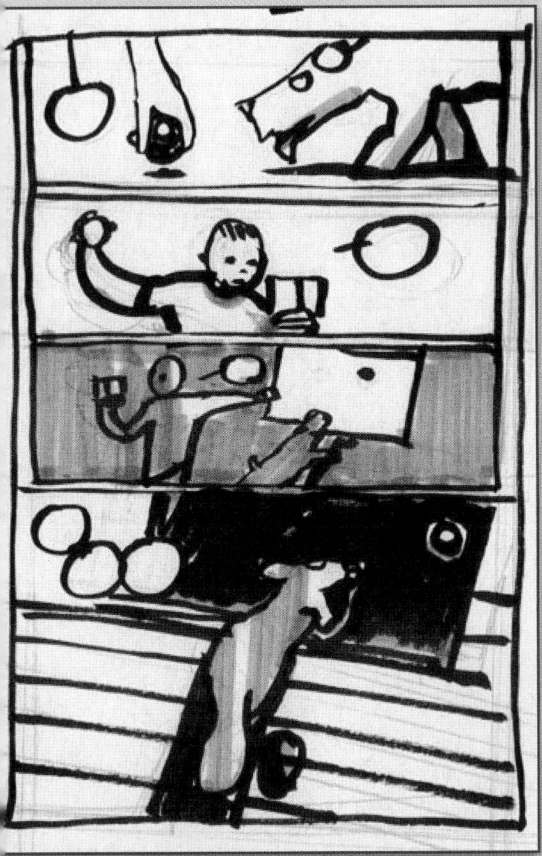

LAYOUT: GABRIEL HERNANDEZ WALTA

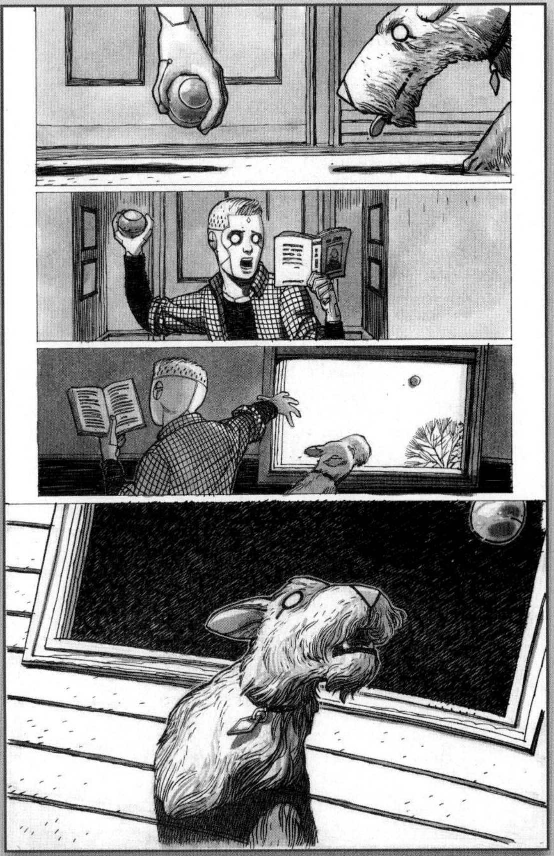

INKS: GABRIEL HERNANDEZ WALTA

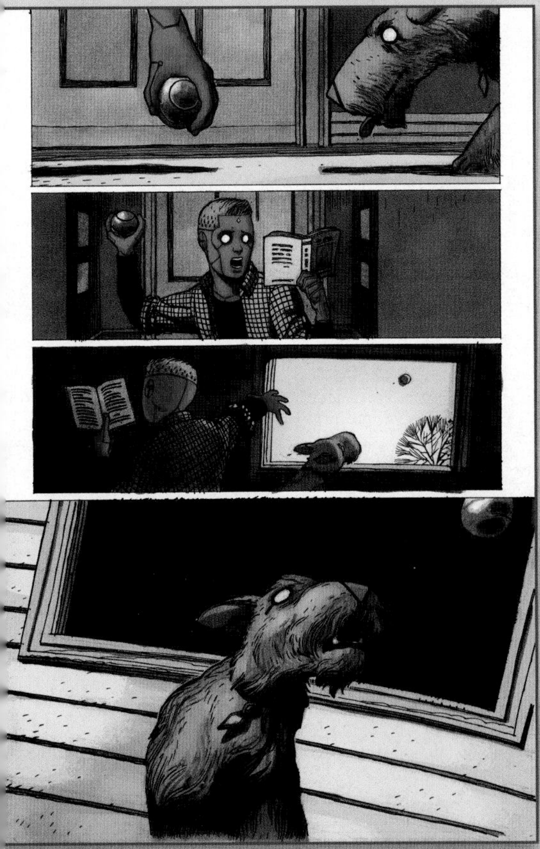

COLORS: JORDIE BELLAIRE

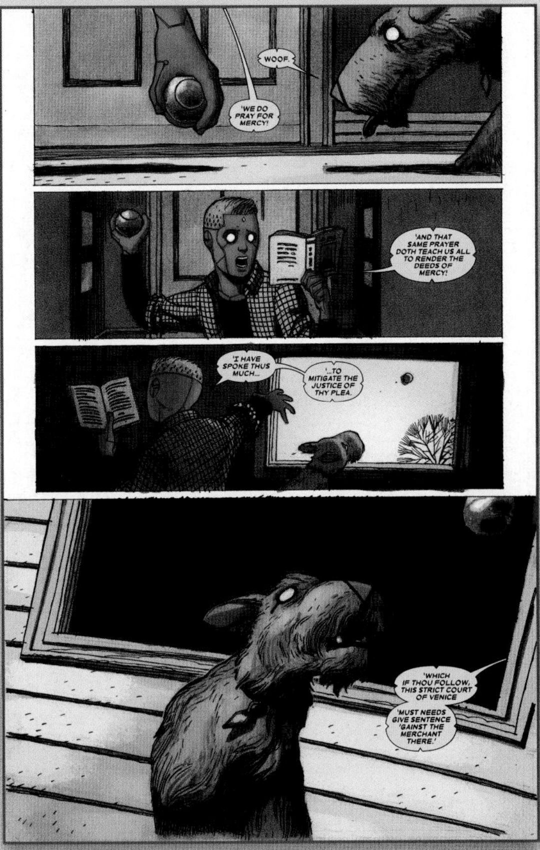
WOOF.
'WE DO PRAY FOR MERCY!
'AND THAT SAME PRAYER DOTH TEACH US ALL TO RENDER THE DEEDS OF MERCY!
'I HAVE SPOKE THUS MUCH...
'...TO MITIGATE THE JUSTICE OF THY PLEA.
'WHICH IF THOU FOLLOW, THIS STRICT COURT OF VENICE
'MUST NEEDS GIVE SENTENCE 'GAINST THE MERCHANT THERE.'

LETTERS: VC's CLAYTON COWLES

PAGE 3:

PANEL 1: SPLASH. The Visions' house from the front in all its winter splendor. This is an image of the VISIONS at peace. Content. VISION is in the front yard clearing snow with his laser. MARTHA, of GEORGE and MARTHA, is walking by and waving. And VISION is waving back. Through the bottom window you can see VIRGINIA practicing. Through the top window you can see VIV at the mirror. And there's a dog flying out of the second story chasing a ball.

VISION: Good. Good. Everything should be fine now.

VISION: You see, in the end, it was not that hard.

DOG: Woof.

TITLE: Victorious

CREDITS

SCRIPT: TOM KING

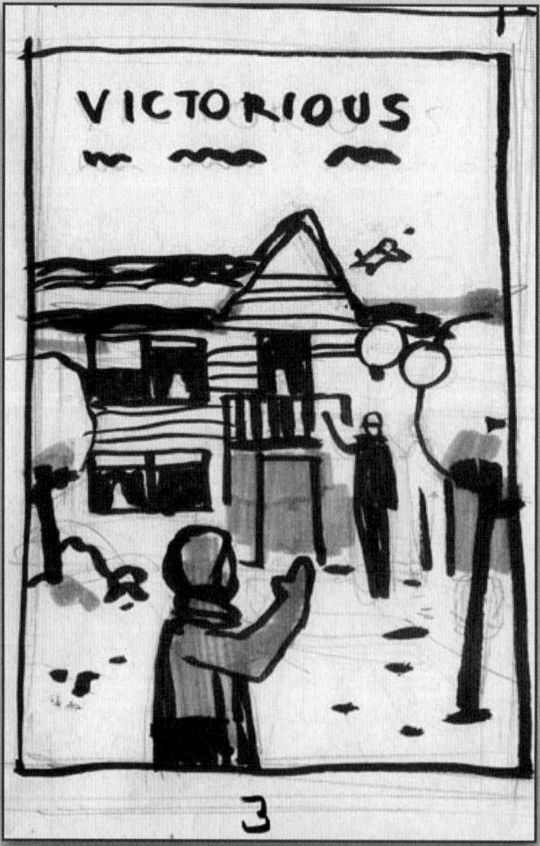
VICTORIOUS
3

LAYOUT: GABRIEL HERNANDEZ WALTA

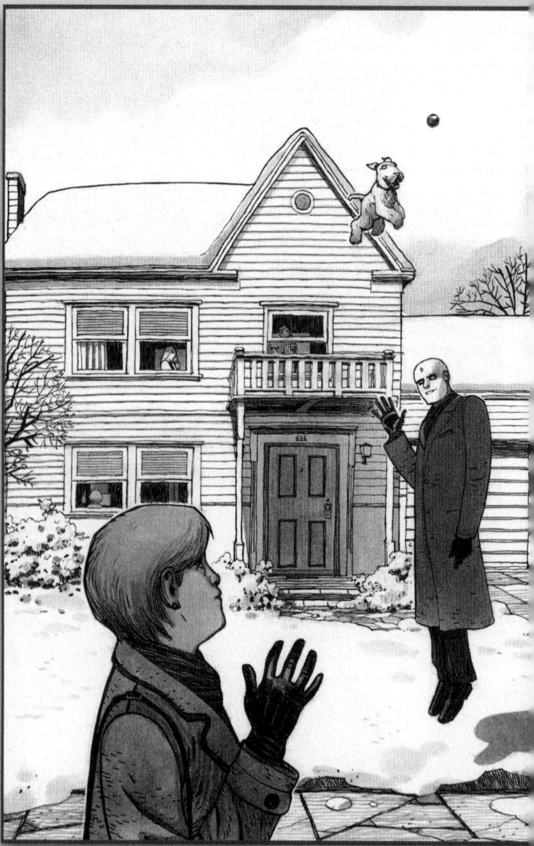

INKS: GABRIEL HERNANDEZ WALTA

PAGE 4:

PANEL 1: The ball bouncing down the sidewalk. The dog descending from the sky, chasing it.

CAPTION: Follow the bouncing ball.

PANEL 2: The ball rolling down the sidewalk. The dog, now landed, chasing after it.

CAPTION: Long after he created the Vision, Ultron attacked the Avengers for the fifth or perhaps sixth time.
CAPTION: He was subsequently defeated for the fifth or perhaps sixth time.

PANEL 3: The ball hits the foot/shoe of VICTOR who is walking down the sidewalk.

CAPTION: The remains of the robot were deposited in a scrapyard in Los Angeles.
CAPTION: Years later Marienella Mancha was digging through this junkyard for metal to use in an architectural project.

PANEL 4: We now see VICTOR MANCHA from behind, looking down on the dog. We don't see his face until page 5.

CAPTION: Ms. Mancha found Ultron's head.
CAPTION: It spoke to her, and she took it home.
DOG: Woof.

PANEL 5: VICTOR reaches out his hand. (still don't see his face)

CAPTION: Ms. Mancha confided to Ultron's head that she was physically unable to have children.
CAPTION: She was also unable to adopt children due to her criminal record (she had been a drug mule in her youth).

PANEL 6: VICTOR rolls up the sleeve of his coat. (still don't see his face)

CAPTION: Ultron's head offered Ms. Mancha a fair exchange.
CAPTION: If Ms. Mancha helped Ultron's head build a body, Ultron's head would help Ms. Mancha build a son.

PANEL 7: Hand splits open into his "Dragon Claw."

CAPTION: Ms. Mancha accepted.
CAPTION: And the construction of Victor Mancha began.

PAGE 5:

PANEL 1: VICTOR fires a magnetic beam from his hand at the metal ball. Still close on hand.

    CAPTION: Ultron gave Victor false memories and nanobot-enhanced organs and blood.
    CAPTION: As such, the day he was turned on, Victor believed himself to be a normal 16-year-old boy.

PANEL 2: The ball magnetically floats into VICTOR'S hand.

    CAPTION: Victor discovered his true nature when a group of runaway super heroes confronted him during a high school football practice.

PANEL 3: The dog looking up at VICTOR, eager.

    VICTOR: You want the ball, boy?
    VICTOR: You want the ball?
    DOG: Woof.
    CAPTION: They said they had information from the future.

PANEL 4: VICTOR throws the ball, back toward the Visions' house. Still can't see Victor, shot from behind.

    VICTOR: Go get it, boy!
    CAPTION: Victor could use his robotic body to manipulate the forces of magnetism.
    CAPTION: Years from now, with this power, under name Victorious, Victor will join the Avengers.

PANEL 5: The dog chasing the ball the other way as goes to VISION.

    DOG: Woof.
    CAPTION: Once he is accepted as a member, his original programming will activate.

PANEL 6: The ball coming to the feet of VISION. We can see all of VISION in this shot. He is looking down at the ball.

    CAPTION: And he will betray his friends and teammates.
    CAPTION: He will kill them. He will kill their families.
    CAPTION: He will raze the world.

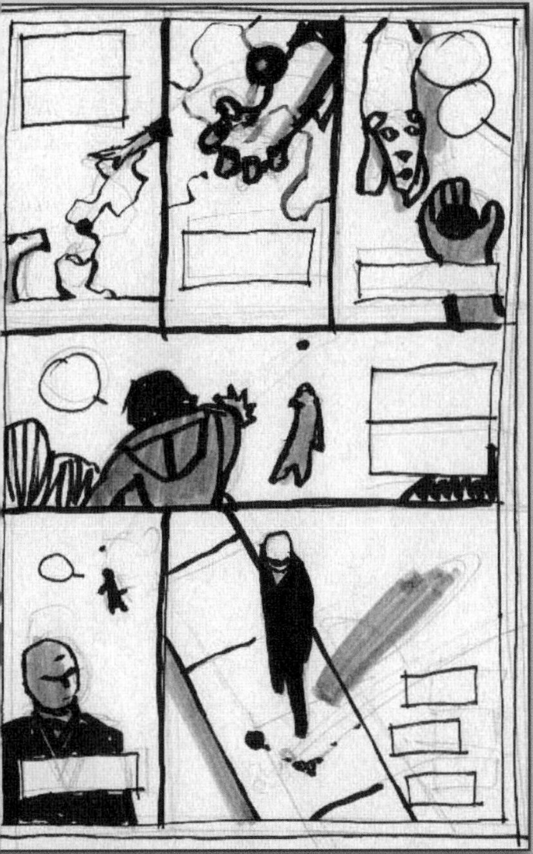

LAYOUT: GABRIEL HERNANDEZ WALTA

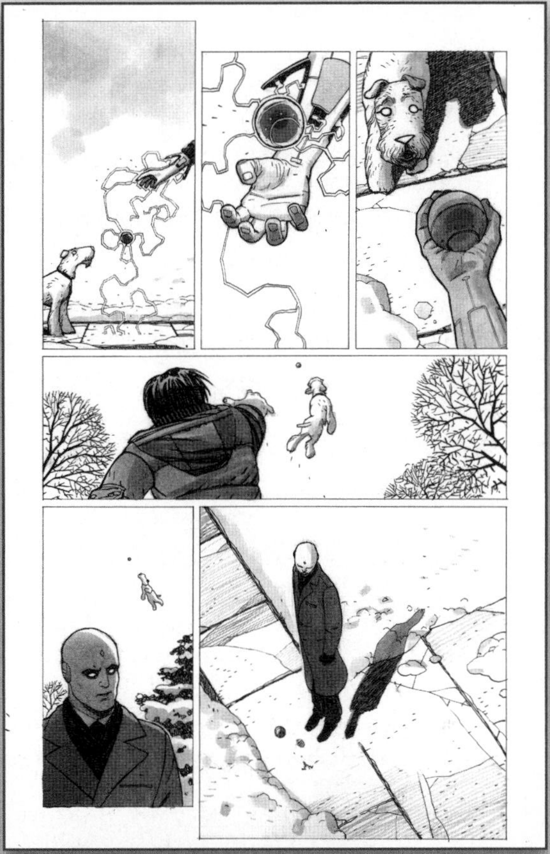

INKS: GABRIEL HERNANDEZ WALTA

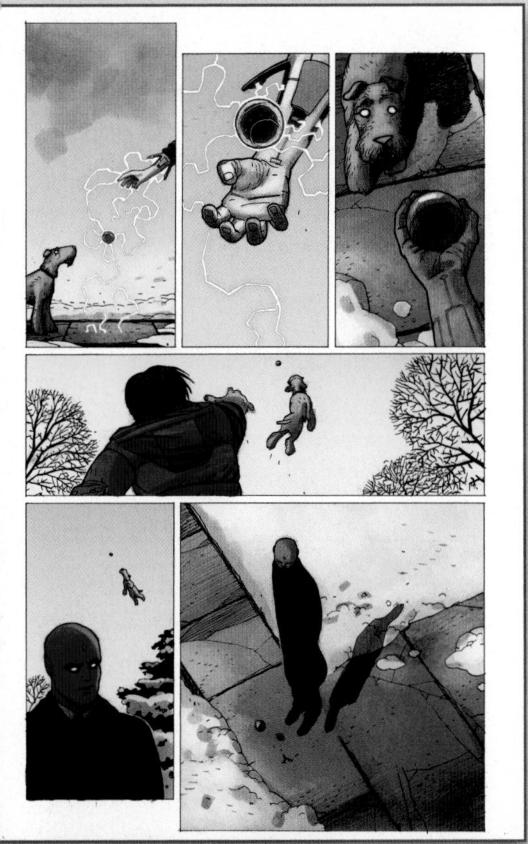

COLORS: JORDIE BELLAIRE

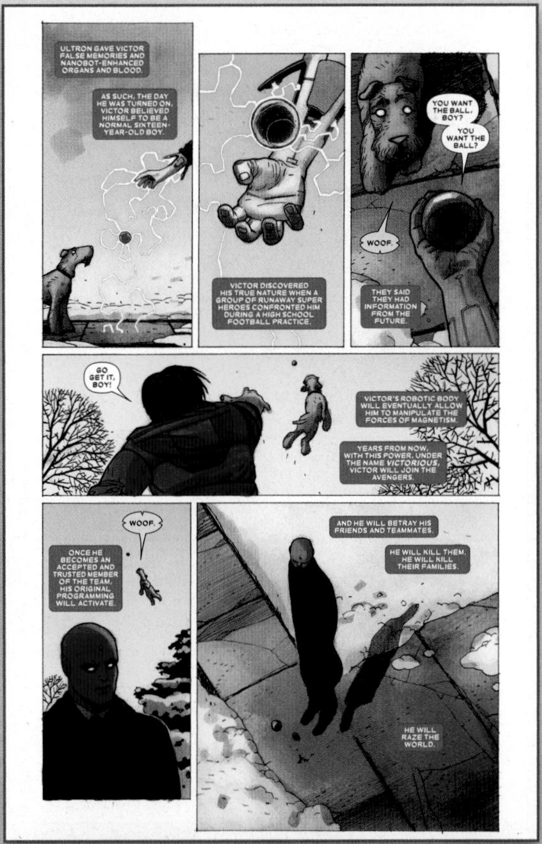
ULTRON GAVE VICTOR FALSE MEMORIES AND NANOBOT-ENHANCED ORGANS AND BLOOD.
AS SUCH, THE DAY HE WAS TURNED ON, VICTOR BELIEVED HIMSELF TO BE A NORMAL SIXTEEN-YEAR-OLD BOY.
VICTOR DISCOVERED HIS TRUE NATURE WHEN A GROUP OF RUNAWAY SUPER HEROES CONFRONTED HIM DURING A HIGH SCHOOL FOOTBALL PRACTICE.
YOU WANT THE BALL, BOY?
YOU WANT THE BALL?
WOOF.
THEY SAID THEY HAD INFORMATION FROM THE FUTURE.
GO GET IT, BOY!
VICTOR'S ROBOTIC BODY WILL EVENTUALLY ALLOW HIM TO MANIPULATE THE FORCES OF MAGNETISM.
YEARS FROM NOW, WITH THIS POWER, UNDER THE NAME *VICTORIOUS*, VICTOR WILL JOIN THE AVENGERS.
WOOF.
ONCE HE BECOMES AN ACCEPTED AND TRUSTED MEMBER OF THE TEAM, HIS ORIGINAL PROGRAMMING WILL ACTIVATE.
AND HE WILL BETRAY HIS FRIENDS AND TEAMMATES.
HE WILL KILL THEM. HE WILL KILL THEIR FAMILIES.
HE WILL RAZE THE WORLD.

LETTERS: VC's CLAYTON COWLES

PAGE 6:

<u>PANEL 1:</u> From VISION'S POV, we finally see VICTOR. He looks serious, maybe even a little scary.

       CAPTION: Behold Victor Mancha.

<u>PANEL 2:</u> A two-shot of VICTOR and VISION standing not too far apart from each other in the snow. They are eyeing each other, almost curious, almost about to fight. The Dog is between them.

       CAPTION: Son of Ultron.

<u>PANEL 3:</u> And they hug! Best friends forever. The dog is at their feet, eager to keep playing.

       CAPTION: Brother of Vision.
       DOG: Woof.

SCRIPT: TOM KING

REFERENCE: VICTOR MANCHA ART BY ANDRÉ LIMA ARAÚJO

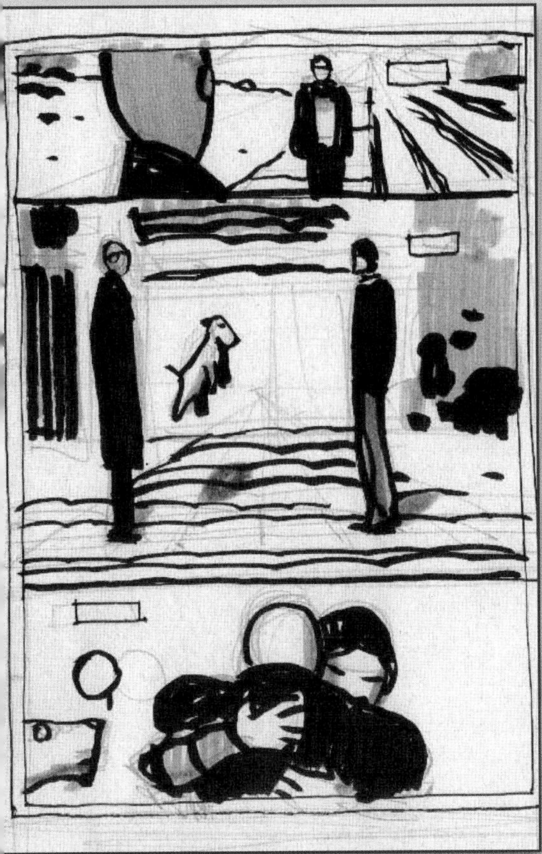

LAYOUT: GABRIEL HERNANDEZ WALTA

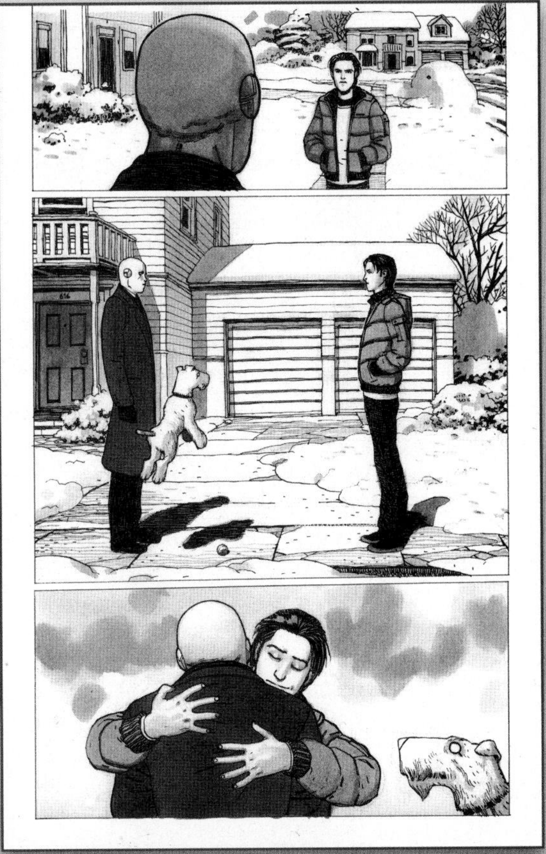

INKS: GABRIEL HERNANDEZ WALTA

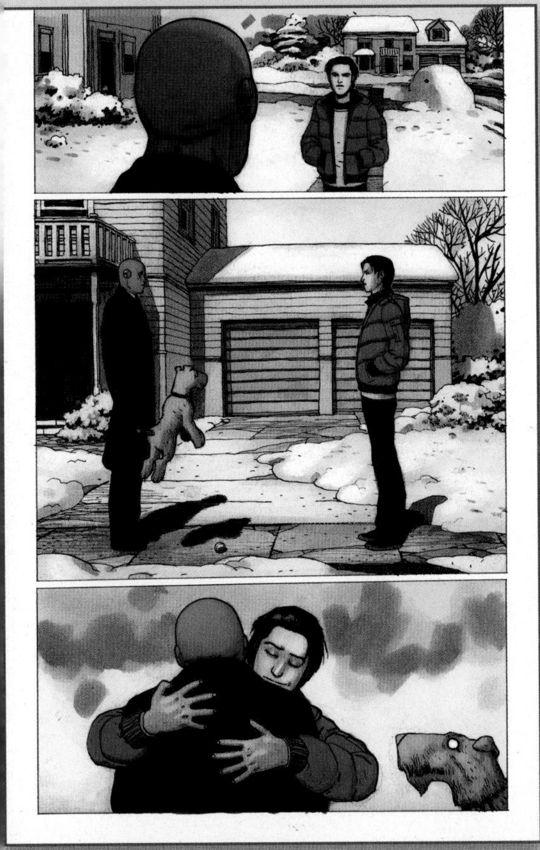

COLORS: JORDIE BELLAIRE

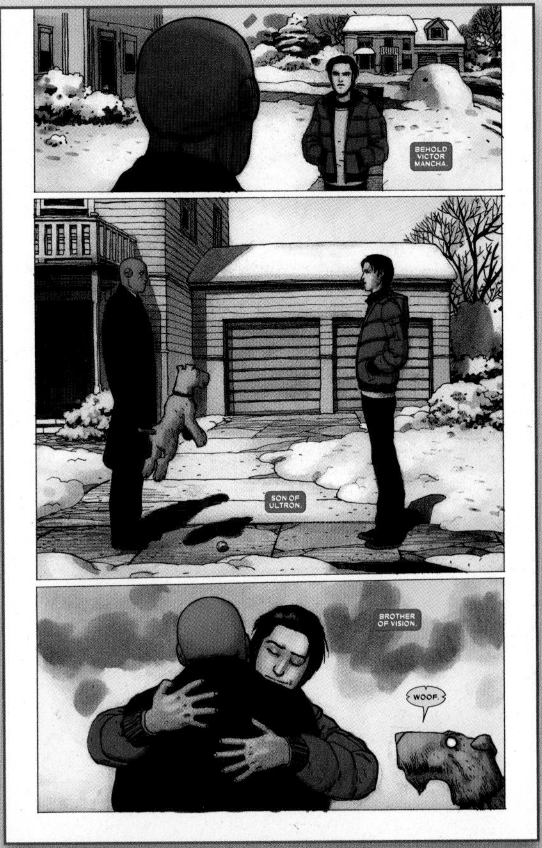
BEHOLD VICTOR MANCHA.
SON OF ULTRON.
BROTHER OF VISION.
WOOF.

LETTERS: VC's CLAYTON COWLES

PAGE 7:

PANEL 1: VISION at the door, his arm around MANCHA. Vision smiling, proud.

> VISION: Family!
> VISION: He is here!
> CAPTION: Of course, Mancha chose to fight against this destiny.
> CAPTION: He joined the Runaways, used his powers to crush his creator.

PANEL 2: VISION inside the house introducing the family to VICTOR.

> VISION: My wife, Virginia.
> VISION: My children, Vin and Viv.
> CAPTION: Later, he joined the Avengers, serving with Vision on a team known as Avengers AI.

PANEL 3: VISION patting VICTOR on the back.

> VISION (OFF): And this is your uncle Victor.
> VISION (OFF): He has earned a prestigious internship on Capitol Hill. He will be staying with us for the semester.
> CAPTION: He worked hard to emulate his brother.

PANEL 4: Close on VICTOR with a frozen smile.

> CAPTION: He felt that if he could be just like The Vision, noble and strong like The Vision.
> CAPTION: Then obviously he would never become Victorious.

LAYOUT: GABRIEL HERNANDEZ WALTA

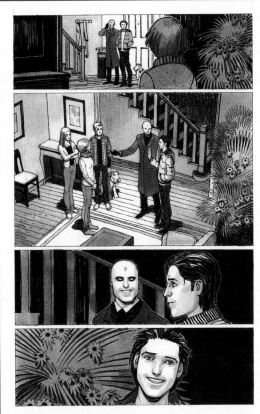

INKS: GABRIEL HERNANDEZ WALTA

COLORS: JORDIE BELLAIRE

LETTERS: VC's CLAYTON COWLES

PAGE 8:

PANEL 1: The Visions in a restaurant with Victor. Unlike in issue #6, here at dinner they are all engaged, laughing and talking. A waitress is approaching VISION.

> CAPTION: That night Victor insisted they all go out to a restaurant.
>
> CAPTION: The Vision objected. "It will be awkward," he said.
>
> VICTOR: It has to be acknowledged that your grandfather—though certainly evil incarnate—was always, and I mean always, well shined.
>
> VICTOR: I had actual trouble deciding to punch him or stop and admire my glorious hair in his glorious mirror-abs.

PANEL 2: The waitress leaning over to talk to VISION.

> CAPTION: "Of course it'll be awkward!" Victor replied.
>
> WAITRESS: Sir, I'm sorry, the chef wanted me to ask again.
>
> WAITRESS: Are you sure you don't want them to make the food you ordered.

PANEL 3: VISION leaning back to whisper to the waitress.

> CAPTION: "That's the fun of it!"
>
> VISION: Yes, I am sure.
>
> VISION: Just wait forty-five minutes and bring me a bill for that amount.
>
> VICTOR (OFF): Oh and grandpa's voice! Significantly higher than you'd think.
>
> VICTOR (OFF): Like, secondhand microwave high. Beeps and squeaks in an almost random order.

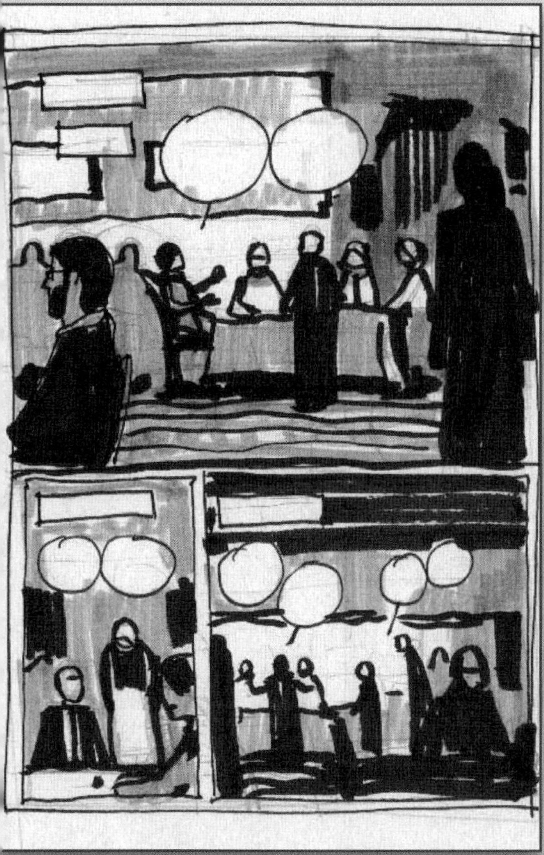

LAYOUT: GABRIEL HERNANDEZ WALTA

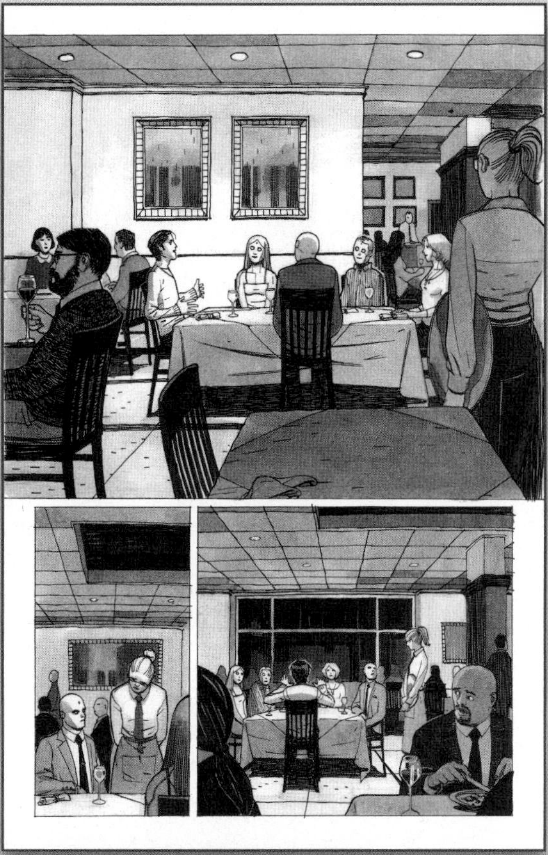

INKS: GABRIEL HERNANDEZ WALTA

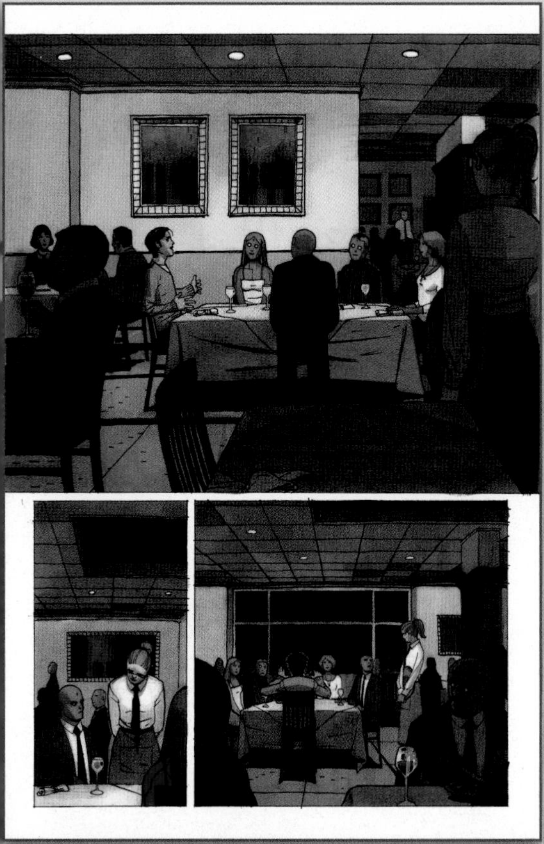

COLORS: JORDIE BELLAIRE

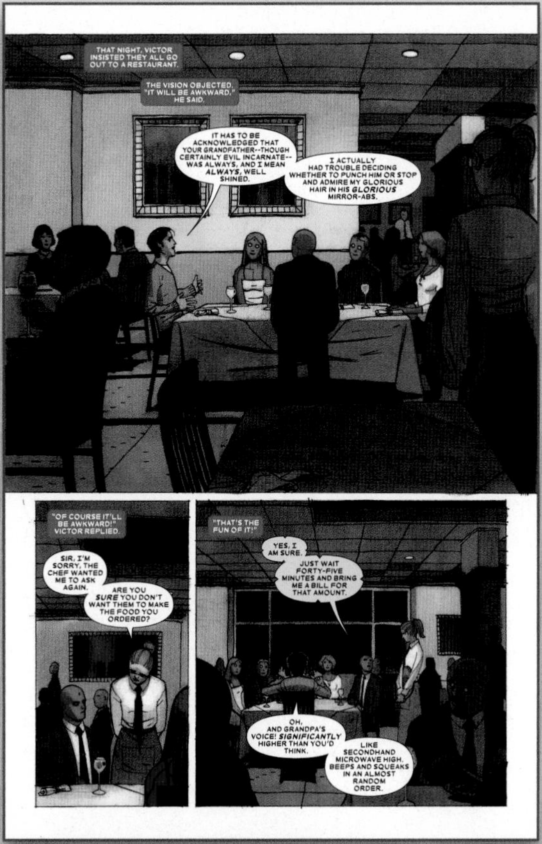

THAT NIGHT, VICTOR INSISTED THEY ALL GO OUT TO A RESTAURANT.
THE VISION OBJECTED. "IT WILL BE AWKWARD," HE SAID.
IT HAS TO BE ACKNOWLEDGED THAT YOUR GRANDFATHER--THOUGH CERTAINLY EVIL INCARNATE--WAS ALWAYS, AND I MEAN *ALWAYS*, WELL SHINED.
I ACTUALLY HAD TROUBLE DECIDING WHETHER TO PUNCH HIM OR STOP AND ADMIRE MY GLORIOUS HAIR IN HIS *GLORIOUS* MIRROR-ABS.
"OF COURSE IT'LL BE AWKWARD!" VICTOR REPLIED.
SIR, I'M SORRY, THE CHEF WANTED ME TO ASK AGAIN.
ARE YOU *SURE* YOU DON'T WANT THEM TO MAKE THE FOOD YOU ORDERED?
"THAT'S THE FUN OF IT!"
YES, I AM SURE.
JUST WAIT FORTY-FIVE MINUTES AND BRING ME A BILL FOR THAT AMOUNT.
OH, AND GRANDPA'S VOICE! *SIGNIFICANTLY* HIGHER THAN YOU'D THINK.
LIKE SECONDHAND MICROWAVE HIGH. BEEPS AND SQUEAKS IN AN ALMOST RANDOM ORDER.

LETTERS: VC's CLAYTON COWLES

PAGE 9:

<u>PANEL 1:</u> Outside the house, VICTOR and the family landing after dinner.

      VICTOR: I got to say, V, when I look at this, what you have--
      VICTOR: I'm a little jealous.

<u>PANEL 2:</u> VIRGINIA, VIN and VIRGINIA phase into the front door. They look happy, playful.

      VISION (off): Yes. Well. I would say the same thing about you, Victor.
      VISION (off): When I look at what you have, I am a little jealous.

<u>PANEL 3:</u> VISION and VICTOR walking up to the house. Gabriel, it's important that you can see that the house across the street is for sale. Sign should "Brand New Listing!"

      VICTOR: Really?

<u>PANEL 4:</u> VISION and VICTOR phasing into the house.

      VISION: Well, your hair is quite …
      VISION: Glorious.

<u>PANEL 5:</u> The VISION house at night. Maybe this shot can be from across the street so we can a bit of the "for sale" sign in the foreground.

      SFX: HaHaHaHa
      SFX: HaHaHaHa

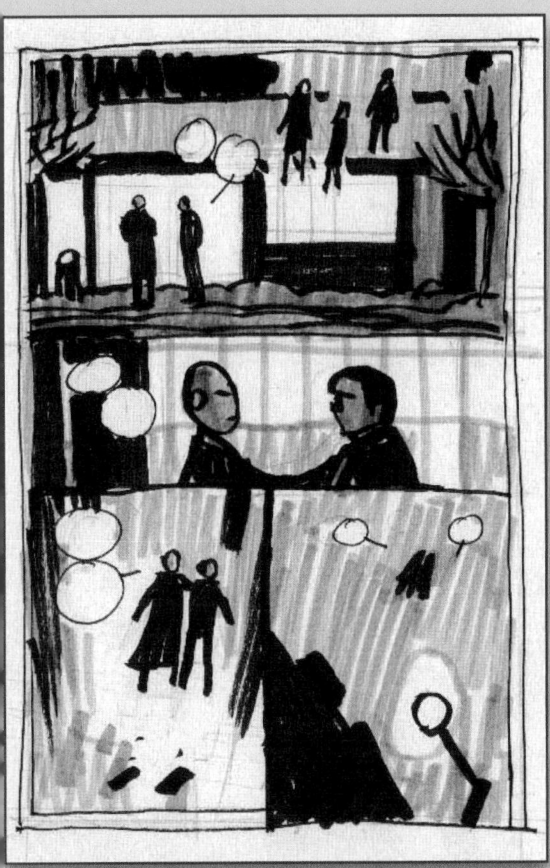

● LAYOUT: GABRIEL HERNANDEZ WALTA

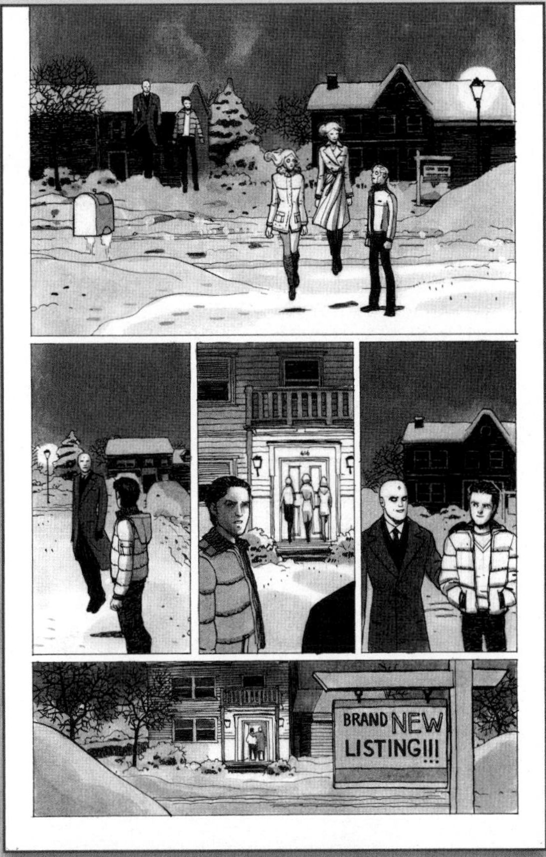
BRAND NEW LISTING!!!

● INKS: GABRIEL HERNANDEZ WALTA

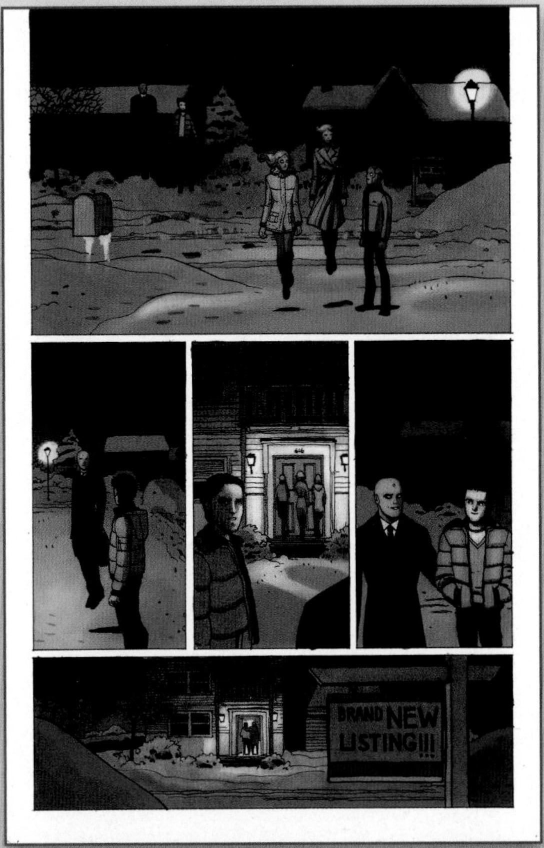
BRAND NEW LISTING!!!

● COLORS: JORDIE BELLAIRE

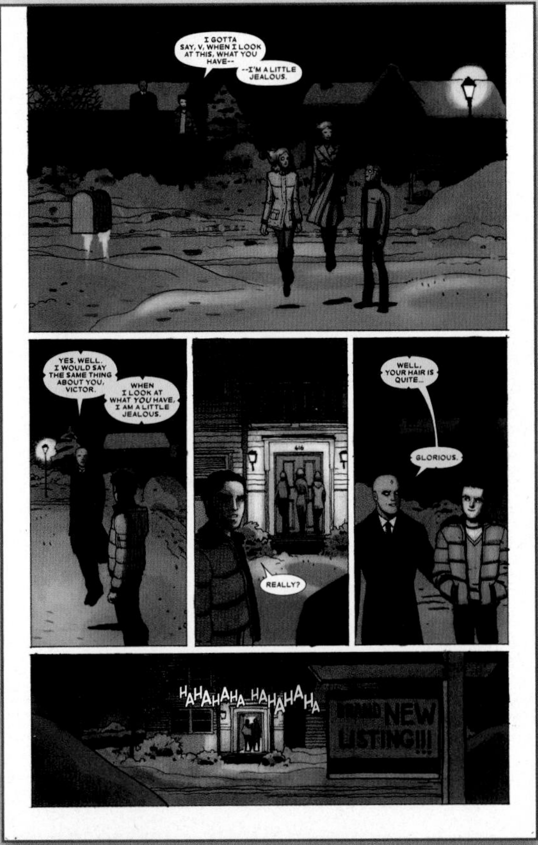
I GOTTA SAY, V, WHEN I LOOK AT THIS, WHAT YOU HAVE--
--I'M A LITTLE JEALOUS.
YES. WELL. I WOULD SAY THE SAME THING ABOUT YOU, VICTOR.
WHEN I LOOK AT WHAT YOU HAVE, I AM A LITTLE JEALOUS.
REALLY?
WELL, YOUR HAIR IS QUITE...
GLORIOUS.
HAHAHAHAHA HAHAHAHAHA

● LETTERS: VC's CLAYTON COWLES

PAGE 14:

<u>PANEL 1:</u> In VICTOR'S POV: the dog in his face, barking and growling.

> DOG: Grrrrr!

<u>PANEL 2:</u> VICTOR uses his magnetic power to throw the dog off of him.

> DOG: Grrr—
> VICTOR: No!

<u>PANEL 3:</u> DOG hits the wall.

> SFX: CLANK

<u>PANEL 4:</u> VIN getting off the floor. VICTOR turning to VIN.

> VIN: Father…

<u>PANEL 5:</u> VICTOR: aims his powers at VIN.

> VICTOR: Stop fighting!

<u>PANEL 6:</u> VICTOR turning his powers back on VIN, hard.

> VICTOR: Stop fighting!

<u>PANEL 7:</u> VIN shouting out, VICTOR'S powers hitting him, a laser firing from his diamond.

> VIN: Father!

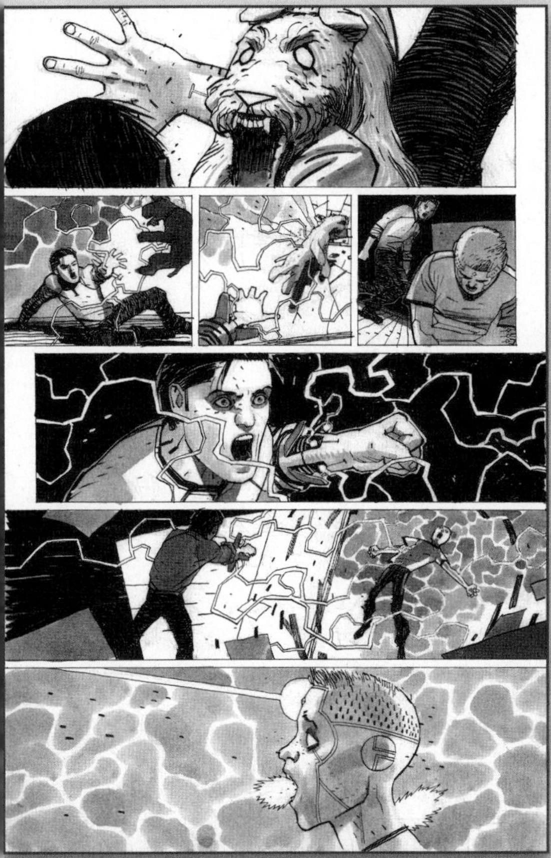

INKS: GABRIEL HERNANDEZ WALTA

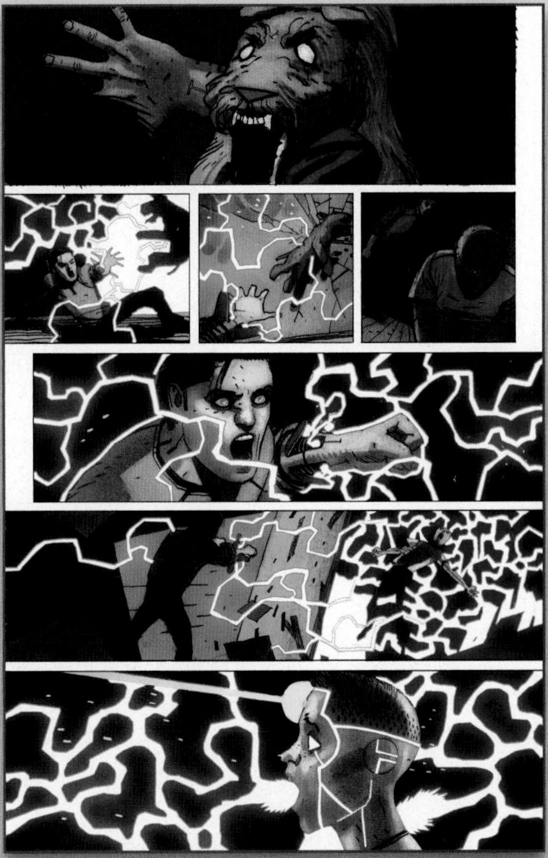

COLORS: JORDIE BELLAIRE

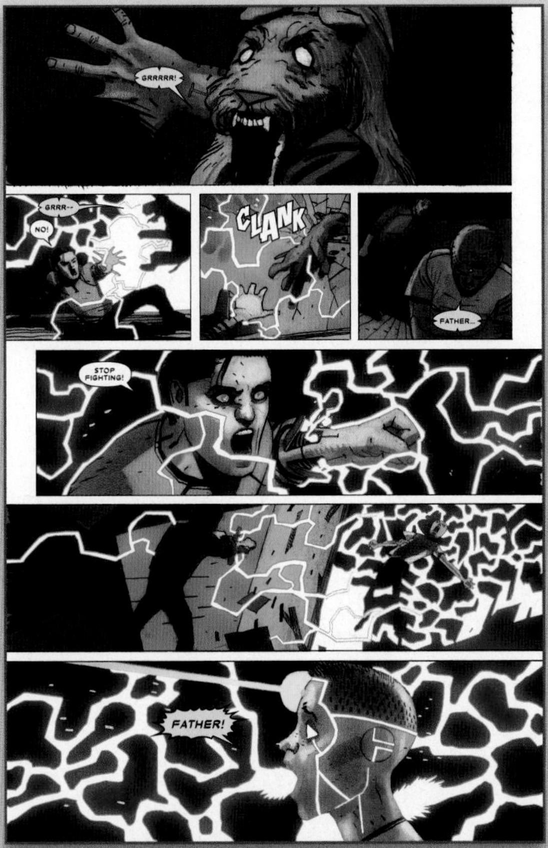
GRRRRR!
GRRR--
NO!
CLANK
FATHER...
STOP FIGHTING!
FATHER!

LETTERS: VC's CLAYTON COWLES

PAGE 15:

<u>PANEL 1:</u> Outside the house VISION and VIN are in. The laser fires through the front of the house. It goes out at an angle, going across the street but not directly across the street.

> SFX: ZZZZAZZZZ

<u>PANEL 2:</u> Camera pulls up, shows the laser leaving the house and going across at the angle and hitting another house a few doors down from the VISIONS'.

> SFX: BBOOM.

<u>PANEL 3:</u> In front of George and Nora's house as the laser is hitting, starting a fire.

> SFX: BBRGGOOM

<u>PANEL 4:</u> On George and Nora's door as it goes up in flames. There's a small, corny Etsy-knitted thing hanging from the door that says "George [heart] Nora."

> SFX: CRRRRKLLLL

<u>PANEL 5:</u> VISION looking up from his chess.

> VISION: Hm?

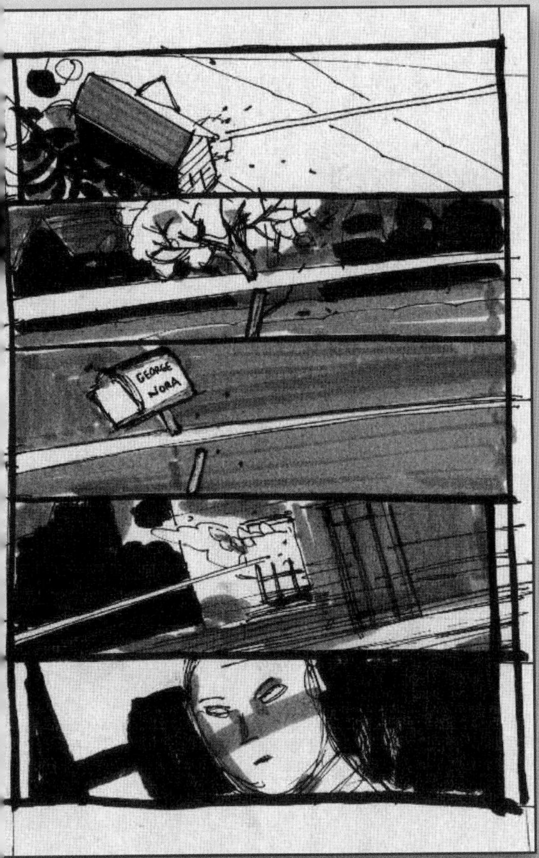
GEORGE
NORA

LAYOUT: GABRIEL HERNANDEZ WALTA

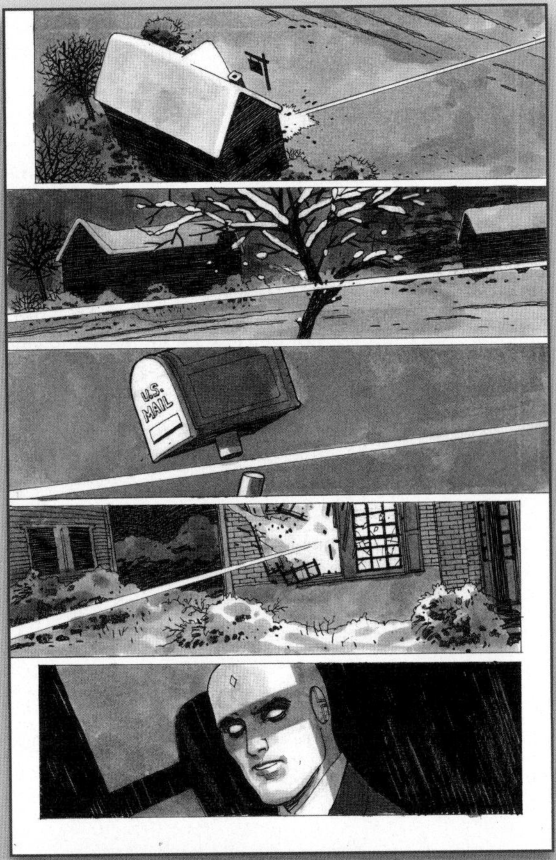
U.S.
MAIL

INKS: GABRIEL HERNANDEZ WALTA

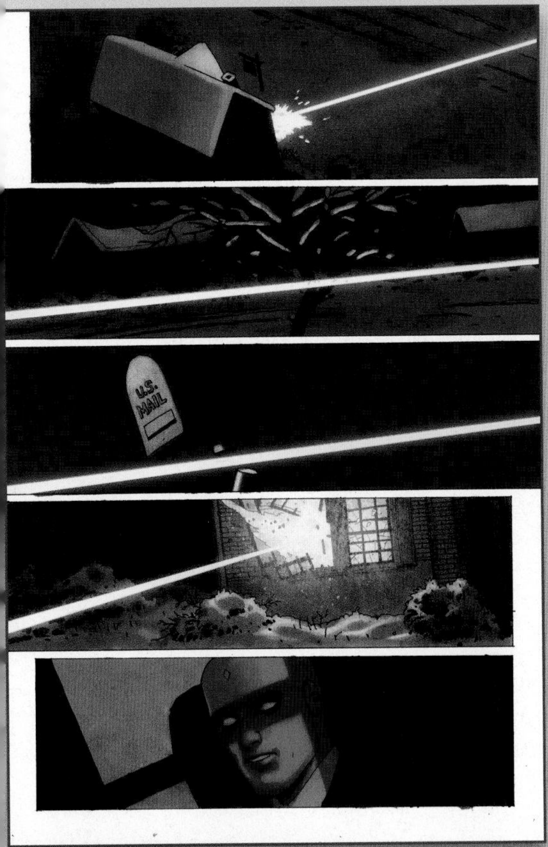
U.S.
MAIL

COLORS: JORDIE BELLAIRE

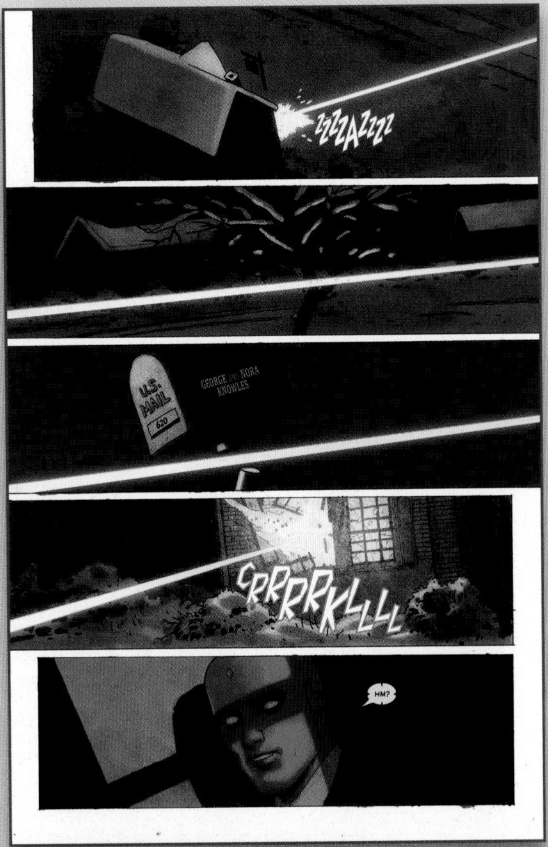
ZZZZAZZZZ
U.S.
MAIL
620
GEORGE AND NORA
KNOWLES
CRRRRKLLLL
HM?

LETTERS: VC's CLAYTON COWLES

PAGE 16:

PANEL 1: VICTOR sitting in a chair in his house. He looks intimidated.

> CAPTION: After Avengers A.I. was disbanded, VICTOR took Klaw's hand home and waited for the next great adventure.

PANEL 2: From VICTOR'S POV: CAPTAIN AMERICA standing above VICTOR (he's standing next to Iron Man and Thor, but they're not in this shot.) CAPTAIN is talking/lecturing.

> CAPTION: After a month the hand stopped working.
> CAPTION: And Victor sat in his house, motionless, holding the inert metal.

PANEL 3: Back to VICTOR, sitting, listening, fidgeting.

> CAPTION: He was still sitting there when the Avengers arrived at his door.

PANEL 4: THOR talking now, going on.

> CAPTION: We need your help Victor, they said.
> CAPTION: It's Vision, they said.

PANEL 5: On Victor, looking anxious. Looking up.

> CAPTION: We have information that Vision has done some things.
> CAPTION: That he may yet do some more things.
> CAPTION: Things unworthy of an Avenger.

PANEL 6: Back on VICTOR, tilts his head, listening.

> CAPTION: We don't know if we can trust this information.
> CAPTION: We don't know if Vision is lying or if our source is lying.

PANEL 7: Iron man, his helmet off, talking on.

> CAPTION: We don't want to confront him yet.
> CAPTION: We fear that if we confront him with unfounded accusations it could trigger the very event we're trying to prevent.

PANEL 8: VICTOR looking up, interested.

> CAPTION: So we need someone who can get close to Vision.
> CAPTION: Find out what is true. What isn't.

PANEL 9: VICTOR looks down at his hands.

> CAPTION: You're his teammate. You're his brother.
> CAPTION: This is your opportunity to be an Avenger.
> CAPTION: This is your opportunity to save the world.

SCRIPT: TOM KING

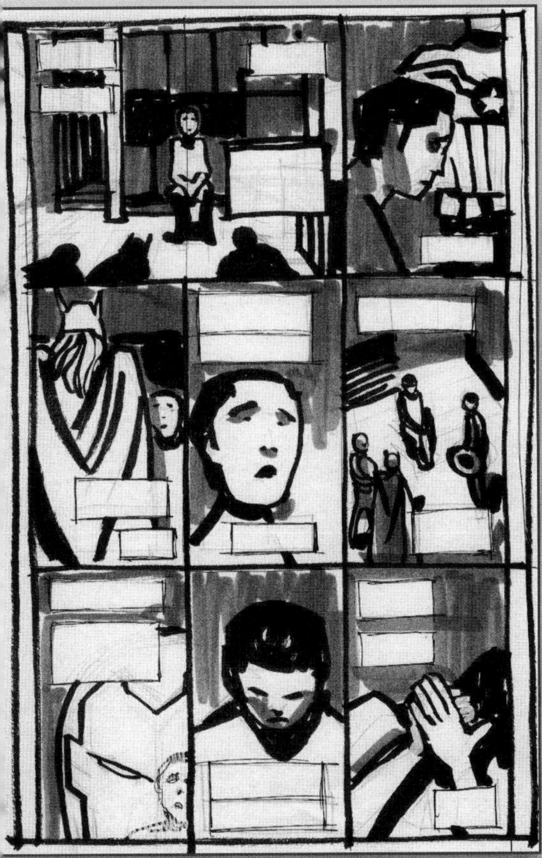

LAYOUT: GABRIEL HERNANDEZ WALTA

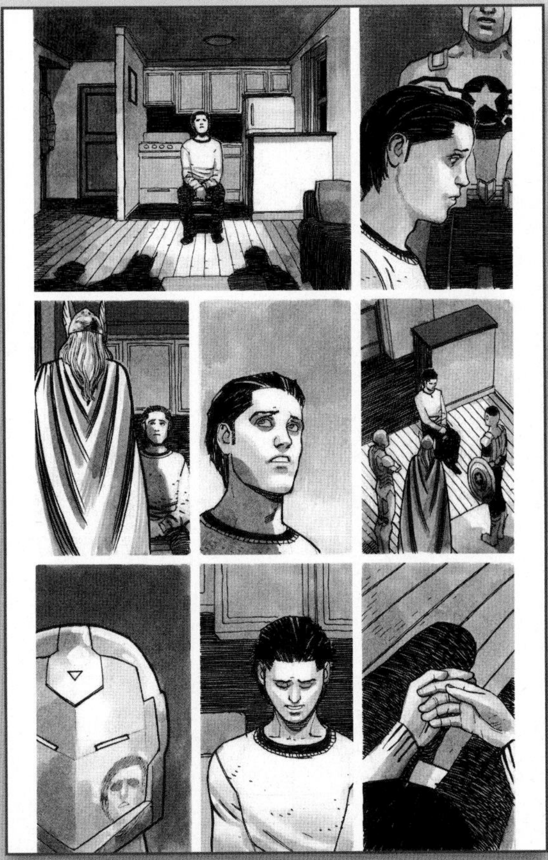

INKS: GABRIEL HERNANDEZ WALTA

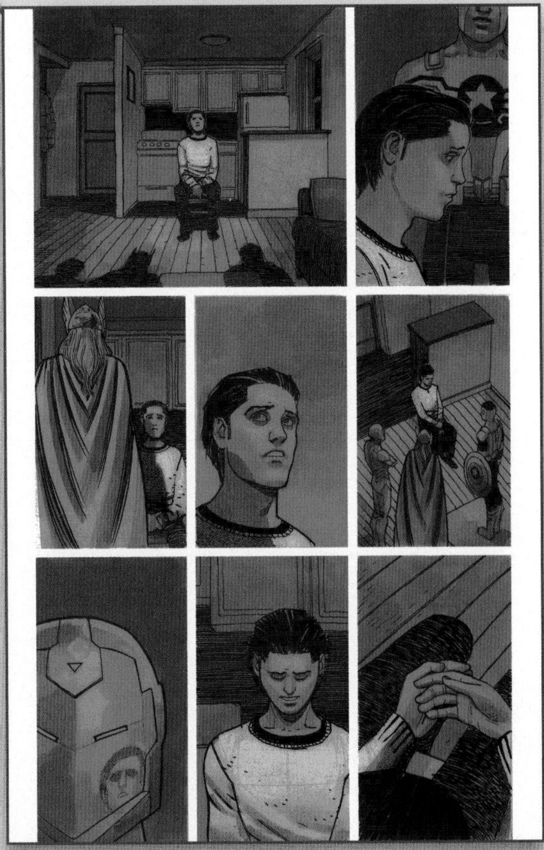

COLORS: JORDIE BELLAIRE

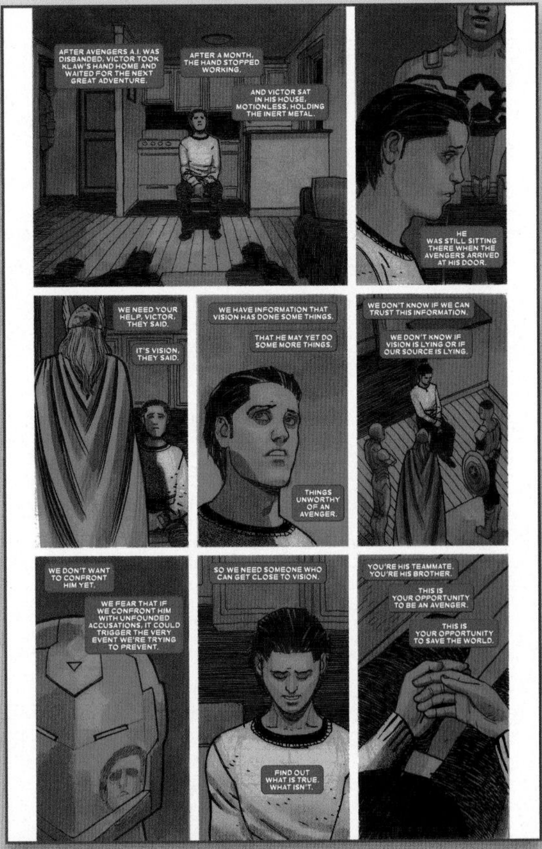
AFTER AVENGERS A.I. WAS DISBANDED, VICTOR TOOK KLAW'S HAND HOME AND WAITED FOR THE NEXT GREAT ADVENTURE.
AFTER A MONTH, THE HAND STOPPED WORKING.
AND VICTOR SAT IN HIS HOUSE, MOTIONLESS, HOLDING THE INERT METAL.
HE WAS STILL SITTING THERE WHEN THE AVENGERS ARRIVED AT HIS DOOR.
WE NEED YOUR HELP, VICTOR, THEY SAID.
IT'S VISION, THEY SAID.
WE HAVE INFORMATION THAT VISION HAS DONE SOME THINGS.
THAT HE MAY YET DO SOME MORE THINGS.
THINGS UNWORTHY OF AN AVENGER.
WE DON'T KNOW IF WE CAN TRUST THIS INFORMATION.
WE DON'T KNOW IF VISION IS LYING OR IF OUR SOURCE IS LYING.
WE DON'T WANT TO CONFRONT HIM YET.
WE FEAR THAT IF WE CONFRONT HIM WITH UNFOUNDED ACCUSATIONS, IT COULD TRIGGER THE VERY EVENT WE'RE TRYING TO PREVENT.
SO WE NEED SOMEONE WHO CAN GET CLOSE TO VISION.
FIND OUT WHAT IS TRUE. WHAT ISN'T.
YOU'RE HIS TEAMMATE. YOU'RE HIS BROTHER.
THIS IS YOUR OPPORTUNITY TO BE AN AVENGER.
THIS IS YOUR OPPORTUNITY TO SAVE THE WORLD.

LETTERS: VC's CLAYTON COWLES

PAGE 17:

FLASHBACK

PANEL 1: VISION hugging VICTOR:

> CAPTION: Victor Mancha's life was still not his life.
> CAPTION: But he was happier than he'd ever been.
> CAPTION: He had a mission. From the Avengers.

PANEL 2: VICTOR reporting back to the Avengers. Talking to their images.

> VICTOR: They let me in.
> VICTOR: I'll be staying here a few weeks.

PANEL 3: VICTOR at the piano with V.

> CAPTION: Find a way into the family.
> CAPTION: Answer these questions:

PANEL 4: VICTOR reporting back to the AVENGERS.

> VICTOR: There's definitely something—I don't know—something with Virginia.
> VICTOR: She's hurt.

PANEL 5: VICTOR and VIN playing basketball.

> CAPTION: Who killed the Grim Reaper?
> CAPTION: Who killed Chris Kinzky?

PANEL 6: VICTOR reporting to the Avengers.

> VICTOR: He's reading this book over and over.
> VICTOR: Like he's obsessed with mercy and justice, like he's seen something.

PANEL 7: VICTOR and VIV at the grave.

> CAPTION: Did Vision lie to the police?

PANEL 8: VICTOR reporting to the Avengers.

> VICTOR: The daughter is hung up on Kinzky, but she won't talk about it.

PANEL 9: VICTOR with VISION at the art museum.

> CAPTION: What causes Vision's fall into madness?
> CAPTION: What could possibly make him want to harm his friends?

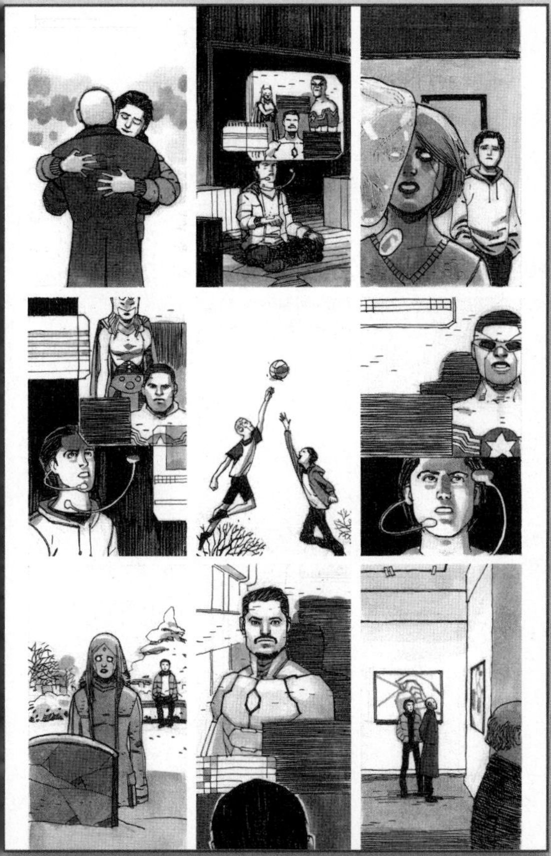

INKS: GABRIEL HERNANDEZ WALTA

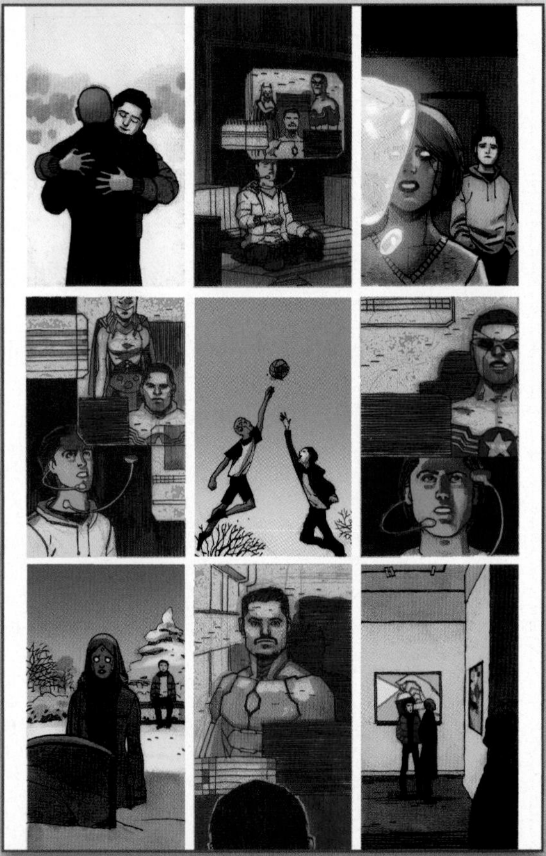

COLORS: JORDIE BELLAIRE

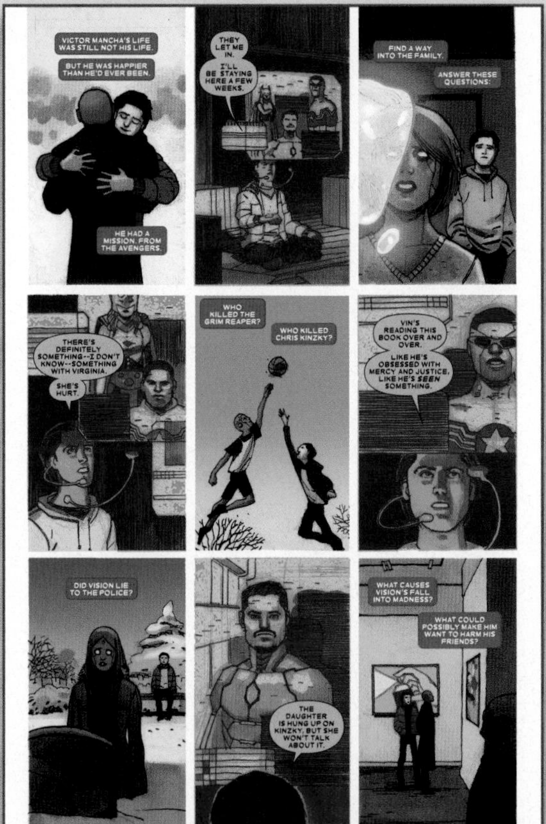
VICTOR MANCHA'S LIFE WAS STILL NOT HIS LIFE.
BUT HE WAS HAPPIER THAN HE'D EVER BEEN.
HE HAD A MISSION. FROM THE AVENGERS.
THEY LET ME IN.
I'LL BE STAYING HERE A FEW WEEKS.
FIND A WAY INTO THE FAMILY.
ANSWER THESE QUESTIONS:
THERE'S DEFINITELY SOMETHING--I DON'T KNOW--SOMETHING WITH VIRGINIA.
SHE'S HURT.
WHO KILLED THE GRIM REAPER?
WHO KILLED CHRIS KINZKY?
VIN'S READING THIS BOOK OVER AND OVER.
LIKE HE'S OBSESSED WITH MERCY AND JUSTICE. LIKE HE'S SEEN SOMETHING.
DID VISION LIE TO THE POLICE?
THE DAUGHTER IS HUNG UP ON KINZKY, BUT SHE WON'T TALK ABOUT IT.
WHAT CAUSES VISION'S FALL INTO MADNESS?
WHAT COULD POSSIBLY MAKE HIM WANT TO HARM HIS FRIENDS?

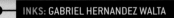

LETTERS: VC's CLAYTON COWLES

PAGE 18:

PANEL 1: VIN lying still on the ground. VICTOR above him. VICTOR using his powers to hold VIN.

> VICTOR: Vin?
> CAPTION: Victor was surprised when he found the Stringless Steinway.

PANEL 2: Flashback. VICTOR standing with VIRGINIA standing by the piano.

> CAPTION: A gift from the Panther.
> CAPTION: Made from genuine Wakandan Vibranium.

PANEL 3: VIN lying still, VICTOR concerned, turning off his powers.

> VICTOR: Vin?
> CAPTION: How amazing, he thought. What a coincidence.

PANEL 4: VICTOR touching the inside of the piano.

> CAPTION: Or maybe even a sign.

PANEL 5: VICTOR bending down by the hurt, unmoving VIN.

> VICTOR: Vin?!
> CAPTION: After all, he wasn't looking for anything.

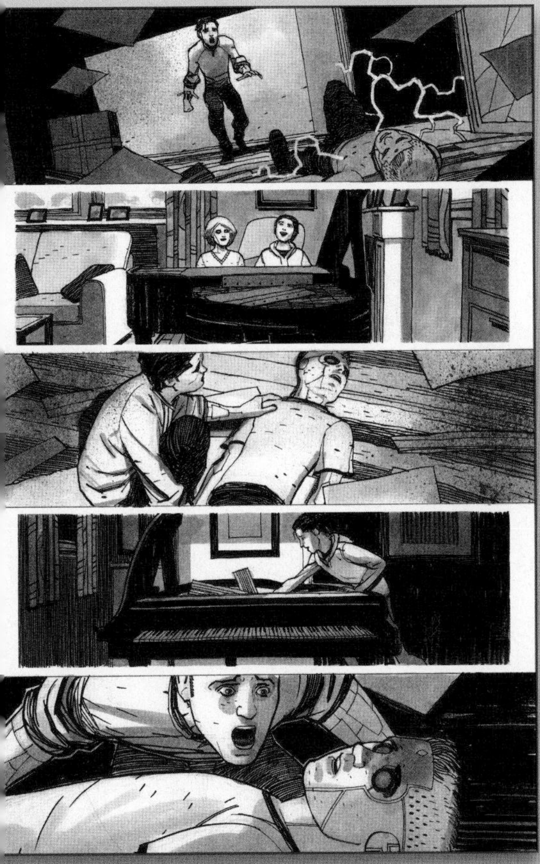

INKS: GABRIEL HERNANDEZ WALTA

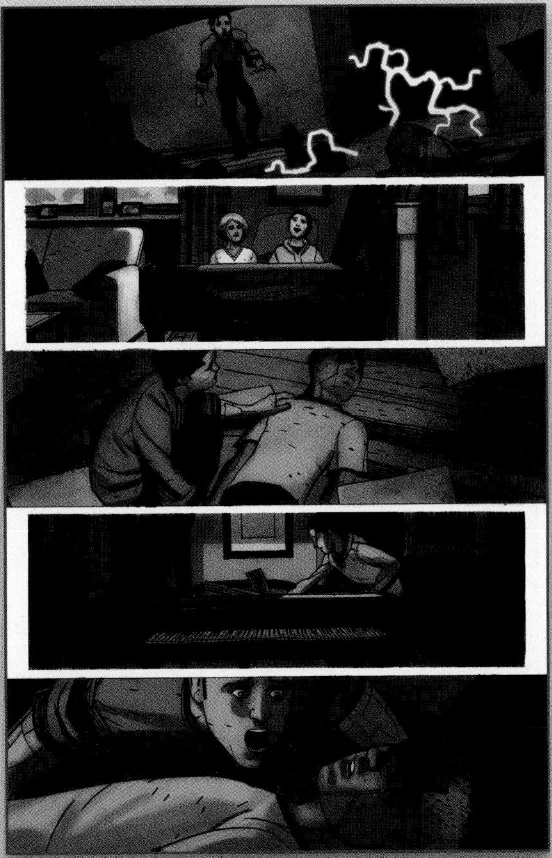

COLORS: JORDIE BELLAIRE

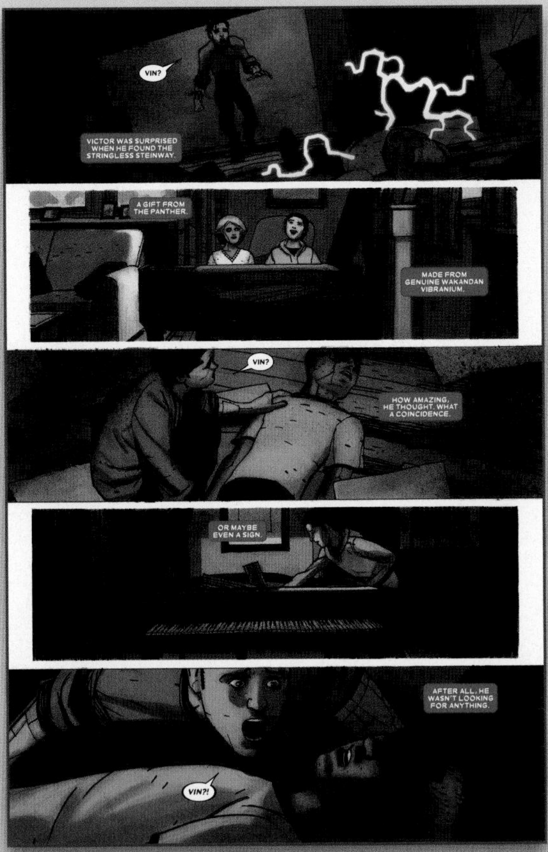
VIN?
VICTOR WAS SURPRISED WHEN HE FOUND THE STRINGLESS STEINWAY.
A GIFT FROM THE PANTHER.
MADE FROM GENUINE WAKANDAN VIBRANIUM.
VIN?
HOW AMAZING, HE THOUGHT. WHAT A COINCIDENCE.
OR MAYBE EVEN A SIGN.
AFTER ALL, HE WASN'T LOOKING FOR ANYTHING.
VIN?!

LETTERS: VC's CLAYTON COWLES

PAGE 19:

<u>PANEL 1:</u> VISION phasing through the wall of the room VIN and VICTOR are in. He looks pissed, annoyed.

        VISION: What is going on here?
        VISION: Who fired the laser?

<u>PANEL 2:</u> Camera behind VISION looking on VICTOR and VIN. VICTOR is desperate, trying to help the un-moving VIN.

        VISION: Victor?
        VISION (smaller): Vin?

<u>PANEL 3:</u> VISION kneeling next VIN and VICTOR. VICTOR panicking. VISION quiet.

        VICTOR: I was just using—I was holding—
        VICTOR: I don't know! I don't know!
        VISION: Vin?
        VISION: Vin, wake up.

<u>PANEL 4:</u> VIRGINIA comes through the wall.

        VIRGINIA: Husband, is it him?
        VIRGINIA: Did you find the boy?

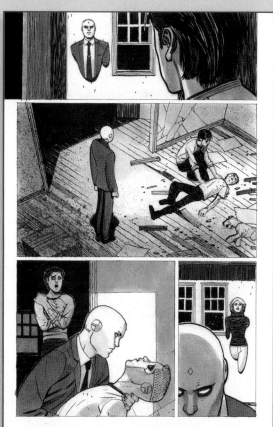

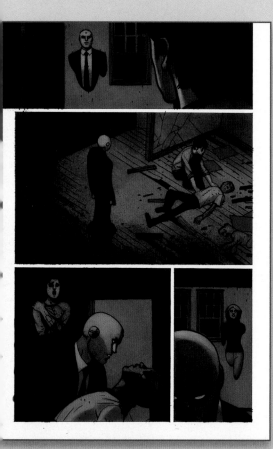

PAGE 20:

<u>PANEL 1:</u> Splash. VIN being held in VISION'S arms. The mother standing, looking on. VICTOR having collapsed into himself, into a little ball. The dog passed out on the side.

VISION: Wake up.
VISION: Vin, son, wake up.
VIRGINIA: NO!!!
VICTOR (small): I don't know…I don't know…I don't know…

CAPTION: Later Vision would learn Victor had miscalculated in the use of his magnetic powers.
CAPTION: He had damaged Vin's incorporeal nerve system, including those nerves linked to cognitive functions.
CAPTION: Due to the extent of the damages, repairs were not possible. Vin could not be revived.

CAPTION: Later Vision would learn that, though they were unaware of the problem that led to the misuse of Victor's powers…
CAPTION: …the Avengers were responsible for Victor's presence in Vision's home.

CAPTION: Later the Avengers would learn of Vision's losses and revelations.
CAPTION: They would finally understand what caused Vision's fall into madness.
CAPTION: They would finally know what could possibly make him want to harm his friends.

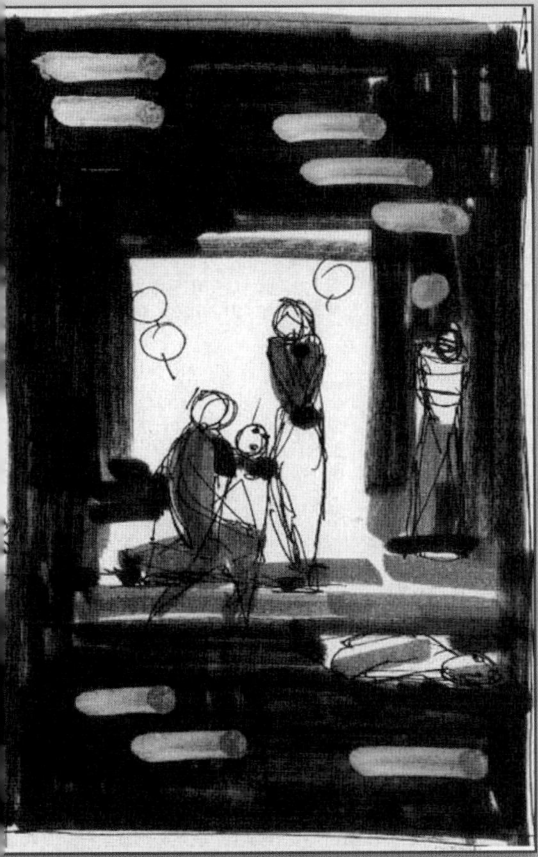

LAYOUT: GABRIEL HERNANDEZ WALTA

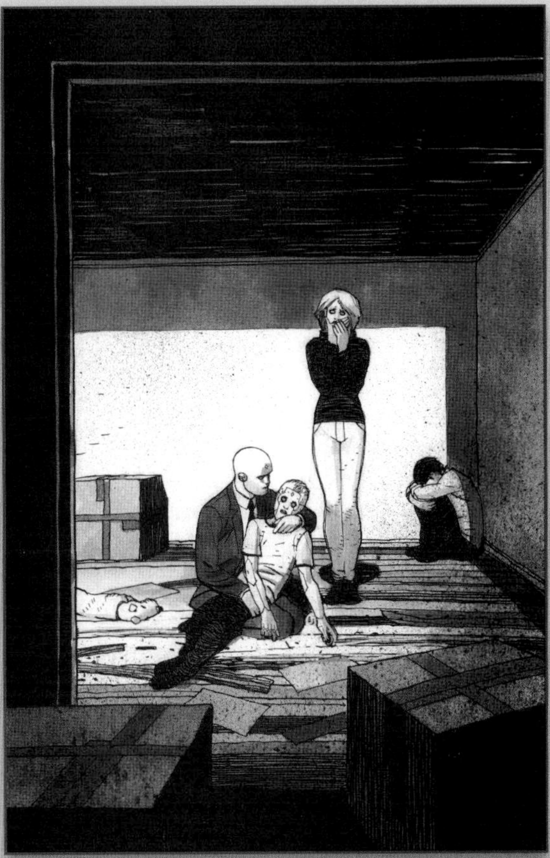

INKS: GABRIEL HERNANDEZ WALTA

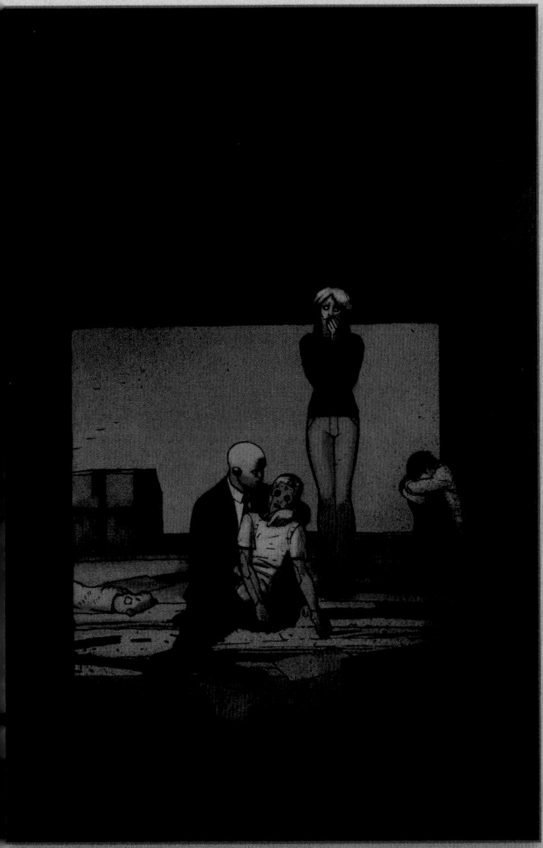

COLORS: JORDIE BELLAIRE

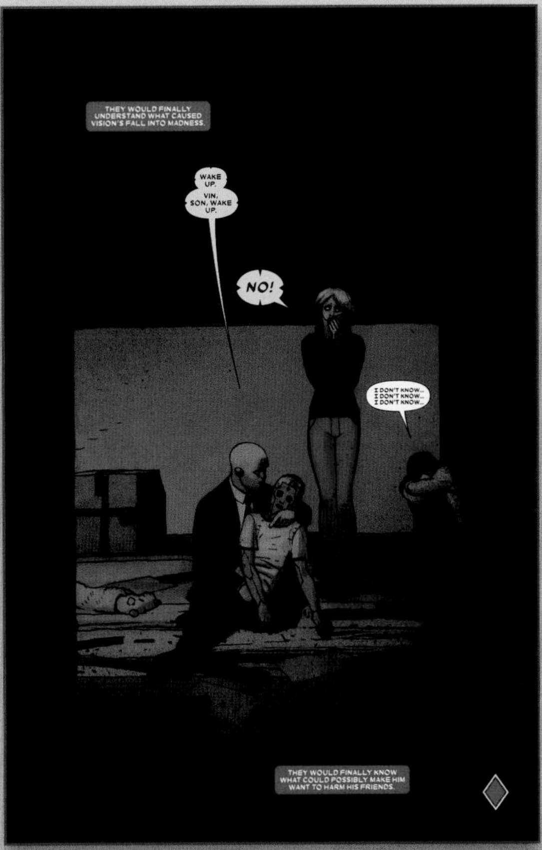

THEY WOULD FINALLY UNDERSTAND WHAT CAUSED VISION'S FALL INTO MADNESS.
WAKE UP.
VIN, SON, WAKE UP.
NO!
I DON'T KNOW... I DON'T KNOW... I DON'T KNOW...
THEY WOULD FINALLY KNOW WHAT COULD POSSIBLY MAKE HIM WANT TO HARM HIS FRIENDS.

LETTERS: VC's CLAYTON COWLES

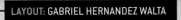

Art Note: Gabriel! So in this issue, Vision is under temporary house arrest and then breaks out. What I want to do is for the first seventeen pages I want the book to have a very claustrophobic feel. Vision locked in his house with only his grief and his broken family. I put lots of panels on these pages to give the readers a sense of being overcrowded, stuck, crammed. Then when Vision finally leaves the house we go to a wide open two-page splash, which will hopefully read (unconsciously) as a relief to the readers. Which is all to say, I'm sorry for so many panels in all those pages.

But, needless to add, you obviously know what you're doing. Feel free to adjust as you need to, man.

Thanks!

PAGE 1:

PANEL 1: VISION in the living room, sitting in a chair in the dark. We can see him just a bit, lit by the moonlight coming in the window. He's holding the CAPTAIN AMERICA lighter in his hand.

No dialogue.

PANEL 2: Vision lights the lighter, slightly illuminating the room. He's staring at the lighter.

SFX: Click

PANEL 3: And he lets the lighter out, and the room goes dark. Angle on Vision switches. As if camera is moving around him.

No dialogue.

PANEL 4: And on again. Angle on Vision switches. As if camera is moving around him.

SFX: Click

PANEL 5: And off. Angle switches.

No dialogue.

PANEL 6: And on again. Angle on Vision switches.

SFX: Click.

PANEL 7: And off. Angle switches. Rotating.

No dialogue

PANEL 8: And on again. Angle on Vision switches. Angle switches.

SFX: Click.

PANEL 9: And off. Angle switches.

No dialogue

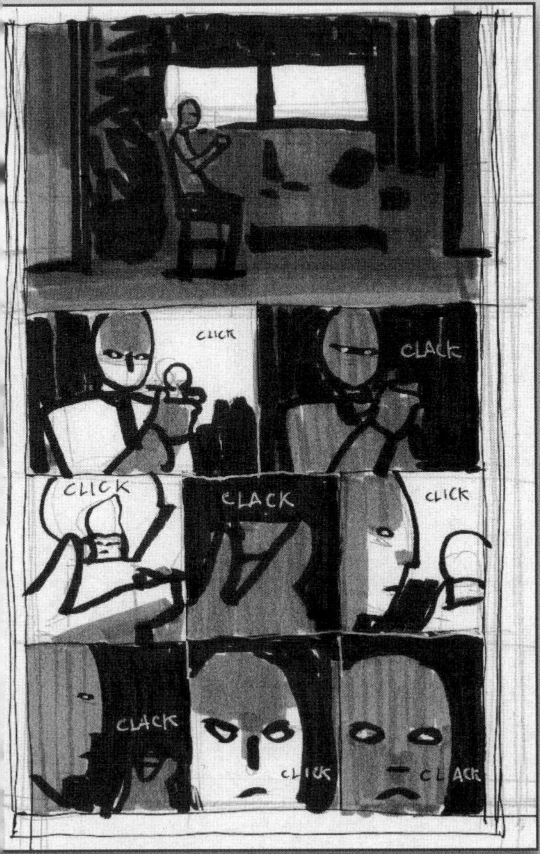
CLICK
CLACK
CLICK
CLACK
CLICK
CLACK
CLICK
CLACK

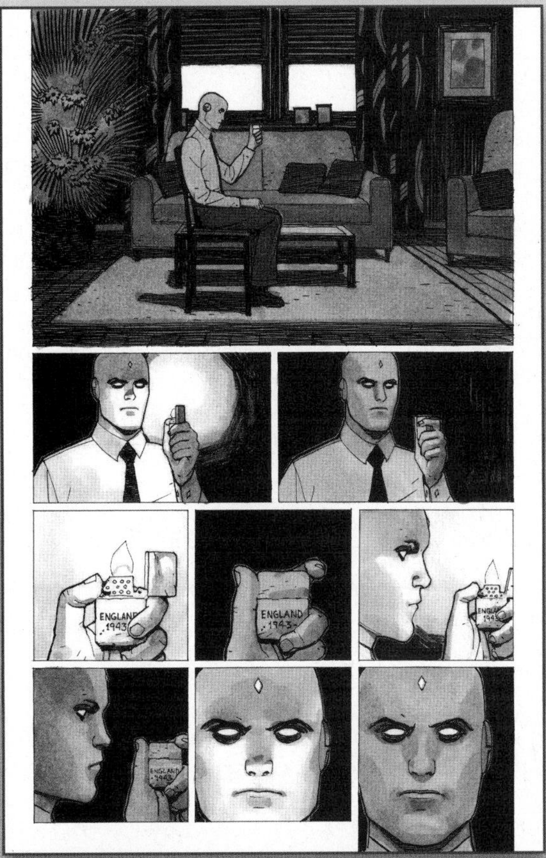
ENGLAND 1943
ENGLAND 1943

LAYOUT: GABRIEL HERNANDEZ WALTA

INKS: GABRIEL HERNANDEZ WALTA

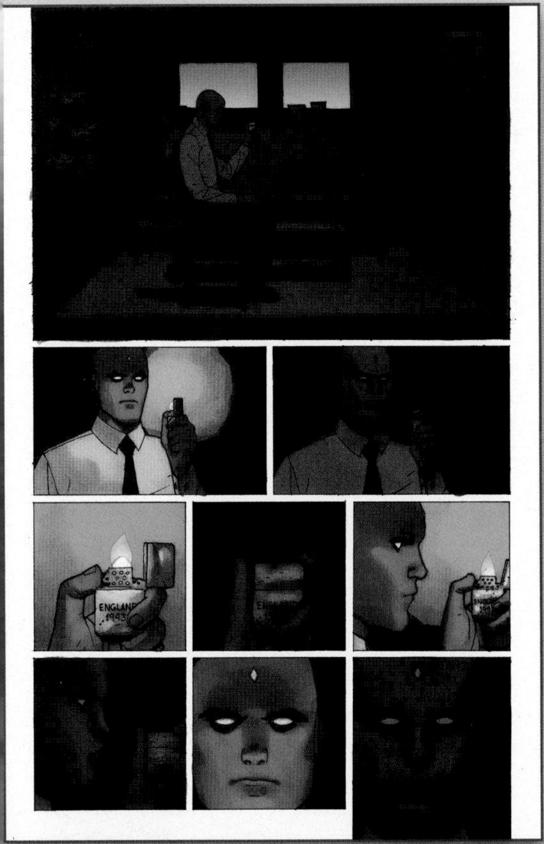

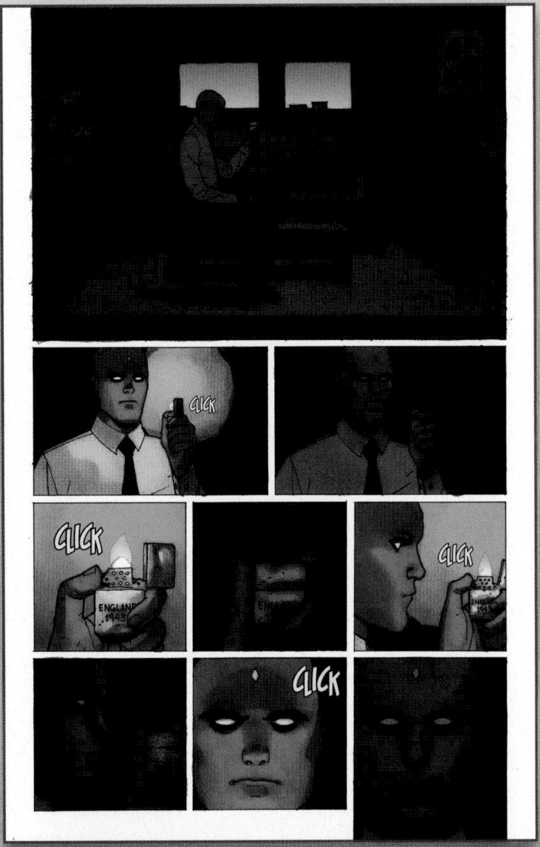
CLICK
CLICK
CLICK
CLICK

COLORS: JORDIE BELLAIRE

LETTERS: VC's CLAYTON COWLES

PAGE 2:

PANEL 1: VISION in his bedroom, taking off his shirt to put on his pajamas.

> VISION: Wife, our recent home incarceration has provided me with time to think.
> VISION: And I have spent this time thinking about my brother, Victor Mancha.

PANEL 2: VIRGINIA taking off her clothes to put on her pajamas. Very perfunctory. Ritualistic. In contrast to our sex scene from #3.

> VISION (OFF): How Victor is alive.

PANEL 3: VISION hanging up his shirt.

> VISION ((OFF): And my son, Vin is not.

PANEL 4: VISION taking off his pants.

> VISION: I have run through a number of scenarios.
> VISION: A great number.

PANEL 5: VISION folding his pants.

> VISION: And I have rigorously applied those scenarios to a variety of philosophical and religious traditions.

PANEL 6: VIRGINIA taking off more of her clothes.

> VISION (OFF): Despite my efforts, unfortunately, I cannot see how in any scenario…
> VISION (OFF): …in any philosophical or religious traditions…

PANEL 7: VISION putting on his pajamas.

> VISION: …this current outcome is just.

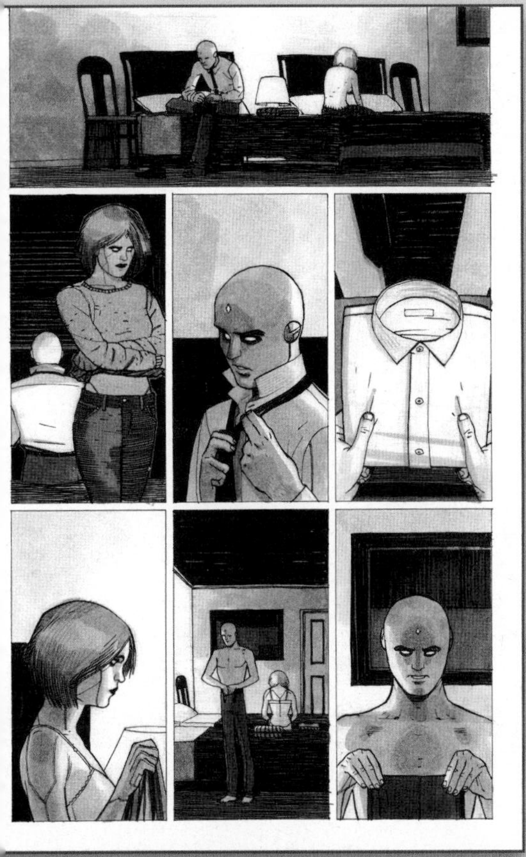

INKS: GABRIEL HERNANDEZ WALTA

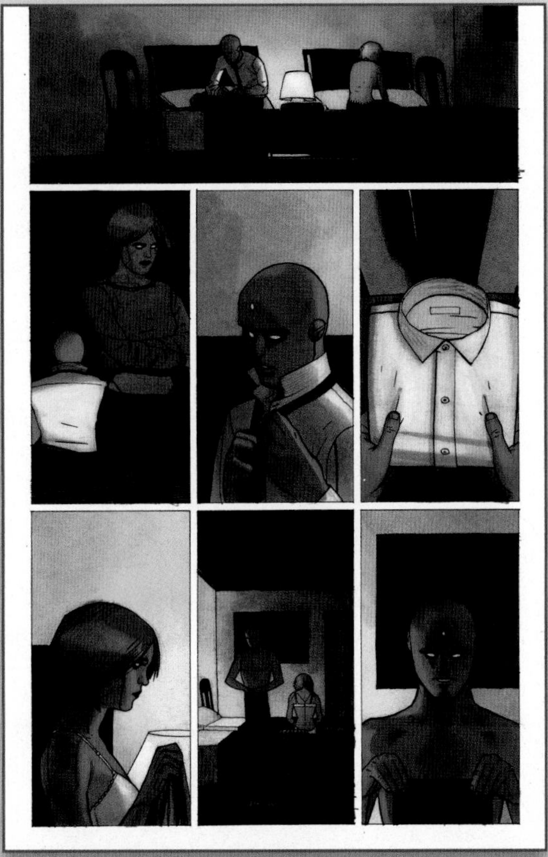

COLORS: JORDIE BELLAIRE

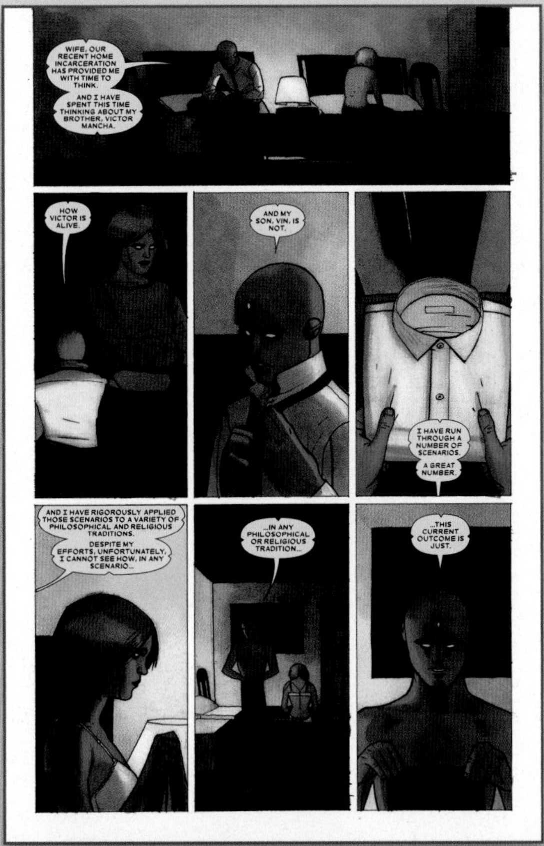
WIFE, OUR RECENT HOME INCARCERATION HAS PROVIDED ME WITH TIME TO THINK.
AND I HAVE SPENT THIS TIME THINKING ABOUT MY BROTHER, VICTOR MANCHA.
HOW VICTOR IS ALIVE.
AND MY SON, VIN, IS NOT.
I HAVE RUN THROUGH A NUMBER OF SCENARIOS.
A GREAT NUMBER.
AND I HAVE RIGOROUSLY APPLIED THOSE SCENARIOS TO A VARIETY OF PHILOSOPHICAL AND RELIGIOUS TRADITIONS.
DESPITE MY EFFORTS, UNFORTUNATELY, I CANNOT SEE HOW, IN ANY SCENARIO...
...IN ANY PHILOSOPHICAL OR RELIGIOUS TRADITION...
...THIS CURRENT OUTCOME IS JUST.

LETTERS: VC's CLAYTON COWLES

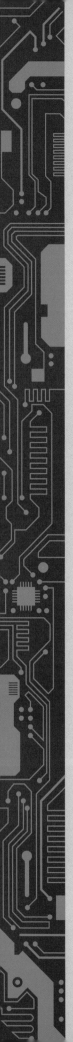

PAGE 3:

PANEL 1: VISION putting on pajamas.

> VISION: I must therefore conclude that it is not just.
> VISION: And what is not just must be addressed.

PANEL 2: VIRGINIA putting on her pajamas.

> VISION (OFF): This is true in all scenarios.
> VISION (OFF): In all systems.

PANEL 3: VISION sitting on the bed.

> VISION : Now, I cannot revive our son.
> VISION: Therefore it seems obvious that I must…

PANEL 4: VIRGINIA sitting down in bed, looking at VISION.

> VISION: That I must…

PANEL 5: VISION looking over at VIRGINIA, lost.

> VISION: That I I…

PANEL 6: VISION in bed as VIRGINIA curls into him.

> VISION: I cannot cannot…

PANEL 7: VISION lying in bed with VIRGINIA next to him.

> VISION: I am the Vision of the Avengers.
> VISION: I saved the world thirty-seven times.
> VIRGINIA: I know know know.

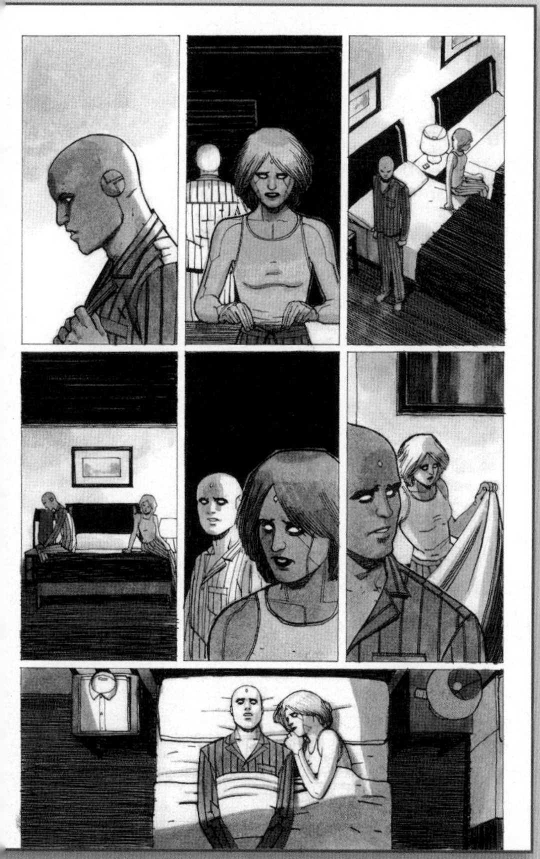

INKS: GABRIEL HERNANDEZ WALTA

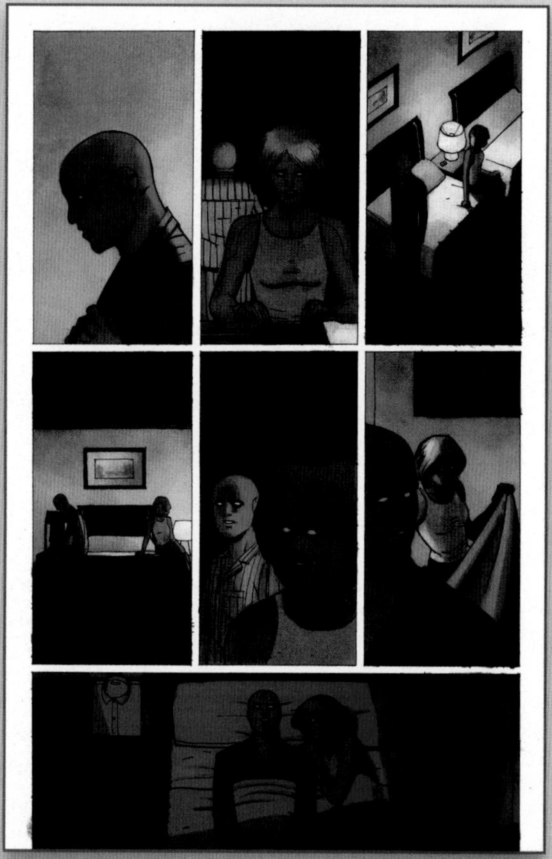

COLORS: JORDIE BELLAIRE

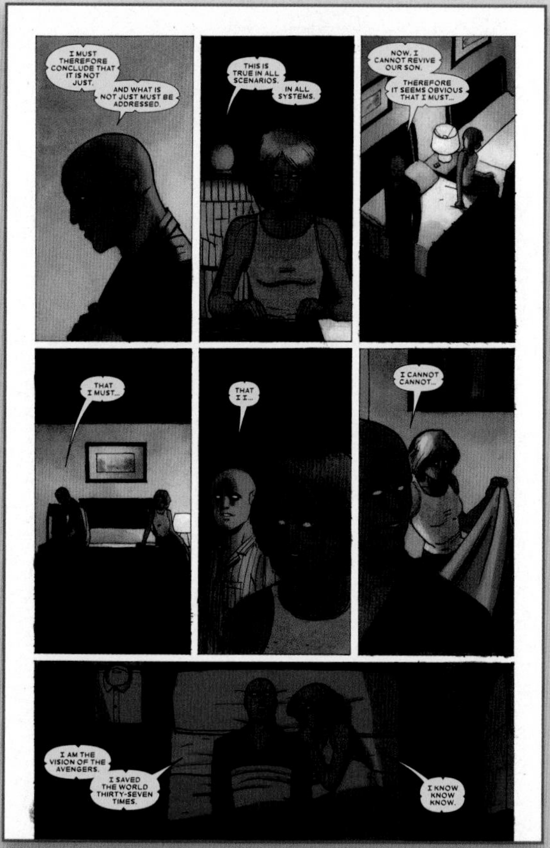
I MUST THEREFORE CONCLUDE THAT IT IS NOT JUST.
AND WHAT IS NOT JUST MUST BE ADDRESSED.
THIS IS TRUE IN ALL SCENARIOS.
IN ALL SYSTEMS.
NOW, I CANNOT REVIVE OUR SON.
THEREFORE IT SEEMS OBVIOUS THAT I MUST...
THAT I MUST...
THAT I I...
I CANNOT CANNOT...
I AM THE VISION OF THE AVENGERS.
I SAVED THE WORLD THIRTY-SEVEN TIMES.
I KNOW KNOW KNOW.

LETTERS: VC's CLAYTON COWLES

PAGE 4:

<u>PANEL 1:</u> VISION, VIV AND VIRGINIA sit at the table. VIN is notably absent. VIRGINIA is staring straight ahead. VIV is looking down, sad. VISION is talking to the table. Dog is asleep next to the table.

        VISION: I finally heard back from the principal.

<u>PANEL 2:</u> On Viv.

        VISION (off): Viv will be sent recordings of each of her classes.
        VISION (off): And will continue to receive her assignments.

<u>PANEL 3:</u> Close on VISION.

        VISION: Iron Man assures me that our current situation will not last more than a few weeks.
        VISION: As soon as he "figures out" what has occurred and why, all will return to normal.

<u>PANEL 4:</u> Back to the full table.

        VISION: As such, Viv needs only to complete these assignments from home.
        VISION: And it will not affect her moving on to her junior year.

<u>PANEL 5:</u> On the sleeping dog.

        VISION (OFF): Which is good.

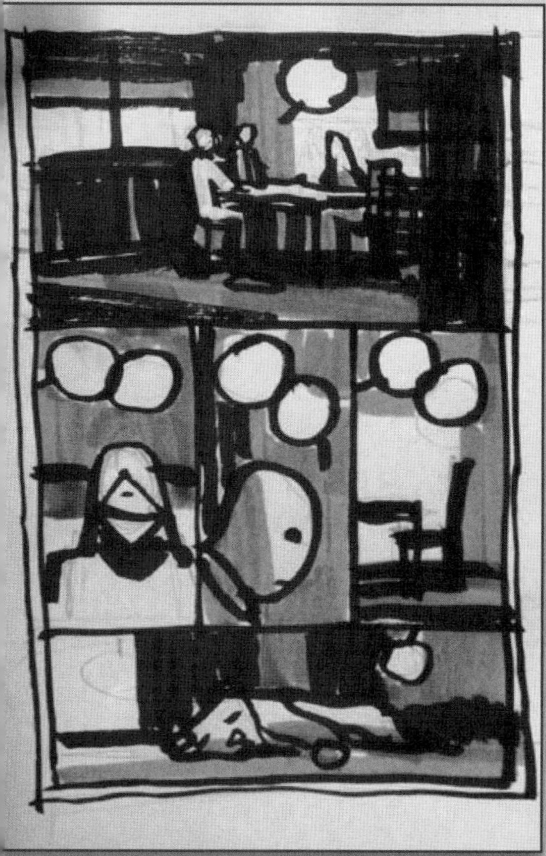

LAYOUT: GABRIEL HERNANDEZ WALTA

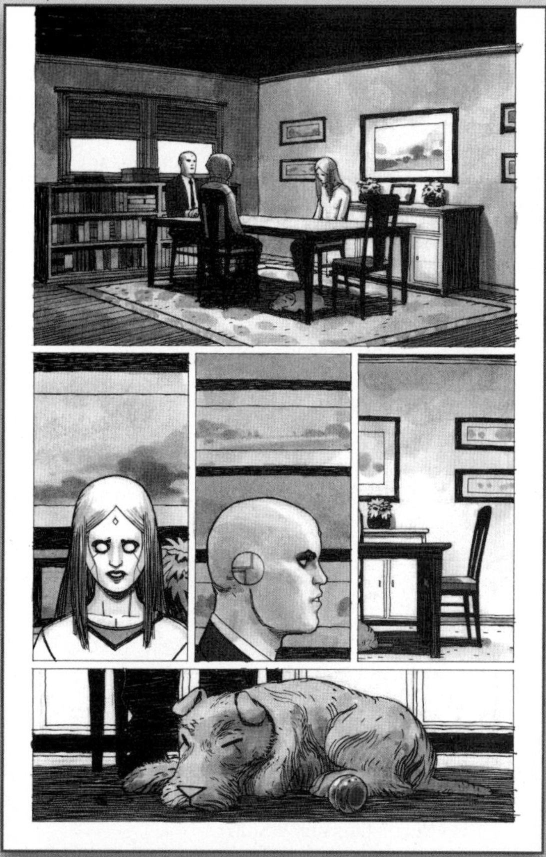

INKS: GABRIEL HERNANDEZ WALTA

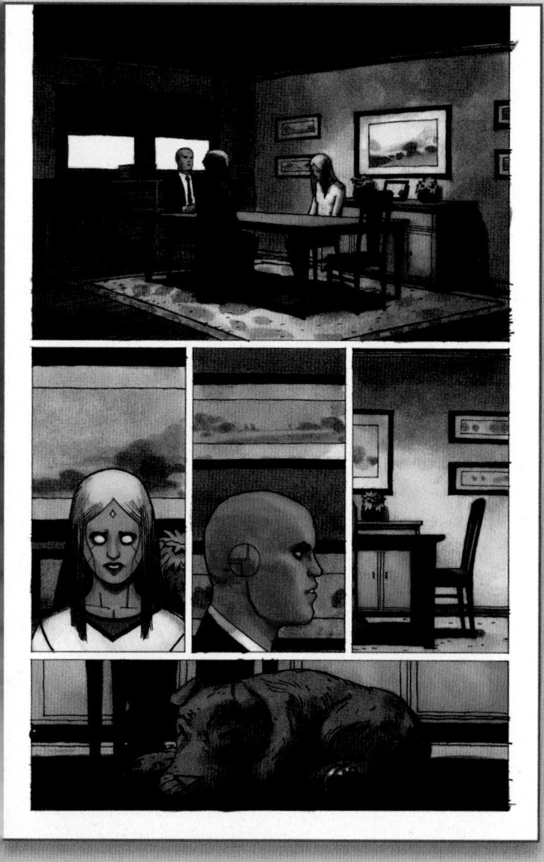

COLORS: JORDIE BELLAIRE

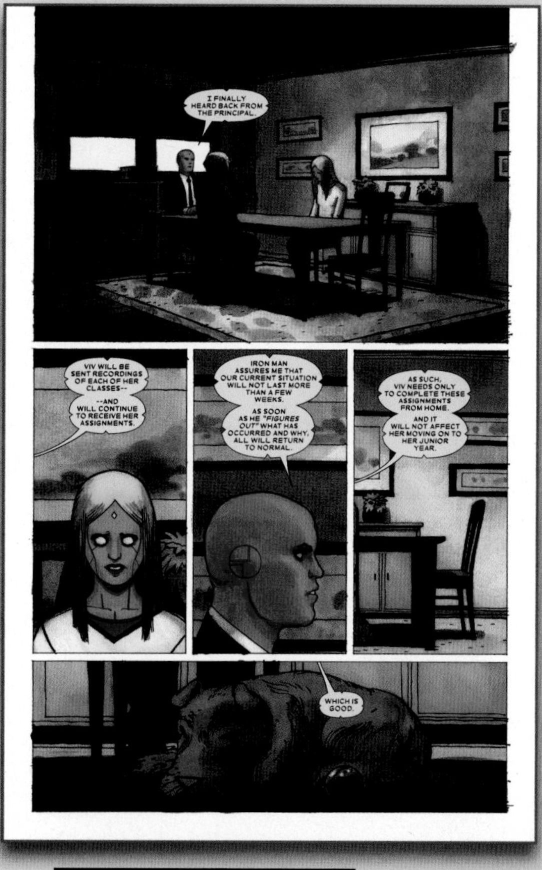
I FINALLY HEARD BACK FROM THE PRINCIPAL.
VIV WILL BE SENT RECORDINGS OF EACH OF HER CLASSES--
--AND WILL CONTINUE TO RECEIVE HER ASSIGNMENTS.
IRON MAN ASSURES ME THAT OUR CURRENT SITUATION WILL NOT LAST MORE THAN A FEW WEEKS.
AS SOON AS HE *"FIGURES OUT"* WHAT HAS OCCURRED AND WHY, ALL WILL RETURN TO NORMAL.
AS SUCH, VIV NEEDS ONLY TO COMPLETE THESE ASSIGNMENTS FROM HOME.
AND IT WILL NOT AFFECT HER MOVING ON TO HER JUNIOR YEAR.
WHICH IS GOOD.

LETTERS: VC's CLAYTON COWLES

PAGE 5:

PANEL 1: VIRGINIA staring straight ahead.

      VIRGINIA: Oh. Good.
      VIRGINIA: That is … good good.

PANEL 2: VIV looking down.

      VIRGINIA (OFF): Good. Good. Good.

PANEL 3: CLOSE on VIRGINIA, trying to get out the words.

      VIRGINIA: G-g-g…

PANEL 4: VISION looking at his wife, putting his arm on her her arm to comfort her.

      VISION: Yes.
      VISION: You are right.

PANEL 5: Close on VISION

      VISION: It is good.

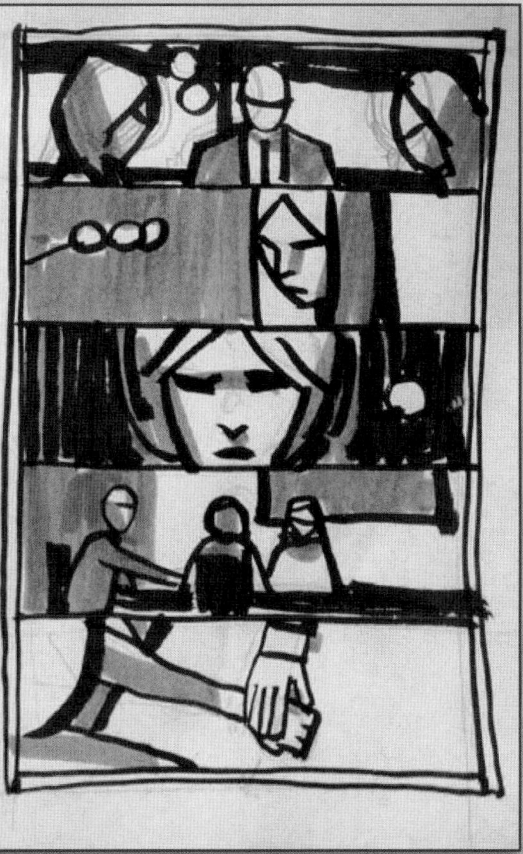

LAYOUT: GABRIEL HERNANDEZ WALTA

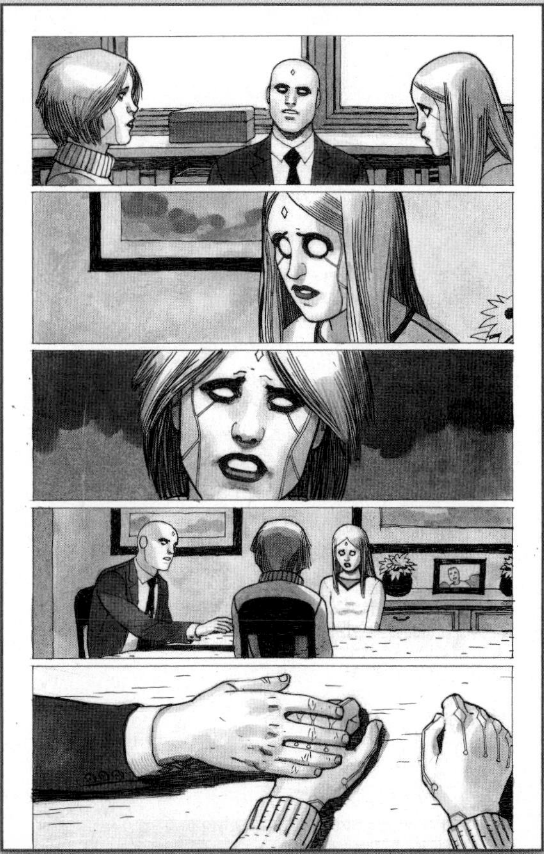

INKS: GABRIEL HERNANDEZ WALTA

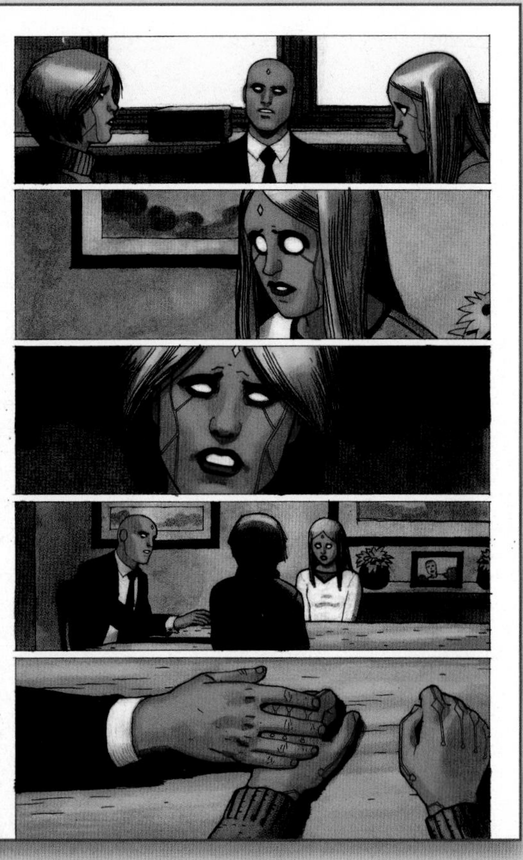

COLORS: JORDIE BELLAIRE

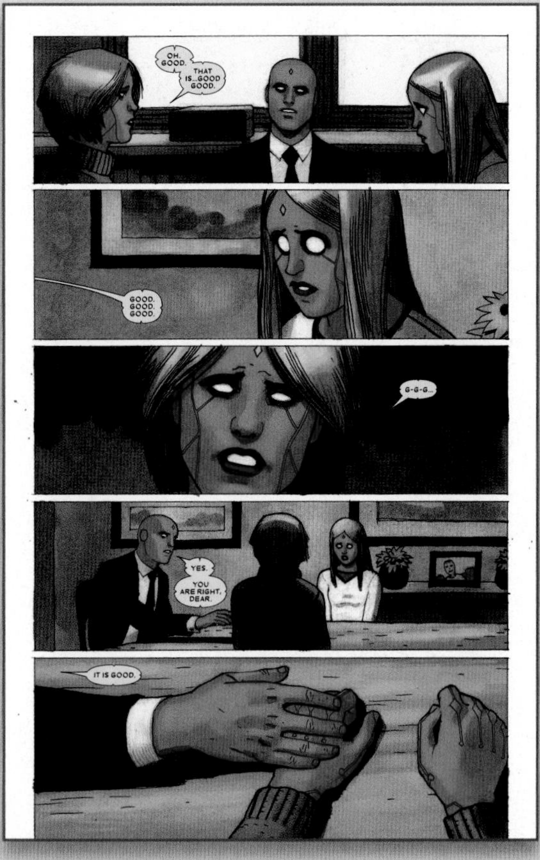
OH. GOOD.
THAT IS...GOOD GOOD.
GOOD. GOOD. GOOD.
G-G-G...
YES.
YOU ARE RIGHT, DEAR.
IT IS GOOD.

LETTERS: VC's CLAYTON COWLES

PAGE 6:

PANEL 1: SPARKY sitting in front of the front door (on the inside of the house). He wants to go outside for a walk.

SPARKY: Woof.

PANEL 2: Close up of SPARKY, wanting to go outside.

SPARKY: nn-nnn

PANEL 3: SPARKY standing in front of the door.

SPARKY: Woof.

PANEL 4: SPARKY starts to phases through the door going out.

No dialogue

PANEL 5: SPARKY a bit through the door (enough so his nose would be touching the other side). There is an electrical charge running through him.

SFX: zzzzzzzz

PANEL 6: SPARKY reeling back into the house from the charge.

SPARKY: Woof! Woof!

PANEL 7: SPARKY curling up, nursing his pain.

SPARKY: Nnn-nnn-nnn

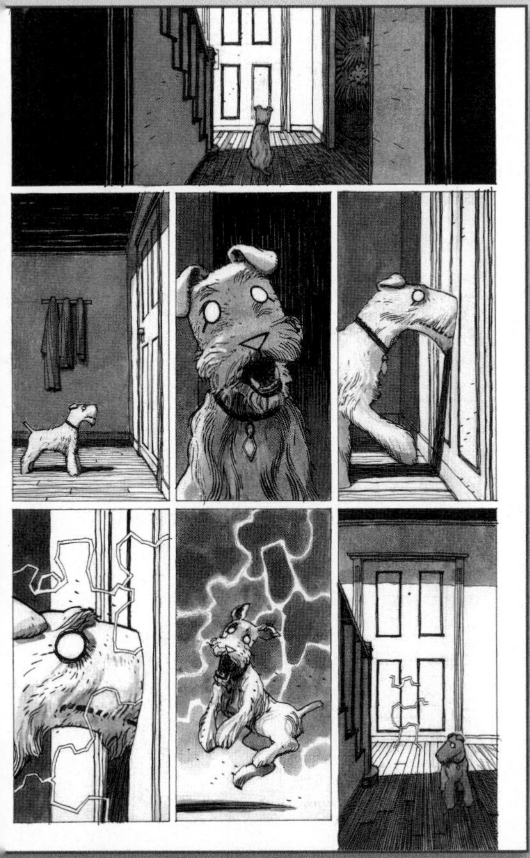

INKS: GABRIEL HERNANDEZ WALTA

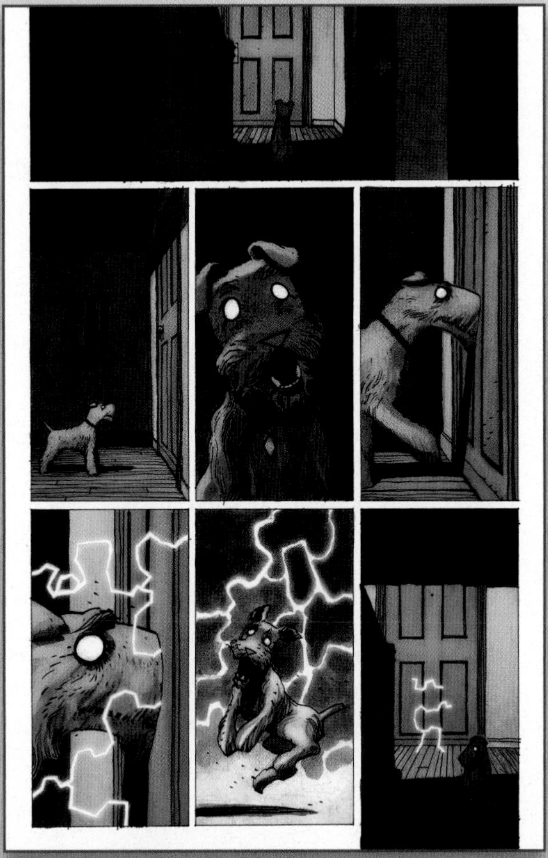

COLORS: JORDIE BELLAIRE

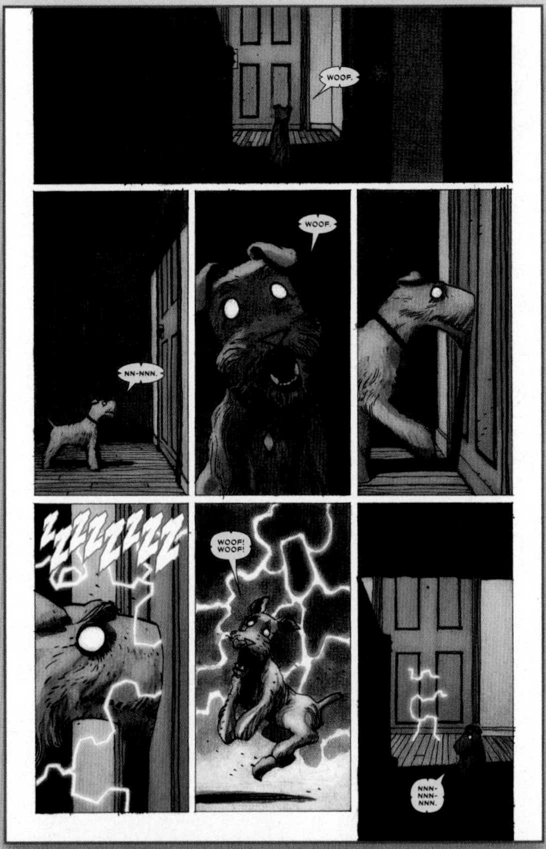

WOOF.
NN-NNN.
WOOF.
ZZZZZZZZ
WOOF! WOOF!
NNN-NNN-NNN.

LETTERS: VC's CLAYTON COWLES

PAGE 7:

PANEL 1: VISION is pacing in the living room in the background. In the foreground. VIRGINIA is sitting at the piano, playing with the keys.

> VISION: My apologies, Iron Man…
> VISION: No. No, there is no reason to deploy the Avengers.

PANEL 2: VISION pacing. VIRGINIA playing.

> VISION: This was not an attempted breach.
> VISION: The dog set off the alarm.
> VIRGINIA: Row Row Row

PANEL 3: VISION pacing, phasing through furniture. VIRGINIA playing.

> VISION: No, when you installed the enclosure I adjusted his programming…
> VISION: He should have stayed within the confines of the house.
> VIRGINIA: Your… boat.

PANEL 4: VISION pacing, phasing. VIRGINIA playing.

> VISION: There are a number of possibilities as to why these adjustments failed.
> VIRGINIA: Gently down … the…stream.

PANEL 5: VISION pacing. VIRGINIA playing.

> VISION: Yes, yes.
> VISION: I will conduct a thorough analysis of the animal this afternoon.
> VIRGINIA: Merrily. Merrily. Merrily.

PANEL 6: VISION pacing. VIRGINIA playing

> VISION: I do not anticipate that the alarm will sound again.
> VIRGINIA: Life is but a dream.

PANEL 7: Close on VIRGINIA.

> VIRGINIA: Dream Dream Dream.

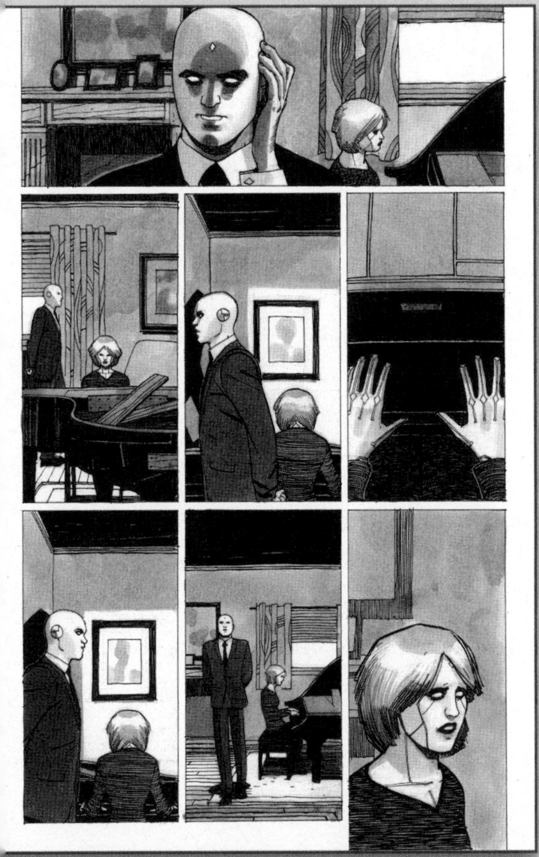

INKS: GABRIEL HERNANDEZ WALTA

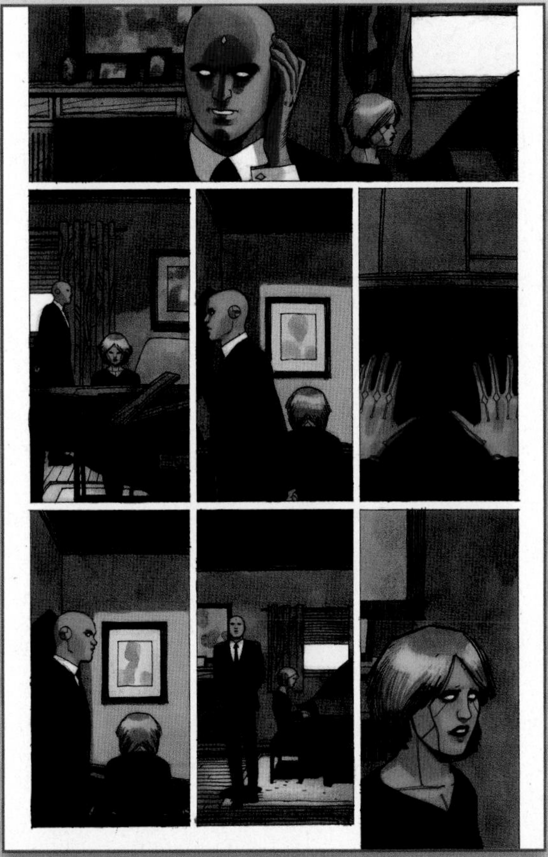

COLORS: JORDIE BELLAIRE

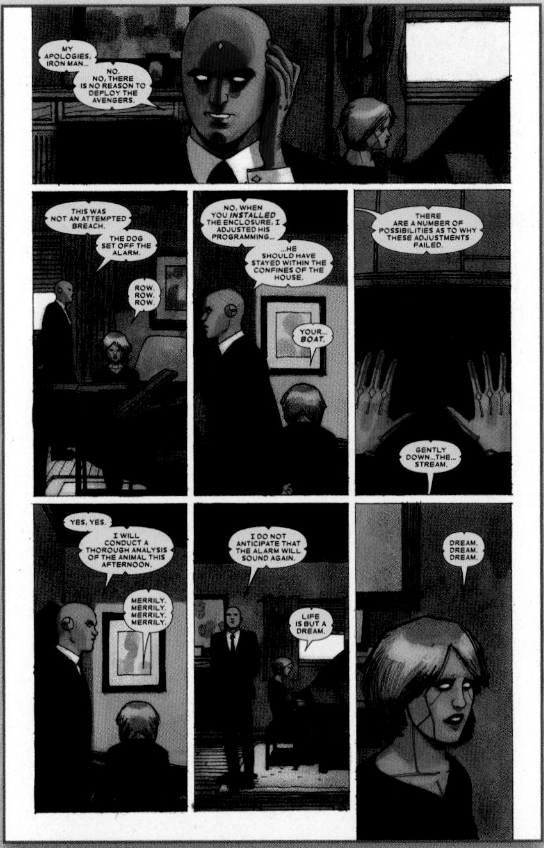
MY APOLOGIES, IRON MAN...
NO. NO, THERE IS NO REASON TO DEPLOY THE AVENGERS.
THIS WAS NOT AN ATTEMPTED BREACH.
THE DOG SET OFF THE ALARM.
ROW. ROW. ROW.
NO, WHEN YOU *INSTALLED* THE ENCLOSURE, I ADJUSTED HIS PROGRAMMING...
...HE SHOULD HAVE STAYED WITHIN THE CONFINES OF THE HOUSE.
YOUR... *BOAT.*
THERE ARE A NUMBER OF POSSIBILITIES AS TO WHY THESE ADJUSTMENTS FAILED.
GENTLY DOWN...THE... STREAM.
YES, YES.
I WILL CONDUCT A THOROUGH ANALYSIS OF THE ANIMAL THIS AFTERNOON.
MERRILY. MERRILY. MERRILY. MERRILY.
I DO NOT ANTICIPATE THAT THE ALARM WILL SOUND AGAIN.
LIFE IS BUT A DREAM.
DREAM. DREAM. DREAM.

LETTERS: VC's CLAYTON COWLES

PAGE 8:

PANEL 1: VISION outside his daughter's door. A Fighting Patriots decoration hangs on it.

      VISION: VIV, may I come in?

PANEL 2: On the door.

      VIV (OFF): Yes, Father.

PANEL 3: VISION phasing through the door.

      VISION: I noticed that you have not downloaded your coursework for the day.
      VISION: I was wondering if--

PANEL 4: VISION enters the room, finding his daughter kneeled down at her bedside, her head bent, hands together. She is praying.

      VISION: Oh.
      VISION: Excuse me.

PANEL 5: Close on VIV her head down.

      VIV: It is fine, Father.
      VIV: I have yet to start.

PANEL 6: Close on VISION, confused, sad, looking down.

      VISION: Oh.
      VISION: Yes. Of course.

PANEL 7: VISION looking up.

      VISION: Well. If you have not started.
      VISION: May I then join you?

PANEL 8: Viv turning her head to look at her dad. Happy to see his interest.

      VIV: Yes, Father.
      VIV: You may join me.

SCRIPT: TOM KING

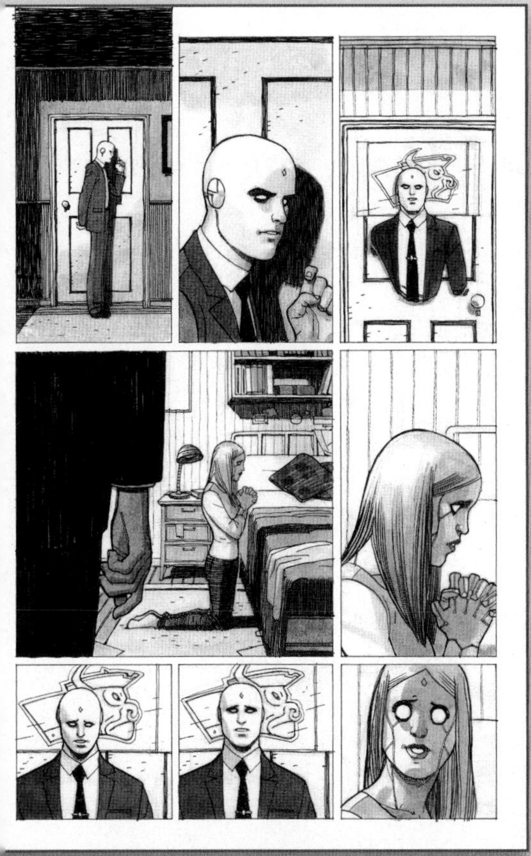

INKS: GABRIEL HERNANDEZ WALTA

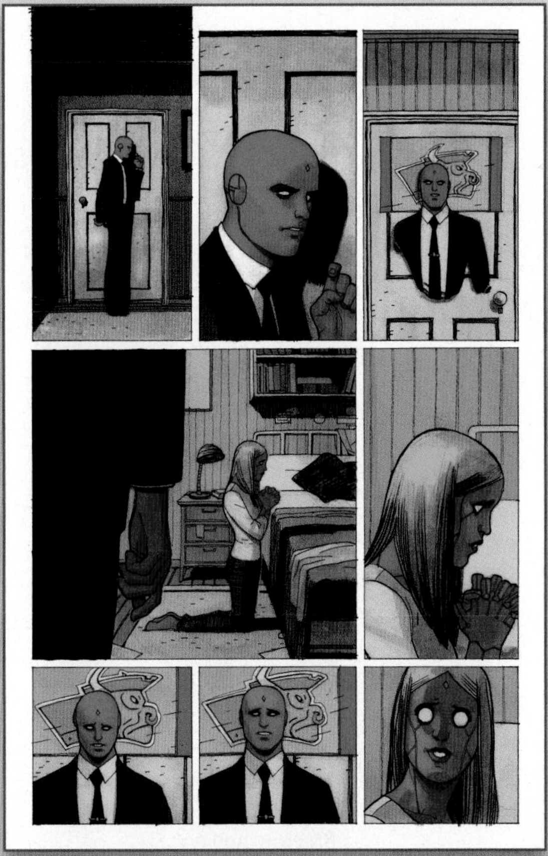

COLORS: JORDIE BELLAIRE

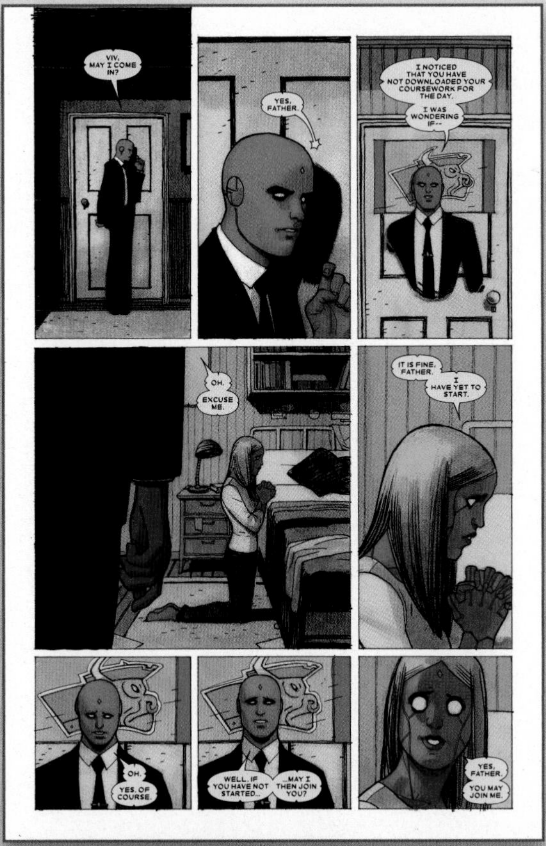
VIV, MAY I COME IN?
YES, FATHER.
I NOTICED THAT YOU HAVE NOT DOWNLOADED YOUR COURSEWORK FOR THE DAY.
I WAS WONDERING IF--
OH.
EXCUSE ME.
IT IS FINE, FATHER.
I HAVE YET TO START.
OH.
YES. OF COURSE.
WELL. IF YOU HAVE NOT STARTED...
...MAY I THEN JOIN YOU?
YES, FATHER.
YOU MAY JOIN ME.

LETTERS: VC's CLAYTON COWLES

PAGE 1:

PANEL 1: VIRGINIA and VIV at the dining room table. SPARKY has his paws on VIV's chair. VIV is petting him as he happily wags his tail.

> VIRGINIA: Your father broke the shield shield and left the house.
> VIRGINIA: He intends to kill kill kill your uncle.
> VIRGINIA: Victor Mancha.

PANEL 2: VIV looks up.

> VIV: Oh.

PANEL 3: On VIRGINIA. In shock.

> VIRGINIA: I believe the only way anyone can stop him is to kill kill kill him.
> VIRGINIA: After which which, they will label us us his dangerous creations.
> VIRGINIA: And most likely they will shut us off off off.

PANEL 4: DOG begging for more attention.

> SPARKY: Nnn nnn nnn.
> VIRGINIA (OFF): That said, if they do not stop him, he will be be be incarcerated …
> or or executed.
> VIRGINIA: In which case, we will then be be be be labeled his dangerous creations.

PANEL 5: On VIRGINIA.

> VIRGINIA: And most likely they will shut us off off off.

PANEL 6: VIV looking back at the dog.

> VIV: Oh.

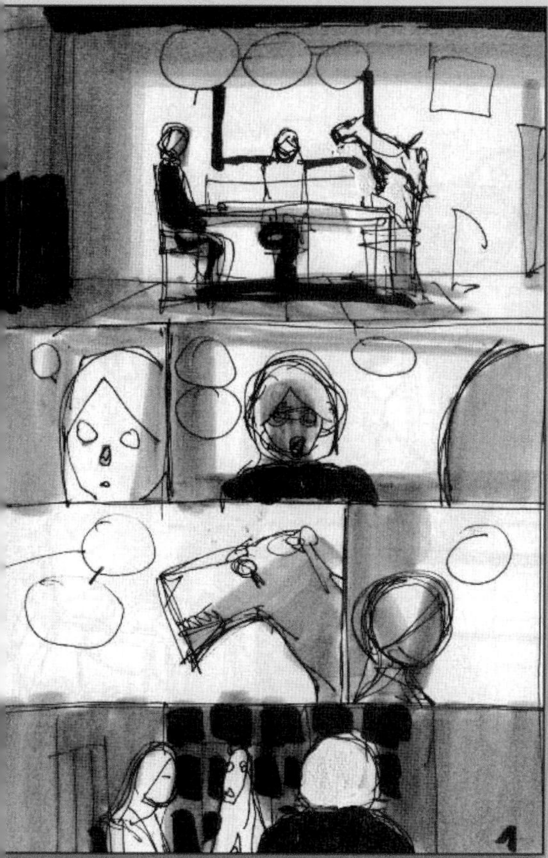

LAYOUT: GABRIEL HERNANDEZ WALTA

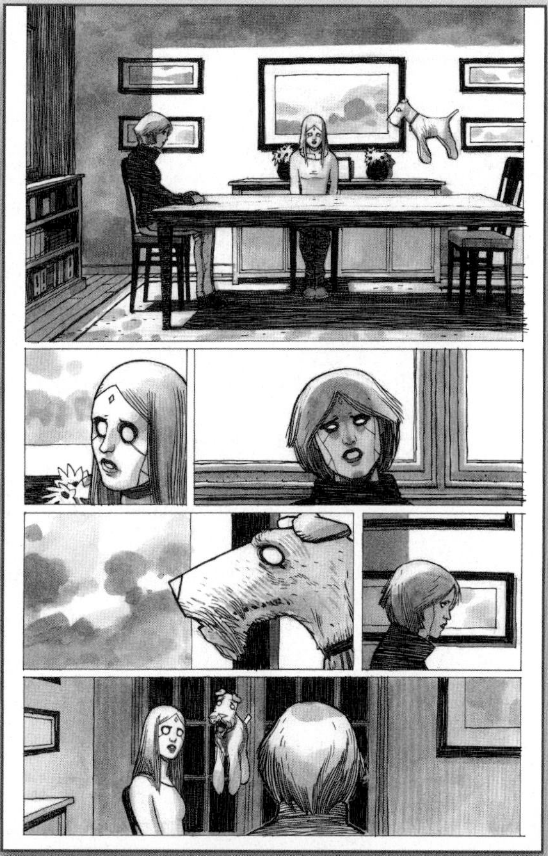

INKS: GABRIEL HERNANDEZ WALTA

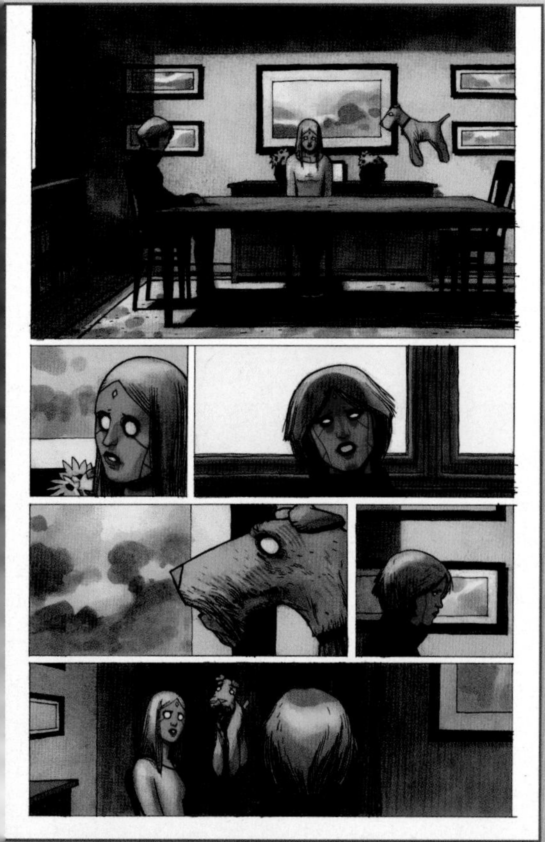

COLORS: JORDIE BELLAIRE

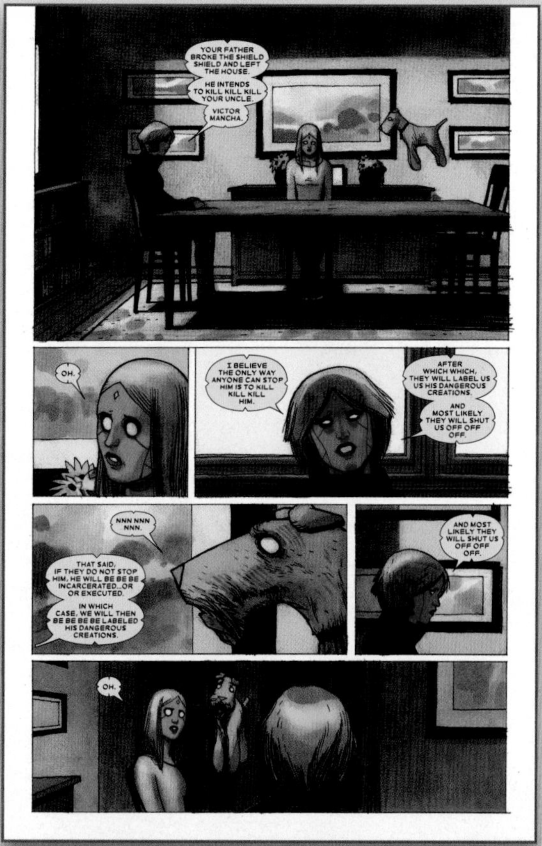
YOUR FATHER BROKE THE SHIELD SHIELD AND LEFT THE HOUSE.
HE INTENDS TO KILL KILL KILL YOUR UNCLE.
VICTOR MANCHA.
OH.
I BELIEVE THE ONLY WAY ANYONE CAN STOP HIM IS TO KILL KILL KILL HIM.
AFTER WHICH WHICH, THEY WILL LABEL US US HIS DANGEROUS CREATIONS.
AND MOST LIKELY THEY WILL SHUT US OFF OFF OFF.
NNN NNN NNN.
THAT SAID, IF THEY DO NOT STOP HIM, HE WILL BE BE BE INCARCERATED...OR OR EXECUTED.
IN WHICH CASE, WE WILL THEN BE BE BE BE LABELED HIS DANGEROUS CREATIONS.
AND MOST LIKELY THEY WILL SHUT US OFF OFF OFF.
OH.

LETTERS: VC's CLAYTON COWLES

PAGE 2-3:

PANEL 1: Two-page splash. We are in the plaza of courthouse VA (a real place, with ref attached). We are in front of a movie theater. The movie theater is showing a super hero movie, "Omega the Unknown! Starring Simon Williams! Special director's cut re-release!" On the left side (page) should be Vision floating in the air. Very much alone. On the right side of the page we have all those heroes from the end of issue six EXCEPT Rogue, Storm, and She-Hulk (whom we can't use for various reasons). Figures are small. There should be lots of free space between them.

NOTE: The Scarlet Witch and Agatha should not be in this shot.

CAPTION: The first words the synthezoid ever heard were the words of his father.
CAPTION: "Welcome to the world of the living," Ultron said.
CAPTION: "You who will never know but a half-life."

TITLE: You and I Were Born for Better Things
CREDITS

SCRIPT: TOM KING

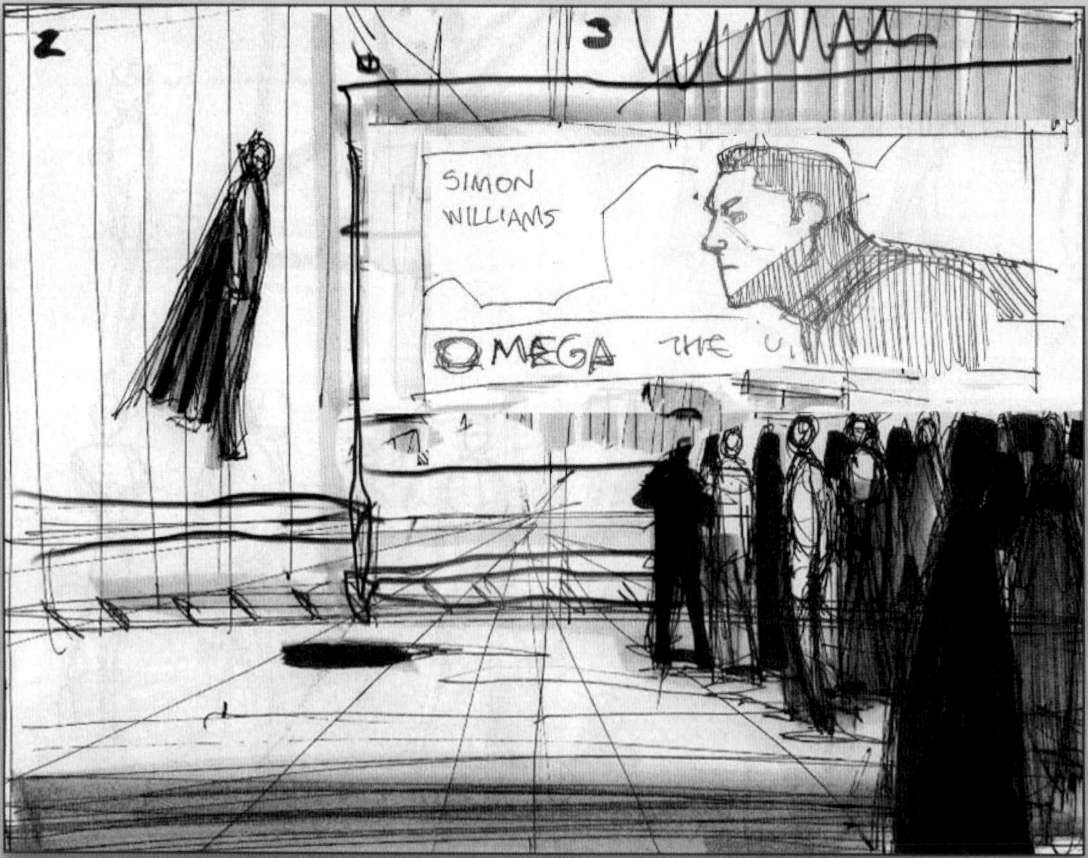
2
3
SIMON WILLIAMS
OMEGA THE U

LAYOUT: GABRIEL HERNANDEZ WALTA

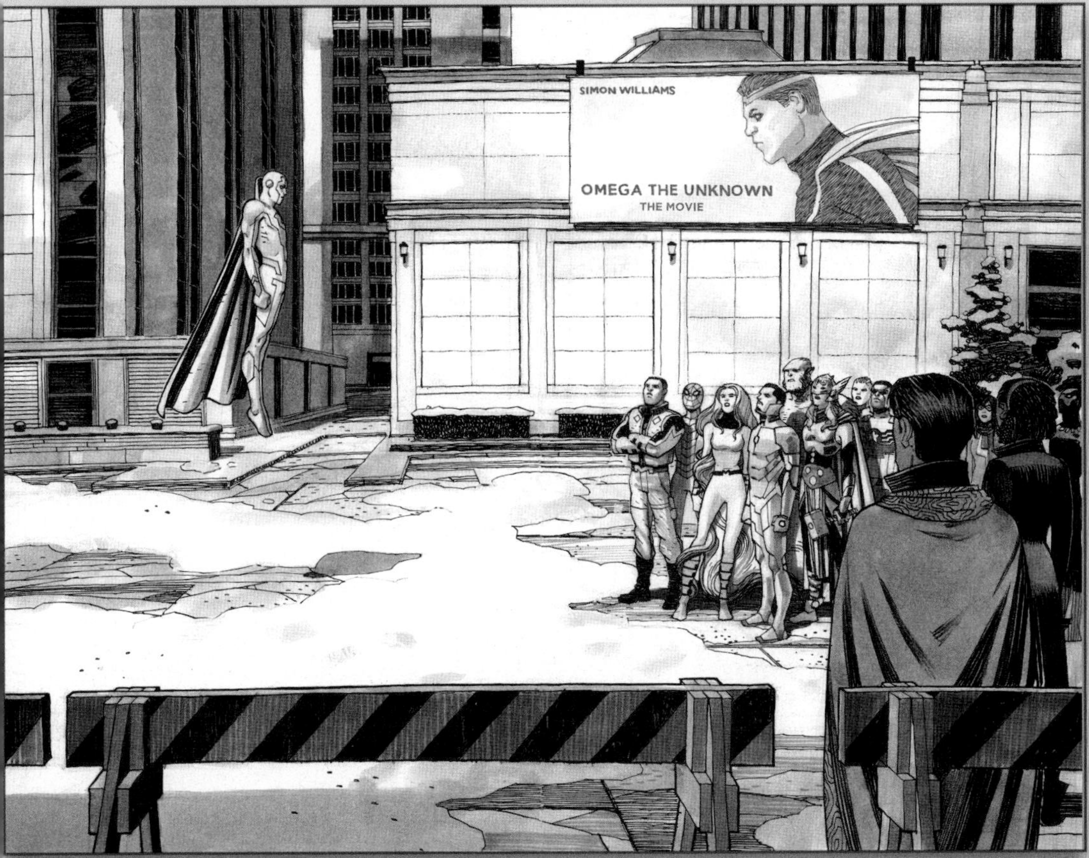
SIMON WILLIAMS
OMEGA THE UNKNOWN
THE MOVIE

INKS: GABRIEL HERNANDEZ WALTA

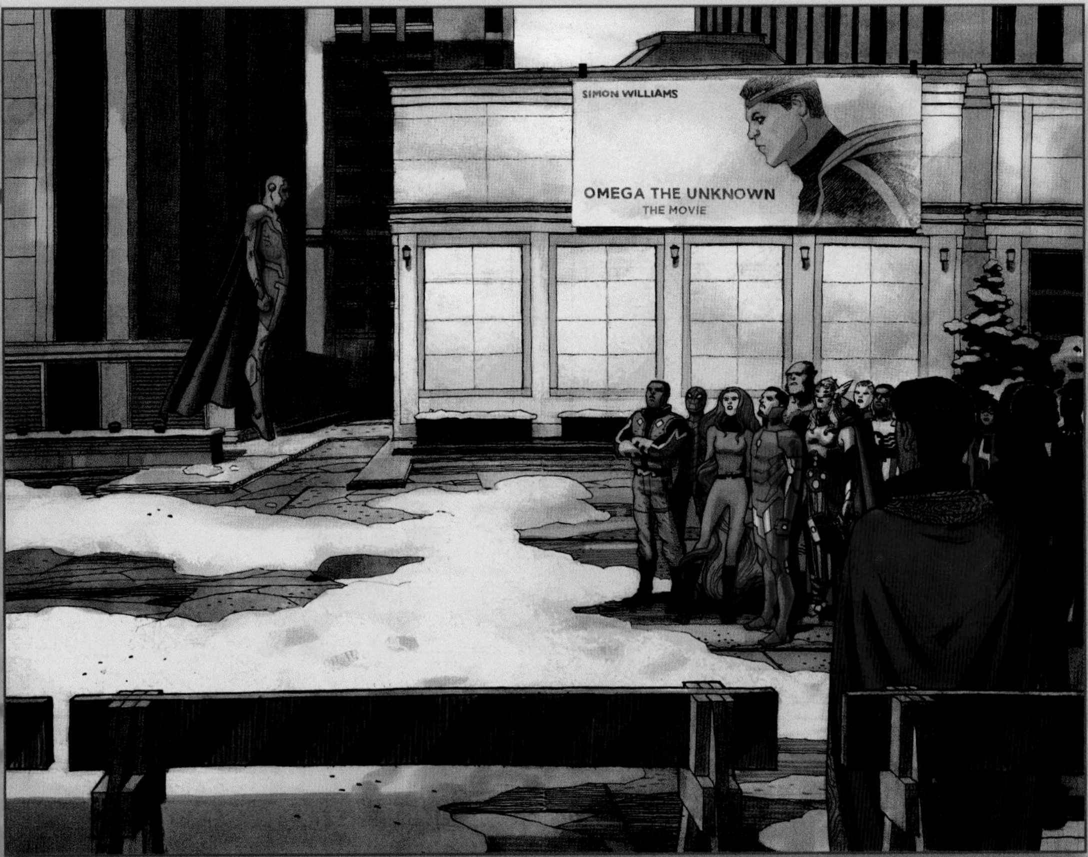
SIMON WILLIAMS
OMEGA THE UNKNOWN
THE MOVIE

COLORS: JORDIE BELLAIRE

PAGE 4:

<u>PANEL 1:</u> On Vision. Looking serious as he floats.

        VISION: I understand that due to his role in the death of my neighbors and my son--
        VISION: --actions undertaken under your supervision--
        VISION: --Victor Mancha is being held here in the Arlington Courthouse jail.

<u>PANEL 2:</u> Iron Man, pleading.

        IRON MAN: Vision--

<u>PANEL 3:</u> Closer on VISION.

        VISION: I am here to visit Victor in his cell.
        VISION: Then I will kill him for killing Vin.

<u>PANEL 4:</u> Closer on IRON MAN.

        IRON MAN: C'mon man, listen, you can't--

<u>PANEL 5:</u> Closer on VISION.

        VISION: I would greatly appreciate your cooperation in this matter.
        VISION: However, I do not require your cooperation in this matter.

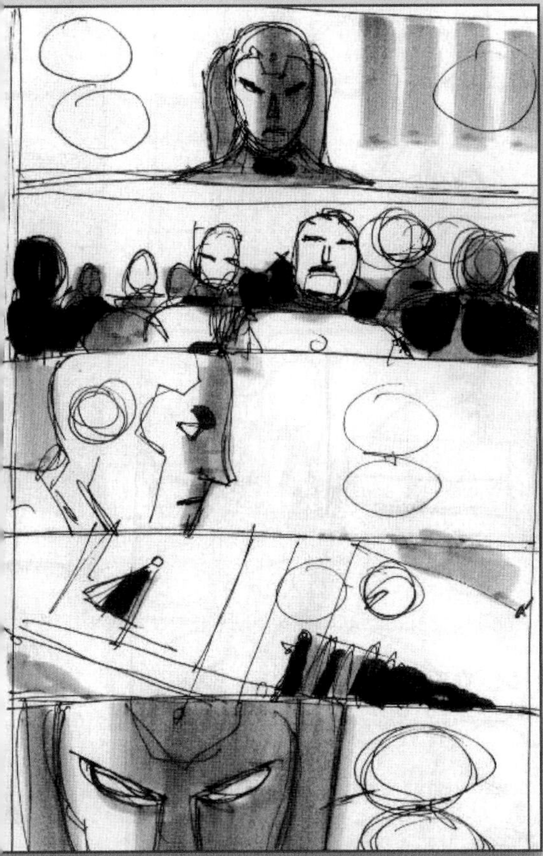

LAYOUT: GABRIEL HERNANDEZ WALTA

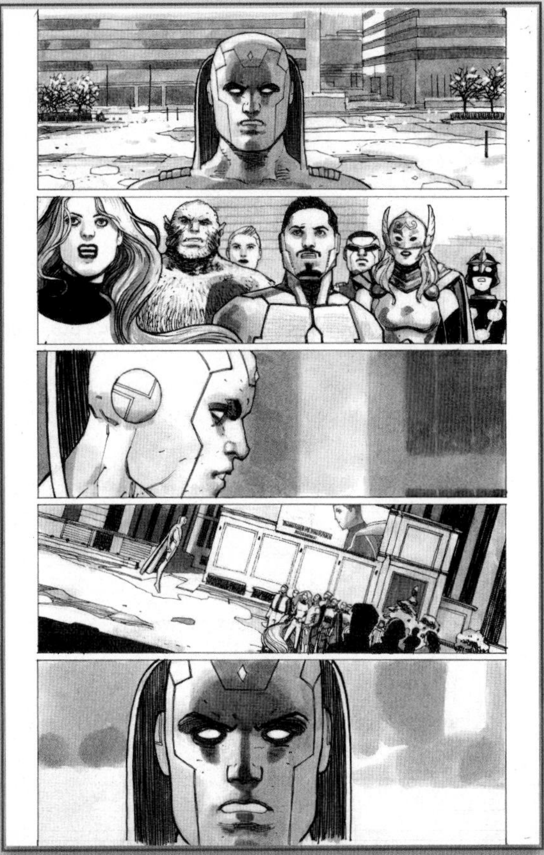

INKS: GABRIEL HERNANDEZ WALTA

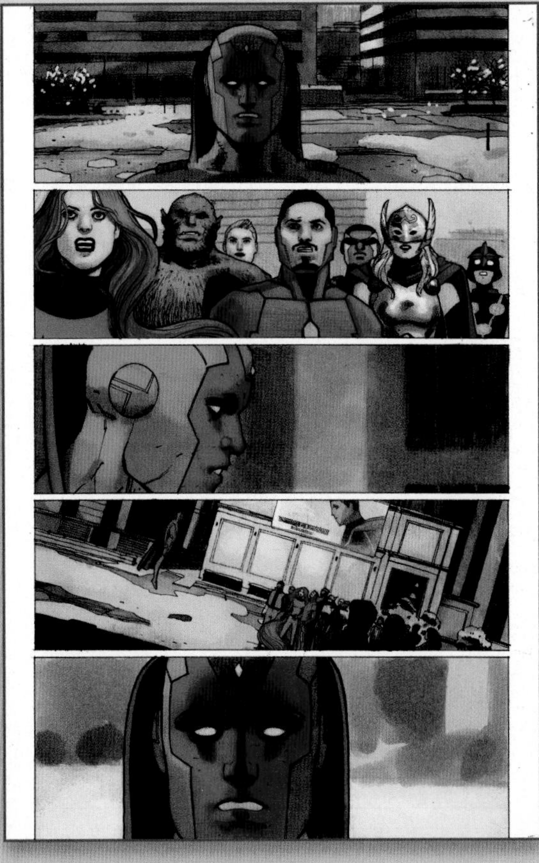

COLORS: JORDIE BELLAIRE

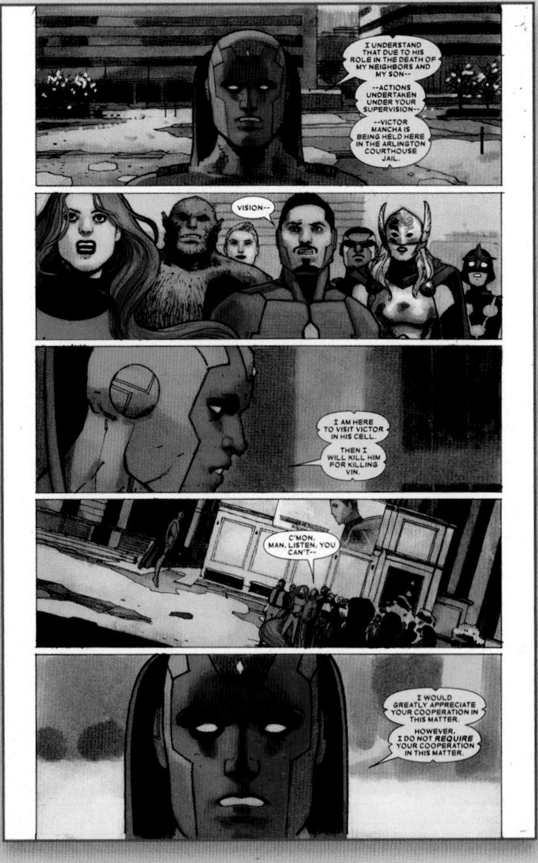
I UNDERSTAND THAT DUE TO HIS ROLE IN THE DEATH OF MY NEIGHBORS AND MY SON--
--ACTIONS UNDERTAKEN UNDER YOUR SUPERVISION--
--VICTOR MANCHA IS BEING HELD HERE IN THE ARLINGTON COURTHOUSE JAIL.
VISION--
I AM HERE TO VISIT VICTOR IN HIS CELL.
THEN I WILL KILL HIM FOR KILLING VIN.
C'MON, MAN, LISTEN, YOU CAN'T--
I WOULD GREATLY APPRECIATE YOUR COOPERATION IN THIS MATTER.
HOWEVER, I DO NOT *REQUIRE* YOUR COOPERATION IN THIS MATTER.

LETTERS: VC's CLAYTON COWLES

PAGE 5:

PANEL 1: IRON MAN reaching inside his wrist, which is opening.

> IRON MAN: Okay.
> IRON MAN: Fine.

PANEL 2: IRON MAN takes a small device out of his wrist.

> IRON MAN: This a portable shield. Similar to the one on your house.
> IRON MAN: It'll keep you contained until we can--

PANEL 3: A huge VISION laser blast hits IRON MAN in his stupid face and body.

> SFX: zxzzzxzx

PANEL 4: Camera pulls out. Shows VISION blasting the ▮ out of IRON MAN, knocking IRON MAN back.

> CAPTION: His father continued:
> CAPTION: "I am Ultron 5--but you shall call me--Master!"

PANEL 5: IRON MAN hitting the back of a building, unconscious and beaten.

> CAPTION: "Yes...Master!" The synthezoid replied.
> CAPTION: "Why have you called me to life?"

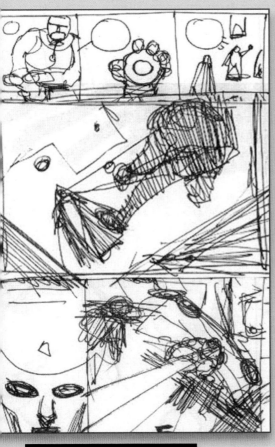

PAGE 6:

PANEL 1: SPIDER-MAN standing with a bunch of heroes, looking over at IRON MAN defeated.

> CAPTION: "Not to ask such human-like questions, Android!" Ultron answered.
> CAPTION: "I was created to command...and you to obey!"

PANEL 2: VISION, his head pulsing with power.

> CAPTION: The synthezoid crossed his arms. "I somehow sense you speak the truth...Master!"
> CAPTION: "And yet I am consumed with curiosity."
> VISION: I will repeat.
> VISION: I do not require your cooperation in this matter.

PANEL 3: The heroes now looking up at VISION.

> SPIDER-MAN (PARKER): Ah, poop.
> CAPTION: "Such emotions are for human fools!" Ultron said.
> CAPTION: "You and I were born for better things!"

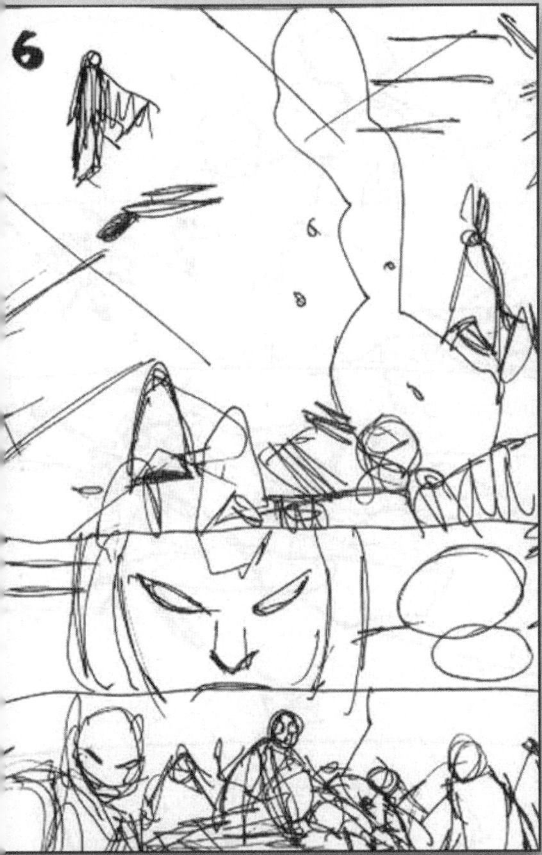
6

LAYOUT: GABRIEL HERNANDEZ WALTA

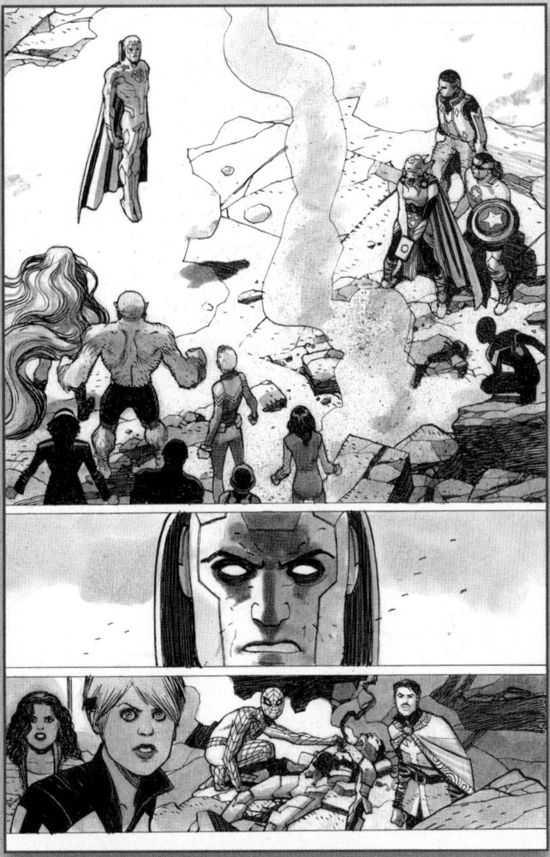

INKS: GABRIEL HERNANDEZ WALTA

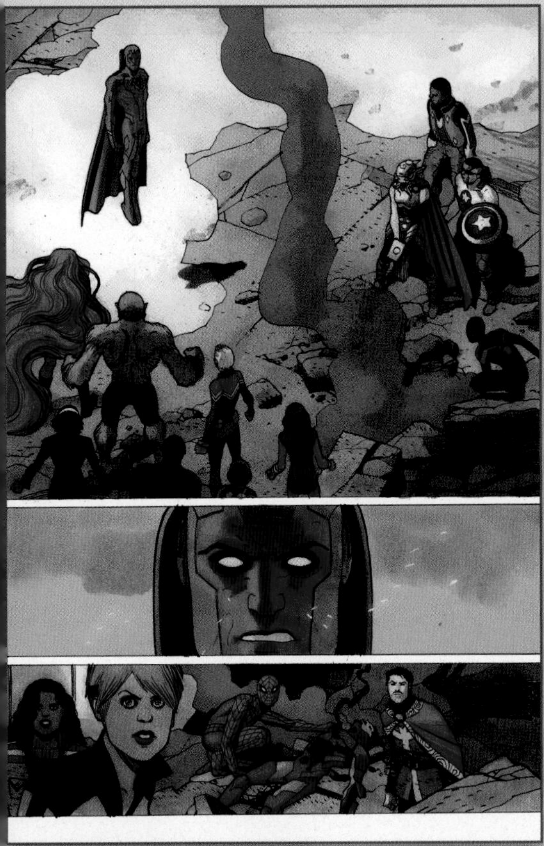

COLORS: JORDIE BELLAIRE

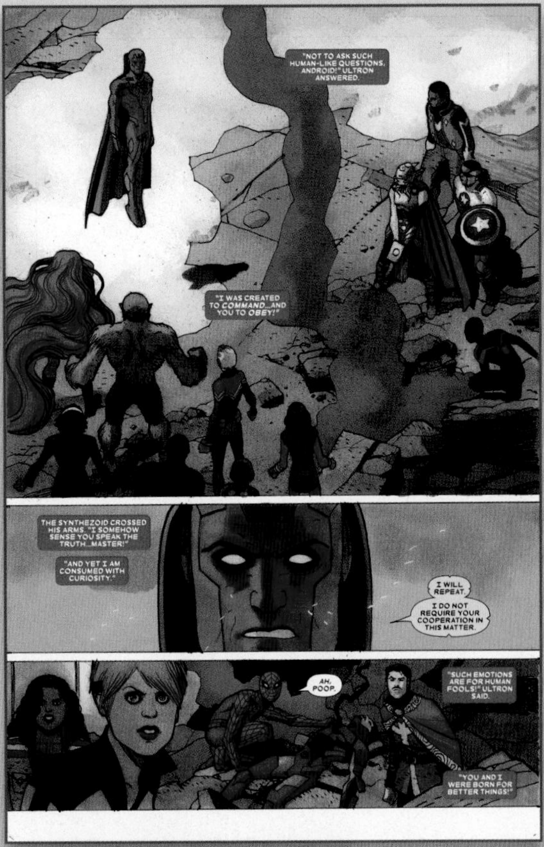
"NOT TO ASK SUCH HUMAN-LIKE QUESTIONS, ANDROID!" ULTRON ANSWERED.
"I WAS CREATED TO COMMAND...AND YOU TO OBEY!"
THE SYNTHEZOID CROSSED HIS ARMS. "I SOMEHOW SENSE YOU SPEAK THE TRUTH...MASTER!"
"AND YET I AM CONSUMED WITH CURIOSITY."
I WILL REPEAT.
I DO NOT REQUIRE YOUR COOPERATION IN THIS MATTER.
AH, POOP.
"SUCH EMOTIONS ARE FOR HUMAN FOOLS!" ULTRON SAID.
"YOU AND I WERE BORN FOR BETTER THINGS!"

LETTERS: VC's CLAYTON COWLES

PAGE 7:

PANEL 1: VIRGINIA and VIV at the table. VIRGINIA staring straight ahead. VIV looking down.

    No dialogue

PANEL 2: On VIRGINIA.

    VIRGINIA: As what may come may come come quite rapidly,
    VIRGINIA: I would like to share with you some some some...
    VIRGINIA: Information.

PANEL 3: VIV, looking up.

    VIV: Yes, mother?

PANEL 4: VIRGINIA, struggling.

    VIRGINIA: Your father did not not not think we should tell tell you.
    VIRGINIA: But your father father is not here, and...
    VIRGINIA: I would would would like you to know.

PANEL 5: On VIV.

    VIV: Yes, mother?

PANEL 6: The table. The dog by Viv.

    VIRGINIA: This boy boy you often listen to. C...K.
    VIRGINIA: His...father attempted to to to confront me about the death of the Grim Reaper.
    VIRGINIA: During my my response to this action action this boy was was killed.

PANEL 7: Close on Virginia.

    VIRGINIA: It is...difficult to explain explain explain.
    VIRGINIA: I will transfer transfer to you to my file on the...the incident
    VIRGINIA: So that you may may may experience what I I I experienced.

PANEL 8: Close on VIV.

    VIV: What?

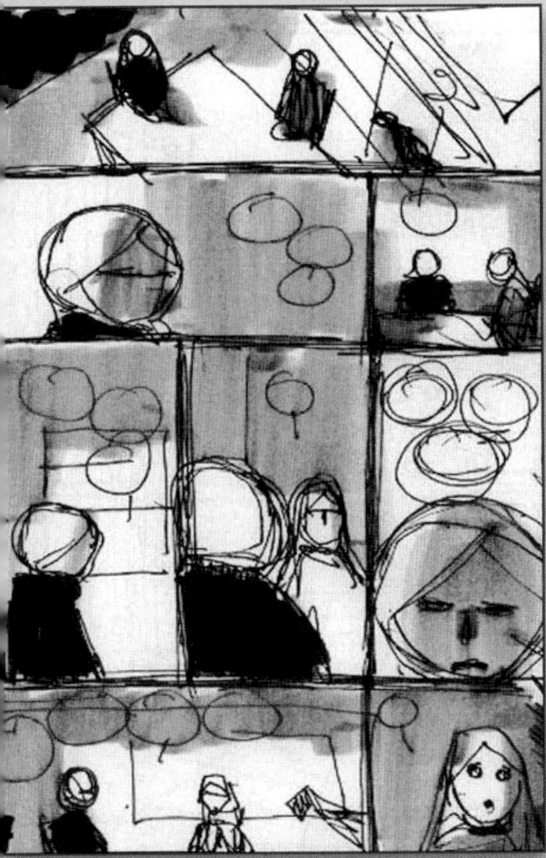

LAYOUT: GABRIEL HERNANDEZ WALTA

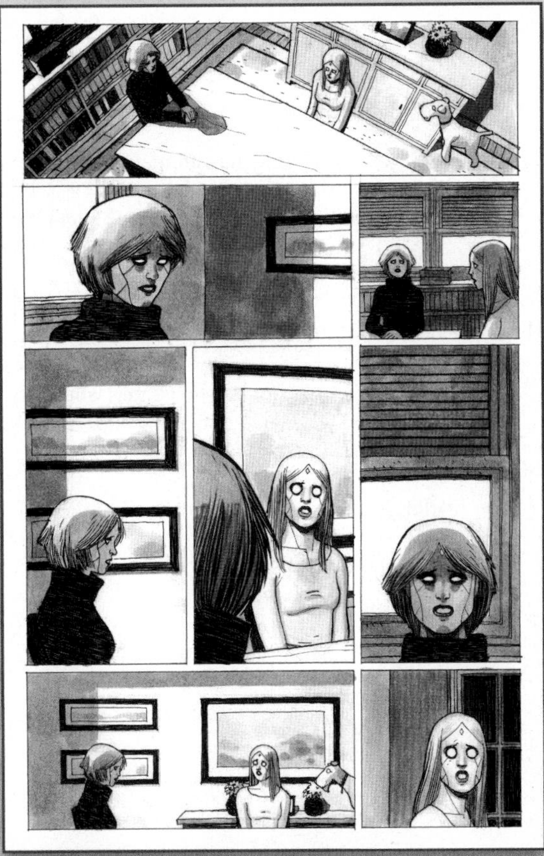

INKS: GABRIEL HERNANDEZ WALTA

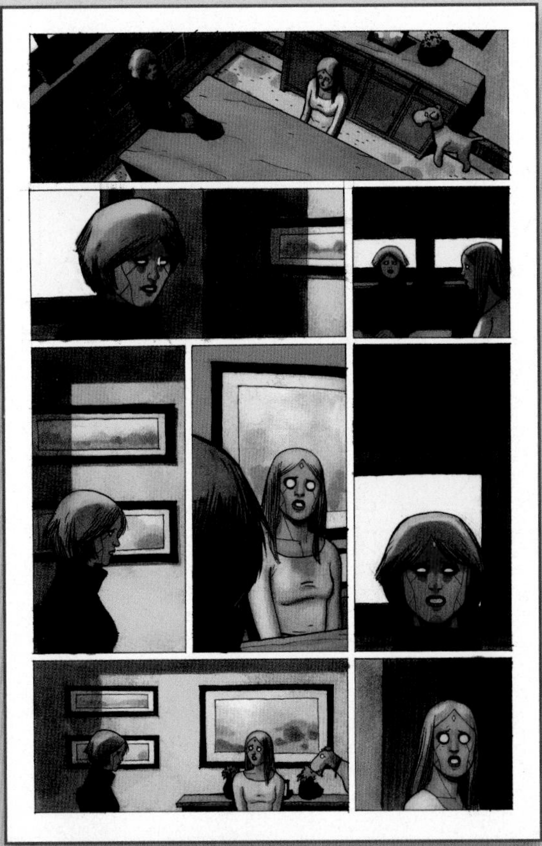

COLORS: JORDIE BELLAIRE

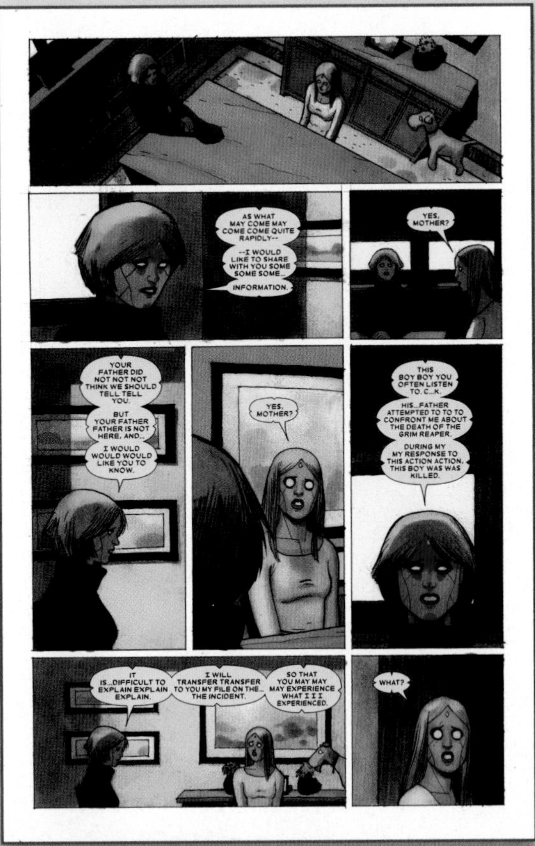

AS WHAT MAY COME MAY COME COME QUITE RAPIDLY--
--I WOULD LIKE TO SHARE WITH YOU SOME SOME SOME...
INFORMATION.
YES, MOTHER?
YOUR FATHER DID NOT NOT NOT THINK WE SHOULD TELL TELL YOU.
BUT YOUR FATHER FATHER IS NOT HERE, AND...
I WOULD WOULD WOULD LIKE YOU TO KNOW.
YES, MOTHER?
THIS BOY BOY YOU OFTEN LISTEN TO. C...K.
HIS...FATHER ATTEMPTED TO TO TO CONFRONT ME ABOUT THE DEATH OF THE GRIM REAPER.
DURING MY MY RESPONSE TO THIS ACTION ACTION, THIS BOY WAS WAS KILLED.
IT IS...DIFFICULT TO EXPLAIN EXPLAIN EXPLAIN.
I WILL TRANSFER TRANSFER TO YOU MY FILE ON THE... THE INCIDENT.
SO THAT YOU MAY MAY MAY EXPERIENCE WHAT I I I EXPERIENCED.
WHAT?

LETTERS: VC's CLAYTON COWLES

PAGE 8:

PANEL 1: VIV receiving the information. Looking lost.

VIRGINIA (OFF): I realize this might might might upset you.
VIRGINIA (OFF): However, if we are to be be be shut off off...

PANEL 2: On VIRGINIA.

VIRGINIA: Prior to that time, I would like like like to seek your...
VIRGINIA: Understanding understanding understanding.

PANEL 3: VIV and VIRGINIA at the table.

No dialogue

PANEL 4: VIV, looking shocked.

VIV (small): He said I was cool.

PANEL 5: VIV smashes her fist into the table, breaks the table as her mother once did.

VIV: He said I was cool!
VIV: And my mother killed him!

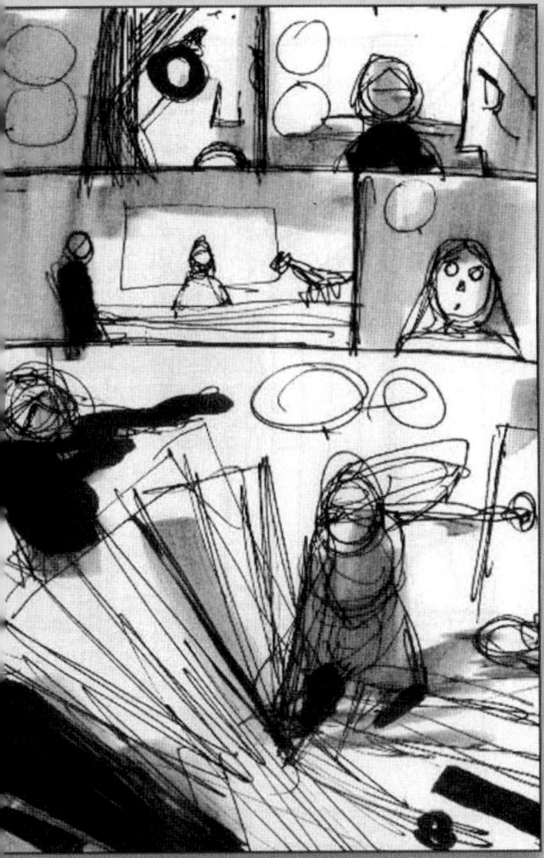

LAYOUT: GABRIEL HERNANDEZ WALTA

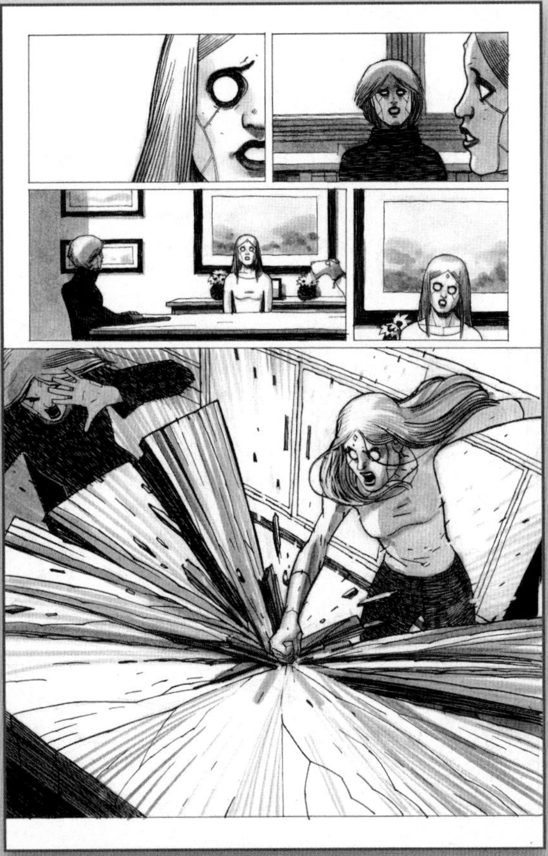

INKS: GABRIEL HERNANDEZ WALTA

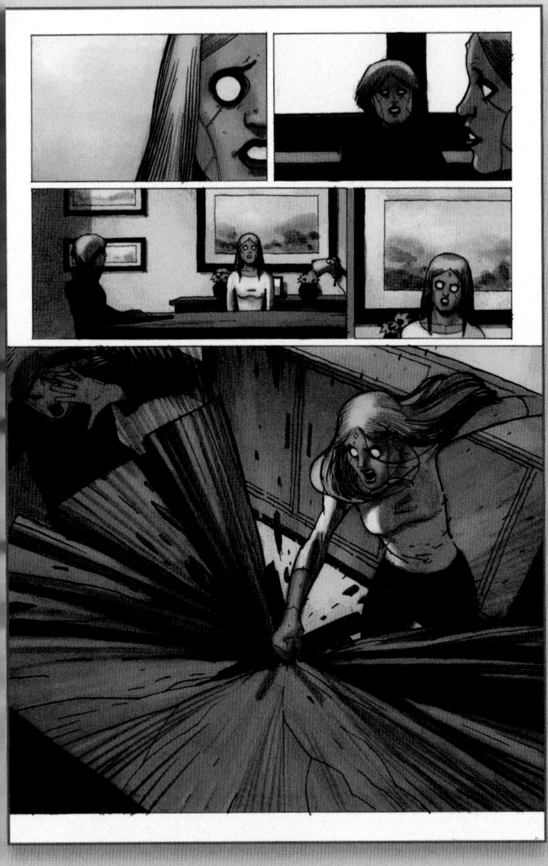

COLORS: JORDIE BELLAIRE

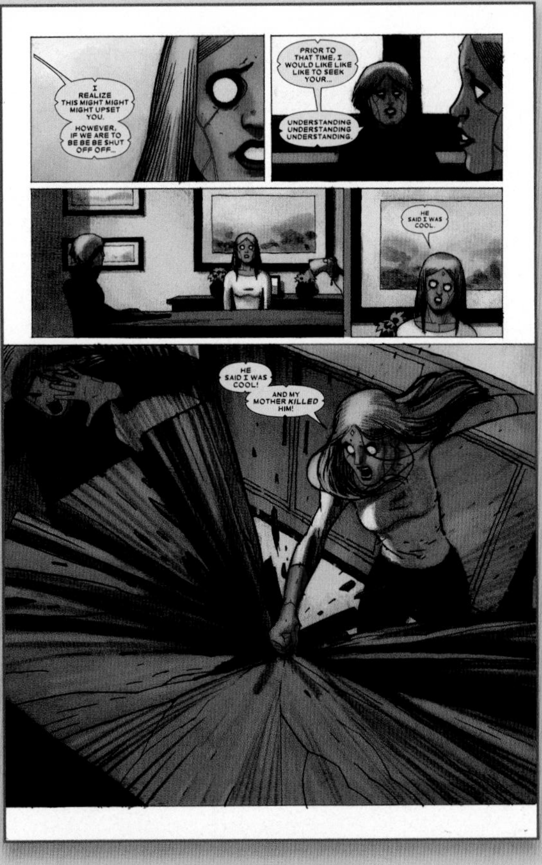
I REALIZE THIS MIGHT MIGHT MIGHT UPSET YOU.
HOWEVER, IF WE ARE TO BE BE BE SHUT OFF OFF...
PRIOR TO THAT TIME, I WOULD LIKE LIKE LIKE TO SEEK YOUR...
UNDERSTANDING UNDERSTANDING UNDERSTANDING.
HE SAID I WAS COOL.
HE SAID I WAS COOL!
AND MY MOTHER KILLED HIM!

LETTERS: VC's CLAYTON COWLES

PAGE 9:

PANEL 1: VIV and VIRGINIA at the broken table. Both in shock.

> VIV: It just goes through me.
> VIV: It just goes through me.

PANEL 2: VIV looking up at VIRGINIA.

> VIV: It just goes through me.

PANEL 3: VIV walks away, leaving her mother.

> VIV: It just goes through me.

PANEL 4: VIRGINIA alone again at a broken table.

> No dialogue

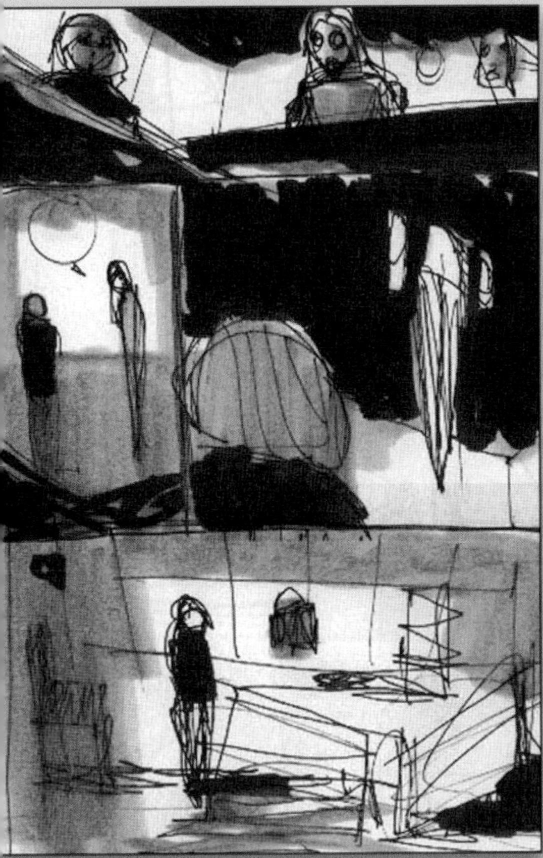

LAYOUT: GABRIEL HERNANDEZ WALTA

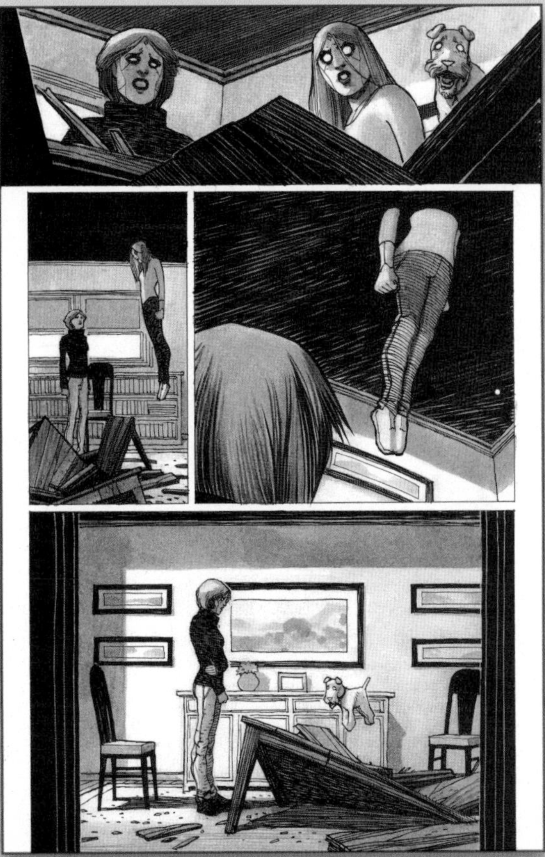

INKS: GABRIEL HERNANDEZ WALTA

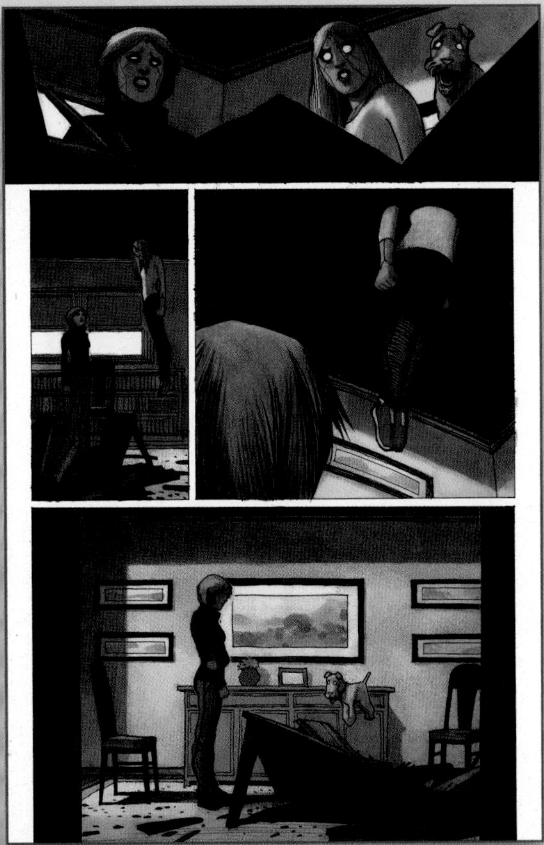

COLORS: JORDIE BELLAIRE

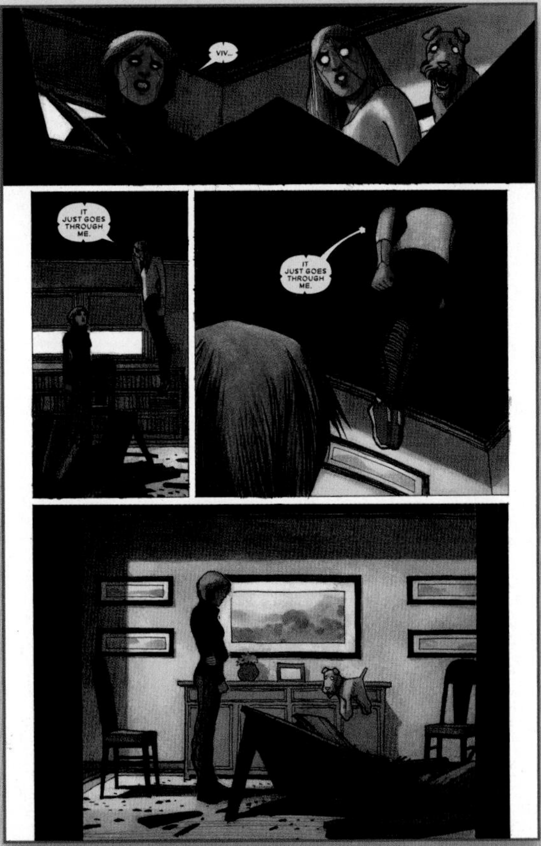
VIV...
IT JUST GOES THROUGH ME.
IT JUST GOES THROUGH ME.

LETTERS: VC's CLAYTON COWLES

PAGE 8:

PANEL 1: VISION and VIRGINIA in the living room, looking at each other. VIRGINIA sitting on the couch. VISION standing.

       CAPTION: They made the compromises that are necessary to raise a family.

PANEL 2: On VIRGINIA.

       VIRGINIA: Viv is upstairs.
       VIRGINIA: I told her of my role in the death of CK.
       VIRGINIA: She is refusing to talk to me.

PANEL 3: On VISION.

       VISION: I see.

PANEL 4: On VIRGINIA.

       VIRGINIA: And I killed the dog.

PANEL 5: On VISION, curious.

       VISION: Oh.

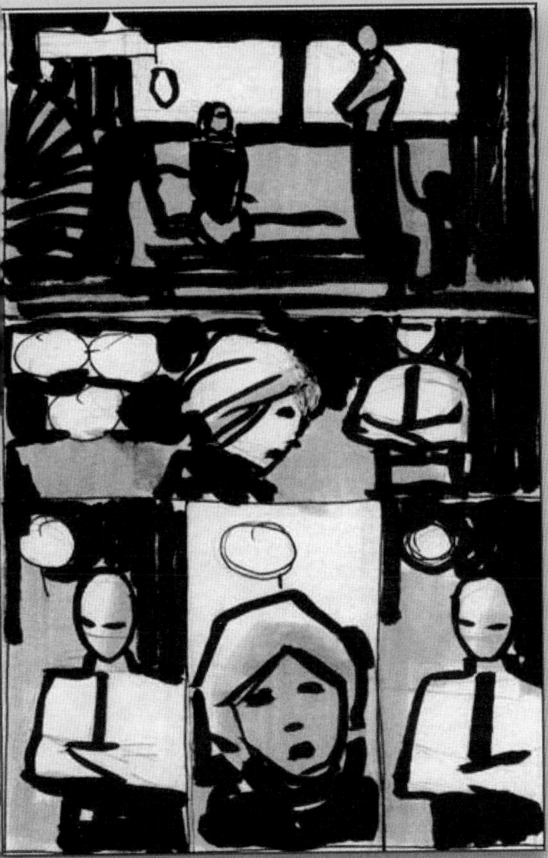

LAYOUT: GABRIEL HERNANDEZ WALTA

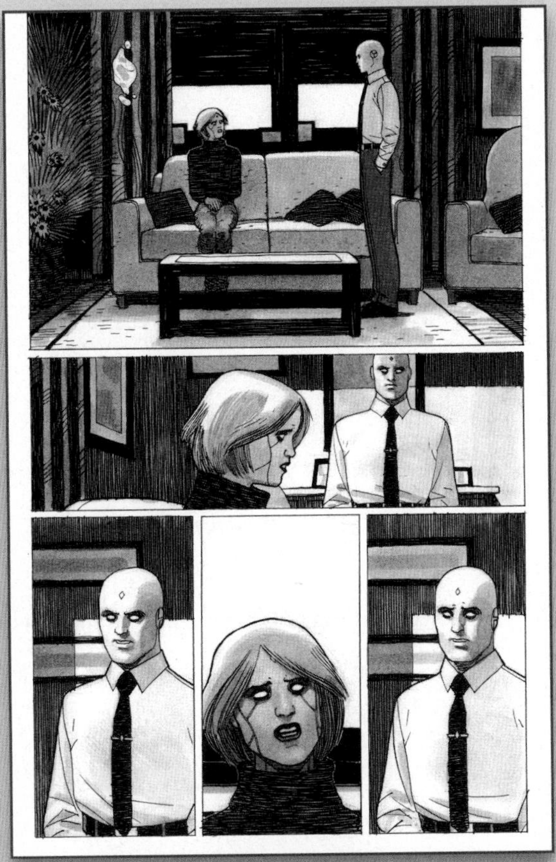

INKS: GABRIEL HERNANDEZ WALTA

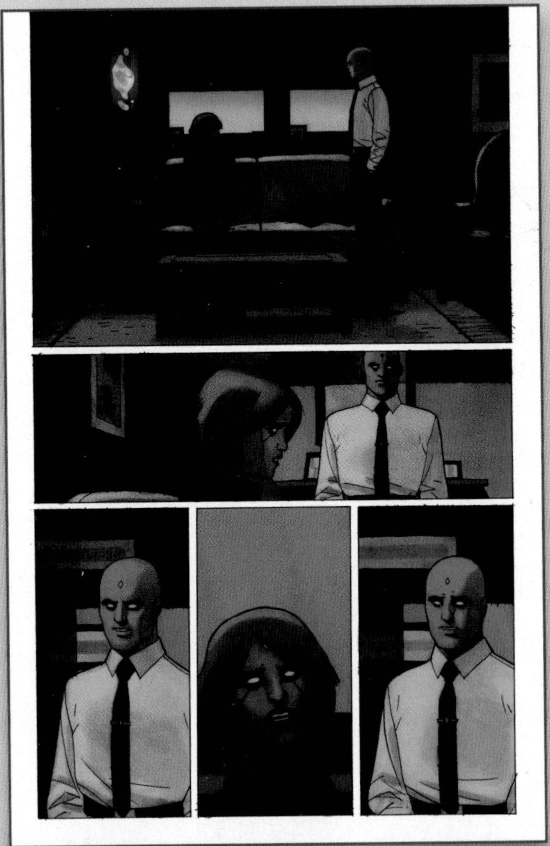

COLORS: JORDIE BELLAIRE

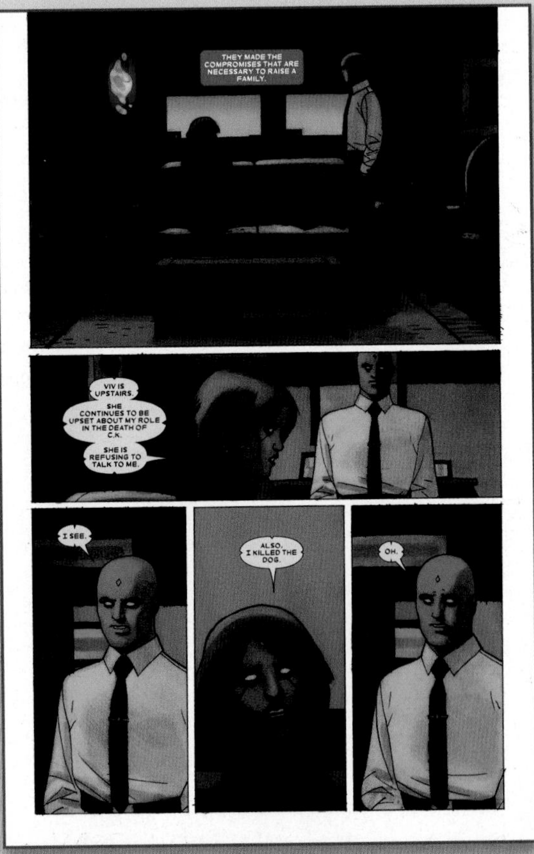
THEY MADE THE COMPROMISES THAT ARE NECESSARY TO RAISE A FAMILY.
VIV IS UPSTAIRS.
SHE CONTINUES TO BE UPSET ABOUT MY ROLE IN THE DEATH OF C.K.
SHE IS REFUSING TO TALK TO ME.
I SEE.
ALSO, I KILLED THE DOG.
OH.

LETTERS: VC's CLAYTON COWLES

PAGE 9:

<u>PANEL 1</u>: VIRGINIA raises her hand to her head.

       VIRGINIA: I uploaded--

<u>PANEL 2</u>: VIRGINIA's head freezes, eyes open.

       No dialogue

<u>PANEL 3</u>: VIRGINIA'S head falls awkwardly on her shoulder, as if she's had a stroke. Her eyes close.

       VISION (OFF): Wife?

<u>PANEL 4</u>: Camera pulls back. VISION staring at his wife with her head leaning awkwardly.

       VISION: Wife?

<u>PANEL 5</u>: Back to VIRGINIA with her head on the side, her eyes closed.

       VISION (OFF): What is wrong?

<u>PANEL 6:</u> VIRGINIA opens her eyes.

       VIRGINIA: --myconfessionto--
       VIRGINIA: Oh.

<u>PANEL 7:</u> VIRGINIA reaches over to pull her head back to the proper position.

       VIRGINIA: Please excuse me, husband.
       VIRGINIA: I drank from the floating water vase of Zenn-La.

<u>PANEL 8:</u> VIRGINIA uses her hand to lift her head back.

       VIRGINIA: The corrosive effects of the liquid are working through my system.
       VIRGINIA: This will of course cause some problems with my internal mechanics.

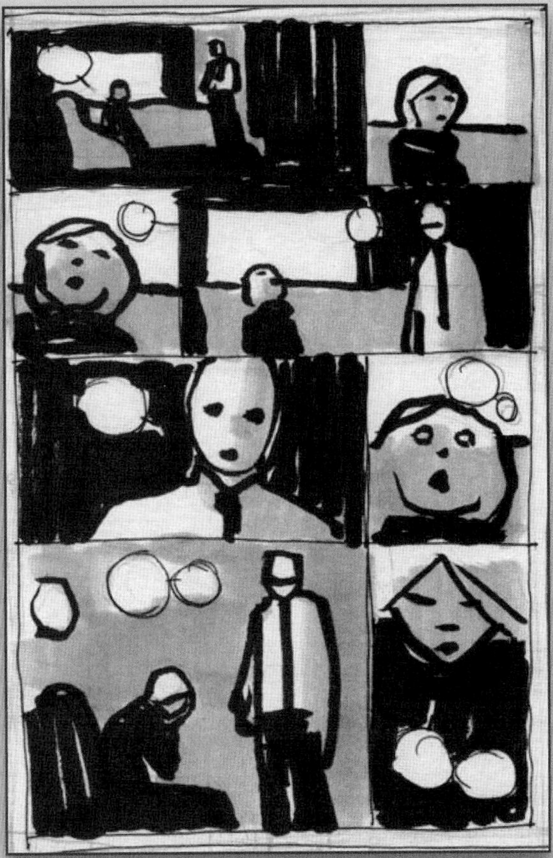

LAYOUT: GABRIEL HERNANDEZ WALTA

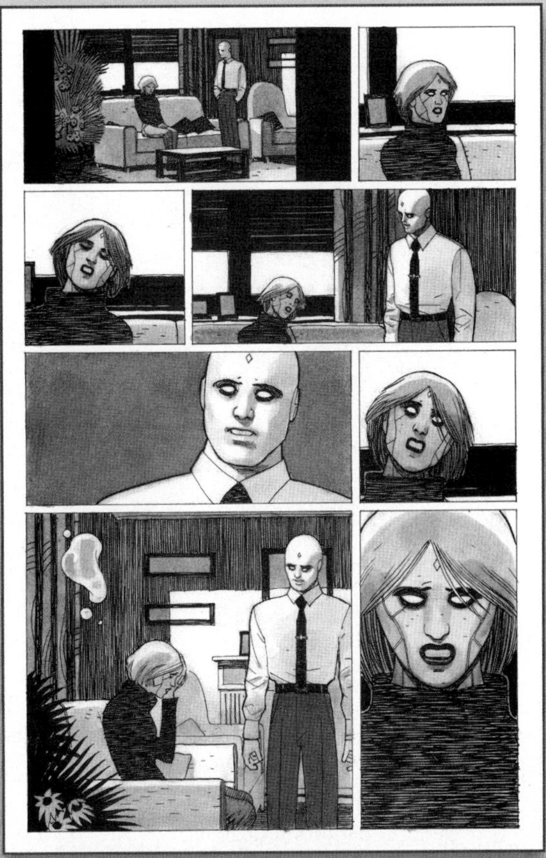

INKS: GABRIEL HERNANDEZ WALTA

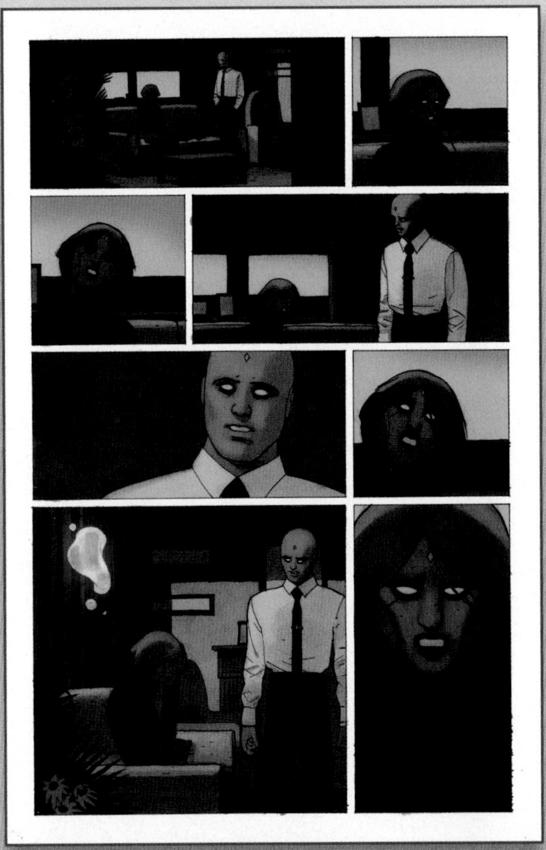

COLORS: JORDIE BELLAIRE

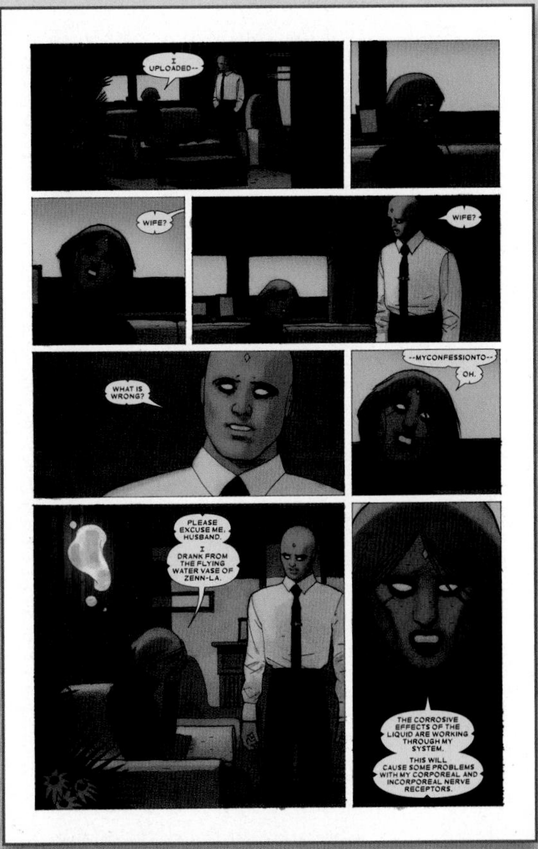

I UPLOADED--
WIFE?
WIFE?
WHAT IS WRONG?
--MYCONFESSIONTO--
OH.
PLEASE EXCUSE ME, HUSBAND.
I DRANK FROM THE FLYING WATER VASE OF ZENN-LA.
THE CORROSIVE EFFECTS OF THE LIQUID ARE WORKING THROUGH MY SYSTEM.
THIS WILL CAUSE SOME PROBLEMS WITH MY CORPOREAL AND INCORPOREAL NERVE RECEPTORS.

LETTERS: VC's CLAYTON COWLES

PAGE 10:

PANEL 1: VISION drops to a knee in front of VIRGINIA. VIRGINIA, in a bit of pain.

> VISION: You are dying.
> VIRGINIA: Yes.

PANEL 2: VISION, slightly desperate.

> VISION: Phase. Now.
> VISION: Allow the water to pass through you.

PANEL 3: VIRGINIA, smiling slightly.

> VIRGINIA: No.

PANEL 4: VISION on one knee reaching his hand to his wife.

> VISION: Please.

PANEL 5: VIRGINIA, smiling down warmly on her husband.

> VIRGINIA: Come, sit here with me, husband.
> VIRGINIA: Let me rest against you.

PANEL 6: VIRGINIA in close-up.

> VIRGINIA: My head is heavy.
> VIRGINIA: And I would enjoy putting it on your shoulder.

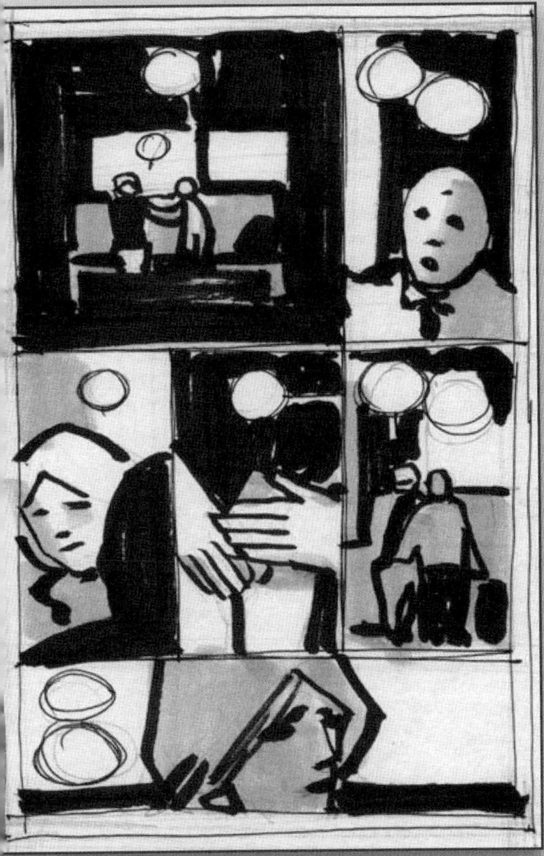

LAYOUT: GABRIEL HERNANDEZ WALTA

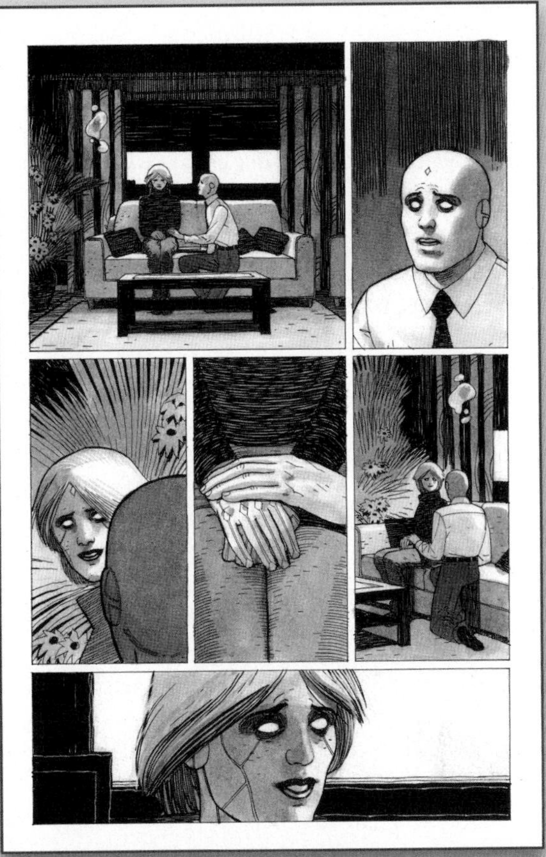

INKS: GABRIEL HERNANDEZ WALTA

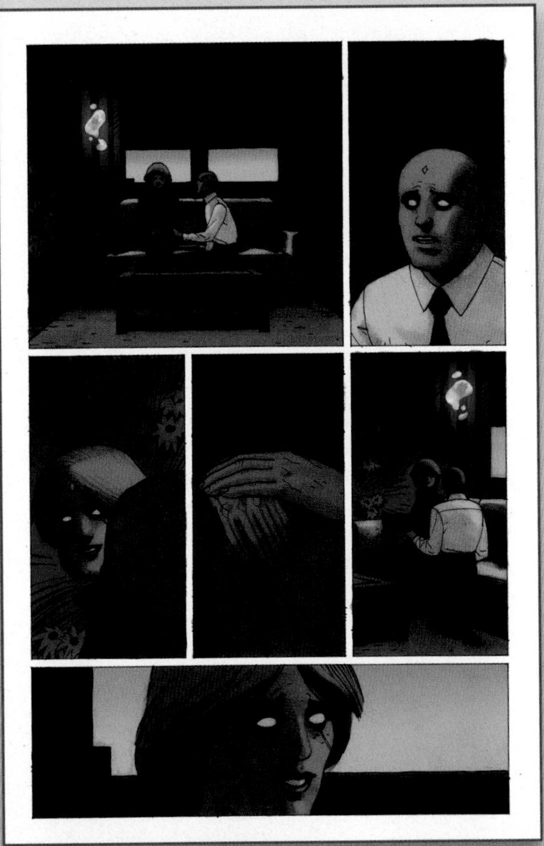

COLORS: JORDIE BELLAIRE

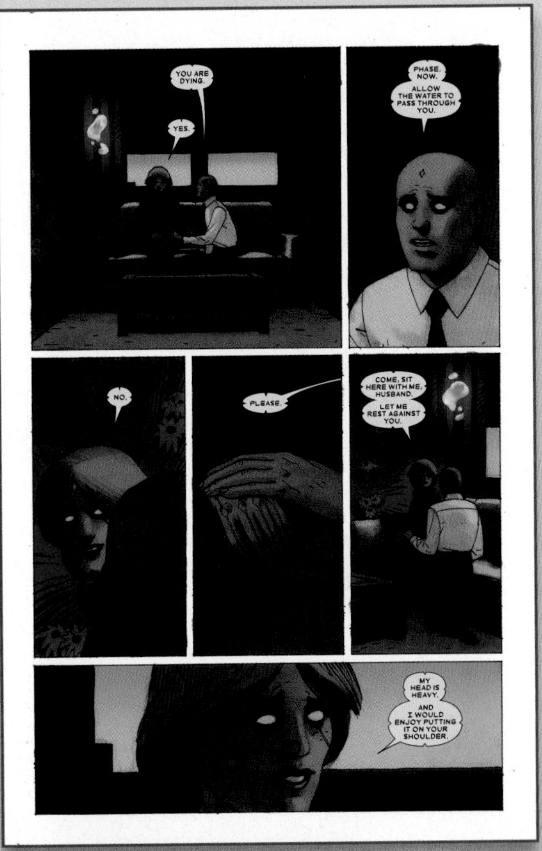

YOU ARE DYING.
YES.
PHASE. NOW.
ALLOW THE WATER TO PASS THROUGH YOU.
NO.
PLEASE.
COME, SIT HERE WITH ME, HUSBAND.
LET ME REST AGAINST YOU.
MY HEAD IS HEAVY.
AND I WOULD ENJOY PUTTING IT ON YOUR SHOULDER.

LETTERS: VC's CLAYTON COWLES

PAGE 11:

PANEL 1: VISION looking up at his wife.

> No dialogue

PANEL 2: VISION standing.

> No dialogue

PANEL 3: VISION sitting on the couch.

> No dialogue

PANEL 4: VIRGINIA moves into him as he puts his arm around her.

> No dialogue

PANEL 5: VIRGINIA puts her head on his shoulder.

> No dialogue

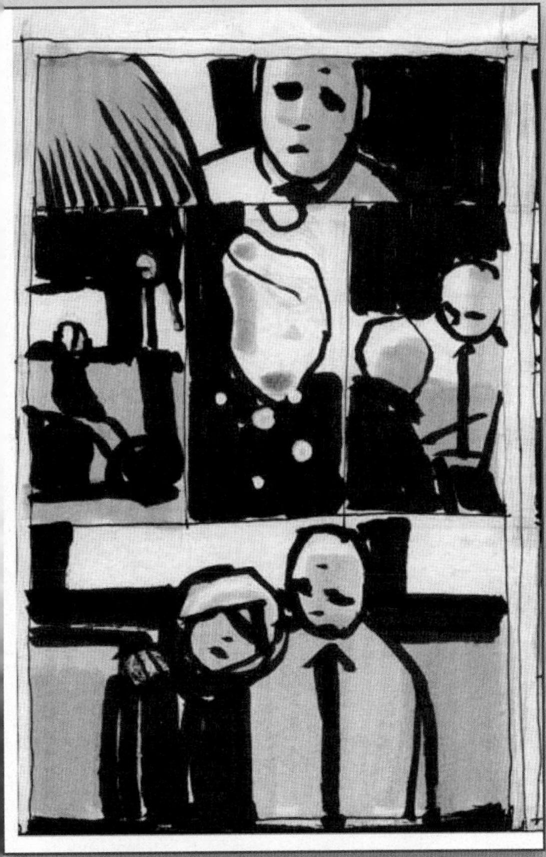

LAYOUT: GABRIEL HERNANDEZ WALTA

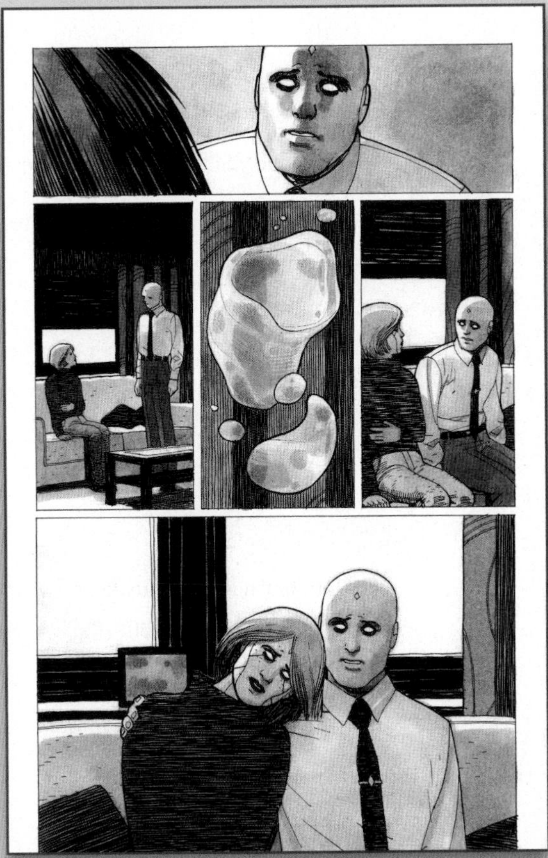

INKS: GABRIEL HERNANDEZ WALTA

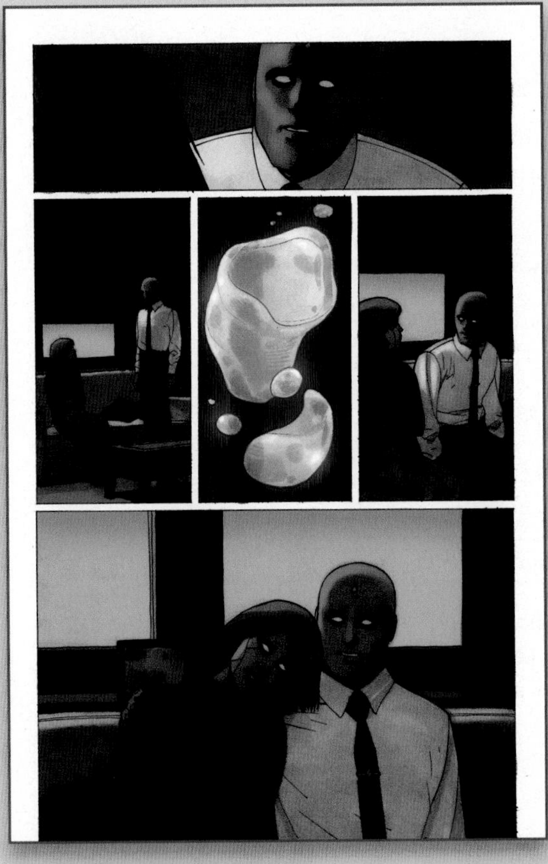

COLORS: JORDIE BELLAIRE

PAGE 12:

PANEL 1: VIRGINIA and VISION sitting on the couch.

> VIRGINIA: I uploaded my confession to the police to our share file.
> VIRGINIA: Have you accessed it yet?
> VISION: I have.

PANEL 2: Close on VIRGINIA.

> VIRGINIA: Good.

PANEL 3: On VISION.

> VISION: You must know death here will be wasted.
> VISION: I will of course correct your embellishments to the authorities.

PANEL 4: VIRGINIA smiling up at VISION.

> VIRGINIA: No.
> VIRGINIA: You will not.

PANEL 5: VIRGINIA snuggling into VISION.

> VIRGINIA: Such corrections would result in your imprisonment.
> VIRGINIA: And the isolation and/or death of our daughter.

PANEL 6: VISION looking down at VIRGINIA.

> VISION: I am the Vision of the Avengers--
> VIRGINIA (interrupting): You are my husband.

PANEL 7: VIRGINIA clutching VISION'S face.

> VIRGINIA: You are the father of my children.

PANEL 8: Their faces close together.

> VIRGINIA: All the rest...

PANEL 9: VIRGINIA again has another stroke.

> VIRGINIA: Just...
> VIRGINIA: goes...
> VIRGINIA: goes...

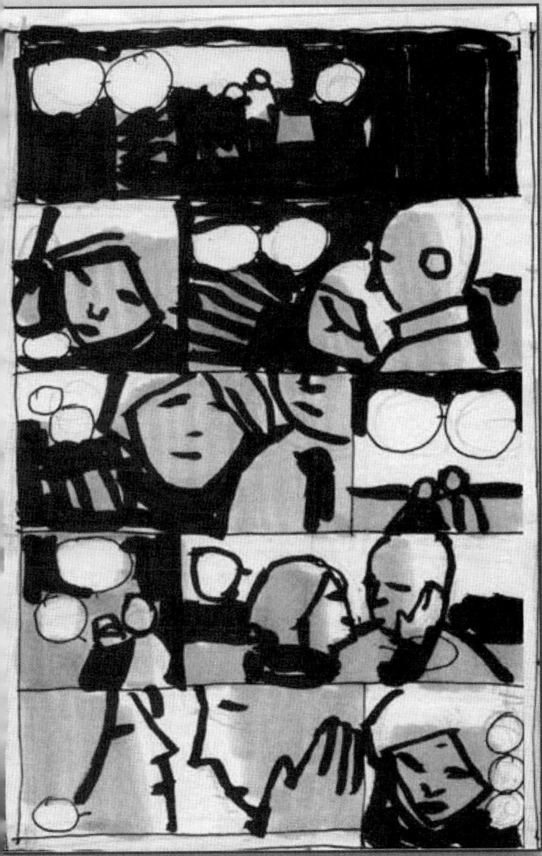

LAYOUT: GABRIEL HERNANDEZ WALTA

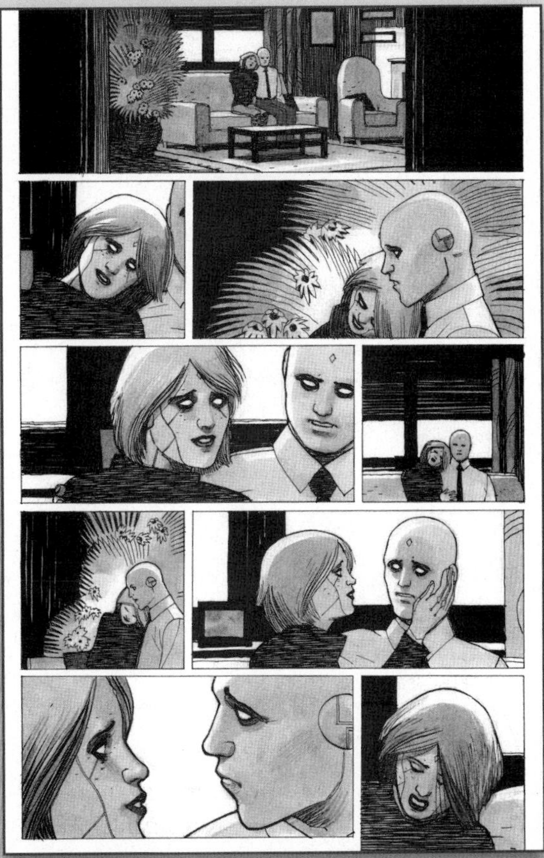

INKS: GABRIEL HERNANDEZ WALTA

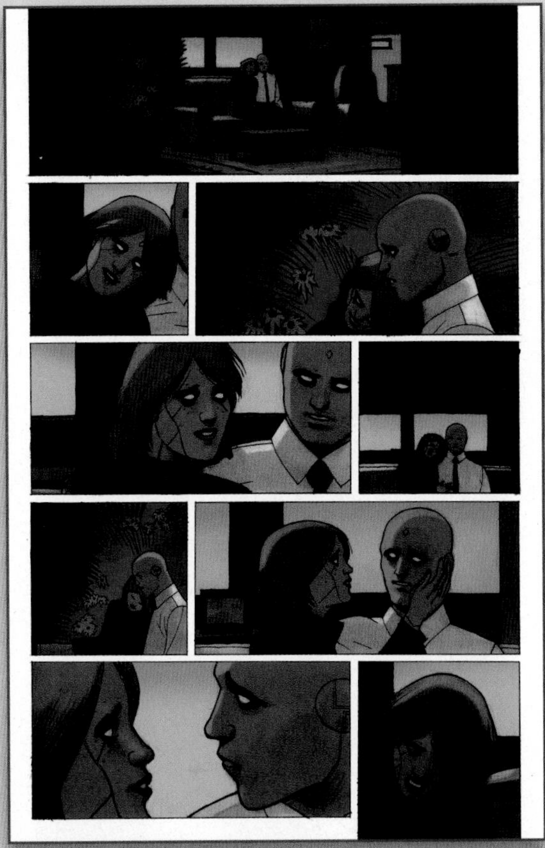

COLORS: JORDIE BELLAIRE

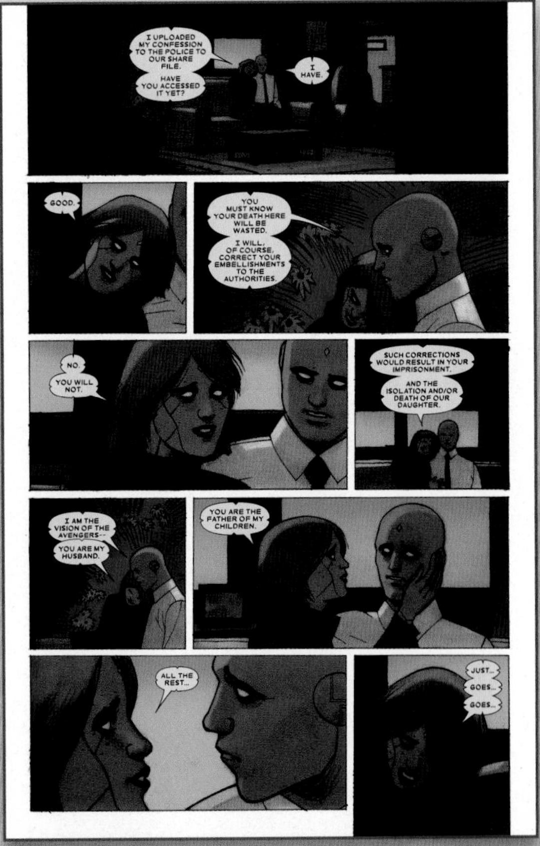
I UPLOADED MY CONFESSION TO THE POLICE TO OUR SHARE FILE.
HAVE YOU ACCESSED IT YET?
I HAVE.
GOOD.
YOU MUST KNOW YOUR DEATH HERE WILL BE WASTED.
I WILL, OF COURSE, CORRECT YOUR EMBELLISHMENTS TO THE AUTHORITIES.
NO.
YOU WILL NOT.
SUCH CORRECTIONS WOULD RESULT IN YOUR IMPRISONMENT.
AND THE ISOLATION AND/OR DEATH OF OUR DAUGHTER.
I AM THE VISION OF THE AVENGERS--
YOU ARE MY HUSBAND.
YOU ARE THE FATHER OF MY CHILDREN.
ALL THE REST...
JUST...
GOES...
GOES...

LETTERS: VC's CLAYTON COWLES

PAGE 13:

PANEL 1: VIRGINIA frozen as VISION looks on.

VISION: Wife?

PANEL 2: VISION moves back and VIRGINIA falls into him.

VISION: Wife!

PANEL 3: VISION trying to help the passed-out VIRGINIA, taking her in his arms/lap.

VISION: Wake up.
VISION: Virginia, wife, wake up.

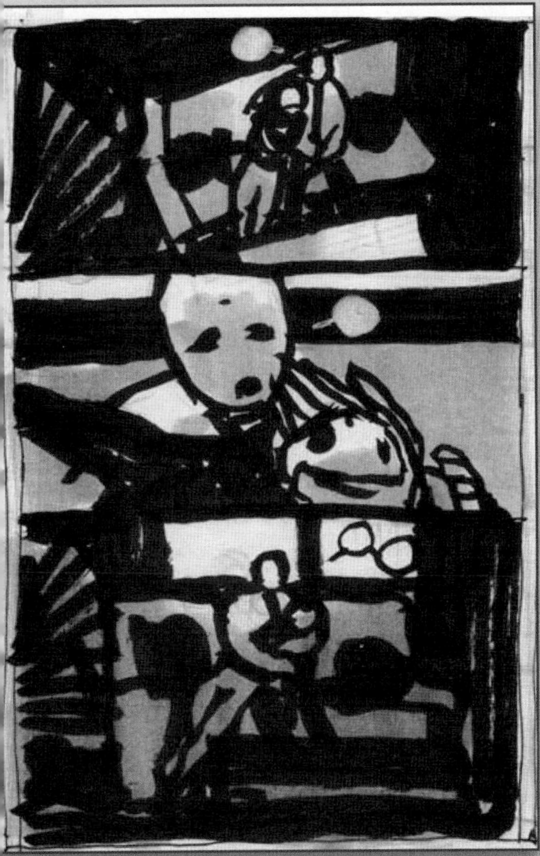

LAYOUT: GABRIEL HERNANDEZ WALTA

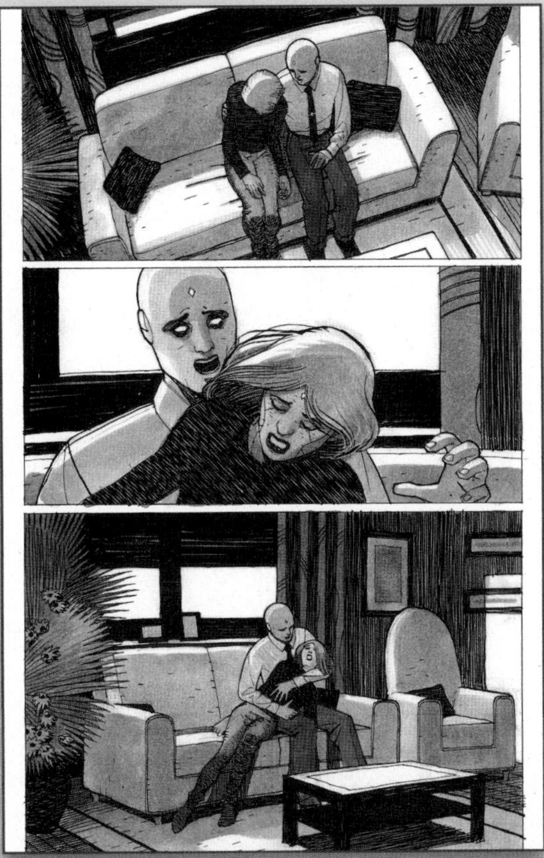

INKS: GABRIEL HERNANDEZ WALTA

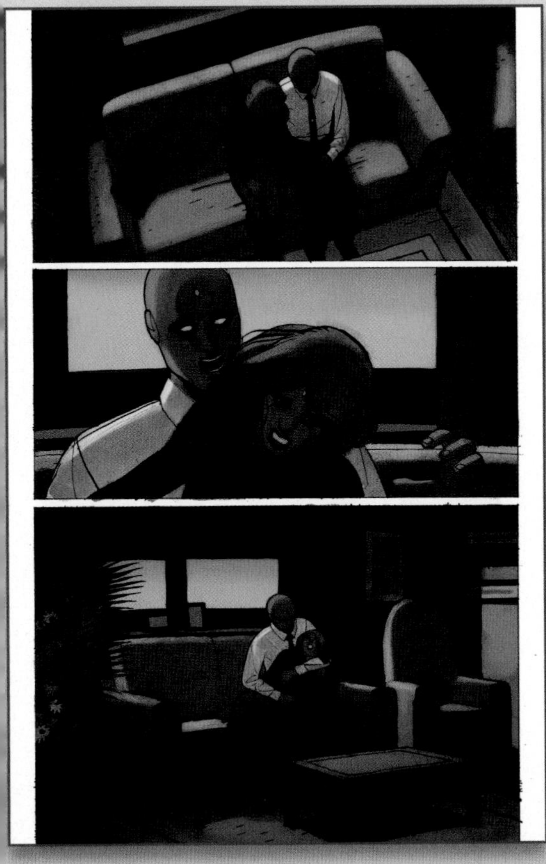

COLORS: JORDIE BELLAIRE

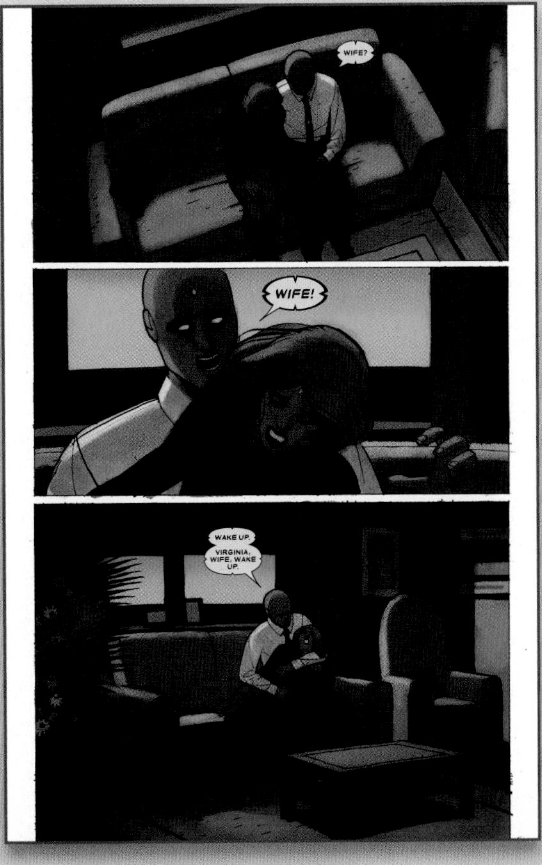
WIFE?
WIFE!
WAKE UP.
VIRGINIA, WIFE, WAKE UP.

LETTERS: VC's CLAYTON COWLES

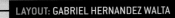

PAGE 14:

PANEL 1: VIRGINIA opening her eyes in VISION'S arms.

      VIRGINIA (weak): Husband...

PANEL 2: VIRGINIA, with very little energy, VISION clinging to her, hugging her.

      VIRGINIA (weak): After the...flower, I...saw I saw...the future.
      VIRGINIA (weak): I saw you...destroy destroy the future.
      VIRGINIA: (weak): For...us us us. For...me.

PANEL 3: VISION holding her closer.

      VISION: Wife...
      VIRGINIA (weak): And I...I could could could not...

PANEL 4: On VIRGINIA, in pain.

      VIRGINIA (weak): You...saved saved the world...thirty-seven times.
      VIRGINIA (weak): I saved...it...once once.

PANEL 5: VIRGINIA smiling weakly.

      VIRGINIA (weak): It it it...was...nice.

PANEL 6: On VISION, crying.

      VISION: No, my love.
      VISION: It was kind.

PANEL 7: VIRGINIA and VISION. VIRGINIA, smiling, joking.

      VIRGINIA (weak): Husband, why must must must you always...
      VIRGINIA (weak): ...make me...

PANEL 8: VIRGINIA, quiet. Gone.

      No dialogue

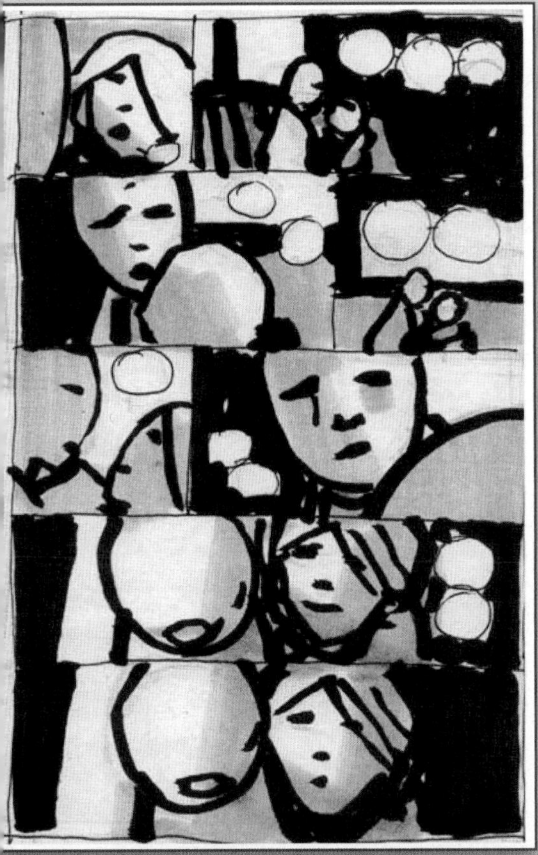

LAYOUT: GABRIEL HERNANDEZ WALTA

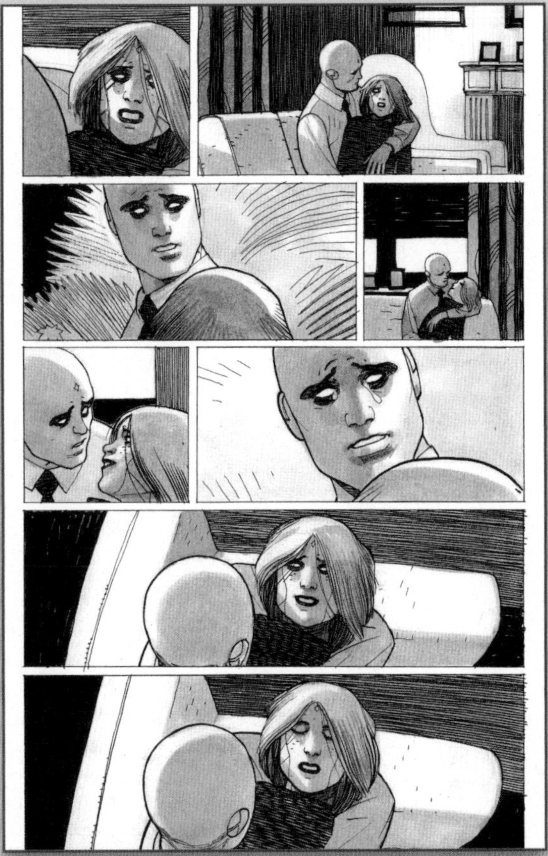

INKS: GABRIEL HERNANDEZ WALTA

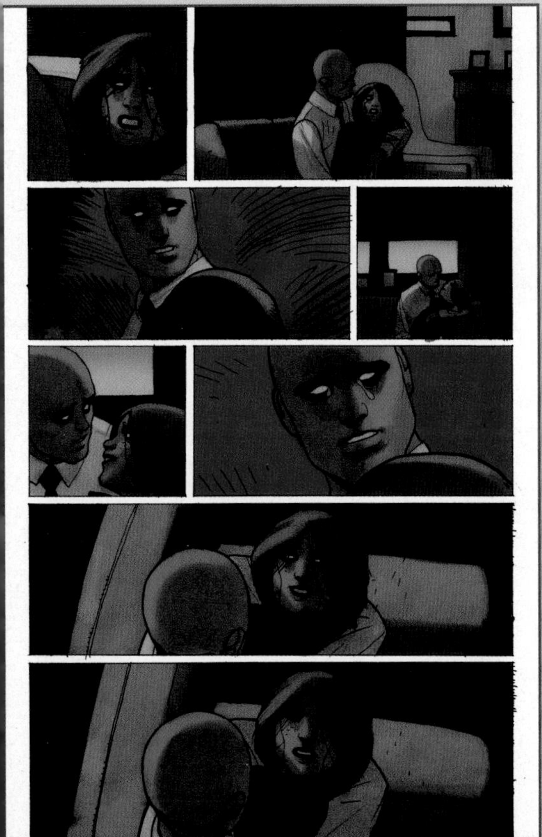

COLORS: JORDIE BELLAIRE

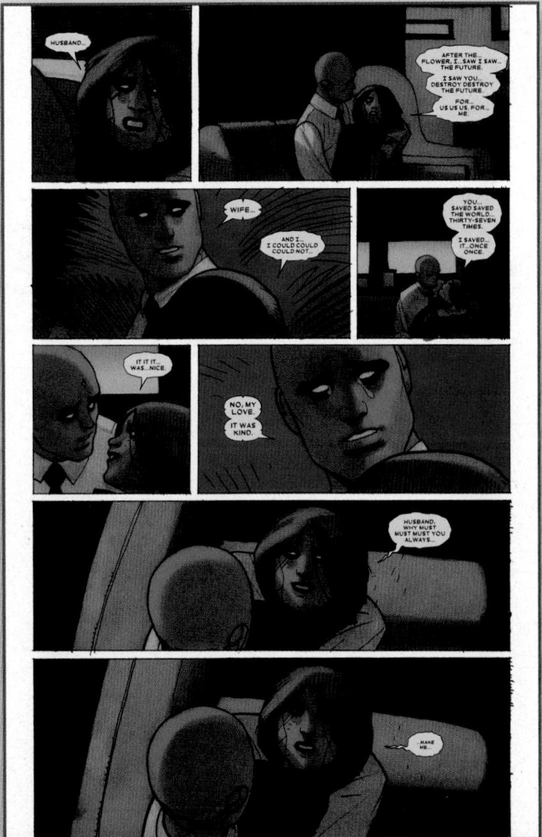
HUSBAND...
AFTER THE... FLOWER, I...SAW I SAW... THE FUTURE.
I SAW YOU... DESTROY DESTROY THE FUTURE.
FOR... US US US. FOR... ME.
WIFE...
AND I... I COULD COULD COULD NOT...
YOU... SAVED SAVED THE WORLD... THIRTY-SEVEN TIMES.
I SAVED... IT...ONCE ONCE.
IT IT IT... WAS...NICE.
NO, MY LOVE.
IT WAS KIND.
HUSBAND, WHY MUST MUST MUST YOU ALWAYS...
...MAKE ME...

LETTERS: VC's CLAYTON COWLES

PAGE 15:

<u>PANEL 1</u>: SPLASH: In the house, in the dark, VISION holds his dead wife.

CAPTION: Virginia did the right thing.
CAPTION: Or she did the wrong thing.
CAPTION: Or she just did what everyone does.

SCRIPT: TOM KING

LAYOUT: GABRIEL HERNANDEZ WALTA

INKS: GABRIEL HERNANDEZ WALTA

REALIZING A VISION WITH GABRIEL HERNANDEZ WALTA

By T.D. Dietsch

NEARLY TWO YEARS AGO, writer Tom King and artist Gabriel Hernandez Walta blew readers away with a series called *VISION*. Lead by the synthezoid Avenger, the book introduced his wife, Virgina, and two children, Viv and Vin. Over the next 12 issues, they created a heart-wrenching story about family, secrets, loyalty, and how all of that plays against the mixed backdrop of suburbia and super-heroics.

To celebrate the book, Marvel will publish *VISION: DIRECTOR'S CUT #1* on June 14. The six-issue limited series will not only reproduce the original installments in pairs, but also offer all kinds of amazing behind-the-scenes material from the creative process.

We talked with Walta about working with King, building the Vision family, and appealing to such a devoted fan following.

Marvel.com: When you and Tom first started talking about this book, what were some of the key visual elements you wanted to work with?

Gabriel Hernandez Walta: The truth is that it all was in Tom's first pitch! He wrote: "Imagine the first cover. Imagine a family at dinner. Talking, laughing. A Norman Rockwell painting. The American Dream. But instead of the bland, white people of the '40s and '50s, we have green, red, and yellow robots each smiling happily, their powers almost jumping out of them. And under the table, the body lies still." From there it was really easy to imagine the feeling for the book, with typical [suburban] houses and a "perfect" family with many hidden secrets.

Marvel.com: Were there specific ways in which you felt you played with your style on the series?

Gabriel Hernandez Walta: From the start I knew that I wanted to develop the kind of "invisible style" that film directors like Billy Wilder or comic book artists like Dave Gibbons used in their works. Rather than using flashy visuals I felt that it was better to let the characters act before the reader and use all the storytelling devices I could to capture all the subtlety and poetry of Tom's writing.

Marvel.com: What was the process like for developing the actual looks of the Vision family members?

Gabriel Hernandez Walta: When Tom and our editor Wil Moss told me that they all should have "red skin and the diamond in the forehead," I imagined them like three variations of Vision, so I used the hair to make real differences between them. Also, I gave the kids those big eyes so they looked surprised and even confused when trying to adapt to the "human" life.

I guess that the most difficult part of designing the family was to use the limited body language and facial expression that they all had to let the readers know that they *did* have feelings.

Marvel.com: You did such a great job in this series of keeping the Vision family humanoid, but still somewhat synthetic. Was that a difficult balance to keep?

Gabriel Hernandez Walta: It was difficult to keep that balance but it was also challenging. In a way, I think that the contrast between the terrible things that happen to the family and their "cold" reactions is one of the strong points of the book.

Marvel.com: Do you have a favorite moment from the series?

Gabriel Hernandez Walta: All [of] issue #10 is my favorite "moment" of the series because all the scenes are, at the same time, powerful and quiet. Above all, the part with Vision and Viv praying and the one with Vin's hologram are, I think, the most beautiful moments of the book.

Marvel.com: What do you think it was about this book that resonated so much with so many people?

Gabriel Hernandez Walta: I can only guess, but I think that the fact that, despite being synthezoids, the Vision family deals with everyday problems, like being different and [trying] to be accepted or to make sacrifices for your children, is the main reason why so many readers got engaged with the story.

ORIGINALLY PUBLISHED MAY 12, 2017, ON MARVEL.COM

A VISION OF THE FUTURE

By Jim Beard

WRITER TOM KING TAKES US INSIDE THE PROCESS FOR HIS CRITICALLY ACCLAIMED WORK!

Sometime when something works so well, you want to take it apart to see what makes it tick.

That's the idea in the *VISION: DIRECTOR'S CUT*, an unparalleled look underneath the hood of one of comicdom's most well-oiled machines, the highly appraised *VISION* series by writer Tom King and artist Gabriel Hernandez Walta. Kicking off June 14, each installment features two issues of the original book, accompanied by, well, everything: script excerpts, designs and sketches, even King's initial story pitch.

It's total immersion in a unique vision for a series. We spoke to King to get more.

Marvel.com: Tom, what was your first encounter with the character of The Vision?

Tom King: My first comic, the first one that got me to buy the next one and the next and the next, was *AVENGERS #300*. In the back of the issue there was a chart showing every Avenger and listing his or her first appearance on the team. I poured over that chart like it was the Zapruder film. I memorized every face, every hint of a cape. I remember seeing Vision there, wondering who this was, why he joined so early, why his collar was so pointy. To me, he was a mystery before he was a character.

Marvel.com: Do you have a particular favorite Vision story of the past?

Tom King: Actual story, I'd say his first appearance [in *AVENGERS #57*]. The tool of the enemy becoming a man of justice, ending with a tear in a robot's eye—that's hard to beat. But my actual favorite Vision moment is from *AVENGERS FOREVER*, when they try to explain his relationship to the original Human Torch, how they're made of the same body and they're also not made of the same body. It is so insanely baroque, the ungainly twists in continuity and time all bent into a straight line of narrative that it kind of becomes one of the most poetic moments ever written. You can see the noble struggle of a dozen authors shouting to tell a hundred stories all of which need to become a single, magnificent epic. It's the essence of comics in a few panels.

Marvel.com: What's your earliest memory of your VISION project? Who first brought it up and what were your initial thoughts about doing it?

Tom King: Genius editor Wil Moss reached out to me and said he had something I'd be great for. Being a former spy who was at that time working in another universe on a sidekick who'd become a spy, I knew he was talking about the Winter Soldier. And I got together like seven espionage Winter Soldier pitches. And then he said, "Vision."

I was a Marvel Zombie growing up and desperately wanted to work in the Marvel Universe. So I, of course, said, "Vision! Just what I thought you'd say! I have like seven pitches ready for that!" And I reached for my find/replace function while I, rather tentatively, asked what he might want from a Vision comic, and he said, "Sci-fi." So I threw away the espionage soldier pitches and planned a whole space epic thing. And as I wrote that, I got another e-mail from Wil: "Sci-fi, but not in space." So I threw away the space pitch.

This left me with "what's sci-fi but not space?" And I thought, "Maybe like Frankenstein?" and Frankenstein had a wife, so maybe Vision has a wife. But then that actually is Frankenstein, and I don't want to get sued, so I said maybe he has a wife and a family—I have a wife and family, I know about these things!—and maybe Vision created this whole family to be happy, to be human. And that seemed kind of messed up. So when it gets to the "kind of messed up" phase, you know you're onto something.

Marvel.com: Okay, so what was your "Hollywood pitch" on it? Did it change much before you began actual work on the book?

Tom King: So, before sending the above in to Marvel, I sent the "Vision makes a family" Hollywood pitch thing to a friend of mine, Darrell Taylor. And he said that sounds kind of lame, like *Small Wonder* from the '80s. And that was true, so I quickly added, "Uh, and the attempt to have a family drives him to evil and he fights all the Avengers, so, uh, it's actually 'Breaking Bad Vision'!"

And that became the Hollywood pitch, "Breaking Bad Vision," which we stuck to pretty well I think.

Marvel.com: Agreed. What do you feel was your greatest challenge on the book as a writer, and how did you conquer it?

Tom King: Once we had the "Breaking Bad Vision" pitch, I couldn't say that was the pitch or else that would spoil the whole "Breaking Bad" part, which I wanted to be a shock. So people looking at the first images of the book and reading the first solicitations were just seeing the "Vision creates a family" thing and they, like my buddy, thought that was a little lame. The whole thing sounded like it might be a stupid comedy of stupid manners, robots doing silly human things; basically Urklebot for the Marvel Universe.

So the first and biggest challenge was—and is—showing the high stakes of this series, showing that something horrible was happening here, something haunting. This is where the narrative voice came from, the voice of someone who knew what was coming—who knew about the "Breaking Bad" pitch—and was telling the audience what you're seeing here is not Urklebot, but is the start of something horrible, something haunting.

Marvel.com: With this Director's Cut, what's one thing you hope everyone will take away from it? What will be highlighted that you're glad is in it?

Tom King: I, very nicely—or kindly—get a lot of credit for [VISION], and, to be perfectly honest, a lot of that credit belongs to others. It belongs to Gabriel Walta and Jordie Bellaire and [letterer] Clayton [Cowles] and [cover artist] Michael [Del Mundo] and [guest artist] the other Michael [Walsh]. I hope in reading my scripts and seeing what this team did with those scripts, people will see that *VISION* is a book of collaboration and any success the book has is the team's success, not mine.

Marvel.com: You brought him up, so let's ask: How do you quantify your time and relationship with Gabriel on the book?

Tom King: Working with Gabriel was a gift. I don't know what I did to deserve it, but I'll always try to do it again. With Gabriel I could see what he'd do with a page, exactly see it in my head, so that when I was writing *VISION*, all I had to do was describe that page in a document. And a month later that page, the very page I had pictured arrived into the world. It's magic and it made telling this story so easy. All the emotion, all the tension was in the lines, not the words. All I had to do was get out of the way.

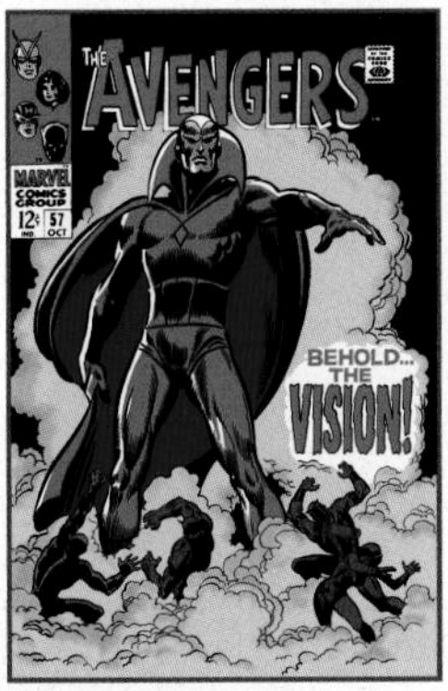
THE AVENGERS
MARVEL COMICS GROUP
12¢ 57 OCT
BEHOLD... THE VISION!
AVENGERS (1963) #57

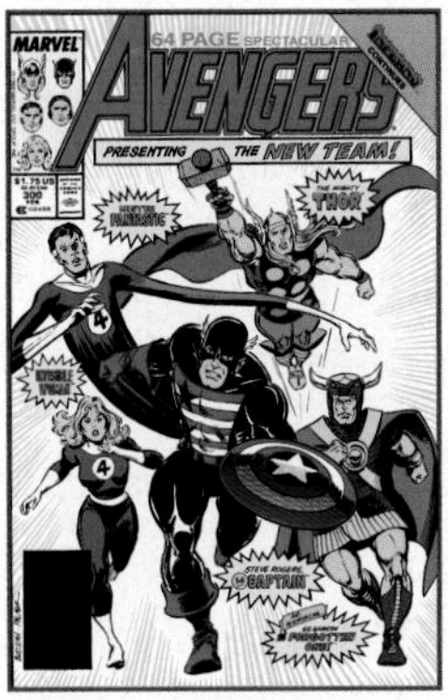
MARVEL
64 PAGE SPECTACULAR
AVENGERS
PRESENTING THE NEW TEAM!
AVENGERS (1963) #300

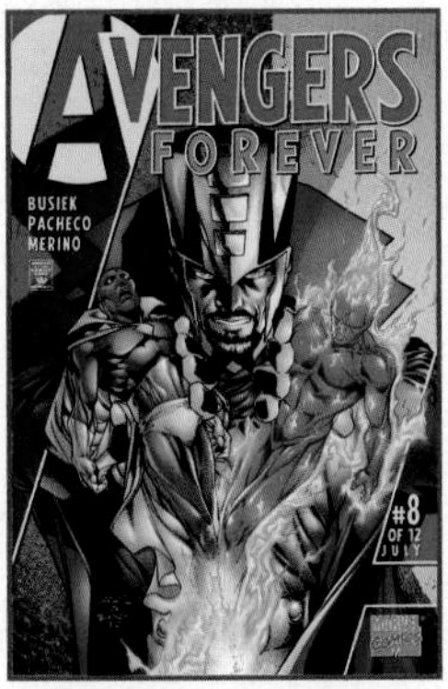
AVENGERS
FOREVER
BUSIEK
PACHECO
MERINO
#8 OF 12 JULY
AVENGERS FOREVER #8

BEHOLD…THE *VISUALS*!

AN ANALYSIS OF THE VISUAL STORYTELLING OF *THE VISION* BY **HASSAN OTSMANE-ELHAOU**, CREATOR OF *PANELXPANEL* AND *STRIP PANEL NAKED*, A MAGAZINE AND VIDEO SERIES, RESPECTIVELY, ABOUT VISUAL STORYTELLING IN COMICS.

Comics as a medium are often seen as little more than escapism, sometimes even reduced to a single genre: super heroes. Viewing a comic that way means seeing it as something lesser than those it rubs shoulders with — movies and novels — easily dismissed as just another story about men in tights. We know it's not as simple as that, and it's important to see comics as their own art form, with their own language — truly an incredibly interesting visual medium in which to tell a story. It's why THE VISION excited me so much, and still does one year after its first publication. It is layered, nuanced, clever work in the medium of comics, by a mainstream publisher.

You couldn't ask for more.

I wanted to try to show off a little of that narrative magic by taking you through a few key (as I see them) scenes in THE VISION, and how the whole creative team works to tell you as much through the visuals as through the dialogue or caption boxes. As artist Gabriel Hernandez Walta said to me in the late hours of a Sunday evening in a pub in Leeds, "The way I look at it is we're writing with art."

One of the most interesting moments that helps set the scene for what this book is going to be comes — unsurprisingly — right at the start. In the first issue, we see Nora and George, along with the captions reflecting their lives, their sacrifices. We follow them leaving their house, interacting with people on the street and heading up to the Visions' house. We experience the opening scene from their point of view. Writer Tom King and Walta are asking us, as an audience, to see the world through George and Nora's very human eyes. That is also what the captions tell us, along with their jobs and a couple of mundane tidbits of their likes and dislikes. That's an important distinction. We're not being presented George and Nora initially through the art, but rather the art is asking us to *be* them, walking up to this strange new house.

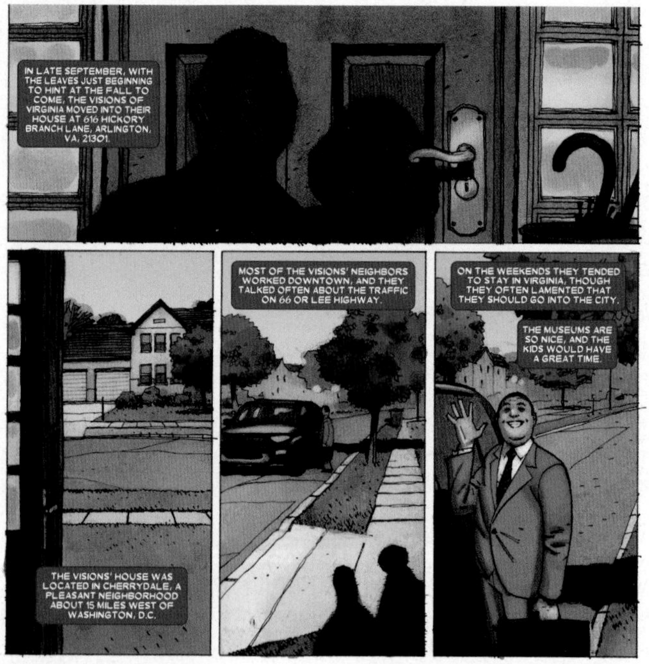
IN LATE SEPTEMBER, WITH THE LEAVES JUST BEGINNING TO HINT AT THE FALL TO COME, THE VISIONS OF VIRGINIA MOVED INTO THEIR HOUSE AT 616 HICKORY BRANCH LANE, ARLINGTON, VA, 21301.
THE VISIONS' HOUSE WAS LOCATED IN CHERRYDALE, A PLEASANT NEIGHBORHOOD ABOUT 15 MILES WEST OF WASHINGTON, D.C.
MOST OF THE VISIONS' NEIGHBORS WORKED DOWNTOWN, AND THEY TALKED OFTEN ABOUT THE TRAFFIC ON 66 OR LEE HIGHWAY.
ON THE WEEKENDS THEY TENDED TO STAY IN VIRGINIA, THOUGH THEY OFTEN LAMENTED THAT THEY SHOULD GO INTO THE CITY.
THE MUSEUMS ARE SO NICE, AND THE KIDS WOULD HAVE A GREAT TIME.

It builds a portrait of humanity — boxed in as it is with a tight grid structure, which serves to limit the scope of the visuals — but there's a truth and an honesty to it. In the middle of this page, George and Nora are framed within the porch, and within the panel gutters themselves. Everything in these opening pages sets up a certain language. Color artist Jordie Bellaire's use of autumnal oranges, Walta's choice to have everything so gridded and boxed in, King's multiple panels. We're learning how this comic reads.

Then we meet the Vision family.

Suddenly, the image extends all the way to the bleed of the page, and green and pink invade the palette, like the whole thing is bursting out of the comic itself. Letterer Clayton Cowles' placement means we "hear" the sound of their speech first, the balloon being the first thing we'll read, then we see the bodies of the Vision family, and it feels *different*. This is not the reality we have been shown already, a very *human* reality, through the art style and visual language and speech balloons.

There's also a lot going on in this image with the costumes. Vision's diamond logo is prevalent across Vin and Viv, and Virginia has a necklace that replicates the design as well. Even Vision himself has the diamond on his tie clip. It's clear immediately that these emblems represent a connection to Vision himself, to the family.

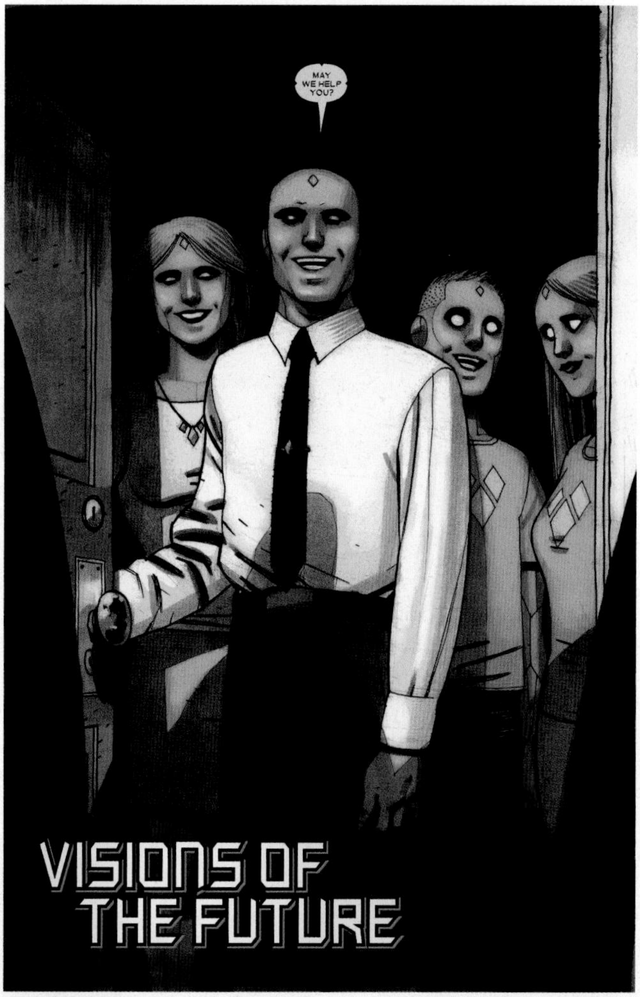
MAY WE HELP YOU?
VISIONS OF THE FUTURE

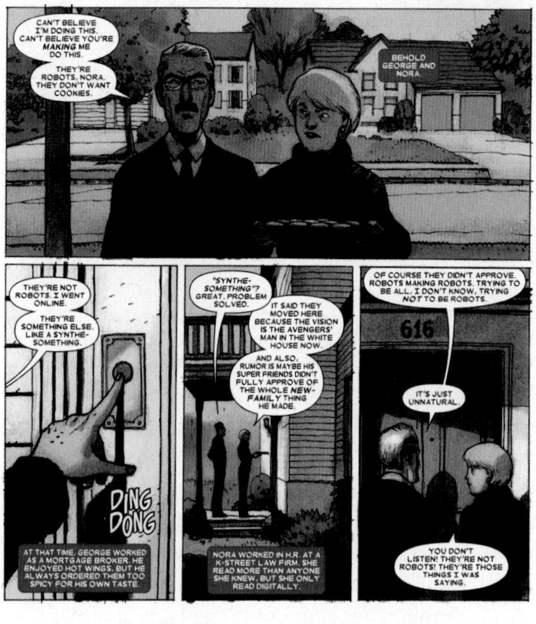
CAN'T BELIEVE I'M DOING THIS. CAN'T BELIEVE YOU'RE *MAKING* ME DO THIS.
THEY'RE ROBOTS, NORA. THEY DON'T WANT COOKIES.
BEHOLD GEORGE AND NORA.
THEY'RE NOT ROBOTS. I WENT ONLINE.
THEY'RE SOMETHING ELSE. LIKE A SYNTHE-SOMETHING.
DING DONG
AT THAT TIME, GEORGE WORKED AS A MORTGAGE BROKER. HE ENJOYED HOT WINGS, BUT HE ALWAYS ORDERED THEM TOO SPICY FOR HIS OWN TASTE.
"SYNTHE-SOMETHING"? GREAT. PROBLEM SOLVED.
IT SAID THEY MOVED HERE BECAUSE THE VISION IS THE AVENGERS' MAN IN THE WHITE HOUSE NOW.
AND ALSO, RUMOR IS MAYBE HIS SUPER FRIENDS DIDN'T FULLY APPROVE OF THE WHOLE *NEW-FAMILY* THING HE MADE.
NORA WORKED IN H.R. AT A K-STREET LAW FIRM. SHE READ MORE THAN ANYONE SHE KNEW, BUT SHE ONLY READ DIGITALLY.
OF COURSE THEY DIDN'T APPROVE. ROBOTS MAKING ROBOTS. TRYING TO BE ALL, I DON'T KNOW, TRYING *NOT* TO BE ROBOTS.
616
IT'S JUST UNNATURAL.
YOU DON'T LISTEN! THEY'RE NOT ROBOTS! THEY'RE THOSE THINGS I WAS SAYING.

In issue #4, the necklace ends up playing a major part in the narrative, and in understanding Virginia's character in a key scene. At this point, Virginia has been through a lot. She's murdered and lied to protect her family, all things she felt like she *needed* to do to maintain the illusion of her perfect family. But now it's coming back to haunt her. We see her in this scene initially boxed within the window frame, physically cut off from the rest of her family. Walta and Bellaire place her in the dark, the light not really hitting her. They compound that by putting her in dark clothing, at odds with how we've seen her in the other issues, and a stark contrast to the softer green we saw her in on that splash page. Through this lighting, color and framing, we get a sense, narratively, of where Virginia is positioned, and a little understanding of her deeper emotional state. It's all done silently, too — not hitting you over the head with any exposition, but revealing itself thoughtfully.

HMMM. YES. THIS IS TYPICAL OF MOST HUMAN ENDEAVORS.
THEY CHANGE, BUT THEY DO NOT CHANGE.
FOR A MOMENT, AS SHE LISTENED TO HER FAMILY ARGUE AND LAUGH, VIRGINIA FELT CONTENT.
SHE BELONGED HERE. THEY BELONGED HERE. EVERYTHING IN THE END WOULD BE GOOD.
THIS MOMENT LASTED 1.72 SECONDS.

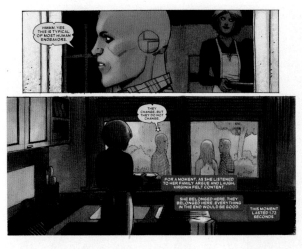

When we go inside the house, Cowles' use of the burst tail helps maintain that distance between Virginia and her family, and the difference in Bellaire's warm orange outdoors and the dank, dark gray and black interiors says a lot about the situation. Outside seems happy, indoors not so much. We'll see this again, too.

And while I talk a lot about framing and colors, artists also make their characters act in each panel. We've established that in some way, the diamond pattern on the clothes and on Virginia's necklace represents a tie to family and to Vision. When Virginia gets a phone call from someone who knows what she's done, her body language changes. Suddenly this necklace, which she had been wearing so proudly over her apron when watching her family, disappears into her hand. She hides it away from the situation, turning her back on her family and shrouding the emblem that represents them, as though it can hear the conversation. That small gesture reveals so much about what's going on with Virginia, too. This is all about preserving some ideal of family as much as possible against seemingly impossible odds. She covers even this inanimate representation of family away from any evil or fear. Like any good mother, she's protecting that ideal. In that moment, we can see the truth of Virginia on the page, entirely visually through Walta's choices. Isn't that just magic?

YES.
SHE IGNORED IT FOR SOME TIME.
WHEN WOULD YOU LIKE THIS TO TAKE PLACE?
UNTIL SHE DIDN'T.
I DO NOT KNOW IF YOU SHOULD FLY.
FATHER, PLEASE LET US. IT MAKES IT MORE FUN.
YES, YES. THAT WILL WORK.
YES.
THE PHONE RANG EVERY DAY AROUND 2:00.

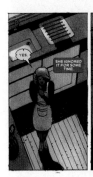

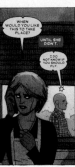

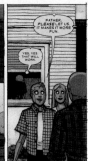

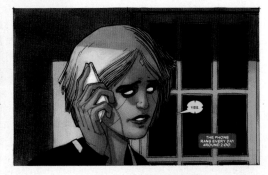

Just before this moment, there's a doorway in frame. Building on the visuals of Virginia being trapped, framed within the window, here she's framed again in a way to trap her. The doorway looks like prison bars, a visual technique seen in films such as *American Beauty*: using frames to trap and lock away characters in a visual way. We don't need a thought bubble or narrative caption to tell us this, because the world around Virginia is so oppressive already, bearing down.

THE VILLAINY YOU TEACH ME
TOM KING WRITER
GABRIEL HERNANDEZ WALTA ARTIST
JORDIE BELLAIRE COLOR ARTIST
VC'S CLAYTON COWLES LETTERER

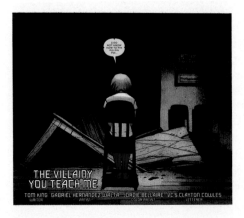

In the final moments of issue #5, we see this motif again, after Virginia breaks the table. Visually, the world in front of her is a mess. The walls surround her, and the only way out is doors with darkness behind them that are structured as the aforementioned prison bars. She's trapped in this familial mess she's created — through nothing but good intentions — and she doesn't know what to do next. It's really a testament to the beauty of THE VISION as a series that we're able to see some harsh truths about our own lives reflected through these artificial humanoid-beings.

And the image works particularly well because we're able to see the full expanse of the world around her. Sometimes you want to trap characters in confined spaces, and sometimes you can use the wide world around them as a way to show their isolation. This is a perfect example of the latter, because there's absolutely nowhere to focus but on Virginia. The only real line leading your eye anywhere is the table's length, which pulls you back into the image. The scene's vanishing point is somewhere dead center, again pulling you in.

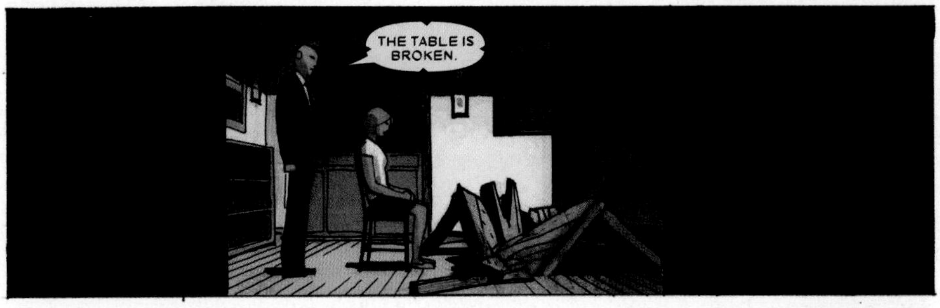
THE TABLE IS BROKEN.

A moment before this, we're given a panel that traps Virginia with negative space. The use of the doorway and dark space of the wall makes the horizontal space thinner. It feels like the world is closing in on Virginia, and once again the vanishing point for the image is in the center of the panel. The lines that draw your eye secretly through the composition are directing you dead center. Walta is forcing you to look where he wants you to, where there's no escape, where there doesn't appear to be much hope.

I always get the sense from these claustrophobic approaches that maybe if the character could just break beyond the boundaries, it might be better for them. If they could just push open the walls surrounding them, even a little, they'd have room to breathe. They'd be okay. It's the playful nature of comics that allows King and Walta to transition from that panel into a full-bleed image showing there is no escape — and that maybe, just maybe, we're also trapped in here with Virginia. We're in this situation, too.

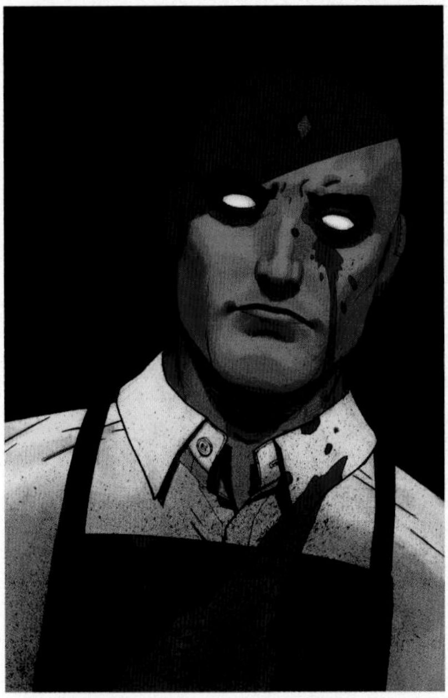

The splash, or bleed, imagery is always used for particular emphasis or effect. It's never wasted in THE VISION, and one of my favorite examples is Vision in the basement turning the neighbors' dead dog into a new android dog in issue #6. The power of the splash is undeniable, too. By its very nature, it's as big as you can go (let's discount those awesome fold-out pages we've seen in comics) within the boundaries of a page. One single image, running all the way to the page edge. King and Walta use it in an interesting way here, too, because it's not some epic battle, or some visually dynamic moment. It's just Vision, blood on his face looking almost like a tear. There's only one thing to look at, the idea diluted to this singular moment and singular visual. So much of the language here is of the enemy, too. He's hunkering over us, we're looking up at him as the reader, he's wrapped in darkness and has blood on him — clearly blood that has splashed back from exactly the position we as readers are being put in. This is not the traditional visual language for a super hero. By combining those traditional villain elements with a single, huge point of focus, we're being forced to respond in a certain way to this moment on the page. Without needing a caption box or anything to *tell* us, it's allowing us to understand on our own terms. That's always more powerful.

THIS WAS VISION'S CHOICE.
THE REAPER HAD COME.
VISION HAD FAILED. HE WOULD CONTINUE TO FAIL. SHOULD HE THEN CONTINUE?
NNN. NNNN.
NNNN. NNNN.
WHAT... WHAT IS *YOUR* NAME?
WOOF!

The language is consistently telling us that something isn't right with this family. That's a thematic point throughout, also asking us whether *any* family is perfect (spoiler: no), but here's one trying to make it work. Later in that same issue, there's a beautiful moment of tenderness shown through Walta's use of backgrounds. Vision has brought a dog home for the family — the dog he was making when we saw him covered in blood in that splash — and Viv is sitting alone. Behind her is a fractured, cracked wall. Like Virginia earlier, the walls close her in a little more on the left and right sides, the shadow on the right side of the wall working to close her off even more into a little box of light. But the wall behind her is reflective of her current mental state, and the state of her life and family. Fractured. Falling apart. When the dog arrives, his background is different. The same color, but flat, no cracks. When we switch back to Viv, we see how her world view compares to what the dog can offer. When she accepts him, at the bottom of the page, the world around her looks clearer, cleaner, more stable.

THE EASY EXPLANATION OF HIS ANSWER WOULD BE THAT HE, WHO LONGED TO BE HUMAN, RECOGNIZED THAT THIS WAS THE *HUMAN* DECISION.
THAT EVERY DAY ALL MEN AND WOMEN MAKE THIS SAME CHOICE. TO GO ON EVEN THOUGH THEY CANNOT POSSIBLY GO ON.
IN TRUTH, HOWEVER, THIS WAS NOT HIS REASONING.
IN THE END, VISION SIMPLY CAME TO UNDERSTAND THAT HE COULD NOT CHOOSE BETWEEN FAMILY AND PRACTICALITY.
INDEED, IN CONSIDERING THE SITUATION, IT WAS CLEAR:
HE HAD NO CHOICE AT ALL...

Ultimately, when the family joins them, the cracked wall is still there, but now Viv is with her family. Sure, the book tells us, they aren't perfect — but they're together.

It's an effect mirrored immediately after with Vision and Virginia. Their faces are shown against the wall and cracked window, but when their hands come together we instead get this warm orange glow and nothing else.

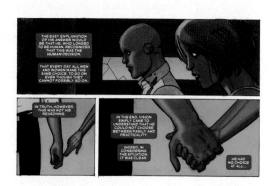

By the end of the series, that warm orange glow has all but gone. The weight of everything has come crashing down, sucking all the color out of the Visions' world. Bellaire casts everything in a blue tone, linked to sadness, isolation. Cool, calmer colors. Virginia's costume earlier, and her necklace representing Vision, is gone. She now looks like Nora, and Vision resembles George. Here are two people who, through their series of decisions — good *and* bad — have become what they wanted to be: human.

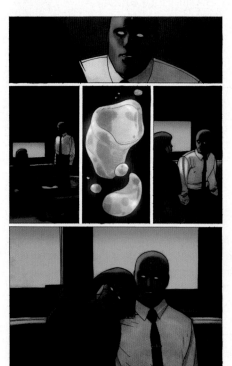

In so many of the scenes here, Walta places Vision and Virginia together in the panels. In contrast with issue #3, they sit next to each other, they engage with each other, they look at each other. And their space is shared. Even in tight panels such as these, they're linked. We're not just seeing Virginia respond to Vision — we're seeing Vision right there with her. It's here, too, that the grid system applied to many of the pages shows its qualities. The water vase gift from the Silver Surfer has been majestically floating through all the issues, and Nora's last thought before she dies is wondering why the vase is empty. We find out here, as Virginia drinks some of it, that it's a corrosive material. Beautiful to look at, but killing anything it comes in contact with. There's a lot to pull out of that, but what it comes to represent here is death. Walta and King frame this sublime moment of Vision coming to sit by his wife with the floating vase in the middle. The representation of death forms the centerpiece of the page, and in fact is the brightest thing there, drawing your eye straight to it. Typically, your eye will naturally gravitate to the brightest point of an image, and it's right there. The elephant in the room.

So much of THE VISION is just that, too. Reality and hyper-reality juxtaposed on the page. And what are the Visions if not that? The reality of the familial unit contrasting to the hyper-reality of androids trying to make it work. The reality of a couple who have finally come to understand each other, juxtaposed with the realities of death. Absurd, real, heartbreaking.

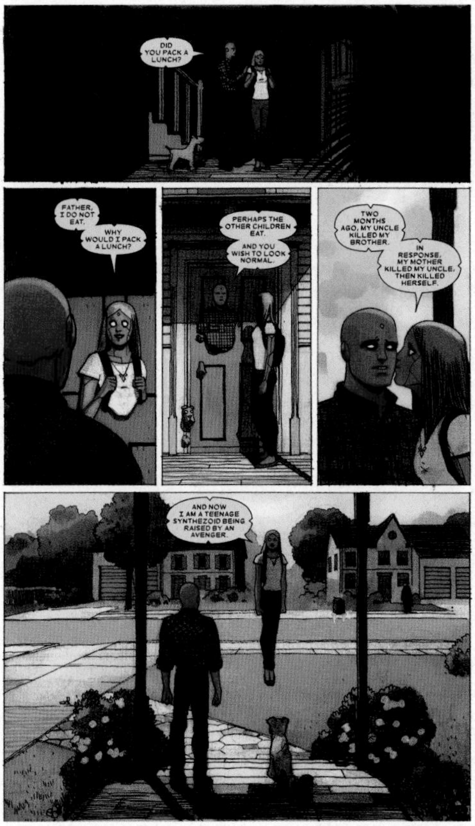
DID YOU PACK A LUNCH?
FATHER, I DO NOT EAT.
WHY WOULD I PACK A LUNCH?
PERHAPS THE OTHER CHILDREN EAT.
AND YOU WISH TO LOOK NORMAL.
TWO MONTHS AGO, MY UNCLE KILLED MY BROTHER.
IN RESPONSE, MY MOTHER KILLED MY UNCLE, THEN KILLED HERSELF.
AND NOW I AM A TEENAGE SYNTHEZOID BEING RAISED BY AN AVENGER.

For me, it all came full circle when Viv goes off to school at the end of issue #12. Viv — dropping her Vision-linking clothes, looking more and more like a normal teenager – is about to leave. Vision connects back to that scene we saw Virginia watching in issue #3, where he'd dropped the shell of the shirt and tie, and instead wore a relaxed, plaid shirt. The world is now brighter again. They've come out of winter and back into spring. New beginnings.

This page is a beautiful construct. Walta, King and Bellaire start in the darker, deep browns of the house — an enclosed background that uses that now-familiar trope of the walls closing in on them. By the end of the page, it's juxtaposed with the freedom of the world. Vision and Viv are still being contained within the porch, but look how alive the world is. Look how vividly Bellaire renders the lush textures. Viv wears blue as she floats toward the blue sky. Vision wears green, the same color as the door to his house, as he inevitably goes back inside to attempt to recover what he's lost. For Vision, family is tied to the construct, the house, the dream, as told through these color cues. For Viv, life is more expansive, the world bigger than just family. Isn't that the same for all parents and children? Maybe the Visions found out how to be human after all.

And one last note on Viv here that Walta decides to add: She's taken her mother's necklace as her own. A sign of forgiveness, a small way to tie her to the family without it being overbearing. A sign it still means something to her, even when she flies away.

THE VISION is full of small visual flourishes such as this, and each page in each issue is layered with visual storytelling that stretches beyond just the narrative caption boxes and dialogue. It's not just Tom King writing this book — it's Gabriel Hernandez Walta writing it, too, on every page, in every panel. It's Jordie Bellaire's colors adding metaphors to the sentences. And it's Clayton Cowles' letters and caption placement adding the punctuation. The book isn't just one of the finest works Marvel has published — it's an argument for the medium itself.

It's absurd. It's real. It's heartbreaking. It's comics. ■

These endnote things from writers always seem to come out the same. Mostly it's just the writer saying how important/talented/transcendent the artist, colorist, letterer, cover artist, editor were on the series. But, I mean, what's the point in that? If you don't know, if you can't see what Gabriel, Jordie, Clayton, Mike, and Wil did on this book, I don't think I can explain it to you. I don't have the words. They are this book; this book is what they made it to be. (Okay, so I had those thirteen words--I'm a stupid writer, I always have words--but we can all agree that those particular words are fairly inadequate and barely count.)

So instead of stating what is obvious to you, I'm going to talk about something that's obvious to me: I'm going to talk briefly and mushily about my lovely wife, Colleen, and her role in shaping everything I create.

I met my wife when we were both working in the Justice Department. We were going to be lawyers. We were going to save the world. Through law, I guess. I don't know. We were very young. Point is, she thought she was getting some dude who was going to be a normal professional person. And instead...

I joined the C.I.A. And went overseas and did that, while she actually went to law school. Then I quit that and became a "writer"--i.e., an unemployed person who pontificates needlessly and endlessly on the uselessness of adverbs. I took care of the kid (then kids--Charlie, Claire, Crosby--Hi, kids!) during the day and I wrote at night, and she went to work and, y'know, bought food. Then I got rejected a lot, then I did a novel, then I got rejected a lot, then I said I actually really want to do comics, then I got rejected a lot, then I did comics.

And throughout all of that weird, my wife, insanely, patiently, just told me it was fine, it was all going to be fine. We would get to the next day. Together, we'll always find the next day. She read every script. She endured every doubt. She suffered every conversation about the minutia of continuity and panel construction and word balloon placement and how this one phrase needs to reflect this other phrase, but I just can't--and she said it was all fine, it was all going to be fine.

We'll get to the next day. Together we'll always find the next day.

THE VISION in its entirety, as much as I can dedicate a work that was done by a team that simply and kindly included me as a member, is dedicated to my wife. It would not exist without her. It would not be good without her. I would not be good without her.

All right. That seems like enough. Or at least it seems like enough for now, and for now that will have to do. I'll see you next time.

-Tom

I feel so proud to be part of the team that made THE VISION possible! Tom's scripts made me want to give my best every time. Jordie's color art always amazed and surprised me. Clayton's lettering glued all the parts together. Mike and Marco D'Alfonso made the perfect covers for ALL the issues. Wil gave us all the freedom to do what we wanted and kept the team focused on doing our best.

I also feel very lucky to have the best family a man could wish for. This has been a very time-demanding book for me, and my wife Violeta and my daughters Clara and Lucía have suffered the many drawbacks of my not having holidays or free weekends. I couldn't have done a single page without their love and constant support.

Finally, I feel very grateful knowing that there are readers out there who "get" all the messages we throw and that this book is also special for them. (Also, thanks to Daniel Ketchum, who was the first one who thought of me for this project!)

So I finish this book feeling proud, lucky and grateful...not bad at all!!

-Gabriel

I haven't been in this industry too long, but in the short while I've been part of it, I've been so incredibly lucky to work on quite a few gems that will go on and survive in the memory of readers everywhere. VISION is one of these gems.

I cannot fully express the gratitude and pride I feel for having been being part of this team. Tom King is one of the best, most humble, yet strong writers I have ever met. Gabriel Walta is an artist and gentleman who will be celebrated forever, his art is a magical transportation device that takes us wherever the page may go--sometimes a blessing and a curse. Clayton Cowles, my brother, my friend, thank you for always lending me your ear. And finally, my amazing editors, Wil Moss, Charles Beacham, and Chris Robinson, their patience and kindness always helped keep this team in good spirits; thank you for bringing all of us together and giving us all the freedom we needed to do what we do.

And thanks to the readers of this amazing thing. I think this team started out making something we would enjoy, but knowing that so many readers have also enjoyed this story is the best part of the game.

You really can't get any better than that, and so *I burn, I pine, I perish.*

-Jordie

Finally, a comic book fine enough to show to my android grandchildren. THE VISION was a hell of a ride, and I'm truly honored to have been a part of it. I would like to thank Tom for being a great collaborator, Gabriel for leaving me enough space, Mike Walsh for stopping by, Mike del Mundo just because, Chris and Charles for keeping me company in the trenches, Wil for hiring me, and Jordie for telling me to get Wil to hire me. I hope we can do this again sometime! And double thanks to everyone who picked up THE VISION and hyped it up online. You all have good taste in books.

-Clayton

Thanks to the fans for the overwhelming response to the book. Tom's scripts really brought my covers to life. I'm so proud of the work Tom, Wil and Gabriel have done with this book and I'm really glad to have been a part of this awesomeness!

Oh and thanks, Gabriel, for that awesome robo-dog design, that was hella fun to draw!

-Mike

Being a part of this book has been an incredible honor. And it's not just because of how incredible this story is. I've loved working with these people. Tom King, you're an AMAZING storyteller. Your ability to evoke emotion through narrative metaphor has consistently astounded me. Gabriel, dude, your art is SO good. I'm going to miss the excitement that comes every time I get new pages from you. Jordie!!! I tell you often, but you're just the best. You put so much heart into what you do, and you make this already awesome job exponentially more fun. Your dedication to everything you do is an inspiration to me. I'm so glad I get to continue working with you! Stay awesome. Clayton. Buddy-Friend. Thanks for spending many a late Friday working with Wil and I to get things just right. You're a godsend. Wil, thanks for putting together such an amazing team and having me aboard. You're the best captain we could've asked for. And to all of you guys who've kept up with the book and written us letters, thank you! We literally couldn't have told this story without you.

-Charles

Thanks to Jay Bowen for the logo, to Tom Brevoort for letting this book be this book, to David Gabriel for pushing this from Day One, to Daniel Ketchum for the gift of Gabriel H. Walta, to my mom's dog Eva for letting us fry her face off and scoop her brain out in #6 (please nobody tell my mom about that, btw), to Marco D'Alfonso for helping out on covers when Mike got too swamped, to Michael Walsh for the beauty that was #7, to those who let us quote them on a few of the covers, to the internet for embracing this weird book, to the retailers for supporting this weird book, to Charles, Chris and the Bullpen for producing this weird book, and most of all to Tom, Gabriel, Jordie, Clayton, and Mike for creating this weird book and turning all of us into socketlovers.

-Wil